THE ROUTLEDGE COMPANION TO ETHICS

The Routledge Companion to Ethics is an outstanding survey of the whole field of ethics by a distinguished international team of contributors. Over 60 entries are divided into six clear sections:

- The history of ethics
- Meta-ethics
- Perspectives from outside ethics
- Ethical perspectives
- Morality
- Debates in ethics.

The *Companion* opens with a comprehensive historical overview of ethics, including entries on Plato, Aristotle, Hume and Kant, and the origins of ethical thinking in China, India and the Middle East. The second part covers the domain of meta-ethics, including entries on cognitivism and non-cognitivism, explanation, reasons, moral realism and fictionalism. The third part covers important challenges to ethics from the fields of anthropology, psychology, sociobiology and economics. The fourth and fifth sections cover competing theories of ethics and the nature of morality respectively, with entries on consequentialism, Kantian morality, virtue ethics, relativism, morality and character, evil, responsibility and particularism in ethics among many others. A comprehensive final section includes entries on the most important topics and controversies in applied ethics, including rights, justice and distribution, the end of life, the environment, poverty, war and terrorism.

The Routledge Companion to Ethics is a superb resource for anyone interested in the subject, whether in philosophy or related subjects such as politics, education, or law. Fully indexed and cross-referenced, with helpful further reading sections, it is ideal for those coming to the field of ethics for the first time as well as readers already familiar with the subject.

John Skorupski is Professor of Moral Philosophy at the University of St Andrews, Scotland. His books include *Ethical Explorations* (1999) and *The Domain of Reasons* (forthcoming in 2010).

ROUTLEDGE PHILOSOPHY COMPANIONS

Routledge Philosophy Companions offer thorough, high quality surveys and assessments of the major topics and periods in philosophy. Covering key problems, themes and thinkers, all entries are specially commissioned for each volume and written by leading scholars in the field. Clear, accessible and carefully edited and organized, *Routledge Philosophy Companions* are indispensable for anyone coming to a major topic or period in philosophy, as well as for the more advanced reader.

The Routledge Companion to Aesthetics, Second Edition
Edited by Berys Gaut and Dominic Lopes

The Routledge Companion to Ethics
Edited by John Skorupski

The Routledge Companion to Philosophy of Religion
Edited by Chad Meister and Paul Copan

The Routledge Companion to the Philosophy of Science, Second Edition
Edited by Stathis Psillos and Martin Curd

The Routledge Companion to Twentieth Century Philosophy
Edited by Dermot Moran

The Routledge Companion to Philosophy and Film
Edited by Paisley Livingston and Carl Plantinga

The Routledge Companion to Philosophy of Psychology
Edited by John Symons and Paco Calvo

The Routledge Companion to Metaphysics
Edited by Robin Le Poidevin, Peter Simons, Andrew McGonigal, and Ross Cameron

The Routledge Companion to Nineteenth Century Philosophy
Edited by Dean Moyar

The Routledge Companion to Phenomenology
Edited by Søren Overgaard and Sebastian Luft

The Routledge Companion to Philosophy of Language
Edited by Gillian Russell and Delia Graff Fara

Forthcoming:

The Routledge Companion to Philosophy and Music
Edited by Andrew Kania and Theodore Gracyk

The Routledge Companion to Epistemology
Edited by Sven Bernecker and Duncan Pritchard

The Routledge Companion to Seventeenth Century Philosophy
Edited by Dan Kaufman

The Routledge Companion to Eighteenth Century Philosophy
Edited by Aaron Garrett

The Routledge Companion to Philosophy of Mental Disorder
Edited by Jakob Hohwy and Philip Gerrans

The Routledge Companion to Social and Political Philosophy
Edited by Gerald Gaus and Fred D'Agostino

The Routledge Companion to Theism
Edited by Charles Taliaferro, Victoria Harrison, and Stewart Goetz

The Routledge Companion to Philosophy of Law
Edited by Andrei Marmor

The Routledge Companion to Islamic Philosophy
Edited by Richard C. Taylor and Luis Xavier López-Farjeat

PRAISE FOR THE SERIES

The Routledge Companion to Aesthetics

"This is an immensely useful book that belongs in every college library and on the bookshelves of all serious students of aesthetics." – ***Journal of Aesthetics and Art Criticism***

"The succinctness and clarity of the essays will make this a source that individuals not familiar with aesthetics will find extremely helpful." – ***The Philosophical Quarterly***

"An outstanding resource in aesthetics ... this text will not only serve as a handy reference source for students and faculty alike, but it could also be used as a text for a course in the philosophy of art." – ***Australasian Journal of Philosophy***

"Attests to the richness of modern aesthetics ... the essays in central topics – many of which are written by well-known figures – succeed in being informative, balanced and intelligent without being too difficult." – ***British Journal of Aesthetics***

"This handsome reference volume ... belongs in every library." – ***Choice***

"The *Routledge Companions* to Philosophy have proved to be a useful series of high quality surveys of major philosophical topics and this volume is worthy enough to sit with the others on a reference library shelf." – ***Philosophy and Religion***

The Routledge Companion to Philosophy of Religion

" ... a very valuable resource for libraries and serious scholars." – ***Choice***

"The work is sure to be an academic standard for years to come ... I shall heartily recommend *The Routledge Companion to Philosophy of Religion* to my students and colleagues and hope that libraries around the country add it to their collections." – ***Philosophia Christi***

The Routledge Companion to Philosophy of Science

"With a distinguished list of internationally renowned contributors, an excellent choice of topics in the field, and well-written, well-edited essays throughout, this compendium is an excellent resource. Highly recommended." – ***Choice***

"Highly recommended for history of science and philosophy collections." – ***Library Journal***

"This well conceived companion, which brings together an impressive collection of distinguished authors, will be invaluable to novices and experience readers alike." – ***Metascience***

The Routledge Companion to Twentieth Century Philosophy

"To describe this volume as ambitious would be a serious understatement. … full of scholarly rigor, including detailed notes and bibliographies of interest to professional philosophers. … Summing up: Essential." – ***Choice***

The Routledge Companion to Philosophy and Film

"A fascinating, rich volume offering dazzling insights and incisive commentary on every page … Every serious student of film will want this book … Summing Up: Highly recommended." – ***Choice***

The Routledge Companion to Metaphysics

"The *Routledge Philosophy Companions* series has a deserved reputation for impressive scope and scholarly value. This volume is no exception … Summing Up: Highly recommended." – ***Choice***

THE ROUTLEDGE COMPANION TO ETHICS

Edited by
John Skorupski

LONDON AND NEW YORK

First published 2010 by Routledge
First published in paperback 2013 by Routledge
2 Park Square, Milton Park, Abingdon, Oxon, OX14 4RN

Simultaneously published in the USA and Canada
by Routledge
711 Third Avenue, New York, NY 10017

Routledge is an imprint of the Taylor & Francis Group, an informa business

Typeset in Goudy by Taylor & Francis Books

British Library Cataloguing in Publication Data
A catalogue record for this book is available from the British Library

Library of Congress Cataloging in Publication Data
The Routledge companion to ethics / edited by John Skorupski.
p. cm. – (Routledge philosophy companions)
Includes bibliographical references and index.
1. Ethics. I. Skorupski, John, 1946–
BJ21.R68 2010
170–dc22 2009050204

Hbk ISBN 13: 978-0-415-41362-6
Pbk ISBN 13: 978-0-415-41516-3
Ebk ISBN 13: 978-0-203-85070-1

CONTENTS

ILLUSTRATIONS

Figures

Tables

CONTRIBUTORS

Peter Adamson is Reader of Philosophy at King's College London. His main areas of interest are ancient philosophy (especially Neoplatonism) and medieval philosophy (especially in Arabic). He is the author of *The Arabic Plotinus*, and has published articles on Plotinus, al-Kindi, al-Farabi, Avicenna and other figures from Greek and Arabic philosophy.

Robert Audi is Professor of Philosophy and David E. Gallo Chair in Ethics, University of Notre Dame. He writes on epistemology, philosophy of action and philosophy of religion as well as on moral and political philosophy. His recent books include *Religious Commitment and Secular Reason* (2000), *The Architecture of Reason* (2001), *The Good in the Right: A Theory of Intuition and Intrinsic Value* (2004), *Practical Reasoning and Ethical Decision* (Routledge, 2006), and (as editor) *The Cambridge Dictionary of Philosophy* (1995, 1999).

Thomas Baldwin is a Professor of Philosophy at the University of York, having been previously a lecturer in philosophy at Cambridge University. He is currently editor of *Mind*.

Christopher Bennett is a lecturer in the Department of Philosophy, University of Sheffield. His work has mainly concerned the moral emotions, punishment and criminal justice.

Simon Blackburn is Professor of Philosophy at the University of Cambridge, and Research Professor at the University of North Carolina, Chapel Hill. His books include: *Spreading the Word* (1984), *Essays in Quasi-Realism* (1993), *The Oxford Dictionary of Philosophy* (1994), *Ruling Passions* (1998), *Think* (1999), *Being Good* (2001), *Lust* (2004), *Truth: A Guide* (2005), *Plato's Republic* (2006) and *How to Read Hume* (2008).

Andrew Brennan is Professor and Chair of Philosophy at La Trobe University, Melbourne, Australia, having previously been Professor and Chair of Philosophy at the University of Western Australia and Reader in Philosophy at the University of Stirling, Scotland.

Samantha Brennan is Professor of Philosophy and Chair of the Department of Philosophy at the University of Western Ontario. She works in contemporary normative ethics and political philosophy, including feminist approaches to both. Brennan co-edited, with Anita Superson, *Feminist Philosophy in the Analytic Tradition*, a special Issue of *Hypatia* (2005), and edited *Feminist Moral Philosophy*, a *Canadian Journal of Philosophy* supplementary (2003).

Tom Campbell is Professor Fellow at Charles Sturt University and Convenor of the Centre for Applied Philosophy and Public Ethics, an Australian Research Council Special Research Centre. He has written extensively on law and legal philosophy. He is author of *Adam Smith's Science of Morals* (1971), *The Left and Rights* (1983) and *Justice* (1988, 2nd edn forthcoming in 2010). His Routledge book, *Rights: A Critical Introduction*, was published in 2006.

Erik Carlson is Professor of Practical Philosophy at Uppsala University. His areas of research include axiology, measurement theory, normative ethics, the problems of free will and determinism, and decision theory. He has published one book, *Consequentialism Reconsidered* (1995), and about thirty papers in journals and anthologies.

Alan Carter is Professor of Moral Philosophy at the University of Glasgow. He is the author of numerous articles and three books: *A Radical Green Political Theory*, *The Philosophical Foundation of Property Rights* and *Marx: A Radical Critique*. He is also joint editor of the *Journal of Applied Philosophy*.

Maudemarie Clark is Professor of Philosophy at the University of California–Riverside. She is the author of *Nietzsche on Truth and Philosophy* (1990), co-translator and -editor of Nietzsche's *On the Genealogy of Morality* (1998), and co-author of a work in progress on Nietzsche's *Beyond Good and Evil*.

Stephen R. L. Clark is Professor of Philosophy at the University of Liverpool. His most recent book is *G. K. Chesterton: Thinking Backward, Looking Forward* (2006), and his present work deals with the third-century Neoplatonist, Plotinus.

Randolph Clarke is Professor of Philosophy at Florida State University. He is the author of *Libertarian Accounts of Free Will* and of numerous articles on agency, free will and moral responsibility.

Matthew Clayton is Associate Professor of Political Theory at the University of Warwick. He works on issues concerning distributive justice and liberal political thought. His recent work includes *Justice and Legitimacy in Upbringing* (2006) and he has co-edited *The Ideal of Equality* (2002) and *Social Justice* (2004).

John Cottingham is Professor Emeritus of Philosophy at the University of Reading, Professorial Research Fellow at Heythrop College, University of London, and an Honorary Fellow of St John's College, Oxford. He is (since 1993) editor of the journal *Ratio*. His books include *The Rationalists* (1988), *Western Philosophy* (2nd edn 2007), *Philosophy and the Good Life* (1998) and *The Spiritual Dimension* (2005), and his edited collections include (with Brian Feltham) *Partiality and Impartiality* (forthcoming in 2010).

Stephen Darwall is the Andrew Downey Orrick Professor of Philosophy at Yale University. He has written broadly on the history and foundations of ethics. His books include *Impartial Reason, The British Moralists and the Internal "Ought," Philosophical Ethics, Welfare and Rational Care* and most recently *The Second-Person Standpoint: Morality, Respect, and Accountability*. With David Velleman, he is a founding co-editor of *The Philosophers' Imprint*.

Fred Feldman, University of Massachusetts at Amherst. Author of *Introductory Ethics* (1978), *Doing the Best We Can: An Essay in Informal Deontic Logic* (1986), *Confrontations with the Reaper: A Philosophical Study of the Nature and Value of Death* (1992), and *Pleasure and the Good Life: On the Nature, Varieties, and Plausibility of Hedonism* (2004).

Andrew Fisher is Lecturer in Philosophy at the University of Nottingham. His research is primarily in meta-ethics and he has published in this area. He teaches a large number of students on a wide range of subjects including meta-ethics. He is co-editor with Simon Kirchin of *Arguing about Metaethics* (Routledge, 2006).

R. G. Frey is Professor of Philosophy at Bowling Green State University and Senior Research Fellow in the Social Philosophy and Policy Center there. He is the author (and editor) of numerous books and articles in normative and applied ethics.

John Gardner is Professor of Jurisprudence and a Fellow of University College, Oxford. An occasional Visiting Professor at Yale Law School and a Bencher of the Inner Temple, he was formerly Reader in Legal Philosophy at King's College London (1996–2000). He serves on the editorial boards of the *Oxford Journal of Legal Studies, Legal Theory, Law and Philosophy, The Journal of Moral Philosophy, The Journal of Ethics and Social Philosophy, The Journal of International Criminal Justice* and *Criminal Law and Philosophy*.

Bernard Gert is Stone Professor of Intellectual and Moral Philosophy, Emeritus, Dartmouth College. He is the author of *Morality: Its Nature and Justification* (revised edn, 2005), *Common Morality: Deciding What to Do* (2004) and *Hobbes: Prince of Peace* (2010); first author of *Bioethics: A Systematic Approach* (2006), and editor of *Man and Citizen* (1972, 1991).

Michael B. Gill is Associate Professor of Philosophy at the University of Arizona. He received his PhD from the University of North Carolina at Chapel Hill and is the author of *The British Moralists on Human Nature and the Birth of Secular Ethics* (2006). He has also published numerous articles in the history of philosophy, meta-ethical theory and medical ethics.

Knud Haakonssen is Professor of Intellectual History and Director of the Sussex Centre for Intellectual History, University of Sussex. He has published extensively on early modern moral, legal and political philosophy and edits a large series of natural law works.

Vinit Haksar is a Fellow of the Royal Society of Edinburgh and an Honorary Fellow, School of Philosophy, Psychology and Language Sciences, University of Edinburgh. His publications include *Equality, Liberty and Perfectionism* (1979), *Indivisible Selves and Moral Practice* (1991) and *Rights, Communities and Disobedience: Liberalism and Gandhi* (2003).

James A. Harris is Senior Lecturer in Philosophy at the University of St Andrews. He is the author of *Of Liberty and Necessity: The Free Will Debate in Eighteenth-Century British Philosophy* (2005). He is the editor of the forthcoming *Oxford Handbook of British Philosophy in the Eighteenth Century*, and (with Aaron Garrett) of the "Enlightenment" volume of *A History of Scottish Philosophy* (general editor Gordon Graham).

Christopher Heathwood is Assistant Professor of Philosophy at the University of Colorado at Boulder. He is the author of several articles on welfare and other topics in ethics.

Thomas E. Hill Jr, Kenan Professor at University of North Carolina, Chapel Hill, is the author of *Autonomy and Self-Respect*; *Dignity and Practical Reason in Kant's Moral Theory*; *Respect, Pluralism, and Justice*; and *Human Welfare and Moral Worth*. He edited the *Blackwell Guide to Kant's Ethics* and, with Arnulf Zweig, co-edited *Kant's Groundwork for the Metaphysics of Morals*. Recent essays concern Kantian constructivism, duties to oneself, virtue, revolution, humanitarian interventions, and the treatment of criminals.

Brad Hooker is Professor of Moral Philosophy at the University of Reading. His book *Ideal Code, Real World: A Rule-Consequentialist Theory of Morality* appeared in 2000. He has published articles on intuitionism, Kantianism, particularism, human rights, desert, world hunger, impartiality, the demandingness of morality and friendship. His research monograph will be on fairness.

Tony Hope is Professor of Medical Ethics at the University of Oxford, Honorary Consultant Psychiatrist, and Fellow of St Cross College. He founded the Ethox Centre. He has carried out research in basic neuroscience, Alzheimer's disease and clinical ethics. His books include the *Oxford Handbook of Clinical Medicine* (editions 1–4); *Manage Your Mind*; *Medical Ethics and Law*; *Medical Ethics: A Very Short Introduction*; and *Empirical Ethics in Psychiatry*.

Nadeem J. Z. Hussain is an Associate Professor of Philosophy at Stanford University. He specializes in meta-ethics and the history of late nineteenth-century German philosophy. He assessed the resurgence of fictionalism in contemporary meta-ethics in "The Return of Moral Fictionalism" in *Philosophical Perspectives* (2004), and defended a fictionalist interpretation of Nietzsche in "Honest Illusion: Valuing for Nietzsche's Free Spirits," in *Nietzsche and Morality* (2007).

T. H. Irwin is Professor of Ancient Philosophy in the University of Oxford and a Fellow of Keble College. From 1975 to 2006 he taught at Cornell University. He is the author of Plato's *Gorgias* (translation and notes 1979), Aristotle's *Nicomachean Ethics* (translation and notes 1999), *Aristotle's First Principles* (1988), *Classical Thought* (1989), *Plato's Ethics* (1995) and *The Development of Ethics*, 3 vols (2007–9).

Richard Kraut is the Charles E. and Emma H. Morrison Professor in the Humanities at Northwestern University. He is the author of *Socrates and the State* and *How to Read Plato*, and has edited *the Cambridge Companion to Plato* and *Plato's Republic: Critical Essays*.

Rahul Kumar is an Associate Professor of Philosophy at Queen's University, Canada. He is a co-editor of *Reasons and Recognition: Essays on the Philosophy of T. M. Scanlon* and is the author of several papers on Scanlonian contractualism.

James Laidlaw is a Fellow of King's College, Cambridge, and a University Le cturer in the Department of Social Anthropology, University of Cambridge. He has conducted research in India, Inner Mongolia and Taiwan. His publications include *Riches and Renunciation* (1995); a two-volume collection of the writings of the social anthropologist Edmund Leach, *The Essential Edmund Leach* (2001); and two collections, both jointly edited with Harvey Whitehouse: *Ritual and Memory* (2004) and *Religion, Anthropology, and Cognitive Science* (2007).

Michael LeBuffe is Assistant Professor at Texas A&M University. His recent work includes "Spinoza's Normative Ethics," in *Canadian Journal of Philosophy* (2007), and "The Anatomy of the Passions," in the *Cambridge Companion to Spinoza's Ethics* (forthcoming).

Anthony J. Lisska, Maria Theresa Barney Professor of Philosophy at Denison University, has published *Aquinas's Theory of Natural Law* and essays and reviews on natural law. Past President of the American Catholic Philosophical Association, he received the Carnegie National Professor of the Year award.

A. A. Long is Professor of Classics, Irving Stone Professor of Literature, and affiliated Professor of Philosophy at the University of California, Berkeley. He is author and editor of many books on ancient philosophy, including most recently *Epictetus: A Stoic and Socratic Guide to Life* and *From Epicurus to Epictetus: Studies in Hellenistic and Roman Philosophy*.

Norva Y. S. Lo is Lecturer in Philosophy at La Trobe University, Melbourne, Australia, having previously worked at the University of Hong Kong and the Chinese University of Hong Kong.

Mary Kate McGowan is Class of 1966 Associate Professor of Philosophy at Wellesley College. She has published in metaphysics, philosophy of language, philosophy of law and analytic feminism and she is especially interested in free speech issues in their intersection.

Sean McKeever is Assistant Professor of Philosophy at Davidson College, North Carolina. He is interested in contemporary moral theory, the history of ethics and political philosophy. He is the author, with Michael Ridge, of *Principled Ethics: Generalism as a Regulative Ideal* (2006), which critiques moral particularism while developing and defending a generalist alternative.

Alexander Miller is Professor of Philosophy at the University of Birmingham. He is the author of *An Introduction to Contemporary Metaethics* (2003), *Philosophy of Language* (Routledge, 2nd edn 2007) and co-editor (with Crispin Wright) of *Rule-Following and Meaning* (2002).

Tim Mulgan is Professor of Moral and Political Philosophy at the University of St Andrews. He is the author of *The Demands of Consequentialism* (2001), *Future People* (2006) and *Understanding Utilitarianism* (2007).

Stephen Mulhall is Professor of Philosophy at New College, Oxford. His current areas of research include Nietzsche, Sartre, Heidegger and Wittgenstein, the philosophy of religion, and philosophy of literature. Recent publications include *The Wounded Animal: J. M. Coetzee and the Difficulty of Reality in Literature and Philosophy* (2009) and *The Conversation of Humanity* (2007).

Thomas Pogge received his PhD from Harvard. He is Leitner Professor of Philosophy and International Affairs at Yale University, Professorial Fellow at the Australian National University's Centre for Applied Philosophy and Public Ethics, Research Director at the Oslo University Centre for the Study of Mind in Nature, and Adjunct Professor at the Faculty of Health and Social Care of the University of Central Lancashire.

Jesse Prinz is Distinguished Professor of Philosophy at the City University of New York Graduate Center. His research areas are philosophy of psychology, philosophy of mind, aesthetics, consciousness and cognitive science. His books include *The Emotional Construction of Morals* (2007), *Gut Reactions: A Perceptual Theory of Emotion* (2004) and *Furnishing the Mind: Concepts and Their Perceptual Basis* (2002).

Peter Railton is John Stephenson Perrin Professor of Philosophy at the University of Michigan, Ann Arbor. His main research has been in ethics and the philosophy of science, focusing especially on questions about the nature of objectivity, value, norms and explanation. A collection of some of his papers in ethics and meta-ethics, *Facts, Values, and Norms*, was published in 2003.

Andrews Reath is Professor of Philosophy at the University of California, Riverside. He has worked extensively on Kant's moral philosophy and is author of *Agency and Autonomy in Kant's Moral Theory* (2006). He has co-edited two anthologies: with Barbara Herman and Christine Korsgaard, *Reclaiming the History of Ethics: Essays for John Rawls* (1997); and with Jens Timmermann, *A Critical Guide to Kant's Critique of Practical Reason* (2010).

Michael Ridge is Professor of Moral Philosophy at the University of Edinburgh. His main research is in moral and political philosophy, though he also has substantial research interests in action theory, the philosophy of mind and the history of philosophy. He is the author, with Sean McKeever, of *Principled Ethics: Generalism as a Regulative Ideal* (2006).

Simon Robertson is a Postdoctoral Research Fellow working on the Nietzsche and Modern Moral Philosophy project at the University of Southampton. His main research interests lie at the intersection of normative ethics, meta-ethics and practical reason.

David Rodin is Senior Research Fellow at the University of Oxford, where he co-directs the Oxford Institute for Ethics, Law and Armed Conflict, and Senior Fellow at the Carnegie Council for Ethic and International Affairs in New York. His publications include *War and Self-Defense* (2002), which was awarded the American Philosophical Association Sharp Prize, as well as of articles in leading philosophy and law journals and a number of edited books, including *Preemption* (2007) and *Just and Unjust Warriors* (2008).

Frederick Rosen is Professor Emeritus of the History of Political Thought and Honorary Research Fellow at the Bentham Project, University College London. He was formerly Director of the Bentham Project and General Editor of *The Collected Works of Jeremy Bentham*. He is currently writing a book on the moral and political philosophy of John Stuart Mill.

Michael Ruse is Lucyle T. Werkmeister Professor of Philosophy at Florida State University. He is the author of many books on the history and philosophy of science, including *Monad to Man: The Concept of Progress in Evolutionary Biology*, *Can a Darwinian be a Christian? The Relationship between Science and Religion* and most recently *Science and Spirituality: Making Room for Faith in the Age of Science*.

Alan J. Ryan was Warden of New College, Oxford, from 1996 to 2009. He is currently a Visiting Scholar at Princeton University. Professor Ryan has written extensively on liberalism and its history, on theories of property, and on issues in the philosophy of the social sciences; among his books are *Liberal Anxieties and Liberal Education* (1998), *John Dewey and the High Tide of American Liberalism* (1995) and *Russell: A Political Life* (2003).

Julian Savulescu is Uehiro Chair in Practical Ethics and Director of the Oxford Uehiro Centre for Practical Ethics at the University of Oxford. He is also Director of the Oxford Centre for Neuroethics and of the Program on the Ethics of the New Biosciences at the University of Oxford. Professor Savulescu is the author of over 200 publications and has given more than 100 international presentations.

Geoffrey Scarre is Professor of Philosophy at Durham University, UK, where he teaches and researches mainly in the areas of moral theory and applied ethics. He has recently published books on death and on Mill's *On Liberty*; his most recent book is *On Courage* (Routledge, forthcoming in 2010).

Henry Shue is Senior Research Fellow at Merton College, Oxford, and Professor of Politics and International Relations. His research has focused on the role of human rights, especially economic rights, in international affairs, and, more generally, on institutions to protect the vulnerable. He is best known for his book on international distributive justice, *Basic Rights*.

John Skorupski is Professor of Moral Philosophy at the University of St Andrews. His books include *John Stuart Mill* (Routledge, 1989), *Ethical Explorations* (1999) and *The Domain of Reasons* (forthcoming in 2010).

Michael Slote is UST Professor of Ethics at the University of Miami. He has recently been working at the intersection of virtue ethics, care ethics and moral sentimentalist thought, and has just published three books: *Moral Sentimentalism* (an account of normative ethics and meta-ethics in sentimentalist terms); *Essays on the History of Ethics* (containing discussions of both ancient and modern views); and *Selected Essays* (a collection of published articles and some new papers).

Craig Smith is Lecturer in Philosophy at the University of St Andrews. He is the author of *Adam Smith's Political Philosophy: The Invisible Hand and Spontaneous Order* (Routledge, 2006), and is book review editor of the *Adam Smith Review*.

Robert Stecker is Professor of Philosophy at Central Michigan University. He is the author of *Artworks: Definition, Meaning, Value*; *Interpretation and Construction: Art, Speech and the Law*; and *Aesthetics and the Philosophy of Art: An Introduction*.

Philip Stratton-Lake is Professor of Philosophy at the University of Reading. His main research interests are Kant, ethical intuitionism, meta-ethics and normative ethics. His book *Kant, Duty and Moral Worth* was published by Routledge in 2000.

Nicholas L. Sturgeon is a Professor of Philosophy at Cornell University. He has published a number of articles on foundational issues in meta-ethics and on the history of modern moral philosophy.

John Tasioulas is Reader in Moral and Legal Philosophy at the University of Oxford and Fellow of Corpus Christi College, Oxford. His research interests are in moral philosophy, legal philosophy, and political philosophy. He is currently engaged in a project on the philosophy of human rights funded by a British Academic Research Development Award.

Christopher Taylor is Emeritus Professor of Philosophy, Oxford University, and an Emeritus Fellow of Corpus Christi College, Oxford.

Suzanne Uniacke is Reader in Applied Ethics at the University of Hull. Before moving to the United Kingdom in 2001 she taught philosophy in Australia. She has published widely in normative moral theory, applied ethics and philosophy of law.

Jonathan Webber is a lecturer in Philosophy at Cardiff University. He is the author of *The Existentialism of Jean-Paul Sartre* (Routledge, 2009), and numerous philosophical articles on moral psychology and applied ethics.

Henry R. West is Professor of Philosophy at Macalester College, Saint Paul, Minnesota. His publications on Mill include *An Introduction to Mill's Utilitarian Ethics* (2004), *The Blackwell Guide to Mill's* Utilitarianism (2006) and *Mill's* Utilitarianism: *A Reader's Guide* (2007).

Kenneth R. Westphal is Professor of Philosophy at the University of Kent, Canterbury. He has published widely on both Kant's and Hegel's theoretical and practical philosophies, in both systematic and historical perspective. He edited *The Blackwell Guide to Hegel's Phenomenology of Spirit* (2009).

Allen W. Wood is Ward W. and Priscilla B. Woods Professor at Stanford University. He has also been on the faculty of Cornell University and Yale University, has held visiting appointments at the University of Michigan and the University of California, San Diego, and has held fellowships from the Guggenheim Foundation and the National Endowment for the Humanities. He is author and editor of numerous books and author of numerous articles, chiefly on topics in ethics and on the philosophy of Kant, Fichte, Hegel and Marx.

Yang Xiao is Associate Professor of Philosophy at Kenyon College, USA. He has published essays on Confucian moral psychology, philosophy of language in early Chinese texts and Chinese political philosophy. He is currently working on a book manuscript on early Chinese ethics.

Michael J. Zimmerman is Professor of Philosophy at the University of North Carolina at Greensboro. He is the author of both books and articles on the conceptual foundations of human action, moral responsibility, moral obligation and intrinsic value.

PREFACE

A companion to ethics should be a companion for two kinds of inquirers. The first consists, of course, of students and teachers of philosophy. The second comprises a much wider group – anyone who is interested in the state of philosophical ethics today, and the history of how we got to where we are.

Philosophical ethics is only a small part of the general ethical discussion that goes on in any society at any time. However, it can and should make a vital contribution to that wider discussion. Furthermore this is especially true in the case of ethics, for various reasons that do not apply, or do not apply as much, to other parts of philosophy. To be sure, some cogent philosophical questions about ethics are quite abstract, and cannot so easily be made accessible to wider ethical discussion. Philosophy does, after all, have an obligation to follow wherever its questions lead. A comprehensive companion to ethics should try to convey what is currently being said about such questions. Yet it should also, as one of its main aims, engage with the wider discussion, and be as helpful as possible to anyone seriously interested in ethical questions – across all their width and depth. In designing the structure and content of this *Companion* we have tried hard to keep these aims in mind.

I should mention that we have in the end been unable to obtain two chapters that we would very much like to have had: in Part I, on medieval ethics, and in Part VI, on ethical questions about the beginning of life. We regret this and hope to include chapters on these topics in future editions.

My personal thanks must go in the first place to our authors, for their patience and diligence. Apart from anything else, I have learnt an enormous amount about ethics and its history from their work. Tony Bruce at Routledge suggested the idea of a *Companion* to Ethics to me, and has been truly helpful and encouraging throughout. I am also very grateful to Adam Johnson and James Thomas for their editorial efficiency and hard work. Finally, my thanks to Roger Crisp, Andrew Fisher and two anonymous readers for Routledge for their sensible advice on my initial ideas about the shape that this *Companion* should have.

John Skorupski
St Andrews

Part I
HISTORY

1
ETHICAL THOUGHT IN CHINA

Yang Xiao

Chinese ethical thought has a long history; it goes back to the time of Confucius (551–479 BCE), which was around the time of Socrates (469–399 BCE). In a brief chapter like this, it is obviously impossible to do justice to the richness, complexity, and heterogeneity of such a long tradition. Instead of trying to cover all the aspects of it, I focus on the early period (551–221 BCE), which is the founding era of Chinese philosophy. More specifically, I focus on the four main schools of thought and their founding texts: Confucianism (the *Analects*, the *Mencius*, and the *Xunzi*), Mohism (the *Mozi*), Daoism (the *Daodejing* and the *Zhuangzi*), and Legalism (the *Book of Lord Shang*). There are two reasons for this choice. First, Chinese philosophers from later periods often had to present their own thoughts in the guise of commentaries on these founding texts; they spoke about them as well as through them. Second, this choice reflects the fact that early China is still the most scrutinized period of the history of Chinese philosophy by scholars in the English-speaking world, and that most of the important texts from this period have been translated into English.

It must be borne in mind that the early period lasted for about 300 years, which may still be too long for such a brief chapter to cover. My goal is not to provide an encyclopedic coverage or standard chronological account of ethical thought in early China. Rather, I want to identify important and revealing common features and themes of the content, style, and structure of ethical thought in this period that have reverberated throughout the history of Chinese philosophy, and have uniquely defined and characterized the tradition as a whole. In other words, this will not be a historian's, but rather a philosopher's, take on the history of Chinese ethical thought.

In this chapter I use terms such as "Chinese philosophy," "Chinese philosophers," and "Chinese ethics," which some scholars may find problematic. There has been an ongoing debate about whether there is "Chinese philosophy" (Defoort 2001 and 2006). Some scholars have argued that Confucianism is not a "philosophy" (Eno 1990), that there is no such thing as "Chinese ethics" (Mollgaard 2005), and that

Confucius is not a "philosopher of ethics" and has no "normative ethical theory" (Hansen 1992). This is obviously a complicated issue. The reality is that in China we can find both normative ethical *theory* and ethical *practices* such as self-cultivation through spiritual exercise. In what follows, I first address the unique problem of style in Chinese ethics; I then discuss the structure of the normative ethical theories of the four main schools of thought. I end with a discussion of the idea of philosophy as spiritual exercise, as well as a brief conclusion.

The problem of style in Chinese ethical thought

One main reason that Chinese philosophical texts are difficult to understand is our unfamiliarity with their styles. For example, when a contemporary reader picks up a copy of the *Analects*, she might find it very easy to understand the literal meaning of Confucius' short, aphorism-like utterances; however, she might still be baffled because she does not know what Confucius is doing with his utterances.

In his theory of interpretation, Davidson argues that an utterance always has at least three dimensions. Besides its "literal meaning," which is given by a truth-conditional semantics, it also has its "force" (what the speaker is doing with it, whether the speaker intends it to be an assertion, a joke, a warning, an instruction, and so on), as well as its "ulterior non-linguistic purpose" (why the speaker is saying what he says, what effects the speaker wants to have on what audience, and so on) (Davidson 1984a, b, 1993). We may say that the literal meaning is the "content" of an utterance, and the force and purpose are the "style" of the utterance. This theory might help us understand that whenever we do not understand an early Chinese text it is often not because the author is an "oriental mystic," but rather because we do not know enough about the historical background to understand what the author is trying to do. We as scholars often misunderstand Chinese philosophers because of our projected expectations about what they must have been trying to accomplish; as Bernard Williams puts it, "a stylistic problem in the deepest sense of 'style' … is to discover what you are really trying to do" (Williams 1993: xviii–xix).

We now know a great deal about the historical background of early Chinese philosophy (Hsu 1965; Lewis 1990; Pines 2002; Lloyd and Sivin 2002; von Falkenhausen 2006); the most important aspect might be that the early philosophers were primarily trying to solve practical problems in the real world that seemed to be governed only by force and violence. To get a concrete sense of how extremely violent their time was, here are some revealing statistics. Confucius, the most important Confucian philosopher, lived around the end of the Spring and Autumn period (722–464 BCE); during the 258 years of the period, there were 1,219 wars, with only 38 peaceful years in between (Hsu 1965: 66). All of the other philosophers discussed in this chapter lived during the Warring

States period that lasted for 242 years (463–221 BCE), during which there had been 474 wars, and only 89 peaceful years (Hsu 1965: 64; also see Lewis 1990). Although there were fewer wars during the Warring States period, they were much longer and intense, and with much higher casualties. As we shall see, this fact has an important impact on how the early Chinese philosophers construct their ethical theories.

However, this turbulent time was also the golden years of early Chinese philosophy. Confucian philosophers such as Confucius, Mencius and Xunzi, the philosopher Mozi (the founder of Mohism), Daoist philosophers such as Laozi and Zhuangzi, and Legalist philosophers such as Shen Buhai, Shang Yang, Shen Dao, and Hanfeizi all lived through great political uncertainties and the brutalities of warfare, and their philosophies, especially their ethics, were profoundly shaped by this shared experience. We can find passages in these thinkers' work that show how they were traumatized by the wars and the sufferings of the people, and it should not come as a surprise that almost all of them saw themselves as "political agents and social reformers" (von Falkenhausen 2006: 11). They traveled from state to state, seeking positions with rulers, such as political advisers, strategists, and, ideally, high-ranking officials. One of the central problems they were obsessed with was the following: What must be done in order to bring peace, order, stability, and unity to the chaotic and violent world? Their solution to the practical problems of their time is a whole package, in which individual, familial, social, economic, political, legal, and moral factors were seamlessly interwoven. In fact, they did not have a distinction between ethics and politics, as we do today. They seemed to take for granted that questions about how one ought to act, feel, and live cannot be answered without addressing questions about what a good society ought to be like. This is why the terms "ethics" and "moral philosophy" should be understood in their broadest sense in this chapter, which includes "political philosophy" as well as "legal philosophy."

The structure of Chinese ethical theories

There are various ways to characterize the structure of an ethical theory. It seems that one way to characterize Chinese ethical theories is to articulate at least three components:

(a) A part that deals with a theory of the good or teleology which indicates what goals or ends one ought to pursue, as well as ideals one ought to imitate or actualize (Skorupski 1999).
(b) A part that provides an account of the factors that determine the moral status of an action (or a policy, an institution, a practice, etc.). They are roughly what Shelly Kagan calls "evaluational factors" or "normative factors" (Kagan 1998). For instance, if one takes the consequences of an action

as the only normative factor to determine its moral status, one would be a "factoral consequentialist."

(c) A part that gives justifications for its normative claims. It often involves a theory of the good, a theory of agency and practical reasoning, or a theory of human nature. This part consists of the "foundation" of an ethical theory (Kagan 1998). It can be read as addressing what Christine Korsgaard calls the "normative question" (Korsgaard 1996). For instance, if one justifies a policy (an action, an institution) by arguing that it is the best or necessary means to the realization of an ideal society, one would be a "foundational consequentialist."

In the next four sections, I discuss the ethical theory of each of the four schools of thought according to the following sequence. First, I discuss (a) its theory of the good on the level of the state, as well as on the level of the individual. Second, I discuss (b) its account of normative factors. Third, I discuss (c) how it justifies its normative claims.

More specifically, when I discuss (b), I pay attention to two issues: First, how it defines virtuous actions, whether it is "evaluational internalist" or "evaluational externalist" (Driver 2001: 68) – that is, whether a virtuous action is defined in terms of factors internal to the agent, such as belief, intention, desire, emotion, and disposition (hence an internalist), or in terms of factors external to the agent, such as the consequence (hence an externalist). We shall use "internalism" as a shorthand for "evaluational internalism" in the rest of this chapter; one should not confuse it with a very different view also labeled "internalism," which can be found in the debate regarding whether reason for action must be internal or not. Second, I shall pay special attention to the issue of whether an ethical theory is "deontological" in the sense that it regards "constraints" (the moral barriers to the promotion of the good) as an evaluational factor (Kagan 1998).

Confucian ethical theory

Let us start with Confucianism (Schwartz 1985: 56–134, 255–320; Graham 1989: 9–33, 107–32, 235–67). The Confucians, most famously Confucius (551–479 BCE) (Van Norden 2002), Mencius (385–312 BCE) (Shun 1997; Liu and Ivanhoe 2002), and Xunzi (310–219 BCE) (Klein and Ivanhoe 2000), have a theory of the good on the level of the state, as well as the level of the individual. With regard to the state, they believe that it is important for a state to have external goods, such as being orderly, prosperous, having an extensive territory, and a vast population. However, the Confucians believe that an ideal state must have "moral character" in the sense that the state should have no other end than the perfection of human relationships and the cultivation of virtues of the individual, and that the morality of the state must be the same as the morality of the individual. This is arguably the most important feature of Confucian ethics, which the Legalists such as Hanfei would eventually reject by arguing that private and public morality ought to be different, and that Confucian virtues could actually be public vices. The Confucian ideal society that everyone ought to pursue should have at least the following moral characteristics:

(1) Every one follows social rules and rituals (*li*) that govern every aspect of life in the ideal society (*Analects* 1.15, 6.27, 8.2, see Lau 1998; *Xunzi* 10.13, see Knoblock 1988).
(2) Everyone in the ideal society has social roles and practical identities that come with special obligations; for instance, a son must have filial piety (*xiao*) towards his father (*Analects* 1.2, 1.11, 2.5–8, 13.18, 17.21), an official must have loyalty (*zhong*) towards his or her ruler (3.19), and a ruler must have benevolence (*ren*) towards his or her people (*Mencius* 1A4, 1A7, 1B5, see Lau 2005; *Xunzi* 10.13). A *junzi* (virtuous person, or gentleman scholar-official) must have a comprehensive set of virtues, such as *ren* (humanity, benevolence, or empathy), *yi* (justice, righteousness), *li* (social rules and rituals internalized as deep dispositions), *zhi* (practical wisdom), *xin* (trust), *yong* (courage), and *shu* (reciprocity, or the golden rule internalized as a deep disposition).
(3) "Benevolent politics" (*ren-zheng*) is practiced when the state adopts just and benevolent policies regarding the distribution of external goods, as well as policies that may be characterized as "universal altruism" in the sense that a virtuous person cares about everyone in the world, including both those who are near and dear and those who are strangers, especially the weak and the poor (*Mencius* 1A4, 1A7, 1B5).
(4) "Virtue-based politics" is practiced when the ruler wins the allegiance and trust of the people not through laws or coercion, but through the transformative power of virtuous actions (*Analects* 2.1, 2.19, 2.20, 12.7, 12.17, 12.18, 12.19, 13.4, 13.6, 12.18, 14.41; *Mencius* 2A3, 3A2, 4A20, 7A12–14).
(5) The unification of the various states in China is not achieved through force and violence, but through the transformative power of virtue (*Mencius* 2A3; 4B16, 7B13, 7B32; *Xunzi* 9.9, 9.19a, 10.13, 18.2).

The central idea here is that it is not enough for a state to be strong and prosperous; it must have moral character, such as justice and benevolence – virtues intimately connected with politics. I shall use the term "virtue politics" (*de-zheng*) in a broad sense to refer to the Confucian ethical-political program as a whole.

On the level of the individual, the Confucians also have a theory of external goods. The external goods include wealth, power, fame, and worldly success. They claim that these external goods are not under one's control, but rather are allotted by fate or Heaven, and they have no intrinsic value, hence one should not be concerned with them (*Analects* 12.5, 14.35; *Mencius* 1B14, 5A6, 5A8, 6A16–17, 7A3, 7A42, 7B24). Furthermore, one's actions should not be motivated by the desire to obtain these external goods (*Analects* 2.18, 15.32, 19.7, 15.32). In sharp contrast to external goods, "virtue," "will," and "true happiness" are not subject to luck, and are under the agent's control (*Analects* 7.30, 9.31, 9.26, 6.11). Virtuous persons take pleasure in doing virtuous actions, even when they live in poverty (*Analects* 6.11).

In general, the Confucians are "internalists" in the sense that they define virtuous actions in terms of factors internal to the agent, such as the agent's intentions, motives, emotions, or deep dispositions, rather than defining them in terms of factors external to the agent, such as external goods or consequences. Among all the Confucians, Mencius might be the most persistent advocate for an internalist definition of virtuous actions. For example, in Mencius, we find an "expressivist" definition of benevolent actions, which is that an action is benevolent if it is a natural and spontaneous expression of one's deep dispositions of compassion for the people (Xiao 2006b). The deep disposition of compassion is what Mencius calls the "heart that cannot bear to see the suffering of others" (2A6):

> The reason why I say that everyone has the heart that cannot bear to see the suffering of others is as follows. Suppose someone suddenly sees a child who is about to fall into a well. Everyone in such a situation would have a feeling of empathy, and it is not because one wants to get in the good graces of the parents, nor because one wants to gain fame among one's neighbors and friends, nor because one dislikes the sound of the child's cry.
>
> (*Mencius* 2A6; see Lau 2005; translation modified)

Mencius believes that this "heart" is innate and universal, and it is what distinguishes a human being from a non-human animal. One might argue that Mencius' account of the virtue of *benevolence* is similar to Michael Slote's account of virtue in his agent-based sentimentalist virtue ethics (Slote 1997, 2007). However, it is not clear whether Slote's theory as a whole applies to Mencius' accounts of other virtues, such as justice, ritual propriety, and wisdom. It might be possible that, in theory, Mencius could have given an account of these virtues in terms of benevolence and empathy, as Slote has done. However, such an account seems to be missing in the *Mencius*.

The Confucians are "deontologists" in the sense that they believe in the existence of constraints on the promotion of the good. Both Mencius and Xunzi use almost the same words to emphasize the existence of such moral barriers to the promotion of the good: "if one needs to undertake an unjust action, or to kill an innocent person, in order to gain the whole world, one should not do it" (*Mencius* 2A2; *Xunzi* 11.1a). Mencius claims that the rulers who send people to die in aggressive wars or take away people's livelihood through heavy taxation are no different from those who kill an innocent person with a knife (*Mencius* 1A3, 1A4, 3B8), and that scholar-officials should not help the rulers make the state prosperous by means other than the virtue politics of benevolence (*Mencius* 4A14, 7A33).

The Confucians have at least two types of justification for their normative claims about virtue and virtue politics: (a) arguments based on a theory of human nature, and (b) pattern-based, consequentialist arguments.

The first type can be found only in the *Mencius*. It relies on what we may call Mencius' perfectionist and expressivist theory of human nature, which consists of two main ideas: (1) everyone's "human nature" (*xing*) is rooted in his or her heart–mind, which is the innate dispositions of virtues such as benevolence, justice, ritual propriety, and wisdom, and this is what distinguishes humans from non-human beasts; (2) human nature is a powerful, active, and dynamic force; it necessarily expresses itself in the social-political world. In other words, the inner nature must manifest itself in the outer (the human body as well as the social world). This is why, for Mencius, virtue politics is not just a *normative* ideal; it is also *real*, and it necessarily becomes reality in human history.

Mencius sometimes uses "*xing*" as a verb, which means to "let *xing* be the source of one's action." He claims that the sages (virtuous persons) always let *xing* be the motivational source of their virtuous actions; their virtuous actions flow spontaneously from *xing*. In other words, when human nature expresses itself as human action, it would necessarily be virtuous action.

This reconstruction of Mencius' view as an argument based on an essentialist theory of human nature is certainly not the only way to interpret the *Mencius*. In fact, some scholars have argued that Mencius does not have an essentialist theory of human nature (Ames 1991). There has been a more general debate about whether the Confucians have rational arguments based on metaphysical theories of human nature, and the debate often takes place in the context of a comparative study of Confucian and Aristotelian ethics (MacIntyre 1991, 2004a, b; Sim 2007; Yu 2007; Van Norden 2007). There has also been a debate about how to understand the concept of human nature (*xing*) in Chinese philosophy, whether it should be translated as "human nature" at all, and whether it is an innate disposition or a cultural achievement (Graham 2002; Ames 1991; Bloom 1997, 2002; Shun 1991, 1997; Liu 1996; Ivanhoe 2000; Lewis 2003; Munro 2005; Van Norden 2007).

The second type of justification, namely the pattern-based, consequentialist mode of arguments, can be found in the *Analects*, the *Mencius*, and the *Xunzi*. The most crucial premise of the argument is based on observations of patterns in social reality, from which the Confucians conclude that virtue politics is the best or necessary means to achieve the Confucian ideal society (*Analects* 2.1, 2.19, 2.20, 12.7, 12.17, 12.18, 12.19, 13.4, 13.6, 12.18, 14.41; *Mencius* 2A3, 3A2, 4A20, 7A12–14). From this premise, it follows that, if one wants to pursue the end of the Confucian ideal society, one ought to (i.e., it is instrumentally rational to) practice virtue politics. In other words, this consequentialist mode can also be labeled as an "instrumentalist" mode of argument. A good example of such a justification is the following passage from the *Mencius*: "If a ruler, equipped with a heart that cannot bear to see the suffering of others, practices a politics of compassion and empathy, he will rule the world as easily as rolling it on his palm" (2A6).

It can be shown that the pattern-based, instrumentalist mode of justification is one of the most popular among all the Chinese philosophers, even though they do not use the technical terms we have been using here, such as "the good," "means," "end," and "instrumental rationality." However, the lack of the general term does not imply the lack of the concept. Confucius, Mencius, and Xunzi were the first in China to use various concrete paradigm cases of instrumental irrationality to talk about people who desire an end, yet refuse to adopt the correct means to the end (*Mencius* 1A7B, 2A4, 4A3, 4A7, 5B7; *Xunzi* 7.5, 16.4). For instance, since Confucius did not have a general term for "rational" or "irrational," when he spoke of a case in which someone desires an end and at the same time does not want to adopt the necessary means to that end, Confucius would say that this person is just like someone who "wants to leave a house without using the door" (*Analects* 6.17).

Mohist ethical theory

Let us now turn to Mohism (Schwartz 1985: 135–72; Graham 1989: 33–64; Van Norden 2007: 139–98). Mozi (480–390 BCE), the founder of Mohism, lived sometime after the death of Confucius and before the birth of Mencius. The founding text of Mohism, the *Mozi*, is a very complex text with many layers. It was certainly not written by a single author; there are at least three sets of ideas, representing the views of three subgroups of Mohists (Graham 1989). Mohism as a school of thought was once the only rival to Confucianism, before the rise of Daoism and Legalism. But Mohism disappeared around the early years of the Han Dynasty (206 BCE to AD 220), until it was rediscovered by scholars in the Qing Dynasty (AD 1644–1911).

Like the Confucians, the Mohist notion of the ideal society is that it must have not only external goods – such as the state being orderly and prosperous (*Mozi* 126–8, see Yi-Pao Mei 1929) – but also moral character. However, their specifications of the moral character of their ideal society are not always the same. Both the Confucians and the Mohists believe in universal altruism, which is that the *scope* of a virtuous person's caring should be universal, which implies that he or she should care about not only those who are near and dear but also those who are strangers. However, they have different views about the *intensity* of the caring: for the Confucians, one should care about the near and the dear more than strangers, but the Mohists insist that one must care about everyone in the world equally and impartially. They are the first ones in China to have argued for the general obligations of "impartial caring" (*jian-ai*) (Wong 1989).

In terms of how to evaluate the moral status of actions and policies, some of the Mohists are factoral consequentialists. Unlike the internalist Confucians, who emphasize internal factors such as emotions and dispositions of the agent, some of the Mohists claim that a policy ought to be adopted if, judging from an impartial point of view, it promotes benefits for all people. Hence, unlike the Confucians, these Mohists are "externalists" in the sense that they define right actions in terms of consequences external to the agent.

Like the Confucians, some Mohists are "deontologists" in the sense that they believe in the existence of moral barriers to the promotion of the external goods. For instance, a ruler should not adopt "unjust" actions or policies such as taking the land that belongs to other states, or "cruel" actions or policies such as killing innocent people (*Mozi* 158). They claim that all aggressive wars are unjust, and that only self-defensive wars can be justified, and they believe it is their obligation to help small states to defend themselves against aggressors (*Mozi* 98–116, 128, and 257–9).

Some of the Mohists have a program for the realization of an ideal society, but their recommendation is not Confucian virtue politics. They do not consider virtue politics to be the best means to achieve their ideal society, and they are the first theorists in China to give a systematic account of how to design political institutions to guarantee peace and civil order. Unlike the Confucians, they do not believe that virtue has transformative power; instead they believe that institutions with a mechanism of reward and punishment need to be created to guarantee that there will be uniformity of opinions about justice and morality, that good deeds will be rewarded and bad ones punished, and that good and capable people will be promoted.

Some of the Mohists justify this program by appealing to their theory of human nature, which is radically different from the Mencian theory of the innate goodness of human nature. The Mohist theory is somewhat akin to a Hobbesian view, which is that human beings naturally seek rewards and avoid punishments. In their justification of the institutional solution to the practical problem of how to bring civil order to the world, the Mohists assume that people's strongest motives are their desire for reward and aversion of punishment, and they believe that people will behave rationally and morally when certain institutions with mechanisms of reward and punishment are in place.

Mohism and Confucianism are similar in terms of their belief in the existence of moral constraints, as well as their conviction that an ideal society must have moral character. As we shall see, both are in sharp disagreement with the Legalists, who deny the existence of any constraints.

Legalist ethical theory

Let us now turn to Legalism (Schwartz 1985: 321–49; Graham 1989: 267–92). Legalism as an ethical theory was not formulated and articulated systematically until Shen Buhai (d. 337 BCE), Shang Yang (d. 338 BCE), Shen Dao (ca. 350–ca. 275 BCE), and Hanfeizi (d. 233 BCE). Here I focus primarily on Shang Yang's version of

Legalism. For twenty-one years (359–338 BCE), Shang Yang was the architect of what was later known as Shang Yang's reform in the state of Qin, abolishing Confucian virtue politics (*de-zheng*) and replacing it with Legalist "punishment-based politics" (*xing-zheng*). Shang Yang was mainly responsible for having made Qin into the most powerful state among the warring states; he laid down the foundation for its eventual unification of China in 221 BCE. Although Legalism was tremendously influential as a political practice, as a school of thought it was not as widespread as Confucianism and Daoism; very few philosophers labeled themselves Legalists.

The Legalists were often powerful officials or advisers to rulers, and their theory of the good is that a ruler ought to pursue only one end, namely the external goods of the state, such as order, prosperity, dominance, and strength (*Book of Lord Shang* 199, see Duyvendak 1963). By a state being orderly, they mean that crimes should be completely abolished (203), and they do not hesitate to punish light crimes with heavy punishments, especially the death penalty. To make their state dominant, they advocate aggressive warfare at the expense of the well-being of ordinary people. In achieving such ends, the Legalists do not care whether the state has moral character, such as whether it has a just legal system.

The Legalists are "factoral consequentialists" in the sense that they determine whether an action or policy ought to be adopted by looking at whether it promotes the external goods of the state. Since what determines the Legalists' evaluation of the moral status of actions is external to the agent, they are "externalists." They deny that there are constraints on a ruler's actions; the ruler can do anything necessary to promote their goals, including adopting policies that are unjust.

The Legalists rely on a theory of human nature to justify their punishment-based politics (*xing-zheng*). The basic idea is that human beings have only two basic desires or emotions: greed and fear, which is why they like rewards and dislike punishment (*Book of Lord Shang* 241). From this Shang Yang claims that the following pattern exists: if a ruler governs by punishment, people will be fearful, and will not commit crimes, out of fear (*Book of Lord Shang* 229–30). In other words, the best means to achieve the legalist ideal society is to rely on physical force, as well as the threat of physical force.

This is in stark contrast with the Confucian belief that the best means to achieve the Confucian ideal society is through virtue, not force. Shang Yang turns the Confucian idea upside down: "Punishment produces force; force produces strength; strength produces awe; awe produces virtue. [Therefore], virtue comes from punishment" (*Book of Lord Shang* 210). And he further concludes, "In general, a wise ruler relies on force, not virtue, in his governing" (243). In the Legalists' justification, they are making two bold assumptions about human nature: first, fear is the strongest moral emotion; second, people's actions can be completely controlled by inducing fear. The Legalists also reject the Mencian idea that human beings' innate dispositions are the only source for morality.

The debate between Confucian *de-zheng* (virtue politics) and Legalist *xing-zheng* (punishment-based politics) is one of the most important and long-standing debates in the history of China, which arguably still has great relevance to the ethical and political life in China today.

Daoist ethical theory

The two main founders of Daoism (Graham 1989: 170–235; Schwartz 1985: 186–254) are Laozi (Csikszentmih and Ivanhoe 1999) and Zhuangzi (Kjellberg and Ivanhoe 1996). Unlike in the case of the Confucians, the Mohists, and the Legalists, it is still disputed by scholars today whether Laozi is a real historical figure. However, it is commonly acknowledged that Zhuangzi might have been a real figure, although we are unsure of his dates (he might have lived before Xunzi). Despite the lack of knowledge of Laozi and Zhuangzi as historical figures, the two texts that are attributed to them, the *Daodejing* and the *Zhuangzi*, have been immensely influential throughout Chinese history. They are read not only by the Daoists but also by the Confucians, and when Indian Buddhism was introduced to China, many Buddhist concepts were first translated into Daoist terms. The later development of Chinese philosophy owes much to both Daoism and Buddhism, although Confucian ideas still remain the core of the philosophical canon.

The Daoists radically disagree with everybody else's notion of the ideal society. Laozi rejects the Legalist regime in which, as Laozi puts it, "the ruler is feared." However, Laozi claims that the Confucian regime, in which "the ruler is loved and praised," is only the second best, and the best is the Daoist state where the ruler is "a shadowy presence to his subjects" (*Daodejing* Ch. 17, see Lau 1964). In other words, like the Confucians, the Daoists are opposed to the Legalists' emphasis on punishment, but they are also opposed to the Confucians' emphasis on virtues and social rules, and they ridicule the Confucians' and Legalists' obsessive aspiration to unify China.

Laozi's justification for the Daoist ideal society and its political program is pattern-based. In fact, almost every chapter of the *Daodejing* contains pattern-statements. Laozi believes that patterns in nature are the best model for understanding patterns in human affairs. Based on his observations of patterns both in society and in nature, Laozi rejects the Confucian idea about the necessity of social rules and rituals; he thinks that the best way to bring about an ideal society is through the power of moral exemplars, or "teaching without words" (*Daodejing* Chs 2, 43, 56).

Laozi's argument against the Legalists' punishment-based politics is also pattern-based. He claims that the empirical patterns actually show that fear of death does not deter people from committing crimes, as the Legalist would have us believe: "When the people do not fear death, why frighten them with death?"

(*Daodejing* Ch. 74). Laozi further says that only Heaven, which he calls "the Master Carpenter," is in charge of matters of life and death, and the state should not kill on behalf of Heaven. And this is because of the following pattern: "In chopping wood on behalf of the Master Carpenter, one seldom escapes chopping off their own hands instead" (*Daodejing* Ch. 74).

Zhuangzi is much more radical than Laozi both in terms of the style and content of his thinking. In terms of style, it is difficult to find straightforward formulations of theory and argument in the *Zhuangzi*. What one finds instead are parables and seemingly strange stories: Zhuangzi himself as a character who dances and sings at the funeral of his wife; a large fish transformed into a bird with wings covering half of the sky; a legendary bandit making fun of Confucius; abstract conceptions such as "Knowledge" becoming human characters, meeting up with the impersonation of "Do-Nothing-Say-Nothing," and so on and so forth. And all of these are told in a distinctly Zhuangzian style that is indirect, ironic, and elusive; it is almost impossible to recover argument and theory from the text. Of course, this has not stopped scholars offering systematic exegesis that assimilates it to philosophical ideas. For example, it has been suggested that Zhuangzi offers an epistemological argument against the Confucian normative claims; his argument seems to be a "sceptical" one, which is that there simply exists no neutral or objective perspective from which one can know which normative claims are valid (Kjellberg and Ivanhoe 1996). It has also been suggested that Zhuangzi is a relativist (Hansen 1992). There are certainly passages that can be easily interpreted to support all of these readings.

It can be argued that Zhuangzi also offers an ontological argument against the Confucian expressivist theory of human nature. He denies that the Confucian virtues and social rules are the expressions of human nature or the essence of humanity. We may attribute to him an anti-expressivist theory of human nature, which is that human beings have no essence or nature, and the true self is empty and without any content, form, or structure, especially not the Confucian hierarchical structure with the heart–mind as the master organ. For Zhuangzi, this is why the Confucian rituals and virtues do not *express*, but rather *cover* and *distort*, humanity (*Zhuangzi* Ch. 2).

If one does not want to attribute any epistemological or ontological theories to Zhuangzi, one may make sense of Zhuangzi by saying that he is trying to articulate a new set of values, of which abstract freedom is the most important. Instead of saying that Zhuangzi holds an ontological view that humanity is empty and without content, we may say that Zhuangzi holds a value judgment, which is that anything concrete and substantive is a limitation on freedom. Zhuang seems to be the first to have discovered what might be called "negativity" or "abstract freedom," to put it in Hegelian terms. If the Confucians could be said to have discovered that one can only become truly human and free when one participates in a concrete and determinate ethical life that consists of social institutions such as family, community, and the state, Zhuangzi could be said to have discovered abstract freedom, which is that one always has the capacity and freedom to renounce any activity, to give up any goal, or to withdraw completely from this world. Zhuangzi sees any perspective or position that has determinate contents as a restriction on one's freedom; similarly, he sees any particularization and objective determination of social life as a restriction or limitation on one's free and purposeless wandering. He instinctively wants to spread his wings and fly away from it.

It has become a cliché these days to say that Confucianism and Daoism complement each other (*ru dao hu bu*). But there is some truth to this popular saying, especially if we also add Buddhism to the mix. The essential tensions between Confucianism and Daoism, between Confucianism and Buddhism, have indeed been a major source of creativity in the history of Chinese philosophy.

Moral psychology and self-cultivation through spiritual exercise

The philosophical texts from early China can be divided into two groups: those that do, and those that do not, contain materials that deal with techniques concerning what to make of oneself, which may be called "self-cultivation," "self management," or "selfhood as creative transformation" (Nivison 1996, 1999; Ivanhoe 2000; Tu 1979, 1985). The Confucian and Daoist texts belong to the first group, and the Mohist and Legalist texts to the second. The reason why the Mohists do not emphasize self-cultivation might have something to do with the fact that they think one's belief can directly motivate actions (Nivison 1996), hence it is enough if one intellectually disapproves of bad desires. In the case of the Legalists, there is no space for self-cultivation in their thinking; they believe that the penal laws set up by the state are enough to produce the correct behaviors (Xiao 2006b).

The Confucian belief in virtue politics implies that it is crucial that one become virtuous through self-cultivation. The Confucians believe that the techniques of self-cultivation go beyond inner mental operation. They involve all aspects of a person's being: intellect, sensibility, imagination, will, as well as the body as a whole. It is in this sense that self-cultivation is not only "intellectual" exercise, but also "spiritual" or "material" exercise (Hadot 1995, 2002; Csikszentmih 2004; Xiao 2006a). For Confucius and Xunzi, it is through observing *li* (social rules and rituals) that one cultivates virtuous desires, and one must be guided by teachers and helped by virtuous friends along the way, hence the internalization and mastery of *li* is essentially a social process (Tu 1979, 1985; Eno 1990; Wong 2004). The goal is to internalize the social rules and rituals so that one naturally has virtuous desires. Confucius calls this process "restraining oneself with social rules and rituals" (*Analects* 6.27, 9.11), "establishing oneself through social rules and rituals" (*Analects* 8.8, 20.3), or self-discipline by submitting oneself to social rules and rituals (*keji fuli*) (*Analects* 12.1). When a student asks about how to engage in *keji fuli*, Confucius replies, "Observe the social rules and rituals in this way: Don't look at anything improper; don't listen to anything improper; don't say anything improper; don't do anything improper" (12.1). Confucius tells us that at seventy he could "follow all the desires of his heart without breaking any rules" (*Analects* 2.4), because all the rules had become constitutive of his self. As a result, all the desires that were fully his ("internal" to him) were now virtuous ones, in the sense that they were always in conformity with social rules and rituals. In other words, he had turned all the improper desires into "external" ones, and all the proper desires into "internal" ones. This is very similar to Harry Frankfurt's view that "there is something a person can do" to turn certain desires into external ones: "He places the rejected desires outside the scope of his preference, so that it is not a candidate for satisfaction at all" (Frankfurt 1988: 67; also see 159–76).

For the Daoists, since they do not make a distinction between the mind and the body, their spiritual exercises include mental as well as bodily exercises such as meditation, chanting, and breathing (Roth 1999). Many later Daoist texts focus mainly on complex techniques for the achievement of the longevity and even the immortality of the body; the early Daoist thought is often reduced to practical manuals for such purposes in later periods (Schipper 1994).

Throughout the history of Chinese philosophy, self-cultivation through spiritual exercise remains a central concern in Confucianism and Daoism, as well as in Buddhism. Partly due to the influence of Daoism and Buddhism, the Neo-Confucian philosophers in the Song Dynasty (960–1279) and Ming Dynasty (1368–1644) developed more elaborated theories, as well as richer techniques, of Confucian self-cultivation (Ivanhoe 2000 and 2002). Wang Yangming (1472–1529) (Ivanhoe 2002), the late Ming Neo-Confucian philosopher, came to reject the views of Zhu Xi (1130–1200), another Neo-Confucian philosopher, who emphasized reading as a spiritual exercise. Wang insisted that to be virtuous one only needed to rediscover what has always been there: the heart/mind that is originally good. Some of Wang's followers pushed the idea to its extreme and claimed that one did not need to engage in any book-learning and *li*-observation; spiritual exercise in the end became pure inner mental activity. Partly as a reaction to this trend, there was eventually a resurgence of the "learning of rituals and social rules" (*li-xue*), which eventually came to dominate the mainstream philosophy in the Qing Dynasty (1644–1911) (Chow 1994).

Conclusion

One of the most distinctive features of Chinese ethical theories is that they do not have a "hierarchical" structure, with the exception of Legalism. I borrow the term "hierarchical" from Julia Annas: "By hierarchical I mean that some set of notions is taken as basic, and the other elements in the theory are derived from these basic notions" (Annas 1993: 7). For instance, although Confucian and Daoist ethical theories have consequentialist justifications of their normative claims about the effective power of virtue, the good is not a basic concept from which other elements are derived. Even though they have a consequentialist justification for their virtue politics or *wu-wei* politics, Confucian and Daoist ethical theories do not define virtue in terms of its consequences.

I believe contemporary moral philosophers can benefit greatly if we take seriously the unfamiliar structure of Chinese ethical theories, for they open up possibilities of new configurations of ethical theory. For instance, the Confucians and Daoists show us that it is possible to take seriously what happens in the external world (i.e., being a consequentialist), while at the same time still defining virtue in terms of factors internal to the agent, not in terms of consequences in the external world.

Now let us compare their theories with Julia Driver's "consequentialism," which is one of the ethical theories that have a hierarchical structure. She takes the good as the basic concept, and defines the concept of virtue in terms of it: "A virtue is a character trait that produces more good (in the actual world) than not *systematically*" (2001: 82). Driver says that her externalist definition of virtue preserves "the connection between the agent and the world," and that "what happens matters to morality, and externalist preserves this intuition" (Driver 2001: 70).

The Confucians and Daoists agree with Driver that what happens in the world matters. However, they also want to preserve the internalist definition of virtue. Their solution for the tension between these two approaches is to look for systematic patterns between virtue and its consequences. This empirical approach allows them to map out the real-world configurations of virtue and consequence, and it leads to fruitful theories such as virtue politics or *wu-wei* politics. It seems plausible to regard the relation between virtue and its effect in the external world as an empirical rather than a conceptual one; the fact that virtue might *systematically* produce good consequences does not imply that their relation must be conceptual.

This chapter has provided the reader with a quick glance at Chinese ethical thought. By exploring styles of ethical theories and practices that are interestingly different from ours, combinations of ethical positions that are surprisingly innovative, as well as radical reconfigurations of familiar structures of ethical theory, I hope we have come to view the global landscape of ethical thought in a new light. To echo something Bernard Williams once said about there being too few ethical ideas in contemporary moral philosophy, we may say that "our major problem now is actually that we have not too many but too few" ethical ideas – and I might add styles and structures as well – "and we need to cherish as many as we can" (Williams 1985: 117).

See also Ethics and sentiment (Chapter 10); Hume (Chapter 11); Hegel (Chapter 15); Ethics and Law (Chapter 35); Reasons, values, and morality (Chapter 36); Consequentialism (Chapter 37); Virtue ethics (Chapter 40); Partiality and impartiality

(Chapter 52); Ideals of perfection (Chapter 55); Justice and punishment (Chapter 57); War (Chapter 67).

References

English translations of early Chinese texts

Duyvendak, J. J. L. (trans.) (1963) *The Book of Lord Shang*, Chicago, IL: The University of Chicago Press.

Knoblock, John (trans.) (1988) *The Xunzi*, Stanford, CA: Stanford University Press. (Cited by book and chapter.)

Lau, D. C. (trans.) (1964) *Tao Te Ching* [*The Daodejing*], London: Penguin Classics. (Cited by chapter.)

——(trans.) (1998) *The Analects*, London: Penguin Classics. (Cited by book and chapter.)

——(trans.) (2005) *The Mencius*, London: Penguin Classics. (Cited by book and chapter.)

Watson, Burton (trans.) (1968) *The Complete Works of Chuang Tzu* [*The Zhuangzi*], New York: Columbia University Press. (Cited by chapter.)

Yi-Pao Mei (trans.) (1929) *The Ethical and Political Works of Motse* [*The Mozi*], Westport, CT: Hyperion Press.

Secondary literature

Due to practical considerations, references to secondary literature are limited to works in English, which implies a regrettable omission of excellent works of scholarship available in Chinese, Japanese, and other languages.

Ames, R. (1991) "The Mencian Conception of Ren Xing: Does It Mean 'Human nature'?" in H. Rosemont Jr. (ed.) *Chinese Texts and Philosophical Contexts: Essays Dedicated to Angus Graham*, Chicago, IL: Open Court.

Annas, J. (1993) *The Morality of Happiness*, Oxford: Oxford University Press.

Bloom, I. (1997) "Human Nature and Biological Nature in Mencius," *Philosophy East and West* 47: 21–32.

——(2002) "Mengzian Arguments on Human nature (Ren Xing)," in Liu and Ivanhoe 2002.

Chow, K. (1994) *The Rise of Confucian Ritualism in Late Imperial China: Ethics, Classics, and Lineage Discourse*, Stanford, CA: Stanford University Press.

Csikszentmih, M. (2004) *Material Virtue: Ethics and the Body in Early China*, Leiden: Brill.

Csikszentmih, M. and Ivanhoe, P. J. (eds) (1999) *Religious and Philosophical Aspects of the Laozi*, Albany: State University of New York Press.

Davidson, D. (1984a) "Communication and Convention," *Inquiries into Truth and Interpretation*, Oxford: Oxford University Press.

——(1984b) *Expressing Evaluations*, Lindley Lecture, Lawrence: University of Kansas.

——(1993) "Locating Literary Language," in R. W. Dasenbrock (ed.) *Literary Theory after Davidson*, University Park: Pennsylvania State University Press.

Defoort, C. (2001) "Is There Such a Thing as Chinese Philosophy? Arguments of an Implicit Debate," *Philosophy East and West* 51: 393–413.

——(2006) "Is 'Chinese Philosophy' a Proper Name? A Response to Rein Raud," *Philosophy East and West* 56: 625–60.

Driver, J. (2001) *Uneasy Virtue*, Cambridge: Cambridge University Press.

Eno, R. (1990) *The Confucian Creation of Heaven: Philosophy and the Defense of Ritual Mastery*, Albany: State University of New York Press.
Frankfurt, H. (1988) *The Importance of What We Care About*, Cambridge: Cambridge University Press.
Graham, A. C. (1989) *Disputers of Tao: Philosophical Argument in Ancient China*, La Salle, IL: Open Court.
——(2002) "The Background of the Mencian Theory of Human Nature," in Liu and Ivanhoe 2002. (The essay was originally published in 1967.)
Hadot, P. (1995) *Philosophy as A Way of Life: Spiritual Exercises from Socrates to Foucault*, trans. Michael Chase, Oxford: Blackwell.
——(2002) *What Is Ancient Philosophy?* Trans. Michael Chase, Cambridge, MA: Harvard University Press.
Hansen, C. (1992) *A Daoist Theory of Chinese Thought*, Oxford: Oxford University Press.
Hsu, C. (1965) *Ancient China in Transition: An Analysis of Social Mobility, 722–222* BC, Stanford, CA: Stanford University Press.
Ivanhoe, P. J. (2000) *Confucian Moral Self Cultivation*, 2nd edn, Indianapolis, IN: Hackett.
——(2002) *Ethics in the Confucian Tradition*, 2nd edn, Indianapolis, IN: Hackett.
Kagan, S. (1998) *Normative Ethics*, Boulder, CO: Westview Press.
Kjellberg, P. and Ivanhoe, P. J. (eds) (1996) *Essays on Skepticism, Relativism, and Ethics in the Zhuangzi*, Albany: State University of New York Press.
Klein, T. C. and Ivanhoe, P. J. (eds) (2000) *Nature and Moral Agency in the Xunzi*, Indianapolis, IN: Hackett.
Korsgaard, C. (1996) *The Sources of Normativity*, Cambridge: Cambridge University Press.
Lewis, M. E. (1990) *Sanctioned Violence in Early China*, Albany: State University of New York Press.
——(2003) "Custom and Human Nature in Early China," *Philosophy East and West* 53: 308–22.
Liu, S. (1996) "Some Reflections on Mencius' Views of Mind–Heart and Human Nature," *Philosophy East and West* 46: 253–79.
Liu, X. and Ivanhoe, P. J. (eds) (2002) *Essays on the Moral Philosophy of Mengzi*, Indianapolis, IN: Hackett.
Lloyd, G. and Sivin, N. (2002) *The Way and the Word: Science and Medicine in early China and Greece*, New Haven, CT: Yale University Press.
MacIntyre, A. (1991) "Incommensurability, Truth, and the Conversation between Confucians and Aristotelians about the Virtues," in E. Deutsch (ed.) *Culture and Modernity: East–West Philosophic Perspectives*, Honolulu: University of Hawaii Press.
——(2004a) "Once More on Confucian and Aristotelian Conceptions of the Virtues," in R. R. Wang (ed.) *Chinese Philosophy in an Era of Globalization*, Albany: State University of New York Press.
——(2004b) "Questions for Confucians: Reflections on the Essays in Comparative Study of Self, Autonomy, and Community," in K. Shun and D. Wong (eds) *Confucian Ethics: A Comparative Study of Self, Autonomy, and Community*, Cambridge: Cambridge University Press.
Mollgaard, E. J. (2005) "Chinese Ethics?," in W. Schweiker (ed.) *The Blackwell Companion to Religious Ethics*, Oxford: Blackwell.
Munro, D. (2005) *A Chinese Ethics for the New Century*, Hong Kong: The Chinese University Press.
Nivison, D. (1996) *Ways of Confucianism: Investigations in Chinese Philosophy*, ed. Bryan W. Van Norden, Chicago, IL: Open Court.
——(1999) "The Classical Philosophical Writings," in M. Loewe and E. L. Shaughnessy (eds) *The Cambridge History of Ancient China*, vol. 1, Cambridge: Cambridge University Press.
Pines, Y. (2002) *Foundations of Confucian Thought: Intellectual Life in the Chunqiu Period, 722–453* BCE, Honolulu: University of Hawaii Press.
Roth, H. (1999) *Original Tao: Inward Training and the Foundations of Taoist Mysticism*, New York: Columbia University Press.

Schipper, K. (1994) *The Taoist Body*, Berkeley: University of California Press.
Schwartz, B. (1985) *The World of Thought in Ancient China*, Cambridge, MA: Harvard University Press.
Shun, K. (1991) "Mencius on *Jen-Hsing*," *Philosophy East and West* 47: 1–20.
——(1997) *Mencius and Early Chinese Thought*, Stanford, CA: Stanford University Press.
Sim, M. (2007) *Remastering Morals with Aristotle and Confucius*, Cambridge: Cambridge University Press.
Skorupski, J. (1999) *Ethical Explorations*, Oxford: Oxford University Press.
Slote, M. (1997) "Agent-Based Virtue Ethics," in C. Roger and M. Slote (eds) *Virtue Ethics*, Oxford: Oxford University Press.
——(2007) *The Ethics of Care and Empathy*, London and New York: Routledge.
Tu, W. (1979) *Humanity and Self-Cultivation*, Berkeley: University of California Press.
——(1985) *Confucian Thought: Selfhood as Creative Transformation*, Albany: State University of New York Press.
Van Norden, B. W. (ed.) (2002) *Confucius and the Analects: New Essays*, Oxford: Oxford University Press.
——(2007) *Virtue Ethics and Consequentialism in Early Chinese Philosophy*, Cambridge: Cambridge University Press.
von Falkenhausen, L. (2006) *Chinese Society in the Age of Confucius (1000–250 BC): The Archaeological Evidence*, Los Angles: Cotsen Institute of Archaeology, University of California, Los Angles.
Williams, B. (1985) *Ethics and the Limits of Philosophy*, Cambridge, MA: Harvard University Press.
——(1993) *Morality: An Introduction to Ethics*, Cambridge: Cambridge University Press.
Wong, D. (1989) "Universalism versus Love with Distinctions: An Ancient Debate Revisited," *Journal of Chinese Philosophy* 16: 251–72.
——(2004) "Relational and Autonomous Selves," *Journal of Chinese Philosophy* 31: 419–32.
Xiao, Y. (2006a) "Reading the *Analects* with Davidson: Mood, Force and Communicative Practice in Early China," in B. Mou (ed.) *Davidson's Philosophy and Chinese Philosophy: Constructive Engagement*, Leiden: Brill.
——(2006b) "When Political Philosophy Meets Moral Psychology: Expressivism in the *Mencius*," *Dao: A Journal of Comparative Philosophy* 5: 257–71.
Yu, J. (2007) *The Ethics of Confucius and Aristotle: Mirrors of Virtue*, New York and London: Routledge.

Further reading

Graham, A. C. (1989) *Disputers of Tao: Philosophical Argument in Ancient China*, La Salle, IL: Open Court. (One of the best introductions to early Chinese philosophy.)
Ivanhoe, P. J. (2002) *Confucian Moral Self Cultivation*, 2nd edn, Indianapolis, IN: Hackett. (One of the best introductions to Confucian virtue ethics and self-cultivation.)
Nivison, D. (1996) *Ways of Confucianism: Investigations in Chinese Philosophy*, ed. Bryan W. Van Norden, Chicago, IL: Open Court. (This collection has some of the most influential essays in the study of Chinese ethics in the English-speaking world since the 1980s.)
Shun, K. (1997) *Mencius and Early Chinese Thought*, Palo Alto, CA: Stanford University Press. (A close study of key concepts and arguments in the *Mencius*, with an emphasis on Mencius' ethics.)
Van Norden, B. W. (2007) *Virtue Ethics and Consequentialism in early Chinese Philosophy*, Cambridge: Cambridge University Press. (A book-length argument that Confucius and Mencius are virtue ethicists, and Mozi a consequentialist.)

2
ETHICAL THOUGHT IN INDIA

Stephen R. L. Clark

Introduction

India, as a geographical entity, incorporates Pakistan, Bangladesh, Bhutan, Nepal, Sri Lanka and the Indian Republic. Even the last includes many different states from Kashmir to Kerala, many religions, many peoples and many language-groups. Its recorded history and literature covers 3,000 years of invasion, development and revolution. Speaking of "Indian ethics" is therefore, most probably, absurd, as absurd as it is to speak of "Western ethics," as if this was the same from Gilgamesh to Harry Potter, Iceland to Iraq. The expression, "Indian ethics, " in practice, usually means "Hindu ethics," with an occasional nod towards the "heterodox schools" which denied the authority of the Vedas: Buddhists, Jains and Carvaka. Even less often it may be acknowledged that there are "tribal" groups and "untouchables" outside the Hindu order, which are still "indigenous" in a way that Islam, Judaism, Christianity, communism and "Western liberalism " are not. Even Hindu Ethics, strictly so-called, is not exactly indigenous, but our chances of disentangling the contribution of the "Aryan" invaders from earlier "Dravidian" thought and practice are minute.

The Vedas, the Upanishads, the Puranas, and the epics Ramayana and Mahabharata lie at the root of India, as Homer, the later Greek poets and philosophers, and the Bible lie at the root of Europe. They are still better known in India than the corresponding texts are known in modern Europe and its colonies, and stories from the epics are still cited in public debate to make some moral point. Studies of Hindu ethics often begin by examining, especially, the Mahabharata, the story of a fratricidal war, and the strange sermon from Krishna, an incarnate god, known as the Bhagavadgita, "the Song of God," that takes place at a crucial battle of that war. That sermon demands that we each do our duty, as defined by status, age and character, and also that we realize that our destiny, our real selves, transcend such duties. More particularly it demands that the virtuous warrior, Arjuna, brace himself to kill his kin.

If these stories lie at the root of India, so also do the gods and demons they imagine, as well as the heroes, saints and villains, slandered wives and subtly dishonest sages. To European eyes it is almost as if the creatures of Greek mythology, gods, titans, monsters, spirits and talking beasts had survived in the imagination of philosophers as well as poets and the common people. One difference is that ritual purity counts for more, and for more people, than it ever did in Greece. Modern secular examination of these practices and stories mostly emphasizes their role in maintaining social order, the divisions of age, gender, caste and sect. Modern theological examination has usually focused on the pantheist or absolutist tendencies of Indian thought, the sense that there is One presence at work in all, one Real transcending all the transient forms. Common hopes are more probably directed at deserving a good life (by living one) than at *transcending* life, though honoring – a little – those who seek, through renunciation and ascetic practice, to transcend.

Do the gods have any more role than they did in Greece so far as requiring or exemplifying moral conduct? Just as in Greece they fight off monsters, and take form as heroes to defend good order. Their requirements, to our eyes, are often ritual more than moral, and even their morality, like Krishna's, seems indifferent to transient pains and pleasures. Romantics tend to emphasize that Hindu art and ritual makes even ordinary pleasures sacred. Cynics may suppose instead that the ruling classes, in India as elsewhere, sought a state monopoly of many desirable things (including sex, via temple prostitution), and also encouraged the elderly to hand their property over to younger and more active householders by praising "renunciation." But some gods, at least, can stand for Justice, Truthfulness and Mercy, as well as Love and Wild Excitement, and the more painful delights of physical endurance. Any stable order, we may suspect, depends in the end on harnessing real emotions, ensuring that we all have something to admire and worship in authority. An order maintained entirely by the threat of violence is unstable: one in which violence is vindicated by its service to the sacred has better hope of lasting. What is intriguing about the Indian experiment in living, even before the secular Indian Republic, is that no single deity is paramount for all. Mainstream, "orthodox" theology, in its most text-oriented forms, identifies Vishnu, Shiva, Devī, Ganesha and Surya as foci of worship, and an abstract Brahman as the underlying reality which is refracted or reflected into various divine personalities. But sectarian worship of Vishnu or of Shiva individually, and family worship of whatever tribal, parochial or professional godling, is more significant. The main problem, both theoretical and political, for India is to reconcile the universalist demand associated with the "golden rule" (to treat others as we would wish ourselves to be treated) with the manifold divisions of gender, caste and personal devotion.

Castes

The first problem, that is to say, is *caste*.

The English term covers two different sorts of grouping. The original division of society dictated in the laws of Manu is into four *varnas*, "colors": Brahmins, Kshatriya, Vaishya (these three being "twice born" through birth and later initiation), and Sudra. The "colors" in question, it should be noted, are more likely those of the three *gunas*, humors (*sattva*, *rajas* and *tamas*: peace, energy and inertia) than skin-colors. Untouchables lie outside the system, and are condemned to such polluting activities as clearing up excrement or tanning leather. Mahatma Gandhi (1869–1948) attempted a redescription of the group as "Harijan," God's children. The great untouchable politician B. R. Ambedkar (1891–1956), with some justice, thought the title patronizing, and instead encouraged all Untouchables, all "Dalits" (currently the term preferred by what have also been called the "scheduled" or the "backward castes," meaning "the oppressed," and including both untouchables and some Sudra), to convert to Buddhism to escape the taint. The Constitution of the Republic, for which Ambedkar was responsible, abolished untouchability, and some Untouchables have achieved high status, politically, educationally and economically. The confusion is not entirely new. The incarnate god, Krishna, was from the Sudra, and the ruling nobility of Kerala were also defined as Sudra by northern Brahmins. But the system, though often in great confusion, still remains.

Even Gandhi, though he sought to encourage even Brahmins to take on the burden of dealing with their own excrement, offered the convenient rationalization that the *varnas* merely distinguish different sorts of person, different goals and motivations – very much as Plato and other Greeks distinguished them. Some people wish to discover a transcendent truth; others seek honor in political or military success; others seek prosperity, or are able simply to serve as laborers (these divisions, perhaps, were not at first hereditary). Other analyses, like that of Louis Dumont (1970), identify the notion of "purity" as the system's source. "Untouchables," outside the system, yet support it, being at the opposite end of a spectrum leading down from Brahminical "purity." Without their practical and symbolic association with *impurity* there could be no "pure." The issue is not only ritual: it is hardly surprising that people condemned to handle human excrement and dead bodies are barred from the society of "cleaner" castes (though the mechanisms for cleansing any impure element are not entirely medical). It may be that it is *technology* that is needed to transform the system, not merely appeals to proper human feeling.

But the "castes" which have more definite and daily reality are not the four *varnas*, but the many thousand *jāti*s, which are both kinship and – by tradition – professional groupings, to be found among Muslims, Christians and Untouchables as well as Hindus. On the one hand, membership of such a *jāti* will make it difficult to marry outside it, or to take on work belonging to a different *jāti*. On the other, it provides support to individuals, even when far from home. Such groups may move up and down the social and economic scale, and even – over many generations – between *varnas*. Those like Ambedkar or Ilaiah (see Ilaiah 2001) who have suffered oppression or contempt for their membership of a low-ranking *jāti* may understandably and justly be enraged, but at least the groupings provide some sense of fellowship and purpose that may be lacking in a more individualist society. Recognizing that people are indeed born into familial and professional groupings may sometimes have some merits: any more *egalitarian* society may, in practical fact, be imposing the values and inhibitions of one historically dominant group on all. In Britain, for example, it has been said that "middle-class values" (of educational attainment, deferred gratification, individual choice) may not be shared at all by the poorer classes (who have good reason to doubt that "education" does them any good or that there is a point in putting off attainable enjoyments, and value family solidarity far more). And British imperial sentiment, which allowed the existence of many differing cultures (as long as all admitted that the British were on top), may have, in a way, been less oppressive than French imperial sentiment (which sought to turn everyone else into good French citizens). Egalitarian or meritocratic individualism, in short, is not necessarily the best or only answer to the human problem. Established castes, clans, classes and professions embody a plurality of values, a diversity of practice and opinion that may really be humane.

Or at any rate such a diversity of castes, clans, classes and professions is a human possibility that has been realized in many times and places. Doing one's best in the station that God or Nature has assigned may sometimes be the best policy – unless the particular system of such stations is maintained chiefly by contempt and the threat of violence against those who step out of line (which is, unfortunately, still the case in many parts of the world, not only India).

Kāma, artha, dharma

It is common Indian doctrine that there are four broad human goals: sensual pleasure, public success, morality – and "freedom." Something very like the first three goals (or maybe the first two and an amalgam of morality and freedom) were also the standard ways of life in Greek common sense. The question for modern European moralists has usually been whether the third goal, morality, takes precedence over the others. More ancient European moralists have been readier to acknowledge that it is the fourth which must take precedence, agreeing in this with most Hindu sages. I shall address the issue in the next section. It is first necessary to consider the first three, *kāma*, *artha*, *dharma*, and consider whether *dharma* is indeed equivalent to morals.

That most of us desire or are glad to enjoy both sensual pleasure and success is obvious and expectable. That any of us desire, really, to be "moral" or "just" is more contentious. Morality, often enough, has been defended simply as a second best: all of us would really prefer to do and enjoy exactly what we want (whatever that is) regardless of our station or the needs of others. Unfortunately, in this age of the world, at least, no more than a handful of the very rich or very powerful (if they) can have this comfort – and they must live in fear of dispossession. Better treat others as we would ourselves be treated, since we can rarely count on any special luck or talent. From this we can infer at least a handful of universal virtues: kindness, honesty, common prudence. Maybe we can go a little further. Richard Lannoy summarizes the "three essential moral predicates" as *dāna*, "to give others their due"; *daya*, "to sympathize with one's fellow creatures'; *dama*, "to restrain one's passions" (Lannoy 1971: 295). At the very least, let us do no harm (*ahimsa*). It does not follow that we will do others very much good: there is a limit to the costs we'll bear in order to be beneficent. But each of us may have to take on some responsibilities: it is expected of us. And each of us may have to acknowledge "rights of property" (though these may not be individual rights), defining what is "ours" or "theirs."

These other rights and responsibilities aren't universal. Whatever our station, status and profession we will have particular duties. So our duty, *dharma*, isn't only to do what is required of *everyone*, but rather what is required of *us*. Perhaps we're warrior aristocrats, like Homer's heroes, who have been given honor and support by all our tribe and must, in honor, now fight bravely. Arjuna, appalled at the prospect of his slaughtering kin, for a moment seeks to withdraw, surrender, give the Kauravas the throne – and is advised by the incarnate God to do his duty. This is the price of sovereignty, that he cannot do just what he pleases, even if his pleasure is in peace. But not everyone is a warrior aristocrat, nor adult, nor a male. Our duties, our *dharma*, are individual, or rather, depend on the many functions we fulfill. This doctrine too is not so distant from the old European model: the virtue of good women is not that of good men, even if the same words are employed. Good servants don't make good masters; good warriors aren't good scholars (or at any rate, if they are, it is because they have more virtues than their kind requires).

Schematically, Hindu ethics identifies four stages of virtue: student, householder, "forest-dweller" (who can keep their spouses) and renouncer (though whether all good Hindus really go through the foursome may be doubted). What we are required to do will differ with our time of life, as well as with our gender and our station. None of us should do harm: we should not steal or cheat or injure others. But what counts as theft or injury or wrongful death depends again on what each agent and patient of the action is, and their particular *dharma*. We should not positively lie, perhaps, but not everyone deserves to be told the truth, and neither is it everyone's job to tell it. Famously, the sage Kausika who told the truth to brigands (and so doomed their victims) is condemned to hell.

These moral duties, universal and particular, are grounded (maybe) in our shared desires for peace and plenty: we cannot afford to be "self-seeking" and neglectful of the rightful claims of others. The gain is not only social. Áyurvedic medicine "advocates a code of conduct that includes respect for elders, holding to the truth, 'nonviolence, avoiding anger, avoiding indulgence in alcohol, sex, excessive labor, keeping peaceful', humble, kind, studious, self-restrained, sensitive to weather and balanced sleep" (Crawford 2003: 82, after the Caraka Samhita [third century BC], the oldest of the Áyurvedic texts), and thereby enjoying a long and happy life. But most moralists, in Europe as in India, will also identify "right conduct" as correct whether or not we can gain peace or plenty from it. There are things we must do, whether all of us or only some, even if they cost us, even if they cost us all. There are things we have no right to do, even if we could, in a way, do so quite safely. Only the really honest *merit* heaven – a claim which does not depend on there really being a heaven to be personally enjoyed. Heroes and saints "go to heaven" at least in the same sense that they may be written into the constellations or the history books as worthy exemplars of virtue. They are to be admired no matter what. Indeed, they are to be admired even for their good intentions, their good characters, even if the actual outcome isn't what we hoped. The father who dives into a stormy sea to save his child is no less to be honored if he "fails" (at least as long as it was not his own incompetence that caused it). This thought, of course, becomes a paradox: how can we do what we do merely as our duty, without caring about its fruits, its outcome, when our duty is exactly to intend, as much as we can, one outcome. The father who doesn't *care* whether he saves his child will likely not jump in – and if he jumps the action is perverse! The answer perhaps is that he is to act without the thought of himself as acting well: to be absorbed in saving.

Roy Perrett, commenting on this advice (it is the incarnate God's to Arjuna) in his *Hindu Ethics* (1998), interprets the suggestion merely to say that we should not form habits, even virtuous habits, nor judge what we do as either good or bad. The father jumps as his fatherliness demands, but without a moral judgement that he is doing right, that this is the desire he *ought* to have. The Greek skeptics had a similar recipe, abandoning moral or epistemic judgement and doing all and only what they felt called to do. They were seeking, in this, the same serenity that other philosophers found by dogma. But Krishna's advice has a dogmatic background: the slaughter does not matter in the end, because *souls* live forever. We must play our parts, but be no more affected by them (no less affected by them) than by any drama where we play the hero or the villain or the victim. That consolation may also serve to support us when we ourselves, or we our ordinarily waking selves, *are* victims. But in that case how is morality a serious matter? Why is it wrong to do another harm, if no one really is ever harmed by what we do?

Moksha, Kārma, reincarnation

Moksha is liberation from the pains and duties of this mortal life. Whereas the goal of modern European ethics (or so it is often supposed) must be to "make the world a better place," or at least (more commonsensically) not to harm others and to alleviate whatever ills we can, the ultimate goal of Indian ethics (or Hindu, Jain and Buddhist, at the least) is to escape the world. For this reason anyone may expect to withdraw from social and familial duties once these have been completed, and some will dedicate themselves to fierce ascetic practices which both exalt the imagination and cut off all ordinary fulfilments. Even the ordinary civil life is best at least in part because we are not then slaves of passion. The point of morals is to *purify* (as Plotinus also taught).

Sociologically or psychologically, *moksha* is the cutting of all ties. Philosophically, it is liberation from the cycle of birth and death. In that cycle all pleasures are transient, and have their disappointments and their painful costs; all achievements are also transient, and trivial when viewed against the backdrop of the ages. Europeans tend to inhabit only a brief history: even the educated rarely think much further back than the third millennium BC (except when thinking of the long prehuman ages), and one of the scandals of the seventeenth century, long preceding the revelations of geology, was that *Indian* records spoke of tens or hundreds of millennia of the human past, in which the "present day" lost its significance. Ancient European philosophers had generally supposed, like those of India, that that past was infinite, but they had no stories to tell of it which reached much further back than ours. Indian storytellers were less inhibited (that is, they made them up). It was also axiomatic that each of us had played some part in those past stories: each of us is a reincarnating soul. Even without that gloss the mere imagination of past wars, kingdoms, empires and catastrophes must direct attention either to the riches of the present moment or to eternity (or both). If each of us has been forever, changing roles, castes, genders, then our attachments here-and-now have all the charm of transience.

The law that determines which lives we shall lead is known in the West as *kārma*, which actually just means action. Actions have consequences not only for the outer world but for our souls. The notion was not unknown in Europe. "There is no accident in a man's becoming a slave," Plotinus wrote, "nor is he taken prisoner in war by chance, nor is outrage done on his body without due cause, but he was once the doer of that which he now suffers; and a man who made away with his mother will be made away with by a son when he has become a woman, and one who has raped a woman will be a woman in order to be raped" (Plotinus, *Enneads*, Ennead 3, treatise 2 [47], ch. 13, lines 11ff., see Armstrong 1966–88). The humane implications are that each of us has been where others are, and that we'll suffer ourselves the things we do to others. The less humane implication is that those who suffer now deserve it. So those who are born into the oppressed castes must be held, for their own souls' sake, to do their duty, however dire that is. Those who would *relieve* them of those duties really do them harm. The third twist in this dialectic is that even if it is understandable that they should suffer, those who inflict that suffering are themselves at fault.

Freedom is possible only for human beings. That is, to interpret the claim sociologically or psychologically, only human beings have the capacity to transcend their *dharma*, turn aside from what comes naturally, change their station (none of which they should do until they have paid their dues). But the self that turns aside is of no different nature than the selves that inhabit animals. Indian, far more than European, thought has retained the knowledge that there is no absolute divide between human and non-human nature. The gods may be incarnate as non-humans as easily as humans. Some animals, such as oxen and monkeys, are particularly sacred, as embodying or symbolizing gods. Gandhi identified "Care of the Cow" as Hinduism's special contribution to humanity, uniting proper gratitude and compassion. It does not necessarily follow that animals are treated well in India: once again, the inhumane inference may be that "animals" like dogs deserve their fate. And it is as easy in Hindu ethics as in European to rationalize their suffering on the plea that "human beings" come first. Strangely, the very fact (if it is one) that humans can transcend their given natures and their accustomed duties – by compassionate concern for those not of our kind – is made a reason for them not to do so.

How are we to reach "freedom"?

Kārma, jñāna, bhakti: satyagraha

There are three routes to freedom: *bhakti*, *kārma* and *jñāna*. The route of action (*kārma*) is, as before, to do one's duty, as that is defined by gender, caste, age and circumstance. Its disinterested or non-ego-driven performance will not incur the sorts of consequences that bind one to rebirth. It might well seem to follow that good Hindus should have accepted the British Raj (as their ancestors might have accepted earlier invasions). Even the efforts of the British to subvert such inconvenient or loathsome practices as *suttee*, or untouchability, did not really disturb the Hindu decencies. And it was not *these* subversions to which Gandhi objected (indeed, he shared the British wish to do away with the offenses). One obvious root of the campaign for "independence" was the wish to live as Europeans were supposed to live: as equal citizens with equal rights to make commercial profit and defend themselves. What Gandhi learnt – in fact from G. K. Chesterton – was that the only real Indian Independence must come from Indian roots. What he envisaged was not another Western "liberal" state, but a realm of properly self-sufficient villages, working to achieve an Indian peace. He did not, perhaps, entirely get his wish.

Nonetheless, the way of "action" as he practiced it is its own contribution to human, not only Indian, history. What matters is our hold on truth:

"*satyagraha* is the force which is born of truth and love of non-violence" (Gandhi 1938: 172). Truth, for Gandhi (and of course also for many Western theists), is God, and we testify to that Truth by laying our life on the line in its service. His critics, not entirely wrongly, reckoned that his fasts and protests were "non-violent" only in appearance, that his success depended on the very real *threat* of violence, and that his ideals (of self-sufficient villages using only the simplest of technology) were both patronizing and unworkable. But *satyagraha* has still been a force for justice, as well as a personal route to freedom. There may even be some congruence between Gandhi's ideals and the ideal of "Dalitization" proffered by Ilaiah (2001): to the pure all things are pure – including excrement and dead bodies.

Jñāna, the route of knowledge, especially appeals, in principle, to scholars or ascetics: by bringing ourselves to *realize* the truth, we are released from bondage. The truth we need to realize is, roughly and with many caveats, that there is One presence masquerading in its many masks and projections. The doctrine is not that far from several European philosophies, including many modern ones: after all, if we are to understand ourselves as the corporeal products of neo-Darwinian evolution and a quantum-mechanical cosmos what room is there to suppose that we are "real individuals?" We are as much a part of the single whole that is the cosmos as rocks and grass. If some recent speculative cosmologists are correct, even the whole expanding universe is no more than a bubble in an infinite manifold, and everything that happens here and now has happened, in essence, infinitely many times before in infinite variations. In one mood this may seem dispiriting: in another, it is exalting. Neither mood has any solid basis: what matters is to know (if all this is correct) that there are no gaps in nature.

These scholarly or philosophic meditations are not for everyone: some of us may find them quite implausible, and few even of the believers can sustain that sense for long. The third alternative is *bhakti*, devotion to some deity (as it might be Krishna): such devotion may release us from habitual self-concern. What matters in devotional ecstasy is not the image we have of our own biological or social life but an image of the god. Such gods are not, like us, susceptible to boredom, fear or weariness. Even if the god requires us to continue in our station, our service is then *chosen*, and so (perhaps) is joyful.

There need be no more agreement among Indian "ethicists" than there is among European. Contemporary moral and political problems (abortion, vivisection, climate change, the role of women) may be as vigorously debated in India as in Europe, and such debates may often be couched in very much the same terms as they would be in Europe (human rights and human welfare; rules, consequences, virtues). When Indian poets and politicians cite the ancient epics they may do so without real attention, or else intend only a nod to nationalistic sentiments (a disease with European roots). But it is also possible for Indian moralists to draw on a tradition that is closer to the *ancient* European norm, and to remind us all of factors that more modern Europe has forgotten.

Willy-nilly, we are born into particular lives and stations. Seeking always to "better" ourselves (to increase wealth, health, knowledge and reputation) is to forget our sense of self. It is also to ignore reality, the complex, ever-changing world that incorporates both nature and human fantasy. On the one hand we have our duties, and our pleasures. In this context, we should at least obey the golden rule, to treat others (and not only human others) as we would wish ourselves to be treated. On the other hand, we may come to see this panorama as a play, and not be so attached to anything here–now as to forget our larger destiny.

See also Ethics, science, and religion (Chapter 22); Virtue ethics (Chapter 40); Respect and recognition (Chapter 47); Ideals of perfection (Chapter 55).

Acknowledgments

My thanks to Christopher Bartley, Jonardon Ganeri and Ananda Wood for their advice and commentary.

References

Armstrong, A. H. (trans.) (1966–88) *Plotinus: The Enneads*, London: Loeb Classical Library.

Crawford, S. Cromwell (2003) *Hindu Bioethics for the Twenty-First Century*, Albany: State University of New York Press.

Dumont, Louis Homo (1970) *Homo Hierarchicus: The Caste System and Its Implications*, London: Weidenfeld & Nicolson.

Gandhi, M. (1938) *Satyagraha in South Africa*, Madras, India: S. Ganesa.

Ilaiah, Kancha (2001) *Why I Am Not a Hindu: A Sudra Critique of Hindutva Philosophy, Culture and Political Economy*, Calcutta, India: Bhatkal & Sen.

Lannoy, Richard (1971) *The Speaking Tree: A Study of Indian Culture and Society*, New York: Oxford University Press.

Perrett, Roy W. (1998) *Hindu Ethics: A Philosophical Study*, Honolulu: University of Hawaii Press.

Further reading

Bilimoria, Purushottama, Prabhu, Joseph and Sharma, Renuka (eds) (2007) *Indian Ethics*, vol. 1: *Classical Traditions and Contemporary Challenges*, Aldershot, UK: Ashgate; vol. 2: *Gender, Justice and Ecology* (forthcoming). (A collection of essays on many contemporary and traditional issues.)

Keown, Damien (2001) *The Nature of Buddhist Ethics*, 2nd edn, Basingstoke, UK: Palgrave. (A revisionist account of Buddhist ideals, drawing on Aristotelian thought.)

McEvilley, Thomas (2002) *The Shape of Ancient Thought: Comparative Studies in Greek and Indian Philosophies*, New York: Allworth Press. (A philosophical and historical study of the connections between the Mediterranean and Indian milieux.)

3
SOCRATES AND PLATO

Richard Kraut

Socrates and Plato distinguished

The dialogues of Plato, composed nearly 2,400 years ago, fill more than 1,600 pages in the most recent English edition of his complete writings, and many of the works in his oeuvre are devoted to fundamental ethical and political matters – questions about how any human being should live, and how we, as members of political communities, should live together. No previous philosopher in the West had examined ethics and politics so deeply and comprehensively, and so he is rightly regarded as the founder of systematic moral and political philosophy. His writings reveal his engagement with the issues that faced Athens (of which he was a citizen) in the fifth and fourth centuries BC, but the questions he raises continue to resonate over the centuries, and Western philosophy has produced no author who has matched his ability to dramatize abstract ethical questions in works of enduring literary value.

He approached philosophical questions in the medium of a literary form – the dialogue – that is meant to signal to readers that face-to-face discussion should be the principal tool by which philosophy, including moral philosophy, is to be learned. Although Plato's dialogues are devices by which he advocated his own point of view, they are also meant to convey his conviction that we cannot gain greater ethical understanding by uncritically reading books and accepting whatever they have to teach. We must take up the issues of moral philosophy by exposing our own ideas, in conversation, to the cross-examination of others. Plato intends his dialogues to be focal points of such conversations, not substitutes for them.

The principal interlocutor of many of the dialogues is Socrates, who did not himself write anything, but occupied himself with ethical questions solely by means of conversations in small groups. A vivid portrait of Socrates' way of life is presented in Plato's *Apology of Socrates*, which purports to be the speech Socrates gave in court when he was accused of having acted impiously by not believing in the gods of the city, but introducing new gods, and thereby corrupting the young. (In Greek, *apologia* means "defense" – Socrates was not apologizing for anything.) Socrates' defense was unsuccessful: he was convicted and sentenced to death. In many of Plato's writings, the folly and injustice of this conviction are not far from the surface of the text. The death of Socrates, he suggests, tells us something not only about Athenian democracy but more generally about human nature: widespread resistance to unsettling ethical reflection is one of the defects to which human beings are prone.

Because Plato never speaks to his readers directly in his own voice, but instead portrays a leading speaker (in most cases, Socrates) and one or more other interlocutors, we might ask whether the point of view endorsed by a dialogue is original to Plato or whether he inherits it from Socrates. In fact, it is legitimate to ask an even more fundamental question: Why assume that Plato's dialogues endorse any point of view at all? Why not instead take Plato to be doing nothing more than reporting some interesting conversations he has heard? The answer is that certain doctrines are consistently presented in a favorable light in many dialogues. Plato seems to be recommending them as doctrines that are worthy of consideration because of their great plausibility.

To renew our question: Are these doctrines Plato's ideas or did he take them over from Socrates? There is no doubt that Plato makes Socrates the principal interlocutor in so many of his dialogues because he takes himself to be working out Socratic insights. Because his writings reveal him to be a literary artist and creative thinker in his own right, not a mere recording medium for the unaltered presentation of what he heard from Socrates, we can be sure that every sentence in his dialogues is shaped by his understanding of what it would be best for someone to say at this point in the conversation. Even the *Apology* must be regarded as Plato's rendition of what Socrates should have said – based, in ways that we cannot recover, on what he did say, but nonetheless, not a mere repetition of words heard.

In what follows, I sometimes speak of what Socrates says, and sometimes of what Plato believes. Although one is making a significant inference when one attributes to Plato a belief on the basis of what Socrates says, that inference is, I believe, often justified. The remainder of this chapter will examine what I take to be Plato's contribution to moral and political philosophy, as conveyed to us by the words he puts into the mouth of Socrates.

Early, middle, and late dialogues

We can make some educated guesses about the order in which Plato composed his dialogues, and it is best to pay attention to that order, because we should be open to the possibility that his ideas developed as he worked them out. One common device used by students of Plato is to divide his works into three groups: early, middle, and late dialogues. The *Laws* can be safely taken to have been written late in his career, and it shares many stylistic affinities to several other dialogues: *Sophist*, *Statesman*, *Philebus*, *Timaeus*, and *Critias*. So these six are generally regarded as belonging to his late period.

Furthermore, there is a group of short dialogues whose content is primarily ethical and whose principal goal seems to be the demonstration of the difficulty of an issue rather than its solution. In several of them, Socrates asks a question of the form, "What is – ?" and then argues that all of his interlocutors' proposed answers are inadequate. These works correspond closely to the portrait Socrates paints of himself in the *Apology*, for he emphasizes in his defense speech that he himself knows little or nothing, and has aroused hostility because his interlocutors often dislike having their claims to knowledge overturned. Among the shorter ethical dialogues that end in perplexity are *Charmides*, *Euthyphro*, *Ion*, *Laches*, *Lysis*, *Hippias Major*, *Hippias Minor*, *Protagoras*. (These are listed alphabetically; we can only guess their chronological relationship within this group.) They are often called "Socratic" dialogues – a term that carries the suggestion that in them Plato is more indebted to Socrates than he is in other works. It is likely that many of them were in any case written at an early stage of Plato's career, and that the *Apology*, *Crito*, and *Gorgias* were also composed during this early period.

Between these early compositions and the six late dialogues, many scholars place the *Phaedo*, *Phaedrus*, *Republic*, and *Symposium* (to list them alphabetically). Like the early dialogues, these four have a strong ethical content, but unlike those early dialogues, they combine ethics with a serious dose of metaphysics. This mixture of subjects, based on the assumption that ethical investigations must be anchored in a conception of the nature of reality, has its roots in some of the early dialogues (particularly the *Euthyphro*), but that assumption is not fully developed until Plato's middle period. There is a distinctive other-worldliness that pervades Plato's writing during his middle period, missing from the works that are considered early. He no doubt thought that the perplexity-filled conversations of the short ethical works point the way towards an other-worldly metaphysics. In the *Meno*, Socrates holds that we must take the soul to be separate from the body and to have enjoyed a prenatal vision of the truth, if we are to understand how it is possible to make progress in an inquiry regarding the nature of virtue. This feature of the *Meno* is generally taken to mark it out as a transitional work, one in which Plato begins to combine the study of ethics with the examination of metaphysical and epistemological issues.

Ethical thought in the early dialogues

Plato's writings do not contain any single word or phrase that corresponds to our word "moral," and although "ethical" has its origin in the Greek word, *êthê* ("character"), he does not use that word as a device for marking off a distinctive subject matter. (Here he differs from Aristotle, who does mark off ethics as an autonomous field of investigation within the broader framework of a study of politics.) When Socrates tells his listeners what it is that particularly interests him, he speaks in terms of virtue or excellence (both words can be used to translate *aretê*), or specific virtues (justice, courage, wisdom), or what is good, or what is fine (*kalon*: it can also be translated as "beautiful" or "noble").

One of the persistent themes of the early dialogues is that such virtues as justice, wisdom, and courage have a value that gives them absolute priority over all other goods. A good illustration of what this means is presented in the *Crito*. Socrates' friend, Crito, reveals that he can arrange for Socrates' escape from jail, and argues that Socrates owes it to his friends and family not to end his life, as he is legally required to, but ought instead to continue his activities in exile. Before Socrates examines the question whether life in exile would have any of the advantages Crito imagines, he insists on a principle – one he says has always been accepted in their previous conversations – that must never be violated, regardless of any benefits that violation might bring: one must never act unjustly. Accordingly, if it can be shown that were Socrates to evade his punishment that would be unjust, the matter will be decisively settled, even if escape would bring all the benefits that Crito has in mind. The rest of the dialogue proceeds to argue both that escape would be unjust, and that the benefits Crito has referred to are illusory.

Why must one never act unjustly? Socrates does not say. But at one point he claims that acting unjustly is bad for the unjust individual, and that idea is consonant with the point, made several times in other early dialogues, that it is contrary to one's interest to have *any* of the vices, and in one's interest to have the virtues. A virtue or excellence is, after all, a good quality, and it seems obvious to Socrates that it must therefore be good *for* the person who has it. Many students of Plato take Socrates to be saying (and Plato to be agreeing) that the ultimate justification for everything one does must be one's own good, and that one should treat others well only if doing so can be shown to be in one's own interest. (That thesis is sometimes labeled "egoism.") But although we have grounds for taking him to be assuming that a *necessary* condition for a quality being a virtue is that it benefits the person who has that quality, it is less clear that this is also a *sufficient* condition. He might think instead that what makes a quality a virtue is that it benefits both its possessor and his community.

Another theme that runs through the early dialogues is an analogy Socrates draws between possessing such virtues as justice, courage, and wisdom, on the one hand, and ordinary practical skills like medicine, carpentry, and shoemaking, on the other. An expert crafts worker, he assumes, has some articulate knowledge that he can call upon to explain why he performs his job in one manner rather than another. A skilled doctor, for example, has some understanding of health and disease – he does not merely have a record of success in healing people (that might be due to a string of good luck) but draws upon an investigation he has conducted of the human body and its vulnerability to disease. In several early dialogues, and particularly in the *Gorgias*, Socrates proposes that we should think of a virtuous person as someone who has the analogue of a doctor's knowledge of medicine. Accordingly, a just person is someone who has made a study of justice, and has thereby learned something about the human soul that is comparable to what a doctor learns about the body. (When the early dialogues allude to the human soul, they are simply making the innocuous assumption that we can attribute psychological – the Greek word for soul is *psyche* – properties to human beings: thought, emotion, deliberation, sensation, and the like. The soul is simply whatever is responsible for these mental states. Socrates does not, in these works, venture any thoughts about how the soul is related to the body, thus leaving it open that the soul might be a special kind of body, as some of his contemporaries believed. That is an issue that Plato takes up for the first time in the *Phaedo*.)

As I noted above, several of the early dialogues pursue questions about how the virtue terms are to be defined. They ask: What is piety? (*Euthyphro*), courage? (*Laches*), moderation? (*Charmides*), beauty? (*Hippias Major*), friendship? (*Lysis*). That definitional quest is not abandoned in Plato's later works. He seeks definitions of justice (*Republic*), knowledge (*Theaetetus*), statecraft (*Statesman*), and sophistry (*Sophist*). It is important to see that these questions are not requests for mere synonyms or any of the easy linguistic equivalents that might be entered into a dictionary. When Socrates asks what *to hosion* (piety) is, for example, he is not looking for a phrase that conveys what any competent speaker of Greek already knows. He is seeking something far more difficult to acquire: he wants to know why pious acts or pious people are grouped together as belonging to the same kind. What is this property, piety, that they all share, and by virtue of which they are pious? To answer that question, one must have a deep understanding of the rationale that justifies our practice of sorting people and acts into the pious and the impious. To have that insight into piety would be an accomplishment as great or greater than the achievement of a doctor who has a comparable understanding of physical health. It would be to have a full theory of piety, not mere facility in using the word.

Socrates is presupposing that there can be such a thing as moral expertise – that is, a mastery of such concepts as justice, goodness, and virtue that would enable one to apply them in a wide range of particular cases, and to know how to justify (to others, not only to oneself) one's beliefs about them. Such a person would be a recognized guide to and teacher of virtue, provided that competent and willing students of the subject are available. Socrates does not claim such expertise for himself; on the contrary, he insists that he falls far short of the mark. His special kind of human wisdom, as he says in the *Apology*, lies in his realization that this is an ideal all human beings must strive to achieve, and in his awareness of his great distance from that ideal. He is critical of his fellow Athenians because they rest content with unexamined assumptions about the virtues and their application to people and actions. They think that because they have learned how to convey their beliefs and desires by using such terms as "good" and "virtue," they know all that they need to know about what goodness and virtue are.

The human error that Socrates despises is comparable to the mistake someone would make if he thought that he knows what heat is, or what a rainbow is, simply because he can more or less correctly apply the words "heat" and "rainbow." There is a scientific theory of heat and other meteorological phenomena, and one cannot acquire it unless one makes a special study of these subjects. Socrates is, in this sense, searching for a science of ethics. His dictum, proclaimed in the *Apology*, that the unexamined life is not worth living, means that human beings must strive for a deeper understanding of the concepts by which they govern themselves. The *Apology* beautifully conveys Socrates' sense of exasperation with the folly of his fellow citizens: after all, is it not obvious that nothing could be more worthwhile than improving one's understanding of the ultimate ends of human life?

The early dialogues take it for granted that genuine fields of expertise – medicine, navigation at sea, farming – owe their success to their discovery of effective means to some single goal. Their deep understanding of that goal, which organizes everything done by the expert, explains their ability to find the best means to it. Socrates assumes that since each of the crafts is organized around a single well-understood end, a virtuous person will similarly aim at and achieve one ultimate goal. What might that goal be? It would be unilluminating to reply: "knowledge." For that tells us nothing, unless we can say: knowledge of what? If we reply that the virtuous person has knowledge of virtue, we have spoken the truth, but this too is an unilluminating truth, because it does not give us a sufficiently concrete target by which we can guide our actions. (These issues are most fully rehearsed in the *Charmides*, *Meno*, and *Republic* Book 1.) It is understandable that the early dialogues typically end in failure. Socrates is asking his interlocutors to draw upon their inner mental resources to find a formula for living well that is both philosophically defensible and concrete enough to serve as a practical guide. No easy task.

In the *Protagoras*, he tries out the idea that pleasure might serve as such a guide. The thematic question of this dialogue (and the *Meno* as well) is whether virtue can be taught – a question that is really a way of asking whether there is such a thing as moral expertise. The issue of the teachability of virtue is then connected to the further question whether virtue is a unitary phenomenon; presumably these questions are linked because Plato assumes that any genuine field of expertise is a single subject with a single domain of study. In the closing pages of the dialogue, Socrates induces Protagoras to accept the common idea that we should make all our decisions by calculating how much pleasure each of the alternatives would bring, and choosing the course of action that would, on balance and over the long run, bring us the greatest amount of pleasure. That is the *kind* of criterion of decision-making that Socrates seeks in other early dialogues, and in fact one important tradition in moral philosophy (with advocates in both the ancient and modern periods) agrees that pleasure is the ultimate goal of all action. But does the Socrates of the *Protagoras* mean that pleasure is the good?

Or is he merely saying that we need some goal that plays the role that pleasure occupies in many people's deliberations? Scholars are divided on this issue. In any case the Socrates of other dialogues is unequivocally opposed to the thesis that pleasure should be our ultimate goal. That idea is decisively rejected in the *Gorgias*, the *Republic*, and the *Philebus*.

One of the greatest contributions to ethical reflection made in the early dialogues can be found in a marvelously succinct passage in the *Euthyphro*. The topic is the virtue whose public enforcement led to Socrates' death – piety. One of the definitions proposed by Socrates' conversational partner (Euthyphro) is that piety is whatever all of the gods love. Through a series of questions and distinctions, Socrates leads Euthyphro to see the difference between two ways of interpreting that proposed definition: the gods might love anything and anyone whatsoever, and that loving attitude would confer on those objects the status of being pious; or the gods might love certain acts and people because they have a property that makes love the appropriate reaction to them. Euthyphro plausibly opts for the second alternative: the love that the gods have for pious people and their actions is their appropriate response to some attribute that merits love. The upshot is that piety must be defined in terms other than the love of the gods. The definition must pick out what makes piety lovable and therefore deserving of love.

That suggests that the attitudes of gods can at best play a secondary role in our ethical reflections and deliberations. The Socrates of the *Republic* consistently endorses the idea that the gods demand and desire only what is good for human beings, and so if we want to live in a way that honors and pleases them, we need to figure out, on our own, what is good for us. Plato has no doubt that religious ceremonies play an important role in human life and that the political community rightly promotes and regulates these festivals. (He most fully expresses these ideas in the *Republic* and the *Laws*.) But he is not tempted by the idea that religious experience or priestly authority might be sources of ethical knowledge. He had an opportunity to explore these ideas, because Socrates is portrayed in the *Apology*, the *Euthyphro*, and several other works as someone who answered to a divine inner voice. But the early dialogues treat that religious phenomenon as a Socratic idiosyncrasy and nothing more. The epistemological assumption made throughout the early dialogues is that ethical knowledge is to be acquired in the same way that all craft-knowledge is acquired: by sustained and careful reasoning that draws upon and organizes our experience.

Ethical thought in the middle and late dialogues

In the *Phaedo*, Socrates offers several arguments for the immortality of the soul, and portrays the body as a prison in which the soul has temporarily taken up residence. The soul is not itself made out of any material, and is therefore not vulnerable to decay or decomposition. Its incorporeal nature marks its kinship to another kind of entity that now comes to play a central role in Plato's thinking: what he calls forms or ideas. His positing of forms arises from a distinction drawn in the *Euthyphro* between the many things that are pious and piety itself. Piety is a property; pious people and actions have that property, but are not identical to it. Forms are simply properties. The Socrates of the *Phaedo* conceives of them as eternal, changeless, incorporeal objects that can be grasped by the soul but not the body. In fact, the soul would be better able to arrive at a full understanding of these properties if it were not hindered by the body. That is why death is not an evil; it is instead an opportunity for the soul to escape its confinement and thereby improve its understanding of the forms.

A later tradition of Platonists, sometimes called "Neoplatonists," who took their lead from the writings of the third-century AD philosopher, Plotinus, looks to this other-worldly component of the middle and late dialogues as the foundation of ethics. But the Platonic dialogues, including those written in his middle and late periods, are as attentive to our social responsibilities and current emotional needs as they are to the soul's eventual release from the body. Death holds the promise of a better world, but while we are embodied we have to learn how to make the best possible use of our sexual desires, our social emotions, and our deliberative skills. In our worldly existence, we can achieve some degree of understanding of the forms, and in fact doing so will give us a chance to make our embodied condition and our political community vastly more livable. Someone who can grasp what the forms of justice, beauty, and goodness are will be far better able to see what must be done to enhance the justice, beauty, and goodness of the everyday world. That is the thought that underlies much of the moral philosophy of the middle and late dialogues. It is most fully developed in the *Republic*, a dialogue that depicts an ideal society ruled by philosophers in the light of their understanding of the most important form of all – the form of the good.

Unlike many of the early dialogues, which fail to find satisfactory definitions of the virtues, the *Republic*, beginning with Book 2 (it is divided into ten books), claims success. (Book 1, by contrast, refutes several proposed definitions but does not offer a positive account of what justice is.) One of the key steps that leads to a successful outcome is the thesis that the human soul is not inherently unitary but is composed of three parts – reason, spirit, and appetite – that will be at war with one another unless each is trained to play its proper role in relation to the others. Reason is the part that is capable of looking after the good of the whole soul, and so it should govern the rest. Spirit, which houses our propensity to seek social distinction (victory, honor, angry domination), must be trained to become an ally of reason. The third part of the soul, by virtue of which we seek food, drink, sex, and the means for their satiation (including and especially wealth), must be tamed in a way that makes us healthy, vigorous, and restrained. In the *Phaedrus*, the tripartite nature of the human personality is depicted by means of the image of a charioteer trying to control two horses, one manageable (spirit) and the other unruly (appetite). As this image suggests, reason, though not inherently inert, can get nowhere on its own; to move ahead, it needs to enlist the massive energies of our emotional and appetitive nature. And yet it must have its own notion of where to go – it cannot simply take its directional cues from the two horses. Implicit in this analogy is the thesis that our lives cannot be lived well unless our highest aspirations are recommended to us not by their emotional appeal or the pleasures of their fulfillment but because reason shows them to be good.

Where does justice fit into this picture? Socrates prepares the way for answering this question by portraying an ideal society in which each citizen contributes as best he can to the common good, receiving in turn the care that other citizens can best give him. A perfectly just city would be one bound together by these ties of reciprocity, and each citizen's recognition of his indebtedness to others would foster a sense of unity sufficient to overcome all of the divisive tendencies of human nature. What it is for a city to be a good city, in fact, is precisely this unification of its parts. The best division of labor, Socrates says, would put philosophically trained lovers of the common good in charge of decision-making. A second group of citizens would be specially trained to defend the city against enemies; and a third would be devoted to the production of material resources. That threefold division of the ideal social world corresponds to the tripartite structure of the human soul. As a city is just when its three parts are unified, each doing its own, so too is the human soul: justice precisely is each doing its own.

But is justice good? – good, that is, for the person who develops this virtue? Is it good for someone even apart from the rewards it often confers in this life (a good reputation and the advantages that brings) and a future life (favorable treatment by the gods)? One of the most remarkable features of the *Republic* is its insistence that this question deserves an answer. It is not enough that a social arrangement be shown to be just; that would not by itself give us enough reason to adopt it. It must be shown to be good – and good not only because there are advantages in being treated justly, but also because it is by itself good to have justice in one's soul.

To answer this question fully, Socrates needs to say not only what justice is, but also what goodness is. And Plato seems to acknowledge this burden, for when Socrates describes the educational program that will best inculcate justice and the other virtues, knowledge of the form of the good is portrayed as the highest form of knowledge. The *Republic* refrains from proposing a definition of goodness, and instead relies on an analogy between the importance of the sun to visible objects and the importance of the good in the realm of the forms. But the dialogue suggests that what makes any complex object good is the order or harmony achieved by its parts. That proposal reappears in the *Philebus*, one of the late dialogues. In the *Laws*, which depicts a second-best city (one ruled by law rather than philosophers), we are again told that what makes for a good community is social harmony. Plato's idea, then, is that if we were to carry out a full inquiry into what goodness is, we would confirm the hypothesis that justice, being a harmony of parts of the soul, is inherently good for the soul, because goodness is itself a proper balance or proportion among parts.

Plato's identification of goodness with order, harmony, measure, and kindred notions has not been universally accepted – far from it. Aristotle, for example, insisted that Plato sought the good at too high a level of abstraction, and recommended instead that we focus our attention on the *human* good. But two other Platonic claims have been accepted by a long tradition of moral thinking, which continues to this day: First, in everything we do, we should strive to achieve something that is good; it is not enough that what we do is something we want to do – it must pass a critical test, by being worthy of our desire because it is good. Second, for this reason, we had better make sure we know what goodness – the property that good things have in common – is.

See also Ethical intuitionism (Chapter 39); Virtue ethics (Chapter 40).

Further reading

Ahbel-Rappe, S. and Kamtekar, R. (eds) (2006) *A Companion to Socrates*, Malden, MA: Blackwell. (Thirty essays on Socrates as portrayed both by his contemporaries and by philosophers of later periods.)

Irwin, T. (1995) *Plato's Ethics*, New York: Oxford University Press. (A systematic and comprehensive discussion, with emphasis on the early dialogues and the *Republic*.)

Vlastos, G. (1991) *Socrates: Ironist and Moral Philosopher*, Cambridge: Cambridge University Press. (A study of Socratic method, emphasizing differences between the early and middle dialogues.)

4
ARISTOTLE

Christopher Taylor

Aristotle's ethical writings belong to his practical philosophy. He states at *Nicomachean Ethics* (*NE*) (see Bywater 1894) 1103b26–28 that his ethical enquiries are not undertaken for the sake of theoretical understanding as the others (such as metaphysics or natural philosophy) are, since the aim of the investigation is not to know what goodness is, but to become good. That would lead us to expect a manual on the art of living, containing detailed practical advice of the kind familiar from agony columns, but in fact, as he repeatedly emphasizes, most of his arguments and conclusions are stated in outline only, leaving the details to be determined by experience, while among the questions thus answered in outline the most fundamental is precisely the question "What is goodness?" Aristotle's point in the passage cited above is that understanding what goodness is is not the ultimate aim of the enterprise, but an intermediate aim. The ultimate aim of studying ethics is indeed to become a good person, but in order to achieve that aim one has to understand what goodness is, or in other words what it is to be a good person.

Underlying Aristotle's thought here is an assumption which he shares with Plato, that the fundamental question in ethics is "How should one live?" This question is not to be understood as "What is the morally best way to live?" since a possible answer to it is that one should cast off the restraints of morality in the pursuit of one's own interest. Rather, the sense of the question is "How can one achieve the best possible life?," where "best" is understood both as "best from the point of view of the agent's interest," as distinct from, e.g. "best from a standpoint of total impartiality," and "best objectively," as opposed to "best in the agent's own opinion." The standpoint of self-regard is therefore fundamental to Aristotle's ethics, as it is to Plato's, though it is a form of self-regard which seeks to make room for altruism (i.e. concern for another for the other's sake) and for self-sacrifice.

In the *NE* Aristotle addresses that fundamental question by beginning from the starting point of a goal of action; he seeks to show that, as every rational activity aims to realize some goal which is seen as good, there is some goal which stands in that relation to human life as a whole, which can therefore be identified as the good for humans, or the supreme good. Everyone, he says (1095a17–20), agrees on the name of the supreme good, namely *eudaimonia* (i.e. happiness, flourishing, or well-being), and that what that name means is "living well and doing well," but people differ on what living well consists in, e.g. some people think it consists in getting as much enjoyment as possible, others that it is a life of political achievement, others that is the life of the intellect. A possible response to that situation would be a subjectivist one, according to which living well is nothing other than getting out of life what you want, whether that is enjoyment, political achievement, or whatever. Aristotle does not consider that response; he takes it for granted that the different conceptions which he has identified are in conflict with one another, and that it is the task of philosophy to settle that conflict by declaring a winner, whether one of the suggested candidates or some other still to be identified.

He first seeks (Bk 1, ch. 7) to confirm the universal belief that the supreme good is *eudaimonia* by establishing that *eudaimonia* alone satisfies two conditions which the supreme good must satisfy, first that it is sought for its own sake and for the sake of nothing else, and secondly that it is by itself sufficient to make life "choiceworthy and lacking nothing" (1079b15). Both conditions have been held (e.g. by Ackrill 1974) to point towards an "inclusive" conception of *eudaimonia*, i.e. a conception of the supreme good as a life in which the best possible combination of specific goods is achieved. An alternative view (maintained e.g. by Kenny 1975–6) sees Aristotle's conception rather as "dominant," i.e. as the conception of a life devoted as far as possible to the pursuit of a single specific good. While the formal specification of *eudaimonia* as sought for its own sake and self-sufficient seems to point towards the inclusive conception, that conception is not sufficient for Aristotle's project of adjudicating between the specific claimants to the title of the supreme good. For the formal conception already includes the conception of the best possible combination of specific goods, which commits Aristotle to offering a substantive account of which combination of goods is the best possible.

The first step towards that account is given by an argument from the function (*ergon*) of human beings. Here extensive controversy must be bypassed (see Lawrence (2001) for an account of the issue, with a substantial bibliography of the literature). It suffices to observe that Aristotle's aim is to move towards a substantive account of the best life for humans from consideration, in terms of his philosophy of nature, of what kind of life human life is. Humans are a kind of animals, specifically rational animals. Hence a distinctively human life is a life of rational activity, and a good human life is one in which rational activity is well employed. But what counts as employing rational activity well? Here a number of complications arise. The first complication arises from Aristotle's view, developed in more detail in Book 1, chapter 13, that the rational element in the human personality is twofold, consisting first in the intellect, which is rational *per se*, and secondarily in the appetites, which are not rational *per se* (since wanting is not as such an exercise of the intellect), but which are derivatively rational in that, unlike the desires of non-rational animals, they are responsive to reason. Hence the notion of employing rationality well is not a simple one, but must find room for the good employment of the intellect on the one hand and of the rationally responsive appetites on the other. Aristotle clearly has this point in mind in the definition of the supreme good which results from the *ergon* argument: "the human good turns out to be activity of the soul in accordance with excellence, and if there are several kinds of excellence, in accordance with the best and the most *teleion*" (i.e. "the most complete," "the most perfect," or "the most final"; 1098a16–18). The first half of the sentence states that the supreme good for humans is the excellent employment of rationality, the second modifies this claim by considering the consequence of the hypothesis, which Aristotle believes to hold, that there are more ways than one in which rationality is excellently employed. Partisans of the inclusive interpretation interpret it as "in accordance with the best, i.e. the most complete," understanding the reference to be to the exercise of rationality considered comprehensively as including both the activity of the pure intellect and that of the rationally responsive appetites. Those who favor the dominant view interpret it as "in accordance with the best (sc. the best among those just mentioned), i.e. that which most has the character of a final end," understanding the reference to be exclusively to the excellent employment of the theoretical intellect, which is described in Book 10 (1177b1–15) as the only human activity employed for its own sake alone. While the latter seems to me clearly the more natural reading of this particular sentence, we have to note that Aristotle has still taken only the first step towards his goal of a substantive specification of the best life. Whether that consists in the excellent employment of rationality in all its forms, or in one only, or in some compromise between those extreme positions, he has still not told us what are the ways in which rationality is excellently employed. The *ergon* argument still leaves it open for the partisans of the various kinds of lives mentioned earlier to claim that their favored lifestyle and it alone constitutes the excellent employment of rationality.

In the succeeding chapters (8–10) Aristotle considers the contribution to *eudaimonia* of external goods such as health and prosperity. His final conclusion is that while the best life must have the excellent employment of rationality as its central goals, since no life can be satisfactory which does not have that aim, nevertheless external goods are necessary for a fully worthwhile life. A full account of *eudaimonia*, then, is that it is a life of excellent rational activity "sufficiently equipped with the external goods, not for any chance period, but over one's life as a whole" (1101a14–16). While this may look like a significant modification of the conclusion of the *ergon* argument, that the supreme good is excellent rational activity, there is in fact no real tension between the two accounts. Excellent rational activity, which it is up to the agent to engage in or not, is what one should aim at in one's life, while the external goods, which it is not in the agent's power to guarantee, are the extra conditions which one hopes for in order to make one's life completely worthwhile. The full account of *eudaimonia* thus contains both inclusive and dominant aspects, since its dominant aim is excellent rational activity, while it also includes the external goods. It remains to establish whether that compromise position applies to rational activity itself (see below).

In Chapter 13 Aristotle sets out the psychological basis of his distinction of types of excellent rational activity. Since rationality belongs essentially to the intellect, and derivatively to the appetites, the types of excellence are the excellence of the intellect and the excellence of rationally responsive appetite. These types of excellence interpenetrate via the practical function of the intellect. The intellect is employed not merely in speculative thought, but in the direction of conduct, and it performs its practical role by shaping and directing the appetites. And the appetites are excellently shaped insofar as they respond appropriately to the directions of practical reason. The stage is thus set for Aristotle to expound his account first of the excellence of rationally responsive appetite and then of reason, both theoretical and practical. The first type of excellence is the topic of Books 2–4, and is completed by the account of justice (also counted by Aristotle a virtue of character) in Book 5. Excellence of intellect is the topic of Book 6.

Aristotle defines virtue of character in general as a stable state of character which is in a mean relative to us, a mean determined by the reason or reasoning by which the person of practical wisdom would determine it (1106b36–1107a2). By a state of character in a mean relative to us Aristotle means a certain stable state of responsiveness to a given motivation or motivations (e.g. courage to fear and boldness, temperance to the desires for bodily pleasures), namely the state of being neither excessively swayed by that motivation nor insufficiently responsive to it. Excessive and insufficient responsiveness is not a simple matter of intensity of a given feeling; there are many ways in which one may manifest excess or deficiency in feeling and in action, e.g. by feeling angry or acting angrily at the wrong time, with the wrong people, for the wrong reasons, etc. (1106b18–24). Yet it is the quantitative notion of the mean relative to us which captures what goodness and badness of character consists in; every specific motivation may be felt and acted on too much, too little, and to the right extent, and getting it right consists in being neither too given nor insufficiently given to that motivation. But the specification of excess and deficiency in terms of the wrong time, person, etc. shows that the quantitative concept of the mean cannot have the analytic priority which Aristotle's theory requires. What is wrong with someone who is consistently angry for the wrong reasons, thereby being angry when he should not, and failing to be angry when he should, is neither that he is excessively given to anger nor that he is insufficiently given to it, but that he lacks the proper sense of appropriate reasons for anger. Aristotle is right to think that goodness of character requires the right fit between reason and motivation, but wrong to think that that fit has to be characterized, or even that it is best characterized, quantitatively.

The definition of the ethical mean stated above raises the question of what is the standard which determines correct practical reasoning. Aristotle poses this question explicitly at the beginning of *NE* Book 6 (1138b29–34), but does not appear to answer it explicitly in that work. If his view is that the ultimate standard of practical reasoning is the promotion of some goal external to that reasoning itself, specifically theoretical excellence, as some commentators have found suggested by the final chapter of the *Eudemian Ethics* (*EE*; see Gauthier and Jolif 1958/9: Vol. 1, 29* [of the introduction], vol. 2, 560–3), then he can be seen as attempting to provide an external grounding for his theory of virtue, one provided, ultimately, by his metaphysics. If, on the other hand, the correct standard of practical reasoning is internal to the practice of practical reasoning itself, his theory of virtue will be ultimately self-standing. That is the view of some influential writers sympathetic to Aristotle (especially McDowell 1995, 1996; also Wiggins 1995; Woods 1986), who urge that the attempt to justify or ground a substantive moral theory from any external standpoint is mistaken in principle, and count it a merit rather than a defect in Aristotle that, as they interpret him, he eschews any such attempt. This question has been extensively discussed; my own view (see Taylor 2008a) is that Aristotle's texts are indecisive on this crucial issue.

Aristotle discusses intellectual excellence in Book 6, in which a central topic is the distinction between *phronēsis*, practical wisdom, the excellence of the practical intellect, whose task is the organization of all aspects of the agent's life "with a view to living well as a whole" (1140a25–28) and *sophia*, the excellence of the theoretical intellect. In the final chapter of the book (Bk 6, ch. 13) he sets out the respective contribution of these excellences to the agent's overall good, i.e. *eudaimonia*. The situation is complex: both kinds of excellence are intrinsically valuable, in that each is the excellence of the appropriate part of the soul (by which Aristotle appears to mean the practical and theoretical intellect respectively), but (a) they are not equally valuable, since *sophia* has higher intrinsic value than *phronēsis*, (b) in additional to its intrinsic value *phronēsis* has an instrumental role in promoting *sophia*, analogous to the role of medicine in promoting health. The claim of *sophia* to higher intrinsic value and its implications for Aristotle's view of the best life for humans is spelled out in Book 10: ultimately *sophia* is the best excellence attainable by humans because the theoretical intellect is the aspect of human nature which most closely approaches divine nature, and its excellent exercise the nearest humans can come to living the divine life, i.e. to "assimilate to the divine as far as possible" (1177b33). But that does not imply that the best kind of human life is a life devoted exclusively to theoretical thought; since human beings are embodied creatures who require a social environment in which to achieve their full development, a life devoted exclusively to the theoretical intellect is simply not possible for them. Rather, the best form of human life is one in which the exercise of intellectual excellence is the principal focus of the agent's interests and energies, as e.g. excellent playing is the principal focus of the life of a concert pianist. Since that life has to be lived in a social context it requires the exercise of the social virtues, i.e. the virtues of character, but it does not follow that the value of those virtues is the purely instrumental one of promoting theoretical excellence. Since, as stated in Book 6, Chapter 13 *phronēsis* has intrinsic value in addition to its instrumental value in promoting *sophia*, the virtues of character which it directs enhance the value of the theoretical life directly, as well as promoting intellectual excellence instrumentally. From the fact that the most valuable human activity is theoretical thought (*theōria*) it does not follow either that one should seek to maximize the amount of *theōria* in one's life, irrespective of what one might have to sacrifice in so doing, nor that anything else is of value in one's life only instrumentally, nor does Aristotle make those claims. Given the primacy of *theōria* in the best human life, Aristotle leaves it indeterminate how that primacy is to be achieved, in conformity with his general policy of stating principles in outline only, leaving the details to the educated judgement of the person of practical wisdom. It may well have been his view that there are a number of different ways in which the best life can be lived. He is, however, unambiguous in his view that a life focused not on intellectual excellence, but on virtue of character, though a good life, is less good than the intellectual life, however the latter is lived (1178a9–10). As distinct from his specific account of virtue of character, Aristotle's overall account of human value is undoubtedly grounded in his metaphysics, and is thereby unambiguously committed to an intellectual elitism which not only differentiates it from modern theories but makes it distasteful to modern sensibilities. Goodness of character does not itself in his view require high-level intellectual capacity, though it does require a substantial degree of practical intelligence; but goodness of character, though a good thing, is not the best thing in human life.

Apart from the two types of excellence and their contribution to the overall good life the topics which receive most extended treatment in Aristotle's ethical works are pleasure and friendship. I shall therefore conclude with a necessarily brief discussion of those two topics.

Aristotle's starting point in the treatment of pleasure is commitment to the thesis that it is a necessary part of the best life. In the *EE* he begins from the unargued claims that the good is *eudaimonia* and that *eudaimonia* is the finest, best, and pleasantest of all things (1214a1–8). In the *NE* the identification of *eudaimonia* as the good is first established by universal consent (1095a17–20), then argued for as described above, and finally confirmed by arguments to the effect that it possesses agreed marks of the good life, one of which is that it is intrinsically pleasant (1099a7–28). Given this commitment to pleasure as a constituent of the best life, Aristotle has first to rebut arguments which purport to show that pleasure cannot have that role, either because it is bad, or at least because it is not good; that rebuttal will require a positive account of pleasure as a way of showing that the opponents of pleasure are wrong about what pleasure is. Further, his own account should provide further arguments in support of pleasure's place in the best life. That account is contained in two treatments of the topic, *NE* Book 7, chapters 11–14 and Book 10, chapters 1–5, which have some overlap in subject matter, but no cross-references; they are clearly independent discussions which owe their position in the text of the *NE* to an editor, probably not Aristotle himself, and since *NE* Book 7 is one of the three books common to both versions of the *Ethics* it is likely that that discussion was originally written for the *EE*.

Both passages contain criticism of a certain view of pleasure, familiar from well-known passages of Plato (see *Gorgias* 494–7, *Republic* 585d–e, and *Philebus* 31–32), and seen as foundational to many of the arguments which Aristotle is seeking to refute. This is the view of pleasure as a perceived process of replenishment of a natural lack, and thereby a return from a state of deficiency to one of equilibrium and normal function. The paradigm cases are those of pleasures in the satisfaction of bodily appetites, especially those for food, drink, and sex. Bodily appetite is either identified with or seen as arising from bodily deficiency, which is experienced as unpleasant; this unpleasant experience prompts the agent to make good the deficiency, and the process of filling up the deficiency is experienced as pleasant. This model has a general feature which makes it unsuitable for the defense of the place of pleasure in the best life; pleasure is seen as something essentially remedial, as bound up with the process of getting rid of an imperfect and undesirable state. Since it is at best an alleviation of the troubles of the human condition it is hard to see how it could have any role in the ideally good life, much less be a necessary feature of it. It is not, then, surprising that in his defense of the necessary role of pleasure in the best life Aristotle proposes an alternative model.

On this model the factor common to all pleasures is the exercise of natural capacities in the appropriate conditions. Pleasures are specific to the different species of animals; every species has capacities for activities which constitute its specific life, and when those capacities are exercised in the appropriate conditions their exercise is pleasant to the individual member of the species (1176a3–8). Human life is constituted by the capacities shared with animals, namely growth, reproduction, nutrition, perception, and locomotion, with the addition of the specifically human capacity for thought; hence some human pleasures, notably those in food, drink, and sex, are kinds of pleasure which animals also enjoy, while intellectual pleasures are specific to humans. This analysis has the advantage of applying both to cases which fit the deficiency/replenishment analysis and to cases which do not, because in them no deficiency can be identified (e.g. enjoying a beautiful view does not presuppose that prior to seeing it one was suffering from the lack of seeing that, or any, view). In the case of pleasures which do fit the deficiency/replenishment model, such as the pleasures of satisfying hunger and thirst, the crucial point is that those drives belong to a natural pattern of animal activity, which, since humans are a kind of animal, is *ipso facto* part of the natural pattern of human activity. Satisfying one's hunger and slaking one's thirst are perfectly genuine cases of pleasure, insofar as they fall under the general classification of the appropriate exercise of natural capacities. That point signals a major divergence from the view of Plato, who maintains that pleasures which involve the replenishment of a deficiency (which include most bodily pleasures) are not in fact pleasures at all, but processes of escape from distress, which people mistake for genuine pleasures from lack of experience of the latter (*Republic* 583c–585a). That view involves a major confusion: even if it is granted that the state of bodily deficiency is unpleasant and that the state of having got rid of the deficiency is neither pleasant nor unpleasant (both assumptions are in fact highly dubious) it does not follow that the process of transition from the state of deficiency to the state of repletion is not genuinely pleasant. Aristotle's analysis allows him to escape this error: the process of transition is the process in which the natural capacity is appropriately exercised, and is therefore genuinely pleasant.

This analysis is perfectly adapted to Aristotle's project of vindicating the place of pleasure in the best life. Since that life consists in the excellent exercise of specifically human capacities, above all the capacity for speculative thought (see above), it immediately follows that it must be intrinsically pleasant, i.e. pleasant just in virtue of being the kind of life that it is; "their life (i.e. the life of those who exercise rational capacities excellently) has no need of pleasure as a kind of adornment, but it has pleasure in itself" (*NE* 1099a15–16). At the same time the wide diversity of human capacities and activities, answering to a corresponding diversity of human interests, readily explains the diversity of kinds of pleasure, and of the fact that what is pleasant to one person may be unpleasant or neutral to another. On the other hand it faces the problem whether the specification of the conditions appropriate for the exercise of a natural capacity must include the condition that the activity is *pleasant* to the agent undertaking it, thereby including the *analysandum* in the analysis. (For fuller discussion see Taylor 2008b.)

Just as the starting point of the discussion of pleasure is the generally accepted belief that pleasure is inseparable from the best life, the treatment of friendship starts from the truism that "no-one would choose to live without friends, even if he possessed all the other goods" (*NE* 1155a5–6) and seeks to give an account of friendship which will explain why that is so. It is obvious enough that we enjoy doing things in the company of friends, and that it is good to have friends to call on in times of trouble, but these truths do not get to the heart of the matter, for it is accepted that "one must want good things for a friend for his sake" (1155b31), i.e. that one must show regard for one's friend irrespective of one's own interests, and it is at least questionable how far that condition is satisfied by friendships based on pleasure and on utility. Aristotle has sometimes been taken to say that in those kinds of friendship one does not really value one's friends in themselves at all, but only the pleasure or utility one gets from them, in which case these would not be genuine kinds of friendship. It is more plausible that he thinks that in those cases one does indeed value, not just the pleasure or the utility, but one's partners in those relations (e.g. one does indeed want one's tennis or business partners to do well, and is concerned when things go badly for them), but that that regard is contingent upon the continuation of the relationship, so that when the partnership breaks up one does not retain an interest in the good of one's former partners. Hence these are inferior kinds of friendship, since one's regard for the other is contingent on superficial factors, whereas in the best kind of friendship one values the other *for themselves*, as opposed to valuing them as a good tennis partner or business colleague (1156a10–12, 16–19). Aristotle assumes without argument that valuing one's friend for his or her self is identical with valuing them for their good character, from which it immediately follows that the best type of friendship is possible only between good people (1157a16–20). That assumption is problematic; there is a complex relation between caring for a person because he or she is *that individual* and valuing them because they are the kind of person that they are, and that complexity allows faults as well as virtues to contribute to the unique mix of characteristics which makes someone lovable for his or her self. Given that assumption, Aristotle has the problem of explaining why friendship based on character is necessary for the ideal life; i.e. why is the friendship of other good persons among the external goods which have to be added to the individual's excellence of character and intellect in order to achieve *eudaimonia*? The answer is a blend of common sense and the philosophy of mind. Common sense says that (a) one manifests one's goodness by treating other people well, and it is better to treat friends well than strangers (1169b10–12), (b) we like being with other people, especially like-minded people (1169b16–21), (c) it is easier and pleasanter to undertake worthwhile activities in company than alone (1170a5–13). From his philosophy of mind Aristotle argues that since *eudaimonia* consists in excellent activity, and we are better able to observe the actions of others than our own actions, intimate association with other virtuous people gives us a special access to *eudaimonia* (1169b30–1170a4, 1170a13–b13). This obscure doctrine is connected with the ideas that a friend is another self (1166a31–32) and that in some sense the disinterested regard which is central to friendship derives from one's regard for oneself (1166a1–2). Aristotle seems to be suggesting that the excellent actions of others are, insofar as they are someone else's, specially apparent to us, and, insofar as they are a friend's, in a way our own. It does not seem to me that this argument has anything to add to the truths of common sense.

The primacy of the self-regarding standpoint in Aristotle's ethics gives rise to the famous puzzle of whether it allows for genuine altruism. In *NE* Book 9, Chapter 8, he tries to reconcile the common belief that the good person will sacrifice themselves for their friend with his thesis that in the appropriate sense the good person is a "self-lover." The virtuous agent will sacrifice everything, including life itself, for their friends and their country, and will even resign to their friend the opportunity of doing fine things, instead of doing them themselves, but even this supreme sacrifice has the paradoxical feature that "the good man appears to assign more of the fine to himself," since it is "finer to cause one's friend to do them (i.e. fine things) than to do them oneself" (1169a33–b1). It thus seems that for Aristotle the *ultimate* point of self-sacrifice for the virtuous agent is not that it promotes one's friend's good for its own sake, but that promoting one's friend's good for its own sake gives the agent's life the right kind of shape. Aristotle's virtuous agent is not totally selfless; it may be that he would regard total selflessness, even if psychologically possible, as an abnegation of one's primary responsibility for shaping one's own life.

See also Socrates and Plato (Chapter 3); Later ancient ethics (Chapter 5); Virtue ethics (Chapter 40).

References

Ackrill, J. L. (1974) "Aristotle on *Eudaimonia*," *Proceedings of the British Academy* 60: 333–59; repr. in A. O. Rorty (ed.) *Essays on Aristotle's Ethics*, Berkeley, Los Angeles and London: University of California Press, 1980, and in *Essays on Plato and Aristotle*, Oxford: Clarendon Press, 1997.

Bywater, I. (ed.) (1894) *Aristotelis Ethica Nichomachea*, Oxford: Clarendon Press.

Gauthier, R. A. and Jolif, J. Y. (1958/9) *L'Éthique à Nicomaque: Introduction, traduction et commentaire*, 2 vols. in 3 parts, Louvain: Publications Universitaires de Louvain; and Paris: Éditions Béatrice-Nauwelaerts.

Kenny, A. (1965–6) "Happiness," *Proceedings of the Aristotelian Society* 66: 93–102; repr. in J. Feinberg (ed.) *Moral Concepts*, Oxford: Oxford University Press, 1969, and as "Aristotle on Happiness," in *The Anatomy of the Soul*, Oxford: Blackwell, 1973, and in J. Barnes, M. Schofield and R. Sorabji (eds) *Articles on Aristotle*, vol. 2: *Ethics and Politics*, London: Duckworth, 1977.

Lawrence, G. (2001) "The Function of the Function Argument," *Ancient Philosophy* 21: 445–75.

McDowell, J. (1995) "Eudaimonism and Realism in Aristotle's Ethics," in R. Heinaman (ed.) *Aristotle and Moral Realism*, London: UCL Press, pp. 201–18.

——(1996) "Deliberation and Moral Development in Aristotle's Ethics," in S. Engstrom and J. Whiting (eds) *Aristotle, Kant, and the Stoics: Rethinking Happiness and Duty*, Cambridge: Cambridge University Press, pp. 19–35.

Taylor, C. C. W. (2008a) "Aristotle on the Practical Intellect," in *Pleasure, Mind, and Soul: Selected Essays in Ancient Philosophy*, Oxford: Clarendon Press, pp. 204–22.

——(2008b) "Pleasure: Aristotle's Response to Plato," in *Pleasure, Mind, and Soul: Selected Essays in Ancient Philosophy*, Oxford: Clarendon Press, pp. 240–64.

Wiggins, D. (1995) "Eudaimonism and Realism in Aristotle's Ethics: A Reply to John McDowell," in R. Heinaman (ed.) *Aristotle and Moral Realism*, London: UCL Press, pp. 219–31.

Woods, M. J. (1986) "Intuition and Perception in Aristotle's Ethics," *Oxford Studies in Ancient Philosophy* 4: 145–66; repr. in *Four Prague Lectures and Other Essays*, Prague: Rezek, 2001.

Further reading

Broadie, S. (1991) *Ethics with Aristotle*, New York and Oxford: Oxford University Press. (A perceptive and challenging study.)

Hardie, W. F. R. (1980) *Aristotle's Ethical Theory*, 2nd edn, Oxford: Clarendon Press. (Still the standard commentary.)

Rorty, A. O. (1980) *Essays on Aristotle's Ethics*, Berkeley, Los Angeles and London: University of California Press. (A classic collection of articles.)

Rowe, C. (trans.) (2002) *Aristotle, Nicomachean Ethics*, Oxford: Oxford University Press. (This is the most recent, but there are many excellent translations of Aristotle.)

5
LATER ANCIENT ETHICS

A. A. Long

Historical and cultural context

Plato, under the inspiration of Socrates, and Aristotle, Plato's most illustrious student, made ethics a fundamental subject of philosophical inquiry. Greek moral thought, however, continued to be vibrant and innovative throughout the three centuries following the death of Aristotle (322 BC), during the epoch modern historians call Hellenistic. The schools that Plato and Aristotle had founded at Athens soon found themselves competing for students with newly established philosophies, especially those inspired by Epicurus, whose school was sometimes called the Garden, and by Zeno of Citium (a city in Cyprus), whose followers acquired the name Stoics from the public colonnade (*stoa*) in the center of Athens where Zeno lectured. Ancient ethics later than the work of Plato and Aristotle was dominated by Epicureanism and Stoicism. These Hellenistic schools provided students with two radically different value systems and ways of life. Epicurean ethics is a form of hedonism, with its prescriptions grounded in a social contract theory of justice and the private sentiments of friendship as distinct from the intrinsic value of virtue. Stoicism, by contrast, restricts all goodness to a virtuous character, takes pleasure to be quite indifferent to happiness, and views human beings as naturally sociable and motivated for civic life.

Strongly divergent though Epicureanism and Stoicism are in their defining principles, the two philosophies share many concepts already central to Platonic and Aristotelian ethics. These include the notion of an ultimate end of life, to be identified with happiness (*eudaimonia*), and the presumption that the attainment of this end requires self-sufficiency, a rationally grounded character, and emotional strength. Both Hellenistic theories are egoistic, in the sense that their prescriptions are intended to satisfy persons' correct understanding of their ultimate interests, but they also seek to accommodate a social outlook that attends to the good of others. Like Aristotle and Plato (in his middle and late dialogues), Epicureans and Stoics connect ethics with doctrines concerning the status of human beings within the universe. In all four philosophies the best human life is presumed to be godlike, with the analysis of that bold notion dependent on their respective theologies and cosmologies. As godlikeness implies, Greek ethics in general is perfectionist, an idea also signified by the shared philosophical ideal of achieving "wisdom" (*sophia*).

Like Plato and Aristotle again Stoics and Epicureans justify their ethical theories by arguments they take to be objectively sound. However, these later theories, notwithstanding their differences from one another, lay claim to being empirically or "naturally" valid. This naturalism is a major innovation, which merits detailed consideration. Another shared and equally prominent innovation is the promise of Stoicism and Epicureanism to deliver tranquility to their practitioners.

Historians have sometimes explained the Hellenistic philosophers' therapeutic goals as a response to supposedly unsettled social conditions and alienation, brought about by the decline of autonomous city states in a world now governed by the monarchies established by Alexander the Great. Unlike Aristotle, neither Stoicism nor Epicureanism specifies participatory politics as a main context of ethics. However, tranquility was already an ideal for Democritus, writing at the end of the fifth century, and he was a prime influence on Epicurus. Socrates too, whom the Stoics appropriated as an exemplary figure, was renowned for his emotional strength and equanimity. Tranquility was not a peculiarly Hellenistic desideratum. Moreover, in both Stoicism and Epicureanism tranquility derives its ethical rationale from reflection on troubling psychological, rather than external, conditions, such as the unhappiness generated by anger or fear. Much original thought went into the Hellenistic philosophers' therapeutic arguments, and many of the syndromes they sought to relieve are endemic to the human condition, such as fear of death and loss of loved ones.

It would be a big mistake, though, simply to assimilate the social context of Stoicism and Epicureanism to the classical Greece of Socrates, Plato, and Aristotle. The polis culture of the latter was rife with chauvinism and sexism, complacent about slavery, and contemptuous of menial work. As the Hellenistic world developed and eventually merged into the Roman Empire, more ecumenical attitudes became prevalent in the intellectual elite. Zeno and Epicurus could not have fully anticipated these changes, but the main doctrines of their ethics are applicable to any time or place, irrespective of status, gender, or race. You do not need to bracket their views on women or slaves or manual work or non-Greeks, as you do when reading Aristotle. In this respect Hellenistic ethics is thoroughly timeless. We can thus understand why it influenced such early modern philosophers as Hobbes, Butler, and Kant, in ways that did not happen in the case of Plato or Aristotle.

Epicurean ethics

"We must rehearse the things that produce happiness, seeing that when happiness is present we have everything, while when it is absent the one aim of our actions is to have it." Epicurus made this statement at the beginning of his *Letter to Menoeceus*, which is the best surviving account of his ethical doctrines (see Long and Sedley 1987: 155). Presentation of his ideas in epistolary form suited the role he assumed within his school as a benevolent mentor to individual acolytes, reflecting the great importance he attached to friendship. The "things that produce happiness" are the cardinal doctrines of his philosophy. They were encapsulated in "the fourfold remedy," the terms of which are as follows: "God presents no fears, death no worries. And while good is readily attainable, bad is readily endurable" (see Long and Sedley 1987: 156). To grasp the principal thrust of Epicurean ethics, we need to understand why Epicurus enunciated these four propositions together with the concept of remedy and its relation to happiness and the lack thereof.

God presents no fears

According to classical Greek religion the world is full of divine beings. The most powerful and prominent of these divinities (e.g. Zeus and Poseidon) were endowed with human form and mentality. Unlike human beings, however, these gods were taken to be immortal and to have dominion over such parts of the world as the sky and weather (in the case of Zeus) and the sea and surface of the earth (in the case of Poseidon). They were deemed to demand worship, and, if affronted, to respond not simply with anger but by bringing about catastrophes such as floods and earthquakes.

Epicurus made a two-pronged attack on this theology. First, he argued that basic and generally acknowledged attributes of divinity, especially blessedness, were incompatible with myths concerning the gods' interventions in the world or interests in humanity. A divine life must be a life of supreme happiness, free from all care and disturbance. For his second line of attack Epicurus invoked the atomistic physics that he appropriated from Democritus and greatly elaborated himself. If everything in the universe is ultimately reducible to matter in motion, there is no reason to refer any phenomena to divine causation. Atomistic physics, when properly understood, is sufficient to explain happenings that had been credulously attributed to gods. According to Epicurus gods do exist, but they live carefree lives and leave human beings completely alone. Hence we need not fear them.

One may reasonably ask two questions about this first proposition of the fourfold remedy. Were Epicurus's contemporaries so oppressed by superstitious fears, and, apart from the answer to that question, does his focus on divinity limit the historical interest of his ethics? In the interests of brevity I propose the following approach to both questions. "God presents no fears" is tantamount to the intriguing claim that an emotionally robust life requires a correct understanding of the world's basic structure; for if we can give compellingly naturalistic explanations of phenomena, they should have no secure purchase on our fears of the unknown. Beyond that, Epicurus's negative theology undermines any justifications for action that appeal to divine authority or command.

Death presents no worries

Greek mythology included stories about the fate of the soul after death, and Plato had ended several of his dialogues with myths concerning *post-mortem* rewards and punishments. Such ideas presupposed the intervention of divine beings. Epicurus had already disposed of that possibility, as we have just seen, but the fears of death he primarily sought to combat did not presume the soul's afterlife. On the contrary, he asked people who are afraid of death to accept the soul's necessary mortality and find that fact liberating. How so?

Like the body, the soul, which confers life on a body, consists of atoms. Death occurs when such a body/soul compound disintegrates. The atoms of the former body and soul persist, because they are essentially indestructible, but the person whom they constituted ceases to exist. The cessation of the person entails the absence of a self to experience anything, including death, which is therefore painless once it has occurred. As to the anticipation of death, we may dispose of its fearfulness by recognizing that the non-existence it will entail is precisely parallel to our condition before we were born. Past events did not trouble us because we did not exist as perceiving subjects. By parity of reasoning, we should not be troubled by the prospect of a future that we shall not experience. Being dead, then, will be no worse than not yet having been born.

Is it not reasonable, however, to want to live a long life or at least avoid a premature death? Epicurus responded to such challenges by arguing that once a person achieves the goal of a fully pleasurable life, happiness is complete and could not be enhanced by an infinite lifespan, which is the implicit goal of those who fear death. This concept of pleasure's limit is fundamental to Epicurean ethics as will become evident when we consider the remaining two propositions of the fourfold remedy.

According to Lucretius, Epicurus's great Roman publicist, fear of death is responsible for numerous crimes and manifestations of human misery including actions done by those who profess to be free from such anxiety (*De rerum natura* [*On the Nature of the Universe*] Bk 3, lines 41–86, see Lucretius 1994: 68–9). His acute observation brings out the full significance of this philosophical concern with death. Acceptance of mortality can acquire moral as well as psychological significance if it discourages the irrational belief that a life that sets a premium on achieving wealth and power at all costs can mitigate the inevitability of death.

Good is readily attainable, and bad is readily endurable

The remedial tenor of Epicurean ethics emerges clearly from the two previous propositions rebutting fear of divinity and fear of death. We are to take it that these fears are quasi-ailments infecting people's minds and sullying their prospects of happiness. With the third and fourth maxims of the fourfold remedy (highlighted above, p. 54) Epicurus provided resources for happiness that he claims to be congenital. His ethical project gives nature correct authority over the recipe for a good life with the presumption that culture is to blame for inculcating fear of the divine and fear of death (topics copiously treated in Homeric epic and Attic tragedy). Culture is equally culpable for misrepresenting the essential items people need in order to live as well as possible.

"As soon as every animal is born, it seeks after pleasure and rejoices in it as the greatest good, while it rejects pain as the greatest bad and, as far as possible, avoids it; and it does this when it is not yet corrupted, on the innocent and sound judgment of nature itself." This is the Roman philosopher Cicero's lapidary formulation of Epicurean hedonism (*De finibus* [*On Ends*] Bk 1, §29, see Long and Sedley 1987: 112). Epicurus grounded this doctrine in what has been called "the cradle argument." If you want to know a creature's *natural* desires and aversions, you need to study it in its earliest life before training or culture has intervened. On this basis Epicurus defended a doctrine of psychological hedonism, meaning that human beings naturally and unavoidably identify the good with pleasure and the bad with pain.

The criterion for these natural judgments is sensation, not reason. But Epicurus assigned a fundamental role to reason in elaborating his hedonism. While every pleasure as such is good and every pain as such is bad, the Epicurean life requires people to calculate the long-term advantages and disadvantages of the types of pleasure and pain that are available to them. Guidelines to this end include a threefold division of desires between "natural and necessary," merely "natural," and "empty." Objectives of the first category are items essential to the preservation of life, those of the third category are exemplified by luxuries. Desire for the latter is empty in the sense that a gourmet meal is presumed to be no more effective at removing pangs of hunger than an adequate but simple diet. In addition, the gourmet meal may have consequences that are more painful than the pleasure it generates, and it may well have a deleterious effect on people's characters, inclining them to be dissatisfied with simple fare.

But surely, one may object, a plain meal is less pleasurable to the palate. Epicurus's response to this challenge indicates the special features of his hedonism. "The pleasure we pursue is not just the one that … gratifies our senses with its sweetness; the pleasure we hold to be greatest is what we feel when all pain has been removed" (Cicero, *De finibus* Bk 1, §37). According to this doctrine, nothing is more pleasurable than the experience of a completely painless condition. With the satisfaction of desire, a state of tranquility supervenes that we are presumed to experience as the essence and limit of happiness. In order to live the Epicurean life, we are required to limit our desires to those that we can fulfill without the risk of incurring a greater pain. Epicurus assumes, in the terms of his fourfold remedy, that the means of satisfying natural and necessary desires are generally at hand, and that persons committed to this way of life will be generally capable of achieving a preponderance of pleasure over pain.

Contrary, then, to what the English term *epicure* signifies (under the influence of a common misrepresentation of his philosophy), Epicurus himself advocated a simple lifestyle. While his hedonism acknowledges the desirability of sensual pleasures, it lays much greater emphasis on the pleasures of the mind. Through memory and anticipation the mind is capable of extending pleasurable consciousness beyond momentary experience. That consciousness, most importantly, is taken to comprise the tranquility that ensues from learning why neither divinity nor death is something to be feared. It will also comprise a mentality that accepts the rationale for a lifestyle that is not only frugal but also disinclined to engage in any activities, such as competitive politics, that could put tranquility at risk.

As presented thus far, the Epicurean way of life will probably seem too self-centered and individualistic to provide a plausible rationale for social well-being. Epicurus sought to counter this charge by the importance he attached to justice and friendship. He endorsed a social contract theory according to which practices are just if and only if the persons undertaking them abide by an agreement to refrain from injuring one another. The mutual benefits that result from such contractual behavior constitute "nature's utility." Justice as so construed is not an absolute principle nor are its particular terms invariant. The constant in Epicurean justice is its mutual utility for those contracting to its provisions. If what is mutually useful changes, what was previously deemed just loses its rationale. This conception of justice suits Epicurean hedonism because Epicureans want to do everything to avoid pain. Therefore they should support social practices that minimize the risk of being subject to injury.

As to personal relationships, Epicurus took friendship to be an essential component of happiness. We are presumed to make friends in the first instance under the promptings of benefit to ourselves, but later, with sentiment deeply supervening, friendship can become not only intrinsically pleasurable but even something on behalf of which an Epicurean will endure great pain. The material on friendship is too complex to be adequately summarized here. Readers may find it worthwhile to read Cicero *De finibus* Bk 1, §§65–70 and then ask whether the great importance Epicureans attached to friendship is compatible with the egoistic emphasis of their ethics in general.

A related question arises concerning the role of virtue in this theory. Epicurus claimed that it is impossible to live pleasurably without living virtuously, but what gives virtue this necessary connection with the hedonistic life? The official answer is that virtue and pleasure are linked together "by nature," but that linkage, far from assigning equal worth to virtue, makes it no more than a means to pleasure. Ancient critics of Epicureanism found this instrumental status of virtue too weak to guarantee its efficacy in potential conflicts with pleasure. Stoic philosophers in particular, to whom I now turn, argued that the best human life is constituted solely and completely by virtue, with pleasure, as already stated, relegated to the status of complete indifference.

Stoic ethics

The standard Stoic formula for happiness, or the *summum bonum*, is living in agreement with nature. Nature in this expression includes both the human constitution and the structure of the world at large. The two natures are connected by sharing in reason (*logos*). Reason is the primary distinguishing feature of the human species, while the world is taken to be a physical continuum, shaped and energized throughout by a principle called cause, reason, mind, soul, and Zeus.

Stoicism is thus a form of pantheism, according to which natural entities owe their existence to a supremely intelligent and providential divinity that permeates all matter. Human beings are presumed to stand at the head of the natural scale of beings. Our species is a sign of divinity's benevolent creativity, and it is distinctly marked as such by the fact that we alone in the order of living beings are endowed with the divine attribute of reason. However, we start our lives as merely potential reasoners, and even as adults our rationality just by itself is too defective to assure our happiness and goodness. What we need, in order to live fully in agreement with nature, is wisdom, signifying a character that will equip us to act with knowledge of the values appropriate to a consistently rational life in a world where we can never completely control the way things will turn out. The attainment of such a character is equivalent to achieving rational perfection and conforming one's emotions to the divinely determined course of events.

Unlike Epicurean physics, then, Stoic cosmology is founded on the idea of divine and providential purpose. What Stoics make of their lives requires them to believe that they are living in the best of all possible worlds. Socrates had probably endorsed this idea and it is strongly canvassed in Plato's later dialogues. If divinity is presumed to care deeply for human beings, big questions immediately arise concerning why natural disasters occur or why material prosperity and virtue do not go hand in hand. While Epicurus, with his detached gods, had neatly avoided such questions, the Stoics attended to them in ways that echo the position of Socrates in Plato's *Apology*. In his concluding words to the Athenian jurors, after being sentenced to death, Socrates had said (*Apology* 41d): "Nothing can harm a good man either in life or after death and his fortunes are not a matter of indifference to the gods." Stoic ethics provides the systematic theory to justify the values implicit in Socrates's position. As we now come to the details, readers may like to ask whether this theory is plausible in its own right, or whether, to accept it, one needs to endorse providential theology and determinism. What can be said, irrespectively, is that Stoic ethics provides the rationale for a life whose goodness and success depend minimally on the external state of the world and maximally on the outlook and mentality of oneself.

Like Epicurus the Stoics looked to the actions of newborn creatures for evidence of what instinctual desires and aversions can reveal concerning *natural* values. Rather than identifying the primary objective with pleasure, they proposed self-preservation, finding support for that proposal in a survey of animal behavior from the moment of birth. An inverted tortoise struggles to regain its upright position, fledglings flutter their wings, and so forth. On the basis of such evidence, the Stoics concluded that animals are born with an elementary sense of their specific identity. This furnishes them with the desire to live accordingly, desiring what will preserve them and avoiding the opposite. Stoics did not deny that creatures enjoy pleasure and dislike pain, but in their theory such experiences are subordinate to self-preservative drives. This survey of animal behavior led the Stoics to propose that all animals, including young children, naturally seek after the things that suit their specific ways of life. It was reasonable, then, to characterize such items as primary valuables.

In Epicureanism it is assumed that pleasure maintains its status as the congenital and only *per se* desirable throughout a person's life. In Stoicism, by contrast, the function of the "cradle" argument is not to settle the essence of goodness but to establish a foundation for ethics in the notion of self-preservation. Whatever is conducive to that end, we are to take it, is *naturally* valuable. Yet between infancy and maturity the human self undergoes such significant development that concomitant changes occur in a person's understanding of the natural desirables. One such development, also ascertainable in other animals, is the emergence of parental instincts. From these instincts the Stoics derived the human motivation for social life and for other-regarding actions in general.

Still more important for human selfhood in its mature manifestations is the development of reason. As we reflect on our constitution, including our bodily organs and senses and our capacities to secure health and avoid danger, we are presumed to recognize the providential workings of nature. What is natural, under this perspective, manifests not only utility but also structure and order. Further, we are presumed to recognize and appreciate that these properties are also present in our minds as functions of reason and understanding. Ultimately, so the Stoics claimed, we should come to see that these properties of reason and understanding are so much superior to everything else that even the primary valuables cannot compete with the attractions of reason and understanding (see Cicero, *De finibus* Bk 3, §§16–21).

In valuing reason, then, Stoics value their selves, or rather, their normative selves, on the basis of what they take to be essential to mature human nature. Aristotle had already specified rationality as the distinctively human function, but he did not regard the perfection of reason as either the only good or as the only determinant of happiness. The Stoics make both claims. Why so?

Common sense suggests (A): that a healthy life equipped with adequate material resources should be preferred to one that lacks these provisions. If, moreover, the goal of ethics is to specify the necessary and sufficient conditions of happiness, it seems reasonable to propose (B): that sickness and impoverishment detract from happiness. The Stoics count good health and wealth as primary valuables because they help to preserve our lives. Hence they endorse (A). However, they reject (B), and so deny that these primary valuables are strictly good or essential to happiness. Critics from antiquity onwards have complained of a double standard here. If health as such is naturally "preferable" to sickness, why is health not "better" and therefore something that a rational agent, committed to "natural" values, should want in all circumstances and be distressed about if absent? The Stoic answer to this challenge brings us to the heart of their system and to its chief significance for the history of ethics.

Everything that accords with nature, they posit, has value, but we need to distinguish between the contingent benefit of natural valuables such as health or wealth and the essential benefit of correct reasoning and understanding. The latter is always beneficial and dependent on nothing outside a person's mentality and character. Health or wealth, by contrast, can be misused (i.e. do material harm to oneself or others), and may not be available. Hence, taking goodness to signify essential benefit, these things, though naturally valuable, lack goodness. Correspondingly, ill health or poverty, though contrary to nature in themselves, will be well used by a perfectly rational agent and therefore not harmful. The Stoic wise agent will always, given the option, prefer natural valuables to their opposites, but he will do so not because his happiness depends upon actually securing health or wealth but because it is rationally appropriate to value these things and to make good use of them, when given the opportunity. If, on the other hand, such an agent falls sick or suffers some material loss, reason equips him to make equally good use of these adverse circumstances and to accept the fact that such things, given the nature of the world, are bound to occur. In this way the ideal Stoic lives in agreement with his own nature (as ruled by reason) and with the world's nature (the external course of events, which falls outside one's control). The virtues that guide his actions are dispositions of how to act consistently with the knowledge of this system of values.

The Greek Stoics summarized their ethics with the statement: "Only the *kalon* is good." The word *kalon* can be variously translated: beautiful, noble, or fine are common renderings, but what the Stoics had in mind is best captured by the Latin translation *honestum*, meaning honorable. It makes no sense to call health or wealth noble or honorable. By confining goodness to the *kalon*, the Stoics went a long way towards anticipating Kant's moral philosophy with its ideas concerning what is good without qualification, the restriction of such good to rational beings, and its independence from material well-being and the consequences of action. Unlike Kant, however, the Stoics maintained that conformity with reason is the essence not only of the moral life but also of human happiness or welfare, when this latter is properly understood as entirely equivalent to a virtuous character.

A further affinity to Kant is evident in the Stoics' analysis of "appropriate" actions, exemplified by caring for parents, siblings, and friends, or honoring one's country. These are actions that reason prompts people to perform, but they only count as excellent when performed on the basis of a virtuous character, and without reference to their outcome. Appropriate actions typically aim at securing for oneself or other people the natural valuables, which, though always *prima facie* preferred objectives, are never counted as essential constituents of happiness. Stoic ethics, then, lays all its emphasis on goodness of intention as distinct from consequences, and relegates successful outcomes to the status of indifference.

Here, however, a deep problem arises. Stoic parents will do everything possible to secure their children's welfare, but if a child dies their system of values requires them to accept this occurrence without grief or diminution of happiness. Grief is not a justified emotion because it involves the false judgment, from the Stoic point of view, that one has experienced something harmful. Indeed, emotions as generally understood, including anger, fear, and desire, are taken to be indications of an imperfect character because they involve the false judgments that external and indifferent things are actually bad (harmful) or good (beneficial). In place of such emotions the ideal Stoic experiences "rational affects" typified by joy, well-wishing, and caution. These mental states are marks of a mentality that never allows itself to be mastered by external circumstances.

By distinguishing, as they did, between material valuables and the goodness of right action or virtue, and by treating the latter as a special kind of value, the Stoics come closer than any other ancient philosophers to the Kantian idea of a good that is purely moral. But as proponents of happiness as the supreme good, they face objections that Kant avoids thanks to his sharp distinction between actions performed solely from duty and actions done from desire for happiness. Is it plausible, though, to think with Kant that human beings are capable of motivations that totally bracket the way they perceive their interests? Not so, according to the Roman Stoic Epictetus, who said:

> If I am there where my volition is, thus and only thus shall I be the friend and son and father that I should be. For this will then be my interest – to preserve my integrity ... and to preserve my human relationships. But if I place myself in one scale and the honorable in another, then the doctrine of Epicurus wins, which states that the honorable is either nothing at all or only reputable opinion.
>
> (*Discourses* Bk 2, ch. 22, §20, see Long 2002: 199)

The idea that moral goodness is supremely in one's interests had already been advanced by Plato and Aristotle. Yet neither these philosophers nor their later ancient successors went along with the Stoics in proposing that virtue on its own is sufficient to ensure complete happiness, no matter what one's material circumstances may be. Stoic theory even maintained that there are no degrees of virtue or happiness and that everyone who is not virtuous is equally defective and unhappy. Rather than trying to mitigate such paradoxes, we should view them as a sign of the school's absolutism, which is vividly illustrated by its doubts of whether any human being had ever fully achieved Stoic wisdom. Stoic ethics, then, is not an account of people's actual moral language and beliefs, but a theory of what a human life governed by perfect rationality would be like. To the charge of their setting the bar too high, Stoic philosophers gave robust responses by emphasizing the practicality of trying to progress towards their perfect model. To cite Epictetus again: "It is impossible to be free from error. What is possible is to be constantly on the alert with a view to not erring; for we should be content if we avoid a few errors by never relaxing our attention to this objective" (*Discourses* Bk 2, ch. 12, §19, see Long 2002: 33).

See also Socrates and Plato (Chapter 3); Aristotle (Chapter 4); Ethics and reason (Chapter 9); Kant (Chapter 14); Consequentialism (Chapter 37); Virtue ethics (Chapter 40); Welfare (Chapter 54); Ideals of perfection (Chapter 55).

References

Long, A. A. (2002) *Epictetus: A Stoic and Socratic Guide to Life*, Oxford: Oxford University Press.

Long, A. A. and Sedley, D. N. (1987) *The Hellenistic Philosophers*, vol. 2: *Greek and Latin Texts with Notes and Bibliography*, Cambridge: Cambridge University Press.

Lucretius (1994) *On the Nature of the Universe*, trans. R. E. Latham, London: Penguin Books.

Further reading

Algra, K. A., Barnes. J., Mansfeld J. and Schofield, M. (eds) (1999) *The Cambridge History of Hellenistic Philosophy*, Cambridge: Cambridge University Press.

Annas, J. A. (1993) *The Morality of Happiness*, Oxford and New York: Oxford University Press.

Long, A. A. (1986) *Hellenistic Philosophy: Stoics, Epicureans, Sceptics*, Berkeley and Los Angeles: University of California Press.

6
THE ARABIC TRADITION

Peter Adamson

Texts of various kinds belong to the history of ethics in the Islamic world. A widely cast net could take in ideas from the Koran itself, reports about the sayings and deeds of the Prophet, jurisprudential literature, books of religious guidance like al-Ghazali's *Revival of the Religious Sciences*, and speculative theology or *kalām*. To give a couple of examples from this last area, the two *kalām* schools known as the Mu'tazilites and Ash'arites clashed over what would nowadays be called the "divine command" theory of ethics, defended by the Ash'arites, and over Mu'tazilite claims about the conditions under which an agent can be considered morally responsible. In particular, they claimed that agents must have power over their actions in order to be justly punished for those actions by God. These and other issues have been covered in more comprehensive studies of ethics in Islam (especially Fakhry 1994). But for reasons of space and continuity with the previous chapters in this volume, I will focus on the ethical reflections of those who practiced *falsafa*, which as the name implies was the direct appropriation of and response to Greek *philosophia* in Arabic.

This may seem an unpromising approach, given that *falsafa* is not particularly known for its contributions to ethics. For instance, Avicenna (d. 1037) was the greatest Muslim philosopher, and had an incalculable influence on later philosophers of all three faiths, in Arabic, Hebrew and Latin. Yet, while it would be an exaggeration to say that Avicenna wrote nothing about ethics, his main contributions were in areas like logic and metaphysics. In general, the most prominent debates in the Arabic philosophical tradition concern such issues as proofs of God's existence, the eternity of the world, and the nature of intellect. To the extent that practical philosophy comes to the fore, the main topics are the ideal political ruler and the relation of religious practice to demonstrative philosophical understanding. These problems aren't exactly "ethical." Often they are discussed under the rubric of "political" philosophy, but even this concept is usually applied to only a small number of Muslim authors, especially al-Fārābī (d. 950) and Averroes (d. 1198).

Of course these generalizations admit of exceptions, and one notable exception is the production of a large number of ethical works during the formative period of philosophy in Arabic, prior to Avicenna. It is on this fertile period of ethical reflection that I will focus here, even though there are also major ethical thinkers from later periods (for instance Fakhr al-Dīn al-Rāzī, on whom see Shihadeh 2006; for a broader treatment of Greek-inspired ethics in Arabic, see Gutas 1990). I will also focus mostly on Muslim thinkers, even though a great deal of medieval Jewish philosophy was written in Arabic, the *lingua franca* of the Muslim empire. The period I will discuss here includes the work of Saadia Gaon (d. 942), whose work takes in ethical themes. A comprehensive survey of ethics in Arabic would include him and, indeed, the whole history of philosophical ethics among Jews. I will not attempt to sketch this history here, but it is worth emphasizing that the authors discussed below worked alongside and sometimes in collaboration with Christians and Jews. A case in point is the one non-Muslim author I will discuss, the Christian Yaḥyā ibn 'Adī (d. 974). As we will see, interfaith disputation played a role in his writings on ethics, and his collaboration with Muslim colleagues helps to put the controversy in context.

The earliest philosopher I will mention is al-Kindī (d. c. 870), who was the first to present himself as a "philosopher [*faylasūf*]" writing in Arabic. He wrote an extensive body of works on practical philosophy, but these are mostly lost, which leaves us with a few distinctively "ethical" works. The best-known and most influential of these is *On Dispelling Sadness* (Ritter and Walzer 1938; see Adamson 2007a: Ch. 6). We have numerous works touching on ethical topics by al-Fārābī, which as mentioned above often place ethics within a political context. Al-Fārābī also wrote a commentary on Aristotle's *Ethics*, but this is lost. His student Yaḥyā ibn 'Adī authored a work called *Refinement of Character* (*Tahdhīb al-Akhlāq*, ed., trans. Griffith 2002). The same title was used by Miskawayh (d. 1030). His *Refinement* provides a remarkable synthesis of themes from both Greek texts which he knew in translation, and from previous authors who wrote in Arabic (Miskawayh 1966, trans. Zurayk 1968). For example, Miskawayh's *Refinement* ends with a long quotation from al-Kindī's *On Dispelling Sadness*. A final author to be treated here is Abū Bakr al-Rāzī, a great doctor and defender of several notorious philosophical theses, not least his alleged denial that certain humans are singled out to receive a revelation from God. The two extant philosophical works of al-Rāzī are both on ethics: the *Spiritual Medicine* (trans. Arberry 1950) and the *Philosophical Way of Life* (trans. McGinnis and Reisman 2007; both works ed. in al-Rāzī 1939).

In ethics as in other areas of philosophy, the main authority for most of these thinkers was Aristotle. His *Nicomachean Ethics* was translated into Arabic with substantial alterations such as an extra "seventh book" (see Akasoy and Fidora 2005). Greek commentaries on Aristotle were also important: for instance, Miskawayh was able to consult Porphyry's lost commentary on the *Ethics*. Plato's influence was important too, though there were few if any complete translations of any Platonic dialogue. He was mostly known indirectly, through what was probably Galen's paraphrase version of the *Laws* and reports on such works as the *Republic* and *Symposium* (see Rosenthal 1940; Gutas 1988). Galen himself was extremely influential in ethics, which may surprise readers who associate him exclusively with medicine. His work on "treating" the passions of the soul became an important model for several of our authors, as we will see below.

Intellectualism and "pre-philosophical" ethics

In part because the Arabic reception of Aristotle was filtered through the Greek Neoplatonic tradition, there is a strong tendency towards intellectualism in Arabic ethical works. One form of intellectualism is inspired by Plato's doctrine of the tripartite soul, according to which humans have rational, spirited, and appetitive aspects. These are called "parts" or sometimes even distinct "souls" (Ibn 'Adi discusses this terminology explicitly: Griffith 2002: Pt 2, §1). As in the *Republic*, to be virtuous is to have one's reason "ruling" one's soul. Our authors frequently use a version of Aristotle's "function argument" to motivate this Platonic thought. Since reason is the faculty which is distinctive to humans, the excellent human is one whose reason is fully developed and in charge of the entire soul, whereas the base human has fallen to the level of an animal. Indeed the lower two soul faculties, especially the appetitive, are often called "bestial." This is related to a common conflation of Plato's tripartite soul with Aristotle's threefold distinction between the rational, sensitive and vegetative faculties, since animals possess only the lower two faculties. Also Aristotelian is the idea that excellence with respect to our distinctive human function will constitute "happiness" for humans. The Arabic texts are squarely within the "eudaimonistic" tradition which sees ethics as the study of how humans can be happy. As with Aristotle, virtue comes into the story simply because it turns out that the excellent, and hence happy, human is the virtuous human.

But what does it mean to say that virtue is the rule of reason over spirit and appetite? Since our authors again follow Aristotle in dividing reason and philosophy into "theoretical (*naẓarī*)" and "practical (*'amalī*)" sides, it would seem that the perfection of reason must involve both theoretical and practical philosophy. Two questions now arise: first, what falls on the "practical" side of this divide, and second, how does the perfection of practical rationality translate into virtuous action? The first question is answered differently by different authors. Al-Fārābī says in numerous works that practical philosophy deals with those subjects which have a bearing on action, while theoretical philosophy deals with whatever is unrelated to action. But al-Rāzī distinguishes philosophy into "knowledge" and "action" (*'ilm* and *'amal*) and seems to put abstract reflection on ethical subjects into the former class. He even says that his authorship of the *Philosophical Way of Life* is a proof of his own competence in *'ilm* (al-Rāzī 1939: 108). It would seem that for him the "practical" part of philosophy involves only the actions themselves, and not grasping the ethical principles which are put into practice.

The more typical view, though, is that of al-Fārābī, so that our second question can be put more sharply as follows: When we grasp principles of practical reasoning, how are these then deployed in virtuous action? This is, notoriously, a difficult issue already in Plato and Aristotle, and it is no different in the Arabic tradition. On the one hand, al-Fārābī has a strikingly optimistic view of ethics as a science, and unlike most Aristotelians thinks that ethics can be demonstrative (see Druart 1996a). On the other, he and other authors are emphatic in saying that knowledge of the good does not guarantee virtue. In fact al-Fārābī contrasts someone who has all the right philosophical beliefs but acts badly to someone who lacks those beliefs but acts well, and claims that the latter man is closer to being a true "philosopher" (al-Fārābī 1961: §93; ed. al-Fārābī 1993: §98). The Socratic view that knowledge of the good is sufficient for virtuous action loses out in the Arabic tradition to the Aristotelian idea that habituation and practice are vital for achieving practical virtue. When Ibn 'Adī and Miskawayh write about "refining one's character," they have in mind mostly this sort of habituation, and not the study of universal ethical precepts.

Caution is needed here, though: several of our authors do seem to think that virtue is largely a matter of grasping universal truths, and that it is relatively straightforward to apply them to particular cases. In al-Fārābī this is the role of practical wisdom (*ta'aqqul*, which renders the Greek *phronêsis*). But all our authors give a central role to the closely allied function of *rawiyya*, "deliberation." There seems to be little danger that we will deliberate badly, unless the lower faculties or souls hinder our practical reasoning. Thus the role of habituation and training is not so much to develop a context-sensitive kind of ethical "perception," as in some readings of Aristotle, as to gradually weaken the lower soul and strengthen the rational soul. The reason these works advise us on the process of habituation rather than laying out universal principles may be that, although a universal ethical science is possible, the works in question are not attempting to lay out such a science. Rather, as Thérèse-Anne Druart has suggested, these texts might best be understood as "pre-philosophical ethics" (she has defended this interpretation for works by al-Kindī, al-Fārābī, and al-Rāzī: see respectively Druart 1993, 1996a, 1997). Certainly this is true of, for instance, al-Fārābī's *Directing Attention to the Way of Happiness* (trans. McGinnis and Reisman 2007), which tells us that it is to be read before the logical works which form the first part of al-Fārābī's philosophical curriculum. Yet it is often unclear how much philosophical "theory" is presupposed by our authors when they write about ethics. For instance, al-Kindī's *On Dispelling Sadness* consists largely of persuasive exhortation by means of anecdotes and practical "devices" that could benefit even a philosophical neophyte. But it opens by dismissing the value of physical things, and affirming that only intelligibles are truly valuable. It is unclear why a neophyte reader would accept this – or even accept that there *are* intelligible objects to be valued. And a reader who does not will have no obvious motivation for following the advice given in the rest of the work (see Adamson 2007a: Ch. 6).

Asceticism

This brings us to another form of intellectualism, which has to do not with the psychology of virtue, but with the objects valued by the virtuous person. The idea is that things in the physical world are to be devalued in favor of intelligible objects. In its extreme form this sort of intellectualism amounts to a rigorous asceticism. Asceticism is a frequent topic in our texts. Most famously, al-Rāzī's *Philosophical Way of Life* is a response to detractors who accuse him of failing to imitate his "Imam" Socrates by not adhering to an ascetic lifestyle. Here it is important to realize that in Arabic literature Socrates is often conflated with Diogenes the Cynic – so that we get stories about him living in a barrel and delivering cutting put-downs to passers-by (see Alon 1991; Strohmaier 1974; and on Greek "wisdom literature" more generally, Gutas 1981). This version of Socrates appears in al-Kindī's collection of sayings about him, which contains material repeated in *On Dispelling Sadness*. But al-Rāzī claims that Socrates abandoned asceticism as he grew older, and adopted the path of moderation instead. This echoes an ancient debate. The ancient Stoics and Cynics both took Socrates as a philosophical paradigm, but whereas the Cynics adopted a rigorous asceticism, the Stoics had a more moderate view according to which only virtue is truly valuable in itself, but physical or "external" goods are rationally choice-worthy as "preferred indifferents."

We find a range of positions on this issue in Arabic ethics. As we just saw, al-Kindī is emphatic that only intelligible objects are worth valuing, because they are invulnerable from change or destruction. In this he is followed by Miskawayh, especially in his *Shorter Healing* (see Adamson 2007b). But they could still accept the Stoic position, where one accepts external goods like wealth so long as one realizes their lack of intrinsic value. As al-Kindī says, one should welcome them as a king welcomes guests, enjoying their presence but not regretting their absence. A roughly similar view can be found in al-Rāzī, who supports the life of moderation with his theory of pleasure (see Adamson 2008). Taking up a view that goes back to Plato, he argues that pleasure occurs only when some deficiency in us is restored to a "natural state" of balance. For instance, if one is insufficiently moist, one will take pleasure in drinking. Because of this, pleasure is not intrinsically good, but merely the removal of a harmful state as one returns to a "neutral" state which is neither pleasant nor painful. On the other hand, for the same reason there is no reason to *avoid* pleasures, so long as they do not themselves inflict some further harm (as one might do if one restored moisture by getting drunk). This seems to be the theoretical basis for the moderate lifestyle recommended in al-Rāzī's *Philosophical Way of Life*.

Among our other authors, Ibn 'Adī has the most ambivalent relationship to asceticism. On the one hand, his *Refinement* mostly recommends the life of moderation implied by Aristotle's doctrine of the mean. Thus when he comes to address the virtue of "abstinence ['*iffa*]," Ibn 'Adī says that it is "the soul's control of the appetites, and the constraint of them to be satisfied with what furnishes the body with the means of subsistence and preserves its health, and no more," adding in an Aristotelian spirit that desires should be indulged "in a measured way [*'alā l-qadr*]" (Griffith 2002: Pt 3, §2). On the other hand, Ibn 'Adī wrote a separate work on the topic of *'iffa*, here specifically referring to abstinence from sex (see Mistrih 1981; Griffith 2006; Druart 2008). He defends the life of chastity on the basis that, even if sex is not intrinsically bad, it is a distraction from the pursuit of happiness; for happiness lies ultimately in the perfection of our intellect. Here, intellectualism apparently becomes the enemy of a life of moderation and the ally of asceticism. Part of the reason for this is that Ibn 'Adī is defending a Christian position against an unnamed opponent who is most likely Muslim – during this period, Muslims were frequently critical of the Christian ideal of chastity.

But there is also a philosophical rationale for Ibn 'Adī's position. He says that while chastity is defensible for some, it is not obligatory for all. Some are called to an ascetic lifestyle, and are admirable for that lifestyle, but this does not mean that those who engage in sex are vicious (after all, as he admits, the propagation of the human race depends on the fact that most people are *not* chaste). If we extrapolate from this discussion of sexuality, we might suppose that Ibn 'Adī would endorse a "monastic" lifestyle of social isolation for those with the best, most intellectual natures. But he could accept that some people attain happiness by less radical means. Such a differentiated view is indeed implied also in his *Refinement*, which frequently states that a given character trait is appropriate for some people, but not for others (for instance, "love of splendor" is good for kings, but bad for monks, Griffith 2002: Pt 3, §43).

Thus we might speak of a "two-level" ethics, according to which some spurn pleasures and physical goods in favor of the theoretical life, while others lead a life of moderation and practical virtue. Both groups are virtuous, even if the former are superior. This can be seen as a reaction to tensions already present in the Greek tradition. In particular, it's frequently wondered how Aristotle meant the theoretical life praised in *Ethics* Book 10 to relate to the life of virtuous practical engagement. Does the truly virtuous life include both kinds of excellence? For Ibn 'Adī, the answer would seem to be that the two lives are indeed incompatible, and that the theoretical life is better, even if both lives are virtuous. A similar view is endorsed by Miskawayh, who in the third section of his *Refinement* distinguishes between two levels of happiness, which correspond to the two aspects of human nature: material body and immaterial soul. Earlier in the *Refinement* he has rejected asceticism (Zurayk 1966: 29–30), and here we see why. So long as we are still in our bodily state, one should live a life of moderation. But this is not true, perfect happiness – for the same reasons mentioned by al-Kindī, regarding the vulnerability of goods in the physical world. Perfect happiness is achieved only in the afterlife, when our existence will be purely intellective, because the rational soul will survive while the lower parts of the soul die with the body. Al-Kindī shares this view, as can be seen not only from *On Dispelling Sadness* but also from his *Discourse on the Soul*, which ascribes to several ancient philosophers an opposition between the rational soul and the lower souls, and speaks of the freedom the soul will achieve upon death, when it goes to "the world of the intellect" to dwell in the "light of the Creator." Even during this life, we should seek to free ourselves from the body insofar as is possible.

Spiritual medicine

This idea that perfect happiness is attained by freeing the soul from the body is a Neoplatonic inheritance, so it is unsurprising that it is found in the most Neoplatonic of our authors, al-Kindī and Miskawayh. But al-Rāzī, too, emphasizes the bliss that can be achieved in the afterlife if one pleases God during one's earthly life. He also explicitly ascribes to Plato the view that the disembodied life is perfectly happy (see al-Rāzī 1939: 30). In all three authors, a favorable depiction of the afterlife is in part designed to forestall the fear of death, which is one of the greatest potential sources of unhappiness for man. They emphasize that this is an irrational fear, arguing, for instance, that only pain is fearful and there can be no pain without the body (a point emphasized especially by al-Rāzī), or that since mankind is essentially mortal, to wish that one is immortal is incoherent (an argument used by both al-Kindī and Miskawayh). Al-Rāzī also goes to the trouble of providing arguments against the fear of death that could be accepted even by someone who does not believe in the afterlife. These arguments, tailored to the needs of the recipient, illustrate the therapeutic approach adopted by our philosophers when they discuss fear, sorrow and vice. These are taken to be sicknesses of soul, which can be cured much as medicine cures sicknesses of body. The parallel between medicine and ethics is perhaps most obvious in al-Rāzī, whose main ethical treatise is after all entitled *Spiritual Medicine*. But the point holds for all our authors.

Again, there is Greek precedent for this "medical" way of seeing ethics. We can go back at least as far as Plato, who at *Charmides* (156–7) has Socrates speak of Thracian doctors who believe one should not cure the body without also curing the soul. But the chief Greek model for this approach is Galen. There were translations of his treatise on the passions of the soul and another treatise on ethics which in Arabic is labeled as dealing with "character traits [*al-akhlāq*]," as in the title *Tahdhīb al-Akhlāq* used by both Ibn 'Adī and Miskawayh (on Galen's work see Walzer 1949 and Mattock 1972). Galen is a direct source for much of al-Rāzī's *Spiritual Medicine*. In one case, for instance, he recommends having friends itemize one's shortcomings, so that one knows the areas in which one needs to improve. This bit of advice is rejected by Miskawayh, on the basis that enemies would be at least as good for the job as friends. He goes on to quote what he sees as a superior method from al-Kindī, which focuses instead on self-criticism. Still, Miskawayh embraces the broader Galenic project of "curing" one's psychological ills as a way of achieving happiness.

Indeed, it would be fair to say that al-Kindī's *Dispelling Sadness*, al-Rāzī's *Spiritual Medicine* and Miskawayh's *Refinement* all present eliminating psychological ills – which means subduing the non-rational appetites – as the primary way of attaining happiness. Like Galen, they emphasize the importance of diagnosing natural temperament (e.g. whether one is prone to passivity or anger) and the importance of training, which plays a role analogous to diet and physical exercise. Again, one might hypothesize that their prescriptions deal with the elimination of vice, rather than the cultivation of wisdom, not because that is all there is to ethics but because these works are pre-philosophical. The project is to prepare one's soul to seek wisdom, rather than to confer that wisdom. This goes hand-in-hand with the "two-level" ethics we have observed in Ibn 'Adī and Miskawayh. The "medical" ethical project, perhaps, will suffice to bring us to earthly or bodily happiness, whereas the more perfect intellective happiness is achieved only through philosophy.

Al-Fārābī agrees that medicine is a good model for ethical instruction and training: this is a leitmotif in his ethical works. But he carries the idea further by putting the medical model to work in a political context. For him, the perfect ruler is analogous to a doctor, who prescribes laws the way that the doctor prescribes remedies. This analogy dominates the *Aphorisms* (*Fuṣūl Muntaza'a*), a work which claims to collect passages from ancient authors "about the way one must govern cities and make them live, and improve the way of life of their people and direct them towards happiness" (trans. al-Fārābī 1961; ed. al-Fārābī 1993 [note that the section numbers in these two versions are not identical]). Here it is significant that al-Fārābī has chosen the title *Aphorisms* (*Fuṣūl*) for his work: this is an allusion to the medical *Aphorisms* of Hippocrates. The first section duly describes virtue as the health of the soul. Al-Fārābī goes on to expound what seems to be Aristotle's doctrine of the mean, using the idea of a balance of humors in the body: the goal of the ruler is to confer "a balanced character [*i'tidāl al-akhlāq*]" on his subjects (al-Fārābī 1993: §3). He compares the city to a body which needs to be treated holistically (§25–6), an analogy that appears in other works as well (e.g. al-Fārābī 1985: §15, 4, which compares the ruler to the "heart" of the body of the city).

All this might seem to leave ethics behind and move into "political philosophy," but this appearance is somewhat misleading. For one thing, al-Fārābī follows Aristotle in seeing the ethical and the political as two aspects of a single discipline. He says therefore that someone who can only make himself virtuous, but not bestow virtue on others, has a "deficient political art" (al-Fārābī 1993: §27). The capacity for political rule is the ultimate exercise of the capacity for practical reasoning, so that political rule becomes part of the ruler's own happiness – as we saw above, happiness consists in the realization of both the theoretical and the practical intellect (see al-Fārābī 1993: §53, 1964: §55). This would constitute al-Fārābī's answer to the Platonic puzzle of why the philosopher would "return to the cave" and consent to rule his fellow citizens: a fully realized practical intellect involves not only being perfect in one's own actions, but also perfecting the actions of others. Thus the best ruler is the same person as the philosopher, that is, a philosopher who has the ability to put his knowledge into practice in the context of a city (see e.g. *Attainment of Happiness*, in al-Fārābī 1962: §57, 1985: §15, 10–11).

Al-Fārābī's further pronouncements on the subject of political rule concern themselves not with detailed proposals for how to run a city – such as we find in Plato's *Republic* or *Laws* – but with the qualities possessed by the perfect ruler and the second-best strategies that need to be adopted in cities where no such ruler is available (see Gutas 2004). So in this sense too his focus remains ethical, insofar as he wants to describe the conditions under which citizens achieve good states of character and, thus, happiness. In yet another use of the medical analogy, he compares the different kinds of cities to the different sorts of climate, which respectively have an effect on one's ethical dispositions and one's bodily temperament (al-Fārābī 1993: §92). The happiness ultimately in view here is, as in our other authors, to be had in the afterlife. Al-Fārābī thus cites the ancients' calling the attainment of virtue in this life our "first perfection," and our blessedness in the afterlife our "utmost perfection" (§28).

Religion

In conclusion, a few words about how these ethical writings relate to the religious faiths of their authors. We have already seen that the Christian commitment to the value of chastity gave rise to a work by Ibn 'Adī on that topic. But it is perhaps more telling that his better-known and more general *Refinement* bears no obvious traces of Christian authorship. Only rarely do our authors appeal explicitly to religious teachings in defending their ethical theories. Some of the ideas that may seem "religious" to us in fact cut across confessional divides, and can even be seen as part of the inheritance of Greek pagan philosophy. For instance, the claim that perfect happiness is found only in the afterlife is often defended not with reference to any revealed text, but as the result of a Platonist theory on the nature of the soul and the malign influence of the body. Equally, though, authors like al-Kindī and Miskawayh would be keen to stress the agreement between Islam and this originally pagan Greek theory.

Ironically, among our authors the one who gets closest to a religious foundation for ethics is al-Rāzī, who is renowned for his skeptical critique of prophecy. In light of this critique it is usually thought that he is at best nominally a Muslim. But he is the only one of our authors to suggest that certain actions are choiceworthy precisely because they are preferred by God, or imitate God's generosity. For example, he argues for benign treatment of other humans and animals on the basis that God hates pain and suffering (al-Rāzī 1939: 103). He also says at the end of his *Spiritual Medicine* that one need not fear death so long as one has followed "the true law (*sharī'a*)"; indeed one can even expect forgiveness if one errs, since God is merciful (al-Rāzī 1939: 95–6). Though this reference to the true law has been taken to be a coded allusion to philosophy (Druart 1996b: 255), I think it is more likely that al-Rāzī is endorsing the ethical prescriptions of Islam and perhaps other religions.

By contrast, al-Fārābī does leave room in his practical philosophy for revelation: prophecy is the final requirement placed on the ideal ruler. But revelation is not required for the ruler to grasp the good. As we've already seen, al-Fārābī's ideal ruler does this by means of a perfected intellect, and it is never claimed that the ruler achieves this perfection by supernatural means. Rather, the purpose of prophecy is that the ruler may convey the truths he understands to his fellow citizens, in a way that they will find persuasive (see his *Book of Religion*, trans. in al-Fārābī 1981). In his discussions of religion, al-Fārābī clearly has Islam specifically in mind. For instance, he explains the role of jurisprudence (*fiqh*) in interpreting and extrapolating from the teachings of the ideal ruler. But in a strikingly pluralist move, he also allows for a multiplicity of "virtuous religions" which could be handed down as prophecies by a multiplicity of ideal rulers – their theoretical knowledge will always be the same, but their revealed religions will be tailored to the needs of their different citizens. Again, the medical analogy is relevant here: the doctor similarly tailors his prescriptions to the needs of each patient.

It should be stressed that al-Fārābī is unusual in subordinating religion to philosophy in this way. He is followed by Averroes (d. 1198) in the latter's *Decisive Treatise* (trans. in McGinnis and Reisman 2007). More typical is a commitment to the agreement between philosophical ethics and religion, without necessarily broaching the question of which is ultimately charged with determining the truth. For instance, Miskawayh's *Refinement* occasionally makes room for *sharī'a* within its fundamentally *falsafa*-based ethics, as when he says that the law is what reforms the character of the young (Zurayk 1966: 35). Ibn 'Adī's treatment of chastity provides another example. Even if he is trying to defend a specifically Christian position, he does so by appealing to an intellectualism that could be, and was, accepted by Muslims.

This is not to say, of course, that our authors would have nothing to contribute to debates that raged within Islamic theology. Consider the examples cited at the beginning of this chapter: the divine command theory of ethics and the relation of free will to moral responsibility. As we just saw, al-Rāzī is the only one to flirt with something like a divine command theory. But even in his case, the operative notion is actually the *imitation* of God – which goes back to the Greek tradition, ultimately to Plato's *Theaetetus* (see Sedley 1999). As for free will, al-Fārābī mentions frequently that the domain of ethics is actions that are subject to choice (*ikhtiyār*), and both he and Ibn 'Adī defend the reality of choice and genuine possibility in response to *kalām* authors (see Adamson 2010). Such examples show that our authors were aware of theological controversy. But they did not engage in it directly. Rather, they explored ethics within *falsafa*, an enterprise common to Muslims, Christians and Jews and continuous with the Greek tradition, even if that tradition was rethought to accommodate religious concepts like chastity, divine will and revelation.

See also Socrates and Plato (Chapter 3); Aristotle (Chapter 4); Later ancient ethics (Chapter 5); Ethics and reason (Chapter 9); Freedom and responsibility (Chapter 23); Virtue ethics (Chapter 40).

References

Adamson, P. (2007a) *Al-Kindī*, New York: Oxford University Press.

——(2007b) "Miskawayh's Psychology," in P. Adamson (ed.) *Classical Arabic Philosophy: Sources and Reception*, London: Warburg Institute, pp. 39–54.

——(2008) "Platonic Pleasures in Epicurus and al-Rāzī," in P. Adamson (ed.) *In the Age of al-Farabi*, London: Warburg Institute, pp. 71–94.

——(2010), "Freedom and Determinism," in R. Pasnau (ed.) *The Cambridge History of Medieval Philosophy*, 2 vols, Cambridge: Cambridge University Press, vol. 1, pp. 399–413.

Akasoy, A. and Fidora, A. (2005) *The Arabic Version of the Nicomachean Ethics*, Leiden: Brill.

Alon, I. (1991) *Socrates in Mediaeval Arabic Literature*, Leiden: Brill.

Arberry, A. J. (trans.) (1950) *The Spiritual Physick of Rhazes*, London: John Murray.

Druart, T.-A. (1993) "Al-Kindī's Ethics," *Review of Metaphysics* 47: 329–57.

——(1996a) "Al-Farabi, Ethics and First Intelligibles," *Documenti e Studi sulla Tradizione Filosofica Medievale* 7: 403–23.

——(1996b) "Al-Razi's Conception of the Soul: Psychological Background to his Ethics," *Medieval Philosophy and Theology* 5: 245–63.

——(1997) "The Ethics of al-Razi," *Medieval Philosophy and Theology* 5: 47–71.

——(2008) "An Arab Christian Philosophical Defense of Religious Celibacy against its Islamic Condemnation: Yaḥyā ibn 'Adī," in N. Van Deusen (ed.) *Chastity: A Study in Perception, Ideals, Opposition*, Leiden: Brill, pp. 77–85.

Fakhry, M. (1994) *Ethical Theories in Islam*, Leiden: Brill.

al-Fārābī (1961) *Fuṣūl al-Madanī: Aphorisms of the Statesman*, ed., trans. D. M. Dunlop, Cambridge: Cambridge University Press.

——(1962) *Philosophy of Plato and Aristotle*, trans. M. Mahdi, Ithaca, NY: Cornell University Press.

——(1964) *The Political Regime [al-Siyāsa alMadaniyya]*, ed. F. M. Najjar, Beirut: Imprimerie Catholique.

——(1981) *The Political Writings: The "Selected Aphorisms" and Other Texts*, trans. C. E. Butterworth, Ithaca, NY: Cornell University Press.

——(1985) *Mabādi' Ārā Ahl al-Madīna al-Fāḍila* [*On the Perfect State*], ed., trans. R. Walzer, Oxford: Oxford University Press.

——(1993) *Fuṣūl Muntaza'a*, Beirut: Dār al-Mashriq.

Griffith, S. H. (ed., trans.) (2002) *Yaḥyā b. 'Adī: The Reformation of Morals*, Provo, UT: Brigham Young University Press.

——(2006) "Yaḥyā b. 'Adī's Colloquy On *Sexual Abstinence and the Philosophical Life*," in J. E. Montgomery (ed.) *Arabic Theology, Arabic Philosophy*, Leuven, Belgium: Peeters, pp. 299–333.

Gutas, D. (1981) "Classical Arabic Wisdom Literature: Nature and Scope," *Journal of the American Oriental Society* 101: 49–86.

——(1988) "Plato's *Symposion* in the Arabic Tradition," *Oriens* 31: 36–60.

——(1990) "Ethische Schriften im Islam," in W. Heinrichs (ed.) *Orientalisches Mittelalter: Neues Handbuch der Literatur Wissenschaft*, vol. 5, Wiesbaden, Germany: AULA-Verlag, pp. 346–65.

——(2004) "The Meaning of *Madanī* in al-Fārābī's 'Political' Philosophy," in E. Gannagé, P. Crone, M. Aouad, D. Gutas and E. Schütrumpf (eds) *The Greek Strand in Islamic Political Thought: Proceedings of the Conference held at the Institute for Advanced Study, Princeton, 16–27 June 2003*, Special issue, *Mélanges de l'Université Saint-Joseph* 62: 259–82.

Mattock, J. N. (1972) "A Translation of the Arabic Epitome of Galen's Book *Peri Ethon*," in S. M. Stern, Albert Hourani and Vivian Brown (eds) *Islamic Philosophy and the Classical Tradition*, Oxford: Cassirer, pp. 235–60.

McGinnis, J. and Reisman, D. R. (ed., trans.) (2007) *Classical Arabic Philosophy: An Anthology of Sources*, Indianapolis, IN: Hackett.

Miskawayh (1966) *Tahdhīb al-Akhlāq*, ed. C. Zurayk, Beirut: American University of Beirut Press.

Mistrih, V. (1981) "Traité sur la continence de Yaḥyā ibn 'Adī, édition critique," *Studia Orientalia Christiana* 16: 1–137.

al-Rāzī (1939) *Rasā'il Falsafiyya* [*Opera philosophica*], ed. P. Kraus, Cairo: Imprimerie Paul Barbey.

Ritter, H. and Walzer, R. (1938) *Uno Scritto Morale Inedito di al-Kindī*, Rome: Reale Accademia Nazionale dei Lincei.

Rosenthal, F. (1940) "On the Knowledge of Plato's Philosophy in the Islamic World," *Islamic Culture* 14: 387–422.

Sedley, D. N. (1999) "The Ideal of Godlikeness," in G. Fine (ed.) *Plato*, vol. 2, Oxford: Oxford University Press, pp. 309–28.

Shihadeh, A. (2006) *The Teleological Ethics of Fakhr al-Dīn al-Rāzī*, Leiden: Brill.

Strohmaier, G. (1974) "Die arabische Sokrateslegende und ihre Ursprünge," in P. Nagel (ed.) *Studia Coptica*, Berlin: Akademie Verlag, pp. 121–36.

Walzer, R. (1949) "New Light on Galen's Moral Philosophy," *Classical Quarterly* 43: 82–96.

Zurayk, C. (ed.) (1966) *Miskawayh: Tahdhīb al-akhlāq*, Beirut: American University of Beirut Press.

——(trans.) (1968) *Miskawayh: The Refinement of Character*, Beirut: American University of Beirut Press.

Further reading

Adamson, P. and Taylor, R. C. (2005) *The Cambridge Companion to Arabic Philosophy*, Cambridge: Cambridge University Press.

Druart, T.-A. (1993) "Al-Kindī's Ethics," *Review of Metaphysics* 47: 329–57.

——(1996) "Al-Fārābī, Ethics and First Intelligibles," *Documenti e Studi sulla Tradizione Filosofica Medievale* 7: 403–23.

——(1997) "The Ethics of al-Rāzī," *Medieval Philosophy and Theology* 5: 47–71. (A series of articles on prominent early figures in the Arabic tradition.)

Fakhry, M. (1994) *Ethical Theories in Islam*, Leiden: Brill. (Broad study of ethical themes, including theological as well as philosophical sources.)

Gutas, D. (1990) "Ethische Schriften im Islam," in W. Heinrichs (ed.) *Orientalisches Mittelalter*, Special issue, *Neues Handbuch der Literatur Wissenschaft* 5: 346–65. (Very useful summary of ethical works in the Islamic world, organized by genre.)

Hourani, G. F. (1971) *Islamic Rationalism: The Ethics of 'Abd al-Jabbār*, Oxford: Clarendon Press. (Study of ethics in a major theological figure.)

Leaman, O. and Nasr, S. H. (1996) *History of Islamic Philosophy*, London: Routledge. (Collection of general articles on figures and themes of philosophy in the Islamic world.)

McGinnis, J. and Reisman, D. C. (ed., trans.) (2007) *Classical Arabic Philosophy: An Anthology of Sources*, Indianapolis, IN: Hackett. (A valuable collection of primary sources on philosophy in Arabic; by far the most complete available in English, with several texts concerning ethics.)

Shihadeh, A. (2006) *The Teleological Ethics of Fakhr al-Dīn al-Rāzī*, Leiden: Brill. (Important study of a later philosophical theologian's take on ethics.)

7
EARLY MODERN NATURAL LAW

Knud Haakonssen

Early modern versus modern natural law

In contemporary parlance, "natural law" most commonly refers to a core doctrine of the Catholic Church and its educational institutions, according to which God has imbued nature, including human nature, with certain fundamental values or purposes which humanity can understand and which are consonant with the values taught by the Christian revelation. (See Contemporary natural law theory [Chapter 42].) The most important Catholic articulation of this idea is ascribed to the great thirteenth-century philosopher Thomas Aquinas, and accordingly it is known as "Thomistic" natural law. In modern philosophical ethics and philosophy of law, "natural law" refers to the more general idea that there is a "higher" norm, or law, that is not the work of human action, such as legislation, and by means of which the latter can be assessed, indeed, has to be assessed in order to be considered "valid" law. In other words, naturally given law is distinguished from "positive" law that is made (posited) by human authorities.

Whatever their contemporary philosophical significance, these neat doctrines have at best very limited relevance for understanding natural law ideas in the early modern period, from the Reformation to the end of the Enlightenment period in the late eighteenth or early nineteenth century. In fact, the tendency to bring our own concepts to bear upon the past has in this case, as in many others, played havoc with the appreciation of an important phase in the history of ethics. In post-Reformation Protestant countries, especially those in whose universities natural law had been transferred from the theology to the law and philosophy faculties, a form of natural law emerged whose main concern was with peace and sociability under civil government rather than with divine law. This aroused significant hostility in Catholic countries and universities and led to a certain wariness of a subject that might be seen as distinctive for Protestant culture. It was only with the so-called Catholic revival in the late nineteenth century that Thomistic natural law doctrine was invigorated to become the prominent flagship for Catholic moral engagement that it has been during the twentieth and twenty-first centuries. Furthermore, the general philosophical idea of a natural law as the master norm and test of legal validity cannot be clearly and uniformly applied to characterize early modern thinking on the subject, especially in Protestant states where the "new" natural law tended to converge with positive civil law. In fact, this idea of a "higher" natural law has been one of the major stumbling blocks for our understanding of significant thinkers of the period in question.

The problem here, as so often in the history of ideas, is the tendency to assume that there is a core meaning of central concepts, such as natural law, and that we can trace the occurrences of these ideas in the course of history. Whether or not this ever makes sense is outside the present brief. This chapter is concerned to show, however, that natural law ideas in the early modern period can best be understood as a string of intellectual episodes that may be said to have varying degrees of family resemblance when they are considered as an intellectual and literary genre and an institutionalized resource for education, public debate and policy-making in quite different contexts. This amorphous character of natural law ideas does not detract from their significance, though that significance may be different from what is commonly expected.

The formation of early modern natural law

Modern developments in economics, politics and religion all had a formative influence on natural law theories. The growth of domestic trade between country and city, of European trade and, most dramatically, of transoceanic trade and colonialism all required an ever greater ability to deal with other people outside one's cultural, moral and, often, political and religious community who yet had status as personal agents. What is more, such persons often had to be dealt with collectively as artificial persons in the form of merchant houses, trading companies, city corporations, overseas tribes, etc. To these purposes the abstract juridical person, characterized in terms of ownership-relations with the natural world and contractual relations with each other, was well suited. Similarly, the gradual emergence of the territorial state with a centralized system of government and administration was accompanied by an obvious tendency to conduct its business by means of rules rather than personal relations. This was desired not least because so few European states were based on ethnic nationality, most being conglomerates of different peoples, sometimes very different. Another political circumstance that nourished the idea of a natural law was the need for a law of nations, often closely associated with the growth in international trade and associated conflicts. Last, but not least, with the Reformation Europe was divided into several Christian confessions, not only between countries, but in many cases within existing states. The ensuing relentless warfare underlined more than anything the need for some sort of moral-legal theory that was not dependent upon religious confession.

However, it is important to appreciate that such theorizing was itself seen as, and hence became, a sectarian religious-political tool, which has to be understood as much in that perspective as in terms of its universalist claims.

During the two and a half, or nearly three, centuries we are dealing with, these factors obviously changed dramatically, but they indicate the demands that early modern theorists of natural law had to meet. To do so, these theorists invoked a wide range of intellectual means. Fundamental was Roman law with the commentaries on it that had been made over many centuries, and this was buttressed with ancient history and other classical literature. It should here be pointed out that the early Protestant lawyers were also humanist scholars who brought the full panoply of classical and textual learning to bear upon the law. Closely associated with Roman civil law was the moral and legal philosophy of scholasticism, especially in the Aristotelian form whose doctrine of man's rational and sociable essence would play a role in the early Protestant natural law of Hugo Grotius and keep recurring much later. Ancient history was increasingly supplemented by modern, and, not least, by the growing information (in many genres) about non-European cultures. Over time, the historical and ethnographic understanding of humanity fed into the Enlightenment's anthropological theories of human nature, so that natural law theories often became seedbeds for the more specialized explanations of human nature and its behavior that we see in retrospect as proto-social sciences: political economy, demography, linguistics, social psychology, and others.

By these and similar means, thinkers tried to assemble a body of law that could be said to belong to humanity as such and which might be substantial enough to provide guidance in solving the problems in economic, political, international and religious matters that we indicated earlier. However, these ambitions were of course not philosophically or theologically neutral, and Protestant natural law was in fact characterized by quite fundamental divisions that were fought over with considerable vehemence. Most fundamental, at least at the time, was the question how the kind of historical and comparative method outlined above could have any authority, for it relied on human nature as it was after the Fall of Adam and Eve, i.e. on the sinful and changeable humanity of common experience, not on any transcendent moral essence. Orthodox scholastic theologians of various stripes, but not least Catholics and Lutherans during the seventeenth and early eighteenth centuries, argued that the law of nature had to be derived from human nature in the pristine form presented in scripture and still present in mankind's rational nature or essence. This tended to make natural law into a political weapon rather than a means of resolving conflict, and much of the criticism of orthodox natural law consisted in pointing this out, especially by highlighting the difficulties and dangers in relying upon scriptural authority or metaphysics in worldly matters, an issue we will return to.

Another problem in the humanist approach to the search for natural law was that this method, of course, often seemed to yield the exact opposite of what natural lawyers aimed at. From Montaigne in the late sixteenth century, through Pierre Bayle in the late seventeenth, to *philosophes* such as Diderot in the high Enlightenment, the historical variety of humanity had been used also to show its moral pluralism, and irrespective of how skeptical the intentions of these thinkers actually were, there was a perception that such arguments undermined the possibility of a common morality. However, often such skepticism, apparent or real, was met by ideas of natural law that were equally unpalatable to religious orthodoxy. Those were "minimalist" theories of morals, that is, attempts to specify the absolute minimum of moral notions that must be assumed in order for it to be intelligible how people can live together and which therefore can be taken to be universal to humanity as we know it.

Hugo Grotius and Thomas Hobbes

The earliest such attempt of real consequence was that of the Dutch humanist scholar and lawyer, Hugo Grotius (1583–1645; see Grotius 2005/1625), who posited the idea that any form of social interchange can be understood in contractual terms, contracts being understood as the bargaining of rights, and rights as natural properties (or their derivatives) of each person. The most extreme case of such supposedly contractual relations was that of slavery, in which the basic right to liberty would have been exchanged for some other good, such as being left alive, given sustenance, offered protection, etc. A very common case was the commercial exchange of goods. However, such a theory depended upon the sense in which rights could be said to be natural properties of persons. Grotius thought of rights as powers, so that personal liberty and property in land or chattel are powers over one's person, one's land and one's movables. On this basis he at first denied that the open sea could be owned, for nobody could have power over it, and consequently shipping and commerce had to be free (2004/1609; he later changed his mind, see 2005/1625: Bk 2, ch. 3). However, he did not follow this line of thinking to its radical end, for he thought that in exercising our moral power, or asserting our rights, we must have insight into the objective rightness of our action, i.e., into its accord with our sociable nature and its role in maintaining social relations with others. In other words, the moral openness of the subjective rights idea was curtailed by the traditional idea (neo-stoic or scholastic) of a moral law of justice to which we are obligated simply through our rational insight (though the interpretation is disputed).

It was left to Thomas Hobbes (1588–1679) to follow the idea of purely subjective rights to a much more radical conclusion. Arguing along lines similar to those of Epicureanism, Hobbes maintained (at least in the final statement of his political philosophy, *Leviathan*, Hobbes 1991/1651) that humanity was universally characterized by limitless passions, thus potentially laying claim to, or asserting rights to, anything and everything. Only the artifice of government and positive law could prevent the state of natural conflict by curbing our limitless natural rights, and the law of nature was a rule of prudence arising from the rational insight that it was necessary to lay down all our rights (except that to self-defense when directly threatened on our life) in order to achieve a sociable life enforced by an absolute sovereign. In this way Hobbes tried to solve the problem of obligation by modern political means, in contrast to Grotius's reliance on moral intuition. According to Hobbes, natural law was to be made obligatory, not by God, but by the will of the political sovereign. It is difficult not to see this as a response to the crises of the English civil war and of the violent change of church and government that followed. Hobbes tried to pay his respects to religion by pointing out that natural law conceived in this way had divine backing, in the sense that it was part of God's creation like everything else about humanity. However, that could hardly conceal that here natural law had been entirely deprived of any meaningful metaphysical standing, religious or otherwise.

Baruch Spinoza and Richard Cumberland

Hobbes's provocation had a shaping influence on subsequent moral and political thought, not least in the genre of natural law. Four names stood out in the period immediately after Hobbes, all born in the same year: the Englishmen Richard Cumberland (1632–1718) and John Locke (1632–1704), the Jewish-Dutch Baruch Spinoza (1632–77), and the German Samuel Pufendorf (1632–94). Of these, Spinoza stretched one central Hobbesian theme to such an extent that he is rarely counted as a natural lawyer at all (1989/1670). As part of a unitary metaphysical conception of the world-and-God, Spinoza dispensed with the idea of a divine will in the ordinary meaning and explained the laws for human behavior as the scientific "laws" of physics and psychology that bind the world together. In such a scheme the question of obligation to natural law simply did not arise. Rather, methodical explanation, or rational insight, made justification irrelevant. This "scientific" ambition was also meant to provide a basis for ethics that was beyond traditional religion and which thus was immune to its confessional divisions, a tolerationist standpoint of particular relevance to Spinoza's own situation and to Dutch society in general.

While Cumberland (2005/1672), too, had scientific ambitions, they were very different from those of Spinoza, and they were in the service of formulating a natural law theory that would suit Anglican preconceptions and give a response to Hobbes. In analogy with Descartes's notion of the physical world as full, i.e., as a system in which every part in some way was connected with every other part, Cumberland sought to show that the good of each individual person is bound up with that of the whole of the human community, so that sociability is a natural duty. Furthermore, we can see that this natural duty is imposed by

God as an obligatory law, because the sanctions of the law of sociability can be scientifically discerned in the world; punishment for transgression is found in the form of psychological and physical misery, reward in the form of peace and happiness. Although endlessly varied by circumstances as far as the scientific garb is concerned, this basic idea remained pervasive in much Protestant thought, both clerical and lay, for a very long time: natural law prescribed social morality as a natural duty that we could discover through empirical investigation of humanity considered as a coherent moral system, and it was disclosed through similarly ascertainable signs in our world as an obligatory law issued by divine will.

John Locke and Samuel Pufendorf

Locke and Pufendorf are often considered as the classic representatives of modern Protestant natural law theory because they combine several of the central ideas of their predecessors into forceful formulations of great clarity. They share with all of them the view of humanity as constitutionally dominated by a desire for self-preservation and concerned with sociability as a means in this regard. They also have the ambition to articulate a basic moral law and its implications that can be established by means of modern science and thus lift ethics above the uncertainties of confessional religion. However, their ideal of science was not that of Grotius's comparative anthropology, nor that of Cumberland's empirical collection of flowers in humanity's present and projected moral gardens. Rather, they aimed at a demonstrative science which differed from that of Spinoza by being a matter of piecemeal or procedural deductive proofs of the relations between concepts derived from experience, rather than the Dutchman's attempt to establish a closed metaphysical world-system. At the root of this was an idea that Locke and Pufendorf had in common with Hobbes, namely the fundamentally anti-scholastic one that morality was not inherently part of the natural world or human nature, but was somehow superimposed upon or introduced into nature. The immediate cause of morality was human action, and consequently Hobbes, Locke and Pufendorf thought that moral ideas were singularly open to certainty, for we know that which we ourselves make in a way that we do not know anything else. Here the three differed as to why this was the case, but that had much less impact than the underlying idea of morals as the outcome of human activity in the natural world, namely our striving to live safely and, hence, sociably.

While Hobbes in *Leviathan* saw the institution of political authority as the fundamental moral implementation of the law of nature, Locke (1954/1663–4, 1997/1686–8, 1975/1690: esp. Bk 2, ch. 28, 1988/1690) thought about morality in much more legalistic terms. No human activity had any moral character unless it was related to some prescriptive law, but there were several different forms of law that were aimed at making mankind live sociably. There was the "political law" made by political authority and enforced by courts; there was the "law of opinion," i.e. the social norms of the various groups in which we live; and as a basis for all, there was the divine law prescribed by the deity. This last was a natural law in as much as human reason alone could prove the existence of the divine legislator and his imposition on us of duties towards the world and each other, namely the basic duty of preservation and the more specific duties and rights that this entailed: individual property rights delimited by duties to the common good, rights to self-governance in the service of peace and safety, etc. However, natural reason could not in the same way demonstrate our obligation to the divine law of nature, for it could not prove the immortality of the soul and hence the certainty of eternal sanctions for the law in the form of eternal life or punishment. Like his contemporaries, Locke understood obligation in terms of effective motivation, which he explained in hedonistic terms as a matter of pleasure and pain. In order for obligation to the ultimate norm, the law of nature, to be absolute, the pleasures of compliance and pains of disobedience must be certain. So Locke shifted his idea of explanation from that of demonstration to that of calculating probabilities, and on the latter approach he thought that it was in the highest degree rational to believe that scripture is God's word revealed to various witnesses. Furthermore, the pleasures and pains that sanction God's law were a rational choice of guidance in comparison with any alternative pleasures and pains.

If Locke was willing to incorporate God's revealed word into natural law on the basis of rational probability in order to solve the problem of obligation to the law, Pufendorf sidestepped the issue of obligation altogether by a strikingly radical line of argument (forthcoming/1672, 2003/1673). Like Locke, he thought that we could have rational knowledge of the existence of a divinity who created this world with a purpose and who would judge humanity beyond it. However, in line with his fideist anti-metaphysical style of Lutheran belief, Pufendorf distinguished sharply between the divine will, the effects of which we could observe in creation, and God's reason, from which he thought that humanity was completely excluded. Consequently we could not have rational or "natural" access to any law of nature that set out God's intentions for us here and in the hereafter; these could only be the subject of faith. Since faith varied endlessly and, notoriously, provided the basis for conflict rather than peace, social living on the basis of Christian belief was impossible in the long run (and, in recent European experience, also in the short). Whatever we believed that God's intentions with our earthly life might be, their pursuit required our preservation, but experience showed that we were too weak to live individually, yet too aggressive to live sociably unless sociability was secured by the force of political government. There was nothing more, or less, to natural law and its obligation than the adoption of social roles, including those of the citizen or subject, that would enable us to live in sufficient peace with our neighbors to pursue whatever goals we happen to have. In this theory, natural law is clearly made independent not only of confessional religion, but of any substantial metaphysics. The law is a matter of cultivating those social personae that are likely to work in a given historical circumstance, without some ultimate basis in a "natural" person, let alone features shared with the divinity.

This secular (though not irreligious) and anti-metaphysical approach to natural law was further pursued by the major German Enlightenment thinker Christian Thomasius (1655–1728), who likewise wanted to keep religion and politics apart (forthcoming/1705/1688, 2007). Pufendorf's and Thomasius's context was one in which Lutheran Germany (and Scandinavia) was dominated by an orthodox theology according to which religious faith was concerned with our innate ideas of God's nature, which had been obscured by original sin so that the clergy had the special role of guiding us in earthly life. It was the task of theologians and clergy to extract the law of nature from the original human condition before the Fall, when humanity could understand the divine prescriptions that derived from God's essence which, just like in scholastic thinkers, was called the eternal law. For Pufendorf and Thomasius this kind of orthodox teaching dangerously mixed up two entirely different aspects of human life: religion, which was humanity's quest for living with God, and politics, which was people's striving to live with each other in this world. The orthodox clergy seemed to claim a special vantage point outside of historical society from which they could judge the latter.

Gottfried Wilhelm Leibniz and Christian Wolff

On this basic point orthodox theologians were in agreement with a broad trend in philosophy, which offered a radically different kind of natural law theory from that of the great voluntarists (Latin "voluntas" = will) we have considered. During the early modern and modern periods, there were throughout Europe thinkers who – with inspiration from ancient and medieval philosophies, especially Platonist, Aristotelian and Thomistic – developed metaphysical theories to deal with often very different "local" challenges, but which nevertheless have some crucial features in common. The main figures were, in Germany, Gottfried Wilhelm Leibniz (1646–1716) and Christian Wolff (1679–1754); and in England, the Cambridge Platonists, such as Benjamin Whichcote (1609–83), Henry More (1614–87), Ralph Cudworth (1617–89) and Nathaniel Culverwell (1619–51), and the "ethical rationalists," such as Samuel Clarke (1675–1729) and William Wollaston (1660–1724). These and many similar thinkers are often called "rationalists" because they assumed a structure to be inherent in reality that is consonant with and, hence, accessible to rational understanding. They are also called "realists," because they thought that values in some sense are inherent in nature, part of the structure of ultimate reality, as opposed to superimposed upon it through conventions or acts of will. Further, they insisted that the value that people and their actions have (virtues, rightness, justice) must be understood and judged in terms of their contribution to the communities of activity in which they occur, ultimately to the system of moral beings as a whole. As a consequence, natural law was seen as an explication and prescription of that which is inherently good according to this criterion.

The greatest and most famous thinker in this vein was Leibniz, whose ambition was to articulate a "universal jurisprudence" that set out the relations of justice between all moral agents from humans, through angels to God (1988). Justice is the "charity of the wise," which is based upon pleasure in the happiness of others, and since this pleasure arises from perfection, the system of justice is in fact an ideal of spiritual perfectibility through cognitive insight. Working from similar metaphysical foundations, Christian Wolff maintained that the perfectibility of ourselves and of the parts of the world within our grasp was the basic law of nature (1740–8, forthcoming/1749). Perfectibility consisted in the gradual realization of our natural abilities in mutual harmony with others, and this was the same as progress in happiness guided by the divine ideal of perfect happiness and signaled to us through experience of pleasure. In this way the law of nature was supposed to provide us with a moral norm that is objective also in the sense of being independent of God's will. We were under an obligation to the law because our intellection of perfection with rational inevitability would draw our will towards this goal, and moral freedom in fact consisted in our insight into this condition of our life.

If Pufendorf and Thomasius claimed natural law for the jurists and legal historians within the law faculties who could advise rulers about the historically given circumstances in which social peace and security were to be sought; and if the orthodox Lutherans wanted natural law to be the tool of the faculty of theology with which it could guide public policy; then Leibniz and in particular Wolff were the protagonists for the professional metaphysicians of the faculty of philosophy as the intellects behind the leaders of the modern territorial state. In Germany these states often had centralist ("absolutist") governments with ambitions of reform that required control and hence expertise; natural law was the foundation course for the training of experts. In addition, natural law remained intimately connected with the development of the law of nations, playing a central role in the European state system as its dynamics changed under the influence of trade. Here the Swiss Emer de Vattel (1714–67; see 2008/1758) was of particular importance.

Enlightenment rights theory

This does not, however, complete the broad picture of natural law theory in the Enlightenment. At various points during the whole of the early modern period, the attempt to deal with crises in religion or politics through a stable "natural" basis for morality concentrated on finding this basis in the individual person, rather than in some law imposed upon individuals. The two approaches were by no means entirely separate, for it was common to see a person's apprehension of obligation to the law of nature as an internalization of the law that enabled the person to make moral judgements. But to the extent that the emphasis was on natural morality as a feature, a faculty, of the individual, we are approaching what we would call a rights theory. We have met two different ideas of natural rights in Grotius and Hobbes, but it was not least in the version presented by Locke that it had significance in the eighteenth century. Locke found the basis for morality in divine law, but a crucial feature of our obligation to the law was that we must apprehend it by our own natural reason, for God's authority could not be mediated by others, such as priests or church traditions. So the total freedom of mind to assent to God's word was required. This was the right of conscience, and when that was exercised concerning all aspects of the conservation of God's creation, as demanded by his fundamental law of nature, we had the basic rights of individual liberty and property.

According to Grotius and Hobbes, rights were completely alienable, and the two thinkers used this to explain the legitimacy of absolutist government. With Locke, rights became a divinely appointed shield against government. It was this Lockean idea that was elaborated and disseminated as part of a similarly voluntarist theory of natural law by the Huguenot refugee Jean Barbeyrac (1674–1744; see his forthcoming/1706, 2002/1716), and subsequently by the Swiss Jean Jacques Burlamaqui (1694–1748; see his 2006/1747). Barbeyrac saw conscience as the core of our moral ability to live socially and as the basis for political government. Its freedom had to be tolerated as a right and hence as a limitation on sovereignty, which should be understood as a contractual device for protection and, in extreme conditions, as subject to a right of resistance. The special status of the right to conscience was due to the fact that it was an unavoidable right, a right that God had imposed on us as moral agents who had to judge for ourselves. In other words, this basic right was in fact a divine duty which could neither be given away nor taken from us; it was inalienable. Furthermore, in exercising our right to conscience we were under the obligation to follow the law of nature, and this meant that there was a right and a wrong way of using that right and its derivatives.

This line of argument was transposed into a moral sense theory by the Scottish philosopher Francis Hutcheson (1694–1747; see his 2008/1725, 2007/1747/1742, forthcoming/1755). According to him, the human mind is issued with a moral sense, analogous to the external senses, by means of which we perceive virtuous and vicious behavior, which is characterized by its tendency to promote happiness or unhappiness. However, like other senses, the moral sense is fallible and must be subjected to correction by the law of nature, which is an injunction to maximize happiness, or minimize unhappiness, in God's creation. When the moral sense is guided by natural law it is in fact our conscience, and Hutcheson agreed with Locke, Barbeyrac and Burlamaqui that we must have a right to conscience and that it is inalienable.

In other words, in this rights tradition, which often refers back to Grotius, we end up with a fundamental ambiguity between right as a sphere of moral freedom and right as morally rightful (or obligatory) action. Since rights were the common basis for contractarian theories of social relations, including civil society and sovereignty, this ambiguity had wide-ranging implications. At one extreme was the notion that society was an artificial construction by individuals trading in their subjective rights or liberties; at the other, the view of society as part of the implementation of a naturally given moral vision for humanity at large. The rights tradition from Barbeyrac, through Hutcheson and Burlamaqui, to the American revolutionary thinkers (e.g., James Madison) and beyond was closer to the latter extreme, and this calls into question its continuity with modern secular ideas of human rights.

See also Hobbes (Chapter 8); Ethics and reason (Chapter 9); Ethics and sentiment (Chapter 10); Contemporary natural law theory (Chapter 42); Rights (Chapter 56).

References

Barbeyrac, Jean (2002/1716) "Discourse on the Benefits Conferred by the Laws," in Pufendorf 2002/1673, pp. 331–60.

——(Forthcoming/1706) "An Historical and Critical Account of the Science of Morality," editorial annotation, in Pufendorf forthcoming/1672. (Also editorial annotation in Pufendorf 2002/1673 and Grotius 2005/1625.)

Burlamaqui, Jean Jacques (2006/1747) *The Principles of Natural and Politic Law*, trans. T. Nugent, ed. P. Korkman, Indianapolis, IN: Liberty Fund.

Cumberland, Richard (2005/1672) *A Treatise of the Laws of Nature*, trans. J. Maxwell, ed. J. Parkin, Indianapolis, IN: Liberty Fund.

Grotius, Hugo (2004/1609) *The Free Sea*, ed. D. Armitage, trans. R. Hakluyt, Indianapolis, IN: Liberty Fund.

——(2005/1625) *The Right of War and Peace*, 3 vols, ed. R. Tuck, Indianapolis, IN: Liberty Fund.

Hobbes, Thomas (1991/1651) *Leviathan*, ed. R. Tuck, Cambridge: Cambridge University Press.

Hutcheson, Francis (2007/1747/1742) *Philosophiae Moralis Institution Compendiaria, with A Short Introduction to Moral Philosophy*, ed. L. Turco, Indianapolis, IN: Liberty Fund.

——(2008/1725) *An Introduction into the Original of Our Ideas of Beauty and Virtue*, ed. W. Leidhold, rev. edn, Indianapolis, IN: Liberty Fund.

——(Forthcoming/1755) *A System of Moral Philosophy*, ed. K. Haakonssen, Indianapolis, IN: Liberty Fund.

Leibniz, Gottfried Wilhelm (1988) *The Political Writings*, ed., trans. P. Riley, Cambridge: Cambridge University Press.

Locke, John (1954/1663–4) *Essays on the Law of Nature*, ed., trans. W. Von Leyden, Oxford: Clarendon Press.

——(1975/1690) *An Essay Concerning Human Understanding*, ed. P. H. Nidditch, Oxford: Clarendon Press.

——(1988/1690) *Two Treatises of Government*, ed. P. Laslett, Cambridge: Cambridge University Press.

——(1997/1686–8) "Of Ethic in General," in Locke, *Political Essays*, ed. M. Goldie, Cambridge: Cambridge University Press, pp. 297–304.

Pufendorf, Samuel (2002/1673) *The Whole Duty of Man, According to the Law of Nature*, trans. A. Tooke, ed. I. Hunter and D. Saunders, Indianapolis, IN: Liberty Fund.

——(Forthcoming/1672) *The Law of Nature and Nations*, trans. W. Kennet, ed. K. Haakonssen, Indianapolis, IN: Liberty Fund.

Spinoza, Baruch (1989/1670) *Tractatus Theologico-Politicus*, ed., trans. S. Shirley, Leiden: Brill.

Thomasius, Christian (2007) *Essays on Church, State, and Politics*, ed., trans. I. Hunter, T. Ahnert and F. Grunert, Indianapolis, IN: Liberty Fund.

——(Forthcoming/1705/1688) *Institutes of Divine Jurisprudence; with Selections from Foundations of the Law of Nature and Nations*, ed., trans. T. Ahnert, Indianapolis, IN: Liberty Fund.

Vattel, Emer de (2008/1758) *The Law of Nations, or, Principles of the Law of Nature, applied to the Conduct and Affairs of Nations and Sovereigns, with Three Early Essays on the Origin and Nature of Natural Law and Luxury*, trans. anon., ed. B. Kapossy and R. Whatmore, Indianapolis, IN: Liberty Fund.

Wolff, Christian (1740–8) *Jus Naturae Methodo Scientifica Pertractatum*, 8 vols, Frankfurt, Leipzig and Halle: Renger.

——(Forthcoming/1749) *The Law of Nations according to the Scientific Method*, ed. T. Ahnert, trans. J. H. Drake, Indianapolis, IN: Liberty Fund.

Further reading

Haakonssen, K. (1996) *Natural Law and Moral Philosophy: From Grotius to the Scottish Enlightenment*, Cambridge: Cambridge University Press. (Analysis of seventeenth-century natural law and its implications for the Enlightenment.)

Hochstrasser, T. (2000) *Natural Law Theories in the Early Enlightenment*, Cambridge: Cambridge University Press. (The use of history and eclecticism in German natural law.)

Hunter, I. (2001) *Rival Enlightenments: Civil and Metaphysical Philosophy in Early Modern Germany*, Cambridge: Cambridge University Press. (The opposition between the voluntarist and the metaphysical schools of natural law; natural law and Kant.)

Tuck, R. (1999) *The Rights of War and Peace: Political Thought and the International Order from Grotius to Kant*, Oxford: Oxford University Press. (Overview of the whole period under consideration above.)

8
HOBBES
Bernard Gert

Misinterpretations of Hobbes

Although Hobbes is acknowledged as the founder of English moral and political philosophy, until recently the standard interpretations of his account of human nature and of his moral and political views made it difficult to understand why he was taken seriously at all. Hobbes was interpreted as a psychological egoist, that is, as holding that every action of every person was motivated by self-interest. On this interpretation it is hard to understand how Hobbes could be offering any non-skeptical account of morality. Many did explicitly claim that Hobbes did not offer any such account, but rather that he reduced morality to enlightened self-interest, completely distorting what we normally regard as morality. Many of Hobbes's contemporaries interpreted him in this way and their criticisms were passed on to succeeding generations by Bishop Butler's criticisms of him. Some of these criticisms were the result of Hobbes's rhetorical style, but most of the criticisms stemmed from the fact that Hobbes was considered an atheist, providing an account of morality that did not depend upon God or even belief in God. Hobbes was not an atheist, but he did hold what is now the standard view of morality in English-speaking countries, namely that morality is independent of religion. Indeed, it is quite likely that Hobbes is one of those responsible for the fact that almost all English-speaking philosophers hold that morality does not depend on religion.

Morality concerned with virtues and vices

Hobbes follows Aristotle in regarding morality as being concerned with traits of character, i.e. virtues and vices, rather than with particular acts. Hobbes presents a list of moral virtues, e.g. justice, gratitude, and equity, and vices, e.g. arrogance and cruelty, that not only would have been accepted by his contemporaries but also would be accepted by most people today. What troubled many of his contemporaries about his moral theory, and still troubles many today, is that Hobbes argues that there is a close relationship between the moral virtues and self-interest. The power of this argument derives from the fact that Hobbes holds that what is most in a person's self-interest is avoiding an avoidable death. He does not hold that maximizing the satisfaction of one's desires is necessarily in one's self-interest, especially if one has desires that conflict with self-preservation.

Even when self-interest is interpreted as self-preservation, Hobbes still did not reduce morality to self-interest. Rather, he puts forward a commonly accepted account of morality; indeed, for Hobbes, the moral virtues simply are those traits of character that all persons praise (1994/1651, *Leviathan*, *L* Ch. 15, para. 40, 1991a/1651/1647/1642, *De Cive*, *DC* Ch. 3, §32). Hobbes then argues that anyone who thinks carefully about these universally praised traits of character will conclude that it is in a person's self-interest to develop and act on these traits of character that are the moral virtues. Hobbes was engaged in the philosophical task of justifying morality. His justification did not depend on God or belief in God, but on a concept of reason that he regards as universally accepted, namely, that reason teaches everyone to avoid an avoidable death (*DC* Dedication, p. 93). Hobbes holds that it is irrational not to develop and act on those traits of character that are the moral virtues, because these virtues are essential for achieving and maintaining peace, and peace is essential for self-preservation (*L* Ch. 15, para. 38, *DC* Ch. 3, §29).

Rationality and human nature

Hobbes regards it as a conceptual truth that everyone ought to follow reason, that is, that no one ever ought to act irrationally. He does not argue for this claim, nor does he argue for the claim that unless one has very strong reasons to the contrary, it is irrational to act in ways that significantly increase one's chances of death. These two claims, which he expected to be universally accepted and which seem to me to be correct, are the foundation of his moral and political theories. He does argue for his claim that reason requires acting morally (*DC* Ch 3, §32). A major element in his justification of morality is his attempt to point out some indisputable facts about human nature that prove that reason requires acting morally (*L* Ch. 13, paras 1–10, *DC* Ch. 1, §12). The two most important facts are that all persons are vulnerable, i.e. any person can be killed by other people, and that all persons have limited knowledge and are fallible, i.e. all people make mistakes. Also important is that most, if not all, people sometimes act on their emotions even when this leads them to act irrationally.

Other important facts are not truths about every human being but truths about populations (*DC* Preface, p. 100). He holds that in any large population, (1) some people hold false views about what is morally acceptable behavior, and (2) some people do not care about acting morally, but are only concerned with benefiting themselves, their family, and their friends. Hobbes's moral theory is an attempt to provide a description, explanation, and justification of morality that would persuade those people holding false moral views to change their views. Hobbes's political theory is an attempt to provide a guide for constructing a government that can protect its citizens from both those who hold false moral views and those who do not care about morality.

Justification of morality

Hobbes is attempting to prove that reason requires developing and acting on the moral virtues. Therefore it is essential that he put forward a traditional list of moral virtues, namely, justice, gratitude, modesty, equity, and mercy, and of the moral vices, namely, injustice, ingratitude, arrogance, pride, and iniquity (*L* Ch. 15, paras 38, 40). It is also essential that Hobbes provide a generally accepted account of these virtues and vices, for he is trying to provide an explanation of traditional morality. In fact, Hobbes's list of moral virtues and vices is remarkably close to what, even now, are generally regarded as moral virtues and vices. His only modification of the traditional list of moral virtues and vices is that he does not include fortitude, prudence, and temperance as moral virtues (*DC* Ch. 3, §32, *L* Ch. 15, para. 34). He does regard them as virtues, but personal virtues rather than moral ones. This is an important point, for it shows that Hobbes does not regard moral virtues merely as those traits of character that lead to an individual's preservation. The "laws of nature" dictate courage, prudence, and temperance as virtues because they tend to the preservation of the person who has them. However, other people need not praise the person who has these virtues, for a person that has these virtues need not act in ways that benefit them (1991b/1658, *De Homine*, *DH* Ch. 13, §9). Only those traits of character that all rational persons praise are moral virtues.

For Hobbes, no trait of character is a virtue unless it is dictated by reason, and so tends to the preservation of the person who has it. A virtue is a trait of character that all persons insofar as they are rational want to have, but being dictated by reason is not sufficient to be classified as a moral virtue. Moral virtues do not merely lead to one's own preservation; by leading to peace they lead to everyone's preservation. Hobbes calls the virtues that lead to peace, moral virtues because they are the traits of character that all people praise. His explanation of why all people praise the moral virtues is that these traits of character benefit everyone, not only the person who has them. They do this because they are the traits necessary for people living together in a peaceful and harmonious society (*L* Ch. 15, para. 40). All of this fits together in a remarkably clear and coherent way, and without distorting the sense of what is meant by moral virtue.

Distinguishing between justice and morality

Currently, common interpretations of Hobbes's moral theory are that it is a form of social contract theory, that is, morality is regarded as the result of an agreement among people about the kind of moral code that they want to govern their behavior. On this account, different societies can have different moralities, so Hobbes is sometimes interpreted as an ethical relativist, that is, as holding that different societies do indeed have different moralities. This is an improvement over earlier interpretations of Hobbes as holding that might makes right, that is, that the sovereign determines what is moral or immoral and that there is no universal standard of morality independent of the sovereign. Both of these kinds of interpretations are the result of failing to distinguish between justice and morality.

Hobbes does hold that justice depends upon a prior giving up of one's right to decide how to act, and hence obliging oneself to act as someone else decides (*L* Ch. 15, para. 2). This right can be given up by a contract between equals who agree to abide by the rules, i.e. laws, that are set up by whomever they choose to make those laws: a single person, as in a monarchy, a small group of people, as in an aristocracy, or all the people, as in a democracy (*L* Ch. 19, para. 1). Or it can be given up by a free gift of that right to someone who has sufficient power to kill one if one does not accept the rules, i.e. laws, that this person puts forward (*L* Ch. 14, para. 7). The former way of giving up a right results in what Hobbes calls sovereignty by institution; the latter way he calls sovereignty by acquisition (*L* Ch. 20, paras 1–2). If sovereignty by institution were concerned with morality rather than justice it would provide some support for the interpretation of Hobbes as a social contract theorist. If sovereignty by acquisition were about morality rather than justice, it would provide some support for the view that Hobbes holds that might makes right. But Hobbes consistently distinguishes between justice and morality. Justice is only one of many moral virtues, and although it is crucial for Hobbes's political theory, it plays no special role in his moral theory.

Hobbes does say that in the state of nature there is no place for justice (*L* Ch. 13, para. 14). But this is because the state of nature, by definition, is that state in which no one has given up their right to decide for themselves how to act. It is the state in which everyone retains what Hobbes calls the "right of nature," namely, the right to decide on their own what ways of acting best conduce to their preservation (*L* Ch. 15, para. 1). Hobbes never says that in the state of nature there is no place for morality. On the contrary, he insists that morality, which the laws of nature dictate, is eternal (*L* Ch. 15, para. 26, *DC* Ch. 3, §29). Hobbes claims that we should always want to act morally and should always act morally when we can do so safely (*L* Ch. 15, para. 36, *DC* Ch. 3, §27).

Hobbes's concept of reason

Hobbes is, in fact, a natural law theorist, but differs from most other natural law theorists in that God does not play a crucial role in his theory. He modifies the natural law theory of Grotius, but agrees with him that the laws of nature are the dictates of reason. This interpretation of Hobbes's moral theory has not achieved the acceptance it deserves because many contemporary philosophers, inspired by Hume, hold an account of reason as purely instrumental (Gauthier 1969). On this modified Humean account of reason, which is far more plausible than Hume's, reason does not merely tell one how to satisfy each particular desire; rather, it tells one how to achieve the maximum satisfaction of all of one's desires, whatever they happen to be. Hobbes agrees that one function of reason is to help one to satisfy one's desires, and the continuing satisfaction of one's desires is what he calls felicity (*L* Ch. 6, para. 58). However, he holds that the most important function of reason is to promote its own end, i.e. self-preservation (*DH* Ch. 11, §6). He regards it as contrary to reason or irrational to act on those desires that conflict with this goal of reason.

Hobbes follows Aristotle, not only in regarding morality as concerned primarily with traits of character rather than particular acts, but also in holding that reason has its own goals and does not merely aid the passions in gaining their goals. The failure to appreciate that Hobbes holds that reason has its own goal is partly due to the fact that Hobbes denies that there is a *summum bonum*, or greatest good, that can serve as the goal of reason (*L* Ch. 11, para. 1). Rather, for Hobbes the goal of reason is a negative one, avoiding an avoidable death (*DC* Dedication, p. 93). As long as one does not act irrationally, Hobbes counts all ways of acting as rationally acceptable. This results in Hobbes holding a surprisingly liberal view, that is, as denying that the sovereign has a duty to promote any way of acting that is not related to the security of the state.

Hobbes does not use the word "reason" to refer only to natural reason, that is, to that reason which dictates self-preservation. He also uses "reason" to refer to the faculty of reasoning with words, that is, to reckoning the consequences of general names, as in geometry and politics, both of which Hobbes regards as sciences. Reason, in this sense, is not natural, but is "attained by industry" (*L* Ch. 5, paras 2, 17). It is natural reason that dictates self-preservation and that Hobbes is referring to when he describes the laws of nature as dictates of reason. It is this natural reason that plays the crucial rule in Hobbes's moral theory. However, given Hobbes's concern with language, it is quite likely that he regards reason as complex, concerned with ends, means, and with the reasoning that is used to go from the means to ends. That is, Hobbes seems to hold that there are several ways of acting irrationally, namely, pursuing the wrong ends, using the wrong means, and reasoning incorrectly, but it is only the first that he consistently regards as irrational.

The laws of nature and the right of nature

Hobbes's moral theory, that is, his attempt to describe, explain, and justify morality, is put forward in his discussion of the laws of nature. Understanding his account of the laws of nature is crucial for understanding his moral theory. Hobbes defines a law of nature as a "dictate of right reason, conversant about those things which are either to be done or omitted for the constant preservation of life and members, as much as in us lies" (*DC* Ch. 2, §1, *L* Ch. 14, para. 3). The laws of nature are the dictates of reason; they require that we act in those ways that are necessary for our preservation. Given this, it is troubling that Hobbes says about the right of nature that it allows us to do whatever we believe to be necessary for our preservation (*L* Ch. 14, para. 1). How can we be allowed to do whatever we believe to be necessary for our preservation and at the same time be required to do what is necessary for our preservation?

Hobbes's solution to this problem is to point out that everyone agrees that reason dictates the achieving of peace, for everyone agrees that without peace no one is likely to live very long (*L* Ch. 14, para. 4). But when peace cannot be achieved then people may do whatever they believe is best for their preservation. The first part requiring us to seek peace yields all of the laws of nature; the second, which applies when peace is not available, is the right of nature (*L* Ch. 14, para. 4). The right of nature, or rather, giving up the right of nature, is basic to Hobbes's political theory, but it does not play the same basic role in his moral theory. Hobbes incorporates his political theory into his moral theory by showing that the laws of nature dictate that all people give up their right of nature and that they keep the obligations, primarily to obey the law, that are the result of giving up their right of nature (*L* Ch. 14, para. 5, Ch. 15, para. 7). Morality, which the laws of nature dictate, is necessary for creating and maintaining a civil society, and a civil society is necessary for achieving that preservation that reason requires. Failure to realize the primacy of morality to politics is one reason that many philosophers have claimed that Hobbes has no way for people to get out the state of nature. If morality starts with the making of contracts to achieve a civil state, then there can be no moral reason for entering into a civil state by making contracts. But if morality, which is eternal, not only requires keeping contracts but also requires making those contracts that create a civil society, there is no problem.

Moreover, Hobbes is not writing for people who are in a state of nature but for people who are already in a civil society. Thus it is a mistake to interpret him as offering advice about how to get out of the state of nature. Rather he is providing arguments to members of his society about why they should not act in ways that might lead to civil war, for civil war leads to a state very similar to a state of nature. Because the state of nature is that state in which everyone retains his right to decide about the best way to preserve himself, emerging from the state of nature must involve everyone giving up their right of nature in some way, either by contract, covenant, or free-gift (*L* Ch. 17, paras 13–15). This means that everyone must have transferred to the sovereign the right to decide how to act. This being the case, everyone in a civil society is obliged to obey the laws of their society. To fail to obey the law is to be guilty of injustice. His strong statements about the horrors of the state of nature, e.g. that in it "the life of man is solitary, poor, nasty, brutish, and short" (*L* Ch. 13, para. 9), are used by him to support his claim that no one can reasonably hope to survive for long in such a state. This is then used to support his conclusion that in entering into a civil state everyone must be "contented with as much liberty against other men, as he would allow other men against himself" (*L* Ch. 14, para. 5).

Equality and impartiality

This introduction of equality and impartiality, right at the beginning of Hobbes's statement of the laws of nature has been generally overlooked, and may account for why some have held that Hobbes does not put forward a genuine moral theory, one that describes, explains, and justifies our common morality. But equality and impartiality are central to Hobbes's account of morality; the ninth law of nature prohibiting pride and the tenth prohibiting arrogance explicitly require acknowledging equality and acting impartially. He even summarizes the laws of nature by using the negative version of the golden rule, "*Do not that to another, which thou wouldst not have done to thyself*" (*L* Ch. 14, para. 35, *DC* Ch. 3, §26). That equality and impartiality are central to Hobbes's account of morality is not surprising, for they are central to almost all accounts of morality. What may be surprising is that Hobbes tries to motivate the introduction of equality and impartiality into his account of morality. His description of the horrors of civil war, which returns people to a state similar to the state of nature, is designed to show that avoiding such a state is in everyone's best interests. Thus everyone has the same strong reasons for obeying the law, and no one has sufficient reason to claim any special rights or privileges.

Hobbes holds that avoiding civil war is more important for everyone's preservation than any improvement in the administration of the commonwealth. Given his historical situation, this is precisely the view that Hobbes should be expected to hold. Hobbes is not claiming that the sovereign knows better than anyone else about how the civil society should be run to maintain peace and harmony in the society. Hobbes holds that we should obey the laws no matter who is sovereign, so it would be inconsistent for him to hold that we should obey the law because the sovereign's decisions are better than those of private citizens. Rather, his argument is that we can best avoid civil war by reaching agreement on whose decision on how to act everyone must follow. If each person – whether acting on egoistic concerns, or religious beliefs, or on her own views about what counts as the rational or moral way to act – were to retain the right to act on her own decisions, rather than on those of the sovereign, the result would be anarchy and civil war.

Moral argument for obeying the law

Anarchy and civil war are a greater threat to a person's preservation than almost anything that happens in a stable civil society. The only way to avoid anarchy and civil war and maintain a stable civil society is for everyone to understand that they have given up their right to act on their own decisions and have therefore obliged themselves to act on the decisions of the sovereign, i.e. according to the laws of the commonwealth. Not to obey the law is to be guilty of injustice. Thus, whether a person is concerned only with her own preservation, or of her family's, or with the preservation of all, obeying the law, is both morally and rationally required.

Hobbes's argument is not egoistic. It has equal force to someone with an impartial concern for the preservation of everyone in the society as it does to an egoist. This argument does not require accepting that the sovereign is correct about the best way to maintain a civil society. It may be that some individual citizen's decision as to the best way to maintain a civil society and thus to guarantee everyone's long-term preservation would be better than the sovereign's, if everyone were to accept it. In fact, there may be indefinitely many ways of acting that are better than that chosen by the sovereign; and there probably are. However, except for the laws of nature, there is usually no way to know for certain what is the best way to maintain a civil society. Even if there were, it is extremely implausible that it would be sufficiently clear and obvious that everyone would see and accept it but that the sovereign would not.

Hobbes shows that if individuals and groups believe that they are morally and rationally allowed to act on the decisions they personally regard as best, not accepting the commands of the sovereign, i.e. the laws, as the overriding guide for their actions, the result is anarchy and civil war. He is not content to show that it is unjust not to obey the law; he also wants to show that the best way to guarantee everyone's long-term survival is for everyone to recognize that they have obliged themselves to accept the decision of the sovereign, i.e. the laws, as their guide. Except in rare and unusual cases, e.g. when one is confronted with an immediate threat to one's life, uniformity of action following the decision of the sovereign is more likely to lead to long-term preservation than diverse actions following diverse decisions. This is true even if each one of the diverse decisions, if accepted by the sovereign as its decision, would be more likely to lead to everyone's long-term preservation than the actual decision made by the sovereign. By this argument Hobbes has not only shown that obeying the law is a moral requirement, he has also shown that this moral requirement, i.e. justice, is a law of nature, that is, a dictate of reason concerning the best way to preserve one's life.

Hobbes's argument in favor of all people giving up their right of nature is uniquely a political argument. It involves an individual's relationship to his government, not an argument that applies to one individual in his dealings with another. It is an argument for accepting the laws of one's country as the guide to one's actions even when one believes that a particular law requires actions that are not in the best interest of its citizens. It is a powerful argument against autonomy, if autonomy is taken as acting on one's own decisions rather than on the decisions of someone else. It is not primarily a prudential argument against autonomy; it is mainly a moral argument against autonomy. If one is impartially concerned with the welfare of everyone then, except in extraordinary cases, one should obey the law rather than act on the dictates of one's own conscience. Because we know that people's consciences often tell them to act in different ways, the actual result of people following their own consciences will almost certainly be worse for everyone than if everyone obeys the law. The most surprising conclusion is that this is true even if each of these different consciences tells them to act in some way that, if it were put forward by the sovereign, would have better results than obeying the present law.

This is an extraordinarily powerful argument for accepting the sovereign's decisions or obeying the law even when it goes against one's conscience, especially in those cases where one knows people's consciences differ. One reason that its force has not been appreciated is due to the rhetorical power of autonomy. Most philosophers and political scientists have become so entranced by autonomy that they find it hard even to consider, let alone to accept, an argument showing that complete autonomy is a bad thing. It may be because Hobbes has an argument against autonomy and for obeying the law, that many have concluded that he does not put forward a genuine moral theory. However, Hobbes's argument is clearly a moral argument, one that should be accepted by completely impartial rational persons who are concerned with protecting the welfare of all persons. No doubt Hobbes's emphasis on the fact that most persons are selfish and emotional plays some role in leading his readers to overlook the moral character of his argument against autonomy, but this cannot be the whole story. Many people take morality to require autonomy, but if autonomy means that morality requires each person to always act on her own decisions concerning what is best even when this is against the law, Hobbes is decidedly and correctly anti-autonomy.

Because Hobbes devotes so much space to discussing the law of nature dictating justice many have taken his discussion of justice to be central to his discussion of morality. His arguments for obeying the law are so powerful that it is easy to think that Hobbes regards morality as consisting simply in obedience to the law. Hobbes does regard justice, that is, obeying the law, as the primary moral virtue of citizens. But the very next law of nature that Hobbes discusses is the one that dictates the virtue of gratitude. Gratitude is the primary moral virtue of those in government. Morality requires them to act in such a way that the citizens will not repent that they have given up their right to decide how to act to the government. Gratitude is a moral virtue for the same reason that justice is; it is a trait of character that everyone calls good because it is conducive to the preservation of all. Every moral virtue that Hobbes says is dictated by the laws of nature, e.g. justice, gratitude, modesty, equity, and mercy, has the same justification; all people call them good because by leading to peace they are conducive to the preservation of all.

Morality does not depend on religion

The first nine (*Leviathan*) or ten (*De Cive*) laws of nature require developing and acting on the traditional moral virtues, which make clear that he is describing traditional morality. By showing that each of these traditional moral virtues is a necessary means to peace, he explains why these traits of character are universally praised and thus regarded as moral virtues. His justification of morality consists in showing that peace is necessary for preservation, thereby showing that reason requires morality. All of these points are made clearly and explicitly in his summary remarks in *Leviathan* about the laws of nature. "The laws of nature are immutable and eternal; for injustice, ingratitude, arrogance, pride, iniquity, acception of persons, and the rest can never be made lawful. For it can never be that war shall preserve life, and peace destroy it" (*L* Ch. 15, para. 38, *DC* Ch. 3, §29). Here Hobbes clearly expresses his view that since war destroys life, and that vices lead to war, the laws of nature prohibit the practice of vice and prescribe the practice of virtue. Two paragraphs later he makes clear that the moral virtues "come to be praised, as the means of peaceable, sociable, and comfortable living" (*L* Ch. 15, para. 40).

Hobbes views the laws of nature as simultaneously the dictates of reason concerning preservation, the laws commanding those practices necessary for peace and civil society, and the moral law commanding the practice of virtue. In contemporary terms, this means that Hobbes holds that rationality, which requires acting in ways that promote one's preservation, turns out to require acquiring those traits of character that lead to peace and the maintenance of a civil society, and these traits of character turn out to be the moral virtues. Although this is an impressive philosophical accomplishment, Hobbes was not primarily an academic philosopher, and wanted, rather, to have political influence. Since most people in Hobbes's time were considerably influenced by religious considerations, Hobbes spends much space showing that the Bible supports the same account of morality that he proposes (*DC* Ch. 4). I am not claiming that Hobbes did not really believe that the Bible supported his account of morality, only that his other more powerful arguments in favor of his account of morality do not involve God at all. Although it is quite likely that his appeal to the Bible is part of his practical attempt to influence as many people as possible to accept his moral and political views, religious thinkers should take this aspect of his account of morality seriously. However, for philosophers, God and religion are completely dispensable to his moral theory. Indeed, distinguishing morality from religion and providing a justification for the former that does not depend on the latter may be Hobbes's most important contribution to moral philosophy.

See also Early modern natural law (Chapter 7); Ethics and reason (Chapter 9); and Contemporary natural law theory (Chapter 42).

References

Gauthier, David P. (1969) *The Logic of Leviathan*, Oxford: Clarendon Press.

Hobbes, T. (1991a/1651/1647/1642) *De Cive*, in *Man and Citizen*, Indianapolis, IN: Hackett. (Cited as *DC*.)

——(1991b/1658) *De Homine*, in *Man and Citizen*, Indianapolis, IN: Hackett. (Cited as *DH*.)

——(1994/1651) *Leviathan*, Indianapolis, IN: Hackett. (Cited as *L*.)

Further reading

Gert, Bernard (2010) *Hobbes: Prince of Peace*, Cambridge, UK: Polity Press. (Provides a fuller version of the account of Hobbes presented here.)

Hampton, Jean (1986) *Hobbes and the Social Contract Tradition*, New York: Cambridge University Press. (Provides Social Contract account of Hobbes.)

Kavka, Gregory S. (1986) *Hobbesian Moral and Political Theory*, Princeton, NJ: Princeton University Press. (Modifies Hobbes's egoism.)

Strauss, Leo (1952) *The Political Philosophy of Hobbes*, trans. E. M. Sinclair, Chicago, IL: University of Chicago Press. (Shows Hobbes's dependence on Aristotle.)

9
ETHICS AND REASON

Michael LeBuffe

Descartes (1596–1650), Spinoza (1632–77), and Leibniz (1646–1716) are commonly, and rightly, considered to belong to a single school of thought in metaphysics and epistemology. Although they arrive at different conclusions, they share a set of concerns and methodological principles. Each is interested in proving the existence of God and describing God's relation to the world; in giving an account of the human being; and in describing the nature and limits of knowledge. Descartes, Spinoza, and Leibniz differ among themselves about what the most basic principles of reason are and how they are rightly applied. However, it is also generally true that each approaches these subjects as ones that can be understood better by means of human reason rather than by uncritical trust in the senses. For these purposes, then, the label "rationalist" can be a useful and tolerably accurate one.

That label is probably not as useful in ethics. Descartes, Spinoza, and Leibniz do hold some ethical views in common. Moreover, some of their most interesting differences do arise from their positions in metaphysical and epistemological debates. These philosophers' aims and influences in ethics also vary in many respects, however, and it would be misleading to underemphasize this point here. Descartes's moral theory shows the influence of Stoicism, and recasts ancient views about the passions and their control in light of his own account of the human being, human physiology, and psychology. The views that Descartes expresses are tempered by a reverence for ecclesiastical and civil authority together with a well-justified concern that his enemies would be very likely to find in a complete ethical theory, and, in particular, in a detailed normative ethics, effective means of damaging his reputation and security. As a result, even his most complete moral work, *The Passions of the Soul*, leaves one with the sense that some important consequences of the theory are left unwritten. Spinoza addresses Descartes and the Stoics in his own account of the passions and their control in the *Ethics*. However, Spinoza also clearly addresses a number of authors, notably Hobbes, Maimonides, and Aristotle. The themes of Spinoza's moral theory include Cartesian themes, but only as an important part of the whole view. Spinoza, moreover, states his view in a bold, uncompromising, and thorough treatise: his moral theory is much better developed than the views of either Descartes or Leibniz. Leibniz, although his remarks on ethics show careful attention to Spinoza and Descartes, addresses other traditions as well, especially the tradition of natural law theory. Leibniz does give accounts of virtue, happiness, and perfection that, while quite short and unsystematic, clearly respond to concerns of the sort that also moved Descartes and Spinoza. His most distinctive and important ethical ideas, however, the notions of charity and of the moral community of minds, which he calls the City of God, address a moral concern – how we should act toward others – that is only a passing concern for Spinoza and that Descartes entrusts to higher authorities. There is, then, a common set of themes addressed in these theories. The authors' various concerns and perspectives suggest, however, that these similarities amount to an interesting development of the tradition of virtue ethics rather than to a single, readily defined school of rationalist ethical thought.

Descartes

In the preface to the French translation of *Principles of Philosophy* (1647), Descartes writes (1969, AT IXB 14):

> Thus all philosophy is like a tree, the roots of which are metaphysics, the trunk is physics, and the branches which grow from the trunk are all the other sciences, which may be reduced to three principal ones, namely, medicine, mechanics, and morality – I mean the highest and the most perfect morality, which presupposes a complete knowledge of the other sciences and is the highest level of wisdom.

While Descartes is often presented as non-naturalist, his commitment to the view that morality is a part of a single body of knowledge together with the other sciences shows that, in a sense, he is a naturalist: his methods in the study of morality do not differ dramatically from his methods in other sciences, and he takes the results of other sciences, particularly his account of the nature of the human being, to have implications for his moral theory.

It is unsurprising, then, that positions of importance to Descartes's account of morality are to be found throughout his philosophical writings, including, notably, the *Discourse on the Method* (1637), the *Meditations* (1641), and the *Principles on Philosophy* (1644). Late in his life, however, in July of 1645, Descartes entered into a correspondence with Elisabeth, Princess of Bohemia, that began with a study of Seneca's *On the Happy Life* and issued in Descartes's *The Passions of the Soul* (1649). The *Passions* and the correspondence with Elisabeth supplement the positions that Descartes develops in his other works and together form his most detailed account of morality. In its broadest outlines, that theory may be understood to comprise an ideally virtuous state, consisting of some degree of knowledge and a will that is steadily guided by that knowledge; an account of provisional morality, the means by which in general we should work to attain virtue; and an account of the passions. Descartes's account of the passions describes the principal barriers to the constancy of will and the means of overcoming them. We can attain happiness (*contentement*) by bringing ourselves to act only on our best understanding of the good, and felicity (*felicité*) by acting in this way from knowledge.

In describing the ideal human condition, Descartes emphasizes the importance of a will that pursues our understanding (however imperfect) of the good without being distracted by appetite or passion, but he mentions also the ideal of a genuine knowledge of the good. His emphasis on the will is clear in the *Discourse*, where he writes (AT VI 28):

> Because our will tends neither to pursue nor to avoid anything but what our understanding represents as good or bad, judging well suffices for acting well and judging as well as we are able suffices also for acting for the best.

In the *Discourse*, his correspondence with Elisabeth, and the *Passions*, Descartes emphasizes the importance of constancy in will and, on the other hand, the harmful influence of passion and appetite, which cause us to follow momentary impulses rather than our best considered convictions about the good. He characterizes virtue in these terms, for example, in a letter to Elisabeth (4 August 1645, AT IV 265):

> [Each person] should have a firm and constant resolution to carry out all that reason recommends without being turned away by his passions or his appetites; and it is in the firmness of this resolution that, I believe, virtue consists.

Constant adherence to an imperfect understanding of the good, of course, may produce actions that are less than optimal, a problem that Descartes recognizes in the same letter. It is there that, most clearly, Descartes adds to his ideal the notion of a true knowledge of the good (AT IV 267):

> [V]irtue alone is sufficient to make us content in this life. But this point notwithstanding, if it is not enlightened by understanding, virtue can be false, that is to say, will and the resolution to do well can bring us to evil things, when we think them good; happiness which comes in this way is not solid. … [T]he right use of reason, by giving a true knowledge of the good, prevents virtue from being false.

Perhaps Descartes typically emphasizes the perfection of free will rather than knowledge because he takes man to resemble God most closely in possessing a will that, like God's, is unlimited. Descartes may, however, also have reason to emphasize the value of a constant will rather than the value of perfect knowledge of the good if the possibility of very bad actions arising from an imperfect understanding can be mitigated by a kind of conservatism in one's commitments. On this view, if I follow the most modest views of others, then whatever misunderstanding I may have can do little harm. Certainly such conservatism is part of the provisional moral code of the third part of the *Discourse* (AT VI 23–8):

(1) "To obey the laws and customs of my country, holding constantly to the religion in which by God's grace I had been instructed from my childhood, and governing myself in all else according to those opinions that were the most moderate and the furthest from excess."
(2) "To be as firm and resolute in my action as I was able, and to follow even the most doubtful of my opinions, once I had put faith in them, with no less constancy than if they had been quite certain."
(3) "To try always to conquer myself rather than fortune, and to change my desires rather than the order of the world."
(4) "To make a review of the various occupations that men have in this life in order to choose the best. ... I thought that I could do no better than ... to direct my whole life to the cultivation of reason, and to advance as far as I could in the knowledge of the truth."

The code of the *Discourse* does include the requirement that I advance as far as I can in the knowledge of the truth. Presumably, where the first and fourth maxims conflict, gains in genuine knowledge of good and evil would require one to abandon an otherwise steadfast adherence to ill-grounded understandings of the good. Descartes's code, however, clearly emphasizes resolution in action and changes to oneself, the third maxim, as a means of bringing about such resolution. These are the themes that he develops in detail in the *Passions*.

Passions can cause a person's will to be unsteady because they influence it in ways that depend upon the body's circumstances. Descartes characterizes the passions as forces that give us a tendency to want what is useful to us which is concomitant with the body's action (*Passions*, Art. 52, AT XI 372):

> The function of all of the passions consists in this alone, that they dispose the soul to want those things that nature says are useful for us and to persist in this volition; and the same agitation of the spirits that customarily causes them also disposes the body toward those movements which serve the fulfillment of the desires.

Passions can influence us in ways that tend to distract us from our best judgment of the good, then, not because they are evil – Descartes argues that they are fundamentally good at Article 211 – but because, through the influence of the body on the soul, they tend to distort the apparent value or disvalue of the ends they concern (*Passions*, Art. 74):

> The utility of all of the passions consists in this: they fortify and make more durable in the soul thoughts that it is good for the soul to preserve and that might otherwise easily be erased. Likewise all the harm that they can cause consists in this: they fortify and make more durable some thoughts more than is needed, or they fortify and make more durable others on which it is not good to dwell.

In the *Passions* Descartes continues to emphasize steadfastness in our judgments about good and evil as a means of resisting the distracting influence of the passions; however, he is also more explicit about the importance of the knowledge of good and evil, as opposed to mere steady opinion. At Article 48, he writes:

> What I call [the soul's] proper weapons are firm and determinant judgments concerning the knowledge of good and of evil, which guide a soul that is resolved to manage the actions of its life.

This article emphasizes steadiness of will in the same way that Descartes has done in the *Discourse*, but it incorporates the view that steadiness in judgments following from knowledge is what is desirable, a point that Descartes emphasizes in Article 49 of the *Passions*: "The power of the soul is not sufficient without knowledge of the truth."

Whether Descartes takes most people to be capable of attaining a high degree of knowledge of good and evil and whether such knowledge would make one still more virtuous on his account are not well-settled issues. The kind of knowledge most important to virtue, on Descartes's account in the *Passions*, is clear, however; it is knowledge of the fact of one's own free will and of its importance to morality. Together with a steadfast will, such knowledge gives a person generosity (*generosité*), a kind of perfect emotional state that the soul can produce in itself and that gives a person well-founded self-esteem (Art. 153):

> I believe that true Generosity which makes a man's self-esteem as great as it can legitimately be, consists entirely in this: in part, in his knowledge that nothing truly is his but this free control of his own will, and that he should be praised or blamed for nothing except its good or bad use; and, in part, in his feeling in himself a firm and constant resolution to use this same thing well.

Whether or not other knowledge of good and evil would make one still more virtuous, the knowledge that generosity includes is essential to virtue.

Descartes does not, in Article 153, insist that one's judgment about what is best be veridical, in order to be a component of genuine generosity. Knowledge of one's nature as an agent that wills freely is all the knowledge that is necessary, then, both for the most perfect pursuit of virtue and for the complete control of passion, a demand that, in its modesty, makes Descartes's moral theory egalitarian. Indeed, Descartes writes in Article 154 that generosity consists in part in the recognition of the fact that any other person has or can have such perfection.

Spinoza

Like Descartes, Spinoza takes metaphysics and epistemology to be a source of moral theory; Spinoza's catalog of the passions derives from a Latin translation of Descartes's *Passions*; Spinoza is a virtue ethicist and a perfectionist; and his account of virtue emphasizes self-knowledge and self-esteem. Arguably, however, the influence of Descartes's moral theory on Spinoza is most evident in Spinoza's criticism of two of Descartes's central doctrines. Spinoza rejects the Cartesian conception of the human mind and with it the view that we possess a free will. He develops instead a notion of freedom compatible with his conviction that human beings and all things are bound by necessity and universal determinism: a human mind is more free to the extent that it is the cause of its own actions. His accounts of the human being and human freedom lead Spinoza to conclude that, while we can become the cause of more (or less) of what we do, we cannot become completely free. So he also strongly and explicitly rejects the Cartesian doctrine that we can completely master passion.

The characteristic causal activity of any singular thing Spinoza calls its *conatus* or striving to persevere in being (a term of importance also to Descartes and Hobbes, among others). Spinoza describes striving in several propositions at the beginning of Part 3 of the *Ethics* (Spinoza 1925a):

> 3p6: Each thing, as far as it is in itself, strives to persevere in its being.
> 3p7: The striving by which each thing strives to persevere in its being is nothing other than the actual essence of the thing.

Although Spinoza moves quickly to an account of the human being, 3p6 and 3p7 show the thoroughgoing naturalism of his ethical theory. Spinoza attempts to explain human action as something similar in kind to the action of any other thing in nature.

Spinoza pursues an account of the human being on which *conatus* may be explained equally well either in completely psychological or in completely physical terms, a commitment that has profound implications for his moral theory. Generally, we may be said, as bodies, to strive for life and its means and, as minds, to strive for knowledge. The human body strives to persevere in the sense that any of its actions can be understood as actions that, were they efficacious, would maintain what Spinoza calls the characteristic ratio of the motions of the body's various parts, that is, of maintaining its life. Spinoza's characterization of striving in mental terms, which he emphasizes in Part 3, makes perseverance also a kind of knowledge:

> 3p9: The mind, both insofar as it has clear and distinct ideas and also insofar as it has confused ideas, strives to persevere in being; it does so for an indefinite duration; and it is conscious of this, its striving.

Any effect that a mind has insofar as it has clear and distinct, or adequate ideas, will be another adequate idea, so what it means to persevere from adequate ideas is clear: it will be to gain knowledge. How the mind acts from its confused ideas is still widely debated, but it is important to the proper understanding of Spinoza, for passions, in his account, are confused ideas.

Spinoza understands passions in terms of his *conatus* doctrine. At 3p11, he defends the claim that changes to the power of acting of the body correspond to changes in mind:

> Whatever increases or decreases, aids or represses our body's power of acting, the idea of this same thing increases or decreases, aids or represses our mind's power of thinking.

Then, in a scholium to the proposition, Spinoza relabels such changes as changes in perfection, and defines them as human passions:

> We see, then, that the mind can undergo great changes, and can pass now to a greater, now to a lesser perfection, passions that certainly explain to us the affects of happiness [*laetitia*] and sadness [*tristitia*]. By "happiness," therefore, I shall understand in what follows a passion by which the mind passes to a greater perfection; by "sadness," however, a passion by which it passes to a lesser perfection.

Any given passion, then, will be for Spinoza at the same time a change in the body's power to preserve its life and in the power of the mind's ideas. Later in the *Ethics* (3p58), Spinoza suggests that some changes to the mind are not changes that, strictly speaking, the mind undergoes; rather they are changes that the mind causes in itself. Just as generosity, in Descartes's account, is an emotional state that the soul brings on itself, so the best emotional states in Spinoza's account, self-contentment, nobility, tenacity, and the love of God, are states that we cause in ourselves. So he uses the term "affect" (*affectus*) to refer to changes generally, and reserves "passion" (*passio*) to refer only to changes that the body undergoes.

As Spinoza's identification of changes in power with changes in perfection at 3p11 and 3p11s shows, he associates a thing's perfection with its power. A given mind or body cannot ever be perfect, then, just because it cannot, as one singular thing in the world alongside many other similar things, be completely powerful. Spinoza emphasizes this point at the end of his account of the passions, at 3p59s:

> With this, I judge that I have explained and demonstrated through their first causes the principal affects and the vacillations of mind that arise from the three primitive affects, desire, happiness and sadness. From which it is clear that we are driven about in many ways by external causes and, like waves on the sea driven by shifting winds, we toss about, ignorant of our fortune and fate.

As a sailor may become better at pursuing a course, we may become better at navigating among the forces that surround us, but we can never be entirely free of their influence. Unlike the Cartesian ideal, the ideal of human perfection as Spinoza understands it is not something that can be attained except in a greater or lesser degree.

Spinoza defines the good, then, in terms of an increase in power, greater perfection:

> 4d1: By "good" I shall understand this, what we certainly know to be useful to us [as a means of becoming more perfect].

Because he takes passions themselves to be either increases or decreases in power, Spinoza differs from Descartes in taking some passions, namely, all forms of sadness, to be at least *pro tanto* evil. Forms of happiness, on the other hand, are *pro tanto* good; however, like Descartes, Spinoza takes passions to represent things to us as good or evil and to do so in a way that typically misleads us. Passionate forms, both of happiness and sadness, are therefore best overcome by understanding and active forms of affects.

Those particular goods which are not themselves affects tend to reflect the duality in Spinoza's account of human striving. At 4p39 he describes goods, in general, for the body:

> 4p39: Things that cause the conservation of the ratio of motion and rest that the human body's parts have to one another are good. Those that bring about a different ratio of motion and rest among the body's parts are evil.

A number of other propositions in the *Ethics* describe in more detail what such goods are like, and it is with respect to these goods that Spinoza's theory of value most closely resembles that of Hobbes. Spinoza's accounts of political goods, such as this passage from his *Theological-Political Treatise*, reveal this affinity (Spinoza 1925b: Vol. 3, 59, lines 13–27):

> Society is very useful not only for securing one's life against enemies, but also for lightening the many tasks that must be done. Indeed, it is necessary for this. For unless men were willing to give work to each other, anyone would lack both the skill and the time to be able to provide for his own sustenance and survival. Indeed, all are not equally suited to all tasks, and no one alone could provide the things which he most needs. Each alone would lack both the strength and the time, I say, to plow, to sow, to reap, to grind, to cook, to weave, to sew, and to do all the many things which must be done to sustain life – not to mention the arts and sciences, which are absolutely necessary to the perfection of human nature and to blessedness. We see, then, that those who live barbarously without a state lead a miserable and almost brutish life.

Arguably, however, even in this passage, Spinoza places a greater emphasis on intellectual goods, and some passages in the *Ethics* (such as 4p26 and 4p28) suggest that indeed only intellectual goods are rightly sought for their own sake. Perhaps this emphasis suggests that corporeal goods are goods only instrumentally or, as he writes, only insofar as they are "necessary to the perfection of human nature."

In Part 5 of the *Ethics* Spinoza offers his account of human freedom, or of the extent to which we can overcome the influence of the passions and pursue virtue rationally. The account includes both a popular account, like Descartes's, that makes some degree of virtue available to all of those who pursue it and also an elitist, highly intellectualist account of a kind of virtue that is not often obtained. In the first half of Part 5, Spinoza describes rules by which we can come to understand our passions or, where we cannot understand them, minimize their influence by cultivating opposed, active affects. He suggests at 5p10s that such techniques are available to all:

> One who observes these maxims carefully (indeed they are not troublesome) and practices them, will in a short time be able to direct his actions for the most part according to the command of reason.

The second half of Part 5, a notoriously difficult part of the *Ethics*, describes the eternity of the mind and suggests that some people, by knowing God, can attain a kind of salvation, a state that brings the best forms of active affects – blessedness and the love of God – and allows them, if not a complete control, a more secure command over their passions than one can ordinarily attain. In holding this view, which is most clearly present in the passage that concludes the *Ethics*, Spinoza introduces a kind of elitism that is absent in Descartes:

> Even if the way that I have shown to lead to these things seems very hard now, still it can be found. And, of course, what is so rarely obtained is bound to be hard. Indeed, if salvation were at hand and it could be obtained without great effort, how could it be that nearly everyone neglects it? But all excellent things are as difficult as they are rare.

Leibniz

Leibniz emphasizes virtue, perfection, and, as a central component of both, knowledge, and he does so in ways that clearly show a debt to Descartes and Spinoza. Descartes and Spinoza might be brought, to some degree, into a discussion of the other major subject of Leibniz's moral theory, his anti-voluntarist account of natural law. Leibniz read Spinoza's *Theological-Political Treatise* carefully and regarded Spinoza's political theory as very like that of one of his principal targets, Hobbes. Moreover, Leibniz rightly mentions Descartes as an important source of the view that most troubles him about voluntarism, the doctrine that God creates eternal truths. However, this influence is less direct. Leibniz's natural law theory directly addresses Grotius, Pufendorf, Hobbes, and Locke and is therefore best understood in the context of those authors' ideas.

Leibniz's accounts of virtue and perfection vary in his writings, and his account of perfection, in particular, is complicated by the importance of that concept to his metaphysics (according to which, as for Spinoza, human minds and other finite beings cannot be absolutely perfect). Among Leibniz's major works, important discussions of the topics occur in his *New Essays on Human Understanding* (1704), *Theodicy* (1710), and *Monadology* (1714). Perhaps the clearest concise statement of his view, however, is the short essay, "Felicity" (Riley, 83–4; see Leibniz 1972), a numbered series of connected moral views and definitions that Leibniz wrote and rewrote in the late 1690s. On that account, moral perfection increases with the knowledge of eternal truths:

> 8. Knowledge of reasons perfects us because it teaches us universal and eternal truths, which are manifested in the perfect Being.

Thus stated, Leibniz's moral perfectionism resembles the intellectualist strains of Spinoza's moral theory: the more that I understand God, the more perfect I become. Leibniz's theory of virtue, however, blends this intellectualism with an account of the value of pleasure, love, and justice. Virtue relates to perfection, in Leibniz's account, as the application to practice of the knowledge that we possess. Leibniz defines virtue in terms of wisdom:

> 1. Virtue is the habit of acting according to wisdom. It is necessary that practice accompany knowledge.

Wisdom is the knowledge of what brings felicity or, as Leibniz wrote later in "Meditation on the Common Concept of Justice" (1702–3), "our own good" (Riley, 57). This, however is just knowledge of the perfection of ourselves or others which, in turn, "flows from ... the absolutely perfect Being." So virtuous action follows from the knowledge of God.

The most important kind of virtue, on Leibniz's account, is justice or charity. In "Felicity," Leibniz defines the term in such a way that it introduces a guide to right action:

> 6. Justice is charity or a habit of loving conformed to wisdom. Thus when one is inclined to justice, one tries to procure good for everybody, so far as one can, reasonably, but in proportion to the needs and merits of each.

Although they are the same thing, one might find different emphases in the labels "justice" and "charity." Justice is a notion of central importance to Leibniz in his development of a natural law theory in the "Meditation" and in "Opinion on the Principles of Pufendorf" (1706, in Riley): voluntarism cannot be right because it makes justice a thing that God wills without reason rather than an immutable manifestation of God that is worthy of our love. Charity (*caritas*), loving conformed to wisdom, is, like Descartes's generosity, the proper state of a virtuous agent. Leibniz's account of charity, the right kind of love, is the most important moral idea in Leibniz's theory. It has two notable implications.

First, whereas Descartes emphasizes will as the respect in which we resemble God, Leibniz emphasizes the possession of a mind. To be a mind, for Leibniz, is to be capable of knowledge of universal truths of the sort described in "Felicity." From at least the 1690s Leibniz writes that this makes us members of a moral kingdom. The doctrine is perhaps put most boldly in the "Monadology" (Ariew and Garber, 224; see Leibniz 1989):

> 85. ... The collection of minds must make up the City of God, that is, the most perfect possible state under the most perfect monarchs.
> 86. This city of God, this truly universal monarchy, is a moral world within the natural world.

This notion helps Leibniz to explain what love conformed to wisdom in a charitable person is: it is loving as one citizen of God's city to another.

Second, the content of ethics, God's law for us, is largely understood by Leibniz through his perfectionism. To be a mind, is to be capable of knowing and loving God, and to be a better mind, is to know and love God more. Therefore, to act charitably toward another, to possess a good will, is to try to advance these ends in him or her. Leibniz writes in his "Memoir for Enlightened Persons," an essay from the 1690s (Riley, 105):

> To contribute truly to the happiness of men, one must enlighten their understanding; one must fortify their will in the exercise of virtues, that is, in the habit of acting according to reason; and one must, finally, try to remove the obstacles which keep them from finding truth and following true goods.

Leibniz conceives, then, of moral laws as laws of the legislator of a moral kingdom of minds and as laws that direct us to improve the faculties of others, especially understanding and reason. In these respects his synthesis of earlier conceptions of virtue and perfection anticipates Kant.

See also Hobbes (Chapter 8); Kant (Chapter 14); Virtue ethics (Chapter 40); Contemporary natural law theory (Chapter 42); Ideals of perfection (Chapter 55).

References

Descartes, R. (1969) *Oeuvres de Descartes*, ed. Charles Adam and Paul Tannery, 11 vols, Paris: Libraire J. Vrin. (Cited as AT, by volume and page.)

Leibniz, G. W. (1972) *The Political Writings of Leibniz*, trans., ed. Patrick Riley, New York: Cambridge University Press. (Cited as Riley.)

——(1989) *Philosophical Essays*, trans. Roger Ariew and Daniel Garber, Indianapolis, IN: Hackett. (Cited as Ariew and Garber.)

Spinoza, B. (1925a) *Ethica*, in *Spinoza Opera*, ed. Carl Gebhardt, 4 vols, Heidelberg: Carl Winter. (Cited by part, followed by d, definition; p, proposition; s, scholium – e.g. 4d1, Pt 4, definition 1.)

——(1925b) *Tractatus Theologico-Politico*, in *Spinoza Opera*, ed. Carl Gebhardt, 4 vols, Heidelberg: Carl Winter.

Further reading

Curley, E. (1988) *Behind the Geometrical Method*, Princeton, NJ: Princeton University Press. (An accessible introduction to Spinoza, including his moral theory.)

Jolley, N. (ed.) (1995) *The Cambridge Companion to Leibniz*, New York: Cambridge University Press. (An introduction to Leibniz that includes two useful entries on his moral theory.)

Shapiro, L. (ed., trans.) (2007) *The Correspondence between Princess Elisabeth of Bohemia and René Descartes*, Chicago, IL: University of Chicago Press. (An English translation that includes Elisabeth's letters.)

10
ETHICS AND SENTIMENT
Shaftesbury and Hutcheson

Michael B. Gill

Introduction

In the eighteenth century, a number of British moral philosophers – the most notable of whom were Shaftesbury (1671–1713), Hutcheson (1694–1746), Hume (1711–76), and Adam Smith (1723–90) – developed a position that has come to be known as "moral sentimentalism," or the moral sense theory. These philosophers disagreed about some things, but they all believed that there is a crucially important respect in which *non-selfish affection* is essential to morality.

The sentimentalists' insistence on an essential moral role for non-selfish affection constituted a rejection of the two other main contending moral theories of the day. One of those positions was *egoism* – the view that morality is based entirely on self-interest. The other was *moral rationalism* – the view that morality originates in reason alone. In this chapter, I will explicate the views of Shaftesbury and Hutcheson, who were the first to set this sentimentalist course.

I will first describe Shaftesbury and Hutcheson's anti-egoist arguments. I will then turn to their anti-rationalist arguments. In-between, I will briefly discuss Joseph Butler (1692–1752), whose views will serve as an illustrative transition between discussion of the sentimentalists' attacks on egoism and on rationalism. I will conclude with some very brief remarks about Shaftesbury and Hutcheson's influence on later sentimentalists.

Shaftesbury and Hutcheson's attack of egoism

According to egoism as Shaftesbury and Hutcheson understood it, all of one's actions have as their ultimate goal the promotion of one's own happiness, and all of one's normative judgments are based in self-interest as well. So, according to egoism, whenever I form a positive moral judgment about others' conduct, it is because I think their conduct benefits me; and whenever I form a negative moral judgment about others' conduct, it is because I think their conduct harms me.

Shaftesbury and Hutcheson thought egoism was a dangerous doctrine, not merely false but pernicious. Belief in egoism, they thought, promotes religious error, leading people to heed God's commandments only because of his power to reward and punish rather than to love and emulate him because of his intrinsic goodness. Belief in egoism damages political society, as it leads people to believe that peace can be bought only at the price of (Hobbesian) absolutism or (Mandevillean) manipulation. And belief in egoism destroys moral character, as believing that people always act selfishly can lead one constantly to regard others through a lens of jealous suspicion as well as deter one from ever trying to act non-selfishly oneself. The belief that self-interest underlies all human conduct can become a corrupting self-fulfilling prophecy.

To combat what they took to be these catastrophic consequences of egoism, Shaftesbury and Hutcheson launched a battery of arguments to show, first, that we judge people to be virtuous when we think they are motivated by concern to benefit humanity as a whole and not merely when we think their conduct advances our own selfish interests; and to show, second, that people can and sometimes do act out of truly non-self-interested concern to benefit others.

To combat the egoist claim that all of our moral judgments are based in self-interest, Hutcheson argued that there are in fact many things we think promote our self-interest that we nonetheless do not judge to be virtuous. Inanimate objects can be just as advantageous to us as human beings, but we never judge inanimate objects to be virtuous (1725, *Beauty and Virtue* 117–18). Nor do we judge people to be virtuous if we believe their motives are selfish, no matter how much we may benefit from what they do (119, 124). A foreign traitor may benefit our country as much as the most valorous hero, but we still do not think the traitor virtuous (130). Moreover, at times we ourselves may have the option of performing actions that harm others, but coming to believe that those actions will be to our own advantage will not necessarily lead us to think that they are virtuous (126–7). And when we give in to temptation and do things that benefit ourselves while harming others, we may continue to morally condemn what we have done even after we have reaped the benefits (127).

A non-egoist account of moral judgment also better explains the fact that there are many things that we think do *not* promote our self-interest that we nonetheless *do* judge to be virtuous. We judge to be virtuous people who have done good deeds long ago in distant lands, even though there is no chance that their actions will have any bearing on our own welfare (117, 121). We judge to be virtuous people who have attempted to benefit others, even if, as a result of circumstances outside of their control, no good whatsoever came of their actions (123). Indeed, it is not uncommon for us to judge to be virtuous people who have performed actions that actually conflict with our self-interest, such as someone with good intentions who harms us by mistake, or a "gallant Enemy" who serves his country well even though it damages our own cause (120, 130, 133).

So according to Shaftesbury and Hutcheson, we judge people to be virtuous when and only when we think they act from ultimately benevolent motives. But it could still be the case that no one ever acts on such benevolent motives – that no one ever acts in a truly virtuous way. Shaftesbury and Hutcheson argued against this possibility, however, contending that egoist accounts of motivation did a manifestly worse job than non-egoist accounts of explaining the wide spectrum of observable activities humans engage in.

Shaftesbury ridiculed egoistic interpretations of "civility, hospitality, humanity towards strangers or people in distress," arguing that it is much more natural to explain such conduct simply by positing real sociability and benevolence (1999, *Characteristics* 55). Human conduct, according to Shaftesbury, is better explained by supposing that people are often motivated by "passion, humour, caprice, zeal, faction and a thousand other springs, which are counter to self-interest" (54; cf. 247–57). The only way the egoist view of motivation can be plausibly maintained is if it is construed tautologically, i.e. if self-interest is defined so as to encompass as a matter of definition everything we pursue. But such a view is empty.

In a similar vein, Hutcheson argued that all egoist attempts to reduce or assimilate our seemingly benevolent conduct to the pursuit of self-interest are miserable failures (*Beauty and Virtue* 145, 155). One of Hutcheson's principal examples was the benevolence parents exhibit toward their children, which can lead them to act in ways that don't seem to be in their self-interest at all (155–8). Egoists try to explain away such cases by attributing all sorts of selfish motives to parents who benefit their children. But, Hutcheson plausibly argued, such interpretations either tacitly presuppose that parents have a disinterested, ultimate desire for the happiness of their children, mistake metaphors for literal truths, or define "selfishness" in a way that makes the claim that parents act selfishly a mere tautology. Hutcheson clinched the point with the following thought experiment: Imagine that God has declared that a person is about to be "suddenly *annihilated*, but at the Instant of his Exit it should be left to his Choice whether his Friend, his Children, or his Country should be made happy or miserable for the future, when he himself could have no Sense of either Pleasure or Pain from their State" (1753, *Beauty and Virtue* [5th edn] 147). Would such a person lack the motive to promote his children's happiness? Of course not. If anything, a person's motivation to promote the future well-being of his children grows stronger as his death draws near. Nor is it only a child whose happiness one may care about for its own sake. At "the instant of his Exit," one may be motivated to promote one's friends' long-term happiness as well. Indeed, this benevolent motive is readily apparent in many actual human interactions. We often act benevolently toward "Neighbours" even when we have "receiv'd no good Offices" from them, and we desire the happiness of our fellow citizens even when we are not in any position to share in it (1725, *Beauty and Virtue* 158). We care about the happiness of people in the "*most distant* parts of the Earth," as is evident from the distress we feel on hearing of the misery of people in faraway lands and the joy we feel on hearing of their good fortune (159).

Butler: against egoism, non-committal on sentimentalism vs. rationalism

In their battles against egoism, Shaftesbury and Hutcheson had a powerful ally in the person of Joseph Butler, Bishop of Durham (1692–1752). Butler endorsed anti-egoist arguments similar to those found in the work of Shaftesbury and Hutcheson. Butler also developed an additional argument that was particularly incisive (Butler's presentation of this argument can be found in Raphael 1991: 332–6 and 363–73).

According to Butler, the egoist view that our desire for our own happiness leaves no room for any truly benevolent motives is based on a misunderstanding of what desire for one's own happiness truly is. The desire for one's own happiness, which Butler called "self-love," is not the desire for any particular substantive thing. Rather, the desire for happiness is a general, second-order desire that our substantive, first-order desires be fulfilled. Happiness consists of the fulfillment of our first-order desires; it is not a single particular thing itself. But what sorts of things do we have first-order desires for? What are the objects of our particular, substantive affections? Some of these are for things that concern only ourselves or our own pleasures. But observation of ourselves and others plainly reveals that many other of our particular substantive affections are for things that are non-selfish or disinterested. And the crucial point to realize, according to Butler, is that these non-selfish desires are not in conflict with self-love (properly conceived) but rather are the first-order components of which happiness consists. Egoists who say that everything we do is based on self-interest are then either saying something true but compatible with truly benevolent desires – namely, that the fulfillment of our first-order desires contributes to our happiness (where "happiness" is taken to be just the term we use to encompass the satisfaction of our first-order desires). Or they are saying something incompatible with truly benevolent desires – namely, that all of our substantive, first-order desires are for our own selfish pleasure – but false.

But while Butler was on Shaftesbury and Hutcheson's side in their fight against egoism, he did not align himself with all of their views. Butler thought that virtue involved a wider array of character traits than just benevolence, while Shaftesbury and Hutcheson often identified virtue entirely with benevolence (see Raphael 1991: 383–6). And – particularly important for our discussion – Butler did not equate the source of our moral distinction with a non-rational sense. Like Hutcheson and Shaftesbury, Butler believed that our moral judgments and actions are based on a non-selfish principle internal to every human mind. Like Shaftesbury and Hutcheson, Butler claimed that that principle is distinct from self-interest. But Shaftesbury and Hutcheson also held that this principle was affective, not rational. And on this point Butler remained resolutely non-committal, explicitly refusing to side either with those who claimed the moral faculty should be taken to be "moral reason" or with those who claimed the moral faculty should be taken to be "moral sense." Perhaps, Butler said, the moral faculty should be "considered as a sentiment of the understanding, or as a perception of the heart" (Raphael 1991: 379), a turn of phrase that gracefully sidesteps the dispute between rationalists and sentimentalists.

One explanation for Butler's not committing to one side or the other of this dispute was his belief that a resolution of it was irrelevant for his overriding practical purpose, which was to make people more virtuous. Defeating egoism was crucial to this purpose, as belief in egoism can destroy political, religious, and moral character. But it seems that Butler thought this purpose could be equally well-served by a rationalist or sentimentalist account of the internal non-selfish moral faculty.

Shaftesbury and Hutcheson shared Butler's primary goal of defending the cause of virtue, and they too thought the most important aspect of this was to show that we had truly non-selfish concerns for others. Whether the origin of that concern was rational or affective was of secondary importance. Shaftesbury and Hutcheson did maintain from the start that morality was based on a moral sense, but their initial emphasis was on the *moral* part of that term, not on the *sense* part.

Eventually, however, Shaftesbury and Hutcheson's differences with moral rationalism would come to the fore (albeit pretty much after Shaftesbury had concluded his philosophical career). Let us examine these differences now.

Shaftesbury and Hutcheson on moral rationalism

Moral rationalism has a long and varied history, but the rationalist views most current in Shaftesbury and Hutcheson's day were well-represented by Ralph Cudworth, Samuel Clarke, John Balguy, and Gilbert Burnet. The claim that is often taken to be essential to moral rationalism is that morality originates in reason alone, and Cudworth, Clarke, Balguy, and Burnet did certainly hold to that. But on closer inspection we find that this is not a single claim but actually encompasses a cluster of at least the following three ideas.

(1) The rationalist ontological claim: there are purely rational moral properties that are independent of all human minds.
(2) The rationalist epistemological claim: humans apprehend morality through the use of reason alone.
(3) The rationalist practical claim: humans act morally when they are motivated by purely rational considerations.

It is especially important to keep in mind the differences between these when examining Shaftesbury, as it turns out that his views are consistent with (1), conflict with (2), and stand in a complicated, hard-to-quickly-summarize relationship to (3).

Shaftesbury and moral rationalism

Shaftesbury never denied the rationalist ontological claim. He believed that good and evil existed independently of human sentiments (*Characteristics* 150, 168, 175, 266–7). This affinity with the rationalists is, however, decidedly absent in Shaftesbury's account of the *conduct* of the virtuous moral agent.

Shaftesbury holds that the moral status of persons' conduct is based entirely on their motives. Indeed, Shaftesbury's contention that moral worth is based on motive is as uncompromising and emphatic as Kant's (see *Characteristics* 169–71; 174–7; cf. Kant 2002: 199–201). Where Shaftesbury differs from Kant – what makes him a sentimentalist and not a rationalist – is his belief that only affections can motivate to action. But because he believes only affections motivate, and because he thinks moral status is based entirely on motive, Shaftesbury is led to the conclusion that moral status is based entirely on affection (*Characteristics* 171, 174, 192). For Shaftesbury, the essential difference between virtuous conduct and non-virtuous conduct is that the former is motivated by one kind of affection and the latter is not. This is clearly inconsistent with the rationalist practical claim.

A crucially important related aspect of Shaftesbury's view is his belief that virtue is a subset of goodness – that all who are virtuous are good but that not all who are good are virtuous. A creature is good, according to Shaftesbury, if its affections promote the well-being of the system of which it is a part, and non-human animals are just as capable of possessing this type of affection as humans. Goodness is thus within the reach of all sensible creatures, not only humans but also non-human animals, such as tigers. "Virtue or merit," on the other hand, is within the reach of "man only" (*Characteristics* 172). That is because virtue or merit is tied to a special kind of affection that only humans possess. This special kind of affection is a second-order affection, an affection that has as its object another affection. We humans experience these second-order affections because we, unlike non-human animals, are conscious of our own affections. Not only do we possess affections, but we also reflect on or become aware of the affections we have. And when we reflect on our own affections, we develop feelings about them. Imagine, for instance, you feel the desire to help a person in distress. In addition to simply feeling that desire, you may also become aware that you are feeling that desire. And when you become aware of that, you may experience a positive feeling (or "liking") toward your desire to help. Or imagine you feel the desire to harm a person who has bested you in a fair competition. In addition to simply feeling the desire to harm, you may also become aware that you are feeling that desire. And when you become aware of that, you may experience a negative feeling (or "dislike") toward your desire to harm (172). Shaftesbury calls this capacity to feel second-order affections the "sense of right and wrong" or the "moral sense" (179–80). The moral sense is that which produces in us feelings of "like" or "dislike" for our own (first-order) affections. When the moral sense is operating properly, it produces positive feelings toward affections that promote the well-being of humanity and negative feelings toward affections that detract from the well-being of humanity. The second-order feelings that the moral sense produces can themselves motivate to action. And humans – who alone possess the powers of reflection necessary for consciousness of their own affections and thus alone possess a moral sense – are virtuous if they act from those second-order feelings (175–6).

Shaftesbury held that this moral sense is the basis of the moral judgments we typically make in day-to-day life. If I conduct myself in a way that leads you to think I am motivated to benefit (or harm) humanity, your moral sense will lead you to approve or "like" (or disapprove or "dislike") me. And these approvals (and disapprovals) are the basis of the moral judgments you form about me. In addition, the approvals and disapprovals of your moral sense are the basis of your assessment of which conduct open to you is virtuous or vicious. As Shaftesbury writes,

> In these vagrant characters of picture of manners, which the mind of necessity figures to itself and carries still about with it, the heart cannot possibly remain neutral but constantly takes part one way or other. However false or corrupt it be within itself, it finds the difference, as to beauty and comeliness, between one heart and another, one turn of affection, one behaviour, on sentiment and another, accordingly, in all disinterested cases, must approve in some measure of what is natural and honest and disapprove what is dishonest and corrupt.
>
> (*Characteristics* 173)

Such an account of moral judgment conflicts with the rationalist epistemological claim, as it implies that our judgments of morality involve the moral sense – that our judgments that something is virtuous (or vicious) are based on the second-order affection of approval (or disapproval).

Elsewhere, however, Shaftesbury suggests that we can apprehend morality through reason alone. When presenting his philosophical account of goodness in the *Inquiry* – and this account is the foundation of his views of morality as a whole – Shaftsbury does not seem to take himself to be relying on sentiment at all. It seems that he thinks the nature of goodness is something that he can discern and establish through the use of reason alone (*Characteristics* 167–9). In other works, moreover, he suggested that we can apprehend the eternal and immutable standards of morality through something like *a priori* rational intuition (*Characteristics* 68).

What is the relationship between Shaftesbury's apparently rationalist account of the nature of goodness and his sentimentalist account of the moral judgments we make in everyday life? It seems that Shaftesbury took the rationalist and sentimentalists accounts to be parallel – coexistensive but not in interaction with each other. But it's far from clear that such a combination can be made philosophically coherent. However that may be, for a fully fledged and uncompromising expression of the sentimentalist position – a position that unequivocally rejects all three aspects of moral rationalism – we have to turn to Hutcheson.

Hutcheson's arguments against moral rationalism

Hutcheson's most important anti-rationalist arguments occur in his *Illustrations on the Moral Sense*, which was published in 1728. Following Shaftesbury, Hutcheson held there that virtuous conduct is conduct that has as its ultimate end or motive the promotion of the welfare of humanity (a view that, in Hutcheson's hands, became one of the most important precursors to utilitarianism). Hutcheson also held that all of our judgments that another person is virtuous are based on our having the positive reaction of approval toward the benevolent motives of that person. But the truths that reason alone informs us of are insufficient to give rise to such benevolent motives or to our approvals of them. Reason alone can play only an instrumental role in our moral conduct and judgments (1728, *Moral Sense* 139, 213–14, 217; Burnet and Hutcheson 1971: 209, 227). It tells us what the effects of an action will be – whether an action will promote certain ends or frustrate them – but it is incapable of favoring (in the sense either of approving or of motivating to pursue) one ultimate end over any other (*Moral Sense* 139). Our favoring of ultimate ends must therefore involve the operation of non-rational mental principles.

Hutcheson called these non-rational mental principles "internal senses," a terminological choice warranted by what he took to be the phenomenological similarities between the experience of the external sensations of sight and touch and the experience of benevolent motives and approvals (*Moral Sense* 134, 154–5). The sense that gives rise to benevolent motives to actions Hutcheson called the "public sense," and the sense that gives rise to approvals of benevolent motives Hutcheson called the "moral sense."

The rationalists, of course, claimed that reason alone can give rise to ultimate ends and our moral judgments of them – that Hutcheson was wrong to limit reason to a purely instrumental role. According to Hutcheson, however, in making this claim the rationalists relied on vague formulations that, when made more precise, are false or fail to support moral rationalism in the slightest.

Rationalists sometimes maintained, for instance, that the "Morality of Actions consists in *Conformity to Reason, or Difformity from it*" (*Moral Sense* 136). But if something's conforming to reason means simply that "true propositions" apply to it, then this characteristic cannot distinguish morality from immorality, as there are as many true propositions that apply to immoral conduct as there are that apply to moral conduct (*Moral Sense* 137–8; see also 144–5, 148, 154). If an action's conforming to reason means that the action will achieve the end at which it is aimed, the rationalists are no better off, for one action can be just as effective at achieving the vicious end of harming humanity as another action can be at achieving the virtuous end of helping (138–40). Then again, when people say that an action is conformable to reason they may sometimes mean simply that they approve of it. But since this approval presupposes a moral sense the rationalists still have not made any headway (144; cf. 160). (Hutcheson makes similar arguments against the rationalist view that morality is based on the eternal and immutable relation of fitness; see Hutcheson's *Moral Sense* (155–60) for discussion of this issue.)

Another rationalist tack was to hold that it is rationally self-evident that certain ends ought to be pursued over other ends. Burnet, for instance, claimed that it was self-evident that the happiness of humanity as a whole is a more reasonable or fitting end than the happiness of a single individual. Hutcheson agreed that we morally ought to pursue the happiness of humanity rather than our own selfish interests. But he denied that this idea can be construed in a way that is both self-evident and supportive of the rationalist cause, arguing that one makes no purely rational mistake if one prefers the happiness of the few to the happiness of the many. This will look to be a mistake only to those who have a prior preference for the happiness of the many (Burnet and Hutcheson 1971: 211; cf. 213, 228–9, and *Moral Sense* 222–3).

Hutcheson also argued that the only way the moral principles his rationalist opponents advanced could be rightly thought of as rationally necessary is if they were construed tautologously. Clarke, for instance, contended that the following is a self-evident, rationally necessary truth: "whoever first attempts, without the consent of his fellows, and except it be for some public benefit, to take to himself more than his proportion, is the beginner of iniquity" (Raphael 1991: 218). Similarly, William Wollaston contended that it is a self-evident, rationally necessary truth that it is wrong for a man to live "as if he had the estate which he has not" (Raphael 1991: 242). What Clarke and Wollaston are saying is that reason alone tells us that we ought to respect others' property – that the principles of morality that condemn theft are rationally necessary. Hutcheson did not deny the self-evidence of Clarke and Wollaston's statements of the morality of respect for property and the immorality of theft. He maintained, however, that if these statements are self-evident, it is only because the positive moral status of respect for property and the negative moral status of theft have been smuggled into the descriptions of the relevant actions. Clarke said that it was wrong, all things being equal, for someone to take more than is "*his*." Wollaston said that it is wrong for someone to make use of something "which he *has* not." But Clarke's "his" and Wollaston's "has" presuppose the morality of respect of property and the immorality of theft. So their principles are rationally necessary only because they are circular or tautologous (see *Moral Sense* 160, 213–14, 228–30, 272–3, and Burnet and Hutcheson 1971: 213).

An important rationalist criticism of his moral sense theory that Hutcheson addressed was that the deliverances of the senses are too uncertain and unstable to serve as the foundation of morality. According to the rationalists, we do not as a matter of course simply accept our sentimental reactions as decisive of whether something is virtuous or vicious, because we know that our sentimental reactions are very often swayed by deceitful appearances. Rather, we hold our initial sentimental responses up to some standard before we properly pass judgment, and we then correct our judgments accordingly. But since we do this (so the rationalists maintained), we must be relying on some standard that is independent of our sentimental responses, as we use that standard to assess and correct our sentimental responses themselves.

Hutcheson responded by pointing out that we correct many of our initial sensory impressions of external objects while its still being the case that our judgments about the objects in question essentially involve sensation and cannot be funded merely by reason alone (*Moral Sense* 138–41, 147, 149). Under unusual lighting conditions, something may appear to us to be one color and yet we will judge (because we are cognizant of how the thing would appear under normal lighting conditions) that it is actually another color. But the fact that we correct our initial visual impression does not show that we have some purely rational, non-sensory standard of visual judgment. Similarly, I may sometimes feel negative emotions when I first consider an action or character, but then, after calm reflection on the action's actual tendencies or the actual features of the character, come to form a positive judgment about it. But the explanation for this correction of my initial reaction is that my moral judgment is based on the emotion I feel when I calmly reflect (just as my visual judgment is based on the visual impression I would have under normal lighting conditions), not that I refer to some purely rational moral standard.

Conclusion

Just as Hutcheson clarified and extended Shaftesbury's moral sentimentalist ideas, so too did David Hume and Adam Smith refine and in some cases alter Hutcheson's sentimentalist ideas. Both Hume and Smith agreed with Hutcheson that morality originates in sentiment – where that claim is taken in a metaphysical, epistemological, and practical sense. But Hume and Smith also both believed that Hutcheson's account of the sentiments at the origin of morality was overly simplistic. While Hutcheson maintained that the moral sentiments were based in an explanatorily basic, divinely implanted moral sense, Hume and Smith argued that these sentiments were the end result of more basic and naturalistically explicable mental processes. And while Hutcheson maintained that benevolence was the single taproot of morality, Hume and Smith argued that other kinds of sentiment were also of fundamental moral importance. There is no doubt, however, that Hume and Smith's moral theories – as well as the sentimentalist theories of a myriad contemporary moral philosophers – grew out of

Shaftesbury and Hutcheson's initial insight into the crucial moral role of non-selfish affection.

See also Hobbes (Chapter 8); Ethics and reason (Chapter 9); Hume (Chapter 11); Adam Smith (Chapter 12); Non-cognitivism (Chapter 27); Error theory and fictionalism (Chapter 28).

References

Burnet, Gilbert and Hutcheson, Francis (1971) "Letters between the Late Mr. Gilbert Burnet, and Mr. Hutchenson, concerning the true Foundation of Virtue or Moral Goodness" in *Illustrations on the Moral Sense*, ed. Bernard Pearch, Cambridge, MA: Belknap Press.

Hutcheson, Francis (1725) *An Inquiry into the Original of our Ideas of Beauty and Virtue*, 1st edn, London: J. Darby. (Cited as *Beauty and Virtue*; see Hutcheson 1753. Unless otherwise specified, references are to the 1725 edn.)

——(1728) *An Essay on the Conduct of the Passions and Affections with Illustrations on the Moral Sense*, London: J. Darby; repr. in facsimile edn, 1971, by Hildesheim: Georg Olms. (Pt 2, cited as *Moral Sense*.)

——(1753) *An Inquiry into the Original of our Ideas of Beauty and Virtue*, 5th edn, London: J. Darby.

Kant, Immanuel (2002) *Groundwork for the Metaphysics of Morals*, trans., ed. Thomas E. Hill and Arnulf Zweig. Oxford: Oxford University Press.

Raphael, D. D. (1991) *British Moralists 1650–1800*, vol. 1, Indianapolis, IN: Hackett.

Shaftesbury, Anthony Ashley Cooper, 3rd Earl of (1999) *Characteristics of Men, Manners, Opinions, Times*, ed. Lawrence E. Klein, Cambridge: Cambridge University Press. (Cited as *Characteristics*.)

Further reading

Gill, Michael B. (2006) *The British Moralists on Human Nature and the Birth of Secular Ethics*, Cambridge: Cambridge University Press. (For further discussion of the moral sentimentalism of Shaftesbury and Hutcheson.)

Griswold, Charles L. (1998) *Adam Smith and the Virtues of Enlightenment*, Cambridge: Cambridge University Press. (For further discussion of the moral views of Adam Smith.)

Penelhum, Terence (1986) *Butler*, London: Routledge & Kegan Paul. (For further discussion of the moral views of Butler.)

11
HUME

James A. Harris

Hume's moral philosophy is to be found in Book 3 of *A Treatise of Human Nature* (published a year after the first two books, in 1740) and in *An Enquiry concerning the Principles of Morals* (1751). Also important to a full understanding of Hume's ethics are some of the essays that he published in various collections from the 1740s onwards. Four essays on the views of the ancient schools concerning the nature of human happiness ("The Epicurean," "The Stoic," "The Platonist," and "The Sceptic") are especially significant, for there Hume appears decisively to distance himself from the didactic, "improving" agenda of both ancient moral philosophy and most of his contemporaries (see Harris 2007). The essay "Of the Standard of Taste," as its title suggests, is primarily a work of aesthetics, but its explanation of how principles of judgment develop out of sentimentalist first principles has been found useful by some modern Humeans as a means of rebutting excessively "subjectivist" readings of Hume's theory of moral judgment (see Wiggins 1998). The essay "On Suicide" provides a rare case of Hume directly addressing a question in practical ethics. In that essay Hume makes clear a deep antipathy to the moral code of the Christianity of his day. Passages in other writings on religion, notably the final sections of the *Natural History of Religion*, manifest the same hostility to religion considered as a basis for moral thought.

There are a number of contexts for Hume's ethics, but the most significant is perhaps the debate begun by Hobbes and then renewed by Bernard Mandeville about whether there is a foundation in human nature for moral judgment and moral motivation (for other approaches, see, e.g., Haakonssen 1996; Schneewind 1998; Gill 2006). Ridiculing Shaftesbury's picture of virtue as a natural development of innate dispositions, Mandeville, notoriously, had portrayed morality as a confidence trick played on the multitude by scheming politicians. Human beings are always and only selfish, Mandeville claimed, and they are only persuaded to behave as if with a concern for the interests of others in return for the flattery of praise from their superiors and their peers. Mandeville's views excited an extensive debate. His most important critic was Francis Hutcheson (see Ethics and sentiment [Chapter 10]). Hume's moral philosophy is best seen as an attempt to negotiate a path between Mandeville and Hutcheson. Letters he wrote to Hutcheson (see Hume 1932: Vol. 1, 32–5, 36–40, 45–8, letters of 1739 and 1740) make it clear that he found elements of the older philosopher's position impossible to accept, and there are frequent soundings of Mandevillean notes in his moral writings. Nevertheless, Hume rejected the view that all actions are done out of self-love, and accepted a foundation in human nature for at least some moral distinctions.

Hume's approach to the issues raised by the debate between Mandeville and Hutcheson is self-consciously detached and, as we might say now, scientific. He presents himself as an anatomist of human nature, who brings to moral philosophy the methods of the "experimental" natural philosophy of Isaac Newton. He makes it clear that the success of his theories is to be assessed in terms of a combination of elegance and explanatory power. At the end of the *Treatise* he says that it would take an entirely different kind of book to demonstrate that the virtuous life is a life of happiness and dignity. The anatomist may assist the painter in the production of alluring portraits of virtue, but his work is very often in itself disturbing at best and hideous at worst. The distinction between anatomy and painting is explored at greater length in Section 1 of *An Enquiry concerning Human Understanding*. There Hume describes the ambition of the anatomical moral philosopher in terms of the discovery of "some general principles, into which all the vices and virtues were justly to be resolved" (Hume 1975/1748: 15). Yet, like any good apologist for the inductive method, Hume warns his reader of the dangers of an excessive concern for theoretical simplicity: there is no reason to think that all of morality can be resolved into "one general principle." To pretend otherwise has been the error of much previous writing in ethics. Hume's project is to apply the experimental method to the basis of the distinction between virtue and vice in a more precise and sensitive way than forebears such as Shaftesbury, Mandeville, Butler, and Hutcheson. (For reliable and thorough treatments of Hume's moral philosophy, see Ardal 1966; Baier 1991; Mackie 1980; Norton 1982.)

Treatise, Book 3: artificial virtues

Book 3 of the *Treatise* is structured around a distinction that Hume makes between those virtues that are "natural" and those that are "artificial." Unlike Mandeville, Hume accepts that there are virtues that are approved of immediately and without reflection: Hume's examples are "meekness, beneficence, charity, generosity, clemency, moderation, equity" (Hume 1978/1739–40: 578). These virtues are discussed in Part 3. In Part 2 Hume focuses on virtues approval of which arises only in the context of conventions established in order that social life be possible for creatures such as we are, limited in our benevolence, and living in conditions of scarcity. These are the "artificial" virtues of justice (defined in terms of rules determining property and its transfer), promise-keeping, and allegiance. Such practices are not immediately recognizable as worthy of moral approbation. They only appear in that light when their utility for society at large becomes obvious. Hume displays some anxiety that he be properly understood when he terms these virtues "artificial": he does not mean that they are *unnatural*, for justice (for example) is so obvious and necessary an invention that it was inevitable that human beings would come up with it. "Tho' the rules of justice be *artificial*," he remarks, "they are not *arbitrary*" (Hume 1978/1739–40: 484). They may, in fact, be called *laws of nature*, in the sense of being practices that are absolutely necessary to beings who need, as we do, to live in society with each other. Still, they are the result of artifice, and are not, contrary to what Hutcheson had claimed for all virtues, practices that we instinctively appreciate as morally valuable.

Part 2 is by far the longest of the three parts of Book 3 of the *Treatise*, and there was surely a polemical point to treating the artificial virtues before the natural ones. Book 3 begins, however, with an airing of an issue that had been vigorously discussed in the first decades of the eighteenth century, whether moral distinctions are made by reason or by sentiment. Hume's case against the rationalism of philosophers such as Samuel Clarke and William Wollaston is rather cursory, and does little more than restate arguments that had already been made at greater length by Hutcheson. Hume raises the issue only to dismiss it as unimportant. Once rationalism is shown to be hopeless, and sentimentalism is left as the only sensible option, the real questions can be addressed: namely, whether moral sentiments are in every particular case "produc'd by an *original* quality and *primary* constitution" (as Hutcheson had claimed, and as Hume thinks is obviously absurd); and whether, having answered this question in the negative, we should go on to look for more general explanatory principles in human nature or "in some other origin" (Hume 1978/1739–40: 473).

Hume thinks he has a decisive argument to show that approval of justice, promise-keeping, and allegiance is not a function of any innate principle of human nature. He begins by laying it down as a maxim that the estimation of the moral worth of an action is always based on the motive upon which the agent acted. He then argues that no action is approved of simply on account of having been done out of a sense of duty. There has to be some additional source of value for the action: that is, there has to be something that explains why actions of that kind are what duty requires. And, according to the maxim laid down at the outset, that something would seem to have to be a motive to such actions, a motive that could be called *natural* in so far as it is, precisely, not a pure regard for duty as such. The problem is that actions done out of respect for justice, or out of respect for the importance of a promise, do not seem to have a motive over and above a regard for what duty requires. Hume considers three possible kinds of motive – self-interest, benevolent regard for society at large, and benevolent regard for particular individuals – and argues that in each case it is quite implausible to think that acting on that kind of motive could be what gives just or honest acts their moral value. These three kinds of motive exhaust the possible *natural* sources for ascribing moral value to justice, promise-keeping, and also allegiance. Therefore the motive which is praised in the case of these virtues must be non-natural, raised in us by processes of inculcation and education that Hume proceeds to explain.

There are two stages to that explanation. The first presents a series of conjectures as to how human beings came to invent such things as rules determining property and its transfer, the practice of being bound by utterances of the words "I promise," and institutions of government. In each case, according to Hume, the key to explanation is self-interest. These practices developed as rational individuals figured out ways of coping with the problem that human beings need to live in society with each other while having good reason to think that other people will take advantage of them if the occasion presents itself. The needs that we all have make it rational for us to foster the convention of respect for the property of others. Hume emphasizes the role of rationality in the development of conventions regarding property: faced with the problem of the combination of our natural selfishness and the difficulty with which we extract what we need to survive from our physical environment, he says, "nature provides a remedy in the judgment and understanding, for what is irregular and incommodious in the affections" (Hume 1978/1739–40: 489). This is a reminder that Hume is very far from denying that reason has any role to play in the construction of morality.

Hume also emphasizes that a convention is something different from a promise. In fact, he argues, promise-keeping is itself a kind of convention, developed in order to facilitate exchanges of goods or services where there is a time delay built into the exchange. As an example of a convention as distinct from a promise, Hume, famously, gives the example of two men who get into a boat together in order to row it to where they both want to go. There is no need for the men to make promises to each other in order for them each to have reason to do his part in the rowing. Hume's thesis that rational self-interest drives the development of conventions is, however, susceptible of more than one interpretation. On one way of reading Hume, conventions such as the rules of justice are the product of enlightened reflection on the part of most or all members of a society about what is necessary to peace and stability of that society; on another reading, such conventions emerge as the unintended consequence of the interactions of agents thinking only about their own local and short-term interests.

What remains to be explained is how following the conventions that enable social life comes to be regarded as a distinctively *moral* matter. This is what is accounted for in the second stage of Hume's treatment of the artificial virtues. The key to Hume's account is the notion of *sympathy*. Sympathy attunes us to the harm done to victims of injustice and dishonesty, and the feeling of uneasiness which is the result of this sympathy is simply constitutive of moral disapprobation – so long as that feeling survives general reflection about the consequences of that kind of action for society at large. Hume says more about how sympathy is brought to the level of generalized concern for all of society in Part 3. Part 2 leaves it as something of a puzzle as to how the invocation of sympathy solves the problem of the nature of the motive that is the object of moral judgment with respect to justice, promise-keeping, and allegiance. It certainly looks as though the motive for, for example, just actions cannot be anything other than self-interest, but it seems implausible that Hume's view is that the virtuousness of the just person lies in his or her prudence (but see Gauthier (1992) for a version of such a view). Some commentators have argued that with the emergence and embedding of conventions there arises a new kind of motive, the disposition to act in accord with conventions, and that that is the motive that is morally approved of (e.g., Darwall 1995: 207–43). Others have suggested that in the end Hume surrenders the supposed maxim that the virtue of an action lies in its motive, in favor of a broadly consequentialist approach to moral estimation (see Mackie 1980: 79–81; see also Cohon 1997).

Relevant to this puzzle is the striking fact that in his application of sympathy to the development of distinctively moral sentiments Hume several times expresses skepticism about the capacity of sympathy to *motivate* agents to act in line with its deliverances (see Hume 1978/1739–40: 500–2, 523, 533–4). More often than not, it would seem, we are just and honest and loyal because of a combination of the artifices and threats of politicians, how we have been educated, and a concern for our reputation. These passages hint at the fundamentally Mandevillean character of Hume's treatment of the artificial virtues, but also suggest that there is reason to see Hume as in fact uncomfortable with the traditional idea that a virtue such as justice is primarily a virtue of individuals. He appears to be moving towards the more distinctively modern view that justice is rather a virtue of institutions, approved of on account of their socially beneficial consequences.

Treatise, Book 3: natural virtues and natural abilities

Natural virtues are those that are recognized as such without need for the prior construction of conventions. They are the subject of Part 3 of Book 3 of the *Treatise*. Hume's first move is to fill out his conception of the role of sympathy in moral judgment, and as he does so it becomes apparent that the natural virtues are not really approved of immediately and directly. On Hutcheson's view we are naturally disposed to be pleased by benevolence without needing to take into account the consequences of benevolent action. Actions done out of benevolent motives do of course tend to have beneficial consequences, but that is not why we approve of them (though it is why God has instilled in us the tendency to approve of them). Hume, by contrast, believes that there is good reason to believe that it is with the estimation of natural virtues as it is with the estimation of artificial virtues (and also with the estimation of beauty): character traits, or "qualities," such as benevolence and generosity and clemency "acquire our approbation, because of their tendency to the good of mankind" (Hume 1978/1739–40: 578). That is, he believes that the fact that such character traits do have a tendency to the good of mankind is what explains our moral approval of them. This is something that most of Hume's contemporaries found objectionable. They wanted to believe, with Hutcheson, that what we morally approve of is recognized as *good in itself*, irrespective of its consequences. Hume in effect rejects both the notion of the good in itself and the notion of our possessing a faculty able somehow to detect it.

Sympathy, then, replaces the Hutchesonian moral sense as the faculty of moral approbation and disapprobation. Hume goes on to argue, by a form of inductive enumeration, that all moral judgment can be analyzed into consideration of just four kinds of good: utility to self and to others, and agreeableness to self and to others. All character traits that we call virtues are approved of because they have one of these four tendencies. The difference between natural and artificial virtues is that benevolence, for example, is always agreeable to behold, whereas the exercise of an artificial virtue such as justice might in particular instances give us pain. The virtue of just acts is brought out only in so far as our focus is the consequences of general adherence to the convention considered as a whole. Hume considers and answers two objections to his theory. The first is that, while our capacity for sympathy with others varies according to the closeness of our relation to them, our moral judgments do not change in the same way: "we give the same approbation to the same moral qualities in *China* as in *England*" (Hume 1978/1739–40: 581). Hume replies that while it is of course true that our sentiments fluctuate in response to alterations of relation, we need to prevent the continual disputes that would arise if we always judged on the basis of our sentiments. So "we fix on some *steady* and *general* points of view; and always, in our thoughts, place ourselves in them, whatever may be our present situation" (Hume 1978/1739–40: 582). It is not perfectly clear, however, whether what Hume means is that we are able to correct our sentiments by such reflection, or whether what is corrected is simply the language we use to express our sentiments. The second problem Hume raises for his sympathy theory is that we can regard someone as virtuous even if his circumstances prevent him from actually doing anything either useful or agreeable. Hume replies that, given enough experience of them in other situations, the usual tendencies of character traits are sufficient for moral approval. This is an instance of the influence of "general rules" on our judgments.

In the second half of Part 3 Hume's attention moves from the distinction between artificial and natural virtues to the distinction usually made between *virtues* and *natural abilities*. Natural abilities are such traits as intelligence, knowledge, wit, eloquence, and even, it seems, cleanliness. Hume extends his sympathy-based theory of approval to these traits, and claims that in every case they, too, meet with approbation on account of their usefulness or their agreeableness. The pleasure wit excites is of course different in kind (not just in degree) from the pleasure that is excited by benevolence; but then the pleasure that benevolence excites is different in kind (not just in degree) from the pleasure excited by justice. There is, Hume concludes, no deep division to be drawn between moral virtues and natural abilities. The question of whether or not natural abilities should be counted as virtues on a footing with justice and benevolence is, Hume says, "merely a dispute of words" (Hume 1978/1739–40: 606).

Hume of course knows that for many moralists the crucial difference between virtues and abilities is that an exercise of the former is supposed to involve choice and freedom of the will. So Hume uses his discussion of the matter to supplement the case made in Book 2 of the *Treatise* for the irrelevance, indeed harmfulness, of the notion of free will to understanding the basis of moral approbation and disapprobation (see Hume 1978/1739–40: 407–12). The concept of virtue, he argues, has no essential connection with the concept of the voluntary. No such connection was made by "the ancients," who were happy to include among the virtues such "involuntary and necessary" qualities as constancy, fortitude, and magnanimity. Furthermore, moral distinctions arise simply from feelings of pleasure and pain, and, Hume says he believes, "no one will assert, that a quality can never produce pleasure or pain to the person who considers it, unless it be perfectly voluntary in the person who possesses it" (Hume 1978/1739–40: 609). And, as Hume reminds the reader, in order for an action to be taken as a genuine expression of someone's character, there has to be the kind of constant conjunction between character and action that is what Humean necessitation amounts to, and that positively excludes freedom of the will. (For discussion of Hume on liberty, necessity, and the moral sentiments, see Russell 1995.)

An Enquiry concerning the Principles of Morals

Utility and agreeableness, considered as the determinants of moral judgment, are the main theme of the second *Enquiry*. (For accounts of the relation of the second *Enquiry* to Book 3 of the *Treatise*, see Abramson 2001 and Baier 2008.) Hume says that the goal of the book is to analyze "that complication of mental qualities, which form what, in common life, we call Personal Merit," in order to discover "those universal principles, from which all censure or approbation is ultimately derived"; and the conclusion reached is "that Personal Merit consists altogether in the possession of mental qualities, *useful* or *agreeable* to the *person himself* or to *others*" (Hume 1975/1751: 173, 268). In Section 1 Hume emphasizes that this is a "question of fact," and that therefore "we can only expect success, by following the experimental method, and deducing general maxims from a comparison of particular instances" (Hume 1975/1751: 174). What he seeks to establish through following the experimental method is not simply that it is true that benevolence, justice, and the rest of the virtues are either useful or agreeable. This no one denies. Rather, he wants to show that these things, and these things alone, are the origin of the merit ascribed to these qualities. Again, the target throughout is the idea that there are character traits and actions which are good in themselves, and known to be such without consideration of consequences. Hume himself uses the language of Roman philosophy in this connection: he says he wants to show that the analysis of personal merit can be conducted solely in terms of the *utile* and the *dulce*. What is implied by this way of describing his agenda is that there is no place in his moral philosophy for the notion of the *honestum*, what is good in itself, good even if no one actually regards it as good.

Throughout the second *Enquiry* Hume works at presenting his ideas in such a way that the reader is not distracted by their more unsettling implications. The distinction between artificial and natural virtues, for example, is not mentioned in the main body of the text. The section on justice restricts itself to proving that "utility is the *sole* origin of justice, and that reflections on the beneficial consequences of this virtue are the *sole* foundations of its merit" (Hume 1975/1751: 183). It is only in an appendix that Hume returns to the question of how conventions regulating property emerged amongst self-interested individuals, and even then the thought that justice might properly be regarded as *artificial*, in the sense merely of being the work of "reason, forethought, design, and a social union and confederacy among men," is introduced in a footnote (Hume 1975/1751: 307). The distinction between moral virtues and natural abilities is also relegated to an appendix, as are discussions of the reason–sentiment controversy and the issue of the extent of human selfishness. The impression given is that Hume wants to move moral philosophy on beyond the debates of the early eighteenth century, and towards a properly scientific treatment of the principal question, that concerning the basis of the distinction that is ordinarily made between virtue and vice. Almost all of Hume's contemporaries were as a result able to recognize that his main thesis was that utility plays a central role in the definition of virtue and vice.

Some readers of Hume detect a painterly and moralistic tone in the second *Enquiry* that is absent from the *Treatise*. And it might be thought that a book that describes how all of the virtues are either useful or agreeable could indeed do something to recommend virtue to those of its readers unsure whether virtue is always worth pursuing. But when in the final section of the book Hume raises the question of the nature of our obligation to act virtuously, it does not occur to him to frame that question in any other terms than those of self-interest, and the upshot of his answer is that, in fact, it is not possible always to show that acting virtuously is in our interests. This is obvious, Hume says, in the case of the virtue of justice. The "sensible knave" who free-rides on the generally law-abiding proclivities of his fellow citizens cannot be shown to be acting irrationally. If his heart really does not rebel at the thought of his own viciousness, there is nothing that argument can do to persuade him to change his ways. It is on this rather disquieting note that the second *Enquiry* ends. (For discussion of the sensible knave, see Gauthier 1992; Baier 1992.)

Hume's legacy

Hume's reputation as a moral philosopher was shaped in the first instance by his deployment of the concept of utility. Adam Smith, for example, regards Hume's appeal to utility as the defining feature of his ethics (see Smith 1984/1759: 179–93, 327). Some of his contemporaries, including Thomas Reid, understood him to be a latter-day Epicurean, even though it was obvious, as Reid himself acknowledged, that Hume rejected the Epicurean claim that all action is motivated by self-interest (see Reid 1969/1788: 401–3). The secular character of Hume's ethics did attract some criticism, but not from his more philosophically sophisticated contemporaries, almost all of whom, even if they accepted the truth of Christianity, held that it was the task of the philosopher to look beyond religion for a grounding of the obligation to morality. What worried philosophers such as Reid and Henry Home, Lord Kames, was that demonstrating the basis of moral obligation did not seem to be among Hume's concerns – something that was shown clearly, they thought, by his treatment of the sensible knave. They believed that it was incumbent on the philosopher to vindicate the commonsensical belief that there are some things that are absolutely obligatory and others that are absolutely forbidden, and this Hume failed to do. To claim that virtue could be reducible to the useful and agreeable was in effect to give up on the notion of inviolable rights and perfect duties. It was found striking that the language of rights and duties is almost completely absent from Hume's writings on moral philosophy. This, of course, is precisely what recommended him to Jeremy Bentham, who gave credit to Hume for the discovery of the principle of utility (see Bentham 1988/1776: 51). Throughout the nineteenth century Hume was portrayed as an originator of utilitarianism, by both that school's advocates and its critics.

More recently Hume's main contribution to moral philosophy has been supposed to lie in "meta-ethics." Hume's importance, it was thought for much of the twentieth century, lies in his arguments against "realism" and his delineation of a form of subjectivist non-cognitivism. More recently still, Hume has been claimed by proponents of "virtue ethics" as the chief early modern exponent of the idea that the primary concern of philosophical ethics is not consequences or duty but rather defining the kind of character necessary to living a full and flourishing human life. The concept of virtue is of course at the very center of Hume's moral philosophy, and he certainly rejects the thought that the core notion of morality is that of duty. He also rejects important aspects of consequentialist ethics, including the idea that outcomes can be given a ranking along a single scale of value. He has an interest in the complexities of character that is shared by many modern virtue ethicists. Yet Hume's sense of the many aspects of morality which are the work of human invention and artifice should not be downplayed. Much of morality is not in any sense "second nature" to us. On the contrary, it is the product of a long and complex negotiation between human beings and their circumstances, and, despite its history, needs constantly to be reinforced by social pressure and the more brutally coercive power of the magistrate.

See also Ethics and reason (Chapter 9); Ethics and sentiment (Chapter 10); Adam Smith (Chapter 12); Utilitarianism to Bentham (Chapter 13).

References

Abramson, K. (2001) "Sympathy and the Project of Hume's Second Enquiry," *Archiv für Geschichte der Philosophie* 83: 45–80.

Ardal, P. (1966) *Passion and Value in Hume's Treatise*, Edinburgh: Edinburgh University Press.

Baier, A. (1991) *A Progress of Sentiments: Reflections on Hume's Treatise*, Cambridge, MA: Harvard University Press.

——(2008) "The Relation between the Second *Enquiry* and Book III of the *Treatise*," in E. Radcliffe (ed.), *A Companion to Hume*, Oxford: Blackwell.

Bentham, J. (1988/1776) *A Fragment on Government*, ed. Ross Harrison, Cambridge: Cambridge University Press.

Cohon, R. (1997) "Hume's Difficulty with the Virtue of Honesty," *Hume Studies* 23: 91–112.

Darwall, S. (1995) *The British Moralists and the Internal "Ought": 1640–1740*, Cambridge: Cambridge University Press.

Gauthier, D. (1992) "Artificial Virtues and the Sensible Knave," *Hume Studies* 18: 401–27.

Gill, M. (2006) *The British Moralists and Human Nature: The Birth of Secular Ethics*, Cambridge: Cambridge University Press.

Haakonssen, K. (1996) *Natural Law and Moral Philosophy: From Grotius to the Scottish Enlightenment*, Cambridge: Cambridge University Press.

Harris, J. (2007) "Hume's Four Essays on Happiness and Their Place in the Move from Morals to Politics," in E. Mazza and E. Ronchetti (eds) *New Essays on David Hume*, Milan, Italy: Franco Angeli.

Hume, D. (1932) *The Letters of David Hume*, ed. J. Y. T. Greig, 2 vols, Oxford: Clarendon Press.

——(1975/1751/1748) *Enquiries concerning Human Understanding and concerning the Principles of Morals*, ed. L. A. Selby-Bigge, 3rd edn, rev. Peter Nidditch, Oxford: Clarendon Press.

——(1978/1739–40) *A Treatise of Human Nature*, ed. L. A. Selby-Bigge, 2nd edn, rev. Peter Nidditch, Oxford: Clarendon Press.

Mackie, D. (1980) *Hume's Moral Theory*, London: Routledge.

Norton, D. F. (1982) *David Hume: Common-Sense Moralist, Sceptical Metaphysician*, Princeton, NJ: Princeton University Press.

Reid, T. (1969/1788) *Essays on the Active Powers of the Human Mind*, Cambridge, MA: MIT Press.

Russell, P. (1995) *Freedom and Moral Sentiment: Hume's Way of Naturalizing Responsibility*, New York: Oxford University Press.

Schneewind, J. (1998) *The Invention of Autonomy: A History of Modern Moral Philosophy*, Cambridge: Cambridge University Press.

Smith, A. (1984/1759) *The Theory of Moral Sentiments*, ed. D. D. Raphael and A. Macfie, Indianapolis, IN: Liberty Fund.

Wiggins, D. (1998/1991/1987) "A Sensible Subjectivism?," in *Needs, Values, Truth: Essays in the Philosophy of Value*, 3rd edn, Oxford: Oxford University Press.

Further reading

Baillie, J. (2000) *Hume on Morality*, London: Routledge.

Bricke, J. (1996) *Mind and Morality: An Examination of Hume's Moral Psychology*, Oxford: Clarendon Press.

Cohon, R. (2004) "Hume's Moral Philosophy," in E. Zalta (ed.) *Stanford Encyclopedia of Philosophy*, <http://plato.stanford.edu/entries/hume-moral/>

——(2008) *Hume's Morality: Feeling and Fabrication*, New York: Oxford University Press.

Fieser, J. (2006) "David Hume (1711–76): Moral Theory," in J. Fieser and B. Dowden (eds) *The Internet Encyclopedia of Philosophy*, <http://www.utm.edu/research/iep/h/humemora.htm>

Gill, M. (2006).*The British Moralists on Human Nature and the Birth of Secular Ethics*, New York: Cambridge University Press.

Mackie, J. (1980) *Hume's Moral Theory*, London: Routledge & Kegan Paul.

Stroud, B. (1977). *Hume*, London: Routledge & Kegan Paul.

12
ADAM SMITH

Craig Smith

Adam Smith (1723–90) is familiar to most people as the father of economics. As the author of the groundbreaking *An Inquiry into the Nature and Causes of the Wealth of Nations* (1776) his name is still widely invoked in discussions of political economy. But Smith was first and foremost a moral philosopher. His economic interests developed from the lecture course that he gave as Professor of Moral Philosophy at the University of Glasgow (1752–64). Smith's moral philosophy is to be found in his *Theory of Moral Sentiments* published in 1759. The *Theory* is a book-length development of ideas that Smith had worked on during his time as a student at Glasgow and Oxford, as a freelance lecturer in Edinburgh and as a professor at Glasgow. It went through six editions in his lifetime: the second (1761) and sixth (1790) of these show substantial revisions, indicating that Smith continued to work on the ideas throughout his life.

Smith's moral thought is clearly framed by his interaction with contemporary British moral philosophy. His teacher Francis Hutcheson's response to Bernard Mandeville through his moral sense theory and proto-utilitarianism were clearly a major influence. So too was the skeptical response to this theory in the work of his close friend David Hume and the development of the notion of conscience in the writings of Bishop Joseph Butler. Smith was dissatisfied by the existing state of moral philosophy for one overwhelming reason: he did not believe that any of the theories of ancient or modern philosophy had developed an accurate model of what it is to experience moral judgment. In his view the attempts to ground morality in self-interest by some (Mandeville) and benevolence by others (Hutcheson) led to unrealistic models of human moral experience. While he admired Hume's attempt to move beyond this and to provide an account of the natural history of moral beliefs, he thought that his friend leant too heavily on the notion of utility for his moral psychology to be satisfying. Similarly, while there are many parallels between Smith's thought and that of his successor at Glasgow Thomas Reid, he does not develop a notion of an innate "common sense" regarding the content of moral judgments in response to Hume's skepticism.

Smith sets himself the task of providing an accurate theory of the everyday experience of moral thinking. What results is one of the most subtle works of moral psychology in all of philosophy. Smith's moral thought is not intended to reveal the nature of the virtues, nor is it meant to identify right and wrong in a didactic manner. Instead it is intended to provide an account of how human beings come to be moral creatures. To do this Smith proceeds in the Humean mode of applying empirical science to morals (Campbell 1975). Smith's evidence is largely grounded in examples from everyday moral experience that allows the reader to follow through his points in terms close to their own experience. The vivacity of Smith's examples means that most, if not all of them, remain easily accessible to the reader who is instantly familiar with the sorts of thoughts and feelings being described from their own everyday lives.

In his early essay *The Principles which Lead and Direct Philosophical Enquiries; Illustrated by the History of Astronomy*, Smith argued that the purpose of philosophy was to dispel wonder by explaining the hidden chains that connect nature. Philosophy is "that science which pretends to lay open the concealed connections that unite the various appearances of nature" (Smith 1980: 51). It addresses itself to the imagination and calms the mind that is disturbed by the apparently inexplicable. Wonder is a disturbing emotion and humans possess an emotional need, or natural propensity in Smith's terms, for understanding that compels us towards inquiry. Philosophers seek to dispel unease through explanation. Or as Smith puts it: "Who wonders at the machinery of an opera-house who has once been admitted behind the scenes" (Smith 1980: 42). The philosopher provides the backstage tour that allows us to grasp how the machinery of the mind operates.

Sympathy

In moral philosophy Smith finds the hidden chains in the notion of moral sentiment. This is not a moral sense, a unique cognitive capacity that is innate to all humans, like that proposed by Hutcheson. Instead it is an attempt to give an account of the nature of moral experience through human emotions and in particular a human propensity for fellow-feeling. Like the propensity to seek explanation and the propensity to trade explored in the *Wealth of Nations*, Smith regards sympathy as a universal feature of human nature. He distinguishes these natural propensities from the passions which motivate our actions and addresses his attention to the psychology of moral judgment rather than to the content of moral beliefs.

Smith develops a particular notion of sympathy that he believes grounds moral experience in our imagination. We need to be clear what Smith means by sympathy. He does not mean what we today mean when we say that we sympathize with people. Instead he has in mind a complex imaginative process where we are able to place ourselves in the position of another and come to understand how they are feeling. Smith's notion of sympathy is not as narrow as the present usage which evokes pity or commiseration. It refers to empathetic "fellow-feeling"

(Smith 1976:10) with "any passion whatever" (Smith 1976:10). By focusing on this empathetic propensity Smith is able to develop a model of how it is that people come to develop normative beliefs about moral notions such as good and evil. The point that Smith wanted to make was that the generation of a set of shared common beliefs about ethics was possible without an (actively) supernatural apparatus and without recourse to a single overarching explanatory principle.

Smith begins from the observation that morality cannot be reduced simply to selfishness or benevolence. Human moral experience is richer than many of his predecessors' theories would allow. While self-interest and benevolence form two of the passions that can motivate human activity, they are not sufficient to explain moral judgment. Human beings, no matter how hardened, are interested in their peers. They are also by no means driven by so extensive an interest in others as to render universal benevolence a satisfactory description of the core principle of morality.

Smith believes that mankind is naturally sociable and that this sociability is a fact that colors how we operate on an emotional and moral level. Social life is not simply the arena within which morality plays out, it is also responsible for generating morality itself. Human beings experience life as members of a group and it is their interaction with their fellows that is the basis of Smith's account of the generation of morality. Humans are acutely aware that they are the subject of the attention of their peers, they are also universally in possession of an emotional need for approval, and these two features come together to provide a theory of socialization that underwrites Smith's book. We adapt our behavior in an attempt to gain the approval, approbation in Smith's terminology, of our peers because we gain pleasure from the concurrence of our feelings with those of our peers. This occurs at the same time as we ourselves judge our fellows and both parties enjoy the pleasure of "mutual sympathy" (Smith 1976: 13). Smith believes that this facet of the human mind explains why we feel relief in close emotional relationships and find social interaction therapeutic.

Smith's account of morality in terms of feelings is combined with his belief in the central role of imagination in human moral experience. Morality is the product of an imaginative process because, if we cannot feel what others feel, the only path to understanding we have is through observation and imagination. Morality is a felt experience, but our judgment of others is conducted through imagined experience of their situations. The process of judgment that Smith has in mind is one that checks the propriety of behavior against our imagination's model of how we would react in similar circumstances. If the behavior observed fits with that which we imagine ourselves as experiencing in a like scenario, then we approve of it because it is how we would feel. Moral judgment is judgment of the appropriateness of behavior undertaken through an imaginative process allowing us to step into the situation of others. Smith stresses that there is a reflective element in this process. He does not regard sympathy as a purely mimetic contagion. While we can recognize and are attracted by smiling faces, it is only once we have become aware of the situation that has brought about the smile that we are able to "enter into" the happiness of the person smiling and engage in the sympathetic process of judgment that generates approval. In this sense the completeness of our sympathy is restricted by the level of our knowledge of the situation.

Smith's sympathy is thus capable of allowing us to enter into the position of people very different from ourselves. It is even capable of allowing us to sympathize with the dead (Smith 1976: 12). Obviously the dead cannot feel, but we are capable of imagining what death might be like, the absence of feeling, removal from one's loved ones and loss of the pleasures of life. We are thus able to conceive that this situation is undesirable and to approve of the grief felt by those who have lost someone close to them and to pity the unfortunate situation of the deceased. Continuing with the theme of bereavement Smith gives the example of a man who approaches us weeping. Initially we might be disturbed by this emotional display, but our approbation is forthcoming when we learn that he has just had news of his father's death (Smith 1976: 17–18). We are able to conduct an imaginative process that allows us to suppose how we would feel in his shoes and to pass judgment on the propriety of his reaction accordingly. Similarly, if a man approaches weeping uncontrollably and we learn that he has just lost a game of golf we can undertake the sympathetic process and conclude that his behavior is not in line with our assessment of an appropriate response, and so we will be disposed towards disapprobation. Judgment through imagination is the essence of moral experience.

Propriety

The experience of reflective moral judgment demands that we attempt to exercise spectatorship on the situation of others. As attentive spectators we attempt to assess as much of the available information about the circumstances of the person observed as possible. It is only after we have done this that we are able to generate a lively picture in our mind of the complete situation. Smith's point is not just that we imagine ourselves in the shoes of another, but the stronger claim that I imagine myself to be that other. The imaginative process invoked is intended to allow us access to how that person is experiencing their situation. The problem here is obviously that this remains an imaginative process. We never fully enter into the person of those whom we observe. Instead we can only ever, for epistemic reasons, develop a partial sympathy. We can imagine how it would feel to lose a close relative, but we "know" that we have not. As a result the emotions generated are of a lower "pitch" (Smith 1976: 22) of intensity. Smith then explains how the observed person knows this to be the case, from his own moral experience, and so restricts his outward display of emotion accordingly. He lowers the pitch of his feelings to that which experience tells him will be acceptable to the spectators. This adjustment in our display of emotion is not effected with the intention of securing some material benefit: it is directed solely at gaining the approval of our fellows.

Smith regards this moderation process as one of the great causes of tranquillity of mind. He is aware that we are able to generate more perfect sympathy with those who are close to us, and it is in the presence and approbation of friends and family that we are able to indulge our strongest feelings and expect the greatest understanding. But we are also subject to the judgment of the impartial spectator, one who is not partial enough to indulge our strongest feelings, and who cannot enter into our passionate experience as fully as those who are familiar with us. While such a figure may enter into our experience of serious misfortunes, like the death of a loved one, he is less willing to indulge our disappointment at matters of smaller account.

This marks the first appearance of Smith's idea of an impartial spectator. In this context the spectator is an actual individual, one who is disinterested in the situation, but who observes and passes judgment. The weeping golfer is subject to disapprobation because his display of emotion is judged to be inappropriate by an impartial spectator. The golfer, keen to secure the approval and sympathy of his peers, realizes this and alters his behavior. Thus morality becomes synonymous with "self-command" over the passions that drive our actions. It is our restriction of our emotions within the bonds of what we regard as socially acceptable that accounts for the phenomenon of moral experience. Society is the "great school of self-command" (Smith 1976: 145). This also highlights that Smith's psychological use of sympathy is very far from being a defense of excessive sensibility. "Extreme sympathy" (Smith 1976: 140) understood as excessive "commiseration" is an unhealthy disposition.

It is control of our emotions in line with assessments of appropriate behavior that characterizes the operation of sympathy rather than emotional incontinence. "Mediocrity" of "pitch" (Smith 1976: 27) in emotional display coalesces into a set of habituated standards or expected forms of behavior that are the basis of moral rules – what Smith calls propriety. Situational propriety differs in accordance with the circumstances of the individuals involved. For instance, Smith describes how we come to form different expectations of individuals engaged in different professions. To use an example, though not one of Smith's, we would be shocked and disapprove of a laughing undertaker, but not a laughing barman. Appropriateness of conduct is assessed in line with the socially generated norms applied to a given situation and these norms have their origin in the experience of passing moral judgment in specific cases.

There is clearly much common ground here between Smith and Rousseau's views on the centrality of emotion and the development of social norms in his *Discourse on the Origins of Inequality*. But Smith does not follow Rousseau in preferring some supposed "genuine" emotional experience to socially generated norms. Instead, and this accounts for those who read Smith as greatly influenced by the Stoics, the ability to control one's emotional experience is the hallmark of the development of moral maturity.

Smith sets out an account of the assessment of merit and demerit based on our experience of the process of judging and being judged in turn by our peers. The urge to judge explains the generation of social phenomena of punishment and reward. We see punishment as the proper reaction to behavior that generates strong disapproval, and reward as the proper reaction to that which generates approval. Punishment is the result of "sympathetic indignation" (Smith 1976: 76) where we enter into the indignation of the sufferer and pass judgment on the person who inflicted suffering. Our assessment must, however, be made with the conviction that the person concerned is responsible. The intervention of fortune affects our judgment of the appropriateness of a punishment in the sense that we add to our imaginative assessment a consideration of how responsible the individual is for a given set of outcomes.

Justice

This leads Smith into an important distinction between two virtues. Justice and beneficence are both produced by the moral psychology that Smith describes. But it is in the instantiation of our reactions to them in terms of punishment that they are distinguished. Beneficence attracts our approbation and we assess it as meritorious, but its absence does not raise our disapprobation to the level where we are willing to extend blame into punishment. The virtue of justice applies to those situations where our indignation is such that we are moved not just to assign demerit, but to act on that judgment. Smith believes that this is because justice concerns itself with cases of real injury that generate more resentment than failure to act with beneficence. Both are proper objects of demerit, but justice concerns itself with more serious matters like deliberate injury and so we regard force as a suitable means of assuring compliance.

This leads Smith to his strictly negative understanding of justice. If justice concerns itself with refraining from injury, then one may be just by "sitting still and doing nothing" (Smith 1976: 82). Such a person may be subject to assessments of moral demerit concerning a lack of proper beneficence, but their behavior is perfectly just. Smith stresses that the concept of justice is limited in its application and is not coextensive with that of moral merit, but he wants to be very clear that it is absolutely necessary for society to persist, and so may be extorted by coercion. Beneficence is necessary for a developed moral experience, but can only be compelled through informal social judgments. As Smith puts it: "The rules of justice may be compared to the rules of grammar; the rules of the other virtues, to the rules which critics lay down for the attainment of what is sublime and elegant in composition" (Smith 1976: 175). We must learn to write grammatically and we should aspire to write beautifully.

The impartial spectator

However, Smith is not yet satisfied that he has captured all of the dimensions of moral reflection. His next step involves examining the internalization of the process of spectatorship. To achieve this he extends the idea of *an* impartial spectator into that of *the* impartial spectator. The idea is that we internalize the process of judgment that provides us with an impartial assessment of others and apply it to our own behavior. Thus I am able to reflect on my behavior while stripping out my own partiality. I imagine how my behavior would appear to an impartial onlooker and thus am able, through my socially acquired knowledge, to generate expectations of likely reactions. I become a spectator of my own conduct. This process of psychologically splitting into two persons and dispassionately examining our own conduct becomes habitual to us as we learn about the reactions of others. We internalize a notion of propriety from the reactions of our peers and are then able to draw on it imaginatively before we act. We are thus able to restrict our behavior to avoid real disapprobation. Once we have learned this process we are able to exercise self-command in line with our understanding of socially acceptable behavior.

It is this internalized habit of self-assessment that lies behind Smith's account of conscience. According to Smith: "Man naturally desires, not only to be loved, but to be lovely; or to be that thing which is the natural and proper object of love" (Smith 1976: 113). This is extended into a desire to be not only praised, but also praiseworthy. This step marks Smith's notion of sympathy in moral judgment apart from that of many of his contemporaries (notably Hume). It explains, together with the impartial spectator, how it is that we come not just to recognize the shared moral beliefs of our peers, but also to internalize them as standards that we regard as valuable. It would, up to this point, be possible to accuse Smith of leaving open the possibility that morality was not a truly reflective activity, but rather operated purely by social conformity. The appearance of virtue would, by this reading, be sufficient to secure approbation from our peers. But the development of the self-reflective mechanism of the impartial spectator as conscience means that, in addition to assessing our behavior before we act, we also develop a habit of passing judgment on ourselves. It is this that represents the crucial step in Smith's account of moral psychology. We practice self-judgment to such a degree that we are dissatisfied with approbation unless we, as judges of our own behavior, are satisfied that we are worthy of such approbation. We "turn our eyes inwards" (Smith 1976: 115) and find that approbation that results from deception simply does not cut it for us. I may enjoy the praise of my peers, but that praise will not be forthcoming from my own conscience which has access to the knowledge that I am undeserving. It is this notion, the desire for praiseworthiness, that underpins our nature as moral beings capable of self-reflection. Indeed, Smith goes so far as to state that it is the love of this self-approbation through conscience that is the love of virtue.

Conscience will haunt the "coxcomb" who pursues the appearance of virtue without its substance.

This sophisticated and naturalistic model of the development of moral thinking leads Smith to identify duty with the dictates of the "higher tribunal," of the impartial spectator, "the man within the breast, the great judge and arbiter" of our conduct (Smith 1976: 130). Human psychology has produced moral reflection from the unfolding of our emotional natures and conscience allows us to make judgments in a swift and accurate manner. Our reflections lead us to generate rules of proper conduct that are the formal rendering of our imaginative and emotional assessment. The "general rules of conduct" (Smith 1976: 160) are the outward manifestation of our moral beliefs. They represent generalizations drawn from actual judgments and are a product of the natural propensity to assess the conduct of our peers.

Once again, though, Smith wants to distinguish his view from mere social conformity and to stress its developmental nature. He is aware that his model also helps to explain how it is that we can develop the belief that the established moral rules of our society are mistaken. We can consult the impartial spectator and form a judgment as to the proper course of action in a given situation, and this assessment can lead us to decide that existing social beliefs are mistaken (Griswold 1999). So strong is the authority of conscience, so thoroughly have we internalized the thought process, that we accept it as the final court of appeal and are willing to stand up to established social norms if we feel they do not agree with the assessment of our internal impartial spectator.

Smith believes that there are a number of psychological factors (greed and self-delusion being among the most prominent) that have the potential to misdirect our moral sentiments, but that the process of moral reflection embodied by consultation with the impartial spectator allows us to identify the true, "natural," principles of morality. This allows Smith to posit a process of social change where the shared moral beliefs of a society gradually evolve in line with reflective judgments on emotional responses to specific situations. Smith's awareness of the historically embedded nature of this reflective process leads him to accept the factual existence of different moral beliefs in different cultures while continuing to maintain that the universality of the propensity to sympathize leaves open the project of identifying universally valid moral rules. The identification of these rules becomes the subject matter of a moral science akin in form to the practice of comparative law outlined in his *Lectures on Jurisprudence*.

Smith's focus on the social aspect of moral reflection explains why he views it as giving us a sense of the "real littleness" (Smith 1976: 137) of our own concerns and passions. We realize that our behavior ought to be guided by imaginative reflection rather than by our own selfish desires and this is achieved without the intervention of philosophy or religion. Smith believes that our moral reflection is developed in everyday life; it is not enhanced, indeed it can be perverted, by seclusion and excessive solitary reflection. It is also only at this point that God begins to make a significant appearance in Smith's thought as something more than a divine instigator of a providential order. Smith had a complex and highly ambiguous attitude to religion. He was notoriously unwilling to commit himself on controversial matters and the place of religion in his thought remains a contested issue. What we can observe here is that he frames the relationship between religion and morality in naturalistic terms. Religious belief emerges as a part of human psychological development and becomes associated with the process of moral reflection and the rules that it generates. This provides an additional sanction that ensures our adherence to moral rules before the slow development of conscious reflection through philosophy.

Utility

After laying out his own theory Smith undertakes a survey of other significant moral philosophies that highlights their relative insufficiencies and the superiority of Smith's account. He includes a section that explains why he differs from his close friend Hume. Smith disagrees with Hume on the operation and relative relationship between utility and sympathy. For Hume morality, and justice in particular, is a product of calculations of utility applied to experience which comes to gain force as a sympathy with the public interest develops. Smith accepts that judgments of utility play an important part in moral experience. But they do not explain the process of moral judgment. This is an emotional, sympathetic process, not a calculative process. Utility is "plainly an after-thought" (Smith 1976: 20) and not the principle that directs our moral assessment. It is an explanatory tool of philosophers, and not a principle that we would admit rings true of our everyday moral judgments. Smith reverses Hume's account of sympathy and utility and he is able to do this because of his more sophisticated notion of reflective sympathy. This also helps us to understand why Smith does not develop his interest in utility into a systematically applied principle of moral assessment. Indeed it leads us to a recurring theme in Smith's work, that the sphere of action open to individuals is limited by the extent of their ability to affect practical outcomes. Smith regards questions relating to what we might call global-level moral outcomes to be beyond the capabilities of individuals.

Part VI of the *Moral Sentiments* is a consideration of some of the implications of this theory of moral sentiment for the character of virtue. Smith's description of the prudent man represents an extension of the ideas of self-command and moderation that are to be found throughout the book. The prudent man will accept that he has duties towards others. These are more extensive to those closely related to us, and extend gradually outward to the level of adherence to the impartial rules of justice regarding strangers. The "weakness of his powers" (Smith 1976: 237) restricts the arena in which any person can act efficiently to affect the happiness of others. This confinement of attention will be accepted by the prudent man as the true arena of moral activity. The prudent man will not measure his moral worth by excessive displays of meaningless empathy. Instead self-command, due regard for propriety, and careful activity within our sphere of influence characterize the man of virtue. This is not a theory that vaunts the heroic virtues. Instead it seeks to account for the everyday moral beliefs of the great body of humanity.

The Adam Smith problem

The Adam Smith problem is the name given to a view first expressed by nineteenth-century German readers of Smith who thought that they detected a contradiction between the stress placed on sympathy in *The Theory of Moral Sentiments* and the focus on self-interest in the *Wealth of Nations*. The contradiction could perhaps be explained by Smith changing his mind between writing the two books, but as we have seen they both have their origins in the same course of lectures and, moreover, Smith continued to work on *Moral Sentiments* even after he had completed *Wealth of Nations*. This problem is now widely viewed as a non-problem based on a flawed understanding of what Smith meant by sympathy and self-interest. Smith's economic writings focus on one particular aspect of human character as it is expressed in the world of production and exchange. Nothing in this contradicts the theory of moral experience developed in *The Theory of Moral Sentiments*. Indeed the notion of self-interest is present throughout in the guise of prudence and plays an active role in the generation of moral behavior. Once we realize that Smith has a particular, technical understanding of sympathy as a part of his explanatory model the problem dissolves. Indeed Smith uses the same explanatory model, with a focus on the significance of unintended consequences, throughout his work (Otteson 2002). The fact that the Adam Smith Problem has been rejected by serious readers of Smith's thought does not prevent some from adopting the superficially "profound" view that Smith's moral thought in some sense contradicts his influence on the development of economics. But this says more about economists' references to Smith than it does about his actual thought. Adam Smith provides a subtle and wide-ranging examination of the nature of the experience of moral judgment that takes humanity as he finds it and attempts to illustrate the principles operating in moral reflection.

See also Ethics and sentiment (Chapter 10); Hume (Chapter 11); Utilitarianism to Bentham (Chapter 13).

References

Campbell, T. D. (1975) "Scientific Explanation and Ethical Judgement in the Moral Sentiments," in Andrew S. Skinner and Thomas Wilson (eds) *Essays on Adam Smith*, Oxford: Clarendon Press, pp. 68–82.

Griswold, Charles L., Jr (1999) *Adam Smith and the Virtues of Enlightenment*, Cambridge: Cambridge University Press.

Otteson, James R. (2002) *Adam Smith's Marketplace of Life*, Cambridge: Cambridge University Press.

Smith, Adam (1976/1759) *The Theory of Moral Sentiments*, ed. D. D. Raphael and A. L. Macfie, Oxford: Oxford University Press.

——(1980/1795) *Essays on Philosophical Subjects*, ed. W. P. D. Wightman, Oxford: Oxford University Press.

Further reading

Campbell, T. D. (1971) *Adam Smith's Science of Morals*, London: G. Allen & Unwin. (Smith as moral scientist.)

Haakonssen, Knud (1981) *The Science of a Legislator: The Natural Jurisprudence of David Hume and Adam Smith*, Cambridge: Cambridge University Press. (Smith's relationship to natural law.)

——(ed.) (2006) *The Cambridge Companion to Adam Smith*, Cambridge: Cambridge University Press. (Latest collection of essays on Smith.)

Smith, Adam (1976/1776) *An Inquiry into the Nature and Causes of the Wealth of Nations*, ed. R. H. Campbell, A. S. Skinner and W. B. Todd, Oxford: Oxford University Press.

——(1982) *Lectures on Jurisprudence*, ed. R. L. Meek, D. D. Raphael and P. G. Stein, Oxford: Oxford University Press.

13
UTILITARIANISM TO BENTHAM

Frederick Rosen

Utility and utilitarianism

Both consequentialism and hedonism, two elements of modern utilitarianism (Quinton 1973: 1), were, as Baumgardt (1952: 35) suggests, "probably as old as human thought itself" and well-known to ancient philosophers. Opinions have differed as to the origins of modern utilitarianism. It is possible to see elements of the doctrine in Thomas Hobbes and John Locke (Plamenatz 1958: 1–21, 161–2; Stephen 1876: Vol. 2, 80ff.), though other scholars trace its origins variously to Richard Cumberland's *De Legibus Naturae* (see Albee 1902: 11; Quinton 1973: 16) or to John Gay's "Dissertation" (see Halévy 1952: 7), while recognizing the importance of David Hume (see Moore 1994, 2002) in its development. Recent scholarship has emphasized the significance of the idea of utility in the ancient and modern Epicurean traditions, the latter of which began in the seventeenth century with Pierre Gassendi (see Scarre 1994: 219–31; Rosen 2003: 19ff.). Gassendi wrote:

> Therefore to speak properly Right or natural Equity is nothing else but what is mark'd out by Utility or Profit, or that Utility which, by common Agreement, hath been appointed that Men might not injure one another, nor receive any wrong, but live in security, which is a real Good, and therefore naturally desired of every one.
>
> (Gassendi 1699: 315)

In Gassendi's account of the relationship between utility and justice, a number of arguments were stated and developed that influenced the way utilitarian ethical thought was later conceived. First, he dismissed the role of retaliation in justice, as it brought increased pain into the system. He also did not assume that justice was desirable in itself (as its operations were painful), though it became desirable in so far as it secured the basic tie without which a society could not exist (Gassendi 1699: 308ff.). Second, Gassendi argued that for a law or practice to be just, it not only had to be useful, but it also had to be "prescribed and ordained by the common Consent of the Society" (Gassendi 1699: 315). Among the consequences of this position was a relative account of morals. A given law or practice could be just in one society though not in another or just and then unjust in the same society when circumstances changed. These changes in the justice of various practices did not depend on the perception of individual profit from moment to moment but on whether the practices more objectively secured the lives, liberties, and happiness of the members of a society and prevented some from harming others. The foundation of these criteria was developed by Gassendi as follows:

> In a word, a thing is and ought to be reputed Just, or to have the Qualities of Just in a Society, *if its usefulness respects all the Individuals associated*; but if it be not so 'tis not properly to be called Just, nor deserves to be so esteemed.
>
> (Gassendi 1699: 316, italics added)

For Gassendi, what made utility the basis of justice was not that "the wise" or the rich or the poor found a law useful and had the power to adopt and enforce it, but that all members of a society found it useful by common consent or that its utility was such that the law or practice "respects all the individuals associated." On this account there was no opposition between utility and justice and no sacrifice of some for the sake of a greater overall utility. After Gassendi and throughout the eighteenth century, prior to Hume and Jeremy Bentham, theories of utility and the social contract happily co-existed. Furthermore, utility itself was a distributive principle, involving compact or agreement, and defined what counted as just or unjust. What made it distributive was that it was grounded in the common consent of all members of society, ultimately on their pains and pleasures, and applied equally to all in that society. Utility, then, became in Gassendi's account of Epicurean justice a technical term, referring to the nature and distribution of pains and pleasures and providing criteria to assess the justice of law and morality.

Gassendi also introduced a new way of looking at nature in both science and morality. Although he rejected the Stoic and Thomistic doctrines of natural law, and founded society on utility, he grafted the new concept of nature on to the idea of common utility and found that this foundation in utility warranted the term "natural." In this respect he believed that Epicurus' view of the compact, even though based on convention, did not necessarily contradict the idea of natural justice found in Plato and Aristotle.

One might ask how Gassendi could deal with the unjust person in society who derived great pleasure from his or her injustice. He rejected the view that the unjust person could be happy, and called attention to the disordered *psyche* suffered by such individuals following an act or acts of injustice: "full of Troubles, Jealousies and Fears, Gripings of Conscience and Anxieties of Mind" (Gassendi 1699: 333, originally in italic). Thus, members of society resisted the temptation to be unjust, because of the anxieties surrounding discovery and punishment which persisted even where there was no serious possibility of punishment.

Although utilitarian arguments featured in numerous debates in the eighteenth century, utilitarianism as a system of thought appeared later in the century in the writings of William Paley (1743–1805) and Bentham (1748–1832) (see Sidgwick 1906: 225ff.). Both recognized the importance of earlier writers with Paley in *The Principles of Moral and Political Philosophy* (Paley 1819: Vol. 1, lxiii–lxiv) acknowledging the influence of Abraham Tucker's *The Light of Nature Pursued* and Bentham referring most often to Claude Adrien Helvétius, Cesare Beccaria, Joseph Priestley, and Hume (see Baumgardt 1952: 37ff.). The greatest happiness principle, itself, the foundation of Bentham's system (see Rosen 1983: 200–20), has been traced to Beccaria (1766: 3, 1767: 2), Priestley (1768: 17), Hutcheson (1725: 163–4) and even to Leibniz (Hruschka 1991: 165–77) (see Shackleton 1972; Stephen 1900: Vol. 1, 177–9).

William Paley

Paley is often classed among the religious or theological utilitarians, such as Gay, John Brown, Soame Jenyns, Edmund Law, and Tucker (see Crimmins 1998: 7). While his theology, like that of many writers from the mid-eighteenth century, was mainly Lockean (see Rivers 2000: 332–3), his morals and politics drew their inspiration from Hume. Like Bentham and William Godwin, for example, Paley followed Hume in rejecting the doctrine of the social contract (see Schofield 1996: 106–7). Like Hume, he also gave utility a more foundational role in his ethics than it had been given by Locke (see Rivers 2000: 338–9). In addition, Paley was a hedonist, and as early as 1765 in his Member's Prize essay, written at Cambridge, he took the side of Epicurean philosophy over that of Stoicism, though in the end he preferred Christianity to both (Barker 1948: 199, 230; Clarke 1974: 10). Nevertheless, the association of Paley, as well as Hume and Bentham, with a sympathy for Epicureanism provides an important link between the three writers, and enables one to look elsewhere for differences between Hume and Bentham, on the one hand, and Paley, on the other. The main difference can be found in an inattention to individual liberty in Paley's thought (as opposed to Hume and Bentham) and, particularly, to the varying ways that individuals perceived and acted on pleasure and pain. Unlike many writers in the modern Epicurean tradition from Hume to Mill, Paley did not fully accept the links established between utility, justice, and liberty. In place of an emphasis on individual liberty, Paley turned to God's will.

If Hume believed that one could separate Christian theology from ethical theory, Paley did not. In Paley's view secular ethics should have a place for rewards and punishments after death, as these were necessary to keep human beings on the path of virtue. Although both Hume and Paley sought to advance human happiness, they differed in that, for Hume, in some circumstances, the pursuit of virtue was self-regulating, with the punishment of vice in serious misdemeanors left to justice. Besides finding little empirical evidence for "the light of nature," Hume believed that the passions themselves could deliver virtue. The passions and self-interest provided sufficient conditions to recommend virtue in so far as virtue "is attended with more peace of mind than vice and meets with a more favourable reception from the world" (Hume 2000: 105).

Paley, however, questioned whether Hume's account could contain "lust, revenge, envy, ambition, avarice; or to prevent the existence of these passions" (Paley 1819: i.40). He obviously thought that the threat of punishment after death was necessary to do so. But Hume would regard the prevention of the existence of passions and, particularly, sexual passion and the social passions that fueled revenge, envy, ambition, and avarice to be a hopeless task. He was also well aware of how the passions themselves could create virtue and hence happiness. In an economic system envy and ambition might prove not to be vices, and a modified form of revenge might prove to be the passion at the foundation of a system of justice. Lust, as Paley called it, might give pleasure and satisfaction as well as form the basis of a social institution like the family. The fact that Paley even wrote of preventing passions might place him among Hume's "austere pretenders," "enemies to joy and pleasure" who were either rejected as "hypocrites and deceivers" or allowed in the train of virtues, ranked "among the least favoured of her votaries" (Hume 1998: 79–80). Like many of Hume's critics, Paley seemed uneasy with the lack of individual effort required by Hume's account of virtue (see Rivers 2000: 308).

In suggesting that the key difference between Hume and Bentham on the one hand and Paley on the other rested with their respective attitudes towards the passions, one is stating only part of the story. The reason that Hume and Bentham were more accepting of the passions was that their theories were underpinned by a conception of individual liberty. Despite Paley's acceptance of the principle of utility and hedonism, the starting point was the will of God, and the will of God revealed the dictates of utility. Individuals were enjoined by duty to conform to the common interest in which the happiness of the community and that of the individuals comprising it were to be found.

Paley can be regarded as a strong advocate of civil liberty and religious toleration. But in the sphere of self-regarding actions, including those between consenting adults, he recognized no obvious sphere of liberty. He placed his emphasis on duties, developed a utilitarianism based on rules, and noted at one point that "every duty is a duty towards God, since it is his will which makes it a duty" (Paley 1819: Vol. 1, 293). Even though duties towards God should not conflict with utility and should advance human happiness, the focal point was taken away from the individual's direct experience of pleasure and pain. Who determined if fornication brought less pleasure (as Paley seemed to believe) than the cultivation of a cucumber? Paley did not leave the choice of pleasures to the estimation of ordinary people. This choice was the essence of human liberty in the modern utilitarian tradition. It underpinned a number of elements in utilitarianism from the concept of an interest to the idea that happiness generally could not be distinct from the happiness of particular individuals in society. While Paley believed that his aim was human happiness and that this was best determined through duties discernible from the will of God, the consequence of his "surer road" to happiness was a general disinclination to trust humanity on its own to choose the right pleasures, and to appreciate the way ordinary passions could support the public good when channeled through liberty and justice.

Jeremy Bentham

There have been two serious obstacles to understanding Bentham's ethics. The first was the posthumous publication of a work on ethics in 1834, entitled *Deontology*, and edited by Bentham's literary executor, John Bowring (Bowring 1834). Like many other contemporaries, J. S. Mill believed that the work was not an accurate reflection of Bentham's views, and, additionally, was "a book scarcely ever, in our experience, alluded to by any admirer of Bentham without deep regret that it ever saw the light" (Mill 1963–91: Vol. 10, 98; see Vol. 10, 90). Only in 1983 did a new version, based on Bentham's own manuscripts, appear as a volume in the new edition of *The Collected Works of Jeremy Bentham* (Bentham 1968–, 1983c).

The second obstacle has been the critique of Bentham by Mill that appeared in his essays on Bentham published in the 1830s (see Mill 1963–91: Vol. 10, 3–18, 499–502, 75–115). Criticizing Bentham's belief in the predominance of self-regarding interests or feelings over the social or public interest in "Remarks on Bentham's Philosophy," he wrote characteristically and somewhat dramatically that "I conceive Mr. Bentham's writings to have done and to be doing very serious evil" (Mill 1963–91: Vol. 10, 15). The effect of this evil was, in part, to turn "enthusiastic and generous minds" against all of his ideas and, additionally, to prevent progress in making ethics and politics the subjects of precise philosophical thinking. The effect on those not shocked or repelled by Bentham's thinking was to pervert "their whole moral nature." "It is difficult," wrote Mill, "to form the conception of a tendency more inconsistent with all rational hope of good for the human species, than that which must be impressed by such doctrines, upon any mind in which they find acceptance" (Mill 1963–91: Vol. 10, 15). In the essay, "Bentham," Mill compounded his critique of Bentham's ethics by first praising his work in the philosophy and practice of law

("He found the philosophy of law a chaos, he left it a science": Mill 1963–91: Vol. 100). By contrast, Bentham's work in ethics was made to appear fairly worthless. The effect of Mill's understanding of Bentham's ethical thought was to limit its study and lead to a confusion of important ideas that Bentham had developed from Hume and Helvétius and in fact passed on to Mill whose debts to Bentham's ethics are greater than his early criticisms first suggest.

For example, like other writers in the Epicurean tradition, Bentham believed in higher and lower pleasures. This belief has been ignored or rejected by many moral philosophers. They have tended to mistake Mill's critique of Bentham's views on taste with Bentham's conception of pleasure and have combined this with a misleading account of Bentham's limited attempts to quantify pleasures within certain categories. Additionally, following Mill, they have taken Bentham's criticism of state funding of the arts in *Rationale of Reward* (Bentham 1838–43: Vol. 2, 253) as evidence of a simplistic quantitative approach to pleasure in ethics (Mill 1963–91: Vol. 10, 113: "quantity of pleasure being equal, push-pin is as good as poetry"). Bentham, himself, stressed the importance of education to moderate what he called "inordinate sensuality" or the "pleasures of sense" in favor of intellectual pleasures. As Bentham put it,

> the greater the variety of the shapes in which pleasures of an intellectual nature are made to present themselves to view, and consequently the greater degree of success and perfection with which the mind is prepared for the reception of intellectual pleasures, the greater the chance afforded of security from the pains by which sensual pleasures are encompassed.
> (Bentham 1983a: 23)

Bentham's first important discussion of ethics appeared in the final chapter (17) of *An Introduction to the Principles of Morals and Legislation*, where he attempted to distinguish private ethics from the spheres of government and legislation. As the bulk of this work was originally conceived as an analytical introduction to a penal code, and although Bentham touched on numerous ethical issues in its chapters, he felt it necessary to distinguish the sphere of the legislator from that more appropriate to the realm of private ethics. By ethics generally he meant "the art of directing men's actions to the production of the greatest possible quantity of happiness, on the part of those whose interest is in view" (Bentham 1996: 282). In the midst of his discussion, Bentham referred to other adults and animals with which both legislation and private ethics should be concerned. In a footnote one finds his remarks about the tyrannical treatment of slaves and other animals, and, particularly, his famous attack on the Aristotelian legacy regarding the human treatment of animals: "the question is not, Can they *reason*? nor Can they *talk*? but, Can they *suffer*?" (Bentham 1996: 283n). As for private ethics, he referred to "the art of directing a man's own actions" in terms of the "art of self-government" (Bentham 1996: 282). He also developed some fundamental distinctions between prudence, probity, and beneficence that underpinned his discussions here and elsewhere in his writings (see Bentham 1983b: 396–7, 1983c). Prudence was conceived as the art of discharging one's duties to oneself. At another point he distinguished between self-regarding and other-regarding prudence as it affected oneself and others respectively (see 1983b: 397). In so far as ethics was concerned with directing one's duties to others, it was distinguished into probity (forbearing to diminish the happiness of others) and beneficence (positively increasing the happiness of others) (Bentham 1996: 284). These logical distinctions between the various categories of virtue underpin the discussions of virtue in Bentham's later writings, and, particularly, in his major ethical work, *Deontology* (see Bentham 1983c).

When Bentham considered the motives to develop these other-regarding virtues, he could see "no occasions in which a man has not some motives for consulting the happiness of other men." He referred to what he called the "social motive" of sympathy or benevolence and the "semi-social motives" of love of amity and love of reputation. The two kinds of motives operated differently on the individual: sympathy, according to the way the individual responded to pleasure and pain (i.e. the bias of one's sensibility) and the semi-social motives, according to a number of circumstances, e.g. "the strength of his intellectual powers, the firmness and steadiness of his mind, the quantum of his moral sensibility, and the characters of the people he has to deal with" (Bentham 1996: 284–5).

Bentham is well-known for his remarks concerning the doctrine of natural rights: "Natural rights is simple nonsense: natural and imprescriptible rights, rhetorical nonsense, nonsense upon stilts" (Bentham 2002: 330). He insisted that the language of ethics had little need for a doctrine of rights, but a great deal for that concerned with duties. Rights, he believed, were more appropriate to law, as they could only rise above the nonsensical by being enforceable legal rights (Bentham 1983c: 171ff.). He found no role for rights (i.e. natural rights) that were supposed to have existed prior to the creation of civil society or government, and thought that general rights to life, liberty, and property were meaningless, unenforceable, and tended to lead to social strife in bringing individuals (through their claims to such rights) into direct conflict with government, when such conflict might well have been avoided. If one had a right to the use of one's property, for example, it was because others were under a legal obligation not to interfere with or obstruct one in the use of it (Bentham 1983b: 188). As for moral rights, Bentham characteristically added: "A thick cloud envelopes the discourse, under it endless confusion reigns – wherever they are confused with *legal rights*" (Bentham 1983b: 188).

In order to avoid the confrontational character of moral or natural rights (and the confusion involved in their use), Bentham chose to write of "securities for appropriate aptitude." He conceived of securities as functioning on a different level and in a different manner than was customary with rights. Instead of the individual standing in direct opposition to the sovereign power of the state, securities operated indirectly, providing incentives for rulers to restrain their agents from behaving immorally or illegally. For example, by insisting on widespread publicity and transparency in government and other institutions, corruption and oppression might be reduced without the threat of civil strife and revolution (see Rosen 1983: 57–8; Bentham 1990: 23ff.).

With the rejection of natural and moral rights, one can appreciate more Bentham's concentration on duties which, as we have seen, he transformed into a theory of virtue. This theory of virtue was developed in numerous respects in the manuscripts on deontology written mainly in 1814 and 1815 (see Bentham 1983c). One finds here an extensive critique of the Aristotelian account of virtue which Bentham hoped to replace with his own theory (see Bentham 1983c: 154ff.). He also developed a number of ideas in an attempt to link virtue with utility. The test of virtue was understood to be the conduciveness of its exercise to happiness (conceived in terms of pleasure and the absence of pain). Such actions were deemed by Bentham to require effort as a condition for being called virtuous, at least at the outset. He provided an example of the purchase of a loaf of bread for one's dinner which brought utility to oneself and to the shopkeeper in the profit from the sale of the loaf. But there was no obvious exercise of virtue here, unless in other circumstances surrounding earning the money and eating the loaf. But if upon encountering a starving person, one gave him or her the loaf and went without dinner, the effort required produced virtue, in this case, beneficence. Much virtuous action, however, by habit ceased to require effort, as when one became moderate through the habitual exercise of prudence.

Included in *Deontology* (Bentham 1983c: 345–63) is an essay on Hume's virtues, where Bentham criticized the language Hume employed in his radical revision of the traditional Aristotelian virtues. From both the tone and context of the essay, Bentham clearly approved of the direction Hume was taking in ethics, but sought to impose on it a logical order and clarity that Hume eschewed. If Hume was criticized by some of his contemporaries for belittling the instinct of natural modesty, or a sense of honor or pride related to it, in connecting modesty only to public utility (see Anon. 1753: 34–5; Rosen 2003: 55), Bentham went further to question whether or not modesty should be regarded as a virtue at all. "Constipation," he wrote at one point, "is a virtue of the same quality as chastity" (Bentham 1983c: 362).

Bentham also redefined other virtues, and an instructive example is courage. Courage was important for Hume both in itself and because of his admiration for the heroes of antiquity who became models for a later age and enabled one to display a capacity for widespread and deep sympathy. Bentham also admired courage but noted that its meaning had changed in modern times. He thought that strenuous exercise and self-denial were not necessarily parts of the virtue: "the old days were days of force; these are the days of fraud. Formerly, it was the powers of the body, now those of the mind. ... Formerly it was physical force; now it is mental fraud" (Bentham 1983c: 360). For Bentham, therefore, courage must be redefined to incorporate honesty and integrity in advocacy (see Rosen 2003: 55–6).

As we have seen, Bentham's main concern in his various discussions of ethics was to provide logical accounts (based on his theory of bifurcation or logical division and his ontological distinctions between real and fictitious entities) within an overall philosophical system. These tended to be more concerned with mental clarity than with moral uplift. In *Chrestomathia* (1816–17), where his newly coined term, "deontology," first appeared in a published work (cf. *Oxford English Dictionary*, see OUP 1989), he developed a map of all the arts and sciences as an improvement on Diderot's map conceived to accompany the *Encyclopédie*. Following a complex series of divisions, Bentham first distinguished ethics from aesthetics with the former concerned with volition and the latter with taste. Within ethics, he distinguished between expository ethics, which he associated with Hume, and deontology, which determined "what is *proper* to be done" and took its inspiration more from Helvétius (Bentham 1983a: Table 5, opposite 179). Deontology was then divided into state-regarding and private ethics. In the work entitled *Deontology*, Bentham further distinguished between theoretical and practical, and political and private deontology. These distinctions were worked out with great care, but underpinning all of it was Bentham's deeply held belief:

> That, being the best judge for himself what line of conduct on each occasion will be most conducive to his own well-being, every man, being of mature age and sound mind, ought on this subject to be left to judge and act for himself: and that every thing which by any other man can be said or done in the view of giving direction to the conduct of the first, is no better than folly and impertinence.
>
> (Bentham 1983c: 251)

Bentham stood for liberty of taste and action where such action was between consenting adults and caused no (mainly physical harm) to others. This liberty enhanced both public and private ethics. For example, Bentham questioned the large number of established criminal offenses concerned with religious heterodoxy and sexual diversity, where no actual harm was done and where the penalties traditionally associated with them were severe (see Boralevi 1984: 37–81; Crompton 1985: 19ff., 251–83). In this respect he differed from Paley in insisting on individual freedom (as opposed to God's will) in the choice of pleasures (see Rosen 2003: 131–43). He also differed from Mill who acknowledged Bentham's emphasis on liberty of taste but insisted that a person's tastes were important for estimations of character, an important foundation of society. For Mill, one needed to determine if a person was "wise or a fool, cultivated or ignorant, gentle or rough, sensitive or callous, generous or sordid, conscientious or depraved" (Mill 1963–91: Vol. 10, 113). For Bentham, many of these aspects of taste might be incorporated within the virtues of prudence, probity, and benevolence. But he still upheld liberty of personal taste, even if, in an individual's estimation of his or her own pleasures, poetry might not be regarded as enjoyable as push-pin.

Another element of Mill's critique of Bentham concerned the latter's emphasis on self-regarding motivation and interests over benevolence and sympathy. But Bentham's emphasis on self-regard was not a simple matter. At one level he insisted on the foundational status of self-regarding interests, even with respect to the cultivation of sympathy. In a well-known remark, he asserted that if Adam thought only of Eve and Eve only of Adam, the human race would have perished within twelve months (Bentham 1983b: 119). At the same time he could write:

> To give increase to the influence of sympathy at the expense of that of self-regard, and of sympathy for the greater number at the expense of sympathy for the lesser number, – is the constant and arduous task, as of every moralist, so of every legislator who deserves to be so.

However, he followed this remark with the qualification that the less that sympathy was assumed to be prevalent in human nature and in various institutions, the more likely it was that sympathy would actually be increased. This was due to the fundamental principle that

> whatsoever evil it is possible for man to do for the advancement of his own private and personal interest ... at the expense of the public interest, – that evil, sooner or later, he will do, unless by some means or other, intentional or otherwise, prevented from doing it.
>
> (Bentham 1983b: 119)

There is, therefore, at one level a healthy self-regard that must exist if human life is to continue. At another level, self-regard, unless checked by ethics, education, and law, could lead to numerous evils. Hence the virtues concerned with prudence, probity, and beneficence had an important role to play in reducing evil self-regard and linking with healthy self-regard. In developing this theory, Bentham was aware of a widespread "false consciousness" among many members of society (for example, in willingly neglecting self-regarding interests in going off to war and facing possible death) inculcated by religion, the military, politicians, and other ruling elites. Moralists and politicians who understood the role of self-regarding interests in human life had, in Bentham's opinion, to oppose these views that led ordinary people astray. He was thus skeptical of criticisms of self-interest in morality and politics, not because he sought to celebrate human depravity, but because he sought to increase virtue in all of its forms.

See also Hume (Chapter 11); John Stuart Mill (Chapter 16); Consequentialism (Chapter 37); Virtue ethics (Chapter 40); Rights (Chapter 56); Justice and distribution (Chapter 58).

References

Albee, E. (1902) *A History of English Utilitarianism*, London: Swan Sonnenschein.

Anon. (1753) *Some Late Opinions Concerning the Foundation of Morality, Examined. In a Letter to a Friend*, London: R. Dodsley and M. Cooper.

Barker, E. (1948) *Traditions of Civility: Eight Essays*, Cambridge: Cambridge University Press.

Baumgardt, D. (1952) *Bentham and the Ethics of Today*, Princeton, NJ: Princeton University Press.

Beccaria, C. (1766) *Traité des Délits et des Peines, Traduit de l'Italian*, trans. A. Morellet, Paris.

——(1767) *An Essay on Crimes and Punishments; Translated from the Italian; with a Commentary Attributed to Mons. De Voltaire, Translated from the French*, London: J. Almon.

Bentham, J. (1838–43) *The Works of Jeremy Bentham*, 11 vols, ed. J. Bowring, Edinburgh: William Tait.

——(1968–) *The Collected Works of Jeremy Bentham*, vols 65–8, ed. J. H. Burns, J. R. Dinwiddy, F. Rosen and P. Schofield, London: Athlone Press; and Oxford: Clarendon Press (in progress).

——(1983a) *Chrestomathia*, ed. M. J. Smith and W. H. Burston, Oxford: Clarendon Press.

——(1983b) *Constitutional Code, Volume I*, ed. F. Rosen and J. H. Burns, Oxford: Clarendon Press.

——(1983c) *Deontology together with A Table of the Springs of Action and Article on Utilitarianism*, ed. A. Goldworth, Oxford: Clarendon Press.

——(1990) *Securities against Misrule and Other Constitutional Writings for Tripoli and Greece*, ed. P. Schofield, Oxford: Clarendon Press.

——(1996) *An Introduction to the Principles of Morals and Legislation*, ed. J. H. Burns and H. L. A. Hart, with a new introduction by F. Rosen, Oxford: Clarendon Press.

——(2002) *Rights, Representation, and Reform, Nonsense upon Stilts and Other Writings on the French Revolution*, ed. P. Schofield, C. Pease-Watkin and C. Blamires, Oxford: Clarendon Press.

Boralevi, L. (1984) *Bentham and the Oppressed*, Berlin and New York: Walter de Gruyter & Co.

Bowring, J. (1834) *Deontology; or, The Science of Morality*: In Which the Harmony and Coincidence of Duty and Self-interest, Virtue and Felicity, Prudence and Benevolence, Are Explained and Exemplified: *From the MSS of Jeremy Bentham*, London: Longman, Rees, Orme, Browne, Green & Longman; and Edinburgh: William Tait.

Clarke, M. L. (1974) *Paley, Evidences for the Man*, London: Society for Promoting Christian Knowledge.

Crimmins, J. (1998) *Utilitarians and Religion*, Bristol: Thoemmes Press.

Crompton, L. (1985) *Byron and Greek Love: Homophobia in 19th-Century England*, London: Faber & Faber.

Gassendi, P. (1699) *Three Discourses of Happiness, Virtue, and Liberty. Collected from the Works of the Learn'd Gassendi, By Monsieur Bernier*, London: Awnsham & John Churchill.

Halévy, E. (1952) *The Growth of Philosophic Radicalism*, trans. M. Morris, London: Faber & Faber.

Hruschka, J. (1991) "The Greatest Happiness Principle and Other Early German Anticipations of Utilitarian Theory," *Utilitas* 3: 165–77.

Hume, D. (1998) *An Enquiry concerning the Principles of Morals*, ed. T. Beauchamp, Oxford: Clarendon Press.

——(2000) *An Enquiry concerning Human Understanding*, ed. T. Beauchamp, Oxford: Clarendon Press.

Hutcheson, F. (1725) *An Inquiry into the Original of Our Ideas of Beauty and Virtue in Two Treatises*, London: J. Darby.

Mill, J. S. (1963–91) *The Collected Works of John Stuart Mill*, 33 vols, ed. J. M. Robson, Toronto: University of Toronto Press.

Moore, J. (1994) "Hume and Hutcheson" in *Hume and Hume's Connexions*, ed. M. A. Stewart and J. P. Wright, Edinburgh: Edinburgh University Press.

——(2002) "Utility and Humanity: The Quest for the *Honestum* in Cicero, Hutcheson and Hume," *Utilitas* 14: 365–86.

OUP (Oxford University Press) (1989) *Oxford English Dictionary*, 2nd edn, Oxford: Oxford University Press.

Paley, W. (1819) *The Works of William Paley, D.D. with A Life by Alexander Chalmers, Esq.*, 5 vols, London: F. C. & J. R. Rivington.

Plamenatz, J. (1958) *The English Utilitarians*, 2nd edn, Oxford: Basil Blackwell.

Priestley, J. (1768) *An Essay on the First Principles of Government; and on the Nature of Political, Civil and Religious Liberty*, London.

Quinton, A. (1973) *Utilitarian Ethics*, London: Macmillan.

Rivers, I. (2000) *Reason, Grace, and Sentiment: A Study of the Language of Religion and Ethics in England, 1660–1780*, Vol. 2: *Shaftesbury to Hume*, Cambridge: Cambridge University Press.

Rosen, F. (1983) *Jeremy Bentham and Representative Democracy: A Study of the Constitutional Code*, Oxford: Clarendon Press.

——(2003) *Classical Utilitarianism from Hume to Mill*, London and New York: Routledge.

Scarre, G. (1994) "Epicurus as a Forerunner of Utilitarianism," *Utilitas* 6: 219–31.

Schofield, P. (1996) "Utilitarian Politics and Legal Positivism: The Rejection of Contractarianism in Early Utilitarian Thought," in *Positivism Today*, ed. S. Guest, Aldershot: Ashgate, pp. 99–118.

Shackleton, R. (1972) "The Greatest Happiness of the Greatest Number: The History of Bentham's Phrase," *Studies in Voltaire and the Eighteenth Century*, 90: 1461–82.

Sidgwick, H. (1906) *Outlines of the History of Ethics for English Readers*, 5th edn, London: Macmillan.

Stephen, L. (1876) *History of English Thought in the Eighteenth Century*, 2 vols, London: Smith, Elder & Co.

——(1900) *The English Utilitarians*, 3 vols, London: Duckworth & Co.

Further reading

Baumgardt, D. (1952) *Bentham and the Ethics of Today*, Princeton, NJ: Princeton University Press. (Major study of Bentham's ethics.)

Harrison, R. (1983) *Bentham*, London: Routledge & Kegan Paul. (Valuable guide to Bentham's philosophy.)

Rosen, F. (2003) *Classical Utilitarianism from Hume to Mill*, London and New York: Routledge. (Philosophical study of modern utilitarianism concentrating on ethics.)

14
KANT
Thomas E. Hill Jr

Kant's writings on ethics followed his monumental *Critique of Pure Reason* (1950/1781). There he tried to show that all previous metaphysical theories failed because they did not begin with a critical assessment of the powers of reason. His own critical study attempted to revolutionize metaphysics and synthesize the best from the rationalist and empiricist traditions. A major conclusion relevant to ethics was that theoretical reason cannot prove the existence of God, immortality, or freedom of the will, though it leaves room for faith. In his later ethical writings he argued that nevertheless from *practical* reason we can establish the supreme principle of morality and the freedom of choice that it presupposes. At least, he argued, these can be shown to be valid for purposes of deliberation and action. These are major themes of his classic *Groundwork for the Metaphysics of Morals* (2002/1785). Here he also defends his *a priori* method for the foundations of ethics, draws a sharp contrast between moral and non-moral "ought" judgments, and articulates several versions of the supreme moral principle. Shortly after, in his *Critique of Practical Reason* (1997/1788) he reaffirms his previous conclusions but modifies his argument. Here he also offers moral reasons for faith that God exists and hope for immortality, but not as a basis or motive for morality. Later Kant published *The Metaphysics of Morals* (1996/1797–8), which (in Part 1) presents his theory of law and justice and (in Part 2) explains how his ethical principles apply to recurrent moral issues. Contemporary philosophers have interpreted Kant's ethical writings in many different ways. This chapter simply highlights some of the main themes, inviting readers to explore them further for themselves.

A *priori* method for basic questions

When addressing the most fundamental questions, Kant argues, moral philosophy should be "pure" and not based on empirical generalizations. For example, the validity of its basic principle should not depend on how altruistic or selfish human beings are naturally inclined to be. In Kant's view, pure moral philosophy aims first to discover the most basic and comprehensive moral principle inherent in ordinary thought about moral duty and morally worthy actions. This requires what he called an *analytic* mode of argument, which is a matter of examining our concepts carefully to see what further ideas they presuppose. The conclusion of such arguments is always conditional. For example, in *Groundwork* 2, Kant argues *not* that the supreme moral principle (which he calls "the Categorical Imperative") is rationally binding for us, but only that *in believing* that we have genuine moral duties *we are necessarily committed* to the Categorical Imperative as a rationally imperative moral principle.

Pure moral philosophy also aims to determine whether or not conformity to the basic moral principle is necessarily *rational*, and this is not a question that can be settled by empirical studies of how people actually behave. Even polls about what people *say is rational* would be inconclusive because the claim that violations of moral requirements are contrary to reason is a *normative* claim. It is a claim about what we have *good and sufficient reason* to do, which is more than a prediction about what most people would say if asked. To establish that the basic moral principle is rationally binding, Kant says, requires a different type of argument, one that proceeds *synthetically*. This is what he attempts in the notoriously dense reasoning in *Groundwork* 3. Here the question is not about what is *presupposed* by our common moral beliefs but about whether we have sufficient reason to regard those beliefs as true. Both questions, in Kant's view, call for an *a priori* method. *Groundwork* 2 uses an *a priori* analytical argument to show that our moral beliefs presuppose that moral requirements are rational, but *Groundwork* 3 uses a different ("synthetical") *a priori* procedure to show that this presupposition is not an illusion.

None of this implies, however, that ethics is completely independent of empirical facts. Most obviously, we cannot make judgments about what we ought to do on a particular occasion without some information about the situation. Even general principles of the sort Kant presents in *The Metaphysics of Morals* depend on at least general facts about the human condition. Kant does defend the controversial claim that some principles (for example, the prohibitions of lying) are binding regardless of the particular circumstances, but he acknowledges that the application of other principles (for example, those regarding giving aid, developing one's talents, and even retributive punishment) may vary with the situation. When moral philosophy focuses on empirical facts, such as the conditions that facilitate moral education, he calls it *moral anthropology*.

The special features of moral judgments

In Kant's view, it is crucial to distinguish between morality and prudence. Too often, in theory and in practice, we confuse moral reasons with self-serving reasons. Philosophers mistakenly urge us to be moral as a means to happiness, and in daily life we make exceptions of ourselves by treating our strong self-regarding desires as excuses. At the heart of Kant's moral theory is his explanation of the contrast between moral and non-moral "ought" judgments. The former express (or are based on) *categorical imperatives* whereas the latter express (or are based on) *hypothetical imperatives*. All imperatives (in Kant's sense) have two features: they are (at least conditionally) *rational* to follow and they are *expressed in terms appropriate for those who can follow them but might not* ("ought," "should," "must," "Do it!"). *Categorical* imperatives are said to be unconditionally necessary "commands" of reason that prescribe an act as good in itself. They express the idea that we (rationally) must do as prescribed whether or not it will contribute to our happiness or serve the particular ends we happen to have. *Hypothetical* imperatives, by contrast, are "counsels of prudence" or "rules of skill" that prescribe an act as (conditionally) good to do if or because it serves as a means to our happiness or particular ends we happen to have. Strictly speaking, Kant argues, there is only one Categorical Imperative – the most basic principle of rational morality (to be discussed shortly) – but he also used the term for strict requirements that are based on this basic principle.

Characteristic examples of specific categorical imperatives, in Kant's view, include "One must not make false promises," "Do not treat anyone as worthless," and "Adopt the happiness of others as an end." The idea is that failing to conform to these moral principles is contrary to reason ("irrational" or "unreasonable," we might say) and, in Kant's view this is not because these failures would make us unhappy or unable to achieve what we want. Examples of hypothetical imperatives might include "One ought to floss one's teeth if one aims to avoid gum disease," "Work out harder!" (assuming you aim to be successful in sports), "Since you want to be happy, you should avoid dwelling on past troubles," and "Save something for a rainy day!" (where the implicit reason is that you will be unhappy otherwise). The idea in these cases is that it is one's particular aim or general concern to be happy that explains why it is rationally necessary to act as the hypothetical imperatives prescribe – unless there is a compelling (perhaps moral) reason not to.

Why are certain facts reasons to act and others are not? Kant treats facts as reasons insofar as they would fit appropriately into a pattern of reasoning governed by a general principle of rational choice. In the case of hypothetical imperatives the general principle seems to be something like this: You ought, if you aim for a certain end, to take the necessary means to it – or else give up the end. This principle picks out certain facts as reasons to act – or at least to modify one's plans. For example, it identifies as reasons the (joint) facts that you aim to be successful at sports and exercising harder is needed to accomplish that goal. These reasons do not make the exercise absolutely mandatory, of course, because you may have good reason to give up your plan to succeed at sports. Our natural desire for happiness (lasting contentment and achieving our desire-based ends) cannot be altogether given up, Kant thought, but we can choose not to pursue happiness as our end on particular occasions when there is sufficient reason (for example, a moral imperative) to choose otherwise. In addition, Kant reminds us, how we conceive of our happiness is vague and our understanding of how to achieve it is uncertain. Prudence, then, only gives us conditionally rational "counsels," not strict "commands," which are only given by categorical imperatives.

When we turn to categorical imperatives, what is the rational principle that identifies compelling reasons to act? Kant thinks that there must be such a principle and it must be a basic Categorical Imperative in the strictest sense – an absolutely unconditional and non-derivative rational principle. His thought is that the existence of particular moral requirements, which we all recognize, presupposes that there is such a principle. How else, for example, could it be (as he assumed) that there are unconditional commands of reason not to make false promises for profit, to commit murder for revenge, or to ignore the welfare of others? The main aims of the *Groundwork* were to articulate and vindicate our reliance on this presupposed rational principle, the Categorical Imperative.

Universal law formulas of the categorical imperative

Given Kant's *a priori* methodology and arguments so far, this supreme moral principle must have compelling credentials as a necessary form or standard that should shape all rational deliberation and choice about practical matters. Too often rationalist theologians and philosophers had uncritically declared their substantive moral dictates to be the voice of reason, but the aim of Kant's critical philosophy was to expose false pretensions in such claims to rational authority and, when possible, to vindicate the proper use of practical reason. The supreme moral principle, however, must also be plausible as a standard presupposed in common moral thought, for example, in our general understanding of the differences between duty and self-interest and in our ability to distinguish right from wrong in particular cases. Because the Categorical Imperative must be the supreme principle of practical reason as well as of morality, we should not be surprised, even if initially disappointed, to find that what it prescribes is essentially that we fully respect the development and exercise of the powers of practical reason in each person. The formulations of this requirement vary as analysis reveals its more specific meaning.

The most general idea Kant is working with here is that good (moral and rational) choice is constrained and guided by the necessity "to conform to universal law." "Universal law" here is by definition a necessary requirement of reason that guides the conduct of any fully rational agent and, in imperative form, is an inherent standard unavoidably recognized by all imperfectly rational human beings. So assuming that there are universal laws, the imperative "Conform to universal law" in this sense should be uncontroversial. In two controversial moves, however, Kant argues that from this basic idea we may infer his famous *formula of universal law:*

> (FUL): "*Act only on that maxim by which you can at the same time will that it should become universal law.*"
>
> (Kant 2002/1785: 4:421)

This is followed immediately by a variation, the *formula of a universal law of nature*:

> (FULN): "*Act as though the maxim of your action were to become by your will a universal law of nature.*"
>
> (4:421)

Kant illustrates the use of FULN, and so (indirectly) FUL, with four examples: suicide to escape a troublesome life, borrowing money with a lying promise to ease financial problems, not doing anything to develop one's useful talents, and refusing to give any help to others in trouble. Agents can determine the wrongness of these acts and omissions, Kant argues, by using FULN to test the *maxim* (intention or policy) on which they propose to act.

Scholars differ on how exactly these formulas are supposed to guide moral deliberation. It is clear, however, that any application must begin by identifying the maxim of a proposed act. This is meant to be an honest articulation of what one intends to do and why: for example, "I intend to do this (e.g. borrow money that I know I cannot repay) for certain purpose (e.g. to pay for an expensive holiday) because I care more for my pleasure than the rights and interests of the lender." Problems arise because there may be several different ways of expressing the maxim, but in any case the next step is to try to conceive of the maxim as a universal law (or law of nature). This has been variously interpreted as a teleological law, a psychological law, or a law of permission: that is, we are to conceive of a possible world in which one's purposeful act *fits into a system of natural purposes*, a world where everyone *does act on* the maxim, or a world where anyone *may* do so. Maxims that cannot without contradiction be conceived as universal laws in the appropriate sense are deemed wrong to act on. Some maxims, however, can be *conceived* as universal laws but not *willed* as universal laws. Kant's examples are neglecting one's talents and refusing to give aid to those in dire need. Acting on these maxims too is deemed wrong, though Kant calls the duties to develop one's talents and help those in need "imperfect duties" by contrast to "perfect duties" such as not to make lying promises.

Kant's followers and critics have long debated whether proper application of FUL and FULN really leads to moral judgments that are correct and compatible with common understanding. Many scholars now doubt that it is important to Kant's basic moral theory that these formulas function as explicit decision-guides regarding particular cases. As Kant sometimes suggests, they may serve as heuristic aids to help us see more clearly that what we propose to do is contrary to principles we already accept and apply to others. Because we are tempted to make illegitimate exceptions for ourselves, reflecting on a world where everyone does (or may) act as we intend can help to expose our self-deceiving excuses. Another idea is that the formulas (with later formulations of the Categorical Imperative) provide a framework or perspective for thinking about very general moral principles rather than deciding particular cases. These would be, for example, the ethical principles of the sort Kant proposes in *The Metaphysics of Morals*: "Do not violate the (legal) rights of others," "Respect every human being as a person," "Seek your own natural and moral perfection," and "Promote the happiness of others."

Regarding the importance of examples, Kant repeatedly insists that the basic moral principle cannot be identified or established as rational by appeal to examples, but he also expresses confidence that ordinary people have a basic knowledge of right and wrong that implicitly relies on the ideas expressed in his formulations of the Categorical Imperative. For this reason Kant suggests that careful use of his formulas in moral judgment would "clarify" and "strongly confirm" his claims about the supreme moral principle (4:392).

The formula of humanity as an end in itself

The universal law formulas are concerned with the "form" of moral maxims, but Kant's next formulation of the Categorical Imperative concerns their "matter" or "end." He states this *formula of humanity as an end* as follows:

> (FHE) "*Act in such a way that you treat humanity, whether in your own person or in any other person, always at the same time as an end, never merely as a means.*" (4:429)

The idea of expressing the essential features of morality in terms of means and ends was not original to Kant but he used it in a way that contrasts with many traditional moral theories. These "teleological" theories tried to describe the ideal end or goal of a moral life and viewed specific virtues and constraints as necessary means to achieve that goal (and as sometimes constitutive elements presupposed in the goal itself). For Kant, rational nature ("humanity") in each person is an *end in itself* in a special sense, not as a goal to be achieved but as a status to be respected. It limits the legitimate pursuit of personal and social ends, Kant argues, by prohibiting the use of certain means (for example, lying promises and revolution) and also by requiring us to adopt and pursue certain moral ends (the perfection of oneself and the happiness of others).

Specific interpretations of this formula vary. For example, some understand FHE as just a different way of expressing the same requirement as the universal law formulas, that is, a maxim is permissible only if it can be willed consistently as universal law by anyone whether they are on the "giving" or "receiving" end of a transaction. For example, the maxim of a lying promise would have to be rationally acceptable, not only to the deceiver, but also to the person deceived. Often the formula of humanity is assumed to be an intuitive guide to be used case by case, ruling out proposed acts that seem not to respect each person as a rational agent. A more formal reading treats the formula as an abstract requirement to honor the rational ("lawmaking") will in each person, as later understood through the "formula of autonomy" and the "formula of the kingdom of ends." Any principle's alleged exceptions need to be ultimately justifiable from a perspective that takes appropriate account of the rational will of every person, especially those who are harmed or thwarted in their pursuits for the sake of others. In discussing ethical duties in *The Metaphysics of Morals* Kant seems to appeal to a more substantive standard, suggesting that to treat humanity as an end implies strong (though not always absolute) presumptions in favor of preserving, developing, exercising, and honoring rational capacities in oneself and others.

The formulas of autonomy and the kingdom of ends

From the previous formulations, Kant says, a third one follows. This *formula of autonomy* is expressed in several ways, including:

> (FA): " ... the supreme condition of the will's harmony with universal practical reason is the Idea of *the will of every rational being as a will that legislates universal law* ... [; and] every human will is *a will that enacts universal laws in all its maxims.*"
>
> (4:431–2)

This formula of autonomy, Kant says, leads to the "very fruitful concept" of a kingdom (or commonwealth) of ends, and he uses this concept to re-express the idea of autonomy in a variation often understood as a separate principle – the *formula of a kingdom of ends*. Kant expresses this as follows:

> (FKE): "A rational being must always regard himself as lawgiving in a kingdom of ends made possible through freedom of the will ... [; and] all maxims which stem from autonomous lawgiving are to harmonize with a possible kingdom of ends and a kingdom of nature."
>
> (4:434–6)

FKE, like FULN and FHE, is supposed to express the supreme principle in a manner "closer to intuition (by means of a certain analogy) and thus nearer to feeling" (4:436). In the *Groundwork* Kant suggests that for purposes of judgment we should rely primarily on FUL or FA (4:436–7), but in *The Metaphysics of Morals* he appeals most often to the idea of humanity as an end in itself (FHE).

Interpretations vary but the basic analogy is with an ideal commonwealth in which all members legislate the laws and are subject to them. The members of a kingdom of ends are conceived, in abstraction from personal differences, as rational agents with private ends and as ends in themselves who autonomously legislate universal laws (4:433ff.). The "laws" here are ethical principles rather than enforceable state laws, and the lawmakers are not influenced by biases and irrationalities as state legislators often are. The analogy with the laws of a commonwealth suggests that the legislators do not legislate the supreme moral principle itself – the constitution, as it were, specifies the basic framework under which they make laws. Rather, they adopt more specific moral principles while being guided and constrained by ideas inherent in the supreme principle (autonomy, rationality, universality, and the dignity of legislators as ends in themselves). If this reading is correct, when Kant says without explicit qualification that we are *subject only to laws we give ourselves* (4:432), then, the "laws" here refer to the more specific universal ethical principles that we "legislate" with the authority, guidance, and constraints of the basic "law" of practical reason and morality (the Categorical Imperative). The basic law must be self-imposed in a different sense by, for example, being authoritative for us because it is the fundamental principle of our own shared practical reason, not because of "alien causes," natural sentiments, alleged intuitions, or even divine commands. Kant does not develop FKE further or propose examples to show how it might be applied to practical issues. Instead, his treatment of specific ethical principles in *The Metaphysics of Moral* mostly appeals to FHE. In addition, some passages suggest that members are conceived of as making the laws, not together in a common legislative session (as the analogy suggests), but simply by always choosing in practice to act only on maxims they can will as universal laws in the sense of FUL.

Freedom and arguments for the categorical imperative

The most difficult and controversial aspects of Kant's writings on ethics are his treatments of freedom of the will and how they figure in his defense of his claims about the Categorical Imperative. The main theses for which he argues in *Groundwork* 2 and 3 and the *Critique of Practical Reason* are: (1) He has identified the basic, comprehensive principle implicit in common moral thought, and it is expressed in FUL and equivalent formulas; and (2) common morality *presupposes* that this basic principle is the one and only Categorical Imperative in the strict sense. To be the Categorical Imperative in the strict sense a principle must be a universal and necessary principle of practical reason and not a particular hypothetical imperative or the general requirement of coherence among one's ends and means (the Hypothetical Imperative). What Kant needs to show, then, is that common morality relies on the principle expressed in his formulas and that the principle is an unconditionally rational requirement. Kant argues analytically for the first claim in *Groundwork* 2 and 3, trying step by step to reveal FUL as implicit in the ideas of a good will and duty. Passing over details, the main steps are these: Common morality accepts that only a good will could be good without qualification, or worth preserving in all situations. We express a good will when our ("morally worthy") acts are both in accord with duty and done out of duty. So the essence of the basic principle of a good will is not that it must bring about desirable consequences, or even aim to do so, but that we must do what is morally required by maintaining an attitude of respect for the (moral/rational) law. By analyzing the essential motive or attitude of a good will, the argument is supposed to reveal that *the basic principle of a good will is "Conform to universal law"* and from this Kant infers FUL.

In *Groundwork* 2 Kant tries to draw out the presuppositions of the common idea of duty, and the mains steps can be paraphrased as follows. By contrast to what we ought to do for prudential or pragmatic reasons, a moral duty is what we ought to do for compelling reasons not based on our personal aims and desire to be happy. We could have duties, understood this way, only if they are backed by a fundamental principle of reason that identifies these compelling reasons without appealing to prudence or rationally optional aims. In other words, duty must be based on a Categorical Imperative in the strict sense. From the concept of a Categorical Imperative, Kant argues, the only principle that could qualify is (to paraphrase): *it is rationally necessary to conform to universal law*. From this (again) Kant infers (with little explanation) that FUL is the Categorical Imperative.

These arguments, Kant dramatically points out, leave open the theoretical possibility that morality might be an illusion. They only reveal what common morality presupposes, not what it is necessarily rational to accept. In *Groundwork* 3 Kant confronts this challenge, arguing that the presupposition that the supreme moral principle is unconditionally rational is valid for all purposes of deliberation and choice. As rational agents, Kant argues, we "cannot act except under the Idea of freedom" (4:448). This is an essential aspect of the standpoint of practice. In deliberation, choice, and acting for reasons we take ourselves to be free in a negative sense – able to cause events "independently of alien causes determining it" (4:446). Negative freedom, however, is inseparable from positive freedom or autonomy, "the property that a will has of being a law to itself" (4:447). In order to make sense of the idea that we can act for reasons independently of our inclinations and sentiments, we must suppose that we can govern ourselves by standards inherent in our nature as rational agents. And, again assuming negative freedom, these rational standards must give us prescriptions that are not relative to our inclinations and sentiments. In sum, when we act as rational agents we necessarily take ourselves to have autonomy of the will, and *Groundwork* 2 is supposed to show that the Categorical Imperative is the standard of rational agents *if* they have autonomy of the will. The upshot is that in taking a practical standpoint we inevitably and rationally take ourselves to be subject to the Categorical Imperative.

In Kant's view, freedom of will is an idea that we must use in practical thinking but cannot comprehend. Theoretical reason, empirical and speculative, can neither prove nor disprove that we have such freedom. Arguments in the *Critique of Pure Reason* are supposed to show that all empirical phenomena are subject to natural laws of cause and effect, but Kant held that the idea of free will presupposed by morality cannot be defined empirically or explained by natural laws. He embraced the apparent consequence, however obscure, that we must think of moral agents as "free" members of an "intelligible world" to which our spatial and temporal concepts do not apply. Perhaps few philosophers today follow Kant's thinking this far, but his idea of autonomy has inspired some to develop and use related concepts.

Justice and the moral obligation to obey the law

Our moral choices are inevitably made in a context that includes a particular legal system and complex international relations. We can conceive of a "state of nature" but this remains a mere idea for most practical purposes. In Part 1 of *The Metaphysics of Morals* Kant presents his theory of law and justice, and earlier in *Perpetual Peace* (2006/1795) he offers recommendations for international justice and global peace. Exactly how Kant's moral theory is related to his theory of law and justice remains controversial, but some points seem clear. For example, Kant's theory of law and justice is a part of his official (published) "metaphysics of morals," and he held that it is an "indirect ethical duty" to obey the law. An exception, rarely mentioned, is that one should not do anything "intrinsically immoral" even if ordered to do so by the government in power. Law makes determinate rights of property, contracts, and status, and its officials have a juridical (and so indirectly ethical) duty to enforce the law justly. They must not, for example, use punishment simply as a means to promote general welfare. Thus even if the Categorical Imperative of the *Groundwork* is only meant as the appropriate standard for individual choices, and not for institutions, the requirements of law and justice are inevitably relevant to individual ethical decisions.

Law and justice, according to Kant, are concerned with the "external freedom" and enforceable rights of persons, not moral motivation. The "universal principle of right" (or justice) is a "postulate" similar in some respects to the universal law formula of the Categorical Imperative (FUL). This principle of right says: "Any action is right if it can coexist with everyone's freedom in accordance with a universal law, or if on its maxim the freedom of choice of each can coexist with everyone's freedom in accordance with a universal law" (Kant 1996/1797–8: 6:231). A corollary of the principle, Kant says, is that coercion to serve as a "hindering of a hindrance to freedom" is consistent with right (6:231). He assumes a fundamental right to freedom, equality, and independence, and develops from this an account of "private law," which includes rights of property, contract, and status. Anyone in a state of nature, Kant argues, would have a duty to join and maintain a system of "public" law necessary for "a juridical condition." This is not because of the brutality or inconveniences of a state of nature emphasized by Hobbes and Locke, but because "rightful" or just relations among persons are impossible without an authoritative way to settle disputes. Full justice, Kant argues, requires republican government with separation of powers, abolition of hereditary political privilege, and freedom to criticize the government. Full republican justice, however, is only a standard for gradual reform, for we must obey the law even in very imperfect (even "despotical") legal systems. Scholars have argued, however, that "rogue states," such as Nazi Germany, fail to meet even Kant's minimum conditions for being a legitimate legal order that is owed obedience.

Regarding international justice, Kant argues that, although a world government would be ideal in some respects, a voluntary federation of sovereign states would be the best hope for peace, at least in a world of diverse cultures and languages. States should recognize a cosmopolitan right of non-citizens to trade and visit peacefully, and they should not exploit indigenous peoples.

Ethics and religion

Ethics is concerned directly with the question "What ought I to do," but Kant also addresses the question "What can I hope for?" This belongs primarily to his philosophy of religion, but it deserves mention here because his answer depends on his ethical theory.

In Kant's view, knowledge of right and wrong is not based on religion. He held instead that our moral knowledge provides the only basis for religious faith. In the *Critique of Practical Reason* Kant presents moral arguments for belief in God and immortality even though the *Critique of Pure Reason* established that we cannot strictly prove or even understand these "Ideas" beyond all possible experience. Religion cannot provide the basis for moral knowledge because in order to identify as morally authoritative any supernatural power or even any supposed exemplar of perfection (such as Jesus) we would already need to have an understanding of right and wrong. The moral arguments for faith are based on two prior moral ideas: that we must seek virtue independently of happiness and that the highest good (to be hoped for) would be perfect virtue combined with well-deserved happiness. In his late work *Religion within the Boundaries of Mere Reason* (1998/1793), Kant argues that morality also provides the limits of a rationally acceptable religious faith. We should see moral duty *as if* commanded by God, but certain doctrines are ruled out as contrary to morality: For example, extreme doctrines of innate and incorrigible human depravity (as opposed to a willful *propensity* to evil), divine cruelty and partiality, and the efficacy of prayer for material rewards. The kingdom of ends discussed earlier has a God-like "head" that has unlimited powers but, like a traditional political sovereign, is not *subject* to laws made by others. The head wills the same rational laws as the members do, however, and is not *subject* to the will of others just because it is independent and has no needs. The most basic principles for any rational being, human or divine, are essentially the same, although they become imperative for human beings who are finite and imperfectly rational.

See also Ethics and reason (Chapter 9); Ethics and sentiment (Chapter 10); Hume (Chapter 11); Hegel (Chapter 15); Reasons for action (Chapter 24); Contemporary Kantian ethics (Chapter 38); Morality and its critics (Chapter 45); Respect and recognition (Chapter 47); Responsibility: Intention and consequence (Chapter 50); Partiality and impartiality (Chapter 52); Moral particularism (Chapter 53); Justice and punishment (Chapter 57); .

References

Kant, I. (1950/1781) *Critique of Pure Reason*, trans. N. K. Smith, New York: Humanities Press.

——(1996/1797–8) *The Metaphysics of Morals*, trans. M. J. Gregor, Cambridge: Cambridge University Press. (Cited by the marginal, Academy edn volume and page.)

——(1997/1788) *Critique of Practical Reason*, trans. M. J. Gregor, Cambridge: Cambridge University Press.

——(1998/1793) *Religion within the Boundaries of Mere Reason*, trans. A. W. Wood and G. di Giovanni. Cambridge: Cambridge University Press.

——(2002/1785) *Groundwork for the Metaphysics of Morals*, ed. T. E. Hill and A. Zweig, trans. A. Zweig, Oxford: Oxford University Press. (Cited by the marginal, Academy edn volume and page.)

——(2006/1795) *Perpetual Peace*, trans. P. Kleingeld, New Haven, CT: Yale University Press.

Further reading

Guyer, Paul (ed.) (1998) *Kant's Groundwork of the Metaphysics of Morals: Critical Essays*, Lanham, MD: Rowman & Littlefield.

Hill, Thomas E., Jr (ed.) (2009) *The Blackwell Guide to Kant's Ethics*, New York and Oxford: Blackwell-Wiley Publishers.

Timmons, Mark (ed.) (2002) *Kant's Metaphysics of Ethics: Interpretive Essays*, New York: Oxford University Press.

Wood, Allen (ed.) (1999) *Kant's Ethical Thought*, Cambridge: Cambridge University Press.

15
HEGEL

Kenneth R. Westphal

Hegel's main work in moral philosophy, *Elements of the Philosophy of Right, or Natural Law and Political Science in Outline* (1821, *Rph*), has been condemned from Marx to Cassirer and Popper as totalitarian, because e.g. Hegel rejected atomistic individualism, the social contract, and open democratic elections. The assumption that Hegel's rejection of these views results in totalitarianism rests on dichotomies Hegel criticized and rejected (Kaufmann 1951; Wood 1990: 8–14, 36–42; Westphal 1993: 234–44, 2002). Recent scholarship demonstrates that Hegel's social theory "is unsurpassed in its richness, its philosophical rigor, and its insights into the nature of good social institutions" (Neuhouser 2000: 1). Hegel belongs to the classical or "civic" republican tradition (see Lovett 2006) and espouses collective liberalism, as do Rousseau, T. H. Green, and John Dewey.

Some theoretical context of Hegel's moral philosophy

Hegel treats moral philosophy as a genus comprising two coordinate species: ethics and theory of justice, a conception which predominated from the Greeks through the nineteenth century and remains prevalent on the European Continent, because many of the most basic conditions required for individuals to engage with ethical issues are social, political, and legal, and conversely, one of the most vital tasks of any society is to empty the nursery and to populate the commons with able, responsible adults. Hegel agrees with the ancient Greeks that the best way to raise a virtuous child is within a city with good laws (*Rph* §173R). Recent historical experience should make this plain even to those most committed to the primacy of individual ethics over political philosophy.

Hegel realized that the standard distinction in social ontology between atomistic individualism and monolithic collectivism is not exhaustive. He developed an intermediate view, which may be called "moderate collectivism," comprising three theses: (1) Individuals are fundamentally social practitioners because everything a person does, says, or thinks is formed in the context of social practices that provide material and conceptual resources, objects of desire, skills, procedures, techniques, and occasions and permissions for action, etc.; (2) What any individual thinks or does depends on his or her own responses to his or her social and natural environment; (3) There are no individuals – no social practitioners – without social practices, and vice versa, there are no social practices without social practitioners, that is, without individuals who learn, participate in, perpetuate, and who modify social practices as needed to meet their changing needs, aims, and circumstances (including procedures and information). Hegel argues that individual human beings and the social groups to which they belong are mutually interdependent for their existence and characteristics; both aspects are mutually irreducible and neither is primary. Hegel's moderate collectivism supports the comprehensive conception of moral philosophy noted above and is consistent with "methodological individualism," the thesis that all social phenomena must be understood in terms of individuals' behavior, dispositions, and relations (Westphal 2003: §§32–7).

Hegel rejected open democratic elections for three basic reasons. First, such elections require a well-informed and sufficiently republican citizenship of a kind not found in Hegel's day in Prussia, a period of intensive liberal reform of largely feudal conditions antedating the Prussian *Restauration*, which Hegel saw on the horizon but which occurred a decade after his death. Without that kind of citizenry, the mere procedural institutions of democratic elections inevitably produce illiberal, anti-republican and unjust outcomes due to tyranny of the majority (or of the vocal minority) or through demagoguery. Second, open elections do not insure that each socio-economic sector of society is represented in the electoral process. Third, by basing representation on geographical regions rather than on socio-economic sectors of society, open elections divorce political life from civil and economic life, thereby undermining the political process (*Rph* §303R). (Hegel's alternative system of political representation is indicated below)

Hegel rejected the social contract model primarily because any social contract must be based on contractors' manifest beliefs, attitudes, preferences, or feelings, etc., which alone can provide grounds for elective choice (regardless of whether the choice to contract is implicit, explicit, or hypothetical). Hence a tenable social contract model must meet three requirements: (1) To identify a positive contribution of voluntary agreement – distinct from justifying reasons as such – to the identification or justification of basic social norms and institutions (see O'Neill 2000); (2) To identify such a contribution which does not reduce to group preferences or attitudes, thus conceding too much to conventionalism or to relativism; (3) To provide adequate criteria or procedures to preclude individual social contractors from neglecting or denying relevant grounds of other-regarding duties. If to the contrary there is no such constitutive role for elective choice in identifying or justifying norms of public conduct, including social principles, procedures, or institutions, then the justifying reasons for these latter carry the full justificatory burden and contractual choice is otiose (O'Neill 2000; Westphal forthcoming a). Like other non-contractualist modern natural lawyers – most prominently Hume (Buckle 1991; Westphal 2010), Rousseau, and Kant – Hegel accordingly distinguished the task of identifying and justifying basic norms of conduct as such from the task of justifying them to individual members of a society. The latter task involves bringing citizens to understand the results of the first task.

An important task of any social philosophy is to determine the extent to which the requirements of enlightened self-interest coincide with moral requirements. Though this extent is large, by the nature of the case the coincidence is imperfect. Contractarian (or also "contractualist") strategies for justifying basic social norms confront a severe problem justifying moral norms to egoists and to moral skeptics. However, if (as Hegel contends) basic norms of conduct can be identified and justified independently of any form of contractarian agreement, this provides a significant basis for re-analyzing egoism and moral skepticism as failures of understanding, perhaps resulting from failures of moral education (see Green 1999). If Hegel is correct, any reasonably just society can require egoists or moral skeptics either to abide by its norms of conduct, to emigrate, or to face social sanctions (legal or otherwise) for violating those norms.

Hegel agrees with Kant, against utilitarianism, that the right is prior to the good, though he also holds that fully achieving justice requires achieving the common good (*Rph* §§114, 129, 130, 336). Hegel's concern that Kant's moral principles cannot guide specific actions – the infamous charge that Kant's moral theory is an "empty formalism" (*Rph* §135R) – addresses an important though widely neglected feature of Kant's moral philosophy. Throughout his moral writings, Kant insists that his system of "pure" or "metaphysical" moral principles requires for its application to human circumstances and action appeal to "practical anthropology," a systematic body of information regarding human capacities and incapacities for thought and action, due to our finite form of human agency or to our circumstances of action. Though his examples and analyses provide much relevant information, Kant assigned "practical anthropology" to an unwritten "appendix" to his moral system. Yet on Kant's (1996, Part 2, §45) own account, his *a priori* system of moral principles as such, without this "practical anthropology," is empty, void of implications for the human condition. A central, express task of Hegel's analysis of "ethical life" (*Sittlichkeit*), the concluding part of the *Philosophy of Right*, is to provide the practical anthropology required to obtain determinate, justified, legitimate normative prescriptions, including principles, procedures, and institutions, from Kant's basic normative principles and procedures (Westphal 1995, 2005, 2007). To do so Hegel pays unprecedented and unparalleled attention to how the modern market economy and a series of non-governmental authorities – taken together, these constitute "civil society" – contribute to individual freedom (Westphal 1993).

Freedom: legal, personal, moral, and social

In contrast to Hobbes' view that freedom consists in the silence of the law – a central component of the liberal, negative conception of individual liberty (Skinner 1984, 2006), especially pronounced in libertarianism – Hegel recognized (as do civic republicans, jurists, and practicing lawyers) the vast extent to which the principles and institutions of justice, including statutory law, are *enabling conditions*: only because certain legitimate principles and institutions are established within a society can we as individual members of that society engage in a vast range of activities which otherwise can be neither specified nor executed; neither could we benefit from the many kinds of actions by others which likewise are possible only due to legal institutions. Examples of this range from the simplest purchases using currency to commercial contract, provisions for public safety, voting, petition of government, or trial at constitutional court. Hegel thus agreed with Hume's key insight that

> Though the rules of justice be artificial, they are not arbitrary.
>
> (*Treatise*, Bk 3, pt 2, §1, para. 19)

Social practices and institutions are literally artifices. Hegel also agreed with Hume that the artifice of justice is necessary to human society (and so "not arbitrary") because it is necessary for social coordination, but he further argued that the principles and practices of justice are rationally justifiable because they are required to establish, protect, and promote the rational freedom of individual agents (Neuhouser 2000; Westphal 2007, 2010).

Central to Hegel's analysis of civil society and the grounds it provides for legitimate statutory law is the sociological "law of unintended consequences," according to which groups of interacting individuals can collectively produce results unintended by any or all members of that group, e.g. Smith's "invisible hand" of the market. These consequences may be good or ill; Hegel's point is that a host of civil and political institutions are responsible for monitoring such unintended consequences of group behavior, to curb those which undermine legitimate free individual action, and to encourage or when needed to legally protect those which support or enhance legitimate free individual action. In brief, this is Hegel's basis for legitimate statutory law.

Hegel identifies three forms of individual freedom, which may be called "personal," "moral," and "social" freedom (Neuhouser 2000). Each of these is a form of free rational self-determination of one's own conduct. Personal freedom is the freedom to pursue one's elective ends; it is a form of self-determination because one elects one's own ends to pursue. This form of freedom is common to liberal individualism, though Hegel argues that we now enjoy a distinctly modern version of this form of freedom, not only to choose one's own profession, but more broadly to modify various socially available roles, especially professional ones, or to create new ones to suit one's own character, talents, and interests. (Social roles have never strictly determined their occupants' actions, though in the Occident they now tend to allow much more room for individual innovation than, say, three centuries ago.) Exercising personal freedom legitimately also requires avoiding unjust interference with others. Understanding what counts as "unjust interference," why it is proscribed, and why it ought to be avoided requires richer reflections and a richer form of self-determination than is afforded by the simple pursuit of elective ends because it requires moral reflection on practical norms and principles of action. Hence personal freedom must be augmented by moral freedom.

Moral freedom, a richer conception of rational agency, involves evaluating and affirming moral principles that inform one's behavior in pursuit of one's elective ends, in respecting others as moral agents, and in pursuit of the moral good. As noted, Hegel contends that moral subjectivity, as articulated by Kant's moral theory, does not suffice to generate a genuine, non-arbitrary, though sufficiently concrete conception of the right or the good to guide individual action. So doing is a collective undertaking ultimately involving social freedom.

Social freedom involves consciously participating in social institutions which expressly protect and promote personal, moral, and social freedom. Such participation is itself an act of freedom: once rationally understood, such institutions and practices (etc.) can be rationally endorsed on the basis of their sufficient justifying reasons in a way which allows and encourages members to affirm the principles, aims, procedures, and institutions of their (reasonably just) society. In this way, these social institutions contribute to constituting and specifying individuals' identities as free rational agents. Social institutions which perform these functions provide an objective form of social freedom in which individuals participate and through which they recognize each other as free rational contributing members.

Hegel's account of social freedom involves both objective and subjective aspects. Objectively, rational laws and institutions must provide social conditions required to realize the freedoms of all citizens, including satisfying the conditions of justice; subjectively, rational laws and institutions must allow citizens to affirm them as good because they are just and because they facilitate and achieve both freedom and welfare, so that citizens can regard the principles which inform their social involvements as coming from their own wills. Personal freedom to elect and to pursue one's ends requires social and legal protection to restrict unjust interference of others. A social order which supports moral freedom is one which both encourages and withstands critical assessment of the reasons which justify its principles, procedures, and institutions. No social institution, procedure, or practice can be fully justified or legitimate, Hegel argues, unless it meets these stringent requirements. Yet actualizing individual freedom further requires the subjective aspect of freedom involved in citizens recognizing that, and how the structure, institutions, procedures, and practices of their society achieve, promote, and protect individual rational freedom (of all three kinds). Pursuing one's elective ends with full cognizance of the necessity and legitimacy of such provisions and restrictions is a richer and more adequate form of self-determination – of rational freedom – than is the mere pursuit of elective ends.

Like Kant's, Hegel's moral philosophy provides rational standards for legitimate actions and institutions which are not restricted to any particular society or group of societies. In this crucial regard, Hegel is not a communitarian, despite other commonalities. Yet Hegel's account of the social and historical circumstances required to specify and to implement those rational standards acknowledges that societies in different circumstances can legitimately devise distinctive ways to satisfy universal standards of normative legitimacy. Hegel's practical philosophy is an ethical theory insofar as it aims to show why it is obligatory to act in accord with and on the basis of the legitimate principles, procedures, and institutions (familial, civil, legal, and political) within a modern market society which has civil and political institutions performing the functions his theory specifies.

The structure of Hegel's analysis in the *Philosophy of Right*

Some important features of Hegel's moral philosophy are revealed by considering Hegel's strategy for identifying and for justifying the various principles, procedures, and institutions he advocates. Hegel identified in and adopted from Kant's moral philosophy precisely the kind of "constructivism" identified by Onora O'Neill (O'Neill 1989, 2003a; Westphal 2007). Like Kant's, Hegel's method of proof is regressive: starting from an accepted claim, he argues that this claim can only be justified or satisfied if further conditions for its possibility are also justified and satisfied.

In Part 1 of the *Philosophy of Right*, "Abstract Right," Hegel's analysis begins with an important basic requirement for human action: acquiring a possession. This point of departure is common in the modern natural law and the social contract traditions and is central to the individualist views Hegel criticizes. Against many natural law theories of property (including Locke's), though with Hobbes, Hume, Rousseau, and Kant, Hegel argues that possession is not natural, it is a social institution because the point of possession is to be left in peace by others to use one's possessions; such provisions require socially established institutions. Like Kant, Hegel argues that taking outer resources into possession is only possible and is only legitimate on the basis of mutual recognition of compossible rights to possession. The mutual recognition of rights to possession is only possible on the basis of correlative acceptance of mutual obligations to acknowledge and respect others' rights to possession. This system of abstract right governs rights of possession, use, and exchange. It suffices to specify various kinds of injustice, from non-malicious wrong to fraud, extortion, and theft. However, the system of abstract right as such cannot distinguish in theory or in practice between legitimate punishment (a pleonasm) and mere revenge. In principle, punishment is legitimate only on the basis of two kinds of impartial, proto-juridical judgments: whether an injustice has in fact been committed and if so, exactly what kind and extent of compensation or punishment is appropriate. Such impartial normative judgments require *moral* judgment, not necessarily of motives or character (though these pertain to distinguishing non-malicious from malicious wrong), but of outward actions.

The system of abstract right as such also cannot minister to the upbringing and education of persons who understand the system of abstract right to be a system of justice and who aspire to maintain the system of possession, exchange, and contract because it is just. No such system can be maintained solely through enforcing civil and criminal law. The requisite system of upbringing and education is itself both a moral and a social institution, and such a system is necessary for the proper functioning of the system of abstract right. In these three regards (juridical decision, upbringing and education, and the character of mature agents who affirm and abide by basic principles and practices of justice), morality is a necessary condition for any legitimate, also for any stable – in sum, for any *possible* – system of property. The very point of a system of property is to stabilize the legitimate possession, use, and exchange of goods; hence no such system can dispense with whatever legitimate conditions are required to achieve that stability (*Rph* §§103, 104).

In Part 2, "Morality," Hegel argues for two complementary points. First, he argues that moral reflection (understood primarily in Kantian terms) is unconditionally necessary for the moral integrity, freedom, and autonomy of individual agents as persons who can effectively and impartially judge issues of morality, justice, and conduct, whether their own or others', and who seek to uphold a legitimate system of morality and justice as such. Second, he argues that, though informed by Kant's pure metaphysical principles of morals, moral reflection by itself is insufficient either to identify or to justify moral norms, including principles of justice (*Rph* §258R). (The "morality" Hegel criticizes holds that moral reflection suffices in this regard.) Instead, identifying and justifying such norms also requires moral reflection on our actual interrelations and interactions, which we collectively develop through history in the form of social practices, namely, the customs and institutions we develop on the basis of our human capacities, limits, skills, and abilities, together with our material and social resources for action. Some of these core customs were considered very abstractly in "Abstract Right" in the form of the system of private law governing possession and exchange. Through our collective, historical life we learn in detail what kind of finite human beings we are. (In this regard, Hegel's theory of justice is more deeply rooted in the modern natural law tradition than is Kant's.) Through our collective historical life we also solve the basic quandary of human existence, that "although it is the essential nature of human beings to be free, freedom does not come naturally" to us (Neuhouser 2000: 149).

This brief sketch highlights the core strategy of Hegel's argument to show that the conditions for the very possibility of abstract right and of morality are given only within his account of ethical life (*Sittlichkeit*), the third and final part of his book. Likewise, this sketch indicates the core strategy of Hegel's argument that also in modern times, regardless of whether we realize it, we human beings are *zoon politikon*. Throughout, the structure and strategy of Hegel's justificatory argument is regressive and constructivist in Kant's senses of these terms.

Among the unintended consequences of individual economic behavior is that a society's economy develops various economic sectors distinguished by the kind of production involved and by the geographical regions in which each form of production occurs. Such developments are especially pronounced in industrialized market economies. In order to counteract the financial and political split between management and labor, Hegel advocated a system of "corporations," one per economic sector, which includes both management and labor and provides (*inter alia*) social recognition of their individual contributions to their sector of the economy, and through that to the economy as a whole, and also of the legitimacy of members' obtaining their self-satisfaction through their trades and professions. In order to insure that each sector of the economy is recognized and involved in the political process, and to insure that all economic agents are adequately informed about economic and political factors (both regional and national) bearing on their economic sector, Hegel advocated a system of political representation based on these corporations, each of which provides representatives to the legislature. Only such an arrangement, Hegel argues, can integrate our economic and political lives, both individually and collectively. Hegel indicates that the prime function of corporate representation is educational. This education is essential for individuals as moral agents to understand and act effectively within their socio-economic and political context. The structure of Hegel's analysis makes plain that this education is essential to developing the kind of informed, republican citizenry mentioned above. Once such a citizenry develops, Hegel's system of corporate representation can easily be converted to an electoral system. The prescience of Hegel's critique of democratic elections behoves us to take seriously his alternative system of representation.

Like other modern natural lawyers, Hegel placed greater confidence in the rationality embedded in social practices than in the *a priori* ratiocinations of philosophers. Because human beings act collectively to promote their freedom (regardless of whether they realize it), a central question of modern political philosophy, on Hegel's view, is: How and to what extent do existing institutions fulfill these functions? Hegel realized that understanding what a social institution *is* requires understanding what it *ought* to be in view of its functional role(s) within society and how these functions facilitate, secure, or promote free rational individual action. Examining extant institutions, whether Prussian *circa* 1820 or elsewhere or more recently, highlights what is already clear in his text (to any moderately charitable reader), namely, that Hegel's account of civil and political institutions is thoroughly normative; the closest approximations to social institutions which fulfill the functions Hegel advocates would be found today in Scandinavia or the Nordic countries.

Social freedom and role obligations

Central to Hegel's analysis of the legitimacy of social institutions are their justifying reasons. Elective, as it were contractualist, agreement plays no constitutive role; it is replaced in Hegel's account by what may be called a "reflective acceptance" model (Hardimon 1994b), guided by the kinds of reasoning just summarized from the three parts of Hegel's *Philosophy of Right*. Hegel's approach enables him to analyze a common and important form of obligation which reflects an important structure of our moral agency, namely, our role obligations and the many aspects of our individual agency which consist in undertaking and sustaining our various social roles. These obligations and these dimensions of our agency are very poorly understood, if understood at all, on a contractual model. In part this is because some roles and the obligations they involve are undertaken involuntarily, for example, filial obligations to one's siblings or parents or obligations as a citizen. Yet the contract model also fails to illuminate many important elective role obligations. This is because the very point of electively undertaking many kinds of roles is to become and to be the kind of person who performs that role (or those social functions). As Hegel notes most directly, the marriage contract is a contract to transcend the standpoint of contract by the married couple integrating themselves into one moral person (*Rph* §163R). Although my employment contract requires me to conduct research and to teach students, my employment contract has much more to do with where and when I perform these activities than whether I do so: I research philosophy because I am a philosopher, I teach students because I am a teacher. These are two of my primary roles in life and they are two primary, integral aspects of who I am. I am directly obligated and motivated to perform my duties as a researcher and as a teacher by my being who I am; my professional integrity is a core aspect of my personal integrity. My contractual obligation to perform my professional obligations parallels these more basic grounds of obligation; contractual considerations may be adduced to justify requiring or motivating me to do better if my professional commitments were to waver. However, it is seriously misleading to suggest, as the contractual model must, that I am obligated to perform my professional duties simply and solely because I agreed to do so (within a legitimate employment contract).

These same points pertain also to one's obligations as a citizen. Most adults acquire obligations as citizens simply by maturing within a reasonably just society.

Their resulting obligations are non-contractual role obligations. Reflective adults may superimpose on those obligations voluntary, elective commitment to their country and to their obligations as citizens. These latter grounds of obligation, however, supplement rather than replace the former. Even naturalized citizens who pledge their allegiance to a new country pledge themselves to become and to be full-fledged citizens by adopting and developing their roles as citizens. If this pledge were to be understood as a contract (though this too would be a misunderstanding), it would again be a contract to transcend the standpoint of contract by actually becoming a citizen who is directly obligated to his or her adopted country and who is motivated directly by that obligation, regardless of whatever allegedly contractual obligation may stem from his or her pledge of allegiance.

The reflective acceptance of principles, obligations, roles, social practices, or institutions requires assessing their functions, benefits, burdens, and above all their justifying reasons and endorsing them insofar as they are sufficiently justified by those reasons. Hence there is no question of Hegel's social theory simply endorsing any social status quo. By focusing on reflective acceptance rather than on contractual agreement, Hegel's moral theory lets justifying reasons speak for themselves, as it were, while recognizing that egoists, skeptics, or recalcitrant contractarians may cavil about them endlessly. Though Hegel does not at all restrict or reduce our moral lives to our social roles, by highlighting our social roles and role obligations, Hegel's moral theory highlights the morally important phenomenon of our adopting and identifying with the various social roles we undertake. This allows his theory to emphasize how we transform ourselves by adopting and developing ourselves by undertaking various social roles. Emphasizing these phenomena allows Hegel's moral theory to highlight an important kind and source of obligation occluded by social contract models, the direct motivation to perform an act of the kind required by one's social role. Additionally, Hegel's moral theory shows how these features of individual moral character and obligation can be understood as an aspect of individual rational autonomy, thus showing that they are not the sole province of communitarians and conservatives.

Individual autonomy and social reconciliation

Like Kant (O'Neill 2003b, 2004a, b), Hegel holds that individual rational autonomy is the capacity to regulate one's own thought and conduct by assessing and, when identified, guiding one's thought and action on the basis of sufficient justifying reasons (Westphal forthcoming b). Like Kant, Hegel also holds that reason is normatively autonomous because by using the resources of Kant's constructivism about moral principles and Hegel's account of ethical life, reason suffices to identify and to justify legitimate principles, practices, and institutions for solving basic problems of social coordination and for guiding right individual action. Yet we are very much finite, dependent beings; we depend in myriad ways on both natural and social resources, whether conceptual, procedural, or material. Left unanalyzed, combining our rational autonomy with our myriad dependencies may appear to reduce "freedom" to insight into acting by necessity. How can we act freely and autonomously if we are so manifestly and manifoldly interdependent creatures? This question appears inherently paradoxical only on the assumption of a strong individualism of a kind exposed and superseded by Hegel's moderate collectivism, mentioned above. This point of principle is a prelude to Hegel's substantive answer to the question. In brief, the basic victory of human freedom over nature is that very few and only very general needs or ends are given us by human biology and psychology. Typically our manifest desires and ends are much more specific because they have been literally *customized* within one's society to be desires or ends for meeting broad natural needs in ways specific to one's culture and to one's own taste and proclivities, whereby any strictly natural needs are also supplemented by myriad acquired needs. In this way, we collectively come to give ourselves our own needs, desires, and ends. The basic victory of individual human freedom over the social context of individual action lies in recognizing the myriad ways in which we have collectively made our social life to be as it is, so that we collectively share the benefits and burdens of our collective social life and we collectively share the obligation as well as the prospect of preserving or modifying it as we need, in view both of our collective circumstances of action and of the basic principles of justice explicated by Kant's constructivism. We can act autonomously in view of the social and natural bases of our own individual action once we recognize how these bases provide the necessary enabling conditions of our own individual free rational action. Explicating this thesis is a central aim of Hegel's *Philosophy of Right* (Westphal 1993; Neuhouser 2000). By explaining how our modern social world facilitates individual action, Hegel explains how our social world is not and need not be regarded as recalcitrantly foreign to ourselves, at least insofar as our social institutions perform the functions Hegel assigns them. To the extent we can recognize that and how our social institutions perform these functions, we can be reconciled with our society rather than alienated from it (Hardimon 1994a). If we now have Weberian concerns about the self-aggrandizing, disenfranchising character of powerful social and especially political institutions, we should consider the extent to which these unfortunate developments occurred because contemporary institutions did not develop within the tightly integrated framework Hegel advocated to curtail such developments, in part by providing comprehensive channels for mutual oversight. Such concerns about present social institutions do not reflect ill on Hegel's moral philosophy; rather, they underscore how strongly normative and prescient it is.

See also Ethics and reason (Chapter 9); Ethics and sentiment (Chapter 10); Hume (Chapter 11); Kant (Chapter 14); Sidgwick, Green, and Bradley (Chapter 17);

Pragmatist moral philosophy (Chapter 19); Ethics and Law (Chapter 35); Contemporary Kantian ethics (Chapter 38); Contractualism (Chapter 41); Contemporary natural law theory (Chapter 42); Respect and recognition (Chapter 47).

References

Buckle, Stephen (1991) *Natural Law and the Theory of Property*, Oxford: Clarendon Press.

Green, Thomas F. (1999) *Voices: The Educational Formation of Conscience*, Notre Dame, IN: University of Notre Dame Press.

Hardimon, Michael (1994a) *Hegel's Social Philosophy: The Project of Reconciliation*, Cambridge: Cambridge University Press.

——(1994b) "Role Obligations," *Journal of Philosophy* 91, no. 7: 333–63.

Hegel, G. W. F. (1991) *Elements of the Philosophy of Right*, ed. A. Wood, trans. H. B. Nisbet, Cambridge: Cambridge University Press. (Abbreviated "*Rph*," cited by main sections, §, or by Hegel's published Remarks, §*n*R.)

Kant, Immanuel (1996) *Metaphysics of Morals*, in *Practical Philosophy*, trans. M. Gregor, Cambridge: Cambridge University Press, pp. 353–603.

Kaufmann, Walter (1951) "The Hegel Myth and Its Method," *Philosophical Review* 60, no. 4: 459–86.

Lovett, Frank (2006) "Republicanism," in E. N. Zalta (ed.) *Stanford Encyclopedia of Philosophy*, http://plato.stanford.edu/entries/republicanism/

Neuhouser, Frederick (2000) *The Foundations of Hegel's Social Theory: Actualizing Freedom*, Cambridge, MA: Harvard University Press.

O'Neill, Onora (1989) *Constructions of Reason*, Cambridge: Cambridge University Press.

——(2000) "Kant and the Social Contract Tradition," in F. Duchesneau, G. Lafrance and C. Piché (eds) *Kant actuel: Hommage à Pierre Laberge*, Montréal, Canada: Bellarmin, pp. 185–200.

——(2003a) "Constructivism in Rawls and Kant," in S. Freeman (ed.) *The Cambridge Companion to Rawls*, Cambridge: Cambridge University Press, pp. 347–67.

——(2003b) "Autonomy: The Emperor's New Clothes," *Proceedings and Addresses of the Aristotelian Society* 77, no. 1: 1–21.

——(2004a) "Autonomy, Plurality and Public Reason," in N. Brender and L. Krasnoff (eds) *New Essays in the History of Autonomy*, Cambridge: Cambridge University Press, pp. 181–94.

——(2004b) "Self-Legislation, Autonomy and the Form of Law," in H. Nagl-Docekal and R. Langthaler (eds) *Recht, Geschichte, Religion: Die Bedeutung Kants für die Gegenwart*, der *Deutsche Zeitschrift für Philosophie*, Special Volume 9: 13–26.

Skinner, Quentin (1984) "The Idea of Negative Liberty: Philosophical and Historical Perspectives," in R. Rorty, J. Schneewind and Q. Skinner (eds) *Philosophy in History*, Cambridge: Cambridge University Press, pp. 193–221.

——(2006) "The Paradoxes of Political Liberty," in D. Miller (ed.) *The Liberty Reader*, Boulder, CO, and London: Paradigm Publishers, pp. 183–205.

Westphal, Kenneth R. (1993) "The Basic Context and Structure of Hegel's *Philosophy of Right*," in F. C. Beiser (ed.) *The Cambridge Companion to Hegel*, Cambridge: Cambridge University Press, pp. 234–69.

——(1995) "How 'Full' Is Kant's Categorical Imperative?" *Jahrbuch für Recht und Ethik/Annual Review of Law and Ethics* 3: 465–509.

——(2002) "Rationality and Relativism: The Historical and Contemporary Significance of Hegel's Response to Sextus Empiricus," *Esercizi Filosofici* (Trieste) 6: 22–33.

——(2003) *Hegel's Epistemology: A Philosophical Introduction to Hegel's Phenomenology of Spirit*, Cambridge, MA: Hackett.

——(2005) "Kant, Hegel, and Determining Our Duties," in S. Byrd and J. Joerden (eds) *Philosophia practica universalis: Festschrift für Joachim Hruschka, Jahrbuch für Recht und Ethik/Annual Review of Law and Ethics* 13: 335–54.

——(2007) "Normative Constructivism: Hegel's Radical Social Philosophy," *SATS – Nordic Journal of Philosophy* 8, no. 2: 7–41.

——(2010) "From 'Convention' to 'Ethical Life': Hume's Theory of Justice in Post-Kantian Perspective," *Journal of Moral Philosophy* 7, no. 1: 105–32.

——(Forthcoming a) "Constructivism, Contractarianism and Basic Obligations: Kant and Gauthier," in J.-C. Merle (ed.) *Reading Kant's Doctrine of Right*, Cardiff: University of Wales Press.

——(Forthcoming b) "Urteilskraft, gegenseitige Anerkennung und rationale Rechtfertigung," in H.-D. Klein (ed.) *Ethik als prima Philosophia?*, Würzburg: Königshausen & Neumann.

Wood, Allen (1990) *Hegel's Ethical Thought*, Cambridge: Cambridge University Press.

Further reading

Brooks, Thom (2007) *Hegel's Political Philosophy: A Systematic Reading of the Philosophy of Right*, Edinburgh: Edinburgh University Press.

Chitty, Andrew (1996) "On Hegel, the Subject and Political Justification," *Res Publica* 2, no. 2: 181–203.

D'Hondt, Jacques (1988) *Hegel in His Time: Berlin 1818–1831*, trans. John W. Burbidge, Peterborough, ON, Canada: Broadview.

Knowles, Dudley (2002) *Hegel and the Philosophy of Right*, London: Routledge.

Neuhouser, Frederick (2008) "Hegel's Social Philosophy," in F. C. Beiser (ed.) *The Cambridge Companion to Hegel and Nineteenth Century Philosophy*, Cambridge: Cambridge University Press, pp. 204–29.

Peperzak, Adriaan (2001) *Modern Freedom: Hegel's Legal, Moral, and Political Philosophy*, Dordrecht and Boston: Kluwer.

16
JOHN STUART MILL

Henry West

John Stuart Mill was the foremost British philosopher of the nineteenth century, and *Utilitarianism*, his short work on the foundations of morals, is the most widely read presentation of utilitarian ethical philosophy. Mill was heir to a utilitarian tradition stemming from Jeremy Bentham (1748–1832). Mill's father, James Mill (1773–1836), was a disciple of Bentham and home-schooled Mill on the Benthamite doctrine. John Stuart Mill's ethics is hedonistic utilitarianism. In *Utilitarianism* Mill states his position as follows: "The creed which accepts as the foundation of morals, Utility, or the Greatest Happiness Principle, holds that actions are right in proportion as they tend to promote happiness, wrong as they tend to produce the reverse of happiness. By happiness is intended pleasure and the absence of pain; by unhappiness, pain and the privation of pleasure" (Mill 1969/1861: 210). This statement shows that Mill is a "consequentialist," founding the morality of actions on their probable consequences, and that he is a "hedonist," judging the consequences that count to be pleasure and pain.

Mill revised Bentham's ethics with (1) a distinction between qualities and quantities of pleasures and pains; (2) a more complex theory of motivation and of the sanctions of morality; (3) an attempt at a sort of "proof" of the principle of utility; and (4) a clearer statement of the relationship between utility and rights, including a theory of moral rights. But he continued to be a utilitarian in the tradition of Bentham. These revisions of Bentham's utilitarianism will be discussed in what follows. There remain, however, some ambiguities in Mill's statement of the utilitarian "creed."

By "actions" does Mill mean *types* of actions or does he mean particular, individual actions in unique circumstances? And by "tend" does he mean the probable consequences of types of actions based on past experience or does he mean the balance of pleasure over pain or vice versa of a particular action? Mill has been interpreted both ways, and Mill probably means both. Mill's principle of utility is "that pleasure, and freedom from pain, are the only things desirable as ends; and that all desirable things (which are as numerous in the utilitarian as in any other scheme) are desirable either for the pleasure inherent in themselves, or as means to the promotion of pleasure and the prevention of pain" (Mill 1969/1861: 210). He called this a theory of life on which his theory of morality is grounded. Mill regarded morality as only one branch of what he calls the "art of life" that includes "the Right, the Expedient, and the Beautiful or Noble in human conduct and works" (Mill 1974/1843: 949). Mill's hedonistic theory of value is to guide conduct in all of these areas, not just morality, and many of the decisions regarding expediency may be decisions of what will have the best consequences in the particular case.

Another controversial assumption in Mill's statement of his creed is his saying: "By happiness is intended pleasure and the absence of pain; by unhappiness, pain and the privation of pleasure" (Mill 1969/1861: 210). This seems contrary to the use of these terms in ordinary English. Isn't happiness more than that, more than just the good and bad feelings in one's life? Mill analyzes happiness as "an existence made up of few and transitory pains, many and various pleasures, with a decided predominance of the active over the passive, and having as the foundation of the whole, not to expect more from life than it is capable of bestowing" (Mill 1969/1861: 215). This analysis includes slightly more than an existence in which episodes of pleasure predominate over episodes of pain. There is also an attitudinal dimension – in requiring that one not expect more from life than it is capable of bestowing, Mill implies that to be happy one must have an attitude towards one's life that finds the existence satisfying, but this could be given an analysis in terms of pleasure – one must find pleasure and not pain in reflecting on one's existence.

Act-utilitarianism vs. rule-utilitarianism

In the twentieth century a distinction between "act-utilitarianism" and "rule-utilitarianism" became explicit. Act-utilitarianism, at least in one of its formulations, is the doctrine that the consequences of each act are to be compared with alternatives to determine correct action by the act that maximizes utility. Rule-utilitarianism, in one of its formulations, is the doctrine that it is the consequences of the practice or recognition of rules or precepts that are to be compared with alternative rules or precepts to determine the ideal moral code, and conformity with the best rules are to determine correct action. Mill sometimes writes as if he were an "act-utilitarian," but at least in the *moral* sphere he was not. He did not regard any action that failed to produce the greatest utility to be a morally wrong action. He limited morality to those actions that deserved sanctions, leaving other actions to the free judgment of individuals. He had an important place in morality for rules and rights, sometimes overriding actions that individually might produce greater utility in the particular case. He also had a place for supererogatory actions, actions going beyond the call of duty, deserving praise for their performance but not blame in their omission.

In regard to morality, Mill's statement of the "creed" is best interpreted as referring in the normal case to action types. Mill thinks that our knowledge of the tendencies of types of actions has provided the foundation for moral rules. In answer to the objection "that there is not time, previous to action, for calculating and weighing the effects of any line of conduct on the general happiness," Mill replies: "The answer to the objection is, that there has been ample time, namely, the whole past duration of the human species. During all that time mankind have been learning by experience the tendencies of actions; on which experience all the prudence, as well as all the morality of life, is dependent" (Mill 1969/1861: 224). After giving an analysis of pleasures and pains, Mill says: "This, being, according to the utilitarian opinion, the end of human action, is necessarily also the standard of morality; which may accordingly be defined, the *rules and precepts* for human conduct, by the observance of which an existence such as has been described might be, to the greatest extent possible, secured to all mankind; and not to them only, but, so far as the nature of things admits, to the whole sentient creation" (Mill 1969/1861: 214, emphasis added).

Many commentators have interpreted Mill as an "act-utilitarian" with regard to the criterion of what is morally *right*, but a "rule-utilitarian" with regard to a *strategy* or *decision procedure* for how best to maximize morally right actions. This is to regard the moral rules as "rules of thumb" to save time in calculating for the particular case, to avoid making decisions prejudiced in one's own favor, and to coordinate behavior so that others can know what to expect of one. However, Mill says that the tendencies of actions that are injurious to human happiness should be codified as moral rules, taught to the young, and enforced by sanctions. In Chapter V of *Utilitarianism* he even says: "We do not call anything wrong, unless we mean to imply that a person ought to be punished in some way or other for doing it; if not by law, by the opinion of his fellow creatures; if not by opinion, by the reproaches of his own conscience. This seems the real turning point of the distinction between morality and simple expediency" (Mill 1969/1861: 246). Thus the application of sanctions, based on rules, justified by their utility, seems to be definitive of moral right and wrong. There is a social dimension to moral rules that make them more than rules of thumb for the individual utilitarian agent's choice of action case by case. But Mill does recognize that there may be unusual cases where the rules can be overridden. Regarding the prohibition of lying, he says that

> the violation, for a present advantage, of a rule of such transcendant expediency, is not expedient … Yet that even this rule, sacred as it is, admits of possible exceptions, is acknowledged by all moralists; and the chief of which is when the withholding of some fact (as of information from a malefactor, or of bad news from a person dangerously ill) would preserve some one (especially a person other than oneself) from great and unmerited evil, and when the withholding can only be effected by

> denial. But in order that the exception may not extend itself beyond the need, and may have the least possible effect in weakening reliance on veracity, it ought to be recognized, and, if possible, its limits defined.
>
> (Mill 1969/1861: 223)

This looks like the application of a more complicated rule, but elsewhere he says:

> It is not the fault of any creed, but of the complicated nature of human affairs, that rules of conduct cannot be so framed as to require no exceptions, and that hardly any kind of action can safely be laid down as either always obligatory or always condemnable. There is no ethical creed which does not temper the rigidity of its laws, by giving a certain latitude, under the moral responsibility of the agent, for accommodation to peculiarities of circumstances.
>
> (Mill 1969/1861: 225)

In conclusion, whether Mill is a consistent "rule-utilitarian," a consistent "act-utilitarian," or allows both "act-utilitarian" and "rule-utilitarian" moral reasoning is difficult to determine.

Consequentialism

Mill presents little argument for the most fundamental characteristic of utilitarianism, that it is what is today called a "teleological" or consequentialist theory, judging the right or wrongness of actions by their consequences. Mill's theory of action is "teleological": he says that all action is for some end, and rules of action take their character from the end to which they are subservient. He thus does not take seriously alternative non-consequential ethical theories, such as deontology (basing ethics on duty independent of consequences), virtue ethics (basing ethics on the character traits of agents), theories that regard rights as fundamental, not derived from utility, and some forms of intuitionism. He also assumes that "there ought to be one principle or law, at the root of all morality, or if there be several, there should be a determinate order of precedence among them" (Mill 1969/1861: 206). This statement is made in the context of criticizing intuitionist theories, but it would also seem to rule out consequentialist theories that have pluralistic theories of value.

Mill regarded his chief opponents to be intuitionists who supported moral rules by assuming that we have a moral sense. Mill criticizes the theory by claiming that it regards the received rules of morality, when supported by the moral sense, as not subject to criticism. Utilitarianism, making the consequences of actions an empirical matter, can be progressive, reforming morality. Mill's *Subjection of Women* is an example of criticism of existing moral attitudes.

Qualitative hedonism

One of the most distinctive features of Mill's philosophy in comparison with Bentham's is Mill's introduction of the notion of higher and lower *qualities* of pleasures. Bentham had analyzed an experience of pleasure or pain as two-dimensional – having a certain duration in time and having a certain intensity at each moment. Mill thinks that this is overly simple. In answer to the objection that the utilitarian philosophy is a doctrine worthy only of swine, Mill says that the accusation supposes human beings to be capable of no pleasures but those of which swine are capable. On the contrary, Mill says, "Human beings have faculties more elevated than the animal appetites and, when once made conscious of them, do not regard anything as happiness which does not include their gratification" (Mill 1969/1861: 210–11). Mill says that the pleasures of the intellect, of the feelings and imagination, and of the moral sentiments have a much higher value, as pleasures, than those of mere sensation. To explain this, Mill says:

> Of two pleasures, if there be one to which all or almost all who have experience of both give a decided preference, irrespective of any feeling of moral obligation to prefer it, that is the more desirable pleasure. If one of the two is, by those who are competently acquainted with both, placed so far above the other that they prefer it, even though knowing it to be attended with a greater amount of discontent, and would not resign it for any quantity of the other pleasure which their nature is capable of, we are justified in ascribing to the preferred enjoyment a superiority in quality so far outweighing quantity as to render it, in comparison, of small account.
>
> (Mill 1969/1861: 211)

And Mill claims that the pleasures of higher quality are those that employ our distinctively human faculties.

In arguing for the superiority of the distinctively human pleasures, Mill seems to be claiming that on every occasion of choice, people who have experienced pleasures of sensation and pleasures of the intellect consistently prefer pleasures of the intellect. If that is his claim it is absurd. But that need not be his claim. He is not necessarily saying that his competent judges on every occasion prefer the higher pleasure. He claims that they would not resign a *manner of existence* that includes that kind of pleasure for any amount of the other. It may be true that "few human creatures would consent to be changed into any of the lower animals for the promise of the fullest allowance of a beast's pleasures" (Mill 1969/1861: 211); but it does not follow that on every occasion a competently experienced human being desires distinctively human pleasures more than the gratification of an animal appetite.

I believe that introspection of pleasurable and painful experiences does lead one to say that they have different pleasurable and painful qualities. There is not some common quality that all pleasures have that makes them "pleasures." They may only have "family resemblances" that make them all pleasures or pains. The pain of a toothache feels different from the pain of a stomach ache. But that does not disqualify them from both being pains. However, I think that Mill is mistaken to think that distinctively human pleasures and pains are consistently more desirable or undesirable than those to which our animal natures are subject. A rich life includes both.

Some commentators have claimed that in introducing qualitative distinctions between pleasures and pains, Mill has assigned intrinsic value to the exercise of the distinctively human faculties, independent of the pleasure derived from them, and thus deserted a strictly hedonistic theory of value. This is not the most plausible interpretation of Mill. Mill is not asserting that it is the exercise of the human faculties as such that has intrinsic value but only that the pleasures derived from that exercise have superior value. In some passages, especially in *On Liberty*, Mill speaks of the need for a recognition of the value of "individuality" and of allowing individuals to develop their capacities in various ways. This has been taken to be inconsistent with the hedonism of *Utilitarianism*, but if qualitative hedonism is taken seriously, then Mill's high evaluation of these ideals of individuality and autonomy can be regarded as essential sources of his higher pleasures.

Sanctions and moral motivation

Another way in which Mill expanded Bentham's utilitarianism was in his analysis of sanctions. Mill, following Bentham, uses the word "sanctions" to refer to the sources of motivation, in this context motives to be moral. Mill classifies them as "external" and "internal." Under the former heading are hope of favor and fear of displeasure from our fellow creatures and from the Ruler of the Universe (if one has a belief in the divine). These are the motives that Bentham analyzed as the political, the moral or popular, and the religious sanctions. Bentham made a distinction between the enforcement of morality by law and public policy, carried out by judges and others specifically designated for the office (the political), and the enforcement of morality by popular opinion (the moral or popular). In each case these are "external" sanctions. Even if there were no other motives to be moral, these would operate, and these are consistent with utilitarianism. It is useful to have laws prohibiting theft and murder and other crimes, although the utilitarian would want to have these subjected to critical analysis to see if they are the best possible laws and public policies. Furthermore, utilitarians would want public opinion to enforce useful moral rules. So utilitarians do not differ from others in seeking to have the political and popular sanctions enforce some forms of behavior. If people believe in the goodness of God, those who think that conduciveness to the general happiness is the criterion of the good must believe that this is what God approves. Thus utilitarianism has available to it these external sanctions. Mill points out that we also have sympathy with and affection for other people and may have love or awe of God as well as hope or fear of favor or disfavor.

But it is the "internal" sanction that really interests Mill. This is the feeling of pain, attendant on the violation of duty, which is the essence of conscience. Mill thought that Bentham ignored this important sanction enforcing morality. Mill believed that conscience is an internalization of the external sanctions, complicated by other associated feelings, but he sees no reason why it may not be cultivated to as great an intensity in connection with the utilitarian as with any other rule of morals. In comparison with Bentham, Mill also held a more complex theory of motivation. Bentham thought that action is always motivated by the prospect of pleasure or pain. Mill thought that the motivation may be a pleasure or pain which precedes the act. One may be deterred from a wrong act by the pain of contemplating the doing of the act, not just the calculation of pain or pleasure following the act. And through conditioning, he thought that habits can be formed such that we continue to will a certain kind of act without any reference to its being pleasurable.

Mill's "proof" of the principle of utility

Perhaps the most controversial chapter of Mill's *Utilitarianism* is the one in which he discusses "Of What Sort of Proof the Principle of Utility is Susceptible." Mill says that it is impossible to give a proof of the principle of utility in the ordinary or popular meaning of the term, but in Chapter 4 of *Utilitarianism* he gives an argument that he claims is "capable of determining the intellect either to give or withhold its assent to the doctrine: and this is equivalent to proof" (Mill 1969/1861: 208). He claims that the only possible evidence that anything is desirable is that people do actually desire it. All persons, so far as they believe it to be attainable, desire their own happiness; so happiness is one desirable kind of thing. He then proceeds to argue that many desires for things as ends which do not appear at first sight to be desires for happiness, such as the desire for virtue or the miser's desire for money, have been acquired through their association with pleasure. They are all "parts of happiness." He says that he now has an answer to the question, of what sort of proof the principle of utility is susceptible. "If the opinion which I have now stated is psychologically true – if human nature is so constituted as to desire nothing which is not either a part of happiness or a means of happiness, we can have no other proof, and we require no other, that these are the only things desirable" (Mill 1969/1861: 237). So happiness is inclusive of all that is of value, and "the promotion of it the test by which to judge of all human conduct; from which it necessarily follows that it must be the criterion of morality, since a part is included in the whole" (Mill 1969/1861: 237).

Mill's statement of the proof has led many commentators to accuse him of various fallacies. He has been said to have defined the desirable as the desired, but this is to misread him. He says that the only *evidence* it is possible to produce that something is desirable is that it is desired, not that the desirable *means* the desired. He says that it is "a question of fact and experience, dependent, like all similar questions, upon evidence. It can only be determined by practised self-consciousness and self-observation, assisted by observation of others" (Mill 1969/1861: 237).

A more plausible accusation is that Mill has committed a fallacy when he says that "each person's happiness is a good to that person, and the general happiness, therefore, a good to the aggregate of all persons" (Mill 1969/1861: 234). This would be a mistake if Mill meant the general happiness to be anything more than the sum of individuals' states of happiness, or the good to the aggregate of all persons to be anything more than the sum of what is good for the individuals involved. But that he did not mean anything more than that is indicated in a letter referring to that passage: "I merely meant in this particular sentence to argue that since A's happiness is a good, B's a good, C's a good, etc., the sum of all these goods must be a good" (letter to Henry Jones, 13 June 1868, in Mill 1849–73: Vol. 16, 1414). Mill views states of pleasure or happiness to be capable of aggregation: if two persons are equally happy, then there is twice as much happiness in the world as if only one were happy. And because he locates intrinsic value in happiness, the values of two individuals' lives are also capable of aggregation.

Mill's theory of justice and moral rights

In Chapter V of *Utilitarianism*, Mill attempts to answer the objection that justice is something independent of utility and can sometimes conflict with the greatest utility. In the end Mill claims "that justice is the name for certain moral requirements, which regarded collectively, stand higher in the scale of social utility, and are therefore of more paramount obligation, than any others" (Mill 1969/1861: 259).

Mill first gives an analysis of justice. In this analysis, he says: "In the first place, it is mostly considered unjust to deprive any one of his personal liberty, his property, or any other thing which belongs to him by law … it is just to respect the *legal rights* of any one" (Mill 1969/1861: 241). But Mill asserts that the legal rights of which the person is deprived, may be rights which *ought* not to have belonged to the person; in other words, the law which confers these rights, may be a bad law. Therefore, he argues, law is not the ultimate criterion of justice. A second case of injustice consists in taking or withholding from any person that to which the person has a *moral right*. In this concept Mill seems to have introduced another difference from Bentham, who seemed to have no place for *moral* rights. Mill makes this concept the primary defining characteristic of justice and injustice. The general idea of moral wrong is that it deserves punishment, if not by law then by the opinion of fellow creatures; if not by opinion by the reproaches of one's conscience. What sets off justice from other moral obligations is that a correlative *right* resides in some person or persons. "Justice implies something which it is not only right to do, and wrong not to do, but which some individual person can claim from us as his moral right" (Mill 1969/1861: 247).

Mill's account of justice also has an account of a sentiment of justice as well as a rule of action for what counts as justice. This sentiment of justice, he says, is the desire to punish a person who has done harm, and the knowledge or belief that there is some definite individual or individuals to whom harm has been done. He claims that it is a spontaneous outgrowth from the impulse of self-defense and the feeling of sympathy. The impulse of self-defense, he says, is common to all animal nature. Humans, however, have more extended capacities for sympathy: "a human being is capable of apprehending a community of interest between himself and the human society of which he forms a part, such that any conduct which threatens the security of the society generally, is threatening to his own, and calls forth his instinct (if instinct it be) of self-defence" (Mill 1969/1861: 248). Mill concludes that from the social sympathies the sentiment derives its morality; from the instinct of self-defense it derives "its peculiar impressiveness, and energy of self-assertion" (Mill 1969/1861: 250).

Having given this account of the concept and sentiment of justice, Mill is prepared to subordinate these to utilitarianism. "To have a right, then, is, I conceive, to have something which society ought to defend me in the possession of. If the objector goes on to ask why it ought, I can give him no other reason than general utility. If that expression does not seem to convey a sufficient feeling of the strength of the obligation, nor to account for the peculiar energy of the feeling, it is because there goes to the composition of the sentiment, not a rational only but also an animal element, the thirst for retaliation; and this thirst derives its intensity, as well as its moral justification, from the extraordinarily important and impressive kind of utility which is concerned. The interest involved is that of security, to every one's feelings the most vital of all interests" (Mill 1969/1861: 250–1). The enforcement of moral and legal rights protects security, the most significant kind of utility. Thus Mill thinks that he has shown that justice is not in conflict with utility but is a most important application of it.

Mill's liberalism

Much of Mill's thinking was preoccupied with social and political questions. With growing democracy, Mill was fearful of the "tyranny of the majority," not only through government coercion but through the informal social control of opinion and attitudes. His essay *On Liberty* attempts to draw a line as to what is appropriate for social interference and what should be left to individual choice. He is against paternalistic interference with adult behavior when it is not harmful to the legitimate interests of others. The thesis of *On Liberty* is that the only aim for which mankind is warranted in interfering with the liberty of action of any individual is to prevent harm to others. The individual is the best judge of his or her own welfare, and, if there is no harm to others, the individual should be left free from coercion, even if the behavior is judged by others to be harmful to that individual. When asked to defend this principle, Mill says that he can give no other reason except "utility in the largest sense, grounded on the permanent interests of man as a progressive being" (Mill 1977/1859: 224). Mill does not use the terminology in *On Liberty*, but qualitatively superior pleasures play an important role. One of the assumptions is that when people are compelled to conformity to custom or to the likes and dislikes of others, they are not exercising their higher faculties. Only when they are permitted to exercise free choice, to be original and creative, to make decisions about the truth of theoretical and practical matters, to engage in voluntary associations with other individuals and so on, can they obtain the greatest happiness. The greatest happiness, according to Mill, is not the satisfaction of *existing* desires, if these are uninformed. The greatest happiness is satisfaction of desires for pleasures measured by both quality and quantity, the qualitatively higher ones coming from the full development of individual capacities. He therefore advocates compulsory education to enable children to develop the capacity for the higher pleasures and he opposes those who would attempt to force a conventional lifestyle on people who want to experiment with alternative ways of living. Those who live uncustomary lives may be obtaining higher pleasures that the majority are incompetent to judge.

In *On Liberty* Mill argued vigorously for freedom of thought and discussion as a way of eradicating false doctrines and discovering and keeping alive true ones. One of the arguments is that the utility of truth is its benefits to society, but another is that it is its benefits to the minds of individuals.

In *Representative Government*, Mill defended representative government as the best way to protect the interests of the most numerous class, although he had reservations about the judgments of that population until it had become better educated. His economic views tended in the direction of greater equalitarian distribution of wealth and income. He said in his *Autobiography* that the social problem of the future would be how to unite the greatest individual liberty of action with a common ownership in the raw material of the globe and an equal participation of all in the benefits of combined labor.

In *Subjection of Women*, he advocated perfect equality in the marriage relationship, first-class citizenship and greater economic opportunities for women. While serving in Parliament, he introduced a bill to give women the right to vote on the same basis as males. It failed to pass.

Much can be said in support of Mill's position. The total subservience of one person to others, as in slavery, is contrary to happiness and individual development. The lack of freedom of religion or of freedom from religion has perpetuated superstitions that have worked against human welfare and development, and genuine freedom to criticize supernatural beliefs would be liberating. On the positive side, compulsory education of children, and freedom of adults to practice artificial birth control, have given people greater control over their lives with resulting greater happiness and fulfillment. Mill's utilitarianism and liberalism are controversial but worthy of serious thought and discussion.

See also Utilitarianism to Bentham (Chapter 13); Consequentialism (Chapter 37); Ethical intuitionism (Chapter 39); Virtue ethics (Chapter 40); Conscience (Chapter 46); Responsibility: Intention and consequence (Chapter 50); Partiality and impartiality (Chapter 52); Moral particularism (Chapter 53); Welfare (Chapter 54); Ideals of perfection (Chapter 55); Rights (Chapter 56); Justice and punishment (Chapter 57); The ethics of free speech (Chapter 64).

References

Mill, John Stuart (1969/1861) *Utilitarianism*, in J. M. Robson (ed.) *Essays on Ethics, Religion and Society*, vol. 10 of *Collected Works of John Stuart Mill*, Toronto: University of Toronto Press, pp. 203–60.

——(1972/1849–73) *The Later Letters of John Stuart Mill 1849–1874*, ed. Francis F. Minka and Dwight N. Lindley, vols 14–17 of *Collected Works of John Stuart Mill*, Toronto and Buffalo: University of Toronto Press.

——(1974/1843; 8th edn 1871) *A System of Logic: Ratiocinative and Inductive*, vols 7–8 of *Collected Works of Johns Stuart Mill*, Toronto: University of Toronto Press.

——(1977/1859) *On Liberty*, in J. M. Robson (ed.) *Essays on Politics and Society*, vols 18–19 of *Collected Works of John Stuart Mill*, Toronto and Buffalo: University of Toronto Press, vol. 18, pp. 213–310.

Further reading

Donner, Wendy (1998) "Mill's Utilitarianism," in John Skorupski (ed.) *The Cambridge Companion to Mill*, Cambridge: Cambridge University Press, pp. 255–92. (An excellent summary of Mill's ethics.)

Skorupski, John (1989) *John Stuart Mill*, London and New York: Routledge. (Contains critical discussions in chapters on "Utilitarianism" and "Liberalism.")

West, Henry R. (2004) *An Introduction to Mill's Utilitarian Ethics*, Cambridge: Cambridge University Press. (A book-length treatment of Mill's ethics.)

17
SIDGWICK, GREEN, AND BRADLEY

T. H. Irwin

Bentham's and Mill's utilitarianism

Sidgwick and Green were near-contemporaries, and they shared common philosophical interests and concerns, though they developed them in different directions. Sidgwick belongs to the British tradition in moral philosophy. Though he draws heavily on Kant, he looks back primarily to the British rationalists, sentimentalists, and intuitionists of the seventeenth to the nineteenth centuries. Green and Bradley are among the British idealists who were influenced by both Kant and Hegel, and therefore took a critical attitude to the main tendencies in earlier British philosophy. Bradley belongs to the next philosophical generation after Green and Sidgwick. He defends Green's position, with some significant alterations, and supports it with sharp criticism of Sidgwick.

Sidgwick's main work, *The Methods of Ethics*, was first published in 1874 (see Sidgwick 1907, *ME*). It was examined in an elaborate essay by Bradley, "Mr Sidgwick's Hedonism" (1935b/1877). The first edition of Bradley's *Ethical Studies* appeared in 1876, and was reviewed by Sidgwick. (The second edition appeared posthumously, in 1927 [see Bradley 1927, *ES*].) Green's *Prolegomena to Ethics* was published posthumously in 1883; it was based on lectures delivered in the 1870s (see Green 2003, *PE*). Green refers often to Mill and Sidgwick, though not to Bradley. Sidgwick discussed Green on several occasions, most fully in *The Ethics of Green, Spencer, and Martineau* (based on his lectures; see Sidgwick 1902, *EGSM*). He revised some parts of *Methods* to take account of, and to answer, the criticisms of Bradley and Green. This process of statement, criticism, and revised statement makes it useful to study some of the main issues on which Sidgwick and the idealists disagree.

Sidgwick and Green define their views in relation to the utilitarianism of Bentham and Mill. Bentham sets out a simple and rather crude utilitarian doctrine that relies on some clear but controversial basic claims: (1) He holds a hedonist account of the good, so that he identifies a person's good with maximum pleasure, whatever the objects of the pleasure may be. (2) He holds an instrumental conception of the right, so that he takes the right action to be fixed by reference to maximum total pleasure for everyone, no matter how it is distributed over the people affected. (3) He holds an egoist conception of motivation and rationality; each person ultimately aims at maximum pleasure for herself and has overriding reasons to aim at it.

According to Bentham's third claim, an individual has no reason to be concerned with what is morally right for its own sake. I have a reason to do a morally right action only in so far as I take it to maximize my own pleasure. But I have no reason to suppose that the actions, sometimes difficult and costly, required by morality will maximize my pleasure.

We might acknowledge that morality in its own right gives me no reason to care about it, but we connect morally right action with external sanctions – reward, punishment, praise, and blame. If society can attach enough pleasure to morality and enough pain to immorality, these artificial sanctions may give a rational individual sufficient reason to follow the requirements of morality. This seems to be a practical solution within the limits of Bentham's basic principles.

But the practical solution may seem unsatisfactory, for two reasons: (1) It may well seem practically inadequate. Any system of sanctions leaves loopholes, and hence leaves opportunities for undetected immorality. (2) Even if the system of sanctions leaves no loopholes, it does not seem to justify us in trying to be morally good people. We do not want to be surrounded by people who always need an external sanction to make them do the right actions.

John Stuart Mill departs from the orthodox Benthamite position. (1) He believes that pleasures differ in quality as well as quantity, and that qualitative differences should be considered in fixing the ultimate good. (3) He believes it is possible and desirable for people to be attached to morality for its own sake. His conception of utility helps us to see that common-sense morality expresses "secondary principles" that tell us how to achieve utility.

Mill's critics are not convinced that this revision of Bentham is really a utilitarian doctrine. John Grote, for instance, believes that Mill really adopts a pluralist conception of the good, and that he abandons any appeal to utility as an independent criterion for right action (see Grote 1870, *An Examination of the Utilitarian Philosophy*, *EUP*). It would provide an independent criterion if we could decide what maximizes pleasure without reference to our antecedent moral convictions, but Mill's qualitative hedonism prevents any such decision.

At this point in the arguments about Bentham and Mill, Green and Sidgwick enter the debate. Green believes that Mill is right to alter Bentham, and that Mill's critics are right to suppose that Mill has thereby abandoned utilitarianism. In Green's view, the next step is to abandon utilitarianism, and to incorporate Mill's insights in a different sort of theory. Sidgwick also agrees with the critics of Mill who believe that Mill has abandoned utilitarianism; but he infers that Mill altered Bentham's position in the wrong way. Sidgwick believes that we need to retain Bentham's first two claims, and that we can do this if we replace his third claim with a better account of reason and morality.

This dispute between Sidgwick and Green about the content of a moral theory is connected with a further dispute about the proper aims of such a theory. Both believe that moral theory is practically relevant, because it should offer some guidance to the appropriate direction of social and political reforms. But they understand this guidance quite differently. Sidgwick believes that a moral theory should be the basis of an effective method of moral decision. An adequate theory will tell us exactly what empirical information we need to decide whether a given course of action is right or wrong; since it may be very difficult to find the relevant information, our moral theory may leave us with unanswered moral questions, but the lack of an answer will not be the fault of our theory. Sidgwick takes this criterion of adequacy for a moral theory so seriously that he uses it to criticize all theories that provide no effective method.

Sidgwick's revision of utilitarianism

The main points of Sidgwick's revised version of utilitarianism are also the main points on which Green differs from Sidgwick. We can survey them as follows:

(1) *Hedonism.* Sidgwick rejects Bentham's psychological hedonism. But he still affirms prudential hedonism; that is to say, though he does not believe that everyone necessarily pursues her own pleasure as her ultimate end, he affirms that each person's good consists in her maximum pleasure (see *ME* Bk 3, ch. 14).
(2) *Quantitative hedonism.* Sidgwick rejects Mill's modification of Bentham's quantitative hedonism. He returns to Bentham's position.
(3) *Why accept utilitarianism?* Having rejected psychological hedonism, Sidgwick defends utilitarianism on non-egoistic grounds. He believes he can show the principle of utility is ultimately reasonable because it follows from two basic principles: (a) It is rational to pursue my own good, and therefore to treat my whole life impartially, with no bias towards the short-term good over the longer-term good. (b) As Kant argues, it is rational to treat other people equally with oneself. Since these principles are ultimately reasonable, but the second is non-egoistic, they provide a non-egoistic defense of utilitarianism (*ME* Bk 3, ch. 13).
(4) *Dualism.* Sidgwick does not affirm that the impartial rationality of the utilitarian position overrides the egoistic rationality of concern for one's own maximum pleasure. He affirms that both the impartial and the egoistic principle are ultimately reasonable, and that we cannot find any third rational point of view from which we can decide which principle overrides the other. Hence we face a dualism of practical reason (*ME* Concluding chapter).

Sidgwick believes that this position meets his criterion of adequacy for a moral theory, because it provides an effective method of decision. He applies this criterion at two main points in his argument: (1) It is one of his main reasons for preferring prudential hedonism over non-hedonist accounts of a person's good. He finds non-hedonist accounts insufficiently clear and precise, because they do not tell us what empirical information we need to decide whether something is or is not good for us. (2) It is one of his main reasons for preferring utilitarianism over pluralist theories that recognize several distinct grounds of rightness (justice, benevolence, generosity, loyalty, etc.) with no overriding ground. These pluralist theories cannot tell us what information we need to decide questions about rightness.

The idealist alternative

The idealists offer an alternative to Sidgwick on the main points we have picked out. For these purposes it will be easiest to draw on both Green and Bradley, since each throws some light on the other.

(1) *The good as self-realization*. Green rejects Sidgwick's prudential hedonism, and argues that a person's good consists in "self-satisfaction" or "self-realization" (Green, *PE* §§118–29). In Sidgwick's view, this conception of the good is too vague to be of any practical use (*ME* Bk 2, ch. 7). Is he right?

When we aim to cook a meal, or climb a mountain, or write a book, we aim at some future result (the cooked meal, etc.). But we also, in the idealist view, aim at a future state of ourselves; we seek to realize ourselves as having achieved these results. To see that this is a non-trivial claim, we may notice that we do not simply try to achieve isolated future results. If I want a degree in dentistry, but I want to be a carpenter rather than a dentist, I have some reason to revise my plans; they do not seem to fit together in a plausible conception of the future self I want to bring into existence. The claim that I want self-satisfaction is not the trivial claim that I want to satisfy my desires. Green means that I want to be satisfied as a whole self; the end I aim at includes a conception of a whole self with its aims coherently and systematically satisfied.

We might suppose that the idealists believe we have reason to aim at self-satisfaction because we want it, and because it partly specifies what the satisfaction of desire consists in. But that is not what Green and Bradley mean. Self-realization consists in more than coherent satisfaction of desires. If we tried to reduce our desires to a minimal level, we could satisfy them harmoniously and coherently without any difficulty. But Bradley denies that we would have realized ourselves. It is no human ideal to lead the "life of an oyster," even if we could modify our desires to the level of an oyster's desires (*ES* Ch. 2)

What is wrong, then, with the life of an oyster, if someone is perfectly content with it? Bradley believes that a plan to lead such a life would be irrational, because it would ignore many aspects of ourselves that we have good reason to try to realize. If we were giving someone else advice about what to do, we would not simply ask ourselves what would result in their maximum satisfaction; we would also want to give them an opportunity to develop and fulfill aspects of themselves that might be ignored if satisfaction of desire were the only goal. For this reason Bradley's term "self-realization" is less misleading than Green's usual term "self-satisfaction" as a name for the end that they both describe. They argue, not surprisingly, for their conception of the end by reference to our aims, because these aims express our intuitive convictions about the good; but they do not argue that their conception of the good is correct because it satisfies our desires. On the contrary, desires are correct in so far as they aim at self-realization.

If we are inclined to agree with Green and Bradley on these points, they have raised a reasonable doubt about Sidgwick's hedonism. If we care about living lives that do some justice to the different aspects of ourselves, we do not care simply about achieving some quantity of pleasure. We also care about the structural aspects of our lives, and about how they are related to the structure of our selves. These concerns are distinct from the concern for pleasure, and we may argue that they are plausible elements of our good.

(2) *Self-realization and morality*. But even if we agree with Green and Bradley on this point, we may doubt whether they have told us anything useful about morality. A saint, an entrepreneur, and a gangster may all have coherent plans for their lives; if they carry out these plans, do they not all realize themselves, and do they not all achieve their good? Why suppose that morality realizes the self more than immoral or amoral plans of life realize it?

Green and Bradley argue that morality is not simply one way of realizing the self, but is essential to self-realization. According to Green, we realize ourselves only by recognizing our good as non-competitive, as a common good (*PE* §199–217). It would be unrealistic and unreasonable to think of realizing ourselves as beings without social attachments and concerns; everyone forms such attachments in growing up, and no plausible conception of self can leave out our attachments to parents, family, and friends. If we tried to envisage a self without these attachments, we would find that such a conception could realize only part of a self.

Though Green recognizes that these elementary attachments to others do not meet the requirements of morality, he believes they are the right starting point for understanding morality, which is simply a reasonable extension of these social aspects of self-realization. To see the point of morality, we have to see that our own self-realization requires us to think of ourselves as deserving certain kinds of treatment from others who equally deserve it from us. If we have the right conception of ourselves, we think of ourselves as deserving something from others, not because we are especially useful to them or they especially admire us or enjoy our company, but because we are persons. If this is why we think we deserve something from them, we must acknowledge that persons equally deserve something from one another. We have now accepted the Kantian principle of treating persons as ends in themselves, and not simply as means.

On this basis, Green believes that he can incorporate a Kantian conception of morality, as embodied in principles that prescribe respect for persons as ends, within his conception of the good as self-realization. Hence he sums up his argument in the claim that we achieve our good in the good will. This good will aims at the common, non-competitive good (*PE* §§218–45).

In Green's view, this argument overcomes the dualism that Sidgwick claims to find in practical reason. It rejects both Sidgwick's account of egoism and his account of morality. (a) The prudent person aims not at the accumulation of his own pleasure, but at his self-realization. Hence he pursues an end that does not in principle exclude the good of others. (b) He does not simply pursue quantity of pleasure; he is concerned about himself as a persistent rational agent. (c) Morality does not enjoin the sacrifice of one person's good to secure a higher total quantity of good, and so it does not demand the extreme self-sacrifice that utilitarianism demands. (d) And so morality and prudence do not conflict. On the contrary, when we understand the implications of each, we see that they imply each other. Belief in a dualism results from an incomplete grasp of prudence and morality.

Objections to idealism

Sidgwick examines Green's views at some length, and criticizes them effectively. In his view, the criticisms show that Green does not offer a viable alternative to utilitarianism.

His most serious criticism attacks Green's conception of the relation between the good and the good will. In some places Green appears to identify them, as though a person's good consisted entirely in having and acting on a morally good will. If the two could be identified, my good consists entirely in the exercise of virtues that promote the same good in others. Sidgwick sees that this conception of the good removes the dualism of practical reason at too high a price (*EGSM* 94). Two objections are especially serious: (1) The complete identification of the good with the good will seems to conflict with any plausible conception of the good as self-realization. If we try to fill in a conception of self-realization by reference to the fulfillment of a person's capacities, we seem to include many elements of self-realization that go beyond capacities for moral virtue. (2) Green supposes that virtuous people should aim at the good, and hence the good will, of others. If A tries to promote the good will in *B*, A needs some conception of the good will in *B*. But if the good will in *B* is simply the will to promote the good will in C, we still do not know what the good will in *B* is until we know what the good will in C is, and so on *ad infinitum*. Green normally ignores these self-defeating implications of his conception of the good.

He assumes that virtuous people aim at the benefit of fellow-citizens, and that they will therefore try to secure the supply of food, shelter, health, and public amenities. They do not care exclusively about making other people virtuous.

If we try to modify Green's view, so as to allow non-moral components of the good, another part of his argument seems to unravel. His extreme moralizing conception of the good tries to avoid the dualism of practical reason. If he modifies his position, he recognizes that some elements of the good are non-moral and open to competition. Your moral goodness does not reduce the possible supply of moral goodness available to me; and so moral goodness is a non-competitive good. But, if there is a finite supply of food, the food that is given to you is taken away from me; and hence food is a potentially competitive good.

If both competitive and non-competitive goods belong to the overall good, which goods take priority? Even if Green removes any sharp opposition between my good and the good of others, this may not help him much. For the opposition is simply transferred to the opposition between the competitive and the non-competitive elements in my good. The persistent dualism in Green's view is clear, once we see how his conception of the good needs to be modified.

These features of Green's position reinforce Sidgwick's objection that Green's idealism is practically useless. According to Sidgwick's criterion, a moral theory should be definite enough to tell us precisely what empirical information we need in order to decide what to do. The idealist theory fails this test at three main points: (1) If we are trying to achieve self-realization, we need to know what its elements are; but Green does not specify them fully enough. (2) Even if we knew what the elements of self-realization are, we would still not know how they are to be weighed in a plan for achieving one's own self-realization. (3) Even if we knew how to weigh them in an individual life, we would not know how to weigh one person's self-realization in comparison with others, and so we would not know how to answer moral questions.

Defenses of idealism

Sidgwick's criticisms show that Green's position is unsatisfactory. But do they show that any attempts to modify it will be futile? Sidgwick believes that any modification that removes the main flaws will have to abandon the main aims of Green's theory. Is he right about this?

Is the conception of the good as self-realization hopelessly vague? To show that it is not, we may turn to one of John Grote's objections to utilitarianism. In Grote's view, utilitarianism gives us the wrong account of what is wrong with slavery. What matters in deciding about the rightness of slavery is the human nature of slaves (*EUP* 319–26). We ought to see that because slaves are human beings, they have human powers and capacities that they have good reason to develop, and that slavery is open to objection because it prevents this development. Though we may not have an agreed and exhaustive list of elements of self-realization, we can understand some of them well enough to reach some practical conclusions. If a plausible conception of self-realization can be used to support Grote's anti-utilitarian conclusion, Sidgwick can hardly be right to say that it is completely empty and practically useless.

Sidgwick might observe that an argument to show that slavery is bad because it interferes with the self-realization of slaves is less than rigorous. A quantitative hedonist begins with an identifiable experience of pleasure and argues empirically about what courses of action maximize pleasure. But one cannot begin with a similarly identifiable condition of self-realization. To show that, for instance, control over one's life is an aspect of self-realization for a rational being, one has to rely on premises that are not wholly uncontroversial, and that may require decisions on some points of ethical difficulty. As Sidgwick puts it, our method of argument has to be "intuitionist," in so far as it requires us to balance different apparently plausible considerations without any definite rule for how to balance them (*ME* Bk 3, ch. 1, 11).

This may not be a devastating objection, however. Rather than object to idealists for their appeal to self-realization, perhaps we should question Sidgwick's demand for clarity and determinacy. While we may agree that these are virtues in a moral theory, we may doubt whether Sidgwick is right to elevate them to the status of a criterion of adequacy. It may be unreasonable to demand a particular degree of clarity and determinacy in advance of our examination of different moral theories.

This doubt about Sidgwick's criterion may be reinforced if we ask about its point. We might suppose that if we can remove uncertainty in moral principles, and reduce our uncertainty to empirical uncertainty, our theory will be more useful for guiding action. But this may not be so. For if the empirical uncertainty cannot, and our moral uncertainty can, be resolved, it may be easier to apply less determinate principles to practice. If, for instance, the utilitarian case against slavery relies on some doubtful and uncertain claims about pleasure, whereas we are confident that slavery is wrong because slaves are human beings, our less precise non-utilitarian theory gives us more definite answers than we can find from the more precise utilitarian, and so the less precise theory may be more useful in practice. If Sidgwick's criterion is open to objection, idealists need not be worried if their theory violates his criterion.

This defense of idealism does not answer Sidgwick's main criticism of Green on the good and the good will. Green would be well advised to affirm clearly what he sometimes implies, that the good is the composite composed of the good will and the non-moral competitive goods that the good will regulates. Green gives morality a regulative role that relies on Kant's "formula of humanity." Since the common good is the good of rational agents, they all deserve respect as ends in themselves. This basis constrains the distribution of resources that can be objects of competition. If idealists can support these claims, they need not agree that Sidgwick's criticisms are devastating. Once we see that Green's more plausible conception of the good does not exclude all possibility of competition and conflict, we see that he needs to face some of the questions that lead Sidgwick to affirm the dualism of practical reason. But idealists need not follow Sidgwick all the way to a dualism. If they can argue that one's own self-realization requires the treatment of oneself as deserving respect simply as a person, they can acknowledge the claims of Kantian morality within a plausible conception of self-realization.

On this point we might have expected Bradley's discussion of self-realization to be helpful to Green. But it is less helpful than it might have been, because Bradley departs from Green at this point. Green argues that the Kantian Categorical Imperative, properly understood, has significant moral implications, because it is expressed in the formula of humanity; Bradley treats Kantian morality from a less sympathetic and more overtly Hegelian point of view, as simply a one-sided and mistaken conception of the self (*ES* Ch. 4). Bradley's initial account of morality relies on only one side of Green's conception of self-realization. He argues that since one's social role ("my station and its duties") forms one's conception of oneself, and hence one's conception of the self to be realized, and since one's social role includes moral demands, rights, and expectations, morality forms the self to be realized. We cannot therefore realize the socially defined self without accepting the moral outlook that defines our stations and their duties (*ES* Ch. 5).

This conception of morality allows Bradley to express his hostility to abstract moral theory, to critical and reforming attitudes to morality, and to casuistical reasoning that tries to defend particular actions by appeal to general principles. All these attitudes undertake the hopeless task of abstracting morality from stations and their duties.

Bradley acknowledges that his conception of morality as consisting simply in stations and duties is too simple. Not every station or social role realizes the self of its occupant (*ES* 202–6). To decide which roles are self-realizing for their occupants and which roles are oppressive, we need critical morality that takes a point of view outside a particular set of stations and duties.

Here Green's Kantian outlook seems to offer something that is missing from Bradley's more explicitly Hegelian view. For Green argues that the relevant critical morality has to rest on Kantian principles requiring respect for rational agents as ends. Since he includes these principles within his conception of self-realization, he has a reasonable reply both to Kant and to Bradley.

We may still doubt, however, whether Green has an answer, or the basis for an answer, to the dualism of practical reason. Even if we agree that Kantian morality is a part of self-realization, we may still ask how important a part it is. If morality has a minor role in self-realization, its requirements may often have to give way to other aspects of self-realization; and so it will not support a reliable commitment to morality. Admittedly, Sidgwick cannot support a reliable commitment to morality either, since he cannot resolve the dualism. But even if the idealists have a sufficient *ad hominem* reply to Sidgwick, we may reasonably be dissatisfied with their position if they cannot offer any better reply.

To show that they have a better reply to offer, the idealists need to defend two aspects of their position: (1) According to Green, the outlook of Kantian morality is not simply a part of self-realization, but an essential part of a true conception of the self to be realized. The other ends that we aim at are worthwhile ends for us as self-respecting agents who respect ourselves simply as rational agents, and therefore rely on a basis for respect that applies to other rational agents in the same way. (2) In so far as the moral outlook is essential to a true conception of the self to be realized, it cannot be turned on and off on different occasions; it has to regulate our other commitments and concerns.

While these aspects of the idealist position need both clarification and defense, they offer some prospect of overcoming the dualism of practical reason; for they help to explain why moral commitments determine the appropriate extent of non-moral commitments. They do not absolutely guarantee that we could never have any sufficient reason to violate a particular moral requirement for the sake of a non-moral aim. But we may doubt whether it is reasonable to demand that every acceptable theory of morality should provide such an absolute guarantee.

The idealist contribution to moral theory

Many twenty-first-century moral philosophers regard Sidgwick as a significant moralist from whom we can still expect to learn something about moral theory. (See e.g. Parfit 1984, *Reasons and Persons*.) This is not because they believe the main points of his moral theory; hedonistic utilitarianism is a rather unpopular view, perhaps partly because Sidgwick has made its implications so clear. Many would nonetheless praise Sidgwick's treatment of many of the main questions in moral philosophy. Green and Bradley have not fared as well in later moral philosophy. While various reasons may be given for this relative estimate of Sidgwick and the idealists, it is nonetheless difficult to justify. Sympathetic readers will soon see that some central aspects of the idealist position need modification; but the same is true of Sidgwick's utilitarianism. Further reflexion suggests that it is easier to construct a defensible position from idealist views than from Sidgwick's version of utilitarianism.

The relative neglect of the idealists may have contributed to the crude, but still popular, assumption that moral theorists need to choose between "deontological" and "consequentialist" views. (Some treat "virtue theory" as a third option.) Hence, those who reject utilitarianism believe that the most plausible option is either Kantian or intuitionist (as set out by e.g. Ross 1930, *The Right and the Good*). Idealism deserves some discussion partly because it casts doubt on this simple division, and tends to undermine the view that it provides us with exhaustive and exclusive options. Green's position includes a crucial deontological aspect, in so far as it accepts Kant's formula of humanity as a basic constraint on self-realization. But in so far as it aims at the achievement of both individual self-realization and a common good, it is teleological (though not wholly consequentialist). The position that results is more complex than those that are firmly utilitarian or firmly Kantian. But this complexity may not be so bad.

See also Kant (Chapter 14); Hegel (Chapter 15); Respect and recognition (Chapter 47); Ideals of perfection (Chapter 55).

References

Bradley, F. H. (1927) *Ethical Studies*, 2nd edn, Oxford: Oxford University Press; 1st edn, 1876. (Cited as *ES*.)

——(1935) "Mr Sidgwick's Hedonism," in *Collected Essays*, Oxford: Oxford University Press, vol. 2, ch. 2; originally published, 1877.

Green, T. H. (2003) *Prolegomena to Ethics*, ed. D. O. Brink, Oxford: Oxford University Press. (Cited as *PE*.)

Grote, J. (1870) *An Examination of the Utilitarian Philosophy*, Cambridge: Deighton Bell. (Cited as *EUP*.)

Parfit, D. A. (1984) *Reasons and Persons*, Oxford: Oxford University Press.

Ross, W. D. (1930) *The Right and the Good*, Oxford: Oxford University Press.

Schultz, B. (ed.) (1992) *Essays on Henry Sidgwick*, Cambridge: Cambridge University Press.

——(2004) *Henry Sidgwick: The Eye of the Universe*, Cambridge: Cambridge University Press.

Sidgwick, H. (1876) Review of *Ethical Studies*, by F. H. Bradley, *Mind* 1 o.s.: 545–49; repr. as Ch. 22 of *Essays on Ethics and Method*, ed. M. G. Singer, Oxford: Oxford University Press, 2000.

——(1902) *The Ethics of Green, Spencer, and Martineau*, London: Macmillan. (Cited as *EGSM*.)

——(1907) *The Methods of Ethics*, 7th edn, London: Macmillan. (1st edn, 1874.) (Cited as *ME*.)

Wollheim, R. A. (1969) *F. H. Bradley*, rev. edn, Harmondsworth: Penguin Books.

Further reading

Bentham, J. (1970) *An Introduction to the Principles of Morals and Legislation*, ed. J. H. Burns and H. L. A. Hart, London: Athlone Press.

Bradley, F. H. (1935) *Collected Essays*, 2 vols, Oxford: Oxford University Press.

Brink, D. O. (2003) *Perfectionism and the Common Good: Themes in the Philosophy of T. H. Green*, Oxford: Oxford University Press.

Green, T. H. (1997/1885–8) *Complete Works*, 5 vols (incl. 2 additional vols), ed. P. Nicholson, Bristol: Thoemmes; 3 vols, repr. from *Works*, ed. R. L. Nettleship, 3 vols, London: Longmans, Green & Co.

Mill, J. S. (1985) *Utilitarianism*, vol. 10 of *Collected Works of John Stuart Mill*, Toronto and Buffalo: University of Toronto Press; originally published 1863.

Rashdall, H. (1924) *Theory of Good and Evil*, 2 vols, 2nd edn, Oxford: Oxford University Press; 1st edn, 1907.
Schneewind, J. B. (1977) *Sidgwick's Ethics and Victorian Moral Philosophy*, Oxford: Oxford University Press.
Sidgwick, H. (2000) *Essays on Ethics and Method*, ed. M. G. Singer, Oxford: Oxford University Press.

18
NIETZSCHE

Maudemarie Clark

This chapter will focus on two interconnected elements of Nietzsche's philosophy that are the most important for understanding his place in the history of ethics and his relevance to contemporary theorizing about morality: his critique of morality and his naturalistic account of the origins and development of morality.

Nietzsche's most striking contribution to ethics is his self-proclaimed "denial of morality." Claiming to be an "immoralist," indeed the "first immoralist," he not only denies that morality has a right to our adherence but also insists that morality is something bad that ought to be overcome. He thus denies both the authority and the value of morality. It is his articulation and defense of this immoralist stance that establishes Nietzsche's distinctive place in the history of ethics, and will therefore be the focus here. His account of the origins and development of morality will be the other main topic of discussion because questions about both the scope and the substance of his critique of morality are best answered by considering this account, which is also of independent importance as a sophisticated example of what it is to naturalize morality that stands in some contrast to other attempts to show that we can understand morality's existence without supernatural or metaphysical assumptions.

The scope problem

The first thing we need to know about Nietzsche's anti-morality stance concerns its *object or scope*. Is it really morality itself that he rejects, or is it only a particular morality or type of morality, say, Christian morality? Some have chosen the latter option, wondering how one could coherently question the *value* of morality. If moral values are defined as those that are overriding, as some have claimed, then they cannot be coherently questioned or rejected. But in most relevant passages, Nietzsche seems to be rejecting morality itself, and he makes explicit in at least one passage that the object of his suspicion is "all moralities" (1998/1887, *Genealogy of Morality*, GM Preface). Philippa Foot was one of the first of recent interpreters to take Nietzsche at his word here. But because he insists that morality is bad, and not just that it lacks authority (that we have no reason to abide by it), Foot concluded that he himself must be arguing against morality from the viewpoint of some other species of value. She found a basis for taking Nietzsche at his word that he was an immoralist rather than a "special kind of moralist" by seeing him as willing "to throw out justice in the interests of producing a stronger and more splendid type of man" (Foot 1978: 166), for she saw justice, but not the production of splendid humans, as conceptually tied to morality. She took Nietzsche's admiration for such splendid beings as analogous to aesthetic evaluation and its judgments of beauty or sublimity. But Foot overlooked Nietzsche's claim that "higher moralities" are, or ought to be, possible (1973/1886, *Beyond Good and Evil*, *BGE* §202), with its suggestion that Nietzsche rejects the value of morality from the viewpoint of such a "higher morality." We can still make sense of his claim to reject "all moralities" if he is using "morality" in two different senses, and this is exactly what he implies in *BGE* §32, where he makes explicit that it is only morality "in the narrower sense" that he seeks to overcome.

Bernard Williams' distinction between ethics and morality gives us a helpful way of formulating Nietzsche's implicit distinction between the wide and narrow sense of "morality." Some use "morality" to mark off a part of the larger domain of the ethical, namely, the part having to do with duty and obligation, and believe that they are following Williams in doing so. But Williams treats morality as an instance rather than as a part of the ethical. What counts as an *ethics* for Williams is "any scheme for regulating the relations between people that works through informal sanctions and internalized dispositions" (Williams 1995: 241), dispositions to accept the *legitimacy* of demands made upon one by the system. Morality, on the other hand, is a particular ethical orientation, or a "range" of such outlooks, which is "so much with us," according to Williams, "that moral philosophy spends much of its time discussing the differences between these outlooks, rather than the difference between all of them and everything else" (Williams 1985: 174). Yet, all of these different moral outlooks are variations on a particular kind of ethical orientation that Williams thinks we would be "better off without."

This is precisely Nietzsche's position. He thinks that what we call "morality" (or at least did call "morality" when he was writing) is "so much with us" because it presents itself as the only possible form of ethical life. He is an immoralist, only if one is using "morality" in the narrower sense; he does not reject all regulatory systems that rely on "informal sanctions and internalized dispositions." Yet he does reject both the authority and the value of the form of ethical life that now goes by the name "morality" and which he thinks claims to be the only form of ethical life. What Foot missed about Nietzsche's position when she tried to ground it in the priority of aesthetic values was the possibility that his rejection of morality was part of a defense of an alternative ethical orientation. At the very least, she shows no signs of appreciating that Nietzsche took morality to be only one of the possibilities for ethical life, perhaps because she herself took it to be the only one.

Defining morality

What we need next is a definition or specification of morality, the form of ethical life that Nietzsche seeks to overcome. Unfortunately, this is not easy to provide, and Nietzsche tells us why, namely, that it is impossible to define anything that has a complicated history. One might try to sidestep this problem, as Brian Leiter influentially attempts to do, by going directly to Nietzsche's critique of morality, constructing the object of Nietzsche's critique from his objections to it. Leiter calls this object "morality in the pejorative sense" (MPS), which he offers as a heuristic category rather than an historical one. Leiter constructs the norms that belong to MPS from Nietzsche's "disparate critical remarks – about altruism, happiness, pity, equality, Kantian respect for persons, utilitarianism, etc." (Leiter 2002: 129). An MPS is thus an ethical system that has a pro-attitude towards, among other things, happiness, altruism, and equality. Although this approach has some appeal – after all, what we want to know is what Nietzsche is against – it also has a downside. For we also want to know if it is really morality that Nietzsche is attacking, and Leiter's account leaves it unclear whether Nietzsche's alleged objections to MPS are actually objections to morality. Leiter takes Nietzsche's objection to MPS to be that "a culture in which such norms prevail as morality will be a culture which eliminates the conditions for the realization of human excellence – the latter requiring, on Nietzsche's view, concern for self, suffering, a certain stoic indifference, a sense of hierarchy and difference, and the like." Leiter's most plausible example of how this can work concerns happiness. A culture permeated with a pro-attitude towards happiness and a con-attitude towards suffering will make it more difficult for creative human beings, great artists and thinkers – Nietzsche's higher human types, according to Leiter – to fulfill their potential: to endure and even welcome the suffering necessary for the realization of that potential, instead of squandering themselves in the pursuit of happiness. But does morality actually embrace happiness as a norm, or create a culture that does? Although contemporary secular culture embraces happiness as a norm, it seems to be the antithesis of a moral culture, which would seem to promote the fulfillment of duty and the striving to be a good person, not the striving for one's own happiness. So granting that one of Nietzsche's major criticisms of morality is that it produces the contemptible "last man" who cares only about happiness, it is difficult to gather from Leiter's account how *morality* is supposed to be responsible for this. It is also difficult to understand why Nietzsche is so horrified by morality. Even if it does work against the existence of higher types, that doesn't seem enough to account for the sense one gets from Nietzsche that morality is "against life" and has turned humanity itself into a diseased and botched species.

Nietzsche's *Genealogy of Morality*

For an understanding of these matters, the best approach is to consult Nietzsche's *On the Genealogy of Morality* (*GM*), which offers a genealogy of the form of ethical life that he seeks to overcome. It does so, in part, because Nietzsche thinks genealogy is the only way to clarify the concept of morality, to get clear on what that particular form of ethical life is. In a late stage of development, he claims, the concept of any practice that has a history will involve "an entire synthesis of 'meanings'" that have "finally crystallize[d] into a kind of unity which is difficult to dissolve, difficult to analyze, and – one must emphasize – is completely and utterly undefinable" (*GM* Treatise 2, §13). But if we are thus unable to "define" morality, establishing necessary and sufficient conditions for a set of practices to count as an instance of this concept, Nietzsche proceeds to point out an alternative way of analyzing it: to look back to earlier stages of its development, where "that synthesis of meanings still appears more soluble, also more capable of shifts," and one can "still perceive" how the elements of the synthesis change their valence and rearrange themselves accordingly. The concept is thus like a rope, held together by the intertwining of its strands, so that analyzing it is not a matter of isolating a core or essence, but of disentangling its various strands so that one can see what is actually involved in it. This is what Nietzsche aims to do in *GM*. By going back to an "earlier stage," he attempts to sort out various strands that are synthesized into our concept of morality and to explain how they came to be synthesized in this way.

GM contains three treatises, each of which traces a particular strand of the concept of morality back to an earlier form. In a postcard to his friend Overbeck (4 January 1888, in Risse 2001: 55), Nietzsche explains that in *GM*, "it was necessary, for the sake of clarity, to isolate artificially the different roots of the complex structure that is called morality." Nietzsche thus indicates that the object for which he is attempting to provide a genealogy is a "complex structure," a synthesis of several distinct elements, and that *GM* deals with these elements in abstraction from their actual involvement with each other in the development of morality. The remainder of the postcard makes clear that Nietzsche is well aware that *GM* leaves out several elements that are involved in the synthesis that is morality, in particular, the "herd instinct," which he calls "the most essential one," and that it does not put them together to provide "a final account of morality." This has important implications for how we should understand *GM*.

The slave revolt in morality

The first treatise (*GM* 1) is infamous for its claim that our morality is the product of a "slave revolt" fueled by *ressentiment* directed towards the nobles of the ancient world. The French "*ressentiment*" is close to the English "resentment," which is a human reaction to feeling slighted. According to Nietzsche's analysis, resentment becomes grudge-laden and poisonous among those who are powerless and therefore unable simply to shake off the (occasional) slight or to discharge the resulting resentment by standing up to the offender and demanding proper treatment or lashing out at him. The slave revolt he posits took place over a long period of time, and was originally led not by slaves, but by religious leaders who considered themselves good, and felt envious of and slighted by the nobles who ruled them with all too much self-confidence in their own superiority. Unable to assert themselves directly against the nobles, they lashed out at them in the only way they could, by devaluing them. The ultimate upshot is a *revaluation* – a reversal – of the noble values. The poor, meek and humble are declared "the good," and the nobles are claimed to be "'the evil, the cruel, the lustful, the insatiable, the godless, [who] will eternally be the wretched, accursed, and damned.'" Nietzsche claims that the slave revolt began with the Jews, but eventually led to the proclamation of the Christian beatitudes. Qualities that slaves needed to develop, such as meekness and humility, came to be seen as virtues (leading eventually to the view that altruism is the essence of virtue), whereas pride, the ultimate noble virtue (even in Aristotle), came to be seen as evil and the essence of sin – not because anyone admired the slavish virtues or wanted to exemplify them, but out of hatred towards and a need for revenge against the nobles, a need to "bring them down," if only in imagination.

However, it is important to recognize that it is not our entire morality – e.g. our notion of right and wrong – that Nietzsche takes to be a product of a slave revolt, but only our idea of goodness or virtue. *GM* 2 argues on etymological grounds that "good" was originally equivalent to "noble" in a purely political sense. It was used by ancient ruling groups to designate themselves as members of the politically superior class, in opposition to commoners and slaves. At this point, it is not an ethical term, much less a specifically moral one. It becomes an ethical term when it evolves into an idea of nobility (i.e. superiority) of soul, so that its contrasting term is equivalent to "bad" in our sense, and not merely "common." This happens because of the nobles' self-affirmation, which shows through in the words they use to describe themselves. Happy with their own existence, they naturally experienced their own lives as superior to the lives of those they ruled. Accordingly, "good" begins to express their sense of their own superiority, as do the other terms they use to distinguish themselves from commoners. For instance, they are not only "the good," but also "the rich" and "the powerful." The nobles' conception of what distinguishes them from commoners is fairly crude at first, but later begins to center on traits of soul or character, such as loyalty, truthfulness, and courage. They are "the truthful," for instance, as "distinct from the *lying* common man" (*GM* 1, §5). In this process, Nietzsche claims, "good" eventually loses all connection to political class and becomes a purely ethical notion, equivalent to virtuous or superior of soul. It is unclear, however, whether this is supposed to have actually happened already, or is being held out as a possible future development of the good/bad distinction. What is clear is that good/bad is not intended by Nietzsche as a moral distinction in the narrow sense. To call someone "bad" is certainly to call him a bad or inferior person, and not simply a commoner, and is therefore an ethical judgment. But it is not to call him "morally bad" or "evil."

The brilliance of Nietzsche's psychological analysis and the fact that his story has the leaders of the slave revolt exhibiting some of the same characteristics they themselves condemn make it tempting to locate his criticism of morality in his claim about its origins in resentment. But this would be an instance of the genetic fallacy, which he repudiates (1974/1887, *Gay Science*, *GS* §345). That humility was first put forward as a virtue by priests who were far from humble or that love was praised out of hatred does not show that humility and love are not virtues. And Nietzsche's whole approach makes clear that Christian virtues might be valued today for very different reasons than they were in the beginning.

The slave revolt plays such a central role in Nietzsche's account of the development of morality because it creates a *moralized* conception of a good person and a corresponding idea of an "*evil one*" (*GM* 1, §10), of a person who is not merely bad, but evil. To judge someone to be "bad," as Nietzsche is using that term, is to judge them to be inferior, but it does not imply that they are responsible for being inferior, much less that they deserve punishment for it. The appropriate response is pity or contempt, not condemnation. When "bad" is moralized into "evil," on the other hand, the person is held responsible for being the kind of person he is and condemned for it. This is how virtue and its opposite become connected to reward and punishment, which makes sense only on the assumption that we actually choose to be the kind of person we are, hence that we have free will in what Nietzsche calls "the superlative metaphysical sense," in which one is "*causa sui*," cause of oneself (*BGE* §21). This is the aspect of the slave revolt that Nietzsche most clearly criticizes. When he demands that the philosopher "take his stand beyond good and evil and leave the illusion of moral judgment beneath himself" (1954/1888, *Twilight of the Idols*, "Improvers," §1), he is referring to the judgment of persons in the moralized terms of good and evil. And his most obvious reason for taking such judgments to involve "illusion" is that they presuppose free will in a sense that he considers absurd, namely, that we are *causa sui* (*BGE* §21). But even if this is true – and many philosophers deny that morality requires free will in that sense – it does not explain why Nietzsche denies the *value* of morality, for he insists that "even if a morality has grown out of an error, the realization of this fact would not as much as touch the problem of its value" (*GS* §345). Explaining that the value of a "thou shalt" is independent of "opinions about its origin, religious sanction, the superstition of free will, and things of that sort," he concludes that "nobody up to now examined the value of that most famous of all medicines which is called morality: and the first step would be – for once to *question* it. Well then, precisely this is our task."

Cruelty and bad conscience

We must dig deeper into the matter, therefore, if we are to understand Nietzsche's critique of morality. We need especially to understand why he calls morality a "medicine." The best text for this purpose is the second treatise of *GM*, which does for moral right and wrong what *GM* 1 does for good and evil, tracing it back to a pre-moral version. Nietzsche calls this version the "morality of custom" (*Sittlichkeit der Sitte*), which is a system of mores and laws that regulated behavior in ancient communities. It was not an ethical system, much less an instance of morality, because it does not work through what Williams calls "informal sanctions and internalized dispositions," but only through punishment and the fear of it. Nietzsche assumes that the disposition to obey the rules has an older source than fear of punishment, namely, the herd instinct, the disposition to conform one's behavior to what those around one do, which he calls the "most essential" aspect of morality in the postcard quoted previously (p. 207). Customary practices thus constituted a kind of norm even before the institution of formal punishments. The disposition to conform one's behavior to customary practices would not count as an "internalized disposition," however, because it is purely a matter of instinct and does not yet carry with it ideas of authority or legitimacy. Rules obeyed only out of fear or instinct are not yet perceived as moral rules by those who are disposed to obey them. The main question Nietzsche pursues in *GM* 2 concerns how such non-moral rules, laws and customs were transformed into moral ones.

His basic answer is that this happened through the development of guilt. Rules and practices have the status of moral rules for those who take those who violate them to be guilty. But what is guilt? Nietzsche's complicated answer has two sides, one conceptual, the other explanatory or causal. First, he argues, partly on etymological grounds, that "the central moral concept 'guilt'" originates in "the very material concept 'debt'" (*GM* 2, §4) – indeed, in German, the same word (*Schuld*) is used for both; second, he traces a process that transformed debt into guilt. His account begins on the conceptual side. The relationship between the community and its members was taken to be analogous to a creditor/debtor relationship. Obedience to the rules necessary for community life was conceived of as something one *owes* the community, a debt one incurs in exchange for the advantages of community life. This is the original idea of *obligation*. It is a primitive ethical idea because it is connected to ideas of legitimacy and fairness, as

Nietzsche brings out by claiming that one who disobeys the rules is conceived of as "a debtor who not only fails to pay back his creditor, but also even lays a hand on his creditor; he therefore not only forfeits all of these goods and advantages from now on, as is fair, – he is now also reminded *how much there is to these goods*."

> The anger of the injured creditor, of the community, gives him back again to the wild and outlawed condition from which he was previously protected: it expels him from itself, and now every kind of hostility may vent itself on him. At this level of civilization "punishment" is simply the copy, the *mimus* of normal behavior towards the hated, disarmed, defeated enemy, who has forfeited not only every right and protection, but also every mercy.
>
> (GM 2, §21)

So this "punishment" (the harm inflicted on the offender beyond banishment) is not yet thought of as something the offender deserves. It is simply what one is permitted to do to those who are not part of the community. This does not yet give us the thought that one who fails to live by the rules of the community is guilty, that he deserves blame and punishment.

That idea begins to come into view only when the community grows stronger, so that violations of its rules are no longer as dangerous to the "continued existence of the whole." Becoming "more humane," the creditor finds a way to separate the criminal from his deed, allowing him to remain in the community by offering him a substitute way of paying off his debt. Just as Shylock is permitted by law to take a pound of flesh as a substitute for the debt he is owed in *The Merchant of Venice*, the community extracts from those who have violated their agreement to abide by the rules a substitute payment in the form of the offender's suffering. Punishment is now no longer a mere venting of hostility on a defenseless "enemy of the people," but is a way in which one pays off one's debt to society. We have here the beginning of the idea that the offender *deserves* his punishment, which is also an *ethical* idea because of its connection to ideas of fairness and legitimacy. The offender did the deed, thereby breaking the rules and reneging on his promise; therefore it is fair that he be punished. But if we can therefore say that he is judged to be *guilty*, this is primitive guilt, still just a debt that can be paid off, and not the moralized idea of guilt that Nietzsche is after. To see how he thinks debt or guilt become moralized, it is necessary to consider the other side of his story.

Note first that Nietzsche's account of punishment as a way to pay off one's debt assumes that human beings find satisfaction in the suffering of others. It would otherwise make no sense that they accept someone's suffering as a substitute payment for obeying the community rules. This aspect of his theory is often connected to his idea of the will to power, but it is controversial how large a role this idea actually plays in his philosophy (Clark 1990; Reginster 2006) and there is no need to bring it in to understand the point at issue here. It is difficult to deny that violence and cruelty have played a huge part in human history, and Nietzsche's theory attempts to explain why. The key point here is that a stable society is impossible without restrictions on the expression of aggressive impulses. Such impulses, a product of natural selection because of the advantages they confer in the wild for hunting and dealing with predators, cannot be directed towards other members of the community, at least not in their original form. Nietzsche thinks societies discourage such behavior both by punishments and by providing alternative outlets for aggressive impulses. Among these are various hierarchical arrangements, including military organizations, athletics and other contests, and the spectator sports of ancient Rome, in which the tendency of human beings towards cruelty is particularly apparent. This tendency towards cruelty is what allows the idea of paying one's debt to society through one's own suffering to make sense. But Nietzsche need not say that human beings are cruel by nature, nor deny that they have altruistic impulses by way of natural selection. His point is that cruel impulses develop under the influence of living in society because of the various things that happen to aggressive impulses, which human beings also have by means of natural selection, under the pressure of the need to suppress them and the further stimulation these impulses receive through the development of alternative means for satisfying them. These are ideas that were developed further by Freud.

Nietzsche is particularly interested in aggressive and cruel impulses because the redirection of these impulses back against the self is the other side of his story concerning the development of guilt. He presents bad conscience, the "consciousness of guilt" (GM 2, §4), as having its origin in the sudden imposition of the constraints of peaceful society on a previously nomadic population (GM 2, §16). Because it happened so suddenly, there was no time to develop new instincts through natural selection or new means of satisfying the old instincts through culture. There was only one way of satisfying such instincts, which was to internalize them, to turn them back against the self. Not all internalization of hostile or aggressive impulses involves a sense of guilt. The animal "that beats itself raw on the bars of his cage" (GM 2, §16) may be internalizing aggressive impulses, but is not feeling guilty or exhibiting a bad conscience. It is only when one internalizes (adopts against oneself) the hostile attitude of one who thinks you *owe* him something, in particular that you deserve to suffer for what you owe him, that it starts to be recognizable as guilt. The process that turns debt into moral guilt is one in which human beings learn to use the idea of having reneged on a debt or obligation, and therefore being deserving of punishment, to take a stand against themselves, to criticize themselves, hence to cause themselves "pain after the *more natural* outlet for this *desire to cause pain* was blocked" (GM 2, §22). When this process is completed, one has an internalized disposition to obey the rules. One has installed in oneself a critical faculty (like Freud's superego) that is on guard against violations of the rules, and that judges one to be guilty (at least blameworthy and often deserving of punishment) if one violates them anyway. The rules have the status of categorical or moral imperatives for those who have developed this critical faculty. They are motivated to obey the rules not out of mere instinct or fear of punishment, but because of the values they themselves hold.

What, then, is Nietzsche's objection to morality? Recall that his "task" is to evaluate morality as a "medicine," and that his immoralism implies that he does not consider it very effective medicine. We can understand this in the following terms: The "sickness" for which morality is a medicine is the bad conscience, the need to internalize aggression and cruelty, the "will to self-maltreatment" (*GM* 2, §18). Such internalization doesn't happen automatically; some kind of reason or basis for it is necessary. Indeed, Nietzsche portrays those who are prevented from expressing aggressive impulses externally but who lack a basis for internalization as suffering from "physiological depression" and "listlessness" (*GM* 3, §§17–20). In the case at issue, if I am going to criticize and hold myself accountable for my behavior, there has to be some standard for correct behavior, and this is what morality supplies. But what, then, is the problem? Why isn't the moralization of guilt a perfect way of providing a safe channel for the expression of aggressive and even cruel impulses while at the same time giving a much-needed incentive for obedience to community standards?

If a "safe channel" is one that does not do damage to human beings and their potential, and morality provided such a channel for the expression of aggressive impulses, Nietzsche would have no objection. Contrary to the impression he makes on some readers, he does not wish to return us to the level of acting on brute instinct. He says that bad conscience is a sickness, "but a sickness as pregnancy is a sickness" (*GM* 2, §19), which means that he looks forward to the new birth to which it can lead, not backwards to a previous stage. But he believes that the moralization of guilt produced by the will to self-maltreatment leads to the infliction of gratuitous suffering, on self and others, in fact, that it promotes an endless cycle of aggression against self and others, which undermines vitality and creativity, and prevents human beings from realizing their highest potential. To get some idea of why he thinks this, we will consider all too briefly the role of the ascetic ideal in his account of morality.

The ascetic ideal

The ascetic ideal puts forward the life of self-denial as the ideal life. By devoting *GM* 3 to this ideal, Nietzsche indicates (as we can infer from the postcard quoted earlier, p. 207) that he considers it one of the main strands of morality. We can make sense of this in light of his claim that the moralization of guilt occurred through the "entanglement of the bad conscience with the concept of god"

(GM 2, §21), i.e. through the use of the concept of god for turning aggression back against the self, if we recognize that the concept of god in question is an ascetic one. Whereas the Greek gods were reflections of what the Greeks valued in themselves, according to Nietzsche, the Judeo-Christian God is the projection of a value human beings can never come close to attaining, a being who is the opposite of our own "inescapable animal instincts." This conception of the divine reflects the ascetic ideal and functions to internalize cruelty.

Nietzsche's idea is that contemplative types, originally priests, are the experts in internalizing aggressive impulses because their own nature disinclines them towards externalizing them. They therefore developed practices of self-denial and cruelty to self, which helps them to avoid the depression and listlessness that Nietzsche thinks would otherwise have afflicted them. But they needed a conscious reason to adopt the practices and found it in the ascetic ideal, which promotes the life of self-denial on the grounds that our life as animals, as part of "nature," has no value in itself, that it receives value only if "it were to turn against itself, *to negate itself*" (GM 3, §11), thus becoming a mere means to another mode of existence that is its opposite (e.g. nirvana, heaven). The ascetic life has no intrinsic appeal to most people. Nietzsche's suggestion is that ascetic priests taught non-reflective types, who were prevented from externalizing aggressive and cruel impulses almost exclusively by fear of punishment, how to use the idea of debt to internalize these impulses. They took over from non-ascetic or pagan priests the teaching that we owe a debt to some divine being and must pay it off with sacrifices or risk terrible consequences. The sacrifices demanded are material, e.g. the best cuts of meat (of which the priests make good use), although things can get much more serious, as when Agamemnon must sacrifice his own daughter to ensure the success of his fleet. The ascetic ideal is not at work here; there is no implication that the sacrifice is demanded because nature is of no value or that sensuality is to be overcome. But that is the implication when ascetic priests insist that we must sacrifice our nature as animal and therefore desiring beings. Ascetic priests use this framework to explain to the people the source of their suffering (which actually comes from having no way to organize and discharge instinctual drives): God is punishing them for disobeying him, indeed for rebelling against him. Their rebellion is a matter of affirming their "inescapable animal instincts," for God, as pure spirit, is the opposite of such instincts. In affirming them, as our nature inclines us to do, we are in effect saying that we do not need God, that "this life" is enough, which is pride, the essence of sin. We therefore deserve punishment. But the debt we therefore owe cannot be paid off, even in principle, because it is rooted in our very nature and connected to our worth as persons (Clark 2002, 1994). This is what makes it moral guilt as opposed to primitive guilt or mere debt. And the debt that cannot be discharged gives rise to the idea of eternal punishment, in which Nietzsche sees "a kind of madness of the will in psychic cruelty that has absolutely no equal: the *will* of man to find himself guilty and reprehensible to the point that it cannot be atoned for ... his *will* to erect an ideal – that of the 'holy God' – in order, in the face of the same, to be tangibly certain of his own unworthiness." Adding "Oh, this insane sad beast man," Nietzsche suggests that our ideas became "bestial" to the extent that we were prevented from acting like beasts (*GM* 2, §22).

Granting that the "self-crucifixion" at issue here is sad and insane, we may still wonder if this is really a problem for morality, for even if the ascetic ideal functioned to moralize guilt, secularized contemporary morality seems to get on quite well without it. Isn't Nietzsche's objection only to a particular and old-fashioned conception of morality, one that demands sacrifice of our natural instincts? He would deny this. The ascetic ideal seems absent from secularized morality because of factors that belong only to the exterior or appearance of the ideal – e.g. belief in God and an explicit demand for the denial of sensuality. But Nietzsche insists that the ascetic ideal itself is responsible for this situation, and that its work is far from over once these factors are gone. It was an ever-deepening cruelty to self and demand for self-denial, imposed by the ascetic ideal on higher or more spiritual types in the form of a "will to truth" (*GM* 3, §§23–8), that led to the "sacrifice [of] everything comforting, holy, healing" in the ascetic ideal, "all hope, all faith in a concealed harmony, in a future bliss and justice" (*BGE* §55), thus everything that appeals to less spiritual people. Now all that remains for higher culture to do is to devote itself to destroying more and more of its own basis, which, according to Nietzsche, is the desire for higher states of soul, which in fact cannot be possessed by everyone. Using the conception of virtue derived from the slave revolt in morality as a basis for further internalization of cruelty, it turns against the desire for and belief in distinction, thereby depriving higher culture of much capacity to inspire, and depriving less spiritual types of any belief in the possibility of a higher type of human than they themselves are. Lower culture becomes unleashed from the ascetic ideal, becoming cruder and more oriented towards material things. Morality is now reduced to "herd animal morality," based largely on prudence and conformity. The reign of the "last man" threatens because we now lack any ideal that could inspire us to care about much beyond our own happiness.

Does Nietzsche have an alternative in mind? No doubt. His critique of morality, the attempt to show how morality and its "medicine" have gotten us into this depressing situation, is only part of his project, the no-saying part. There is also the yes-saying part, which is the attempt to show us glimpses of a new life-affirming ideal that could play the same kind of role in a new form of ethical life that the ascetic ideal played in bringing about the moralized form. Such an ideal cannot be adopted at will, but can only emerge in the new ways of seeing and feeling that come from thinking through the old ideal and its role in making us who we are now. Nor would a new ideal have to create a new form of ethical life from scratch. Nietzsche's genealogy of morality shows us that there are important ethical resources on which it can rely, e.g. pre-moral notions of virtue, obligation, and guilt. Synthesizing these notions in a new way would be an important part of its task (Clark 2002), as would pointing us towards new sublimated ways of dealing with the instinctual impulses that the ascetic ideal has directed back against the self. This is a major function of Nietzsche's books and goes a long way towards explaining why he writes the way he does.

See also Morality and its critics (Chapter 45).

References

Clark, M. (1990) *Nietzsche on Truth and Philosophy*, Cambridge: Cambridge University Press.

——(1994) "Nietzsche's Immoralism and the Concept of Morality," in R. Schacht (ed.) *Nietzsche, Genealogy, Morality: Essays on Nietzsche's Genealogy of Morals*, Berkeley: University of California Press.

——(2002) "On the Rejection of Morality: Bernard Williams's Debt to Nietzsche," in R. Schacht (ed.) *Nietzsche's Postmoralism*, Cambridge: Cambridge University Press.

Foot, P. (1978/1973) "Nietzsche: The Revaluation of Values," in *Virtues and Vices*, Berkeley, CA: University of California Press; originally published in R. Solomon (ed.) *Nietzsche: A Collection of Critical Essays*, New York: Doubleday.

——(1994/1991) "Nietzsche's Immoralism," in R. Schacht (ed.) *Nietzsche, Genealogy, Morality: Essays on Nietzsche's Genealogy of Morals*, Berkeley, CA: University of California Press; originally published in *New York Review of Books* 38: 11, 18–22.

Leiter, B. (2002) *Nietzsche on Morality*, London: Routledge.

Nietzsche, F. (1954/1888) *Twilight of the Idols*, trans. W. Kaufmann, in *The Portable Nietzsche*, New York: Viking Penguin.

——(1973/1886) *Beyond Good and Evil*, trans. R. J. Hollingdale, London: Penguin Books. (Cited as *BGE*.)

——(1974/1887) *The Gay Science*, trans. Walter Kaufmann, New York: Vintage. (Cited as *GS*.)

——(1998/1887) *On the Genealogy of Morality*, trans. M. Clark and A. Swensen, Indianapolis, In: Hackett. (Cited as *GM*.)

Reginster, B. (2006) *The Affirmation of Life*, Cambridge, MA: Harvard University Press.

Risse, M. (2001) "The Second Treatise in *On the Genealogy of Morality*: Nietzsche on the Origin of the Bad Conscience," *European Journal of Philosophy* 9, no. 1: 55–81.

Williams, B. (1985) *Ethics and the Limits of Philosophy*, Cambridge, MA: Harvard University Press.

——(1995) "Moral Luck: A Postscript," in *Making Sense of Humanity*, Cambridge: Cambridge University Press.

19
PRAGMATIST MORAL PHILOSOPHY

Alan J. Ryan

To borrow a very old joke, writing about pragmatist moral philosophy is like writing about snakes in Ireland. There are no snakes in Ireland. It will be objected that Dewey published a very substantial volume entitled *Ethics*, and that this was no youthful error, but a work first published in 1907 when Dewey was 42 years old and republished in revised form in 1932, when he was 73 (Dewey 1932/1907). The response to that objection is the subject of this chapter. I rely here on the distinction between what I describe in a wholly friendly fashion as *pragmatist moralizing* (by which I mean the articulation of the morality implicit in pragmatism) and *moral philosophy* – by which the pragmatists discussed here understood the attempt to uncover by philosophical means the foundations of morality. The paradigms of moral philosophy so understood are the moral theories of Plato and Kant, the main targets of Dewey's complaints against "apart thinking." Pragmatist moralizing is philosophical in the extended sense that it implies a view both about what is wrong with moral theorizing in a Kantian or Platonic vein and about what should replace it. In the same way as Wittgenstein's later philosophy, pragmatist reflection on ethics attempts to abolish (one part of) philosophy by philosophical means, and induces the same anxiety about how to describe the activity that is not philosophy in the disapproved sense but looks very like a form of philosophy.

Here, pragmatism is represented by the work of William James, John Dewey, and Richard Rorty. Indeed, it is really represented by the work of James, with a *coda* picking up the ways in which Dewey and Rorty are unlike James and one another. This slights others, but these three cover a sufficient range. What fol lows is writer-by-writer rather than topic-by-topic. In the light of James's obse rvation that the genesis and acceptance of philosophical doctrines have much to do with the temperament of the philosopher who puts them forward or accepts them, we should recall that these three thinkers were temperamentally dissimilar. We should also recall that a disbelief in the value (or existence or possibility) of moral philosophy may lead to many different destinations. Be rnard Williams's cutting observation that moral philosophy had taken as its main task that of making the world safe for well-intentioned persons could not have been uttered by Dewey. Contempt for the well-intentioned would have offended Dewey's democratic sensibilities. Dewey had his own complaints against moral philos ophers; moral philosophy had not set out to make the world safe for well-intentioned persons but to replicate the authority relations of priest and congregation in the relations of the enlightened philosopher and the "plain man." James, conscious of his heritage as a Boston Brahmin, thought that the upper classes owed to society at large a duty to think seriously about the moral and political challenges their society faced, but, as his frequent invocations of the poetry of Whitman suggest, it was a duty the advantaged owe to the less advantaged in a democracy, not the transmission of arcane knowledge to the ignorant.

I

A short historical excursus may be useful. The origins of pragmatism are disputed. Conventionally, accounts begin with C. S. Peirce's 1878 article on "How to Make Our Ideas Clear," but Peirce was unhappy with his own formulations of pragmatism and unhappier still with the use that James – a lifelong friend – made of the term; Peirce finally described his own view as "pragmaticist," on the grounds that "pragmaticism" was too ugly a term for anyone else to steal. Peirce had no time for Dewey when he taught him as a graduate student at Johns Hopkins, nor thereafter. He cared little for the issues that attracted moral and political theorists. The key thought in Peirce's formulation is that we become completely "clear" about a concept, or attain what he called the third level of clarity, only when we can give an account of its bearing on experimental situations. Knowing what entity a concept picks out is "knowing what would happen to it if … ." It is a form of experimentalism. Peirce attacked ontology-obsessed forms of metaphysics and hoped to replace questions about the ultimate constituents of reality with questions about what we could infer from repeatable experiments. James, on the other hand, described pragmatism as "a new name for some old ways of thinking," and dedicated *Pragmatism* to the memory of John Stuart Mill, whom he "liked to fancy as our leader" (James 2000: 3). (The dedication reads "to the memory of John Stuart Mill from whom I first learned the pragmatic openness of mind and whom my fancy likes to picture as our leader were he alive today.") Much in J. S. Mill lies easily enough alongside pragmatist epistemology; the empiricism of Mill's analysis of mathematics is radical enough for any radical empiricist, prefiguring as it does Quine's insistence that even the truths of mathematics and logic were revisable if experience should call for their revision. In an American context, the fact that Mill was the great critic of the "philosophy of the conditioned" that Sir William Hamilton constructed in the first few decades of the nineteenth century and that James McCosh had taken with him to the College of New Jersey in Princeton drew a useful dividing line.

James famously had no philosophical training. Born in 1842 to a Swedenborgian pastor of eclectic theological tastes, James was educated at the Lawrence Scientific School. Although his enormous *Principles of Psychology* relies on the results of introspection too much for twentieth-century tastes, both in execution and intention it is a scientific work. James moved more easily than we between an interest in what we in fact believe, which later writers would have thought unequivocally a matter of psychology, and an interest in our right to believe what we believe, which later writers would have thought a matter of logic or epistemology. The famous paper on *The Will to Believe* would – James later agreed with some of his critics – have been better entitled *The Right to Believe*. Austere critics have always said that a well-controlled will to believe is a will to believe only what is true, or well-attested, and that our right to believe extends no further than the right to believe what is true, or well-attested. James turned the thought around. What is true is a matter of how a belief stacks up against our purposes. Particular purposes are to be judged by how they stack up against our wider and well-considered purposes; this is very far from the thought that we may believe any old nonsense that we find either consoling or inspiring. The notion that we should believe what is most fruitful for the achievement of our purposes is non-scandalous when set against the background of an evolutionary perspective that says that the human race would have been very ill-advised to see no difference between poisonous and non-poisonous plants, or between animals that we might eat and those that might eat us. The difficulty lies in knowing what evolutionary or quasi-evolutionary pressures operate in the present. I say "quasi-evolutionary" to cover such practices as scientific experimentation or democratic voting, which are intended to eliminate error. Popper thought that the scientific community provides by artifice an environment designed to ensure the survival of the epistemically fittest views of reality; James and Dewey thought of everyday life itself as having an experimental character, though what this entailed is something to be scrutinized more carefully than we can do here. The presumption is not that we are licensed to believe whatever we choose but that the beliefs that underpin a psychologically healthy, happy, and harmonious existence are properly praised as "true."

Naturalism – in this sense – was a central feature of pragmatism. James appears to have been led there by his own temperament, which was as it should have been, given his view of philosophy as an expression of the philosopher's temperament. This was less true of Dewey. Born seventeen years after James, Dewey was initially immersed in the intuitionism of McCosh's disciples, and in the self-abnegating Congregationalist faith of his mother. Although he was a graduate student at Johns Hopkins during C. S. Peirce's brief stay there, he got nothing out of Peirce, and followed the dilute intuitionism of G. S. Morris. During this period, which ended in the mid-1890s, he wrote some interesting papers on such topics as the relationship between poetry and morality and the relationship between Christianity and democracy. At this stage of his life, Dewey certainly wrote moral philosophy, no matter how one glosses the term. His views were very like T. H. Green's. In terms of his non-philosophical allegiances, he largely remained a communitarian liberal. Like Green, he disliked the collectivist implications of a thoroughgoing Hegelianism, and insisted that ideals must be realized by individuals. But the individual was not an abstraction from society. To be an individual was to be an individual in relationship to other individuals and to the cultural world they collectively created and drew on to find a meaning in their lives. He later complained that critics exaggerated the Hegelianism of his subsequent work, but admitted that Hegel had left a permanent residue in his thought. This is true enough in the sense that Hegel had repudiated the "either–or" of Kant's division of the world into the phenomenal and the noumenal and Dewey was deeply hostile to what he termed "apart thinking," which for him was typified by the Kantian dichotomy between the is and the ought, the sensory world and the noumenal world of ends. It is not surprising that much of Dewey's early ethical writing – not only his moral philosophy but his work on politics, community activism, the role of the church in a secular age, and even on the contribution of poetry to ethics – reflected this liberal communitarianism.

One final parenthesis is needed. Some of Dewey's most interesting ideas about practical matters were not, on his own account, pragmatist. This is true of much that he wrote after 1910. The explanation is simple. Dewey insisted that pragmatism was a theory of truth. This sounded bleaker than he intended, because Dewey did not insist on drawing a sharp line between a theory of meaning and a theory of truth; his insistence that a proposition's truth was a matter of what difference it made to the conduct of life and thus to future experience is close to Wittgenstein's insistence that we should look to the use we make of propositions in everyday life. Dewey's critics accused him and other pragmatists of saying that propositions about the distant past were "really" about the future; but when James and Dewey said that the meaning of a proposition was to be found in the difference it made to our practice, it was more nearly a banality than an outrage. A man who believes that the battle of Naseby occurred at a particular place and time takes his metal detector to the appropriate place expecting to find artifacts from the seventeenth century rather than the thirteenth.

Dewey eventually placed the enhancement of experience rather than truth at the center of his concerns. *Art as Experience* is aimed at enhancing our ability to derive from the experience of works of art all the artist has, wittingly and unwittingly, put in front of us. Indeed, it is characteristic of Dewey's discussion of art that he readily assimilates such things as the movements of a cat or the ease with which Mohawk Indian scaffolders worked on top of New York skyscrapers to the made and intended art objects that hang on the walls of galleries. The implications for Dewey's view of ethics are not wholly clear, but his hostility to the very idea of the "specialness" of art suggests how strongly Dewey felt that what was wanted was close attention to "the problems of men" rather than "the problems of philosophy." One implication, made much of by Richard

Rorty towards the end of his life, was that the philosopher should not stand apart from her or his society. There is a great deal that might be said about James's aristocratic ambitions for "the college educated," as against Dewey's more determinedly democratic approach and Rorty's occasional suggestion that almost anyone other than the philosopher might help us to realize our better natures; but the crux is that in practical matters we are in the thick of events, and that philosophers should try to assist their fellows to lead productive and interesting lives, and not seek to deliver a message about transcendental truths. The thought is as old as Aristotle's complaint against Plato that Plato looked for the truth, but that ethics should be studied for the sake of action.

II

Reading James is such a pleasure that it is tempting to provide a few paragraphs of direct quotation and leave James to speak for himself; of all philosophers, he stands least in need of an interpreter. Still, there are two or three features of James's work that will bear emphasis. First, he was an indeterminist. He thought that our conviction that we face genuine choices, and that these are not antecedently determined, was both unshakeable and justified by our experience of reality. This view is unusual in modern philosophy, but was shared by Isaiah Berlin among others. It sits naturally with a second distinctive feature of James's philosophy, which was a radical pluralism. The thought that the universe is plural has puzzled many commentators; its motivation is less puzzling. James was, for complicated reasons, anxious to espouse an inclusive rather than an exclusive ontology; the world could contain the insights of physics along with the insights of poetry and religion. One suspects that he was pressing hard on the reactions of readers when insisting that "God is real," but the thought is less shocking than the expression. Given that the universe does not reveal itself to us with an account of how it wishes to be characterized, an indefinite number of descriptions of how things are may be fruitful, some of which may invoke the thought of a deity presiding over our destinies. Diehard atheists like myself resist the thought that we cannot say, "however useful God-talk may be to some people, there is not and never has been any such entity as God." But even the diehard has to accept that *arguing* believers out of their faith is a fruitless occupation, while *weaning* them off it is altogether more possible. James's pluralism is more unassimilable than Nietzsche's perspectivalism, since we manifestly do see the world from multiple different vantage points and what we say about it reflects how it appears from those vantage points. The thought that the world is itself plural is less easy to grasp.

One way of doing some justice to the thought rests on a third thing to notice about James, and Dewey too. They are anti-reductive inasmuch as they do not suggest that one account of how things are has priority over all others. There has been a tendency within empiricism since Locke to think that the world "really is" as it is described in the language of physics – possessed only of Lockean primary qualities – and everything else we see, hear, and feel in our encounters with the world is plastered onto the underlying reality by ourselves. The pragmatist view was closer to what we find in Collingwood and Oakeshott. The "world" is not an underlying entity but our generic term for whatever is the object of experience. The austerities of the physical sciences do not better represent reality than the rhapsodies of the poets and painters; they merely abridge experience severely to handle particular aspects of it with the tools of mathematics. These are claims that can be made without delving far into James's views about truth and verification, but a fourth point is that James was inclined to use the term "true" to embrace not only "truth to fact" but "value in action." We are not, therefore, obliged to ask or answer the question of what facts about the world a poem expresses or a painting depicts.

What, then, is the upshot for James's view of moral philosophy? He answered the question in the essay that formed a chapter of *The Will to Believe*. In "The Moral Philosopher and the Moral Life," James emphasizes the role of experience in ethics and denounces any attempt to construct "an ethical philosophy dogmatically made up in advance" (James 2000: 242). He distinguishes three sorts of questions in ethics: *psychological*, *metaphysical* and *casuistic*. The first concerns the origins of out moral ideas and moral judgments, the second the meaning of terms such as "obligation" and the third the appropriate "measure" of the goods and evils of human life on the basis of which a philosopher "may settle the true order of human obligations" (243). One may wonder whether a philosopher has any particular standing in this matter, and James himself ends the essay with the claim that the ethical philosopher "whenever he ventures to say which course of action is best, is on no essentially different level from the common man." What James in fact does in the essay is something that only a philosopher could be imagined doing, but it is done with an informality and easiness of delivery appropriate to its original setting as a talk to students; this has not stopped critics trying to make it yield something more sophisticated than James intended.

At the simplest level, James commits himself to an empiricist view of his subject matter. Or rather, he follows Mill in holding that the objects of ethical interest must be objects of desire, and that much of what we think worth pursuing has become so by the association of ideas. In a less Millian vein, he also claims that some things present themselves to us as worthwhile simply as the deliverances of consciousness, probably because something in our brains sparks the attraction. Moreover, James does not assimilate all desire to a desire for happiness as Mill does. Indeed, although he talks about achieving the maximum satisfaction of our desires or of minimizing the obstruction of one desire by another – very much as Russell later did – he is not interested in pursuing a felicific calculus. The thought is more interesting. In a world with only one occupant, there would be no room for ethics. It is not quite clear that James should have said this on his own premises, because he frequently treats the question of which of our own individual goals to pursue and at what cost as an ethical question. Nonetheless, it is clear enough where the argument is headed. A world with more than one individual is a world in which the aims of two or more different persons exist. These aims may diverge in such a way that they cannot both be satisfied at once. This is familiar territory. The interesting aspect of James's development of the argument is the thought that even then there may be no "ethics" in the situation. The ethical perspective comes into existence only when one agent takes the other agent's aims into account when framing his own decisions.

That raises the "casuistic" question. How should we take each other's aims into account, to rank our claims alongside theirs, and the urgency of some of our claims over others? James's views are mostly negative; that is, he denies – almost – that there can be the sort of perspective that Sidgwick described as "the point of view of the universe" which would yield the answer that a wholly rational agent would accept as binding on himself. Because of his respect for what it is that human beings actually desire and for its diversity, James follows Mill as far as insisting that ideals must be desired, then diverts towards the negative formulation described above, of thinking we should try to minimize the obstruction of one desire by another. The crucial thing is that success is always provisional. Just as every "truth" is revisable in the light of further experience, all ideals are provisional and open to revision. The distinctively Jamesian thought – in the light of which we must qualify the claim that James does not seek to occupy "the point of view of the universe" – is that, as he says elsewhere in *The Will to Believe*, we may imagine ourselves under the eyes of a God who sees the world as it truly is and ranks states of affairs as they truly should be ranked.

This adds nothing cognitively, but it encourages in us a "strenuous" attitude. This is part and parcel of James's preference for a universe which is not predeterminedly as good as it can be, but requires the active cooperation of human beings to make it better. The thought of a God who grasps all at once and all of a piece the goodness, badness, and potentiality for improvement of the world is not cognitively precise. That is no drawback. Cognitive precision is worth having for some purposes, but not always in practical life. When Matthew Arnold tried to capture the essence of religion, his notion of God was Jamesian: "an eternal power not ourselves that makes for righteousness" (Arnold 1873). "Righteousness" was too protestant a term for James, but the thought that we are cooperating with a force that sustains our efforts to behave well was not very different. It was, more surprisingly, not very different from Mill's reflections in *The Utility of Religion* and *Theism*. It is not moral philosophy as practiced in the analytical tradition since 1900, and a modern reader will find foreign its concern for the impact of moral reflection. James was anxious about what he saw as a form of moral exhaustion, especially in the young people training to be teachers to whom much of his popular writing was addressed. This is not the place for even a thumbnail sketch of the anxieties current in late nineteenth-century American higher education, but there was a widespread sense that well-educated young people, and especially women, were uncertain of their role in modern America. This was exacerbated by the diminishing hold of traditional religion, but much of it stemmed from the opening up of new career opportunities for educated women and the familiar first-generation uncertainty about whether to have a career at all, what ambitions to entertain, how to juggle domestic and career demands.

At all events, three features of James's writings on ethics distinguish his moral vision from that of Mill, whom he otherwise resembles as closely as he hoped. The first of the three features is the boldness with which James accepts that a central part of ethical commitment is in the last resort a matter of *taste*. Socrates's pleasures are not, *pace* Mill, pleasanter than those of the fool or the pig; rather, they are pleasures that we would wish to have because we would not wish to be fools or pigs. It is an exaggeration to say this is wholly unlike what Mill says, since Mill's early thoughts on the matter in his essay on Bentham and in the *System of Logic* are squarely based on the thought that it matters not only what we do but what manner of person we are. It is nonetheless very different from Mill's argument in *Utilitarianism*.

The second is James's insistence on allowing into the discussion as much of the ordinary ethical experience of humanity as possible. Mill was concerned to reform the way his readers thought about ethics, and therefore set out to do a lot of tidying up. James was hostile to premature tidiness in any field of inquiry, and may have thought that ethics was a field where tidiness came a poor second to richness of sympathy. This view has had a new lease of life since the 1950s in the work of writers such as Stuart Hampshire; the idea that different ideals pull us in different directions and that no uniquely rational resolution of the conflict is to be had is a Jamesian thought. Mill, for all his emphasis on the need for humanity to develop in innumerable contradictory directions, nonetheless thought that at the end of the day a rational consensus would obtain. Finally, James's openness to the thought that the universe might contain a spiritual reality with which we were intermittently in touch was much greater than Mill's. Mill offers a glimmer of light for anyone who wants to believe that there *might* be a deity, well-intentioned but far from omnipotent, but it is faint. Nor was that all; Mill's bleakness about the hospitality of nature to human existence was greater than James's. James's assurance that "all is well" was un-Millian. Mill was more inclined to emphasize the fact that nature kills us, tortures us with disease, kills our loved ones, and behaves in ways that, were they those of a sentient being, would be disgusting and sadistic. James was slow to contrast the human will for good with the obdurate resistance of Nature. And the James who longed for the psychical researchers to come up with something credible to show that we are in touch with a transcendent reality wanted the possibility that there are more things in heaven and earth than are dreamed of in our philosophy to remain both open and inspiring.

III

Dewey, for all his own and others' attempts to assimilate him to James, was a very different sort of moralist. He was a Heideggerian who decided that the quest for Being was a waste of everyone's time. At the heart of reality there is no mystery, and things are as careful investigation shows them to be. In a non-mysterious world, there is sufficient beauty and interest to engage any moderately well-attuned heart, but the attuning of those hearts is, for Dewey, a social and political as much as an individual and moral matter. Dewey wrote over a sixty-five-year period, and his earliest work is often pious and timid, and written in an intuitionist or Hegelian mode hard for a modern reader to penetrate. Even then, his less philosophically elaborate writing is infused with democratic utopianism. What follows is a short sketch of Dewey's thoughts on ethics, or rather Dewey's thoughts on intelligent action. One feature of Dewey's thinking that is disconcerting is that "intelligent action" is, in his little book on *Liberalism and Social Action*, the same thing as modern liberalism; his distaste for "apart thinking" led him to draw no distinction between ethics and politics, and for someone whose life was so bound up with public education, he was surprisingly uninterested in the way institutions structure our roles and duties. However, we shall not come to grief if we first consider what Dewey did when he wrote about ethics, essentially as part of the inescapable instruction of philosophy students, and secondly consider what Deweyan "moralizing" amounted to. To the extent that there are problems about this way of proceeding, they stem from the fact that Dewey left a great deal of the infilling of the second part of the *Ethics* to his old colleague James Tufts; but Tufts's views and Dewey's were just about indistinguishable. They had worked together in Chicago, and thought very similarly thereafter.

The first part of *Ethics* is a conventional analysis of moral concepts; conventional in the fashion of early twentieth-century American philosophy. It is not touched by the Vienna Circle austerities that were about to arrive in the United States. That means that to a late twentieth-century eye, the analysis moves disconcertingly back and forth between the linguistic and the psychological. Unlike post-1945 moral philosophers who would, for instance, have taken the analysis of the concept of obligation to require an account of when and why we feel linguistically constrained to say "I was obliged to do X" rather than "I should have done x," Dewey tries, as had Mill, to account for the origins of the sense that we are sometimes constrained more tightly by a duty than we are at other times, and pick out those times by saying "I am obliged" rather than "I should." The tone of the discussion is very different from the more pious tone struck by some of Dewey's little essays of the 1880s (e.g. 1969/1884), but the discussion belongs to nineteenth-century moral psychology. The framework is broadly evolutionary, which is again not surprising, since Dewey always subscribed to the view that there had been a slow process of enlightenment in the course of which humanity had gradually acquired a scientific understanding of the world. This understanding was fallibilist, tentative, always being remade; the hankering after the certainties of religion was probably ineradicable but in any event unhelpful. What we take for certainties are, on a pragmatist view, only those beliefs that we cannot think of any reason to question. They are not the deliverances of a deity or of any philosophical stand-in for a deity.

This returns us to the crucial point about the ways in which Dewey was and was not a moral philosopher at all. To the extent that any two terms encapsulate Dewey's thought, they are "problem-solving" and "growth." As he said during the First World War, he wanted philosophers to turn from the problems of philosophy to the problems of men. The problems he wanted them to explore were, mostly, the problems of "associated living." The enhancement of experience, which a work such as *Art as Experience* aimed at, was not placed in this problem-solving perspective, but books for teachers such as *How We Think* certainly were, even though the problem-solving they were concerned with was much more straightforwardly a matter of solving problems about cause and effect. "Growth," which was the key idea of Dewey's account of education, was left undefined, and deliberately so. To a tidy-minded reader, this is extremely irritating, but it was part and parcel of Dewey's insistence on the unfinishedness of experience. One might, after all, become more and more adept at something that after a decade one sees to be a complete waste of time and effort. What had seemed like growth would have turned out to be anything but. Dewey's response to demands for a tidy story about growth was that we know it when we see it. If education is like gardening, no single description of a flourishing plant is going to meet the case, especially when education is unlike gardening in the crucial respect that human beings do not belong to fixed species and genera. It is thus unsurprising that commentaries on Dewey's ethics almost always turn out to be commentaries on Dewey's conception of democracy, since "democracy" was defined by Dewey in terms of an intelligent society's attempts to think its way through the problems of associated living.

IV

Dewey's best-known, most imaginative, but most misleading disciple was Richard Rorty. Rorty carried Dewey's claim that what he was doing was in some sense post-philosophical to an extreme. It sometimes seemed that Rorty thought that almost everyone other than philosophers could contribute usefully to the discussion of the problems of associated living, and that poets, novelists, and ordinary citizens would do perfectly well if it were not for philosophers. The underlying thought was, however, exactly the same as it has always been in pragmatism: philosophy has no subject matter of its own. This is not an original thought with pragmatism, but it formed the centerpiece of the pragmatist insistence that philosophers could not supplant nor supervise shoemakers, boatbuilders, and car mechanics. It was what lay behind Dewey's urge that we should turn from the problems of philosophy to the problems of mankind; and it fueled the deconstructive urge in Rorty's reflections, not only on ethics and politics but science too.

In Rorty's work, the argument took a linguistic turn in the sense that the key idea was – often – that human beings tell stories about the world, organize those stories into connected wholes that they label "fact" and "fiction," "science" and "religion," and that these stories do not, singly or collectively, "mirror nature." The question whether they are constrained by the way the world really is is not completely intelligible; certainly, they are constrained twice over by the relationships we call logical and those we call evidential. In that sense, it is absurd to wonder whether there is a world "out there," since the wondering itself presupposes that there is. But, the philosopher is not called on to confer an epistemological blessing on, let us say, Newtonian mechanics. Physicists tell the stories they do; if they tell stories that, as James had it, are good in the way of belief, bridges stay up, spacecraft dock with space stations, and we understand why a car that hits an obstacle does it more than twice as much damage as it would have done at half the speed.

Just as we happily call many statements "true" without having or needing a theory of "Truth," so we can call actions and states of affairs good without having or needing a theory of Goodness or "The Good." Decently brought-up people flinch from cruelty without thinking that absent a philosophical theory of the evil of cruelty, their behavior is irrational. We can, and probably it is only philosophers, anthropologists, social psychologists, and evolutionary biologists who would spend a great deal of time doing it, look for explanations of why we have these revulsions, how they get ingrained in us, what good it does the species to have us flinch in this way, and so on. These explanations, however, are no more relevant to our moral judgments than the physiological explanation of my ability to ride a cycle to my riding of this bike here and now to the place to which I am riding it. What is relevant to them is the capacity of poets, novelists, plain persons, and first-order descriptive critics of a state of affairs to induce in us a change of heart or a change of perspective. Nobody supposes that when Shylock asks, "If you prick me, do I not bleed," the proper response is "So what?" Even if Shylock rather undermines our sympathies by going on to exult in the revenge he is about to take.

This emphasis on the role of rhetoric and on the importance of the devices of poets and playwrights in getting us to see the world in one way rather than another is the other face of an important observation that Rorty often made. Changes in belief do not generally come by processes that would stand up to scrutiny in a class on formal logic; people are "joshed" out of their previous convictions, or simply find that they have forgotten why they ever held them and that they have different beliefs from the ones they had before. By parity of reasoning, moral beliefs are in the same boat; if physics is, as Rorty claimed, politics all the way through, then so is ethics. These are less alarming claims than one might think; given a naturalistic view of reasoning and argument, it follows that all methods of changing minds, from a swift blow to the side of the head to an elaborate education in the intricacies of quantum mechanics, are just that – methods of changing minds. The virtues of the latter method as compared with the former are to be understood in terms of the quality of the conviction produced, the depth and detail of the resulting capacity to tell the "story" of twentieth- and twenty-first-century physics. Once all this is clearly understood, the seemingly shocking account of truth, beauty, and goodness that Rorty offered becomes less shocking, and can be appreciated as what Dewey claimed that philosophy had now become – or perhaps what philosophy *should* now become – which is to say the criticism of culture, or the criticism of cultural criticism. This is not to say that once we appreciate Rorty's desire to be a cultural critic rather than a philosopher in the sense in which he had been trained to be one, we should uncritically accept everything he had to say about ethics, literature, or contemporary American politics. It is to say that meeting his pragmatism with the assertion of pre-pragmatist pieties about Truth or Goodness is unlikely to be fruitful.

By way of a conclusion to this these thoughts, I should make good on the claim above that Rorty's claim to be a disciple of Dewey was misleading. Rorty held, perhaps somewhat tongue in cheek, that the three great philosophers of the twentieth century were Dewey, Wittgenstein, and Heidegger. The contrast between Dewey and Heidegger, however, was about as great as can be imagined. For Heidegger, the question of Being was inescapable; for Dewey, the impossibility of grounding the being of humanity in Being was something to shrug one's shoulders at and ignore. All the same, there was a residue in Dewey's psyche of the hankering for the Absolute that had led him into intuitionism and Hegelianism in his youth. It was something to which Rorty was oddly tone-deaf. To put it crudely, Dewey always hankered after an integrated culture within which the individual could feel that his life and that of the social whole within which he moved were one, not in conflict, and where in tension productively so and on the way to a higher or richer synthesis. Late in life, Dewey said he wished he had written more about the individual, and it is easy to see what he meant. But Rorty was sociologically unenchanted in a way that Dewey was not. Rorty could and did say that there was no reason why one could not be a Nietzschean or a Foucauldian about the private self, while being devoutly communitarian in public.

I think that as a matter of fact he is right, and that Foucault's own life demonstrates it. But it was not what Dewey thought. For Dewey, immersion in the culture of a successful modern society is the happiness of the earthly heaven. One might, with a great deal of pushing and tugging, contrive to argue that the transgressive and the deeply bizarre might manifest themselves as aspects of a fundamentally harmonious universe, or at least a universe that might be seen in a harmonious light; but such an exercise is quite at odds with the "integrative" style of Dewey's thinking. He did not need the reassurance that Being might be recaptured or might envelop us if we were quietly attentive; but he certainly wanted to believe that what could not be guaranteed by the reasoning of the philosophers might be accomplished by social and cultural reconstruction. Commentators frequently suggest that this hankering after harmony is an echo of Dewey's youthful piety when his devoutly Congregationalist mother did her best to bring him up in her own faith. That is easily exaggerated. Dewey's own account of his loss of faith suggests strongly that one day in his early twenties, he discovered that he did not after all believe in the existence of a Christian deity, and discovered at the same moment that "it didn't matter." The sense in which it did not matter was that the hypothesis of a deity who would guarantee the ultimately harmonious quality of experience was unnecessary. All the harmony that was to be had was latent in the world around us. *Latent* is important; as Dewey told an interviewer, he was a terrific optimist about things in general but a terrible pessimist about everything in particular. This was not simple incoherence; it was the affirmation of a confidence that the universe was in a broad way friendly to the human project, and a great deal of skepticism about our ability to realize that project. If one seeks a common thread in the ethics of James, Dewey, and Rorty, it is perhaps to be found in this combination of optimism in the large and exasperation in the detail; and more negatively in the refusal to be trapped by the philosophical conventions of the day.

See also Hegel (Chapter 15); John Stuart Mill (Chapter 16); Sidgwick, Green and Bradley (Chapter 17); Ethics, science, and religion (Chapter 22).

References

Arnold, Matthew (1873) *Literature and Dogma*, London: Smith Elder.

Dewey, John (1907/1932) *Ethics*, ed. James H. Tufts, New York: Holt.

——(1969/1884) "The Obligation to Knowledge of God," in *Collected Works*, vol. 1, Southern Illinois University Press.

James, William (2000) *Pragmatism and Other Essays*, New York: Penguin Books.

20
EXISTENTIALISM

Jonathan Webber

Since it gained currency at the end of the Second World War, the term "existentialism" has mostly been associated with a cultural movement that grew out of the wartime intellectual atmosphere of the Left Bank in Paris and spread through fiction and art as much as philosophy. The theoretical and other writings of Jean-Paul Sartre, Simone de Beauvoir, Albert Camus, and Frantz Fanon in the 1940s and 1950s are usually taken as central to this movement, as are the sculptures of Alberto Giacometti, the paintings of Jean Dubuffet, and the plays of Samuel Beckett from this time. Existentialism is frequently viewed, therefore, as an aesthetic movement rooted in certain philosophical thoughts and as supplanting surrealism at the center of European artistic fashion. This is the existentialism of black clothes and jazz clubs, coffee and cigarettes.

The term has also been applied retrospectively to various thinkers whose concerns and ideas chime with this movement. Most notably, the nineteenth-century philosophers Søren Kierkegaard and Friedrich Nietzsche are usually taken to be the key early existentialists. One a devout Christian, the other an ardent atheist, these thinkers are united by their emphasis on the individual rather than society as a center of concern and value. Since there are similar themes in the work of Fyodor Dostoevsky, Gabriel Marcel, Karl Jaspers, and more controversially Martin Heidegger, these thinkers are also often found in surveys of existentialism. Beyond this core, many other candidates have been named. Some scholars find existentialist themes and ideas in the works of William Shakespeare, for example, and many Christian theologians have argued for an existentialist understanding of certain passages in the New Testament.

This trend for admitting thinkers into the existentialist fold regardless of whether they would have described themselves in this way seems to have been started by journalists and critics but swiftly endorsed by Sartre himself in his lecture *Existentialism Is A Humanism* delivered in October 1945 and subsequently published as a book (Sartre 1956). After complaining that this term being used to describe his work was so nebulous as to be meaningless, he went on to contribute to the confusion: he described certain Christian thinkers as existentialists but then claimed that existentialism is a form of atheism, and he enlisted

Heidegger as a fellow existentialist only for Heidegger to publicly repudiate the label a couple of years later in his "Letter on Humanism" (1998/1947). Camus also refused to be classified as an existentialist, in an interview in 1945, on the grounds that his thought had little if anything in common with Sartre's, though in his case Sartre had not said otherwise and he was concerned to counter only the media image of his work (Camus 1968/1945: 345).

Rather than try to define existentialism with reference to the concerns and ideas of such a diverse collection of thinkers, a set whose membership is anyway contentious, it seems wiser to follow the lead of Camus and Heidegger and understand the term primarily as a name for Sartre's philosophy as he expounded it in that lecture and in *Being and Nothingness*, which the lecture seeks to defend. That lecture is, after all, the earliest text in which a leading proponent of this purported movement attempts to define the term. (Sartre had accepted the label for the first time a year before in a brief article entitled "A More Precise Characterization of Existentialism" in the underground newspaper *Action*, but did not there define it.)

Taking this as our model of existentialism, we can understand the works of others, and indeed the later works of Sartre himself, to be more or less existentialist according to the degree to which they fit its contours. Before describing this model, however, we should consider the relation between *existentialism* so understood and the broader notion of *existential philosophy*. Drawing this distinction will help us to see quite why such a diverse array of cultural products have been described as existentialist and to see the conceptual connection between these two closely related terms.

Existential philosophy is concerned with the kind of existence we have, as opposed to the kind of existence had by rocks, plants, and animals. Many existential philosophers reserve the very word "existence" for the way in which we exist, using "being" as the more general term to capture the existence that rocks, plants, animals, and humans have in common. Awkward though it sounds in English, according to this usage humans *exist* but, so far as we know, all other things merely *are*. This is not to rule out the possibility of discovering another species in the universe that exists as we do, just to say that no such species has yet been found. Existential philosophy is the attempt to articulate the nature of this existence.

Central themes of existential thought therefore include the reliability of our everyday views of ourselves and other people, the relation between objective facts and subjective experience, the significance of the temporality and mortality of life, the basic nature of relationships between people, and the role of society in the structure of the individual. The urge to consider these issues is not confined to any particular phase or movement in intellectual history, of course – be it wartime Paris or any other. These are clearly perennial questions arising from the very human condition they ask about, though as William Barrett makes clear in his masterly study of existential thought, *Irrational Man*, their sense of urgency is heightened and lessened by historical circumstances and the framework within which they are addressed varies with other aspects of culture.

This list of central themes makes clear, moreover, that existential thought is not another branch on the philosophical tree along with metaphysics, epistemology, aesthetics, ethics, and politics, but rather a lens through which these topics can be viewed. The nature of reality and the limits of knowledge are important, according to this approach to philosophy, only insofar as they enlighten us about the structure of our own existence. The nature and significance of beauty and art cannot be understood without reference to the sort of existence had by those who find pleasure and solace in them. How we should treat one another and organize our societies depends upon the kinds of things we all are.

Existential philosophy encompasses all the classic philosophical problems, therefore, but with the distinctive twist that they should be understood in relation to a single overarching question: What is it to exist as a unique individual person? In asking what it should profit a person to gain the whole world and lose his own soul, Jesus was posing the question at the heart of existential thought, as was Hamlet when he pondered whether to be or not to be, but it is a mistake to categorize Jesus or Shakespeare as existentialists purely on these grounds. Focusing on the human individual in this way, moreover, has led many existential thinkers to see the social and material worlds as at best dimensions of the individual, at worst a threat to each of us. This explains why artworks that focus on isolated and lonely figures, such as many of Giacometti's more famous sculptures or the classic movies of the film noir genre, have often been described as existentialist: they fit a standard conception of existential thought, a notion often conflated with existentialism.

Existentialism, as Sartre defines it, is an ethical theory. It is a form of humanism, which means that it takes humanity as the central ethical value. But it is distinguished from other forms of humanism in the way it understands humanity. What is valuable is not simply the empirical fact of human existence. Our ethical aims should not be to increase our numbers, lengthen our lives, satisfy our desires and preferences, or improve on our achievements. What distinguishes existentialism – or, more precisely, existential humanism – as an ethical theory is its view that all that is intrinsically valuable is the nature or structure of our existence, the kind of thing we are. The relation between existentialism and existential philosophy therefore justifies the similarity of the two terms: existentialism seeks the flourishing of the human individual, where this is understood as the unfettered realization of our most fundamental nature (see Sartre 2007: 52–3).

Existentialism therefore has much in common with the ethical theory propounded by Aristotle in his *Nicomachean Ethics*. Both see the aim of ethics as promoting human flourishing, and both understand this as requiring that we first ascertain the underlying nature of human existence. Aristotle argues that we are essentially rational animals, so sees flourishing in terms of the good exercise of our rational faculties, and understands ethical virtue as the set of dispositions manifested in this exercise (2002: Bk 1, ch. 7). This is the central inspiration for the tradition that has become known as virtue ethics, according to which the center of our ethical concern should not be the intentions with which individual actions are performed or the consequences of those actions but rather the character traits that we possess and that are manifested in our thoughts, feelings, perceptions, and actions.

The ethical theory Sartre propounds is along these lines. What matters is that we possess and express the single overarching virtue of authenticity: the disposition to recognize and promote what is most genuinely our own, the fundamental nature of our existence (see 2007: 50–1). Any theory that places authenticity at the center of ethics can fairly be described as a form of existentialism, whether or not it concurs with Sartrean existentialism on the fundamental nature of human existence. This does not include Aristotelian ethics, however, since authenticity is primarily a matter of *recognizing and promoting* the deep structure of humanity wherever it is found, whereas for Aristotle flourishing consists primarily in *manifesting it eminently*.

Sartre's argument for authenticity being the cardinal virtue takes us deeper into his philosophy. The values and significances that we find in the world, he argues, do not exist independently of our awareness, but rather reflect our own aims and purposes, themselves a filter through which we see the world. It might seem to us that our desires simply react to what is objectively good and bad, attractive and unattractive, but in fact things seem good, bad, attractive, or unattractive only because of the goals we are already pursuing. As soon as we realize this, Sartre thinks, we can no longer choose to pursue any goal without also promoting the underlying cause of the significance that goal has. Since our goals are freely chosen and pursued, this means that once we understand this aspect of our existence we cannot value anything without also valuing "freedom as the foundation of all values" (2007: 48).

Just how this argument is supposed to work is a matter of some controversy. It is clearly alluding to a similar argument given by Immanuel Kant in Section 2 of his *Groundwork of the Metaphysics of Morals* (1998/1785). Kant argues that the value we find in most of our goals is really only relative to our needs and desires, but since we do take our endeavors seriously we must therefore ascribe intrinsic value to whatever lends relative value to our goals. Since our goals are grounded in our rational nature, the argument runs, we cannot consistently value anything unless we also admit that rational nature itself is intrinsically valuable. Hence the injunction to treat rational creatures always as ends and never as means. Where Kant talks about rationality, it might seem, Sartre has simply substituted freedom.

These two arguments seem to face the same objection: surely the conclusion is, at best, that I should value *my own* rationality or freedom as the source of my other values, not that I should value rationality or freedom wherever it is found. Controversy over just how each of these arguments should be understood is partly generated by the attempt to obviate this objection. But the parallels between these arguments should not be overplayed. They occur in quite different contexts, giving them quite different meanings. Kant is presenting a normative account of practical reason, of the ways in which we are rationally required to think. Sartre, on the other hand, seems to be making a psychological claim about what it is to recognize the actual relation between our values and the goals we pursue. It would be misleading, therefore, to describe Kantian ethics as a form of existentialism, despite Sartre's obvious debt to Kant.

Rather than follow Kant's emphasis on rationality, as we have seen, Sartre understands our values to be rooted in our freedom. This aspect of his philosophy is widely misconstrued and misrepresented. The confusion is largely due to his use of the language of choice. He describes our values as freely chosen, the ways in which we see the world as freely chosen, and even the ways in which we think about and emotionally respond to the world as freely chosen. He is often taken to be saying that when we confront any situation, we choose there and then how we will construe it, how we will feel about it, and what to think about it.

Such a theory would be palpably false. Although it is true that we can have a certain amount of voluntary control over how we see certain images, such as the famous duck–rabbit picture, such control is remarkable precisely because we usually understand the things around us without making decisions. Our emotional responses similarly seem to us utterly spontaneous: we are pleased or angered directly and immediately by the situation as we see it, not after some consideration about how to feel. And an obvious regress threatens any theory that claims that we do not make a decision without first deciding how much weight to assign to each consideration. What is more, this idea that we simply choose how to see things and think and feel about them sits uneasily with other key aspects of Sartre's early philosophy, such as his famous view that we generally hide our freedom from ourselves, and the idea that we might need the help of an existentialist psychoanalyst to uncover our true motivations.

Sartre uses the language of choice to emphasize his claim that the ways in which we see things, the relative importance each consideration has for us when we deliberate, and our emotional responses to events are all determined by the projects that we have adopted and that we can change. Such projects may have become so habitual that it is no longer obvious to us that we are pursuing them, or their very pursuit might even require that we do not acknowledge that we are doing so, but they are projects we have chosen and can revise nonetheless. The deepest roots of our perceptions, thoughts, and feelings, therefore, are neither fixed facts about us due to our genetic inheritance or early childhood nor the mechanical effects of our material and social environment, but rather the goals that we choose to pursue and can choose to abandon. Sartre allies this teleological understanding of character with an indeterminist theory of freedom. Nothing can determine which goals we adopt, according to Sartre, and nothing can determine whether we continue to pursue a given goal or abandon it altogether. Freedom is radical in the sense that it is freedom over the deepest roots of our behavior, and causal determinism is incompatible with this freedom.

Despite his own protestations to the contrary, these two aspects of Sartre's account of the structure of human existence seem to be separable. We can agree that the kind of person you are is determined by the goals that you are freely pursuing without also agreeing that your freedom over these goals is incompatible with determinism. Perhaps one can revise or abandon a specific goal only if one is sufficiently motivated to do so by one's other projects. Some philosophers think this would not really be freedom, since our initial goals would come about without our control and then ultimately determine whatever else we did. Others argue that it is rather Sartre's indeterminist picture that leaves our fates beyond our control, by leaving entirely to chance whether or not we continue to pursue a given project at any given moment. This is just an application of the general debate over the compatibility of freedom and determinism, however. Wherever you stand on that issue, therefore, you can still agree with Sartre on the role of our projects in determining the ways in which we see the world, think and feel about it, and thereby behave in it.

Thus we can classify as a form of existentialism any philosophical theory that broadly agrees with Sartre on the role our goals play in our overall outlook, regardless of whether that theory also embraces an incompatibilist notion of freedom. One way to read Nietzsche's philosophy, particularly as set out in *Beyond Good and Evil* (2001/1886), takes him to support the belief that we each see the world through the lens of our projects that in turn manifest the unruly will-to-power that underlies everything including ourselves. Nietzsche would therefore be recommending an existentialist theory of our relation to the world, albeit one that does not include an indeterminist freedom. This reading is, however, contentious. Rival scholarship contends that Nietzsche only employs this view as part of a dialectical argument for rejecting the entire enterprise of metaphysics and epistemology within which it might gain any sense or significance. If this is right, then it seems that Nietzsche has very little in common with Sartre and so, existential though his thought is, perhaps it should not be understood as existentialist at all.

Sartrean existentialism, the paradigmatic form of existentialism, is the ethical theory that we ought to recognize that our values are rooted in the projects we freely pursue and so promote the freedom of all to pursue their projects. This is not, however, simply the liberal view that each person should be allowed to pursue whatever they see as good so long as this does not infringe on the similar freedom of someone else, but rather the more stringent view that the only acceptable goals are those pursued "in the name of freedom" (2007: 50). Opponents have argued that this is inconsistent. If values are rooted in projects, the argument runs, there cannot be any objective ethical injunction at all: Why should anyone value authenticity unless they are already pursuing projects that generate this value? This is the charge that existentialism is at best a form of moral relativism, at worst a form of nihilism according to which nothing really matters at all.

The lecture *Existentialism Is A Humanism* was partly aimed at rebutting these criticisms, but few have found the responses Sartre gave there convincing. He claims that any attitude other than authenticity is based on falsehood and inconsistency (2007: 47–8). The first of these seems obviously right: authenticity is, after all, supposed to be the recognition of the actual nature of human existence. The second seems to rest on the idea that it is inconsistent to value anything without valuing the freedom in which that valuing is itself rooted. But even if we grant that this is so, we might well ask what is wrong with falsehood and inconsistency. Within the account of valuing that Sartre has given, that is, we might ask why someone has to care about truth or consistency.

To be fair to Sartre, we ought to take seriously his comment that to give a popular presentation of a philosophical theory is to "agree to dilute our thinking in order to make it understood" (2007: 55). We should understand his talk of truth and consistency as summarizing an argument presented in full elsewhere. What he condemns as false and inconsistent is bad faith (see 2007: 47–8). So we should look more closely at his theory of bad faith, detailed in *Being and Nothingness*, to see just what is so bad about it. Bad faith is the project of deceiving ourselves about the nature of our existence. Since a deceiver must know the truth being hidden from the deceived, and must also hide the intention to deceive, it is difficult to see how deceiver and deceived could be the same person. Sartre's attempt to address this issue is one of his most widely discussed contributions to moral theory. But we need not consider it here, since we are looking for a reason to prefer the correct view of ourselves irrespective of how our incorrect views might come about.

Quite which incorrect views Sartre thinks we prefer is a matter of debate. Some commentators find in his writing two forms of bad faith: one in which we deny our freedom, another in which we identify wholly with it. We consider our outlook and behavior to be strictly determined by our genetic inheritance, childhood experiences, or social position, on this view, or we deny that these form any part of ourselves. But this reading does not sit well with Sartre's claim that the recognition of our freedom, and the responsibility it brings with it, is unpleasant. The desire to escape the anguish of this recognition is, he tells us, "the basis of all attitudes of excuse" (2003/1943: 64). Other commentators therefore claim that there is only one form of bad faith in Sartre's philosophy: seeing one's outlook and behavior as rooted in a fixed nature determined by inheritance, upbringing, or socialization.

However that dispute is to be resolved, it seems that Sartre has not given an account of what is wrong with bad faith, at least by the time of the popular lecture, unless we take his theory of interpersonal and social relations to provide that account. This theory is the subject of further exegetical disagreement. Some read it as the pessimistic view that we can only ever misunderstand one another and must inevitably struggle to dominate one another. Certain limitations on the ways in which we see the world mean, according to this reading, that we cannot avoid categorizing other people in ways that they find alienating, but the only way in which they can react against this is to constrain us in turn in categories that we find alienating. A struggle for supremacy is therefore built into the very fabric of human relations: each individual wants control of their own image and this requires their control over the images of those around them. The famous line from the end of Sartre's 1943 play *Huis Clos* – "Hell is … other people!" – is taken to encapsulate this pessimism (Sartre 2000).

Some commentators argue that the limitations on our views of one another that lead to this conflict are not the necessary result of the structure of consciousness, according to Sartre, but are rather the manifestation of our contingent bad faith. The claim that "conflict is the original meaning of being-for-others" (2003/1943: 386), therefore, is not the claim that human relations are necessarily conflictual, but that bad faith condemns us to such relations. This certainly seems to be the view that Sartre held soon after the publication of *Being and Nothingness*. In his work on anti-Semitism, written in 1944, he portrays bad faith as the root of all racial hatred: it is "fear of the human condition" manifested in a social outlook (1948/1945: 54; see also 71n). According to this reading of Sartrean existentialism, therefore, what is wrong with bad faith is the impact it has on our relations with other individuals and with society at large.

For someone happy to live in perpetual struggle for domination, of course, this consequence of bad faith would provide no reason to abandon it. So if this construal of Sartre's ethical theory is to make sense, it must involve the idea that nobody could be happy with a life led in bad faith. To remain consistent with the claim that our values are rooted in our projects, and that these in turn are chosen and changeable, we cannot appeal to any necessarily held values that are frustrated by the life of bad faith. The argument must rather be that bad faith restricts the goals that one can pursue in one's relations with other people while at the same time ensuring that none of the goals that can be pursued can actually be achieved. Sartre's lengthy discussions of personal relationships, particularly his discussion of sexuality, do have this flavor: each project is frustrated, leading inevitably to a new project that is in turn frustrated.

Beauvoir characterizes existentialism this way in her essay "Existentialism and Popular Wisdom," published a couple of months after Sartre gave his famous lecture. The touchstone of existentialism, she explains, is the idea that we are better off if we accept that people do not have unchangeable natures than we are if we continue to pretend that they do. After attacking the popular but pessimistic view that humans are by nature self-interested and that the fate of each of us is determined by the fixed facts of our personalities, she proclaims that the aim of existentialism is to save us "from the morose disappointments and sulking that [this] cult of false idols brings about" (2004b/1945: 216).

There is quite some scholarly discussion over the relation between the philosophies of Beauvoir and Sartre. As lifelong intellectual as well as personal companions since they met as students in 1929, they must have influenced each other immeasurably through critique of one another's writings and through casual conversation. Sartre dedicated *Being and Nothingness* to Beauvoir, but his publications do not acknowledge any specific debts to her influence. Beauvoir's writings of the 1940s, on the other hand, clearly develop moral and political theories within the framework of Sartre's account of human existence, bad faith, and authenticity, but do so independently of Sartre's own applied moral and political writings. Her treatises *Pyrrhus and Cineas* (2004a/1944), *The Ethics of Ambiguity* (1986/1947), and *The Second Sex* (1993/1949) should therefore all be counted as paradigmatically existentialist writings. Her other works, like Sartre's other works, should be understood as existentialist to the degree to which they affirm the existential theory of *Being and Nothingness*.

The extent to which we should consider the works of Fanon to be existentialist is a much more complicated question. It is not simply the case, as it seems to be with Camus, that he was labeled an existentialist because of his personal association with Sartre rather than because of any deep connection between his works and Sartre's. His first book, *Black Skin White Masks* (1986/1952), is very much influenced by Sartre's account of relations between people as developed in *Being and Nothingness* and applied in *Anti-Semite and Jew*. What is more, it is a clear example of the kind of socially engaged literature that Sartre urges writers to produce in his essay *What Is Literature?*: Fanon mixes philosophical reflection, literary criticism, political polemic, and poetry to address issues of identity and interaction with the goal of liberating us all from the constraining, distorting, oppressive influences of colonialism and racism (Sartre 1950/1947).

Fanon is not, however, simply applying Sartrean philosophy. His work draws on a wide range of other sources, including psychoanalytical work on the unconscious that Sartre considered to be based on a confused and somewhat arbitrary understanding of human motivation and behavior. Fanon criticizes Sartre's discussion of encounters between people for failing to take account of the backdrop of prejudices and power relations against which they occur, moreover, and sees his own encounter with Sartre's works in just this way: as the experience of a black man from a French colony reading the works of a white man from France who dominated the francophone intellectual scene at the time. The precise nature and extent of Sartre's influence on Fanon's thinking is therefore an intricate issue but one that seemingly must be addressed if we are to fully understand *Black Skin White Masks*, or indeed his later book *The Wretched of the Earth* (2001/1961).

The example of Fanon's writings should make clear that problems can be generated by classifying a thinker as an existentialist. We should not treat this label as a guide to interpreting any particular works, as though we could resolve exegetical issues by considering what "an existentialist" would say at that point.

There has been something of a tendency to distort the works of the various thinkers grouped under this label by emphasizing their agreements, downplaying or even denying their deep differences, and ignoring their debts to thinkers not accorded the same label. Perhaps this has been necessary to bring these diverse and often extensive works into the purview of anglophone intellectual life, but if we are to sharpen our focus on them we need to guard against the continuation of this tendency. Whether a particular work counts as existentialist, and the ways in which it does so, are now questions to be answered only after we have understood that work.

Should we think of the writings of Kierkegaard, for example, as existentialist? There are undeniably existentialist themes in his philosophy, such as his theory in *The Sickness unto Death* (1980b/1849) that we are aware that we perpetually remake ourselves through our ongoing commitments but prefer not to face this truth, and his related discussion in *The Concept of Anxiety* (1980a/1844) of this aversion to our freedom. Perhaps these aspects of his work influenced Sartre and others in such a way as to justify the common description of Kierkegaard as "the father of existentialism." But even if so, we should not allow this to blind us to other strands of his sophisticated and subtle writings.

Treating the idea of existentialism in this way might well have the further benefit of affording us insightful perspectives on works not previously grouped under this label. This might improve our understanding of those works or enhance their relevance to our present concerns. Perhaps we should find existentialist themes in the philosophy of Karl Marx, for example, as Sartre suggested (1985/1944: 157), or in the writings of the Stoic philosophers to whom Sartre and Beauvoir refer so often, or indeed in myriad other places.

See also Aristotle (Chapter 4); Kant (Chapter 14); Nietzsche (Chapter 18); Heidegger (Chapter 21); Virtue ethics (Chapter 40).

References

Aristotle (2002) *Nicomachean Ethics*, ed. S. Broadie and C. Rowe, Oxford: Oxford University Press.

Barrett, W. (1958) *Irrational Man: A Study in Existential Philosophy*, Garden City, NY: Doubleday.

Beauvoir, S. de (1986/1947) *The Ethics of Ambiguity*, trans. B. Frechtman, New York: Citadel Press.

——(1993/1949) *The Second Sex*, trans., ed. H. M. Parshley, London: David Campbell Publishers, Everyman's Library.

——(2004a/1944) *Pyrrhus and Cineas*, trans. M. Timmerman, in *Philosophical Writings*, ed. M. A. Simons, Champaign: University of Illinois Press.

——(2004b/1945) "Existentialism and Popular Wisdom," trans. M. Timmerman, in *Philosophical Writings*, ed. M. A. Simons, Champaign: University of Illinois Press.

Camus, A. (1968/1945) "No, I Am Not an Existentialist … ," in A. Camus, *Lyrical and Critical Essays*, trans. E. Kennedy, ed. P. Thody, New York: Alfred A. Knopf.

Fanon, F. (1986/1952) *Black Skin White Masks*, trans. C. L. Markmann, London: Pluto Press.
——(2001/1961) *The Wretched of the Earth*, trans. C. Farrington, London: Penguin Books.
Heidegger, M. (1998/1947) "Letter on Humanism," in *Pathmarks*, trans. W. McNeill, Cambridge: Cambridge University Press.
Kant, I. (1998/1785) *Groundwork of the Metaphysics of Morals*, ed., trans. M. Gregor, Cambridge: Cambridge University Press.
Kierkegaard, S. (1980a/1844) *The Concept of Anxiety*, ed., trans. R. Thomte and A. B. Anderson, Princeton, NJ: Princeton University Press.
——(1980b/1849) *The Sickness unto Death*, ed., trans. H. V. Hong and E. H. Hong, Princeton, NJ: Princeton University Press.
Nietzsche, F. (2001/1886) *Beyond Good and Evil: Prelude to a Philosophy of the Future*, ed. R.-P. Horstmann, trans. J. Norman, Cambridge: Cambridge University Press.
Sartre, J.-P. (1948/1945) *Anti-Semite and Jew*, trans. G. Becker, New York: Schocken Books.
——(1950/1947) *What Is Literature?* trans. B. Frechtman, London: Methuen.
——(1985/1944) "A More Precise Characterization of Existentialism," trans. R. McCleary, in *The Writings of Jean-Paul Sartre*, vol. 2: *Selected Prose*, ed. M. Contat and M. Rybalka, Evanston, IL: Northwestern University Press.
——(2000) *Huis Clos and Other Plays*, trans. K. Black and S. Gilbert, London: Penguin Books.
——(2003/1943) *Being and Nothingness: An Essay in Phenomenological Ontology*, trans. H. E. Barnes, rev. edn, London: Routledge.
——(2007) *Existentialism Is a Humanism*, trans. C. Macomber, New Haven, CT: Yale University Press.

Further reading

Flynn, T. R. (2006) *Existentialism: A Very Short Introduction*, Oxford: Oxford University Press.
Sartre, J.-P. (2007) *Existentialism Is A Humanism*, trans. Carol Macomber, New Haven, CT: Yale University Press.
Webber, J. (2008) *The Existentialism of Jean-Paul Sartre*, New York: Routledge.

21
HEIDEGGER

Stephen Mulhall

This chapter will focus exclusively upon Heidegger's early philosophical work, as that finds expression in his masterpiece *Sein und Zeit* (hereafter *Being and Time* – published in 1927). Even though it is perhaps easier to appreciate the relevance to ethics of the various phases of his later thought (Young 2002), their basic structure and motivation are essentially indebted to that first major work, even when most explicitly critical of its limitations. Hence, any real understanding of Heidegger's significance for ethics must take its initial bearings from *Being and Time*.

There are various difficulties in doing so, however. Even if we set aside (what I judge to be ultimately uncompelling) claims that elements of *Being and Time* propel us on a trajectory that terminates in the ethico-political values of Nazism, there is another standing assumption that must be confronted before we can hope to read this book on its own terms. That is the assumption that Heidegger's early work is a species of existentialism – a gesture much encouraged by the knowledge that Sartre's version of existentialist philosophy (as encapsulated in *Being and Nothingness*) was in large part inspired by his reading of *Being and Time*. Heidegger himself famously resisted this categorization, even if from a philosophical perspective he attained only after taking decisive steps beyond his early masterpiece (Heidegger 1977). But even if (as we shall see) there is nonetheless some reason to align his early work with existentialist patterns of thinking, we cannot take such an alignment for granted at the outset, because it is far from obvious what it means to categorize anyone's thinking as "existentialist." Such a contestable concept can hardly help to orient us at the very beginning of our attempt to understand Heidegger's way of philosophizing.

A third obstacle is harder to dismiss, since it emerges from *Being and Time* itself; and that is Heidegger's repeated denial that the analyses contained in his book should be taken as having any particular ethical implications. His immediate ground for this denial is not far to seek. Insofar as we define "ethics" as a theoretical study of one aspect of human beings and their common life, it counts as what Heidegger calls an ontic science; like anthropology or biology, it aims to construct a body of knowledge about a distinct domain of reality. In doing so, however, any ethical theory necessarily presupposes a particular way of demarcating that domain, of conceptualizing the phenomena encountered within it, and of constructing and defending the theories it advances about them. What Heidegger calls ontological inquiry is the very different task of identifying and interrogating such presuppositions; and that ontically neutral enterprise is his exclusive concern in *Being and Time*.

More precisely, his sole aim is to provide an existential analytic of "Dasein" (his term for the distinctively human way of being). Individual human beings engage in a wide variety of activities in a wide variety of ways; and the various aspects of their nature that are made manifest in these ontic possibilities can be systematically studied. But Heidegger's existential analytic is concerned with what kind of being a human being must be if it is so much as possible to study it in such ways; and that requires giving an account of what makes it possible for human beings to be in any of their distinctive states, or to engage in any of their distinctive patterns of behavior. Those underlying ontological structures must, by their very nature, be equally manifest no matter what particular state a human being is in or what particular behavior he is engaged in. So Heidegger's inquiry has no interest in, and can provide no grounds for, approving or disapproving of any such state or mode of behavior, let alone proving or disproving any particular theoretical claims about the creatures who manifest them. Hence, if we regard ethics either as a matter of engaging more systematically in a familiar kind of human behavior (that of evaluating ourselves and others in a particular way), or as the enterprise of providing a theoretical account of that distinctive dimension of human life, Heidegger will deny that his analyses have any bearing on ethics. Either endeavor will be of interest to him only insofar as it provides indications of the ontological distinctiveness of the human way of being.

However, the true significance of Heidegger's denial remains questionable. After all, one reason he finds himself repeating that denial so vehemently throughout his book is that the basic terminology through which he articulates his ontology of the human appears to be blatantly evaluative. Terms such as "authenticity," "the call of conscience," "guilt" and "resoluteness," "fate" and "destiny," are undeniably central to *Being and Time*; and even if they are not all straightforwardly ethical in import, at the very least they insistently evoke a conceptual field in which matters of ethical, political and religious evaluation converge and conjoin. Since he could easily have avoided such terminological connotations altogether, we need to understand why Heidegger should instead choose to activate them so insistently that he is then required, with equal insistence, to cancel them. Might it be that his intellectual project verges sufficiently closely upon matters of (let's say) spiritual significance to require an emphatic denial that it relates to them in any straightforward or conventional way? If so, then Heidegger's denial can only be properly understood if one understands why the impression is nevertheless repeatedly recreated of there being something for him to deny.

Essence and existence

The analysis of Dasein that unfolds in *Being and Time* is oriented from the outset by two central claims about the human way of being, both of which help to determine the relevance of Heidegger's work to ethics. I shall examine the first claim in this section, and the second in the next.

That first claim is that, unlike every other kind of being, the modes of existence distinctive of human beings are not determined by their essence; rather, their essence lies in, is given or determined by, their existence. What is distinctive of the human way of being is that every moment of it can be thought of as posing the question of what the next moment of it will be. I am presently sitting in front of my computer. That this is so is the result of my having decided a moment ago to stay in my seat rather than get up to make a cup of tea, and if I continue to do so, that will be because I have once again decided against making that cup of tea; but each moment in which I prefer writing this entry to rehydrating simply projects me into another moment in which I must decide again either to re-enact that preference or to commit myself to some other existential possibility. The point is not that I make an explicit decision one way or another in every moment of my life; it is rather that whichever possible way of being I realize at any moment is something for which I am ineliminably responsible or accountable, not something determined by factors entirely outside my control.

My responsibility is thus neither absolute nor absent. It is necessarily exercised in situations that are only partly determined by its own previous exercises (my freedom in fixing the deadline for submitting this entry was constrained by the editor and publishers of this volume), and what results from its present exercise is also necessarily conditioned in various ways (by the continued functioning of my computer and my motor nerves, for example); but the way in which it is exercised is never entirely reducible to those conditions. In short, living as a human being is a matter of endlessly confronting, answering and then confronting once again the question of how to live. As Heidegger puts it, Dasein is the being whose being is an issue for it.

Accordingly, whereas the distinctive behavior exhibited by a stone propelled through the air or a seed planted in fertile soil is wholly explicable by reference to their determinate nature as beings of a particular kind, the given nature of human beings (for example, as animals of a certain kind) does not wholly determine how they live, but is better thought of as posing a question to which they must supply an answer, namely: "How is this fact about myself to inform or inflect my life?" For example, human beings must eat if they are to survive: but eating has very different meanings in different cultures, individuals within a single culture may treat eating in very different ways, and some individuals may simply refuse to eat in the name of something they value more highly than their own lives. In other words, the particular answer someone gives to such questions (preferring McDonald's to Le Manoir aux Quat' Saisons, regarding the breaking of bread as a gesture of unavoidable necessity or of hospitality or of divine grace) reflects the particular significance she assigns to whatever is in question, which in turn reflects the values in terms of which she understands herself and her world – values which may differ from person to person, and which are ultimately embedded in a broader vision of what it is to be human (a vision that might be religious or secular, teleological or deontological, and so seemingly endlessly on). And by living one's life in accordance with such a conception of who and what one is, an individual human being thereby contributes to constituting herself as the kind of person, and the kind of being, she conceives herself to be.

Should we summarize this by saying that her existence determines her essence, or rather by saying that her essence consists precisely in her capacity to determine her own essence? In Heidegger's view, the latter formulation is not exactly wrong, but it is profoundly misleading, because it represses the radical nature of the difference between human beings and all other beings at this level. In the context of the ontic sciences, a specification of essence is primarily designed to pick out something that can play an independent and fully determinative role in explanations of the behavior of entities, as with the stone and the seed. But if Heidegger is right, that is the one job that a specification of the human essence cannot do; for the envisaged human capacity for self-determination is only exercisable through the patterns of activity we want to explain, and so determines nothing prior to its exercise in any actual case. Accordingly, rather than presenting that claim in a way which encourages the very misunderstanding it contests, by inviting us to regard human beings and stones as alike in this vital respect, why not choose a mode of presentation that carries this refusal of explanatory expectations on its face?

Even so, however, could one not say that – far from constituting an ethically neutral ontological specification of the human way of being – Heidegger's claim amounts to a substantive ethical vision of humanity, and a distinctively existentialist one at that? In my view, Heidegger's response to such a claim should parallel his response to the claim in the previous paragraph. It is not exactly wrong to describe this aspect of his characterization of Dasein as existentialist: it does after all give a certain kind of priority to existence over essence, which provides a real if minimal justification for employing the term. But it would not, for example, justify attributing to him the view (often ascribed to existentialists) that human beings are possessed of the capacity for absolute freedom, able to define and redefine their own nature from the ground up. On the contrary: for him, human freedom is essentially conditioned or situated, never exercisable except in contexts whose lineaments must in various ways simply be accepted as given; in this sense the nature of human freedom reflects the fundamental finitude of human existence. And acknowledging human freedom as real but finite hardly adds up to an ethical vision of humanity – at least not if that is supposed to imply that it bears comparison with the detailed, elaborate and highly specific views of a Kant or a Mill or an Aristotle.

It would be far less misleading to say that Heidegger's account merely identifies a condition for the possibility of any such ethical vision having an intelligible bearing on individual human beings. For what Kant and Mill and Aristotle each supply is one particular, well worked-out way of taking responsibility for how we lead our lives, one way of exercising our freedom to determine for ourselves the evaluative terms in the light of which we will live. Hence they all presuppose that we are capable both of adopting such an evaluative vision, and of holding ourselves answerable for that choice in the face of its contestation by adherents of other visions. In this sense, ethics makes sense if and only if human beings are free (free to have done otherwise, and hence to be subject to ethical praise and blame at all, and free to answer for the particular terms of ethical evaluation they employ when judging themselves and others). But this is precisely what Heidegger means when he talks of Dasein as the being whose being is an issue for it. For if we were not beings whose existence poses a question to us that must, and can only, be answered through that existence – if we were not both capable of and required to enact some particular conception of life's meaning in our own lives – then we could not either realize a specifically Kantian vision of life in their own lives, or debate with one another the relative merits of a Kantian as opposed to an Aristotelian outlook.

Heidegger's work might certainly lead us to ask whether an adherent of any given ethical stance fully acknowledges both the reality and the finitude of the freedom that his judgements presuppose. For example, some might argue that Mill's desire-centered version of utilitarianism risks putting the reality of human freedom in doubt, and others that Kant's conception of human freedom as noumenal verges on the supernatural. And he would also warn against advocating any ethical view in ways that imply that the authority of its recommendations for living flow necessarily from some objective truth about our essential nature (as, say, desiring or rational or social animals); for that risks reintroducing the very model of "essence as determining existence" which threatens the freedom that any ethical recommendations must presuppose. Such theoretical self-subversions are hardly minor matters; but to warn against them hardly amounts to taking a general stand on the relative merits of any given ethical vision, or to urging the adoption of any particular one. Hence, insofar as ethics is understood as essentially a matter of doing either or both of those things, Heidegger's work has no bearing upon it.

Authenticity

The second of the two opening claims that Heidegger makes about human existence in *Being and Time* is that every Dasein is characterized by mineness. This esoteric formulation is initially explicated by reference to the fact that human beings employ personal pronouns when addressing one another, which suggests that Heidegger is emphasizing that every human life is the life of a particular person – it is mine, or yours, or his. But the full significance of this apparently trivial point only emerges as Heidegger develops the conception of authenticity that unfolds from it; and the best way to grasp that conception is to examine his description of its opposite – the condition of inauthenticity which, he claims, most of us inhabit most of the time.

On Heidegger's view, human beings are inherently social creatures. By this he means not just that we typically conduct our lives within social and cultural formations, but that our capacity to stand in a bewildering variety of specific relationships with other human beings is internal to our nature. In Heidegger's terminology, those various concrete existential possibilities indicate that, ontologically speaking, Dasein's nature is Being-with. And the intelligibility of stories such as Robinson Crusoe's actually confirms his point; for only a being inherently capable of social interaction could intelligibly be described as deprived of it, as isolated or alone. If, however, human modes of existence will always involve specific kinds of relations to others, and if, as we have seen, it is through the realization of possible modes of existence that human beings establish a particular, concrete relation to themselves; it follows that, for human beings, one's relations to oneself and one's relations to others are mutually determining. How one relates to oneself will inflect one's relations to others; and how one relates to others will inform one's way of relating to oneself.

The mutually determining significance of these relations is evident in the way most of us inhabit the social world most of the time – an inauthentic mode of existence that Heidegger christens "das Man" (literally, "the one," or the "they"). This mode of existence is not simply a matter of doing what everyone else does – for example, reading the latest winner of the Booker Prize, or queuing to see the new Hollywood blockbuster, or joining in the general condemnation of the government's most recent display of incompetence; what matters is how we comprehend or stand to the fact that we are doing it, as evinced, for example, in what we would say if asked why we were doing it. If we were to say something like "That's what everyone's doing," or "That's just what one does" or "What else is there to read or see or think?," then we would reveal that we are existing in the mode of "das Man."

So we could not exit from that mode of existence by resolving to do the opposite of whatever everyone else is doing, if our reason for so doing were simply and solely that it is the opposite of what everyone else is doing. For in both cases, the "they" is exercising its dictatorship (in the latter case, by negation); in both, my life takes the form it does because of the form that everyone else's life is presently taking. And it is not that these other inhabitants of the "they" are avoiding my inauthentic mode of existence; for insofar as they too exist as "das Man," they are doing whatever they are doing because that is what one does, what everyone does. In that sense, the "others" to whom an individual human being subjects himself in "das Man" are not a group of genuine individuals to whose shared tastes others are subjected; they are just as much subject to the dictatorship of the "they" as I am.

Hence, despite the fact that Heidegger's descriptions of "das Man" emphasize an individual's relations to others, they aim to identify a particular kind of self-relation that both reinforces and is reinforced by a particular kind of relation to others. For if I regard the way in which I live as simply reflecting the way everyone lives, as merely a local instantiation of the way living is done here and now, as if these ways of occupying myself were somehow the only conceivable ways of doing so, then I am living my life as if it were not my own – mine to own, to take responsibility for. To live this way is to disown my life, to deny my responsibility for it; it involves regarding the course of my existence as given, as somehow beyond question, rather than as the enactment of one possible way of living to which there are alternatives, and hence as something for which I am answerable. In the terms of Heidegger's first defining characteristic of Dasein, anyone who inhabits the "das Man" mode of living treats their own existence as if it were not an issue for them, not at issue in every moment of their existence; they manifest the inherent questionability of their existence by failing to put it in question. In terms of his second defining characteristic, such a life indicates the ontological mineness of human existence precisely insofar as it exemplifies an absence or rather a repression of that mineness – a way of living as if my life was not my own, as if I haunted my own existence.

It follows that what I initially presented as two distinct claims about the human way of being are in truth internally related. In effect, Heidegger's sense of the priority of existence over essence for human beings, and his conception of them as manifesting mineness, are different ways of delineating the same distinctive ontological reality. But the second way highlights the potential ethical relevance of these ontological matters. For if what Heidegger means by inauthenticity is an absence or repression of mineness, then authenticity must be a matter of acknowledging or realizing that mineness; and that implies that evaluating any human life in terms of its authenticity means judging the extent to which that life, which is necessarily the life of a particular individual, is genuinely expressive of his or her individuality. Whether or not someone is living authentically is not, then, a matter of what she spends her time doing, or of how many other people spend their time in the same ways, but of how she relates to whatever it is that she spends her time doing. Does she have reasons of her own for doing it, reasons for which she takes herself to be individually answerable? If so, then how she lives is rooted in her individual determination of what is worth doing and why, and so her life makes it manifest that she is, and serves to constitute her as, a distinct individual. If not, then her life makes it manifest that she is relating to herself as if there were no self for her to relate to; her existence embodies an aspiration to deny the ineluctable truth that it is hers, and hers alone, to live.

Two points are worth underlining here. First, the question of whether a person's existence manifests genuine individuality is not restricted to the domain of action, at least not if that domain is regarded as contrasting with the domain of thought, desire and feeling. Such a contrast would certainly be artificial, since human actions necessarily involve thought insofar as they are grounded in reasons, and since thinking could plausibly be regarded as a species of action or activity. But if one draws such a distinction at all, it must be emphasized that human individuality finds expression as much in one's relation to one's thoughts, desires and feelings as in relation to one's actions. Heidegger stresses that the "das Man" mode of existence inflects public discourse as pervasively as it inflects patterns of social action. What we find ourselves discussing and thinking about, what we find ourselves passionately opposing or endorsing, what we regard as horrifying or disgusting or admirable or desirable, can as easily manifest the inherent impersonality of "das Man" as can our patterns of behavior. As always, the critical question is: do we regard ourselves as individually answerable for the particular matters that we are attending to, and for the ways in which we attend and respond to them, whether intellectually, appetitively or emotionally? Is my mind and my heart my own?

In this domain, however, taking responsibility for our responses involves ensuring that those responses aspire to track the real nature of the subject matter. After all, if I take myself to have good reason to be preoccupied with this issue rather than another, and to respond to it in this way rather than another, then those reasons must be grounded in the nature of the issue. Whether it be a controversial prize for artistic achievement, a putative threat to the environment or another's apparently insulting behavior, I cannot take responsibility for my thoughts and feelings about it unless I aspire to make those thoughts and feelings genuinely responsive to the real nature of their objects. In this context, individual authenticity is a matter of aiming properly to acknowledge the reality of things; relating questioningly to oneself requires that one relate questioningly to one's world – as opposed to taking one's bearings from what everyone says or takes to be obvious about it, or from what everyone suddenly finds boring or fascinating about it. In this sense, existing in the mode of "das Man" amounts to repressing one's capacity to grasp things as they really are. To think and feel inauthentically is to participate in forms of life in which the distinction between judgements and evaluations that capture reality and ones which merely seem to do so becomes increasingly difficult to draw, and in which we become increasingly uninterested in drawing it.

The second point to underline is that, if authenticity is a matter of establishing a certain relation to oneself (and hence to others and to the world), it is never something that can be definitively achieved. For even if I do succeed in taking responsibility for something I am presently doing or thinking, I am necessarily then confronted with the task of doing so again in the next moment of my existence, and so endlessly on. Each such achievement simply sets me the task of re-establishing the same self-relation; and for that reason, it would be least misleading to say that being authentic is a matter of endlessly becoming authentic. It is not so much an attainable state to be aimed at as a process or a task that can never be accomplished but can always be abandoned. It is, one might even say, a matter of endlessly overcoming one's tendency to inauthenticity.

Ethics and ontology

Should one then conclude that ethics either can or should take an interest in Heidegger's suggestion that human existence is always and everywhere a matter of either becoming or failing to become an individual?

Here are three plausible ways of articulating its ethical relevance. The first employs terms provided by Kantian ethics. If the moral law – the principles by reference to which we guide and evaluate our actions – must be thought of as at once applying to the self and as originating from the self, then one necessary condition for the possibility of ethics is the actual possession or genuine realization of selfhood; and Heidegger's interest in authenticity is thus an interest in something without which ethics as standardly understood would be unintelligible. But is an interest in a condition for the possibility of ethics an ethical interest? Yes and No. "No," in that it is not an interest in what one might call the content of the moral law, in what is sometimes known as first-order ethical theorizing – the provision of any concrete guidance with respect to any particular ethical problem, let alone of a systematic account of how one ought to live. But "Yes," in that it is an interest in a condition for the possibility of *ethics* (as opposed to some other aspect of human life).

A second attempt might rather say that Heidegger's interest in the realization of individuality is in fact one that surfaces at significant moments in every major variant of first-order ethical theory. In Mill, it emerges in his sense that liberty is threatened by the fact that it mostly does not occur to most of us to have any inclination except for what is customary; in Aristotle, it is registered in his conception of individual character as needing to be formed or cultivated; in Kant, it looms behind his distinction between acting in conformity with the moral law and acting from it – as if making it one's own. On this formulation, authenticity is not a presupposition of ethical thought, but rather a vital preoccupation of any worthwhile variant of it (whether deontological, teleological or neither – Cavell 2004).

A third approach would be to say that Heidegger's position is in fact one species of a relatively neglected genus of first-order ethical theory – that of perfectionism. If so, however, it cannot be essential to perfectionism to claim that facilitating the flourishing of certain exceptional individuals might justify sacrificing the interests of all others in society (the sense in which Nietzsche is often said to be a perfectionist). For Heidegger's perfectionism interests itself solely in a possibility that is open to all individuals insofar as they are human – the possibility of self-realization understood as a process of overcoming inauthenticity and becoming oneself, of realizing (that is, appreciating and enacting) one's answerability for everything one thinks, says and does.

Nothing requires us to choose between these three ways of formulating Heidegger's position; and something speaks in favor of refusing to do so. For to recognize their equal legitimacy amounts to acknowledging that Heidegger's concern with individuality is not simply an articulation of a perfectionist claim, or an issue registered in every serious ethical vision, or an essential presupposition of any ethical theorizing, but rather has an equal claim to be viewed in any (and so in all) of these ways. In short, Heidegger's preoccupations cannot be assigned a single, stable place in the accepted taxonomies of contemporary ethics; and that, I suggest, is because they unsettle the assumptions that those taxonomies reflect. Many suppose, for example, that ethical perfectionism is necessarily elitist; or that an interest in the formation of individual character can straightforwardly be used to distinguish one type of ethical theory (say, the Aristotelian) from others; or that the distinction between an ethical theory and its enabling non-ethical presuppositions can be easily drawn; or that ethics primarily or even exclusively concerns our relations to others (as opposed to our relations to ourselves), and our actions and judgements (as opposed to pretty much anything we might think, feel or do). By forcing us to reconsider just these issues, Heidegger's writings reveal the extent to which contemporary modes of ethical thought regard their inherently questionable ways of demarcating their subject matter as if they were beyond question, and so constitute exemplary instances of inauthentic thinking.

See also Nietzsche (Chapter 18); Existentialism (Chapter 20); Freedom and responsibility (Chapter 23); Ideals of perfection (Chapter 55).

References

Cavell, S. (2004) *Cities of Words*, Cambridge, MA: Harvard University Press.

Heidegger, M. (1962) *Being and Time*, Oxford: Blackwell, trans. J. Macquarrie and E. Robinson.

——(1977) "Letter on Humanism," in D. Farrell Krell (ed.) *Heidegger: Basic Writings*, San Francisco, CA: HarperCollins.

Sartre, J.-P. (1958) *Being and Nothingness*, trans. H. Barnes, London: Routledge.

Young, J. (2002) *Heidegger's Later Philosophy*, Cambridge: Cambridge University Press.

Further reading

Hodge, J. (1995) *Heidegger and Ethics*, London: Routledge. (Interprets *Being and Time* in the light of Heidegger's later thought.)

Mulhall, S. (2005), *Heidegger and* Being and Time, London: Routledge. (Develops the view summarized in this entry in more detail, and as a reading of the whole text.)

Olafson, F. (1998) *Heidegger and the Ground of Ethics*, Cambridge: Cambridge University Press. (Offers a different reading of the ethical implications of Heidegger's conception of Dasein as Being-with.)

Part II

META-ETHICS

22
ETHICS, SCIENCE, AND RELIGION

Simon Blackburn

Ethics is the study of what is of value in general, and morality is the part of ethics that concerns itself with how we may or may not behave. Science and religion impinge upon ethics, and I shall argue that each make good servants to it, but bad governors of it. That is, each of them may bring in their own way views about human nature and the human condition which have implications for what we value and how we ought to behave. Each of them however is apt to harbor ambitions beyond this, presuming to dictate what we are to value and how we ought to behave, usurping and deposing ethics and occupying its throne. In this brief introduction I shall explain why this is a danger and something of how we might wish to think about it.

Ethics and religion

The idea that morality and ethics require a foundation in religion is old and widespread, yet it can appear almost laughably easy to refute it. Plato, although himself at least conventionally religious, put his finger on the problem when Socrates poses the so-called "Euthyphro dilemma": Are things of value because the gods love them, or do the gods love things because they are of value? If we take the first horn, we have to explain how the arbitrary preference of anyone, divine or not, can actually bring it about that something has value. This is hard enough to understand, but worse, it seems to preclude us from praising or admiring the gods for their justice and wisdom and goodness. For if their preferences literally create value, they cannot go wrong, and deserve no credit for whichever preferences they indulge. But if we take the second horn, we acknowledge the prior existence of values, with which the desires of the gods then conform. And that gives value an independent existence, which then needs to be understood in other terms.

Furthermore, the enterprise of coming at ethics by first discovering gods and then interpreting their wishes or commands is multiply fraught. Gods tell different people different things at different places and times. And the enterprise of trying to work out what the gods are like and what they wish us to do, by starting from the world as we have it and as we can best reason about it, leads to nothing. As David Hume put it in his inimitable way (Hume 1999/1748: §11, para. 22),

> While we argue from the course of nature, and infer a particular intelligent cause, which first bestowed, and still preserves order in the universe, we embrace a principle, which is both uncertain and useless. It is uncertain; because the subject lies entirely beyond the reach of human experience. It is useless; because our knowledge of this cause being derived entirely from the course of nature, we can never, according to the rules of just reasoning, return back from the cause with any new inference, or making additions to the common and experienced course of nature, establish any new principles of conduct and behaviour.

With this door firmly closed, the only recourse is to privilege some one revelation: a preferred text or authority to whom the power of dictating ethics is ceded. But such a choice cannot rationally settle the question of whether the confidence is rightly placed, or whether we have to pick and choose from among the dictates that the authority issues. We have to filter those through our own sense of what is good or bad, right or wrong. We may defer to authority, but we retain the power to judge its deliverances.

All this is plain enough, and in the modern world the threat from religion is easier to diagnose and to neutralize than that from science. Indeed, many fire-breathing agnostics and atheists would doubt that human religions can bring anything at all of value to the enterprise of thinking how to live. They might think of religions as outdated, "primitive" attempts at science, better to be retired in favor of the real thing (Dawkins 2006). They might think of the obvious downside: religions as the nurseries of sectarian conflict, and as repositories of bigotry, fanaticism, intolerance, misogyny, xenophobia, and racism. They might think of religions as responsible for the arrogance of human beings, both in their dealings with others who are identified as in need of conversion, and in dealings with the animal world and the natural world, supposed to be there entirely for our benefit. They might see religions as bastions of ignorance and enemies of free inquiry.

All these points must be acknowledged, and they indeed disqualify us from handing ethics over entirely to religious authority. But they need not by themselves disqualify religions from having a voice in the conversations in which we try to discover what to do. They may deserve to do so not as fountains of edicts and commands, but because of their time-tested ability to tap into the emotional and social needs of people (Durkheim 2001/1912). The point here is that we cannot be content to leave it a mystery why religions are so appealing and why they have such staying power. This is something that needs explanation, and the only plausible explanations are likely to tell us important truths about ourselves. Even if religions only flourish because of ignorance and gullibility, as the more patronizing atheists suppose, then we need a politics and a morality contoured to ignorant and gullible people. If more realistically we agree that they speak to emotions such as terror of the unknown, or to our need to cope with common vulnerabilities to distress, sickness, and loss, or to the desire for hope or consolation, then our politics and ethics need to remind themselves that we are fearful and vulnerable people who crave hope and consolation. It will be no good crafting policies suitable only for rational, unemotional, self-sufficient, and self-governing people if the whole course of human history contains unmistakable signs that this is not what we are like. A mature religion will be a repository of social, emotional, and spiritual expressions of a culture. The people will not have been perfect: if they were misogynistic and intolerant and xenophobic then their expressions will reflect that, and will in turn cement and perpetuate the vices. But they will not have been all bad either: if they needed to find ceremonies and words to express togetherness, grief, loss, desolation, hope, reconciliation, then we will need to do the same in our own ways. It is as foolish for ethics to ignore the resources that this makes available as it would be to ignore the rest of the literature, music, architecture, or art of our culture. The path of wisdom will be not to ignore religious expressions, but to discriminate amongst them.

A more interesting functional story will itself consider the relation between religion and ethics. In spite of Plato and Hume, many people find an absence of religious authority disquieting. They fear that it leaves only nihilism, or the loss of values, that it leaves us rudderless and incapable of true principle and true commitment. They resonate to Dostoevsky's dark aphorism that if God is dead, everything is permitted. Well into the modern era the word "atheist" served as a virtual synonym for being amoral, or unprincipled, or a libertine (Berman 1990). Philosophers may patronize all this as a mistake, but if it is a mistake to which people are highly vulnerable, then perhaps one of the most important functions of religion is precisely to serve as a bulwark against the loss of values or the loss of principles. The gods of battle fortify people, and a fighting unit with public rituals whereby each member knows that each of the others makes the right overtures to these deities, is very likely to be better than one in which many are suspected not to do so (and this begins to explain why atheism is so often seen as dangerous and corrosive). It is as if by taking part in the right ceremonies, or hearing ourselves say the right words, we armor ourselves as we need to do against faltering when things become difficult. Still more, by seeing our neighbors simply reciting the ten commandments or singing the right songs, we can be reassured, as we need to be, that they share enough of our own values, that they too can be relied upon or trusted. Religion, then, is a "hard to fake sign of commitment" (Irons 2001). It does not give the source of values, but in many social and political circumstances, helps people to stand by them.

Ethics and science

Religion is visibly in the ethical business of shaping and affirming our practical identities, whereas on the face of it science has a much less intimate relationship with ethics. The office of science is to tell us what the world is like; the office of ethics is to direct how we respond to it. The gap between science and ethics is canonized in the "fact–value" distinction or the "is–ought" gap: closely related or identical ways of reminding ourselves that it is one thing to know how things stand, but another to know what may be done or should be done about them. Science is in the business of cognition, and ethics in the business of conation, or the directions of the will and of choice, attitudes, and emotions.

The difference is sometimes put by denying that we can infer a value from a fact, or by claiming that doing so commits something called the "naturalistic fallacy," but these thoughts are incorrect. Suppose we consider norms or obligations. It is quite in order to infer that we have to do something from the fact that a child is injured and we are the nearest source of help, or to infer that we ought to turn down the music from the fact that a neighbor is trying to sleep. Good people will be guided by the fact to the appropriate belief about what they should do. They would find the inferences as immediate and inexorable as any other. The question is only one of the *kind* of defect on show if a person is not guided as they should be. It is not a question of semantics or meaning: someone could understand the situation in the right terms, but deny the obligation, and they would not therefore convict themselves of some linguistic error. This was what G. E. Moore was concerned to show when he christened the naturalistic fallacy. The fallacy lies not in making the inference, but in supposing that it can be underwritten or compelled simply by a definition. The failure is not a defect of logic either: the person who is not guided in the right way is not on the face of it on the road to contradicting himself, which is the pre-eminent sign of logical failure. Rather the defect is one of what St Augustine called "the pull of the will and of love." In other words, it is a defect of practical coloration or motivation, of failing to be moved or to care as the situation requires. The person who is not moved by the facts of the case as the virtuous person would be is not usually semantically or logically challenged, but simply careless, callous, or selfish: in short, *bad*.

In spite of all this, science has imperialistic ambitions, and it is certainly tempting firstly for scientists to believe that they have something special to offer to ethics, and secondly for philosophers to hope that some of the prestige of science might rub off onto their subject, revealing it as truly objective, empirical, experimental, and therefore authoritative. Indeed, for a long time biology in particular has been a vociferous contributor to the ethical conversation, often exhibiting implications, or supposed implications, of the Darwinian account of evolution for human nature. The discovery that we have to think of ourselves as closely related to other animals, and like them needing to live and breed in jungles red in tooth and claw, could hardly fail to influence interpretations of human nature, generally in the pessimistic direction of seeing ourselves as necessarily characterized by selfishness, deceitfulness, manipulativeness, promiscuity, and a complete lack of expensive emotions including altruism, empathy, guilt, or remorse. But this is a description of a psychopath rather than a normal human being, and science itself has contributed to casting doubt on the misinterpretations of Darwinism that superficially seemed to require it to apply to us. There are circumstances in nature in which less aggressive organisms are more successful than more lethal ones, and in which organisms survive by being parts of wholes within which cooperation is as pronounced as competition. It is then a question of interpreting the history of humanity, and its different manifestations at different times and in different circumstances, to find out which traits come to prevail. So, rather than imposing a monolithic and unalterable "human nature," evolution is better seen as equipping us with functions for absorbing environmental data, and forming the motivational states that eventually move us in response to what we find. Human nature would turn out to be quite plastic, ready to be molded and shaped by experience, including most saliently our experience of other people. Our plasticity enables surrounding culture to mold our sympathies, our capacity for taking another's point of view, our sense of justice and the sources of pride, self-worth, shame, and guilt, just as the plasticity of our linguistic abilities equipped us to pick up any of the mother tongues with which we might have been surrounded.

Currently, however, there is an explosion of interest in a much wider confluence of disciplines: biology, developmental psychology, evolutionary psychology, cognitive science, chemistry, neurophysiology, neurology, game theory, economics, and sociology, hopefully pulling together to generate a truly scientific account of human nature: who we are and how our practical lives should proceed (Hauser 2006; Sinnott-Armstrong 2008). The size of the explosion is partly due to the arrival of new experimental methods. In the brain sciences, there is the relatively recent appearance of neural imaging and the widespread dissemination of hitherto specialist studies of brain damage and its effects (Damasio 1994; Greene 2008). For the first time we can learn, for example, whether the areas of the brain that are excited by emotional events are also excited when we exert moral judgment, or whether a lesion that destroys emotional responses also destroys moral ones. In the social sciences there is the even more recent harnessing of the World Wide Web for cross-cultural research on a scale that was hitherto impossible. For the first time we can learn whether quite complex moral and ethical ideas are confined to our own culture, or whether they have a universal appeal (Hauser 2006; Knobe and Nichols 2008). For example, studies have tested whether the so-called principle of double effect, the idea that it can be permissible to tolerate a foreseen but unwanted event as a bad side effect of a plan, when it would be impermissible to intend the same event as part of the execution of an equivalent plan, is a parochial and variable feature of some moral schemes, or is felt to be compelling across the world. The more widely a principle is found, the more likely it may seem that it is part of our human birthright, perhaps by being a deliverance of an innate "moral module" molded by evolution.

These advances in instrumentation are exciting, and nobody can doubt that they have produced fascinating results. This is compatible with recognizing one or two caveats about their use, of which practitioners are largely aware. One caveat about web surveys is quite obvious. Respondents are self-selected, and only drawn from the admittedly huge community of people who first have access to computers, second have the leisure to fill in questionnaires, and third have an interest in the kind of question being asked. Finally, while they give us a time slice of responses, they do not enable a diachronic look at how human beings might have thought and felt at different times, nor indeed may they be a reliable guide to how they feel, as opposed to how they say they feel, even at the present time. Thus, suppose a survey showed that worldwide nearly everyone who answers the question ticks the box saying they approve of treating animals kindly. We would be ill-advised to see this as a constant of human nature either through time or even in the present, in the face of abundant evidence of the contrary from history and from the courts. Surveys are better at telling whether people talk the talk, rather than whether they walk the walk.

The idea of an innate moral module, universally programmed to give all human moralities a shared underlying structure, is modeled on Chomsky's similar hypothesis about an innate grammar constraining the form that possible human language may take. The principal argument for Chomsky's innatism was the celebrated "poverty of stimulus": the disparity between what he saw as the meagre input to the infant's learning of a language, and the torrential output, which is the ability to see immediately and without conscious thought the syntactic structure (and the meaning or semantics) of any of the vast number of sentences that can be formed in its native language. Furthermore we have only the haziest idea of how we do it, or how we could write down programs for computing grammaticality, or principles for showing other people how to do it. The moral case bears only a rather distant analogy to this. The perception of meaning is quick, unconscious, inflexible or immune to influence from collateral information, and perfectly certain across a prodigiously wide spectrum. By contrast our moral judgments are often hesitant, articulable in conscious thought, responsive to collateral information, while certainties are far from abundant and far from the norm. Finally the universal features that have been discovered include such things as the principle of double effect, sensitivity to a difference between actions and failures to act (it being worse to kill than to let die), and proximity to harm as increasing moral responsibility. But it is not difficult to see how the ordinary constancies of human life and infant upbringing could bring about a universal sensitivity to these features. The child who is emphatically taught not to eat dirt will only later and probably with less emphasis be told that he is responsible for standing by and letting his little brother eat dirt; and it is cases in which we can most easily see the effects of our actions that form the paradigms and prototypes of bad behavior. A child is inducted in all this by examples, stories, and admonitions as well as by imitating and practicing the activities of allowing and forbidding conduct. So the disparity between the materials with which it learns and what it makes of them is much less marked than in the linguistic case, and there is correspondingly less plausibility to any argument from the poverty of stimulus to a richly structured innate endowment.

A second caveat reverts to the is/ought distinction. Suppose we do have a robust piece of data about how nearly everybody feels about some question. It is still open to the moralist to lament this uniformity as the unfortunate product of a fallen human nature, and indeed there are clear examples where this is a fairly natural response. Utilitarians, for instance, pride themselves on the doctrine that everyone counts for one and nobody for more than one; the "calculus" of happiness has no discounts or multipliers, and it is only the total aggregate of happiness that underwrites value. A sociological result that in fact people do discount for distance, having extremely tribal moralities that separate insiders from outsiders in invidious ways, is saddening no doubt, but it does nothing to impugn utilitarianism as an ideal, or even as a practical value to preach. It may suggest that there will be an awful lot of preaching to be done, or even that while we may be able to move towards the ideal it is unlikely that we will ever reach it. But then sober utilitarians will always have known that. The same structure applies if we find that men are generally more faithless than women, or that people find it more tolerable or permissible to pull a lever whereby someone dies at a distance, than to be in close proximity and push them off a bridge. The natural response is that no doubt we feel like that, and it may be evolutionarily explicable why we do, but we shouldn't.

The widespread interest in the results of the brain sciences has generated work of a different kind, largely hoping to disentangle the various contributions of emotional or "affect" mechanisms from cognitive or rational mechanisms in the formation of moral judgement. The hope is that this work will speak to the old division between sentiment-based approaches to moral philosophy, whose principal figurehead is David Hume, and more ratiocentric approaches, associated above all with Kant, but also with the Platonic tradition in classical thought, whereby it is the privilege of reason to control and direct the otherwise unruly passions. Neither of these positions is merely historical, and they form the two poles around which a great deal of contemporary theorizing revolves. They are however only unfortunately presented as polar opposites: Kant, at least in his later work, pays cautious attention to affective states (Kant 1996/1803), while Hume constantly emphasizes the role of cognition and reason in isolating and distinguishing the entangled morally relevant features of human actions and human characters (Hume 2006/1751). Furthermore, Hume himself does not work with the categories of "affect" or "emotion." His preferred term is the "passions," and he includes a large spread of different states: "desire, aversion, grief, joy, hope, fear, despair and security," not to mention indirect passions, which include "pride, humility, ambition, vanity, love, hatred, envy, pity, malice, generosity, with their dependants" (Hume 1978/1739: 276–7). He is also clear that there are "calm passions" that are not conscious, but more like dispositional or functional states of whose existence we may not be immediately aware. Finding, therefore, that someone may be morally motivated, or inclined to judge a situation, without visible activity in parts of the brain that become excited when heart-pounding emotions such as fear or anger assail us, is not likely to touch this position.

This introduces two important aspects of research into the neural substrates of our psychologies. One is that we can take up positions towards the world – stances and dispositions towards actual and potential doings, for example – without any salient phenomenology. Just as I can build a fence in an unemotional and clinical frame of mind, so I can forbid a course of action or intend to enforce a policy. Our ethics may bubble up emotionally on enough occasions, when sympathy and sorrow, or anger and indignation, or shame and guilt make themselves felt. But it is still there in our cold, calm dispositions and intentions. It is sometimes argued that if a Humean has such an expanded conception of the passions, the view that motivations in general and ethics in particular require passionate engagement with the world becomes a mere tautology, reducing to the triviality that only motives motivate (Nagel 1970). But this is overly pessimistic. In fact dispositions – including attitudes, resolution, and intentions – serve as intervening variables in psychology in exactly the same way that theoretical counterparts such as forces and fields do in physics. They are known by their functions and effects, certainly, but they stand at the service of an indefinite number of predictions and ways of dealing with systems. Hume's insight was that an ethical commitment bears greater resemblance to a practical stance or disposition than it does to more ordinary empirical judgments. Ethics is directly about motivation and practice in a way that empirical judgments are not (Smith 1994; Blackburn 1998).

The other moral to take from this is that brain writing is no easier to interpret than human writing and human behavior, and indeed needs calibrating against the overt practices of people. So if, for instance, an area of the brain associated with problem solving is shown to be active when we work out whether to accept something as subtle as the doctrine of double effect, this confirms that there is indeed working out going on, but it does not tell us whether we are working out a plan or policy, or working out a plain matter of fact, or exercising imagination, or even offline rehearsals of what to feel, or doing something more like a mathematical problem or a crossword puzzle solution. That has to be shown by the resultant behavior, which may include many social expressions, such as writing the distinction into criminal laws, embodying it in soap operas and morality tales for the young, or simply tending to shun more completely those who intend harm as opposed to those who put up with it. It is in the light of all these activities that candidates for the neural substrate of morality have to be interpreted. Even gross neurological disorders, such as that suffered by the unfortunate ventromedial prefrontal cortex patient Phineas Gage, need interpreting as deficits of affect, or of sense of self, or of imagination, or as admixtures of all of these (Damasio et al. 1991; Damasio 1994; Gerrans 2008). The moral is that there is no short cut to exercising interpretative caution; as with medicine, the new tools and shiny modern machinery need human understanding adjoined to them if they are to tell us the things we want to know.

The way forward

The reader may reasonably worry whether we have talked ethics into an impasse. If religious authority does nothing to underwrite it, as the Euthyphro dilemma suggests, and if science itself comes up against the is/ought gap, then the subject may seem to be not so much elusive as chimerical, an exercise of the mind founded on nothing more than an illusion. The old ghosts of nihilism and relativism walk in the darkness. But these fears are groundless. What metaphysics and even physics and its satellite sciences cannot do for us, we can do for ourselves. It is we who bring our affective natures into play when we take up practical stances, and it is we who have to voice our own attitudes and policies, prohibitions and insistencies, as we conduct our lives together. What other sources of authority cannot do for us, we can do for ourselves.

This may seem paradoxical. When thinking about religious authority, we saw that the will of a divine lawgiver seemed an insufficient source for the authority we need in ethics. We could not conceive how the inescapable nature of obligation and duty, or the intransigent demands of justice could result from the arbitrary preferences of any being, however supernatural. So how can we now turn around and say that what even the gods cannot do, we can do for ourselves? Is it not a royal road to the most corrosive collapse of values to think that ethics is nothing but the "banner of the questing will" (Murdoch 1967)?

The answer is to reflect on what is meant by insisting that it is we ourselves who value things and insist on things. We need to do so to enable social life to go on, with its distribution of burdens and benefits, its contracts, promises, rights, government, and laws. We had better make the adjustments carefully, or we risk injustice and we court the resentments and instabilities to which injustices give rise. We are in the domain of practice, but that is not to say that the practice is easy, that our first thoughts will be our best, or that the long experience of human affairs going well or badly has nothing to teach us. Our natures determine many of our likes and dislikes, desires and needs. They also determine what will work in human affairs and what will not. Hence our ethics has indeed to be founded on as much knowledge of human experience as we can muster, and that includes the interpretative sciences of history, law, anthropology, and literature as well as those of psychology and surrounding disciplines.

Fortunately, we know a great deal, and nearly all of what we know is open to view. The qualities of mind and character that help us to succeed in cooperative endeavors are named with words of admiration and praise; others are talked of with dislike or contempt. One of the things we all know, and one of the early things the child in any society learns, is which are which. Ethics is therefore inescapable, and while nihilism and relativism may be specters that haunt theorists in the study, they disappear in the cold light of day.

References

Berman, David (1990) *A History of Atheism in Britain: From Hobbes to Russell*, London: Routledge.

Blackburn, S. (1998) *Ruling Passions*, Oxford: Oxford University Press.

Damasio, A. R. (1994) *Descartes' Error: Emotion, Reason and the Human Brain*, New York: Putnam.

Damasio, A. R., Tranel, D. and Damasio, H. (1991) "Somatic Markers and the Guidance of Behaviour: Theory and Preliminary Testing," in H. S. Levin, H. M. Eisenberg and A. L. Benton (eds) *Frontal Lobe Function and Dysfunction*, New York: Oxford University Press, pp. 217–29.

Dawkins, R. (2006) *The God Delusion*, Boston, MA: Houghton Mifflin.

Durkheim, E. (2001/1912) *The Elementary Forms of Religious Life*, trans. Carol Cosman, Oxford: Oxford University Press.

Gerrans, P. (2008) "Mental Time Travel, Somatic Markers and 'Myopia for the Future'," Philip Gerrans' homepage, <http://homepage.mac.com/philipgerrans/page2/assets/synthese2.pdf>

Greene, J. D. (2008) "The Secret Joke of Kant's Soul," in Sinnott-Armstrong 2008, vol. 3, 35–117.

Hauser, M. (2006) *Moral Minds: How Nature Designed a Universal Sense of Right and Wrong*, New York: HarperCollins.

Hume, D. (1978/1739) *A Treatise of Human Nature*, ed. L. A. Selby-Bigge and P. Nidditch, Oxford: Oxford University Press.

——(1999/1748) *An Enquiry Concerning Human Understanding*, ed. Tom L. Beauchamp, Oxford: Oxford University Press.

——(2006/1751) *An Enquiry Concerning the Principles of Morals*, ed. T. Beauchamp, Oxford: Oxford University Press.

Irons, W. (2001) "Religion as a Hard-to-Fake Sign of Commitment," in *Evolution and the Capacity for Commitment*, ed. R. M. Nesse, New York: Russell Sage Foundation, pp. 292–309.

Kant, I. (1996/1803) *The Metaphysics of Morals*, trans. Mary Gregor, Cambridge: Cambridge University Press.

Knobe, J. and Nichols, S. (2008) *Experimental Philosophy*, New York: Oxford University Press.

Murdoch, I. (1967) *The Sovereignty of Good over Other Concepts*, Cambridge: Cambridge University Press.

Nagel, T. (1970) *The Possibility of Altruism*, Oxford: Clarendon Press.

Sinnott-Armstrong, W. (ed.) (2008) *Moral Psychology*, vols 1–3, Cambridge, MA: MIT Press.

Smith, M. (1994) *The Moral Problem*, Oxford: Blackwell.

23
FREEDOM AND RESPONSIBILITY

Randolph Clarke

We commonly take ourselves and each other to be morally responsible agents. We sometimes blame someone for doing something he should not have done, or praise someone for exemplary behavior. It is generally thought that we are responsible for such things only if we freely do them (or things resulting in them). Two fundamental philosophical questions that arise here are: What is the nature of moral responsibility, and what kind of freedom does it require? Only with answers to these questions can we settle whether we are in fact morally responsible.

Before turning to these questions, it will sharpen our focus to distinguish the topic here from some related things about which we may talk using the words "responsibility" or "responsible." For example, we might say that it is Sue's responsibility to feed the cat, or that she is responsible for seeing to it that the cat is fed. In this case, we would be saying that Sue has a certain obligation or duty, perhaps one that she acquired by promising to take care of the cat. This type of responsibility is often called prospective responsibility. If Sue is someone who takes her obligations seriously and generally carries them out, we might say that she is a responsible person.

But now suppose that, although Sue generally does what she ought to do, and although she has an obligation in this case to feed the cat, she does not in fact do so. We might then blame her for the cat's going hungry. In attributing blame, we would be finding Sue responsible in the sense at issue in this chapter. If Sue is someone who can be responsible in this sense, then she is, in this sense, a responsible agent. This type of responsibility is often called retrospective responsibility.

Retrospective responsibility can be moral or legal. Someone might be morally responsible for something for which, given the existing laws and legal institutions, he is not legally responsible. The offense committed might not be sufficiently important to be considered by the law, and no legal responsibility attaches to ordinary good deeds. One might still be morally praiseworthy for lending one's neighbor a hand with some yard work.

It is, then, retrospective moral responsibility that is our topic. What exactly is it to be responsible for something in this sense?

The nature of moral responsibility

Philosophers have offered several different conceptions of moral responsibility. One core notion has it that responsibility is *attributability*: you are morally responsible for something just in case it is attributable to you as a basis for moral assessment of you (Scanlon 1998: Ch. 6; Watson 2004). The appropriate judgment might be positive (you have acted heroically), negative (you were thoughtless), or neutral, depending on the character of what you did. Writers holding this conception sometimes maintain that our responsibility can extend beyond our actions to our thoughts, feelings, and even failures to think of things (Adams 1985; Scanlon 1998: 21–2; A. Smith 2005). On this view, one can be blameworthy for feeling envious, or having a racist belief, or forgetting a friend's birthday, regardless of whether these things result from, or are influencable by, one's actions, for they may nevertheless disclose moral faults.

A somewhat similar conception is that of *appraisability*: when one is morally responsible for something, there is a mark – positive, negative, or neutral – on one's moral ledger (Zimmerman 1988: Ch. 3). To be culpable for something is for there to be a debit or blemish on one's moral record for that thing; to be laudable is for there to be a credit or luster on one's record. This view differs from the former in holding that, of the variety of moral assessments of agents, only a narrow range are ascriptions of moral responsibility. For example, on this conception, one might be reprehensible for having a bad desire or character trait, or admirable for having a good one, without being culpable or laudable – and so without being responsible – for these things.

Some writers take attributability to include *answerability*: when one is morally responsible for something, one is answerable for that thing (Scanlon 1998: 268). On this view, moral criticism of an individual calls on that person to justify his behavior and, if it is not justifiable, to acknowledge wrongdoing.

When we address such a demand to someone, we are holding that person responsible. We might reproach him for having acted wrongly, and we might express anger or insist on an apology. Sometimes we impose sanctions on a wrongdoer, giving him the cold shoulder or withholding some favor. In the case of praiseworthy action, we might express gratitude or offer a token of thanks or a reward to the meritorious agent.

A conception of responsibility as *accountability* ties it to the appropriateness of responses of these types (Scanlon 1998: 248–67; Watson 2004; Zimmerman 1988: Ch. 5). On this view, one's responsibility for something can permit or require others to administer sanctions or offer rewards (depending on what one has done). It might be said that one who is blameworthy has no grounds for complaint about being treated harshly, or that it is fair that he be punished, or that he deserves to suffer.

Often when we take someone to be responsible for something, we have some type of emotion-laden attitude toward that person. We might be resentful if he has wronged us, or indignant if he unjustifiably harmed others. We might be grateful to someone who has been especially kind to us. One might feel guilty about one's own misdeeds. These emotions are often called reactive attitudes. A widely held conception of moral responsibility has it that to be responsible is to be *an appropriate target of the reactive attitudes* (Fischer and Ravizza 1998: 1–8; P. Strawson 2003; Wallace 1994: Chs 2–4). Some proponents of this view construe some of these attitudes, such as indignation or gratitude, as inherently retributive, as including the thought that the person in question deserves some sanction or reward (P. Strawson 2003). But others who associate responsibility closely with reactive attitudes deny that these attitudes have a retributive element (Scanlon 1998: 276).

Which of these conceptions of moral responsibility is correct? Perhaps several of them are; perhaps there are different types of moral responsibility, as some writers maintain (Scanlon 1998: Ch. 6; Watson 2004; Zimmerman 1988: Chs 3 and 5). In any case, when we encounter arguments about what kind of freedom is required for responsibility, it helps to note what the authors in question take responsibility to be.

The compatibility question

If I am responsible for something I have done, then, it is generally accepted, I must have exercised a certain type of freedom in performing that action, or in doing something that led to my performing that action. A fundamental question about responsibility is whether the required freedom is something that we could exercise even if determinism is true, or whether, on the contrary, its exercise requires indeterminism.

Determinism is the thesis that given the laws of nature, the way the world is at any given point in time completely determines every aspect of how the world is at any later point in time. For example, one aspect of how the world is right now is that you are reading this chapter in *The Routledge Companion to Ethics*. If determinism is true, then given the laws of nature, the way the world was at some point in the distant past, long before any human beings existed, has determined that you are now reading this chapter. (To eliminate the word "determines" from our definition, we can state the thesis as follows: a complete statement of the laws of nature, conjoined with a complete description of the total state of the world at any given point in time, entails every truth about how the world is at any later point in time.)

Might we have the kind of freedom required for moral responsibility even if determinism is true? The position that we cannot is known as *incompatibilism*; the view that we can is called *compatibilism*.

One historically prominent line of argument for incompatibilism holds that one does something with the requisite freedom only if one was able to do otherwise. It is then argued that if determinism is true, no one ever has the ability to do otherwise. The conclusion is that the truth of determinism would preclude our ever being morally responsible. For example, according to this line of argument, if determinism is true, and if I told a lie on a certain occasion, then I could not have done other than tell a lie then; and I cannot be responsible for telling the lie if I could not have done otherwise.

Would determinism really preclude our being able to do other than what we in fact do? One of the strongest arguments for an affirmative answer to this question is *the consequence argument*. It observes that, if determinism is true, then our current actions are consequences of the past and the laws of nature. It is not up to us what the laws of nature are, nor is it now up to us what happened in the past. Hence the consequences of these things are not now up to us. And if our actions are not up to us, then when we perform them, we are not able to do otherwise (van Inwagen 1983: Ch. 3).

The consequence argument is hotly contested. (For discussion of the debate, see Fischer 1994: Chs 1–5; Kapitan 2002.) But many defenders of compatibilism seek to bypass it. At issue with the consequence argument is whether, if determinism is true, we might still be able to do other than what we in fact do. But does moral responsibility for having done a certain thing require that one was able to do otherwise?

The thesis that it does is known as the principle of alternate possibilities, or PAP. Though PAP might strike one as obviously correct, a number of philosophers reject it. If that principle is false, then whatever freedom is required for responsibility does not include the ability to do otherwise. And if that is so, then even if determinism precludes the ability to do otherwise, it does not thereby preclude our being morally responsible.

One challenge to PAP focuses on cases of pre-emptive overdetermination, cases in which an agent does something on his own, without being forced to do it, but in circumstances in which some ensuring condition would make the agent do that very thing, were he not to do it on his own. It is stipulated that the agent is unaware of the ensuring condition, and that this condition does not in fact influence what happens. It seems, then, that the agent could be responsible for what he does. But given the circumstances, he could not have done otherwise (Frankfurt 2003).

Suppose, for example, that Albert considers whether to steal an apple, decides to do so, and steals an apple. Suppose that, unbeknownst to Albert, Betty was monitoring his deliberations (she has the means to do this), and if he had given serious thought to refraining from stealing the apple, Betty would have detected that fact, she would have intervened, and she would have seen to it that Albert decided to steal the apple and carried out that decision. Albert did not give serious thought to refraining from stealing the apple, and Betty did not intervene; she did not have to. Albert did what Betty wanted him to do, but he did it entirely on his own. It seems that if anyone can be responsible for anything,

Albert can be responsible for stealing the apple. But it also seems that, given Betty's readiness to intervene, Albert could not have done other than steal the apple. (Such situations are commonly called *Frankfurt scenarios*, after the author who introduced them into the literature on responsibility.)

Whether such a scenario really undermines PAP is a disputed matter. (Widerker and McKenna [2003] covers the debate.) But suppose that PAP is false – responsibility does not require the ability to do otherwise. Does that show that responsibility is compatible with determinism?

Several writers advance incompatibilism without appealing to PAP. Being morally responsible for something, they hold, requires that one be a source of that thing in a way that is ruled out if determinism is true. One cannot be such a source, it is said, if one's action is determined by something over which one has no control (Pereboom 2001: 2–6; Stump 1996; Zagzebski 2000). But why think that responsibility requires this sort of sourcehood?

Source incompatibilists (as these writers are called) sometimes appeal to a design argument in response to this question. Suppose that some thirty years ago a very resourceful agent, Gaia, wanted a certain very specific sequence of deeds done thirty years hence. Gaia had available to her the materials necessary to create any of a vast number of different human zygotes in Petri dishes. She had the power to ensure that whichever one she created would develop in a deterministic manner, and that its life would unfold entirely deterministically, and Gaia could foresee exactly how each life would unfold. She picked certain materials and combined them precisely because she knew that the resulting individual, and only that one, would do exactly the deeds thirty years later that she wanted done then. Her product is Robert. His deeds are all determined in exactly the way that Gaia foresaw, though in all other respects he is like us. Today Robert does precisely the things that Gaia created him to do. What are we to say of Robert's moral responsibility for these actions?

Source incompatibilists think that we should deny that Robert is responsible for what he does. Further, they argue, if determinism is true, there is no difference, with respect to responsibility, between Robert and the rest of us. Granted, we are not created by Gaia. But, they claim, whether we are products of such a being is not something on which our responsibility could hinge. If our lives unfold as deterministically as Robert's does, then even if we are not created in the same way as he is, we are no more responsible than Robert is. (Mele [2006: 188–95] sets out an argument of this sort but does not endorse it; Pereboom [2001: 110–17] advances a similar argument.)

A key premise of the argument is the denial that Robert is responsible for what he does. Would it be outrageous to reject this claim, to maintain that Robert can indeed be responsible for his deeds? The plausibility of that response depends on what responsibility is. Suppose that it is just attributability. Robert does perform his actions (Gaia does not – she might no longer be around), and we can make various moral assessments of Robert on the basis of his behavior, for example, that he is considerate, or clueless, or cruel. On the other hand, it may be less clear that Robert is culpable or laudable for his actions; it might seem inappropriate to respond with indignation toward him; and we might not find it credible that Robert deserves to suffer for his misdeeds, that he has it coming, or that justice demands that he suffer so.

If there are different kinds of moral responsibility, then perhaps we should say that Robert could have some of them but not others. Then, we might say, determinism is compatible with some types of responsibility but not with others.

Compatibilist accounts

If responsibility is compatible with determinism, then determinism is compatible with our exercising the freedom required for responsibility. What account can be given of this freedom? That is what a compatibilist theory of moral responsibility should tell us.

The required freedom can be characterized, in part, negatively, as freedom from certain kinds of responsibility-undermining conditions. Responsibility might be precluded if one's behavior results from hypnosis, brainwashing, or (if such a thing is possible) the direct implantation of thoughts into one's mind. Responsibility can be undermined by compulsion or addiction to a drug (particularly if one is not responsible for having become addicted). Freedom from these conditions is compatible with determinism; the truth of determinism would not entail that all of us are all the time hypnotized or brainwashed or suffering from compulsions or addictions.

The required freedom can be given a positive characterization as well. One reason why, it seems, we human agents are responsible for what we do, while non-human agents such as cats and chimps are not, is that we have certain rational capacities that they lack. We can, for example, take certain considerations to be reasons favoring or disfavoring a possible course of action. Among the reasons that we so recognize are moral reasons, considerations showing that one or another course of action is, in some respect, morally better or worse. Further, we can deliberate about what to do, assessing reasons, judging which are weightier, and making up our minds on the basis of such deliberation. In this process, we often have an awareness of ourselves carrying out these deliberations, and we can reflect on how well we are doing so, altering the process on the basis of this reflection.

A capacity to engage in such reflective deliberation, and to act on the basis of it, would seem to be required for moral responsibility. Is the possession of any such capacity compatible with determinism? Compatibilists contend that a deliberative process of this sort can be a deterministic process (Arpaly 2006: Ch. 2; Dennett 1984: Ch. 2). But suppose that on some occasion I do not in fact engage in any significant deliberation about what to do; the thought of making a hurtful remark occurs to me, and I make the remark. Or suppose that I deliberate about whether to make the remark and I make it on the basis of my deliberation. If determinism is true, might I have been capable of deliberating, or of deliberating differently, and refraining from making the remark on the basis of that process?

Some compatibilists offer a conception of rational capacities, and of capacities to act on the basis of practical reasoning, on which even if determinism is true we can, on a given occasion, possess capacities of these sorts that we do not in fact exercise then. The conception draws our attention to dispositions, such as fragility or solubility. Consider a difference between a lump of sugar and a hunk of lead. The sugar is disposed to dissolve in water, the lead is not; in a clear sense, the sugar can dissolve in water, while the lead cannot. This difference between sugar and lead is not eliminated if determinism is true; it remains true of sugar that it can dissolve in water. And this remains true of a particular lump of sugar that is not now in water and is not now dissolving.

Now, the account contends, the rational capacities required for moral responsibility – those that constitute the required positive freedom – are (or are composed of) dispositions. Just as sugar that is not now dissolving nevertheless can dissolve, even if its not now dissolving is determined, so a human agent who makes a hurtful remark on some occasion normally has a capacity then to deliberate and act otherwise on the basis of that deliberation, even if his actual behavior is determined. The positive freedom required for responsibility, these compatibilists contend, is thus compatible with determinism (M. Smith 2003; Vihvelin 2004).

An alternative compatibilist theory focuses on the mechanisms (or processes) within agents that generate their behavior and requires, for responsibility, that these mechanisms possess a certain disposition-like feature, responsiveness to reasons. A process issuing in action on a certain occasion (for example, deliberating about what to do) is said to have the required responsiveness just in case, with that type of process operating, the agent would display a certain pattern of behavior in a range of possible situations. Suppose, for example, that Albert's theft of an apple was produced by a mechanism of type M. Consider all the possible scenarios in which an M-type mechanism might operate in Albert and there was sufficient reason for him not to steal an apple. What is required is that, among these possibilities, there is an understandable pattern of cases in which Albert would recognize the reasons – including moral reasons – not to steal an apple, and there is at least one such scenario in which he would refrain from stealing on the basis of that recognition (Fischer and Ravizza 1998).

Notice that an action-producing mechanism might possess the required responsiveness even if, given the circumstances in which an action is performed, the agent cannot do other than what he actually does. For example, the process that issues in Albert's theft of an apple might be appropriately reasons-responsive even though, with Betty prepared to intervene, Albert cannot refrain from stealing. Since Betty does not in fact influence what Albert does, in judging whether the mechanism that generates his behavior is suitably responsive, we include among the possible scenarios to be considered situations in which Betty is absent. And it might well be that in many of these situations, if there were sufficient reason not to steal an apple, Albert would refrain.

Proponents of this mechanism-based approach, then, take Frankfurt scenarios to show that the ability to do otherwise is not required for responsibility. They then argue that even if determinism precludes the ability to do otherwise, it is compatible with our having the freedom required for responsibility.

However, there is an interesting difference between Frankfurt scenarios and the way things are if determinism is true. In the former cases, it is allowed, nothing in the actual process by which the action is produced precludes the agent's being able to do otherwise. It is the presence of the ensuring condition – something that does not actually affect what happens – that rules this out. But if the consequence argument is sound, then, given determinism, the nature of the actual processes by which our behavior is produced itself precludes our ever being able to do otherwise. We are, in that respect, like Robert. One might then find that, even if we have capacities to act otherwise, and even if the mechanisms that issue in our actions are reasons-responsive, we are not morally responsible for what we do, for we are not in an appropriate sense the sources of our behavior. One might draw this conclusion if one holds that responsibility entails a strong form of desert. Or one might find that, while the freedom characterized by one or another of these compatibilist accounts suffices (as far as freedom is concerned) for some type of moral responsibility – attributability, say – it does not suffice for some other type, such as accountability.

Incompatibilist accounts

If moral responsibility – or some type of moral responsibility – is not compatible with determinism, would indeterminism of any sort allow for it? Theorists who think that we can be responsible if, but only if, indeterminism is true offer incompatibilist (or libertarian) accounts of the requisite freedom.

Some such accounts take free actions to be entirely uncaused and hold that they need not themselves consist of one thing's causing another – they can lack internal causal structure. Proponents of these theories maintain that we have an active power, and the exercise of this power is a free action. Basic exercises of active power are simple uncaused events, such as decisions (Ginet 1990; Goetz 1997; McCann 1998; Pink 2004: Chs 7–8). A free decision is explained by some feature of that decision itself, and not by anything that brings it about (nothing brings it about).

A second kind of incompatibilist theory points out that causation need not be deterministic. One event can bring about another even though, until it does, there remains a chance that the effect will not occur. Causal laws might be probabilistic; there might, for example, be a probability of .6 that, given an event of a certain type, it will cause an event of a certain other type. Proponents of this kind of view hold that free actions are caused but not determined. A free decision might be nondeterministically caused (and explained) by the deliberative process leading up to it (Kane 1996; Nozick 1981: 291–316).

Suppose, for example, that a businesswoman is on her way to an important meeting when she sees someone being mugged in an alleyway. She considers stopping to call for help, realizing that if she does, she will likely miss her meeting. She sees reasons both for stopping and for proceeding to work. Suppose that until she makes her decision, it remains undetermined which decision she will make. If she decides not to stop, that decision will be caused (and explained) by her recognition of the importance of getting to the meeting. But it will have remained open to her to decide otherwise. (If she had, that decision to help would have been caused and explained by her recognition of the reasons for stopping.) Whichever decision she makes, then, she will have been able to do otherwise (Kane 1996: 126–7).

A third type of account takes literally the idea of being a source of, or originating, one's behavior. We act with the freedom required for responsibility, on this view, just in case *we* cause our behavior and our doing so is not determined. The required causation by an agent – agent-causation – is said to be different from, say, causation by one's recognition of reasons, or by the deliberative process leading to one's action, or by one's beliefs or desires. It is causation by oneself, the agent who performs the action. An action belongs to one in the way required for moral responsibility, it is held, only if one is in this way its source, its uncaused cause (O'Connor 2000; for discussion, see Clarke 2003: Chs 8–10; Pereboom 2001: Chs 2–3).

Whether indeterminism of any of these types actually exists is, of course, debatable. But even apart from that question, there is a powerful challenge to each of these incompatibilist accounts. If, until some event occurs, there remains a chance that it will not occur, then it would seem to be in some sense a matter of luck whether that event occurs. If our decisions or other actions are undetermined, then they, too, would seem to be subject to this sort of luck. And to the extent that something is a matter of luck, that thing is not under anyone's control. But how can we be responsible for what we do if it is not under our control?

This problem is perhaps most pressing on the first, noncausal type of incompatibilist account, but it bears on the others as well. Consider the agent-causal view. Suppose that the businesswoman agent-causes a decision not to stop, and until she does there remains a chance that she will instead agent-cause a decision to stop. There is, then, a possible world with the same laws of nature, and with the same pre-decision history, in which she decides to stop (and agent-causes that decision). There is no difference between the actual world, in which the woman agent-causes the decision not to stop, and that alternative world, in which she agent-causes a decision to stop, that can explain the difference between her doing the former and her doing the latter; nothing explains that difference. It is, then, just a matter of luck. And if the difference between the woman's agent-causing a decision not to stop and her agent-causing a decision to stop is just a matter of luck, then, it seems, she is not morally responsible for the decision she in fact makes (Haji 2004; Mele 2006: Ch. 3).

Whether the luck argument undermines this type of incompatibilist account hinges on whether agent causation, if it exists, constitutes our originating or being the sources of our decisions in a way that suffices for our deciding freely. If it does, then the difference between the actual world and the other possible world in question is a matter of how the businesswoman exercises her freedom. The difference is then not just a matter of luck. But it is unclear how we are to settle whether agent-causation does, in the way suggested, constitute the exercise of freedom. Answering that question would seem to require that we know more about what agent-causation is supposed to be.

Is moral responsibility impossible?

Some authors hold that some possible type of indeterminism (for example, one including agent-causation), if it existed, would allow for responsibility, but that we have good evidence that the required indeterminism does not exist, and hence that we are not morally responsible agents (Pereboom 2001). Others maintain that responsibility is impossible, whether determinism is true or not.

One argument for the latter view observes that actions for which we are responsible are (at least typically) things we do for reasons. When one acts for a certain reason, one does what one does because of the way one is, mentally speaking. In order to be responsible for what one does, then, one must be responsible for being the way one is. But in order to be responsible for being that way, one must have brought this about, and one must be responsible for having brought it about. But in bringing this about, one will have acted for reasons; one will then have acted because of the way one then was, mentally speaking. Responsibility for that action will require that one was responsible for how one then was; and so on, without end. In order to be responsible for anything, then, one must have completed an infinite sequence of actions for which one was responsible, thereby creating oneself, with respect to how one is mentally. But such self-creation is impossible, at least for finite beings such as ourselves. Moral responsibility, then, is impossible, at least for beings like us (G. Strawson 2002).

Proponents of such an argument sometimes emphasize that what they claim to be impossible is ultimate responsibility, something that could make an agent deserving of eternal reward in heaven or eternal damnation in hell

(G. Strawson 2002: 451–2). However, even if it is not possible for us to possess this type of responsibility, it remains an open question whether we might have what is called attributability, or appraisability, or even a type of accountability on which we can deserve certain sorts of treatment in response to our behavior, even if never heaven-or-hell rewards or punishments. Again, we see, whether we are responsible depends on what responsibility is, or on which type of moral responsibility is at issue.

See also Blame, remorse, mercy, forgiveness (Chapter 48); Responsibility: Intention and consequence (Chapter 50); Responsibility: Act and omission (Chapter 51); Justice and punishment (Chapter 57).

References

Adams, R. M. (1985) "Involuntary Sins," *Philosophical Review* 94: 3–31.

Arpaly, N. (2006) *Merit, Meaning, and Human Bondage: An Essay on Free Will*, Princeton, NJ: Princeton University Press.

Clarke, R. (2003) *Libertarian Accounts of Free Will*, New York: Oxford University Press.

Dennett, D. C. (1984) *Elbow Room: The Varieties of Free Will Worth Wanting*, Cambridge, MA: MIT Press.

Fischer, J. M. (1994) *The Metaphysics of Free Will: An Essay on Control*, Oxford: Blackwell.

Fischer, J. M. and Ravizza, M. (1998) *Responsibility and Control: A Theory of Moral Responsibility*, Cambridge: Cambridge University Press.

Frankfurt, H. G. (2003) "Alternate Possibilities and Moral Responsibility," in G. Watson (ed.) *Free Will*, 2nd edn, Oxford: Oxford University Press.

Ginet, C. (1990) *On Action*, Cambridge: Cambridge University Press.

Goetz, S. (1997) "Libertarian Choice," *Faith and Philosophy* 14: 195–211.

Haji, I. (2004) "Active Control, Agent-Causation and Free Action," *Philosophical Explorations* 7: 131–48.

Kane, R. (1996) *The Significance of Free Will*, New York: Oxford University Press.

Kapitan, T. (2002) "A Master Argument for Incompatibilism?," in R. Kane (ed.) *The Oxford Handbook of Free Will*, New York: Oxford University Press.

McCann, H. J. (1998) *The Works of Agency: On Human Action, Will, and Freedom*, Ithaca, NY: Cornell University Press.

Mele, A. R. (2006) *Free Will and Luck*, New York: Oxford University Press.

Nozick, R. (1981) *Philosophical Explanations*, Cambridge, MA: Harvard University Press.

O'Connor, T. (2000) *Persons and Causes: The Metaphysics of Free Will*, New York: Oxford University Press.

Pereboom, D. (2001) *Living Without Free Will*, Cambridge: Cambridge University Press.

Pink, T. (2004) *Free Will: A Very Short Introduction*, Oxford: Oxford University Press.

Scanlon, T. M. (1998) *What We Owe to Each Other*, Cambridge, MA: Harvard University Press.

Smith, A. M. (2005) "Responsibility for Attitudes: Activity and Passivity in Mental Life," *Ethics* 115: 236–71.

Smith, M. (2003) "Rational Capacities, or: How to Distinguish Recklessness, Weakness, and Compulsion," in S. Stroud and C. Tappolet (eds) *Weakness of Will and Practical Irrationality*, Oxford: Clarendon Press.

Strawson, G. (2002) "The Bounds of Freedom," in R. Kane (ed.) *The Oxford Handbook of Free Will*, New York: Oxford University Press.
Strawson, P. F. (2003) "Freedom and Resentment," in G. Watson (ed.) *Free Will*, 2nd edn, Oxford: Oxford University Press.
Stump, E. (1996) "Libertarian Freedom and the Principle of Alternative Possibilities," in D. Howard-Snyder and J. Jordan (eds) *Faith, Freedom, and Rationality: Philosophy of Religion Today*, Lanham, MD: Rowman & Littlefield.
van Inwagen, P. (1983) *An Essay on Free Will*, Oxford: Clarendon Press.
Vihvelin, K. (2004) "Free Will Demystified: A Dispositional Account," *Philosophical Topics* 32: 427–50.
Wallace, R. J. (1994) *Responsibility and the Moral Sentiments*, Cambridge, MA: Harvard University Press.
Watson, G. (2004) "Two Faces of Responsibility," in *Agency and Answerability: Selected Essays*, Oxford: Oxford University Press.
Widerker, D. and McKenna, M. (eds) (2003) *Moral Responsibility and Alternative Possibilities: Essays on the Importance of Alternative Possibilities*, Aldershot, UK: Ashgate.
Zagzebski, L. (2000) "Does Libertarian Freedom Require Alternate Possibilities?," *Philosophical Perspectives* 14: 231–48.
Zimmerman, M. J. (1988) *An Essay on Moral Responsibility*, Totowa, NJ: Rowman & Littlefield.

Further reading

Fischer, J. M. (ed.) (1986) *Moral Responsibility*, Ithaca, NY: Cornell University Press. (An excellent anthology of contemporary articles on responsibility.)
Fischer, J. M. and Ravizza, M. (eds) (1993) *Perspectives on Moral Responsibility*, Ithaca, NY: Cornell University Press. (Another excellent, and more recent, anthology of articles on responsibility.)
Watson, Gary (ed.) (2003) *Free Will*, 2nd edn, Oxford: Oxford University Press. (An excellent anthology of articles on free will.)

24
REASONS FOR ACTION

Robert Audi

Reasons for action are central in understanding persons and in describing their moral obligations. We begin by outlining the main kinds, using chiefly examples in which a reason might be the basis of a moral obligation. Following that outline, we can see important points about the relation between reasons and other elements in which they play a major role, particularly moral motivation, moral judgment, and the explanation of action.

Three overlapping categories of reasons for action

Reasons for action come in at least three overlapping kinds. There are normative reasons – which include moral reasons as a major subset – motivational reasons, and explanatory reasons.

Normative reasons are reasons (in the sense of objective grounds) there *are* for doing something, for instance, to avoid lying and to wear a coat in the cold. Examples such as the former are commonly considered moral reasons, the latter, prudential reasons. Some normative reasons *for* – roughly, counting in favor of – an action are reasons for any normal human being. Other normative reasons, however, are *person-specific*: reasons there are *for* a specific person. That doing an errand would help *my* friend can be a reason for me to do it. This can hold even if neither I nor anyone else realizes the errand would help.

Motivational reasons constitute a second broad category. These are *possessed reasons*: reasons someone *has* to do something, such as my reason to write a check, a reason I have because I promised to support a cause. Reasons we have can and often do motivationally explain our action. Normally, if my reason to write a check at least partly explains why I do so, it is motivat*ing*, and not merely motivational in kind. But the reason is potentially motivational even if I never act on it.

Many reasons we have belong to a third main category: that of *explanatory reasons for action*. These are reasons *why* someone acts, say, why I make amends for an injury. But a reason why I act need not be motivational even in kind.

Something very different, say, depression or brain manipulations, might explain why I do something, such as hang my head, without being motivational or constituting a reason I have. We might, then, call depression merely a reason *why an action occurs,* rather than a *reason for action.* Explanatory reasons for action, however, are typically not just causal grounds of it, but motivating. Motivating reasons are a complex kind. They are *reasons for which* we do something and thereby ground a motivational explanation of our doing it. They are explanatory, possessed, and, when the motivating reason genuinely counts in favor of the action, also normative. A normative reason need not motivate but is at least possibly motivating.

Motivating reasons are also the kind for which we act when we act on the basis of practical reasoning, as where we must decide how to fulfill an obligation. Moreover, Kantians and others hold that an action has moral worth only if performed "from duty," which entails being performed *for* some morally appropriate kind of reason, say, to fulfill a promise.

When a reason one has to act is based on a desire, in the sense that the action will satisfy the desire, the reason may be called *internal* to contrast it with normative reasons viewed as having reason-giving force *independently* of the agent's wants and other attitudes. Normative reasons, such as moral reasons not to kill people, are in that sense external. But "internal" and "external" can mislead. First, some possessed (thus internal) reasons are also normative, as where writing a check both fulfills a promise *and* satisfies a desire; secondly, normative reasons, though external, must be *potentially* possessed and hence capable of being internal. A reason we possess may or may not be an actual basis of action. When we act for such a reason, it is not only motivational in kind, but (as noted above) motivating: it plays an explanatory role. The paradigm of a reason's motivating action is one's doing something *in order to* realize a desired state of affairs.

A natural way to refer to any of the three kinds of reasons for action – normative, motivational, and explanatory – is with infinitive clauses expressing the content of an intention or other motivational element, such as "to pay a debt," or with that-clauses expressing the content of an instrumental belief, say "that writing the check will help Oxfam." Strictly speaking, the objects designated by such clauses are abstract: in the case of contents of beliefs and other cognitive attitudes, they may be considered propositions; in the case of the contents of desires and of other conative attitudes, they may be considered states of affairs, encompassing actions as special cases.

Using this conception of reasons strictly conceived, we can see an important point about normative reasons. Since, by counting in favor of action, these have a certain kind of authority, it should be no surprise that they are *factive*: when a normative reason is propositional, the proposition constituting it is in fact true; when it is not propositional, it in some way corresponds to a truth. Take, for instance, a normative reason based on a change in the weather and expressed using the infinitive, "to wear a coat." This reason corresponds to a truth, say, that I would suffer without a coat. The existence of this normative reason does not require that I *realize* the relevant truth; and, on some views, until I do, the reason is not one I *have*. However that may be, reasons one has are (1) *expressible* by articulating one's intentional states, such as a desire to avoid a chill or a belief that this requires a coat, and (2) *possessed* in virtue of being the contents of some such appropriate psychological state. These states may or may not exercise causal power on conduct. We may have a reason to wear a coat and not do so. Even apart from weakness of will, we do not act on all our reasons or fulfill all our intentions, and any of these attitudes may come and go without behavioral traces.

In ethical theory, a main focus of analysis is normative reasons for action. These are also called *practical reasons;* they include moral reasons, and they determine what we ought (hence have some normative reason) to do. They also determine what we have *adequate* reason to do, as where we have a practical reason to do something *and* no such reason not to. (The notion of its being *ir*rational *not* to do a particular thing yields a concept of a *compelling* reason, but I leave this notion aside here.)

If we conceive of reasons as *contents* of such propositional attitudes as desires and beliefs, we must explain why it is natural to say, in answering "What was your reason for doing that?" things like "I wanted to help," where we cite a desire (one whose content coincides with the reason). For one thing, this reply *both* provides a reason and indicates that it was mine (*I* wanted to help). For another, "I wanted" contrasts with expressions of different attitudes I might have had that express the same practical reason; for instance, feeling obligated to show appreciation or hoping to show it. Where "reason" designates a desire (or other attitude) that expresses the sort of abstract element constituting a reason, I speak of *reason states*. By virtue of their content, these attitudes *provide* reasons; those contents *constitute* the reasons.

Desires are often thought to provide all three kinds of reason for action, but some types of desire cannot provide normative reasons. Irrational desires, even if they motivate, provide no normative reasons. Suppose an agent (S) could readily see (but does not believe) that the desired object, say, levitating, is impossible. An irrational desire of this sort does not provide any normative reason for action aimed at satisfying it. A normal desire, by contrast, say, to support Oxfam, can provide a normative reason, at least *for* certain people. The reason may or may not be motivating.

On what are sometimes called Humean instrumentalist theories of reasons for action, normative reasons are ultimately *desire-based*: roughly, to have a reason for an act is for it to be a means (or probable means) of satisfying a basic desire one has (a "passion" in Hume's terminology). There is wide agreement that this condition is sufficient for one's having a *motivational* reason (at least where one can see that the action is a means); but there is controversy concerning whether even restricting the basic desires to (e.g.) those one would retain on clear and informed reflection is sufficient to enable them to ground *normative* reasons. Suppose, for instance, that a neurologically implanted desire to be burned resists elimination by such reflection. Ineliminability does not confer normative authority. Such cases seem to show that normative reasons are tied to standards for what is *worth* desiring. (Detailed examination of instrumentalism is provided in chapter 5 of Audi 2001.)

Like certain kinds of desires, certain kinds of beliefs can provide all the kinds of reason noted, either for further belief or for action, though they may do so for action only because of what one does or should want or otherwise be motivated to do, where the "should" is that of rationality. To be sure, beliefs do not express normative reasons in the way wants do. This is apparently because, apart from what, in some presumably objective sense, we *should* want to do, there cannot *be* reasons for action. Roughly, if there is nothing worth wanting, there is nothing worth doing. Even if, e.g. a belief that contributing to charities is obligatory provides, by itself, a reason to do it, it also provides a reason to want to contribute, and it could not yield the former reason apart from yielding the latter. By contrast, a belief can express a reason for a further belief quite apart from what one wants or should want; and this *evidential* role of beliefs is usually taken to be their primary reason-giving function.

Reasons, moral judgments, and motivation

It is not unnatural to think that *believing* one has a normative reason to A entails *having* a motivational reason to A. Similarly, on the plausible assumption that holding the judgment that one ought (on balance) to A normally implies having a belief of roughly the former kind, it may seem that holding such a judgment entails having some degree of motivation to A. This last entailment thesis is a generic form of *motivational internalism*. Motivational internalism is supported by the idea that "actions speak louder than words," which is commonly taken to imply that the motivation expectable from our overall ought-judgments must be exhibited in our deeds. The view is especially important in ethics because, as Hume brought out, if motivation is intrinsic to holding moral judgments but extrinsic to holding factual ("descriptive") judgments, then moral judgments are not factual and do not strictly speaking admit of truth or falsity.

Motivational internalism is highly controversial and is often defended only with major qualifications. Several forms have been examined in detail by Parfit (1997) and in papers by Audi and others in Cullity and Gaut (1997). Here we can only note three points important for appraising it.

First, motivational internalism is not entailed by morality's providing *action-guiding* reasons. Even on the assumption that morality guides agents through their making self-addressed moral judgments indicating what they ought to do, the relevant implication is only that such judgments can and often do produce motivation to act on them. This is largely uncontroversial, but does not entail that these judgments are *necessarily* motivating.

Second, motivational internalism is stronger than the more plausible view that agents who are *fully rational* and judge that they (on balance) ought to *A* must have *some* motivation to *A*. This thesis about practical rationality is, however, also controversial and, even if true, leaves open the possibility that acting against such a judgment is not always *irrational*. The agent may have a stronger self-interested motive even if the moral motivation is strong.

Third, motivational internalism is sometimes restricted to morally sound agents or, more modestly, to agents who are fully moral at the time the judgment is entertained. There are many ways to characterize morally sound agents and "fully moral" agents. The same holds for fully rational agents. Enough has been said to indicate that the important relations holding among reasons of various kinds, ought-judgments of various sorts, and motivation, are both numerous and a challenge to philosophical reflection.

The relation between reasons and facts

I have described reasons for action as contents of propositional attitudes, including desires. The contents of desires are not true or false and are often best represented by infinitive clauses, say, "to meet an obligation," whereas contents of beliefs (of the kind in question) are best represented by truth-valued propositional clauses. One may wonder how this view accounts for two points that may suggest a univocal view of reasons for action – the *facticity view* that all reasons are facts. This question is important because, if reasons are facts then, far more often than is generally realized, people are mistaken in thinking they have reasons or have acted for reasons. This, in turn, would imply that either people need excuses more often than is generally thought or actions not based on reasons can often be rational or even praiseworthy.

To see the case for the facticity view, note first that reasons for action are always expressible in a propositional mode, as well as infinitivally; and, when propositionally expressed, they *seem* subject to a facticity constraint: if, e.g. it is false that drafting females for military service would be unfair, then it is at least odd to call it someone's reason for opposing the practice. Moreover, when we give reasons for actions by simply citing a proposition – say, that drafting females would be unfair – we normally believe the proposition. We also typically assume that others' reasons given in propositional form are true. We regard our own propositional reasons – whether we offer them in explaining beliefs or actions – as true; and we tend to give others credit for getting such things right unless we have cause to think otherwise.

These pragmatic points about our linguistic practices do not establish the facticity view. Indeed, they are sufficient to explain why, even if the view is false, it is odd to say such things as that his reason for believing that (e.g.) there has been life on Mars (*p*) is that there was once water there (*q*), where we think *q* is false. We want to say something like "His reason is that – as he sees it – *q*. But notice that *he* – taking as we commonly do in giving our reasons – might properly say his reason is simply *that q*. This explanation is equivalent to the proposition that he believes *p* (wholly) on the basis of *believing* that *q and* to the proposition that the reason for which he believes *p* is that *q*. But the former, employing the basis locution, clearly does not imply that *q* is true. If so, neither does the latter, which will not even seem odd where we consider *q* true. The best explanation of the data is again that pragmatic considerations heavily influence what reason-ascribing locutions we use and that, as not uncommonly holds for equivalent locutions in English, some ascriptions are odd where their equivalents are not.

Furthermore, on the facticity view, if I am asked for what reason I believe *p*, and I sincerely say that my reason for believing it is *q*, I can be corrected – told that *q* is not my reason – (1) without being thought insincere or wrong about why I believe *p* and (2) on the ground that *q* is false. But this would be a mistaken way to correct self-ascriptions of (explaining) reasons for believing. We normally presuppose that others (apart from self-deception and other special cases) are correct when they sincerely offer their reasons for believing or doing something, and we do not properly take the falsehood of a stated reason to falsify this presupposition of self-knowledge. Suppose a credible person tells me *q* is false. Assuming that I now doubt that *q* but do not immediately cease to believe *q*, I will *not* now doubt that *q* is the reason for which I have believed *p*, but rather will think that perhaps I *ought* not to have believed, and should not now believe, *p* on the basis of *q*. I may also come to cease believing *p*.

A second difficulty for the facticity view is this. Suppose that, on the basis of *reasoning* from *q*, I form a belief that *p* (or perform an act A). I will find it especially strange to think that my believing *p* (or my A-ing) is not based on some reason (in this case, *q*); but *q*, being false, is, on the facticity view, not a reason. Still, my reasoning might be valid, hence formally good. In one terminology, the trouble with my reasoning (hence with my inferential ground for *p*) is external; the trouble is mistaken *inputs* to my reasoning, not their rationalizing capacity. This defect does not preclude my conclusion's being reason-based.

To hold that propositions constituting reasons for action (or belief) need not be true is not to deny an important point about discourse concerning reasons. It may well be that in second- and third-person *ascriptions* of reasons for belief or action, whether of (a) reasons for anyone at all to believe *p* or to A, or (b) reasons for a specific person to believe *p* or to A, or (c) reasons *for which* a particular person *does* believe *p* or perform A, *a (defeasible) presupposition of truth predominates*. Hence, if we think *p* false, we normally do not cite it as someone's reason for holding the belief that *q*, or for A-ing, unless we cancel the truth presupposition, for example, saying "that – as he claims – *p*." Take the question, "What reason does Sally have for supporting Jonathan?" We usually would not say "that he is the best candidate" if we disbelieve this – though we might cite the corresponding reason state, saying that she *believes* he is the best candidate. If we are thinking of *p* as false and only as a subjective or a motivating reason, or both, we are likely to say, "She believes that *p*," or to use "as she sees it," or in some other way distance ourselves from the objectivity presupposition.

It may help in understanding such cases to notice that, where the inquirer presumably seeks an objective and external reason, the normative notion of a *reason there is to believe p* seems to be operating. Such an external reason must indeed be true (factive). Suppose, however, that one could have a reason to believe *p* or for a deed *A only* if one had an external one – which is factive. Now consider my having an excellent basis for closing a valve, say, that it will prevent a flood, for which I have evidence that would lead any rational person to believe this (though it is false). We would have to conclude that I have *no* reason to close it. This holds even if genuine evidence must be true (on the plausible assumption that some evidence is inductive and does not entail the truth of what it supports).

On my view, we must acknowledge that (1) a reason one has, a possessed reason, *q*, need not be external – a reason there *is* to believe *p* (or to A) – and (2) reason-ascriptions for beliefs tend to presuppose truth and so, apart from qualifiers like "as she sees it," which select subjective (or at least internal) reasons for *p*, are odd and misleading where the ascriber disbelieves *q*. But granting these points sacrifices nothing: for many truths, there are some contexts in which any unqualified affirmation of them is odd or misleading.

Reasons for action, instrumental beliefs, and action-explaining desires

Consider the most general kind of ascription of a reason for action: the kind employing the purposive "in order to." Every intentional action for a further end (every one not performed "for its own sake") – and arguably every intentional action – admits of an in-order-to explanation in which S's reason is expressed by the infinitive clause. We raise our hands in order *to greet others*, open books in order *to find information*, etc. In-order-to locutions imply both a desire, in a wide sense encompassing intending and (except possibly where the action is basic for S) an instrumental belief connecting the act with realizing the desire. But these locutions do not presuppose that the instrumental belief is true. Thus, even if an equivalent explanation can normally be given by citing the belief, for instance, by saying she opened the book because she believed it had a map of Florence, this equivalence would not hold if that mode of explanation presupposed a true belief.

Connected with these points are other untoward consequences of taking reasons for action – not just objective or sound or "external" reasons for action – to be factive. Consider the practical case (reasons for belief – "theoretical" reasons – function similarly). If my reason for action must be factive, say, constituted by some truth connecting my action with its goal, at least two untoward consequences follow. First, I could not know what my reasons are without knowing the relevant propositions to be true, say, could not know that my reason for signing a check is that it will discharge a debt (where the check will be stolen). Second, others who see that my relevant belief is false can tell me that I had no reason or acted for no reason. But both implications seem mistaken. If, for instance, you take a medicine in order to relieve a headache, I may not say to you, simply on the ground that the medicine will not help, either that you had no reason for taking it or that you were not acting for a reason. I can perhaps say that despite appearances, there was no *good* reason to take it, where I invoke the notion of an objective reason, an external reason there is, for an action. But this is neither the only notion of a reason for action nor – even more important – the only kind that bears on the rationality of action. The contrast between good reasons and those only appearing to be good may incline us to take "good reason" to entail truth, but ordinarily the notion of a good reason includes inductive grounds and is not this narrow.

Reasons and the causal explanation of action

During the years when the controversy over whether reasons are causes raged, reasons for action were taken to be intentional attitudes or, not infrequently, desire–belief combinations of the kind Davidson (1963) called *primary reasons*. More recently, reasons, as described above, have been conceived as the *contents* of such attitudes (or, where the contents are true propositions, as the corresponding facts). This content view seems more natural. The most basic specification – though not the only proper specification – of a reason to act apparently has the form of "to *x*," the kind of infinitive that follows "in order" when an action is explained as performed in order to bring something about. The most basic specification of a reason for belief, by contrast, has the form of "that *p*." It is true, however, that we can properly say, in answering "What was your reason?," "I want to … ," "I intend to … ," and "I believe … ." This shows why we should distinguish *reason states* from *reasons proper*. Confusion can arise because "reason" is commonly used for both. But the former are intentional attitudes, the latter their contents (sometimes called their *objects*). Thus, asked for a reason for driving rather than flying, I can say, "I wanted to take heavy luggage," or "to take heavy luggage," or even "I believed I had too much luggage to fly," or simply "I had too much luggage." This distinction between reason states and reasons proper cuts across the one initially introduced: normative, possessed, and explanatory reasons may all be contents of reason states and may often quite naturally be indicated by citing those states, as where a normative reason is indicated by saying the agent *realized* (a cognitive state) *that A-ing was his obligation* (a reason).

Often, citing the reason state is taken as equivalent to citing the reason proper; these types of ascription are in practice sometimes interchangeable, but ascribing the reason state is often preferable where one is uncertain of the truth of a proposition constituting a reason proper, for instance, unsure whether one was correct in thinking there was too much luggage. If we distinguish between reasons proper and reason states, we can leave open whether reasons in either sense are causes, though few if any would argue that the contents of intentional attitudes are the right sorts of things to be causes.

Reasons of all the kinds described here can explain an action: citing the reason can indicate *why* the agent performed it. But apart from the case of a mere reason why an action occurred, such as brain manipulation, the reason must be possessed. The mere existence of a normative reason for A-ing does not explain it. That cutting an exposed power line will save a life might be a good reason for S to cut it; but what explains the action may be S's believing it blocks a lawnmower. The action would then not be performed from duty, and one might say that, though right, it is not morally creditworthy (Kant might say it had no "moral worth").

Even citing a reason the agent had to A may fail to explain the action. To explain the action, the reason – say, that cutting the line will clear the mower's path – must be the content of a reason state, such as an instrumental belief, *and* that state must be at least part of what explains the agent A-ed. It must be the case that we can truly say that S A-ed *because* (e.g.) S believed this would clear the mower's path. This "because" seems causal. There is disagreement over whether it is. Here it suffices to say that it can be causal without being *deterministic* in subsuming the action explained under a universal law of nature. For those who take freedom and moral responsibility to be incompatible with determinism, then, reason states can be causes of actions without undermining their freedom.

Reasons and rational action

We have seen that any possessed reason can provide a motivational explanation of action. But are all motivationally explainable actions rational? What if the explaining belief or explaining desire is not rational? One view is that, if S A-s on the basis of the belief that it will maximize S's desire satisfaction, the action is rational even if both the belief and the desire are irrational. Here one might speak of *subjective rationality*. If, however, A's being rational is a positive normative status – and not just a matter of intelligibility – it is plausible to say that A-ing must, on S's *rational* beliefs, be (1) at least a possible way of realizing the explaining desire(s) in question and (2) any desire of S's that is necessary for motivating A-ing is rational. There are other conceptions of rational action, and both of these need qualification, but they are indicative of major strong and weak conceptions.

A related issue is whether reason states in the light of which an action is rational must bear some generative or sustaining relation to it. One way to put the question is to ask whether an action rational on account of a reason the agent has for it must be performed at least in part *for* that reason. In Kantian terms, the question is whether an action merely in conformity with the agent's reason but not performed *from* it is thereby rationally creditworthy. A plausible answer is that where there is no appropriate causal connection in virtue of which A-ing is at least in part based on the reason state, A-ing is at most *rationalizable* by appeal to the reason, rather than rational on the basis of it.

We have now seen how reason states can play an explanatory role in relation to act-tokens – concrete actions by specific agents at a particular time. There is also an important connection between reasons proper, which are abstract, and act-types, which are also abstract. One way to see this is to focus on hypothetical explanations and justifications. It is sometimes important to know whether a reason a person had or might have had, say, to make a large profit, *would* explain or justify an action. Suppose S suddenly flies to Rio at the cost of failing to do some expected good deed as a volunteer reading to children. That doing so would produce a huge profit on a sale of stock would explain this and might justify it, i.e. the concrete act, S's flying to Rio, would be explained, and might be justified, by that reason. If we shift to the relation between the abstract items, we may say that (in the circumstances) the truth of the reason statement – here, that the flight would produce a huge profit – provides a *rationale* for the act-type, flying to Rio at the cost of failing to do the reading. Its doing this yields a sense in which it both explains and justifies that type (for any agent): it makes the type intelligible as a kind of response appropriate in the context, and it justifies the type for S, in the sense of showing how tokening it *for* the reason in question would be justified for S. Thus, where S A-s for a reason good enough to render A-ing rational in the circumstances, the reason, as abstract content, is sufficient in those circumstances for the rationality of the type, A-ing.

Reasons for action, then, take many forms and play many roles. Whether in moral contexts or in others, they may motivate, explain, rationalize, and justify. The term "reason" may designate either the abstract elements that constitute the contents of such psychological states as beliefs and desires or the states themselves. Those states may bear generative and sustaining relations to concrete actions; their contents may bear normative relations to act-types, which are abstract. Even when both these categories and their interconnections are recognized, however, there remain competing criteria for both the rationality of actions and the adequacy conditions for their explanation, their freedom, their obligatoriness, and their moral worth.

See also Ethics and reason (Chapter 9); Ethics and sentiment (Chapter 10); Ethics and psychology (Chapter 32); Reasons, values, and morality (Chapter 36); Moral particularism (Chapter 53).

References

Audi, Robert (2001) *The Architecture of Reason: The Structure and Substance of Rationality*, Oxford: Oxford University Press.

Cullity, Garrett and Gaut, Berys (eds) (1997) *Ethics and Practical Reason*, Oxford: Oxford University Press.

Davidson, Donald (1963) "Actions, Reasons and Causes," *Journal of Philosophy* 60: 685–700.

Parfit, Derek (1997) "Reasons and Motivation," *Proceedings of the Aristotelian Society* Supplementary Volume 77: 99–130.

Further reading

Audi, Robert (2001) *The Architecture of Reason: The Structure and Substance of Rationality*, Oxford: Oxford University Press. (A comprehensive account of reasons, rationality, and reasonableness for beliefs, actions, desires, and values.)

——(2006) *Practical Reasoning and Ethical Decision*, London: Routledge. (A theory of practical reasoning and its relation to reasons for action, rationality in action, and moral judgments, with background accounts of Aristotle's, Hume's, and Kant's views on the same problems.)

Cullity, Garrett and Gaut, Berys (eds) (1997) *Ethics and Practical Reason*, Oxford: Oxford University Press. (A wide-ranging collection of papers in ethics and the theory of reasons for action and its explanation; it includes most of the topics of this chapter.)

Davidson, Donald (1963) "Actions, Reasons and Causes," *Journal of Philosophy* 60: 685–700. (An influential, widely discussed account of reasons for action viewed as causative desire–belief combinations.)

Davis, Wayne A. (2005) "Reasons and Psychological Causes," *Philosophical Studies* 122: 51–101. (A detailed account of the nature of reasons and their role in explaining actions.)

Goldman, Alvin I. (1970) *A Theory of Human Action*, Englewood Cliffs, NJ: Prentice-Hall. (A comprehensive theory of the nature and explanation of action.)

Hume, David (1888) *A Treatise of Human Nature*, ed. L. A. Selby-Bigge, Oxford: Oxford University Press.

Kant, Immanuel (1948) *Groundwork of the Metaphysics of Morals*, ed. J. J. Paton, London: Hutchinson.

Parfit, Derek (1997) "Reasons and Motivation," *Proceedings of the Aristotelian Society* Supplementary Volume 77: 99–130. (An account of reasons as facts, with critical discussion of motivational internalism and a positive treatment of the relation of rational beliefs to the rationality of action.)

25
THE OPEN QUESTION ARGUMENT

Thomas Baldwin

G. E. Moore and *Principia Ethica*

The "open question" argument aims to establish that ethical claims and questions have an irreducible significance of their own. The argument gets its name from G. E. Moore's presentation of it in his book *Principia Ethica* (Moore 1993). His argument takes the form of a critical thought experiment which his readers are invited to perform when they are offered a definition of goodness, which Moore takes to be the fundamental ethical property. Moore takes the example of a hedonist definition of goodness in terms of pleasure:

> But whoever will attentively consider with himself what is actually before his mind when he asks the question "Is pleasure (or whatever it may be) after all good?" can easily satisfy himself that he is not merely wondering whether pleasure is pleasure. And if he will try this experiment with each suggested definition in succession, he may become expert enough to recognise that in every case he has before his mind a unique object, with regard to the connection of which with any other object, a distinct question may be asked.
>
> (Moore 1993: 68)

Moore's argument here is that a hedonist definition of goodness implies that the question "Is anything which is pleasant good?" has the same meaning as the question "Is anything which is pleasant pleasant?"; for the phrasing of the questions differs only in that where the first has the word "good" the second has the word "pleasant," which should not alter the overall meaning of the question if the hedonist definition of goodness, that to be good just is to be pleasant, is correct. But these questions are obviously distinct: the former raises a substantive ethical question concerning the value of pleasure whereas the latter is manifestly trivial. As he puts it, to equate these questions is to hold that what looks to be a substantive ethical question is not really serious at all so that doubts concerning the value of pleasure can be swept aside with the comment:

> This is not an open question: the very meaning of the word decides it: no one can think otherwise except through confusion.
>
> (Moore 1993: 72)

Thus the main thesis of the "open question" argument is that proposals to define ethical terms such as "good" inevitably misrepresent some fundamental ethical claim as a proposition which is true merely by definition when in fact its truth remains an open question for those who understand the terms employed in it.

Moore's argument obviously has many assumptions concerning the nature of definitions and the questionability of ethical claims. Before discussing these, however, it is worth saying a little about the history of the argument and its role in Moore's ethical theory. Moore maintains that his thesis that basic ethical terms such as "good" are indefinable represents a major advance in ethical theory which was anticipated only by Sidgwick. This is doubly incorrect: on the one hand, Sidgwick did in fact propose a definition of goodness (I discuss this in the second section, "Definitions"); on the other hand, Moore's claim concerning the indefinability of basic ethical terms, and his way of arguing for it, was anticipated by the eighteenth-century English moralist Richard Price (Selby-Bigge 1897: 162–3). Price in fact argued for the indefinability of moral obligation, rather than goodness, and this emphasis is characteristic of most of those who have affirmed the distinctiveness of ethics. Thus what is unusual about Moore's position in *Principia Ethica* is the emphasis he places on the indefinability of goodness, which is enhanced by the fact that he defines moral obligation in terms of goodness:

> the assertion "I am morally bound to perform this action" is identical with the assertion "This action will produce the greatest amount of good in the Universe."
>
> (Moore 1993: 197)

This last aspect of Moore's position was criticized by Russell, using the technique of Moore's own open question argument (Russell 1904). The question whether the action which will produce the greatest amount of good in some situation is the action which one is then morally obliged to perform is, Russell argued, an open question, which will be answered in the negative by many moral philosophers; it is certainly not a question to be settled just by defining moral obligation in the way that Moore does. Moore accepted Russell's criticism and thereafter accepted that ethics involves two fundamental indefinable terms, "good" and "ought" (or "right") (Moore 1942: 558).

Going back to *Principia Ethica*, however, there is a further aspect of Moore's position which needs to be introduced. Moore used the conclusion of the open question argument to support the claim that there is a fallacy in those ethical theories which maintain that ethical questions can be settled by reference to "natural" facts. Moore called this fallacy "the naturalistic fallacy" and he took it that in showing that goodness is indefinable he had refuted naturalistic ethics. In thinking about this, however, almost everything turns on what is assumed about the meaning of "natural" and cognate terms such as "nature" and "naturalistic." If it is assumed that an understanding of what is natural should not involve any ethical considerations, then a definition of goodness in naturalistic terms will immediately be exposed to Moore's open question argument. Yet there are plenty of respectable ethical theories which reject the assumption that an understanding of what is natural should not include any ethical considerations: one has only to think of the conceptions of "natural law" and "human nature" in medieval and early modern philosophy to recognize positions of this kind. To support his position Moore offers two different accounts of what is natural. In one he simply refers to "the subject-matter of the natural sciences and also of psychology" (Moore 1993: 92), as if it was obvious that the natural sciences and psychology are inherently value-free. But this is just the presumption which ethical naturalists reject on the grounds that a comprehensive understanding of human nature, and perhaps also of natural ecology, has an irreducible ethical aspect. Perhaps this thesis is mistaken, but its truth needs to remain an open question in the absence of an argument (which Moore does not provide) to demonstrate that it is untenable. In addition, however, Moore proposes a metaphysical account of natural properties, to the effect that natural properties are those which are fundamental in the sense that "they are in themselves substantial and give to the object all the substance that it has" (Moore 1993: 93). This proposal is somewhat detached from our ordinary understanding of nature and cognate terms, but it is interesting for its own sake since it is indeed plausible to hold that goodness is not a fundamental property in this sense; I return to it in the third section, "Supervenience."

Moore combined his critique of ethical naturalism with a similar critique of what he called "metaphysical ethics" such as the thesis that human morality is to be defined by reference to the will of God. Moore's critical arguments here are much the same as before, and he says that metaphysical ethics is equally guilty of the naturalistic fallacy. He then adds, revealingly, that "the root of the naturalistic fallacy" is that naturalistic philosophers and metaphysicians both think that "Every truth … must mean somehow that something exists" (Moore 1993: 176), when in fact, he maintains, the truth of fundamental ethical propositions is independent of questions about what exists, be it a natural object or property or metaphysical ones: whatever properties or objects exist, he writes, "it still remains a distinct and different question whether what thus exists is good" (Moore 1993: 176). In the light of this remark the best way to express the content of Moore's "ethical non-naturalism," as Moore's meta-ethical position is often called, is as a rejection of a correspondence conception of truth for ethical propositions: truth for fundamental ethical propositions, unlike those of the natural sciences and metaphysics, is not a matter of correspondence with some reality, even an ideal metaphysical reality. Instead the truth of fundamental ethical propositions is a matter of the impossibility of believing otherwise, since even though they are not true by definition these propositions are self-evident (Moore 1993: 192–4). In this respect, therefore, Moore's position is rationalist in inspiration and comparable to that of Kant. Indeed, like Kant, Moore thinks that fundamental ethical truths are synthetic *a priori*; but unlike Kant, Moore has no conception of practical reason or critical judgment to vindicate the possibility of these *a priori* truths and thereby facilitate reasoned debate about fundamental ethical questions. Instead, for Moore, each of us has to fall back on our "intuitions," those judgments which for us capture our deepest ethical convictions. This position can appear liberating, as it did to Moore's young friends in the Bloomsbury Group such as Lytton Strachey and Maynard Keynes. But it equally implies that those who disagree profoundly will find that they have nothing constructive to say to each other, as Moore famously found when he was confronted at dinner by D. H. Lawrence (Moggridge 1992: 137i). The result is that there is a dialectical nihilism at the heart of Moore's ethics. To my mind this is profoundly unsatisfactory, but it provided an important starting-point for the ethical non-cognitivism which became such an important feature of ethical theory as the twentieth century progressed.

Definitions

Moore's open question argument is intended to establish the indefinability of goodness. It rests on the assumption that the substitution within a complete question of the definition of a term for the term itself does not alter the meaning of the question. Yet once one applies this assumption to definitions themselves, the result seems wrong. For example, the definition of a second cousin is someone with whom one shares a great grandparent but not a grandparent; but if one uses this definition to carry out a substitution within the definition itself, all one ends up with is the trivial thesis that the definition of a second cousin is a second cousin; and generalizing this result implies that all definitions, or analyses, are trivial (this result is known as "the paradox of analysis," and was discussed as such by Moore himself in the 1930s). The way to avoid this conclusion is to reject the initial assumption concerning the results of substitution where a claim about the meaning of a word or phrase is being made, as in definitions; for the significance of a definition depends precisely on the fact that the same meaning can be expressed in two different ways. Nonetheless, where one is dealing with a question such as "Is Jane your second cousin?" which concerns the world and not our ways of describing it, using the definition of a second cousin to clarify the question is plainly legitimate. Someone who, on being shown that she shares a great grandparent but not a grandparent with Jane, continued to doubt whether they are second cousins would just show that she did not understand what it is to be someone's second cousin.

This line of thought indicates that we should be wary of relying on Moore's use of definitional substitution to criticize the hedonist definition of goodness in terms of pleasure on the grounds that it implies that the apparently substantive question "Is whatever is pleasant really good?" is as trivial as the question "Is whatever is pleasant really pleasant?" For this line of argument closely resembles that which led to the conclusion that all definitions are trivial; hence it is preferable to concentrate on applications of a proposed definition. So suppose it is accepted that living the comfortable life of a celebrity is very pleasant; nonetheless many will question whether such a life is for this reason a good life. Is such a question comparable to wondering whether Jane is one's second cousin despite the fact that she shares a great grandparent but not a grandparent with one? Surely not, the Moorean will reply: the critic of the celebrity lifestyle does not fail to understand the term "good"; she just questions the hedonist thesis that the pleasantness of this lifestyle suffices to make it a good one. This remains, for her, an open question.

Although this Moorean response seems right, one needs to ask why this is so when there is no problem about defining what it is to be a second cousin. It is clear that what makes this latter definition possible is the fact that the term "second cousin" belongs within a network of interdependent kinship terms constructed around the begetting relationship between parents and their children. In the case of "good" there is a comparable cluster of terms such as "worth," "ought" and "value," and Moore himself is ready to characterize intrinsic goodness as the kind of goodness which belongs to things which are "worth having purely for their own sakes" (Moore 1993: 237) or "ought to exist for their own sake" (Moore 1993: 33). The purpose of these characterizations seems to be to elucidate "good" in a way which does not define it, but even if one were to treat them as definitions they would not pose a significant threat to the conclusion of Moore's open question argument. For that argument is directed against definitions of goodness in terms (unlike these ones) whose understanding does not involve evaluative or normative considerations.

This point does not, however, explain what is distinctive about "good" and why the question of what things are good persists as an open question even if it is agreed what is good. One influential approach to this issue explains this phenomenon by the hypothesis that our value-judgments are essentially expressive and not descriptive; through these judgments we express our approval and commend things to others, but we do not thereby describe them. On this account, therefore, the attempt to provide a definition of goodness in terms of pleasantness fails because the expressive role of value-judgments cannot be subsumed within the descriptive role of judgments concerning what is pleasant; and the persisting openness of questions concerning what is good reflects the fact that the attitudes expressed in value-judgments are not rationally required by our descriptive judgments. One objection to this approach is that the contrast between the descriptive and the expressive roles of language is not exclusive, in that there are plenty of terms which combine these roles, such as "rude." An expressivist will, however, respond that what is distinctive of "thin" value-judgments concerning goodness (as opposed to "thick" value-judgments such as that concerning rudeness) is precisely that they are purely expressive and lack all descriptive content. But this position undermines the central role of judgments concerning what is good in practical deliberations since by means of these judgments we provide ourselves and others with reasons for a decision, and to play this role these judgments need to have a content which is not just an expression of the speaker's positive feelings.

This last point suggests that it is this reason-providing role of judgments concerning goodness which undermines definitions of goodness such as the hedonist definition. The suggestion is that the judgment that whatever is pleasant is good implies that something's pleasantness is a reason for favoring it, but that this implication will be lost if goodness is defined as pleasantness; for even if pleasantness is a reason for favoring what is pleasant, saying of what is pleasant that it is pleasant does not convey that content. The question which now arises is whether this provides a definition of goodness, to the effect that to be good just is to be something whose properties constitute reasons for choosing (favoring, promoting) it, as has been proposed by Scanlon (Scanlon 1998: 96). Since this definition is formulated in normative terms it is not incompatible with Moore's general approach – indeed, it can be regarded as an interpretation of his characterization of goods as things which "ought to exist for their own sake." It is not possible to deal here with the issues raised by this influential proposal (for a good discussion, see Stratton-Lake and Hooker 2006), but I am myself skeptical about it. A typical problem concerns the evaluation of reasons themselves: on Scanlon's proposal good reasons are reasons whose properties provide us with reasons for choosing (etc.) these reasons. But we do not normally choose reasons nor do we seek reasons for our reasons. Hence I prefer Mackie's proposal (Mackie 1977: 55–6) that to be a good thing of some kind is to fulfill to a high degree the requirements appropriate for the kind of thing in question; a good pen is one which amply fulfills the requirements for pens as instruments for handwriting, and a good reason is one which amply fulfills the requirements for reasons such as relevance and evidence. Where something amply fulfills the appropriate requirements, this fact often provides a reason for choosing (favoring, promoting) it which is dependent upon its properties. But the fact that it has these properties is not by itself the reason for choosing it; what matters is that it is in virtue of having these properties that it amply fulfills the requirements for things of its kind, and it is this fact which the value-judgment captures. Again, there is no essential disagreement here with Moore since requirements are inherently normative; and the definition readily accounts for the persisting openness of accounts of what is good by reference to the fact that it always makes sense to reflect critically concerning the requirements for things of some kind.

But there is a different approach to the definability of goodness which needs to be addressed. The suggestions considered so far have involved proposals intended to define goodness in a way which analyses our ordinary understanding of it. But it is also possible to clarify the meaning of a term, and thereby define it, by a more external approach which draws on an established body of knowledge about the things denoted by the term. A typical case of this is the way in which the development of chemistry has made it possible to define salt and water as NaCl and H_2O. The starting point here is the fact that our ordinary understanding of these substances includes the presumption that they each have a distinctive underlying structure which is responsible for their observable properties, such as the solubility of salt in water. Hence when there is a reliable body of knowledge about these underlying structures our ordinary understanding can be extended by defining the substances in a way which identifies their structure. Definitions of this kind are commonly called "synthetic" in order to distinguish them from the more familiar "analytic" definitions, and we need to consider whether it makes sense to suppose that there could be a synthetic definition of goodness which avoids the objections based on the open question argument (Putnam 1981: 206–8).

If the comparison with the definitions of salt and water is to work, it needs to be assumed that goods constitute a determinate kind whose underlying nature is responsible for their role in human life, and the rationale of a synthetic definition of goodness is to be that it identifies this underlying nature in such a way that this role is explained in the light of human psychology. Since the role that is primarily characteristic of goods is that we choose (favor, promote) the good, a satisfactory synthetic definition of goodness should help to explain this role. The most plausible suggestion of this kind is not the hedonist proposal that goodness be defined in terms of pleasure, since this confronts the well-entrenched objection that many pleasures are not goods, but the suggestion that goodness be defined as what is desirable, in the sense that things which are good are things which would satisfy our desires. For defining goods in this way provides an obvious explanation of the fact that we choose the good. Equally, however, there are obvious problems: on the one hand, there are activities which would be good for us but which we do not want to undertake, such as taking more exercise; on the other hand, we have desires which are trivial, foolish or perverse, and which are therefore such that satisfying those desires would not be a good thing. The standard response to this issue is that proposed by Sidgwick (1907: 110–11; see also Rawls 1999: 366–71), namely that goodness is to be defined by reference to the desires of an ideal agent who is fully informed about the alternatives available to him, capable of making their consequences imaginatively apparent to him, and resolute in directing his desires in the light of all this rich information. This response certainly helps, but the key issue is whether the idealization of the agent imputes to him knowledge of the good or other ethical dispositions. Since the aim here is provide an explanatory definition of good it would be self-defeating to idealize the agent in this way; but without it the proposed definition rests on the assumption that an ordinary agent with perverse desires and a disinclination to realize the good can be transformed into a lover of the good just by adding non-evaluative knowledge and dispositions. This assumption is surely unwarranted; it is not just ignorance of matters of fact and a lack of determination which deflects people from wanting what is good (for a fuller discussion of this approach to defining goodness, see Brink 2008).

The fact that this proposal is not convincing does not prove that there could not be a satisfactory synthetic definition of goodness; but it does indicate why the task of finding one is so difficult. The merits of a synthetic definition depend on its capacity to contribute to a satisfactory explanation of the role of goods in human life, so the fact that this latter role is mediated by value-judgments which withstand analytic definition in non-evaluative terms entails that a convincing synthetic definition has to provide an explanation of human conduct robust enough to withstand criticism from those for whom the truth of the synthetic definition remains an open question and who therefore doubt that their own motivations are explained by it. While those with doubts about the definition of water as H_2O can be brought around once the underlying theory is explained, it is unlikely that the same applies to those with doubts about a definition of goodness if it implies that they do not understand their own motivations.

Supervenience

I mentioned above (in the introductory section) that one of Moore's reasons for holding that goodness is not a natural property was that it is not a "substantial" property. In later writings Moore developed this thought as the thesis that something's intrinsic value is not itself an intrinsic property of it but depends on its intrinsic properties in the sense that, where the intrinsic values of two things differ, this difference is dependent on other intrinsic differences between them in virtue of which one is better than the other (Moore 1922). This point is easily understood if something's goodness is characterized as suggested above in terms of fulfillment of the requirements for the kind of thing involved; for where things differ in this respect there must be some other difference between them in virtue of which one fulfills the requirements in question but the other does not.

Although Moore himself did not use the term, this feature of values is generally now called "supervenience": a thing's goodness is said to "supervene" on its other properties, where supervenience is a kind of necessary dependence. In the second section, I alluded to the thesis that goodness is a "thin" property by contrast with "thick" evaluative properties such as rudeness, and this thesis is often associated with the further thesis that goodness is quite generally dependent on the thick "good-making" properties of that which is good. Since being a thin property and not being a substantial property are intuitively equivalent one might well suppose that the supervenience of values is just a reformulation of the considerations which lead to this thesis. But there are complications here. The forms of dependence involved in the supervenience of goodness go well beyond those which are intuitively characteristic of the relationship between goodness and good-making properties. As we shall see below, the supervenience of goodness can be taken to imply its dependence on physical properties, the properties which are the concern of physics; but the typical good-making properties of a good act are properties such as its being kind, considerate, courteous, compassionate, etc., which are themselves evaluative and not the concern of physics. Furthermore these properties are themselves subject to the requirement of supervenience: it cannot be that two remarks are exactly similar except that one is courteous and the other not. So if the supervenience of courtesy is to be understood on the model of the dependence of goodness on good-making properties, there must be some thicker "courtesy-making" properties on which the courtesy of a courteous remark depends. But it can be doubted if there are such properties: for it is impossible to articulate in a non-circular way where the acceptable limits of humor lie and thus what makes one remark discourteous where another was not; in learning how to be courteous we learn from examples and each other's reactions without learning a formula which identifies general courtesy-making properties (McDowell 1979). Thus although the dependence of goodness on thick good-making properties implies a form of supervenience, supervenience as such is a broader concept. It is a requirement of consistency which states that something's value is globally dependent on the totality of its properties but which does not by itself require the existence of a subset of value-making properties which explain quite generally the differences between the value of different things.

This conception of the global, unspecific, supervenience of something's value on its other properties is difficult to grasp, though the considerations which Moore employs to promote his thesis that some goods are "organic unities" can be used to support it (Moore 1993: 79–82). But setting aside further discussion of its defensibility, I want to discuss its implications, in particular whether the way in which goodness supervenes on other properties provides the basis for a synthetic definition of goodness – contrary to the conclusion of the previous section. An argument to this effect runs as follows (Jackson 1998: Ch. 5): let us suppose that something x_1 is good in some way and that its properties comprise the complex bundle B_1 of properties. Then anything (actual or possible) with that same bundle of properties B_1 must be good in the same way: for if it were not good it would violate the supervenience principle that things which differ in value must differ in some of their other properties. A similar line of thought can be pursued for other things x_i which are good in the same way but do not have the same bundle of properties: the supervenience of goodness implies that anything exactly similar to x_i, i.e. which also has x_i's bundle of properties B_i, must also be good. And since anything which is good must have a bundle of properties on which its goodness depends, it follows that goodness is necessarily equivalent to satisfying the indefinite disjunction of all these bundles of properties B_1 or … or B_i or … .

It will be clear that this conclusion does not in fact provide the kind of synthetic definition discussed in the previous section; all that the argument demonstrates is the necessary equivalence between goodness and an open-ended disjunction of bundles of the properties of the things which are good. This disjunction will typically not be stateable and as such will not generate a definition that could be of any use to us in determining whether something is good or explaining the role of goods in human life. Nonetheless this conclusion does give rise to an important challenge to Moore's position. To present this challenge one needs to restrict the properties on which goodness is taken to supervene: so let it be supposed that these are just physical properties. On this supposition the supervenience of goodness is the thesis that things which are exactly similar in all physical respects have the same value; and although this can be questioned, it is difficult to construct a plausible counter-example. The previous argument now implies that something's goodness is necessarily equivalent to its satisfying a disjunction of bundles of physical properties; and even though this conclusion does not provide a helpful definition of goodness it does strongly suggest that goodness is in principle reducible to physical properties. One way to make this suggestion vivid is to ask whether, in the light of the equivalence between goodness and these bundles of physical properties, a God who creates a physical universe with these bundles of properties needs to do anything more to add values to his universe. If not, then it would seem to follow that goodness is not a metaphysically fundamental aspect of the world. In truth, however, matters are more complicated than is assumed in this last reasoning. All that the supervenience of goodness on physical properties by itself implies is that there is some disjunction of bundles of physical properties equivalent to goodness, but the constitution of these bundles is determined by reference to the physical properties of the things which are in fact good. So, to continue the theological analogy, God does need to do something to add values to his physical universe, namely to attach values to some bundles of properties and not to others. Hence the fact that goodness supervenes on properties of good things does not imply that goodness is directly reducible to these properties, for the identity of the properties which are equivalent to goodness depends on what is good.

Conclusion

This discussion provides a qualified endorsement of Moore's open question argument. The argument points to a defect in definitions of goodness that are couched in terms of the kinds of thing which are good. This defect is easily understood once one appreciates the normative role of value-judgments; and although this role implies that goodness is dependent on properties of other kinds, it does not imply that goodness is reducible to these properties.

See also Sidgwick, Green, and Bradley (Chapter 17); Ethics, science, and religion (Chapter 22); Non-cognitivism (Chapter 27); Reasons, values, and morality (Chapter 36); Ethical intuitionism (Chapter 39).

References

Brink, D. (2008) "The Significance of Desire," in R. Shafer-Landau (ed.) *Oxford Studies in Metaethics*, Oxford: Oxford University Press, vol. 3, pp. 5–45.

Jackson, F. (1998) *From Metaphysics to Ethics*, Oxford: Clarendon Press.

Mackie, J. L. (1977) *Ethics: Inventing Right and Wrong*, Harmondsworth: Penguin Books.

McDowell, J. (1979) "Virtue and Reason," *Monist* 62: 331–50.

Moggridge, D. E. (1992) *Maynard Keynes*, London: Routledge.

Moore, G. E. (1922) "The Conception of Intrinsic Value," reprinted in Moore 1993, pp. 280–98.

——(1942) "A Reply to my Critics," in P. A. Schilpp (ed.) *The Philosophy of G. E. Moore*, La Salle, IL: Open Court.

——(1993) *Principia Ethica*, rev. edn, ed. T. Baldwin, Cambridge: Cambridge University Press.

Putnam, H. (1981) *Reason, Truth and History*, Cambridge: Cambridge University Press.

Rawls, J. (1999) *A Theory of Justice*, rev. edn, Oxford: Oxford University Press.

Russell, B. (1904) Review of *Principia Ethica*, by G. E. Moore, *Independent Review* 2: 328–33.

Scanlon, T. S. (1998) *What We Owe to Each Other*, Cambridge, MA: Harvard University Press.

Selby-Bigge, L. A. (1897) *British Moralists*, vol. 2, Oxford: Clarendon Press.

Sidgwick, H. (1907) *The Methods of Ethics*, 7th edn, London: Macmillan.

Stratton-Lake, P. and Hooker, B. (2006) "Scanlon versus Moore on Goodness," in T. Horgan and M. Timmons (eds) *Metaethics after Moore*, Oxford: Clarendon Press.

Further reading

Horgan, T. and Timmons, M. (eds) (2006) *Metaethics after Moore*, Oxford: Clarendon Press. (A stimulating collection of papers: see especially those by Rosati, Stratton-Lake and Hooker, and Thomson.)

Moore, G. E. (1993) *Principia Ethica*, rev. edn, ed. T. Baldwin, Cambridge: Cambridge University Press. (Moore's classic presentation of the open question argument occurs in §§13–15; Moore's later Preface to the second edition provides a helpful review of the argument.)

26
REALISM AND ITS ALTERNATIVES

Peter Railton

Traditional debates over realism concerned the existence of things in their own right, "things-in-themselves," whose existence does not depend upon being perceived or conceived by a mind. Most of us are realists about the external world in this sense, though the "things" in question need not be concrete entities. Platonists, for example, were realists about universals, which they saw as eternal and independent of any mind or mental activity. Those who deny the existence of a realm of entities, like skeptics about the world or nominalists about universals, are *anti-realists*.

But there is also a third position. Nineteenth-century idealists saw realists and skeptics about the external world as sharing the mistaken view that our talk of "the world" must be understood as referring to an experience-transcendent entity. Instead, they argued, the world is really a *thought object* – a mental construct used in describing patterns in our experience. To them, the debate between realists and skeptics was as misguided as worrying about whether we could know the home address of "the average German." While realists about the external world accept an *order of explanation* in which a self-subsistent world is the source of our experience, idealists explain things the other way around: experience is sufficient unto itself, and the proper foundation for any theory of being – including the being of what we call "the world." A view like this is called *irrealism* about the external world rather than anti-realism because it treats our ordinary talk of the world as perfectly well-grounded, just as talk of the "the average German" is perfectly well-grounded, once we see what it really amounts to. The only error is the philosophers' tendency to *reify* or *project* such thought objects as "things-in-themselves." As we will see, the debate among realists, anti-realists, and irrealists about morality takes a rather similar form.

That sounds odd. How could moral realists maintain that morality (of all things!) is a "thing-in-itself," independent of mind? This is, however, a misleading way of putting it. Realism is not a stand-alone philosophical view, like empiricism or rationalism. We need to know: realism about *what*? And to understand what realism about X involves, we must ask what sort of "things" X's would be if they *were* real. Mental substance, for example, if it were real, could hardly be independent of mind. But it could be independent of what we think about it, and so not dependent upon any actual perception or conception. What, then, is realism about X when X = morality? That is no simple question, but one short answer is: there are genuine *facts* about what is morally right or wrong – facts that are independent of what anyone, or any society, thinks is morally right or wrong.

It is fair to say that most of the great moral philosophers down through history have been realists in this sense. Though they have differed over which moral qualities are basic, rightness or goodness, they have agreed that there are genuine facts about what we morally ought to do and about what sort of life is best, and that these are *not* mere matters of opinion, or incapable of being true or false. There have been few moral skeptics or anti-realists (such as the nihilists and, perhaps, Nietzsche) and still fewer moral irrealists (though this *might* be the right way to understand some post-Kantian idealists and Hume). Today, things are different. While moral skepticism remains rare, there has been a dramatic increase in moral irrealism, starting with the "linguistic turn" in philosophy at the beginning of the twentieth century. With that turn, the focus of ethical theory broadened from the first-order questions about the right and the good to include second-order questions about what it *means* to call something right or good. This opened up the possibility into which irrealism has inserted itself, namely, accepting our first-order moral talk of acts as right or wrong, or outcomes as good or bad, but then saying at the second order that no "moral facts" are needed to make these claims true. In recent years, many variants of this idea have emerged, and this chapter is meant both to characterize moral realism and introduce a wide range of alternatives in contemporary meta-ethics.

Some moral philosophers question whether meta-ethical debates have any real importance for actual moral thought and practice. However, although contemporary meta-ethics can become quite technical and seemingly arcane, the underlying concerns at stake are familiar to any thinking person. Social customs differ across societies and times in countless ways, and individuals show still greater diversity in moral views – all claiming to be closest to getting things right. There seems to be no way to resolve such differences, even among reasonable people. Worse, in comparison with many other areas of human inquiry, we seem unable to say much about what it would amount to for one or another moral opinion to be the right one. Although some moral injunctions appear nearly universal – prohibitions of murder, assault, and theft, or requirements of keeping one's word, caring for one's offspring, and showing loyalty to family and friends – this might reflect nothing more than broad similarities in human nature and broad commonalities in the human condition. Perhaps morality isn't all it's cracked up to be.

To address this question, we need to ask what morality *is* cracked up to be. Most philosophers agree that the following five features, at least, are central to morality as we know it.

(F1) *Cognitive form.* Although we worry about truth and knowledge in morality, still, we certainly *talk* as if such things were possible. We regularly call moral claims true or false, justified or unjustified. And we speak of our moral convictions as *beliefs*, of children coming to *understand* the difference between right and wrong, and of criminal psychopaths failing to *know* this difference. This is mirrored in the grammar and logic of moral claims, which look and act just like ordinary factual statements. When we argue about right and wrong, we hold ourselves and each other to the same logical rules, the same standards of consistency, as we do when reasoning about ordinary factual matters. Indeed, moral statements and factual statements seamlessly interweave in thought and speech.

(F2) *Objective purport.* Moral statements behave like ordinary factual statements in another way as well. Though we might fear that morality is merely "subjective," we nonetheless make a clear distinction between moral judgments and expressions of preference. Suppose that you and I have just finished listening to a speech by the President announcing new taxes for people in our income bracket. If I say to you, "Well, I'm not happy about this," I am merely reporting my personal response, not purporting to speak for anyone else. If you reply, "Really? I'm actually glad to see it," you, too, are speaking only for yourself. Even though your attitude is in some sense the opposite of mine, and could lead you to behave differently from me, our opposition in attitude remains "subjective," a matter of preference not principle. Indeed, nothing either of us has said actually contradicts the other, and we could both accept that what the other says is true. But suppose I had said instead, "This is a clear injustice, we're paying enough!" Then I would be staking a claim in conversational space that extends beyond my personal corner – it speaks to the question of how you, or anyone else, *should* respond, regardless of personal preferences. And had you replied, "What? It's a matter of simple fairness," you would not be describing your own reaction, but laying a counterclaim to the very same conversational space, *contradicting* what I said, and calling for a response. We would have a principled difference in attitude. Although any such difference is in *some* sense "subjective" and "personal" in *origin* and *location*, still, the *purport* of these attitudes is objective, independent of our personal perspective, even universal. In contrast to the first case, neither of us can fully accept what the other has said and leave it at that. The issue is *not* a matter of intensity of feeling. Even if our feelings were mixed, indeed, even if I felt nothing and were speaking insincerely, we would nonetheless contradict one another. Whatever our states of mind, there is an objective conflict in the *meaning* or *content* of what we said.

(F3) *Supervenience.* Some forms of valuation are conventional, like *price*. Others are personal, like *attachment* or *affection*. Two hammers might be identical in every respect – same shape, size, materials, strength, durability, etc. – and yet one is priced higher than the other, or, being a gift, is the object of greater personal attachment than the other. Other forms of valuation are not like this. The two hammers will be equally *good hammers*, regardless of how we price or prize them. Their quality as hammers is said to *supervene* upon their physical constitution. Now consider a murder trial. If the jury concludes that the non-legal facts concerning defendant *A* and defendant *B* are just the same – the same circumstances, intentions, acts, effects on others, etc. – then the jury cannot properly conclude that one is guilty of murder and the other not. There is a norm at work here: a jury must *treat like cases alike*. Legal assessments are said for this reason to *supervene* upon the facts – once all the facts are settled, so is the guilt or innocence of a defendant. Moral valuation, and putative moral properties, follow these same patterns of supervenience. If two acts of promise-breaking are the same in every factual respect, then if one of them is wrong, so must the other be; if one of them is to be judged blameworthy, so must the other. In particular, mere differences in who is involved cannot change things. The supervenience of moral valuation helps to explain a very important fact of our moral life. Even though moral controversies persist, moral debate is not anarchic. Whatever reasons we treat as relevant in assessing others, we must acknowledge apply equally to ourselves. We must present our cases *impartially*, attempting to give reasons with a certain *generality*, whose relevance could be recognized from viewpoints other than our own.

(F4) *Categoricalness.* As we noted in discussing (F2), objective purport, moral judgments are intended to apply to agents regardless of their personal preferences. Kant pointed out that this gives moral injunctions the form of *categorical* rather than *hypothetical* imperatives. Thus, if I judge that eating meat is inhumane, I am not saying, "If you care about animals, you ought not to eat meat," but rather, "You ought not to eat meat, period. If you do not now consider the suffering of animals, you *should*." Moral demands are not made in the name of a rationally optional goal, and apply even in the face of contrary inclination.

(F5) *Practical import.* (F1) and (F2) make it clear how much moral language resembles ordinary descriptive or fact-stating language, and (F3) makes it clear how closely moral judgment is tied to the facts. Even so, moral language seems to be more than a more colorful way of describing the world. It also has a *practical* or *prescriptive* character. We shift to moral language in trying to decide what to do, or how others should act. Moral language is suited to these "action-guiding" functions because it abounds in normative and evaluative concepts, allowing us to ask not only how things are, but how they *should* be, or whether it is *good* that they are so. Ordinary factual judgments do not in the same way purport to guide action. If I face a moral quandary, then even a long string of well-considered factual judgments would still not constitute "making up my mind" or deciding what, in light of these facts, is the thing to do. Moral thought also functions to guide action *after* I have made up my mind. You care about convincing me that I should pay higher taxes, say, because you believe that if I can be convinced, this will shape not only what I believe, but also how I will go on to act. If you have convinced me, then when I next find myself in the voting booth, I will feel some inner pressure not to reject a candidate just because she supports higher taxes. This pressure does not appear to arise from any source other than my moral conviction, and will be felt even if I still don't *like* the idea of paying more. Should I yield to selfish impulse and vote against this candidate, I will feel some measure of guilt or dissatisfaction with myself for doing so, as well as a sense of "inconsistency" between my words and my deeds. Just how moral judgment is linked to the guidance of action, and whether it is always motivating, is far from obvious. But it is obvious that we normally expect some such link, and tend to doubt the sincerity of a speaker's moral declaration if, when push comes to shove, it has no effect on how he acts or feels.

If (F1)–(F5) give us an idea of what morality is cracked up to be, it becomes clear why it is difficult, or perhaps impossible, to show how morality could live up to its billing. For example, the most straightforward way of accommodating cognitive form (F1) and objective purport (F2) is to say that moral judgments behave like factual judgments because they *are* factual judgments – judgments of *moral facts* – and express beliefs capable of truth or falsity. That is a typical moral realist position. But this makes it difficult to see how to capture categoricalness (F4) or practical import (F5). Take a case of an ordinary factual belief, say, my belief that there is a pitcher of water on the table before me. In order for you to know how this belief will affect my behavior, you need to know what I want – Am I thirsty? Do I want to offer you a drink? Any such desire or aim seems to be an entirely separate state from my belief about the pitcher, which, in itself, appears to be practically "inert." Hume offered an explanation of why this is so. Beliefs function to *represent* the world, and "add nothing" to their object. For this reason, a belief that *p* is true exactly when *p* itself is true. Put in modern terms, beliefs have a "mind-to-world" direction of fit: a belief that *p* successfully performs its function of representing that *p* just in case *p is* true, i.e. just in case the content of the belief "fits" the state of the world – there really is a pitcher of water before me. By contrast, states of mind with inherent motivational force, like a desire to drink or be polite, cannot be mere representations of the world. To desire to drink is not to take it *as true* that I am drinking – that would make the desire self-satisfying, and no goad to action at all. Rather, it is to take drinking as something *to be made true*. Desire thus has a "world-to-mind" direction of fit: a desire that *p* functions to motivate the individual to find a way of making *p* happen, and it successfully performs its function (the desire is "satisfied") only when *p* does happen, say, I quench my thirst. Now, if moral judgments have practical import (F5), it would seem that they, like desires, must have a world-to-mind direction of fit – they present an idea of how things *are to be*. Moreover, if this import is categorical (F4), they must motivate in their own right, without need for any additional desire. But then, it seems, moral judgments cannot simply be factual beliefs, as (F1) and (F2) suggest. For how could one state of mind have *both* directions of fit? (For discussion, see Lewis [1988, 1996] and Smith [1994].)

The difficulty of reconciling (F1)–(F5) is a problem for any theory of morality that seeks to avoid skepticism while taking ordinary morality at face value. To be sure, an interpretation of morality need not take every aspect of actual morality uncritically. For example, it is a hallmark of realism to have a substantial view of truth, and to allow for the possibility that even our best-established current views are in error. Realists thus tend to be *fallibilists*, who note that our views in nearly every area of inquiry have undergone dramatic changes historically – and morality is no exception. However, any interpretation of morality must perform a delicate balancing act, striving to be faithful to the facts but also no more than *modestly revisionist* about morality, lest it simply change the subject. Different ways of achieving this balance have led to a proliferation of forms of moral realism, anti-realism, irrealism, "quasi-realism," etc. in contemporary ethics. Can we find any orderly way of describing the complex landscape of contemporary meta-ethics, and the issues at stake?

Here's one approach. Consider a series of questions that confront any full-scale interpretation of morality, each an important cross-road or choice-point in the meta-ethical landscape. At each such point, a *yes* answer (given in **boldface**, in Figure 26.1) takes the interpretation one step further along the path toward greater realism. *No* answers at these choice-points generate a fairly natural taxonomy of alternatives to realism. Some of these alternatives will be seen to travel a good distance down the path toward moral realism before parting ways. (I am indebted to Gideon Rosen for first introducing me to this strategy for laying out debates over realism. Replacing "moral" with the variable *X* in the diagram below yields a taxonomy for debates over realism in many domains. Of course, Rosen should not be held responsible for any of the particular features of this diagram.)

(Step 1) *Do moral statements have cognitive content?*

In the early twentieth century, logical empiricists sought to give a "rational reconstruction" of all knowledge to place it upon a sounder foundation. Knowledge claims that could not be verified by logic or tested in experience were rejected as *cognitively* meaningless – "pseudo-propositions" that might have rhetorical force, but could not be true or false. Moritz Schlick and A. J. Ayer (1946) applied this criterion to *moral* statements, and concluded that moral language served a *dynamic* rather than descriptive function, enabling people to express their positive and negative sentiments toward certain courses of action, and thereby to influence the behavior of others. According to these *emotivists*, a judgment like "Torture is always wrong," though cognitive in form (F1), does not state a fact – not even the fact that the speaker abhors torture. Instead, when uttered sincerely, it *expresses* the speaker's revulsion at torture – a categorical (F4) *con-attitude*. By expressing this revulsion in moral language, the speaker hopes to discourage torture, an emotive rather than rational effect. The intractability of moral disputes is attributed to differences in people's most basic feelings, which

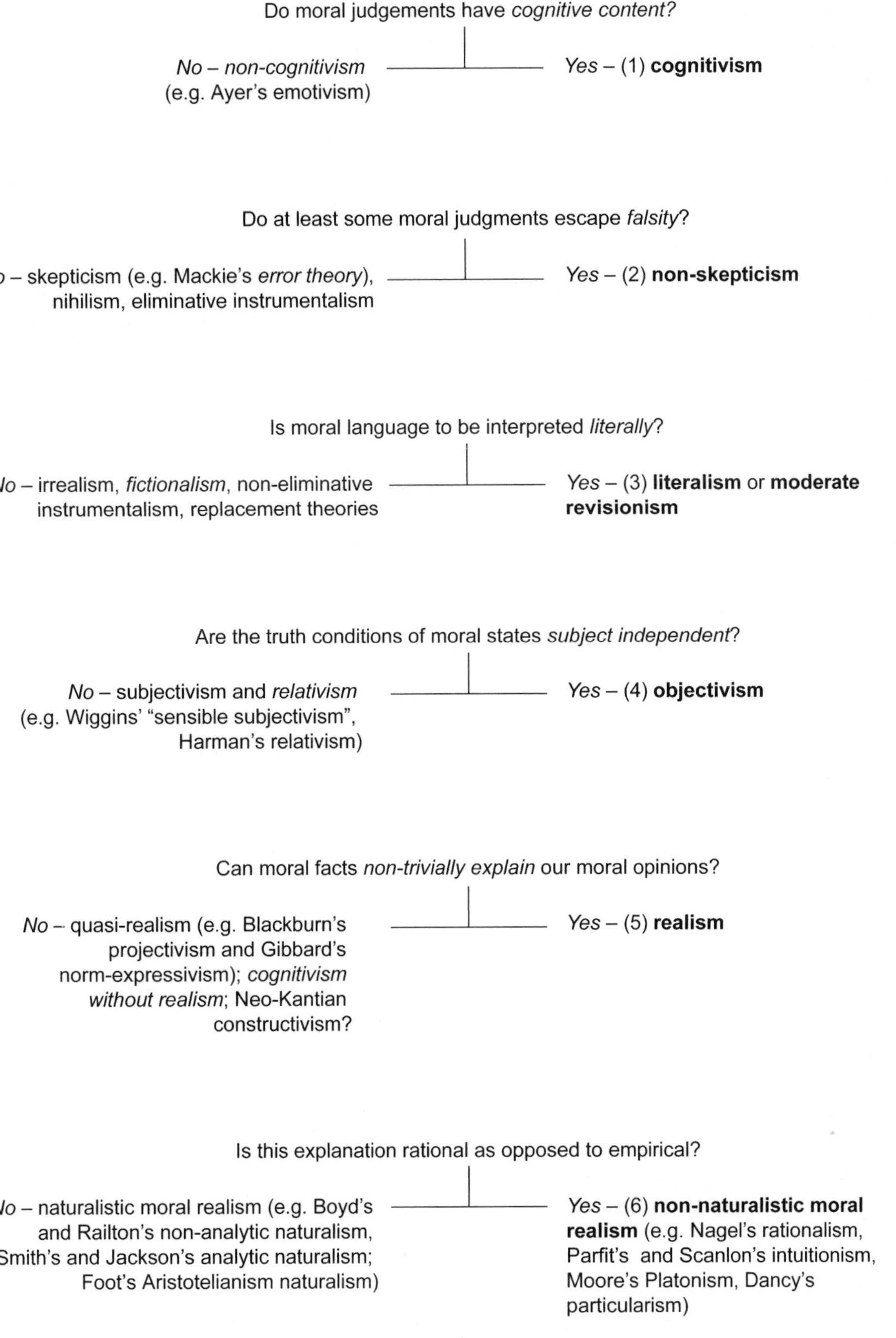

Do moral judgements have *cognitive content?*
No – *non-cognitivism*
(e.g. Ayer's emotivism)
Yes – (1) **cognitivism**
Do at least some moral judgments escape *falsity*?
No – skepticism (e.g. Mackie's *error theory*),
nihilism, eliminative instrumentalism
Yes – (2) **non-skepticism**
Is moral language to be interpreted *literally*?
No – irrealism, *fictionalism*, non-eliminative
instrumentalism, replacement theories
Yes – (3) **literalism** or **moderate**
revisionism
Are the truth conditions of moral states *subject independent*?
No – subjectivism and *relativism*
(e.g. Wiggins' "sensible subjectivism",
Harman's relativism)
Yes – (4) **objectivism**
Can moral facts *non-trivially explain* our moral opinions?
No – quasi-realism (e.g. Blackburn's
projectivism and Gibbard's
norm-expressivism); *cognitivism*
without realism; Neo-Kantian
constructivism?
Yes – (5) **realism**
Is this explanation rational as opposed to empirical?
No – naturalistic moral realism (e.g. Boyd's
and Railton's non-analytic naturalism,
Smith's and Jackson's analytic naturalism;
Foot's Aristotelianism naturalism)
Yes – (6) **non-naturalistic moral**
realism (e.g. Nagel's rationalism,
Parfit's and Scanlon's intuitionism,
Moore's Platonism, Dancy's
particularism)

Figure 26.1 Branching taxonomy of meta-ethical positions with respect to questions of realism. Note: The positions indicated in **boldface** correspond at each branch-point to the path leading toward greater realism.

are not subject to any sort of rational adjudication. The practical purport (F5) of moral judgments follows directly: revulsion, praise, endorsement, outrage, etc., are feelings that directly shape how the speaker is disposed to act.

Emotivism soon became very influential, but, starting in the 1950s, it fell to sustained philosophical attack. Peter Geach (1960) argued that if moral statements functioned solely to express emotion, there would be no explanation of how we use them in *conditional* reasoning. Even supposing that "Stealing is always wrong" expresses a con-attitude toward stealing, no such attitude is expressed by "If stealing is always wrong, then Robin Hood behaved wrongly," which can be asserted with equal sincerity by someone who approves or disapproves of stealing. Emotivism thus fails a fairly basic test for a theory of meaning for a statement – it should be able to explain how that statement contributes to the meaning of the compound statements or embedded contexts in which it appears. Worse, we can clearly understand the following argument: *If stealing is always wrong, then Robin Hood behaved wrongly. But Robin Hood did what's right. So stealing is not always wrong.* Moreover, we can see at once that this argument is *logically valid* – that it would be flatly inconsistent to accept both premises but reject the conclusion. There must be some cognitive content in moral language after all, since there is no logical inconsistency in having conflicting *emotions* about stealing – on the contrary, having mixed feelings about stealing might be a mark of good sense, as cases like Robin Hood's show. Noncognitivism thus appears unable to make sense of how moral claims function in reasoning. This has come to be dubbed the *Frege–Geach Problem.*

Philippa Foot (1978, 2001) and others then pointed out that not just any unconditional pro- or con-attitude will count as a *moral* attitude. Infants, for example, are able to express unqualified pro- and, especially, con-attitudes well before we are inclined to say that they have acquired moral concepts. Moreover, when translating the language of another culture, we will find ourselves confronted with a number of different terms used to express unconditional disapproval. Unless we know something about what sorts of situations or actions these different terms are attached to, we will not know which foreign term to translate as *wrong*, as opposed to *imprudent*, or *impolite*, or *illegal*, or *cowardly*, or *tacky*, etc. Most ethical concepts are *thick*, that is, they carry definite descriptive criteria of application as well as normative force. Thus I convey to you quite different information if I praise a friend as courageous as opposed to conscientious. These criteria also give structure to moral reasoning and discussion since they shape the sorts of reasons that can be given on behalf of making a certain moral judgment. I cannot defend my claim that an individual is fair-minded and courageous by saying that she is wealthy and influential, even though these latter traits might cause me to feel a pro-attitude toward her.

For these and other reasons, few contemporary philosophers think noncognitivism could possibly give the best account of the meaning of moral judgments, and so most accept Step 1 realism about morality: moral judgments have some measure of cognitive content, and are answerable to ordinary norms of reasoning and justification. Indeed, even contemporary descendants of emotivism now accept this.

(Step 2) *Do at least some moral judgments escape falsity?*

Cognitivism might be a necessary condition for moral realism, but it is far from sufficient. For it is compatible with cognitivism that all affirmative moral statements are *false*: nothing is ever really good or bad, and no act is ever really right or wrong. How could that be? Two possibilities are most salient. First, there might be a logical contradiction or conceptual confusion within moral thought that makes it impossible for moral judgments ever to be true. We have already seen an example of this in discussing the difficulty of jointly satisfying (F1)–(F5). J. L. Mackie (1977), for example, claimed that any putative moral value would have to be "objective" (F2) and cognizable (F1), and possess categorical "to-be-pursuedness" (F4)–(F5). Merely recognizing this value would necessarily motivate the agent, *whatever* her personal desires or goals might be. This seemed to Mackie impossibly "queer." Moreover, he added, if there were such values, wouldn't they "impel" humans to much greater consensus in morality? Mackie thus adopted an "error theory" of morality.

The other salient possibility for skepticism is that morality has some very definite conditions of applicability, which as a matter of fact or metaphysical necessity are not met. Nietzsche thought that morality required the existence of a kind of free will that no natural being, and certainly no human, could ever have. And some philosophers have thought that, if God does not exist, then neither does right or wrong.

Few moral philosophers, however, are tempted by skepticism of either sort. Most contemporary philosophers believe that we can give an account of human freedom sufficient to support attributions of moral responsibility, and moreover believe that morality does not depend in any essential way upon divine will or sanction. Beyond this, philosophers divide into those who think moral judgments are subject to notions of correctness or assertability that lie on a different dimension from truth or falsity – so, *a fortiori*, moral judgments cannot be systematically false – and those who argue that, under an interpretation that satisfies *enough* of (F1)–(F5), at least some moral judgments are true. How much is enough? Here is one thought. Even if we think (F1)–(F5) capture something essential to morality, still, we are much more confident that betraying a friend or torturing for pleasure is wrong than we are in the details of (F1)–(F5). Indeed, no sooner had Mackie cast morality aside as erroneous than he began recommending a system of norms remarkably similar to basic morality, which he deemed essential for our collective well-being. But why isn't this morality under another name? We might see Mackie as an *eliminative instrumentalist* about morality: we should dispense with traditional, objectivist moral notions as erroneous, and candidly accept a more subjectivist substitute.

Most would say, however, that the error lies not in morality, but in an exaggerated interpretation of (F1)–(F5) – these conditions can be met *well enough* to obviate eliminativist worries. How? Typically, one of the following three approaches is adopted.

(i) *Motivational judgment internalists* take the key distinguishing feature of moral judgment to be its "practicality" (F5) – a necessary, conceptual ("internal") connection between judging and being motivated to act accordingly. These internalists divide into several groups.

Contemporary *expressivists*, like Allan Gibbard (1990, 2003) and Simon Blackburn (1993, 1998), have picked up where the emotivists, the first expressivists, left off. Like the emotivists, contemporary expressivists give a *non-representational* or *non-descriptivist* account of moral language. They approach meaning indirectly, via the question, "What sort of psychological state is expressed in sincere moral judgment?" For emotivists, this state of mind is non-cognitive, a feeling. For contemporary expressivists, by contrast, the state has cognitive content as well as motive force. Gibbard has proposed the attitudes of endorsing a norm, or accepting a plan. Such states of mind are not beliefs, but they do support "logics" of permission and prohibition, inclusion and exclusion, that exhibit a number of parallels with ordinary propositional logic and at least partially address the Frege–Geach problem. Gibbard, for example, has most recently argued that a judgment, "Stealing is always wrong," expresses acceptance of a plan, *In all circumstances, refrain from stealing*. Suppose we accept this plan. Then we have, in effect, given ourselves a categorical (F4) imperative. It is universal in scope because in moral reasoning we ask ourselves ("plan") what we'd do in others' shoes as well as our own. Suppose we reflect, "What would I do in Robin Hood's circumstances?," and find ourselves judging that what he did was the thing to do. We thus accept the plan, *In Robin Hood's circumstances, steal just like him*. But now we are caught in a mental fix that simulates *modus tollens* – we must either give up our starting point, the general plan never to steal, or change our mind about the specific judgment of Robin. This model explains patterns of inference (F1) and intra- and inter-personal disagreement (F2) by appeal to the mutual inclusion or exclusion of plans, without appeal to truth. Moreover, unlike mere beliefs, plans have practical import (F5) – part of what it is to *accept* a plan is to have some tendency to carry it out, or to feel at odds with oneself if one does not. Can this sort of expressivist account *fully* capture the logic and objective purport of moral thought? Thus far, no complete expressivist solution exists for the Frege–Geach problem and other difficulties in capturing the full logic and semantics of cognitive discourse (*see* Schroeder 2008), but perhaps we begin to see how expressivism might come close enough to count as, at worst, moderately revisionist.

Other motivational judgment internalists, such as John McDowell (1985) and David Wiggins (1998), take the opposite tack from expressivists, and argue that moral judgments express propositional beliefs. But these are beliefs with a special sort of *response-dependent* content, so that they are linked in a necessary way with motivation (F5). Consider a parallel. A person with wit is alive to the ironies of life, and for her there is an "internal" connection between *recognizing* the humor in a situation (a cognitive state) and being *amused* by it (an affective state, with motive force). Indeed, these seem not to be two states, but two aspects of the same state, namely, *seeing* the humor, "getting it." To explain this there is no need to posit queer facts of "to-be-amusedness" – a sense of humor and a mind alert to ordinary facts will suffice. Moreover, within a culture human humor sensibilities overlap sufficiently to make possible "communities of judgment" grounded in familiar forms and practices of shared humor – irony, sarcasm, joke-telling, comedy, etc. – that play a basic role in our everyday lives. We can describe this community as centered on a response-dependent property – that which people of actual human wit find amusing – in much the same way as our common language of color is centered on the shared color sensibilities of the human visual system. Neither humor nor color judgments will be merely "subjective." One cannot simply declare oneself an authority on what is funny or what is red – such authority must be earned by showing excellence in wit or color-discrimination.

Now consider the concept of a *need* and a moral virtue like *kindness*. A kind person has a distinctive way of seeing the world, a sensibility that attunes her not only to the feelings of others, but also to their needs. She can, in one, unified response to a situation, *see* that someone is in need (hungry, cold, discouraged, grieving) and *feel* moved to help him – no additional desire or aim is needed (F4). There is nothing mysterious here, no facts of "to-be-doneness," just reactions of a kind with which we are all familiar. Insofar as we possess kindness, then, we see instances of need as *calling for* a certain response – a fact that exists on the human plane, as obvious as humor and as objective as color. Is that objective enough to capture the full objective purport of morality (F2)? We will consider a worry about this, below. But if we understand moral concepts as response-dependent in this way, and moral communities as built upon such shared sensibilities, the result is a challenge to neo-Humean strictures about "direction of fit" – arguably, cognition (F1) and motivation (F5) can combine within moral judgment in a way that can be called *seeing things aright*.

(ii) *Motivational judgment externalists* also seek to capture cognitive form (F1) and objective purport (F2) by showing that moral statements express genuine propositions, but they argue that the link between moral judgment and motivation is *psychological* rather than conceptual. People normally have a strong motivation to act well, and to be seen as acting well. There is a strong internal pressure, or felt need, to see ourselves in a good light, and as consistent in thought and action. The positive self-image that psychically underwrites this link between judgment and action can, however, break down – for example, in chronic depression. When this happens, an individual can find that thinking he ought to do something evokes no impulse to action. Has this person become amoral, or lost his understanding of moral language? Or is he simply a victim of flattened affect and withered motivation?

The externalist maintains that motivational internalists have conflated the conceptual connection between moral judgment and *normative* force with a connection to *motive* force. The depressed individual who judges his self-destructive behavior wrong may lack motivation to overcome it, but will certainly agree that he *ought* to be so motivated, that there are *reasons* to change. Are externalists therefore committed to reasons as "intrinsically normative" facts, above and beyond ordinary facts? They divide on this point, roughly into naturalists and non-naturalists.

Naturalistic motivational externalists attempt to show how reasons and values can *be* ordinary facts, thus securing (F1) and (F2) directly. Two strategies predominate. *Non-analytic naturalists* (Richard Boyd [1988], Peter Railton [1986]) distinguish normative *concepts* from normative *facts* and *properties*. They accept the long tradition of arguments, from Hume on *is* vs. *ought* to Moore's (1903) "open question" test (*see* The open question argument [Chapter 25]), showing that normative and natural concepts are categorially distinct). But, they argue, this does not require the positing of irreducible normative facts and properties – for these normative concepts might function to represent natural facts or properties in a special way, rather than to refer to a separate realm of facts or properties. Debilitating pain, for example, is an intrinsically aversive psychological state, but it is therefore also a bad thing for the person experiencing it, and something she has reason to avoid, other things equal. This badness or reason-givingness is not an additional fact – it is constituted by the very nature of such pain, affording a direct explanation of supervenience (F3). Normative language has the distinctive "job" of presenting the natural aversiveness of pain *as* bad, a "mode of presentation" that can enter directly into evaluation, deliberation, and choice (F5) (see Railton [1993] for an account of the meaning of moral concepts along these lines).

For example, medical procedures differ in their painfulness, duration, efficacy, and so on. We need a way of representing these various features that permits weighing them against one another. The language of value or reasons permits just that – not because these different features share some uniform non-natural property, but because each in its own way *is* a reason, or a harm or a benefit of a certain strength, connected to motivation (F5) through psychology rather than semantics. Non-analytic naturalists typically give a *functional* characterization of normative properties – e.g. goodness as a matter of conducing to lives found to be intrinsically rewarding, rightness as a matter of practices conducing to social relations that promote intrinsically rewarding lives – and argue that facts about what would, or would not, satisfy these functions can be objective (F2) and known through experience, history, and natural and social science. What is called "moral intuition" might be the result of millennia of human experience, not a special, extra-empirical insight into an *a priori* moral order. Moreover, our moral intuitions continue to be shaped by experience and the growth of knowledge – witness fundamental changes in intuitions about the justness of slavery, the subjugation of women, and the treatment of animals.

Analytic naturalists (Frank Jackson [1998], Michael Smith [1994]) may agree with much in the non-analytic naturalists' program, but believe that a similar strategy can yield a yet stronger result: outright naturalistic definitions of normative concepts. Relying upon a technique developed by analytic functionalists in the philosophy of mind, analytic naturalists about morality start out with our going normative theories about what is right or good, and then idealize to the form normative theory will take when it is fully developed and ideally justified. This ideal theory can be seen as laying down complex functional roles or "job descriptions" for key moral concepts. Since the supervenience of the normative upon the non-normative, (F3), is *a priori*, we know in advance that, unless nihilism is true, there will be some, possibly complex natural properties that satisfy these job descriptions. These complex natural properties will be necessarily coextensive with the corresponding normative concepts, and so afford a way of *defining* those concepts. Such definitions would likely be functional, and far from obvious – the complex natural properties involved could lack any explanatory unity of the kind the non-analytic naturalists seek. But these definitions would at least establish that we need not be committed to any metaphysical extravagance by our use of normative concepts, and that normative truths can have an objective natural foundation, (F1)–(F2). Because these functional definitions are generated from ideal normative theory, an immediate answer is available to the question whether we have reason to think that what satisfies these functions would have normative import, (F5). Insofar as we could ever answer that question definitively, it would.

Non-naturalistic motivational externalists do not share the naturalists' sense that non-natural properties, intuited *a priori*, are dubious. They argue that much of our firmest knowledge is "non-natural" and known by *a priori* means, e.g. mathematics, geometry, and logic. Moreover, like the claims of mathematics, fundamental moral truths have an air of *necessity* about them. There may be possible worlds in which anti-gravity exists, or where people grow from seeds, but is there a possible world in which debilitating pain is, in itself, what it is to live well? Or in which imposing great suffering on many to provide slight benefit to a privileged few is, in itself, a paradigm of acting justly? Such things are manifestly impossible, the non-naturalist argues, and we can know this without needing to run experiments or await the verdict of history. Moreover, this knowledge is not merely tautological or "analytic," since it has implications about how to live or act. To recognize such obvious truths is just what it is to have a "synthetic *a priori* rational intuition" – so the idea is not so mysterious, after all. Cognitivism (F1) and objective purport (F2) thus are in hand.

Intuitionists can point out that all systems of rational thought must rely on something like intuition at some point. Ordinary factual beliefs might appear to be based solely upon experience and reasoning, not "intuition," but consider the basic principles we rely upon in drawing inferences or learning from experience. We cannot, without circularity, appeal to inference or experience to justify *these*. Instead, we claim that the fundamental rules of logic or principles of induction are "self-evident," e.g. "*p* & *q* implies *p*" and "If one has reason to believe that *p* & *q*, one also has *pro tanto* reason to believe that *p*." And it is just this sort of self-evidence that the non-naturalist is claiming for fundamental moral truths. Historically, some intuitionists, like Sidgwick, thought that intuitions of moral truths were always "accompanied by a certain impulse to do the acts recognized as right," and thus might accept a form of motivational judgment internalism. This, however, spoils the analogy with logic or norms of inference, since it involves not just recognition of a fact, but necessary motivation on its behalf. Most modern non-naturalists (Derek Parfit [2006], T. M. Scanlon [1998]) reject this motivational thesis, and point out, as we noted above, that what is needed is a connection between moral judgment and recognition of *reasons to act*, not motivational impulse. They therefore have no need for "queer" facts that are motivating simply to recognize. All they need to show is that we can intuit facts that constitute reasons to act (F5). And, as the example above of "conjunction elimination" in inference shows, reasons may be just the sort of thing *a priori* intuition can deliver.

(iii) *Kantians* seek a different path to synthetic *a priori* moral truths, via the notion of *practical reason*, i.e. reasoning concerning action. For them, *the* question about whether morality is what it's cracked up to be – and not, as Kant put the worry, a "high-flown fantasticality" – is whether there are categorical practical reasons (F4), reasons to act that would bind all rational beings as such, regardless of any contingent variation in motivation or aim (F5). They take the perspective of the deliberating agent, and argue that such an agent must take herself to be free in the special sense of being regulated by *choice* rather than mere causes, and that choice is only intelligible as such if it is based upon reasons. But reasons by their nature are general, of a kind recognizable by any rational being. The result is that acting for a reason is acting as if upon a universal principle, i.e. a principle binding upon all rational beings. Here, then, we find the "categorical imperative" that lies at the foundation of morality: we should act only upon maxims we could at the same time will to be universal laws. All this is held to be inescapable from the deliberative perspective, affording a *practical* rather than metaphysical conception of the objectivity of moral judgment (F2). As a result, Kantians today typically reject the label "moral realist" and prefer to speak of themselves as *constructivists* (*see* Rawls 1980 and Korsgaard 1996). Though they insist that there are genuine facts about what is right or wrong (F1), these are "facts of reason" arising within and through the exercise of agency, not independently existing natural or non-natural facts that antecedently determine how agency is to be exercised.

(Step 3) *Is moral language being interpreted literally?*

Thus far the interpretations we have discussed have been aimed at capturing enough of (F1)–(F5) to avoid skepticism. But that is a tall order. We can expect any bit of natural language, normative or non-normative, to reflect a complex and contentious history, and to be too wrinkled to fit within the skin of a perfectly smooth account. Our earlier discussion of eliminative instrumentalism suggests a possibility. Why not instrumentalism without the elimination? That is, why not take a page from the Kantians and place primary normative emphasis on the practical function of morality, its action-guiding role, (F5), but then show that this can be achieved without needing to take moral talk literally? If this were possible, then the upshot would be that we can continue to think and act *as if* (F1)–(F5) held, without worrying that morality will be a massive mistake if these conditions cannot literally be satisfied. After all, if morality is essential to human flourishing, should we discard it in an excess of meta-theoretical purism?

This line of thought suggests the strand of irrealism known as *moral fictionalism* (*see* Error theory and fictionalism [Chapter 28]). Fictionalists allow that moral claims might well be false if literally interpreted, but suggest that literal interpretation is beside the point. Consider an actual fiction, say, *Huckleberry Finn*. To enter a fiction is not to think that anything goes, but to enter *the world* of the fiction, within which there are many facts, and truth and falsity function pretty much as usual, e.g. it is true that Huck Finn is a boy and therefore not a girl, and that Pap Finn is a vicious man and therefore not a model father.

It might be objected: there is no *real* boy or father, no *real* abuse, so none of these things could be true. But such literal-mindedness is simply obtuse. What matters for understanding a novel is what is *fictional*, or true within the world of the novel. To treat morality fictionally would be to treat ourselves as cohabiting – collectively enacting in thought, words, and deed – a moral world, where there are facts of right and wrong with categorical action-guiding force. Fictionalism is an attractive option in any domain whose concepts and principles are useful, or even indispensable, but where metaphysical commitments seem either beside the point (recall "the average German") or so incomprehensible that they might as well be ("free will as agent causation"). However, while it might be true that metaphysics is beside the point for many moral concerns, it is hard to believe that our moral convictions, or the point of going on as we do in morality, would be essentially unchanged if we came to think that *freedom*, *responsibility*, *benefit*, *harm*, and *fairness* are a shared pretense, and nothing real. Moreover, if (F1)–(F5) involve incoherencies, then we will have made no real progress by going fictional, since in order to act *as if* (F1)–(F5) held true we'd have to enact an incoherent world. Finally, fictionalism about the normative might bring incoherencies of its own. What would it mean to say that we should keep talk of *value* and *reasons to act* as useful fictions? "Useful" sounds like a claim about value, and "should keep" sounds like claiming the existence of a reason to act. Can fictionalism about the normative swallow its own tail and not choke?

To stay on the path to realism, as we argued, one's interpretation of morality must be literal, or near enough – no more than moderately revisionist. What this amounts to is, of course, is a source of endless debate. Expressivists see motivational judgment internalism as the essence of normative concepts, and so see motivational judgment externalists as immoderate revisionists with regard to (F5). Some motivational judgment externalists return the favor, and see motivational judgment internalists as immoderately revising (F5) by replacing objective reasons to act with the speaker's motivational tendencies. Among externalists, non-naturalists tend to see naturalists as immoderately revising moral thought by dispensing with the idea of irreducible, intrinsically normative moral facts. And so on. Such debates over revisionism occur in every area of higher-order philosophical reflection – epistemology, semantics, philosophy of mind, etc. – and appropriately so. Every attempt to introduce clarity and coherence into living human thought will involve some tidying-up, and deciding how much is too much is a matter of weighing costs and benefits. In what follows, I will assume that all of the major interpretive tendencies that present themselves as non-revisionary, or only modestly revisionary, can reasonably make this claim, and thus count as Step 3 realisms. I submit the liveliness of the current debate itself as evidence.

(Step 4) *Are the truth conditions of moral statements subject-independent?*

Many philosophers take objectivity (F2) to be the core issue in discussions of moral realism. As we have seen, "objectivity" has multiple senses, but they share a root idea, *subject-independence*. In the metaphysical sense, objectivity is a matter of existence that is experience- and opinion-independent. In the epistemic sense, objectivity is a matter of beliefs or methods that are free from, or tend to reduce, the influence of subjective perspectives or interests. And in the practical sense, objectivity is a matter of requirements or reasons to act that apply to all rational agents alike, independent of any subject-to-subject variation in standpoint or goals. What about the *moral* sense? On Kantian views, the objectivity of morality just *is* practical objectivity. But on other accounts of morality, the answer is less straightforward. After all, morality has to do with subjects, that is, beings capable of experience or agency, so no blanket exclusion of facts about subjects could be right. Rather, what makes a given interpretation of moral discourse objective or subjective is *how* facts about subjects and their views or viewpoints enter into the meaning or truth conditions of moral claims.

Moral subjectivists hold that moral judgments function rather like judgments of *legality* – they contain a (usually implicit) reference to the norms of the relevant community. *Within* a given community, there will be facts about what is legal or illegal, and what is right or wrong. These facts will depend upon what the community's laws and courts, or shared moral principles and practices, permit or prohibit. But apart from *all* communities, the question "What is legally required?" or "What is morally right?" simply has no answer. Moral subjectivists differ concerning how the relevant moral community is determined, and how homogenous or wide it must be – could it, for example, be a community of one? – but they share the idea that dependence upon community norms is *built into* the meaning of moral judgments, when properly interpreted.

As a result, subjectivists have difficulty accounting for a key manifestation of objective purport (F2), namely, the existence of moral disagreement and criticism across differences in moral communities. When defenders of human rights declare that "Torturing people for their opinions is wrong," they take themselves to be making a claim that applies equally to all societies, including in particular those that *do not* accept this norm. Indeed, it seems to be the peculiar office of moral language, e.g. the language of human rights, as opposed to legal language or the language of custom, to permit the expression and application of normative claims that apply across cultures and over time. (Although quite different from subjectivism, expressivism can face a similar difficulty in dealing with fundamental moral disagreement, since the expressivist "proxy" for a shared subject matter in moral judgment is an *overlap in attitudes* – e.g. in the fundamental norms or plans individuals accept – that provides enough common ground among individuals to give their moral pronouncements normative relevance to each other. Absent such overlap, and strategic considerations aside, it is unclear what authority or applicability one individual's moral pronouncements could have for others.)

Wiggins' "sensible subjectivism" seeks to remedy the sort of opinion-dependence or social relativism that afflicts older subjectivisms by rigidly fixing the meaning of moral terms to a *non*-variable index: the responses of *actual* moral sensibilities. Should our sensibilities or culture change, this would not alter what is right or wrong, just as the colors of objects would not change if our visual systems or color-naming conventions changed. However, an inability to capture certain potentially important forms of criticism or disagreement lingers. Two cultures with different fundamental sensibilities will typically end up speaking two different moralizing languages, each anchored in a different set of canonical actual responses – just as Martians and humans, if they possessed different perceptual systems with different canonical normal responses, would end up with different color concepts. If someone were to ask whether Earthling or Martian concepts pick out the *real* colors – "Which group gets things right?" – the only thing to say is that this is not a sensible question. Nothing objective is at stake, and in any event, neither one's color discourse is a live option for the other. Something similar, we are told, holds in the case of asking, as between two cultures with fundamentally different sensibilities, which one has the *right* conception of a good or virtuous life – "Which one gets things right in the moral realm?" A way of life founded upon a sensibility we can neither enter into nor understand is not a live option for us, it is claimed, neither could it pose a genuine challenge to the authority of our own responses. This response, however, seems a great deal less compelling in the moral case, for something objective *does* seem at stake. Perhaps a population dominated by a xenophobic warrior ethic and code of male honor cannot readily enter into or understand the sensibility of a modern population dominated by more pacific, benevolent, gender-neutral, and universal norms, and vice versa. But history has witnessed the gradual transition from the former to the latter in numerous lands, so an option *can* exist despite difficulties in mutual understanding, and it would be hard to say that nothing objective has thereby been gained, or that less xenophobic and more gender-neutral norms are no closer to getting things right about the moral significance of our fellow humans. Moreover, reflecting upon such examples of dramatic historical improvement, we can meaningfully ask whether *our* own actual moral sensibilities might also need dramatic change. Actual sensibilities, then, do not seem to play the role in fixing our moral concepts that "sensible subjectivists" imagine.

Recently there has been reawakened interest in forms of *moral relativism* that afford a somewhat different way of saying *no* at Step 4. For many years, moral relativism was dismissed as incoherent, since it seems to make universal assertions about what is right or wrong – e.g. that in any society S, what S's norms and customs approve is right – while at the same time denying that such statements are capable of truth or falsity. This quick refutation depended, however, upon seeing the relativist as making normative judgments rather than advancing a meta-ethical position. So contemporary philosophers impressed with the phenomenon of seemingly intractable moral diversity and with the difficulty of identifying "objective reasons" have sought to formulate a coherent meta-ethical relativism. Aware of the failings of subjectivism, some "new relativists" reject the idea that there is a culture-dependent element in the *meaning* of moral concepts, and locate the connection to cultural norms in the *truth-conditions* of moral judgments (see Harman 1996). According to such views, "Burning heretics is wrong" itself makes no reference to any particular group of subjects or set of norms, and thus means the same thing whether uttered in twenty-first-century Spain or thirteenth-century Castile. However, relativism enters in identifying the frame of reference with which to evaluate the truth or falsity of particular moral judgments – e.g. modern vs. medieval moral standards. By analogy, consider the claim, "*x* is in motion." This has a definite, constant meaning regardless of one's choice of reference frame, even though *which* bodies are in motion or at rest will depend upon which coordinate system one fixes upon. In the case of motion, relativists argue, we have learned to accept the idea that no such coordinate system is privileged, or "objectively at rest" – so that there simply are no facts about "absolute motion." They want us to learn the same lesson about morality. If someone asks, "Well, who's right about whether to burn heretics, medieval or modern

Europeans?" we should no more expect an absolute, objective, frame-independent answer than we do if someone asks, "Well, is the sun in motion or at rest?" This sort of relativist need not deny the objective purport of ordinary moral judgments (F2), but she will claim that there is nothing in reality that answers to it beyond truth *relative to a standard*. And no standard is, in itself, objectively privileged or absolute. The result is at best a "relative realism," which, they claim, is sufficient to capture all the "objectivity" actually found in moral practice.

As a claim about the actual meaning of our moral terms, moral relativism seems false, or radically revisionist. As a claim about moral truth, it seems in conflict with morality's objective purport. But as a claim about how morality works in practice – namely, that people tend to refer moral questions to their own attitudes or those prevalent in their society – it may have more plausibility. Even so, this socio-psychological observation has less force than might at first appear. After all, in much the same sense, people tend to refer *all* their judgments, ordinary factual judgments included, to their own attitudes or those prevalent in their "reference group." Indeed, many fundamental factual disagreements across individuals and cultures seem quite intractable, too, and we may find ourselves unable to identify non-question-begging "objective epistemic reasons." If we are to allow ourselves to be pushed by facts about diversity and intractability into *moral* relativism, it is hard to see why we would stop there.

Naturalist and non-naturalist cognitivists characteristically reject moral and factual relativism alike, and give an account of the content of moral judgments and factual judgments alike in terms of propositions or representations with classical truth conditions, not relativized to speaker or culture (though see Horgan and Timmons [1991] for worries that some naturalists will end up as "cross-world" relativists). In the last two decades, however, an alternative, non-classical way of thinking about the truth of moral judgments has begun to have an effect on debates over realism. According to a *minimalist* conception of truth (*see* Horwich 1998), to say that a theory – factual or moral – is true is just to say that everything the theory says is true, and that, given the Tarski schema – "p" is true iff p – is just to assert the theory. The truth predicate does not correspond to a "word/world" relationship or require a substantive account of "propositions," "representation," "reference," or "truth conditions." Instead, it simply is a linguistic device that gives us a rule for shifting from first-order talk of cabbages and kings to second-order talk about sentences concerning cabbages and kings. Otherwise, talk of truth adds no content, and assumes no metaphysics.

Minimalism has enabled expressivists to reclaim truth for themselves. Suppose that I judge that torture is always impermissible. According to the expressivist, this is an expression of my attitude of accepting a norm or plan that rules out torture in all situations, by anyone and for any reason. According to the minimalist, once I judge that torture is always impermissible, nothing more is needed for me to say that "Torture is always impermissible" is true. I do not need to give you a metaphysical theory explaining what sort of "fact" or "truth" this is, or worry that I have only explained what it is to *judge* this, and not given its "truth-conditions." True is true – it just doesn't amount to much more than a device for quotation and disquotation. Indeed, once we see how this is done, we can see how minimalists might accept the notion of *fact* as well: to say that "It is a fact that *p*" is just to say that "*p*" is true, which in turn is just to say that *p*. So, as long as the expressivist is prepared to judge that torture is always impermissible, she would have every right to insist this is a "moral fact."

Assuming that worries about the Frege–Geach problem and other syntactic and semantic worries facing expressivism can be met, is this sort of expressivism a new form of moral realism? Yes, but one that we need to distinguish from earlier forms of realism that took truth to be a substantive relation of word to world, and therefore worried about how to give substantive truth-conditions for moral judgments. Thus, this "expressivist realism" is usually called *quasi-realism* or *minimal realism*. To be clear, the true-blue minimalist *doesn't* think he is being at all *quasi* about truth or facts – he is just giving "truth" and "fact" their literal meaning, which turns out to be very minimal. According to the quasi-realist, then, there never was an alternative of "*real* realism" that "takes truth more seriously" – there simply were people calling themselves "*real* realists," trapped in an illusion of what truth must be. It would be taking sides on a contentious debate over the nature of truth to dismiss the quasi-realist's position. Let us therefore say that quasi-realists can attain Step 4 moral realism right alongside older realisms, and join them in passing on to the next choice-point.

(Step 5) *Can moral facts non-trivially explain our moral opinions?*

Realism, as we noted at the beginning, favors a certain "order of explanation." It is concerned with developing an understanding of the world that is more than just the shadow cast by what we think. The world predates us, often resists our efforts to impose our views or will upon it, and sometimes rewards us with success when we get something right. This is an instance of the generic realist scheme: we appeal to the fact that *p*, or the truth of *p*, as part of an explanation of how we have come to believe that *p*. Why do we believe that the continents move? Here is a non-trivial answer: because we found ways – through seismic, geological, and biological observation and experiment – to discipline our thought to the behavior of these large land masses. Here is a trivial answer: because continental drift is the hegemonic view within the scientific establishment, and that's what it *is* for it to be a fact.

We have seen an example of non-trivial explanation of normative beliefs in the case of the non-analytic naturalists' theories of a human well-being – the very facts that constitute this well-being have, through history and experience, shaped our thinking about what well-being consists in. An analytic naturalist can give essentially the same sort of functionalist account (although some parts of this explanation are truistic, the whole will not be). Functionalist explanations face some well-known difficulties, especially the threat of underdetermination, as too many candidates – including some rather perverse ones – may exist for satisfying a given function. But these are problems for functionalism generally, and so no special reason to deny both forms of moral naturalism the status of Step 5 realisms.

A neo-Aristotelian naturalism can also afford non-trivial explanations – at least if, as Aristotle himself would have held, the essential *proper human* functions and sensibilities that afford the groundwork for morality can come to be known to us through reflection and experience. Aristotle himself thought essences could be identified through an understanding of the teleology of nature, but modern Aristotelians tend to adopt a less metaphysical, and more frankly normative, practice-based account. These accounts are avowedly circular, since they allow us at the start to help ourselves to normative truths. But if the circularity of such accounts can be shown not to be vicious, then neo-Aristotelian naturalism can give a non-trivial explanation of our moral opinions in terms of moral truths, and so reach Step 5 realism (*see* Foot 2001).

Naturalist explanations have tended to invoke a substantive notion of truth, but what of the minimal notion of moral truth advocated by the quasi-realist? Could the minimal truth of "*p*" afford a non-trivial explanation of how we have come to believe that *p*? It seems not – that the one is simply a relabeling of the other. Blackburn himself has adopted the label "projectivism" for his view, reversing the realist "order of explanation." But minimalism is typically intended to leave our moral discourse and practices undisturbed, i.e. to be a form of *quietism*. And indeed, once one gives up the notion of a fact as freighted with metaphysical significance, there is no harm in saying that Southern apologists were "unable to disguise the fact of slavery's injustice." In this way, a rather thin notion of moral explanation is allowed – "quasi-explanation," perhaps. Not enough for Step 5 realism, but perhaps enough to leave ordinary talk of moral reality unperturbed.

It remains to ask about non-naturalism. At first blush, it is difficult to see what it would mean for non-natural moral facts – facts that are not themselves part of the causal order, not situated in space and time – to explain our moral opinions. But this is simply to privilege causal explanation over other forms. Consider a realm many would see as paradigmatically non-natural: logic and mathematics. Does the fact that arithmetic is incomplete explain our belief that it is? Certainly, that belief rests squarely upon a mathematical practice that found a way, through proof, to discipline our mathematical thought by the very facts that are its object. Thus Gödel's proof, and many subsequent proofs, account for our belief that arithmetic is incomplete. To be sure, this way of putting things skates over difficult questions concerning the epistemology of proof and the metaphysical status of logical and mathematical facts. And it presupposes that our thoughts, words, and symbols can come to represent or refer to *abstracta*. But the case for saying that, in Gödel's proof, we have a non-trivial explanation of the right sort, is intuitively very strong.

The moral case seems much harder for non-naturalists, however, since in ethics we have nothing like logical proof to play the explanatory role. Instead, we must resort directly to the idea that certain claims about what reasons we have for acting, and what morality requires, are self-evident. But, as we saw earlier, appeals to self-evidence at the *fundamental* level appear to be found in all forms of rational inquiry. Is the fact that debilitating pain is a *prima facie* reason for acting, or that promises *prima facie* ought to be kept, any less self-evident than the excluded middle? After all, logicians have had a long-running debate over the excluded middle that seems clearly normative in character. Logicians and mathematicians, especially those in the "classical" camp, have *vindicated* their assumptions many times over, with the development of a vast, powerful, coherent, useful, and beautifully intelligible body of self-reinforcing results. We have nothing so grand in the moral case, and, Kantians to the contrary, the amount of ethics that is self-evident, or follows logically from what is self-evident, is disappointingly small. Moreover, the moral non-naturalists have had much less to say than philosophers of logic and mathematics by way of a theory of the epistemology and metaphysics of non-natural facts, or how we might gain semantic or epistemic access to them. But some moral non-naturalists would note that such higher-order worries do nothing to undermine the authority of our firmest moral convictions, the fruit of centuries of wise reflection. The non-naturalist can stake her claim here, arguing that moral facts – not accident, prejudice, individual idiosyncrasy, or social custom – have indeed played the right sort of role in the formation of some of our most deeply held moral opinions. Hence she, too, can occupy Step 5 moral realism. A slightly different strategy is pursued by *particularist* non-naturalists, like Jonathan Dancy (1993), who argue that it is not general, abstract principles – which always seem to admit of exceptions – but judgments about what reasons to act we have in particular, concrete cases that have true self-evidence.

Conclusion

By posing a series of questions about realism, we can generate a nearly complete taxonomy of contemporary meta-ethics, and this is reason to think of realism as a central question in moral philosophy. But such a claim should not leave the impression that "the question of realism" is *one* question. Instead, as we have seen, it is a host of questions – semantic, epistemic, metaphysical, and normative – that reflect the many ways in which we can be concerned over whether there really is a fact of the matter about how we ought to live together, and whether we have any business claiming what it might be.

See also Non-cognitivism (Chapter 27), Error theory and fictionalism (Chapter 28), Cognitivism without realism (Chapter 29), Relativism (Chapter 30), Reasons, values, and morality (Chapter 36), Ethical intuitionism (Chapter 39).

References

Ayer, A. J. (1946) "A Critique of Ethics," in *Language, Truth and Logic*, London: Gollanz, pp. 102–14.
Blackburn, Simon (1993) *Essays in Quasi-Realism*, Oxford: Oxford University Press.
——(1998) *Ruling Passions*, Oxford: Oxford University Press.
Boyd, Richard (1988) "How to Be a Moral Realist," in G. Sayre-McCord (ed.) *Essays on Moral Realism*, Ithaca, NY: Cornell University Press, pp. 181–228.
Dancy, Jonathan (1993) *Moral Reasons*, Oxford: Blackwell.
Foot, Philippa (1978) *Virtues and Vices*, Oxford: Blackwell.
——(2001) *Natural Goodness*, Oxford: Clarendon Press.
Geach, Peter (1960) "Ascriptivism," *Philosophical Review* 69: 221–5.
Gibbard, Allan (1990) *Wise Choices, Apt Feelings*, Cambridge, MA: Harvard University Press.
——(2003) *Thinking How to Live*, Cambridge, MA: Harvard University Press.
Harman, Gilbert (1996) "Moral Relativism," Pt 1 of *Moral Relativism and Moral Objectivity*, by Gilbert Harman and Judith Jarvis Thomson, Oxford: Blackwell.
Horgan, Terrance and Timmons, Mark (1991) "*New Wave* Moral Realism Meets Moral Twin-Earth," *Journal of Philosophical Research* 16: 447–65.
Horwich, Paul (1998) *Truth*, 2nd edn, Oxford: Oxford University Press.
Jackson, Frank (1998) *From Metaphysics to Ethics*, Oxford: Oxford University Press.
Korsgaard, Christine (1996) *The Sources of Normativity*, Cambridge: Cambridge University Press.
Lewis, David (1988) "Desire as Belief," *Mind* 97: 323–32.
——(1996) "Desire as Belief II," *Mind* 108: 303–13.
Mackie, J. L. (1977) *Ethics: Inventing Right and Wrong*, London: Penguin Books.
McDowell, John (1985) "Values and Secondary Qualities," in T. Honderich (ed.) *Morality and Objectivity*, London: Routledge & Kegan Paul, pp. 110–29.
Moore, G. E. (1903) *Principia Ethica*, Cambridge: Cambridge University Press.
Parfit, Derek (2006) "Normativity," in R. Shafer-Landau, *Oxford Studies in Metaethics*, Oxford: Clarendon Press, pp. 325–80.
Railton, Peter (1986) "Moral Realism," *Philosophical Review* 95: 163–207.
——(1993) "Noncognitivism about Rationality: Benefits, Costs, and an Alternative," *Philosophical Issues* 4: 36–51.
Rawls, John (1980) "Kantian Constructivism in Moral Theory," *Journal of Philosophy* 77: 512–72.
Scanlon, T. M. (1998) *What We Owe to Each Other*, Cambridge, MA: Harvard University Press.
Schroeder, Michael (2008) *Being For: Evaluating the Semantic Program of Expressivism*, Oxford: Oxford University Press.
Smith, Michael (1994) *The Moral Problem*, Oxford: Blackwell.
Wiggins, David (1998) "A Sensible Subjectivism?," in *Needs, Values, Truth*, 3rd edn, Oxford: Oxford University Press.

Further reading

Brink, David O. (1989) *Moral Realism and the Foundations of Ethics*, Cambridge: Cambridge University Press. (An externalist naturalism.)
Dworkin, Ronald (1996) "Objectivity and Truth: You'd Better Believe It," *Philosophy & Public Affairs* 25: 87–139. (A spirited defense of non-natural realism.)
Nagel, Thomas (1986) *The View from Nowhere*, New York: Oxford University Press. (A non-natural realism of Kantian inspiration, an alternative to Kantian constructivism.)

Railton, Peter (2003) *Facts, Values, and Norms*, Cambridge: Cambridge University Press. (A naturalistic realism extended to questions of normativity.)

Shafer-Landau, Russ (2005) *Moral Realism: A Defence*, Oxford: Oxford University Press. (A contemporary intuitionist approach.)

Street, Sharon (2006) "A Darwinian Dilemma for Realist Theories of Value," *Philosophical Studies* 127: 109–56. (An epistemic critique of contemporary non-naturalist realisms.)

27
NON-COGNITIVISM

Alexander Miller

Introduction

Ethical non-cognitivism claims that moral judgements do not express beliefs or mental states apt to be assessed in terms of truth and falsity. Alternatively, it can be characterized as claiming that moral sentences do not have a propositional logical form or fact-stating semantics: such sentences are not in the business of expressing propositions or attempting to describe some moral reality, but have a non-propositional logical form and non-fact-stating semantic function. Or again, it can be characterized as claiming that sincere utterances of moral sentences do not serve to make genuine assertions, but are conventionally used to perform different kinds of speech-act. For the purposes of this chapter, we will not differentiate between these various characterizations. In the second section, we give a brief characterization of a famous form of non-cognitivism, emotivism. We'll see that a large part of the motivation for emotivism comes from an application of G. E. Moore's open question argument, and suggest in the third section that the open question argument actually threatens emotivism itself. In the fourth, we'll give a brief outline of a contemporary form of non-cognitivism defended by Simon Blackburn, quasi-realism. In the fifth, "A *priori* objections to non-cognitivism," we'll outline a couple of problems – the "contaminated response" and "disentangling" problems – raised for quasi-realism by John McDowell. In the sixth, "Towards synthetic non-cognitivism," we'll argue that non-cognitivism is threatened by the open question argument and the other objections described in the fifth section, only if it is put forward as an *analytic* thesis. Drawing on an analogy with Peter Railton's defense of a naturalistic cognitivist account of moral judgement, we'll suggest that contemporary versions of non-cognitivism can be viewed as putting forward a *synthetic* thesis about the nature of moral judgement, thereby bypassing the open question, contaminated response and disentangling objections.

Emotivism

In chapter 6 of *Language, Truth and Logic* (1946/1936) A. J. Ayer argues that moral judgements express *sentiments* or *feelings* of approval and disapproval. Since these sentiments and feelings, unlike beliefs, do not aspire to describe reality, the judgements which express them are not apt to be assessed in terms of truth and falsity. Compare one's belief that Jones is six feet tall with one's feeling of revulsion towards his having stolen Grandmother's purse. The belief that Jones is six feet tall has a descriptive function: it aspires to describe the world, and it is true if and only if the world actually is as it describes it. The feeling of revulsion, on the other hand, is not the kind of mental state that can be assessed in terms of truth and falsity: unlike the belief, it does not aspire to describe reality. As Ayer puts it:

> If I say to someone, "You acted wrongly in stealing that money," I am not stating anything more than if I had simply said, "You stole that money." In adding that this action is wrong, I am not making any further statement about it. I am simply evincing my moral disapproval about it. It is as if I had said, "You stole that money," in a peculiar tone of horror, or written with the addition of some special exclamation marks. The tone, or the exclamation marks, adds nothing to the literal meaning of the sentence. It merely serves to show that the expression of it is attended by certain feelings in the speaker.
>
> (Ayer 1946/1936: 107)

It follows that moral judgements are not apt to be assessed in terms of truth and falsity:

> If I now generalise my previous statement and say, "Stealing money is wrong," I produce a sentence which has no factual meaning – that is, expresses no proposition that can be either true or false.
>
> (1946/1936: 107)

Ethical cognitivism views moral judgements as expressing beliefs, and therefore views moral disagreement between two people as consisting in their holding contradictory beliefs. If Smith says "Stealing money is wrong" and Jones says "Stealing money is not wrong," they are *contradicting* each other in the sense that if what Smith says is true, what Jones says is false, and vice versa. Emotivism, by contrast, has a radically different model of moral disagreement: moral disagreement is a matter of a *clash of feelings* rather than a matter of contradictory beliefs (Ayer 1946/1936: 111).

Ayer argues for emotivism by developing a dilemma for cognitivism. Naturalistic cognitivism, according to which moral judgements express beliefs about natural properties, is undermined by G. E. Moore's open question argument (Moore 1993/1903). For example, Ayer argues against utilitarian analyses of "*x* is good" as follows:

> [S]ince it is not self-contradictory to say that some pleasant things are not good, or that some bad things are desired, it cannot be the case that

> the sentence "*x* is good" is equivalent to "*x* is pleasant," or to "*x* is desired." And to every other variant of utilitarianism with which I am acquainted the same objection can be made.
>
> (1946/1936: 105)

Non-naturalist cognitivism such as that espoused by Moore himself, according to which moral judgements express beliefs about non-natural and *sui generis* properties, is rejected because its metaphysical and epistemological commitments are intolerable. The non-naturalistic cognitivist has no plausible account of the nature of moral properties, their relationship to non-moral properties, or our means of epistemic access to them. Emotivism, by contrast, is free of any expensive metaphysical or epistemological debts: since it denies that there *are* moral facts, it is under no obligation to give an account of their nature, of the relationship they stand in to non-moral facts, or our means of epistemic access to them.

Emotivism and the open question argument

It has been noticed that the version of Moore's open question argument that Ayer uses against naturalistic cognitivism can actually be deployed against emotivism itself (Smith 2001; Miller 2003). The naturalistic cognitivist Ayer and Moore argue against holds that moral properties are identical to natural properties in virtue of an analytic relationship between moral predicates and naturalistic predicates. For example, according to the utilitarian view above, the property of being good is identical to the property of being pleasant in virtue of the fact that "is good" and "is pleasant" are synonymous or analytically equivalent (by "is pleasant" we here mean something like "maximizes the amount of pleasure felt in the world"). The open question argument then proceeds:

> (1) Suppose that "is good" is analytically equivalent to the naturalistic predicate "is pleasant."

Then:

> (2) It is part of the meaning of "*x* is pleasant" that "*x* is good."

But then:

> (3) Anyone who asks "Are pleasant things good?" would contradict themselves or betray some conceptual confusion.

However:

(4) "Are pleasant things good?" is an open question: of any act that maximizes the amount of pleasure felt in the world it can be sincerely asked without self-contradiction or betrayal of conceptual confusion whether it is good.

So:

(5) "is good" is not analytically equivalent to "is pleasant."

So:

(6) The property of being good is not identical to the property of being pleasant.

Since the same holds no matter what naturalistic predicate we enter in place of "is pleasant," we can conclude that there is no natural property with which the property of being good can be identified.

An open question argument can be directed against Ayer's emotivism in virtue of the fact that Ayer himself sees the emotivist view as the product of *conceptual analysis*:

> A strictly philosophical treatise on ethics should … make no ethical pronouncements. But it should, by giving an *analysis* of ethical terms, show what is the category to which all such pronouncements belong.
> (1946/1936: 103–4, emphasis added)

Thus, even though the emotivist does not claim that an analytic equivalence obtains between "Murder is wrong" and e.g. "Jones disapproves of murder" (this would be a *subjectivist* view treating the judgement that murder is wrong as expressing a *belief* about Jones's sentiments), he *does* claim that an analytic equivalence obtains between "Jones judges that murder is wrong" and "Jones expresses a sentiment of disapproval towards murder." This allows the following argument to be developed:

(7) Suppose that "Jones judges that murder is wrong" is analytically equivalent to the sentence "Jones expresses a sentiment of disapproval towards murder."

Then:

(8) It is part of the meaning of "Jones expresses of sentiment of disapproval towards murder" that "Jones judges that murder is wrong."

But then:

(9) Anyone who asks "Jones expresses a sentiment of disapproval towards murder but does he judge that murder is wrong?" would contradict themselves or betray some conceptual confusion.

However:

(10) "Jones expresses a sentiment of disapproval towards murder but does he judge that murder is wrong?" is an open question: one can ask without betraying conceptual confusion whether Jones, in expressing the sentiment, is making a moral judgement, or an aesthetic judgement, or a prudential judgement, or some other judgement of taste.

So:

(11) "Jones judges that murder is wrong" is not analytically equivalent to "Jones expresses a sentiment of disapproval towards murder."

So:

(12) The judgement that murder is wrong does not express a sentiment of disapproval towards murder.

Although the open-question argument in the strong form utilised by Moore has largely been discredited, descendants of the argument still exert a high degree of influence in contemporary meta-ethics (see Darwall et al. 1992; Miller 2003: Ch. 2). Is there a form of non-cognitivism not susceptible to an open question-style argument? We'll return to this question in the sixth section.

Quasi-realism

Blackburn's quasi-realism is a form of non-cognitivism designed to cope with a number of standard problems for emotivism.

Ordinary moral practice seems to have many features that are inconsistent with emotivism. For example, as far as syntax is concerned, "Murder is wrong" is on a par with "Murder is a daily occurrence in some cities." In general, though, predicates have the semantic function of standing for properties. However, according to emotivism, when we utter "Murder is wrong" we are not attempting to ascribe a property of wrongness to murder, because there is no such property: rather, we are expressing a sentiment towards acts of murder. The problem for emotivism is to explain why this does not convict ordinary moral practice of a widespread *error* or *mistake* (Blackburn 1984: 170–1). If we speak and think as if "wrong" and "good" are predicates, as if they stand for properties of wrongness and goodness, why doesn't the emotivist view that "wrong" and "good" are not genuine predicates imply that our speaking and thinking in this way is simply *flawed?*

A thorny instance of this worry is provided by what has come to be known as the "Frege–Geach" problem. Consider the argument:

(13) Murder is wrong.

(14) If murder is wrong then getting Peter to murder people is wrong.

So,

(15) Getting Peter to murder people is wrong.

According to the emotivist, the meaning of "Murder is wrong," as it appears in (13), is expressive: its meaning isn't given in terms of a state of affairs whose obtaining is necessary and sufficient for its truth, but in terms of a sentiment of disapproval. The problem is that it is very difficult to see how the meaning of "Murder is wrong," as it appears in the antecedent of (14), can be given in terms of this sentiment. An utterance of (13) may be construed as expressing disapproval towards murder, but someone uttering (14) expresses no such sentiment (I don't disapprove of honesty, but I can still utter "If honesty is wrong, then getting Peter to act honestly is wrong" in perfectly good faith). This suggests that the emotivist has to view "Murder is wrong," as it appears in (13), as meaning something different from what it means when it appears in the antecedent of (14), and the problem is then that this renders the argument from (13) and (14) to (15) invalid in virtue of a fallacy of equivocation. Again, this suggests that the emotivist has to convict ordinary moral practice, which regards the argument from (13) and (14) to (15) as valid, as guilty of an error.

Blackburn makes a number of ingenious attempts to deal with this worry (Blackburn 1993: Essays 6 and 10), but here we will focus on the attempt outlined in Blackburn (1984).

A moral sensibility is a set of dispositions to have attitudes in response to perceptions, beliefs and other attitudes. Blackburn suggests that we construe the utterance of (14) as expressing approval of moral sensibilities that combine disapproval of murder with disapproval of getting Peter to murder people. Using [B! (*x*)] to represent the sentiment of disapproval ("Boo!") towards *x* and [H! (y)] to represent the sentiment of approval ("Hurrah!") towards *y*, and the semicolon to mark the holding of both sentiments flanking it, the logical form of the argument from (13) and (14) to (15) can now be represented as:

(16) B! (murder)

(17) H! ([B! (murder)]; [B! (getting Peter to murder people)])

So,

(18) B! (getting Peter to murder people).

The validity of the inference is captured by the fact that someone who accepted the premises but rejected the conclusion would fail to have a combination of attitudes of which he himself approves, and would be prey to a "clash" of attitudes. Such a person:

> [H]as a fractured sensibility which cannot itself be an object of approval. The "cannot" here follows not ... because such a sensibility must be out of line with the moral facts it is trying to describe, but because such a sensibility cannot fulfill the practical purposes for which we evaluate things.
>
> (1984: 195)

And there is no worry about equivocation here, as the meaning of "Murder is wrong" as it appears in (14) is given in terms of the sentiment of disapproval it expresses in (13).

However, Blackburn's idea that the "clash of attitudes" involved here is sufficient to capture the logical validity of the inference has not convinced many, nor have his other attempts to deal with the Frege–Geach worry (see Miller [2003] for a survey). For our present purposes we can note that if Blackburn's attempt works, it shows that the emotivist or non-cognitivist can avoid convicting ordinary moral practice of error when it designates inferences such as that from (13) and (14) to (15) as valid. And if this strategy works in general, it will show how the non-cognitivist can earn the right to all of the linguistic constructions usually taken to require a cognitivist account of moral judgement. (For a similar strategy see Gibbard 1990, 2003.)

A *priori* objections to non-cognitivism

As it stands, quasi-realism appears vulnerable to the version of the open question argument that haunted emotivism in the third section:

(19) Suppose that "Jones judges that murder is wrong" is analytically equivalent to the sentence "Jones expresses the sentiment [B! (murder)]."

Then:

(20) It is part of the meaning of "Jones expresses the sentiment [B! (murder)]" that "Jones judges that murder is wrong."

But then:

> (21) Anyone who asks "Jones expresses the sentiment [B! (murder)] but does he judge that murder is wrong?" would betray some conceptual confusion.

However:

> (22) "Jones expresses the sentiment [B! (murder)] but does he judge that murder is wrong?" is an open question: one can ask without betraying conceptual confusion whether Jones, in expressing the sentiment, is making a moral judgement, or an aesthetic judgement, or a prudential judgement, or some other judgement of taste.

So:

> (23) "Jones judges that murder is wrong" is not analytically equivalent to "Jones expresses the sentiment [B! (murder)]."

So:

> (24) The judgement that murder is wrong does not express the sentiment [B! (murder)].

In his recent book-length defense of quasi-realism, Blackburn makes a number of suggestions as to the distinctive kind of sentiment expressed by moral judgements (Blackburn 1998) but arguably none of these escape the reapplication of the open question argument or one of its more sophisticated descendants (see Miller 2003: 88–94). We'll now introduce two further problems for Blackburn's quasi-realism that have been developed by John McDowell, before considering whether there is a way the non-cognitivist can avoid all three of the *a priori* objections.

First, the problem of the "contaminated response." Blackburn's quasi-realism is a form of *projectivism*, where:

> We project an attitude or habit or other commitment which is not descriptive onto the world, when we speak and think as though there were a property of things which our sayings describe, which we can reason about, know about, be wrong about, and so on.
>
> (Blackburn 1984: 170–1)

We speak and think as if "wrong" denotes a genuine feature of reality, although it doesn't: when we say things like "Murder is wrong" what we are really doing is projecting a sentiment of disapproval onto a world which contains no such feature. Quasi-realism, if successful, shows that projectivism needn't force us to view ordinary moral practice as "diseased" or "flawed":

> Projectivism is the philosophy of evaluation which says that evaluative properties are projections of our own sentiments (emotions, reactions, attitudes, commendations). Quasi-realism is the enterprise of explaining why our discourse has the shape it does, in particular by way of treating evaluative predicates like others, if projectivism is true. It thus seeks to explain, and justify, the realistic-seeming nature of our talk of evaluations – the way we think we can be wrong about them, that there is a truth to be found, and so on.
>
> (Blackburn 1984: 180)

McDowell argues that the projectivist aspect of Blackburn's project imposes a constraint that moral quasi-realism cannot meet:

> The point of the image of projection is to explain certain seeming features of reality as reflections of our subjective responses to a world which really contains no such features. Now this explanatory direction seems to require a corresponding priority, in the order of understanding, between the projected response and the apparent feature: we ought to be able to focus our thought on the response without needing to exploit the concept of the apparent feature that is supposed to result from projecting the response.
>
> (1998b/1987: 157)

In some cases, the requirement of explanatory priority of projected response to apparent features may be met. Take the sentiments of *disgust* and *nausea*: McDowell concedes that "we can plausibly suppose that these are self-contained psychological items, conceptualizable without any need to appeal to any projected properties of disgustingness or nauseatingness" (1998b/1987: 157). We can conceptualize the subjective response associated with nausea without having to rely on the concept of the nauseating: we don't have to conceptualize the subjective response as a reaction to the property of being nauseating. But McDowell suggests that the required explanatory priority is absent in the philosophically contentious cases, such as ethics, and he argues that our thought and talk about the comic provides an example where priority of response to projected feature fails:

> What exactly is it that we are to conceive as projected onto the world so as to give rise to our idea that things are funny? "An inclination to laugh" is not a satisfactory answer: projecting an inclination to laugh would not necessarily yield an apparent instance of the comic, since laughter can

> signal, for instance, embarrassment just as well as amusement. Perhaps the right response cannot be identified except as amusement; and perhaps amusement cannot be understood except as finding something comic. If this is correct, there is a serious question whether we can really *explain* the idea of something's being comic as a *projection* of that response … . Surely it undermines a projective account of a concept if we cannot home in on the subjective state whose projection is supposed to result in the seeming feature of reality in question without the aid of the concept of that feature, the concept that was to be projectively explained.
>
> (1998b/1987: 158)

If – as seems likely – the same holds true in the case of the ethical, projectivism about morals will face the same problem.

Second, McDowell's "disentangling" objection to non-cognitivism. Philosophically sophisticated forms of non-cognitivisim construe our uses of moral language, not as mere "sounding off," but as manifestations of *conceptual* competence, as part of a practice of "going on *doing the same thing*" (McDowell 1998a/1981: 201). McDowell argues that Wittgenstein's reflections on rule-following establish that non-cognitivism makes presuppositions that commit it to a false view of that conceptual competence and of what the ability to "go on doing the same thing" consists in.

We saw earlier that in his attempt to solve the Frege–Geach problem, Blackburn makes use of the notion of a moral sensibility. A moral sensibility is in effect a type of input–output function:

> We can usefully compare the ethical agent to a device whose function is to take certain inputs and deliver certain outputs. The *input* to the system is a representation, for instance, of an action, or a situation, or a character, as being of a certain type, as having certain properties. The *output*, we are saying, is a certain attitude, or a pressure on attitudes, or a favouring of policies, choices, and actions. Such a device is a function from input to output: an ethical sensibility.
>
> (Blackburn 1998: 5)

The notion of an ethical sensibility is serviceable only if it is in principle possible for us to distinguish between the input and output of the function. So, McDowell argues, the non-cognitivist is committed to the idea that "when we feel impelled to ascribe value to something, what is actually happening can be disentangled into two components. Competence with an evaluative concept involves, first, a sensitivity to an aspect of the world as it really is … and, second, a propensity to a certain attitude – a non-cognitive state that constitutes the special perspective from which items in the world seem to be endowed with the value in question" (McDowell 1998a/1981: 200–1). McDowell argues that this idea "implies that the extension of the associated term, as it would be used by someone who belonged to the community, could be mastered independently of the special concerns that, in the community, would show themselves in emulation of actions seen as falling under the concept" (1998a/1981: 201). This, McDowell suggests, is of a piece with a conception of rule-following according to which "it is in principle discernible, from a standpoint independent of the responses that characterize a participant in [a rule-following] practice, that a series of correct moves in the practice is really a case of going on doing the same thing" (1998a/1981: 203). And this conception of rule-following as consisting in the grasp of a practice-transcendent item has, according to McDowell, been decisively refuted by the later Wittgenstein (McDowell 1998: §3, *passim*).

Towards synthetic non-cognitivism

In this section we will develop a framework within which the non-cognitivist can bypass the *a priori* objections outlined in the fifth section. We can get started by introducing Peter Railton's distinction between methodological naturalism and substantive naturalism:

> A methodological naturalist is someone who adopts an a posteriori, explanatory approach to an area of human practice, such as epistemology, semantics, or ethics.
>
> (1993: 315)

> Substantive naturalism is ... a view about philosophical conclusions. A substantive naturalist advances a philosophical account of some domain of human language or practice that provides an interpretation of its central concepts in terms amenable to empirical inquiry.
>
> (1989: 156)

Consider again the naturalistic cognitivism that is the target of Moore's open question argument: "good" is interpreted as denoting a property, the property of e.g. being pleasant, dealt with by an empirical science (psychology). Since this is established via an *a priori philosophical analysis*, this view is substantively naturalist but not methodologically naturalist.

Railton defends a form of naturalistic cognitivism that is by contrast both methodologically naturalist and substantively naturalist. Eschewing *a priori* analysis, this view proposes a *reforming definition* of "right": it suggests, for example, that "right" be interpreted as standing for a naturalistic property N, and argues that the identification of rightness with N contributes to the *a posteriori* explanation of features of our experience (Railton's own suggestion is that rightness be identified with what is "instrumentally rational from a social point of view" (Railton 1986: 200)). Since there is no suggestion that "right" is analytically equivalent to some naturalistic predicate "N" Moore's open question argument simply fails to get a grip. Thus "our naturalist's central claims are, at bottom, synthetic rather than analytic" (1989: 157). Railton's methodological naturalism consists in his proposing a reforming definition of moral concepts, a definition which must be vindicated by the capacity of the reforming definition to contribute to the *a posteriori* explanation of features of our experience. Whether or not a reforming definition is ultimately acceptable is an *a posteriori* matter.

We'll now suggest that the non-cognitivist can adopt Railton's "reforming definition" strategy to his own ends, and thereby avoid the objections of the fifth section.

Recall that emotivism and quasi-realism appeared vulnerable to an open question-style argument because of their claim that "Jones judges that murder is wrong" is analytically equivalent to the sentence "Jones expresses the sentiment [B!(murder)]." The synthetic non-cognitivist, in contrast, can avoid this worry entirely by proposing "Jones expresses the sentiment [B! (murder)]" as a *reforming definition* of "Jones judges that murder is wrong."

How might the identification of Jones's judging that murder is wrong with Jones's expressing the sentiment [B!(murder)] contribute to the *a posteriori* explanation of features of our experience? Some of the arguments that Blackburn proffers in favor of non-cognitivism can be viewed as answering this question. Take the argument concerning moral motivation (Blackburn 1984: 187–9). Suppose that Jones judges that murder is wrong. Suppose that Jones is asked by his lover to poison his wife. If this judgement expressed a belief, then, in order to explain Jones's motivation to refrain from murdering his wife, we would need to ascribe some desire to Jones in addition to the judgement (because according to the Humean view of motivation accepted by Blackburn, motivation always requires the presence of both a belief and a desire). But no such supplementary desire need be present: the judgement on its own suffices for the relevant motivation. On the other hand, if this judgement expressed the sentiment [B!(murder)] all that would be required to explain Jones's motivation would be the ascription to him of the belief that poisoning his wife would be an act of murder. And this ascription does seem plausible.

Although this argument is of course controversial, what it shows, if it is cogent, is that the *reforming definition* of "Jones judges that murder is wrong" as "Jones expresses the sentiment [B! (murder)]" contributes to the *a posteriori* explanation of moral motivation (and does so in a manner superior to ethical cognitivism).

The reforming definition strategy also defuses McDowell's "contaminated response" objection. Recall that McDowell's objection to taking an inclination to laugh to be the state expressed by a judgement that a thing is funny was that "projecting an inclination to laugh would not *necessarily* yield an apparent instance of the comic, since laughter can signal, for instance, embarrassment just as well as amusement" (McDowell 1998b/1987: 158). The synthetic non-cognitivist about the comic can agree that it is an open question whether projecting an inclination to laugh constitutes making a judgement about comedy, but argue that the judgement that a thing is funny be taken to express an inclination to laugh (or whatever) on *a posteriori* explanatory grounds. And the synthetic non-cognitivist about morals can do likewise.

If the non-cognitivist can make out the required kind of *a posteriori* case, then he will also have done enough to see off McDowell's "disentangling" objection. Having good empirical grounds for accepting a particular kind of sentiment as the sentiment expressed by a moral judgement in effect disentangles, in a competent moral judger, the non-cognitive attitude expressed by the moral judgement and the naturalistic feature of the world that prompts that expression. So the distinction between the input and output of a moral sensibility can be preserved on *a posteriori* grounds. And there seems to be no reason to think that making such an *a posteriori* case requires the idea that an agent from a form of life radically different from our moral practices might grasp the sense of a moral predicate.

Synthetic non-cognitivism is thus well placed to see off the objections of the fifth section. However, our conclusion here is modest. We have shown only that there is theoretical space for a form of synthetic non-cognitivism, but we have not even begun to show that that space can be convincingly occupied. The task of distinguishing moral from other kinds of sentiment via empirical considerations has not even been started in this chapter. So the non-cognitivist has some very substantial empirical work cut out for him. However, this is a far cry from the idea that there are compelling *a priori* reasons why no form of non-cognitivism can ever hope to succeed.

See also Ethics and sentiment (Chapter 10); The open question argument (Chapter 25); Realism and its alternatives (Chapter 26); Error theory and fictionalism (Chapter 28); Cognitivism without realism (Chapter 29).

References

Ayer, A. J. (1946/1936) *Language, Truth and Logic*, 2nd edn, London: Gollancz.

Blackburn, S. (1984) *Spreading The Word*, Oxford: Oxford University Press.

——(1993) *Essays in Quasi-Realism*, Oxford: Oxford University Press.

——(1998) *Ruling Passions*, Oxford: Oxford University Press.

Darwall, S., Gibbard, A. and Railton, P. (1992) "Toward *Fin de Siecle* Ethics: Some Trends," *Philosophical Review* 101: 115–89.

Gibbard, A. (1990) *Wise Choices, Apt Feelings*, Cambridge, MA: Harvard University Press.

——(2003) *Thinking How To Live*, Cambridge, MA: Harvard University Press.

McDowell, J. (1998a/1981) "Non-Cognitivism and Rule-Following," repr. in his *Mind, Value and Reality*, Cambridge, MA: Harvard University Press.

——(1998b/1987) "Projectivism and Truth in Ethics," repr. in his *Mind, Value and Reality*, Cambridge, MA: Harvard University Press.
Miller, A. (2003) *An Introduction to Contemporary Metaethics*, Cambridge: Polity Press.
Moore, G. E. (1993/1903) *Principia Ethica*, rev. edn, Cambridge: Cambridge University Press.
Railton, P. (1986) "Moral Realism," *Philosophical Review* 95: 163–207.
——(1989) "Naturalism and Prescriptivity," *Social Philosophy and Policy* 7: 151–74.
——(1993) "Reply to David Wiggins," in J. Haldane and C. Wright (eds) *Reality, Representation and Projection*, Oxford: Oxford University Press.
Smith, M. (2001) "Some Not-Much-Discussed Problems for Non-Cognitivism in Ethics," *Ratio* 14: 93–115.

Further reading

Fisher, A. and Kirchin, S. (eds) (2006) *Arguing about Metaethics*, London: Routledge. (Contains reprints of many sources cited above.)
Miller, A. (2003) *An Introduction to Contemporary Metaethics*, Cambridge: Polity Press. (Chapters 3–5 survey forms of non-cognitivism.)

28
ERROR THEORY AND FICTIONALISM

Nadeem J. Z. Hussain

Perhaps the easiest way to come to understand what contemporary philosophers mean when they call a theory about ethics an error theory, or a form of fictionalism, is to begin with nihilism. Nihilism about morality is the view that in fact nothing really is right or wrong. Many of us do have moral beliefs; many of us believe, for example, that torture is wrong. According to nihilism all such moral beliefs are false.

One main motivation for such a radical position is the worry that in the world as described by modern science there seems to be no place for rightness or wrongness. The universe, to simplify somewhat, is made up of elementary particles in a void with properties like charge or charm. Despite these evocative names, such properties are evaluatively neutral. In other words, saying that an electron has positive charge is not *ipso facto* a positive assessment; it is not saying that there is something good about being this way. Neither is it a normative assessment; it is not saying that the electron should be this way. All the properties that physics and, supposedly, the rest of the sciences ever mention are similarly neither evaluative nor normative. If reality is as the sciences claim, then it is evaluatively and normatively neutral. Our moral beliefs, however, are essentially evaluative and normative; they assess states of affairs as good or bad and actions as right or wrong. Since nothing in reality lives up to these beliefs, these beliefs must be false. Or so the nihilist argues.

Not surprisingly, when nihilism is motivated in this manner, it is natural for it to spread. Many claims that we may not think of as moral are, nonetheless, evaluative or normative. Consider claims of prudential goodness: eating more vegetables is good for me. Or aesthetic claims: the painting is beautiful. Once on this path, the grand conclusion that everything is without value and that there is nothing that one should do in life can seem inevitable. Such global nihilism about the evaluative and the normative is often what is being expressed in nihilistic declarations that life is meaningless.

Nihilists, famously, have disagreed about how one should respond to either nihilism about morality or to such general nihilism about the evaluative and the normative (Nietzsche 1974/1887: 239, 241–2, 1982/1889: 501; Sartre 1995/1946: 270–4). Should one somehow continue believing in morality or should one adopt a radically different way of going on? Or, as Camus famously asked, should one commit suicide? (Camus 1991/1942)

Contemporary philosophers in the "Anglo-American" or "analytic" tradition do not in general use the label "nihilism." In this tradition, meta-ethics has emerged as the subfield that attempts to provide an account of what is going on when we make moral or ethical claims. Within contemporary meta-ethics there is a family of theories that does claim, in some sense or the other, that nothing is really right or wrong and that therefore our moral beliefs are false. These are the theories that are usually classified as forms of error theory or fictionalism. Contemporary philosophers have, however, tried to provide more precise specifications of the different ways in which one could accept some form of the view that nothing is really right or wrong. They have also proposed a range of different ways of going on in the light of such a realization. The resulting taxonomy of positions is quite complicated and sometimes surprising. One surprise will be that some positions plausibly classified as error theories or forms of fictionalism do not quite seem to be forms of nihilism.

Error theory

To understand the taxonomy of error theories and fictionalisms we need to understand their place in the larger taxonomy of meta-ethical theories in general. The sincere utterance of an indicative sentence, say, "The Eiffel Tower is in Paris," is normally taken to be an expression of the speaker's commitment to the truth of the proposition that the Eiffel Tower is in Paris. Philosophers call such commitments "beliefs." (This is somewhat of a term of art since in ordinary language we sometimes reserve talk of beliefs to cases in which we – speakers or observers – are in fact not fully committed to the truth of the proposition.) The belief is either true or false depending on whether it is indeed a fact that the Eiffel Tower is in Paris. Not all utterances express beliefs so understood. Commands are an obvious case. The command that the Eiffel Tower be in Paris does not express the commitment that it is already true that this is the case.

Meta-ethical theories can differ on whether they take utterances of sentences involving moral terms to be expressions of belief. Despite the use of an indicative sentence, perhaps the utterance of "Torture is wrong" actually expresses a command and not a belief at all. Such views have often been called non-cognitivist views. The error theorist begins by claiming that the utterances of such sentences do express corresponding beliefs. When someone says sincerely that "Torture is wrong," he or she is expressing her belief that torture is wrong. Like beliefs about towers in Paris, these beliefs too are true or false depending upon the facts – now the moral facts. If it is a fact that torture is wrong, then the belief that torture is wrong is true.

One form of error theory then proceeds to argue that in fact nothing is right or wrong. Since nothing is right or wrong, or good or bad, or just or unjust, and so on, all moral beliefs are false. A belief that is false is a belief that is in error. Since such a theory posits widespread error it deserves to be called an error theory.

Taking moral utterances to express moral beliefs allows us to recognize a distinctive, epistemic form of error theory. Beliefs, after all, can be unjustified even if they are true. Thus the belief that extraterrestrial creatures regularly abduct humans is unjustified, given the evidence, even if it turns out to be true. In the moral case, a certain kind of error theorist could think that the best explanation for why we believe certain moral propositions is, for example, that such beliefs help our group or class perpetuate itself. They are part of an ideology. She could then argue that this explanation undermines the claim that these moral beliefs are the result of careful consideration of the relevant evidence for the truth of the moral beliefs. She would thus be positing a widespread epistemic error: our moral beliefs are unjustified; they are not grounded on good evidence. This would be a form of error theory that would be consistent with its still being the case that, in fact, actions are really right or wrong. We should distinguish therefore between such *epistemic error theories* and the *metaphysical error theories* we began with.

Metaphysical error theories, recall, were theories according to which nothing is really right or wrong, good or bad, and so our moral beliefs are all false. This simple way of putting the matter avoids some important complications.

First, there are different ways in which it could be the case that nothing is right or wrong. To see these different ways, consider two expressions: "is a dodo," "is a twenty-meter-tall human" and "is a square circle." Dodos being non-existent, there is not anything that is a dodo, and so if someone believes of some particular bird that it is a dodo or believes that there are dodos, then those beliefs are false. Thus, if there were a community that regularly went around believing that there are dodos, we would accept a metaphysical error theory about that community's talk of dodos. However, it is not as though it is impossible for dodos to exist; indeed, they did exist. One way of putting this point is to say that there is nothing wrong with the property of being a dodo. It is just that this property is not instantiated now. Contrast all of this with the case of "is a square circle." Here we might well think that the very idea of a square circle is incoherent and so there is no property of being a square circle. Arguably the property of being a twenty-meter-tall human falls between these two cases. It is not logically impossible for there to be such a person, but given the fundamental biological and physical facts of our world, it is no accident of history that nothing instantiates this property.

Second, the belief that it is not true that rape is wrong is a moral belief, but this is a belief that – putting aside the worry that the properties in question are so strange that talk of them may, in some sense, be incoherent – error theorists will have to grant is true. Thus the error theorist will want to restrict his claim about the general falsehood of moral beliefs to some more restricted domain of "positive" moral beliefs – those beliefs that "positively" claim that some action, say, is right or wrong.

Metaphysical error theories can thus come in different flavors. An error theory could claim that the very idea of wrongness is incoherent; that given the way the actual world is there are, in some sense, deep reasons why nothing can be right or wrong; or, less plausibly, that as a matter of contingent fact nothing happens to be right or wrong. Depending on the kind of claim made, different kinds of arguments will have to be given for the error theory in question.

Arguments for error theories

We have already seen some suggestions for arguments for metaphysical or epistemic error theories. One can read Marxist theories of ideology as arguments for an epistemic error theory (Marx 1978b/1845–6: 154–5, 172–4, 1978a/1848: 482). Similarly Nietzsche can be interpreted as providing a genealogy of our moral practices that undermines the purported justifications of moral belief: our moral beliefs are best explained as being the descendants of various revolts against the values of traditional dominant, ruling classes. These revolts inverted traditional, and perhaps more natural, aristocratic values (Nietzsche 1989/1887). Finally, some have appealed to theories of evolution to argue for error theory. Our moral beliefs are best explained by their usefulness in helping our ancestors reproduce rather than by any abilities we might have to track moral truths (Joyce 2001: 135–74; Joyce 2006; Street 2006).

As this last example makes clear, the details of these explanations are important. After all our perceptual beliefs are the result of perceptual capacities which presumably can be explained by evolution; it would be odd to give an evolutionary explanation of morality but not of these capacities. However, in the case of perception, evolutionary explanations are not generally undermining. The fact that the capacities that produce a set of beliefs are to be explained by evolutionary usefulness does not immediately show us that they are epistemically unjustified. Similar points hold for other kinds of genealogies.

What such arguments have to show is that the purported explanations of our moral beliefs, or our capacities for moral beliefs, are not compatible with seeing these beliefs, or capacities, as tracking, more or less, the moral facts. Evolutionary explanations have to be supplemented, in general, by an account of what the moral facts are like or what moral truths would have to be like in order to exist. One then argues that given that moral truths are this way, the explanations given of our moral beliefs are not compatible with the claim that we are tracking the moral truths with our moral beliefs.

Direct arguments for metaphysical error theories attempt to show that there is something incoherent in the very ideas or concepts of purported normative and evaluative properties. Or perhaps that such concepts are inconsistent with what we confidently take to be basic truths about fundamental reality. One interpretation of John Mackie's well-known defense of error theory falls into this category (Mackie 1977). Mackie argued that normative concepts like "right" and "wrong" involved the idea of "objective, intrinsic, prescriptivity," the idea that objective features of the world could somehow issue authoritative commands to us (35). He then argued that we know that the fundamental constituents of the world just are not the kinds of things that can issue authoritative commands.

Epistemic arguments can seem like metaphysical arguments. After all, if one concludes that, say, all moral beliefs of the form so and so is obligated to do such and such are false, then we may well conclude that it is rational to believe that there are no obligations. Consider an analogy. Imagine that we have an argument to show that all beliefs about unicorns can be explained by bad reasoning from observations of narwhal tusks and certain notions of virginal purity. With such an argument in hand, one might well conclude not just that current beliefs of the form such and such is a unicorn are unjustified, but also that one should positively believe that there are no unicorns. This is compatible with granting that unicorns could have existed or that we could be wrong – as future evidence might show. But such a position is not agnosticism: it is not the position that involves having no belief about the matter of the general existence of unicorns at all. Precisely stating the conditions under which such inferences are rational is not straightforward; nonetheless, it is plausible to think that sometimes one can draw the metaphysical-sounding conclusion that there are, say, no obligations from epistemic arguments about beliefs about obligations.

Revolutionary fictionalism

Were a fifteenth-century inquisitor to conclude that there are no witches because there is no such thing as sorcery, then we would expect him to stop engaging in the practice of figuring out who is a witch. He would stop looking for witches, because such practices require believing that there actually are witches. On the other hand, consider Santa Claus. Most of us stop believing in Santa Claus at some point, but many of us replace our belief in Santa Claus with an elaborate pretense involving imagining him coming down chimneys and living at the North Pole. This seems quite unobjectionable, presumably in part because nothing too serious is at stake – unlike the torture of supposed witches.

It would seem that accepting an error theory about our moral beliefs would, given the seriousness of the issues at stake, be more like the case of witches than of Santa Claus. Our moral beliefs are the basis of decisions, individual and collective, that have significant impact. If it is not true that anything is right or wrong, then it would seem we should simply stop our current attempts to figure out what is right or wrong. After all, we know that our resulting moral beliefs will be false or unjustified. And making decisions, often life-or-death decisions, on the basis of such beliefs seems quite irrational. Of course, if the error theory includes the normative claims of rationality, then we cannot truly say this. We can still say, though, that if moral beliefs are simply false, then there seems to be nothing irrational or wrong with simply doing whatever we want.

Such amoral conclusions might seem the obvious ones to draw from an error theory. However, many of those attracted to error theory have not in fact drawn these conclusions. For them accepting an error theory about morality is more like accepting an error theory about Santa Claus than about witches. There may well be good reasons to continue with calling things right or wrong, though we may have to do it in something like the spirit of pretense. It may be true that when we realize, for example, that the belief that rape is wrong is false or unjustified, either we may not psychologically be able to continue to have that belief or it may be irrational for us to continue to have that belief. Nonetheless, we could continue to pretend that rape is wrong. Just as we accept the fiction of Santa Claus, we could accept the fiction that certain actions are wrong. Our reasons for doing this would presumably be different. To simplify, it is the pleasure of the pretense in the case of Santa Claus that is our reason to take this pretense up once we have given up the belief. In the case of morality, the reason often given is that without the practice of calling things right or wrong, social order would collapse (Joyce 2001: 175–231).

Such theories that accept an error theory about our current moral beliefs, but recommend going on in something like a pretense, are often classified as forms of *revolutionary fictionalism*. "Fictionalist" because they recommend treating morality as a fiction and "revolutionary" because they recommend a dramatic revolution: a revolution that gives up the error-ridden business of actually believing that things are right or wrong and replaces it with a pretense that things are right or wrong.

Such a view faces some problems. The appeal to, for example, social order as a reason to start pretending that rape is wrong seems to require that this normative claim – the claim that this consideration is a reason – is not one of the normative claims that the error theoretic part of revolutionary fictionalism has been shown to be false or unjustified. As we saw at the beginning, certain motivations for an error theory about moral claims in particular, such as the concern that the world the sciences show us is evaluatively and normatively neutral, also motivate an error theory about evaluative and normative claims in general. However, if all claims about reasons are false, then the claim that maintaining social order is a reason to pretend that murder is wrong is also false and so in fact there is no reason to pretend that murder is wrong. The global revolutionary fictionalist then cannot give us a reason to adopt the proposed revolution.

A revolutionary fictionalist may insist that the error theoretic part of his theory only applies to some limited domain of normative and evaluative claims: the normative truths about what reasons we have to adopt the proposed fiction are not threatened by the arguments for the error theory. This requires that the errors in question cannot be the result just of the fact that moral claims are evaluative and normative.

Another option for such a global revolutionary fictionalist is to claim that when he says that social order is a reason to adopt the proposed fiction, this claim itself is put forth already as part of a pretense. The global revolutionary fictionalist is already engaged in a pretense that there are reasons, and then, as part of this pretense, he is pretending that there is a reason to adopt the proposed pretense of morality. Though such a position may be consistent, it does involve an admission by the revolutionary fictionalist that in fact there is no reason to accept the proposed fiction.

This highlights a further problem. We often think of morality as imposing constraints on us: a strong desire to cheat is kept in check by a belief that doing so would be morally wrong. Indeed, in the error theoretic part of their theories revolutionary fictionalists often refer to this functional role of moral beliefs to explain why we have them in the first place despite the fact that they are false. However, once we replace the belief that doing something is morally wrong with the pretense that it is wrong, it is not obvious that a pretense can play the same role. One can worry that such pretenses would easily be overridden by our desires. Our commitment to morality seems no longer to be serious enough.

Assuming revolutionary fictionalism can adequately deal with these concerns, there is one sense in which it is not committed to nihilism. It is not committed to simply doing without morality – or without whatever normative or evaluative practice is its focus. It is recommending a related replacement practice, namely, a fictionalist one.

Hermeneutic fictionalism

If asked where Sherlock Holmes lived, most of us would say Baker Street, London. It would be a mistake though to think that we believed that there was an actual human being named Sherlock Holmes. According to a more plausible account, we are all engaged in a collective pretense that there was such a person as Sherlock Holmes. Consider as evidence the fact that attempts to track down his living relatives would leave us quite perplexed. The hermeneutic fictionalist thinks that there is analogous evidence for the conclusion that our practice of morality is also a collective pretense. The claim is not that our current moral practices involve beliefs that are mistaken, but rather that we never believed that murder was wrong but were all along pretending that murder is wrong. Fictionalism is proposed as a correct interpretation of our current moral utterances rather than as a revolutionary proposal for replacing moral belief with moral make-belief (Kalderon 2005).

The purported evidence for this interpretation is controversial. Recall one of the motivations for error theory: the suggestion was that it was hard to see how rightness or wrongness would fit into the world as described by modern science. The fictionalist suggests that in fact most of us go along in our moral practices quite unconcerned by such matters, and, indeed, the fictionalist insists, it takes some effort to get us worried about these metaphysical issues. Our natural, initial response is to find these worries themselves perplexing – perplexing just in the manner we would find the search for Holmes's relatives perplexing. We should conclude, claims the fictionalist, that we were never really committed to such properties actually being instantiated anyway. We were just, in some sense, pretending they were.

However, it does not feel to most people that they are pretending. The hermeneutic fictionalist attempts to undermine this counter-evidence by pointing to other cases in which we do not believe what we apparently literally say but still do not consciously think of ourselves as pretending: Juliet can be the sun without incinerating Verona. The first-person reports of participants are only one source of evidence that needs to be weighed against other sources of evidence such as our purported puzzled reactions to philosophers' inquiries about whether there really are moral facts.

The hermeneutic fictionalist may claim that he does not face the worry about seriousness that faced the revolutionary fictionalist. After all pretense is what we have been engaged in all along and so it can be serious – or at least as serious as morality actually is for us. This reply will not do by itself. If indeed we are not fully conscious of the pretense we are engaged in, then bringing it to full consciousness might well have an effect. Explicitly being aware that it is a pretense might undermine our commitment. The hermeneutic fictionalist will have to show that it does not, if he wants to fully vindicate our existing practices. To the degree that he succeeds, there is, once again, one important sense in which hermeneutic fictionalism is then not a form of nihilism.

On the other hand, the hermeneutic fictionalist can always insist that, though becoming aware of the fictional nature of the practice would undermine it, this does not show that the account is false. Even on this version, he might insist that he is not a nihilist in any interesting sense. Someone who points out that Sherlock Holmes does not really exist is not giving us news. It is odd to think of all of us as nihilists about Sherlock Holmes. We never did believe in his existence and so there is not some pre-existing commitment about which we could come to be nihilists.

Non-cognitivism and error theory

We come finally to a set of more sophisticated distinctions and a corresponding range of theoretical possibilities. Recall that error theory was introduced as a theory according to which sincere utterances of "Torture is wrong" express the belief that torture is wrong. This belief is an attitude, a commitment to the truth of the proposition, that torture is wrong, towards which it is directed.

As we have just seen in the case of fictionalism, there seems to be space for a position that replaces the attitude of a belief with a different attitude, an attitude of pretense or make-belief. The proposition towards which the attitude is directed is, however, the same as in the case of a simple error theory, namely, the proposition that torture is wrong. The proposition can be false without our attitude, and thus without us, being at fault since the attitude is not one of belief and so not a commitment to the truth of the proposition.

There is a wide range of attitudes towards propositions that we seem to posit in our everyday language. We can imagine something, hypothesize it, assume it, consider it, wonder about it, and so on. In the appropriate context, an utterance of a sentence that we might claim normally expresses a belief can express one of these other attitudes. Imagine a detective trying to reconstruct a crime scene: "The house is dark, our suspect can't see the glass partition, so he bumps into it." We would theoretically distinguish these attitudes by giving different accounts of their function within our thinking. For many of these attitudes – and others we could hypothesize – it may well turn out that the truth of the proposition towards which the attitude is directed is not crucial to the functioning. The fictionalist thus potentially has a wide range of attitudes that he can posit. The attitudes we have been considering so far – pretense, imagining, or make-belief – may not be the best for the fictionalist. After all, first, these are attitudes which, as we have seen, we are arguably conscious of being in when we are in them, and, second, these attitudes suggest a certain lack of seriousness in our commitment. Both features of these attitudes can be a problem for the hermeneutic fictionalist in explaining our lack of awareness that we are pretending and our apparent strong commitment to our moral practices. By appealing to a different attitude, the hermeneutic fictionalist may have an easier time explaining our current practices (Kalderon 2005: 130–6).

Similarly, a revolutionary fictionalist may also prefer proposing a shift to an attitude that does not have the same apparent lack of seriousness that pretense and imagining do and that is yet still directed at the same proposition at which our existing beliefs are directed.

Most of these alternatives to belief are attitudes that do not directly have the role of keeping track of the truth. Thus they could all be called non-cognitive attitudes, and theories that propose them as the attitudes expressed by some discourse could be regarded as non-cognitivist accounts of that discourse. However, traditionally, the label non-cognitivism has been applied in a more restricted manner. A non-cognitivist account of moral language is not standardly construed to take such language as playing the role of expressing attitudes other than belief but that nonetheless have a moral proposition as their content (Kalderon 2005: 89–90). Rather, the attitude expressed is a motivational attitude directed towards a non-normative or non-evaluative proposition. A crude account that would count as non-cognitivist by these traditional standards is, for example, an account according to which an utterance of "Killing innocents is wrong" expresses a desire that innocents not be killed. The attitude expressed may well be a propositional one, but the proposition towards which it is directed is not the apparent moral proposition. Traditionally error theories have been defined as forms of cognitivism, that is as theories that take moral language to express beliefs. Thus, given these traditional understandings of the relevant labels, one could not be both an error theorist and a non-cognitivist. However, it is important to see that there are some senses in which a non-cognitivist could be an error theorist.

First, a non-cognitivist could hold the view that once we come to see that our practices are, in some sense, merely in the business of expressing motivational attitudes we will give them up. They will have turned out not to live up to our expectations, and so, in some sense, such a non-cognitivist theory could be taken as identifying an "error" in our current practices. It should be emphasized that most extant non-cognitivist theories deny that their accounts undermine in any such way.

Second, for a non-cognitivist account to stand any chance of being plausible it must deal with what is called the Frege–Geach puzzle (see the entry on Non-cognitivism [Chapter 27]). Solving this puzzle, arguably, requires that the non-cognitivist leave open the possibility that speakers can sensibly say things of the form "It is true that torture is wrong." That is to say, the non-cognitivist needs to provide a non-cognitive account of what is going on when someone makes such an utterance. The same point holds for utterances of the form "It is false that torture is wrong," "Our belief that torture is wrong is not justified," and so on. Most extant non-cognitivist theories take themselves as succeeding in doing this while still remaining non-cognitivist. Whether they succeed is an important question (see, again, the chapter on Non-cognitivism). In any case, this means that a plausible non-cognitivism apparently has to be such that one could both be a non-cognitivist and say, "Our moral beliefs are systematically false," or "Our moral beliefs are systematically unjustified." It follows, then, that there is a perfectly sensible sense in which a non-cognitivist could also be an error theorist, and an error theorist that says very much what a traditional error theorist would say.

See also Nietzsche (Chapter 18); Existentialism (Chapter 20); Non-cognitivism (Chapter 27); Biology (Chapter 33).

References

Camus, A. (1991/1942) "The Myth of Sisyphus," in *The Myth of Sisyphus and Other Essays*, New York: Vintage Books, Random House.

Joyce, R. (2001) *The Myth of Morality*, New York: Cambridge University Press.

——(2006) *The Evolution of Morality*, Cambridge, MA: MIT Press.

Kalderon, M. E. (2005) *Moral Fictionalism*, Oxford: Clarendon Press.
Mackie, J. L. (1977) *Ethics: Inventing Right and Wrong*, London: Penguin Books.
Marx, K. (1978a/1848) "Manifesto of the Communist Party," in R. C. Tucker (ed.) *The Marx-Engels Reader*, 2nd edn, New York: Norton.
——(1978b/1845–6) *The German Ideology* in *The Marx-Engels Reader*, New York: Norton.
Nietzsche, F. W. (1974/1887) *The Gay Science*, New York: Vintage Books.
——(1982/1889) *Twilight of the Idols* in *The Portable Nietzsche*, New York: Viking Penguin.
——(1989/1887) *On the Genealogy of Morals*, New York: Vintage Books.
Sartre, J.-P. (1995/1946) "The Humanism of Existentialism," in C. Guignon and D. Pereboom (eds) *Existentialism: Basic Writings*, Indianapolis, IN, and Cambridge, MA: Hackett.
Street, S. (2006) "A Darwinian Dilemma for Realist Theories of Value," *Philosophical Studies* 127: 109–66.

Further reading

Blackburn, S. (1993) "Errors and the Phenomenology of Value," in *Essays in Quasi-Realism*, Oxford: Oxford University Press.
——(2003) "Quasi-Realism No Fictionalism," in M. E. Kalderon (ed.) *Fictionalism in Metaphysics*, Oxford: Clarendon Press.
Hussain, N. J. Z. (2004) "The Return of Moral Fictionalism," *Philosophical Perspectives* 18: 149–87.
Lewis, D. (2003) "Quasi-Realism Is Fictionalism," in M. E. Kalderon (ed.) *Fictionalism in Metaphysics*, Oxford: Clarendon Press.
Nolan, D., Restall, G. and West, C. (2005) "Moral Fictionalism versus the Rest," *Australasian Journal of Philosophy* 83: 307–30.

29 COGNITIVISM WITHOUT REALISM

Andrew Fisher

> The question is not whether ["true" and "false"] are in practice applied to ethical statements, but whether, if they are so applied, the point of doing so would be the same as the point of applying them to statements of other kinds, and if not, in what ways it would be different.
>
> (Michael Dummett, quoted in Lynch 2001: 273)

When I claim that "my bike is dirty" or that "the dinner is burning" what makes it the case that what I say is true or false? One intuitive answer would be that the statements are true if, as a matter of *fact*, my bike *is* dirty or the dinner *is* burning. Considering our day-to-day talk reveals that we believe there are facts which *make* our common-or-garden-variety statements true. We don't of course believe that we *know* all such facts but nevertheless we still believe that if what we say is true then some fact *makes* it so.

Consider an uncontroversial statement:

(A) "Peeling the skin off babies is morally wrong."

Surely this is true; and if moral talk is just like other talk, then we seem committed to the existence of *moral facts*. If we grant that (A) is true and if we grant that what *makes* things true are appropriate facts, then there must exist the moral fact that *peeling the skin off babies is wrong*.

What is more, we think that the "truth-making" facts of common statements are *not* constituted by us. They exist whether or not we have any beliefs about them. They are not dependent on how we feel, what we believe, how informed we are. My bike is dirty, my dinner is burnt, even if I am asleep, drunk, or if I radically change my beliefs, etc. So given moral claims are analogous, moral facts such as *the wrongness of peeling the skin off babies* remain the same even if we were asleep, were drunk, radically changed our beliefs, etc.

So, if – and as we'll see it is a big "if" – there are no good reasons to distinguish moral discourse from common-or-garden-variety discourse then, hey presto, we have an argument for moral realism; the view that there are moral facts in the world which are mind-independent.

You won't be surprised to know that few have been swayed by this line of argument. After all, we don't think this way of proceeding works in other domains. For example, talk of elves looks like talk of dogs. But whereas dogs exist, we know that elves don't. It is thus a mistake to conclude merely from the way the word "elves" functions that there are such things as elves. *We can't simply pull an ontological rabbit out of a semantic hat.*

Putting some flesh on these bare bones will create the conceptual space for cognitivism without realism.

When we make a claim about bikes, food, chairs, tables, etc., it seems that we are expressing a *belief*: I *believe* that my bike is dirty, that my dinner is burnt, that the chair is under the table, etc. *Cognitivism* is the view that we express beliefs when making statements. It is uncontroversial, then, that we are cognitivists about our everyday statements.

As such there is a presumptive argument in favor of moral cognitivism. For it seems that we are expressing moral beliefs when we make moral statements and as such the burden-of-proof is on the *non*-cognitivist who believes that we are doing something *different* when we make moral statements (see the chapter on Non-cognitivism [Chapter 27]).

Putting non-cognitivism to one side, if cognitivism is true, 'what is a belief?' Importantly some cognitivists who reject moral realism – in particular, Horgan and Timmons – think cognitivists haven't properly considered this question. I return to this issue below.

A belief is typically thought to be a *propositional attitude* towards a proposition which represents the world as being thus-and-so. Our belief that there is a duck on the football pitch represents the world as being such that it has a duck on the football pitch. So, if *moral* cognitivism is true, and moral judgements express beliefs, when we judge that peeling the skin off babies is wrong, we represent the world as containing a certain value – the wrongness of flaying babies.

Representation allows the cognitivist to explain the common assumption that moral judgements can be true or false (the feature sometimes referred to as *truth-aptness*). For in representing the world as being a certain way, the world could fit (true) or fail to fit (false).

The move to reject realism typically follows from questioning the nature of *truth* and the nature of *facts*. One way to understand cognitivism without realism (though not in the way we'll be concerned with here) is as follows. Given that moral judgements express beliefs that represent the world, then the truthfulness of our moral practice is hostage to the fortunes of what the world actually contains. Unfortunately, the world couldn't contain such facts. As Mackie (1977: esp. Ch. 1) famously states, moral facts if they existed would require two opposing features, making moral facts "queer." They would have to be both *independent* of us, for we don't believe that we can change whether something is right by just thinking differently; and yet to motivate they would have to be closely related to our psychology. Mackie asserts that no such fact could possibly exist. Moreover, he argues that even *if* they did exist, given that they are queer, we could never *know* about them. We are forced to conclude then that when we make moral judgements we are systematically and uniformly mistaken. This is *error-theory* (a more recent alternative is *fictionalism* – see Error theory and fictionalism [Chapter 28]).

Most meta-ethicists find so much error unsatisfactory. After all, most of our primary commitments are to the *truth* of claims such as: "Peeling the skin off babies is morally wrong." Let's put error-theory to one side and merely note that it is *a* version of cognitivism without realism, though distinct from the position which we are concerned with.

What we have developed so far is a series of intuitive but conflicting thoughts.

(1) Moral judgements express beliefs.
(2) Moral judgements are truth-apt.
(3) Moral judgements are sometimes true.
(4) Moral facts are strange, unknowable and cannot be part of our ontology.

What makes cognitivism without realism attractive is that it *can* accept (1–4); it *is* consistent with this full set of intuitive claims. To see how, we need to consider a key assumption that has been implicit in the preceding discussion: *the correspondence theory of truth*.

I have suggested a correspondence theory *seems* quite plausible, we are happy to say things like, it is the *fact* that my bike is dirty *corresponds* to my claim that "my bike is dirty" that makes it the case that I am speaking the truth. However, arguably this is plausible only because "corresponds" is being used in a colloquial and non-technical way; crucially though, this is *not* the way correspondence theorists mean it. If there is this "non-technical" correspondence and a "technical" correspondence, then cognitivists who reject realism can accept that a factual proposition is true only if the substantial fact that it is says obtains does obtain; without thereby committing themselves to the more sophisticated correspondence theory; one that says that every proposition states that some fact obtains.

So, to try and draw some thoughts together, cognitivists who reject realism claim that moral judgements express beliefs, that moral judgements are truth-apt (though not necessarily in virtue of their expressing beliefs), and that moral judgements are sometimes true but not in virtue of any moral *facts*. The issues get very complicated quickly, but this is at the heart of such positions.

There are a number of questions which will have occurred to the attentive reader. For instance, "If there is a rejection of the correspondence theory, what *do* cognitivists who reject realism mean by truth?," "What do cognitivists who rejects realism mean by fact?," "What do they mean by belief?"

To start to answer these questions and in turn develop a few of the common features of cognitivism without realism, it will be beneficial to consider two accounts: Skorupski's (1999a, b, 2002, 2006), and Horgan and Timmons' (2000, 2006). Let's consider these in turn.

To return to a theme from above, we might worry that rejecting moral realism simply ignores how we talk. Skorupski argues that "fact" has two meanings and that as such we can *respect* how we talk without thereby committing ourselves to any particular ontological view.

For Skorupski in our everyday "fact" talk, for example, "it's a *fact* that it is raining," we are talking about *substantial, worldly* facts. Spelling out what this means is complicated. However, the important point is that some of our "fact" talk *doesn't* refer to worldly facts; *moral* talk, for instance, is about *nominal facts* – put simply it is about what propositions are true. Skorupski puts it like this:

> Nothing in the world *makes* [moral] propositions ... true or false. There are no *worldly facts* in virtue of which pure normative propositions are true when they are true. There is no special sector of reality which they describe, "represent," or "fit"; they have no "truth-makers"; there is nothing to which their truth "corresponds."
>
> (1999b: 437, emphasis mine)

So, according to Skorupski, we can happily talk about moral *facts* without being moral realists; for realists rely on facts being worldly. He argues that such a distinction between *types* of facts can be justified if we consider the *epistemology* of normative as against factual discourse.

> [T]he very idea of a *worldly fact* is the idea of a fact that can only be known to obtain by *receptive* awareness ... [cognitivism without realism] about the normative says that normative knowledge of fundamental normative propositions *rests on no receptive awareness*. The only capacity it requires is the non-receptive cognitive capacity of rationality, a capacity which involves *spontaneity* and regulation by the universality of reasons, *not receptivity*.
>
> (*Ibid.*: 136, emphasis mine)

There are a number of technical ideas here, such as the "universality of reasons"; however, this need not detain us. The key point is that *receptivity* and *spontaneity* are Skorupski's way of distinguishing between worldly and nominal facts. What, then, is "spontaneity?"

> [Spontaneity] does not mean "acting without thinking." Rather, a spontaneous act is an act that comes in the right way from me. Such an act can issue from profound reflection. The critical point is its source; it must be the product of a disposition to that very act which is "really mine." A spontaneous act is a self-originating, not a purely receptive, act. Connectedly, "spontaneous" contrasts with "factitious": a factitious as against a truly spontaneous response ... is one that is accepted

> uncritically into one's thinking from others, or one that results from a wish to please or to annoy ... and so on. Finally "spontaneous" also contrasts with "conventional." For example my disposition to drive on the left in Britain is not spontaneous; it registers my awareness of a convention. However following the convention itself always involves the exercise of spontaneity – there is spontaneity in the judgement that a convention rule applies in such-and-such a way to a particular case.
>
> (Skorupski 2002: 39)

So spontaneity arises from us, it isn't conventional nor does it mean accepting uncritically; whereas knowing something through receptive awareness requires things being *presented* to us, it results from something external affecting our present cognitive state.

But now we can't ignore the issue of truth any longer. For if knowledge of the truth of a moral judgement derives from *spontaneity*, then *when* is a moral judgement true? After all, wasn't it one of the attractions of a *worldly* conception of moral facts that it provided a ready account of what makes moral judgements true when they are? If, in contrast, we hold that knowledge of moral truth is best understood in terms of *spontaneity*, then isn't this just a way of saying that it is a matter of what we *will*? And presumably such a conclusion would make cognitivism without realism a whole lot less plausible; do we really want "Peeling the skin off babies is morally wrong" to be true simply because people have decided it is?

However, this isn't the conclusion forced on Skorupski. For him, although what *makes* a moral judgement true is, strictly speaking, *nothing*, this doesn't mean all moral judgements are equally good. There is a *possibility* of truth as spontaneous judgements can be "wrong" if, for instance, they don't cohere with other judgements (for more see Skorupski 2006).

This is *not* the view that the fact that there is consensus *makes* normative judgements true; this would be smuggling the correspondence theory in through the back door. It is, rather, that consensus allows Skorupski to develop and take account of what *warrants us* in making moral judgements, and of how we can discover when we are wrong. But this *isn't* to be committed to a further *reduction* of truth to claims about warranted assertibility.

We might ask "Why stop at cognitivism without realism in *ethics*?" "Why not hold a global cognitivism without realism and be done with the worldly notion of fact altogether?" Or, "Why not get rid of the *nominal* notion of fact and go for global cognitivism *with* realism?" Answering these questions will help us to further clarify Skorupski's cognitivism without realism.

The key is to hold onto the thought that metaphysics and semantics are distinct. Semantics requires the notion of truth, but not the notion of a worldly fact. And recall that it is the difference in the *epistemology* of spontaneity and receptivity which allows Skorupski to keep hold of worldly facts. So the answer to the questions rely on a coherent epistemology.

This though is the Achilles' heel of the position. For if we *can't* clearly distinguish receptivity and spontaneity, then this version of cognitivism without realism fails. And, although this isn't the place to pursue this worry in detail, there are some problems worth noting.

Contrary to what Skorupski thinks, don't we know about moral facts through something like a *receptive* awareness? Turning the corner the moral wrongness of the mugging is *presented* to us. The phenomenology of moral experience seems to be of moral facts which are there to be experienced. This means that, if Skorupski's characterization of facts is correct, *moral facts* are actually *worldly facts* and he is a *moral realist*.

Furthermore, we might think that our knowledge of worldly facts requires us to *actively* conceptualize the world. We *aren't* presented with a world of chairs, slugs and cars; we *bring* these categories to the world. If this is the case, then perhaps Skorupski's notion of "receptivity" is too passive to adequately capture our understanding of worldly facts and consequently he is actually an idealist.

Another recent version of cognitivism without realism has been developed (and is still evolving and changing) by Horgan and Timmons (e.g. 2000, 2006). For them it is "belief," rather than "fact," which is key. They claim that moral judgements can express *truth-apt beliefs* but that these *beliefs do not describe or represent anything*.

Horgan and Timmons (2000, 2006) claim that *any* sentence with the grammatical, phenomenological and logical trappings of *assertion* have *genuine cognitive content*; furthermore, moral sentences do have these features and hence have genuine *cognitive content*. Let's briefly consider why they say this about moral sentences.

Moral sentences can figure in logical inference, we say things like: "*if* torture is wrong, *then* the troops torturing prisoners is wrong; torture is wrong; therefore, troops torturing prisoners is wrong." In terms of the phenomenology, moral judgements are experienced as psychologically involuntary. For instance, if we were witness to a violent mugging we would be *presented* with its wrongness and we don't *infer* the wrongness (this then seems in direct contrast to Skorupki's "spontaneity" discussed above). Given these features Horgan and Timmons claim moral statements are *cognitive*. But notice that this is only a minimal commitment. In particular this isn't to hold that moral claims are *descriptive*. In fact, for Horgan and Timmons to make this further claim would be a mistake, for some beliefs are *non-descriptive*. In other words, to move from the claim that moral statements are cognitive to their being descriptive requires a further argument, one which, they suggest, need not be given. To see their reasoning, consider an example:

(1) Andy *will* clean his bike.
(2) Andy *ought* to clean his bike.

(1) and (2) have overall *cognitive* content, but this differs. Judgements expressed by (1) are *is-commitments* to a core descriptive content (Andy cleans his bike). Judgements expressed by (2) are *ought-commitments* to the *same* core content. However, and this is key, is-commitments are *representational* whereas ought-commitments are *not*. So, (1) and (2) have different *overall* cognitive content. Horgan and Timmons claim that given this distinction, moral sentences can have an overall declarative cognitive content without being descriptive.

If there is no descriptive cognitive content in moral claims, then Horgan and Timmons need to give us some account of truth. The problem is that, given the subtle and evolving nature of their work, it is hard to get a sense of what they mean by moral truth – here though is a rough characterization. Similar to Skorupski, Horgan and Timmons argue that there are truth-*conditions* for moral claims but not truth-*makers*; and that these truth-conditions should be characterized in terms of correct and incorrect assertability.

For Horgan and Timmons correct assertability is explained in terms of the rules for our language use; what they call the *semantic norms*. For them there are two types of semantic norms: *tight* and *loose*. In our everyday talk about chairs, bikes, etc., the semantic norms are *tight*. They: "conspire with the world itself to confer determinate correct-assertability or correct-deniability status on the statements in the discourse" (Horgan 1996: 892). This contrasts with *moral claims*. In this case the semantic norms are *loose*. Moral claims are: "made from within an *engaged stance* in which they reflect certain features of that stance itself – e.g. certain attitudes or preferences, or the acceptance of certain non-semantic norms" (*ibid.*: 893, emphasis mine).

Thus, the claim: "Peeling the skin off babies is wrong," is true, not because the semantic norms conspire with *the world*; there isn't anything objectively determining correct-assertability. According to Horgan and Timmons, there is a "slackness" in moral claims which is taken up by the *attitudes of the speaker*. So we can talk about moral truth without needing a substantial notion of moral facts. Furthermore, like Skorupski, Horgan and Timmons are *not* reducing correct-assertability to warranted-assertability. It is worth ending this discussion of Horgan and Timmons' position by quoting at length a recent discussion of moral truth by Horgan:

> From a certain morally detached perspective – the perspective of theoretical inquiry – there is no moral truth (or falsity), since semantic standards alone do not conspire with THE WORLD to yield correct assertability or deniability status to moral statements. Truth is correspondence to THE WORLD … and moral statements, being non-descriptive in their assertoric content, cannot enter into a relation of language/WORLD correspondence. … But from an engaged perspective, "true" as predicated of moral statements results in a metalinguistic claim that is a fused semantic/moral assertion rather than a detached

> semantic assertion. But ways of employing the truth predicate are legitimate in context because of the contextual variability of the semantic standards governing the notion of truth. One can properly use truth talk either way, but not in the same breath.
>
> (Horgan 2001: 90)

How much we can make sense of these different semantic norms and this account of moral truth, I will leave to the reader. I do though want to end with one issue.

Consider the example from above:

(3) I believe Andy *will* clean his bike.
(4) I believe Andy *ought* to clean his bike.

For Horgan and Timmons (3) and (4) have *overall cognitive content*, but crucially they claim that they differ in cognitive content. However, from what they say, it isn't clear why this should be true.

Belief is a propositional attitude – it is a mental state in which a subject has a specific *attitude* or *orientation* towards a *proposition*. So, to have the belief that Andy will clean his bike is to take the belief attitude towards the proposition, *Andy will clean his bike*. The *content* of the belief is the proposition that *Andy will clean his bike*. Likewise, to have the belief that Andy ought to clean his bike is to have the belief attitude towards the proposition, *Andy ought to clean his bike*.

Horgan and Timmons argue that the belief-attitudes in (3) and (4) are different. The belief-attitude in (3) is an "is"-commitment whilst the belief-attitude in (4) is an "ought"-commitment. But hold on – are we talking about *commitment* or *content*? Why should we think that "is"-commitments and "ought"-commitments produce *different* kinds of cognitive content? Recall that Horgan and Timmons want to claim that we can have *non-descriptive* beliefs. But they are talking about the content – the proposition – of the belief.

So, it remains possible on Horgan and Timmons' account that the content differs in (3) and (4) but both are *descriptive*. (3) *describes* Andy as someone who will clean his bike, (4) *describes* Andy as someone who ought to clean his bike. Something has gone wrong somewhere.

It seems then that Horgan and Timmons need a further claim *linking* the different kinds of belief-attitude they postulate with claims about the representational nature of the propositions believed. For it is only with this in place that they could claim that if the commitment is an "is"-type *then* the content is descriptive, whereas if the commitment is an "ought"-type *then* the content is non-descriptive. But what this link could be is, to me at least, unclear.

For Horgan and Timmons, different kinds of belief-attitude are distinguished by different commitments, descriptive and non-descriptive. But belief-attitudes are psychological states and are not the sort of thing we would typically think of as either descriptive or non-descriptive. It is then unclear why Horgan and Timmons think they can motivate a non-descriptive cognitivism by *starting* from the idea of different kinds of belief. Should the starting point not be a distinction between different types of *proposition*, i.e. belief-*content*? I will leave it up to the reader to figure out what is going on here.

If cognitivism without realism can be successfully defended then it is a very attractive position. Not least because it captures a set of intuitive thoughts: cognitivism, truth-aptness, truth, and the apparent ontological strangeness of moral facts. However, a number of complicated and problematic issues have arisen in this chapter concerning such things as the *meaning* of "belief," "proposition," "facts," "representation," etc. Thus I suspect that the plausibility of cognitivism without realism, along with further developments in meta-ethics, will depend on meta-ethicists taking a look at the domain they are working in and trying and agree on some terminological foundation. A bit disconcertingly, then, it seems that to make things clearer and thus progress, meta-ethicists should become meta-meta-ethicists!

See also Realism and its alternatives (Chapter 26); Non-cognitivism (Chapter 27); Error theory and fictionalism (Chapter 28); Contemporary Kantian ethics (Chapter 38).

References

Horgan, T. (1996) "The Perils of Epistemic Reductionism," *Philosophy and Phenomenological Research* 4: 891–7.

——(2001) "Contextual Semantics and Metaphysical Realism: Truth as Indirect Correspondence," in M. Lynch (ed.) *The Nature of Truth: Classic and Contemporary Perspectives*, Cambridge, MA: MIT Press, pp. 67–95.

Horgan, T. and Timmons, M. (2000) "Nondescriptive Cognitivism: Framework for a New Metaethic," *Philosophical Papers* 2: 121–53.

——(2006) "Morality without Facts," in J. Drier (ed.) *Contemporary Debates in Moral Theory*, Oxford: Blackwell.

Lynch, M. (2001) *The Nature of Truth: Classic and Contemporary Perspectives*, Cambridge, MA: MIT Press.

Mackie, J. (1977) *Inventing Right and Wrong*, New York: Penguin Books.

McDowell, J. (1996) *Mind and World*, Cambridge, MA: Harvard University Press.

Skorupski, J. (1998) "Rescuing Moral Obligation," *European Journal of Philosophy* 6, no. 3: 335–55.

——(1999a) *Ethical Explorations*, Oxford: Oxford University Press.

——(1999b) "Irrealist Cognitivism," *Ratio* 12: 436–59.

——(2002) "The Ontology of Reasons," *Topoi* 21: 113–24.

——(2006) "Propositions about Reasons," *European Journal of Philosophy* 14: 26–8.

Timmons, M. (1999) *Morality without Foundations: A Defense of Ethical Contextualism*, New York: Oxford University Press.

Further reading

Devitt, Michael (1984) *Realism and Truth*, Oxford: Basil Blackwell. (A classic discussion of the links between truth and realism.)

Engel, Pascal (2002) *Truth*, Montreal, Canada: McGill–Queen's University Press. (A clear discussion of the main theories of truth.)

Skorupski, John (1999) "Irrealist Cognitivism," *Ratio* 12: 436–59. (A clear and succinct statement of cognitivism without realism.)

Wright, Crispin (1992) *Truth and Objectivity*, Cambridge, MA: Harvard University Press. (A classic discussion of the links between truth and realism, but defending a contrary position to Devitt's *Realism and Truth*.)

30
RELATIVISM

Nicholas L. Sturgeon

One difficulty for any attempt to explain and assess moral relativism is that so many different doctrines, even mutually incompatible ones, have gone under this name, not just in popular discussions but also in the debates of academic philosophers. My aim here is to distinguish some of the most important doctrines that have been called relativist, to lay out their motivation, and to note some problems they face. It is possible, of course, to be a relativist about topics other than morality: in that case, moral relativism can be just one application of a more general (and, of course, controversial) doctrine. Here, however, I shall focus almost entirely on more selective relativisms, ones that take a relativist line about morality (and perhaps, a bit more generally, about values), but not about other issues. Partly, this limitation is to keep my discussion manageable; but it is also justified by the fact that this sort of selective relativism – a version of the idea that the sciences are hard, values soft – has had a considerable influence in popular thought and among some philosophers.

Arguments for the main forms of relativism are often said to begin from the existence of moral disagreement, especially disagreement that proves rationally irresolvable (Brandt 1967: 75). As we shall see, this cannot be quite right. But it will do for now to say that the standard forms of relativism are a response to the *appearance* of irresolvable disagreement; I will make this more precise below. What relativists maintain, characteristically, is that in these deep disagreements, as I shall call them, there is some sense in which both sides can be *right*. In taking this to be the central relativist idea, I am taking two stands worth mentioning. First, I am understanding relativism to be a doctrine that one might apply to some moral disagreements – the deep ones – but not to all of them. Some discussions treat moral relativism as if it had to apply to all moral issues: and, of course, it will look that way even on my characterization to someone who holds that all moral claims are subject to deep disagreement. But some defenders of relativism have seen it as applying selectively even within morality, and I formulate it so as to leave that possibility open (Wong 1986; Foot 2002). (Of course, the doctrine becomes more interesting when it is claimed to apply to central, controverted moral issues, not just peripheral ones; so I shall assume that we are talking about a doctrine aimed at central issues.) Second, my characterization puts to one side some doctrines that have sometimes been called relativist. An alternative response to irresolvable disagreements, for example, would be to declare not that both sides are right but that neither is, in that there is no truth, no fact of the matter, about such issues. This is an important view that merits discussion in its own right – it is sometimes called moral nihilism, or an "error theory" – but I do not count it as a form of relativism. Neither do I call relativist the expressivist view that the function of moral discourse is primarily to express pro and con attitudes rather than to express beliefs that might be true or false. In its classical versions this view held that, in moral disagreements, no one is right. In more recent formulations, its proponents allow that we may call moral statements true or false as a way of agreeing or disagreeing with them, but they avoid calling true the statements of both sides in a moral disagreement: so they aren't, on my account, relativists.

Relativism comes in both social and individual forms. Sometimes the deep disagreements are between individuals, sometimes between the outlooks of different historical societies. Social versions need an explanation of what it is for a group to have an outlook. Unless they take this to be more than possession of the outlook by all the individuals in the group, they are unlikely to differ much in their implications from individual versions. For this reason I shall assume that they hold that a society can believe something even if not all its members do. Most of my discussion will be of individual versions, since many points come out more easily that way, but I shall say a bit about social versions too.

Beyond this distinction between social and individual forms of relativism, standard philosophical discussions differ quite a bit in how they distinguish versions of the view. One very helpful distinction, introduced by David Lyons, is between *agent* and *appraiser* forms of relativism – where an agent is someone performing an action, an appraiser someone forming a moral judgment about someone's action (Lyons 1976: 109–10). Agent relativism takes the moral quality of an agent's act (for simplicity in my examples, always its rightness or wrongness) to be determined at bottom by some feature that can vary across agents. In the simplest version this is just the agent's belief about the action, so that whether the action is right or wrong just depends on whether the agent thinks it is right or wrong; I say something below about how this story might be amended. Appraiser relativism, by contrast, sees the truth conditions for moral judgments made by a given appraiser as determined at bottom by some feature that can vary from appraiser to appraiser – such as, again, the appraiser's moral beliefs. Thus, again in the simplest (and individual) version, the mere fact that an appraiser believes a certain action (whether by herself or by someone else) wrong is enough to insure that the appraiser's belief is correct. We shall see how we might depart from the simplest version.

One reason for distinguishing these two sorts of views – roughly, that we ought to judge others by their own beliefs, and that we ought to judge them by ours – is that they get conflated in popular and anthropological discussions (though typically not in philosophical ones). Another is that, insofar as it can keep them distinguished, popular thought tends to be drawn more towards agent relativism, a view that has not had many philosophical defenders; when philosophers take relativism seriously, as some do, it is most commonly the appraiser version that they have in mind. I will say something about both versions, beginning with agent relativism.

Agent relativism

Start then with the way in which agent relativism tries to capture the idea that both sides in a deep disagreement can be right. Agent relativism does not say that whenever I disagree with you (deeply) about a question of right and wrong, my belief is correct. What it says, at least in the simple version I have mentioned, is that if you and I have a deep disagreement in which you think it would be right for you to act in a certain way and I disagree, you are right and I am mistaken. The way in which we can both be right, at least in a crucial application of our views, comes out in a different sort of case. Suppose that I think that lying in a certain set of circumstances is wrong, whereas you think that it is right (that is, permissible) in those circumstances, and suppose that this is a deep disagreement, the sort where relativism is supposed to take hold. Then, according to the simplest version of individual relativism, it follows that it would be wrong for me to lie in those circumstances but permissible for you to do so.

Individual agent relativism is thus the view that, in cases of deep disagreement, people ought to live by their own moral standards, as represented in their moral beliefs. Some of its attraction surely comes from the common-sense resonance of this view. Of course, this particular attraction is not obviously shared by social versions of agent relativism, which say that in such cases agents ought to follow the beliefs of their society. Also, one should keep in mind, agent relativism is a single-minded view: it does not treat the injunction to follow one's own moral beliefs as one principle among others to be balanced against others in cases of deep disagreement, but as the only basic principle. It can thus lead to some quite counter-intuitive implications. No doubt many slave owners over the centuries have thought buying and selling slaves quite permissible, but few of us would find it plausible that this actually made it right for them to buy and sell slaves – indeed, it is quite certain that they themselves did not believe that what made it right for them to buy and sell slaves was just that they thought it right. And similar points can be made about the numerous other terrible practices that humans have at various times endorsed. In reply, a relativist might of course just dig in her heels and accept these unconventional verdicts. But one should here note a point about debates in ethics. It is standard practice in thinking about normative theories such as utilitarianism or Kantianism to evaluate these theories in part by considering the plausibility of their implications for cases. But agent relativism is a normative theory competing with these other normative theories – it is one view that is sometimes called "normative relativism" – so it seems apt for evaluation in the same way. If it is commonly taken to count against utilitarianism that there are conceivable circumstances, even if no actual ones, in which it would permit slavery, it is hard to see how it could not count against agent relativism that it would condone many of the actual systems of slavery that have existed. One would expect a similar objection to any ethical theory that implies, as Gilbert Harman once argued that his version of agent relativism does, that it was not wrong of Hitler to order the Holocaust (Harman 1975).

(Noting that agent relativism is itself a controversial normative theory, I can now explain why I have not had the doctrine say that deep disagreements in ethics are actually irresolvable. The reason is that if we cannot settle controversial issues in normative ethics, then one thing we cannot settle is whether agent relativism is correct; whereas, if we can determine that it is correct, then the deep disagreements are settleable after all – on the basis of agent relativism. What defenders will say about these disagreements, however – this is the improved formulation I promised – is that they are not resolvable on any other grounds.)

A more interesting reply that a proponent of agent relativism might make is that I have so far oversimplified the doctrine. I have made the determinant of an action's rightness or wrongness the agent's own belief about whether it is right or wrong. But, besides leading to troubling implications about slavery and other issues, this also has the implausible general implication that there is no room for error in the judgments we form about the rightness or wrongness of our own actions. (Certainly, that is not how it feels when we form such a judgment but also wonder whether we might be mistaken.) This general implication can be avoided, and perhaps some of the problems about cases like slavery as well, if we make the rightness or wrongness of the agent's actions depend not on her actual moral beliefs but on some other property of her. We need to be careful here, because of a well-known problem in formulating agent relativism. This is that while it is obviously a version of agent relativism to hold that it is agents' various moral beliefs about their actions that makes them right or wrong, it is not in any interesting sense relativist to say about many other variable circumstances of agents that they can have this effect. For example, it is not controversial that an action may be right in one circumstance but wrong in another because of differing promises the agent has made, or because of differences in the two cases in the alternatives to the action and their consequences. (Sometimes the view that this can happen is called "circumstantial relativism": but, then, everyone is a circumstantial relativist.) So what is special about the variable circumstances that a version of agent relativism will appeal to? I think that the answer is that this can include not just the agent's moral beliefs but also other states of the agent that are *like* beliefs in that they are normally thought of as appropriate responses to the rightness and wrongness of actions. These can include standards for forming moral beliefs (if these are not beliefs themselves), and they can include moral emotions such as disapproval (so one agent relativist view might say that an action is wrong just in case the agent disapproves of it, or would disapprove after a certain kind of reflection). Some versions of agent relativism also say that right and wrong depend on convention: but since the relevant conventions will always be ones that the agent or the agent's society thinks (or, would after appropriate reflection think) it morally appropriate to adhere to – or else disapproves of, or would disapprove of, violating – I do not treat this as an alternative to appealing to the agent's moral beliefs or emotions.

In any case, the amendment a proponent of agent relativism might suggest, in response to my objections, is to say that what at bottom makes an action right or wrong is not necessarily the agent's actual belief about the action, but instead the assessment the agent would have of it after reflection that corrected for various kinds of mistakes: misinformation or incomplete information about the nonmoral facts, and for various kinds of bad reasoning. (There need be no suggestion that stubborn agents would be willing to engage in this kind of reflection; the test is a counterfactual one about what would happen if, however implausibly, they did engage in it.) Different relativists might defend different versions of this proposal, advocating different degrees of idealization; all that matters here is that they would agree in making right and wrong depend on what we might call the agent's corrected response rather than his or her actual belief. This would quickly block the objection that relativism leaves no room for error in an agent's assessment of her own action, for my actual belief about my action may certainly differ from my corrected belief.

The proposal would also allow the relativist to say that some people who approved of slavery nevertheless acted wrongly in supporting it, on the grounds that their actual approval of slavery depended on correctable mistakes; and so for similar examples. However, the amended proposal also comes at some cost to the relativist. For one thing, to an extent that depends on the degree of idealization asked for, it puts strain on the idea that, according to agent relativism, agents are always right about what they should do; it says instead that they would be right if their response was the corrected one. A corollary of this point is that agent relativism will lose its intuitive appeal in some cases. For part of the attraction of the unamended version was that it promised to respect acting on conscience in cases where it can seem plausible (and not just to relativists) that that is the right thing to do. For example, it would say of someone committed to pacifism that it would be wrong of them to participate in a war. But the revised version no longer guarantees this result, for a deeply held conviction might nevertheless fail the kind of test we were proposing for those defenders of slavery. The concession that our moral beliefs are subject to correction, though extremely plausible, also opens the door to someone who wants to claim that these contested issues are actually rationally resolvable; a relativist will deny this, maintaining that different agents in situations otherwise alike would still differ in their corrected responses, but this is not nearly so obvious as that people disagree in their actual moral beliefs. And many will find implausible the relativist's continued insistence that buying and selling slaves, for example, was right for some agents.

Confusions

These are some of the difficulties besetting agent relativism. Philosophers often note in addition that much popular support for the view is based on misunderstanding. One common example involves confusing moral relativism with moral fallibilism: with the view, that is, about some moral belief or beliefs we hold, that they might be mistaken (Schlesinger 1989). This is obviously a different doctrine from agent relativism (which, as we have seen, needs to be adjusted even to allow for the possibility of our being wrong about what we ourselves should do), and also from appraiser relativism (which, as we shall see, is formulated precisely to allow that our opponents may be right without our own view being in any way mistaken). All that the doctrines have in common is some kind of modesty, very different in the different cases, about one's own moral beliefs; though it is no doubt also a misfortune that the name "absolutism" is used sometimes for the denial of fallibilism, sometimes for the denial of relativism, so that someone attracted to fallibilism may think that in rejecting absolutism in one sense she must also have rejected it in the other, and so ended up a relativist. An even more common confusion is the popular conception that agent relativism supports toleration. This seems clearly to be a mistake: relativism simply tells agents to live by their moral views, or by their corrected moral views, and whether this will involve any support for toleration of different moral views or moral practices depends entirely on what the agent's moral views, or corrected moral views, are. The thought that agent relativism supports toleration most likely arises from the belief (a) that it will label as morally required any action by an agent following his own moral views, together with the principle (b) that if someone's action is morally required, it is morally wrong for others to interfere to prevent the action. But (a) is false about our amended version of relativism, which will call an action right only if it conforms to what the agent's moral beliefs would be as corrected; and, more important, though some principle like (b) is quite plausible, it is a principle that any agent relativist will have to reject. For relativism cannot guarantee this kind of coordination between requirements on different agents: my moral obligations depend on my moral beliefs (possibly, as corrected), your moral obligations on yours, and there is nothing in this account to preclude my being required to do something while you are required to prevent me.

Social versions of agent relativism, about which I have said little to this point, also derive support partly from misunderstanding. They are often defended by pointing to various goods, including social cohesion, that are promoted by conformity to a society's moral norms. But (a) it takes an exceptionally high estimate either of the value of these goods or of the fragility of a society to argue that no one could ever be justified in departing from those norms; and (b) in any case, an argument appealing to the goods promoted by conformity to the accepted norms looks to rely at bottom on some kind of consequentialism rather than relativism. An interesting special case is what we might call a "rule of the road" case. The two accepted (literal) rules of the road are that everyone should drive to the left and that everyone should drive to the right. It's obvious (i) that, abstractly, there is nothing to choose between these equally good rules, but (ii) there are powerful reasons for wanting everyone in a given region to abide by the same one of them and so (iii) there is also good reason for conforming to whichever already prevails locally. Despite its vaguely relativist sound ("When in Rome, drive as the Romans drive"), this is a position that will be endorsed by anyone who thinks, on entirely non-relative grounds, that we ought to promote safe and efficient transportation. It is not, in any interesting sense, relativism. (Note, for one thing, that although there are two equal-best rules, there are numerous bad ones – "Randomize," "Left if your birth date is odd, otherwise right" – that would have no claim on an agent even if some society had been unwise enough to implement them.) It is a fascinating question whether there might be equal-best but incompatible patterns of moral life, each requiring widespread conformity, developed, for example, by different historical civilizations, and such that agents raised in one could never successfully adapt to the other. If this were so, it would be an important complexity for moral thought; but I think that it would not be, in any interesting sense, moral relativism.

Appraiser relativism

As I explained above, agent relativism must be distinguished from appraiser relativism. The difference can be illustrated with an example borrowed from Lyons (Lyons 1976: 107–8). Suppose that Alice and Barbara are considering whether Claudia may have an abortion, and suppose that this is what I have called a deep disagreement. Alice thinks abortion wrong – that is, not permissible – in cases like this, whereas Barbara thinks it permissible (and these are their "corrected" views as well). Agent relativism says that to know whether Alice or Barbara is right, we need to know something we haven't yet been told, what Claudia's views (or corrected views) are on the matter. Appraiser relativism, by contrast, says that no matter what Claudia thinks, Alice is right to think abortion impermissible for Claudia and Barbara is right to think it permissible.

The example brings out clearly one problem for appraiser relativism. This is that it appears to endorse contradictions, a philosophically embarrassing stance in ethics as much as in any other area of thought. Alice thinks abortion impermissible for Claudia and Barbara thinks it permissible: how can both be right? The standard relativist response is to interpret Alice's and Barbara's views so that they do not after all contradict one another. Proposals differ in details, but the general idea is to interpret what Alice and Barbara are saying as containing an implicit reference to themselves, the appraiser. For example, a relativist might maintain that when Alice says, "Abortion would be impermissible for Claudia," what her statement means, more fully, is, "Claudia's having an abortion would conflict with *my* corrected moral views," whereas what Barbara is saying amounts, when spelled out, to, "Claudia's having an abortion would be permitted by *my* corrected moral views." (A social version of appraiser relativism might take the implicit reference to be to "my *group's* views"; but I shall confine my discussion of appraiser relativism to individual versions, since all the points transfer pretty straightforwardly to social versions.) On this understanding of what they are saying, it is easy to see how Alice and Barbara could both be right. Each is simply talking about how her own standards apply to Claudia. There is no contradiction. But now there is another problem. This is that it is also clear on this understanding that Alice and Barbara are not really disagreeing: they are simply talking about different subjects. Hence my remark above, that it is misleading to say that moral relativism rests on the assumption of irresolvable deep disagreements. For agent relativism, that is because the disagreements turn out to be resolvable; for appraiser relativism, it is because they turn out not actually to be *disagreements*.

But almost everyone, including relativists, finds that an implausible implication. Relativists standardly argue that we must accept it even so, on the grounds that the alternatives are even less plausible. The argument is that if we do *not* interpret moral claims about deeply disputed issues relativistically, then those disagreements will indeed be genuine, but also irresolvable. (So the existence of irresolvable disagreements, on an understanding of them that the relativist proposes to reject does play a role in the argument.) But that, according to the relativist, would force us to nihilism about this issue – to the view that neither Alice nor Barbara is right, because there is no fact of the matter about the morality of Claudia's abortion – and so for every other issue on which there is (on a non-relativistic understanding of the discourse) irresolvable disagreement. And that in turn would require any non-relativist to stop making, and stating, judgments about these issues; relativism, it is said, can, by contrast, "save the discourse" by providing a subject matter for Alice and Barbara's judgments (Wong 1986: 109). It may also be said to provide a respectful interpretation of Alice and Barbara's statements, in that it credits them with being right about something, when their moral judgment matches what their corrected judgment would be.

There are many ways in which one might find this argument unpersuasive. For one thing, expressivism is a competing view that also promises to save the discourse in the face of irresolvable disagreements by providing a point (if not a subject matter) for Alice and Barbara's judgments; and it will count their disagreement as a genuine "disagreement in attitude" rather than as a case in which they talk past one another. So the relativist needs an argument for dismissing expressivism: too large an issue to explore here, but one on which she might find some allies among non-relativists who also reject expressivism. For another thing, it is not so clear why the discourse needs to be saved. Even putting expressivism to one side, it is not as if our only choices were to keep using moral discourse as before (while understanding it as a relativist would) or to say nothing; there is also the option of speaking in a more subjective way, of what matters to us and why. In addition, it is surely debatable whether Alice and Barbara would find a relativist understanding of their positions respectful, even if they knew as much as (according to the relativist) we do; for, even if we imagine them acknowledging that their dispute is irresolvable, they could easily find quite dismissive the suggestion that they are simply talking about their own views and are not really in disagreement. In addition, some relativists hold, as I have mentioned, that their doctrine does not apply to all moral disagreements. They mean it to apply to the ones that would be irresolvable if treated as genuine, but not to others that are rationally resolvable. But this makes even more pressing the question why we should want to save the rest of the discourse. Doing so in the relativist manner will yield a strikingly disjoint account of moral judgments, some made true by whatever it is that makes some of them objectively true, others made true simply by the appraisers' beliefs (or corrected beliefs). And it can seem very misleading, to say the least, to propose that we go on talking in the same objective-sounding way about issues whose status is said to be so different.

Resolving disagreements

As should be clear, I do not count as relativist the bare thesis that some moral disagreements, even central moral disagreements, are irresolvable, for it is compatible with views that are not relativist. But some form of this thesis – as the proposal that the disagreements are irresolvable except by appeal to agent relativism, or as the proposal that they are irresolvable unless interpreted as an appraiser relativist would interpret them – is nevertheless central to a relativist outlook, so I should say something about it. It raises an enormous and difficult issue; here I shall only say a couple of things to keep it in perspective. First, the selective relativists we are considering of course contrast ethics, in which they see central debates as irresolvable, with other areas, such as the sciences, where disagreements get settled. But it is widely agreed among philosophers that few scientific issues (some say: none) are resolvable with certainty. The best that can be hoped is that evidence and argument will weigh, objectively, more on one side than on the other. But, then, to maintain the contrast, the selective relativist must deny not just that moral disagreements can be settled with certainty, but also that they can receive this more modest form of resolution – a far less obvious thesis. Second, the relativist will need a realistic account of science. For a good part of the twentieth century many philosophers accepted a largely positivist picture on which scientific disputes were resolved by seeing how competing hypotheses fared against empirical evidence described in theory-neutral language we know *a priori* to be appropriate, according to an equally *a priori* "inductive logic"; and it was fairly easy to argue that ethical views do badly by this test. But this account of scientific procedure has been widely criticized, often on the ground that there are fewer *a priori* standards in science than it claims; and this, again, can make it harder than it once seemed to argue that scientific and ethical reasoning are not on a par (Boyd 1988).

See also Non-cognitivism (Chapter 27); Error theory and fictionalism (Chapter 28).

References

Boyd, Richard (1988) "How to Be a Moral Realist," in Geoffrey Sayre-McCord (ed.) *Essays on Moral Realism*, Ithaca, NY: Cornell University Press.
Brandt, Richard B. (1967) "Ethical Relativism," in Paul Edwards (ed.) *The Encyclopedia of Philosophy*, New York: Macmillan, vol. 3, pp. 75–8.
Foot, Philippa (2002) "Moral Relativism," in *Moral Dilemmas*, Oxford: Clarendon Press.
Harman, Gilbert (1975) "Moral Relativism Defended," *Philosophical Review* 84: 3–22.
Lyons, David (1976) "Ethical Relativism and the Problem of Incoherence," *Ethics* 86: 107–21.
Schlesinger, Arthur Jr (1989) "The Opening of the American Mind," *New York Times Book Review*, 23 July.
Wong, David (1986) "On Moral Realism Without Foundations," *Southern Journal of Philosophy* 24 (suppl.): 95–113.

Further reading

Foot, Philippa (2002) "Moral Relativism," in *Moral Dilemmas*, Oxford: Clarendon Press. (Sympathetically defends moral relativism against some objections, but in the end does not endorse it.)
Sturgeon, Nicholas L. (1994) "Moral Disagreement and Moral Relativism," *Social Philosophy and Policy* 11: 80–115. (An overview, with arguments against [mainly] appraiser relativism.)
Wong, David (1984) *Moral Relativity*, Berkeley: University of California Press. (A systematic defense of appraiser relativism.)

Part III

IDEAS AND METHODS FROM OUTSIDE ETHICS

31
SOCIAL ANTHROPOLOGY

James Laidlaw

Many classic ethnographies in social anthropology have consisted at least in part of descriptions and analyses of diverse forms of moral life. Yet until recently, theoretical debate in the discipline has hardly been concerned with, or affected by, questions of the general understanding or comparative analysis of morality; and occasional attempts to set out an intellectual agenda that might place such questions centrally in the discipline (e.g. Westermarck 1932; Firth 1951, 1953; Read 1955; Edel and Edel 1959; Fürer-Haimendorf 1967; Gluckman 1972; Wolfram 1982; Pocock 1986; Fiske and Mason 1990; Howell 1997) have had limited impact on the general direction of inquiry and debate. Attempts by non-anthropologists to draw systematic conclusions for the understanding of ethics from ethnographical data and analyses (MacBeath 1952; Ladd 1957; Hatch 1983; Moody-Adams 1997; J. D. Cook 1999) have been similarly uninfluential. During the last two decades, however, something like a concerted field of enquiry has developed in the anthropology of ethics, with a series of conceptual innovations finally directing ethnographic inquiries, which have in turn informed further debate. Progress has depended on some success in transcending two limitations of vision that have hitherto constrained anthropological engagement with ethics: a tendency to equate ethics or morality with the social, conceived in law-like terms, and a particularistic conception of distinct moralities embodied in plural cultures or societies. Ideas from ethnographically minded philosophers have been helpful in developing this anthropological approach.

Conceptions of the social as an order of reality superordinate to "the individual" come in many forms, but Émile Durkheim's formulation has been exceptionally influential. Durkheim (1915/1912, 1953/1906, 1973/1899, 1979/1920) argued that the power of both morality and "the sacred" to compel and constrain human action, manifest in their being simultaneously both obligatory and desirable, derives from the fact that they represent "society": "a moral being qualitatively different from the individuals it comprises," and the source of the latter's better qualities – everything that distinguishes them from amoral bundles of natural appetites. The implicit recognition of this is the explanation for both religion, which is the veneration of society symbolically transfigured, and morality, which is the authority of society manifested in "its imperative rules of conduct." On the one hand, Durkheim's powerful vision appears to recognize the constitutive importance of morality in social life, as a reality not reducible to material interests, but on the other it simply equates morality with the collective; and people following moral rules, like the rest of a social structure, is conceived as the more-or-less mechanical functioning of a natural causal system. Morality is central, but at the same time almost invisible, because there is nothing true of it that is not equally true of society.

Many anthropologists accepted enough of this Durkheimian framework to think that understanding morality was a matter of explaining "why custom binds" (Fortes 1959, 1977), and if successive generations found Durkheim's own account unsatisfactory, and looked to psychoanalysis, hermeneutics, cognitive science, Marxism, or phenomenology for better answers, they have rarely considered that anything distinctive about ethical choice, dilemma, judgment, or conduct, anything that sets the ethical apart from the rest of culture, ideology, discourse, and so on, might be central to the understanding of social life.

When anthropologists explained patterns of peasant insurgency and resistance, for instance, in terms of "moral economy" (Scott 1977), the force of the term "moral" was just that ideas of entitlement that motivate political action are collectivist rather than individual; and cross-cultural comparisons of the "morality" of market exchange turned on equating morality with society and the long term, as opposed to the self-interest, the individual, and the short term (Parry and Bloch 1989). For Marxists, morality was identified sometimes with a ruling ideology (Bloch 1989) and sometimes with proletarian insight into the truth behind such ideology (Taussig 1980); in both cases, indistinguishably, with collectively shared ideas that mandate and motivate collective cohesion.

Durkheim's nephew Marcel Mauss, in his classic 1938 lecture, "The Category of the Person" (1985), provides a Durkheimian counterpart to Nietzsche's *Genealogy of Morality* (1994/1887). Like Nietzsche, Mauss describes the stages in the emergence of a distinctively modern moral agent. Mauss's is a more benign narrative, of the social production of the conscious, responsible individual who is the bearer of rights. In line with the Durkheimian opposition between the moral-collective and the natural-individual, Mauss begins by declaring a disjunction between socially constituted categories of person (*personne*), whose history he proposes to reconstruct, and the sense of physical and spiritual individuality of the self (*moi*), which he suggests people have always possessed and, he implies, therefore has no history. Michael Carrithers (1985) rightly insists that this disjunction is invalid and that there is a history to be written of senses of self (*moi*) which is connected with that of the person. He distinguishes *personne*-theories, which conceive of persons in an ordered social collectivity, from *moi*-theories, in which selves are conceived in cosmological and spiritual contexts, interacting as moral agents, and he emphasizes that organized reflection on the self is not a parochial Western concern. Indeed, north India in the fifth century BC, with the development of Buddhism and other organized projects of self-formation, was the site of a decisive step in human thought and practice relating to the self, comparable to that which Mauss identifies, in relation to the person, in Roman law. Mauss misses the significance of these developments, and also those in China, because his narrative is structured by the *telos* of the morally inviolate legal individual, so the elaborate institutionalized projects for the analysis and refashioning (including the decomposition) of the self developed there are dismissed as historical dead-ends. But forms of life and techniques of self-fashioning have been widely and pervasively influential, including in Europe, over many hundreds of years. During the last century the mutual influencing and interchange of ideas and practices intensified as traditions such as Buddhist *vipassana* meditation and yoga were reformulated and commoditized in globalizing movements (Alter 2004; Strauss 2005; J. Cook forthcoming).

Carrithers' proposal for a complement to Mauss's narrative provides the basis for bringing anthropological analysis into dialogue with other accounts of the genealogy of the moral subject, whether Nietzsche's or more recent philosophical-historical and Europe-focused accounts (Taylor 1989; Rose 1990, 1996; Seigel 2005). But little has so far been accomplished here, partly because it has been unusual for anthropologists, including those who have departed more or less radically from the Durkheimian understanding of the moral/social, to paint on such a broad historical and comparative canvas. Instead, where anthropologists have sought to interpret something like Durkheim's insistence on the centrality of the moral in a less reductive way than he did, they have most often declared the irreducible diversity of moral life among what they represent as distinct and separate cultures or societies.

Thus when Edward Evans-Pritchard described societies as "moral systems" (1962) he meant not, as Durkheim had, that the content of morality varies in predictable ways with different social structures, but rather that it is underdetermined by any such causal forces. The anthropologist cannot explain the choices and actions people make; the ambition must be to render them intelligible by translating the categories and concepts in which they are made, always in more-or-less explicit contrast with "the West" or "us." Many fine ethnographic studies in this interpretive manner have characterized local societies by their dominant moral values and concepts (Evans-Pritchard 1937, 1956; Lienhardt 1961; Campbell 1964; Beidelman 1971; James 1988; Howell 1997), but whenever attempts have been made to generalize in this vein beyond "local moralities" to regions or cultural areas – with honor and shame in the Mediterranean (Peristiany 1965) or hierarchy and purity and pollution in South Asia (Dumont 1980) – problems have been exposed which cast doubt on the original method (Herzfeld 1980). The assumptions of holism and internal homogeneity, and indeed the very concept of plural "cultures" as natural units existing in the world, awaiting description and comparison, have come increasingly to be rejected in anthropology (for just one influential line of argument, see Strathern 1991).

Yet expressions of cultural and moral "relativism," which plainly only make what sense they do on the basis of such assumptions, have played like a leitmotif through the history of anthropology. Edward Westermarck's magisterial two-volume study on *The Origin and Development of Moral Ideas* (1906) puts forward a simple argument: our moral reactions are rooted in natural emotions, but the content of our moral ideas is arbitrary and accepted largely without reflection. A comparative study that demonstrates this will lead us to question and revise those opinions. The followers of Franz Boas developed the idea of cultures each embodying in their socially approved habits a distinctive moral philosophy (Benedict 1935), and these anthropologists' sympathetic portraits of radically "other" moralities were designed as support of moral reform at home (Mead 1928), a rhetorical form later called "cultural critique" (Marcus and Fischer 1986). This was partly in reaction to evolutionary views correlating stages in the development of technology or socio-political forms with advances in moral maturity (Marett 1911; Fürer-Haimendorf 1967), and such views do continue to be advanced (Hallpike 2004). The contradiction involved in seeking to advance non-relative causes and claims by means of assertions of relativism has however caused strain. Nancy Scheper-Hughes is only unusually forthright in asserting both that the primacy of anthropologists' ethical responsibilities should lead them to reject cultural relativism (1995), but also that in order to meet the challenge of exposing ethically objectionable practices (her example being commercial traffic in human organs) "anthropologists must intrude with our cautionary cultural relativism" (2000: 197). Relativism being thought of as a sort of anthropologists' union card has inhibited serious intellectual engagement with ethics.

In much of the above the object of analysis has been conceived of as "local moralities": distinctive moral philosophies embodied in and therefore coextensive with sociocultural entities. Recent writings under the rubric of the anthropology of ethics have begun, by contrast, from the conviction that when people pursue, or act in the light of, conceptions of human excellence or the good, certain distinctive things (including reflective thought) may be going on, that these processes are pervasive and constitutive in human social life, that such diversity as they give rise to may not coincide with what are thought of as societies or cultures, and that prevalent conceptions of society and culture may not readily capture them. To acknowledge and accommodate the prevalence of ethical choice, dilemma, judgment, and conduct, some fairly thorough rethinking may be required of some central concepts in social theory, such as structure, culture, and agency. Many, though not all, of the authors in this field have been influenced by virtue ethics (including Aristotle, especially as interpreted by Alasdair MacIntyre) and/or by the later writings of Michel Foucault.

Michael Lambek (2000, 2002, 2008), for instance, has insisted on what he calls the "ubiquity" of the ethical: the pervasive significance in human life of reflective striving for the good and cultivation of good dispositions; such dispositions being embodied, but at the same time more than mere habit, and requiring the exercise of judgment or practical reason, which he distinguishes insistently from mere acts of choice. Much influential recent anthropological theory, going under the broad designation of "practice theory," has sought to achieve some kind of synthesis between a recognition that human beings are brought to act in the ways they do because of some kind of social or cultural causation on the one hand, and on the other of how they are to some degree autonomous agents (paradigmatic statements include Bourdieu 1990 and Ortner 2006). Lambek has interpreted Aristotle's conception of practical reason as achieving a genuine synthesis between the poles of unthinking habit and self-interested calculation, where practice theory merely oscillates (see Keane 2003). He has suggested that we find distinctive, culturally variable forms of reflective striving for the good embodied in practices, such as spirit possession, which, like ritual in general (Humphrey and Laidlaw 1994), involve "displacements of intentionality," and where, for instance, individuals may make use of culturally authorized media in which to speak in the voice of a conception of the general good.

MacIntyre (1981, 1988) characterizes virtue as the purposeful cultivation of goods that are intrinsic to complex, culturally instituted practices (so "strategic intelligence" in the case of chess, as distinct from the extrinsic wealth or fame one might achieve as a result of success at chess). Thomas Widlok (2004) has suggested that we study ethnographically the way virtues are not bound to "cultures" but manifested wherever the varied practices that embody them are undertaken for their own sake. His analysis of sharing draws analogically on the anthropology of art as skilled performance to show how the distribution of food by San hunters in Namibia can be understood as striving towards a virtue in MacIntyre's sense, one that is at the same time embodied in certain specific practices yet not confined within the boundaries of social or cultural groups. A number of anthropologists have also found helpful MacIntyre's rethinking of the concept of tradition, with Talal Asad (1986) influentially arguing that it is preferable to any conception of plural "cultures." Anand Pandian (2008) has observed that MacIntyre's conception of a tradition, as a set of ongoing arguments embedded and transmitted in practices, relieves us of the false choice of seeing traditions as either unchanging and unquestioned premises on the one hand, or, if not this, somehow inauthentic and "invented"; and he has adapted MacIntyre's conception to interpret aspects of ethical practice in agricultural communities in rural south India as a "fragmented" tradition. MacIntyre makes clear that the arguments that constitute a tradition are not only internal but also with rival traditions, and this gives us a way of understanding positive engagements between hitherto separate traditions, which might as a result either merge or else modify themselves to mimic the other while remaining distinct (Laidlaw forthcoming). These adaptations of ideas from virtue ethics have in common an insistence on the irreducibility of the ethical, in particular its not being comprehensible in terms of the application of social rules and norms or self-interested competition, and a striving to escape the problem situation of ethical relativism.

In his later writings on "the genealogy of ethics," Foucault (1985, 1986, 2000, 2005) explicitly repudiated the idea, with which he had come to be associated, of power as systematic domination, "that leaves no room for freedom." Except at the limit, power relations are always to some extent reciprocal and create possibilities for action on both sides. Indeed, it is only possible properly to speak of power relations insofar as subjects are free (2000: 292). Thus under the single term "subjectivation" (*assujetissement*), Foucault included both interactive processes whereby certain kinds of social subjects are formed in power relations, and practices of self-constitution and self-transformation. This has implications for how one might study systems of morals. Foucault distinguished morality or moral codes – rules that might be imposed, followed, or resisted – from ethics, which are projects for making oneself into a certain kind of person. He argued that from classical antiquity through the rise of Christianity not much changed in the content of prescriptive moral codes (so he rejects the idea that the ancients were "more relaxed" about sex, for example), but ethics, the ways people were enjoined to work on and fashion themselves, changed profoundly: from an aesthetics of existence – an active cultivation of qualities so as to achieve a restrained excellence, in particular in wielding power over others – to a hermeneutics of the subject – a searching, interpretive investigation of one's actions, thoughts, intentions, and desires (1985, 1986, 2005).

Foucault's delimitation of the ethical is not the only one that is of interest to contemporary anthropologists, and nor is his distinction between ethics and morality. Bernard Williams (1985) used the same vocabulary to make an equally useful but different distinction. For him, ethics is any answer to the question, "How ought one to live?" and morality is one particular subset of such answers: those ethical theories (paradigmatically Kantianism, but also, though he did not mention this, Durkheim's theory) that place peculiar stress on notions of obligation, the voluntary, and sentiments of blame (see also Skorupski 1998). So whereas for Foucault "ethics" describes an aspect of morality, for Williams morality is a special case of the broader category of ethics. Both Foucault and Williams were indebted to Nietzsche (1994/1887) in making these different distinctions, and in both cases part of the motivation lay in wishing, as Nietzsche did, to liberate themselves and their readers from the parochialism of equating one kind of value system – in Nietzsche's case specifically self-denying asceticism – with ethics as such. Both distinctions are likely to be of enduring usefulness in an anthropology of ethics that extends beyond the Western traditions to which Foucault and Williams largely confined their attention (Laidlaw 2002), and just because they are different, cross-cutting distinctions, neither should easily rigidify into merely technical jargon, but perhaps in the end different vocabulary will be needed to make these important distinctions.

A further distinction between morality and ethics is proposed by Jarrett Zigon (2007, 2008: 162–6). Zigon characterizes morality as normally taking the form of unconscious habit, such that our conduct is neither thought out beforehand nor even consciously registered as it is gone through. Ethics, by contrast, is brought about by circumstances of "moral breakdown," when some event or person "intrudes" into one's everyday life, requiring reflection and conscious decision on whether and how to act. The end of such "ethical moments" is to enable a return to "the unreflective and unreflexive dispositions of morality," but this requires the creation of new, even if only very slightly new, dispositions, and therefore an altered moral self. Although he associates this account with Foucault's discussion of "problematization," Zigon's ideas are importantly different. Foucault's ethics–morality distinction does not imply separate subject matters; so he described ethics as "another side of the moral prescriptions, which most of the time is not isolated as such" (2000: 263). Problematization is therefore not an isolated or occasional event or episode; it is an aspect of any ongoing form of life. Foucault reflected that his studies of madness, criminality, and sexuality seemed in retrospect to be variously successful attempts to examine each of these phenomena along the three axes that characterize any "matrix of experience" (2000: 204): as domains of knowledge, as systems of institutionalized rules, and as models of the relation one has to oneself. Where he had erred was in underemphasizing the third of these dimensions. Different forms of morality vary not in whether or how intensely problematization occurs, but in the particular form it takes. Throughout late antiquity as described in Foucault's later lectures and books, the forms of problematization vary considerably, but there is no time at which nothing is problematized. And crucially, the point of the many techniques of the self he described is to fashion the self in terms of a particular current problematization. Foucault postulated no state of untroubled tranquility such as Zigon holds to be "our everyday way of being." The latter idea seems to owe more to Bourdieu's (1990) concepts of "habitus" and "doxa," according to which the crucial determinants of human conduct are unavailable to consciousness, and indeed social systems can only function because and insofar as subjects are systematically ignorant or mistaken about them. Zigon's distinction – which unlike Foucault's and Williams' is a dichotomy between mutually exclusive terms – reduces ethics once again to a merely functional role in the reproduction of a society/culture to which, in "everyday" circumstances, the reflective practice of freedom is at best incidental.

Foucault suggested that techniques of the self have existed in every civilization (2000: 87), and proposed a four-part analytical framework for the comparative study of ethical projects (2000: 263ff.). He distinguished the part of the self that is the object of ethical attention (ontology), from the mode in which that attention is directed (deontology), the techniques used to work on the self (ascetics), and the state of the self the project is directed towards realizing (teleology). If only a few studies (e.g. Laidlaw 1995; Rabinow 1996; Faubion 2001a, c) have made systematic use of this framework, Foucault's highlighting of ethical projects as objects of description has been formative. In addition to studies of religious traditions that have highlighted diverse or changing ethical projects embedded in ostensibly or assertively unchanging moral codes (Asad 1993; Laidlaw 1995; Lester

2005; Mahmood 2005; Hirschkind 2006; Mair 2007; J. Cook forthcoming), anthropologists have described techniques of the self in diverse forms of ethical life: Mongols living under Maoist repression choosing human exemplars as reference points in making life decisions (Humphrey 1997); the Urapmin people in Papua New Guinea, recently converted to Pentecostal Christianity, coping with the moral torment of two mutually condemnatory moral codes which they experience as simultaneously applicable to them (Robbins 2004, 2007); and scientists engaged in the reflective cultivation of distinctive kinds of subjectivity, by practicing and as means to achieving distinctive forms of detachment and engagement (Daston and Galison 2007; Candea forthcoming). And Faubion (2001c) has persuasively argued that while kinship systems always involve some degree of subjection, with relationships and statuses appearing as given or naturalized in various ways, they are never this exclusively, and kinship relations are typically also media and means of self-cultivation. Indeed, the apparent relative securities of kinship may appeal all the more forcibly the more the self, as in liberal societies or cosmopolitan situations, is not merely able but positively obliged to "make something of itself."

Such ethical projects exist only insofar as prevalent modes of domination leave room for some reflective practice of freedom. While Foucault insisted that the ubiquity of power indicated that we are always to some extent free (2000: 167), we are certainly not all equally free. And he proposed an image for the possibility, however remote, of the space for ethics being wholly extinguished. A slave who lived under total domination, so that his or her every act could be only as someone else's agent, would have no ethics (2000: 286). While this is not incompatible with Lambek's stress on the "ubiquity" of ethical judgment, it usefully raises as an ethnographical question the scope and resources people have, in particular contexts, to engage in projects of self-constitution and to exercise ethical judgment. But the notion of degrees of freedom or of scope for choice, while indispensable, is in itself insufficient and even hazardous. It is too easy to think of liberal societies as affording just more freedom of choice than their predecessors or alternatives. As Asad points out, discussing the reconfiguration of law and ethics in colonial Egypt, many new legal restrictions were introduced (state regulation of age of marriage, restrictions on polygamy, registration of marriage and divorce, etc.) and some social relations (such as those with children) became subject to new forms of anxiety and administrative regulation (2003: 226). The liberal notion of "private life" is not just an increase in a homogeneous "room for choice," but a new kind of ethical space, one in which we are not just permitted but enjoined and even legally obliged to exercise freedom and self-government (see also Rose 1999). Anthropology can describe how freedom comes not only in degrees but also in qualitatively different, historically constituted forms (Laidlaw 2002).

Two ethnographic studies have discerned sophisticated ethical projects of self-constitution in apparently authoritarian schools of religious "fundamentalism." These are respectively Faubion's (2001a) study of a follower of the Branch Davidian sect, conducted in the aftermath of the Waco massacre, and the separately published but collaboratively produced studies by Mahmood (2005) and Hirschkind (2006) of Islamic reformist revivalism in Cairo. Both draw substantially on Foucault's writings on ethics; Mahmood and Hirschkind also on MacIntyre's on tradition. Thus far similar, these studies also pose interesting questions for each other.

Faubion (2001b, following Foucault 2000: 298–9), makes a convincing case for pedagogy as the foundational ethical relationship and although all such relationships begin with subordination and proceed through constraint, he offers as a criterion for genuinely ethical pedagogic relationships that their trajectory be one in which the pupil is led towards autonomy from the teacher. His understanding of the engagement his principal interlocutor has had with Branch Davidian millennialism as constituting ethics turns substantially on his estimation of her achievement of autonomy, in spite of considerable adversity (Faubion 2001a). The importance placed on autonomy in this general argument needs to be clarified and qualified. There are many institutionalized ethical projects whose *telos* is some kind of ascetic ideal of autonomy – eremitical ideals of purity, cutting of worldly ties and affections, and so on, some of which are realizable only with death (Laidlaw 2005) – but nothing of the kind is necessarily intended here. In myriad social contexts, autonomy may be and much more usually is achieved through and not in spite of relations with others (an exceptional study is Riesman 1977/1974). For a student to attain autonomy through a pedagogical relationship does not imply or require ending that relationship, or ending relations of dependence on others. In addition, as virtue ethicists, following Aristotle, have emphasized, periods of intense dependence, including in childhood, sickness, and old age, are a normal part of the human condition. So it is a mistake to build accounts of ethics on the image only of a young adult in perfect health (Hursthouse 1999; MacIntyre 1999). Nevertheless, it is equally true that these periods of dependence are developmentally connected to ideals of autonomy, and Faubion's criterion for genuine pedagogy has at least *prima facie* plausibility. Yet Mahmood and Hirschkind both emphasize that the projects they describe, although they begin with reflective decisions on the part of those who join these movements, are directed towards making submission an unreflective, embodied disposition, a pre-subjective and pre-conscious "instinct." For many (women especially) success in pursuing these projects will preclude rather than enable their ever joining or being peers of their teachers. If this is so, does their *telos* include the eradication of precisely that practice of freedom which was its precondition? So does this show, as Mahmood and Hirschkind might claim, that Faubion's (and Foucault's) criterion is ethnocentric? Or should we query Mahmood and Hirschkind's claim that the end as well as the beginning of these projects is properly speaking ethical?

T. M. S. Evens' account of "anthropology as ethics" (2008) attempts to realize anew the Durkheimian ambition of showing how the ethical is constitutive of the human condition. Anthropology's attempts to grasp this have been hampered by what Evens calls a dualist ontology, an intrinsically anti-ethical but pervasive feature of Western culture, which he identifies with the legacy of Greek science. Anthropology can transcend this by being itself an ethical enterprise, which, following Levinas (1998/1991), Evens understands as openness to the other. This theme is developed most particularly through a reading of the meaning of sacrifice in Judaic, Christian, and certain African religious traditions. Thus anthropology, like ethics, is engaging with and taking the perspective of the other: a self-transcending engagement that does not involve a return to how one was (an Exodus rather than an Odyssey); and a sacrifice, insofar as it involves a "self-deconstruction on behalf of the other." Evens concludes with the admirable thought that "the endeavour to learn *about* another culture needs to be founded, directly and knowingly, on the endeavour to learn *from* that culture" (2008: 284), although this ambition is not one that anthropology can claim exclusively (Kupperman 1999). And there may be ways of achieving something of this kind, without depending on the problematical concept of "another culture," and without the despite-itself intensely dualist ascetic self-abasement before the other.

For instance, Williams (1993) uses reflection on Greek ideas of responsibility and agency, as embodied in epic and tragedy, to alert us to the fact that our reflective thought, practical judgment, and experience are richer and more subtle than some of our own philosophical theories about responsibility and agency would indicate. Williams employs a genealogical method – in which the form of life studied is not conceived as exclusive of, and contrasted with, the ethical horizon of the analyst (and reader), but as a means by which to reflect upon and enlarge it. This may be contrasted with that deployed in a classic paper by Kenneth Read (1955) on the concept of the person among the Gahuku Gama of Papua New Guinea. Read's is in many ways an insightful portrait of moral life, but is structured as a contrast between "them" and "us"; our ethics being characterized as "moral universalism," as "exemplified by Christianity." Among "them" obligations are recognized, but only "distributively," by which Read means that obligations only arise, as it were, relationship by relationship. Since there is no notion of the "invariant ethical value" of each individual, and no obligations that bind simply in virtue of this, there is "no moral universalism" and this means, Read assumes, that there is no notion of obligation that is properly speaking moral. Of course, what Read is comparing Gahuku-Gama practice to is not "our" practice but a descriptively poor and prescriptively disabling brand of moral theory that would require us to regard our obligations to our closest family and friends as no greater than those to people we have never met, and would hold that our preference for the former is simply an absence of morality. We could equally well deploy Read's perceptive description of Gahuku-Gama life, in the manner of Williams, to highlight ways in which our reflective practice resembles theirs, and how we conduct ourselves in ways that are more complex and sophisticated than some of our theories tell us we do or should. That would be one non-relativist way to learn from as well as about "others." Placing ourselves in a genuinely pedagogical relationship to the ethnography would lead, as Faubion suggests pedagogical relationships in general should, to overcoming the heuristic opposition between self and other, making the study of other forms of ethical life itself a form of self-fashioning.

See also Ethical thought in China (Chapter 1); Ethical thought in India (Chapter 2); Aristotle (Chapter 4); The Arabic tradition (Chapter 6); Kant (Chapter 14); Nietzsche (Chapter 18); Freedom and responsibility (Chapter 23); Relativism (Chapter 30); Virtue ethics (Chapter 40).

References

Alter, J. S. (2004) *Yoga in Modern India: The Body between Science and Philosophy*, Princeton, NJ: Princeton University Press.

Asad, T. (1986) *The Idea of an Anthropology of Islam*, Washington, DC: Center for Contemporary Arab Studies, Georgetown University.

——(1993) *Genealogies of Religion: Discipline and Reasons of Power in Christianity and Islam*, Baltimore, MD: Johns Hopkins University Press.

——(2003) *Formations of the Secular: Christianity, Islam, Modernity*, Stanford, CA: Stanford University Press.

Beidelman, T. O. (ed.) (1971) *The Translation of Culture: Essays to E. E. Evans-Pritchard*, London: Tavistock.

Benedict, R. (1935) *Patterns of Culture*, London: Routledge.

Bloch, M. (1989) *Ritual, History, and Power*, London: Athlone.

Bourdieu, P. (1990) *The Logic of Practice*, Oxford: Polity Press.

Campbell, J. K. (1964) *Honour, Family, and Patronage: A Study of Institutions and Moral Values in a Greek Mountain Village*, Oxford: Oxford University Press.

Candea, M. (Forthcoming) "'I Fell in Love with Carlos the Meerkat': Engagement and Detachment in Human–Animal Relations," *American Ethnologist*.

Carrithers, M. (1985) "An Alternative Social History of the Self," in M. Carrithers, S. Collins and S. Lukes (eds) *The Category of the Person: Anthropology, Philosophy, History*, Cambridge: Cambridge University Press, pp. 234–56.

Cook, J. (Forthcoming) *Meditation and Monasticism: Making the Ascetic Self in Thailand*, Cambridge: Cambridge University Press.

Cook, J. D. (1999) *Morality and Cultural Differences*, New York: Oxford University Press.

Daston, L. and Galison, P. (2007) *Objectivity*, Brooklyn, NY: Zone Books.

Dumont, L. (1980) *Homo Hierarchicus: The Caste System and Its Implications*, Chicago, IL: University of Chicago Press.

Durkheim, E. (1915/1912) *The Elementary Forms of the Religious Life*, London: Allen & Unwin.

——(1953/1906) "The Determination of Moral Facts," in *Sociology and Philosophy*, London: Routledge: 35–62.

——(1973/1899) "Individualism and the Intellectuals," in *Emile Durkheim on Morality and Society*, ed. R. Bellah, Chicago, IL: University of Chicago Press, pp. 43–57.

——(1979/1920) "Introduction to Ethics," in W. S. F. Pickering (ed.) *Essays on Morals and Education*, London: Routledge, pp. 77–96.

Edel, M. and Edel, A. (1959) *Anthropology and Ethics: The Quest for Moral Understanding*, Cleveland, OH: Press of Case Western.

Evans-Pritchard, E. (1937) *Witchcraft, Oracles, and Magic among the Azande*, Oxford: Clarendon Press.
——(1956) *Nuer Religion*, Oxford: Clarendon Press.
——(1962) *Essays in Social Anthropology*, London: Routledge.
Evens, T. M. S. (2008) *Anthropology as Ethics: Nondualism and the Conduct of Sacrifice*, Oxford: Berghahn Books.
Faubion, J. D. (2001a) *The Shadows and Lights of Waco: Millennialism Today*, Princeton, NJ: Princeton University Press.
——(2001b) "Toward an Anthropology of Ethics: Foucault and the Pedagogies of Autopoesis," *Representations* 74: 83–104.
——(ed.) (2001c) *The Ethics of Kinship: Ethnographic Inquiries*, Lanham, MD: Rowman & Littlefield.
Firth, R. (1951) "Moral Standards and Social Organization," in *Elements of Social Organization*, London: Athlone, pp. 206–24.
——(1953) "The Study of Values by Social Anthropologists," *Journal of the Royal Anthropological Institute* 53: 146–53.
Fiske, A. P. and Mason, K. F. (eds) (1990) *Ethos* 18, no. 2. (Special issue on ethical relativism.)
Fortes, M. (1959) *Oedipus and Job in West African Religion*, Cambridge: Cambridge University Press.
——(1977) "Custom and Conscience in Anthropological Perspective," *International Review of Psycho-Analysis* 4: 127–54.
Foucault, M. (1985) *The Use of Pleasure*, vol. 2 of *The History of Sexuality*, New York: Random House.
——(1986) *The Care of the Self*, vol 3 of *The History of Sexuality*, New York: Random House.
——(2000) *Essential Works*, vol. 1: *Ethics*, Harmondsworth: Penguin Books.
——(2005) *The Hermeneutics of the Subject: Lectures at the Collège de France 1981–1982*, New York: Palgrave Macmillan.
Fürer-Haimendorf, C. von (1967) *Morals and Merit: A Study of Moral Values and Social Controls in South Asian Societies*, London: Weidenfeld & Nicolson.
Gluckman, M. (ed.) (1972) *The Allocation of Responsibility*, Manchester, UK: Manchester University Press.
Hallpike, C. R. (2004) *The Evolution of Moral Understanding*, London: Prometheus.
Hatch, E. (1983) *Culture and Morality: The Relativity of Values in Anthropology*, New York: Columbia University Press.
Herzfeld, M. (1980) "Honour and Shame: Problems in the Comparative Analysis of Moral Systems," *Man*, n.s. 15: 339–51.
Hirschkind, C. (2006) *The Ethical Soundscape: Cassette Sermons and Islamic Counterpublics*, New York: Columbia University Press.
Howell, S. (ed.) (1997) *The Anthropology of Moralities*, London: Routledge.
Humphrey, C. (1997) "Exemplars and Rules: Aspects of the Discourse of Moralities in Mongolia," in S. Howell (ed.) *The Anthropology of Moralities*, London: Routledge, pp. 25–47.
Humphrey, C. and Laidlaw, J. (1994) *The Archetypal Actions of Ritual: A Theory of Ritual Illustrated by the Jain Rite of Worship*, Oxford: Clarendon Press.
Hursthouse, R. (1999) *On Virtue Ethics*, Oxford: Clarendon Press.
James, W. (1988) *The Listening Ebony: Moral Knowledge, Religion, and Power among the Uduk of Sudan*, Oxford: Clarendon Press.
Keane, W. (2003) "Self-interpretation, Agency, and the Objects of Anthropology: Reflections on a Genealogy," *Comparative Studies in Society and History* 45: 222–48.
Kupperman, J. J. (1999) *Learning From Asian Philosophy*, New York: Oxford University Press.
Ladd, J. (1957) *The Structure of a Moral Code: A Philosophical Analysis of Ethical Discourse Applied to the Ethics of the Navaho Indians*, Cambridge, MA: Harvard University Press.

Laidlaw, J. (1995) *Riches and Renunciation: Religion, Economy, and Society among the Jains*, Oxford: Clarendon Press.

——(2002) "For an Anthropology of Ethics and Freedom," *Journal of the Royal Anthropological Institute* 8: 311–32.

——(2005) "A Life Worth Leaving: Fasting to Death as Telos of a Jain Religious Life," *Economy and Society* 34: 178–99.

——(Forthcoming) "Whose Virtues? Which Forms of Knowledge? Ethical Choices for Contemporary Jains," in D. Ali and A. Pandian (eds) *Ethical Life in South Asia*, Bloomington, IN: Indiana University Press.

Lambek, M. (2000) "The Anthropology of Religion and the Quarrel between Poetry and Philosophy," *Current Anthropology* 41: 309–20.

——(2002) "Nuriaty, the Saint and the Sultan: Virtuous Subject and Subjective Virtuoso of the Postmodern Colony," in R. Werbner (ed.) *Postcolonial Subjectivities in Africa*, London: Routledge: 25–43.

——(2008) "Value and Virtue," *Anthropological Theory* 8: 133–57.

Lester, R. J. (2005) *Jesus in Our Wombs: Embodying Modernity in a Mexican Convent*, Berkeley: University of California Press.

Levinas, E. (1998/1991) *Entre Nous: Essays on Thinking-of-the-Other*, New York: Columbia University Press.

Lienhardt, R. G. (1961) *Divinity and Experience: The Religion of the Dinka*, Oxford: Clarendon Press.

MacBeath, A. (1952) *Experiments in Living: A Study of the Nature and Foundation of Ethics or Morals in the Light of Recent Work in Social Anthropology*, London: Macmillan.

MacIntyre, A. (1981) *After Virtue: A Study in Moral Theory*, London: Duckworth.

——(1988) *Whose Justice? Which Rationality?* London: Duckworth.

——(1999) *Dependent Rational Animals: Why Human Beings Need the Virtues*, London: Duckworth.

Mahmood, S. (2005) *Politics of Piety: The Islamic Revival and the Feminist Subject*, Princeton, NJ: Princeton University Press.

Mair, J. (2007) "Faith, Knowledge and Ignorance in Contemporary Inner Mongolian Buddhism," PhD diss., University of Cambridge.

Marcus, G. E. and Fischer, M. M. J. (1986) *Anthropology as Cultural Critique: An Experimental Moment in the Human Sciences*, Chicago, IL: University of Chicago Press.

Marett, R. R. (1911) "Rudimentary Ethics," in J. Hastings (ed.) *Encyclopaedia of Religion and Ethics*, Edinburgh: T.&T. Clark.

Mauss, M. (1985/1938) "A Category of the Human Mind: The Notion of the Person; The Notion of Self," in M. Carrithers, S. Collins and S. Lukes (eds) *The Category of the Person: Anthropology, Philosophy, History*, Cambridge: Cambridge University Press, pp. 1–25.

Mead, M. (1928) *Coming of Age in Samoa*, New York: Morrow.

Moody-Adams, M. M. (1997) *Fieldwork in Familiar Places: Morality, Culture, and Philosophy*, Cambridge, MA: Harvard University Press.

Nietzsche, F. (1994/1887) *On the Genealogy of Morality*, Cambridge: Cambridge University Press.

Ortner, S. B. (2006) *Anthropology and Social Theory: Culture, Power, and the Acting Subject*, Durham, NC: Duke University Press.

Pandian, A. (2008) "Tradition in Fragments: Inherited Forms and Fractures in the Ethics of South India," *American Ethnologist* 35: 1–15.

Parry, J. and Bloch, M. (1989) *Money and the Morality of Exchange*, Cambridge: Cambridge University Press.

Peristiany, J. G (ed.) (1965) *Honour and Shame: The Values of Mediterranean Society*, London: Weidenfeld & Nicolson.

Pocock, D. (1986) "The Ethnography of Morals," *International Journal of Moral and Social Studies* 1: 3–20.

Rabinow, P. (1996) *Essays on the Anthropology of Reason*, Princeton, NJ: Princeton University Press.

Read, K. E. (1955) "Morality and the Concept of the Person among the Gahuku-Gama," *Oceania* 25: 233–82.

Riesman, P. (1977/1974) *Freedom in Fulani Life: An Introspective Ethnography*, Chicago, IL: University of Chicago Press.

Robbins, J. (2004) *Becoming Sinners: Christianity and Moral Torment in a Papua New Guinea Society*, Berkeley: University of California Press.

——(2007) "Between Reproduction and Freedom: Morality, Value, and Radical Cultural Change," *Ethnos* 72: 293–314.

Rose, N. (1990) *Governing the Soul: The Shaping of the Private Self*, London: Routledge.

——(1996) *Inventing Our Selves: Psychology, Power, and Personhood*, Cambridge: Cambridge University Press.

——(1999) *Powers of Freedom: Reframing Political Thought*, Cambridge: Cambridge University Press.

Scheper-Hughes, N. (1995) "The Primacy of the Ethical: Propositions for a Militant Anthropology," *Current Anthropology* 36: 409–20.

——(2000) "The Global Traffic in Human Organs," *Current Anthropology* 41: 191–224.

Scott, J. (1977) *The Moral Economy of the Peasant: Rebellion and Subsistence in South-East Asia*, New Haven, CT: Yale University Press.

Seigel, J. (2005) *The Idea of the Self: Thought and Experience in Western Europe since the Seventeenth Century*, Cambridge: Cambridge University Press.

Skorupski, J. (1998) "Morality and Ethics," in E. J. Craig (ed.) *Routledge Encyclopedia of Philosophy*, London: Routledge.

Strathern, M. (1991) *Partial Connections*, Walnut Creek, CA: Rowman & Littlefield.

Strauss, S. (2005) *Positioning Yoga: Balancing Acts Across Cultures*, Oxford: Berg.

Taussig, M. J. (1980) *The Devil and Commodity Fetishism in South America*, Chapel Hill, NC: University of North Carolina Press.

Taylor, C. (1989) *Sources of the Self: The Making of the Modern Identity*, Cambridge: Cambridge University Press.

Westermarck, E. (1906) *The Origin and Development of the Moral Ideas*, London: Macmillan.

——(1932) *Ethical Relativity*, London: Kegan Paul.

Widlok, T. (2004) "Sharing by Default: Outline of an Anthropology of Virtue," *Anthropological Theory* 4: 53–70.

Williams, B. (1985) *Ethics and the Limits of Philosophy*, London: Collins.

——(1993) *Shame and Necessity*, Berkeley: University of California Press.

Wolfram, S. (1982) "Anthropology and Morality," *Journal of the Anthropological Society of Oxford* 13: 262–74.

Zigon, J. (2007) "Moral Breakdown and Ethical Demand: A Theoretical Framework for an Anthropology of Moralities," *Anthropological Theory* 7: 131–50.

——(2008) *Morality: An Anthropological Perspective*, Oxford: Berg.

Further reading

Heintz, M. (ed.) (2009) *The Anthropology of Moralities*, Oxford: Berghahn Books. (A conference collection containing a mixed bag of contributions – not all of them in harmony with the editorial prospectus – exemplifies the range of approaches currently being developed: some brilliant and original proposals are explained and illustrated.)

Pandian, A. (2009) *Crooked Stalks: Cultivating Virtue in South India*, Durham, NC: Duke University Press. (The Piramalai Kallar caste was formally designated a "criminal tribe" in late colonial times. Ethical life among them today has been shaped by various governmental schemes designed to implement moral "development," but also draws on a rich range of indigenous resources. A complex tradition of "cultivation" is embedded in everyday practices, including agricultural labor.)

Rogers, D. (2009) *The Old Faith and the Russian Land: A Historical Ethnography of Ethics in the Urals*, Ithaca, NY: Cornell University Press. (A community of refugee religious dissenters – Old Believers – in a small town in the Urals has drawn with remarkable persistence on an "ethical repertoire" of sensibilities, dispositions, and expectations, through three centuries of Tsarist repression, Soviet anti-religious campaigns and forced collectivization, and post-Soviet religious revival and economic and political turbulence.)

32
ETHICS AND PSYCHOLOGY

Jesse Prinz

Historically, philosophers have had a great deal of interest in science. Thinkers as diverse as Aristotle, Descartes, and Berkeley made important contributions to a range of scientific fields. In more recent times, however, philosophers have often had an anti-scientific (or perhaps trans-scientific) orientation. Nowhere is this attitude more keenly felt than in moral philosophy. Here, it is sometimes suggested that the very nature of the subject matter defies empirical inquiry. Morality is normative. It describes how things should be, not how they are. And moral rules, like rules of logic, are necessary, unlike the contingent regularities with which scientists are typically preoccupied. Kant (1998/1785: Preface) expresses this attitude in an influential passage:

> Now it is only a pure philosophy that we can look for the moral law in its purity and genuineness. ... That which mingles these pure principles with the empirical does not deserve the name of ... moral philosophy, since by this confusion it even spoils the purity of morals themselves, and counteracts its own end.

Despite this widespread view, social scientists have recently taken a serious interest in morality. Whatever one wants to say about normativity, there are obviously aspects of human behavior that issue from the moral values we hold dear, and these can be empirically investigated. Philosophers who study this work (and, at times, contribute to it) are coming to realize that psychological findings may actually bear on philosophical theories (Flanagan 1991; Doris 2002; Nichols 2004; Sripada and Stich 2005; Prinz 2007; Sinnott-Armstrong 2009/2008). That will be the claim defended and illustrated in this chapter.

The subject of moral philosophy has traditional subdivisions. Some study moral psychology (the way people think about the moral domain), others study meta-ethics (the ultimate metaphysical basis of our moral claims), and others study normative ethics (the question of what we ought to do or how we ought to be). Now it might be taken as obvious that scientific psychology can contribute to moral psychology. But even here there is some resistance, as we will see. Less obvious is the contention that scientific psychology can contribute to meta-ethics, since meta-ethics concerns what, if anything, makes our moral convictions true, not the convictions themselves. And equally controversial is the claim that scientific psychology can contribute to normative ethics, because psychology is in the business of description, not prescription. I will try to show that scientific psychology contributes to all three subdivisions, though I will spend most of the discussion on the first. My claim will not be that philosophy should be replaced by psychology. Rather, I think the two work in concert. To echo Kant in another context, theory without data is empty, and data without theory are blind.

Internalism, externalism, and empirical inquiry

Moral psychology is the study of psychological states associated with morality. Broad topics include moral motivation, emotion, deliberation, and development. Many of these are studied in psychology. For example, there is a massive literature on moral development, which has clear connections to philosophy: Aristotle writes about moral development, and the most influential psychologist in the area, Lawrence Kohlberg (1984), argued that children progress through a series of developmental stages that mirror major theories in normative ethics (from Aristotle to Mill to Kant). But there are also some topics in moral psychology that have been dominated by philosophical discussion, and, in some of these cases, there is an implicit assumption that empirical psychology may not be especially helpful. This is especially the case when issues in moral psychology turn on conceptual claims. It is philosophers, not psychologists, who purport to specialize in conceptual analysis. Claims in moral psychology that have a conceptual dimension have, therefore, been approached without drawing heavily on empirical evidence. I think this is a mistake.

To make this case, I will focus on a central controversy in moral psychology: the debate between motive externalists and motive internalists. A motive externalist says that motivation is independent from moral judgment, so that when one makes a moral judgment one is not, thereby, motivated to act in accordance with that judgment. Motive internalists, on the other hand, say that there is a necessary connection between moral judgment and motivation. Sometimes this connection is presented as the view that moral judgments are intrinsically motivating: if I judge that charity is good, I am thereby in a motivational state that disposes me to give to charity. This link may be defeasible, because there may be countervailing interests that prevent one from acting on or even experiencing one's moral motivations. But, barring weakness of will or other forms of practical irrationality, moral judgments compel action, according to the internalist (Smith 1994).

On the face of it, this may look like a straightforward empirical debate. Either moral judgments motivate, or they do not, and whether they do can be tested in a psychology lab. But philosophers who have weighed in on the debate have rarely looked at empirical psychology. Let's put aside the possibility that philosophers are lazy, methodologically reckless, ill-equipped to understand psychology, or irrationally biased against other fields. Philosophers think there are two good reasons to approach the debate from the armchair. First, they note that the debate is conceptual. Internalists claim that there is a *necessary* connection between morality and motivation; one *could not* make a moral judgment without being disposed to act. This modal claim is supposed to derive from a conceptual truth – something about our moral concept. The concept of moral goodness is supposed to entail something relating to motivation, and conceptual truths are best discovered using conceptual analysis, rather than empirical observation. Call the view expressed in the last sentence the conceptual thesis.

The second reason for resisting empirical approaches is that the opposing views may make similar empirical predictions. Externalists admit that moral judgments are typically associated with motivational states. Most of us desire to act in accordance with morality, so when we make moral judgments we are motivated. They simply claim that this link is causal rather than constitutive. Likewise, internalists admit that we are not always practically rational. As a result, the motivational states that should come along with moral judgments can fail to arise. The connection is dispositional and the dispositions are not realized in every case. Thus, empirical evidence showing that motivations arise in the context of moral judgment would not entail internalism, and evidence to the contrary would not entail externalism. Call this the empirical intractability thesis. The conceptual thesis relates to the empirical intractability thesis in the following way. According to the conceptual thesis, the debate between internalists and externalists is a conceptual or semantic debate, concerning the meaning or moral concepts. Psychology tells us about causes and correlations, not conceptual constituency. Therefore, psychological findings just can't settle the debate.

Let me address these two concerns in turn. First, consider the conceptual thesis, which says that the debate in question should be investigated using conceptual analysis rather than empirical methods. This is problematic for two reasons. First, the contrast between conceptual and empirical matters is a version of the analytic/synthetic distinction. To say that a debate is conceptual is to say that it is a debate about the analytic entailment of a concept. Since Quine's (1953) critique, the notion of analyticity has been called into question. While it is often the case that people understand one concept by appeal to another, these associations are characteristically revisable in light of empirical evidence. Thus, scientific discoveries might lead me to believe that aardvarks are not animals (perhaps they are robots sent to spy on us from another planet), red is not a color (rather it is an experience caused in me by a colorless world), and some bachelors are not male (there may be people with XX chromosomes who look and act male, but are really women). Concepts are something like mini-theories that correspond to our best guess about how the world is, and they are subject to revision. If my theory of morality specifies that moral judgments are motivating, this is not an analytic truth, but a conjecture that, like any other belief about morality, might be empirically challenged. If this view of concepts is right, conceptual analysis cannot resolve the debate about internalism.

Now suppose Quine was wrong and there are analytic entailments. The second problem with the conceptual thesis is that it mistakenly presupposes that conceptual truths should be studied using non-empirical methods. I claim, in contrast, that conceptual questions *are* empirical questions. The reason is simple: concepts (according to the majority view in the philosophy of mind and cognitive science) are mental representations, and mental representations can be empirically studied. Indeed, there is a massive research area in psychology that studies concepts, and there is absolutely no reason for thinking these research methods can't be applied to moral concepts. If we want to discover what a given concept entails, we can ask ordinary concept users or we measure their behavior when those concepts are being used.

Someone might object that pure philosophical methods are *better* for studying concepts than psychological methods. Philosophers are adept at devising carefully constructed thought experiments, and these can be used to distinguish those features that are merely associated with a given concept and those that are really essential to it. Against this move, I offer three remarks: first, philosophical methods *are* a form of empirical psychology, namely introspective psychology. Philosophers report their intuitions about cases, and intuitions are arrived at by observing one's own psychological states. Second, philosophical thought experiments can be given to untutored subjects and doing so has some advantages over philosophers reporting their own intuitions. Philosophers' intuitions are not theory neutral, which is one reason why philosophers seem to have different intuitions about the same cases, and, even if philosophers can miraculously free themselves from bias, they will be reporting a sample of one, rather than attaining statistical significance by measuring responses in a population. Third, reporting intuitions about what a given concept entails is a measure of our *beliefs* about conceptual entailments, rather than the entailments themselves. To know what a concept entails, the real question is not what I believe it entails, but what features are necessarily applied when the concept is actually used. One can think about concepts as structured entities that contain other concepts (or "features") as parts. My beliefs about what features are part of a given concept may be mistaken. A measure of what features get deployed when the concept is used (rather than reflected upon) would be informative. Psychological methods are useful for that.

Let me turn, now, to the empirical intractability thesis. Psychological research is best equipped to study correlations and causal relations. Now suppose that psychology discovers that people enter motivational states when they make moral judgments: this would not entail internalism. And the opposite discovery would not entail externalism. Is there a way out of this impasse? One thing to notice is that empirical science obeys different rules of evidence than some areas of philosophy. The gold standard here is argument to the best explanation. Suppose that motivational states accompany moral judgments most of the time. Suppose this even happens in people who are (like most of us) selfish. Suppose too that it even happens in laboratory situations where the opportunity for action is limited and the cases are hypothetical. This would be *predicted* by internalism. Externalists might suppose that most people are motivated to act morally, but, because motivation is external to moral judgment on this view, motivational states are not predicted to arise when action is not an option.

Second of all, there may be a couple of ways to tease the two accounts empirically apart. For one thing, suppose that the induction of motivational states that have no connection to morality actually influence a person's judgment about what is morally good or bad. This is consistent with internalism, for internalists say that moral judgments essentially involve motivational states. Influencing such states might, on such a view, influence emotions. By comparison imagine an internalist view of humor judgments according to which such judgments essentially involve states of amusement. If such views are correct, then tickling someone should influence their assessment of how funny something is, because it amplifies feelings of amusement. Now suppose that externalism is true. If so, assessments of moral goodness and badness are independent of emotion. Most of us are motivated to act on such judgments, but that motivation is not part of the judgment. Thus, induction of motivational states should affect willingness to act, not the content of evaluation. Likewise, if an externalist theory of humor judgments is correct, then tickling should not influence how funny things seem, only how much we laugh.

Another way to empirically tease apart externalism and internalism is to consider what happens in cases of motivational impairment. If externalism is true, a profound deficit in motivation should not undermine the capacity to make moral judgments. If internalism is true, such a disruption is not entailed (the link between judgment and motivation is defeasible), but it would be predicted (motivational dispositions are part of conceptual competence).

In summary, even if some empirical findings can be accommodated by both internalists and externalists, one of these accounts may offer the better overall explanation. In addition, some empirical findings may be extremely difficult for one of the two accounts to accommodate. One of these accounts could turn out to provide the *only* explanation.

Empirical evidence for internalism

To empirically investigate the debate between internalism and externalism, it is important to gain some clarity on the notion of "motivation." How, according to internalists, do moral judgments motivate? The standard answer is that they motivate by means of emotions. Emotions are motivating states, and many philosophers propose that moral concepts have an emotional foundation (e.g., Hume, Adam Smith, Ayer, Stevenson, Williams, Blackburn, Gibbard, to name a few). So the hypothesis that moral judgments are motivating can be tested by investigating the more specific claim that moral judgments essentially involve emotions.

There are various ways to address this question empirically. One strategy is to find an empirical test for a conceptual link between moral judgment and motivation (recall my assertion that conceptual analysis can be done empirically). Toward this end, I designed such a study, in which subjects read two vignettes. One involved a student, Frank, in a fraternity who verbally insists that he thinks marijuana smoking is morally wrong, but never feels badly when he or others smoke. The other vignette involves a student, Fred, in a fraternity who insists that marijuana smoking is morally permissible, but feels badly when he or others smoke. The question is, do either Fred or Frank believe that marijuana smoking is bad? In both cases, my subjects overwhelmingly tracked the emotions. They said Frank thinks marijuana smoking is fine, because he doesn't feel badly about it, and Fred thinks marijuana smoking is bad, despite his verbal testimony. Also consider a study by Nichols (2002). He found that people would not attribute an understanding of morality to a mathematician who lacked emotional responses. Subjects did attribute moral understanding to a psychopathic killer who was described as lacking emotions, but, Nichols reasons, this may derive from their strong desire to see the killer punished. In an unpublished follow-up study, I described a psychopath who lacks emotions and commits a very minor crime. Few of my subjects attributed moral understanding. These studies may not be decisive, but they suggest that our ordinary intuitions strongly link emotions to morality: we generally attribute moral judgments when and only when emotions are present. Limitations on this generalization could be brought out by further studies.

Above I said that our intuitions may not reveal what processes actually take place when people make moral judgments. Here, again, empirical research is helpful. For example, there are now numerous neuroimaging studies showing that, when people make moral judgments, brain areas associated with emotion are active. Greene et al. (2001) gave people moral dilemmas and non-moral dilemmas and found emotion areas active during reflection on the former, not the latter. Moll et al. (2002) asked subjects to make moral or factual wrongness judgments, and found emotional activations during the moral cases. Heekeren et al. (2003) showed people morally significant photographs and found that emotion areas light up. The pattern has been consistent in this research. The intuition that emotions arise in the context of moral judgment is empirically confirmed.

Such results are not predicted on externalist theories, because the cases involved are hypothetical. Subjects are not expected to act (quite the contrary), and there is no reason to think that a general desire to do what morality demands would lead to emotional responses in cases where morality demands nothing of us – passive reflection on imaginary situations. The results are even difficult to square with some forms of internalism. Consider internalist theories that posit a rational as opposed to causal relationship between moral judgments and emotions; such theories say moral judgments *warrant* or *merit* emotional responses (McDowell 1985; Smith 1994). It's far from clear why a hypothetical scenario should warrant an emotion, given that emotions are primarily useful in orchestrating actions. The empirical results may be best explained by those theories that posit a *causal* or *constitutive* link between moral judgments and emotions (Hume 1978/1739; Prinz 2007). Such theories entail that moral judgments will result in emotional responses even when we consider hypothetical cases, just as the evidence suggests. The fact that emotions arise when considering cases that don't rationally require emotions, because they are merely hypothetical, may be taken as evidence for the conclusion that the deployment of moral concepts causes or contains emotions. Thus, empirical findings can help adjudicate between competing versions of internalism.

At this point the externalist might cry foul. Surely the fact that emotions arise when people make moral judgments in hypothetical cases is not *sufficient* to refute externalism. The externalist can introduce theory-saving auxiliary assumptions. For example, ordinary people care about morality, as, consequently, through heavily practiced associations, we tend to get emotional when we consider moral cases, even in the abstract. Alternatively, we may even be the kind of people who like to exhibit moral concern; getting bent out of shape in these hypotheticals conveys how much we care about morality. I think such moves border on being *ad hoc*, but, even if they can be used to block the empirical results mentioned so far, others may be more damaging.

First consider the fact that emotions can influence moral judgment. On the auxiliary hypothesis just considered, emotions are a consequence of moral judgment, not a cause. But the causal arrow can go the other way. For example, Schnall et al. (2008) conducted a study in which they induced disgust in a number of ways: recalling disgusting events, showing disgusting films, and sitting subjects down at a filthy desk, or spraying fart spray in a nearby trash can. In all these cases, some subjects rated moral vignettes as more wrong than subjects in non-disgusting control conditions. This outcome is predicted by internalist views that say emotions are component parts of our moral concepts. If tokens of the judgment that φ-ing is wrong contain a negative emotion toward φ-ing, then prior induction of negative emotions should amplify one's judgment that φ-ing is wrong. Not so if emotions are mere consequences of moral judgment as externalist and some internalist theories would have it.

In response, externalists might concede that emotions are components of some moral judgments in ordinary folks, while insisting that there *could be* moral judgments in the absence of emotion. This modalizing move makes an empirical prediction. If we remove emotions, somehow, the capacity to make moral judgments should remain intact. This empirical prediction is difficult to test in healthy subjects, because there is no way to prevent healthy people from having emotions. But there are clinical populations where emotions are very deficient. One such population is psychopaths. Externalism predicts that psychopaths should be able to make moral judgments. Empirical evidence suggests otherwise. Evidence suggests that psychopaths don't understand what moral judgments are. They do not distinguish them from mere conventions (Blair 1995). Psychopaths score as being in the earliest stage of moral development (Campagna and Harter 1975). Like young children, they know that they might be punished for doing certain things, but, beyond that, they cannot articulate what is wrong with violating moral rules.

An externalist might, at this point, concede that emotions are necessary for some moral rules, while holding out that others can be acquired and applied without the benefit of emotions. There is even some empirical evidence that has been interpreted in this way. Koenigs et al. (2007) studied, not psychopaths, but individuals with a lesion in ventromedial prefrontal cortex, which has been associated with the ability to assign emotional significance to events. They found that this patient made moral judgments, but his judgments tended to be consequentialist in nature. When given a choice between taking one life and saving five, he said take the life. They think such judgments may be made without the benefit of emotions. Unfortunately, this is not an ideal test. Such patients do have emotions. They just have difficulty using one emotion to override another. Perhaps the desire to help five people, backed up by anticipatory pleasure and empathetic concern, drives them to choose an option where they can save lives, even if doing so involves harming another. The sting of harm cannot override the reward of helping. There is, as yet, no decisive empirical demonstration of moral judgments being made successfully, without rote memorization, in the absence of emotions.

The existing empirical evidence seems to support internalism and count against externalism. Indeed, I think the evidence offers best support for the view that emotions are component parts of moral judgments (Prinz 2004), because such views offer the most straightforward explanation of the fact that emotion induction influences moral judgment. Other theories can accommodate the data, but they do so only by introducing auxiliary assumptions, which can themselves be empirically assessed. Whether internalism is said to be a thesis about what moral concepts logically entail or a thesis about what occurs when moral judgments are made, I think empirical findings are clearly relevant and clearly support the internalist.

The externalist might hold out hope that there is some way of possessing a moral concept that does not in any way involve the emotions, but this modal claim, which may appeal beyond the reach of empirical testing, is vulnerable to a tidy refutation (see Prinz 2006). If our ordinary moral concepts are linked (perhaps constitutively) to emotional responses, then why think hypothetical moral concepts that lack such a link qualify as moral concepts at all? Such concepts would clearly be very different in their cognitive significance from ordinary moral concepts, and on most accounts, two concepts that differ in their cognitive significance are conceptually distinct. If externalism amounts to the view that there are possible concepts distinct from ordinary moral concepts that lack a link to motivation, then the thesis loses much of its interest.

I conclude that the prospects for empirically settling the internalism/externalism debate are quite high. Current evidence favors internalism, and compensatory refinements to the theories or novel interpretations of the data can be used to generate new empirical predictions and new tests.

Meta-ethics and normative ethics

I have been arguing that a central debate in philosophical moral psychology can be advanced by looking at empirical research. This flies in the face of standard philosophical practice, but, on reflection, it may not seem very surprising. The internalism/externalism debate concerns the nature of moral judgments and moral judgments are real psychological events that can be empirically investigated. Much harder to defend is the claim that empirical research bears on meta-ethics and normative ethics. Before concluding, I want to briefly indicate how these subfields may have empirical dimensions as well.

First consider meta-ethics. This is the study of what sorts of facts our moral judgments refer to, if any. I have argued that moral concepts are linked to the emotions. More specifically, I suggested that moral concepts contain emotions, which means judgments are felt attitudes towards actions. When we verbally express our judgments, we are expressing how we feel. This sort of position has been traditionally associated with a particular meta-ethical view, expressivism, according to which moral statements do not have truth conditions; they simply express feelings (Stevenson 1937; Ayer 1952; Blackburn 1984; Gibbard 1990). But there are other meta-ethical positions consistent with the discovery that moral judgments contain emotions. Another possibility is that these emotions track mind-independent objective moral properties, just as physical disgust might track the objective property of being a noxious contaminant. A third possibility is that moral emotions represent mind-dependent subjective properties. By analogy, the concept of deliciousness uses gustatory pleasure to track things that are pleasing to the taster, even if no things are delicious to all. The idea that moral concepts represent such subjective properties has been defended by philosophers such as Wiggins (1987) and McDowell (1985). A fourth possibility, put forward by Mackie (1977), is that moral concepts aim to refer to objective properties but fail, because no objective properties fit the bill.

How can we settle this debate in meta-ethics? One answer is that we can use empirical methods. Do people take their moral concepts to be referring? Why not ask them? Positive answers to this question would tell against expressivism.

Are there objective properties that moral concepts refer to? Why not look? Failure to find a common essence unifying the things we regard as moral or as immoral would tell against objectivism. Do moral concepts fail to refer if there is no objective essence to morality? Why not see whether ordinary people are committed to objectivism? If not, the Mackie's error theory does not follow. Do moral concepts refer to responses-dependent properties? Why not see if people use moral concepts in ways that parallel concepts that seem to designate response-dependent properties, such as beautiful, delicious, or funny? Parallels would favor a subjectivist meta-ethics. Research relevant to all these questions has been conducted. It is beyond the scope of this chapter to review that research here, but I hope these questions have made it clear that meta-ethics can be approached in an empirical way. What our concepts refer to depends on (a) our semantic policies in using them, and (b) what exists out there in the world. Both of these issues can be addressed empirically.

Finally, what of normative ethics? Is Kant right that descriptive psychology cannot contribute to prescriptive morality? Here, again, the answer may be negative. Consider three examples. First, Flanagan (1991) endorses the dictum that ought implies can, and he argues that empirical psychology can constrain normative ethics by studying what we can in fact do. For example, if we are psychologically incapable of impartiality, an ethics that requires impartiality can be rejected. Second, normative theories sometimes postulate capacities that do not, in fact, exist. Doris (2002) and Harman (1999) reject standard virtue ethics on this ground. Virtue ethicists say that the proper subject of morality is the cultivation of good character traits, but Doris and Harman argue on empirical grounds that character traits do not exist in the sense required. Social psychologists have shown that circumstances drive behavior, not enduring, broad-based, causally robust inner traits. Thus, they try to rule out a normative theory by exposing false empirical assumptions. Similarly, one might try to undermine Kantian ethics by arguing that the will is not capable of autonomy in the sense Kant requires, or one can criticize Millian ethics by arguing that Mill misconstrues the nature of happiness. Millgram (2000), for example, argues that happiness registers an upward change in status rather than overall well-being, and, thus, actions that maximize happiness might paradoxically lead to diminished happiness as goals are achieved. Third, if subjectivist meta-ethical theories can be empirically defended, then it follows that the good is that which a moral judge takes to be good. When asked what should I do, morally speaking, the answer given by subjectivists is that I should do what I take myself to be obligated to do. One might also alter a person's subjective sense of what morality requires by presenting empirically informed genealogical studies of that person's deeply held values (Prinz 2007). If subjectivism is true, then such empirical critiques literally alter normative demands.

These examples are controversial, of course, but they illustrate a wide range of ways in which empirical findings could have an impact on normative ethics. A philosophical purist, like Kant, might argue that empirical findings cannot deliver a complete normative ethical theory. Kant tries to move outside the empirical sphere by offering an armchair analysis of the concept of the good. I have already argued that conceptual analysis is best construed as an empirical enterprise, so Kant's conceptual move does not forestall more empirical approaches. It's hard to imagine any aspect of normative ethical theory that is immune to empirical assessment.

Conclusion

I tried to show that empirical psychology is highly relevant to philosophical ethics. I focused on a debate in moral psychology, but the points made in addressing that debate expose a broader role for empirical findings, and I concluded that meta-ethics and normative ethics may benefit from psychological research as well.

Does this mean that philosophy will eventually give way to psychology, and science will solve all moral problems? Such a conclusion would be gravely mistaken. For one thing, science needs philosophy, just as philosophy needs science. Philosophy poses the questions that science investigates; philosophy generates theories, and systematizes evidence. Experiments are essentially arguments with empirical premises, and philosophers are trained to assess how good these arguments are. Moreover, even if science can reveal what our moral values are and what their metaphysical basis is, we use those values to make decisions and guide action. Figuring out what follows from our values involves the kinds of reasoning that philosophers, above all others, are in the business of carrying out. Construed as the study of what existing moral values demand of us, pure normative ethics retains an important place in moral deliberation. But it would be grotesquely misguided to infer from this important fact that empirical psychology has no bearing on morality.

See also Ethics and sentiment (Chapter 10); Hume (Chapter 11); Adam Smith (Chapter 12); Contemporary Kantian ethics (Chapter 38); Virtue ethics (Chapter 40).

References

Ayer, A. J. (1952) *Language, Truth, and Logic*, New York: Dover.

Blackburn, S. (1984) *Spreading the Word: Groundings in the Philosophy of Language*, Oxford: Oxford University Press.

Blair, R. J. R. (1995) "A Cognitive Developmental Approach to Morality: Investigating the Psychopath," *Cognition* 57: 1–29.

Campagna, A. and Harter, S. (1975) "Moral Judgment in Sociopathic and Normal Children," *Journal of Personality and Social Psychology* 31: 199–205.

Doris, J. M. (2002) *Lack of Character*, Cambridge: Cambridge University Press.

Flanagan, O. (1991) *Varieties of Moral Personality: Ethics and Psychological Realism*, Cambridge, MA: Harvard University Press.

Gibbard, A. (1990) *Wise Choices, Apt Feelings*, Cambridge, MA: Harvard University Press.

Greene, J. D., Sommerville, R. B., Nystrom, L. E., Darley, J. M. and Cohen, J. D. (2001). "An fMRI Investigation of Emotional Engagement in Moral Judgment," *Science* 293: 2105–8.

Harman, G. (1999) "Moral Philosophy Meets Social Psychology: Virtue Ethics and the Fundamental Attribution Error," *Proceedings of the Aristotelian Society* 99: 315–31.

Heekeren, H. R., Wartenburger, I., Schmidt, H., Schwintowski, H. P. and Villringer, A. (2003) "An fMRI Study of Simple Ethical Decision-making," *NeuroReport* 14: 1215–19.

Hume, D. (1978/1739) *A Treatise of Human Nature*, ed. P. H. Nidditch, Oxford: Oxford University Press.

Kant, I. (1998/1785) *Groundwork of the Metaphysic of Morals*, ed. Mary J. Gregor, Cambridge: Cambridge University Press.

Koenigs, M., Young, L., Adolphs, R., Tranel, D., Cushman, F., Hauser, M. and Damasio, A. (2007) "Damage to the Prefrontal Cortex Increases Utilitarian Moral Judgements," *Nature* 446: 908–11.

Kohlberg, L. (1984) *The Psychology of Moral Development: Moral Stages and the Life Cycle*, San Francisco, CA: Harper & Row.

Mackie, J. L. (1977) *Ethics: Inventing Right and Wrong*, London: Penguin Books.

McDowell, J. (1985) "Values and Secondary Qualities," in T. Honderich (ed.) *Morality and Objectivity*, London: Routledge & Kegan Paul.

Millgram, E. (2000) "What's the Use of Utility?" *Philosophy & Public Affairs* 29: 113–36.

Moll, J., de Oliveira-Souza, R., Bramati, I. and Grafman, J. (2002) "Functional Networks in Emotional Moral and Nonmoral Social Judgments," *NeuroImage* 16: 696–703.

Nichols, S. (2002) "On the Genealogy of Norms: A Case for the Role of Emotion in Cultural Evolution," *Philosophy of Science* 69: 234–55.

——(2004) *Sentimental Rules: On the Natural Foundations of Moral Judgment*, New York: Oxford University Press.

Prinz, J. J. (2004) *Gut Reactions: A Perceptual Theory of Emotion*, New York: Oxford University Press.

——(2006) "The Emotional Basis of Moral Judgments," *Philosophical Explorations* 9: 29–43.

——(2007) *The Emotional Construction of Morals*, Oxford: Oxford University Press.

Quine, W. V. O. (1953) "Two Dogmas of Empiricism," in *From a Logical Point of View*, Cambridge, MA: Harvard University Press, pp. 20–46.

Schnall, S., Haidt, J., Clore, G. L. and Jordan, A. H. (2008) "Disgust as Embodied Moral Judgment," *Personality and Social Psychology Bulletin* 34: 1096–1109.

Sinnott-Armstrong, W. (ed.) (2009/2008) *Moral Psychology*, vols 1–3, Cambridge, MA: MIT Press.

Smith, M. (1994) *The Moral Problem*, Oxford: Blackwell.

Sripada, C. and Stich, S. (2005) "A Framework for the Psychology of Norms," in P. Carruthers, S. Laurence and S. Stich (eds) *The Innate Mind: Structure and Content*, New York: Oxford University Press.

Stevenson, C. L. (1937) "The Emotive Meaning of Ethical Terms," *Mind* 46: 14–31.

Wiggins, D. (1987) "A Sensible Subjectivism," in *Needs, Values, Truth: Essays in the Philosophy of Value*, Oxford: Blackwell, pp. 185–214.

Further reading

Doris, J. M. (1998) "Persons, Situations and Virtue Ethics," *Noûs* 32: 504–30. (An engaging and careful defense of the view that social psychology refutes standard versions of virtue ethics. The case is developed in more detail in Doris's book, cited above, but the core argument is here, and the paper launched a sizeable secondary literature.)

Doris, J. M. and the Moral Psychology Research Group (eds) (Forthcoming) *The Oxford Handbook of Moral Psychology*, Oxford: Oxford University Press. (Some of the key practitioners of empirical approaches to ethics teamed up to write new papers for this state-of-the-art anthology. Highlights include a compendious paper by Stephen Stich, John Doris, and Erica Roedder reviewing psychological research on altruism: Do people ever really act altruistically or do we always have ulterior selfish motives?)

Nichols, S. (2004) "After Objectivity: An Empirical Study of Moral Judgment," *Philosophical Psychology* 17: 5–28. (In addition to his groundbreaking book, *Sentimental Rules*, Nichols has numerous articles that illustrate how philosophers can use experiments to answer philosophical questions. Here Nichols devises a study to show that people are less inclined to believe that morality is objective than many philosophers have supposed.)

Prinz, J. J. (2007) "Can Moral Obligations Be Empirically Discovered?" *Midwest Studies in Philosophy* 31: 271–91. (In this paper I consider the widely accepted thesis that normative conclusions cannot be derived from merely descriptive premises. I argue that there is a sense in which this conclusion is false, and this gives ethicists another reason to take psychology seriously.)

Roskies, A. L. (2003) "Are Ethical Judgments Intrinsically Motivational? Lessons from Acquired Sociopathy," *Philosophical Psychology* 16: 51–66. (Discussing the central theme in this chapter, Roskies argues that research on brain-damaged patients shows that moral judgment can occur without moral motivation. Her position differs from the one offered here and serves as an informative, well-argued counterpoint, reminding us that much philosophical work is needed to interpret empirical results.)

Sinnott-Armstrong, W. (ed.) (2008) *Moral Psychology*, vols 1–3, Cambridge, MA: MIT Press. (A massive three-volume anthology on empirical approaches to ethics. The volume includes a heretical paper by philosopher-turned-neuroscientist Joshua Greene, who uses brain science to argue that Kantian ethics hinges on emotional intuitions, despite Kant's admonition to extirpate emotions from moral judgment. It also includes papers by Susan Dwyer, Marc Hauser, and John Mikhail on the question of whether morality is an innate capacity.)

33
BIOLOGY
Michael Ruse

Fifty years ago, when the *Origin of Species* (1859) by Charles Darwin was just celebrating its hundredth anniversary, the idea that biology might have anything of significance to contribute to moral philosophy was considered not just wrong, but the philosophical equivalent of a bad smell. How things have changed! Today, even conservative philosophers discuss evolutionary ethics. It may not be right, but at least it is sufficiently interesting to be worth refuting.

The biology of cooperation

In the *Origin*, Darwin's chief mechanism of natural selection promotes change of a particular kind, namely in the direction of adaptive advantage. Organisms have features, adaptations, that aid them in the struggle for existence. They have characteristics – eyes, teeth, noses, penises, vaginas, leaves, bark, roots, fruits, seeds – that help them to survive and (more importantly) to reproduce. Darwin realized at once that behavior was part of the package. There is no point in having the physique of Tarzan if all you have behaviorally are the urges of the philosopher, wanting only to contemplate the eternal verities. But at once, this raises a paradox. Much behavior seems to be social in the sense of working for the benefit of others. The honeybee in the hive is the paradigmatic example, with the sterile female worker devoting her whole life to her relatives. How can this be of reproductive advantage to the bee?

Darwin worried about this problem, never really solving it satisfactorily, either in the *Origin* itself or some years later when he returned to the problem, in the *Descent of Man* (1871), where he discussed the origins of human morality, something which he saw again raises the issues in a big way. Why should the soldier sacrifice his life for his buddies, when it aids his own reproduction not one whit? For various reasons, in the century after Darwin, few took up the challenge of answering this question, either in the realm of the animal or that of the human. Partly the failure to respond was because behavior generally is so much more difficult to study than physical features. Partly it was because of the growth of the social sciences whose practitioners thought that they alone had the right to speak to human issues.

Then, in the 1960s, things changed dramatically. Evolutionary biologists turned in a big way to behavior, especially social behavior. At the theoretical level, new models were devised to explain such behavior, showing that help (what the biologists called "altruism") can indeed benefit the helper. Notable were "kin selection," where an individual helps a relative, namely someone who shares the same genes as you, and whose reproduction thereby helps your genes to have higher representation in the next generation (Hamilton 1964a, b), and "reciprocal altruism," where help given is reciprocated on the "you scratch my back and I'll scratch yours" principle (Trivers 1971). At the empirical level, relatedly, people started to do long-term studies of animals, finding out how exactly it is that altruism occurs and functions. From dung flies (Parker 1978) to red deer (Clutton-Brock et al. 1982), the actions of organisms in groups was looked at in great detail.

In 1975, the Harvard entomologist Edward O. Wilson brought all of the new work together in one overall volume, *Sociobiology: The New Synthesis* (1975). Wilson saw the work as having implications for humankind, and his final chapter as well as a full-length, subsequent book (*On Human Nature* [1978]) devoted themselves to giving biological (that is, Darwinian) explanations of such things as work, play, fighting, language, religion, and moral behavior. This last was no afterthought. In *Sociobiology*, Wilson firmly put ethics at the front of his endeavors. If the title of the first chapter, "The Morality of the Gene," does not flag you, then the opening words surely will:

> Camus said that the only serious philosophical question is suicide. That is wrong even in the strict sense intended. The biologist, who is concerned with questions of physiology and evolutionary history, realizes that self-knowledge is constrained and shaped by the emotional control centers in the hypothalamus and limbic systems of the brain. These centers flood our consciousness with all the emotions – hate, love, guilt, fear, and others – that are consulted by ethical philosophers who wish to intuit the standards of good and evil. What, we are then compelled to ask, made the hypothalamus and limbic system? They evolved by natural selection. That simple biological statement must be pursued to explain ethics and ethical philosophers, if not epistemology and epistemologists, at all depths.
>
> (Wilson 1975: 3)

Expectedly, professional philosophers reacted as though they were virgin aunts to whom an indecent proposition had been made. They immediately argued that even if Wilson's science was right, and many thought it was not, the fact that evolution may have had something to do with the causes of morality has nothing to do with the justification of morality. The fact that we may have evolved to think that we should be good (and, given Hitler, this is a dubious proposition) has nothing to do with whether or not we should be good (like Mother Teresa).

Yet even as the critics wrote, it was clear that some were starting to have second thoughts. Already Wilson's Harvard colleague John Rawls, in his great work *A Theory of Justice* (1971), had suggested that our moral beliefs about things like fairness are a product of our biology. At once Rawls stressed that this says nothing about foundations, but still it was the thin end of a very big wedge. A wedge that by the early 1980s a number of philosophers, including the late John Mackie (1978), the legal philosopher Jeffrey Murphy (1982), and Michael Ruse (1986), were starting to hammer in hard and deep. Wilson and I wrote a piece together (Ruse and Wilson 1986), one which was taken up and much anthologized as a dreadful example of HOW NOT TO DO ETHICS. Philip Kitcher (1993) wrote what seems to have become the official reply, for it is always anthologized along with our piece. In other words, things were taking their normal course. First, you ignore a new idea. Then you say that it is false. Finally, you say that it is true but that you have known it all along.

Social Darwinism

Well, what is it that we have known all along? Let us start with the traditional way of doing evolutionary ethics. This is usually known as social Darwinism, although as a scientist Charles Darwin himself tended not to be too interested in the sorts of things that concern moral philosophers. Far more interested and far more influential was Darwin's fellow English evolutionist, Herbert Spencer (1851, 1879). He did care very much about these sorts of things. At the normative, prescriptive level, Spencer set a pattern of looking at the processes of evolution and then generalizing from them. Since natural selection is brought on by a struggle for reproduction, it seems that morally what one should do is promote a societal struggle, a strenuous form of *laissez faire* economics. Widows and children to the wall, might is right!

However, things are a bit more complex than this. Social Darwinism has a bad name, but taken in its entirety the negative assessment is not entirely justified. Spencer was not a cruel man. He loathed state charity precisely because he felt it kept people down and below the levels to which they were entitled. He was strongly against violence and oppression as such, something that came out fully in his hatred of militarism. He thought conflict between societies was wasteful and inimical to free trade, thus destroying the possibilities of open commercial competition. Spencer's followers also were all over the map in their prescriptions. It is often thought that American business people – notably John D. Rockefeller and Andrew Carnegie – liked Spencer because he justified their rough ways with the working classes. But, generally, people like this much preferred to stress their own successes rather than the failures of others. Carnegie is justly famous for sponsoring the building and running of public libraries. He did this in order that bright but poor children could thereby better themselves. The survival of the fittest not the non-survival of the non-fittest (Bannister 1979).

It is true that some did take up a form of Darwinism and argue that this justifies the worst kind of inter-societal strife. Count General Friedrich von Bernhardi (1912), a member of the German General Staff until they pushed him out for being a bit too open, was a classic social Darwinian of this kind. "War is a biological necessity," and hence: "Those forms survive which are able to procure themselves the most favorable conditions of life, and to assert themselves in the universal economy of nature. The weaker succumb." Everything depends on violent conflict: "Without war, inferior or decaying races would easily choke the growth of healthy budding elements, and a universal decadence would follow" (von Bernhardi 1912: 10).

In recent years, American evangelicals who subscribe to a literal interpretation of Genesis have taken note of this kind of argument, claiming that it led straight to the doctrines of the Nazis (Weikart 2004). However, although there are passages in *Mein Kampf* (Hitler 1925) that do sound like Spencer at his worst, more detailed study shows that Hitler's real fears were the poisoning effect of "the Jew" in society rather than the need for purification of the race through bloody conflict. It is true that this is a kind of biological argument, but it is surely one based on false biology. Truly, evolution was no friend of National Socialism. Not only does Darwin's theory suggest that we all come from monkeys, but also it shows that Aryan, Jew, Black, Gypsy, Slav are siblings under the skin. Not the message that Hitler and his vile crew wanted promulgated (Richards 2008).

Progress

Like the norms of Christianity, a world system that many Darwinians felt their science was replacing, social Darwinism's prescriptions tended to take on the problems and solutions of the day. In the 1930s, we find Julian Huxley (1934) promoting large, science-based, societal-funded works projects. In the 1980s and 1990s, Edward O. Wilson (1984, 1992) was in favor of biodiversity. But rather than delving farther in that direction, ask now about justification. Making uncomfortable the life of the poor, promoting reading programs, fighting one's neighbors (or not), building dams and laying down highways, saving the rain forests – why should one do any of these things? It is here that the traditional philosopher strikes. Suppose, a big supposition but one we can make for the sake of argument, that we do press the poor because our biology makes us do it, that we have genes making us benevolent to would-be readers, and all of the rest. Why does it follow that we should do these things? At this time, G. E. Moore's (1903) "naturalistic fallacy" is invoked. We are trying to equate the "good," a non-natural property, with "this is what evolution produced," a natural property. Relatedly, David Hume (1978) is rolled out and his argument about the illicit moves made from "is statements" to "ought statements" is endorsed and considered definitive. Evolution makes me want to save the rain forests, but does it follow that it is right to save the rain forests? It may indeed be right to save the rain forests, but what has evolution to do with any of this? To assume that the one follows from the other is simply not true.

My experience is that, rightly or wrongly, evolutionary ethicists find this argument profoundly unconvincing. Like the ontological argument, they don't care how clever it is and what it proves, they know it is wrong. Wilson is strong on this. When the claim is made that he is going from "is" to "ought," he agrees cheerfully. However, he points out that this is the sort of thing that is always happening in science. It is known as "reduction." In physics we go from talking about little balls buzzing around in a container to hot gasses pushing to get out of that container. If the velocity/temperature barrier can be bridged, then why not the is/ought barrier?

No doubt traditional philosophers will have an answer and no doubt it too will fail to convince. But there is another argument that can be brought into play here and it is important, logically and psychologically. Ask why the traditional evolutionary ethicists are so convinced that they are right. Each and every one shares a common premise. They do not believe that evolution is a slow process, going nowhere. They believe it has direction. It goes from the simple to the complex, from the valueless to the value full, from (in traditional language) the monad to the man. It is progressive.

Listen to Julian Huxley:

> When we look at evolution as a whole, we find, among the many directions which it has taken, one which is characterized by introducing the evolving world-stuff to progressively higher levels of organization and so to new possibilities of being, action, and experience. This direction has culminated in the attainment of a state where the world-stuff (now moulded into human shape) finds that it experiences some of the new possibilities as having value in or for themselves; and further that among these it assigns higher and lower degrees of value, the higher values being those which are more intrinsically or more permanently satisfying, or involve a greater degree of perfection.
>
> (J. Huxley 1943: 41–2)

Wilson likewise sings the same song. Again and again he stresses progress:

> the overall average across the history of life has moved from the simple and few to the more complex and numerous. During the past billion years, animals as a whole evolved upward in body size, feeding and defensive techniques, brain and behavioral complexity, social organization, and precision of environmental control – in each case farther from the nonliving state than their simpler antecedents did.
>
> (Wilson 1992: 187)

He believes that there have been four pinnacles of social evolution, and that humans have uniquely scaled the last and most important.

The argument therefore is that the evolutionary process itself promotes value, and therefore our ethical duty is to work with and within this process to see that it is realized as fully as possible.

> The teleologically-minded would say that this trend [progress] embodies evolution's purpose. I do not feel that we should use the word purpose save where we know that a conscious aim is involved; but we can say that this is the *most desirable* direction of evolution, and accordingly that our ethical standards must fit into its dynamic framework. In other words, it is ethically right to aim at whatever will promote the increasingly full realization of increasingly higher values.
>
> (J. Huxley 1943: 42)

Progress is not just a biological or a social phenomenon: it is an all-encompassing world philosophy. And the trouble is that there is nothing all that progressive about evolution. The whale descended from land mammals and as it did so, the backbone became very much simpler. Does that make the whale any less biologically worthwhile than the hippo? The HIV virus flourishes whereas in the wild the great apes are in much danger. Does that mean that these viruses are further up the tree of life than the chimps? Even if there was progress, it is not so in such a way as to make for value. The liver fluke is a marvel of complexity as it goes through various forms as it moves from one host (ants) to another (sheep). Is it that worthwhile, morally? Are we to say that birds are morally superior to their parents, the dinosaurs? There is little wonder that the late Stephen Jay Gould wrote of progress that it is a "noxious, culturally embedded, untestable, non-operational, intractable idea that must be replaced if we wish to understand the patterns of history" (Gould 1988: 319). Julian's grandfather, Thomas Henry, was wiser than his descendant on these sorts of things. T. H. Huxley (1893) pointed out that evolution goes for what works rather than what is good, and much of the time the truly moral is fighting the ape or the tiger within us, not with going easily with our emotions.

It is for this reason that traditional evolutionary ethics – social Darwinism – fails. Not so much because the prescriptions are wrong – in this respect, like Christianity, you pay your money and you take your choice – but because the foundation is sand. Evolution is not that progressive and even if it is, it is not morally progressive.

Empirical ethics

So where do we go from here? One important thing that moral philosophers are realizing is that, with respect to the actual beliefs and practices of ethics (the part of the field that is covered by substantive ethics), we need to do a lot better than rely simply on the intuitions of an aging bachelor in East Prussia in the late eighteenth century (Kant 1997) or the gut feelings of a Victorian English gentleman (Mill 1859), however much his wife was nudging him in the right direction. Homosexual relations are not necessarily a gross violation of the categorical imperative, and the greatest happiness principle does not always allow a dishonest pharmacist to sell polluted drugs if the customer is not sufficiently suspicious. We need to turn to the actual practices and feelings of real people, here in our own society and in other societies, in time and place.

In this quest, evolutionary biology is not going to give us all of the solutions, but it might give us some. Mention has already been made of the way in which Rawls spotted this. Rawls particularly pointed out that evolution solves the big lacuna in any social contract approach to morality, namely how did the contract get put in place in the first place? It was not a group of old men around a fire but the genes. "The theory of evolution would suggest it is the outcome of natural selection; the capacity for a sense of justice and the moral feelings is an adaptation of mankind to its place in nature." Rawls continued, "It seems clear that for members of a species which lives in stable social groups, the ability to comply with fair cooperative arrangements and to develop the sentiments necessary to support them is highly advantageous, especially when individuals have a long life and are dependent on one another. These conditions guarantee innumerable occasions when mutual justice consistently adhered to is beneficial to all parties" (Rawls 1971: 502–3). Rawls pointed out that this kind of situation would be precisely what one would expect were a biological mechanism like reciprocal altruism at play.

It is worth stressing that no one thinks that there is a simple connection between genes and behavior. Human nature is far more complex than that. The popular analogy is with language. Clearly the human ability to speak a coherent language is rooted in our evolutionary past. However, which language you speak is a matter of environment.

> We are endowed with a moral faculty that operates over the causal-intentional properties of actions and events as they connect to particular consequences. ... We posit a theory of universal moral grammar which consists of the principles and parameters that are part and parcel of this biological endowment. Our universal moral grammar provides a toolkit for building possible moral systems. Which particular moral system emerges reflects details of the local environment or culture, and a process of environmental pruning whereby particular parameters are selected and set early in development.
>
> (Hauser 2006: 2)

Recently, some moral philosophers – Peter Singer (2005) is a notable case – have been turning to evolution to throw light on some of the knotty problems that seem to bedevil discussions of morality. Consider what I like to call the *Bleak House* problem. Most moral systems do not distinguish between the people whom you should aid. A utilitarian thinks that if a hundred dollars could buy food for ten starving Africans, then you should not spend this money on (say) extra mathematics tutoring for your child. Yet few of us lie awake worrying about this kind of thing. I am not saying we never worry about these things or that we should not be worrying more than we do. What I am saying is that generally we do not, and we do not think of ourselves as moral monsters for not so doing. Despite exhortations by some moralists to love every other human being indifferently, we do not, nor do we often think that we should. "Charity begins at home." I call this the *Bleak House* problem or issue, because in his great novel Dickens is scathing about those who worry about the problems of the starving poor in Africa, when they are indifferent to the problems of the starving poor in England and even to the needs of their own families.

There are clearly good biological reasons why we feel this way. Selection has fashioned us to think first of closest relatives, then more distant ones and friends in our social group, and so on out. Although no evolutionist, Hume spotted this. "A man naturally loves his children better than his nephews, his nephews better than his cousins, his cousins better than strangers, where every thing else is equal. Hence arise our common measures of duty, in preferring the one to the other. Our sense of duty always follows the common and natural course of our passions" (Hume 1978: 483–84).

None of this obviously addresses the issues of whether our feelings and actions are really right or wrong, but much light is thrown on why we think and feel and act as we do. And this is no small thing, even for philosophers.

Foundations?

But what about the question of justification? The simple fact is that evolutionary biology is not going to give it to you. However, there are those – I am one – who think that evolutionary biology might do something equivalent, namely show that there is no justification of morality in the way that philosophers have traditionally sought. In other words, we ought to be moral skeptics or nihilists about foundations. Murphy (1982: 112n) writes:

> The sociobiologist [student of the evolution of social behavior] may well agree with the point … that value judgments are properly defended in terms of other value judgments until we reach some that are fundamental. All of this, in a sense, is the giving of *reasons*. However, suppose we seriously raise the question of why these fundamental judgments are regarded as fundamental. There may be only a *causal* explanation for this! We reject simplistic utilitarianism because it entails consequences

> that are morally counterintuitive, or we embrace a Rawlsian theory of justice because it systematizes (places in "reflective equilibrium") our pre-theoretical convictions. But what is the status of those intuitions or convictions? Perhaps there is nothing more to be said for them than that they involve deep preferences (or patterns of preference) built into our biological nature. If this is so, then at a very fundamental point the reasons/causes (and the belief that we ought/really ought) distinction breaks down, or the one transforms into the other.

The critics (like Kitcher) jump at this point. There is a fallacy here. Surely you are saying: "Substantive ethical beliefs 'like love your children' are adaptive and were brought about by natural selection. Hence they have no foundation." But this no more follows than does: "I believe that a truck is bearing down on me because of my powers of observation brought about by natural selection. Hence the truck's existence has no foundation." Perhaps however there is a difference which is crucial. If the truck does exist, then there may be different ways of sensing it, but you had better have some way. Truck avoiders must end up with the same solution. In the case of morality, given that there is no necessary progress to one best or right solution, we could have very different systems (substantively) and get along – and there seem no reasons why the solutions should be the same. Suppose I adopt what (in honor of President Eisenhower's Secretary of State) I will call the John Foster Dulles system of morality. "Hate your neighbors (especially if they are Russian) but remember they hate you. So get along." How would we ever distinguish between this and: "Love your neighbors and get along"? They both work and there is an end to things. No need for or possibility of any moral grounding beyond the utilitarian.

I offer this argument as one current position and hardly as the view adopted by all. There is one final thing to be said on the topic, however, namely that if substantive morality is to work, then whether or not there is a foundation we had better believe that there is! Something bigger than the both of us. If we do not believe this, then people will start to cheat and before long morality breaks right down. The late John Mackie (1979) spoke of this as the need to objectify and (ugly word though it is) he is right. The big problem with ethical skepticism – what is sometimes known as the "error theory" and sometimes as "non-cognitivism" – is that it seems so unpersuasive. Emotivism, the ethical theory of the logical positivists, could not be right. If I say that "Killing is wrong" I do not mean merely that I disapprove of it. I mean that it is wrong. The evolutionary ethicist of the kind just sketched agrees fully. The meaning of killing is wrong is that killing is wrong. It is just that there is no ultimate foundation for this belief. But there are good psychological reasons why we should have it.

At this point the reader will surely be reminded of David Hume and about how his psychology rescues him from doubt. "Most fortunately it happens, that since reason is incapable of dispelling these clouds, nature herself suffices to that purpose, and cures me of this philosophical melancholy and delirium, either by relaxing this bent of mind, or by some avocation, and lively impression of my senses, which obliterate all these chimeras" (Hume 1978: 269). In the end, what we have with evolutionary moral skepticism is a system that owes much to Hume, brought up to date by Darwin.

This is a good point on which to end. Evolutionary ethicists today are realizing that the findings of philosophers are there to be appreciated and used. Likewise philosophers are realizing that the findings of evolutionists are there to be appreciated and used. That really is progress.

See also Ethics, science, and religion (Chapter 22); The open question argument (Chapter 25).

References

Bannister, R. (1979) *Social Darwinism: Science and Myth in Anglo-American Social Thought*, Philadelphia, PA: Temple University Press.

Clutton-Brock, T. H., Guinness, F. E. and Albon, S. D. (1982) *Red Deer: Behaviour and Ecology of the Two Sexes*, Chicago, IL: Chicago University Press.

Darwin, C. (1859) *On the Origin of Species by Means of Natural Selection, or the Preservation of Favoured Races in the Struggle for Life*, London: John Murray.

——(1871) *The Descent of Man, and Selection in Relation to Sex*, London: John Murray.

Gould, S. J. (1988) "On Replacing the Idea of Progress with an Operational Notion of Directionality," in M. H. Nitecki (ed.) *Evolutionary Progress*, Chicago, IL: University of Chicago Press, pp. 319–38.

Hamilton, W. D. (1964a) "The Genetical Evolution of Social Behaviour I," *Journal of Theoretical Biology* 7: 1–16.

——(1964b) "The Genetical Evolution of Social Behaviour II," *Journal of Theoretical Biology* 7: 17–32.

Hauser, M. D. (2006) "The Liver and the Moral Organ," *Social Cognitive and Affective Neuroscience* 1, no. 3: 214–20.

Hitler, A. (1925) *Mein Kampf*, London: Secker & Warburg.

Hume, D. (1978) *A Treatise of Human Nature*, Oxford: Oxford University Press.

Huxley, J. S. (1934) *If I Were Dictator*, New York and London: Harper & Brothers.

——(1943) *Evolutionary Ethics*, Oxford: Oxford University Press.

Huxley, T. H. (1893) "Evolution and Ethics," in *Evolution and Ethics*, London: Macmillan, pp. 46–116.

Kant, I. (1997) *Lectures on Ethics*, Cambridge: Cambridge University Press.

Kitcher, P. (1993) "Four Ways to 'Biologicize' Ethics" [in German], in K. Bayertz (ed.) *Evolution und Ethik*, Stuttgart: Reclam.

Mackie, J. (1978) "The Law of the Jungle," *Philosophy* 53: 553–73.

——(1979) *Hume's Moral Theory*, London: Routledge & Kegan Paul.

Mill, J. S. (1859) *On Liberty*, London: John W. Parker & Sons.

Moore, G. E. (1903) *Principia Ethica*, Cambridge: Cambridge University Press.

Murphy, J. (1982) *Evolution, Morality, and the Meaning of Life*, Totowa, NJ: Rowman & Littlefield.

Parker, G. A. (1978) "Evolution of Competitive Mate Searching," *Annual Review of Entomology* 23: 173–96.
Rawls, J. (1971) *A Theory of Justice*, Cambridge, MA: Harvard University Press.
Richards, R. J. (2008) *The Tragic Sense of Life: Ernst Haeckel and the Struggle over Evolutionary Thought*, Chicago, IL: University of Chicago Press.
Ruse, M. (1986) *Taking Darwin Seriously: A Naturalistic Approach to Philosophy*, Oxford: Blackwell.
Ruse, M. and Wilson, E. O. (1986) "Moral Philosophy as Applied Science," *Philosophy* 61: 173–92.
Singer, P. (2005) "Ethics and Intuitions," *Journal of Ethics* 9: 331–52.
Spencer, H. (1851) *Social Statics; Or the Conditions Essential to Human Happiness Specified and the First of them Developed*, London: J. Chapman.
——(1879) *The Data of Ethics*, London: Williams & Norgate.
Trivers, R. L. (1971) "The Evolution of Reciprocal Altruism," *Quarterly Review of Biology* 46: 35–57.
von Bernhardi, F. (1912) *Germany and the Next War*, London: Edward Arnold.
Weikart, R. (2004) *From Darwin to Hitler: Evolutionary Ethics, Eugenics, and Racism in Germany*, New York: Palgrave Macmillan.
Wilson, E. O. (1975) *Sociobiology: The New Synthesis*, Cambridge, MA: Harvard University Press.
——(1978) *On Human Nature*, Cambridge, MA: Cambridge University Press.
——(1984) *Biophilia*, Cambridge, MA: Harvard University Press.
——(1992) *The Diversity of Life*, Cambridge, MA: Harvard University Press.

Further reading

Hauser, M. (2006) *Moral Minds: How Nature Shaped Our Universal Sense of Right and Wrong*, New York: Ecco.
Joyce, R. (2007) *The Evolution of Morality*, Cambridge, MA: MIT Press.
Ruse, M. (ed.) (2009) *Philosophy after Darwin: Classic and Contemporary Readings*, Princeton, NJ: Princeton University Press.

34
FORMAL METHODS IN ETHICS

Erik Carlson

Methods and techniques involving mathematics or formal logic have been applied to a wide variety of issues in normative ethics, as well as meta-ethics. With no aim at completeness, we shall consider four areas of research that have immediate connections to ethics and to a large extent utilize formal and mathematical reasoning. These areas are deontic logic, measurement theory, decision and game theory, and, lastly, welfare economics and social choice theory. The last three subjects overlap to a considerable degree, and the boundaries between them are vague.

Deontic logic

Deontic logic is the logic of normative reasoning. (The term "deontic" derives from the Greek word δεου, meaning "that which is binding.") It investigates the logical relations between normative concepts, particularly obligation ("ought," "should," "must"), permission ("may"), and prohibition ("ought not," "must not," "forbidden"). "Standard" deontic logic, henceforth SDL, originating with the work of von Wright (1951), assumes a close structural similarity between the concepts of obligation, permission, and prohibition, on the one hand, and the modal concepts of necessity, possibility, and impossibility, on the other. As a result, SDL can be seen as a branch of modal logic.

SDL is an extension of classical propositional logic. It adds to propositional logic an operator O, usually interpreted as "it is obligatory that." Letting $\Box$ symbolize negation, and p represent a proposition, the operators P, "permissible," and F, "forbidden," are usually defined as $Pp = \Box O \Box p$, and $Fp = O \Box p$, respectively. The most common axiomatization of SDL assumes as axioms, besides the theorems of propositional logic, the two principles $O(p \supset q) \supset (Op \supset Oq)$, and $Op \supset \Box O \Box p$. (The symbol $\supset$represents material implication, i.e. the "if … then" of propositional logic.) Permitted inference rules are *modus ponens* (if p and $p \supset q$ are theorems, then q is a theorem), and the rule that if p is a theorem, then Op is a theorem.

Several problematic features of SDL were soon discovered. Perhaps the most serious difficulty concerns "contrary to duty imperatives" (Chisholm 1974). Suppose that you ought to visit your aunt, and that, if you will not go, you ought to call and tell her. How, then, is the conditional obligation, "if you will not visit your aunt, you ought to call her," to be represented in SDL? Letting v stand for "you visit," and c stand for "you call," there are two natural possibilities. On a "wide scope" interpretation, the conditional obligation is to be formalized as $O(\Box v \supset c)$, while, on a "narrow scope" interpretation, it has the form $\Box v \supset Oc$.

Either possibility is problematic. The wide scope obligation, $O(\Box v \supset c)$, follows in SDL from Ov, whereas the conditional obligation, to call if you do not visit, surely does not follow from the obligation to visit, by itself. Further, $\Box v$ and $O(\Box v \supset c)$ do not in SDL together entail Oc. Hence, we are implausibly debarred from deriving the obligation to call from the conditional obligation, together with the assumption that you will not visit. The narrow scope interpretation fares no better, although it allows us to infer an obligation to call, from the conditional obligation and the assumption that you will not visit. The trouble is that Ov and Oc together imply $O(v \,\&\, c)$. Clearly, you are not obligated to visit your aunt *and* call to tell her that you will not come. Moreover, in SDL v implies $\Box v \supset Oc$. But the conditional obligation obviously does not follow from the assumption that you do visit your aunt.

Another potential problem is that SDL implies that two contradictory propositions cannot both be obligatory. Hence, if Alf promises Beth to go to the party, and also promises Celia not to go, at most one of these promises creates an obligation. Alf cannot be obligated both to go and not to go to the party. Some philosophers claim, however, that there are genuine "moral dilemmas," i.e. situations in which each of two incompatible courses of action is obligatory. It may be that Alf, by making his contradictory promises, lands himself in such a dilemma. Likewise, SDL excludes the possibility that Beth ought to make sure that Alf goes to the party, while Celia ought to make sure that Alf does not go. If such interpersonal "moral conflicts" are genuinely possible, SDL errs in ruling them out.

These and other problems have prompted a search for alternatives to SDL. (See Belzer [1998] for an overview.) No extant alternative system has, however, met with general approval. A more fundamental problem, concerning the very possibility of deontic logic, arises if one believes that normative sentences do not express propositions that can be true or false. According to non-cognitivists in meta-ethics, the primary function of normative sentences is to express attitudes or issue prescriptions, rather than to state propositions. Logical inference, however, is usually understood in terms of preservation of truth. An inference is valid if it is impossible that the premises are true and the conclusion is false. Hence, if normative sentences are neither true nor false, it seems that there can be no deontic logic. As a response to this challenge, there have been attempts to develop a logic of imperatives, understanding inference in terms of preservation of "satisfaction," rather than preservation of truth. As in the case of deontic logic proper, there is no generally accepted system of imperative logic. It should be pointed out, though, that non-cognitivism poses a threat to the possibility of meaningful normative argumentation in general, and not merely to formal deontic logic.

The impact of work in formal deontic logic on ethics in general has not been as great as some of the early investigators predicted. This is partly due to the internal problems with SDL and alternative systems. In addition, many philosophers are suspicious of the attempt to formulate a logic of normative concepts that is neutral as regards the content of moral norms. There may be no *a priori* reasons for believing that adherents of different moral theories should agree on the logical properties of normative concepts. It seems that a consequentialist and a deontologist, for example, could reasonably reach different conclusions regarding the logic of moral obligation. In SDL, $O(p \& q)$ implies Op. This "deontic consequence principle" may be rejected by the consequentialist, on the grounds that realizing $p \& q$ could have a good outcome, while realizing p would have a bad outcome. A much discussed case is that of Professor Procrastinate, who is asked to review a book (Jackson and Pargetter 1986). The best he could do, in terms of consequences for the author and everyone else involved, would be to say yes and then write the review. Hence, consequentialism implies that he ought to say-yes-and-write. Were he to say yes, however, he would not get around to actually writing the review. Saying yes and not writing would have a worse outcome than saying no. Arguably, therefore, consequentialism implies that it is not the case that he ought to say yes. (This verdict is controversial. See Zimmerman 1996.) If so, the consequence principle is not valid.

It can hardly be denied, however, that there are issues in moral philosophy to which the results and methods of deontic logic, and formal logic more generally, can be fruitfully applied. One example is the meta-ethically central and widely discussed principle known as Hume's law, stating that normative conclusions cannot be derived from non-normative premises (Schurz 1997). Furthermore, informal or semi-formal deontic logic plays an important role in influential work on consequentialism, the concept of moral obligation, and other issues (Feldman 1986; Zimmerman 1996).

Measurement theory

There is a long debate in ethics about whether and how goodness can be measured. The general theory of measurement, which is not well known among moral philosophers in general, has obvious bearings on this issue. Measurement is essentially the *representation* of some comparative relation, such as "longer than" or "better than," by means of some mathematical relation, such as "greater than," among numbers or other mathematical objects. A representation is said to be *unique* to the extent that it implies a given type of scale. The stronger the scale implied, the greater the uniqueness of the representation. The most important types of scales are, in order of increasing strength, *ordinal* scales, *interval* scales, and *ratio* scales. An ordinal scale is only order-preserving. The values yielded by the scale simply reflect the ranking of the relevant items. Statements about differences or ratios between values lack meaning. On an interval scale, comparisons of value differences are meaningful. It makes sense to say that the difference in value between *a* and *b* is greater than that between *c* and *d*. The Celsius and Fahrenheit temperature scales are standard examples of interval scales. Ratio scales, finally, make statements about ratios of values meaningful. An important implication of this is that the zero point is fixed. Properties such as mass and length are measured on ratio scales.

Measurability on at least an ordinal scale, with values represented by real numbers, requires that the relation "better than" is transitive and complete. Transitivity of a relation means that if it holds between *a* and *b*, and between *b* and *c*, then it holds between *a* and *c*. Completeness means that the relation holds between any two objects in the relevant domain. These assumptions have both been questioned, as regards "better than." Against completeness, many philosophers have argued that certain items are incomparable with respect to value. That is, neither item is better than the other, nor are they equally good (Raz 1986). Against transitivity, there are alleged examples of intransitive betterness, i.e. cases in which *a* is better than *b*, and *b* is better than *c*, but *a* is not better than *c* (Rachels 1998).

The existence of an interval scale presupposes, besides the assumptions necessary for ordinal measurement, that the value *differences* between items form a transitive and complete ordering, with certain properties. The most important of these properties are "monotonicity," and the "Archimedean condition." Monotonicity says that if the value difference between *a* and *b* is greater than that between a^* and b^*, and the difference between *b* and *c* is greater than that between b^* and c^*, then the difference between *a* and *c* is greater than that between a^* and c^*. The Archimedean condition rules out the possibility of infinitely large or infinitesimally small differences between value differences.

An interval scale permits us to compare ratios of value differences, but in order to speak meaningfully of ratios of individual values, we must be able to define an operation of "concatenation," allowing us to combine individual value bearers into larger wholes. Whether there is such a concatenation operation, with the required properties, depends on our substantial theory of the good. If the value bearers are assumed to be states of affairs or propositions, it is natural to identify concatenation with conjunction. This is problematic, however, since conjunction is idempotent, i.e.

$$(a \,\&\, a) = a,$$

whereas, in measurement structures, concatenating *a* with itself is typically supposed to result in an object different from *a*.

Moreover, a ratio scale requires that the monotonicity and Archimedean conditions hold, applied to individual values rather than to differences. Both conditions are controversial. Monotonicity is incompatible with "organic unities," of the kind famously defended by Moore (1903). An organic unity is a whole whose value is not a function of the values of its parts (although it may be a function of other properties of the parts). Being conscious of a beautiful object is one of Moore's examples of organic unities. Such a state of consciousness has great intrinsic value, according to Moore, although the object itself has little or no intrinsic value, and although mere consciousness does not generally confer great value on wholes of which it is a part. The Archimedean condition rules out the possibility that certain value bearers are infinitely better than certain others. Such infinite differences have been defended by a number of philosophers. Ross (1930) argued, for example, that although virtue and pleasure are both intrinsically good, no amount of pleasure outweighs the smallest amount of virtue.

So far, we have assumed representations to be in terms of real numbers. This is, of course, the standard way to mathematically represent values. From a measurement-theoretical point of view, however, representability by real numbers is not essential. We can define ordinal, interval, and ratio scales by functions with other mathematical entities as values, provided that the usual arithmetical operations, as well as the relations "greater than" and "equal to," are defined for the entities in question. Neither completeness nor the Archimedean property is necessary for measurement on an interval or ratio scale, if we allow the value of an object to be represented by some mathematical object other than a real number. Thus, it can be shown that a kind of ratio scale representation, by means of vectors of real numbers, is possible for structures involving incomparable objects (Carlson 2008). Similarly, structures involving infinite or infinitesimal value differences can be given a ratio scale representation in terms of ordered n-tuples of ordered pairs of real numbers.

In ethics, discussions about the structure and measurability of the good are not seldom unclear or confused, due to ignorance about measurement theory. For example, it is frequently argued that general comparability of value does not hold, on the grounds that goodness is not amenable to "calculation," or that it is not a "quantity" to which arithmetical operations can be applied. Such arguments reveal unawareness of the fact that comparability only requires that the value bearers can be completely ordered, with respect to goodness. A mere ordering does not imply that arithmetical operations on values of items (or on value differences) are meaningful.

Examples like this show that measurement theory is relevant to ethics, at least as a tool to increased clarity and precision. Whether measurement of theoretical results can have a more substantial impact on ethical issues is a vexed question, connected to fundamental meta-ethical problems. Constructivists about value may regard the fact that measurability presupposes certain structural properties, such as transitivity, as a reason for assuming goodness to have these properties.

A realist of a robust kind, on the other hand, is likely to hold that the structural properties of the good must be determined independently of issues of representation and measurement.

Decision and game theory

Decision theory is the study of individual rational decision-making. Its core tenet is that a rational agent maximizes her *expected utility*. Each option in a particular situation of choice is supposed to have a finite set of possible outcomes, exactly one of which will be actual if the option is chosen. For each option, the agent assigns, in a consistent way, a probability to each of its possible outcomes, on the condition that the option is chosen. Further, the agent is assumed to have a complete and transitive preference ordering over the set of possible outcomes. Given that these and certain other axioms hold, it can be shown that there is a "utility function," assigning numerical values to the outcomes in such a way that the agent prefers option a to option b if and only if a has greater expected utility than b. (This was first proved by von Neumann and Morgenstern 1947.) It should be stressed that, in decision theory, "utility" just refers to a representation of a rational person's preferences, and not to some independent value that he seeks to maximize. The expected utility of an option is calculated by multiplying, for each of its possible outcomes, the utility of the outcome with its probability, and then summing these products. Thus, suppose that option a has two possible outcomes, x and y, with utilities 9 and 5, and probabilities 0.3 and 0.7, respectively. The expected utility of a is then $(9 \times 0.3) + (5 \times 0.7) = 6.2$.

Importantly, a utility function contains information not merely about which options are preferred to which, but also about the strengths of the agent's preferences. If the difference between the utilities of outcomes x and y is twice the difference between the utilities of z and w, we can infer that she prefers x to y twice as strongly as she prefers z to w. This amounts to measurement on an interval scale.

Not everybody accepts maximization of expected utility as a criterion of rationality. There are situations where it is far from obviously irrational to violate one or more of the axioms of standard decision theory. Completeness and transitivity of preferences are debatable as universal requirements, and much discussed cases like "Allais' paradox" and the "St Petersburg paradox" cast doubt on other axioms.

Decision theory has had considerable influence on normative ethics, especially on consequentialist theories. Thus, some recently proposed forms of consequentialism maintain that an action is right just in case it maximizes expected value (Jackson 1991). According to such a theory, the value to be maximized is intrinsic or final value, rather than the agent's utility. Nevertheless, the structural part of the theory emulates decision theory. Some utilitarian versions of consequentialism resemble decision theory even more closely, by understanding intrinsic value in terms of the aggregated utilities of everyone affected by the action. Others have proposed the maximization of expected value, not as a criterion of rightness, but rather as a moral decision-making procedure.

Game theory is an extension of decision theory. It studies the outcomes of interaction between rational, i.e. expected-utility-maximizing, agents. (Here, too, the classic source is von Neumann and Morgenstern 1947.) A set of strategies, one for each player, is a "Nash equilibrium" (Nash 1950) just in case no individual can improve her pay-off, by changing her strategy, unless at least one other player also changes his strategy. (Note the similarity to the concept of Pareto optimality, defined in the next section.) Almost all theorists agree that if a game has a unique Nash equilibrium, that equilibrium is the only *solution* of the game. That is to say, it is the outcome that will occur, given that the players are rational. Any "zero-sum" game, in which one player's gain is balanced by the other's loss, has a unique Nash equilibrium. In games that are not zero-sum, however, there may be several Nash equilibria, and there is no general consensus among game theorists about how rational agents should choose among different equilibria.

The type of game that has received most attention by moral philosophers is the "prisoner's dilemma," or PD for short. In its simplest version, this is a two-person game, where each agent has two options. The structure of the game is often illustrated by a story about two accomplices, let us call them Dave and Eve, arrested on suspicion of a serious crime. The prosecutor gives each of them the following offer: "If you confess, and your accomplice remains silent, you will go free, while he will get a long sentence. Similarly, if he confesses and you keep silent, you will have to do the time. If you both confess, I will see to it that you both get early parole. If you both remain silent, I will have to settle for a short sentence for each." The dilemmatic feature of the situation is that it is better for each of Dave and Eve to confess, whatever the other does. If both confess, however, both will be worse-off than if both remain silent. The game is often depicted by the kind of matrix depicted in Figure 34.1, with the numbers representing years in prison for Dave and Eve, respectively.

Dave \ Eve	Confess	Be silent
Confess	8, 8	0, 12
Be silent	12, 0	2, 2

Figure 34.1 A prisoner's dilemma matrix (severity of harms to agents caused by alternative choices).

The only Nash equilibrium, and hence the only solution of this game is each player's confessing. It is easy to show that "agent-relative" moral theories lead to PDs. Consider, for example, a theory that says, in accordance with common-sense morality, that Dave ought to save his own child from a certain harm, rather than save Eve's child from a slightly greater harm, whereas the contrary holds for Eve. Letting the values in the matrix in Figure 34.1 represent the severity of the harms that befall the children, we see that both children suffer more if Dave and Eve both act so as to minimize the harm to his or her own child, than if they strive to minimize total harm. It has been argued that the possibility of such PDs shows agent-relative theories to be "self-defeating," and therefore seriously flawed (Parfit 1979).

Arguably, PDs involving many agents are common in real life. Serious and large-scale problems, such as global warming, may be cases in point. No matter what others do, it might be better for me to continue my present lifestyle, rather than stop travelling by air, use my car only when necessary, etc. If so, the same presumably holds for other, similarly situated individuals. Nevertheless, disaster for everyone might ensue, unless we all substantially change our way of living. Likewise, there may be one-person PDs, where the options are spread over time. If you are a smoker, it might be true of each cigarette that the pleasure it gives you outweighs the health risk it imposes. The combined effect of very many cigarettes could nevertheless be such that it would have been much better for you, had you never started smoking.

The fact that universal pursuance of rational self-interest can result in outcomes that are dispreferred by all, has been taken to indicate that adherence to moral rules, prescribing more altruistic behavior, can ultimately be justified in terms of individual rationality. Thus, several contemporary versions of moral contractualism rely on game-theoretical results and techniques. Contractualism is the view that political institutions or moral norms are justified insofar as rational persons would agree to accept them under suitable conditions. Game theory has been invoked to show that there would, in fact, be agreement under the specified conditions, and also to predict the outcome of the hypothesized negotiations between rational persons (Gauthier 1986). Other applications of game theory concern the *function* of morality. It is sometimes argued that the function of moral norms is to enable agents to cooperate, and coordinate, their actions, thereby achieving an outcome that is better for all, than what would ensue if everybody acted in a purely self-interested way (Ullman-Margalit 1977). A third trend is to use "evolutionary" game theory to explain the emergence of moral norms. On this approach, morality is seen as an unintended side effect of repeated interactions between people.

Functionalism, as well as the evolutionary approach, are sometimes judged to be of rather limited interest to moral philosophers, since these approaches only seek *explanations*, and not *justifications*, of moral norms. The fact that moral norms have a certain function (whatever that means, exactly), or that they have evolved in a certain way does not appear to give us any reason to accept them. Even so, game theory may provide the moral theorist with important insights. For example, the study of games with multiple equilibria indicates that any population will contain rational individuals with different dispositions or character traits. This may give us some reason to doubt that there is a unique set of dispositions, or virtues, that everyone should ideally acquire. (Verbeek and Morris [2004] contains a more extensive survey of applications of game theory in moral philosophy.)

Welfare economics and social choice theory

Welfare economics studies normative issues of resource allocation and policies of distribution, using the powerful mathematical tools of economics. The "old" school of welfare economists assumed interpersonal comparability, i.e. that one person's utility or welfare level can be compared to another's. Roughly since the 1930s, however, "new" welfare economics, eschewing interpersonal comparisons, has been dominant. Proponents of new welfare economics generally accept the "Pareto principle," named after the Italian economist Vilfredo Pareto, according to which a social state is acceptable only if it is "Pareto optimal." Pareto optimality means that nobody can be made better-off, without somebody else being made worse-off. As a sufficient condition of acceptability, Pareto optimality is questionable. Suppose the move from one Pareto optimal state to another would involve a gain for many badly-off people, and a loss for one well-off person. Many would consider the resulting state better than the original one, although both are Pareto optimal.

The necessity of Pareto optimality has also been questioned by moral philosophers. A state with perfect equality of welfare may be judged better than an unequal state, arrived at by making some people better-off, at the cost of nobody. (Note that this example presupposes interpersonal comparability.) Further, Sen (1982) has argued that the Pareto principle is incompatible with the liberal principle that each individual should be allowed to decide in personal matters, such as the color of one's shoes.

Since most economic changes involve winners as well as losers, the Pareto principle is a rather weak criterion of acceptability. Consequently, economists have tried to strengthen it, without invoking interpersonal comparisons, so as to allow judgements about cases involving trade-offs between individuals. Kaldor (1939) and Hicks (1939) proposed "compensation tests," suggesting, roughly, that a change from one social state to another is an improvement if the winners could compensate the losers. The resulting criteria of improvement are stronger than the original Pareto principle, but they are beset with two fundamental problems. First, they sometimes imply inconsistent judgements; one state may be judged better than another, and vice versa. Second, the criteria are ethically dubious, since it is not assumed that the imagined compensations are actually made. This tends to make the criteria biased in favor of the well-off, who are generally willing and able to pay compensation, in order to get what they want.

In the tradition of old welfare economics, Harsanyi (1953) proposed an "impartial observer" argument in favor of utilitarianism. An impartial observer should choose among social states as if she had an equal chance of being anyone in the society under consideration. If she is rational, she maximizes expected utility. According to Harsanyi, this constitutes a vindication of preference-based average utilitarianism. A common objection to Harsanyi's argument is that it illegitimately excludes risk aversion on the part of the impartial observer. Relying partly on another argument by Harsanyi, Broome (1991) aims to show that the social good is a sum of individual goods. This does not necessarily lead to standard utilitarianism, however, since inequality aversion can be included in the individuals' good.

For methodological as well as ideological reasons, economists usually equate welfare with utility or preference satisfaction. Since this conception of welfare is much less of an orthodoxy among moral philosophers, the ethical importance of the results and methods of welfare economics is contested. Broome (1999) has argued that although the preference-satisfaction theory of welfare is mistaken, the formal methods of economics can nevertheless be used to analyze the structure of welfare, or of the good quite generally. Moreover, some economists have proposed alternative conceptions of welfare. A prominent example is Sen's (1992) theory of welfare as capabilities.

Social choice theory is closely related to, but has a wider scope than welfare economics. It is concerned with the relations between individual preferences and values, on the one hand, and collective decision-making and evaluation, on the other. Its most famous result is an impossibility theorem, due to Arrow (1963/1951). Like Nash's work in game theory, Arrow's axiomatic approach set a new standard of clarity and rigor in the theory of social choice. Arrow showed that individual preference orderings cannot in general be aggregated into a rule for social decision or evaluation, given three reasonable assumptions: first, if everybody ranks *a* above *b*, then *a* is better than *b* ("weak Pareto principle"); second, the social ranking of any two alternatives depends only on the individual orderings of these two alternatives ("independence of irrelevant alternatives"); third, there is no individual whose preference ordering determines the social ordering, regardless of the other individuals' preferences ("nondictatorship").

Importantly, Arrow's impossibility result presupposes that each individual's preferences are only measured on an ordinal scale, and that interpersonal comparisons of preference strength cannot be made. If there is interpersonal comparability, certain social orderings, such as those based on the "maximin" principle (Rawls 1971), are possible even if ordinalism is retained. (The maximin principle says that one social state is better than another just in case the worst-off in the former state are better-off than the worst-off in the latter state.)

If, in addition, cardinal measurement of individual preference strength is possible, certain forms of utilitarianism, such as Harsanyi's theory, are also viable.

One particular topic in ethics, where formal methods from social choice theory have significantly advanced the discussion, is "population ethics." This part of ethics concerns choices which affect the number and identity of people who will exist in the future. Systematic philosophical study of these questions began in the 1970s, and the *locus classicus* is Parfit (1984). Parfit observed that total utilitarianism implies the "Repugnant Conclusion," that a huge population of people with lives barely worth living is better than a moderately large but very happy population. Average utilitarianism, on the other hand, implies that a very small but very happy population is better than a large and only slightly less happy one. Thus, total utilitarianism one-sidedly favors "quantity," while average utilitarianism one-sidedly favors "quality." Parfit tried, unsuccessfully on his own account, to find a theory that strikes the right balance between quantity and quality. (He also pointed out other important problems, concerning the import of negative welfare.) The core of the problem is a tension between three intuitively plausible criteria. First, adding people with positive welfare to a population should not result in a worse state. Second, an equality-increasing redistribution of welfare should make a state better, or at least not worse. Third, the repugnant conclusion should be avoided.

Arrhenius (2000) has shown that even quite weak versions of these three criteria are mutually inconsistent, leading to an impossibility theorem for population ethics. Others have rejected or modified the first criterion, given up the second criterion, or accepted the repugnant conclusion. The approach of Parfit's seminal work was quite informal, and it is clear, in retrospect, that many pitfalls and dead-ends could have been avoided, if greater mathematical sophistication had been brought into the debate at an earlier stage.

See also Realism and its alternatives (Chapter 26); Non-cognitivism (Chapter 27); Consequentialism (Chapter 37); Contemporary Kantian ethics (Chapter 38); Contractualism (Chapter 41); Ideals of perfection (Chapter 55); Population ethics (Chapter 61).

References

Arrhenius, G. (2000) "An Impossibility Theorem for Welfarist Axiologies," *Economics and Philosophy* 16: 247–66.

Arrow, K. (1963/1951) *Social Choice and Individual Values*, 2nd edn, New York: Wiley.

Belzer, M. (1998) "Deontic Logic," in E. Craig (ed.) *Routledge Encyclopedia of Philosophy*, London: Routledge.

Broome, J. (1991) *Weighing Goods: Equality, Uncertainty, and Time*, Oxford: Basil Blackwell.

——(1999) *Ethics Out of Economics*, Cambridge: Cambridge University Press.

Carlson, E. (2008) "Extensive Measurement with Incomparability," *Journal of Mathematical Psychology* 52: 250–9.
Chisholm, R. M. (1974) "Practical Reason and the Logic of Requirement," in S. Körner (ed.) *Practical Reason*, New Haven, CT: Yale University Press.
Feldman, F. (1986) *Doing the Best We Can: An Essay in Informal Deontic Logic*, Dordrecht and Boston: D. Reidel.
Gauthier, D. (1986) *Morals by Agreement*, Oxford: Clarendon Press.
Harsanyi, J. (1953) "Cardinal Utility in Welfare Economics and in the Theory of Risk-Taking," *Journal of Political Economy* 61: 434–5.
Hicks, J. R. (1939) "The Foundations of Welfare Economics," *Economic Journal* 49: 696–712.
Jackson, F. (1991) "Decision-Theoretic Consequentialism and the Nearest and Dearest Objection," *Ethics* 101: 461–82.
Jackson, F. and Pargetter, R. (1986) "Oughts, Options and Actualism," *Philosophical Review* 95: 233–55.
Kaldor, N. (1939) "Welfare Propositions and Interpersonal Comparisons of Utility," *Economic Journal* 49: 549–52.
Moore, G. E. (1903) *Principia Ethica*, Cambridge: Cambridge University Press.
Nash, J. (1950) "The Bargaining Problem," *Econometrica* 18: 155–62.
Parfit, D. (1979) "Is Common-Sense Morality Self-Defeating?" *Journal of Philosophy* 76: 533–45.
——(1984) *Reasons and Persons*, Oxford: Clarendon Press.
Rachels, S. (1998) "Counterexamples to the Transitivity of *Better Than*," *Australasian Journal of Philosophy* 76: 71–83.
Rawls, J. (1971) *A Theory of Justice*, Cambridge, MA: Harvard University Press.
Raz, J. (1986) *The Morality of Freedom*, Oxford: Clarendon Press.
Ross, W. D. (1930) *The Right and the Good*, Oxford: Clarendon Press.
Schurz, G. (1997) *The Is–Ought Problem*, Dordrecht: Kluwer Academic.
Sen, A. (1982) *Choice, Welfare and Measurement*, Oxford: Blackwell.
——(1992) *Inequality Re-examined*, Oxford: Clarendon Press.
Ullman-Margalit, E. (1977) *The Emergence of Norms*, Oxford: Oxford University Press.
Verbeek, B. and Morris, C. W. (2004) "Game Theory and Ethics," *Stanford Encyclopedia of Philosophy*, <http://plato.stanford.edu/entries/game-ethics/>
von Neumann, J. and Morgenstern, O. (1947) *The Theory of Games and Economic Behavior*, 2nd edn, Princeton, NJ: Princeton University Press.
von Wright, G. H. (1951) "Deontic Logic," *Mind* 60: 1–15.
Zimmerman, M. J. (1996) *The Concept of Moral Obligation*, Cambridge: Cambridge University Press.

Further reading

Broome, J. (1999) *Ethics out of Economics*, Cambridge: Cambridge University Press. (Collection of essays, applying methods from economics to ethics. Not overly technical.)
Forrester, J. W. (1996) *Being Good and Being Logical. Philosophical Groundwork for a New Deontic Logic*, Armonk, NY, and London: M. E. Sharpe. (Lucid discussion of different systems of deontic logic, from the perspective of moral philosophy.)
Resnik, M. (1987) *Choices: An Introduction to Decision Theory*, Minneapolis: University of Minnesota Press. (Accessible introduction to decision and game theory.)
Roberts, F. S. (1979) *Measurement Theory with Applications to Decisionmaking, Utility, and the Social Sciences*, Reading, MA: Addison-Wesley. (Comprehensive but relatively accessible introduction to measurement theory, with applications relevant to ethics.)

35
ETHICS AND LAW

John Gardner

Does law have moral aims?

Law, unlike morality, is made by someone. So it may, unlike morality, have aims, which are the aims of its makers (either individually or collectively). Not all law has aims, however, because not all law making is intentional. Customary law is made by convergent actions that are performed without the intention of making law, and so without any further intention to achieve anything by making law, i.e. without any aim. There are also some other modes of accidental law-making. However, for the time being we will focus on law that is intentionally made, and therefore is capable of having aims.

Some have thought that law must, by its nature, have certain distinctive moral aims when it has aims at all. If it lacks those aims it is not law. It must aim to be just (Postema 1996: 80), or aim to serve the common good (Finnis 1980: 276), or aim to justify coercion (Dworkin 1986: 93), or aim to be in some other way morally binding or morally successful. The problem with such views is that at least some intentional makers of law have no moral aims. They are entirely cynical. They use law making purely as an instrument of profit, retaliation or consolidation of power. Sure, one may still attribute moral aims to law made by such people if it is intentionally developed or adapted by subsequent officials with moral aims. Later judges, for instance, may interpret a law as having a moral aim, and thereby endow it with one, even when it lacked one at inception. But judges too may, on occasions, be entirely cynical. Whole legal systems may, indeed, be run by cartels of self-serving officials for whom the system is primarily an elaborate extortion racket or a huge joke.

Here law has no moral aims. Yet all legal officials, even in such a system, must at least *pretend* to have moral aims when they act in their official capacities. Or as it is often put, they must at least make moral *claims* on behalf of law (Raz 1979: 28–33; Alexy 1989: 177–82). This doesn't mean, of course, that without moral claims these people will fail in their non-moral aims (e.g. lose their profit or privilege or power base). That may be true, but it is beside the point. The point is that inasmuch as they are law's spokespeople, officials cannot avoid making moral claims for law. These are the very claims that (in combination with certain other criteria) mark these people out as legal officials.

In identifying the claims of law, the place to begin is with the language that legal officials use. In setting out or explaining legal norms, officials cannot but use the language of obligations, rights, permissions, powers, liabilities, and so on. What they thereby claim is that the law imposes obligations, creates rights, grants permissions, confers powers, gives rise to liabilities, and so on. One might think that the claim here need not be a moral claim. Officials need be claiming only that there are *legal* obligations, *legal* rights, *legal* permissions, and so forth, not moral ones. But that cannot be all that their claim for law amounts to. For a legal obligation or right or permission is none other than an obligation or right or permission that exists according to law, and an obligation or right or permission that exists according to law is none other than an obligation or right or permission, the existence of which law claims. So claiming the existence of a legal obligation is simply claiming the existence of what law claims to be an obligation. It is a second-order claim. Officials (and lawyers and legal commentators, and so on) have plenty of reasons and occasions to make such second-order claims, but when they do it they are reporting law's claims, not making them. On pain of vacuity or infinite regress, we still need to attribute to law itself a suitable first-order claim. Legal obligations are claimed to be something, but what are they claimed to be? This is where the idea that law makes a moral claim comes in. "Moral," in this context, is the name given to the kind of obligation that legal obligations are claimed by law to be. Legal obligations are claimed to be obligations that are not merely claimed, and hence that are not merely legal. They are claimed to have a standing beyond law, or to bind (as it is sometimes put) in conscience as well as in law (Finnis 2005).

Does law ever form part of morality?

That law makes a moral claim for itself means that the paradigm or ideal-type of law – the model to which all other law needs to be compared and through which it needs to be understood – is morally justified law (Finnis 1980: 14–15). That is because the paradigm or ideal-type of anything that has aims is the case in which it succeeds in those aims, and the paradigm or ideal-type of anything that makes claims is the case in which it makes those claims sincerely. Law makes moral claims, and when it makes those claims sincerely it has moral aims, and when it succeeds in those aims it is morally justified law. It is law that actually lives up to the moral standards that, by its nature as law, it holds itself out as living up to. It is law's paradigm case.

When law is morally justified – in law's paradigm case – it has the hold that it claims to have over those to whom it applies. Its norms have moral force. This need not always be a matter of being morally obligatory. Some legal norms impose obligations, and when they do so and they are morally justified in doing so, they impose moral as well as legal obligations. But other legal norms confer powers or grant permissions (Hart 1961: 79, 247). When a legal norm confers a power or grants a permission, and the conferral or grant is morally justified, the norm equally confers a moral power or grants a moral permission as the case may be, i.e. it enables the conferee to change someone's moral as well as legal position, or makes some course of action by the grantee morally as well as legally permissible.

When a legal norm is morally justified, to generalize, it becomes part of morality. Now I started by saying that morality, unlike law, is not made by anybody. It has no sources, no officials, and no agency capable of making rulings. But this point now needs to be qualified. Morality does have these trappings to the extent that it is itself constituted by law. When a legal norm becomes part of morality, there is a sense in which law's sources and officials become sources and officials of morality too. There is then a pocket of moral authority. Yet one cannot understand morality as a whole on this model. There can be no general moral authority. Why? Because there is a further condition to be met before a legal norm (or indeed any norm that is made by somebody) becomes part of morality, namely that its application to those to whom it applies must be morally justified. There need to be independent moral standards by which the exercise of authority can be judged in order to determine whether it has the moral force that it claims to have.

There is a hint of paradox, you may think, about the idea that morally justified legal norms become part of morality. Why does morality need them? You may think that inasmuch as they are morally justified they merely duplicate content that morality already has, and so the condition of their becoming part of morality is also the condition of their moral redundancy (Coleman and Leiter 1996: 244). But this is a mistake. Morally justified legal norms need not merely replicate content that morality already has. Morally, for example, I have a reason not to crash my car into yours, namely that I may hurt you. This means that I have a reason to drive my car on the same side of the road – left or right – as you drive yours on. But morality is indifferent as between left and right. It does not matter, morally, whether we both keep left or both keep right, so long as we both do the same. The law can make it a rule that we should keep left rather than right. So long as we are both willing to accept the law's authority, and all else being equal, the law's intervention in this case is morally justified, as it will enable us to do, or to do better, what morally we already have reason to do. Yet it does not merely duplicate morality's existing content. Morality already told us what to do but law added, by its authority, a suitable way to do it (Finnis 1989; Honoré 1993).

Such a case is known as a coordination case and it is one kind of case in which law adds to morality. The need for law to add to morality in such cases comes of the gappiness of morality. On many questions morality is silent. (Left or right on the road?) On others it harbors internal conflicts that it cannot resolve on its own. (Kill one innocent to stop the killing of two innocents?) On still others it is afflicted by conceptual indeterminacy. (Can one be cruel to be kind?) Either way, the morally best solution may sometimes (only sometimes) be whichever solution people can converge on, thereby reducing error and wasteful dispute.

Here law's coordinating ability is called for, or is at least available, to make morality less gappy than it would otherwise be. Law can also help us in other ways to do what morally we have reason to do (Raz 1986: 75). It can help us, from time to time, with extra expertise or extra wisdom. It can also help to strengthen our resolve. In the latter case the legal norm typically replicates the content of a moral norm that exists independently of it but changes the moral consequences of failure to conform to it (i.e. the further moral norms that bear on what is to be done in response to the failure). This is another important way in which law may make morally justified interventions, thereby adding to morality. The important thing to understand, however, is that law's interventions are not automatically morally justified. Often law does not restrict itself to choosing between morally eligible alternatives but chooses instead a morally unacceptable one. All else being equal we should treat law, in such cases, with the contempt or ridicule that it deserves. For it is a long way from claiming moral authority to actually having it.

Does morality ever form part of law?

Morality is gappy and sometimes needs law to help fill in the gaps. But the same is also true in reverse. Often law is gappy and needs morality's help to make it less so. Legal norms, like moral norms, often conflict among themselves, and often such conflicts cannot be resolved using legal norms alone. Indeterminacies of language and intention on the part of lawmakers, moreover, can afflict law in such a way as to frustrate its role as a filler of moral gaps. Legal conflict and indeterminacy require extra-legal resources to overcome them (Raz 1979: 53–77). And the need to overcome them is often pressing in law. Many legal officials, notably judges, are bound by their oaths (or other duties) of office to decide any case before them that falls within their jurisdiction. They cannot suspend their judgment. Whereas the rest of us can often suspend judgment and keep it suspended.

How do judges, the legal officials most publicly afflicted by such legal gaps, bring morality to bear on their legal deliberations? A simple view, sketched by Hart (1961: 124–54), goes like this. First, a judge goes as far as she can with legal norms. Then she has a gap, and a consequent legal discretion. She exercises the discretion by using moral reasons and norms (or indeed any other available reasons and norms) to fill in the gap. By doing this she makes new legal norms. This is the converse of the coordination case discussed above, in which a moral gap exists which law enables us to fill (by choosing left rather than right, for example). But it is rather rare for judges to fill gaps in this quasi-legislative way. In most legal cultures it is a last resort. Instead, judges usually fill gaps by engaging in legal reasoning. They combine existing legal norms with other premises, including moral premises not hitherto recognized by law, to reach new legal conclusions. You may say that this is not really legal reasoning since, by hypothesis, it includes norms not hitherto recognized by law. True, this means it is not reasoning *about* the law. The judge who engages in such reasoning is not working out what the law already says. But it is reasoning *with* (or according to) the law. The law figures non-redundantly in the judge's reasoning even though it does not by itself determine the judge's conclusion (Raz 1994: 326–40).

Here is a typical example of legal reasoning understood as reasoning with (or according to) the law:

(1) Nobody is to be discriminated against in respect of employment on the ground of his or her sex (existing legal rule).
(2) Denying a woman a job on the ground of her pregnancy is morally on a par with denying her a job on the ground of her sex, even though there is no male comparator to a pregnant woman that would allow the denial to count as sex-discriminatory in the technical sense hitherto recognized by law (moral proposal, invoking a moral norm of parity).

Thus (3) nobody is to be denied a job on the ground of her pregnancy (new legal rule).

(4) *P* was denied a job by *D* on the ground of her (*P*'s) pregnancy (finding of fact).

Thus (5) *D* still owes *P* the job she was denied, or some substitute relief (legal ruling).

I included the final steps (4) and (5) to make clear that the ruling in the case (5) is a different legal norm from the rule on which it is based (3), even if the content of the ruling follows from the application of the rule to the facts as found (4). It is a different norm because it has different legal consequences. In particular, it usually allows *P* to access enforcement options which would not be available without the ruling in her favor. It is also worth mentioning that the ruling in the case (5) may bind later officials even if the rule on which it is based (3) does not. Whether the rule (3) binds later officials depends on whether the court engaging in the reasoning is at a level in the court system that allows it to create binding precedents. But the ruling in (5) binds later officials even if the court engaging in the reasoning is the lowest court with jurisdiction, for it is part of the nature of a court that its rulings bind even if its rules do not.

Most misunderstandings center on the status of (2) and the consequent status of (3). Many people worry about where the court gets its license to invoke a moral norm in (2) and thereby change the law to include (3). A common reaction is to try and show that (3) is really already part of the law before the court arrives at it, often by arguing that (2) is already part of the law before the court invokes it (Dworkin 1967: 16–40), or at any rate is covered by some more general law that licenses its use (Coleman 2001: 103–19). Some are even driven to argue that there is a body of law that comes into existence without anyone's ever having announced it, used it, or otherwise interacted with it. This maneuvering is needed only because of a mistaken assumption that judges, while they remain judges, owe all their loyalty to law. On this assumption, the key question is: How, legally, do judges come to be entitled to invoke morality? How can they properly help themselves to premise (2)? But this reverses the proper order of inquiry. The key question about judges is: How, morally, do judges come to be entitled to invoke the law? How can they properly help themselves to premise (1)? For judges are human beings like the rest of us. By virtue of that fact, morality has an inescapable hold over them. Whereas their relationship to the law is escapable. They need a moral reason to hold themselves answerable to law, but they need no legal reason to hold themselves answerable to morality (Raz 2004).

What moral reason do judges have to hold themselves answerable to law? Well of course, they have the same reasons as you and me. They should apply morally justified law because it forms part of morality; it has the moral force it purports to have. But judges, and some other legal officials, have extra-moral reasons going beyond this. They have extra-moral reasons to uphold the law that extend even to some cases of morally unjustified law. For they have undertaken to uphold the law when they took the job, and this gives legal norms extra force in their work that those norms would not have had apart from the undertaking to uphold them. Judges should tolerate some moral deficiencies in the law that they should not have tolerated had they not undertaken, as part of the job, to uphold the law. But they should not by that same token tolerate just any moral deficiency in the law. Invariably, as in the example schematized as (1) to (5) above, they should strive to improve the law, at the very least by filling in its gaps in a morally decent way. Sometimes they should also improve it by reversing or containing immoralities introduced by other officials, inasmuch as they retain the legal power to do so. And just occasionally, in cases of extreme immorality, they should simply disobey the law (while perhaps pretending to uphold it).

In many legal systems the moral commitment to uphold the law that the judge undertakes on taking the job is formalized in an oath of office. The content of such oaths is worth noting. In most legal systems judges take an oath to do "justice according to law," or something like that. This is not an oath to apply the law. On the contrary, it is an oath to do justice, to decide cases in a morally meritorious way. To do so is not to usurp the role of the legislature. For the oath does not authorize judicial legislation. It authorizes judicial changes in the law, to make the law more just, but only when these changes are brought about by legal reasoning, i.e. by reasoning with (or according to) law. That is the "according to law" part of the oath. This explains the sense in which legal reasoning is a kind of moral reasoning. Notice that it remains consistent with the idea that all law is made by somebody. In this case, it is made by somebody (a judge) who makes new law by using a moral norm in her reasoning, a moral norm that thereby becomes legally recognized. Morality does not enter the law of its own accord. By the nature of law, it always takes an official to turn a moral norm into a legal one.

Does law have an inner morality?

Some people are drawn to the idea that nothing is legal unless it passes a moral test. This is quite different from the idea that morality sometimes and somehow passes into law of its own accord, without official intervention. One may accept that nothing enters the law without official intervention, and yet insist that a distinct moral test *also* needs to be passed before any norm qualifies as a legal one. The most enduring versions of this proposal claim that there is a moral value or ideal called *legality*, which is such that a norm qualifies as a legal one only if it exhibits this value (Dworkin 2004: 23–37). Many subscribers to this view add that exhibiting the value of legality is a matter of degree, such that norms can be *more or less* legal.

There is some confusion here. It is true that there is a moral ideal of legality, and that law can approximate to (or depart from) this ideal, and in that sense be more (or less) legal. The ideal, however, applies to law because it is law. It is not that it is law because it lives up to the ideal. If it were not law, to put it another way, it would not be held up to the ideal of legality in the first place and so could not be found wanting relative to that ideal (Finnis 1980: 363–6). So it cannot be the case that if it is found wanting relative to that ideal, it is not law. Actually, this is a slight exaggeration. The ideal of legality can also be used to judge other norms and systems of norms to the extent that they are law-like. But once again this requires their law-likeness to be determined independently of whether they live up to the ideal. Law, then, is always legal in one sense (it always forms part of some legal system) but it can be more or less legal in another sense. It is not an oxymoron, therefore, to speak of illegal law. Its being law is determined without moral argument, just by looking to the agent by whom and the way in which it was made. Its being illegal in the relevant sense is, however, a moral judgment that one can make about it once one accepts that it is law.

What is the ideal of legality? It is the ideal also known as the rule of law or *Rechtsstaat* (MacCormick 1984) or the "inner morality" of law (Fuller 1964). It is an ideal of government (or rule) by law, in which people can be guided by the law itself and by the expectation that officials too will be guided by the law. Its main ingredients are the following norms: legal rules should be prospective, open, clear, and stable; legal rulings should be based on these prospective, open, clear, and stable legal rules; the rules should be administered by an independent judiciary, with review powers over other officials; the courts should be open and accessible; and the principles of *audi alterem partem* ("both sides are to be heard") and *nemo in sua causa iudex* ("nobody is to be judge in his own cause") should be observed (Raz 1979: 214–19).

It is easy to see here why lawyers, who tend to be professionally committed to this ideal of legality, might be morally anxious about judicial legislation, or more generally about judicial law making. For judicial law making may seem to violate several of the norms on the above list. The law that is applied in such cases is not prospectively created, and is not clear at the time when it is violated, and to the extent that it is clear the ruling is not based on it. The law is, in short, unavailable for the guidance of those who are supposed to be guided by it. No wonder some theorists are motivated to find a way of showing that premise (2), in the example of legal reasoning that we set out above, is already part of the law before the judge makes it so.

In fact, however, the ideal of legality does not frown on judicial law making nearly so comprehensively as this line of thought suggests. First, there are inevitably gaps in the law and we cannot avoid leaving judges to fill them. So long as judges avoid legislating and instead fill these inevitable gaps by legal reasoning, they rely on the law in developing the law and do not defeat anyone's expectations of it. So the ideal of legality is not engaged and cannot be frustrated. Secondly, there are conflicting demands within the ideal of legality itself. Some sacrifice of prospective clarity in the law may be warranted to, for example, ensure that everyone gets a fair hearing. Finally, and most importantly, the ideal of legality is not the be-all and end-all of moral success on the part of the law. Its norms may clash with other moral norms that are not part of the ideal of legality. On those occasions the legality of law should sometimes be sacrificed in favor of making other moral improvements in the law. On such occasions, judges may justifiably depart from the law (say, by overruling) even if that defeats people's expectations. The last point is often overlooked. The paradigm of law is law that exhibits all of the moral virtues that can be exhibited by institutions, not just the virtue of legality. When law can exhibit legality only at the expense of other moral virtues, it is by no means a foregone conclusion that legality must triumph.

Is there a moral obligation to obey the law?

We have already encountered two important points about the moral obligatoriness of law. The first is that obligation-imposing legal norms are sometimes morally justified, and when they are they create moral obligations as well. The "sometimes" here should be understood as referring to differences between different legal norms, but also to differences between different applications of one and the same legal norm. A legal rule may be morally justified as it applies to one person and not as it applies to another, or morally justified as it applies to one action and not as it applies to another. A legal rule that forbids driving through a red traffic light has more to be said for it, morally speaking, when the red light is at a busy intersection than when it is in the middle of nowhere. In some cases the traffic light's location may be so stupid as to render the law, in connection with that red light, morally unjustified, so that the legal obligation to stop that it creates does not yield a similar moral obligation. All such matters depend on the details of the case. It is hard to imagine any law that has *all* the moral force that it claims for itself. Even the best of laws encounter cases where they overextend to the point at which their application is morally unjustified, so that ideally they should be reined in.

The second point we have encountered is that people may add to the range of moral obligations that the law gives them by taking oaths or vows of obedience, by promising or undertaking to obey, or by otherwise committing themselves to obedience. By these methods people can bind themselves to follow even morally unjustified laws: overcomplicated laws, futile laws, overextensive laws, although probably not positively immoral laws. The people we already mentioned who typically find themselves in this position are judges. But there are others. New immigrants, police officers, heads of state, and various others often make such commitments. But most people do not make them, and they cannot be made to do so. If someone were to attempt to make them commit themselves, that would already neutralize the moral effect of the act of commitment and so would be a self-defeating intervention.

A long-standing tradition in political philosophy has attempted to extend the reach of such commitment, and hence of the extra-moral obligations to which it gives rise, to everyone to whom the law applies, or at least to every citizen to whom the law applies. Elaborate arguments have been made to show how people who never made oaths or other undertakings to obey the law should nevertheless be treated as having done so. The most interesting question about this long but ill-starred tradition is: Why would it matter so much to show that people have an extensive moral obligation to obey the law, akin to that of judges and police officers? Why would one go to such elaborate trouble to show consent, contract, or other commitment? This is something of a mystery. There seems to be a common anxiety about social disorder, about the breakdown of the rule of law. This anxiety is reasonable. But the existence or not of a moral obligation to obey the law is irrelevant to the prospect of social disorder. At most the avoidance of social disorder gives one a reason to *pretend* to people that they have a moral obligation to obey the law, i.e. to claim for law more moral justification than it actually has. And even this pretense is defensible only if people intent on social disorder will care about (what they believe to be) their moral obligations. But why would they? If they don't already care about their moral obligation not to bring about social disorder, their obligation not to threaten the Rule of Law, why would they care about their supposed moral obligation to obey the law, which seems of only paltry significance by comparison? The same is true of murderers. If they don't already give weight to their moral obligation not to murder, what makes us think that they will give more weight to a moral obligation to obey the law of murder? What such people need to stop them are effective threats of sanctions, and whether the law lays on effective threats is quite independent of whether there is a moral obligation to obey it on the part of the threatened person.

The moral problem of the law is not the problem of how or why it speaks to moral delinquents. The moral problem of the law is the problem of how and why it speaks to morally decent people. Why, morally speaking, should they cave in before the law? Why should they give credence to the say-so of elderly men in wigs, pork-barrel politicians, or burly fellows with riot shields? Is this not a morally irresponsible surrender of moral judgment (Wolff 1970)? We saw already that sometimes it is justified. But there is no reason to think that it always is, or that it typically is, or that it presumptively is. The law should be viewed with a skeptical eye, to see what nonsense (or worse) it is trying to get us to accept by claiming moral authority for itself.

See also Reasons, values, and morality (Chapter 36); Justice and punishment (Chapter 57).

References

Alexy, Robert (1989) "On Necessary Relations Between Law and Morality," *Ratio Juris* 2, no. 2: 167–83.

Coleman, Jules (2001) *The Practice of Principle*, Oxford: Oxford University Press.

Coleman, Jules and Leiter, Brian (1996) "Legal Positivism," in Dennis Patterson (ed.) *A Companion to Philosophy of Law and Legal Theory*, Oxford: Blackwell, pp. 241–60.

Dworkin, Ronald (1967) "The Model of Rules," *University of Chicago Law Review* 35: 14–46.

——(1986), *Law's Empire*, Cambridge, MA: Harvard University Press.

——(2004) "Hart's Postscript and the Character of Political Philosophy," *Oxford Journal of Legal Studies* 24: 1–37.

Finnis, John (1980) *Natural Law and Natural Rights*, Oxford: Clarendon Press.

——(1989) "Law as Co-ordination," *Ratio Juris* 2, no. 1: 97–104.

——(2005) "Aquinas' Moral, Political and Legal Philosophy," in Edward N. Zalta (ed.) *Stanford Encyclopedia of Philosophy*, <http://plato.stanford.edu/entries/aquinas-moral-political>

Fuller, Lon (1964) *The Morality of Law*, New Haven, CT: Yale University Press.

Hart, H. L. A. (1961) *The Concept of Law*, Oxford: Clarendon Press.

Honoré, Tony (1993) "The Dependence of Morality upon Law," *Oxford Journal of Legal Studies* 13: 1–17.

MacCormick, Neil (1984) "Der Rechtsstaat und die Rule of Law," *JuristenZeitung* 39: 65–70.

Postema, Gerald (1999/1996) "Law's Autonomy and Public Practical Reason," in Robert George (ed.) *The Autonomy of Law*, Oxford: Oxford University Press.

Raz, Joseph (1979) *The Authority of Law*, Oxford: Clarendon Press.

——(1986) *The Morality of Freedom*, Oxford: Clarendon Press.

——(1994) *Ethics in the Public Domain*, Oxford: Clarendon Press.

——(2004) "Incorporation by Law," *Legal Theory* 10: 1–17.

Wolff, Robert Paul (1970) *In Defense of Anarchism*, New York: Harper & Row.

Further reading

Lyons, David (1984) *Ethics and the Rule of Law*, Cambridge: Cambridge University Press.

Part IV
PERSPECTIVES IN ETHICS

36
REASONS, VALUES, AND MORALITY

Simon Robertson

Morality is a body of thought and practice focused in the first instance on the normative and evaluative status of actions, especially as they affect others. At one level, it is a social phenomenon involving a range of norms and expectations informing how we are to treat those around us. But the term "morality" is also used more technically to designate a certain style of ethical outlook or theory, one comprising a system of duties regulating relations between people, compliance to which on many accounts is categorically required. This chapter focuses on morality in this more specific sense, examining its connections with normative reasons for action and values. These are wide-ranging topics informed by and bearing on a variety of issues in both normative and meta-ethical theory; they go to the heart of questions about the nature, justification, and foundations of morality. The first section, "Morality as a perspective within ethics," begins by locating morality within normative and evaluative thought more generally. The second, "Moral obligation and reasons," is organized around the theme that morality is "normatively authoritative," and explores different views about moral obligation and reasons for action. The third, "Values and morality," turns to the role of value, both moral and non-moral, in ethical thought.

Morality as a perspective within ethics

On one broad construal, ethical enquiry encompasses the whole domain of evaluative and normative thought as it bears on the good life and how one should live. It is common to view morality more narrowly as either a particular perspective within, or instance of, ethics. Some view it as one compartment of ethical thought that serves to regulate the whole – other compartments including self-interest, excellence, the aesthetic, and so on. On this view, without morality there may be no constraints on how the potentially conflicting interests and needs of different people are to be regulated. Others regard any ethical outlook as essentially regulatory, while treating morality as one particular form of ethical outlook distinguished from others by the notion of obligation integral to it. Either way, morality is a regulative enterprise. Defining it more precisely remains an ambitious task. Nevertheless, we can usefully circumscribe our topic as follows.

First, it is often said that modern morality represents a law-conception of ethics structured through *deontic* concepts like moral *right*, *wrong*, *obligation* and *permissibility*. Many take these to be inter-definable. For instance: "A's doing *x* is morally right" = "A has a moral obligation to do *x*" = "A is not morally permitted not to do *x*"; "A's doing *x* is morally wrong" = "A has a moral obligation not to do *x*" = "A is not morally permitted to do *x*." (These equivalences can be contested, though in this chapter I adhere to them.) Then there are also *evaluative* concepts by which we appraise people's actions, motives, and intentions; these include *good*, *bad*, *better*, *worse*, as well as thicker modes of assessment like *generous*, *cruel*, *unfair*. How the deontic and evaluative connect is controversial; but we may provisionally place them together as forming part of the normative realm.

Second, there are many approaches to characterizing morality – in terms of a supposed (e.g. regulative) function, a distinctive (e.g. other-regarding) content, its formal features (e.g. universalizability), its characteristic sentiments and sanctions (e.g. blame and guilt). Each has its limitations and, arguably, ends up referring back to more basic notions like obligation. In combination, though, they offer a good indication of what morality involves. Let's characterize it as a system of thought and practice regulating relations between people via (generally other-regarding) obligations the violation of which merits blame. On a traditional view, moral obligations are also normatively authoritative and universal. Whether such features are essential to moral obligation remains disputed; we turn to such issues shortly.

Third, while morality's focus on action places it firmly within the *practical* normative sphere, it plausibly extends beyond this to involve those aspects of belief, feeling, and character that bear on conduct – what one is justified in believing one ought to do in light of the available evidence, what it is reasonable to feel in response to wrongdoing, which dispositions of character one should cultivate. The interaction of belief, feeling, and action as they figure in moral thought is a far-reaching topic. The rest of the chapter focuses on issues more closely connected to the authority of morality.

Moral obligation and reasons

It is often said that morality embodies a claim to "objectivity." This can mean many things. In the context specifically of moral obligation, a common idea is that whether a person has a moral obligation does not generally depend on that person's subjective desires, aims, ends, interests, and the like – or, as we may collectively call these, the person's "motives." More precisely, if you have a moral obligation, you have that obligation irrespective of whether doing as it specifies either serves or conflicts with your motives. A further claim is that moral obligations are objective in virtue of being normatively authoritative. This too can mean many things, though a common thought is that morality represents an authoritative standpoint because we necessarily have reason to do as it demands. One way to explicate this generic idea is in terms of the conjunction of the following two claims: first, that moral obligations entail normative reasons to act, in that someone who has a moral obligation has a reason to do what it demands; second, that the person has this reason irrespective of whether doing as the obligation demands either serves or conflicts with the person's motives. For example, if you have a moral obligation to refrain from murder, you have a reason to so refrain irrespective of whether committing the murder serves or conflicts with your own subjective aims or interests. This section examines the normative authority thesis.

To clarify what it involves, let's begin by considering, and contrasting it to, the following thesis:

> (1) A has a moral obligation to do $x \rightarrow$ A has that obligation whether or not doing x serves A's motives.

This is distinct from the idea that moral obligations are normatively authoritative, since it makes no claim about the connection between moral obligation and reasons. By itself, (1) therefore leaves open whether someone who has a moral obligation to do x thereby has a reason to do x. Whether a person does have a reason to do what he has a moral obligation to do depends in part on how we understand the expression "has a moral obligation," for instance, as it figures in the antecedent of (1). (1) could be read as saying "*According to morality*, if A has an obligation to do x, A has that obligation whether or not doing x serves A's motives." However, that could be true even if A has no genuine reason to do x. For it doesn't follow from the fact that some system of norms *claims* you have an obligation to do something that you have a reason to do it. Philippa Foot (1978) makes this point by considering duties derived from norms of etiquette. It might be true, according to etiquette, that women are forbidden from offering their hand when greeting men unless the man first offers his. But if such duties and prohibitions are themselves frivolous nonsense, there may be no reason to comply with them. Similarly, it may be true according to the laws of a fascist state that you are legally required to engage in racist activity; but it doesn't follow from this that you actually have reason to do so. Whether you do have a genuine reason to do what etiquette or the law requires depends on whether the demands they make are demands there is reason to obey in the first place. If they do not provide us with reasons, we might say that the standpoints they represent lack genuine normative authority. Importantly, many who endorse (1) think morality possesses a special kind of authority lacking in other putative requirements – and that this consists in there being an essential connection between moral obligations and what we genuinely ought and have reason to do. Before examining these connections, it will be useful to first introduce the concepts *ought* and *a reason*.

Oughts are typically taken to specify requirements or demands; they are overriding and present conclusive normative verdicts. Thus if you ought to perform some particular action, there is no other action you ought to perform instead. Reasons, in contrast, need not specify requirements: you could have a reason to do something without being required to do it. A reason to perform some action is usually understood as a consideration that counts in favor of doing it (Scanlon 1998: Ch. 1; Dancy 2004: Ch. 2); but a reason can be just one consideration amongst others, with there being many different reasons favoring many different actions, not all of which you ought to perform. Nonetheless, many think there is an intimate connection between oughts and reasons, so that:

(2) If A ought to do $x \rightarrow$ A has a reason to do x,

even though the converse may fail.

If moral obligation has some essential connection with oughts and reasons, we might then say that:

(3) A has a moral obligation to do $x \rightarrow$ A ought to do x,

and/or:

(4) A has a moral obligation to do $x \rightarrow$ A has a reason to do x.

(3) is stronger than (4). It captures a traditional thought that moral obligations are overriding: your having a moral obligation implies not just that you have some reason to do what it demands, but that you ought to do it (this is often labeled the "moral ought" or "ought of moral obligation"). (4) follows from the conjunction of (2) and (3). Many endorse both (3) and (4), though one could accept (4) but reject (3), and hence deny that moral obligations are always overriding. Or one could accept (3) but deny (4), for instance, by denying (2). Alternatively, one could deny both (3) and (4). Here we shall focus on (4) and its denial.

(4) represents a view sometimes called *morality–reasons internalism* (because the connection between moral obligation and reasons it posits is often presented as an internal or conceptual one, whereby it is part of the very nature or concept of moral obligation that it entails reasons to act). Its denial, *morality–reasons externalism*, denies this conceptual connection and holds that A could have a moral obligation to do x but no reason to do x. Both positions offer contrasting views about the nature or concept of morality and its demands – whether, in particular, moral obligations are reason-entailing. There are a number of ways to

understand the connection (4) articulates. On the one hand, it could be read as saying either that the moral obligation to do *x* provides *A* with a reason to do *x*, or that the reason favoring *x* provides *A* with the obligation. On the other hand, (4) could be understood as the claim that facts about moral obligation *determine* facts about reasons, so that by establishing that *A* has a moral obligation to do *x* we have therein established that *A* has a reason to do *x*; or it could be interpreted as a *constraint* on who has what obligations, so that if *A* has no reason to do *x* then *A* has no moral obligation to do it. Since (4) can be interpreted in any of these ways, to deny (4) is to deny each of these interpretations. Those who do deny (4) deny that it is part of the concept of moral obligation that it entails reasons. They hold that it is therefore possible that you have no reason to do what you are morally required to do. This need not be to deny that you have moral obligations, nor therefore that you act morally wrongly by violating them. Nor even is it to deny that you *can* have good reason, indeed moral reason, to do as morality requires. Denying (4) involves denying only that there is a *necessary* connection between moral obligation and reasons; the connection is instead contingent. Many who deny (4) do so because they think that whether people have reason to do as morality demands depends on their having suitably moral sentiments and motives; to the extent most of us do, most of us may have reason to do what we are morally required to do. Nonetheless, this is not guaranteed. To assess the significance of (4) and its denial, it will be useful to introduce one further distinction, this time concerning reasons themselves.

On one view, often called *reasons internalism*, for it to be true that you have a reason to perform some action, acting for that reason must somehow serve your subjective motives. On this view: *A* has a reason to do *x* only if *A* has some motive that would be served by doing *x* (Williams 1981b). Thus, you have a reason to go mountain climbing only if you have some desire, aim, end, or interest that would be served by doing so; if you have no such motive, you have no reason to mountain climb. Similarly, you have a reason to refrain from murder only if you have some motive which would be served by so refraining; if you have no such motive, you have no such reason. (Note that a person's motives can include moral motives, for instance, a desire to do the morally right thing because it is morally right; so reasons internalism does not entail egoism.)

Reasons externalists, in contrast, hold that at least some reasons do not depend on agential motives, so that you could have a reason to refrain from murder irrespective of whether committing the murder would serve or conflict with your motives. Hence, according to reasons externalism:

(5) For some reasons *R*, whether *A* has *R* does not depend on *A*'s motives.

If we combine (4) with the claim that the reasons entailed by moral obligation satisfy (5), we arrive at the thesis that moral obligation is normatively authoritative. Thus the normative authority of moral obligation involves the following conjunction of claims: that moral obligations do entail reasons to act (as in [4]), and that the reasons entailed by moral obligation are reasons the person has irrespective of his motives (an application of [5]). It follows that moral obligation is universal to the extent that one does not escape having a reason to do what one is morally obligated to do merely if or because one lacks suitably moral motives. Furthermore, if we combine (4) with the claim that, whenever a person has a moral obligation the reasons satisfying (5) generate an *ought*, we get one version of the traditional claim that moral obligations present categorical (and overriding) requirements: if you have a moral obligation to do *x*, you ought to do *x* irrespective of whether doing *x* serves your motives. The claim that moral obligation is normatively authoritative can be endorsed by a wide variety of positions within normative ethics: Kantians and intuitionists do generally accept it, but it is also open to utilitarians and others. However, one could reject it in a number of different ways; here are some:

(a) Some deny morality's commitment to both (4) and (5). This is in fact a common approach amongst many contemporary naturalist moral realists (e.g. Railton 1986). Such realists hold that moral facts (including facts about moral right and wrong) are identical to or constituted by natural facts. They therefore accept that moral facts are objective in one sense, since the natural facts they are related to are. Nonetheless, these realists deny that moral obligation has to be objective in the further sense that it is normatively authoritative. Often they deny that moral obligations entail reasons *because* they think that whether a person has reason to do as morality demands depends on whether the person has suitably moral motives (i.e. they often deny [4] because they deny [5]).
(b) One could instead accept morality's commitment to (4) but deny its commitment to (5). If one also accepts a reasons internalist view, this provides a constraint on the scope of moral obligation: you only have a moral obligation and thus a reason to do what it demands, if you have some motive that would be served by doing so (see Williams 1995).
(c) Alternatively, some hold that it is part of our concept of morality that morality is committed to both (4) and (5), but deny on substantive grounds that any reasons satisfy (5). This signals an error theory about morality, or at least those conceptions of it according to which moral obligation is normatively authoritative (e.g. Mackie 1977; arguably Williams 1985). In other words, error theorists might hold that, if there were any moral obligations, these would entail reasons to act irrespective of one's motives; but they deny that there are any such reasons – and they therefore deny that there are any moral obligations thus construed.
(d) Or one could accept (5) (whether accepting [4] or not) but deny that the reasons satisfying (5) are moral reasons. This is one way to be a non-moral perfectionist, i.e. someone who thinks people might have reason to pursue

human excellences irrespective of their motives, but who holds that human excellence is distinctively non-moral.

Since the crux of disagreement between those who do and do not think that moral obligation is normatively authoritative lies in whether they think moral reasons satisfy (5), it will be useful to consider the significance of (5) and its denial.

At one level, the debate between proponents and opponents of (5) is a substantive one, concerning the conditions under which people have reasons and hence who has what reasons. For instance, denying (5) effectively concedes that the sufficiently ruthless and amoral may have no reason to act morally well; moreover, they may even have reason to act in ways most would think decidedly immoral. Many who deny (5), however, argue that, even if reasons are contingent on agential motives, most of us do have suitably moral motives and so do fall within the scope of moral obligation; in which case, the denial of (5) does not *in fact* generate implications as morally objectionable as some claim. Moreover, if there really are people who lack any moral dispositions whatsoever, merely attributing reasons to them will have little practical benefit anyway: it is unlikely to affect their behavior, and they may just be people we have good reason to avoid or protect ourselves against.

At a further level, though, the debate goes to the heart of issues about the nature, justification and foundations of morality. Those who think morality is normatively authoritative often argue that severing the connection between moral obligation and reasons leaves us (at best) with an impoverished conception of moral objectivity (for instance, by reducing moral facts to natural facts arguably lacking any genuine normative significance), or (at worst) fails to account for morality as an essentially normative enterprise (making morality little more than a system of norms on par with etiquette). Skeptics about (5), on the other hand, think the view of reasons underpinning the aspiration to normative authority untenable, often because they think it metaphysically mysterious (Mackie 1977: Ch. 1) or because they find arguments for it systematically unconvincing (Foot 1978; Williams 1995). Many seek thereby to defend an alternative approach to ethics. Some do so by preserving a conception of moral obligation not committed to the supposedly problematic picture of reasons the normative authority thesis presupposes – this is the approach of those who combine naturalist moral realism with reasons internalism. Others jettison moral obligation itself – this is the approach of some virtue ethicists. These debates about reasons therefore have wide-reaching implications. They remain live issues.

Values and morality

We have so far concentrated on connections between morality and reasons. Another central element to morality, on many views, concerns value. In recent moral philosophy debate about value has been extensive and diverse. Here I shall broach three topics.

The first concerns the relation between value and moral obligation. Normative moral theories are often divided into two opposing camps: *deontological* and *teleological*. One influential account of this distinction comes from John Rawls (1972: 24–30). Taking the good and the right as our two main moral categories, Rawls characterizes teleological moral theories as those that first specify the good independently of the right and then define moral rightness as that which maximizes the good. Consequentialist theories are a paradigmatic example of a teleological approach: they hold that certain states of affairs are valuable and that the rightness of an action (say) is determined solely by the value of the states of affairs it brings about as its consequences. Classical utilitarianism, for instance, conceives the good as pleasure and the absence of pain, specifying morally right actions as those producing most overall good given the available alternatives. Strictly speaking (contra Rawls), it is now widely agreed that teleological theories are not committed to a maximizing view. For example, *satisficing* utilitarians hold that you have a moral obligation only to bring about *good enough* outcomes, where this may be less than the best possible; nonetheless, moral rightness is still a function of goodness. Deontological moral theories, in contrast, do not define moral rightness in terms of, or do not think it determined by, an independently specified conception of the good. Different deontologists disagree whether the consequences of an action can be relevant to determining its status as right, wrong, or permissible; but all deontologists think there are factors besides the value of an action's consequences that are relevant to determining this. In particular, they think there are moral constraints on how we are permitted to pursue the good, where such constraints operate independently of the value of outcomes. To take one example: Many forms of consequentialism are arguably committed to the view that it could be required, or at least permissible, to frame an innocent person for a crime if doing so would bring about best overall consequences – if, say, it would prevent significant social disorder. Deontologists, however, would typically think this morally wrong, for instance, because it is unjust or fails to respect the dignity of the innocent person as a free moral agent. Thus even if framing the individual would bring about best overall consequences, the fact that this is unjust (say) may serve as a constraint that prohibits using the person as a means to that end. Teleological and deontological approaches thus represent two rival conceptions of morality distinguishable by the role they assign to value. Both remain leading players in contemporary normative ethics.

A second issue concerns the relation between values and reasons, moral, or otherwise. Many teleologists *and* deontologists think there is indeed an intimate connection between them; but there remains significant disagreement over *how* they are related, in particular whether one is more fundamental than the other. *Value-based* views hold that we have reason to do things *because* they are good;

reasons-based approaches deny this. One prominent reasons-based approach emerges from what T. M. Scanlon (1998: 95–100) calls the "buck-passing" account of (intrinsic) value. This clusters around a number of ideas. First, we construct some biconditional linking values with reasons, a basic version of which might claim that "*x* is intrinsically good if and only if there is reason to *y*," where "*y*" stands for some response to *x* – an action or pro-attitude, say – there is reason to do or have. Second, buck-passers hold that it is not the quality of being good which gives reason to *y*, but certain other (non-evaluative) features of *x*. Third, they claim that to say that *x* is good just is to say that there is reason to *y* with respect to *x*. Thus, for example, to say that mountain climbing is an intrinsically valuable activity is to say that it has certain features (provides opportunity to view stunning landscapes, to experience wilderness and tranquility, to overcome challenges, or so forth) which give people reasons – perhaps reasons to do it or reasons to admire its leading exponents. If defensible, this provides a way by which to analyze value in terms of the more basic notion of a reason and to deny that value is the source of reasons. Combining it with (4) also offers a way to unify the deontic and evaluative domains, since it allows that both deontic and evaluative concepts entail the concept of a reason. Each of the three theses comprising the buck-passing account may be contested, though. Some deny the biconditional. On the one hand, it inherits many similar permutations to those that arose regarding the connection between moral obligation and reasons. Reasons internalists, for instance, could endorse a substantive account of value according to which the value of an action does not depend on agential motives, yet also hold that you have reason to do or to have a pro-attitude towards what is good only if you have some motive that would be served by doing so. On the other hand, some deny the biconditional in the other direction, because they claim there can be reason to do or pro something that is not intrinsically valuable. Suppose that I promise to pay you a vast sum of money for admiring a dreadful musical composition lacking any aesthetic merit; you may, so the objection goes, have good reason to form the attitude of admiration even though the musical composition is not intrinsically valuable. Alternatively, one could accept the biconditional but maintain that we have reasons to do or pro things because they are valuable; value-based approaches do just this and typically hold that it is the quality of being valuable which provides us with these reasons. Thus it may be the fact that mountain climbing is an intrinsically good or worthwhile activity that gives us reason to do it, or to admire those who do. There are, nevertheless, further responses one may make to these objections; both the reasons-based and value-based approaches continue to command adherents.

A third central topic concerns the role of *non-moral* value in moral theory. Granting that there are a variety of non-moral values we have reason to pursue, there emerges the possibility of conflict between the moral and non-moral. A pressing issue for moral theories is whether they can (and to what extent they should) accommodate individuals' pursuits of non-moral goods. The distinction between moral and non-moral values is not always clear-cut; but the latter are typically taken to include the sorts of relationships and personal projects that give our lives meaning and can contribute to our living a good or flourishing life – friendships and emotional attachments, artistic and sporting pursuits, projects embodying personal excellence, and so on. A generic concern is that morality might require us to sacrifice such goods and that this is a bad thing (Williams 1981a, 1985: Ch.10; Wolf 1982). One source of this worry emerges from the idea that the demands of morality represent an impartial standpoint which has priority over the partial and subjective interests of individual agents. For instance, classical utilitarianism may require each person to promote the good of all impartially, since the good of one person is as valuable as the good of any other; yet this may in turn require an individual to forgo the sorts of personal project constitutive of his own good if promoting the good of others will have better overall consequences. Kantian theories may also be susceptible to a version of this objection. For if they require a person to deliberate impartially by abstracting from contingent facts about himself (including his subjective aims, goals, interests, and other motives) when considering what to do, the person's subjective goals may become sidelined and thus eclipsed by the demands of morality. On either theory, if moral obligation is both pervasive and overriding, we may end up continually required to do as morality demands and hence not permitted to pursue our own personal good. Many responses have been offered on behalf of the moral outlooks so accused. Some concede that morality is indeed intrusive and demanding in these respects – but argue that, given that we are indeed able to help those less fortunate than ourselves, we ought to do so even if that requires significant personal sacrifice. Others seek to make morality less demanding, either by accommodating the legitimate pursuit of personal goods within an impartial framework, or by preserving space outside of morality within which to pursue non-moral goods. Thus we might treat moral considerations as presenting just one kind of reason alongside whatever non-moral reasons we have, both of which may be relevant to determining what overall we ought to do. If moral considerations are not always decisive in determining what we ought to do, they needn't generate an unremitting series of obligations. In which case, even if moral obligations are overriding, they need not be pervasive; thus they needn't preclude the legitimate pursuit of non-moral goods.

Much more can be said both about these responses and the other themes the chapter has introduced. By way of conclusion, it should be noted that the objection just raised against obligation-centered moral theories has motivated not only a variety of responses on behalf of morality but also an array of contrasting (notably virtue and feminist) approaches to ethics – approaches that either do away with, or give less emphasis to, the notions of impartiality and obligation that they see as part of the problem. Insofar as the notion of obligation is integral to "morality," these may not be instances of morality in the narrow sense but, rather, alternative *ethical* perspectives. Both styles of approach are explored in the other chapters of Part IV of this volume.

See also Reasons for action (Chapter 24); Realism and its alternatives (Chapter 26); Error theory and fictionalism (Chapter 28); Consequentialism (Chapter 37); Contemporary Kantian ethics (Chapter 38); Virtue ethics (Chapter 40); Feminist ethics (Chapter 43); Morality and its critics (Chapter 45); Partiality and impartiality (Chapter 52).

References

Dancy, J. (2004) *Ethics without Principles*, Oxford: Oxford University Press.
Foot, P. (1978) "Morality as a System of Hypothetical Imperatives," repr. in *Virtues and Vices*, Oxford: Blackwell.
Mackie, J. (1977) *Ethics: Inventing Right and Wrong*, Harmondsworth: Penguin Books.
Railton, P. (1986) "Moral Realism," *Philosophical Review* 95: 163–207.
Rawls, J. (1972) *A Theory of Justice*, Oxford: Oxford University Press.
Scanlon, T. M. (1998) *What We Owe to Each Other*, Cambridge, MA: Belknap Press of Harvard University Press.
Williams, B. (1981a) "Persons, Character and Morality," repr. in *Moral Luck*, Cambridge: Cambridge University Press.
——(1981b) "Internal and External Reasons," repr. in *Moral Luck*, Cambridge: Cambridge University Press.
——(1985) *Ethics and the Limits of Philosophy*, London: Fontana Press.
——(1995) "Internal Reasons and the Obscurity of Blame," repr. in *Making Sense of Humanity*, Cambridge: Cambridge University Press.
Wolf, S. (1982) "Moral Saints," *Journal of Philosophy* 79: 419–39.

Further reading

Cullity, G. and Gaut, B. (eds) (1997) *Ethics and Practical Reason*, Oxford: Oxford University Press. (A collection of essays on different approaches to practical reason and its connections with ethics, with useful editors' introduction.)
Darwall, S. (1997) "Reasons, Motives, and the Demands of Morality: An Introduction," in S. Darwall, A. Gibbard and P. Railton (eds) *Moral Discourse and Practice*, Oxford: Oxford University Press. (Outlines further issues in debates about morality's normative authority.)

37
CONSEQUENTIALISM

Brad Hooker

The definition of consequentialism

A consequentialist theory evaluates things exclusively in terms of consequences. For example, beliefs could be evaluated in terms of the consequences of holding them (an approach often called pragmatism). The most common forms of consequentialism, however, focus on the evaluation of acts and sets of rules. And the rest of this chapter will stick to that focus.

The most familiar kind of consequentialism is the kind of utilitarianism maintaining that an act is morally right if and only if no alternative act has consequences containing greater *welfare* (or net benefit), impartially assessed. In utilitarians' *impartial* assessment of welfare, a benefit (i.e. addition to someone's welfare) or harm (loss to welfare) to any one individual gets the same weight as the same size benefit or harm to anyone else. Thus, benefits and harms to everyone count equally, no matter what his or her ethnic group, religion, wealth, education, political views, talent, or conscientiousness; all that matters is the size of the benefits and harms.

This kind of utilitarianism is *maximizing* in the sense that it calls for an act with unsurpassed consequences (anything less than the best isn't good enough, according to act-utilitarianism). And this theory is *direct* in the sense that the acts are assessed solely and directly by their own consequences (not, for example, by whether the acts are allowed by the rules with the best consequences). Thus the theory is known as maximizing act-utilitarianism.

While maximizing act-utilitarianism is the most familiar form of consequentialism, defining consequentialism so that this is the *only* form is a naive mistake. Many self-described consequentialists explicitly reject maximizing act-utilitarianism. Some consequentialists think *welfare* is not all that matters. Some reject *utilitarian impartiality*. Some reject a requirement to *maximize*. And some deny that acts are to be solely assessed *directly* by their consequences.

Given the disputes among consequentialists, consequentialism must not be characterized in such a way as to imply that all forms of it are welfarist, impartial in the way specified, maximizing, and direct. How should it be characterized? What all consequentialists about the morality of acts agree on is that, where there are differences in the value of consequences, these are always, directly or indirectly, decisive in the moral evaluation of acts.

What makes consequences better or worse?

While the most familiar form of consequentialism is maximizing act-utilitarianism, the oldest form is probably maximizing act-egoism. Maximizing act-egoism evaluates acts in terms of nothing but the consequences *for the agent*. Such egoism is, in terminology made popular by Derek Parfit (1984:143) and Thomas Nagel (1986: 152–3), *agent-relative* in the special sense that *the value of consequences depends on their relation (or connection) to the agent*. Maximizing act-egoism claims that the only consequences that matter are the ones affecting the agent's good.

Just as egoistic evaluation of consequences is agent-relative, so is purely altruistic evaluation. Imagine Jack and Jill each evaluate consequences *only* in terms of what is most beneficial (or least harmful) overall to everyone else. In other words, Jack cares about the consequences for everyone else but not for himself, and Jill cares about the consequences for everyone else but not for herself. Their evaluations of consequences will sometimes diverge, since sometimes what will be best overall for everyone except Jack will be different from what will be best overall for everyone except Jill. (Such divergence is most obvious, of course, when what is most beneficial for Jack is not what is most beneficial for Jill and no one else's welfare is affected.)

Pure egoism seems to be very rare. Nearly everyone would accept that other people's good matters morally *to at least some extent*. Pure altruism might be even rarer.

Indeed, many people accept that each agent is (at least often if not always) allowed to attach greater importance to consequences for himself or herself than to consequences for others. On such a view, while everyone's good matters, the agent's evaluation of consequences may legitimately be somewhat biased in a self-serving direction. Such a view is certainly not *purely* egoistic, but it still contains a large agent-relative component, since this view allows the value of consequences to depend on their connection to the agent. Another view with a large agent-relative component is the view that possible benefits to the agent should be given *some* weight in the agent's practical thinking but need not be given as much weight as the same size benefits to others. This view is altruistic but not purely so.

The most common forms of altruism involve special concern for those with whom one has special connections. Consider a mother who attaches more value to benefits for her own child than she does to the same size benefits for any child that is not hers. The special concern, which again is agent-relative in Nagel's and Parfit's terminology, comes in the priority the mother gives to benefits for *her* child. Many people have such agent-relative concerns for their family, their friends, their colleagues, and members of their community or country.

We have seen that one kind of agent-relativity involves a bias concerning the agent's own good, and another kind comes in special concern for others with special connections with oneself, such as one's family and friends. Yet another kind of agent-relativity focuses on the connection between the agents and their own actions, as the examples below illustrate.

Suppose Jill is in an awkward situation where the only way she can prevent three other people from telling lies is to tell a lie herself. Suppose Stephanie can prevent four other people from stealing only by stealing something herself. Suppose Rae can prevent five other people from killing innocent others only by killing an innocent person herself. Each of Jill, Stephanie, and Rae thinks that her primary duty is not to commit acts of lying, or stealing, or killing, rather than to minimize the number of acts of lying, stealing, or killing in general. Each of them thinks of herself as having agent-relative duties focused on acts of her own doing.

The opposite of agent-relativity (in Nagel's and Parfit's terminology) is *agent-neutrality*. Agent-neutral evaluation of consequences is not biased towards (or against) benefits to the agent or towards benefits to individuals with special connections to the agent. And agent-neutral evaluation of consequences is not biased towards (or against) acts with special connections with the agent (in particular, acts of the agent's doing). Therefore, agent-neutral evaluation should, in principle, be the same for everyone.

The question of what makes consequences better or worse cannot be answered without determining whether the consequences are to be evaluated agent-neutrally or agent-relatively. Most discussions of consequentialism assume that consequences are to be evaluated agent-neutrally. But influential agent-relative forms of consequentialism have been advanced.

On virtually every form of consequentialism yet advocated, at least a large part of what makes consequences better or worse is how much welfare, or net benefit, they contain. But what constitutes net benefit? There are three main views.

Hedonists hold that net benefit consists in pleasure minus pain. Pleasures and pains, or at least the ones that constitute additions to or reductions in welfare, are introspectively discernible and either attractive or aversive to the person experiencing them. Suppose Jack's life project turns out to be a failure but he never finds this out. Furthermore, suppose his pleasures are not reduced in some indirect way by this failure. Hedonists hold that failure of Jack's life project does not reduce his welfare. This is because hedonists think that one's welfare is determined solely by how one's life feels from the inside, and that this depends on whether one believes one's desires have been fulfilled, not on whether they really have been fulfilled.

Another main view of welfare holds that a person's welfare is constituted by the fulfillment of his or her desires, whether or not the person knows the desires have been fulfilled. This view is often called the desire-fulfillment (or preference-satisfaction) theory of welfare.

The main argument in favor of the desire-fulfillment theory over hedonism is that many people's self-interested concern extends beyond their own pleasures and pains, enjoyments and frustrations. For example, many people have stronger self-interested concern for knowing the truth (especially about whether their other desires are fulfilled) than for blissful ignorance. The main argument against the desire-fulfillment theory is that some desires are so whacky that their fulfillment would not itself constitute a benefit for the people who have them (though whatever associated pleasure these people derived *would* constitute a benefit for them). Imagine someone who wants a saucer of mud for its own sake (Anscombe 1957: 70), or to count all the blades of grass in the lawns along a street (Rawls 1971: 432), or to turn on as many radios as possible (Quinn 1993: 236).

A third theory of welfare holds that hedonism is right to hold that pleasure constitutes a benefit but wrong to hold that pleasure is the only thing to do so. This theory proposes that knowledge of important matters, friendship, and significant achievement (and perhaps other things) also constitute benefits. On this theory, a life contains more welfare to the extent that it contains pleasure, knowledge of important matters, friendship, significant achievement, and perhaps some other things. A life where desires were fulfilled but were not for these things would contain little welfare, according to this theory, which Parfit dubbed the objective list theory, but is sometimes called the list theory (Parfit 1984: 493–502; Crisp 1997: Ch. 3).

As well as disagreements about which theory of welfare is best, there are disagreements about whether the amount of overall welfare is all that matters, or whether the pattern of distribution matters as well. Utilitarians hold that consequences are to be assessed only in terms of overall welfare. Many other consequentialists think that an evaluation of consequences should take into account not only how much overall welfare obtains but also its distribution.

Some consequentialists think that the fact that a distribution of welfare is more equal than all others is always a consideration in that distribution's favor (Temkin 1993). Call this view *equality for its own sake*. A prominent objection to equality for its own sake is that there seems nothing attractive about equality where it can be achieved only by "leveling down" better-off individuals to the level of worse-off individuals (Raz 1986: 227; Parfit 1997). To preserve much of the spirit behind equality for its own sake without inviting the objection about leveling down, many consequentialists have moved to the view that, while equality of welfare does not always have something in its favor, benefits to the worse-off always matter somewhat more than the same size benefits to the better-off (Parfit 1997). This view is called *prioritarianism*.

A third prominent view about the distribution of welfare is egalitarian and prioritarian only up to a point. This view holds that the pressure to equalize welfare or choose benefits for the worse-off stops once everyone is above some threshold of welfare. If absolutely everyone has very high levels of welfare, there need be nothing objectionable about some people's having higher levels than others have, according to this view (Skorupski 1992; Miller 1992; Crisp 2006: Ch. 6; cf. Casal 2007). Call those who hold this threshold view *sufficientarians*. Of course there is vagueness, debate, and uncertainty about where the threshold of sufficiency is.

Finally, there is the view that what really matters is not whether consequences increase equality of welfare, not whether consequences bring larger benefits to the worse-off, and not whether consequences would push people up to some sufficiency level of welfare, but instead whether people get what they *deserve* (Feldman 1997: 158–70, 203; Kagan 1999). On this view, undeserved inequalities of welfare are bad, but deserved inequalities of welfare are good.

Thus, there are disagreements among consequentialists about all of the following: (1) whether consequences are to be evaluated in an agent-neutral or agent-relative way, (2) whether welfare is constituted just by net pleasure, or by desire-fulfillment, or by some objective list of items, and (3) whether not only maximum overall welfare but also one or another pattern of distribution guide the assessment of consequences.

Act-consequentialism: maximizing vs. satisficing vs. scalar

Although the most familiar kind of act-consequentialism requires the agent to maximize, much attention has recently been directed at forms of act-consequentialism that do not require maximization. Part of the explanation of the retreat from *maximizing* act-consequentialism is that the most familiar agent-neutral versions of maximizing act-consequentialism seem excessively demanding. The most familiar agent-neutral versions of maximizing act-consequentialism are maximizing act-utilitarianism and versions that conjoin concern for utility with concern either for equality, or for the plight of the worst-off, or for getting everyone up to some level of sufficiency. Each such theory calls on each relatively well-off individual to make huge sacrifices for the badly-off.

There are over a billion people in the world who are very badly-off. As long as there are efficient aid agencies with access to the badly-off, a relatively well-off person could make a small contribution that would be of huge benefit to one of the badly-off. Suppose a relatively well-off person contributes $5 to Oxfam, and this saves someone's life. Well, this relatively well-off person could contribute another $5 and save another life. And again, and again, and again, and many times more. Indeed, the relatively well-off person would have to reduce herself to near poverty before further sacrifices from her would be as large as the benefits for others that her further contributions would produce, or before her sacrifices would no longer be required by egalitarian, prioritarian, or sufficientarian principles.

Such a requirement to come to the aid of strangers requires a huge reduction in the agent's own good, unless the agent is already quite badly-off. This requirement seems excessive. Working assiduously to achieve an optimal outcome in agent-neutral terms will typically require the agent actively to sacrifice more, and more often, than it is reasonable to demand. (For some alternative explanations of what the demandingness objection is supposed to be, see Hooker 2009: §2.)

A related objection to maximizing act-consequentialism is that it leaves the agent vanishingly little moral freedom (Vallentyne 2006: 23–8). According to maximizing act-consequentialism, the set of permissible acts contains only those acts whose consequences are not less good than the consequences of any alternative act. In some situations, there will be two or more acts whose consequences are not less good than the consequences of any alternative act. In such situations, maximizing act-consequentialism leaves the agent morally free to decide among these two or more acts. In most situations, however, there will be only one act with consequences not less good than the consequences of any alternative. So, in most situations, maximizing act-consequentialism will restrict the agent's "choice" to one alternative. In this way, the theory is excessively restrictive.

Satisficing act-consequentialism does not require the agent to produce the best possible outcome. It instead requires the agent to choose acts with "good enough" consequences (Slote 1985, 1992). The main attractions of satisficing act-consequentialism are that it can avoid the charges of being excessively demanding and excessively restrictive. But in order to have these attractions, satisficing act-consequentialism must offer a criterion of "good enough" consequences that typically falls some distance short of "best available consequences."

One of the main lines of objection to satisficing act-consequentialism focuses on the obvious difficulty of finding a stable and non-arbitrary specification of "good enough." Do consequences need to be 50 percent as good as the best available? Or 75 percent as good? Or sometimes 50 percent and sometimes 75 percent, and sometimes 90 percent as good?

The second main line of objection to satisficing act-consequentialism is that this theory allows agents to do *less* than the best for others *even when doing the best for others would involve no greater sacrifice for the agent* (Mulgan 2001: 129–42). Why would morality allow agents to benefit others less when doing more for others would cost the agent not one bit more?

Some consequentialists have developed theories that were supposed to share satisficing act-consequentialism's attractions (satisficing act-consequentialism is neither too demanding nor too restrictive) without permitting agents to choose an act that would benefit others less though some other act would benefit others more and not involve any greater sacrifice from the agents. For example, Douglas Portmore has developed a consequentialist theory that mixes altruistic concern for others' good with agent-relative favoring of benefits for oneself (Portmore 2001, 2003, 2005, 2008). On such a theory, the agent is permitted to choose a lesser benefit for oneself over a greater benefit for someone else, as long as the difference is not too great.

Another kind of theory developed in reaction to the difficulties that maximizing and satisficing share is scalar act-consequentialism. This theory assesses acts in terms of the relative goodness or badness of their consequences but jettisons the categories of "morally required," "morally optional," "morally permissible," and "morally wrong" (Slote 1985: Ch. 5; Railton 1988; Norcross 2006). Because scalar consequentialism jettisons those categories, it absolves itself of the responsibility to identify the boundary between "morally permissible" and "morally wrong" and (within the category of "morally permissible") the boundary between "morally required" and "morally optional."

Is it sensible for a theory of morality to jettison these categories? The concepts of moral guilt and blame, and the categories of morally guilty and morally blameworthy, are of absolutely central importance. And they are parasitic on the concept of moral wrongness. Normally, an agent is morally guilty and his act morally blameworthy only if what he did was morally wrong. So, by jettisoning the concept of moral wrongness, scalar act-consequentialism threatens the concepts of moral guilt and blameworthiness. There would have to be an overwhelmingly powerful argument in favor of this theory in order for us to accept the conceptual purges it dictates.

Actual vs. expected value of consequences

So far, our discussion has presumed to compare the actual consequences of one act with the actual consequences of each alternative act. But this sort of "full-information," God's-eye point of view might seem quite irrelevant to the situation of normal agents, who are usually uncertain what the consequences of an available action would be. One way of dealing with such uncertainty is to think in terms of *expected values* of outcomes.

To calculate the expected value, multiply the value of each possible outcome times the probability of that outcome, and then add together these products. Table 37.1 gives a very simple example, where there are only two available

Table 37.1 Calculating expected values.

	Value of possible outcome	Probability of this possible outcome	Expected value of possible outcome	Expected value for option
Alternative A	20	.5	20 x .5 = 10	10 + 1 = 11
	2	.5	2 x .5 = 1	
Alternative B	4	.7	4 x .7 = 2.8	2.8 + 4.8 = 7.6
	16	.3	16 x .3 = 4.8	

alternatives to choose between, and each of them has only two possible outcomes.

This example is artificial in many important ways. In the example, there are only two possible alternatives. Each alternative has only two possible outcomes. The value of each possible outcome is quantifiable, and the probability of that possible outcome is known. Real life is rarely so simple. Still, understanding often starts with the simplest cases.

In a world of uncertainty, of course, how agents deal with probabilities and risks matters. Agents are blameworthy for taking unnecessary risks of very bad outcomes for others even if the bad outcomes did not in fact come about. In other words, blameworthiness is tied to expected values of choices.

Now wrongness and blameworthiness have close conceptual ties. Given this, wrongness seems to be conceptually tied to expected value rather than to actual value of choices. Admittedly, in many contexts the choice that would actually have had the best consequences is the one we *wish* we had made. Nevertheless, *moral* assessment of choice is more about expected value than about actual outcomes. Maximizing act-consequentialism can take on-board these ideas about moral assessment – by holding that an act is morally wrong if there is some alternative act whose consequences have greater expected value.

Decision procedures

It would be a mistake, however, to think that maximizing act-consequentialism is the view that on every occasion an agent *should decide which act to do* by ascertaining which act has the greatest expected value. Trying to decide what to do on that basis is often not what has the highest expected value, for the following reasons:

(a) People often lack information about the probable effects of their choices and, without such information, could not calculate expected value.
(b) Where they lack this information, they also often lack the time needed to get the information.
(c) Even if they had the information, calculating expected values is typically unpleasant and time-consuming and thus a cost in itself.
(d) Human limitations and biases are such as to make people inaccurate calculators of the expected overall consequences, especially where self-interest interferes.
(e) There would be a breakdown of trust in society if people knew that others, with all their human limitations and biases, were always making their moral decisions by trying to calculate expected values. For if people knew others were deciding in this way, they could not confidently predict that others would routinely behave in certain ways (e.g. not attack, not steal, not break their promises, not lie, etc.).

If maximizing act-consequentialism's recommended procedure for making day-to-day moral decisions is not to try to calculate expected values, what is it? Act-consequentialists say that the right procedure to follow when making decisions is to follow rules against attacking others, stealing, breaking promises, lying, and so on, unless following these rules is more or less certain to result in far worse consequences than breaking them would. Deciding what to do on the basis of these rules has greater expected value than deciding what to do by trying always to calculate expected values.

But now act-consequentialism is in a seemingly paradoxical position. On the one hand, the theory holds that an act is morally permissible if and only if there is no alternative act whose consequences have greater expected value. In its account of moral permissibility, act-consequentialism makes no reference to rules about killing, promise breaking, attending to welfare of others to whom one has special connections, etc. On the other hand, act-consequentialism tells agents to make their day-to-day moral decisions by following such rules. An agent who follows such rules might well feel confused when told that his act was nevertheless impermissible because some other act had a bit more expected value (cf. Parfit 1984: 31–40; Streumer 2003; Lang 2004).

Rule-consequentialism

Rule-consequentialism tells agents to make moral decisions by following certain rules, and the theory ties moral permissibility to these rules. It holds that an act is morally permissible if it is permitted by rules selected for their consequences. So rule-consequentialism does not get itself into the bind of specifying a criterion of moral permissibility that can conflict with its injunction about how to make moral decisions.

Is rule-consequentialism to be formulated in terms of rules with the *best actual consequences* or in terms of rules whose *consequences have the greatest expected value*? For reasons much like those mentioned earlier, rule-consequentialism is best formulated in terms of expected value (Hooker 2000: 72–5).

If rules are to be selected by their expected value, is this expected *agent-neutral* value (such as welfare for everyone, equality, or getting everyone above some threshold of sufficiency) or *agent-relative* value (such as the agent's own welfare and the welfare of those specially connected to the agent)? Well, rule-egoism is a form of rule-consequentialism. But obviously rule-egoism eschews the very attractive idea that rules are to be assessed in terms of the benefits and harms *for everyone*, not merely for the agent or some subset of everyone. Thus, the only kinds of rule-consequentialism discussed in the rest of this chapter are ones that assess rules in terms of agent-neutral value. (However, as will be explained below, the content of rule-consequentialist duties will be mostly agent-relative.)

Sometimes rule-consequentialism has been formulated as holding that an act is morally permissible if general *conformity* with the rule has the greatest expected value. Arguably, however, formulating rule-consequentialism purely in terms of the expected value of conformity with rules pushes rule-consequentialism into "extensional equivalence" with act-consequentialism, which means that though the theories have different criteria of permissibility, they end up selecting exactly the same acts as permissible. Act-consequentialism holds that it is wrong to attack others, or steal, or break a promise, etc., *only* when such acts have less expected value than not doing them has. The objection is that rule-consequentialism would have to agree, because of the benefits of perfect conformity with rules forbidding such acts only when these acts do not maximize expected value.

Although conformity with rules is hugely important, the process of internalizing rules and their ongoing acceptance can have consequences in addition to compliance with them. For one thing, people's knowing that Jack accepts certain rules might lead them to do certain acts or have various feelings, even though Jack never has an opportunity to comply with these rules. For another thing, suppose that, while compliance with rule *A* would have *slightly* greater expected value than compliance with rule *B*, the time, effort, and other costs involved in getting rule *A* internalized would be *much* greater than those involved in getting rule *B* internalized. These additional consequences should be counted in a rule-consequentialist assessment of possible rules. So most philosophers now accept that rule-consequentialism is better formulated in terms of acceptance or internalization than in terms of mere compliance.

Thus formulated, rule-consequentialism holds that an act is morally permissible if it is allowed by the rules whose general acceptance (including the costs of getting them accepted) has the greatest expected value. Usually, "general acceptance" is interpreted as "full acceptance by a large percentage of people." Permissibility is determined by rules selected by the expected value of their acceptance by a collection of people, not merely acceptance by the individual. In this sense, rule-consequentialism is typically put forward as a "collective" rather than an "individual" form of consequentialism.

Rule-consequentialism needs to be formulated in terms of acceptance by a large percentage of people, not in terms of acceptance by every single person (though universal acceptance can be an ideal). The reason not to formulate it in terms of acceptance by every single person is that many moral problems simply would not exist if every single person fully accepted rules against attacking others, stealing, breaking promises, etc. For example, there would not need to be rules about permissible defense against attackers in a world where there were no attackers. Of course, rule-consequentialism would *prefer* for every single person to accept the best rules. But it had better gear its moral rules for a less ideal world.

Rule-consequentialism seems to accord well with widespread views about permissibility. Constraints on attacking others, stealing, breaking promises, lying, and so on can be justified by the fact that acceptance of such constraints by a large percentage of people is crucial for security and thus has high expected value. Duties to be especially concerned about the welfare of those with whom one has special connections can also be justified by their high expected value, since human nature is such that a world without such special concerns is likely to be a miserable place (Hooker 2000: 136–41).

According to standard forms of rule-consequentialism, these constraints and duties of special concern have agent-*neutral justification* but agent-*relative content*. The constraint on attacking others, for example, is the duty not to attack others oneself, not the duty to minimize instances of attacks by agents generally. More obviously, the duty to be especially concerned about the welfare of those with whom one has special connections will require different agents to be concerned about different others.

Such foundationally agent-neutral rule-consequentialism also endorses a more general duty to come to the aid of others, because of the benefits of this duty's acceptance. Now, will the general duty about aid that rule-consequentialism endorses be excessively demanding? General compliance with a more demanding duty to aid has higher expected value than general compliance with a less demanding duty to aid. However, the time and energy and emotional costs in getting a more demanding duty to aid internalized by a large percentage of people will at some point outweigh the added benefits of compliance with the more demanding duty. For this reason, foundationally agent-neutral rule-consequentialism justifies a less demanding duty to aid than agent-neutral act-consequentialism does.

Conclusion

There are forms of agent-relative act-consequentialism and of agent-neutral rule-consequentialism that accord much better with intuitive ideas about constraints, about duties of special concern, and about limits on the duty to aid than agent-neutral act-consequentialism can. But agent-relative act-consequentialism has no place for the attractive idea that moral assessment is foundationally impartial in an agent-neutral way. Of consequentialist theories, only foundationally agent-neutral rule-consequentialism manages to achieve the conjunction of (a) building this kind of impartiality into the foundational level of assessment and (b) justifying the constraints, duties of special concern, and a limit on the more general duty to aid that seem intuitively compelling.

See also Utilitarianism to Bentham (Chapter 13); John Stuart Mill (Chapter 16); Welfare (Chapter 54); Population ethics (Chapter 61).

References

Anscombe, E. (1957) *Intention*, Oxford: Blackwell.
Casal, P. (2007) "Why Sufficiency Is Not Enough," *Ethics* 117: 296–326.
Crisp, R. (1997) *Mill on Utilitarianism*, London: Routledge.

——(2006) *Reasons and the Good*, Oxford: Clarendon Press.

Feldman, F. (1997) *Utilitarianism, Hedonism, and Desert: Essays in Moral Philosophy*, New York: Cambridge University Press.

Hooker, B. (2000) *Ideal Code, Real World: A Rule-Consequentialist Theory of Morality*, Oxford: Clarendon Press.

——(2009) "The Demandingness Objection," in Tim Chappell (ed.) *Moral Demandingness*, London: Palgrave, pp. 148–62.

Kagan, S. (1999) "Equality and Desert," in Louis Pojman and Owen McLeod (eds) *What Do We Deserve?*, New York: Oxford University Press, pp. 298–314.

Lang, G. (2004) "A Dilemma for Objective Act-Consequentialism," *Politics, Philosophy & Economics* 3: 221–39.

Miller, D. (1992) "Distributive Justice: What the People Think," *Ethics* 102: 555–93.

Mulgan, T. (2001) *The Demands of Consequentialism*, Oxford: Clarendon Press.

Nagel, T. (1986) *The View from Nowhere*, New York: Oxford University Press.

Norcross, A. (2006) "Scalar Act-utilitarianism," in Henry West (ed.) *Blackwell Guide to Mill's Utilitarianism*, Boston, MA: Blackwell, pp. 217–32.

Parfit, D. (1984) *Reasons and Persons*, Oxford: Clarendon Press.

——(1997) "Equality and Priority," *Ratio* 10: 202–21.

Portmore, D. (2001) "Can an Act-Consequentialist Theory Be Agent-Relative?," *American Philosophical Quarterly* 38: 363–77.

——(2003) "Position-Relative Consequentialism, Agent-Centered Options, and Supererogation," *Ethics* 113: 303–32.

——(2005) "Combining Teleological Ethics with Evaluator Relativism: A Promising Result," *Pacific Philosophical Quarterly* 86: 95–113.

——(2008) "Dual-Ranking Act-Consequentialism," *Philosophical Studies* 138: 409–27.

Quinn, W. (1993) *Morality and Action*, New York: Cambridge University Press.

Railton, P. (1988) "How Thinking about Character and Utilitarianism Might Lead to Rethinking the Character of Utilitarianism," *Midwest Studies in Philosophy* 13: 398–416.

Rawls, J. (1971) *A Theory of Justice*, Cambridge, MA: Harvard University Press.

Raz, J. (1986) *The Morality of Freedom*, Oxford: Clarendon Press.

Skorupski, J. (1992) "Value and Distribution," in M. Hollis and W. Vossenkuhl (eds) *Moralische Entscheidung und rationale Wahl*, Scientia Nova, Munich: Oldenbourg, pp. 191–207.

Slote, M. (1985) *Common-sense Morality and Consequentialism*, London: Routledge & Kegan Paul.

——(1992) *From Morality to Virtue*, New York: Oxford University Press.

Streumer, B. (2003) "Can Consequentialism Cover Everything?," *Utilitas* 15: 237–47.

Temkin, L. (1993) *Inequality*, New York: Oxford University Press.

Vallentyne, P. (2006) "Against Maximizing Act Consequentialism," in James Dreier (ed.) *Contemporary Debates in Moral Theory*, Boston, MA: Blackwell, pp. 21–37.

Further reading

Kagan, Shelly (1998) *Normative Ethics*, Boulder, CO: Westview Press.

McNaughton, David and Rawling, Piers (1991) "Agent-Relativity and the Doing–Happening Distinction," *Philosophical Studies* 63: 167–85.

Mulgan, Tim (2007) *Understanding Utilitarianism*, Stocksfield, UK: Acumen.

Pettit, Philip (1994) "Consequentialism and Moral Psychology," *International Journal of Philosophical Studies* 2: 1–17.

Smart, J. J. C. and Williams, Bernard (1973) *Utilitarianism: For and Against*, Cambridge: Cambridge University Press.

38
CONTEMPORARY KANTIAN ETHICS

Andrews Reath

Introduction: some main themes in Kant's ethics

Kant's project in ethics is to defend the conception of morality that he takes to be embedded in ordinary thought. The principal aims of his foundational works in ethics – the *Groundwork of the Metaphysics of Morals* and the *Critique of Practical Reason* – are to state the fundamental principle of morality, which he terms the "categorical imperative," and then to give an account of its unconditional authority – why we should give moral requirements priority over non-moral reasons – by grounding it in the nature of free rational agency. Roughly the principle of morality gets its authority from the fact that it is by acting from this principle that we exercise our free agency. In these works Kant develops a distinctive account of the content of moral requirement (which is filled out in his later work, *The Metaphysics of Morals*). According to one version of the categorical imperative, we determine what sorts of actions are permissible or required in various situations by asking whether a principle of action is rationally willed as universal law for agents with autonomy. A second version of the categorical imperative derives the content of morality from the principle that we are to respect "humanity," or "rational nature," as an "end in itself" and never merely as a means. "Humanity" is the capacity for autonomous rational choice, and it includes the capacity to act from one's own judgment of what one has reason to do, to set ends for oneself, and to guide one's actions by values one finds it reasonable to accept. To hold that this capacity is an end in itself is to claim that it has an absolute value – a value that Kant terms "dignity" – that sets limits on the proper treatment of and is the basis of positive duties toward any agent with that capacity. Since, in Kant's view, all normal individuals possess this capacity equally, it grounds the fundamental moral equality of all individuals, in virtue of which they are owed moral concern. The principle of treating humanity as an end in itself and never merely as a means thus bases the content of morality in respect for persons as rational agents with autonomy. It leads to an ideal of moral community in which relations between persons are based on mutual respect for autonomy, an ideal that Kant terms a "realm of ends." Since Kant thinks that rational agents necessarily value the capacity for rational choice and the related capacities for self-governance, this approach to the content of morality also suggests a justification of its authority.

Kant's overall moral theory also suggests a meta-ethical stance. While he thought that moral principles are objective requirements based in reason, he rejects the moral realism of his rationalist predecessors which holds that there are metaphysical facts about right and wrong that are part of the nature of things and whose truth is independent of the operation of our practical reason. He also rejects empiricist accounts that base moral judgments in features of our psychology, e.g. holding that properties of virtue and vice are the tendency of certain actions to elicit feelings of approval or disapproval when we consider them from a general and impartial point of view. Rather, Kant held that the fundamental principle of morality is based in the nature of rational volition, and that particular moral requirements are based in principles that we autonomously impose on ourselves through reason. This aspect of his moral thought is seen in the idea that we determine the content of morality at some level of generality by determining whether a principle of action can be willed as universal law for agents with autonomy, or whether it shows proper respect for humanity as an end in itself – that is, through rational procedures based on commitments that we have as rational agents. Some commentators have termed this feature of Kant's moral theory a form of "moral constructivism": moral requirements do not reflect an order of moral truths that are part of the nature of things, but rather are "constructed" by an idealized rational procedure. The truth or objectivity of a moral principle is explained by the fact that it is justified through this kind of reasoning.

Thus Kant suggests distinctive answers to several different questions in moral theory: What are the basic standards of right and wrong, and what are the fundamental values that drive moral thought? What sorts of claims are moral claims – what are they about and what determines their truth or falsity – and how do we establish them? What explains the special authority of moral requirements? Contemporary Kantian theories, while they may modify or reject many of Kant's specific views, follow Kant's lead in developing answers to some or all of these questions. This chapter will give an overview of Kantian approaches to the content of morality, Kantian constructivism, and Kantian accounts of the authority of morality. But first we begin with a note on Kantian moral psychology.

Kantian moral psychology

Humeans believe that motivation is desire-based – that reasons for action and motivation are ultimately traced back to desires and fundamental preferences that arise in an agent independently of any practical reasoning. If I desire to take a trip to Tahiti and I need to set aside money to afford it, then my desire to take this trip can give me a reason to begin the regime of savings. Furthermore, the realization that saving money is a means to my end can redirect my desire for the end toward the means, thus producing the motivation to begin saving. Because Humeans believe that all motivation is desire-based, they explain moral motivation in terms of some natural desire or psychological mechanism, such as sympathy or natural concern for others, or a tendency to identify with the well-being of others.

Contemporary Kantians reject the Humean view of reasons and motivation because they believe that moral principles are requirements of reason that apply to agents independently of desire. They are committed to holding that human beings can be moved to act by reason alone. Kantians hold that it is part of rational agency that one can be motivated to act by one's application of rational principles and one's judgments about what one has reason to do, without the intervention of any desire or further source of motivation. In the above example, the fact that I need to begin saving money in order to afford my trip is a reason to begin saving, and the judgment that I ought to begin saving money now by itself can motivate me to do so. Likewise the judgment that I ought to take steps now to ensure my well-being later in life can motivate me to do so, without any further felt desire. (Note that the claim is that one *can* be motivated by one's judgment of what one has reason to do – that is not to say that one always *will* be motivated by that judgment.) Since the reasons in these two cases ultimately stem from some desire (e.g. some future desire), the full significance of the Kantian view of motivation comes to light in moral cases. Here Kantians hold that moral requirements apply to us simply as rational beings independently of our desires, and that the judgment that we ought to perform (or refrain from) some action can motivate us to do so, without the stimulus of any further desire. So, for example, judging that I ought to refrain from taking unfair advantage of a competitor or that I ought to help someone in need can motivate me to do so. The Kantian view here is that the application of principles of reason (or the judgment about reasons) produces the motivation to comply with the principle and does not simply redirect or elicit a prior motivational state that exists independently of any reasoning.

Kantian approaches to the content of morality

The component of Kant's moral theory that has had the most influence on contemporary normative ethics is the principle of treating persons as ends in themselves and never merely as a means, and the related ideal of relations between persons based on mutual respect for autonomy. Many theorists have thought that this principle, suitably developed, can ground at least significant portions of the standards of right and wrong.

The Kantian principle may at first seem to say only that we should not "use people" for our own purposes (or "use them without their consent"). But since we use the actions, decisions, and services of others all the time in morally innocuous ways, often without their explicit consent, it must mean more than this. We get more mileage out of the principle by noting that Kantian autonomy is a capacity for self-determination and self-governance that includes the capacity to form one's own judgments about good and bad reasons. Intuitively, we respect the autonomy of individuals, so understood, when we allow their use of these capacities to set limits on how we may treat them. This thought suggests an ideal of justifiability to others, and that is how the principle of respecting persons as ends in themselves is now widely understood at the most general level: to treat persons as ends and never merely as a means – that is, to respect persons as autonomous self-governing agents – is to act from principles that others can freely endorse (as agents with autonomy) and that justify one's actions to them. Or it is to act from reasons that others can reasonably be expected to accept. "Justifiability to others" implies that the justification of an action is to be addressed to those affected by it as rational agents, in light of their fundamental interests. I cannot expect others to endorse or to accept my reasons and principles unless they acknowledge other people's equal moral standing and give adequate weight to their fundamental interests, including their interest in exercising autonomy and self-governance. Since actions that do not meet this standard are off limits, this ideal gives individuals a kind of hypothetical veto power over how others may treat them. In this way, the ideal of respect for the autonomy of individuals, when specified through the idea of what can be justified to others as agents with autonomy, leads to strict principles of conduct that recognize persons as moral equals.

This ideal of justifiability to others needs to be understood in a strongly nonconsequentialist fashion. The specific principles to which it leads set limits on how one may promote desirable outcomes or overall good. They may require some action even when an alternative produces a better overall outcome. Furthermore, the reasons identified by these principles are not simply weighed against competing reasons (such as those based in the desirability of some outcome), but rather can silence them or undercut their force. For example, consider a situation in which some action furthers a desirable outcome, but fails to satisfy the general criterion of justifiability. Perhaps one can advance one's career through an act of deception that will undermine someone else's prospects; or perhaps violating someone's legal rights, or torturing them, may further the security of one's community. In these cases, one cannot expect the person on the receiving end to accept these particular ways of furthering one's ends. (As an agent with autonomy, that person has no reason to endorse these ways of pursing one's ends, since they infringe the person's capacity for self-determination and self-governance.) Normally the fact that an action may promote some good (one's career, national security, etc.) is a reason in its favor. But in these circumstances, that fact has no force as a reason. In other words, one does not just weigh reasons that favor the action based on the desirability of the outcome against reasons that oppose it stemming from its failing the criterion of justifiability. The fact that the action violates an individual's autonomy undercuts and excludes the force of any reasons based in the desirability of the outcome.

Finally, since the resulting principles do not aim at promoting or maximizing some value (such as individual autonomy), they do not underwrite certain forms of reasoning, for example, that some action should be chosen because it leads to fewer overall infringements of autonomy in individuals or because it produces more opportunities for autonomy across individuals. Rather, these principles are required by the ideal of justifiability to others or respect for persons as agents with autonomy. This gives us a way to understand how actions can be right or wrong in themselves. Of course, action on such principles standardly aims at some outcome (protecting an individual from harm or aggression, providing aid that will preserve a person's capacity to exercise her agency, etc.). But they are understood as forms of concern that are owed to persons as such.

The general requirement of justifiability to others as equal autonomous agents readily translates into familiar, more specific moral principles. It leads to requirements to avoid or refrain from gratuitous injury, coercion, deception and fraud, manipulation, exploitation and profiting from the weaker position of others, and so on. The rationale is not simply the generally harmful effects of such actions on individual well-being. Rather, these kinds of actions infringe on individuals' capacities for self-governance and self-determination, and autonomous individuals can reasonably object to such treatment. For similar reasons, it leads to a requirement to avoid paternalistic interference. It leads to requirements to refrain from free-riding and similar forms of unfairness, and to requirements of fidelity, keeping one's word, and not violating trust. Individuals who violate these requirements make an exception for themselves (by failing to do their share in cooperative schemes) or disappoint expectations that they have invited others to form. Because such actions fail to respect others as moral equals in various ways, they are not based on principles that equal autonomous agents can be expected to endorse. Finally, the ideal of justifiability to others grounds positive duties such as beneficence and mutual aid, gratitude, loyalty, special obligations between loved ones and friends, and so on, because such principles are among the social and material conditions needed to support the exercise of rational agency in socially interdependent beings.

In the political sphere, the ideal of justifiability leads to a liberal theory of justice, such as that developed by John Rawls (Rawls 1999/1971). Rawls's theory guarantees all citizens a set of equal basic liberties (such as liberty of conscience, freedom of expression and association, rights of political participation, and so on) and substantively equal opportunity to compete for positions of social and economic advantage. His "difference principle" limits social and economic inequalities to the condition that they benefit those who are worst-off. Rawls understands the basic liberties and opportunities as social conditions needed for citizens to develop and exercise various rational and moral powers (a capacity for a sense of justice and a capacity to develop and pursue a conception of their own good) and to participate fully in social life. The principles of justice taken together establish a framework in which individuals have both the constitutional guarantee and adequate material resources to exercise these capacities and to pursue meaningful conceptions of the good. When the principles of justice are satisfied, the social order can be justified to all citizens, even to those who are worst-off.

These moral and political principles are shared by many normative theories. What distinguishes a Kantian approach is the underlying rationale: they are requirements not because they promote some set of values or good outcomes, but because they express respect for persons as equal autonomous agents and are a condition of relations between persons based on mutual respect.

While many people find this approach to the content of morality compelling, disagreements remain. Consequentialists, of course, insist that standards of conduct be tied to the promotion of certain values or good consequences. Other theorists worry that Kantians overvalue individual autonomy, or that they adopt an overly rationalist picture of human beings. In response to the latter set of worries, it is important that for Kantians autonomy is not, fundamentally, the ability to act on one's preferences whatever they may be, but a capacity for rational self-government that includes the capacity to form one's own judgment about reasons. Its theoretical role is to ground the equal moral standing of persons and to set standards of justification for action and social and political arrangements. Further, like any capacity, the capacity for rational self-government needs to be developed (through socialization, moral education, or interacting with others), it is often realized partially or imperfectly, and it can be diminished by adverse circumstances (psychological, social, or material). Thus, Kantians need not deny the social interdependence of human agents.

Another question is that if rational capacity is the basis of moral standing, can Kantians accord moral standing to children, in whom the capacities remain undeveloped, or to the mentally disabled who will never develop or have lost the capacity? And what about the status of animals and nature? Children are easily included in the Kantian moral universe by noting childhood is a stage in the life of a person who normally develops to autonomy. Children need not be treated as adults (e.g. paternalistic intervention is warranted), but the proper treatment of children should keep in view the rational capacities that they are in the process of developing. Most Kantian theorists hold that the moral standing of mentally disabled or incapacitated human beings comes from their membership in a species in whom rational capacity is the norm. Again, the standards of proper treatment differ from those for fully competent agents, but they will require giving adequate weight to the interests of such individuals and respect for any level of self-government of which they are capable. Regarding animals and nature, to hold that autonomy confers special moral standing on persons is not to deny that there are other forms of value or that other kinds of entities that can make claims on us. Thus Kantians can allow that certain ways of treating non-rational creatures and entities are morally deficient.

Kantian constructivism

Many contemporary theorists influenced by Kant have suggested deliberative procedures for arriving at moral principles that assign a role to reasonable choice or agreement – what principles individuals with a concern for justifiability would choose or agree to. Rawls argues for his principles of justice by showing that they are the rational choice in the "original position" – a construct designed to represent an ideally fair choice between free and equal moral persons tasked with selecting principles of justice to govern their social order. T. M. Scanlon's contractualism explains judgments about right and wrong in terms of principles that could not reasonably be rejected by people motivated to find general principles of conduct acceptable to others with similar motivation (Scanlon 1998). This suggests a method of identifying moral principles that asks whether individuals could reasonably object to being treated in certain ways (i.e. would have reason to reject principles that permitted such treatment). Thomas E. Hill Jr has suggested, as a modification of Kant's notion of a "realm of ends," a framework that assumes idealized Kantian legislators overridingly committed to respecting human dignity who are concerned to give all agents the opportunity to exercise their rational capacities and live as autonomous agents, and who seek principles that all can endorse. The idea is to guide reflection about moral principles by asking what universal principles for regulating conduct such Kantian legislators would choose for themselves (Hill 2000: 33–57). These theories are all forms of moral constructivism – theories that derive the content of morality from an idealized process of rational deliberation.

The term "constructivism" was introduced into moral theory by Rawls, who defines it as the view that moral (and political) principles may be represented as the outcome of a "procedure of construction" that incorporates the relevant standards of practical reason – that is, a process of deliberation aimed at reasonable agreement along the lines described above (Rawls 1996: 89–90). Constructivism is an approach to the justification of moral principles, holding that the rational acceptability of a set of principles is established by showing that they are what individuals would choose for themselves or agree upon through idealized rational deliberation. Constructivists hold further that the "procedure of construction" is the criterion of what is right: that what makes a moral principle correct is that it would result from this idealized process of deliberation. Constructivism contains an approach to meta-ethical questions about the nature of moral claims, the epistemology of moral principles, and their objectivity and truth conditions that is accepted by many contemporary theorists influenced by Kant. Constructivism need not be Kantian. What marks Kantian forms of constructivism is that the process of deliberation is structured not just by self-interested rationality (e.g. the "agents of construction" are not simply concerned to secure their own interests), but is constrained by the aim of reasonable agreement on principles that give due weight to the interests of all, or by the aim of justifiability to each individual.

The distinctive force of constructivism is best illustrated by contrasting it to the account of moral truth and objectivity given by certain forms of moral realism. Moral realists such as the rational intuitionists accept the existence of an order of moral facts or moral properties that is independent of our methods of thinking about them, analogous to a realm of mathematical facts, that can be known or grasped through rational reflection. The objectivity of moral claims comes from this mind-independent order of moral facts: moral judgments about right and wrong are true when they accurately reflect these facts. Constructivists, by contrast, do not appeal to any such mind-independent order of moral facts to ground moral objectivity. A moral judgment is correct not because it accurately reflects the independent moral facts, but because it is arrived at through correct reasoning – i.e. through deliberation that satisfies the constraints that come from practical reason and the aim of reasonable agreement. Thus constructivists can hold that correct moral principles and moral facts are constituted by practical reasoning, in the sense that correct principles are those that would result from this idealized process of reasoning. Facts about right and wrong are a function of the application of these moral principles.

One feature brought out by this last point is that constructivism denies a sharp distinction between our epistemological access to moral principles and their truth conditions. We justify or come to have knowledge of a set of moral principles by seeing that they result from the idealized deliberative process, and of course we can only do that by deliberating as conscientiously as we can. According to constructivism, that process of reasoning also specifies their truth conditions: what makes a principle true or correct is that it follows from correct reasoning.

Constructivism is often described as a form of "moral anti-realism," but that label is misleading insofar as it associates constructivism with non-cognitivism. First, constructivism is not a form of subjectivism or relativism, since the standard of justification is not actual agreement on principles, but ideal agreement. Like cognitivists, Kantian constructivists hold that claims about moral principles can be correct or incorrect, and that they can be the objects of belief and knowledge (and not just the expression of pro-attitudes). Here it is important to realize that constructivism offers a distinctive account of objectivity that is an alternative to various forms of moral realism.

Kantian approaches to the authority of morality

Many people think that moral reasons have special authority in that they apply to us independently of our desires and take priority over competing reasons in cases of conflict. The ideal of respect for persons outlined above has great plausibility on its face, but is it a source of reasons that are necessary and inescapable? Some theorists argue that the evident appeal of some substantive value suffices to explain the authority of morality. Scanlon, for example, argues that the authority of morality can be explained through the value of "mutual recognition" – the value of living with others on mutually justifiable terms (Scanlon 1998: 162). Kantian approaches to the authority of morality go further by grounding it in inescapable requirements of rationality. It is an open question whether such arguments succeed, but they take us into deep questions about practical reason and agency.

One such argument has been made by Thomas Nagel (Nagel 1978). Nagel tries to establish a rational requirement of "altruism" – the principle that the interests of others give us direct reasons for action – by basing it in a metaphysical conception of oneself as one person among others equally real. Rational individuals ascribe value to the satisfaction of their own needs. But recognizing the reality of others requires that what one asserts about oneself can be meaningfully asserted of others, thus that the satisfaction of others' needs has the same value that one ascribes to one's own. An individual who does not acknowledge this requirement of altruism in effect denies the obvious metaphysical truth of the equal reality of others.

More recently, Christine Korsgaard has attempted to ground the authority of morality in the conditions of rational agency. One component of her view is that the formal principles of practical reason – including that of acting from principles that can hold as universal law – are "constitutive principles of rational agency" (Korsgaard 2009). That is to say that it is by following these principles that we constitute ourselves as authors of our actions, and that these principles are tacitly involved in all exercises of rational agency. If so, they are not coherently rejected by any rational agent. To see how these principles are constitutive of agency, consider that action is determining oneself to be the cause of some end. Thus rational action requires a self over and above one's various motives that chooses which motive to act on, and action is the work of the self as a whole, rather than of some force within the self. Korsgaard's argument is that these conditions are achieved by following the formal principles of practical reason. (One makes oneself the *cause* of some end by taking effective means to one's ends, and one makes *oneself* the cause of some end by acting from principles that can be willed as universal laws. We focus here on the second argument.)

First, a rational action is guided by some principle and for an action to be the work of the self as a whole, it must be based on a principle with which one identifies. So self-determination requires identification with some principle of choice. Second, the principle of choice with which one identifies must be a universal principle applying to a range of similar cases. To see why, imagine an agent that identifies with a "particularistic principle" with no implications beyond the case at hand. This agent would wholly identify with the present motive of action.

But in this case, no distinction can be drawn between the self and the various motives within the self, and there is in effect no active self at work. Such a "choice" fails to satisfy a basic condition of action – it fails to constitute an active unified self – and would not count as volition (Korsgaard 2009: §4.4.3). Thus, self-determination involves giving oneself some universal law, and if so, the principle of acting from some universal law is a constitutive principle of action.

Since this is a weak principle that sets almost no limits on one's concrete principles of action, further argument is needed to get the basic principle of morality. A second component of Korsgaard's argument is that rational action involves valuing oneself as a person. Korsgaard holds that reasons for action are based in a "practical identity," or "description under which you value yourself" (Korsgaard 1996: §3.3.1) – that is, a self-conception based on such things as social roles, ties to others, personal ends and projects, and so on, through which one finds certain activities to be worthwhile. Many of our practical identities are contingent, and their hold on us is a matter of our continuing to endorse them. But since we need reasons in order to act and reasons are based in specific practical identities, the need for some practical identities is not contingent. That fact about rational action is the basis of a necessary identity – one's identity as a human being, "a reflective animal who needs reasons to live and act" (Korsgaard 1996: §3.4.7). Our human identity gives us higher order reasons to endorse and to take seriously some practical identities, and in acting on these higher order reasons one values oneself as a human being. Thus, the hold on us of our particular practical identities comes in part from our human identity (our need for some practical identities), and valuing oneself as a human being is a condition of having reasons and finding anything to be worth doing. In endorsing a specific practical identity, one also endorses the reasons that come from one's human identity and values oneself as a human being (Korsgaard 1996: §§3.4.7–9). What follows is that the conditions of agency commit us to valuing ourselves as human beings, and valuing oneself in that fashion commits one to acknowledging the value of all human agents.

To combine these two arguments: you constitute yourself as an agent by giving yourself some universal law. Rational agency also commits you to valuing yourself as a human being in a way that acknowledges the moral standing of others. But if valuing humanity is implicit in all rational choice, then the universal laws by which you constitute yourself as an agent are implicitly laws for rational agents as such, or laws that all rational agents can endorse. In this way, Korsgaard argues that the basic principle of morality gives the basic form of action. This argument grounds the authority of morality in autonomy in the sense that the fundamental principle of morality expresses the conditions of rational agency.

See also Kant (Chapter 14); Realism and its alternatives (Chapter 26); Cognitivism without realism (Chapter 29); Ethical intuitionism (Chapter 39); Contractualism (Chapter 41); Respect and recognition (Chapter 47).

References

Hill, Thomas E. Jr (2000) *Respect, Pluralism, and Justice*, Oxford and New York: Oxford University Press.

Korsgaard, Christine M. (1996) *The Sources of Normativity*, Cambridge and New York: Cambridge University Press. (Referred to by section number.)

——(2009) *Self-Constitution: Agency, Identity, and Integrity*, Oxford and New York: Oxford University Press. (Referred to by section number.)

Nagel, Thomas (1978) *The Possiblity of Altruism*, Princeton, NJ: Princeton University Press.

Rawls, John (1996) *Political Liberalism*, New York: Columbia University Press.

——(1999/1971) *A Theory of Justice*, rev. edn, Cambridge, MA: Harvard University Press.

Scanlon, T. M. (1998) *What We Owe to Each Other*, Cambridge, MA: Harvard University Press.

Further reading

Herman, Barbara (2007) *Moral Literacy*, Cambridge, MA: Harvard University Press. (Explores Kantian approaches to several issues in moral theory.)

O'Neill, Onora (1996) *Towards Justice and Virtue*, Cambridge and New York: Cambridge University Press. (Develops a Kantian constructivist account of universal principles of justice and virtue.)

Velleman, David (2006) *Self to Self*, Cambridge: Cambridge University Press. (Essays by a contemporary philosopher that explore Kantian themes.)

39
ETHICAL INTUITIONISM

Philip Stratton-Lake

Intuitionism is a movement in ethics that dates back to the early eighteenth century. It includes Samuel Clarke (1675–1729), Richard Price (1723–91), Henry Sidgwick (1838–1900), G. E. Moore (1873–1958), H. P. Prichard (1871–1947), W. D. Ross (1877–1971) and A. C. Ewing (1899–1973). The distinctive features of intuitionism are non-naturalist moral realism and the view that basic moral principles are self-evident. Most intuitionists are pluralists about basic moral principles – that is, they believe that there is an irreducible plurality of basic moral principles. However, Sidgwick and Moore were monists, and held that the morality of right and wrong could be subsumed under a single consequentialist principle.

The main features of intuitionism

Intuitionists are moral realists – that is, they believe that moral judgements express beliefs, that many of these beliefs are true, and that what makes them true is the presence of the relevant moral properties in their objects. So beliefs such as the belief that stealing is wrong or that kindness is good are made true by the fact that acts of stealing have (instantiate) the property of wrongness, and the fact that acts of kindness have the property of goodness. Intuitionists took these properties (rightness, wrongness, goodness and badness) to be non-natural properties. It is not always clear precisely what they mean by "non-natural," but the idea is that we cannot define moral properties without including some explicitly moral term, and so they cannot be defined using the terminology of any natural science. So, for example, X's being good cannot be the same as X's being desired by some individual or group of individuals, though it could be understood as what *ought* to be desired. Indeed, this is how Sidgwick and Ewing understood goodness (Sidgwick 1967: 110–11; Ewing 1947). So intuitionists were not only realists, but *non-natural* moral realists. Moral facts and properties, are, for them, real yet non-natural facts and properties.

The intuitionists were also epistemological foundationalists. This means that they maintain that moral knowledge is divided into two kinds – knowledge that is based on some sort of inference, or argument, and knowledge that is not. Moral knowledge that is based on argument is derivative knowledge. It is derivative because the knowledge that we acquire from the conclusion must rest upon a prior knowledge of the premises that support that conclusion. If our knowledge of these premises is based upon an argument, then we must know the premises of that argument, and if this knowledge is based on a further argument, we must know the premises of this argument, and so on. If we are to avoid an infinite regress, some premises must be known directly, i.e. without the need of any argument in support of them. In relation to moral knowledge these basic premises are the self-evident moral axioms upon which all moral knowledge is based. For intuitionists these self-evident axioms are moral principles stating that we ought (or ought not) to do certain acts, or in the case of Ross, that certain acts are *prima facie* right, or wrong.

Intuitionists did not, however, claim that all of our moral convictions count as knowledge, let alone as self-evident knowledge. Ross, for instance, maintained that only basic moral principles can be known. We can never have knowledge of what we ought to do in a particular set of circumstances, for we can never know for certain which principles apply, or in cases of conflicting obligations, which obligation is the more stringent in the circumstances. Furthermore, if the duty of promoting the good applies, we can never be certain which of all the acts we could do would produce the best outcome. All we can hope for in specific cases is mere probable opinion, but that falls a long way short of knowledge. So although intuitionists may appear to make very strong epistemological claims, overall their moral epistemology was rather modest. For them, we have very little moral knowledge.

Intuitionists did not believe that self-evident moral principles have to be obvious to anyone who contemplates them. Consequently, they accept that there may be disagreement about what those self-evident principles are, and about how many there are. Clarke thought that basic moral principles would be assented to by anyone with an adequate understanding of them and who considered the matter in an unbiased way. But, of course, this allows for plenty of disagreement, as some people may not have an adequate understanding of the relevant principle, or their judgement may be biased in some way. So intuitionists acknowledged that there may be disagreement about basic moral principles, which is just as well as there were significant disagreements between the intuitionists about what these principles are.

Some intuitionists, like Sidgwick, for example, were quite unsettled by such disagreement. Sidgwick held that disagreement between thoughtful people should weaken our confidence in the disputed principles. But others, like Ross, seemed unfazed by such disagreement. Ross was well aware that other intuitionists, like Moore, rejected his view that a principle of fidelity to promises has moral significance independently of any good that fidelity produces. But this did not seem to dent his confidence in the view that the principle of fidelity to promises is self-evident.

Intuitionists claimed that proof of basic moral principles is not needed. If it were, then these principles would not halt the regress of justification. But the view that no proof, or argument, is *needed* for belief in a self-evident principle is quite compatible with the view that such arguments *can* be provided. Intuitionists often fail to note this and sometimes mistakenly state that no argument can be provided for self-evident principles. But even where intuitionists deny the possibility of providing arguments for self-evident principles, they nevertheless often provide such arguments. These arguments tend to take the form of thought experiments aimed at drawing out our moral intuitions. Thus, for instance, Ross tried to get us to see that fidelity to promises has a moral significance independently of good consequences, by getting us to imagine a situation in which breaking a promise would produce 1,001 units of good whereas keeping it would produce only 1,000 units of good. If good consequences are the only morally relevant features of acts, then we would be obligated to break our promise here. But, Ross maintains, we cannot accept this conclusion, and this seems to show that we regard fidelity to promises as having independent moral weight (Ross 2002: 34–5).

Ross uses similar arguments against those who think that there is only one thing that is intrinsically good. Hedonists, for example, think that only pleasure is intrinsically good. Everything else is, they maintain, good only when and because it produces pleasure. But we may ask whether a world containing virtuous actions and dispositions would be no better than another world that contains no virtuous acts or dispositions, even if both worlds contained exactly equal amounts of pleasure (both in terms of duration and intensity). If we think that the world containing virtue is better, then it seems that we must reject the view that pleasure is the only intrinsic good, and allow that virtue also has intrinsic value (Ross 2002: 134).

So although intuitionists denied that any form of argument is needed for self-evident principles of what is right and good, they still offered arguments for their self-evident principles. This is quite compatible with their view that these principles are self-evident.

The most significant difference between the various classic intuitionists relates to how many basic, self-evident moral principles there are. Sidgwick, and Moore, maintained that there is one such principle, and that it is consequentialist. They are thus monists about the basic principles of duty. All of the other intuitionists maintained that there is an irreducible plurality of such principles that may conflict with each other in particular cases, and that no explicit priority rules for resolving such conflicts can be provided.

This difference between monists and pluralists appears in their views about the good as well as the right. Sidgwick was a monist about both the right and the good, maintaining that we ought always to produce the best outcome (from an impartial point of view), and that the only good to be promoted is pleasure. Moore agreed with Sidgwick's monism about the right, but rejected his monism about the good. Moore held that there is an irreducible plurality of intrinsically good things, the most important of which is the admiring contemplation of beauty and virtue (1993: 237). In what follows, however, I shall cover only pluralism and monism about the right.

Pluralistic intuitionism

Clarke, Price, Prichard and Ross were all pluralists about the right. Clarke argued that there are what he called eternal relations of fittingness between certain things and relations in which people can stand to each other and certain acts. The propositions expressing these eternal and immutable relations are self-evident in the sense that no one who considered them fairly and with an open mind could fail to assent to them. He argued for his basic principles largely by analogy with basic mathematical or geometrical truths.

Clarke divided these duties into three categories: duties owed to God, those owed to our fellow men, and those we owe to ourselves (1965/1706: 499). In relation to God, the rule of righteousness requires that we:

> keep constantly in our Minds, the highest possible Honour, Esteem, and Veneration for him, which must express it self in proper and respective influences upon all our Passions, and in the suitable direction of all our Actions.
>
> (1965/1706: 499)

This principle follows from the infinite superiority of God to ourselves, and is as clear as that infinity is larger than a point, or eternity longer than a moment. It is, he maintains, self-evident that it is fitting for us to worship and honor such a being. To fail to recognize this duty is, Clarke maintains, like thinking that the effect owes nothing to its cause, or that the whole is no bigger than one of its parts (1965/1706: 491).

The second branch of duty involves two rules of righteousness: equity and universal beneficence. Clarke offers different formulations of the first principle. Sometimes he describes this duty with reference to how we *desire* others to treat us. For instance, he writes that to fail to act in accordance with this duty is to refuse to deal "with every man as he desires they should deal with him" (1965/1706: 491). This formulation makes it look like a version of the Golden Rule. But sometimes he makes no reference to desire in describing this duty, as when he describes it as the requirement that "we so deal with every Man, as in like circumstances we could reasonably expect he should deal with Us" (1965/1706: 500). Here the point seems to be that if in a certain set of circumstances it is reasonable for someone to treat us in a certain way, then it must be reasonable for us to treat them in the same way if the circumstances were reversed – that the identity of the agent is irrelevant. This is not a point about what we want, and so does not seem to be a version of the Golden Rule. It is rather a point about the universality and impartiality of moral requirements, though Clarke describes it as a principle of equity (1965/1706: 500).

Once again, Clarke uses an analogy with mathematics and geometry to make his point compelling. The principle of equity is, he maintains, as evident in moral philosophy as the principle of equity in mathematics and geometry. If one number or line is equal to another, then that other must be equal to it. Similarly, if your standing to me in a certain relation obligates you to treat me in a certain way, then if I stood in the same relation to you I would be obligated to treat you in the same way.

The second of our duties to others is universal love, or benevolence (1965/1706: 502). This principle can, Clarke claims, be seen to follow once we accept that the good is what is fitting and reasonable to be done, and the greatest good is the most fitting. Since the welfare and happiness of our fellow creatures is good (as the goodness of God spreads itself over his creations) then we ought to promote the good of others. In doing this we most nearly imitate the perfections of our creator (1965/1706: 502).

Finally we all have a duty to ourselves, to preserve our being (1965/1706: 504). This involves both temperance not only to preserve our lives, but also to preserve our faculties that are necessary to carry out our other duties. Sidgwick describes this as a purely derivative duty, on the ground that Clarke defends this duty by arguing that it is necessary for us to carry out our other duties (Sidgwick 1967: 384n). But this is not the only reason Clarke provides for why we ought to preserve our lives. He claims also that we ought to do this because our life is something that is given by our creator and is thus not something we have the authority to take away (1965/1706: 504). This seems to make it a basic duty, unless this ground be subsumed under the duty to honor and respect God.

We have seen then that Clarke lists four duties – the duty to honor God, the duty of equity, of universal beneficence, and of self-preservation. From these four duties (or three if the last turns out to be merely derivative) Clarke maintains, all of the particular duties may be derived.

Like Clarke, Price held that certain relations are by their nature such as to make certain actions fitting, and others unfitting. Price agreed with Clarke that we have a basic duty to respect and honor God, and to promote our own and others' good (1974/1758: 178–80), though the duty of equity does not figure among those he lists in the *Review*. But Price adds other duties to Clarke's list, and seems to regard these as self-evident and basic also. For instance, to Clarke's list he adds a duty to respect our superiors (which he held to have the same ground as our duty to God [1974/1758: 178]), as well as the duties of gratitude, veracity and justice.

The duty of gratitude is, he maintains, distinct from any duty to promote the general good. The mere fact that we have received a benefit from another puts us under an obligation to benefit that person. Price goes on to make an important distinction between duties that are owed to fellow men in general, and those that are owed to specific individuals. Whereas universal beneficence falls under the former, gratitude falls under the latter. This duty is, he writes, one of a number of duties that are owed to certain specific individuals (1974/1758: 180). Other instances of such personal duties, or agent-relative duties, include fidelity to promises, private interest, friendship, "and all particular attachments and connections" (1974/1758: 181).

Price also adds the duty of veracity to Clarke's list. This duty includes not only "impartiality and honesty of mind in our inquiries after truth" but also a regard for truth and honesty in everything we say. Unlike later intuitionists, such as Ross, who thought that fidelity to promises is a basic duty, Price argued that this duty is derivative, and grounded in the duty of veracity. To see this we must distinguish between promising and declaring an intention. If I declare an intention to do something, I say that I now intend to do it, whereas if I promise to do it, I am declaring that I *will* do that action at some suitable time in the future. With regard to declaring an intention I utter a falsehood if I do not have that intention at the time of utterance. With regard to promises I utter a falsehood if I do not do the relevant act at the appropriate time. So, Price argues, the duty to keep our promises stems from the fact that when we break a promise we knowingly and wilfully make something we said in the past false (1974/1758: 182). Consequently, breaking promises is the same sort of wrong as knowingly and willingness uttering a falsehood.

The final duty Price enumerates is the duty of justice. By this he means "that part of virtue which regards *property* and *commerce*" (1974/1758: 740). The idea of property is that of a relation to an object or person which makes it fitting for him to do what he wishes with it, and wrong for others to deprive him of it. So this duty stems from the very idea of some object's being one's own.

So Price enumerates more basic duties than Clarke, although he agrees with Clarke that each basic duty is self-evident. Price also emphasizes that these duties can conflict with each other and that there is no higher order principle for deciding what to do in particular cases where they do conflict. So although the abstract ideas of virtue enumerated are all self-evident, universal, and invariant, there will be no self-evident and invariant truths relating to particular cases (1974/1758: 185).

After Price the most important pluralist intuitionists are Prichard and Ross writing at the beginning of the twentieth century. Both Prichard and Ross argued in a more systematic way for pluralism by rejecting the best monistic theories. They both argued that the most plausible monistic theories attempted to derive the right from the good, either from the agent's own good, the intrinsic goodness of our acts, or the impartial good of the consequences of one's acts. They dismissed the idea that moral obligations can be derived from the agent's own good on the ground that this is irrelevant to what we are obligated to do. That some act will benefit us may get us to want to do it, but cannot get us to believe that we are obligated to do it (Prichard 2002b: 9; Ross 2002: 16). They deny that our obligations stem from the intrinsic goodness of obligatory acts, for the only aspect of an action that could be intrinsically good is its motive, but the motive is never part of what we are obligated to do (Prichard 2002b: 11; Ross 2002: 6). So what we are obligated to do can never be *intrinsically* good. This leaves only the consequentialist view that our obligations are grounded in the goodness of their outcomes.

Both Prichard and Ross reject consequentialism mainly because it conflicts with our considered moral convictions. There are, they maintain, plenty of cases in which two acts produce the same amount of good, but our duty is to do only one of them. Prichard gives the example of a situation in which a person could help either a stranger, himself or his father, though the point is made better if we regard a situation where he has to choose only between benefiting his father or the stranger (2002a: 2). Since the good conferred would be equal regardless of who received it, consequentialism must, he argues, say that it does not matter on whom the benefit is conferred. But this conflicts with a strong intuition that the person should, in such circumstances, benefit his father. If this intuition is sound then certain personal relations have moral significance that cannot be subsumed under the impartial promotion of the good.

Ross's argument for the basic duty of fidelity mentioned earlier could be modified to take the same form. It might be that keeping my promise will produce as much good as breaking it would. If the goodness of outcomes is the only thing that is relevant to the rightness of the act, then we should be indifferent between these acts. But, it seems, we cannot bring ourselves to believe that we should be indifferent. So we must reject the thesis that would force us to do this – namely, that the only determinant of right is good outcomes.

The most noticeable way in which Prichard and Ross differed from earlier intuitionists like Clarke and Price is that they do not mention any duty to God. Prichard's and Ross's intuitionism seems, then, to be atheistic, or at least compatible with atheism. The difference between Prichard and Ross is, in contrast, less striking. Their main difference is in relation to the general nature of principles of right conduct. Prichard regarded basic moral principles as stating that we have certain obligations. He thus understands a conflict of duties as a conflict of obligations, a conflict which is to be decided by deciding which of the conflicting obligations is the most pressing.

Ross, however, thought of his moral principles as principles of what he called *prima facie* duty, and distinguished *prima facie* duty from actual duty, or duty proper. An act is *prima facie* right if it has some feature that tends to make it actually right, and is *prima facie* wrong if it has some feature that tends to make it actually wrong (Ross 2002: 19–20). "*Prima facie*" here does *not* mean "at first sight," but means "as far as that goes," or "*pro tanto*" right. It is a consideration that counts in favor of doing the act. Whether an act is actually right or wrong depends on all of the *prima facie* right and wrong features – that is, on *all* of the features that count for and against doing it. If the act has, all things considered, a higher degree of *prima facie* rightness over *prima facie* wrongness, then it is actually right, and conversely if it is more *prima facie* wrong than right, then it is actually wrong.

Thinking of moral conflicts as conflicts of *prima facie* duty has the advantage that it does not force us to think that actions that we ought to do all things considered are to a certain extent morally wrong (though less wrong than any other act). For (actual) rightness and wrongness applies only at the all things considered level. At this level an act can be either right or wrong, but not both. The idea that there may be something to be said against an act that we ought to do is captured by the claim that it is *prima facie* wrong. But this is not to say that it is actually wrong to some degree.

Prichard later came to accept this view, as he found it impossible to accept the view that there is some obligatoriness to a wrong act or some wrongness to a right act, although he preferred to describe conflicts in terms of conflicting claims than *prima facie* duties (Prichard 2002c: 79).

Prichard doesn't offer us a list of basic principles of duties, or claims, but Ross does. Initially he lists seven *prima facie* duties – the duties of fidelity, gratitude, reparation, justice self-improvement, beneficence and non-maleficence (Ross 2002: 21). But he later reduces this list to five, by subsuming the duties of justice, self-improvement and beneficence under the duty to promote the good (2002: 26–7). According to Ross, from these five basic *prima facie* duties all obligations can be derived.

As we have seen, most intuitionists were pluralists about the right. The most important monists about the right were Sidgwick and Moore. Henry Sidgwick rejected earlier pluralist views on the ground that most of their supposed self-evident principles are either mere tautologies, or are not self-evident at all. For instance, the principle of justice states that we ought to give everyone his or her own. But the only way in which "his or her own" may be understood is as "that which it is right he [or she] should have" (1967: 375). So this principle states merely that we ought to give every man what he ought to have, and that is uninformative. Other principles that Sidgwick thought were substantive, such as the principle of fidelity to promises or of honesty, were not self-evident. Such principles, he maintained, present themselves as principles that require rational justification (1967: 383).

But Sidgwick did not reject all self-evident moral principles. He accepted Clarke's principle of equity and universal benevolence as self-evident (1967: 379, 382). He also maintained that it is self-evident that we ought to aim at our own good on the whole, where "good on the whole" involves treating future benefits to ourselves as we would treat equal present benefits – the principle of rational egoism. Indeed, Sidgwick maintained that the principle of rational egoism would sometimes conflict with the principle of universal benevolence, and referred to such conflicts as revealing a fundamental contradiction "in our apparent intuitions of what is reasonable in conduct" (1967: 508). That there is no ultimate reconciliation of utilitarian duty and self-interest is what Sidgwick sometimes refers to as the dualism of practical reason (1967: 404n).

The principle of equity, he maintains, is something that all moral theories must acknowledge. They will differ with regard to when and why it will be right to treat someone in a certain way, but must accept that the same considerations that make it right for me to treat you in a certain way will make it right for you to treat me in the same way (all other things being equal). We may, then, regard this as a formal principle, rather than as a substantive principle telling us *what* we ought to do.

This leaves the principles of rational egoism and universal benevolence. It may seem from this that Sidgwick is after all a pluralist, albeit a pluralist with only two basic principles. But although the principle of universal benevolence and of rational egoism are both principles of practical reason according to Sidgwick, he seemed to regard only the former as a moral principle. For instance, he describes conflicts between these two principles as conflicts between duty and self-interest (1967: 502, 503, 508). So although he lists two substantive (plus one formal) self-evident principles, he seems to think that there is only one basic *moral* principle.

Since Sidgwick identifies my good and the good of others with happiness, and understands happiness to be simply pleasure and the absence of pain, rational egoism will involve producing as much net pleasure for oneself as one can, and universal benevolence will involve producing as much net pleasure in the world as is possible (1967: 402). But in both cases this goal is best achieved indirectly. What he means by this is that we are much more likely to live a pleasant life and produce pleasure in general if we aim at things other than pleasure, such as virtue, truth, freedom, beauty, etc. for their own sake (1967: 405). So his consequentialism requires non-consequentialist motivations and goals. But what justifies these motivations and goals is the consequentialist principle of maximizing good.

G. E. Moore was greatly influenced by Sidgwick, and agreed with him that we ought always to produce as much good as possible. But Moore differed from Sidgwick in several important ways. First, he was pluralistic about the good that is to be promoted. Pleasure will figure in many of those goods, but is not itself of any great intrinsic value, according to Moore, and is certainly not the sole good. Among the many diverse goods Moore held that the admiring contemplation of beauty and pleasures of social intercourse were by far the most important (1993: 237)

A further way in which Moore differed from Sidgwick is that in his *Principia* he argued that "right" *means* "maximises good" (1993: 196). This is quite a surprising thing for Moore to say given that he devoted considerable energy to arguing that "good" is indefinable in his *Principia Ethica*, and the arguments he uses in support of this view about good apply equally well to right. Nonetheless, in *Principia* Moore regarded his consequentialism as true by definition, though he would abandon this view in his later work (*Ethics*) and claim that this principle expresses a synthetic truth.

By the 1930s intuitionism fell into disrepute. The moral realism and epistemology that was so central to intuitionist views was completely eclipsed by the non-cognitivism of Ayer, Stevenson and Hare, and interest in normative moral philosophy waned. Intuitionism remained deeply unfashionable until the 1970s and 1980s when confidence grew that some form of moral realism could be defended after all. Many of these neo-realists were naturalist, but with the rise of naturalist moral realism, the intuitionists' anti-naturalistic arguments became relevant again, and the influence of their views can be found in philosophers as diverse as Wiggins, McDowell, Parfit, Scanlon, Raz, Audi, Hurka and Dancy. Furthermore, in normative moral theory the debate between monists and pluralists – which is independent of the intuitionists' epistemological and meta-ethical views – is as strong as ever. Many current debates about whether the right can be derived from the good, and between impartialist and partialist moral theories, continue to draw on arguments put forward by the intuitionists discussed here, and their influence, significance and relevance to our understanding of morality now seems secured.

See also Ethics and reason (Chapter 9); Sidgwick, Green, and Bradley (Chapter 17); The open question argument (Chapter 25); Realism and its alternatives (Chapter 26); Consequentialism (Chapter 37).

References

Clarke, S. (1965/1706) *A Discourse Concerning the Unalterable Obligations of Natural Religion*, in vol. 2 of *The British Moralists: Being Selections from the Writers Principally of the Eighteenth Century*, ed. L. A. Selby-Bigge, New York: Dover.

Ewing, A. C. (1947) *The Definition of Good*, London: Macmillan.

Moore, G. E. (1993) *Principia Ethica*, ed. T. Baldwin, Cambridge: Cambridge University Press.

Price, R. A. (1974/1758) *Review of the Principal Questions in Morals*, ed. D. D. Raphael, Oxford: Clarendon Press.

Prichard, H. A. (2002a) "What Is the Basis for Moral Obligation?," in *Moral Writings: H. A. Prichard*, ed. J. MacAdam, Oxford: Clarendon Press, pp. 1–6.

——(2002b) "Does Moral Philosophy Rest on a Mistake?," in *Moral Writings: H. A. Prichard*, ed. J. MacAdam, Oxford: Clarendon Press, pp. 7–20.

——(2002c) "A Conflict of Duties (1928)," in *Moral Writings: H. A. Prichard*, ed. J. MacAdam, Oxford: Clarendon Press, pp. 7–20.

Ross, W. D. (2002) *The Right and the Good*, ed. P. Stratton-Lake, Oxford: Clarendon Press.

Sidgwick, H. (1967) *The Methods of Ethics*, London: Macmillan.

Further reading

Moore, G. E. (1966) *Ethics*, London: Oxford University Press.
Stratton-Lake, P. (ed.) (2002) *Ethical Intuitionism: Re-evaluations*, Oxford: Clarendon Press.
Urmson, J. O. (1975) "A Defence of Intuitionism," *Proceedings of the Aristotelian Society* 75: 111–19.

40
VIRTUE ETHICS

Michael Slote

In the ancient world, virtue ethics was the dominant form of ethics, but in modern times, and until fairly recently, virtue ethics was largely forgotten in favor of other approaches to morality like utilitarianism and Kantian ethics. That has changed, however, over the past fifty years. In 1958 Elizabeth Anscombe published "Modern Moral Philosophy," a paper that excoriated Kantianism and (utilitarian) consequentialism and recommended a return to Aristotelian moral psychology. Since then, virtue ethics has steadily revived, and in the past ten years it has come to be considered one of the major forms of contemporary ethical theory.

In what follows, I want to say what virtue ethics is and isn't, and this will involve drawing contrasts between it and other philosophical approaches to morality. I then want to compare and contrast the main kinds of historical and contemporary virtue ethics and shall go on to discuss the major problems, or challenges, that present-day virtue ethics faces. Finally, I would like to describe some interesting similarities and differences between various forms of virtue ethics and other ways of thinking about morality.

What is virtue ethics?

It is perhaps easiest to understand what virtue ethics is by drawing a contrast with Kantian and consequentialist or utilitarian approaches to moral philosophy. For Kantian ethics, rules and fundamental principles play a crucial and (some would say) a foundational role, and consequentialism treats the moral assessment of actions as a function of what can be said about the consequences of those actions. But rules/principles and consequences are not the basis for the moral evaluations virtue ethics makes. The ethical focus, rather, is on character and motive, which are naturally regarded as the key elements in determining whether someone is virtuous or has a particular virtue (like courage or kindness).

Some proponents of virtue ethics (e.g. Leslie Stephen 1882 and Edmund Pincoffs 1986) place so much importance on character and motive that they lose interest in the moral assessment of actions. But almost all contemporary virtue ethicists do want to evaluate actions, and I shall confine our attention to such forms of virtue ethics. However, many philosophers who offer theories of the virtues are not virtue ethicists, and seeing this will help us better understand what virtue ethics, positively, is. For example, both Rawls (1971) and Kant (1964) have a great deal to say about what virtue or particular virtues consist in, and for both virtue involves acting in accordance with certain principles. But to conceive virtue in relation to principles is to treat the principles as ethically (more) fundamental, and, as I characterized virtue ethics above, this isn't virtue ethics. Kant and Rawls, and even some utilitarians, offer us theories of virtue or the virtues; but they aren't virtue ethicists if they don't see virtuous character or motivation as the most important element in (understanding) morality.

One important division *within* virtue ethics concerns the role of theory in moral philosophy. Kantianism and utilitarianism clearly offer us theories of morality, and in the early years of the recent revival of virtue ethics, most advocates of virtue ethics objected to the theoretical character of those two then-dominant traditions and therefore saw virtue ethics as a form of anti-theory. Those advocating the avoidance of theory argued, among other things, that our understanding of ethical phenomena is too complex, too *rich*, to be captured by any unifying theory. Rather than do ethics on the model of science, we should regard it as more like the writing of history or art connoisseurship, disciplines where sensitivity, experience, and judgment would seem to make general theories unnecessary and unhelpful. (The work of Bernard Williams [1985], John McDowell [1979], and Martha Nussbaum [1986, 1990, 1992, 2001] is relevant here.)

More recently, however, virtue ethicists have been increasingly willing to engage in theorizing and theoretical generalizations. This may have been because, given the importance of theoretical approaches like Kantianism and consequentialism in contemporary moral philosophy, it was thought unlikely that any anti-theory could ever be regarded as a serious alternative to them. It was seen that it would take a theory to beat a theory (shades of Thomas Kuhn), and at least three virtue ethicists – Rosalind Hursthouse (1999), Christine Swanton (2003), and I myself (2001) – have produced book-length, theoretical, virtue-ethical work in recent years. (Philippa Foot, who did so much to promote the revival of virtue ethics (1978), doesn't like to be called a virtue ethicist.) I myself believe that virtue ethics is now taken as seriously as it is by ethicists generally because it has been willing to stake out its own territory in theoretical terms that distinctly compete with or criticize other ethical theories like utilitarianism and Kantian ethics (including its contractualist forms).

So some current virtue ethics is anti-theoretical and some is very strongly in favor of theory, but in fact this distinction was not operative or evident in ancient ethical thought. Some ancient ethical thinkers (and I am speaking of classical antiquity, not of ancient Chinese and Indian ethical thought, about which I shall say something just below) were skeptical or nihilistic about values and morals, but the major ethical philosophies of the ancient world – Platonism, Aristotelianism, Stoicism, and Epicureanism – were all quite comfortable presenting themselves as general theories. In addition, all four schools took a fundamentally eudaimonistic approach to ethics, and this stands in marked contrast with most modern forms of virtue-ethical thought.

Eudaimonism is the idea that no trait of character can count as a virtue unless it serves the interests, promotes the overall well-being, of the virtuous individual – "eudaimonia" is, roughly, the Greek word for overall or long-term well-being, or the "good life." Alternatively, and to borrow from Julia Annas (1993), the eudaimonism that is common to all ancient ethical theorizing assumes that the ethical agent's own long-term well-being is the "entry point" for any individual's ethical thinking. That doesn't mean that ancient ethical thought was uniformly "egoistic," that is, favorable to universally selfish motivation. Aristotle, for example, thought that a concern for values beyond the self – e.g. for the good of one's own country or city state – was part of virtuous character, but at the same time he held that an individual who lacked such character would be worse off than one who possessed it (even if that meant giving up one's life for the good of one's country). So Aristotle is a eudaimonist, but is far from recommending that we be selfishly or egoistically motivated.

By contrast, much modern virtue ethics doesn't accept eudaimonism and thinks that a morally virtuous individual may sometimes have to sacrifice her own (greater) good for the good of others. This difference from ancient thought seems at least partly due to the influence of Christianity, with its idealization of Jesus's self-sacrifice on behalf of sinful, suffering humanity. But whatever its historical source, most modern and contemporary virtue ethics stresses our obligations to others at the expense, to some extent, of the well-being of the individual who has the obligations, and in this respect modern virtue ethics resembles Kantianism and utilitarianism more than it does the ancient modes of ethical thought that we have just mentioned. Eudaimonism is not, therefore, part of the definition or concept of virtue ethics. On the other hand, some forms of ancient and modern virtue ethics are avowedly egoistic – Epicureanism and Nietzsche's philosophy being pretty clear examples – and so we can't define virtue ethics as standing *opposed* to egoism any more than we can require it to *be* eudaimonistic.

In addition, not all forms of virtue ethics are rationalistic, i.e. committed to treating reason or rationality as the basis for ethical thought and action. The virtue ethics of classical antiquity is pretty uniformly rationalistic in its assumptions, but ancient Chinese and Buddhist thought in at least some instances stresses the emotional, or sentimental, side of ethics, and both Hume and contemporary virtue ethicists who are influenced by him also regard emotion and feeling, rather than human reason, as the basis of morality. Perhaps the Christian emphasis on love and compassion has made such sentimentalist forms of virtue ethics seem more attractive even to secular modern-day ethicists than it ever was in the period of classical antiquity. But this means, once again, that rationalistic assumptions can't be built into the definition or concept of virtue ethics and that in certain respects rationalistic modes of virtue ethics have more in common with Kantian rationalism than with non-rationalist, sentimentalist, forms of virtue ethics (e.g. Hume's). I will return to this theme later in our discussion, but it is time now to say more specific things about the different forms of virtue ethics that have flourished in the past or more recently.

Forms of virtue ethics

We can't possibly talk about every kind of virtue ethics that has ever been – our discussion needs to be governed by a sense of what is important and what is not so important, and, as a virtue ethicist myself, I am inclined to think that the importance of one or another mode of virtue ethics to contemporary ethical thought gives us some basis for deciding what to emphasize within the history of virtue ethics. In the ancient world, Stoicism, with its emphasis on the "divine spark" in all human beings, was much more popular and influential than Aristotelian ethics, with its clearly aristocratic leanings and commitments. But since Anscombe published "Modern Moral Philosophy" in 1958, reviving virtue ethics has emphasized and followed Aristotle more than any other ethical thinker. Indeed, for the longest time virtue ethics was simply identified with Aristotle's views; but over the past few years it has become evident that other forms of virtue ethics may be viable in contemporary circumstances. As Christine Swanton (2003) has put it, virtue ethics turns out to be a genus, rather than (as some had thought) a species. So I want to begin by speaking of Aristotle and of contemporary neo-Aristotelianism and then go on to speak of the history and present-day development of other kinds of virtue ethics.

For Aristotle virtue is a certain sort of habit or disposition of thinking, feeling, and acting. According to his "doctrine of the mean," virtuous individuals act (and feel) in a way that lies in a mean between extremes, as when a person of courage, when faced with danger, chooses a course of action that is neither cowardly nor foolhardy. Where the mean lies is not given mathematically (it needn't be an exact halfway point between vices); and Aristotle thinks, more generally, that the dictates of virtue cannot be captured in rules or universal principles. In order to be virtuous, rather, a person has to become rationally sensitive to or perceptive about what is morally right in any given situation, and such practical wisdom is acquired as a result of parental training and accumulating life experiences. In addition, he holds that there is a unity to the virtues, that there cannot be conflict among them, so that, for example, courage never calls for one to do an act that is unjust or intemperate.

Aristotle's talk of perception and sensitivity can lead one to think that situationally determined facts about what it would be right or noble to do are independent of any specification of the virtuous individual. In that case, virtue would consist in habitually knowing and appropriately responding to such facts. But Aristotle also says that the virtuous individual is the measure of what it is right to do or feel, and some, though not all, interpreters have understood this to mean that what is right counts as such *because* it would be chosen by a certain kind of, i.e. virtuous, individual. This would entail that one has to specify virtuousness independently of saying what makes an act right and that acts are right because an independently specified virtuous individual would choose them; and it is most frequently assumed that such an independent specification requires one to characterize the virtuous individual as someone leading a life of eudaimonia. There are other interpretive difficulties (and the threat of a circle too) because Aristotle is not entirely clear about whether eudaimonia consists (mainly) in a mix of practical and theoretical virtues or whether only the theoretical virtues are crucial to it.

Aristotle doesn't put much weight on virtues like kindness and compassion, but, quite possibly because of the pervasive cultural influence of Christianity, contemporary (neo-)Aristotelians like John McDowell (1979), Philippa Foot (1978), and Rosalind Hursthouse (1999) all mention kindness as a prime example of a virtue. Recent Aristotelian virtue ethicists also abandon Aristotle's doctrine of the mean, and for good reason, too, because it was that doctrine as much as any other that led to the long-term rejection and eclipse of ethical Aristotelianism beginning in the seventeenth century. At that time, Aristotelianism was seen as unable to accommodate emerging notions of human rights, but it also came to be recognized that virtues like truthfulness, loyalty, and fidelity to promises cannot be seen as involving a mean between extremes, and since modern-day ethicists want to insist on the importance of those virtues, the doctrine of the mean has/had to go.

During the past decade, the most influential work of neo-Aristotelian virtue ethics has been Hursthouse's *On Virtue Ethics*. That book interprets Aristotle, in the second of the two ways mentioned earlier, as understanding right actions in terms of an independently specified notion of the virtuous individual. Hursthouse is definitely engaged in theorizing (at least if Aristotle was), but in work subsequent to the book she has disclaimed any attempt to give a foundational account of virtue. Still, the book emphasizes the ways in which what counts as a virtue depends on considerations about the good of the human species, of the given virtuous individual, and of the community that individual is a member of – though Hursthouse is somewhat non-committal about how these different considerations weigh against one another. In any event, neo-Aristotelianism has had the largest influence, at least till now, within reviving virtue ethics; but there are presently other forms of virtue ethics in play, and I want to mention some of these.

For some reason, one now sees very little virtue ethics inspired mainly by Plato or by the Epicureans, but there are a number of contemporary neo-Stoics, among them Martha Nussbaum and Julia Annas. Nussbaum (along with others) has attempted to revive the Stoic view that emotions are nothing but mistaken or distorted beliefs or thoughts (2001); and Annas has in resourceful ways attempted to show that the Stoic doctrine that equates virtue with happiness or a good life is not as far-fetched as many, over the millenia, have taken it to be. Speaking now of more modern historical influences, there is also work nowadays on Nietzsche-style virtue ethics. Christine Swanton makes use of Nietzschean ideas in her book *Virtue Ethics: A Pluralistic View* (2003); and I myself have discussed (but explicitly rejected) a Nietzschean version of virtue ethics in my book *Morals from Motives* (2001).

On the whole, however, I think the most important non-Aristotelian historical influence on recent virtue ethics has been that of Hume. Hume's *Treatise* (1978/1739) contains an unstable mixture of utilitarian, virtue-ethical, and deontological elements, but Hume lays great stress on the idea that the virtue or rightness of an action depends on the virtuousness of its underlying motive, and this is certainly virtue ethics. Very much unlike Aristotle, Hume also stresses the moral importance of benevolence, and (once again) this reflects the influence of Christianity even for a relatively secular modern moral philosopher. Hume treats considerations of human happiness as underlying considerations of virtue and to that extent anticipates utilitarianism; but his account of promise-keeping and of honesty or justice regarding property is very definitely not (purely) utilitarian in inspiration, and since Hume himself sees the difficulty of explaining just actions, etc., in terms of underlying independent motives, his account of deontology puts an enormous strain on his commitment to virtue ethics. (Hume acknowledges that his ideas seem to go in a vicious "circle.")

For that reason, contemporary neo-Humean virtue ethicists like myself seek to understand deontology and justice in ways that don't run in a circle, but that remain, nonetheless, within the terms and assumptions of virtue ethics. Hume was a sentimentalist who thought morality and virtue depended on feeling and feelingful motivation, rather than on reason or rationality, and neo-Humean virtue ethics takes a similar position. To that extent, I myself have found it useful and necessary to borrow ideas from what is perhaps the most influential of recent sentimentalist approaches to morality, the ethics of care. Deriving ultimately from the work of Carol Gilligan (1982) on the differences between the male and the female moral "voice," care ethics emphasizes connection *to* and caring *about* the welfare of others rather than the considerations of autonomy *from* and rights *against* others that rationalistic Kantian liberalism essentially appeals to. The latter tradition also stresses the importance of acting (rationally) from principles or out of respect for rules, whereas care ethics thinks moral action depends much more on emotional connection with people. Care ethicists soon realized that this distinction in ethical approaches doesn't correlate all that well with gender differences, but they argued that a focus on moral connection rather than separateness/autonomy can work as a much-needed corrective or supplement to traditional rationalist ethical theorizing and may even support a total reconfiguring of previous philosophical thinking about morality (e.g. support thinking of just societies as basically, in some sense, caring societies).

Neo-Humean virtue ethics can usefully borrow from this new ethical tradition while at the same time remaining somewhat separate from it. For example, my own approach to virtue ethics stresses the inherent admirability of caring about others (genuinely caring about others isn't a virtue because it leads to good consequences, but because of the kind of motive it is, namely, one *aiming* at good consequences for others). But care ethics typically understands the value of caring as a motive or virtue as derived from the fact that it plays a role in good caring *relationships* like that between a mother and a child. It asserts that the value of, and in, relationships is the primary or most fundamental ethical value and holds that the moral value of individual traits or actions has to be seen as derivative from the value of certain relationships. By contrast, a neo-Humean virtue ethics of caring wants to say that the character trait of caring has an independent moral value, and it says this in part because even if both caring and being cared for play an essential role in paradigmatically good mother–child relationships, caring has a moral value (and virtue status) *that being cared for clearly lacks*. And this supports the virtue-ethical idea that (the individual trait of) caring is of independent and fundamental moral importance. But since caring is just a folksier way of talking of various forms of benevolence, a virtue ethics of caring remains very much within the sentimentalist Humean tradition (though care ethicists often acknowledge *their* indebtedness to Hume). It is worth adding, however, that for all his talk of benevolence, Hume also places a greater emphasis on self-love than either care ethicists or neo-Humean virtue ethicists would wish to do.

Finally, in this section, I should mention the seemingly virtue-ethical approaches to morality that one finds, historically, in Asian thought and culture. Confucianism and the ethical traditions, in China, that derive from it are often viewed by philosophers here in the West as very similar to virtue ethics in the West; and although analogies with Aristotelian ethics have been most frequently noticed, a number of contemporary scholars think that some forms of Confucian and neo-Confucian thought are actually more analogous to sentimentalist, Humean modes of virtue ethics. In any event, the centrality of compassion within Buddhist ethics clearly calls Hume to mind more than Aristotle, and several scholars are now doing work that seeks to help us all better understand the relations between virtue ethics here in the West and various Asian traditions of ethical thought.

Problems for contemporary virtue ethics

Virtue ethics is no longer moribund or dormant, but it now faces some important challenges. If its approach to morality is to be fully persuasive in present-day circumstances, it needs, I believe, to face up to the most important ethical/philosophical challenges that other traditions have made us aware of and offered their own solutions or responses to. For example, ethicists nowadays recognize that there is a problem about justifying deontology. Almost all people are deeply morally persuaded that it is wrong to kill, say, one innocent person to save the lives of five others, and Kantians rise to the challenge of deontology by trying to account for *why* such killing is wrong. Act-utilitarians and act-consequentialists, for their part, attempt to show why, despite initial strong intuitions, it can be all right and even obligatory to kill one to save five. So although virtue ethics doesn't have to give any other theory's answer to the problem of deontology, it does need to say something persuasive about it. Otherwise, it will be widely seen – at least by philosophers who are not virtue ethicists – as lacking in contemporary relevance.

Unfortunately, however, those who have lately defended neo-Aristotelian and neo-Stoic virtue ethics haven't focused on this problem – even to the extent of saying that our deontological intuitions simply have to be and should be taken at face value. Not surprisingly, my own work (see Slote 2007) does try to say something usefully explanatory (and supportive) about deontology and supererogation, but since I am a Humean, and a sentimentalist, about morality, I don't think what I have done would be of much help to or very persuasive for neo-Aristotelian rationalists. And it is in any event probably also worth mentioning that one advantage of virtue ethics generally over other traditions, like utilitarianism and Kantian ethics, is that it has a more positive view, or more positive views, than these others have of the role of the emotions and of human relationships in the moral life. Virtue ethics revived in some measure because it was seen as addressing these issues in a way that other, more accepted views did not, and so I am far from saying that the burden of relevance to central moral issues is all on the side of virtue ethics.

But let me also add, just briefly, some thoughts about how sentimentalist neo-Humean virtue ethics would propose to address the important issue of deontology. Hume's account of justice/honesty does deal with some important questions about deontology, for example, but, as I suggested earlier, it does so (and Hume acknowledges this) somewhat at the expense of the commitment to virtue ethics. Also, Hume has absolutely nothing to say about the issue of doing vs. allowing (of killing, say, vs. allowing to die) that surfaced above, when I said that almost all of us initially feel it is wrong to kill one person to save five. But this issue is central to deontology and I think a sentimentalist virtue ethics needs to address it. My own contribution here, if it is one, has been to suggest that deontology is just one modality of our partialistic, or perspectival, interactions with good or evil (bad things) in the world. Just as we morally prefer, other things being equal, to alleviate the pain of those immediately visible to us rather than alleviate the pain of someone whose pain we only know *about*, I think we prefer a less immediate causal connection to harm or disaster than a more immediate one.

But to kill is to be in a much more immediate and direct causal connection to a death than it is to merely allow someone to die, and that I think gives us a basis for deontology. Natural human empathy, as studied by psychologists, leads us to be more concerned about potential harm we are perceptually acquainted with than about more distant or merely known-about potential harm, and by the same token we empathically flinch more from the immediate causal connection that is involved in *doing* harm than from merely *allowing* similar harm. Empathy and empathic concern for others are arguably features of our emotional life, of feeling rather than pure or practical reason, so what I have just too briefly sketched is a sentimentalist approach to deontology.

But having said as much, let me bring up a whole other area where virtue ethics of every stripe faces a considerable contemporary challenge: political morality. None of the forms of virtue ethics that flourished in the ancient world advocated an egalitarian or democratic conception of social justice, so any contemporary virtue ethics that bases itself on ancient models runs the risk of appearing hopelessly retrograde in the political sphere or, if it avoids political issues altogether, is likely to seem incomplete and inadequate in comparison with theories like Kantianism and utilitarianism that can offer accounts of both individual and political morality.

In recent years, virtue ethicists have in effect been seeking a way out of this dilemma. Stoicism, with its talk of the "divine spark," is friendlier to democratic/egalitarian ideals than either Plato or Aristotle was, and Martha Nussbaum (1992), for example, has proposed some ways in which Stoicism might be turned in the direction of modern-day democratic theory. But such shifts are also possible within neo-Aristotelian virtue ethics. To be sure, Alasdair MacIntyre has used Aristotle to argue for an anti-liberal conception of political morality, but Martha Nussbaum (1990) has pointed out that Aristotle's *Politics* advocates a rather democratic and egalitarian ideal of social cooperation except for the conditions it attaches to citizenship. To the extent, then, that those conditions depend on now-rejected assumptions about the political incapacity of women, laborers, and non-Greeks, the contemporary neo-Aristotelian might be able to use the *rest* of Aristotle's political views to defend a more contemporary and less retrograde ideal of social justice than Aristotle himself ever contemplated.

Rosalind Hursthouse (1991) also defends the contemporary relevance of Aristotle's political philosophy, though along somewhat different lines. Aristotle held virtuous living to be the main component of eudaimonia or human good and regarded societies as just to the extent they enable their citizens to achieve eudaimonia. And Hursthouse believes that we can derive most modern-day political and civil rights from this Aristotelian conception of social justice rather than treat such rights as the *basis* for understanding justice.

However, neo-Humean virtue ethics can also address issues of social justice in relevantly contemporary terms. Where societies and their governments seek to preserve enormous differences in wealth or (political) power for the benefit of some small elite, there is a pretty clear lack of concern or caring for the good of the country as a whole, and such concern or caring can in fact function as a/the touchstone of social justice for a modern-day sentimentalist theory. (See Slote 1998.) Since religious intolerance and persecution also demonstrate a lack of (empathic) concern for those who differ from one, neo-Humeanism may also be able to vindicate various civil rights in strictly sentimentalist terms (Slote 2007). So in fact the prospects of contemporary virtue ethics within the political sphere are by no means as dim as the previous history of virtue ethics might lead one to fear or suspect, and a virtue ethics that includes an element of "virtue politics" may be as capable as utilitarianism and Kantian ethics of offering a comprehensive account of morality.

Some comparisons

Kantian morality places great weight on the autonomy of the rational individual and seems somewhat ethically atomistic by comparison with Aristotle and Hume, whose ethical views stress the social embeddedness of the individual. The Stoics, however, had a rather individualistic picture of human flourishing, and it is perhaps not surprising that their ideas (are often said to have) influenced Kant's ethics more than the ideas of any other ancient school of thought. In that respect, most virtue ethics, whether ancient, modern, or contemporary, resembles communitarianism (see MacIntyre 1981; Sandel 1982) more than Kantianism does. But utilitarianism, with its commitment to our moral connection to anyone and everyone we are in a position to help or hurt, seems somewhat friendly to communitarian ideals. However, communitarianism has also tended toward a certain relativism and historicism about political/moral values – what is just or good depends on the tradition one grows up in – and to that extent communitarianism differs sharply from Kantianism, utilitarianism, and most forms of virtue ethics – all of which insist on a single universal standard of moral/political evaluation.

The comparisons fall out in a somewhat different way when one considers the distinction between rationalism and sentimentalism. Both Kantian and Aristotelian ethics (and their contemporary embodiments) treat moral thought and action as based in reason or rationality, and both regard explicit moral thinking about what is right/noble or wrong/ignoble as an indispensable element in morally/ethically acceptable or good conduct. By contrast, neo-Humean virtue ethics, care ethics, and (to some extent) communitarianism stress the emotional roots and non-rational justification of morality, and treat explicit or self-conscious moral thinking as ethically less desirable than Kant and Aristotle do. Interestingly, utilitarianism resembles neo-Humeanism more than it resembles Kant or Aristotle in these respects. Some forms of utilitarianism (e.g. Sidgwick's) are avowedly rationalistic, but others (like Bentham 1982) don't defend or seem to depend upon rationalist assumptions, and the latter fact may reflect the immediate historical influence Hume had on Bentham. Similarly, almost all forms of utilitarianism are comfortable with the possibility that explicitly conscientious motives and thinking might have inferior results to those of acting and thinking on the basis of "natural" motives like compassion, gratitude, and even ambition or curiosity. To that extent, utilitarianism once again resembles neo-Humean virtue ethics, care ethics, and communitarianism more than it does Aristotelianism and Kantianism.

However, all these comparisons seem to me, at least, to show how well virtue ethics fits in with the insights and controversies that characterize the historical traditions of ethical thought and contemporary developments of those traditions. Virtue ethics is very much in play now within academic ethical theorizing, and its prospects seem brighter, much brighter, than, in the modern period, they have ever seemed before.

See also Ethical thought in China (Chapter 1); Ethical thought in India (Chapter 2); Socrates and Plato (Chapter 3); Aristotle (Chapter 4); Later ancient ethics (Chapter 5); Ethics and reason (Chapter 9); Ethics and sentiment (Chapter 10); Hume (Chapter 11); Utilitarianism to Bentham (Chapter 13); Kant (Chapter 14); John Stuart Mill (Chapter 16); Nietzsche (Chapter 18); Consequentialism (Chapter 37); Contemporary Kantian ethics (Chapter 38); Contractualism (Chapter 41); Feminist ethics (Chapter 43); Partiality and impartiality (Chapter 52); Moral particularism (Chapter 53); Justice and distribution (Chapter 58); The ethics of free speech (Chapter 64); World poverty (Chapter 66).

References

Anscombe, G. E. M. (1958) "Modern Moral Philosophy," *Philosophy* 33: 1–19.

Annas, Julia (1993) *The Morality of Happiness*, Oxford: Oxford University Press.

Bentham, Jeremy (1982) *An Introduction to the Principles of Morals and Legislation*, London: Methuen.

Foot, Philippa (1978) *Virtues and Vices*, Oxford: Blackwell.

Gilligan, Carol (1982) *In a Different Voice: Psychological Theory and Women's Development*, Cambridge, MA: Harvard University Press.

Hume, D. (1978/1739) *A Treatise of Human Nature*, ed. L. A. Selby-Bigge and P. Nidditch, Oxford: Oxford University Press.

Hursthouse, Rosalind (1991) "After Hume's Justice," *Proceedings of the Aristotelian Society* 91, no. 3: 229–45.

——(1999) *On Virtue Ethics*, Oxford: Oxford University Press.

Kant, Immanuel (1964) *Doctrine of Virtue*, New York: Harper.

MacIntyre, Alasdair (1981) *After Virtue*, Notre Dame, IN: University of Notre Dame Press.

McDowell, John (1979) "Virtue and Reason," *Monist* 62: 331–50.

Nussbaum, Martha (1986) *The Fragility of Goodness*, Cambridge: Cambridge University Press.

——(1990) "Aristotelian Social Democracy," in R. B. Douglass, G. Mara and H. Richardson (eds) *Liberalism and the Good*, London: Routledge.

——(1992) "Human Functioning and Social Justice," *Political Theory* 20: 202–46.
——(2001) *Upheavals of Thought: The Intelligence of Emotions*, Cambridge: Cambridge University Press.
Pincoffs, Edmund (1986) *Quandaries and Virtues*, Lawrence: University Press of Kansas.
Rawls, John (1971) *A Theory of Justice*, Cambridge, MA: Harvard University Press.
Sandel, Michael (1982) *Liberalism and the Limits of Justice*, Cambridge: Cambridge University Press.
Sidgwick, Henry (1907) *Methods of Ethics*, 7th edn, London: Macmillan.
Slote, Michael (1998) "The Justice of Caring," *Social Philosophy and Policy* 15: 171–95.
——(2001) *Morals from Motives*, New York: Oxford University Press.
——(2007) *The Ethics of Care and Empathy*, London: Routledge.
Stephen, Leslie (1882) *The Science of Ethics*, New York: G. P. Putnam's Sons.
Swanton, Christine (2003) *Virtue Ethics: A Pluralistic View*, Oxford: Oxford University Press.
Williams, Bernard (1985) *Ethics and the Limits of Philosophy*, Cambridge, MA: Harvard University Press.

Further reading

Broadie, Sarah (1991) *Ethics with Aristotle*, Oxford: Oxford University Press.
Crisp, R. and Slote, M. (eds) (1997) *Virtue Ethics*, Oxford: Oxford University Press.
Foot, Philippa (2001) *Natural Goodness*, Oxford: Clarendon Press.
Hursthouse, Rosalind (1991) "Virtue Theory and Abortion," *Philosophy & Public Affairs* 20: 223–46.
McDowell, John (1998) "The Role of Eudaimonia in Aristotle's Ethics," repr. in his *Mind, Value, and Reality*, Cambridge, MA: Harvard University Press.
Slote, Michael (1990) *Goods and Virtues*, Oxford: Oxford University Press.
Walker, R. and Ivanhoe, P. (eds) (2007) *Working Virtue: Virtue Ethics and Contemporary Moral Problems*, Oxford: Clarendon Press.
White, Nicholas (1986) "The Ruler's Choice," *Archiv für Geschichte der Philosophie* 68: 24–46.

41
CONTRACTUALISM

Rahul Kumar

What is contractualism?

Contractualism is a non-consequentialist moral theory first advanced by T. M. Scanlon in his influential article, "Contractualism and Utilitarianism" (1982), and later developed in detail in his book, *What We Owe to Each Other* (1998). Its distinctive central claim is that one person morally wrongs another by treating him in a way whose permissibility is not justifiable to him on grounds he cannot reasonably reject.

The name, "contractualism," suggests an account belonging to a tradition of thinking about morality associated with Hobbes. Its animating idea is that valid moral norms are those that can be thought of as the object of a hypothetical agreement, reached through a process of self-interested bargaining, among all those to whom they apply. In this respect, the name is misleading. Scanlonian contractualism's roots lie not in Hobbes, but in the social contract tradition of Rousseau and Kant, one that treats what motivates the parties to the hypothetical agreement as the appeal of living in community with others on a basis of mutual respect for one another, along the lines of what Kant calls a the "kingdom of ends," a "systematic union of different rational beings through common laws" (Kant 1997: 4:433).

This strand of the social contract tradition is one that John Rawls brilliantly develops in his *A Theory of Justice* (1971). Scanlon's contractualism is importantly indebted to Rawls's work, but is not helpfully understood as an extension of it. Rawls's concern is with the nature of justice, and in particular, how a society's basic institutions ought to be regulated so as to enable ongoing social cooperation on terms of fair reciprocity. Contractualism, on the other hand, focuses on a different, and more general, question: What makes it the case that a person is morally wronged by another's treating her in a certain way?

In particular, contractualism has two principal theoretical aims. The first is that of providing a plausible alternative to consequentialist accounts of the subject matter of moral judgments. Consequentialists hold, roughly, that a person's conduct is morally wrong if it is other than the way she ought to conduct herself if she is to best contribute to the promotion of aggregate well-being. Many find some form of consequentialism intuitively compelling, despite the difficulty of defending, on consequentialist grounds, certain familiar moral convictions concerning how it is and is not morally permissible for individuals to treat one another. Contractualism offers itself as an account that is at least as intuitively appealing as any form of consequentialism, but one that provides a better basis for explicating the justification for common-sense moral convictions.

Its second aim has to do with the nature of moral motivation. It is prompted by the thought that knowing a certain way of conducting oneself to be morally wrong is not a kind of esoteric knowledge, to which a person could be blamelessly indifferent. Rather, those who take moral considerations to be important to take into account in their practical deliberations understand them as considerations that anyone capable of being guided by reasons should consider specially important. The question is, can this special importance be defended as appropriate? Part of the contractualist project is to defend a positive answer to this question, one that connects its understanding of the subject matter of moral judgments with the appropriateness of taking such judgments, so understood, to be of special importance.

Contractualism and the value of human life

Key to what contractualism says about both issues is a particular understanding of what respect for the value of human life requires. How this value figures in the account is easily misunderstood if it is simply assumed that the appropriate way to respond to something of value is to take it to be something one should aim to promote, or bring about more of. Reflection on different examples of things of value suggests, rather, that there is no one way of appropriately responding to something of value (Scanlon 1998: 87–103). A correct appreciation of the value of suffering plausibly requires that one strive to decrease the amount of suffering in the world. But it is a misunderstanding of the reasons one has to act, feel, and think in certain ways if one appropriately values friendship to take the appropriate appreciation of its value to require one to aim to bring it about that there are lots and lots of friendships in the world.

This way of thinking about the requirements for a proper appreciation, or respect for, something's value informs the contractualist rejection of the idea, associated with consequentialism, that respect for the value of human life requires taking oneself to have reason to contribute to bringing it about that there is more human life in the world. What it requires, rather, is a recognition, in one's practical thinking, of other human beings as creatures who have reasons for wanting to live and for having their lives go better, and who have a capacity to both assess reasons and justifications and select among the various ways there is reason to want a life to go, enabling them to live actively self-governed lives (Scanlon 1998: 103–7).

Respect for the value of others, then, requires that individuals be sensitive, in their practical thinking, to others' reasons for wanting, caring about, and pursuing certain things. But how exactly does respect for another's value require that another's reason for, say, caring about something figures in one's practical thinking? To paraphrase a point Scanlon makes in another context, a person's reasons for having a decent diet may well entitle him to claim the assistance of others in making that possible, while his equally strong reasons for building a monument to his God do not, even if he is quite willing to forgo the former in order to advance the latter (which is compatible with his still having a claim against others that they not interfere with his building it) (Scanlon 2003: 74).

The contractualist proposal is that how another's reasons, in a particular situation, ought to figure in one's practical thinking is fixed by a principle no one could reasonably reject for the regulation of that type of situation. That part of morality concerned with what we owe to each other as a matter of respect for the value of one another as persons is constituted, on this account, by an indefinite number of such principles, each for the regulation of a certain type of situation. For any situation, the relevant principle will spell out how other individuals are entitled, or may legitimately expect, to have their reasons figure in one's practical thinking, and how one is entitled to have one's own reasons figure in their practical thinking.

Grasping a relevant principle for the regulation of the type of situation one finds oneself in is not a matter of understanding a wholly stable rule that one knows how to apply. Rather, it is to exhibit a complex understanding of the reasons why in general it is important that there be constraints on how persons act in this type of situation. In particular, grasping a principle is a matter of understanding why there are good reasons for requiring that individuals, in determining what it is permissible to do in such situations, take certain reasons into account in their thinking, but not others. Judging a certain course of action permissible or impermissible under the circumstances is, on this account, then, a matter of assessing what there is or is not decisive reason to do, as informed by an understanding (which need not be readily articulable) of the moral rationale that supplies the relevant principle's evaluative point.

Scanlon gives several examples of contractualist principles, such as those regulating promissory obligations (Scanlon 1998: 295–327). Individuals have good reason to want to be able to sometimes assure one another of their future conduct by undertaking a voluntary obligation, like a promise, that binds one to do what one has promised to do unless released by the promisee. Displaying an understanding of the relevant principle in one's practical thinking is a matter of understanding when it is the case that one's normative situation has changed because one has successfully undertaken a promissory obligation; what one has reason to do and not to do because doing, or not doing, so would constitute violating the promise; when the circumstances justify the judgment that one has grounds to take the promise to have lapsed, that one is justified in breaking one's promise, etc.

What respect for the value of others as human beings requires on this account, then, is that individuals regulate their practical thinking by principles no one can reasonably reject. One *wrongs* another, or fails to comply with the requirements of respect for her value as a human being, when one fails to give her interests the kind of consideration in one's practical thinking that the relevant principle for the regulation of the situation requires.

Scanlon is clear in presenting contractualism as an account of the basis of those norms that constitute one important aspect of morality, those having to do with "what we owe to each other"; many moral norms, such as those having to do with the treatment of animals, fall outside this domain (Scanlon 1998: 171–7). This domain restriction is sometimes treated as evidence of contractualism's theoretical modesty. But it should now be clear that it is motivated by the recognition that what contractualism characterizes is just reasoning about what respect for one particularly important value – namely, that of human life – requires. There is every reason to think that the kinds of standards anyone takes to be constitutive of his morality will draw upon not just this value, but also a plurality of other, distinct, values.

Morality's authority and the value of mutual recognition

Why hold that what respect for the value of human life requires is that one be guided in one's practical thinking by principles no one could reasonably reject? A rationale for this connection starts to emerge from reflection on the full statement of the contractualist criterion of moral wrongness:

> An act is wrong if its performance under the circumstances would be disallowed by any set of principles for the general regulation of behaviour that no one could reasonably reject as a basis for informed, unforced, general agreement.
>
> (Scanlon 1998: 153)

No one, that is, who is motivated by a concern to be guided in his practical thinking by principles no one could reasonably reject.

The characterization of valid principles here is as the objects of a *hypothetical*, not actual, agreement between all persons. That the agreement is hypothetical, not actual, does not, however, make the appeal to the idea of agreement spurious. What it draws attention to is an idea that lies at the heart of contractualism: that a person who takes complying with morality's requirements to be specially important is one who attaches importance to his conduct being *justifiable to* any other on grounds that that person cannot reasonably reject.

To care about the justifiability of one's conduct to another is not the same as the concern that others in fact accept one's conduct as justified. That they do so is desirable, but as Scanlon notes, people often accept as justified that which they have good reason not to accept as justified (Scanlon 1998: 155). What principally matters to one who takes his conduct to be justifiable to any other is that others have good reason to accept his conduct as justified, even if they don't see that.

A common criticism frequently pressed against contractualism is that to care about the justifiability of one's conduct to others amounts to nothing more than a concern that one's conduct be morally justified. The crucial question, that of what the criterion is for evaluating moral justifiability, is one contractualism fails to address. But this criticism misses its mark. The central idea of contractualism is not that (a) conduct or a principle that is justifiable to others is so because it is justified, but the striking idea that (b) a principle or conduct that is morally justified is so because it is justifiable to others on grounds no one can reasonably reject. Being *justifiable to others* is itself a substantive view about what moral justification requires.

In particular, for a principle to be justifiable to another on grounds that a person cannot reasonably reject is for that principle to be one that he has reason to *authorize* or *license* others to be guided by in their practical deliberations. What it is for a principle to be one that a person has reason to authorize, or license, others to be guided by in their practical thinking is helpfully fleshed out by the metaphor of principles being the object of a hypothetical agreement. It invites us to think of a valid principle for the regulation of a certain type of situation as one that is worked out through a process in which all those within the moral domain (anyone, on this view, with a capacity for rational self-governance) participate as co-deliberators, each with an equal voice, in working out what the principle ought to be.

In evaluating candidate principles, each compares the implications for himself of each candidate principle being the principle regulating the type of situation in question. But the assessment by each of which principle she has reason to agree to is not based solely on which principle's implications are most favorable to her. Because each cares about the justifiability of his conduct to others, each takes into account in his own assessment of whether a candidate principle is one that he has reason to agree to both his own reasons for favoring or objecting to the principle and the reasons of other individuals for objecting to or favoring it. Convergence on a principle, one that each, as assessed from his or her own point of view, has reason to agree to, is arrived at through a process, one might say, of individuals comparing the strength of one another's objections to different principles. The converged-upon principle will be one of which it is true that the most serious objection that can be pressed from a particular point of view against it is not as strong as the objections, from other points of view, to any other candidate principle.

To say that a principle no one could reasonably reject is one that individuals authorize, or license, one another to be guided by in their practical thinking is to say, then, that the principle is one that any person, assessing it from his or her own point of view, has reason to agree to for the regulation of the type of situation in question. By being guided by such principles in how one relates to others, one's conduct manifests respect for the value of others as human beings. For to be guided by principles that others authorize, or license, one to be guided by is to recognize others in one's practical thought as rationally self-governing creatures, capable of assessing reasons and justifications concerning principles regulating how it is permissible for individuals to relate to one another. As Kant remarked, making an analogous point, the dignity of a human being lies in the fact that he or she stands to the moral law as both subject and legislator.

Though respect for the value of human life requires that one be guided in one's practical thought by principles no one could reasonably reject, it is not this requirement that contractualism identifies as what moves the morally motivated. Rather, it holds that what moves one who takes the justifiability of his conduct to others to be specially important is the appeal of an ideal of moral community in which individuals stand in a relationship to one another of *mutual recognition*, living on terms of "unity with one's fellow creatures" (Scanlon 1998: 154). Individuals stand in this kind of intrinsically valuable relationship to one another when they regulate their conduct by principles justifiable to others on grounds no one could reasonably reject. The pain of guilt that we associate with having wronged another, Scanlon suggests, is best understood as a feeling of estrangement from another as a result of having violated the requirements of this kind of valuable relation with others (Scanlon 1998: 162). Living morally, for those who take doing so to be important, is integral, on this account, to their understanding of what it is to live well.

Assessing a principle's reasonable rejectability

As noted in the previous section, assessing the validity of a particular principle – assessing, that is, whether or not it is a principle that no one can reasonably reject – requires considering the general implications, from different points of view, of individuals being guided in their practical thinking, in the relevant type of situation, by the proposed principle. This is not, however, a matter of imagining what the implications of the proposed principle might be for particular individuals one happens to know. Rather, it is a matter of thinking about the proposed principle's implications from different individual standpoints. A "standpoint" is just an abstract description of a point of view characterized by a certain combination of things that people generally have reason to want and to care about (Scanlon 1998: 202–6). Any particular standpoint could (but need not) aptly characterize some actual person's point of view, and any actual person's point of view will certainly be aptly characterizable by many different standpoints.

So, let's say that what is in question is the validity of a principle that permits deception under certain circumstances. Assessment of its reasonable rejectability will focus, not on the implications for actual people of it being permissible in some circumstances for individuals to deceive one another, but on its implications as assessed from different relevant standpoints, such as: someone who finds himself in circumstances in which deception is permitted, someone not permitted to deceive in circumstances in which he would have good reason to do so were it permissible, someone who stands to be deceived, someone whose interests stand to be affected in certain ways by others being deceived, etc.

One of the defining features of contractualism that starkly distinguishes it from any form of consequentialism is what has come to be known as the *individualist restriction*. It stipulates that the only implications of a principle that are relevant to its assessment are those that could be appealed to from a certain standpoint as implications of the proposed principle for a person being able to live his or her life. Ruled out as irrelevant, then, are the more impersonal kinds of consideration that consequentialists take to be important, such as the implications of a proposed principle for the aggregate value of the outcome that will obtain if it is generally complied with, or the aggregate value of its implications for several individuals. Neither of these is the type of consideration that could be appealed to from the standpoint of an individual objecting to a proposed principle *on his own behalf*.

On the same grounds, a principle's implications for those things a person might, for good reason, care about, but whose importance to him is not properly characterized as being important for his being able to live his life, have no bearing on a principle's assessment. A person with a certain standpoint might, for instance, take it to be important that certain species of wild fauna flourish, quite independently of the pleasure he takes in experiencing their flourishing, but that a principle will have bad implications for those species won't count as a relevant implication from his standpoint of the principle.

Critics of contractualism have forcefully argued that the theory would be more plausible without the individualist restriction. That may be, but the restriction does make sense as a central feature of the account. What it holds matters to the morally motivated person, after all, is that he respond to the value of the lives of others in a way consistent with standing in a relationship of mutual recognition to any other. Whether or not treating another in a certain way is an appropriate response to the value of that person's life is, intuitively, a matter that turns on the ways that he might object that one would be failing to take seriously the implications *for his life* by treating him this way.

Though the individualist restriction limits the range of considerations relevant to a principle's assessment, it is less restrictive than it might at first seem. First, as any principle is for the regulation of a certain type of situation, its assessment will have to take into account not just the implications of certain individuals being guided by it on certain occasions, but those of all individuals over time being guided by it in that type of situation. Second, implications of a principle having nothing to do with how well or badly off individuals will be are also relevant to its assessment. Consider, for example, a principle that licenses a designated authority to periodically force randomly chosen individuals to serve as test subjects for dangerous medical experiments. It is of course relevant to assessing such a principle that it exposes everyone to the risk of serious harm. But a further objection to it that could be pressed from a certain standpoint is that such experiments being permissible undermine the exclusive authority of individuals concerning decisions about how their bodies are to be used (a prerogative that plays a fundamental role in an agent's understanding of his life as his own), turning them into a form of public property. This is a good reason for wanting to reasonably reject a principle that permits the envisioned form of experimentation, even though it has nothing to do with its implications for individual welfare.

That a certain principle has, from some standpoint, seriously negative implications does not, however, warrant the conclusion that, all things considered, it is one that could be vetoed from that standpoint as reasonably rejectable. Whether it can depends on the implications for other standpoints of the alternative candidate principles. If every alternative to the one that, from a particular standpoint, is seriously objectionable has implications for some other standpoint that are even more seriously objectionable, the principle cannot be reasonably rejected.

It cannot be reasonably rejected because standing in a relationship to other individuals of mutual recognition requires that one's rejection of a principle in favor of some alternative to it be justifiable to other individuals – especially to the one who has the most serious objections to this alternative principle. If the alternative to the principle one wants to reject is worse for someone from a different standpoint than the principle being rejected is for oneself, the proposed principle's rejection won't be justifiable to that person. What reason could one offer, after all, for why he should bear a greater burden in order that you are spared a lesser burden that would be compatible with the recognition of his equal value to oneself as a person?

Whether or not a particular principle is in fact reasonably rejectable is a matter of judgment about which morally informed and sensitive individuals may well disagree. Contractualism's aim is not that of providing a method for resolving moral disagreements; what it offers is a characterization of what the question is that conclusions about how it is morally permissible for persons to treat one another answer. But what the correct answer is to that question, in any given instance, may well be contestable.

The problem of aggregation

Part of contractualism's appeal lies in its value as a framework for developing plausible justifications for familiar convictions concerning how it is morally permissible for persons to treat one another that have proven difficult to articulate in consequentialist terms. Consider, for instance, the often-discussed question of the permissibility of killing a healthy individual in order to transplant his organs to five others, whose survival depends on receiving a transplant. The problem for consequentialists isn't in saying something about why doing so is impermissible. It is, rather, that of saying something about why this is so that makes sense of the intuitive idea that its being impermissible has to do with there being something in itself objectionable about one person taking another's life as a means to even a worthwhile end.

Contractualism's strength lies in its ability to make good sense of this thought. On its terms, the question of the permissibility of killing a person for his organs turns on the strength of the reasons that could be pressed from the standpoint of that person against a principle permitting such killings, as compared with the reasons that could be pressed from the standpoint of those standing to benefit from such killings being permitted. Since the number of individuals who stand to benefit if such killings are permitted is not a relevant consideration in contractualist moral argument, it is fairly easy to see how an argument would go for the impermissibility of killing for organs, one that appeals, in particular, to the reasons individuals have for wanting the kind of control over their lives that killing for organs being permitted would undermine.

There are situations, however, in which the number of individuals who stand to be benefited or burdened is clearly morally relevant. Say, for example, you find yourself in a boat equidistant from two tiny islands. There is only one person on one of the islands, but there are six on the other. The tide is rising, so there is only time to reach one of the islands and save its inhabitants before all are drowned. Few doubt that the only morally permissible course of action is to save the six. And since the obligation in question is just an instance of a more general obligation to aid others when one can do so at little cost to oneself, the rationale for doing so ought to be explicable using the resources of the contractualist framework.

Doing so turns out, however, to be surprisingly difficult. Contractualism doesn't count aggregative considerations as morally relevant, so the amount of good that will be done by saving the six can't be appealed to in order to justify a principle that requires the rescuer to do so. Considering what might be justifiable to the standpoint of each of those whose life is at risk, however, leads to the conclusion that the only non-rejectable principle for the regulation of this type of situation is one that requires the rescuer to give each an equal chance of being saved by, for example, tossing a coin to settle the matter. The strength of the reason that each has for having the rescuer save him is exactly the same, after all. How, then, can it be justifiable to the one alone on an island that he not be given the same chance of being saved as each of the many?

Arguably, contractualism is not committed to the counter-intuitive conclusion that one should toss a coin to decide whether to save the many or the one (Scanlon 1998: 229–41). It's true that since there is no reason, *ex hypothesi*, to save any one rather than another, there are no grounds for thinking that a principle no one could reasonably reject for the regulation of this type of situation requires any one, rather than one of the others, be saved. What can be reasonably rejected, though, is any principle that does not require the rescuer to take into account, in deciding whom to save, the reason of each for wanting to be saved. Tossing a coin, or any simple lottery procedure, violates this requirement, for if the rescuer is guided by such a procedure, it will make no difference to his thinking about how to proceed whether the situation is one of the one on the first island and of the six on the other, or two on the first island and twelve on the other.

A plausible principle for the regulation of the rescuer's reasoning in this type of situation that respects this requirement is one that directs the rescuer, in his thinking about how to proceed, to balance the reason to save one person's life against the reason to save the life of another that requires a course of action incompatible with saving the first person. By balancing competing reasons against one another, the rescuer takes into account each person's reason for wanting to be saved. What decides how the rescuer will proceed is the first reason to save someone that is not balanced by an equally weighty opposing reason to save the life of another.

This procedure directs the rescuer to save the six, but not because doing so will do the most good. And though the one who is not saved will no doubt curse his bad luck, the rescuer has not wronged him. The reason to save his life is given exactly the same weight in the rescuer's reasoning as the reasons to save each of the others. He is just unlucky that the reason to save his life happened not to require the same course of action as an equally forceful reason to save the life of another.

Whether this argument is successful as an example of how one can explain, in contractualist, non-aggregative terms, intuitive responses to cases which appear to be hard to make sense of without appealing to aggregative considerations is a contested issue (see Kamm 2007). Doubts have been raised about both the soundness of the above line of argument and, even if it is sound, whether it provides any guidance as to how a contractualist might justify the intuitive relevance of aggregative considerations in cases that do not have the structure of a conflict between equally forceful reasons. Whether contractualism can be defended as a compelling account of what we morally owe one another turns, to a large extent, on the development of convincing contractualist responses to these kinds of questions.

See also Consequentialism (Chapter 37); Contemporary Kantian ethics (Chapter 38).

References

Kamm, F. M. (2007) "Owing, Justifying, and Rejecting," in *Intricate Ethics*, Oxford: Oxford University Press.

Kant, I. (1997) *Groundwork of the Metaphysics of Morals*, ed. Mary Gregor, Cambridge: Cambridge University Press. (The reference is to volume and page of the standard Prussian Academy edn, as given in the margins of this work.)

Scanlon, T. M. (1982) "Contractualism and Utilitarianism," in A. Sen and B. A. O. Williams (eds) *Utilitarianism and Beyond*, Cambridge: Cambridge University Press.

——(1998) *What We Owe To Each Other*, Cambridge, MA: Harvard University Press.

——(2003) "Preference and Urgency," in *The Difficulty of Tolerance: Essays in Political Philosophy*, Cambridge: Cambridge University Press.

Further reading

Kamm, F. M. (2007) "Owing, Justifying, and Rejecting," in *Intricate Ethics*, Oxford: Oxford University Press. (An important and sympathetic discussion of contractualism's credentials as a non-consequentialist account of moral reasoning.)

Scanlon, T. M. (1982) "Contractualism and Utilitarianism," in A. Sen and B. A. O. Williams (eds) *Utilitarianism and Beyond*, Cambridge: Cambridge University Press. (The original paper sketching the contractualist account. A must-read before tackling the book-length treatment of the view.)

Wallace, R. Jay (2006) "Scanlon's Contractualism," in *Normativity and Will*, Oxford: Oxford University Press. (A comprehensive review article that critically discusses most of the major themes of *What We Owe to Each Other*.)

42
CONTEMPORARY NATURAL LAW THEORY

Anthony J. Lisska

Recent work in natural law theory, both in moral theory and jurisprudence, is by any account burgeoning. The last third of the twentieth century witnessed a burst of energy by philosophers sorting out its many-faceted claims.

Natural law, with extensive resources rooted in Aristotle's *Nicomachean Ethics* and with Stoic modifications, was developed and systematized in the thirteenth century by Thomas Aquinas; his *Summa Theologiae* (Ia–IIae, QQ. 90–7, see Thomas Aquinas 1996) became the classical canon for much natural law thinking. The insights of Aquinas focused on the role of the human person possessing a unique essence or nature as a necessary condition for a cogent theory of ethical naturalism and a foundational theory for human law. But since natural law is based on human nature, both the Kantian objections to the possibility of a naturalist moral theory together with Moore's naturalistic fallacy cast a death-knell on natural law philosophy. As a result, through most of the twentieth century ethical naturalism as found in Aristotle and developed in natural law theory was not a vibrant component of significant moral discussions in Anglo-American philosophy. But the tide has changed.

While the concept of natural law plays an essential role in the historical development of Western moral and political theory, nonetheless there is no one theory of natural law. What is common to natural law accounts, for the most part, is that its fundamental principles are in some sense objective, knowable by human reason, grounded in human nature, and not related necessarily although sometimes connected historically with divine command theory. Nonetheless, there are different ways that these principles have been adopted and adapted over the course of the development of Western philosophy.

Resurgence of interest in natural law moral theory and jurisprudence

This resurgence of interest in natural law theory is witnessed in normative ethics, meta-ethics, and jurisprudence. Natural law theory is one philosophical position where moral theory and legal theory intersect. The jurisprudence discussions direct attention to the foundational issues of a justified legal theory and also to the nature and structure of human rights theory. In one sense, events beyond the academy first drove this renewed interest in natural law jurisprudence. The aftermath of the Second World War with the charges of "Crimes against Humanity" brought about the need for clearly elucidated arguments to justify these claims.

Two prominent English-speaking philosophers of law, H. L. A. Hart and Lon Fuller, led the conceptual charge into rethinking how natural law theory might assist in these conceptual muddles and struggles. While both Hart and Fuller took as their foil legal positivism, the then regnant theory of law in English-speaking countries, nonetheless Hart remains closer conceptually to legal positivism than Fuller. Legal positivism, which is reducible to a "command theory," is articulated succinctly in the famous quote from Justinian: "What pleases the prince has the force of law." This theory rooted law solely in the authority of the person or governing body in charge of the community, however large or small this community might be. In his influential *The Concept of Law*, Hart (1961) articulated what he considered the "core of good sense" in natural law theory. The strict positivist claims were countered by what Hart took to be the "natural necessities" that human persons share with one another. These served, Hart argued, as the foundation for what civil laws must consider: "the protection of persons, property and promises."

Fuller argued that the concept of functioning human reason rather than a set of natural necessities was a necessary condition for justified law-making. He argued that there were eight propositions that valid law must meet. His version of natural law is often called "procedural" because Fuller directs his attention towards the rational method – the procedure – that renders law-making valid. Fuller referred to procedural propositions like "Laws ought not to be contradictory, ought not to be retroactive, ought to be made public," etc., which provide the "internal structure of natural law" (Fuller 1964: 106). Articles by both Hart and Fuller – especially their influential 1958 debate in *The Harvard Law Review* – stirred up a flurry of philosophical reflection on how to address theoretically a justification for rejecting positions entailing "genocide" and "crimes against humanity." Natural law jurisprudence argues for a standard against which these heinous crimes might be judged.

A second political spark that contributed to the recovery of natural law centered on the 1960s civil rights movement, especially in the United States, together with the forceful opposition to the United States's engagement in the Vietnam War. Martin Luther King's elegant "Letter from a Birmingham Jail" (King 1963) with its reference to Augustine and Aquinas that "unjust law is no law at all" brought attention to the role that natural law jurisprudence played in legal discussions in much Western thought. What is of particular interest is how these social and political issues moved the philosophical arguments and discussions away from their acceptance of legal positivism and into the more theoretical realm searching for foundational concepts.

On the moral philosophy front as distinguished from jurisprudence, mid-twentieth-century discussions resulted in renewed interest in natural law theory. These arguments developed in both normative ethics and meta-ethics. In Anglo-American philosophy, what stimulated these discussions initially and became the harbinger of the renewed interest in Aristotelian moral theory was Elizabeth Anscombe's essay, "Modern Moral Theory" (Anscombe 1958). Anscombe argued that contemporary moral discussions were bankrupt and needed a new direction; she judged that a fresh look at Aristotelian moral theory was necessary to resolve this vacuum. Furthermore, she called for a reworking of philosophical psychology, a reinterpretation of practical reason, and a return to some version of moral virtue. These three themes, Anscombe argued, were necessary conditions for a constructive renewal of Anglo-American moral philosophy. This would provide a conceptual thrust to refuting various non-cognitivist theories and provide for more direction than the continual rehashing of Mill's teleological utilitarianism based on the principle of utility and Kant's deontological contractarianism rooted in the principle of pure practical reason. Anscombe suggested that the law-centered moral theories established without God contributed to the conceptual implausibility of much modern moral theory.

Entering this moral philosophy discussion some twenty years later came Alasdair MacIntyre with the publication of his paradigm-changing *After Virtue* (MacIntyre 1981). MacIntyre too argued that contemporary moral discussions had reached a dead-end and that a fresh look at Aristotelian ethical theory with a consideration of the nature of the virtue tradition was indispensable to move beyond this impasse with "the continuing clash between various types of Kantian moral philosopher and various types of utilitarian in a series of inconclusive engagements" (Knight 1998: 70). MacIntyre's arguments had a profound effect in redirecting moral philosophy in English-speaking countries. Russell Hittinger, reflecting on the influence of MacIntyre's work, once wrote:

> MacIntyre has been a pioneer figure in … the "recoverist" movement: those who wish to retrieve … the common morality of the West. If nothing else, MacIntyre has made this recoverist project professionally respectable. Less than a decade [now two decades] has passed since its publication, yet many are already prepared to admit that *After Virtue* represents something pivotal.
>
> (Hittinger 1989: 449)

MacIntyre followed *After Virtue* with three other influential texts: *Whose Justice? Which Rationality?* (MacIntyre 1988), his Gifford Lectures, *Three Rival Versions of Moral Enquiry* (MacIntyre 1990), and the Carus Lectures, *Dependent Rational Animals* (MacIntyre 1999).

Another Anglo-American philosopher, Philippa Foot, found insights in Aristotle and Aquinas compelling as a way to transcend the limits of non-cognitivist meta-ethics. Foot wrote: "It is my opinion that the *Summa Theologiae* is one of the best sources we have for moral philosophy, and moreover that St Thomas's ethical writings are as useful to the atheist as to the Catholic or other Christian believer" (Foot 1978: 1–2). With several books and many essays, Martha Nussbaum too brought Aristotelian ethical naturalism to the forefront of normative and meta-ethical discussions. Like MacIntyre, Foot, and Anscombe, Nussbaum is much concerned that English-speaking moral theory was caught up in an overly formalist, Kantian direction that neglected the role of the total human person in moral decision-making. Rather than posing the "obligation question" first – which is a common Kantian approach – Nussbaum suggested that moral philosophers must ask the Aristotelian question first: "What kind of lives should we live?" Like Foot, Nussbaum argued that Aristotelian moral theory – and for similar reasons, natural law normative theories – can provide a necessary corrective to the Kantian approach on the one hand and the utilitarian approach on the other. To varying degrees, Anscombe, MacIntyre, Nussbaum, and Foot called for a rekindled interest in Aristotelian ethical naturalism, of which the natural law tradition is a prominent piece. These philosophers argued against placing the virtue ethics of Aristotle and the natural law philosophers into the meta-ethical dustbin with other theories of ethical naturalism.

In the middle part of the twentieth century, the French Thomists Jacques Maritain and Yves Simon articulated contemporary versions of natural law theory. Both were concerned about the justification of natural rights. Maritain's writings on natural law had an influence on rendering Roman Catholic theologians more conversant with liberal democracy and religious pluralism. Maritain's *Man and the State* (Maritain 1951) proposed a role for natural law theory in the development of a modern democratic state together with a contemporary reconstruction of natural law rights theory. These roots of legal foundational thinking point to seventeenth-century natural law writings about individual natural human rights. Suarez, Las Casas, DiVitoria, and other members of the Salamanca school of "the second scholasticism" in the 1600s articulated this aspect of natural law theory. Of particular interest to these Salamanca philosophers was a justified and cogent defense of the basic rights of the native peoples of the Americas who were then being criminally manhandled by the conquistadors. Historically, natural law theory appears to have a distinctive moral clout in regard to morally traumatic issues. However, neither Maritain nor Simon had much direct influence on Anglo-American moral or legal philosophy.

The important writings of Henry Veatch and Ralph McInerny contributed significantly to the understanding of classical natural law moral theory. However, they approach the writings of Aquinas from different vantage points. McInerny, using classical Thomism as a neo-scholastic paradigm for undertaking philosophical analysis, considers Aquinas as the central player in natural law theory.

Veatch, while arguing for the same conclusion, comes forward from a more secular version of Anglo-American philosophy. He was not a Thomist, but worked seriously with Aquinas's texts in order to address the importance of natural law in developing an adequate account of human rights. *Human Rights: Fact or Fancy?* (Veatch 1986) and *Swimming Against the Current in Contemporary Philosophy* (Veatch 1990) spell out his contemporary reconstruction of natural law. Acknowledging his philosophical method, Veatch wrote: "(M)y own program … (is) a dialectic … directed to the overall purpose of trying to rehabilitate Aristotle and Aquinas as contemporary philosophers" (Veatch 1990: 13).

The central role of the human person in natural law theory

Natural law theory based on Aquinas is rooted in the human person with a dependence on Aristotle's biology in *De Anima*. Aquinas argued that a human person is, by definition, a set of potentialities or dispositions (*inclinationes*). In the *Summa Theologiae* (Ia–IIae, Q. 94, a. 2), Aquinas delineates his famous account of three generic categories of properties that determine human nature (Lisska 1996):

(1) The set of *living* dispositions (what humans share with plants).
(2) The set of *sensitive* dispositions (what humans share with animals).
(3) The set of *rational* dispositions (what renders humans unique in the material world).

Considered briefly, a living disposition is the capacity or drive all living beings share to continue in existence. This capacity is to be protected; hence, a "right" is developed based on the dispositional property of living. Had humans evolved or been created differently, a different theory of rights would be addressed. A right is what it is because human nature is what it is. This living disposition is similar structurally to Hart's natural necessity of "survival." Likewise, one rational disposition Aquinas considered was the drive human persons exhibit to know, which is the common human trait of intellectual curiosity. Aquinas suggested that this disposition was developed only when a human person knew that which is true. Hence, human persons have a "right" to the truth. Again, rights protect what humans are ontologically as human persons. This "rational curiosity" is similar to what Fuller called "communication."

In his *Aquinas*, John Finnis wrote: "The order Aquinas has in mind is a metaphysical stratification: (1) what we have in common with all substances, (2) what, more specifically, we have in common with other animals, and (3) what is peculiar to us as human beings" (Finnis 1999: 81). Columba Ryan analyzed these three general aspects of human nature as "the good of the individual survival, biological good, and the good of human communication" (C. Ryan 1965: 28). Martin Golding referred to the living dispositions as the "basic requirements of human life," the sensitive dispositions as the "basic requirements for the furtherance of the human species," and the rational dispositions as "the basic requirements for the promotion of [a human person's] good as a rational and social being" (Golding 1974: 242–3). Nussbaum's earlier "capabilities approach" articulated eight fundamental properties analogous to the Aristotelian analysis: "we can nonetheless identify certain features of our common humanity, closely related to Aristotle's original list." Nussbaum's eight characteristics are mortality, the body, pleasure and pain, cognitive capability, practical reason, early infant development, affiliation or a sense of fellowship with other human beings, and humor (Nussbaum 1993: 263–4; 2006).

In jurisprudence, natural law based on the human person provides the direction of law-making rooted in the natural necessities. The connection with law-making is that any law, which, all things being equal, hinders the development of a human natural disposition is inherently unjust. Aquinas provided a set of criteria by means of which one might develop a justified theory of law. Philosophers like Ryan suggest that natural law's contribution to jurisprudence is articulating the "possibility" of legitimate law-making. John Haldane referred to this position as "objectivist naturalism," a position that he in principle accepts (Haldane 2004: 136).

Differing natural law theories in the contemporary marketplace

What is interesting and significant about the resurgence of natural law theory in contemporary philosophy is that it is not limited to the traditional followers of Aquinas, usually referred to as "Thomists." If anything, there is more creative philosophical writing on natural law in non-Thomist arenas than in those schools of thought once dominated by classical Thomism. Natural law jurisprudence gained prominence in the contemporary Anglo-American marketplace of ideas with John Finnis's "New Natural Law Theory." His *Natural Law and Natural Rights* (1982), *Fundamentals of Ethics* (1983) and his treatise on Aquinas's moral and political theory, *Aquinas: Moral, Political and Legal Theory* (1999), elucidate and defend a contemporary reconstruction of classical natural law theory.

Finnis appropriated the insights of the American Neo-Thomist philosopher, Germain Grisez. Grisez's seminal article on practical reason is an important hallmark in Finnis's natural law theory (Grisez 1965). Grisez was concerned that any reformulation of natural law needed to bypass the pitfalls of the naturalistic fallacy. Finnis appears to have accepted this set of presuppositions. McInerny once wrote: "Finnis/Grisez accept as good money the naturalistic fallacy and attempt to construct a non-naturalist account of natural law" (McInerny 1998). Finnis's theory depends on a reinterpretation of the role that practical reason plays in ethical decision-making. There are, so Finnis argues, sets of "objective goods" that are self-evident to practical reason. In his *Natural Law and Natural Rights*, Finnis put forward his list of basic human goods: life, knowledge, play, aesthetic experience, friendship, practical reasonableness, and religion (1982). Finnis, however, argues that this set of basic goods is known by practical reason and is not grounded in a philosophical anthropology. In *Fundamentals of Ethics*, Finnis wrote: "(E)thics is not deduced or inferred from metaphysics or anthropology" (1983: 22). This lack of a philosophical anthropology is where the Grisez/Finnis account of natural law theory parts company with Veatch, McInerny and MacIntyre. Robert George, a proponent of Finnis's theory, has published profusely in various arenas defending the new natural law theory.

Finnis's "new natural law theory" has not escaped some rather trenchant criticism, mostly from philosophers generally friendly to natural law thinking. Regarding moral theory directly, Russell Hittinger early on rendered a critique of the Finnis account (Hittinger 1987). Haldane argued that this meta-ethics is reducible to a kind of moral intuitionism similar to W. D. Ross's "prima facie duties" rather than the absolutist position articulated by G. E. Moore. In jurisprudence, Lloyd Weinreb worried lest the Finnis account lack the realist grounding necessary for a theory of justice (Weinreb 1987). Veatch suggested that what Finnis proposed in dismissing philosophical anthropology removed the metaphysical foundation for natural law. Similarly, McInerny argued that Finnis's theory is reducible to "natural law without nature" (McInerny 1998). Several commentators have suggested that the shadow of Kant hovers more heavily on this new theory of natural law than Grisez or Finnis are wont to admit. The advocates of the new natural law account, especially Grisez, deny this connection with Kant.

In *After Virtue*, MacIntyre also denied that a philosophical anthropology – what he called Aristotle's antiquated "metaphysical biology" – was a necessary condition for explaining ethical naturalism. In two later texts, however, McIntyre accepted theoretically the need for a philosophical anthropology in order to justify a moral theory and reconsidered this "metaphysical biology." In *Dependent Rational Animals*, MacIntyre wrote:

> In *After Virtue* I had attempted to give an account of the place of the virtues, understood as Aristotle had understood them, within social practices, the lives of individuals and the lives of communities, while making that account independent of what I called Aristotle's "metaphysical biology." ... I now judge that I was in error in supposing an ethics independent of biology to be possible. ... No account of the goods, rules and virtues that are definitive of our moral life can be adequate that does not explain – or at least point us towards an explanation – how that form of life is possible for beings who are biologically constituted as we are, by providing us with an account of our development towards and into that form of life.
>
> (MacIntyre 1999: x)

This analysis, which MacIntyre calls natural law, points to a major issue in contemporary discussions: is a natural kind ontology sufficient to explain natural law? Jean Porter, Fergus Kerr, and John Rist all argue that while human nature is a necessary condition, it is never a sufficient condition. This discussion leads to a consideration of the relation of theism to natural law theory, which is discussed below.

Natural law, natural rights, and the common good

Often natural law theory serves as the cornerstone in developing natural rights theory. Medieval natural law theory, with particular reference to Aquinas, is considered the theoretical source for natural rights; nonetheless this use must be reconciled with the fact that Aquinas, it would seem, did not consider the concept of natural right explicitly. Veatch and Finnis among others, however, have developed a philosophical derivation of rights from Aquinas's moral texts. Brian Tierney (1997) provides sophisticated analytical and historical analyses of this thicket of medieval jurisprudential issues. Moreover Henrik Syse developed recently an elucidation of a Thomistic theory of rights (Syse 2007).

According to Veatch, one determines a concept of "duty" based on the set of human dispositional properties. A natural right becomes the "protection" of the duties derived from human nature. This derivation, Veatch proposed, limits the present debate on the nature and scope of rights; in effect, this is a response to L. W. Sumner's worrisome claim that "the rhetoric of rights is out of control" (Sumner 1986: 20). Veatch argues for the possibility only of "negative rights," which are protections; he is less certain about the natural law derivation of "positive rights" or "entitlements." A negative right as a protection is exemplified in the rights to property, life, and liberty, which are the "rights not to be interfered with." Positive rights as entitlements, on the other hand, would be the rights to education, health care, retirement benefits, and so forth. One response to Veatch's restriction suggests that human dispositions might justify a limited set of positive human rights. Nussbaum, it would appear, would accept this theoretical direction (Nussbaum 2006). Nonetheless, contrary to most liberal theories of right, a natural law analysis suggests that the concept of right cannot be separated from the concept of the good. What Enlightenment moral and political theory separates, natural law theory more closely links.

Natural law theory argues that the common good – the commonweal – of a society must be part of the enactment of positive or human law rooted in human nature. Finnis renders the common good into English as "the public good." A law is never justified for the private interest of one or a few citizens. Furthermore, the common good of a society must not be neglected arbitrarily by enactment of positive law. Like Aristotle, natural law philosophers argue that a human person, as a social person, achieves one's development – Aristotelian *eudaimonia* – through the auspices of social interaction. Aquinas often emphasized this social nature of human beings. Donne's claim that "No man is an island" rings true to philosophers in the natural law tradition. The communitarian analyses of Michael Sandel (1984) and Charles Taylor (1989) hearken back to natural law leanings suggesting the importance of the common good. The common good, however, is more than the collection of individual goods. It is that set of means instrumentally necessary to maintain the fabric of a just society. The rules for governing society are rooted in the development of the human person and contribute to the commonweal of the society. In his excellent analysis of the common or public good in Aquinas, Finnis argues, for example, that the elements of the common good are "justice and peace," and that "concord – the tranquility of order," and "a sufficiency of at least the necessities of life" are necessary conditions for the common good (Finnis 1999: 226–7). These principles provide a broader role than a reduction of the common good to the combined acquisition of individual goods or virtues. The public good is "instrumental to securing human goods" (Finnis 1999: 246). Accordingly, the role of the *civitas* is limited and instrumental. Finnis even suggests that on law and its role in the *civitas*, Aquinas is close to Mill's analysis in *On Liberty*. Nussbaum's *The Fragility of Goodness* (Nussbaum 1986) and her capabilities approach (2006) develop this concept of the common good. The common good is never reducible to a quantitative amassing of individual goods. Aristotelian to the core, the role of prudence is central to determining how the goods are to be acquired and distributed.

God, theism, and ethical naturalism

In discussing the relation of God to natural law, two conceptually separate issues come to the forefront: (a) Is a secular view of natural law possible? (b) What role does natural law play in moral theology?

More than several philosophers argue that some connection with God is a necessary condition for a sufficient analysis of natural law theory. These philosophers take seriously Alan Ryan's arguments: "Once God was dead, natural law was dead, natural duties were dead, and natural rights were dead," and " … a secular natural-law theory is simply incoherent, and a secular natural-rights theory is therefore incoherent too" (A. Ryan 1985: 180). Pamela Hall and Fergus Kerr suggest that in order to understand Aquinas on natural law, one must understand the role Divine Providence plays. Kerr writes: "Thomas's concept of natural law is thoroughly theological" (Kerr 2002: 106). John Rist argues that it "makes no sense" to remove God from natural law theory (Rist 2002: 153), and Fulvio Di Blasi offers a similar refrain (Di Blasi 2006: 73ff.).

Despite these philosophers who demand the existence of God for establishing a coherent theory of natural law, the central philosophical issue is, to the contrary, the possibility of establishing a natural kind of ontology. If natural law depends fundamentally on a theory of human nature, then for Aquinas, this is a metaphysical issue resolved in terms of ontology, not theology or philosophy of religion; it follows that a consistent account of natural law is independent conceptually of the proposition that God exists. In *Natural Law and Natural Rights*, Finnis offered a similar position: "For Aquinas, there is nothing extraordinary about man's grasp of the natural law; it is simply one application of man's ordinary power of understanding" (Finnis 1982: 400). Therefore, understanding natural law is, in principle, a human activity undertaken in normal human ways of knowing. Even in Aquinas, this knowledge is nothing special beyond one's epistemology.

Natural law discussions in contemporary moral theology

Essays and books written by several late twentieth-century moral theologians in both the Anglo-American and the Continental traditions – both Roman Catholic and Protestant – have brought natural law moral theory into the forefront of moral theological discussions. Among these moral theologians are Jean Porter, Cristina Trainia, Servais Pinckaers, Martin Rhonheimer, and Eberhard Schockenhoff.

Porter argues that scholastic natural law was one of the great achievements of medieval theology (Porter 1999). While probing the philosophical foundations of natural law developed by Aquinas, nonetheless Porter proposes that while Aquinas grounds moral theory in human nature this grounding must be understood theologically. Given this perspective, she argues that a conceptually coherent natural law theory is more precisely a "distinctively theological" account than a philosophical analysis. Nonetheless, the role of reason, Porter argues, is a necessary condition to lay bare the foundation for natural law (Porter 2005). Porter hence provides an analysis of ethical naturalism in both a philosophical and a theological sense. Another theological venue for a contemporary reconsideration of natural law is Cristina Trainia's *Feminist Ethics and Natural Law* (1999). Trainia attempts creatively to blend insights from feminist moral theory with natural law writings, arguing that both positions complement rather than conflict with one another.

Many other theologians and several philosophers suggest that on natural law, Aquinas must be read as a theologian first. Porter and Schockenhoff argue that natural kind theory is conceptually insufficient to explicate natural law moral theory. Kerr notes that the Protestant scholar Ulrich Kuhn developed an interpretation of Aquinas's "theology of law" (Kerr 2002: 111). The French Aquinas scholar, M.-D. Chenu, argued at mid-century that Aquinas must be read more as a theologian than as a philosopher. Etienne Gilson and Henri De Lubac, it appears, ultimately adopt this position, especially regarding Aquinas's ontology. McInerny recently challenged this rendering of Aquinas's work by arguing that this more theological interpretation of Aquinas proposed by Chenu, De Lubac, and Gilson is misdirected (McInerny 2006). Simon Tugwell argues for a more balanced interpretation of this issue (Tugwell 1988).

With the writings of Porter, Rhonheimer, Pinckaers, Schockenhoff, and Trainia, natural law theory returns to current discussion in Christian moral theology. One item of discussion concerns explaining the historical reasons that led to the general dismissal of natural law from serious theological discussion. Certainly the shadow of Karl Barth's fideism, found in Kierkegaard and Luther, hovers over these questions (Schockenhoff 2003). Schockenhoff, furthermore, emphasizes the role historicism, as articulated in the writings of Wilhelm Dilthey, played in these discussions. Schockenhoff accepts this historicism but Porter, for one, does not. In the more intramural theological discussions, Schockenhoff is critical of several Rhonheimer conclusions. Whether philosophers more committed to ethical naturalism will log into this discussion is another question. Nonetheless, these recent natural law writings by both Protestant and Roman Catholic authors suggest that natural law is reconcilable with contemporary Christian moral theology, a position not widely accepted during most of the twentieth century.

A final comment: natural law and Ronald Dworkin

Various treatments of contemporary natural law suggest that Ronald Dworkin's jurisprudential theory is a significant contribution, with reference to his *Taking Rights Seriously* (Dworkin 1977) and "'Natural' Law Reconsidered" (1982) as illustrations. These arguments usually depend on Dworkin's analysis of judicial decision-making, where the moral principles of a society are necessary conditions. However, insofar as Dworkin remains agnostic about the role human nature might play, he does not fit under the umbrella of natural law as discussed in this chapter. Natural law philosophers respond to the contractarianism of Dworkin – and to Rawls and Nozick – by proposing a "thick" as opposed to a "thin" theory of the human good. This natural law account based on a metaphysics of natural kinds poses a foundational query for contemporary rights philosophers adopting a "thin theory" of the human good. Natural law philosophers argue that this lacuna is a theoretical problem with most theories of liberal jurisprudence. The thick theory would also be a response to the "moral fanatic" made famous by R. M. Hare in *Freedom and Reason* (Hare 1965).

In concluding this analysis of the contemporary recovery of natural law, one might with benefit consider Golding's reflections upon the importance of natural law jurisprudence, which offers a response to the limits of liberal jurisprudence. "The lesson of the natural law tradition is that both [legal effectiveness and legal obligation] involve attention to human needs, human purposes and the human good. Whatever the problems of this tradition, we cannot ignore its lesson in trying to understand the law that is" (Golding 1975: 31). The same holds for natural law moral theory.

See also Aristotle (Chapter 4); The open question argument (Chapter 25); Realism and its alternatives (Chapter 26); Ethics and law (Chapter 35); Virtue ethics (Chapter 40); Moral particularism (Chapter 53); Welfare (Chapter 54); Rights (Chapter 56); War (Chapter 67).

References

Anscombe, G. E. M. (1958) "Modern Moral Philosophy," *Philosophy* 33: 1–19.
Di Blasi, F. (2006) *God and the Natural Law: A Rereading of Thomas Aquinas*, South Bend, IN: St Augustine Press.
Dworkin, R. (1977) *Taking Rights Seriously*, Cambridge, MA: Harvard University Press.
——(1982) "'Natural' Law Revisited," *The University of Florida Law Review* 34, no. 2: 165–88.
Finnis, J. (1982) *Natural Law and Natural Rights*, corrected edn, Oxford: Clarendon Press.
——(1983) *Fundamentals of Ethics*, Oxford: Oxford University Press.
——(1999) *Aquinas: Moral, Political and Legal Theory*, Oxford: Oxford University Press.
Foot, P. (1978) *Virtues and Vices and Other Essays in Moral Philosophy*, Oxford: Blackwell.
Fuller, L. (1964) *The Morality of Law*, New Haven, CT: Yale University Press.
Golding, M. (1974) "Aquinas and Some Contemporary Natural Law Theories," in *Proceedings of the American Catholic Philosophical Association* 48: 238–47.
——(1975) *The Philosophy of Law*, Englewood Cliffs, NJ: Prentice-Hall.
Grisez, G. (1965) "The First Principle of Practical Reason," *Natural Law Forum* 10: 168–96.
Haldane, J. (2004) "Natural Law and Ethical Pluralism," in J. Haldane (ed.) *Faithful Reason*, London: Routledge, pp. 129–51.
Hare, R. M. (1965) *Freedom and Reason*, New York: Oxford University Press.
Hart, H. L. A. (1961) *The Concept of Law*, Oxford: Clarendon Press.
Hittinger, R. (1987) *Critique of the New Natural Law*, Notre Dame, IN: University of Notre Dame Press.
——(1989) "Natural Law Theory, Virtue Ethics and *Eudaimonia*," *International Philosophical Quarterly* 29, no. 4: 449–61.
Kerr, F., OP (2002) *After Aquinas: Versions of Thomism*, Oxford: Blackwell.
King, M. L. (1963) "Letter from a Birmingham Jail," *Christian Century* 80 (12 June): 767–73; repr. in R. G. Wright (ed.) *Legal and Political Obligation: Classic and Contemporary Texts and Commentary*, Lantham, MD: University Press of America, 1992.
Knight, K. (ed.) (1998) *The MacIntyre Reader*, Notre Dame, IN: University of Notre Dame Press.
Lisska, A. (1996) *Aquinas's Theory of Natural Law: An Analytic Reconstruction*, Oxford: Clarendon Press.
MacIntyre, A. (1981) *After Virtue: A Study in Moral Theory*, Notre Dame, IN: University of Notre Dame Press.
——(1988) *Whose Justice? Which Rationality*, Notre Dame, IN: University of Notre Dame Press.
——(1990) *Three Rival Versions of Moral Enquiry: Encyclopaedia, Genealogy, and Tradition*, Notre Dame, IN: University of Notre Dame Press.
——(1998) "The Claims of *After Virtue*," in K. Knight (ed.) *The MacIntyre Reader*, Notre Dame, IN: University of Notre Dame Press, pp. 69–72.
——(1999) *Dependent Rational Animals: Why Human Beings Need the Virtues*, Chicago, IL: Open Court.
Maritain, J. (1951) *Man and the State*, Chicago, IL: University of Chicago Press.

McInerny, R. (1998) Electronic review of *Aquinas's Theory of Natural Law: An Analytic Reconstruction*, by A. Lisska, *Medieval Review* 98.01.10, <http://hdl.handle.net/2027/spo.baj9928.9801.010>

——(2006) *Praeambula Fidei: Thomism and the God of the Philosophers*, Washington, DC: Catholic University of America Press.

Nussbaum, M. (1986) *The Fragility of Goodness*, Cambridge: Cambridge University Press.

——(1993) "Non-Relative Virtues," in M. Nussbaum and A. Sen (eds) *The Quality of Life*, Oxford: Clarendon Press, pp. 242–69.

——(2006) *Frontiers of Justice*, Cambridge, MA: Harvard University Press.

Porter, J. (1999) *Natural and Divine Law: Reclaiming the Tradition for Christian Ethics*, Grand Rapids, MI: Eerdmans.

——(2005) *Nature as Reason: A Thomistic Theory of the Natural Law*, Grand Rapids, MI: Eerdmans.

Rist, J. (2002) *Real Ethics*, Cambridge: Cambridge University Press.

Ryan, A. (1985) "Utility and Ownership," in R. G. Frey, *Utility and Rights*, Oxford: Blackwell, pp. 175–95.

Ryan, C., OP (1965) "The Traditional Concept of Natural Law: An Interpretation," in I. Evans (ed.) *Light on the Natural Law*, Baltimore, MD: Helicon Press, pp. 13–37.

Sandel, M. (1984) "Morality and the Liberal Ideal," *New Republic*, 7 May, pp. 15–17.

Schockenhoff, E. (2003) *Natural Law and Human Dignity*, trans. B. McNeil, Washington, DC: Catholic University of America Press.

Sumner, L. W. (1986) "Rights Denaturalized," in R. G. Frey (ed.) *Utility and Rights*, Oxford: Blackwell, pp. 20–41.

Syse, H. (2007) *Natural Law, Religion, and Rights*, South Bend, IN: St Augustine's Press.

Taylor, C. (1989) *Sources of the Self*, Cambridge, MA: Harvard University Press.

Thomas Aquinas (1996) *Summa Theologiae, Ia-IIae, QQ. 90–97*, in A. Lisska 1996, pp. 260–91. (Ia-IIae, part 1 of the 2nd part; Q., question; a., article.)

Tierney, B. (1997) *The Idea of Natural Right*, Atlanta, GA: Scholars Press.

Trainia, C. (1999) *Feminist Ethics and Natural Law*, Washington, DC: Georgetown University Press.

Tugwell, S. (1988) "Aquinas: Introduction,"in S. Tugwell (ed.) *Albert and Thomas: Selected Writings*, New York: Paulist Press, pp. 201–351.

Veatch, H. (1986) *Human Rights: Fact or Fancy?*, Baton Rouge, LA: Louisiana State University Press.

——(1990) *Swimming against the Current in Contemporary Philosophy*, Washington, DC: Catholic University of America Press.

Weinreb, L. (1987) *Natural Law and Justice*, Cambridge, MA: Harvard University Press.

Further reading

Finnis, J. (1999) *Aquinas: Moral, Political and Legal Theory*, Oxford: Oxford University Press. (An excellent account of the "new natural law theory" in moral and legal theory.)

Lisska, A. (2007) "On the Revival of Natural Law: Several Books from the Last Half-Decade," *American Catholic Philosophical Quarterly* 81, no. 4: 613–38. (An extensive review of eight books on natural law from contemporary philosophers and theologians.)

Porter, J. (2005) *Nature as Reason: A Thomistic Theory of the Natural Law*, Grand Rapids, MI: Eerdmans. (An excellent overview of natural law from a philosophical and a theological perspective.)

43
FEMINIST ETHICS

Samantha Brennan

Feminist ethics takes as its normative focus the oppression of women in society at large and the exclusion of women's voices from the development of culture, in particular from the development of moral philosophy. Beyond this general description, a wide variety of approaches to ethics fall under the description "feminist ethics" and it can be a challenge to say what all of these approaches have in common. Feminist approaches to ethics are often distinguished by the kinds of issues and cases addressed. For example, feminist ethics addresses the ethics of sex work, gender-based harassment, workplace discrimination, family life, and reproductive choices. Philosophical work in these areas counts as feminist ethics when the conclusions reached are those that further women's equality or when considerations addressed are issues of importance in women's lives that have traditionally been overlooked by mainstream ethics. But we can also distinguish feminist approaches to ethics, not just by topic, but also by the method employed in theorizing. Distinctively feminist approaches to moral theorizing place a special emphasis on the moral experiences of women and pay special attention to moral practice and political context. Some of these theories focus on a special aspect of women's experience, such as mothering, while others are more generally inclusive of a wide range of women's experiences. We can distinguish feminist approaches to ethics then both in terms of their criticism of traditional approaches on the grounds that such theories exclude the sorts of problems which most affect women, as well as by their approach to moral problems, such as the tools and methods brought to bear on moral problems.

One also finds feminist approaches to ethics which build on or extend traditional moral theories, such as consequentialism, contractarianism, and deontology, in feminist directions (Driver 2005; Hampton 1993; Schott 1997). Recently feminist ethicists have explored problems associated with the traditional core of moral philosophy, such as moral luck (Card 1996) and moral skepticism (Superson 2009). There is also a growing body of work by women moral theorists which is not explicitly feminist (Calhoun 2004). A lively debate exists as to whether that work has any common themes and whether women, as women, have a distinctive voice in the field of ethics. My plan in this discussion of feminist ethics is to lay out some common themes, raise some suggestions about future directions for feminist ethics, and outline some areas of disagreement between feminist ethicists.

Common themes

Feminist ethics began as a sub-discipline of ethics in the 1970s and 1980s, alongside the growth of the second wave feminist movement. While there were much earlier advocates of women's rights, and women's inclusion in the moral and political realm more broadly, earlier authors were not so self-consciously aware of themselves as feminists, nor did they necessarily criticize other approaches to ethics for the exclusion of women and women's concerns. Feminist ethics began by expanding the range of topics considered worthy of moral concern and moral theorizing. Feminists brought ethical considerations to bear on issues such as reproduction, abortion, women's sexuality, sexual harassment, pornography, the role of women in the military, and many others. However, feminist philosophers working in ethics also criticized traditional moral theories for the neglect of women's oppression and typically tied that neglect to the exclusion of women from the development of ethical theories. Feminists criticized traditional approaches to ethics on a variety of grounds: as overly abstract, placing too much emphasis on individuality, overvaluing rationality, focusing on individuals in conflict, rather than on individuals in community, and as caring about autonomy and independence out of proportion to their true moral worth. Some feminists viewed traditional moral theories as reformable, while others thought that an entirely new feminist approach to ethics was required both to adequately address women's oppression and to overcome the male bias in moral philosophy itself.

The early feminist approaches to ethics urged a new approach to moral philosophy, one that put women's experiences in relationships front and center. We were asked to think of ethics in terms of care as well as (or instead of) justice. For a time it looked as if feminist ethics might become synonymous with the ethics of care. After the publication of Carol Gilligan's research on women's moral reasoning in 1982 and Nel Noddings's theoretical articulation of that reasoning in 1984, a decade followed in which the ethics of care predominated as *the* feminist approach to ethics. In more recent years there has been a broadening of concern (feminists are now well known for work on trust, autonomy, and responsibility, to give some examples) but the focus on relationships, if not care, as the sole source of value in those relationships, remains central.

The focus of feminist ethics on relationships takes two forms. First, relationships are central to feminist ethics as a topic of moral evaluation. Feminists argue that mainstream approaches to ethics have focused too much on individuals and ignored the moral significance of human relationships. Second, feminists have argued that the moral concepts developed by mainstream moral philosophy are ill-suited for dealing with persons understood in relation to one another. Instead, feminists have developed alternative relational moral concepts. These concepts are not meant to be used solely in thinking morally about relationships. Rather, it is argued that persons themselves are best understood in relational terms and so moral concepts such as autonomy, rights, and freedom have undergone a relational transformation.

Feminists have also expanded the range of relationships to which ethical demands have been thought to apply. Feminists have been critical of most traditional approaches to ethics as focusing too much on the adult, independent, autonomous person in his interactions with other persons sharing those same characteristics. (Of course not all traditional approaches make this mistake. We need to distinguish "individualist" positions, whether egoist or impartialist, from "relationship-oriented" positions, whether egoist or impartialist, taking care not to paint Artistotle's relationally orientated ethics with the same brush as Kant's individualist moral framework.) On certain traditional views then, morality is conceived of as rules which constrain the behavior of autonomous persons each out to promote his or her own self-interest. But such a way of conceiving of the scope of ethics leaves out our close, personal, loving relationships with others with whom our interests are intimately connected. It also leaves out relationships with dependent others, such as children, the elderly, and the disabled. While some feminists think the problem with traditional ethics has been the range of problems addressed, others think that the problem runs much deeper and that the problem is not with the application of the concepts and tools of moral theory, traditionally conceived; the tools and concepts themselves are flawed. On this view, we need to revise traditional moral concepts in light of relational insights. Some feminists see this as a complete break with the history of moral philosophy, where others see the development of recent feminist insights as offering further support for a relational approach to ethics which has been present all along as a minority voice in the tradition of moral philosophy.

Consider as just one example feminist work in the area of rights. Feminist moral theorists have, in the past, been consistent critics of rights-based moral theories. Feminists have criticized moral rights for a wide variety of reasons but many of those reasons relate to the account of the self to which rights theories have been attached. According to mainstream moral theory, the kind of individual which is assumed to be the bearer of rights is one who is autonomous and independent. This kind of individual is also frequently seen as one who is self-interested and in conflict with others. Caroline Whitbeck, for example, attributes to "the rights view of ethics" the description of people as "social and moral atoms, armed with rights and reason, and actually or potentially in competition or conflict with one another" (Whitbeck 1983: 79). If morality is modeled on rules for self-interested individuals, each pursuing his or her own good, the feminist fear is that we do more than simply reflect such a society, we contribute to the continuation of a society marked by uncaring and conflict.

More recent work by feminist moral theorists suggests a reconciliation between rights and feminist ethics (Brennan 1999; Minow 1990). There are tremendous risks to abandoning rights talk given how entrenched the language of rights is, especially on the international political scene. Martha Minow (1990) and Annette Baier (1985) have argued that rights need not be tied to an atomistic, overly individualistic conception of the self. Jennifer Nedelsky (1993) goes so far as to argue that in the political realm we ought to conceive of rights as tools with which to construct relationships and that we should resolve disputes about rights in terms of thinking about the kinds of relationships we wish to promote. The alternative conception of rights proposed by feminist moral theorists sees rights as relational, rather than individualistic, moral concepts and as connected to concepts and practices of moral responsibility and cooperation.

The focus on morality as lived experience means that feminist moral theorists pay attention to rights as moral practice. People don't just hold rights, they also do things with rights such as claiming, according, and negotiating. Minow describes the claiming of a right as an activity which has the potential to affirm one's commitment to a community. Minow writes: "Although the language of rights, on its surface, says little of community or convention, those who exercise rights signal and strengthen their relation to a community" because "those who claim rights implicitly agree to abide by the community's response and accord a similar regard to the claims of others" (Minow 1990: 294). Feminists will want to reject theories of rights which have built-in assumptions of complete independence and separation, but this still leaves feminists free to develop accounts of rights based upon a relational account of the self.

But this work on relational theories of rights is not the only aspect of morality which feminists have made over in a relational fashion. Feminists have also developed relational accounts of autonomy, of responsibility, and perhaps most importantly, in theories of the self which underpins all of these moral concepts. The feminist relational account does look at persons in their particularities. Persons are not viewed as separate from their histories and relationships. Feminist relational approaches are not limited to particular moral concepts either. Feminist theorists have also advanced relational approaches to applied topics within moral and political philosophy. Minow, for example, advocates relational approaches to social problems related to family law and to the rules governing juvenile courts.

The relational turn in feminist ethics might suggest that feminists are more interested in the ethics of small-scale interaction, such as intimate family relationships, than in ethics on a larger scale. However, this could not be further from the truth. Feminist ethics also has a distinctively political cast, understanding personal relationships in their broader political context. The slogan of the second wave feminist movement, "the personal is political," is especially true in the case of feminist ethics and this can sometimes make it difficult to distinguish feminist ethics from work in feminist political philosophy.

Consider, as an example, the issue of moral agency. Many of the factors which would seem relevant to women's moral agency are themselves political considerations. The early socialization of male and female children into appropriate gender roles would seem to restrict women's choices. Likewise, a self who is raised to want less for herself and to care more for the welfare of others may not be a reliable judge of her own best interests. Issues of character and development and moral agency, which might seem at the outset to be essentially questions about individuals, turn out to have a distinctly political character. Feminist theorists have proposed a theory of the self as relational, where the focus is on the relationships that form and sustain individuals. However, the sorts of relationships that are possible will depend in part on the material circumstances in which one lives. Issues of oppression and of wide-scale social forces are relevant to the formation of the self as well as to the opportunities available to that self. The standard liberal goes wrong in focusing solely on the latter.

Feminist ethicists, whether writing about particular normative concepts, such as rights or responsibility, a concept central to moral psychology such as character or agency, or virtue theoretic conceptions such as goodness or bravery have tended to focus more than traditional sorts of theories on description and practice. The focus on practice is obviously a matter of emphasis and degree for there are mainstream male moral theorists who are also very sensitive to detail and context. Feminists share with other theorists interested in moral psychology a concern with how people come to make moral decisions. A difference may be that feminist theorists, along with others who bring a critical and political perspective to bear on the subject, "ask questions about states of mind, feeling, and action in context of social difference and unequal power and opportunity" (DesAutels and Walker 2004: xiii). Writes DesAutels and Walker:

> Critical social perspectives in moral psychology relate questions of motivation, responsibility, and actions to political possibilities and social identities. They render a significantly more nuanced picture of how our moral communities shape our capacities for moral perception, action, and responsibility, as well as how differently many communities distribute recognition of those capacities to people of different groups and statuses.
>
> (2004: xiii)

Common themes then in feminist ethics include attention to relationships, the development of relational moral concepts, a focus on moral psychology, and the attention paid to the broader political context in which relationships grow and develop and in which individuals negotiate their way morally. These features of feminist approaches to ethics can be seen as well in areas of applied ethics to which feminists have made significant contributions, such as feminist bioethics in the area of reproductive ethics as well as in issues related to family justice.

Some areas of disagreement

(1) How much should we care about the inequalities in income, in job opportunities, in access to education, and in political status of relatively affluent First World women? Feminist philosophers disagree about the moral importance of equality. Two different sets of criticism of the importance of equality as a feminist value have been put forward, both of them quite compelling. Iris Young (1990) has argued that contemporary moral and political philosophy focuses too much on the redistribution of material goods, and not enough on other aspects of oppression. She argues that oppression has "five faces" and that we ought to broaden our scope of moral concern. Claudia Card argues against the feminist focus on women's inequality, which she attributes to the influence of liberal feminism and argues instead for a version of feminist ethics inspired by the politics of radical feminism, which focuses on evils directed at women such as rape and sexual violence. Both argue that feminism's moral tools have been shaped by our focus on the lives of First World women and that moving beyond equality is necessary for feminist ethics and political philosophy to be relevant on the global scene.

(2) Feminist disagreement about issues related to sexuality is notorious. Feminist debate about sex work and pornography raged through the 1980s and persists into the current day. It is also however connected to important issues in moral philosophy regarding choices and oppression, autonomy, women's participation in our own oppression, and the role of women's experiences and first-person narratives of those experiences in ethics. Typically issues related to sexuality divide feminists on liberal versus radical lines but such divisions between kinds of feminism are not so useful when it comes to feminist ethics. All feminist ethicists will agree that coercion and forced participation in harmful work is worth our moral attention. However, difficulties arise once we ask whether all sex work is of this sort. That is, what ought feminists to say about women's participation in pornography and other forms of sex work if such participation is voluntarily chosen? This is an area in feminist ethics in which no consensus exists. Women's choices to take part in pornography – as actors, producers, and consumers – pit advocates of women's autonomy against those feminists who view all such desires and choices to be constructed in a patriarchal society and their fulfillment to be ultimately bad for women. Jessica Spector (2006) notes that feminist liberals tend to treat pornography differently than prostitution and that even with the liberal position there are significant disagreements.

(3) A difficult question for all areas of feminist theory, including feminist ethics, concerns the category of "woman." If feminist ethics is an ethics accountable to women's experiences of moral life, then we need to have some account of "woman" that avoids essentialist claims about "women's nature." Since Simone de Beauvoir feminists have claimed that women are made and not born, and that gender is in some important sense a performative category. How useful

is feminist ethics for thinking about issues of gender and sexual identity? This set of questions is connected to the links between feminist theory and other kinds of critical theory such as queer theory, race theory, and disability studies. To fully understand the nature of interlocking oppressions, how far beyond the resources of feminist ethics do we need to move? Cheshire Calhoun, for example, has argued that feminist theory has failed to adequately represent lesbian concerns (Calhoun 1994). Do feminist ethicists need to "take a break from feminism" as some have suggested (Halley 2008) in order to see the problems clearly? Halley argues that sexuality involves deeply contested and clashing realities and interests, and that feminism helps us understand only some of them. Others argue that feminist ethics can be expanded to address sexual and gender orientation, race, and disability.

Future directions

Women and mainstream moral theorists: blurring the boundaries

One interesting development that affects feminist moral philosophy is the growing number of women working in mainstream moral philosophy. Indeed, if one were asked to name the most important moral philosophers of our time, sex aside, it's likely that that list would include the names of a great many women moral theorists. That list would also include women whose work includes work in feminist ethics, some of which have successfully moved feminist concerns and approaches into the mainstream. Consider the work of Onora O'Neill, Martha Nussbaum, and Christine Korsgaard. Most recently work by women moral theorists has been brought together in an edited collection, Cheshire Calhoun's *Setting the Moral Compass.* While not explicitly feminist in orientation throughout, it brings together a wide range of women philosophers, some best known for their work in feminist ethics, such as Virginia Held, Alison Jaggar, and Margaret Walker; others best known for work in the history of philosophy, such as Elizabeth Spelman, Marcia Baron, and Christine Korsgaard. In the introduction Calhoun comments that she sees common threads and themes in the work of these very diverse theorists. But this raises an interesting challenge for the distinctiveness of feminist ethics. As feminist concerns move into the mainstream and a growing number of moral philosophers, both male and female, incorporate feminist themes and concerns into their work, boundaries blur between feminist ethics and mainstream moral philosophy done well.

Feminism and global justice

What role does feminist ethics have to play in debates about international justice? This is perhaps the area of feminist ethics in which one finds the strongest sense of urgent concern, combined with considerable theoretical disagreement and frustration. While all feminists are concerned about the situation of the world's women, different versions of feminist ethics approach this issue in different ways. A prime area of disagreement is how much we are able to judge, from the outside, how well women are faring in a particular set of social arrangements. Peggy DesAutelsand Whisnant puts the challenge facing feminist global ethics this way: "Can Western feminists theorize approaches to global suffering and injustice without falling prey to imperialist and essentialist ways of thinking, and without viewing women in the developing world as passive victims in need of saving?" (DesAutels and Whisnant 2008: ix). Martha Nussbaum (2000) argues that the danger of inaction, from fear of getting things wrong, is far worse than the risks of making judgments about the lives of women in developing countries. Notable figures writing in this area include, in addition to Nussbaum, Christine Koggell (2006), Uma Narayan (1997), and Onora O'Neill (2000). Issues of global justice of special concern to feminist moral theorists include immigration and the caring labor of women from the developing world who assist First World families with child care, elder care, and housework, the sexual exploitation of women from developing countries and the sexual trafficking of women and girls, the double exploitation of women in the developing world, exploited both by patriarchal customs at home and the global economic order, as well as the unequal distribution of food and other goods, both between rich and poor nations, and between men and women within those nations.

Feminist theories of the good

What is it for a life to go well? Traditionally moral philosophy has divided normative ethics into two separate domains: theories of right action and theories of the good. Feminist moral philosophy has been reluctant to propose distinctively feminist theories of the good life, though there are some notable exceptions. However, one of the strengths of feminist moral philosophy lies in its resistance to drawing a sharp line between the right and the good. Contemporary mainstream moral theorists – consequentialists and deontologists alike – seem to have a common way of thinking about the relationship between the right and the good. Their method assumes that questions about the nature of the good lie on neutral ground. Feminist moral theorists seem not to share this assumption, instead providing us with theories of the good that are closely tied to a theory of right action.

It is most easy to see the strong connection between the right and the good in feminist ethics by looking again at care ethics. Although the ethics of care is no longer synonymous with feminist ethics and there are many rival approaches, care ethics was certainly influential as an early attempt at an explicitly women-centered account of moral theory, one that moved beyond criticizing mainstream ethics for male bias. But what is the "care" in care ethics? Is it a morally required action, hence part of the right? Or is it a component of the good life, something that we ought to promote in our lives and the lives of others? Care is clearly both of these things. Insofar as it is valued it is also valued for two different aspects of caring: caring as activity and caring as attitude. Virginia Held (2004) argues that we should not neglect the activity of care by reducing our analysis of care to care as a virtue. Held's view is that we need to expand the vocabulary of moral evaluation beyond the categories of "good" and "right." The close tie between the good and the right is also evident in mothering approaches to ethics in which the activity of mothering is both a requirement of morality and a thing to be valued. Caring and mothering are both part of the good and the right.

Another example of a feminist moral theory in which the right and the good converge is Martha Nussbaum's (2004) capacity-based account of human rights. In her well-known account of human capacities, Nussbaum provides us with a list of internal capabilities and external conditions required for attaining a good life. An alternative to utilitarian measures of well-being, such as preference theories and hedonism, Nussbaum's account provides an objective but pluralistic account of what makes for a good human life. But unlike accounts of justice which separate the right from the good, and place the right prior to the good, Nussbaum's account links the account of a good life to the requirements of justice.

Critics of feminist ethics have charged feminist moral theorists with conflating the right and the good. But one could see this unified approach to ethics as a strength rather than a weakness of moral theory. However, there is a related danger of which feminist moral theorists ought to be wary. This is the danger of ignoring questions of value which are not tied to the requirements of right action. The field is a relatively young one and this is a recommendation for future feminist moral thought. Feminist moral theorists need to develop a distinctive theory of value.

While feminists have been correct to stay away from conceptualizing the good independent of the account of right action into which it fits, there are dangers for feminists in focusing too narrowly on right action at the neglect of the good. Without a feminist account of the good – to guide lives and moral choices – we risk ceding the language of the good to conservative politicians and theorists. Feminist reservations about engaging in discussion of the good stem from a fear of "others" telling us how best to live our lives and also from the awareness of the danger of Western feminists speaking for others. Standards of good relationships, personal and community flourishing, and the good life abound in political feminist communities. From the early books of the women's movement on women's sexual and physical health, to feminist self-help books on issues of weight, food, and self-esteem, it is clear that feminists have lots to say about the components of a good life. Feminist moral philosophy needs to connect with these lines of thought in the feminist community, articulating an account of the good, even if aspects of that good will lie outside the realm of the morally enforceable. Feminists are obviously critical of the liberal view that the good consists in desire or preference satisfaction because of worries about adaptive preferences and gender socialization. But how far away from desire satisfaction ought feminist ethics to move? Kimberly Yuracko (2003) argues for a feminist version of perfectionism as the best basis for feminist arguments for women's autonomy but it may be that there are revisions to the desire or preference theory which would achieve similar results at a less theoretically weighty price. This area of feminist ethics, feminist theories of well-being, seems to be a rich area for future feminist research.

In conclusion, feminist ethics has undergone a transformation since its early days of serving primarily to criticize masculine bias in mainstream moral philosophy. The issues addressed and the moral theories developed by feminist moral philosophers have branched out in many different directions. And if at times it can be more difficult to see a hard distinction between feminist ethics and mainstream moral philosophy, this is likely all to the good.

See also Ethics and psychology (Chapter 32); Partiality and impartiality (Chapter 52); Rights (Chapter 56).

References

Baier, A. (1985) "What do Women Want in a Moral Theory," *Noûs* 19: 53–63.

Brennan, S. (1999) "Reconciling Feminist Ethics and Feminist Politics on the Issue of Rights," *Journal of Social Philosophy* 30: 260–75.

Calhoun, C. (1994) "Separating Lesbian Theory from Feminist Theory," *Ethics* 104: 558–81.

——(ed.) (2004) *Setting the Moral Compass: Essays by Women Philosophers*, New York: Oxford University Press.

Card, C. (1996) *The Unnatural Lottery: Character and Moral Luck*, Philadelphia, PA: Temple University Press.

——(2002) *The Atrocity Paradigm*, New York: Oxford University Press.

DesAutels, P. and Walker, M. U. (eds) (2004) *Moral Psychology: Feminist Ethics and Social Theory*, Lanham, MD: Rowman & Littlefield.

DesAutels, P. and Whisnant, R. (eds) (2008) *Global Feminist Ethics*, Lanham, MD: Rowman & Littlefield.

Driver, J. (2005) "Consequentialism and Feminist Ethics," *Hypatia* 20: 183–99.

Gilligan, C. (1982) *In a Different Voice*, Cambridge, MA: Harvard University Press.

Halley, J. (2008) *Split Decisions: How and Why to Take a Break from Feminism*, Princeton, NJ: Princeton University Press.

Hampton, J. (1993). "Feminist Contractarianism," in L. Antony and C. Witt (eds) *A Mind of One's Own*, Boulder, CO: Westview Press.

Held, V. (2004) "Taking Care: Care as Practice and Value," in C. Calhoun (ed.) *Setting the Moral Compass: Essays by Women Philosophers*, New York: Oxford University Press.

Koggell, C. (ed.) (2006) *Moral Issues in Global Perspective*, 2nd edn, Peterborough, ON, Canada: Broadview Press.

Minow, M. L. (1990) *Making All the Difference: Inclusion, Exclusion, and American Law*, Ithaca, NY: Cornell University Press.

Narayan, U. (1997) *Dislocating Cultures: Identities, Traditions, and Third-World Feminism*, London: Routledge.

Nedelsky, J. (1993) "Reconceiving Rights as Relationship," *Review of Constitutional Studies/ Revue d'etudes constitutional* 1: 1–26.

——(2004) "The Future of Feminist Liberalism," in Calhoun 2004.

Noddings, N. (1984) *Caring: A Feminine Approach to Ethics and Moral Education*, Berkeley: University of California Press.

Nussbaum, M. C. (2000) "The Future of Feminist Liberalism," *Proceedings and Addresses of the American Philosophical Association* 74: 47–79.

O'Neill, O. (2000) *Bounds of Justice*, Cambridge: Cambridge University Press.

Schott, R. M. (1997) *Feminist Interpretations of Immanuel Kant*, University Park, PA: Pennsylvania State University Press.

Spector, J. (2006) *Prostitution and Pornography: Philosophical Debate about the Sex Industry*, Stanford, CA: Stanford University Press.

Superson, A. M. (2009) *The Moral Skeptic*, New York: Oxford University Press.

Walker, M. U. (1998) *Moral Understandings: A Feminist Study in Ethics*, London: Routledge.

Whitbeck, C. (1983) "A Different Reality: Feminist Ontology," in C. Gould (ed.) *Beyond Domination*, Totowa, NJ: Rowman & Allanheld.

Young, I. (1990) *Justice and the Politics of Difference*, Princeton, NJ: Princeton University Press.

Yuracko, K. A. (2003) *Perfectionism and Contemporary Feminist Values*, Bloomington, IN: Indiana University Press.

Further reading

Cudd, A. and Andreasan, R. O. (eds) (2005) *Feminist Theory: A Philosophical Anthology*, Oxford: Blackwell.

Tong, R. and Williams, N. (2009) "Feminist Ethics," in Edward N. Zalta (ed.) *Stanford Encyclopedia of Philosophy*, <http://plato.stanford.edu/entries/feminism-ethics/> (accessed 15 July 2009).

44
ETHICS AND AESTHETICS

Robert Stecker

Ethics and aesthetics are sometimes conceived of as two different parts of value theory, one concerned with ethical value, the other with aesthetic value. There is some truth in this way of conceiving their relationship. It is plausible that there is such a thing as aesthetic value, and that a subclass of aesthetic judgments are about this kind of value. Ethical judgments are also concerned with value, but in a way that seems different from those aesthetic judgments. Many ethical, indeed moral, judgments are concerned with what *non-moral* value ought or may be realized. Thus, Tolstoy raised the question – surely a moral question – whether great sums of money should be devoted to elaborate artistic productions when not enough money is devoted to famine relief. So even if there is such a thing as ethical or moral value, this kind of value is hardly the exclusive focus of ethics.

On the aesthetics side of the equation, things are also more complex than the initial conception suggests. This is because "aesthetics" refers to two different, though intertwined, philosophical disciplines. One of these was alluded to in the previous paragraph. It rests on the assumption that there is a distinctive kind of value – aesthetic value – and it is about understanding the nature of this value. But "aesthetics" can also refer to the philosophy of art. Aesthetics in this sense is first of all not just a branch of value theory since it faces all sorts of questions about art, which have more to do with metaphysics, epistemology, the philosophy of mind and language. In addition, artworks are not merely aesthetically valuable, but valuable in other ways including being ethically valuable. So a judgment about the value of an artwork might be pluralistic and have an ethical dimension. Finally, many things besides artworks possess aesthetic value: natural objects and environments, non-art artifacts, scientific theories, and mathematical proofs. In fact, aesthetic value pervades every corner of the world of human experience.

In order to take this complexity into account, this chapter will be divided into two parts. The first will explore conceptions of aesthetic and ethical value, and what, if any substantive relations there might be between them or between judgments about them. The second will concern the ethical evaluation of artworks and what substantive connection there might be with a work's artistic value.

Value in ethics

Here are two ways of thinking about the subject matter of ethics.

On one conception, ethics has two parts: one about the right, the other about the good (Ross 1930). The first concerns action: what we may, must, and must not do. The second provides a general theory of value. On this conception, ethics is not about a part of value theory – the part that deals with ethical value. It is the whole enchilada. If there are distinctive kinds of value, or if things are good in distinctively different ways, and if one of those ways is the aesthetic way, then that way is strictly part of the subject matter of ethics on this conception. It appears to be a historically contingent matter that those working in the field of ethics have "outsourced" this part of their field to specialists about aesthetic value. A few, such as Tolstoy (1962) and, in a different way, G. E. Moore (1965: 183–225), have tried to "rectify" this. Alternatively, one might see the part of ethics that is concerned with the good as only providing a general framework for conceptualizing value or ways of being good, while other, more specialized disciplines are responsible for understanding the specific ways. Aesthetics would then be the discipline responsible for understanding the aesthetic way of being good. Not all ways of being good (e.g. being a good knife) require a philosophical or scientific investigation, but aesthetic value is philosophically problematic because some question its very existence while others disagree about its nature.

A second way of conceiving ethics is based on a distinction between broad and narrow focus (Williams 1985). Ethics in broad focus is about what it is to have a good life or about how one should live – the question that Socrates articulated and which seems to drive ancient Greek ethical thought. Ethics in narrow focus is about morality: what is morally permissible, required, and prohibited. The narrow question drives a great deal of modern ethics. This question plausibly coincides with the theory of the right identified in the alternative conception mentioned above. Ethics in narrow focus or a theory of the right has little to do with aesthetic value *per se*, though as already mentioned it might sometimes face the issue of whether aesthetic value ought to be realized on a given occasion. On the other hand, some argue that this part of ethics is relevant to a full understanding of the value of artworks – an issue that will be discussed in the second part of this chapter.

It is plausible that ethics in broad focus will be more concerned with aesthetic value because it is arguable that part of a good life will involve the appreciation of aesthetically good things. However, the relation ethics in broad focus has to aesthetic value is different from the relation a theory of the good has to it. If there is such a thing as aesthetic value, then it is part of value theory – a theory of the good – to understand it. Just because a good life should involve the enjoyment of aesthetic value does not mean that it is part of a theory of the good life to understand what aesthetic value is. It can get that understanding from another discipline, just as those who think health is part of a good life get an understanding of what health is from another discipline – medicine.

The general conclusion of this section is that there is room for aesthetic value on both conceptions of ethics. On one it could be part of the good. On the other it could be a constituent of a good life.

Aesthetic value

I now want to examine the aesthetic way of being good – aesthetic value. What is good in this way and what role do those things play in a good life?

There is a consensus that the concept of the aesthetic came into self-conscious use only in the eighteenth century, where the primary concern is with judgments of beauty and sublimity in nature, art, and other artifacts. There is a line of thought running from Hutcheson through Hume to Kant that emphasizes that judgments of beauty are based on a felt response of pleasure caused by perceiving (or in some other way attending to) properties belonging to the objects of these judgments when we adopt an unbiased or disinterested attitude to the objects. This line of thought begins a tradition in thinking about the aesthetic that emphasizes that aesthetic value lies primarily either in *the experience* of appreciating an object or in *those properties* of objects that we directly cognize in appreciation, and depends in some way on bringing the right sort of attitude to the situation in which the experience occurs or the properties are cognized.

In contemporary thought, this tradition has evolved in the following way. First, we need the broader notion of aesthetic experience instead of simply the experience of the beautiful and sublime, and a broader array of properties appreciated in this experience. The concepts of beauty and sublimity cannot reasonably be supposed to cover the breadth of relevant experiences, nor are the experiences always pleasant even if the value of the experience is positive. Artworks sometimes shock, horrify, dwell on the grotesque. Ordinary objects that are neither beautiful nor sublime nevertheless elicit an aesthetic response, and are made to do so. Concerted criticism of "the aesthetic attitude" and of conceptions of disinterest also led to a much more minimalist view about whether a special attitude is required in aesthetic experience (Dickie 1973). It is no longer thought that the object appreciated, or that the experience it affords, must be of no instrumental value (Beardsley 1958; Carroll 2002). Nor is it now thought that the way one attends to things when aesthetically engaged with them involves anything more than the attention one would give to an object of non-aesthetic interest.

On a widely, if by no means universally, accepted view, aesthetic experience is characterized by two properties, one epistemic, one axiological (Iseminger 2004). One comes to know about some properties of the object of experience in virtue of experiencing them (epistemic property), and one values this experiencing for its own sake (axiological property). One upshot of this is that one can have a qualitatively identical experience induced by a drug or direct brain stimulation, but this would not be an aesthetic experience because it lacks the epistemic property. Also, one can come to know about some experienced properties, but if one remains indifferent to this experience, it is not aesthetic because it lacks the axiological property.

On this view, we can identify two kinds of aesthetic value or two kinds of things that are aesthetically good. There is the value of the experience itself. It is "intrinsically" rewarding (when positive), valued for its own sake. Second, there is the value of the object of the experience, which consists of its capacity in virtue of some of its properties, to deliver the intrinsically rewarding experience. This is a kind of instrumental value, but one that is sometimes called "inherent," because it is intimately related to the intrinsically rewarding experience.

If one is to get a full grasp of the place aesthetic value might have in a good life, one has to realize that, not only the objects of the experience, but aesthetic experience itself characteristically acquires instrumental value of various kinds depending on the context in which it occurs. This instrumental value piggybacks on the intrinsically rewarding experience and considerably enhances it. Consider the aesthetic experience of nature, characteristically the enjoyment of natural beauty. This is valuable in itself, but it can also serve various functions that add to this value by significant increments. It sharpens one's senses, enhancing one's ability and inclination to notice fine-grained features of the environment. It may make one feel closer to, more in tune with, or more immersed in, a natural environment, and that in turn may make one feel more grounded or more psychically stable. These and other beneficial effects won't emerge from a single fleeting experience, but from sustained experiences over a period of time. Similar claims can be made for the aesthetic experience of everyday items such as clothes, adornments, appliances, vehicles, food, and so on indefinitely. While these items less frequently have the great beauty one sometimes finds in nature, and may on occasion leave one indifferent, often enough they please or in some other way excite the senses and lift one's day-to-day existence above the monotony of routines. Such experiences may also make one a more perceptive individual. As we will see when we turn below to value in art, aesthetic experience can be cognitively useful in providing tools, skills, and virtues that are needed in the acquisition of knowledge. Nowhere is this more true than in the realm of ethics.

No one denies that aesthetic experience can have these kinds of instrumental value. People quite divided about whether the instrumental value of such experiences is part of their aesthetic value. (See Beardsley [1958] for a proponent of the view, and Budd [1995] for an opponent.) I am with the proponents. Many fleeting experiences of aesthetic pleasure may seem relatively trivial if they didn't incrementally have such enormous effects on the quality of human lives. It is the multifarious beneficial functions of aesthetic experience in combination with its intrinsic value that make it one of the great human goods.

Art and ethical value

In what ways can art be ethically evaluated? Many, since Plato, have worried about the effects of art, or some artworks, on its audience. Some artworks have had demonstrably bad effects such *The Sorrows of Young Werther* by Goethe, which caused a rash of suicides by people emulating the hero of the story. *The Jungle* seems to have played a positive role in reforming working conditions and sanitation in the meat industry, and unlike the previous case, this result was intended or at least desired by its author, Upton Sinclair. Most artworks don't have such clear large-scale consequences, but inevitably have micro-consequences – effects on the feelings, thoughts, and desires of their audience as they take in the work.

We can also ethically evaluate the means required for the production of works of art. As mentioned above, Tolstoy complained that the considerable resources needed for some artistic productions could have been better directed toward more urgent causes. Some artists have intentionally injured or mutilated themselves in the making of artworks that record them doing so. Is it OK for people to do that to themselves for the sake of art? Surely it would not be OK to do it to others.

In the contemporary literature on the ethical evaluation of art, the main focus has been elsewhere, namely on the ethical value of the content of the work, what is sometimes called a work's intrinsic ethical value. There are two main grounds for evaluating this content. One concerns the attitudes that a work expresses in virtue of its content. The undiluted admiration for Hitler and the Third Reich expressed in Riefenstahl's film, *Triumph of the Will*, is morally dubious (if entirely predictable since it is Nazi propaganda). So is the anti-Semitism expressed in Pound's *Cantos*, some Wagner operas, and Céline's *Journey to the End of the Night*. On the other hand, the condemnation of slavery clearly manifest in *Uncle Tom's Cabin* is morally admirable, especially since it was far more controversial then than now. Such attitudes are not confined to literature. Raphael's painting, *The School of Athens* presents the pursuit of knowledge as a noble activity, one of the highest goods. Rembrandt's 1654 *Bathsheba with King David's Letter* is notable for the compassion it exhibits toward its subject, which distinguishes it from other paintings of the period including another by Rembrandt about the same biblical scene. (For an excellent discussion, see Gaut 2007: 14–25.) Notice that the attitudes that receive ethical evaluation are not merely those of a character or narrator but belong to the work itself.

Whether or not a work manifests an attitude toward its subject matter, it may have a content that explores matters of ethical importance: How should one live (*Anna Karenina*)? What values should one be loyal to (Gottfried Keller's *Green Henry*)? How does one balance material aspirations and spiritual needs (Vermeer's *A Woman Weighing Gold*)? What should one do in the face of a moral dilemma and how should one cope with the aftermath of having faced one (*Sophie's Choice*)? Even when a work does express an attitude toward the issues it raises, we can also inquire into the quality of the exploration of moral content found in a work. Is it sensitive to the complexity of the issues it addresses? Does it look at them in a fresh way? Is it insightful? Does it allow one to feel the pull of both sides of an issue, or to get a sense of what it is like to live according to a set of values? Or is it simple-minded, conventional, opaque, unimaginative, and lacking in insight? So the second main ground for ethically evaluating the content of an artwork concerns the quality of the exploration of the morally significant material.

The ethical evaluation of the attitudes manifest in a work is roughly analogous to the evaluation of a person's character in terms of virtues and vices. An attitude that merely involves an error in judgment about a hard-to-decide matter is much less of an ethical flaw than an attitude that would be indicative of a defect of character when ascribed to a person. Thus even if we decide that Hardy's novels are overly pessimistic about the possibility of human happiness, or Larkin's poems are too misanthropic, these are errors of judgment at worst. An endorsement of racism or fascism in a work more plausibly manifests a defect in character.

The quality of the ethical exploration is also relevant to the moral character of the work, since those explorations we count as fine are indicative of a mind capable of empathy, compassion, subtle investigation, or some other virtue. (None of this is to imply that the actual author of such a work is morally admirable.) Similarly, correctness in moral attitude is consistent with shallowness or some other defect that is exhibited in explorations of lower quality. However, the main ethical importance of an exploration is cognitive. Some argue that artistic exploration can be a source of moral knowledge (Gaut 2007: 133–64; Nussbaum 1990). One may be skeptical about that (Lamarque and Olsen 1994; Stolnitz 1992). Consider one of the best-known attempts to show this: Nussbaum's discussion (1990) of Henry James's novel, *The Golden Bowl*. According to Nussbaum, James exhibits a paradigm of the acquisition of particular moral knowledge – knowledge of what to do in a specific situation – as two of the central characters, Adam and Maggie (father and daughter) become both clear about and "richly responsive" to the nest of circumstances, feelings, and obligations within which they must act (laid out in all the subtly and complexity of late Jamesian prose). In virtue of this, they perceive the right course of action. Supposing that this is the right interpretation of what is represented in the novel, it's worth asking where this leaves the reader with respect to the possession of moral knowledge. The reader may agree that the characters make the right choice, and she may believe that she also perceives its rightness. But this presupposes an Aristotelian model of ethical decision-making (on Nussbaum's interpretation) that James's novel cannot itself show to be correct. That requires independent philosophical argument. Even if the reader actually does come to know that the characters make the right decision, that is a rather slim piece of moral knowledge. Far more substantial would be knowledge of how one goes about reaching the right moral choice, but as just pointed out, the novel by itself can't give one that.

Further, it is not so clear the decision Adam and Maggie reach is as morally perfect as Nussbaum represents it to be. It's true they are incredibly sensitive to each other, but what is left out is their attitude toward and effect on the other two central characters – Amerigo, Maggie's husband, and Charlotte, her faithless friend, who recently had a passionate affair with Amerigo. Charlotte may not deserve much consideration, but the life with Adam in bleak Midwestern America that father and daughter consign her to has at least a touch of sadism. As for Amerigo – an Italian aristocrat who is now willing to devote himself to Maggie – the not so obvious assumption is that everything will be fine between them with Charlotte out of the picture and Maggie's love for him undistracted by her great affection for her father. Once we recognize that these two are more disposed of than richly responded to – something made possible by the power of Adam's great fortune – the quality of the moral decision is more ambiguous.

Whether or not one sometimes acquires moral knowledge from works of art, the chief cognitive value of the ethical explorations one finds in them lies elsewhere. In part, it consists in the conceptions suggested by these explorations – of moral decision-making such as that found in the *Golden Bowl*, but also of values, virtues, right action, moral dilemmas, and so on. In part it consists of skills one may acquire as one imaginatively realizes the contents of fictional worlds and applies the conceptions found therein beyond them. One may acquire skill in achieving the heightened sensitivity endorsed by James in part by reading him and imaginatively occupying the minds of his characters. One may become more adept at seeing things from another's point of view, in detecting emotional responses, or identifying intentions. The ability to consider alternative conceptions and the possession of the skills just mentioned are cognitive virtues. It is the provision of such virtues that is the chief cognitive value of explorations.

Whatever one's interpretation of the moral decision portrayed in the *Golden Bowl*, its cognitive and emotional force will derive from the imaginative experience resulting from entering the intricate conscious lives of these characters. Without this experience, which is a characteristic aesthetic experience provided by literature, one will not gain access to the ethical exploration. In general, the cognitive value of an exploration is dependent upon the quality of the imaginative experience the work is capable of providing. If the imagined world is flat and unconvincing, so will be the exploration. To take one more example, consider one of the main themes in the work of Gottfried Keller, Wittgenstein's favorite novelist. This is the clash between the values associated with an older traditional way of life over which one has little choice and those that come with the modern world, which presents a menu of goods from which one tries to carve out a worthwhile life. Keller wants us to understand the state of mind of being torn between these two ways of life and what a society where some people are so torn is like. To accomplish this he must enable us to have a certain kind of experience where we feel the pull of each system of value. Short of that, one may see that characters are divided but fail to understand why it is hard to choose without loss.

I suggested above that the ethical value of an exploration in a work depends in part on the quality of the aesthetic experience the work is capable of providing. Call that aesthetic–ethical interaction. Does interaction also go in the other direction? Does ethical value of an artwork contribute to its aesthetic value? Do ethical merits in works enhance its aesthetic value; and ethical defects, diminish that value?

One attempt to establish ethical–aesthetic interaction is the merited response argument. We often find that artworks prescribe certain cognitive and emotional responses for their audience. Thus both tragedies and thrillers are concerned about the fate of their protagonists. The former prescribe pity for the protagonists as a result of their fate while the latter prescribe suspense about their fate. Among these prescribed responses are ethically evaluable ones. For example, a work may prescribe the adoption of an attitude manifested by the work. A prescribed response can be merited or unmerited. A lame thriller does not merit the suspense it prescribes and if one were to write a play entitled *The Tragedy of Hitler*, the pity it attempts to elicit for its protagonist would be unmerited if the play is historically accurate. One way a response may not be merited is by being unethical. If a prescribed response is unmerited, that is an aesthetic defect in the work. Hence, ethical defects in works that make prescribed responses unmerited detract from the aesthetic value of works (Gaut 2007: 229–33).

Unfortunately for this argument, some of its premises are just too uncertain to achieve general acceptance. To see the problem, consider the hypothetical *Tragedy of Hitler*. Suppose, as I implied above, that no historically accurate play could succeed representing Hitler as a tragic figure meriting the pity appropriate to such a character. Is that because it is unethical to adopt such an attitude? No. It is because the combination of traits needed to be a tragic figure was just not possessed by the historical Hitler. The imaginary author of the play made an aesthetic error in attempting to present Hitler with the traits he actually possessed in the tragic mode. Those skeptical of this argument with some plausibility reject the premise that one way a prescribed response may not be merited is by being unethical. They argue that in each case where this may seem to be so, the real problem is an aesthetic rather than an ethical choice.

I leave it an open question whether the merited response argument can be salvaged. Nevertheless, it is plausible that the ethical value of a work at least sometimes is part of its artistic value. While there are genres and individual works where moral concerns are either beside the point or suspended, *some* drama going back to ancient Greek tragedy, and *some* novels, stories, poetry, paintings, and cinema virtually require ethical exploration as a component of their content. For works like these, the ethical attitudes they manifest and the quality of the explorations that occur within them are relevant to their value as the artworks they are. This of course does not mean that the mere fact that a work manifests an admirable attitude makes it a good work of its kind. There are obviously many non-ethical considerations that are also relevant. Wagner and

Pound created great opera and poetry, respectively, despite the moral flaws found in some of their work. Though *Uncle Tom's Cabin* expresses, given its historical context, a not merely morally correct but a commendable attitude toward slavery, it is also excessively sentimental, has wooden characters, and is propelled by an implausible plot, which make it on the whole a poor specimen of a novel. However, note that these same features limit its effectiveness as an exploration of the evils of slavery, and so create in it ethical as well as an aesthetic demerit. Nevertheless, it is still true that its admirable condemnation of slavery is *prima facie* relevant to its literary value, and in this case makes it, all things considered, a better novel than one with similar defects but without the redeeming ethical merit.

Those who would reject this claim have to defend a narrower conception of artistic value. Formalists claim that artistic value derives entirely from valuable formal properties of works such as its unity, balance, etc. Formalists have long recognized that the literary arts are hard cases for their view, but more generally formalism has few defenders these days as applied to any of the representational art forms. Somewhat more plausible is an aesthetic criterion of value: that the artistic value of a work is constituted by the valuable perceptual or imaginative experience afforded to those who understand it (Budd 1995). On this view, the fact that a work has an admirable ethical character, that it explores issues in a way that makes it a valuable cognitive tool, or that it is a source of moral knowledge do not in themselves make a work more valuable as art. However, proponents of this view can hold that these features can enhance the value of the experience the work affords and this still leaves a way in which the ethical value of a work can contribute to overall artistic value. So, for example, a work that prompts its audience to experience the way certain important values can come into conflict can make the experience of the work more significant or profound in virtue of its subject matter. In contrast, a work that dwells on more trivial subjects might be found to offer a shallower experience no matter how vividly it brings its subject to life.

While this view is a vast improvement over formalism, in my view, it still provides an inadequate conception of artistic value. Though the experience a work can provide is a core feature of its value as art, one should also take into account what it achieves and what its audience takes away from it after the experience is over. If a work in an appropriate genre provides ethical insight, that is not simply a matter of the experience it provides. It is also a matter of what we possess when we are no longer experiencing the work.

Omissions

This chapter has attempted to pack a large topic of growing interest into a small space. It has inevitably omitted some important issues related to this topic, which I conclude by noting. One issue concerns environmental ethics and aesthetics. Does the interaction noted above between ethical and aesthetic properties in art also hold for nature? Sometimes something that is bad for the environment – an invasive species, pollution – *seems to* make it more beautiful. Vivid sunsets are caused by particles in the atmosphere often produced by pollution. Does recognition of the harm caused by an item (e.g. the pollution) reveal that that natural setting (e.g. the sunset) actually is not more beautiful (Eaton 2001)? On another issue, some have proposed an aesthetic understanding of some ethical properties, e.g. virtue as a kind of beauty (McGinn 1997: 92–122). Finally, the most important issue not discussed here concerns meta-aesthetics in comparison with meta-ethics. I have argued that ethics and aesthetics differ in that the former is concerned with value in general (the good or the good life), while the latter is concerned with a particular kind of value. In contrast, the meta-issues each discipline faces are exactly parallel: realism vs. anti-realism, objectivity vs. subjectivity, cognitivism vs. expressivism, etc. But should they be treated in a parallel way (Railton 1998)? The answer to that must await another occasion.

See also Ethics and sentiment (Chapter 10); Hume (Chapter 11); Realism and its alternatives (Chapter 26); Non-cognitivism (Chapter 27); Cognitivism without realism (Chapter 29); Reasons, values, and morality (Chapter 36); Moral particularism (Chapter 53); The environment (Chapter 63); The ethics of free speech (Chapter 64).

References

Beardsley, M. (1958) *Aesthetics: Problems in the Theory of Criticism*, New York: Harcourt, Brace & World.

Budd, M. (1995) *Values of Art: Pictures, Poetry, Music*, London: Penguin Books.

Carroll, N. (2002) "Aesthetic Experience Revisited," *British Journal of Aesthetics* 42: 145–68.

Dickie, G. (1973) *Art and Aesthetics: An Institutional Analysis*, Ithaca, NY: Cornell University Press.

Eaton, M. (2001) *Merit, Ethical and Aesthetic*, Oxford: Oxford University Press.

Gaut, B. (2007) *Art, Emotion and Ethics*, Oxford: Oxford University Press.

Iseminger, G. (2004) *The Aesthetic Function of Art*, Ithaca, NY: Cornell University Press.

Lamarque, P. and Olsen, S. (1994) *Truth, Fiction and Literature*, Oxford: Oxford University Press.

McGinn, C. (1997) *Ethics, Evil, and Fiction*, Oxford: Oxford University Press.

Moore, G. E. (1965) *Principia Ethica*, Cambridge: Cambridge University Press.

Nussbaum, M. (1990) *Love's Knowledge*, Oxford: Oxford University Press.

Railton, P. (1998) "Aesthetic Value, Moral Value and the Ambitions of Naturalism," in J. Levinson (ed.) *Aesthetics and Ethics: Essays at the Intersection*, Cambridge: Cambridge University Press, pp. 59–105.

Ross, W. D. (1930) *The Right and the Good*, Oxford: Clarendon Press.

Stolnitz, J. (1992) "On the Cognitive Triviality of Art," *British Journal of Aesthetics* 32: 191–200.

Tolstoy, L. (1962) *What is Art? And Essays on Art*, New York: Hesprides.

Williams, B. (1985) *Ethics and the Limits of Philosophy*, Cambridge, MA: Harvard University Press.

Further reading

Carroll, N. (1996) "Moderate Moralism," *British Journal of Aesthetics* 38: 223–37. (One of the first presentations of the merited response argument.)

Jacobson, D. (1997) "In Praise of Immoral Art," *Philosophical Topics* 25: 155–99. (Argues for particularism about the ethical–aesthetic interaction.)

Levinson, J. (ed.) (1998) *Aesthetics and Ethics: Essays at the Intersection*, Cambridge: Cambridge University Press. (A seminal collection of essays on both aesthetic and ethical value and the ethical evaluation of art.)

Part V
MORALITY

45
MORALITY AND ITS CRITICS

Stephen Darwall

Near the beginning of Book 2 of Plato's *Republic*, Glaucon poses the following challenge to Socrates. Most people, Glaucon says, act justly not because they think doing so is good in itself, but only because they want a reputation for justice so that others will act justly toward them. Though they believe taking advantage of others would be best if they could do it with impunity, they nonetheless acknowledge that suffering injustice from others is even worse. So all are willing to

> agree among themselves to have neither; hence there arise laws and mutual covenants; and that which is ordained by law is termed by them lawful and just.
>
> (Plato, *Republic*, 2006: Bk 2, 31)

Ordinary people thus regard justice as a kind of second-best compromise. All would prefer to act unjustly if they could get away with it but realize they often cannot. So justice is widely acknowledged to be a "lesser evil" and "honored by reason of the inability of men to do injustice."

Glaucon makes his point vivid with the myth of a shepherd, Gyges, who discovers a magical ring able to make him invisible at will. With the ring, Gyges acts unjustly to his great benefit. Anyone with such a ring (in the company of others lacking it) would act similarly, Glaucon says. It is only because our powers are sufficiently similar that we accept justice as second best.

Plato (429–347 BCE), speaking through Socrates, answers Glaucon's challenge in a way that will become common in ancient Greek philosophy: ethical conduct benefits the just person not simply through its consequences, but in itself. Justice realizes order and health in the soul, whereas injustice creates disorder and disarray. Ethical people are at one and at peace with themselves in ways the unethical cannot be.

We find versions of this same underlying idea in Aristotle (384–322 BCE) as well as post-Aristotelian philosophers like the Stoics. Aristotle holds that human beings have a distinctive nature, as do all natural creatures, and function well and prosper only when they realize this nature. What distinguishes human nature is the capacity for virtuous activity, so humans realize their nature and flourish when they engage in virtuous activity for its own sake. The Stoics advance a more extreme version of the idea that ethical conduct is intrinsically beneficial. Virtue, they hold, is the only human good (Aristotle 2009).

Glaucon's challenge is not, however, the only criticism of justice (more broadly, of ethics and morality) that Socrates confronts in the *Republic*. Thrasymachus poses an even more radical challenge, arguing that "justice" is simply a label the powerful use for self-sacrificing conduct of the less powerful that is in the interest of the strong. There really is no reason to act other than self-interest, but the powerful speak as though there were, using the term to induce the weak to act against their own real interests and benefit the strong. Socrates's response to this more radical challenge is no different than his response to Glaucon. Whatever one's position of relative power, justice and virtue benefit one intrinsically.

Two things are notable about these ancient criticisms of ethics and the responses to them. First, the defenses of ethics are in terms of the agent's own good. Contrary to claims like Glaucon's and Thrasymachus's, the defenders argue that when we understand the true nature of virtue and our good or interest, respectively, we see that we do not simply *do good* when we act ethically but also *live well* – we realize a life that benefits us most as the kind of creature we are. Justice and virtue are what a good life for human beings involves. Second, ancient critics and defenders seem both to accept that no ethical idea or principle – justice, for example – can provide any reasons to act that are independent of the agent's good. According to Thrasymachus, the strong do indeed speak of justice as though it provided such reasons to the weak to act against their own real interest. But Thrasymachus holds that there really are no such reasons – the thought that there are is an ideology foisted on the weak by the strong. (We will want to bear this idea in mind below when we consider Nietzsche's critique of morality, which shares some of the structure of Thrasymachus's position, but turns it on its head.) And whereas Glaucon holds that the powers of normal human beings are sufficiently similar that no one can reliably impose a Thrasymachean ideology, what this leads people to accept is a system of sanctions and positive laws as a compromise or *modus vivendi*; they *call* this justice, but nonetheless believe that it generates no reasons for acting that are independent of the self-interested considerations created by the sanctions.

The modern conception of morality

Beginning in the seventeenth century, however, a different way of thinking about a part of ethics, at least – what philosophers have come to refer to as *morality* – began to take hold. The key idea was that morality concerns not just what is good or virtuous, but what we are *obligated*, and would be wrong not, to do. Moral obligations involve a distinctive form of responsibility, moreover: we are *accountable* for complying with them in a way we are not for being virtuous or for avoiding (at least some) vice. When we do wrong without excuse, we act *culpably*; we are worthy not merely of disesteem, as, for example, when we gluttonously fail to exercise the ancient virtue of moderation, but of moral blame. From our own point of view, what seems warranted is not, or at least, not simply, shame, but *guilt*. We seem to have violated a kind of law, but one that transcends the actual laws or customs of any society or jurisdiction in which we merely happen to live.

Finally, moral obligations also purport to bind us whether or not it is in our interest to comply with them. Immanuel Kant (1724–1804) famously put the point by saying that moral obligations are *categorical imperatives* (1998). Unlike *hypothetical imperatives*, which tell us what to do in order to realize our aims or interests, and which can give us reasons only "hypothetically," from the perspective of those aims or interests, the moral law obligates and gives us reasons to act whether or not doing so promotes our aims or interests.

Suppose, for example, that we think we are morally obligated not to use torture to try to extract valuable information from someone suspected of terrorism. We need not consider whether this would actually be morally wrong. Just imagine that we believe that it is. What would we then believe? Whether it would be disadvantageous to use torture – say, because of the unreliability of information we would thereby gain or because others might disapprove of us and withdraw their cooperation from us or even because of the intrinsic benefits of relating to others in ways that exclude torture – is one question. Whether we would thereby fall short of our own standards and so act in an ignoble or base way, would be another. But neither would be the very same issue we would take a stand on in thinking that torture violates a moral obligation. Whether we would benefit from such an act of torture or not, we might think, it would nonetheless be wrong and therefore something we should not do, however beneficial it might be. And if, believing this, we were to engage in torture, we would be committed to thinking that there would be warrant to be held responsible and blamed, if only in our own and others' thought and feelings, for example, through feeling guilt ourselves. We would not just have fallen short of some optional standard of noble conduct; we would see ourselves as morally *required* not to torture and therefore as rightly held answerable for not doing so.

These are the distinctive elements of morality as philosophers have sought to defend it (or indeed, like Nietzsche, to criticize it) in what we generally call the "modern" period beginning in the seventeenth century with the modern natural law tradition of Hugo Grotius, Samuel Pufendorf, Hobbes, and Locke. The two major systematic approaches that followed – utilitarian, and more generally consequentialist theories deriving from Bentham and Mill in the nineteenth century, on the one hand, and so-called deontological approaches inspired either by Kant's ideas or by "intuitionist" theories, according to which acts can be self-evidently morally obligatory or wrong simply in themselves, on the other – have by and large shared a common conception of the part of ethics they have been attempting respectively to articulate and defend: Morality consists of a set of norms (or "laws") that are universally binding on all moral agents and which are all responsible for complying with whether or not it is in their interest to do so.

Perhaps the most philosophically acute utilitarian, Henry Sidgwick (1838–1900), remarked that a central difference between ancient Greek ethical thought and "the modern ethical view" is that whereas the ancients took there to be but one fundamental ethical standard – the agent's own good or happiness – modern moral philosophy holds that morality provides a source of reasons that is independent of the agent's own good (Sidgwick 1967: 198). One can look at things from one's own perspective and view them in terms of one's own interest, however inclusive that might be, including whatever intrinsic benefits moral conduct might bring one, on the one hand, or from the "moral point of view," on the other. From the latter standpoint, we are simply one person (or perhaps creature) among others, with needs, interests, and aims no more important or worthy of consideration than those of any other.

Whether or not they agree with ancients like Plato and Aristotle about the intrinsic benefits of the ethical life, modern moral philosophers have been inclined to believe that complying with moral requirements is unlikely to coincide with the agent's interest in every case, and that, whether it does or does not, a moral obligation is a different kind of normative consideration than self-interest. As H. A. Prichard (1912) famously put it, to attempt to argue to a moral obligation on the grounds that compliance is in the agent's interest is to "rest" one's moral philosophy "on a mistake." As in our example of torture above, considerations of self-interest provide a justification of the wrong kind for a moral obligation. That it is imprudent to torture is one thing; that it is wrong is quite another.

By and large, modern moral philosophers have agreed with Glaucon's analysis of the relation between justice (or moral obligation, as they understand it) and agents' interests. Complying with moral obligations, and the consequences for everyone of everyone's compliance or failure to comply, frequently has the same structure as the famous game theory example, a prisoner's dilemma. Suppose, as in a prisoner's dilemma, only two people, *A* and *B*, are involved and that they have made an agreement to exchange certain items, say, a pound of flour for a pound of sugar. *A* and *B* make the agreement because they value, respectively, having another pound of flour or sugar more than retaining all of the sugar and flour with which they begin. It is thus in the interest of each to make the agreement, but is it in the interest of each to keep it? Assume that what each does is causally independent of the other's act and that neither has any way of retaliating against a failure to keep the agreement. It seems clear that this does not affect the moral obligation of *A* and *B* to keep their agreement. Whether or not it is in their interest to keep the agreement, it seems that *A* and *B* are morally obligated to do so (if the other does). Still, both *A* and *B* would benefit most if the other kept the agreement and they did not. *A* would be better off if he could keep his sugar and *also* get a pound of *B*'s flour, and similarly, with appropriate changes, for *B*.

Of course, if we invariably benefit most from acting justly, as Plato and Aristotle believe, then this will not be the case. But even if this were invariably true, we can hardly rely upon being able to persuade others that it is. This seemed especially to be so to philosophers of the early modern period who had experienced violent civil wars, such as the English Civil War in England and the Wars of Religion in France, in which fundamental disagreements of faith seemed to undermine the possibility of finding a basis of social order in controversial visions of the good life, whether sectarian or secular, like that of the ancient Greeks.

There are then four possible scenarios, which we can represent in the matrix seen in Figure 45.1, using K for "keeps agreement" and NK for "does not keep agreement." The number pairs represent the four outcomes, with the first and second numbers referring, respectively, to A's and B's preferential ordering of the outcome ("1" being best, "4" being worst), respectively, A's being on the left and B's on the right.

Thus *A* does best if he doesn't keep the agreement and *B* does, and worst if he keeps the agreement and *B* doesn't. A's second best outcome is when both keep the agreement, and his third best results from both not keeping the agreement. *B*'s situation is the mirror image of A's: she does best when she doesn't keep the agreement and *B* does, and so on. The game theoretic situation then is identical to a prisoner's dilemma. If, for example, *A* is considering whether to keep the agreement, then it seems clear that not keeping it is the rational choice in light of his interests. Again, we are assuming that what *B* will do is causally independent of what *A* does and that this is a "one shot" situation with no future ramifications beyond the above results in this instance. We can then reason as follows. *B* will either keep the agreement (K) or not (NK). If *B* keeps the agreement, then *A* will have done better by not keeping it, since he thereby gets his first- rather than

A \ B	K	NK
K	(2,2)	(4,1)
NK	(1,4)	(3,3)

Figure 45.1 Values of the outcomes of *A*'s and *B*'s choices in a prisoner's dilemma. Note: K = keeps agreement; NK = does not keep agreement.

his second-ranked outcome. Similarly, if *B* doesn't keep the agreement, *A* will have done better by not keeping the agreement, since he will then get his third- rather than his fourth-ranked outcome. Since *B* must do one or the other, *A* will do better by not keeping the agreement whatever *B* does.

However, the situation is exactly the same for *B*. The very same reasoning that convinced us that *A*'s most rational choice in light of his interests is not to keep the agreement, should convince us that not keeping the agreement is the most rational choice for *B* in light of her interests also. But notice now the upshot. If both *A* and *B* do what is most rational in terms of their interests and do not keep the agreement, then both end up with their third-ranked outcome. Both could have ended up better off, with their second-ranked rather than their third-ranked outcome, if they had both kept the agreement. So both do worse if both do what is most rational in light of their own individual interests.

The consequence is that if both had available a way of thinking about their decision, according to which they had reason to keep the agreement whether or not it was in their interest to do so, and had acted on this understanding, then they would both have ended up better off than they do when each pursues his or her self-interest independently. But that is precisely what the idea that they are morally obligated to keep their agreements gives them. It gives them a reason to act as they agreed whether or not it is in their interest to do so. When they both regard themselves as having a conclusive moral reason to keep the agreement, because they are morally obligated, whether or not it is in their interest to do so, they end up promoting the interests of each better.

We have been using a specific example, but a little reflection shows that a similar structure holds with many things we think we are morally obligated to do – helping others in need, telling the truth, and so on. So understood, moral conduct involves a form of reciprocally beneficial cooperation, even when it does not necessarily seem so in the particular case at hand. Consider, for example, moral obligations concerned with truth-telling. Being truthful with others, not purposely misleading them, and so on, is a form of reciprocally beneficial cooperation. Each of us should be prepared to accept the burdens of truth-telling even when it is not in our interest to be honest (of course, within certain domains consistently with retaining a space of privacy, etc.) if that is the cost of others' being truthful with us in their turn; everyone's interest, including one's own, is promoted better if we do.

This may seem to get us no farther than Glaucon. So long as *A* sees himself as having reason to keep his agreement, or one sees oneself as having reason to tell the truth or help others in need, only because it is in *A*'s or one's interests so to see things, then the idea of moral obligation seems no more than a *modus vivendi* or second-best compromise. This defines what might fairly be considered the central problem of moral philosophy. So long as we take Glaucon's position and begin with self-interest, we cannot think our way into the moral point of view. So what grounds morality and moral obligation?

Starting with individual self-interest enables everyone to see that everyone would be better off if all accepted the idea of moral obligation as independently valid and governed themselves by it in situations like those mentioned above. But as Prichard pointed out, there simply is no way of coming to the conclusion that we actually are morally obligated, that moral obligations *validly* constrain self-interest, from premises about our own interest. From the fact that it would be better for me, or for all of us, if we all saw ourselves as morally obligated, it simply cannot follow that we actually are thus obligated. Alternatively, if we start within the moral point of view and take moral obligations at face value and think therefore that there are conclusive reasons to act as we are morally obligated regardless of our individual interest, what guarantees us that these reasons actually exist in fact? What can convince us that the moral point of view is normatively valid, that the reasons for acting that it purports to provide actually exist in fact?

These are the issues with which moral philosophers have wrestled ever since the ideas of morality and moral obligation came to be systematically articulated, beginning in the seventeenth century. One way of putting one of them is in terms of Sidgwick's famous "dualism of practical reason." It seems that we can view our practical lives *either* from our own perspectives as individual agents, seeing things in relation to ourselves and our own overall interest or good, *or* we can view them from an impartial perspective in which we are simply one among others (the moral point of view). Sidgwick claimed that neither perspective is any more intrinsically rational than the other. And no argument exists to get us from one standpoint to the other. There is no argument from premises concerning what will promote one's own good or interest to any conclusion about moral obligation. Likewise, no argument beginning with moral premises seems to lead to rational prudence.

As Sidgwick saw it, the central problem moral philosophers faced once they departed from the ancient idea that happiness or the agent's good is the only fundamental normative standard was that of properly integrating the moral and the prudential points of view and somehow avoiding the consequence that practical reason is not in some kind of irresolvable incoherence when these perspectives conflict. This way of framing the issues takes morality and moral obligation at face value. Philosophers in the modern period have not, however, generally been willing to do that, no doubt because the dialectical situation in which modern moral philosophy begins is one in which its distinctive conception of morality must be defended against the ancient idea that prudence, or as Sidgwick puts it, "egoistic reason" provides the "one regulative and governing faculty" (Sidgwick 1967: 198) (It is an interesting feature of both ancient and modern philosophical discussion that it takes for granted that the agent's own good provides valid reasons for acting. If, however, the reason-giving force of morality can be coherently doubted, so also can that of the agent's good or interest.)

Morality's critics

In any event, the attempt to establish the normative authority of morality has been a central preoccupation of defenders of the modern conception of morality. Critics have argued that nothing could possibly have the kind of authority that moral obligations purport to have. Before we consider the various kinds of defense of morality that philosophers have attempted to provide it may be useful to rehearse, first, some of the central criticisms.

Surely the most radical critique of morality was put forward in the nineteenth century by Friedrich Nietzsche (1844–1900). Like Thrasymachus, Nietzsche argued that morality is an ideology rooted in power (Nietzsche 2006). But Nietzsche's version is developed with enormous subtlety and power, and he turns Thrasymachus's claim that justice is an ideology imposed by the strong on its head. The powerful have no need for subterfuge; after all, they are powerful. To the contrary, Nietzsche argues that the modern idea, that all persons are subject to a universal moral law that all are accountable for complying with, is an illusion that a "priestly caste" who represent the weak advance to subdue the strong.

There are three distinct strands to Nietzsche's critique. The first concerns the "genealogy" of moral ideas, which Nietzsche claims arise as a response to and subconscious replacement for the weak's self-hatred owing to their lower status and their "ressentiment" in reaction to the disregard of the strong. The second is a philosophical critique, namely, that the idea of a moral law necessarily presupposes free will and a fundamental equality and that neither hold. And the third is an ethical critique: moral "values" amount to a denial of natural, life-affirming values; it is literally unhealthy to internalize and try to live by them. To see the force of this last idea, consider qualities we normally admire and wish to emulate in others (at least when we are not in the grip of moral ideas), such as intelligence, beauty, strength, psychic security, generosity, charm, and so on. These qualities are all naturally good, and the weak are not simply less powerful than the strong; they are, Nietzsche thinks, less highly regarded because they are deficient in these qualities. Homeric heroes may be closer to Nietzsche's ideal, but the basic value scheme he describes is not too dissimilar from Aristotle's.

The weak begrudge the strong their position and hate themselves on account of their own impotence. They cannot, however, deal with this directly, for example, by taking out their anger on the strong or by changing their own less valuable qualities. So they respond indirectly, by repressing personal anger and hatred and transforming it subconsciously into a kind of impersonal anger and hatred towards the powerful and the characteristics that make them so. These new impersonal sentiments give rise to new concepts. In the place of the original contrast between "good" and "bad" (in the sense of estimable and contemptible: "noble" and "base"), there develop the concepts of moral good and *evil*. The very features that were originally seen as noble, as objects of a kind of warranted natural esteem, now seem, from this new impersonal "moral" perspective, morally evil. The powerful are "to blame" for their contemptuous treatment of the weak.

The distinctively moral idea that all are answerable for complying with obligations we have as fundamentally equal moral agents does not simply have a dubious genealogy, according to Nietzsche. It also carries philosophically unsupportable presuppositions, for example, a nature-transcending free will. Finally, attempting to live with moral ideas, born in negativity and denial, inevitably saps life of health, vigor, and natural value. In successfully promulgating moral ideas, including to the strong, the weak, and their organizers, has undermined the vitality of culture and the quality of life.

Nietzsche does not call for a simple overthrow of the moral framework in favor of the earlier "aristocratic ethos" of noble and base, however. Only after individuals have lived within the moral framework can they transcend its problematic idea of responsibility, come to take *individual* responsibility for and direct their lives, and thereby become genuinely autonomous. Nietzsche's Übermensch realizes a form of individual creativity that would have been impossible for a pre-modern.

Recent philosophers have picked up and developed one or another element of Nietzsche's critique. For example, Bernard Williams argues that the orthodox conception of morality (as represented most vividly by Kant) amounts to a kind of obsession that threatens to consume all of life and alienate us from the individual projects that give meaning to human life (Williams 1985). And Annette Baier maintains that law-based moral conceptions (again, especially Kantian ones) that are tied to the distinctive form of moral responsibility mentioned above flirt with sadomasochism (Baier 1993). It is better, she argues, to take inspiration from virtue ethics of the kind advanced by David Hume (1711–76). Hume is of course a modern writer, but like the ancients, he stresses virtue over right and is profoundly skeptical of the modern distinction between moral standards that essentially concern the will, e.g., moral obligation, and broader forms of ethical criticism of thought and feeling that may not be subject to voluntary control. What Hume calls "moral sentiments" are actually a broader form of ethical esteem; and when self-directed, the negative version is closer to shame than to guilt.

The relation between virtue ethics and theories of moral right and wrong, such as utilitarianism and Kantianism, has been vigorously debated during the past fifty years. In a famous paper, "Modern Moral Philosophy," published in 1958, Elizabeth Anscombe argued that the modern conception of morality is philosophically unsupportable and should be replaced with a virtue ethics of the sort found in Aristotle (Anscombe 1958). Anscombe stressed the very juridical elements emphasized above – the moral law along with its companion notions of moral blame and responsibility. She argued that there can be no law without a legislator and, therefore, that the only coherent way of grounding moral obligation would be in divine commands. Some seventeenth-century natural lawyers, like Pufendorf and Locke, were indeed theological voluntarists, but modern moral philosophers, perhaps especially those of our own period, have not been. But this means, according to Anscombe, that they thereby reject the only coherent foundations for their subject.

Some proponents of an ethics of virtue, like Anscombe, propose it as a replacement for philosophical accounts of morality, indeed, for the very concept of morality itself. But some advance virtue ethics not to supplant morality, but, as we might say, to "put morality in its place." The ethical life concerns far more than moral requirements and obligations. Important questions of value and virtue, about what to want, feel, think, and do, arise in broad areas of life that are morally optional – not in the sense that there aren't good reasons, even good moral reasons, at issue, but where our moral obligations do not settle the question. So understood, virtue ethics poses no direct threat to morality, and morality's defenders have nothing to fear from it. They should simply agree that it is possible to be overly consumed with moral obligation to the exclusion of other important ethical questions. Nonetheless, they also do well to bear in mind a point Kant insisted on, namely, that it is no less possible (or depressingly familiar) to evade our moral duty and rationalize failure to comply with it by focusing on how good (enough) we are overall (especially, in relation to others).

Defending morality

What would a fully adequate philosophical account of the modern conception of morality and moral obligation look like? What kind of an account is required? Some philosophers employ the strategy John Rawls calls "philosophy as defense." They attempt no positive philosophical foundation or account, arguing that the most we can do is to defend morality against specific criticisms. To try to do more is not only unnecessary, they argue; it can be positively misleading or confused. It can risk giving a reason of the wrong kind, for example, by trying to argue, as Prichard warned us against, that we are morally obligated because we would have happier lives if we so saw ourselves. Perhaps we would, but that can hardly establish that what we take to be moral obligations are genuinely binding on us in the way we take them to be.

Other philosophers attempt to provide a justification of the "right kind" that can avoid the pitfall to which Prichard pointed. The most famous and influential is Kant's argument, and arguments deriving from his, that any rational agent is committed to the moral law by presuppositions that she must accept to deliberate coherently at all (Korsgaard 1996). In my view, such arguments inevitably fail because they cannot capture the distinctive element of responsibility or accountability that is an ineliminable aspect of the concept of obligation. What commits us to this idea, as I see it, is not agency, pure and simple, but *interagency*, that is, making claims on one another's will as we inevitably do in interacting with one another (Darwall 2006). An argument of this kind offers the hope of defending the distinctive law-like aspect of moral obligation that has been under attack by critics from Nietzsche to Anscombe. What we are morally obligated to do is indeed what we are accountable for doing, but this idea does not require the premise of theological voluntarism, that is, a fundamental answerability to God that the weak perhaps project through *ressentiment*. Rather, moral obligations derive from a fundamental accountability we have to one another and to ourselves, an equal authority we have as persons to make claims on and demands of one another.

See also Kant (Chapter 14); Nietzsche (Chapter 18).

References

Anscombe, G. E. M. (1958) "Modern Moral Philosophy," *Philosophy* 33: 1–19.
Aristotle (2009) *Nicomachean Ethics*, trans. David Ross, ed. Lesley Brown, New York: Oxford University Press.
Baier, Annette (1993) "Moralism and Cruelty: Reflections on Hume and Kant," *Ethics* 103: 436–57.
Darwall, Stephen (2006) *The Second-Person Standpoint: Morality, Respect, and Accountability*, Cambridge, MA: Harvard University Press.
Hume, David (2000) *A Treatise of Human Nature*, ed. David Fate Norton and Mary J. Norton, Oxford: Oxford University Press.
Kant, Immanuel (1998) *Groundwork of the Metaphysics of Morals*, ed. Mary Gregor, intro. Christine Korsgaard, Cambridge: Cambridge University Press.
Nietzsche, Friedrich (2006) *On the Genealogy of Morals*, ed. Keith Ansell-Pearson, trans. Carol Diethe, Cambridge: Cambridge University Press.
Plato (2006) *The Republic*, trans. Benjamin Jowett, Mineola, NY: Dover.
Prichard, H. A. (1912) "Does Moral Philosophy Rest on a Mistake?," *Mind*, n.s. 21: 21–37.
Sidgwick, Henry (1967) *The Methods of Ethics*, 7th edn, London: Macmillan.
Williams, Bernard (1985) *Ethics and the Limits of Philosophy*, Cambridge, MA: Harvard University Press.

Further reading

Baier, Annette C. (1993) "Moralism and Cruelty: Reflections on Hume and Kant," *Ethics* 103, no. 3: 436–57.
Nietzsche, Friedrich (2006) *On the Genealogy of Morals*, ed. Keith Ansell-Pearson, trans. Carol Diethe, Cambridge: Cambridge University Press.
Williams, Bernard (1985) *Ethics and the Limits of Philosophy*, Cambridge, MA: Harvard University Press.

46
CONSCIENCE

John Skorupski

Neither the notion of conscience, nor the special importance we place on it, is evident in the moral thinking of all societies. The word "conscience" (from Latin, *conscientia*) originally included in its meaning what we now call "consciousness" and "self-consciousness." It is only in the seventeenth century that it came to be complemented, in English, by these terms, and distinguished in meaning from them. "Conscience" acquired its specialized moral meaning, while its other meanings became obsolete. An influential text in this respect was Locke's *Essay Concerning Human Understanding*. Its German translator distinguished *Bewusstsein* (consciousness) from *Gewissen* (conscience). Pierre Coste, Locke's French translator, tried *conscience* for conscience and *con-science* for consciousness; but in French no such distinction of terms has caught on. (See Andrew 2001.)

Of course the lack of a distinct term does not show the lack of a concept. More would be required to prove the negative about a given society and time – that it has no notion corresponding to what we mean by conscience. One piece of evidence would be absence of philosophical discussion of the distinctive puzzles that the notion raises: absence of such discussion in the ancient world, particularly in light of its philosophical sophistication, is telling. In contrast, philosophical questions about conscience are discussed by Aquinas and other medieval philosophers and theologians (Langston 2008). The hypothesis that *conscience*, in roughly the way we understand it, first acquires salience through Christianity, and rises to a position of special importance with the growth of Protestant and then secular individualism, is at least plausible.

Puzzles about conscience

The special importance that conscience has come to have in modern ethics is both moral and political. To consider conscientiously what moral obligations one may have, and then to act in accordance with that conviction, is taken to be a mark of moral seriousness, perhaps a duty. More strongly, there is the doctrine that one has a moral obligation to act in accordance with one's conscience.

These views in turn are thought to have a political consequence: conscientious objection, or civil disobedience, should be respected and regarded – within much debated limits – as a right.

But we soon run into puzzles, both about the presumed obligation to act in accordance with one's conscience and about the presumed rights of conscientious objection. As to the first, the question is, can I be mistaken in my conscientious conviction as to what I ought to do? Suppose I can be and am. In that case it is false that I ought to do what I conscientiously believe that I ought to do, or again false that something my conscience tells me is permissible is indeed permissible. In general, to say that my conscience errs is to say that something it tells me is obligatory, or permissible, is not so. Hence, if I ought always do what my conscience tells me I ought to do, then my conscience cannot err. And this doctrine seems both implausible, and in social and political terms, potentially dangerous.

At this point we might want to distinguish between what my conscience *really* tells me and what I think, however sincerely, that it tells me. But can we make anything of this distinction? If, alternatively, we simply accept that conscience can be wrong, then why do we place as much emphasis as we do on respecting a person's conscience?

Directly related difficulties arise with conscientious objection. Suppose I am a conscientious pacifist. I refuse to be conscripted. But, in fact, the war we are engaged in is a just war, and fairness requires that I should play my part in fighting it. My conscientious conviction that all participation in war is morally wrong is erroneous. Why then should society acknowledge it as having any special standing? Why should it give me any special status as a conscientious objector? If I am right, none of my fellow citizens should engage in this war. But if I am wrong, I should engage in it along with others. So either society should not have embarked on this war in the first place, or alternatively it should require me to take part in it as a matter of fairness to others, since the costs of a common burden that we are obliged to take up should be fairly distributed amongst all of us.

Or consider someone who carries out a political assassination directed, at least according to his own sincere conviction, by the demands of his conscience. Must we conclude that he did what he ought to have done? On the contrary, common sense says that he may have been wrong. It is, for example, one thing to kill a tyrant, another to kill a democratically elected politician in a state whose democratic institutions continue to function well. Should someone who does the latter, however sincerely he believes himself to be justified, not have known better? Could it really be his conscience that was telling him to do that?

Apart from these questions in moral philosophy, there are also more pragmatically political issues. May not an excessive respect for conscientious objection produce anarchy? Is it not dangerous to give free rein to the conscientious convictions of all, when we know how bizarre such convictions can turn out to be?

And when should a person with a conscientious conviction as to what is right acknowledge and accept a majority's view that it is wrong? May not a person of rock-like integrity be a danger to his or her fellows? Can integrity lead to irresponsibility? It is not surprising that philosophers interested in both ethics and politics have reflected on these questions – Hobbes and Locke with the English civil war in mind, Kant and Hegel with the French revolution and its aftermath.

Two conceptions of conscience

It will be useful before going further to distinguish two conceptions of conscience: as (A) *self-judgement* and as (B) the, or a, *source of moral knowledge*.

According to A, conscience is the power of judging whether what we have done, or are thinking of doing, is in accordance with what we believe to be right. On this conception conscience is not thought of as itself a way of knowing what *is* right. We come to know what is right in some other way.

This conception of conscience fits with the fact that the word "conscience" could originally refer to what we have come to separate off as (self-)consciousness. For, on this conception, moral conscience is consciousness of one's moral convictions on the one hand and one's actions on the other, and thus knowledge of whether one's actions accord with one's convictions. Conscience judges one's actions in the light of one's convictions.

Conception B is more ambitious; here conscience is thought of as the power of knowing what is right and wrong. It is the faculty of moral knowledge, the faculty whereby we know for ourselves what is right, without having to rely on the testimony of others.

B is likely to include A. For if we think of conscience as the faculty of moral knowledge, we can include the capacity to judge oneself in accordance with that knowledge under the notion of conscience too. But A may not include B. For conception B involves the individualistic idea that to have a conscience is to be able to know for oneself, by one's own personal insight, what is right and wrong. Someone might deny that everyone has that power, or any great degree of it, while still accepting that everyone has or can have a conscience in sense A. They might hold, for example, that most people have to rely on others for their knowledge of right and wrong.

On either of these conceptions, the question arises of what role conscience plays in practical deliberation and how it gives rise to action. For we think of conscience not just as a source of knowledge – be it of oneself and one's convictions or also of morality as such – but also as a motivator of action.

One might think of conscience as simply the power of one's moral beliefs to make one act. Some philosophers would reject this on the grounds that beliefs alone cannot make one act. However, even if one holds that beliefs about what one should do often straightforwardly cause action, this purely intellectualist picture of conscience seems a bad one. For what we call conscience clearly has deep emotional constituents; it is, or includes, as John Stuart Mill nicely put it,

> a feeling in our own mind; a pain, more or less intense, attendant on violation of duty, which in properly cultivated moral natures rises, in the more serious cases, into shrinking from it as an impossibility. This feeling, when disinterested, and connecting itself with the pure idea of duty … is the essence of Conscience; though in that complex phenomenon as it actually exists, the simple fact is in general all encrusted over with collateral associations, derived from sympathy, from love, and still more from fear; from all the forms of religious feeling; from the recollections of childhood and of all our past life; from self-esteem, desire of the esteem of others, and occasionally even self-abasement.
>
> (Mill 1969/1861: 228)

Thus a fuller statement of conception A would be as follows. Conscience is the power of seeing into what our moral convictions really are, and how they apply to our actions – as against the tendency to deceive ourselves, when convenient, about what they are and how they apply to what we do. It is also an associated emotional force – of aversion to a contemplated action, or remorse after doing it – that is released by that self-insight, perhaps even when we try to deceive ourselves. It is the ability to judge honestly of one's convictions and their application, together with the emotional disposition that makes it difficult to act against them once one has recognized what they are.

Conception A says nothing about the sources of moral knowledge. Religion may claim to find them in a book, a great religious teacher, the teaching of the church, or a knowledge of God's law that is implanted in human beings by God. Christianity has taken all these approaches. They are consistent with a certain moral individualism and egalitarianism, but also with a certain collectivism and hierarchy, depending on which of these sources of moral authority are stressed. We get to the latter if we stress the moral authority of Christian doctrine as developed over time by bishops and theologians. We get to the former if we stress that anyone can know the teaching of Christ as recorded in the New Testament. However, it is a universal Christian teaching that all human beings have a capacity for moral knowledge implanted by God, taking the form not of revelation but of natural reason. That already generates a tendency, or at least leaves an opening, towards individualism and egalitarianism about moral agency.

Autonomy

This idea of natural reason as a faculty of moral knowledge raises a fundamental issue. What is it that is known? Does natural reason tell us what God lays down that we ought to do, or does it itself, directly, tell us what we ought to do? The very idea of natural *reason* seems to point in the latter direction. Reason is an independent power by which we can test what anyone, divine or human, tells us we ought to do. As Kant famously put it,

> Even the Holy One of the gospel must first be compared with our ideal of moral perfection before we can recognise him as such ... where do we get the concept of God as the highest good? Solely from the *Idea* of moral perfection which reason traces *a priori*.
>
> (Kant 1949/1785: 76)

It is our reason alone, Kant thinks, that tells us what is good, and it is through our ability to apply for ourselves the test of our own reason that we know God to be good. If someone replies that "good" just means "what God tells us to do" then reason can ask why we should do what is good, i.e. what God tells us to do. If, that is, the moral law is simply by definition God's law, we can ask how we know that what God tells us we ought to do is what we ought to do. A religious fideist may shrink from this as an unacceptable question. From a logical point of view, however, it merely rejects a conception of morality as positive command. God or society may command that we act in accord with moral principles, and we ourselves – as "self-legislators" – may command ourselves to do so. Yet, as Kant also put it, no one is the *author* of these moral principles. Their *validity* does not depend on the command of God, or of oneself, or on the prescriptions and conventions of society.

The basic insight here is the "open question challenge." Whoever has laid down a law, I can ask myself whether it is right for me to follow that law. The answer may of course be affirmative; but it is my own reason that tells me it is, if it is. In contrast, it is held, the principles of morality do not admit of that question. If one accepts that an action is morally obligatory, one has already answered whether it is right to do it. Given this point, it is easy to see how an emphasis on telling for oneself develops. It becomes natural to think that having a conscience is being able to tell for oneself, through one's own insight, what is morally right and wrong.

Such insight might be, as rationalists think, the power of pure reason, or it might be, as sentimentalists think, a capacity that is rooted in sentiment or emotional intelligence: a capacity to judge of right feeling. The question of the sources of moral knowledge has been a major debate in modern Western ethics. But the important point to note, for our purposes, is the progress an individualistic conception of moral knowledge has made in the modern world – whether such knowledge is thought of as based in "reason" or "sentiment." In J. B. Schneewind's terms (1998), there has been a great shift over a long period from the "command model" of morality to the "self-governance model."

Accompanying this progress of moral individualism has been a progress of moral egalitarianism. It is a legacy of Christianity that has not faded away, even as the idea that morality is God's law fades away. Post-Christian moral theorizing (which is what most philosophical – and even much theological – theorizing about morality has been since the Enlightenment) has tended to be individualist and egalitarian. An assault on this conception of morality has come to seem an assault on morality itself.

Yet clearly there is also the possibility that true moral insight is a capacity of the few – that the great majority derive their knowledge of right and wrong from others, whether through religious teaching or in some other way. This is consistent with a conception of conscience in sense A. It is consistent with a conception in which the distinctive "pains" associated with conscience, which give the ordinary person a moral compass, are not required by enlightened or rational persons, who act simply from what they see to be right.

In Kant and Mill the idea of conscience seems to be somewhere on the road between A and B. When Kant writes specifically about *conscience*, his conception of it is conception A. Your conscience is infallible only in the sense that you can always tell, by careful self-scrutiny, whether your own past or proposed actions are in line with your own sincere convictions as to what is right. At the same time, however, Kant is a main source of the individualist and egalitarian conception of moral knowledge. The ability to tell for yourself what your moral obligations are, and to act on that knowledge, is what Kant means by *autonomy*, and it is important to him that every human being is absolutely autonomous. One could say that his conception of conscience looks back to some earlier notions of conscience, while his conception of autonomy looks forward.

John Stuart Mill might also be thought to have a somewhat "enlightenment" as against "romantic" conception of conscience, along the lines of A. He takes the utility principle to be the basis of ethics; he thinks of morality as a set of rules that have socially evolved to regulate society for the greater good, but which it may be necessary to revise in the light of the utility principle and up-to-date social science. On this view conscience becomes a psychological resource which is educable in line with enlightened moral principles, but not itself the *source* of our knowledge of these principles. Yet there is also a strong underlying emphasis in Mill's more political writing on the importance of personal moral responsibility, including, it seems, deciding for oneself as to moral rightness. This may be the deepest underlying tension between his utilitarianism and his liberalism.

Conscience and the self

At any rate the B conception of conscience has come to be a dominant force in late-modern ethics. It is a conception of morality as autonomy, or personal integrity, as somehow bound up with one's self-identity. Here are some eloquent statements of this conception. The first is from Hegel:

> Conscience ... is that deepest inner solitude within oneself in which all externals and all limitation have disappeared – it is a total withdrawal into the self. As conscience, the human being is no longer bound by the ends of particularity [i.e. his or her particular interests], so that conscience represents an exalted point of view, a point of view of the modern world, which has for the first time attained this consciousness, this descent into the self. Earlier and more sensuous ages have before them something external and given, whether this be religion or right; but [my] conscience knows itself as thought, and that this thought of mine is my sole source of obligation.
>
> (Hegel 1991/1820: 163 –4)

Note how Hegel connects this conception of conscience with "the modern world," how he equates conscience with "descent into the self," and with the apparent subjectivism of, "this thought of mine is my sole source of obligation." This apparent subjectivism seems even clearer in the following passage:

> *Conscience* expresses the absolute entitlement of subjective self-consciousness to know *in itself* and *from itself* what right and duty are, and to recognise only what it thus knows as the good; it also consists in the assertion that what it thus knows and wills is *truly* right and duty.
>
> (*Ibid.*: 164)

Consider also these representative passages from Heidegger:

> The call of conscience has the character of an appeal to *Dasein* [the distinctively human way of being] by calling it to its ownmost potentiality-for-Being-its-Self. ... Conscience summons Dasein's Self from its lostness in the "they". ... *In conscience Dasein calls itself.* ... "It" calls, against our expectations and even against our will. On the other hand, the call undoubtedly does not come from someone else who is with me in the world. The call comes *from* me and yet *from beyond me.*
>
> (Heidegger 1962/1927: 314, 319 and 320)

Again conscience is withdrawal into the self, this time from "lostness in the 'they'" – that is, the pressures and expectations of the crowd. The apparently subjectivist implication is problematized: "The call comes *from* me and yet *from beyond me.*"

Both Hegel and Heidegger connect conscience with freedom, and freedom with being at one with one's true self. They also both connect it with guilt or at least loss of innocence – awareness of the possibility of doing evil – seeing this as an existential condition of being human. And they think that this existential condition, openness to good and evil, in turn constitutes the freedom and dignity of human being and makes self-governance a "right." This combination of ideas remains a powerful modern conception of the self. Various aspects of it could be examined, but we shall focus on its epistemology, where Hegel will again be a guide.

The epistemology of conscience

At the root of this modern doctrine of conscience is what we can call the *principle of individual moral insight*, or *insight principle* for short: all of us have the power to arrive, by conscientious moral reflection, at our own first-personal knowledge of what is morally right or wrong. We may misuse this power or fail to use it, but we all have it. Careful enough reflection always suffices for moral knowledge. Thus if I come to the wrong conclusion, it must be that I have not thought carefully or sincerely enough. Conscience considered as a faculty of moral knowledge is infallible, though I am not.

Does this insight principle entail moral subjectivism? To see the issue, compare conscience and moral knowledge with perception and perceptual knowledge. In both cases there can be damage to the faculty that gives one that knowledge. Just as one's eyesight or hearing may be damaged in some way, so presumably one's moral faculty may be damaged, say by brain injury or mental illness. In both cases some internal malfunctioning of one's cognitive powers, moral or perceptual, can occur. However, perception is also fallible in *another*, purely external, way, even when it is functioning perfectly well, and the perceiver is making rational judgements on its basis. The light may be poor, atmospheric conditions may distort looks and sounds, etc. Perceptually based judgements are inherently fallible because of these external factors. My perceptual and rational powers may be working faultlessly, and yet I may still reach false conclusions.

Is there any analogue in the case of conscience? Can a sincere conviction, reached without fault, be wrong? The kind of realism that we take for granted about the objects of perception creates the possibility of a purely external mismatch. If it had some analogue in the case of moral knowledge, there would be a similar possibility. But the principle of individual moral insight precludes this possibility: it holds that conscience is infallible in a way that perception is not.

How then can my faculty of conscience be infallible, unless what *makes it true* that an act is morally wrong is that when I conscientiously reflect, it seems to me to be wrong? The insight principle seems to lead to this subjectivism about morality. (One could add that subjectivism then supports a vulgarized "right of conscience": if morality is just a matter of my own convictions, then it's for me to decide what I should do.)

This was the prime issue that concerned Hegel in his classic discussion of conscience. He fully recognized, as we have seen, the individualist modern emphasis on conscience, but he thought conscience could not function in abstraction from the moral common sense of the community. The interplay between conscience and community is crucial to his whole conception of modern morality. Modern morality is the morality of "self-governance," not "obedience," to be sure – but an individual cannot come to moral knowledge outside the context of a shared moral tradition, which provides him with a supporting point even when he is opposed to it. There is a difference between coming to know *for* yourself – i.e. without indoctrination, group pressure, or uncritical acceptance of some positive law – and coming to know *by* yourself. The idea that the latter is possible involves a mistaken abstract individualism which Hegel placed at the door of Kant.

Hegel's account may correct an excessively individualist emphasis, but we can still ask: Does it lead to a kind of *collective* "subjectivism," or community-relativism, about morality? A full discussion would lead us into the metaphysics of morals. It does seem that the kind of realism that applies to perceptual knowledge cannot apply to moral knowledge; but it is by no means clear that subjectivism or relativism are the only alternatives. (This general question of meta-ethics is discussed in Part II of this volume.)

As regards conscience, it is a question of how to reconcile its authority with a reasonable account of moral knowledge – in particular, with proper acknowledgement of the role that discussion with others plays. Dialogue is not a one-way consultation with experts. That would be morality as obedience, not morality as self-governance. In the end you must be able to see for yourself what your moral obligations are. Yet discussion with others is often an essential route to reaching that end: to ignore it is arrogance, not integrity. Self-governance, in short, requires personal moral insight but does not imply that such insight arises only from a private source within the individual.

Ethics and politics of conscience

So a sensible account of conscience should not hold that it is always right to act in accordance with conscientious conviction. Your conviction may be conscientious yet wrong; if it is, you do the wrong thing in acting in accordance with it.

However, whether you are *blameworthy* in so acting is a distinct issue. In various ways a person may do the wrong thing without being blameworthy. Extenuating circumstances may arise, and it may be argued that conscientious conviction is one of them. (The point is recognized by Aquinas in his discussion of conscience.) Furthermore there is an important larger question: Is it not a valuable thing for people to arrive at conscientious convictions and act on them – valuable enough to outweigh the fact that they may sometimes be wrong? Is it not both a personal and social good for people to develop a habit of conscientious action, even if it sometimes leads to error? We should consider both of these points.

First, then, it seems true that you cannot blame people for acting in accordance with their conscientiously arrived at moral convictions, even when these convictions are wrong. On what basis could we blame them? By hypothesis, they have done whatever is required (by way of investigation, reflection, consultation with others) for their conviction to be fully conscientious. Thus we cannot blame them for lack of care. If we nonetheless blame them, it can only be because they should have somehow known that they were not reliable judges of the case. But they could only have known that by leaping out of their skins. Consider a person living in a community from which he derives moral convictions that he sincerely shares about the rightness of slavery. He is, by his best lights, a just and generous slave owner. He could not reasonably be expected to see that the very institution of slavery is morally flawed: he does not have the critical power to see that for himself. (Others may have that power; if so, civil disobedience on their part may be justified.) If we hold that everyone always has absolute Kantian autonomy, and hence the critical power to see for themselves the moral inadequacies of common, received opinion, then this assessment of the conscientious slave owner cannot be right. But if we give up that view, and accept that people may often have important moral blind spots, then although we hold that the conscientious slave owner engages in an immoral practice we may yet agree that he should not be blamed.

At the same time, of course, it is very difficult to judge when blameless conscientiousness falls into blameworthy stubbornness and arrogance. Consider a person who regularly says hurtful things. If he insists that he is merely being honest, that he hates hypocrisy, etc., we may well end up doubting his motives. He is kidding himself: his actions have very little to do with a campaign against hypocrisy, and quite a bit with the pleasures of cruelty. Alternatively, however, we may end up doubting his moral powers. Perhaps he lacks some element of emotional intelligence that is essential for moral competence in this sphere. That would tend to excuse him from blame.

Second, even granting that some modern ideals of conscience involve an untenable romanticism about moral agency, we surely want people to think for themselves and be as self-determining as they can be. Hence we want them to be so educated as to maximize their competence in determining moral issues for themselves. That is important in maintaining a healthy democratic moral and political order, for this kind of order requires inclusive moral discussion in which anyone's voice can be heard. It also requires reasonable acceptance by all that legitimately arrived at collective decisions should be respected by all – unless they are conscientiously held to be so unjust as to require disobedience. But if someone seriously and conscientiously concludes they are unjust, then even if they are in error we should not blame them.

The fact that a person who does the wrong thing from a conscientiously arrived at moral conviction is not blameworthy will be central to an account of civil dissent and disobedience. Of course it is not the only relevant point. There is the possibility that a dissenter is in the right, even though most people hold him to be wrong. On that assumption, the main question is how far he can justifiably take his dissent, taking into account both the costs he will impose and, in a democratic society, the *prima facie* authority of a legitimately arrived at democratic decision.

But let us suppose that the conscientious dissenter is in the wrong. If, for example, we think a war is just, then we will think that conscientious pacifist objections to taking part in it are wrong: in refusing to take part a conscientious objector is being unfair to others, even though he does not intend to be. Here the main case for toleration must be that the objector is acting from a moral conviction conscientiously arrived at, and is therefore blameless. Beyond that, there remains the importance of encouraging robust, sincere moral reflection.

Still, mere sincerity does not make your action right – it does not even make it blameless. It may well be that you should have known better. This obviously applies to particularly outrageous moral convictions, such as the well-worn case of the sincere Nazi, or the ruthless political activist who does not hesitate to kill many people for his cause. With such people we feel that either they must have been capable of seeing that what they were doing was wrong, or that their moral powers are impaired. In the latter case they are indeed to that extent morally blameless – however, that does not mean they should not be brought to trial and imprisoned. A balance of considerations is involved: considerations of deterrence, prevention and safety, as well as considerations of moral guilt. But that leads to a different topic: the philosophy of legal punishment and preventive detention.

See also Kant (Chapter 14); Hegel (Chapter 15); John Stuart Mill (Chapter 16); Nietzsche (Chapter 18); Existentialism (Chapter 20); Heidegger (Chapter 21); The open question argument (Chapter 25); Morality and its critics (Chapter 45); Justice and punishment (Chapter 57); The ethics of free speech (Chapter 64); chapters in Part II.

References

Andrew, Edward G. (2001) *Conscience and Its Critics: Protestant Conscience, Enlightenment Reason, and Modern Subjectivity*, Toronto: University of Toronto Press.

Hegel, G. W. F. (1991/1820) *Elements of the Philosophy of Right*, ed. Allen W. Wood, Cambridge: Cambridge University Press.

Heidegger, M. (1962/1927) *Being and Time*, trans. John MacQuarrie and Edward Robinson, Oxford: Blackwell.

Kant, I. (1949/1785) *Groundwork of the Metaphysics of Morals*, trans. H. J. Paton, New York: Harper & Row.

Langston, Douglas (2008) "Medieval Theories of Conscience," in Edward N. Zalta (ed.) *Stanford Encyclopedia of Philosophy* (Fall 2008 edn), <http://plato.stanford.edu/archives/fall2008/entries/conscience-medieval/>

Mill, John Stuart (1969/1861) *Utilitarianism*, in *Collected Works of John Stuart Mill*, London: Routledge, vol. 10.
Schneewind, J. B. (1998) *The Invention of Autonomy*, Cambridge: Cambridge University Press.

Further reading

Scanlon, T. M. (2008) *Moral Dimensions: Possibility, Meaning, Blame*, Cambridge, MA: Harvard University Press. (Discusses connections between wrongness, blameworthiness and voluntariness.)
Skorupski, John (2010) "Moral Obligation, Blame and Self-Governance," *Social Philosophy and Policy*. (Covers the same ground in a different way.)
Taylor, Charles (1989) *Sources of the Self: The Making of the Modern Identity*, Cambridge: Cambridge University Press. (More on the connections between conscience and self-identity.)

47
RESPECT AND RECOGNITION

Allen W. Wood

The idea of *respect*, especially the more specific idea of *respect for persons*, is an important moral concept – some would contend it is a (or *the*) *fundamental* moral concept. Respect is perhaps most closely associated with the moral philosophy of Immanuel Kant (1724–1804), where it is involved in several other fundamental ideas: *moral obligation, humanity as end in itself, and the dignity of humanity*. The idea of *recognition* (*Anerkennung*) belongs to the same family. Though it was used by Kant (*MS* 6:462), "recognition" is probably best known for its appearance in G. W. F. Hegel's (1770–1831) famous "master–servant" dialectic in the *Phenomenology of Spirit* (Hegel *PhG*, paras 178–96). But it was actually first introduced into this tradition of moral philosophy by J. G. Fichte (1762–1814), where it serves as the foundation of his theory of natural right (Fichte *GNR* 3:30–47). Here I begin by expounding the idea of respect, introducing Kantian and Fichtean claims about respect and recognition when they seem to illuminate it or to provide specific influential philosophical claims about it.

Respect

Etymologically, "respect" derives from "*spectāre*," to look (at). The prefix "re-" might mean *returning the look* of someone, but it could also be taken as an intensifier, implying a repetition, prolongation or persistence of attention in your look. The latter thought links respect with the German word for respect – *Achtung* (as in the exclamation or command *Achtung*! – "(Pay) attention!"). As an ethical notion, what is *respected* is thought of as having a distinctive *value* deserving or requiring our regard.

Respect, in fact, is the appropriate attitude to take toward any *objective value* making a valid claim on us. The opposite of respect is *contempt*, whose proper object is whatever has little or no value or importance, something we can afford to dismiss or ignore. Respect for a *person* is regarding the person as having a value that makes a claim on us: specifically, the claim that their standpoint as a free and self-governing agent is to be taken as seriously as our own. To have respect for myself is to think of myself as having that same value, which makes a claims on me (to live up to this value, and not to permit it to be treated with contempt by others) and on others (that they must not treat it with contempt).

People often think of respect as closely related to *fear*. We are said to *respect* those who can harm us, and to *gain respect* from others by intimidating them or showing them that they cannot intimidate us. Thus after the 2006 war in Lebanon, representatives of Hezbollah claimed that through their successful resistance of the Israeli army, the Arab people had regained their respect (and their self-respect). Respect is also often associated with the possession of other goods – such as wealth or reputation – which enable people to manipulate others or bend them to their will by appealing to their self-interest or their subjective opinions. There is no doubt that this is the way much of the world thinks about human self-worth, but this way of thinking is also extremely questionable. For it is obvious, almost to the point of triviality, that what actually has a value may be quite different from what is commonly supposed to have it; and yet there are sad, deplorable and yet very powerful forces in human nature that lead people to confuse the two. It is fundamental to Kantian ethics, in fact, emphatically to deny that anything like this could be true, and in this Kant is articulating in a modern, secular context a very powerful moral vision that has roots deep in many of our best cultural and religious traditions. We are deeply torn, both in our collective behavior and in our individual attitudes and feelings, between that vision and rival conceptions of self-worth where respect depends merely on the capacity to coerce, manipulate or impress other people. This chapter will develop a fundamentally Kantian conception, as opposed to these rivals.

Respect in Kantian ethics

For Kant, "respect" is most fundamentally the name of a *feeling*, whose proper object is the moral law, or else humanity in someone's person, whose dignity as end in itself is for Kant the value on which the moral law is based. Respect is a complex and even an ambivalent feeling: it is uplifting, insofar as it is an experience of our own dignity and the high moral vocation that goes with it, but it is also painful and even humiliating, insofar as it limits the pretensions of our self-love and strikes down our self-conceited pretension that our point of view is worth more than that of others who are entitled to respect (Kant *KpV* 5:72–81). Kant really has two related concepts of respect, which are distinguished by their Latin names. The first is respect as *reverentia* ("reverence") (Kant *G* 4:402), which could be thought of as the basic attitude or feeling of respect, while the other is *observantia aliis praestanda* (*MS* 6:462), or conduct toward something regarded as standing over against our claims of self-love or our pretensions of self-conceit, and as making claims prior to these, having a rightful authority over our attitudes and actions.

In Kantian ethics, respect is due to the moral law because of the fundamental objective value or "objective end" that underlies the law (*G* 4:427–8). This value is *humanity* or *rational nature* in *persons*, which is an *end in itself* (*G* 4:428–9), which Kant further develops into an even deeper value, the *dignity* of rational nature as having the capacity for universal moral legislation (*G* 4:431–6). True human self-worth is constituted not by success in obtaining the powers or other goods for which people compete, but merely in the capacity to set ends and govern your actions through reason. Looked at in one way, we may think this capacity is not necessarily present in equal degrees in all adult human beings who are responsible agents, since some people are more intelligent, self-controlled, and so on than others. But to regard a self-governing rational being with respect is to treat their standpoint, and their voice, as having an irreplaceable and independent status alongside that of all others, and in that sense, it is to treat all rational beings as equals.

It is sometimes thought that the Kantian notions of respect, dignity and autonomy must rest on ascribing to them some supernatural or metaphysical status as members of a noumenal world. Kant himself is sometimes prone to such thoughts, but their importance for Kantian ethics is often exaggerated, especially by those looking to make Kantian ethics look vulnerable to charges of metaphysical extravagance and supernaturalism. It seems inconsistent with the critical rejection of transcendent metaphysics to think that fundamental moral principles and attitudes depend on such unknowable claims. A more consistent Kantian way to see it is that in recognizing the worth of rational nature in yourself and others, you regard all of them with respect, and that means treating the standpoint of each as having the same absolute and irreplaceable moral status.

The respect owed to humanity as such is closely related to the concept of human *dignity*. The term "dignity" itself means simply "worthiness" or "excellence." It is any quality of a person entitling them to be regarded, respected and honored by others. Originally, in the context of early modern European society, a "dignity" was some high office, usually an office of state, carrying with it certain extraordinary privileges and prerogatives. "Dignities" marked off different levels of aristocrat from each other, and dignity separated all aristocrats from all the plain and ordinary people, who altogether lacked dignity. Nowadays the term "human dignity" strikes us as a platitude. But in the context where Kant and others introduced it "human dignity" amounts to a paradox, a shocking oxymoron, even a subversion (or even – Dare we say it? – a "deconstruction") of the very idea of "dignity" itself. The claim that humanity has dignity is the impudent and defiant assertion that the highest possible status belongs to each and every human being simply as a human being. The Kantian conception of human dignity, however, goes even farther. As a basic conception of value, Kant contrasts "dignity" with "price" (*G* 4:434). What has price has a kind of value that may be rationally sacrificed or traded away for something else having an equal or greater value. The market price of a commodity, for example, is the ratio at which it may be exchanged for other commodities whose value is deemed equal for the purposes of exchange. Dignity, however, is an incomparable or absolute value, which can never rationally be sacrificed or traded away for anything at all, not even for something else having dignity. Though human beings come and go, the value of a human being is absolute and irreplaceable.

This sheds light on the peculiar kind of human *equality* that goes along with the idea of human dignity. This is not an equality of anything measurable or comparable. It is neither something that all human beings are alleged to have in equal quantities, nor something that we are required to dole out to them in equal quantities. Equality is based instead on the fact that since dignity, as a value, is absolute and incomparable, there is no way that any human being could be *unequal* to any other in regard to it. This explains Alan Donagan's observation that although it is quite possible (and even deplorably common) for people to *esteem* themselves too much, it is not possible even in principle for anyone to *respect* himself too much (Donagan 1977: 240).

I have spoken of respect as *the basic attitude toward objective value* (or, as I might more accurately have said, the attitude toward *basic objective value*). But it is not an appropriate attitude at all toward many things people do value, even toward the kind of thing that many philosophical theories portray as the sole conceivable locus of value, namely, *states of affairs* – the good consequences of actions: pleasure and freedom from pain, well-being, desire-satisfaction, and so on. None of these is ever an appropriate object of respect, however valuable we may take it to be. The conclusion I draw from this is not that states of affairs cannot have value (or objective value) – that would be absurd – but rather that their value can never be *basic*. It always rests on an objective value of an altogether different kind – namely, the *dignity of persons* – the persons whose pleasure and freedom from pain, desire-satisfaction and well-being these are.

A corollary of this is that in the structure of moral value, respecting persons is prior to caring about them. The individual instances of respect, of course, are not necessarily more important. Respect for a person may be shown in very minor ways, while caring about a person can involve saving their life or their happiness. Thus it is obviously not the case that all instances of showing respect for a person are lexically ordered in moral value ahead of all instances of caring about them. But as regards our fundamental moral relation to a person, it is more important that we respect them than that we care about them, and caring that occurs in the absence of respect is morally questionable, to say the least. We *respect* a person's human dignity, but we *care about* their welfare. Caring without respect is even morally questionable, and it is unenviable to be cared about by those who do not respect us. Kant is correct, I think, that we do not regard a person as genuinely *loving* another person unless this love rests on respect for the person (Kant *ED* 8:337).

This is related to the fact that the value of persons as objects of respect is not of the same kind as the value of their happiness or welfare, or, more generally, the value of states of affairs as objects of desire or as end-results of actions. This is what Kant meant by saying that humanity in a person is an *end in itself* – or a "self-sufficient" (*selbständig*) end, rather than an "end to be effected" (G 4:429, 437). An *end*, in the most basic sense of the term, is anything *for the sake of which* we act. Ends to be effected – the intended results or consequences of our actions – are ends because we act for the sake of their coming into existence. But a person is something that is already in existence for whose sake we act. And it is the Kantian position that the value of every end to be effected is in some way related to the more basic value of a person. For instance, some pleasure or happiness has value as an end to be effected because it is the pleasure or happiness of a person, for whose sake it has value as an end to be effected. This also means, as we will see presently, that persons as ends in themselves provide us with a very different kind of *reason for acting* from the reason provided by a desirable state of affairs as an end to be effected.

Varieties of respect

So far I have been discussing the general idea of respect, and the more specific idea of respect for persons, by focusing on a very special kind of respect, *respect for human dignity in persons*, and also on a particular (though historically very influential) account of it, namely, Kant's. I am going to continue to focus on this special case because I think respect for human dignity in persons is extremely important and fundamental to morality, and that Kant's account of it is the best one we have. Before proceeding further, however, I had better say more about respect in general, and to locate respect for human dignity in persons on a larger map of kinds of respect.

Stephen Darwall (1977: 36–49) has drawn a well-known distinction between "recognition respect" and "appraisal respect." Recognition respect is a certain status or authority that a person may have that normatively regulates our relations to them. Respect for human dignity in persons is a fundamental kind of recognition respect, but there are other kinds as well, such as respect for a person's expertise (epistemic authority) or for the office they hold (authority within an institutional structure). Appraisal respect is directed toward a person's moral merits or the virtues of their character or conduct. I think there is a species of something like appraisal respect that may have nothing to do with morality, though I think it does have to do with agency. We respect people's accomplishments, for example, even where these involve nothing of moral value. (But I do not think we can properly speak of "respect" merely for a person's talents, for instance, unless we are thinking in some measure of the way the person has developed or successfully exercised them.) Of course, as I have already observed, people often respect others for things that are not deserving of respect – such as their power, wealth or charisma – their capacities to intimidate, bribe, extort, impress or incite foolish adulation. To show such respect, it seems to me, is to display slavishness or sycophancy.

Let us return now to the Kantian conception of respect. Although a Kantian would agree that we can genuinely respect a person's expertise or office, or their moral virtues and non-moral achievements, I take it to be the Kantian position that in so doing we are not (or should not be) respecting *them* – their self-worth, or the worth of their person – which lies entirely in their human dignity. The moral worth of a person's actions and even the goodness of their will is for Kant only an "inner" worth – that is, it is something having worth only by comparison with one's self-given moral law or idea of virtue, never something in regard to which it is fitting to *compare* people, or for one person to command greater respect than another (*G* 4:393–4, 426; *KpV* 5:88; *MS* 6:387, 391, 435; *VE* 27:349, 462). And of course the worth of a person's expertise, office or accomplishments are for Kant always only part of someone's "state" or "condition" (*Zustand*), never part of the worth of their person (*KpV* 5:60–1, 66, 88; *MS* 6:387). To look down on another on the basis of one's (supposed or even real) excellences, merits or accomplishments (even moral ones) is to display the vices of "arrogance" (or "self-conceit") and "contempt." It is "to deny them the respect owed to human beings in general, and is in every case contrary to duty, for they are human beings" (*MS* 6:463). Kant is aware that people do not in fact regulate their conduct and attitudes in this way, and he even acknowledges that it may not harmonize with our own feelings, especially in regard to vicious people and vicious acts. But his clear-sighted and resolute position is the radical one that the only self-worth relevant to people's mutual relations simply as persons is their human dignity; and the concept of dignity, which goes with the attitude of respect, guarantees that it is the same in all (*MS* 6:462–4).

Respect for humanity in persons

When Kant says that it is humanity or rational nature in persons that is an end in itself, there is sometimes the objection that Kantian ethics does not value persons, but only some abstract property of persons, such as "humanity," "personality," or "universal reason." This objection is misguided, because it ignores what "humanity," "personality" and "reason" themselves are, and how they relate to the persons in whom they reside. "Humanity" for Kant is a technical term referring to that side of rational nature that involves the capacity to set ends and combine them into a concept of your own happiness. "Personality" is Kant's name for the related capacity that gives us dignity. This is the capacity to govern one's life rationally in a larger sense, including the capacity to recognize and obey moral laws (*R* 6:26–8; *VA* 7:321–4). "Universal reason" is equivalent to the capacities that permit each of us to have a practical point of view of a human sort, to constitute oneself as a person who is able to make claims, for oneself and for others, based on reasons. These capacities and their determinate exercise are the core of what any person is. It is therefore a false dilemma to think we can (or even must) choose between respecting humanity or rationality and respecting the persons who have them. To respect humanity as an abstract property while showing disrespect for persons who have it would be an abuse, not an exemplification, of respect. It is nevertheless a truth of utmost importance that it is only a capacity for *universal* reason that could adequately serve to constitute any *individual* human personality and a practical point of view, because it is only *universal* reason that could enable our *individual* standpoint to address others in terms of claims and reasons they are required to acknowledge.

This sheds further light on the way in which respecting a person differs from being concerned about their welfare. We may show a lack of respect for a person by failing to take sufficient account of their interests or well-being, but a person's interests or well-being are never themselves objects of respect. Our relation to these goods therefore never constitutes the fundamental relation of respect for a person (or the failure to respect a person). Instead, what we are to respect in a person is fundamentally the person's *point of view* – by returning their "look" in the right way (as the term "respect" perhaps implies). Or, to employ a different (and perhaps even a more apt) metaphor (or synecdoche), we respect someone by listening to their *voice* – by paying the right kind of attention to the claims they make on us or the arguments they address to us. When people do not *listen* to us (our claims, our reasons, our arguments) and we become *invisible* to them – they fail or refuse to see things from our point of view – those are the paradigm cases of being treated with *dis*respect. You might do a lot to further someone's well-being by making inquiries about what would please or gratify them and how best to provide it, but you show them no respect unless you listen to them tell you what they want and permit them to participate in deciding how to get it. It is profoundly false – and even betrays an utterly false sense of moral values – to say that your only (or even your best) reason to listen to them tell you what they want is that this is the *best source of information* about what will make them happy.

Fichte: respect as interpersonal; and recognition as fundamental

This means that the kind of recognition respect that is respect for human dignity in persons is never merely a feeling or attitude of one person toward another, but is always fundamentally a *relation between people*. Respect for human dignity is always in a way *reciprocal*. It is of course possible for you respect my human dignity while I fail (or refuse) to respect yours. But if I demand this respect from you, I am rationally committed to grant it to you, and if I fail (or refuse) to do so, then I am defying a normative requirement that I myself implicitly acknowledge. To demand respect from another is to demand that they respect me for a certain specific reason – namely, for the worth (dignity) of humanity in my person. I cannot demand this except from a being I recognize as having this same humanity (or dignity) and whom I therefore recognize as entitled to the same respect from me. This makes mutual recognition, or rather the objective grounds for this recognition, the true foundation of respect.

The recognitive reciprocity of respect for human dignity is something of which Kant sometimes shows at least peripheral awareness – as in his argument for the Formula of Humanity (*G* 4:429) and his explicit mention of "recognition" (*Anerkennung*) in relation to the duty of respect (*MS* 6:462). But in the Kantian tradition it becomes fully explicit only in the thought of Fichte. Fichte's theory of recognition is developed as part of a transcendental argument that the awareness of other Is is a condition of being aware of one's own I. Our awareness of activity in general requires the concept of an object of that activity – "not-I" contrasting with and resisting this activity. In the same way, our awareness of our free activity as the activity of an individual I also requires the concept of a different kind of object encountered in our experience – an object Fichte calls a "summons" (*Aufforderung*). This translation may mislead; the German term is very broad in its meaning, ranging all the way from "requirement" to "invitation." I think Fichte's basic idea is that in order to see myself as an individual I, I must be able to distinguish actions that are suitable or appropriate to me (to an I in my situation, with my point of view) from actions that are not (Fichte *SL* 4:220–1). In other words, I must encounter what I take to be a reason for acting one way rather than the other. The summons is an object given in my experience that satisfies this condition. But only a being that is itself capable of acting for reasons could provide such an object. Therefore, if there is one I, there must be a plurality of Is, summoning one another to free activity (*GNR* 3:30–40).

Any individual I is therefore aware of other Is, and must posit its own free activity as occupying an external sphere distinct from that of others (*GNR* 3:41–3). Each I must, therefore, be understood as summoned by every other to restrict its action to its own sphere, and to concede every other I its own sphere for free activity. This is the Fichtean concept of reciprocal recognition. To *recognize* another is to treat the other as free, by limiting one's own free activity to one's own external sphere (*GNR* 3:43–4). But "I can expect a particular rational being to recognize me only if I myself treat him as one." So recognition can properly occur only if it is mutual: "One cannot recognize the other if both do not mutually recognize each other, and one cannot treat the other as a free being, if both do not mutually treat each other as free" (*GNR* 3:44). This reciprocal relation of recognition is what Fichte calls the "relation of right" (*Rechtsverhältnis*) (*GNR* 3:41), which grounds Fichte's theory of external rights, justified coercion, and the state.

For our purposes, however, the important point is that Fichte's analysis of mutual recognition can be used to explicate the mutuality we have seen to be involved in the Kantian idea of respect for human dignity in persons: A person is to be seen as a free rational agent who lays claim to respect from other free rational agents in virtue of the dignity of rational nature that they share. To do this is at the same time to grant the basis of the other's claim to the same respect. It is also to do so on the basis of the other's capacity to make that very claim. So the reason for respecting persons – others and also yourself – is best viewed as something created by the very making and accepting of such claims, which is also to be seen as a reciprocal relation, constituted by the mutual *recognition* of persons by one other.

Recognition in Hegel

Hegel's famous master–servant dialectic relies on Fichte's analysis, but ingeniously makes Fichte's point in a strikingly original (indirect) way. Like Fichte, Hegel takes the world for a self-consciousness to require two distinct kinds of objects: (1) *things*, which resist our activity and which we strive to overcome, dominate or "negate" and (2) *other self-consciousnesses*, from which it seeks to obtain *recognition* (*PhG*, paras 172–8). Hegel first imagines what must happen when self-consciousness attempts to obtain recognition from other self-consciousnesses in the same way it gains satisfaction from overcoming or negating things. This leads, first, to a "struggle to the death" in which it either suffers death itself or achieves the death of the other self-consciousness – but in either case, it fails to obtain recognition (*PhG*, paras 185–8). This failure leads, second, to the thought of what would happen if one of the struggling self-consciousnesses, on the point of being killed by the other, should propose to save its life by giving the other recognition without demanding to be recognized in its turn. The victorious self-conscious in this scenario is the "independent" self-consciousness, the lord or master (*Herr*), the vanquished is the "dependent" one, the servant or bondsman (*Knecht*) (*PhG*, paras 189–93).

This outcome, however, has an ironic result: It is the master, not the servant, who remains dependent on the recognition of the other, while the servant has found a way of living independently, without being recognized. "The *truth* of the independent consciousness is accordingly the servile consciousness" (*PhG*, para. 193). The attempt to obtain recognition without giving it is therefore necessarily self-defeating, even incoherent. If we think of the point in terms of respect for humanity, it could be put this way: If you demand this respect from another, you can get what you are demanding only if you think of the other as having the humanity you want respected in yourself; otherwise, you will be denying to the other even the capacity to give you what you are demanding. But if you acknowledge that capacity in the other, then you are tacitly admitting that the other is entitled to the same respect you want for yourself.

In the *Phenomenology*, the master–servant dialectic results only in the free self-consciousness of the stoic sage – who, Hegel points out, is equally free whether, like Marcus Aurelius, he sits on the imperial throne or, like Epictetus, finds himself in the chains of a slave (*PhG*, para. 199). In the *Phenomenology* Hegel does not explicitly draw the Fichtean moral that recognition must be mutual, that it can be truly obtained only in a community of equals. But he does draw this conclusion in the *Encyclopedia* (*EG* §§435–6). In both texts, the outcome is a "universal self-consciousness" that is truly free because it stands in no need of the subordination of another. Or, as Fichte elsewhere puts it: "The only person who is truly free is the person who wishes to liberate everyone around him and who – by means of a certain influence [that of rational education and reciprocal communication] – really does so" (*SW* 6:309).

Conclusions

The discussions of recognition in Fichte and Hegel advance the Kantian idea of respect for human dignity in persons in several ways. I conclude by summarizing them in the following set of claims:

(1) They show how that respect is essentially a reciprocal relation, not merely a one-sided attitude.
(2) They bring to the fore the essentially "second-person" character of respect, and the fact that being addressed by another who demands respect from you provides you with a special kind of reason for action that is basic to a wide range of ethical concepts, values and principles.
(3) Through the Fichtean idea of the summons, we can see that the idea of respect for persons is deeply connected both to the notion of having (being given) a reason for doing something, and to the fact that acting for a reason is something that presupposes the freedom of the agent.
(4) Our being free, and our acting for reasons, are both closely tied to being one person among others, to our recognition of one another as persons and the objective grounds for regarding every person as entitled from every other to respect for their human dignity.

See also Early modern natural law (Chapter 7); Kant (Chapter 14); Hegel (Chapter 15); Freedom and responsibility (Chapter 23); Reasons for action (Chapter 24); Reasons, values, and morality (Chapter 36); Contemporary Kantian ethics (Chapter 38); Contemporary natural law theory (Chapter 42); Conscience (Chapter 46); Blame, remorse, mercy, forgiveness (Chapter 48); Rights (Chapter 56); Torture and terrorism (Chapter 68).

References

Darwall, Stephen (2006) *The Second-Person Standpoint*, Cambridge, MA: Harvard University Press.

Donagan, Alan (1977) *The Theory of Morality*. Chicago, IL: University of Chicago Press.

Fichte, J. G. (*GNR*) *Foundations of Natural Right*, trans. Michael Baur, ed. F. Neuhouser, Cambridge: Cambridge University Press, 2000. (Cited by volume and page.)

——(*SL*) *System of Ethics*, trans, D. Breazeale and G. Zöller, Cambridge: Cambridge University Press, 2006. (Cited by volume and page.)

——(*SW*) *Sämmtliche Werke*, ed. I. H. Fichte, Berlin: deGruyter, 1970. (Cited by volume and page.)

Hegel, G. W. F. (*EG*) *Philosophy of Spirit*, trans. W. Wallace and A. V. Miller, Oxford: Oxford University Press, 1977. Werke, vol. 12.

——(*PhG*) *Phenomenology of Spirit*, trans. A. V. Miller, Oxford: Oxford University Press, 1975. Werke, vol. 3.

——(Werke) *Werke*, Theorie Werkausgabe, Frankfurt: Suhrkamp, 1970. (Cited by volume.)

Kant, I. (Ak) *Gesammelte Schriften*, Royal Prussian Academy of Science edn, Berlin: W. de Gruyter, 1902–. (Unless otherwise noted, writings of Immanuel Kant will be cited by volume and page number of this edition.)

——(Ca) *Cambridge Edition of the Writings of Immanuel Kant*, New York: Cambridge University Press, 1992–. (This edition provides marginal Ak volume and page.)

——(*ED*) *Das Ende aller Dinge*, Ak, vol. 8; trans. as *The End of All Things*, in *Religion and Natural Theology*, Ca, 2001.

——(*G*) *Grundlegung zur Metaphysik der Sitten* (1785), Ak, vol. 4; trans. as *Groundwork of the Metaphysics of Morals*, in *Practical Philosophy*, Ca, 1999.

——(*KpV*) *Kritik der praktischen Vernunft* (1788), Ak, vol. 5; trans. as *Critique of Practical Reason*, in *Practical Philosophy*, Ca, 1999.

——(*MS*) *Die Metaphysik der Sitten* (1797–8), Ak, vol. 6; *Metaphysics of Morals*, in *Practical Philosophy*, Ca, 1999.

——(*R*) *Religion innerhalb der Grenzen der bloßen Vernunft* (1793–4), Ak, vol. 6; trans. as *Religion within the Boundaries of Mere Reason*, in *Religion and Rational Theology*, Ca, 2001.

——(*VA*) *Anthropologie in pragmatischer Hinsicht* (1798), Ak, vol. 7; trans. as *Anthropology from a Pragmatic Point of View*, in *Anthropology, History, and Education*, Ca, 2007.

——(*VE*) *Vorlesungen über Ethik*, Ak, vols 27, 29; trans. as *Lectures on Ethics*, Ca, 1997.

Further reading

Darwall, Stephen (2006) *The Second-Person Standpoint*, Cambridge, MA: Harvard University Press. (A presentation of a wide variety of ethical issues, arguing for the indispensable role in treating them of the second-person standpoint and the distinctively second-person reasons associated with recognition and respect.)

Honneth, Axel (1996) *The Struggle for Recognition: The Moral Grammar of Social Conflicts*, trans. Joel Anderson, Cambridge, MA: MIT Press. (A presentation of Hegel's treatment of *Anerkennung* and its application to issues in moral and social philosophy.)

Wood, Allen W. (2008) *Kantian Ethics*, Cambridge: Cambridge University Press. (A recent exposition of Kantian ethics on a variety of topics.)

48
BLAME, REMORSE, MERCY, FORGIVENESS

Christopher Bennett

Introduction: moral questions about wrongdoing and reconciliation

One night you come back home after an evening out to find the door ajar, the inside in disarray. An intruder has been in your home. Your first thought is: Is he still there? Your hands shaking, you put on the lights, making enough noise to give him plenty of time to escape. The last thing that you want to do is to have to confront him. Then you work your way through the rooms, body tense. Each room has been turned over, carelessly but single-mindedly. Eventually you assure yourself that he has gone. You take a breath and sit down in a chair. But you can't get comfortable. The familiar place now feels somehow different, not quite your own. Then you start to feel angry: How dare he? In your home? Treat it like this? Before you contact the police you need some words of comfort. You phone your mother and some close friends. They are all keen to make sure that you are all right, and tell you they will come over straight away. But at the same time they are outraged that anyone should have done that to you. "Don't let it get to you. You're better than that." The words stay in your mind as you dial the police.

This scenario suggests a number of powerful human reactions to wrongdoing. One is *fear* and a sense of vulnerability, being at the mercy of more powerful others. Another is *violation*, having had one's privacy intruded upon without one's say-so. Another might be *irritation* and *grief* at the loss of precious belongings. We also have reactions that are directed at the wrongdoer, reactions of *anger*, *defiance*, *outrage*, *condemnation*, as well as a readiness to defend oneself against him should he return. In this chapter we will be surveying some moral philosophical questions about these reactions to wrongdoing.

Let's get a clearer idea of the sort of debate I have in mind. So say your call to the police proves immediately productive. They have just picked up a young man leaving your building with a suspiciously large collection of valuables that he cannot adequately account for. Seized by a sudden curiosity to see him, you go outside. He is handcuffed answering questions. He looks over to you and you catch his eye, hold it. You say, "That was my flat, you know." Why do you say that? Perhaps because you want an explanation, you can't understand why this should have happened to you. Before he can help himself he says, "Look – I'm sorry. It wasn't anything to do with you. I needed the money." We can see that if that was *all* that he thought was necessary then it would be an inadequate response. But it is at least an acknowledgment and might be the start of something more significant.

With the coincidence of your meeting the wrongdoer (and having the courage to address him), my tale may be taking on a slightly artificial shape. But the significance of your coming face-to-face with the wrongdoer is that it throws you into some sort of relationship with him. You have to decide on which terms that relationship is able to proceed (cf. Wiesenthal 1998). And thinking about how we might make this decision is a good way to address some of the fundamental questions about how wrongdoing affects the way we think we ought to treat wrongdoers and what we should expect of them. For instance, are you a better person if you are able to be forgiving rather than vengeful – or is it sometimes necessary to take a stand against wrongdoing? How ought *offenders* to react to what they have done? Do offenders have duties to their victims or to others because of their wrongs? What attitude should *third parties* adopt towards the offender? Even if you have no knowledge of anyone involved, would it be adequate to be entirely unaffected by the news of the incident? Related to the question of how unconnected bystanders ought to react is the question of how the *state* should react to such wrongdoing. One influential recent tradition in theory of punishment has taken it that an important role of punishment is the state's expression of condemnation of the offense (Feinberg 1974; von Hirsch 1993; Duff 2001; Bennett 2008).

Moral philosophy and the emotions

In this chapter I will look at the way in which philosophers have tried to address these questions by looking at the *emotions* that are characteristically engaged by situations of wrongdoing: fear, anger, outrage, etc. Contrary to the role they sometimes play in the popular imagination, emotions are not mere psychic disturbances that drive us to act in mysterious and irrational ways. Unlike itches, pains, pangs and so on – but like beliefs – we have emotions in a directed way *about* things. In other words, there is usually something in a situation that brings the emotion about and to which we can recognize it as an intelligent response (I am afraid of … , angry about … , aggrieved that …). For instance, fear is appropriate in our scenario because there is the risk of danger. Anger is appropriate because one's property has been intruded upon without one's say-so. It makes sense to have these emotions only because one understands one's situation in such a way.

Recently Martha Nussbaum has contrasted what she calls an *evaluative* conception of the emotions – according to which emotions are ways in which we evaluate situations – with a *mechanical* conception according to which emotions are brute psychic forces (see e.g. Nussbaum and Kahan 1996). She regards the latter as inadequate to our experience of emotions. Emotions, on the evaluative conception, are partly cognitive states (that is, they involve beliefs about what *matters*). They involve judgements of value: evaluations of our situation as good or bad in certain respects. So rather than being just brute forces that sweep over us, emotions on the evaluative conception embody certain claims about what is important. If we accept this model it means that we can ask whether the judgements that seem to be embodied in our emotions really *are* justified. It is important to make this point, because the issue of responding to wrongdoing is a personal one, involving us in the vagaries of all sorts of awkward emotions. The evaluative conception of the emotions explains why we should still expect to be able to say something philosophically interesting about it. These general claims about assessing the emotions will be more comprehensible once we have looked at some emotions as examples.

The problem of forgiveness

First of all, let's return to our question: How should one respond to wrongdoing? Would one be a better person if one was forgiving rather than holding a grudge against the offender? Forgiveness tends to be regarded in our culture as a virtue, and those who are able to forgive after suffering grave wrongs admired. But is the disposition to forgive always a virtue? Or is it a virtue in some situations but not in others? Forgiving someone for something seems to involve in some way coming to terms with what she has done: "letting the wrong go," stopping it dominating one's life or one's relation with the wrongdoer. The problem of forgiveness is that sometimes this "letting go" might be a refusal to take the wrong fully seriously, a denial of its reality or significance. Forgiveness would represent a refusal to deal with the wrong rather than an admirable state of wider moral understanding.

What is forgiveness? Philosophers have pointed to a number of features that are involved in forgiveness. First of all, forgiving someone seems different from merely *saying* that you forgive. You can say that you forgive but not *really* forgive. So what goes on in real forgiveness? Fundamentally, it seems to involve a change of heart towards the wrongdoer (Calhoun 1992). Jeffrie Murphy (Murphy and Hampton 1988: 14–34), following Bishop Butler (Butler 1967: 120–48), understands forgiveness as "overcoming resentment." Forgiveness involves expunging negative emotions that one might have towards the wrongdoer as a result of the wrong. However, these emotions can be expunged in various ways that wouldn't involve forgiving. One might just forget about the offense (e.g. through suffering amnesia). Or one might realize that the action was not really a wrong (that the agent had some *justification*) or that in some way it was not really the agent's fault (that the agent had a good excuse) and hence that she was not really deserving of resentment in the first place. But in this case you don't need to forgive her. When you forgive, it might be said, you stop feeling resentment towards the wrongdoer and yet you continue to regard her as fully responsible for the wrong action. Furthermore – though it might be more debatable whether this is genuine forgiveness or not – many writers take it that you have not really forgiven if the reason you bring your negative emotions to an end is *therapeutic* (that is, for your own good) rather than as a result of something about the wrongdoer. Forgiveness seems to involve some manner of reconciliation with the wrongdoer despite the full recognition that what they did was wrong.

In the light of this we can see "the problem of forgiveness." The problem is that (1) forgiveness involves overcoming emotions of condemnation towards the wrongdoer; (2) these emotions might themselves have some value as responses to wrongdoing; therefore (3) we should bring these emotions to an end – and hence forgive – only when it is no longer appropriate to condemn. This conclusion is significant because it would mean that if the emotions of condemnation are themselves valuable (and of course that might be disputed) then forgiveness would be only conditionally valuable (though for an opposing view see Garrard and MacNaughton 2002). In short, it would be *wrong* to forgive when one *ought* to condemn. And we would need to investigate the emotions of condemnation in order to understand when it is good to bring these emotions to an end, that is, when it is good and right to forgive (though for the view that this would make forgiveness redundant, see Kolnai 1973–4).

Let me put the problem another way. In an attempt to explain what is going on in forgiveness, writers often quote St Augustine: "hate the sin; love the sinner." In forgiveness we seem to separate the agent from her wrongful action, holding that we can end our negative emotions towards the agent even while keeping it in view that the act was wrong. The problem with this is that it is hard to see how one can do this if the agent was responsible for the action. In general an agent is responsible for an act only if she expresses or reveals herself in that act: the act sheds some light on her character, attitudes, motivations, etc. But if this is the case then it can be no simple matter to separate the agent from her responsible acts. If we ought to condemn responsible wrongdoing then forgiveness will look morally suspect until the agent responds in such a way as to make the condemnation no longer appropriate.

Emotions of condemnation: resentment, indignation, blame

The previous section raises the question of what value these emotions of condemnation have. We will now have a look at a range of such emotions, beginning with *resentment*. While some philosophers see victims' desire to "get even" as an understandable but regrettable part of our psychology, some admire and applaud it. To investigate whether these emotions can be justified we should ask first of all what it is about wrongdoing that arouses these emotions. Jeffrie Murphy argues that as well as causing material harm, wrongdoing involves a "symbolic communication" – like an insult – that the victim is an inferior whom the wrongdoer can use for his own purposes (Murphy 1988: 25). For Murphy we can understand *resentment* (or even vindictiveness: see Murphy 2003) as a reaction that serves to defend our rights to equal treatment against those who would relegate us to inferiority. As long as one has enough self-respect to think that one has such rights, one ought to react with resentment whenever one's rights have been violated. Murphy's emphasis on resentment as the paradigm emotion of a victim's reaction to wrongdoing echoes P. F. Strawson's classic paper, "Freedom and Resentment" (P. Strawson 1982), which itself harked back to eighteenth-century philosophers such as Butler and Adam Smith (Smith 2002).

Although Murphy's view has some intuitive plausibility he doesn't make it clear *why* it is good or right to retaliate after wrongdoing (and hence why resentment is justified). Perhaps the justification on Murphy's view (as on Butler's) is that when we react vengefully in defense of our rights then others are less likely to mess with us in the future. This would be an indirect or instrumental justification of the emotion rather than one that showed the emotion to be *intrinsically* right or *fitting*. It would show that, *if* a policy of retaliating would tend to deter people from wronging us *then*, out of self-interest, we ought to adopt this policy. A problem with this type of instrumental justification is that it seems like changing the subject to ask about the *effects* of having a certain emotion rather than whether the emotion is justified in its own right. Think of a case in which you are deliberating about whether to continue to hold a grudge against your friend for sleeping with your partner behind your back. Murphy tells you that if you have a general policy of holding grudges and retaliating then this will make people less likely to cross you. However, you might think that this doesn't fully answer your question: you want to know, not whether to have an effective policy of self-defense but whether, in this particular case, the person *deserves* begrudging and retaliation for having abused your friendship. The indirect or instrumental justification is silent on this point.

The urge to get even has been given a less flattering diagnosis by Jean Hampton (Murphy and Hampton 1988: 35–87). Hampton makes a distinction between resentment and indignation. She thinks that it is only the former that prompts us to "get even" but that it is tied to a dubious view of human value. Hampton argues that resentment occurs when a victim experiences a wrong as an insult (as on Murphy's view, above), but where the "insult" raises some doubt in her own mind about her true value. In other words, the victim who experiences resentment *fears* that it *may* have been permissible to treat her in that way – but defiantly (as if through an act of will) rejects this possibility. Resentment on Hampton's account is therefore a defiant but slightly insecure reaffirmation of one's value in the face of some act that has called one's value into question, not just in the mind of the perpetrator, but in one's own mind. Resentment leads to retaliation because if the victim believes that she can be diminished by wrongdoing then she probably believes that she can be raised in status by getting even (where she herself defeats the wrongdoer). However, for Hampton, resentment and these retaliatory strategies are always unjustified. This is because they are based on the belief that human value can vary and is the outcome of competitive struggle. If one is a Kantian as one ought to be, she thinks, and regards human value as egalitarian and intrinsic, one will not think that one's value can be put into question in the way the resentful person fears.

Hampton offers a fascinating and unsettling diagnosis of our urge to get even. She thinks that when we want to get even we are really motivated by a false view of human value, a groundless fear that we may really *be* the wrongdoer's inferior. However, she does not think that we should do *nothing* in the face of wrongdoing. As I said above, she contrasts resentment with *indignation*. Indignation is in her eyes a more justifiable emotion: it is a protest against the action whose function is to prevent further abuses in the future. The crucial difference between resentment and indignation, for Hampton, is that the latter is compatible with full confidence in one's value, whereas resentment betrays an insecure uncertainty about whether one really ought to be treated as an equal. Indignation prompts us to defend our values, but not to get even for the sake of it (for discussion see Walker 2006; Hieronymi 2001).

Whether or not resentment and its retaliatory strategies are justified, they cannot be the only emotions of condemnation, or even perhaps the central ones. To see this, try to feel resentment towards *oneself*. Turning resentment on oneself does not seem altogether intelligible. However, when one has oneself done wrong one *does* turn some form of condemnation on oneself: one accepts the condemnation that might be made of you by others. It seems plausible that there should be an emotion that wrongdoers and others *share* when assessing the significance of what has been done.

In the search for such an emotion we can look at what has been written about *blame* (Skorupski 1999). Sometimes blaming is thought of as an action (Smart 1961); at other times an evaluation, as when we judge someone to be blameworthy (for something). However, to blame is to condemn, and to condemn is to *feel* a certain way about something, or at least to regard such feelings as appropriate. So what is blame? We might start with the idea that blaming involves a withdrawal of goodwill (P. Strawson 1982; Skorupski 1999). Why do we feel that such withdrawal is apt when someone has committed a wrong? Sometimes it is said that such withdrawal is a recognition that the wrongdoing has *damaged* the relationship (Duff 2001). But what does this mean? One answer might be that the damage to the relationship makes it prudent to terminate or modify it, since such relationships ought to be based on mutual care and respect (Scanlon 2008: Ch. 4). But while this would explain why we have some reason to engage in blaming, it would not explain what can be wrong with *failing* to blame. A more retributivist account would insist that essential to blame is the recognition that one cannot properly treat the wrongdoer as if nothing has happened – that if one did one would be ignoring, condoning, perhaps even acquiescing in the offense. One cannot properly proceed as if you are "on good terms" with the wrongdoer, so blaming expresses some recognition that what the wrongdoer has done changes the terms of your relationship with her (or if you had no relationship with her previously – as in our example with the thief above – then the relationship you begin is one that is *conditioned* by the wrong, it is a relationship *with a wrongdoer*, and this has to be different from the relationship that you can have with anyone else). Blaming is sometimes thought of as in some way a *punitive* emotion. Perhaps the right way to understand this thought is that blaming involves, not just a negative evaluation of a person, but the thought that one has to impose a certain kind of (normally negative) treatment on that person in order to mark her out as a wrongdoer. Blame involves, not just judging a person, but holding her accountable (cf. Watson 1996).

Regret, shame and guilt

Blame could be a candidate for the emotion of condemnation that is shared by condemnors and condemned. So what is self-blame? Self-blame belongs to the same family of emotions as *regret*. But one can regret all sorts of unfortunate events that have no particular connection with oneself, and are certainly not cause for blame. Bernard Williams has argued that as well as this general regret we have in our range of emotions a particular form of regret that he terms *agent-regret* (Williams 1981). Agent-regret is something we can feel when we have some special connection with an unfortunate event in virtue of its having come about through our agency. However, Williams stresses that we can appropriately feel agent-regret about an event we have caused quite innocently (say, by accident, unknowingly, with good justification, etc.). Thus a lorry driver who was driving carefully in a safe and well-maintained vehicle may unavoidably knock over a child who runs out in front of him. Williams's point is that, while the lorry driver *can* rightly console himself with the thought that it was not his fault, he still should be particularly pained by the fact that it was *his* action that caused it – and he should acknowledge a special responsibility to say sorry and make some amends that a mere spectator to the event would not have.

Williams discusses agent-regret in the course of addressing a wider concern that, if we assume that we are morally responsible only for what is under our control, moral judgement might be swallowed up by luck – for (as Williams believes) very little if anything about us is *ultimately* under our control (cf. Nagel 1979; G. Strawson 1994). Williams argues that at least some of our moral judgements are still in order, since many of our moral emotions about agents (and the judgements they embody) do not assume such control. Developing this argument, Williams has recommended expunging the Kantian elements of our conception of morality and moral assessment and returning to those moral ideas that we share with the ancient Greeks (Williams 1993; cf. Anscombe 1958).

However, agent-regret cannot be the whole story about what we feel when we blame ourselves. Even if Williams is correct that modern moral philosophy (and modern moral thinking in general) has a tendency to overplay the importance of fault in our moral judgements, we should not overlook the important difference between agent-regret and emotions of self-condemnation (Baron 1988). The thing about the case of the innocent lorry driver is that he ultimately has nothing to reproach himself for. However, there is a range of emotions of self-reproach that we take to be fitting in cases in which our actions do show some moral failing. The central case of such an emotion is perhaps *shame*. Shame is an emotion one experiences when one has failed to live up to some standard one has set for oneself, or an aspiration one has (Taylor 1985). One has failed to be as good (at something) as one wishes one could be (or thinks it important that one should be). One can feel shame about many things that have nothing to do with morality: for instance, I can feel shame that I wasn't a good enough singer to make it into the choir. But there is such a thing as moral shame, where one has come to see the importance of the things one harmed or violated, and one's act as wrong. Such awareness is painful because it is an awareness of the distance between where one is and where one would have oneself be.

One can feel shame about failings that one cannot change. In these cases shame disposes us to conceal the fault – or to hide ourselves away when the fault can no longer be hidden (Williams 1993). However, shame can have a more constructive role when the failing is something that *is* amenable to change. In these cases shame can motivate us to reform and self-improvement (Kekes 1988). Many cases of moral shame might be like this, where the failing is some kind of insensitivity, and where one could learn (e.g. to take people's feelings into better account, etc.).

With this typography of regret and shame we can now say something about what self-blame might be. Self-blame seems to be a type of moral shame, in that it involves accepting the blame that says one has revealed some moral failing in one's action. However, if blame involves some withdrawal of goodwill, or at any rate some determination to treat the person as a wrongdoer, then self-blame will also involve imposing such punitive treatment on oneself. We can call this emotion of self-blame *guilt*. (There are competing ways of distinguishing shame and guilt. For instance, it is sometimes said that shame involves the way one is perceived by others while guilt has to do with how one evaluates oneself – e.g. in one's conscience. The problem with this is that one can clearly feel shame when one is making one's own judgement of one's failings. Alternatively, it is sometimes said that shame is about *who one is* while guilt is about *what one has done*. The problem with this interpretation is that when one is responsible for an action it can be hard to separate who one is and what one has done: one reveals who one is *in* what one does.) If one withdraws goodwill *from oneself* when one is feeling guilty then it might also explain why guilt disposes us to atonement or penance. If you feel bad about yourself then the way in which it might make sense to express this is through undertaking some action that you would normally regard as "beneath" you, or as too onerous to be reasonably undertaken.

Reparation

Feeling guilty in this way is an unpleasant, if sometimes necessary, place to be. But there is a way out (one that doesn't involve simply denying or ignoring what one has done). Philosophers (and sociologist and psychologists) have increasingly been paying attention to what goes on in *apologizing*. Apology, it has been claimed, has an almost magical quality about it (Tavuchis 1991). The passing of a few words can rebuild relationships and allow people to go on together after wrongdoing. Without some such social mechanism for bringing about reconciliation it is perhaps hard to imagine how social life would be possible.

Some writers take apologies to have an *instrumental* significance: they are ways in which we announce to others that we are ready to cooperate again, or that we can be trusted again. The thought is that we demonstrate our commitment to cooperation by showing that we are prepared to go through something difficult (like loss of face in apologizing) in order to get the chance to rejoin the cooperative activity. The problem with such instrumental interpretations is that they do not connect (or connect only contingently) with our reasons for feeling bad when we do wrong. For instance, when I give a sincere apology it seems to be an *expression* of my self-reproach. However, on the instrumental interpretation my reason for thinking that I should make amends is a desire to regain trust and cooperation that I could have without in any way feeling guilty.

By contrast an *expressive* or *intrinsic* interpretation of the value of apology might start with the idea of *atonement*. Richard Swinburne has claimed that atonement has four elements: repentance, apology, restitution and penance (Swinburne 1985). If we look at the criteria by which we judge an apology to be sincere, we see the same criteria emerging, and our understanding of blame and guilt can shed light on why these various elements should form a unified response to wrongdoing. Thus we might say that an apology works to restore relations damaged by wrongdoing if it expresses *shame*, that is a remorseful acknowledgment of the wrongness of what one has done, one's own responsibility for it, and a determination to reform so that one does not do it again. If one is remorseful about what one has damaged then one will be motivated to repair it: this is the element of restitution. However, a successful apology also has to show proper recognition of the gravity of what was done. One will withdraw goodwill from oneself to a greater extent the more one regards oneself as having done something serious. Therefore if blaming oneself motivates one to penance then the penance will be greater the more serious the wrong. If penance was not an element of apology then we would have no way of expressing in action our awareness of the gravity of what we did. Overall the story of this paragraph suggests that there might be a non-instrumental way of explaining the significance of reparation.

Conclusion

In this chapter I have given a brief survey of moral philosophical writing on the issue of responses to wrongdoing. One of the fundamental lines of division on this topic is between instrumental and expressive approaches. The instrumental approaches attempt to show how the behavior and attitudes involved in forgiving, resenting, feeling guilty and making reparation can be justified in terms of their good results. The expressive approaches attempt to show how these attitudes and behavior are in some way *intrinsically* fitting to certain situations. One reason for opting for the instrumental approach is if one has the following sort of story in the back of one's mind. Many of our moral emotions are the product of a theological cultural heritage that cannot be reconciled with a secular or naturalistic point of view, since they involve essential reference to e.g. the state of one's soul, or one's relationship to God, etc. However, even if such emotions cannot be justified intrinsically or in their own terms they may still have an important social value – particularly when a susceptibility to such emotions is widely shared. The problem with the instrumental approach, however, is that it seems to involve changing the subject: it does not bear out our sense that these attitudes and behavior are fitting to or "called for" by the situation. The ideal justification of our moral emotions would therefore perhaps be one that does justify our sense of "fittingness." But a challenge for such an expressive account would lie in making sense of the intrinsic value of forgiveness, blame, atonement, etc., in terms that are compatible with naturalism (or that do not rely on supernaturalism). I hope in this chapter to have provided some glimpses of how such an approach might proceed.

See also Ethics and sentiment (Chapter 10); Freedom and responsibility (Chapter 23); Conscience (Chapter 46); Evil (Chapter 49); Responsibility: Intention and consequence (Chapter 50); Justice and punishment (Chapter 57).

References

Anscombe, G. E. M. (1958) "Modern Moral Philosophy," *Philosophy* 33: 1–19.
Baron, M. (1988) "Remorse and Agent-Regret," *Midwest Studies in Philosophy* 13: 259–81.
Bennett, C. (2008) *The Apology Ritual: A Philosophical Theory of Punishment*, Cambridge: Cambridge University Press.
Butler, J. (1967) *Fifteen Sermons Preached at the Rolls Chapel*, ed. W. R. Matthews, London: Bell.

Calhoun C. (1992) "Changing One's Heart," *Ethics* 103: 76–96.
Duff, R. A. (2001) *Punishment, Communication and Community*, Oxford: Oxford University Press.
Feinberg, J. (1974) "The Expressive Function of Punishment," in *Doing and Deserving*, Princeton, NJ: Princeton University Press.
Garrard, E. and MacNaughton, D. (2002) "In Defence of Unconditional Forgiveness," *Proceedings of the Aristotelian Society* 103: 39–60.
Hieronymi, P. (2001) "Articulating an Uncompromising Forgiveness," *Philosophy and Phenomenological Research* 62: 529–56.
Kekes, J. (1988) "Shame and Moral Progress," *Midwest Studies in Philosophy* 13: 282–96.
Kolnai, A. (1973–4) "Forgiveness," *Proceedings of the Aristotelian Society* 74: 91–106.
Murphy J. G. (2003) *Getting Even: Forgiveness and its Limits*, Oxford: Oxford University Press.
Murphy, J. G. and Hampton, J. (1988) *Forgiveness and Mercy*, Cambridge: Cambridge University Press.
Nagel, T. (1979) "Moral Luck," in *Mortal Questions*, Cambridge: Cambridge University Press.
Nussbaum, M. and Kahan, D. (1996) "Two Conceptions of the Emotions in Criminal Law," *Columbia Law Review* 96: 269–374.
Scanlon, T. M. (2008) *Moral Dimensions: Permissibility, Meaning, Blame*, Cambridge, MA: Harvard University Press.
Skorupski, J. (1999) "The Definition of Morality," in *Ethical Explorations*, Oxford: Oxford University Press.
Smart, J. J. C. (1961) "Freewill, Praise and Blame," *Mind* 70: 291–306.
Smith, A. (2002) *The Theory of Moral Sentiments*, ed. Knud Haakonsen, Cambridge: Cambridge University Press.
Strawson, G. (1994) "The Impossibility of Moral Responsibility," *Philosophical Studies* 75: 5–24.
Strawson, P. F. (1982) "Freedom and Resentment," in G. Watson (ed.) *Free Will*, Oxford: Oxford University Press.
Swinburne, R. (1985) *Responsibility and Atonement*, Oxford: Clarendon Press.
Tavuchis, N. (1991) *Mea Culpa: A Sociology of Apology and Reconciliation*, Palo Alto, CA: Stanford University Press.
Taylor, G. (1985) *Pride, Shame and Guilt*, Oxford: Clarendon Press.
von Hirsch, A. (1993) *Censure and Sanctions*, Oxford: Oxford University Press.
Walker, M. U. (2006) *Moral Repair*, Cambridge: Cambridge University Press.
Watson, G. (1996) "Two Faces of Responsibility," *Philosophical Topics* 24: 227–48.
Wiesenthal, S. (1998) *The Sunflower: On the Possibilities and Limits of Forgiveness*. New York: Schocken Books.
Williams, B. (1981) "Moral Luck," in *Moral Luck*, Cambridge: Cambridge University Press.
——(1993) *Shame and Necessity*, Berkeley: University of California Press.

Further reading

Moore, M. (1987) "The Moral Worth of Retribution," in F. Schoeman (ed.) *Responsibility, Character and the Emotions: New Essays in Moral Psychology*, Cambridge: Cambridge University Press.
Murphy, J. G. and Hampton, J. (1988) *Forgiveness and Mercy*, Cambridge: Cambridge University Press.
Taylor, G. (1985) *Pride, Shame and Guilt: Emotions of Self-Assessment*, Oxford: Clarendon Press.
Oldenquist, A. (1988) "An Explanation of Retribution," *Journal of Philosophy* 85, no. 9: 464–78.
Walker, M. U. (2006) *Moral Repair: Reconstructing Moral Relations after Wrongdoing*, Cambridge: Cambridge University Press.

49
EVIL

Geoffrey Scarre

Evil and moral evil

In its widest sense, evil is the antithesis of good: according to the *Shorter Oxford English Dictionary*, "whatever is censurable, mischievous or undesirable." On this broad understanding of the concept, any and all of "life's 'minuses'" (Adams and Adams 1990: 1) count as evils, including even such trivial events as my painfully stubbing my toe on a kerbstone. According to St Thomas Aquinas, because "good properly speaking is something inasmuch as it is desirable," evil, as the opposite of good, "must be that which is opposed to the desirable as such" (Aquinas 1995: 5). The equation of evil with the undesirable is echoed in many later writers, including Hobbes and Sidgwick, and it receives eloquent expression from Josiah Royce:

> By evil in general as it is in our experience we mean whatever we find in any sense repugnant and intolerable. ... We mean [by evil] precisely whatever we regard as something to be gotten rid of, shrunken from, put out of sight, of hearing, or memory, eschewed, expelled, resisted, assailed, or otherwise directly or indirectly resisted.
>
> (Royce 1915: 18)

Amongst "life's minuses" it is traditional to distinguish between *moral* and *natural* evils. By the former is meant the intentional harm or wrong done by moral agents – "sin, wickedness" is the dictionary's gloss – whereas the latter includes such harmful natural contingencies as diseases, famines, earthquakes and floods. (However, since human beings are themselves a part of nature, any intentional harm they cause might itself be classed as a species of natural evil.) "Natural" and "moral" evils typically evoke different cognitive and emotional responses in the victims, only the latter being liable to generate anger or resentment. They also call for different kinds of explanation, since only moral evil raises the question (which has puzzled philosophers from Socrates to the present day) of why any rational being should ever deliberately choose evil in preference to good.

Some recent authors have proposed withholding the label "evil" from purely natural harmful events that involve no moral agency. So Claudia Card has argued that earthquakes, fires and floods that are not the result of human activity are only improperly called "evil" (Card 2002: 7). In a similar vein, Susan Neiman suggests that "modern evil" is primarily envisaged as being "the product of will" (Neiman 2002: 268). Yet if modern history has prompted much intense reflection on man's inhumanity to man, ordinary usage does not (yet) justify looking on the expression "natural evil" as an oxymoron. While it is arguably odd to apply the *adjective* "evil" to events such as the Black Death or the 2004 Asian tsunami, speakers at least of UK English feel no strain in bringing these under the *substantive* "evils."

Evil as a special category?

This chapter will not be further concerned with natural evil, nor with human wrongdoing in general, "moral evil" in the traditional sense. In recent years, the liveliest philosophical discussion of evil has centered on the question of whether the term "evil" has a more particular application to certain specially reprehensible or shocking acts, persons or characters. Should we distinguish, within the deep of human wrongdoing, a lower deep of *evil*doing, in which human beings are at their worst and most depraved? Or, as Luke Russell has put it, is there a point at which wrongdoing moves into the "red zone" and becomes something worse, namely evil (Russell 2007: 92)? This philosophical debate has run in tandem with the striking revival of public discourse about evil since the Second World War, prior to which the concept of evil was becoming relatively unfashionable outside theological circles. To many people reflecting on the Holocaust and other atrocities of the twentieth- and early twenty-first centuries, the language in which we appraise more common-or-garden-variety wrongdoing has seemed inadequate to express the appropriate condemnation of Auschwitz, My Lai, the Cambodian "Year Zero," Srebrenica or the events of 9/11. To talk of Nazi "wrongs" rather than Nazi "evils" sounds mealy-mouthed and insipid to many ears, as if the speaker recognized no difference in kind between genocidal mass murder and stealing apples from the corner shop. When, following the 2001 attacks on New York and Washington, President George Bush told the American people that "Today our nation saw evil, the very worst of human nature," his words resonated with those who saw the attacks as a fundamental assault on American core values and the country itself.

While some philosophers have been sympathetic to the idea of treating "evil" as a moral natural kind term, denoting a category of the morally horrific which is qualitatively and not merely quantitatively different from more ordinary objects of moral indignation, others have been skeptical or hostile. They point out that, however popular it may be with preachers, politicians and tabloid newspaper editors, calling someone or something "evil" – the "most severe condemnation our moral vocabulary allows" (Kekes 1999: 1) – often substitutes for more fine-grained judgement and psychologically illuminating analysis. Worse, it can be used, or abused, to promote dubious political, social or religious agenda, where damning opponents as "evil" puts them beyond the pale of ordinary modes of engagement, representing them as alien, devilish creatures who pose a permanent threat to our security and ideals. As Adam Morton observes, "evil" often figures as "part of the vocabulary of hatred, dismissal, or incomprehension," a word used to divide friends from enemies, us from them (Morton 2004: 4). Phillip Cole similarly complains that the concept of evil "*obstructs* our understanding, blocks our way, brings us to a halt," because its historical associations make it a term of demonization; someone described as "evil" is deemed to be "not *really* human," and so beyond the scope of "communication and negotiation, reform and redemption." In Cole's view, it would be wise to ditch the language of evil, as practically inflammatory and theoretically unilluminating (Cole 2006: 236).

Ironically, both those who defend the use of the language of evil and those who oppose it appeal to a form of moral sensitivity which they accuse their opponents of lacking. Defenders assert that, without it, we would lack an adequate vehicle for expressing our disapproval of and indignation at the worst things that human beings do to one another. Offenses of different moral colors, some in the red zone and some not, would end up indiscriminately lumped together. In contrast, opponents charge that talk of evil too often displaces trying to understand other agents, impugns their humanity and intrinsic value, disregards their interests, and supports a Manichean caricature of a world sharply divided between good and evil. One thing at least seems clear from this debate: that if the term "evil" is to play a legitimate role in our moral appraisals of persons, acts and events, it must be stripped of its more rhetorical overtones and cease to be used as a mere term of dismissal – still less as a firecracker label for sparking fear and hatred.

Modern analyses of evil

Philosophers who agree that the concept of evil has a valuable role to play in moral thought have not all agreed on what that role should be, and there have been numerous proposals about what sets evil people or acts apart from "merely" bad people or acts. It is doubtful, though, whether the word "evil" in ordinary speech possesses the precision of meaning that some theorists attempt to impose on it, and the pretensions of any theory to locate *the* real meaning of "evil" may justly be viewed with some skepticism. As we shall see, the notion of evil has struck different chords in different people, and there is probably little point in trying to force anyone and anything that can be called evil into a single definitional frame. From this perspective, it may be better to read the various accounts on offer for the complementary lights they throw into some of the darker corners of human experience than as rival accounts of the "real meaning" of evil.

Some characterizations of evil have focused on the greater severity of the harm involved in cases of evil than in cases of more ordinary wrongdoing. John Kekes has defined evil as "serious unjustified harm inflicted on sentient beings" (a definition that allows that animals as well as humans can suffer it) (Kekes 1999: 1). On this view, the motives of those who do the harm may be less important than the amount of harm they (intentionally) do in making that harm *evil*. Hannah Arendt's famous conception of "banal evil" might be thought to be an account of this kind, since a central theme in her psychological analysis of Nazi architects of death such as Adolf Eichmann is the chronic thoughtlessness they exhibited when they murdered millions (Arendt 1994). However, what made Eichmann's activities evil, in Arendt's eyes, was not so much the *amount* of suffering they produced as the vast and absurd disproportion between the quantity of harm done and the paucity of his reflection about it.

Comparatively few writers have thought that there is nothing more to evil action than the intentional production of serious harm. Some have not even regarded the causation of *serious* harm as necessary for evil. Those who hold the quintessential feature of evil action to be its origin in malice or misanthropy or moral blindness or some other serious cognitive or emotional fault or deficiency in the agent may class as evil some deeds that cause no harm at all, so long as they stem from an evil-making motivation. (One example here would be the practice of malicious but ineffectual black magic.)

Even if not all evils involve harm on a massive scale, Claudia Card rightly notes that it is atrocities such as the mass murders perpetrated in the Nazi death camps that provide us with our main paradigms of evil. This, she suggests, is for the epistemological reason that "the core features of evils tend to be writ large in the case of atrocities, making them easier to identify and appreciate" (Card 2002: 9; cf. Lara 2007: 25). But an equally important reason may be that, while not all evils are atrocious evils, atrocities are the most horrifying examples of the genre, the ones that make us catch our breath in dismay and incredulity. In a refinement of his earlier view, Kekes observes that the harm involved in evil acts is typically "not just serious but excessive" – as when a robber, having taken his victim's money, proceeds to torture and murder him as well (Kekes 2005: 2). One might quibble that any morally wrong act is "excessive" or "over the top" in so far as it goes beyond the morally permissible, but Kekes, like Card, is drawing attention to the element of gratuitous injury or insult frequently found in those acts we call "evil" – an element which appears to owe more to their agent's hatred or malevolence than to their instrumental rationality. In contrast with more ordinary wrongs, evils inflict suffering not so much (or not only) as a means to an end, but as an end in itself.

Among philosophers who think that the most notable thing about evils is the peculiar malice or nastiness of those who perpetrate or enjoy them are Todd Calder and Daniel Haybron, who point out that there would be something evil about a person who did no harm himself but took sadistic satisfaction in witnessing or contemplating the harm that other human beings inflicted on one another (Haybron 1999: 133–4; Calder 2002: 56). Taking this line further, it would show an evil disposition if a person delighted in watching realistic computer-generated scenes of torture and mutilation where he knew that no actual suffering was going on at all. Eve Garrard likewise places the major emphasis on the bad minds of evildoers, rather than on the amount of harm they bring about. A person who mistreats an animal or gloatingly bullies a terrified child does something *evil*, and not just wrong, she asserts, even though "in the scale of the world's catastrophes the disvalue produced by these actions is pretty insignificant" (Garrard 1998: 45).

Another view focuses less on the harm associated with evils than on the existential impact they have on their victims – though this could be regarded as a special form of mental harm. Some evils attack the things that ground the meaning of people's lives, assaulting their values, beliefs and traditions, and undermining their self-respect. Stephen de Wijze remarks that a common object of evil action is the dehumanization, humiliation and denigration of its victims, making them feel that they and their lives are utterly worthless (de Wijze 2002). Sergio Pérez speaks of evil as a lack of humanity exhibited in acts that are "carried out against human beings or against something meaningful to human beings," observing that some kinds of political oppression may have this result even where they do not impose much physical pain or hardship (Pérez 2001: 189). Having our moral principles ridiculed, our friendships belittled, our projects denigrated, or our religion derided can be as hurtful and damaging as severe physical pain, especially if it causes us to start questioning our own commitments. A related sense of disorientation can be caused by the treachery or desertion of a trusted friend which, even if it should cause only minor concrete harm, may give us a sense that our world is falling apart.

The evil character

Not all evil acts are done by evil agents, i.e. agents whose character is fundamentally attuned to the doing, or enjoying, of evil. Extreme circumstances can generate extreme behavior in people who in normal life would never think of treating others in cruel or debasing ways. Morton remarks that "far more evil acts are performed by perfectly normal people out of confusion or desperation or obsession than by violent individuals or sociopaths" (Morton 2004: 53–4). Such out-of-character evildoing has been the subject of extensive empirical research over recent decades, when it has become increasingly recognized what evil such "ordinary men" as the members of German Police Battalion 101, whose murderous exploits in Western Russia in 1942 were famously studied by Christopher Browning, are capable of when removed from their customary moral and social environment (see Browning 1992). Still, there exist some individuals who display a more consistent and characteristic tendency to cause suffering when they get the chance, and these have attracted considerable attention from both psychologists and philosophers.

Among these are people suffering from innate antisocial personality disorder (APD), whose essential feature, as defined by the American Psychiatric Association, is "a pervasive pattern of disregard for, and violation of, the rights of others," a condition commonly referred to as psychopathy or sociopathy. Subjects of APD "lack empathy and tend to be callous, cynical, and contemptuous of the feelings, rights, and sufferings of others" (see Kekes 2005: 103). Because such people are not responsible for their natures, calling them "evil" might seem unjust; yet to say that someone has an evil disposition need not be read as imputing blame to that person for having it. Many of the serial killers that we know from real life as well as from fiction and film fall into this category, and it would run strongly contrary to everyday usage to deny the epithet "evil" to them on the ground that they could not help their behavior, having the misfortune to have been "born like that."

Thoroughly evil persons – human monsters, if ever there were any – are sometimes conceived of as the diametrical opposites of moral saints. Hume gives us a thumbnail sketch:

> A creature, absolutely malicious and spiteful, were there any such in nature, must be worse than indifferent to the images of vice and virtue. All his sentiments must be inverted, and directly opposite to those which prevail in the human species. Whatever contributes to the good of mankind as it crosses the constant bent of his wishes and desires, must produce uneasiness and disapprobation; and on the contrary, whatever is the source of disorder and misery in society, must, for the same reason, be regarded with pleasure and complacency.
>
> (Hume 1902: 226)

A person who fitted this description would be as bad as bad could be, though Hume is rather outlining a conceivable figure than claiming that any human beings are actually like this. In fact, individuals who are invariably malicious and spiteful, and never wish well to anyone besides themselves, may be as mythical as unicorns. (Moral saints – people who are always as good as good can be, and never slip below the highest standards of virtue – are probably equally creatures of fantasy.) Even some of the worst men and women in history have had their softer sides. Hitler killed millions but was sincerely fond of certain members of his own family; he was also kind to animals and a committed vegetarian.

The Emperor Nero had his mother Agrippina cruelly murdered and delighted to torture prisoners, yet he loved his mistress Poppaea. Some of the most notorious serial killers of modern times have shown themselves capable of an unsimulated affection towards a few favored others.

Central to Hume's idea of the evil character is the malice, the wishing ill (Latin *malum*) to others, which lies at his heart. Several contemporary writers have followed and defended a similar Humean line. Hillel Steiner defines evil acts as "wrong acts that are pleasurable for their doers" and understands the psychology of evildoers in terms of the perverse satisfaction they take when things go wrong for other people (Steiner 2002: 189). Colin McGinn has proposed that the "basic idea" of the evil person is one of a character that derives pleasure from others' pain and pain from others' pleasure (in contrast to the virtuous person, who takes pleasure in others' pleasure and pain in their pain) (McGinn 1997: 62). McGinn instances both real and fictional cases of evil characters, and suggests that for some individuals – such as the malicious master-at-arms Claggart in Melville's novel *Billy Budd* – the distress of others has a primitive psychological attraction; they are, so to speak, wired up to enjoy other people's distress. But McGinn is careful not to claim that *all* evil characters conform to this "basic idea." One common and powerful motive for wanting to harm others is envy of what is perceived to be their better fortune (an attitude that may even be extended to animals on account of their "free, comparatively serene, and unencumbered" lives) (McGinn 1997: 79–80, 82). Even a confirmed sadist may occasionally be driven less by a primitive delight in others' pain than by "a kind of existential envy – a feeling that his life is intrinsically less valuable than other people's," which impels him to reduce them to his own "dismal level" (McGinn 1997: 80). The envious Iago in Shakespeare's *Othello* could be proposed as a type of the existentially dissatisfied person desirous of leveling down those whom he perceives to have been more successful than himself. Such malice born of envy should be distinguished from that more primitive kind which McGinn thinks is grounded in an innate sadistic streak.

Despite the undeniable intuitive appeal of the Humean tradition's analysis of evil character as malicious character, some have thought it overly narrow in implicitly excluding from the category of evil people men such as the SS chief Heinrich Himmler, overlord of the Nazi genocidal project, who inflict terrible suffering on others from a perverse sense of duty and without any special relish for what they do. As Luke Russell notes, on Steiner's theory, Himmler's horrific acts, since they brought no pleasure to their doer, do not qualify as evil: a very counter-intuitive result (Russell 2007: 670). But perhaps it should be allowed that Himmler's deeds, though evil in themselves, do not issue from an evil character. Maybe we should say that Himmler (if we accept his self-description as a reluctant killer) was not evil, but tragically mistaken, in thrall to a false ideology, morally benighted, disastrously inclined to follow his principles rather than be guided by his emotions. But some philosophers (especially those who incline in a more Arendtian direction) prefer to see a man like Himmler – stern and pitiless, ruthless and unbending, exceptionally lacking in the milk of human kindness, unable to recognize the moral "stop" signs that most people respect – as having *one kind* of evil character.

Their position may draw some indirect support from a popular traditional view, espoused by such influential Christian writers as St Augustine and St Thomas Aquinas, that evil is best understood not as some positive thing in itself but in negative terms, as a privation of good. Aquinas illustrated the claim with the example of physical blindness which, though a very real and harmful evil, is nevertheless not a *thing* but an absence, namely the absence of the faculty of sight (Aquinas 1989: 10). The privative theory of evil has often been criticized on metaphysical and empirical grounds, most stridently by Schopenhauer, who thought it absurd to hold that evil was something negative when "evil is precisely what is positive, that which makes itself palpable" (Schopenhauer 1970: 40). Yet the theory does at least nod in the direction of one important insight about evil: that many of the worst things that human beings do to one another are causally associated with some crucial lack or shortfall – of thought, or imagination, or love, or empathy, or the capacity to put oneself in another's shoes. So Himmler's case could be explained in terms of his emotional stuntedness, his inability to grasp what other lives were like from the inside, and his consequent moral blindness to the humanity of his victims. Even in the absence of malice, this lethal combination may not unwarrantably be deemed to constitute his character an evil one.

Some evil agents recognize that their victims' misery provides a reason against mistreating them but refuse to heed it; others, still more morally or psychologically incomplete, may not even see it as a reason. Not all philosophers are willing to call those who come within the latter group "evil"; they may alternatively be regarded as a kind of moral imbecile. But it is people of this description that Arendt was referring to when she spoke about the "banality of evil," and we might accordingly wish to class such killers as Himmler and Eichmann as men of *banally evil* character, in contrast to those whose mainspring of action is malice. When Arendt attended the trial of Eichmann in 1960, the defendant she saw standing in the dock in Jerusalem was not a monster or perverted sadist but a quiet, unimpressive figure who (in so far as he had thought at all) had thought it his duty to obey the will of the Führer to the best of his ability. "The longer one listened to him," Arendt reported, "the more obvious it became that his inability to speak was closely connected with an inability to think, namely to think from the standpoint of somebody else" (Arendt 1994: 49).

An account of evil character in Arendtian vein has been offered by Eve Garrard, who defines the evil agent as someone who cannot hear as reasons the moral considerations telling against certain kinds of act. Evil agents are afflicted by a special sort of moral blindness (in contrast to virtuous ones, who are blessed with a distinctive kind of moral insight). Someone who performs an act that is merely very wrong is aware that there are considerations that tell against the act but allows them to be outweighed by the selfish reasons in favor, whereas for the evil agent "such considerations as the suffering of his victims are silenced. They don't weigh with him at all, not even to be outweighed" (Garrard 1998: 53–4).

Garrard's account has been criticized both for what it includes within the category of evil and for what it excludes. Christopher Hamilton has pointed out that, on this view, Macbeth's treacherous murder of King Duncan very implausibly fails to qualify as evil, or Macbeth as an evil character, since Macbeth has to struggle with his conscience before he can bring himself to commit the fatal deed (Hamilton 1999: 124). Garrard in response has suggested that Macbeth's act was "appallingly wicked" rather than evil, but this appears a forced distinction in the light of ordinary usage (Garrard 1999: 139). Russell has objected that, since Garrard does not insist that evil acts should cause serious harm, she implies that even a minor act of shoplifting would be evil, and show evil character, if the shopkeeper's right to keep his property were not a reason that weighed with the shoplifter (Russell 2007: 673). Garrard might best be able to meet this objection, while preserving her conviction that evil has more to do with the psychology behind the acts done than with the amount of harm produced, by borrowing from the more fully fleshed-out picture of the evil agent presented by Daniel Haybron. On Haybron's portrayal, the evil person is "thoroughly or consistently" vicious and has no redeeming virtues whatsoever (or hardly any). To be evil "is to be disposed to be neither moved nor motivated (positively) by the good to a morally significant extent" (Haybron 2002a: 63, 70). Such a person is unlikely to confine herself to an occasional bout of shoplifting, but will show her obnoxious side consistently and predictably. If the reason why the shopkeeper's right to keep his property fails to weigh with the thief is that such reasons *never* weigh with her, then her act of shoplifting, though minor in itself, will fit into a pattern of evil behavior.

It would be unwise to look for a definitive conception of the evil agent, or to hope to distinguish with precision people who are evil from those who are "merely" very bad. More disturbingly, perhaps, there may be no more than a fuzzy boundary to be drawn between truly evil characters and moral imbeciles. Many doers of gross wrong proceed with a breathtaking disregard of moral considerations or the feelings of others, while displaying no trace of malice. Often in such cases we may think that the agent *could*, and consequently *should*, have paid more attention to the morally significant reasons against acting as he did. To say that Eichmann was a thoughtless man is not to say that he was incapable of thought; and, being able to think, he should have questioned the orders he was given and the principles he honored. His negligence in this regard may persuade us to label him an evil man rather than a moral imbecile. Yet there are further issues that could be raised. Why did Eichmann fail to see the need to raise such critical questions? Did that failure itself result from an innate lack of moral intelligence? If we suspect that the answer might be yes, then we may feel renewed uncertainty how to pigeon-hole him.

Evil and explanation

Finally, is the concept of evil ever useful in explaining why people do the bad things they do? This is doubtful, for two closely related reasons. The first is that, as we have seen, the concept admits of no single, simple or uncontested analysis. It would be dogmatic to claim that such-and-such is the quintessential feature belonging to all those persons, acts and states of affairs that we bring under it (though, as we have also seen, that has not stopped philosophers proffering such claims). "Evil" does not distinguish a unitary motive for doing harm and certainly not some impulse of pure diabolism; moreover, the existence of several contrasting conceptions of evil poses a risk of serious confusion where evil is cited in an explanatory role.

The second reason is that describing someone or something as evil says nothing that cannot be better expressed in more precise and illuminating language. Inga Clendinnen, in her book on the Holocaust, has remarked in rejecting the appeal to evil in the explanation of Nazi atrocities that such appeal is usually "of no use whatsoever in teasing out why people act as they do" (Clendinnen 1999: 88). Calling a deed, an agent, an event, or a state of affairs "evil" is no substitute for articulating the particular psychological, sociological, historical or situational factors that are at work; and those factors in their turn will require explanation. What causes a person to enjoy inflicting pain on others, or to wish to destroy the meaningfulness of their lives or the basis of their self-respect? Why do some agents suffer from the serious cognitive deficiencies to which Garrard alludes, being blind to the reasons against performing certain harmful acts? How is it that prolonged exposure to negative ideological messages sometimes induces such insensitivity even in relatively intelligent and kindly people? Even where we can explain a case of moral blindness, we will still not fully understand the agent's evildoing until we have identified the positive motives that impel him to act in the absence of the usual restraints. In short, evil is usually the *explanandum*, not the *explanans*.

Appealing to evil for an explanation of atrocious or horrifying acts may be mischievous as well as misleading where it is associated with a flawed conception of "a world of simple binary oppositions of Good and Evil" (Bernstein 2005: 50). Many politicians in recent years have played on the dark, if vague, resonances that the term "evil" sets off in many minds, trusting that once people have docketed the enemy as evil, they will feel they know all they need to know to justify his destruction. Thus pseudo-explanation replaces genuine explanation, throttling all but the most superficial reflection and reducing those whom it takes in to a level of thoughtless acceptance of the state or party line indistinguishable from Eichmann's. (Eichmann himself believed that the Jews were evil.) Small wonder that some philosophers and political commentators have suggested that we should jettison the language of evil altogether. But there is no necessity to take that drastic step and discard a mode of discourse that is at least as old as the

Bible, provided that we employ it with due discretion and sensitivity to its ambiguities and limitations.

See also Conscience (Chapter 46); Blame, remorse, mercy, forgiveness (Chapter 48); Torture and terrorism (Chapter 68).

References

Adams, Marilyn McCord and Adams, Robert Merrihew (1990) Introduction to Marilyn McCord Adams and Robert Merrihew Adams (eds) *The Problem of Evil*, Oxford: Oxford University Press.

Aquinas, St Thomas (1995) *On Evil*, trans. Jean Oesterle, Notre Dame, IN: University of Notre Dame Press.

Arendt, Hannah (1994) *Eichmann in Jerusalem: A Report on the Banality of Evil*, London: Penguin Books.

Bernstein, Richard J. (2005) *The Abuse of Evil: The Corruption of Politics and Religion Since 9/11*, Cambridge: Polity Press.

Browning, Christopher (1992) *Ordinary Men: Reserve Police Battalion 101 and the Final Solution in Poland*, New York: HarperCollins.

Calder, Todd (2002) "Towards a Theory of Evil Acts," in Haybron 2002b, pp. 51–61.

Card, Claudia (2002) *The Atrocity Paradigm: A Theory of Evil*, New York: Oxford University Press.

Clendinnen, Inga (1999) *Reading the Holocaust*, Cambridge: Cambridge University Press.

Cole, Phillip (2006) *The Myth of Evil*, Edinburgh: Edinburgh University Press.

de Wijze, Stephen (2002) "Defining Evil: Insights from the Problem of 'Dirty Hands'," *Monist* 85: 210–38.

Garrard, Eve (1998) "The Nature of Evil," *Philosophical Explorations* 1: 43–60.

——(1999) "Evil Revisited – Responses to Hamilton," *Philosophical Explorations* 2: 139–42.

Hamilton, Christopher (1999) "The Nature of Evil: A Reply to Garrard," *Philosophical Explorations* 2: 122–38.

Haybron, Daniel (1999) "Evil Characters," *American Philosophical Quarterly* 36: 131–43.

——(2002a) "Consistency of Character and the Character of Evil," in Haybron 2002b, pp. 63–78.

——(ed.) (2002b) *Earth's Abominations: Philosophical Studies of Evil*, Amsterdam and New York: Rodopi.

Hume, David (1902) *An Enquiry Concerning the Principles of Morals*, ed. L. A. Selby-Bigge, Oxford: Clarendon Press.

Kekes, John (1999) "Evil," in *Routledge Encyclopedia of Philosophy*, Version 1.1, London and New York: Routledge (online).

——(2005) *The Roots of Evil*, Ithaca, NY, and London: Cornell University Press.

Lara, María Pía (2007) *Narrating Evil*, New York: Columbia University Press.

McGinn, Colin (1997) *Ethics, Evil, and Fiction*, Oxford: Clarendon Press

Morton, Adam (2004) *On Evil*, New York and London: Routledge.

Neiman, Susan (2002) *Evil in Modern Thought*, Princeton, NJ, and Oxford: Princeton University Press.

Pérez, Sergio (2001) "Major Offenders, Minor Offenders," in María Pía Lara, (ed.) *Rethinking Evil: Contemporary Perspectives*, Berkeley: University of California Press.

Russell, Luke (2007) "Is Evil Action Qualitatively Different from Ordinary Wrongdoing?," *Australasian Journal of Philosophy* 85: 659–77.

Royce, Josiah (1915) "The Problem of Job," in *Studies of Good and Evil: A Series of Essays upon Problems of Philosophy and Life*, New York: D. Appleton.

Schopenhauer, Arthur (1970) "On the Suffering of the World," in *Essays and Aphorisms*, trans. R. J. Hollingdale, Harmondsworth: Penguin Books.

Steiner, Hillel (2002) "Calibrating Evil," *Monist* 85: 183–93.

Further reading

Bennett, Jonathan (1974) "The Conscience of Huckleberry Finn," *Philosophy* 49: 123–34. (Contains an interesting analysis of the moral psychology of Himmler.)

Morrow, Lance (2003) *Evil: An Investigation*, New York: Basic Books.

Rorty, Amélie Oksenberg (ed.) (2001) *The Many Faces of Evil: Historical Perspectives*, London: Routledge. (A useful anthology of classic and modern texts on evil.)

Russell, Luke (2006) "Evil-Revivalism versus Evil-Skepticism," *Journal of Value Inquiry* 40: 89–105.

Shafer-Landau, Russ (2003) *Whatever Happened to Good and Evil?*, New York: Oxford University Press.

Singer, Marcus G. (2004) "The Concept of Evil," *Philosophy* 79: 185–214. (Surveys the recent literature.)

Tabensky, Pedro Alexis (ed.) (2009) *The Positive Function of Evil*, Basingstoke and New York: Palgrave Macmillan. (Explores the controversial idea that evil may in some contexts make a positive contribution to human life.)

50
RESPONSIBILITY
Intention and consequence

Suzanne Uniacke

We are responsible for the intended consequences of our actions. A critical understanding of this relatively uncontroversial claim requires us to address a range of questions that have important bearing both on what it is to be responsible for something and also on what it is that we are responsible for. The first such question concerns the relevant sense of "responsible" under which we are responsible for the intended consequences of our actions.

In what sense of "responsible"?

"Responsible" and "responsibility" are commonly used in a number of distinguishable and partially overlapping senses. We speak of responsibility for an event or state of affairs in a purely causal sense when we say, for example, that a stone, or the storm, was responsible for the broken window. We also use "responsibility" in a more narrowly defined sense in attributing causal agency to the behavior of animate beings, both human beings and non-human animals, where we might say, for example, that old Tom's aggression was responsible for the fight. In a still narrower, more specific sense, we use the language of responsibility in attributing personal agency, where we say of a particular person that, for example, *he* was responsible for the fight. Ascriptions of purely causal responsibility and of causal agency do not themselves carry any moral implications. (Stones and storms are not morally responsible for what they cause; non-human animals are not morally responsible for what they do.) An ascription of personal agency, however, usually implies that the person responsible was acting as a moral agent: that she acted voluntarily and with understanding of the moral quality of her actions. (Personal agents are not always moral agents. Young children lack moral understanding and psychopaths are said to do so.) Moral agency is the basic necessary condition under which a person is morally responsible for what she does or brings about.

In ascribing responsibility to persons as moral agents we can draw another type of distinction: that between so-called prospective as opposed to retrospective responsibility (Duff 1998; Zimmerman 2001). Prospective responsibility refers to those *responsibilities*, that is, those moral (or legal) duties or obligations that a person has in virtue of her particular role(s), or that she has simply *qua* human being. For instance, as a parent I am responsible for the welfare of my dependent children; as a lifeguard I am responsible for going to the rescue of swimmers on the stretch of beach I patrol; as a citizen I am responsible for paying my taxes and for obeying the criminal law; as a fellow human being I am responsible for not inflicting wrongful injury on other people. Prospective responsibilities may or may not be fulfilled by the person who has those responsibilities. Retrospective responsibility for something, on the other hand, is based on ascription of personal agency for that same thing: under certain conditions we are retrospectively responsible for what we do or bring about. I might be retrospectively responsible, for example, for abandoning my children and for the subsequent hardship they suffer; for neglecting my lifeguard duties and for someone's drowning as a result; for not paying my taxes; for violating the criminal code; or for injuring someone. (Although retrospective responsibility is ascribed for what has passed, it can be conditional and predicted, as in the warning, "Be aware that if you do that you'll be responsible for the outcome.") The examples mentioned above highlight the fact that although prospective responsibility and retrospective responsibility are different, what I am retrospectively responsible for can partly depend on what my prospective responsibilities are (Duff 1998).

The claim that we are responsible for the intended consequences of our actions ascribes retrospective responsibility. All ascriptions of retrospective responsibility, including purely causal ones, invoke a norm or standard against which something or someone is held to be responsible for an event or state of affairs. Something that we identify as the cause of a particular event or state of affairs is a deviation from a norm (Feinberg 1970). Typically, this deviation is a variation or intervention in the usual set of circumstances or a variation from the expected course of events. (In the case of a broken window, it might be a stone hitting the window or the onset of a violent storm.) Ascription of retrospective responsibility can also invoke evaluative norms, including moral or legal principles or obligations. Here the type of responsibility ascribed is moral or legal. For example, I can be morally responsible for the effects of my generous actions and also for the consequences of lying to someone; I am both morally and legally responsible for the injuries that my dependent children suffer because I neglect them.

Our particular concern is with attributions of retrospective moral responsibility for the consequences of our actions, and for intended consequences in particular.

What counts as a consequence?

A basic question for ascription of moral responsibility for consequences is what is to count as a consequence of what a person does. Broadly speaking, a consequence of an action can be any event or state of affairs that results from that action. This broad characterization raises two important questions: On what basis do we distinguish an action from its consequences? At what point can we say that the consequences of a particular action cease?

We speak of being responsible, under certain conditions, for our actions and also for (some of) their consequences. However, a distinction between an action that is described in a particular way, as opposed to one or more of the consequences of that action, is often artificial. For example, in describing my action and its consequences, you might say, "She fired the gun (action) and someone was shot (consequence) and injured (consequence)." Alternatively, these particular consequences can be incorporated into various descriptions of what I did: "She shot someone" (action); "She injured someone" (action). As is frequently noted, the language in which we speak about actions and their consequences is "accordion like" in that it admits of the type of expansion and contraction illustrated in this example (D'Arcy 1963; Feinberg 1970). When asked, "What did she do?," you might answer in the more expansive mode and say that I fired the gun (action) and another person was shot (consequence) and seriously injured (consequence); or you could elide the more basic action (firing the gun) and say that I shot and injured another person.

The elision of more basic actions in more encompassing descriptions of what an agent did is often entirely appropriate and a matter of where our particular interest or focus lies (D'Arcy 1963). For instance, although it would not be wrong to say that someone flipped a switch (action) and the light came on (consequence), we would not normally use this particular description. Rather, we would elide the distinction between the more basic action (flipping the switch) and its consequence (the light going on) and say that someone turned on the light. The less expansive description might be apt in some circumstances, however. It could be appropriate if, for example, we were interested in whether a light came on because someone flipped the switch or because someone or something triggered a remote sensor.

Where a more basic action is itself morally significant, it is inappropriate to elide it in a more encompassing action-description (D'Arcy 1963). For example, if I protect my own life by inflicting serious injury on another person, it is inappropriate simply to say that I protected my own life, thereby eliding the morally significant more basic action (injuring someone else) by which I did this. Here we must explicitly acknowledge that my protecting myself was a consequence of my seriously injuring someone else. Equally, where a more encompassing action-description is morally significant, it can be important to identify the more basic actions involved. For example, the moral significance of my preventing another person from suffering serious injury partly depends on how this came about. (Was it a consequence of a deliberate action on my part, and if so, what was this? Did I perhaps bring it about inadvertently?)

The broad characterization of a consequence of an action given above would encompass events and states of affairs that are too remote from our actions to count as consequences for which we are morally responsible. On what grounds are some consequences too remote in this regard? Initially two types of remoteness might suggest themselves: physical remoteness, where a consequence occurs at a considerable physical distance from the action; and temporal remoteness, where a consequence occurs well into the future. However, a moment's reflection shows that physical remoteness or temporal remoteness is insufficient to disqualify a consequence of an action as something for which the agent could be morally responsible. If I fire a missile that kills people on the other side of the world I can be morally responsible for their deaths; if I trigger a hidden device in 2009 that explodes and kills people in 2030 I can be morally responsible for their deaths. In these two examples, the causal relationship between my action and the particular consequence in question is *direct*. In both cases, it is possible to elide the distinction between my action and its consequence and say that I have killed these people. These are important considerations in the strong ascription of moral responsibility for these consequences despite their physical or temporal remoteness.

This suggests that the relevant type of remoteness arises when the causal relationship between an action, *x*, and a subsequent event or state of affairs, *y*, is *indirect*. A consequence will be indirect in this sense when there is one or more intermediate causal factors between *x* and *y*. Intermediate causal factors can include natural events and also the voluntary actions of other people who are themselves morally responsible for what they do and bring about. Causal indirectness will be a matter of degree since the number and the significance of intermediate causes can vary, and the causal connection between an action, *x*, and a subsequent event or state of affairs, *y*, can be more or less indirect. The suggestion is, then, that when the causal connection between an action, *x*, and a consequence, *y*, is sufficiently indirect, *y* is too remote from *x* to be something for which the agent of *x* is morally responsible.

This suggestion goes in the right direction. However, it does not tell us on what basis a causal connection between an action, *x*, and a subsequent event or state of affairs, *y*, will be sufficiently indirect so as to diminish or eliminate moral responsibility. We can consider a number of possible grounds, one of which is the role of the voluntary actions of another person or persons as intermediate causes between *x* and *y*. If, for example, I generously give you money and you use it to buy a gun with which you shoot someone, your victim's death is not (normally) something for which I am responsible. However, this example also shows why the voluntary intervention of another person does not always "sever" the connection of responsibility between *x* and *y*. This is because I *would* bear some moral responsibility for your actions were they to be a predictable outcome of my giving you the money. People can share responsibility for a particular event or state of affairs and in some circumstances more than one person can be morally responsible for something that is directly due to the voluntary action of a particular person. If I lend you a gun knowing that you intend to kill someone with it and you do so, I bear some moral responsibility for what you do. If I negligently leave a gate open and a toddler wanders into my garden and drowns in my swimming pool, I am to some extent morally responsible for this even if the toddler's parents are principally responsible because they let it roam unsupervised. Notwithstanding the intermediate voluntary actions of other people, we can be morally responsible for those indirect consequences of our actions that we foresee or that we have an obligation to prevent.

In these last examples, my action (lending you the gun; leaving the gate open) is not the principal cause of the consequence in question (a shooting; a child drowning). Nonetheless, the causal connection between my action and the outcome in question is still relatively close. (You might have obtained a gun some other way and killed someone with it, but in fact you killed someone with the gun I lent you. Perhaps the unsupervised child could have got into my pool some other way, but she actually got in through the gate I left open.) We might then consider that the number and range of intermediate causes between *x* and *y* can have a significant bearing on ascription of responsibility. Again this goes in the right direction. If, for example, one of my descendants is a tyrant in 150 years' time, I am not morally responsible for his misdeeds. A significant reason for this must be the number and range of intermediate causal factors, both natural events and also human actions. But here we need to ask why the number and range of intermediate causes should make some consequences too remote from my action for ascription of moral responsibility. I think that the answer lies in what a person intends or what she can reasonably foresee in acting as she does. Whether a moral agent intends or can foresee a particular *direct or indirect* consequence of her action is central to the question of whether, and to what extent, she can be morally responsible for it. We are not normally morally responsible for consequences of our actions that are not reasonably foreseeable. This is because of what it is to be morally responsible for a consequence of one's action.

What is it to be morally responsible for a consequence?

An influential view is that to be responsible for something is to be answerable for it (Duff 1998). On this view, to be morally responsible for a consequence of one's action is to have a moral case to answer for having brought it about. Those consequences for which we can be answerable are those that are morally significant because they infringe a moral norm or appear to do so. If, for example,

I act in a way that harms another person (e.g. I fire a gun and seriously injure her) this is morally significant. If firing the gun was a voluntary act on my part, then I can legitimately be called upon morally to answer for having thereby caused serious injury. I might respond by offering an explanation intended as a moral justification of my firing the gun and the injury this caused. I might claim, for instance, that the person I injured was attacking me and I was acting in self-defense. A justificatory explanation of this type maintains that it was morally permissible for me to act as I did in the circumstances and that the injury I inflicted was not wrongful. (A stronger type of justification, such as the claim that I was defending other people whom I had a duty to protect, would maintain that what I did was morally right.) If I was acting in justified self-defense, then while I am answerable for having caused serious injury to another person I am not morally at fault or to blame for this.

Alternatively, I might offer an explanation intended as an excuse for the injury I caused, as opposed to a justification of it. This purported excuse might be, for example, that when I took aim and pulled the trigger I honestly believed that I was firing a toy gun and meant only to joke with the other person, not injure her. In offering this kind of explanation I am conceding that I caused wrongful injury, but maintaining that since I acted on the mistaken belief that the gun was a toy and I meant no harm, I am not morally at fault or blameworthy on this account. (A third possible way of discharging a moral case to answer is that of claimed immunity [Duff 1998]. This option is not applicable to this particular example, but will be outlined later.)

To regard a person as answerable for a morally significant consequence of his action does not (yet) attribute to him any moral fault on that account (Duff 1998). In some contexts, "morally responsible" is used in imputing moral fault and sometimes blame. (In rejecting my purported excuse above, you might say, "Even if she thought the gun was a toy, I hold her morally responsible for the injury she caused. She should have inspected the gun more closely." Consider also that we think that retrospective responsibility can be a matter of degree. Actions can be voluntary to a greater or lesser extent, and there are also degrees of moral fault and blame, but not I think degrees of answerability.) Nonetheless, it is important to recognize that when we attribute moral fault to someone for a particular consequence of her action we are making a *further* judgment, namely that the case to answer has not been discharged in terms of a satisfactory moral justification or complete excuse. Imputation of moral fault is inappropriate if a person's conduct was morally justified or completely excusable; she remains morally responsible (answerable) for what she did or brought about.

However, in another important respect the view that to be morally responsible for something is to be answerable for it is misleading. This is because we can be morally responsible for good consequences as well as for bad. "Answerable" means having a case to answer, and this implies that the consequences for which we can be morally responsible are only those that call for justification or excuse.

(The view that to be morally responsible for something is to be accountable for it has the same implication.) Ascriptions of moral responsibility for bad consequences invoke deviations from moral norms, for which there is a case to answer. Ascriptions of moral responsibility for good consequences, on the other hand, usually invoke positive deviations from what is morally required of a person that are potentially to her credit (as would be e.g. saving someone else's life). (Ascription of moral responsibility can also invoke a person's conformity with a moral norm where it is to her moral credit to have fulfilled an obligation under extreme pressure or at great cost to herself.) We are not *answerable* for those good consequences of our actions for which we are morally responsible, unless for some reason they infringe a moral norm or appear to do so. (An example of the latter possibility would be where I rescue a child from drowning at the expense of others, or I endanger others as a means of conducting the rescue.)

Some writers maintain that in ascribing responsibility we are only ever concerned with attributing moral fault or blame. This claim might be true of *legal* responsibility (which is perhaps always answerability or accountability), but it provides a lopsided conception of ascription of moral responsibility. In ascribing moral responsibility we are concerned with an appropriate moral appraisal of moral agents for what they do or bring about (Feinberg 1970). This appraisal includes attribution of moral credit for good consequences as well as attribution of fault for bad ones. Just as ascription of moral responsibility underpins any further attribution of moral fault for the bad consequences of our actions, so ascription of moral responsibility underpins attribution of moral credit for good consequences. For example, were I to act in a way that deflects a threat of serious harm from another person, it is relevant to ask whether I am morally responsible for this good outcome.

We are morally responsible for consequences that are attributable to us as moral agents; that is to say, we are morally responsible for those consequences that it is potentially to our moral credit or demerit to have brought about.

How are intention and foresight relevant to moral responsibility?

In assessing the relevance of intention to moral responsibility, we need to be aware that there are wider and narrower conceptions of intention. In some contexts, the criminal law regards as intended any consequence of a person's action that she foresees as certain or highly probable. This means that, for example, someone who plants a bomb in a railway carriage with the aim of killing a particular person also intends the deaths of other people who happen by chance to occupy the same carriage (Duff 1998). There might be good reason for the criminal law to regard such consequences as intended. However, in everyday contexts we conceive of intention more narrowly. Someone who, for example, undergoes chemotherapy as cancer treatment does not intend its concomitant effects of nausea and hair loss. These are foreseen side effects of chemotherapy intended to kill cancer cells. Here we distinguish between a consequence that an agent intends, as opposed to an outcome that, while foreseen as certain or highly probable, is incidental to what she aims to achieve.

Some philosophical opinion to the contrary (Sidgwick 1901: 202), the distinction between what is intended, as opposed to merely foreseen, can be morally significant. For example, a doctor who tells her patient the truth about her poor prognosis does not intend to cause the patient distress, even if the doctor knows that the bad news will have this effect. An additional point to note here is the third possibility, mentioned earlier, of justification in the form of claimed immunity. If the doctor has an obligation to tell her patient the truth, then the foreseen distress this unavoidably causes is something for which she is not morally responsible. In this particular case the obligation is a professional one, but Kant, for instance, maintained that we cannot be responsible for the foreseen bad consequences of compliance with a strict moral duty, since it would be impermissible for us to act otherwise (Kant 1949/1797).

The moral significance of the distinction between intention and foresight is central to the principle or doctrine of double effect (DDE). The DDE originates in Catholic moral theology but it is now more widely accepted as part of a secular non-consequentialist ethics according to which some *types* of acts, such as intentional killing, are impermissible (Uniacke 1998). The DDE sets out conditions under which, in difficult cases, it can be morally permissible to bring about a bad effect of a type that is impermissibly intended (this might be e.g. the death of an innocent person). The term "double effect" refers to the two foreseen effects that an action might have: a good effect which the agent intends, and a foreseen bad effect that is not intended. The DDE could be applicable where, for example, a driver swerves his car in order to avoid hitting a group of children who have run out onto the road (good effect), foreseeing that he will hit a pedestrian on the curb (bad effect). A common misunderstanding is that according to the DDE, a person is not responsible for a foreseen bad effect provided it is unintended and morally proportionate to the intended good effect. This interpretation would imply, for example, that the driver who swerves to avoid the children is not responsible for the foreseen harm done to the pedestrian. The DDE does not say this. The DDE is not a doctrine about moral responsibility. On the contrary, its purpose is to guide decision about the *moral permissibility* of actions of "double effect": it is invoked precisely because in such cases the agent must justify bringing about the foreseen bad effect, and he will be morally at fault if the bad effect is intended or disproportionate to the intended good effect.

I have said that to be morally responsible for a consequence of one's action is for it to be potentially to one's moral credit or demerit to have brought it about. According to some writers, a good consequence of our action can be to our moral credit only if we intend it, whereas a bad consequence can be to our demerit if foreseen or reasonably foreseeable (D'Arcy 1963: 93–129). Whilst I think that this is generally true, the claim that moral credit for a good consequence always depends on its being intended arguably allows a slightly wider conception of intention than the strict notion invoked by the DDE. Consider a case in which I want to achieve a particular outcome, *x*, and I can do this equally well either by means of act *A* or by means of act *B*. If I bring *x* about by means of act *A*, *A* will produce an additional foreseen good effect *y*. Act *B* will not produce *y*. This additional effect of *A*, *y*, is strictly incidental to my purpose, *x*, but *y* would significantly benefit someone else. I choose *A* in preference to *B* as a means to *x*, since *A* will also produce *y* and this will benefit someone else. I think that in this case it is to my moral credit to have brought about *y*. In choosing *A*, did I intend *y*? According to the DDE, to intend a consequence of one's action is to aim at it either as one's end or as a means to achieving one's end in the circumstances. In this sense, arguably I do not intend *y*. On the one hand, were *A* to produce *x* and, contrary to my expectation at the time of action, not produce *y*, then my intention to bring *x* about by means of *A* is unaffected. On the other hand, although *y* is incidental to *x*, *y* is not *merely* a foreseen consequence of *A* since *y* is my reason for choosing *A* over *B*. Irrespective of whether I strictly intend *y*, it can be to my moral credit to bring about a foreseen good consequence that acts as a reason for my choice of action.

We are most fully morally responsible for the intended consequences of our actions, since they are what we aim to achieve in acting as we do (Duff 1998). We are also responsible for consequences that are foreseen or reasonably foreseeable. The conditions of moral responsibility for good and bad consequences differ in this respect, because a bad consequence of our action is potentially to our moral demerit even if it is not part of our reason for acting as we do. If we choose to do an act, *x*, for whatever reason, foreseeing that *x* will bring about a bad consequence, *y*, then we choose to do *x* despite *y*. We are then morally responsible for *y* in the sense that we are answerable for causing *y*, and in the absence of a satisfactory justification or excuse we are morally at fault on account of *y* (Duff 1998).

Our prospective responsibilities include general obligations of due care towards other people, and on this basis we can be responsible for consequences of our actions that we ought to have foreseen, but due to negligence did not foresee. For example, I am responsible for shooting and seriously injuring someone if I should have checked more closely that the gun was a toy before firing it in jest. Ascriptions of responsibility that appeal to prior fault can also include actions that we do under duress where e.g. we freely consort with bullies who then subject us to coercion (Aristotle), and also the consequences of negligent inattention where e.g. a driver hits people on a pedestrian crossing because he is embroiled in conversation.

Ascriptions of responsibility on the basis of prior fault can also raise broader and more fundamental questions about the extent to which we can be responsible for something that is not wholly under our control (Nagel 1979/1976). Consider, for example, two speeding drivers, both of whom foresee or ought to foresee that if a car in front of them were to pull up suddenly, they would be unable to stop in time. One of these drivers is lucky and encounters nothing on the road in front of him. Despite the risks he takes by speeding, he arrives at his destination without harming anyone. The other speeding driver takes exactly the same risks. A car pulls up suddenly in front of him and he is unable to stop in time. He hits the car in front and kills a child in the back seat. These two drivers are equally morally responsible for speeding and for putting the safety of other people at risk. But why is one of them additionally morally responsible for a child's death if the difference between what he did, compared with the other driver, is due to external factors (another car pulling up suddenly; someone in the back seat)? If the point of ascription of responsibility is an appropriate moral appraisal of a person on the basis of his conduct, why should this appraisal go beyond what both drivers culpably risked by speeding, to include in the case of one of the drivers the harm he actually caused? One response might be to say that one engages in certain forms of wrongful conduct, such as driving at speed in a populated area, at one's own moral risk, so to speak. On this view, the driver who harmed no one is lucky, and he ought to consider himself lucky. It does not follow from this, however, that the driver who killed the child is "morally unlucky." His killing the child was due to his speeding: his hitting the back of another car was something that he could reasonably have foreseen and that he voluntarily chose to risk in acting as he did. Given these considerations, the child's death is properly attributable to the driver's wrongful conduct. One speeding driver has a child's death on his conscience; the other driver ought to be grateful that he does not.

See also Responsibility: Act and omission (Chapter 51).

References

D'Arcy, E. (1963) *Human Acts*, Oxford: Clarendon Press.

Duff, R. A. (1998) "Responsibility," in E. Craig (ed.) *Routledge Encyclopedia of Philosophy*, London: Routledge.

Feinberg, J. (1970) "Action and Responsibility," in *Doing and Deserving*, Princeton, NJ: Princeton University Press.

Kant, I. (1949/1797) "On a Supposed Right to Lie from Altruistic Motives," in *Immanuel Kant's Critique of Practical Reason and Other Writings in Moral Philosophy*, trans., ed. Lewis W. Beck, Chicago, IL: University of Chicago Press.

Nagel, T. (1979/1976) "Moral Luck," in *Mortal Questions*, New York: Cambridge University Press.

Sidgwick, H. (1901) *Methods of Ethics*, 6th edn, London: Macmillan & Co.

Uniacke, S. (1998) "The Principle of Double Effect," in E. Craig (ed.) *Routledge Encyclopedia of Philosophy*, London: Routledge.

Zimmerman, M. J. (2001) "Responsibility," in Lawrence C. Becker and Charlotte B. Becker (eds) *Encyclopedia of Ethics*, 2nd edn, vol. 111, New York and London: Routledge.

Further reading

Aristotle (1999) *Nicomachean Ethics*, ed., trans. Terence Irwin, Indianapolis, IN: Hackett.

51
RESPONSIBILITY
Act and omission

Michael J. Zimmerman

We are all in control of the lives of others, of whether they live or die. Few readers of this chapter either have killed, are killing, or will kill another human being, despite the frequent opportunity to do so. Yet all readers not only have allowed but are allowing and will continue to allow many other human beings to die, despite the constant opportunity to save them. Presumably at least part of the explanation for this dramatic divergence in behavior is the widely held belief that, barring exceptional circumstances, it is seriously morally wrong to kill (or, more generally, harm) another human being, so that anyone who chooses nonetheless to do so incurs a high degree of culpability, whereas the same is not true of letting another human being die (or, more generally, letting another person come to harm). But what could account for this alleged asymmetry? Whether one kills another person or "merely" lets that person die, he or she is equally dead. How can one way of behaving be so different, morally, from the other, when the end result is the same in either case?

One answer that is often given to this question is this: to kill is to act, whereas to let die is to omit to act, and action and omission are of such a nature that we bear responsibility for our acts in a way in which we do not bear responsibility for our omissions. It is with this claim, which I will call the disparity thesis, that this article is concerned. To assess its merits, we must begin by examining briefly what responsibility, action, and omission consist in.

Responsibility

The term "responsibility," even when used to refer to moral responsibility in particular, is ambiguous. It has two main senses, one prospective, the other retrospective. In the prospective sense, it is roughly synonymous with "obligation" or "duty." For example, to say that the lifeguard is responsible for the swimmers' safety is, under normal circumstances, to say that it is the lifeguard's obligation or duty to see to it that the swimmers remain safe. (Two modes of obligation are commonly distinguished. Someone has a *prima facie* obligation if he, or she, has some but not necessarily conclusive moral reason to do something; he has an *all-things-considered* obligation if he has conclusive moral reason to do something.) In contrast, retrospective responsibility concerns what has happened, rather than what will or may happen, and has to do with a person's being either laudable or culpable for some past occurrence. Thus, to say that the lifeguard is responsible for the swimmers' deaths is, under normal circumstances, to say that the lifeguard is culpable for deaths that have already occurred.

Given the ambiguity of "responsibility" between its prospective and retrospective senses, there are two corresponding interpretations of the disparity thesis. Insofar as prospective responsibility is concerned, the thesis is roughly this: behaving in such a way that harm results is more seriously wrong if one's behavior takes the form of action than if it takes the form of omission. Insofar as retrospective responsibility is concerned, the thesis is roughly this: culpability for the occurrence of some harm is greater if the harm occurs as a result of an act than if it occurs as a result of an omission. (There is a corresponding proposition, seldom discussed, to which proponents of the disparity thesis might also subscribe: laudability for the occurrence of some benefit is greater if the benefit occurs as a result of an act than if it occurs as a result of an omission.) At this point, though, it would be useful to have a more precise formulation of the thesis. I propose that we understand it as follows:

> *The Disparity Thesis:* Action and omission are of such a nature that, if we can avoid some harm's occurring as a result of some act of ours, then we have a *prima facie* obligation to do so that is, all else being equal, stronger than any *prima facie* obligation we may have to avoid an equally harmful outcome's occurring as a result of some omission of ours. Furthermore, the culpability, if any, that we would incur for failing to fulfill the former obligation is, all else being equal, greater than the culpability we would incur for failing to fulfill the latter.

The opening phrase "Action and omission are of such a nature that … " makes explicit the contention that it is the distinction between action and omission as such that accounts for the alleged moral disparity. The phrase "all else being equal" accommodates the possibility that, due to extraneous reasons, one's responsibility, whether prospective or retrospective, regarding letting someone come to harm is greater than one's responsibility regarding doing harm to someone. (Such extraneous reasons might include, for example, the fact that one has made a promise not to let someone come to harm, or the fact that one has some sort of special relation to the person who is in danger of coming to harm.) Finally, the phrase "if any" allows for the possibility that one may have an excuse for wrongdoing.

Action and omission

Whether the disparity thesis is plausible depends in part, of course, on how action and omission are to be distinguished. Initially, the distinction may seem straightforward: to act is to be active, to omit is to be inactive. But in fact there are several complications, only three of which there is space to note here.

First, a distinction is to be drawn between inactivity in general and omission in particular. If activity consists in "putting hands on," then inactivity consists in not putting hands on. But omission consists, more particularly, in "keeping hands off." The difference is this: one keeps hands off only when one has the opportunity to put hands on and yet fails to do so. Omission consists, then, in the failure to prevent some outcome that one could have prevented. (Perhaps, too, there must be some kind of expectation that one would have prevented it.) Only in such a case has one let the outcome occur or allowed it to occur. For example, if someone dies in such a way that one could not have prevented his death, then, while it is of course true that one did not save him, it would be incorrect to say that one let him die.

Second, as mentioned at the outset, an outcome may be the result either of an act or of an omission. A death, for instance, may occur either as a result of a shooting or as a result of a failure to throw a life preserver into the water. Now, when one puts hands on, one's act may be said to cause the outcome in question (in the sense of contributing causally to it). For example, if one shoots and thereby kills another person, then the shooting has caused the death. But what should we say about the relation between an omission and its outcome? Should we say that the failure to throw in the life preserver caused the death? The matter is controversial. Some writers say that we should indeed say this. Others maintain that the failure to prevent something else (such as a strong undertow) from causing a death does not itself qualify as a cause of death, even though the death is the result of the omission.

Third, perhaps the greatest difficulty in accounting for the distinction between action and omission is the fact that the line between activity and inactivity often gets blurred. First, in many cases whether someone's behavior is to be described in the "positive" terms of activity or the "negative" terms of inactivity seems an arbitrary matter. Is someone who is standing rigidly to attention best described as keeping still or as not moving? Is he acting or omitting to act? Second, often one manages to accomplish an omission by means of performing some act. For instance, one may fail to save someone from death by reaching for a second helping of dessert rather than for one's wallet. Third, there are cases in which it seems that one not only does manage to let something happen by means of performing some act but couldn't manage to do so without some such activity. Suppose, for example, that someone has shot an arrow in your direction; you duck, and the arrow strikes the person next to you, killing him. Have you killed your companion? It seems wrong to say so; the killer is not you but the person who shot the arrow. Have you contributed causally to your companion's death? This is controversial. Did you let him die in your place? So it seems, but you couldn't have saved yourself at his expense without either ducking or performing some other act (such as grabbing him and using him as a shield). Or consider the distinction between "active" and "passive" euthanasia that is often drawn by those who debate the issue. This distinction is supposed to correspond to the distinction between killing and letting die; yet the paradigm of passive euthanasia is that of "pulling the plug" on a respirator, behavior that clearly involves the activity of withdrawing support rather than the mere inactivity of withholding it.

The disparity thesis rejected

Given the difficulties in accounting for the distinction between action and omission, what are we to make of the disparity thesis? Why should we think that the distinction as such is morally significant, especially when it is so hard to draw and appears to break down in crucial cases?

It is no surprise that many writers who acknowledge the initial appeal of the disparity thesis argue that it is nonetheless to be rejected. One argument is highly theoretical. It is based on the premise that, when it comes to determining what is morally right or wrong, all that matters at bottom is what the outcome of one's behavior is and not what form one's behavior takes; it is the "end" and not the "means" that counts. (This claim is characteristic of consequentialism.) An immediate implication of this claim is that the distinction between killing and letting die is itself of no moral significance with respect to what one is morally obligated to do, since (as noted at the outset of this chapter) the person in question is equally dead, regardless of the means by which death has been accomplished. So too, more generally, for the distinction between doing harm and allowing harm.

Another argument is less high-flown. It appeals to "parallel cases," a pair of cases in which everything is, as far as possible, held constant, except that in one case harm occurs as a result of an act and in the other case harm occurs as a result of an omission. It is then contended that this difference between the cases makes no difference, morally, and on the basis of this contention it is concluded that the disparity thesis is false.

It is important to note that those who argue against the disparity thesis do not necessarily deny that responsibility for acts typically differs from responsibility for omissions. Rather, they claim that, if and when such a difference arises, it has nothing to do with the nature of action and omission as such but rather turns on contingent circumstances.

One kind of circumstance has to do with the mental state of the person whose behavior is in question. In behaving in such a way that some harm results, one may be doing so (a) from a good or a bad motive, (b) with or without intending that the harm occur, and (c) with or without foreseeing that the harm will occur. There is disagreement whether these factors affect the moral rightness or wrongness of one's behavior, that is, whether they are pertinent to the question of one's prospective responsibility regarding the outcome (consequentialists typically deny that they are pertinent, whereas many non-consequentialists assert that they are), but it is generally accepted (even by consequentialists) that they can and do affect the degree to which one is retrospectively responsible for the outcome. For example, it is commonly held that, all else being equal, culpability is greater when (a) one's behavior stems from a bad motive rather than a good one, (b) the outcome is intended rather than not intended, or (c) the outcome is foreseen rather than not foreseen. It is then often observed that many instances of doing harm (such as killing) stem from a bad motive and are such that the harm in question is both intended and foreseen, whereas most instances of allowing harm (such as letting someone die) do not stem from a bad motive and are not such that the harm in question is intended, even if it is foreseen. On this basis, many people claim that culpability for doing harm tends to be greater than culpability for allowing harm, even though the disparity thesis itself is false, that is, even though there is nothing about the nature of action and omission as such that accounts for the disparity in responsibility.

A second kind of circumstance has to do with the probability that one's behavior will result in a certain outcome. It seems often to be the case that it is well-nigh certain that a particular person will be harmed if one acts in a certain way (if one pulls a trigger, say, or administers a poison), whereas the probability that a particular person will come to harm as a result of one's omitting to do something (donate blood, say, or contribute to Oxfam) is considerably lower. Again, it is controversial whether such a variation in probability affects the rightness or wrongness of one's conduct, but it is generally accepted that it can affect the degree to which one is culpable for the eventual outcome. On this basis, many people once again claim that culpability for doing harm tends to be greater than culpability for allowing harm, even though the disparity thesis itself is false.

A third consideration concerns the ease with which one can accomplish a certain outcome. There are two respects in which such ease may vary. The first is this: it seems that it is in general easier to avoid doing harm to someone than it is to avoid letting harm come to that person. For example, it is easier to avoid killing someone (by shooting him, say) than it is to avoid letting someone die (by starvation, say). To accomplish the former one need hardly go out of one's way at all, but to accomplish the latter one may have to go well out of one's way. It is commonly held that, when accomplishing a certain worthwhile goal is exceptionally difficult, doing so is supererogatory (that is, above and beyond the call of duty) rather than all-things-considered obligatory. This alone, it is often claimed, helps account for the fact that, although refraining from killing another person is usually all-things-considered obligatory, refraining from letting him die is not. It is also often said that this fact receives further support from the second respect in which the ease of accomplishing an outcome may vary. It is an unfortunate truth that, the world being as it is, the opportunity that we have to prevent harm from coming to others is, as noted at the outset, constant. Thus, even if saving one particular person from death can be accomplished without great difficulty, that person will be immediately succeeded by another who needs saving, and then another, and then another, and so on without end. Clearly, accomplishing such a series of tasks would be immensely burdensome and hence, many maintain, doing so is supererogatory rather than all-things-considered obligatory. The same does not hold true of killing. Refraining from killing anyone, even a great number of people, is very easy; it is killing that takes effort. In light of both these considerations, many hold that, even if the disparity thesis is false, the relative ease with which we can refrain from killing people as opposed to the relative difficulty of saving people from death helps account for the disparity in our obligations on this score.

A final consideration has to do with the fact that the responsibility one bears for having allowed others to die (or to come to some other sort of harm) is typically shared with a great many other people, whereas the responsibility one bears for having killed another is typically not shared nearly so widely, if at all. On this basis, some maintain that one's culpability for any particular death that one has failed to prevent is typically tiny, whereas this is not typically the case for any particular death that one has actively caused, so that, once again, the falsity of the disparity thesis may be seen to be compatible with a wide disparity in responsibility for acts and for omissions.

The disparity thesis restored?

The points raised in the last section are important, but there is reason to doubt that they succeed in disposing of the disparity thesis.

The theoretical premise on which the first argument is based is, unsurprisingly, highly controversial. Whereas consequentialists are happy to accept it, many non-consequentialists assert that the end does not necessarily justify the means.

The success of the second argument is also in dispute, on two counts. First, the inference from "The bare difference between doing and allowing harm has no significance in *this* set of circumstances" to "The bare difference between doing and allowing harm has no significance in *any* set of circumstances" has been challenged. Second, alternative pairs of cases have been proposed in which the only variable is that in one case harm occurs as a result of an act and in the other as a result of an omission and between which, it is alleged, there does appear to be a significant moral difference.

There is, moreover, reason to doubt that the four considerations mentioned succeed in explaining the disparity that is alleged typically to hold between our responsibility for our acts and our responsibility for our omissions; for these considerations seem to be either false or such that their force can be neutralized.

Consider the last consideration first, that which has to do with the sharing of responsibility. The claim is that responsibility shared is responsibility diminished, but this is patently false. Responsibility is not a pie to be divided, so that, the more people seated at the table, the smaller the slice that each receives. Think how simple it would be to reduce one's responsibility! All one would need do is invite others to join in one's misbehavior. Clearly, excuses are not so easy to come by.

Turn now to the third consideration regarding the difficulty of preventing harm from coming to others. This difficulty has been exaggerated. True, it would be exceptionally burdensome to save as many people as one could from death; doing so would require huge adjustments to the way in which one normally goes about one's life. Perhaps this difficulty does indeed render saving as many as one could supererogatory. But we cannot infer from this that saving some lesser number is supererogatory. Often, saving one person, or even several people, is extremely easy: just write a check, put it in a stamped envelope, and mail it. Compare this with braking, swerving, and possibly damaging one's car in order to avoid running someone over. The latter may be much more difficult or burdensome, but we wouldn't say that it was therefore supererogatory.

The second consideration concerning probability is also unconvincing. On one hand, success in one's effort to kill another is often far from guaranteed (one may be a poor shot, or the toxicity of the poison may be uncertain), but that alone seems insufficient to reduce one's culpability for killing another. On the other hand, it can often be well-nigh certain that a donation to charity will indeed save someone from death who would not otherwise survive. Of course, one may not know just who that person is, but that seems irrelevant. Compare poisoning your spouse's drink with poisoning the local water supply. One's ignorance in the latter case concerning just who one's victims will be doesn't serve to reduce one's culpability.

Finally, the consideration concerning the mental state of the person whose behavior is in question is once again unpersuasive. We can simply compare cases of killing with cases of letting die in which the mental state is held constant. For example, if the letting die is not malicious but merely callous, then let us stipulate that this is also true of the killing with which it is being compared. Or again, if the death in the case of letting die is not intended but merely foreseen, then let us stipulate that this is also true of the corresponding killing. We are not in general prepared to tolerate killings that are "merely" callous and ones whose constituent deaths are "merely" foreseen and not intended. Yet we routinely tolerate lettings die that meet this description.

It therefore appears that none of the four considerations mentioned can be relied on to account for the disparity that is alleged typically to hold between our responsibility for our acts and our responsibility for our omissions. Unless some other pertinent consideration has been overlooked that would succeed where these four have apparently failed, the upshot would seem to be that we must have recourse to the disparity thesis after all (or something close to it) if we are to explain the alleged disparity. But what reason do we have to accept this thesis?

One claim that is sometimes made with respect to killing and letting die in particular is that killing is "worse in itself" than letting die because the proper definitions of "kill" and "let die" have an evaluative component that yields this result. Consider, for example, a newborn baby who needs feeding. She's in her crib in the bedroom, crying pitifully. Her father is chatting with his neighbor in a nearby room. A bottle of milk is close at hand. Either man could easily feed the baby, but neither does; they ignore her and carry on chatting. This happens several days in a row, and the baby eventually starves to death. Some people maintain that, although the neighbor's behavior is clearly awful, the father's is even worse. Perhaps the neighbor has ("merely") let the baby die, but it seems somehow inadequate to say this of the father. Through his neglect, his disregard of his duties as a parent, he has killed his child.

There are several points to note here. First, it is dubious that the correct definitions of "kill" and "let die" have any evaluative component, let alone one that warrants this discrepancy in the descriptions of the ways in which the father and the neighbor have behaved. (Contrast "murder," whose definition clearly does make reference to evaluative matters.) On the contrary, whether one should be said to have killed another or to have let another die seems to be purely a matter of how one's behavior is to be described in non-evaluative terms. It seems quite correct to say that the neighbor let the baby die. Since the father behaved in just the same way, it seems equally correct to say this of him, too. The tendency to accuse the father of having killed his child can be attributed to an implicit reliance on the idea that letting die (as opposed to killing) is usually not such a bad thing and, since what the father did was very bad indeed, we had better not say that he "merely" let his child die. But then, of course, the thesis that killing is worse in itself than letting die is being presupposed in the very definitions of "kill" and "let die," in which case these definitions cannot be used to support the thesis. Second, however, even if "kill" and "let die" should be defined in evaluative terms, it is highly dubious that, more generally, "do harm" and "allow harm" should be similarly defined. Third, and most importantly, even if "do harm" and "allow harm" should be similarly defined, this provides no support for the disparity thesis unless, more generally still, the very definitions of "act" and "omit" should be given in evaluative terms. If such evaluatively charged definitions were correct, then (depending on just how they were drawn up) perhaps the disparity thesis could be seen to follow. But that "act" and "omit" should be defined in evaluative terms is extremely dubious. On the contrary, whatever the distinction between the two should be said to be (not an easy question, as noted in the second section, above, "Action and Omission"), it is presumably at bottom non-evaluative.

One way to argue for the disparity thesis that does not appeal to any evaluatively skewed definitions is this. People in general have a "negative" right not to be harmed by others; they do not in general have a "positive" right to be saved from harm. (Such a positive right does sometimes exist, but only if there is a "special" relation between the right-holder and the person against whom the right is held – a relation such as that of child to parent, say.) All else being equal, behaving in such a way that one infringes a right is more seriously wrong than behaving in a way that is similar but involves no infringement of a right. Hence the disparity thesis is true.

It is not clear that this argument is sound. One problem is that it may appear to beg the question. Unless the disparity thesis is presupposed, why think that there is the alleged discrepancy between negative and positive rights? One answer to this question appeals to the principle that "ought" implies "can." People in general have a right not to be harmed by others in part because the latter can refrain from harming the former. People do not in general have a right to be saved from harm because there are millions who need saving and, even if each of these people were such that one could save him or her, one cannot save them all, and there is no good reason to discriminate between them and to ascribe a right to be saved to some but not to others. One problem with this answer is that, even if it is correct, it does not directly support the disparity thesis. On the contrary, it seems to appeal to contingent facts: the fact that one can refrain from harming others (which may hold in general, but to which there would occasionally appear to be exceptions) and the fact that one cannot save all who need saving. Neither of these facts has to do with the nature of action and omission as such.

Another way to argue for the disparity thesis is to note that we just do take being causally complicit in the occurrence of some outcome to be morally significant. Compare a drunk driver, who has run someone over, with another driver, equally drunk, who has luckily escaped running someone over. Our common judgment is that the first driver has done something more seriously wrong than the second driver has, and that the former is more culpable than the latter, in virtue of the fact that the former has a causal connection to harm that the latter lacks, even though the (lack of) connection is entirely fortuitous. (Of course, this judgment can be and has been challenged.) We typically think that even a driver who is driving without fault but who nonetheless unfortunately causes someone harm incurs responsibilities (to make amends, perhaps even to show contrition) that others who have no such causal history lack. That whether and how one is causally related to some outcome can itself be morally significant is a brute fact, and it is this fact that underwrites the disparity thesis.

It is hard to know what to make of this argument. On one hand, it speaks to an intuition that people commonly have. On the other hand, the alleged fact, being "brute," has not been argued for in turn, and one wonders why it should be accepted. Moreover, it seems at best to be pertinent to those cases of omission that consist wholly in "keeping hands off" (such as the withholding of aid) as opposed to involving some way of "putting hands on" (such as the withdrawal of aid), and even then it is pertinent only if keeping hands off does not contribute causally to the eventual result (a matter which, as noted in the second section, is controversial). Finally, there is the suspicion that the alleged fact merely caters to a certain complacency in us and should in actuality be rejected. It is easier for us to get on with our own lives if we are not pricked too sharply by our consciences when we consider the starving masses. But consider the neighbor. Perhaps we can agree that the father had more reason to feed his baby than the neighbor did, but should we not also agree that, given the father's abdication of his responsibility, the neighbor had sufficient reason to feed the child to render him all-things-considered morally obligated to do so? If so, the dramatic divergence in behavior noted in the opening paragraph of this chapter would seem hard to justify.

See also Freedom and responsibility (Chapter 23); Reasons for action (Chapter 24); Consequentialism (Chapter 37); Responsibility: Intention and consequence (Chapter 50); Rights (Chapter 56).

Further reading

Bennett, Jonathan (1995) *The Act Itself*, Oxford: Clarendon Press.
Steinbock, Bonnie and Norcross, Alastair (eds) (1994) *Killing and Letting Die*, New York: Fordham University Press.

52
PARTIALITY AND IMPARTIALITY

John Cottingham

Introduction: partiality within different ethical frameworks

Impartiality is an essential virtue, for example, in judges and administrators, and a good parent is expected to treat her children more or less impartially, without showing favoritism to one over the others. But the virtuous life is not one of complete impartiality. A good lawyer is not required to be neutral as between the interests of his client and those of the opposing party; and we feel serious doubts about the behavior of Mrs Jellaby in Charles Dickens' *Bleak House*, when she becomes so wrapped up in her work for an African charity that she ceases to devote any special attention to her own children. A good person, it seems, is one who cultivates dispositions of impartiality in some of her dealings, or some areas of life, but who is also disposed to have partialistic commitments and preferences in other areas.

It is not just in accounts of the virtues and the good life that difficulties may arise concerning the scope of partiality and impartiality. If we adopt a consequentialist ethical framework, assessing the rightness of actions (or types of action) by reference to the amount of good produced, then similar problems arise. Initially, we may be inclined to suppose that all outcomes should be assessed in a completely impartial manner. So if two people are trapped in a burning building and we can only rescue one, then the person to be saved appears to be the one whose life, assessed from an impartial standpoint, will produce the greater good. This was the approach taken by the utilitarian William Godwin in the eighteenth century. If it was a choice between saving either an archbishop (or some great benefactor of mankind) or a chambermaid unlikely to do much good to anyone, then you should rescue the archbishop. But what if the chambermaid happens to be your mother? Godwin was prepared to bite the bullet and argue that this should make no difference: "What magic," he asked, "is in the pronoun 'my' to overturn the decisions of everlasting truth?" (Godwin 1976/1793: Bk 2, ch. 2). But other consequentialists want to resist such a radical conclusion.

Some, taking an institutional approach, would argue that the decision should depend not just on the balance of good produced in this one case, but on the benefits accruing from established institutions or general patterns of conduct, for example, from the fostering of close family ties such as that between parent and child. So perhaps preferential treatment for one's own parent can be justified as the kind of behavior that tends in general to make for a better society.

A third ethical framework standardly listed alongside virtue theory and consequentialism is that of deontological or duty-based ethics; and here too there are difficult issues about the limits of partiality. Clearly there are cases where we have a duty to be impartial. A public official distributing welfare benefits is obliged to avoid any bias or favoritism and to allocate the relevant resources fairly in accordance with the appropriate rules. But there are other occasions, for example, where the official is spending his own money in his spare time, where it seems quite permissible for him to show favoritism (e.g. by buying a special present for a friend or relative). In yet other contexts, it seems that partiality may be not only permissible but required. A nurse, for example, is arguably not only allowed, but duty bound, to give some degree of special preferential attention to the needs of his or her own patient, notwithstanding the fact that an impartial calculus might show that some other person in some other hospital or some other country was in greater medical need.

So whether we are thinking of how we may live a virtuous life, or of how we can maximize the good, or of what kinds of duties govern our lives, all of us are likely sooner or later to confront the question of the proper limits of partiality or preference towards those to whom we have some special relationship – not to mention what Samuel Clarke called "the natural self-love which everyone has in the first place towards himself" (Clarke 1969/1706: §244).The fact that the issues here are difficult is not in itself surprising, given the complexities of human life, and the puzzles that arise in so many areas of morality. But the problems of partiality and impartiality have a special philosophical significance because they take us to the heart of some central questions about what it means to adopt an ethical perspective in the first place.

Partiality versus the ethical perspective?

There is a widespread conception according to which ethical thinking takes us beyond the "I" to some more impersonal and impartial perspective. The eighteenth-century thinker Adam Smith identified the moral point of view with the perspective of an "impartial spectator" or "indifferent bystander" (Smith 1969/1759: Pt 2, §1, ch. 2; see also Hutcheson 1970/1725: Introduction), and this notion exerted a considerable influence in subsequent ethical theory. From the detached standpoint of an observer looking down on the planet, this particular individual whom I call "me" is simply one among countless others; I may think that I, and my loved ones, are "special," but from the more detached perspective it seems that I have no greater claim to special treatment than anyone else. Psychologically speaking, it may feel to me as if I and those close to me are terribly important; but from an *ethical* point of view – if that means from the standpoint of the impartial spectator – it seems that I am no more important than anyone else. We are back with Godwin's challenge: "What magic is there in the pronoun 'my'?"

The hypothetical notion of an impartial spectator is sometimes seen as a successor to the traditional theistic notion of a benevolent and all-seeing God looking down from heaven upon the doings of humanity. This image has been associated historically with Christian ideals like that of the brotherhood of man, which invite us to reach beyond the particularities of tribal and national allegiance, towards universal justice and respect for all mankind. But while these ideals have undoubted appeal, it is questionable whether the moral point of view should be identified with one that wholly prescinds from particular concerns and commitments, or that any ethical system must require the adoption of a detached and impersonal stance. Christian ethics, for example, certainly does not abstract from particular relationships; on the contrary, the Christ who is depicted in the Gospels appears to have had close personal ties (for example, to his mother, and to the "beloved disciple" who was special to him [see John 19:25–7]). So while all human beings are seen as equally children of God, it seems a distortion to see the Christian morality as requiring us to forswear partialistic concerns and commitments in favor of impersonal detachment. Arguably, the love for one's fellow creatures that forms the core of the Christian message is a love that is often manifested not in some impersonal and detached concern for "humanity in general," but rather in the committed relationships which we forge with those whom we encounter in our individual lives. The situation with respect to Buddhist ethics appears to be rather different, since in Buddhism the very idea of the "self" is regarded as an illusion, and personal ties and commitments are seen as attachments that are obstacles to enlightenment. On some interpretations of this view, the ethically appropriate perspective indeed turns out to be one of impersonal detachment; but many would be unhappy about taking this as the only model for an acceptable system of morality.

Despite the differences of emphasis between Christian and Buddhist ethics, it remains true that both outlooks, and indeed many secular systems such as utilitarianism, tend to contrast morality with selfishness and egoism. In all ethical systems, someone who always puts their own interests before those of their fellows is a paradigm case of an ethically flawed person; and the more ruthlessly someone pursues their self-interest, the more we may be inclined to describe them as immoral. Even here, however, things are not entirely simple, since some significant degree of self-concern seems bound up with what it is to be human, and therefore to be necessary for a flourishing human life. This leads to the question of the ethical status of self-preference – a topic that has been at the core of much recent debate on partiality and impartiality in ethics.

The ethics of self-concern

A strictly impartial perspective might seem to require me, in my ethical deliberations, to accord no special priority to myself or my own concerns as against those of others. But it seems doubtful whether I could function as a human being at all unless the mere fact that a given project was *mine* was allowed to have some weight in my deliberations. If each day I was to consider how every moment could best be spent furthering, for example, global utility, without according any special priority to the fact that certain projects are the ones I have made my own, it seems that I would disintegrate as an individual. For I would be obliged to drop any activity or project in which I was engaged whenever another project presented itself whose contribution to the general utility was marginally greater. In such a case, it seems that I would have no real character – there would be no distinctive pattern to my life. I would simply be, in a phrase of Bernard Williams, a cog in a "satisfaction system" which "happened to be near certain causal levers at a certain time" (Williams 1981: 4).

This line of thought has become associated with what is known as the "integrity argument" – one originally put forward by Williams as an objection to utilitarian ethics. If we apply it to the debate over partiality and impartiality, we may be inclined to draw two possible lessons, a minimal one and a stronger one. At a minimum, it may be argued that each of us must, if he or she is not to disintegrate as an individual, be allowed to accord some priority to their own personal plans and projects. In other words, we must have some kind of "prerogative" to give some weighting to ourselves and our projects in our ethical deliberations. The stronger claim would be that we not only may but should give our own projects extra weight – that such weighting is ethically quite proper and even desirable.

Given the opprobrium with which selfishness is viewed, and the fact that self-sacrifice is widely regarded as admirable, it may seem that an extra weighting for one's own projects is hard to justify from the ethical point of view. But there is at least one moral ideal, namely that of self-development or self-improvement, that seems clearly to require such weighting. Each individual is (from birth and/or upbringing) the possessor of certain talents or gifts, which only they are in a position to develop. And most if not all such talents inescapably require considerable investments of time and energy if they are to come to fruition (consider the time and effort required, for example, to learn to play a musical instrument). One could perhaps object that the development of personal skills and talents is trivial from the ethical point of view, and that they should be sacrificed if the resources needed to foster them can be better utilized to promote some more important good (for example, the relief of global poverty). But most people on reflection would probably find something very counter-intuitive about such an austere picture of how humans should live. Certainly most virtue ethicists would insist that the good life must include the opportunity for developing at least some personal excellences, and that the devotion of time and energy to this end is desirable and indeed praiseworthy. From a deontological perspective too, self-development has generally been regarded as ethically desirable – indeed a duty, albeit (in Kant's classification) an "imperfect" one – that is, duty which allows for a certain discretion in the extent to which it is pursued (unlike the "perfect duties," such as the obligation not to harm others, which apply categorically and without qualification). Finally, even from a consequentialist perspective, self-development appears to be a good whose promotion is incumbent upon each individual. For given that each individual is, as a matter of fact, endowed with a unique set of talents and capacities which only they can develop, the goods in question are ones that are achievable only by the individual in question. So it seems to follow (and this is a thought that might commend itself even from an impartial perspective) that each of us has at least a *prima facie* obligation to make the relevant individual investments of time and energy, without which the opportunities for the realization of the goods in question will be irrecoverably lost.

Such considerations, which speak in favor of a necessary element of self-concern in any plausible model of a good life for human beings, do not of course settle the question of the *extent* to which I may use up time and resources on my own self-development, when these might presumably have been expended on the good of others. Some ethical writers, among them Kant, have argued that there is an unavoidable latitude which each of us has in deciding this matter: "It is impossible to assign determinate limits to the extent [to which I ought to sacrifice a part of my welfare to that of others]. How far it should extend depends, in large part, on what each person's true needs are in view of his sensibilities, and it must be left to each to decide this for himself" (Kant 1996/1797: 156). The phrase "left to decide for himself" may appear to make the amount one should spend on self-development within the arbitrary power of an individual to settle at whim – a procedure that might seem too capricious to carry any normative weight. However, a freedom to decide a question of extent, or degree, does not imply a completely unfettered discretion. As Kant himself puts it, "a wide duty is not to be taken as permission to make exceptions to the maxim of actions, but only as permission to limit one maxim of duty by another – for example, love of one's neighbour in general by love of one's parents" (1996/1797: Introduction, §7). The conclusion, which would seem to match many people's ordinary intuitions, is that partialistic duties (for example, to develop my talents) have to be balanced against more impartially structured duties, such as the duty of general beneficence; the latter remains a genuine and binding duty, which I cannot evade over my lifetime as a whole, even if it may legitimately be subject to limits in any specific instance.

Friends and family

Although a great deal of the preceding section relates to what may be called partiality to self (for example, in each person's developing the gifts necessary or conducive to their fulfilling their human potential), many of the virtues relevant to a good human life involve not just the individual agent but also those to whom he or she is intimately related. Thus, there are virtues (and duties) associated with parenthood, and with friendship, to cite but two central areas of human life, where the partiality involved is often of a highly altruistic kind. Nevertheless, the type of altruism at issue here is, as some philosophers have termed it, "self-referential." I devote special time and energy to promote the interests of this particular child; but her interests are very closely bound up with mine, since she is not just any child, but is *my* daughter. Or again, I take a special interest in the welfare of this individual, and show considerable partiality towards him, but again, not out of general benevolence, but because he happens to be *my* friend.

Aristotle, whose writings on ethics contain extensive discussions of friendship (since ethics is for him about human flourishing, and friendship is clearly a major ingredient in this), highlights the concern we show towards friends by saying the friend is (in Greek) *allos autos* – "another self." Just as one wishes the good for oneself, for one's own sake, the same applies to what one wishes for a friend. Genuine friendships involve affection for the friend for himself, for who he is (Aristotle 1976/*c.* 325 BC: 1156a 10–14). There has been some dispute among commentators about the precise implications of the phrase "another self." The idea that one wishes well for the friend for his own sake, seems partly to prefigure Kant's famous conception of what is owed to all persons, namely to be treated as "ends in themselves," rather than as means to an end; and indeed Aristotle is clear that true friendship cannot be based solely on the pleasure the friend gives me, or any other instrumental benefits provided, but must involve genuine concern for the other's own flourishing as valuable in itself. Nevertheless, we need to be careful not to assimilate the attitudes someone has towards a friend to the kind of impartial Kantian respect for persons that is owed to every rational agent just in virtue of being human. A friendship is a special and intimate relationship which takes a considerable time to cultivate, and involves a close and individualized affection; this explains, for example, why (as Aristotle notes) one cannot have more than a strictly limited number of friends. Unlike *agape*, the love often referred to in the Christian gospels, which is supposed to be felt for any "neighbor" whom one may encounter on the road and who needs to be helped or looked after (Luke 10:25–37), the love between friends (*philia*) involves something much more intimate and personal. All this suggests that although one's concern for a friend is genuinely altruistic, it is not an impartial concern, but is rooted in a sense that the other is one with whom I have a special bond.

Family loyalties provide another central case of ties that are based on close personal commitments, and this again can generate seeming conflicts between impartially assessed needs and considerations based on the particularities of a given relationship. Suppose it costs a certain sum of money to give my child music lessons, or to arrange physiotherapy for my aged parent. From an impartial standpoint, there may be some other, perhaps more talented, child who would derive much greater benefit from the music tuition, or some other geriatric patient who has a greater need for treatment. And, if the money was just "there" on the table, and a benevolent but uninvolved agent was allocating it on the basis of impartially assessed need, it seems clear that the money should not go to my child or my parent but to the more suitable recipients. But if we move from this hypothetical scenario to the actual situation I am confronted with, how are things altered? Although the money may be mine, and thus legally within my control to allocate as I wish, nevertheless, if I know about the needs of those (from an impartial perspective) more worthy recipients, it seems I cannot as a moral agent simply shut my eyes to them. So, if I am morally to justify spending the money on my child's music lessons, or my parent's physiotherapy, it seems that the mere fact that they are related to me must be more than a piece of "magic," as Godwin might have put it, but must carry some genuine moral weight. How could this be?

A possible answer is that I have a debt of gratitude to my parent, or an obligation of responsibility for my child. This suggests that not only may I justifiably favor my relatives but that I have a special duty to benefit them (and conversely they have a right to my help); in other words, such partialism falls within the province of rights and justice, rather than being in tension with it. Similarly, consequentialists might argue that preferring one's own relatives is not in tension with the aim of achieving the best overall outcome, since the good of the world is constituted by the good of the individuals who make it up, and I am in a special position to benefit those close to me (cf. Mill 1962/1861: Ch. 2). Be that as it may, from the point of view of moral psychology it seems that what matters ethically about my attitudes towards my friends and family is not fully captured by the language of impartially justified duties and obligations. Someone who deliberates along the lines "I ought to pay for her lessons, on the grounds that she is my child," or "I have a duty to pay for his treatment on the grounds that he is my father," may strike us as the kind of person who has, in Bernard Williams' telling phrase, "one thought too many" (Williams 1981: 18). In other words, most of us regard partialistic commitments as valuable partly because they stem from free and spontaneous feelings of love and affection, rather than being derived from the sober assessment of reasons for action based on the agent's relatedness to the beneficiaries in question.

Reflections of this kind have often led people to associate partialistic commitments with warm and caring emotions, while the impartial perspective is sometimes seen as implying a certain coldness or remoteness. But while a due acknowledgment of the importance of the emotions in ethics can be a valuable corrective to the over-intellectualized approach to moral problems found among some philosophers, it seems a mistake to suppose that deep emotional responses are the prerogative of the partialist. Notwithstanding William Blake's scathing comment that the "general good" is the "plea of the hypocrite" (Blake 1952/1805: Ch. 3, Plate 55, line 61), is seems quite possible to suppose that some saintly or philanthropic individual, perhaps not involved in normal partialistic ties, could have quite genuine and very passionate feelings about the need to relieve the needs of suffering humanity at large. Nevertheless, it is important to remember that our personal ties, of family, of friendship, are typically associated with strong emotions of affection and concern, without which the ethical landscape would be unrecognizable. Despite the efforts of would-be reformers like Plato to eradicate personal and family ties in favor of general civic solidarity (Plato, *Republic*, 1987/c. 375 BC: 462), our ethical awareness characteristically grows outwards from a core of love and concern which we learn as children from those to whom we are intimately related. The special, partialistic concern we feel for close friends and family members is, in this sense, not something that needs to be explained or justified by reference to some wider ethical concerns; rather, it can plausibly be seen to be bound up with our very formation as beings who are capable of thinking ethically.

Wholesome versus suspect partiality

Despite the central role played by partialistic concern in human ethical development, there are certain kinds of partiality that are widely condemned as ethically suspect. We may allow, or even applaud, the partiality a mother shows towards her children, but tend to be suspicious of clannishness and cliquish behavior. Nepotism (the term is derived from the Latin word for a nephew) is something most people condemn – for what moral grounds could a manager have for promoting a family member over a better qualified candidate (Cottingham 1986)? Sometimes, as noted earlier, it is the context that makes such behavior inappropriate: it may be objectionable to favor a nephew in the workplace, but not to throw a party for him at the weekend. But the public/private distinction does not solve all such problems, since racial preference strikes many people as obnoxious even if it is confined to private associations, and the same goes for gender preference (compare the disapproval many feel for clubs whose rules restrict membership to men).

Patriotism provides an interesting test case here, since although in the past it has often been regarded as a paradigm of an ethically acceptable attitude, and indeed as one of the great virtues, increasing global mobility has led many to re-evaluate how far it is acceptable to subscribe to networks of loyalty and preference that favor one's own nation and its citizens over foreigners or "aliens." The propensity to regard members of one's own group as somehow better than or preferable to others has ancient social and religious roots, but some have argued that ethical enlightenment consists in progressively widening the circle of our concern beyond such boundaries. Thus the Australian philosopher Peter

Singer has famously taken impartialism to the point of envisaging a time when even "speciesism" (preferring *x* over *y* on the grounds that *x* belong to the same species as you) will one day be regarded as just as suspect from the ethical point of view as racism (Singer 1993/1979).

The idea of a favored group is one which has also played a central role in many religious movements. The concept of the Israelites as a "chosen people" is prominent in the Bible (Deuteronomy 7:6), though alongside the apparently partialistic implications of this, there is also a more universalist strand (as when Abraham is told that through him "*all* the nations of the Earth will be blessed" (Genesis 18:18)). Following on from this, the New Testament contains evidence of conflicts in the early Christian community between those who proposed fairly restrictive tests for Church membership and those with a more inclusive approach; compare the reported words of the apostle Peter "In truth I understand that God does not show partiality, but in every nation the one who fears Him and works righteousness is acceptable to Him" (Acts 10:34). Notwithstanding such declarations, the history of much subsequent religious conflict shows the deep-seated tendency of human beings to exclude from the favored group those putative outsiders ("infidels," "heretics," "nonconformists," etc.) who do not satisfy the approved membership tests.

From a philosophical point of view, the key issue arising from such behavior is whether there is a clear criterion for deciding which types of favoritism and group-preference, if any, are acceptable from the moral point of view. A natural place to look for such a criterion might seem to be in the idea of human flourishing. Thus, given the importance of the family in human development, the partialities associated with family preference seem to be benign from an ethical standpoint, while it would be much harder to mount a similar defense of, for example, racist associations. Unfortunately, however, the notion of human flourishing appears to be too indeterminate to provide a clear basis for making judgments in difficult cases. There is no doubt, for instance, that many people find security and comfort in associating themselves with some kind of "club" or group (of class, religion, race or nation) that will afford protection or advantage to them, in contrast to others; and though the inevitable result of this is that many will be left out, and may feel excluded or discriminated against, it would perhaps be difficult to argue that the world as a whole would necessarily be better off, or overall human flourishing necessarily impaired, if all preferences based on such groupings were eliminated.

Conclusion

The intractability of many of the issues discussed above no doubt arises in part from the complexities of human psychology. We might wish that all moral issues could be decided on a purely rational basis, but our so-called ethical "intuitions" are not like the abstract judgments of mathematics, but arise from a complex process of moral acculturation. As each of us, as a child, is inducted into the ethical community, we necessarily develop habits of feeling and action that express our involvement in close partialistic relationships – with family, with friends, and later with colleagues and fellow citizens. We may never be able to stand wholly outside these involvements, but we do have the ability to stand back from them to some extent and reflect on how far the networks in which we are involved might commend themselves to an impartial observer. This suggests the possibility of a "two-tier" approach to the problems of partiality and impartiality: at the ground-floor level, our ethical attitudes and conduct may, inevitably, express our involvement in partialistic networks; but at a more theoretical and abstract level, we may nonetheless retain the ability to take a more impartial look at those networks and consider how they might be modified, or ordered differently. Moreover, many of the issues arising here are of course not just a matter of individual ethical conduct, but have a social and political dimension. Part of what we expect from the modern democratic state is that it will offer various kinds of protection for all, through impartially administered standards of justice and fairness that apply to everyone, irrespective of which groups they belong to. Nevertheless, however much scope for improvement there might be in the preferential networks that structure our lives, and however much they may need to be subjected to an impartial political and legal framework for a just society, a morally ideal world for humanity would surely not be one without any ties of partiality; for such a world would not be recognizably human.

See also Early modern natural law (Chapter 7); Kant (Chapter 14).

References

Aristotle (1976/c. 325 BC) *Nicomachean Ethics*, trans. J. Thomson, Harmondsworth: Penguin Books.

Blake, William (1952/1805) *Jerusalem*, repr. London: Trianon Press.

Clarke, Samuel (1969/1706) *A Discourse of Natural Religion*, excerpted in D. D. Raphael (ed.) *The British Moralists*, Oxford: Clarendon.

Cottingham, John (1986) "Partiality, Favouritism and Morality," *Philosophical Quarterly* 33: 357–33.

Godwin, William (1976/1793) *An Inquiry concerning Political Justice*, repr. Harmondsworth: Penguin Books.

Hutcheson, Frances (1970/1725) *An Inquiry concerning Moral Good and Evil*, repr. in *Collected Works*, Hildesheim: Olms.

Kant, Immanuel (1996/1797) *The Metaphysics of Morals*, ed. M. Gregor, Cambridge: Cambridge University Press; trans. of *Metaphysik der Sitten: Tugendlehre*.

Mill, John Stuart (1962/1861) *Utilitarianism*, ed. M. Warnock, London: Fontana.

Plato (1987/c. 375 BC) *Republic*, trans. H. Lee, Harmondsworth: Penguin Books.

Singer, Peter (1993/1979) *Practical Ethics*, 2nd edn, Cambridge: Cambridge University Press.

Smith, Adam (1969/1759) *The Theory of Moral Sentiments*, in D. D. Raphael (ed.) *The British Moralists*, Oxford: Clarendon.

Williams, Bernard (1981) *Moral Luck*, Cambridge: Cambridge University Press.

Further reading

Baier, Kurt (1958) *The Moral Point of View: A Rational Basis of Ethics*. Ithaca, NY: Cornell University Press.

Mendus, Susan (2002) *Impartiality in Moral and Political Philosophy*, Oxford: Oxford University Press.

Nagel, Thomas (1970) *The Possibility of Altruism*, Oxford: Clarendon Press. (Introduces a distinction between "subjective," or what have later come to be called "agent-relative" reasons for action, and "objective" [or "agent-neutral"] reasons.)

Sidgwick, Henry (1981/1874) *The Methods of Ethics*, 7th edn 1907, repr. Indianapolis, IN: Hackett. (Covers many issues relevant to the partiality debate, including the relation between general benevolence and particular duties, e.g. of loyalty and gratitude.)

53
MORAL PARTICULARISM

Michael Ridge and Sean McKeever

Moral particularists doubt that morality must be understood in principled terms. By contrast, moral generalists defend a prominent role for moral principles. Since no introduction to the philosophical study of morality lasts long before one hears talk of moral principles, this dispute comes as no surprise. Indeed, rival normative moral theories are often individuated by the distinct principles to which they give voice. The principle of utility then squares off against the categorical imperative or the doctrine of double effect or the egoist's dictum that in practical matters it is every man for himself. This familiar picture, however, belies deep disagreements about just what a moral principle is and about the role principles play in morality. Worse yet, it may suggest that moral principles (of some sort) must play an important role (of some sort) in morality and therefore in any plausible effort to understand it. In fact, though, there is a rich debate about these issues that stretches back at least to Aristotle who famously warned against expecting a degree of precision in any theory, including moral theory, which outstrips the degree of precision to be found in its subject matter (Aristotle 1999: 1094b). The contemporary debate between particularism and generalism, to which the present discussion is devoted, is important and independent. It is important because, if true, particularism throws into doubt much of what has passed for sound moral theorizing. It is independent because it is not readily reducible either to familiar debates about the merits of rival normative theories or to more familiar meta-ethical debates about the semantics of moral language and the metaphysics of moral properties.

We suggest that moral particularism is best seen as a name for a family of related views that are united by virtue of taking some negative attitude towards moral principles. They are distinguished by the negative attitude in question and also by their conception of what a moral principle is. Moral generalism is just that family of views that deny moral particularism.

Principles and particularisms

To clarify the issues at stake between particularism and generalism one must first address what a moral principle is. A moral principle must be a generalization, but beyond that agreement may quickly evaporate. Some of this disagreement should be traced to familiar meta-ethical disputes. For example, while J. S. Mill, G. E. Moore, and R. M. Hare all consent to some version of the view that the right thing to do is that which promotes the most good, they would disagree mightily about the proper semantics for such a principle, as well as about the moral metaphysics and epistemology which supports it. In so far as we are interested in generalism, however, we should strive to identify what Mill, Moore, and Hare share in common but without appeal to the normative content of consequentialism. After all, in advocating moral principles, Mill, Moore, and Hare also share something in common with Kant and Aquinas.

Disagreement about what a principle is also arises from the distinct roles principles might be thought to play in morality. Here we can and should be ecumenical. Principles have in fact been asked to play several distinct roles in normative theory and one might be optimistic about the prospects in some cases but not others. Perhaps the most familiar role principles are expected to play is that of a standard. Understood this way a moral principle must provide sufficient conditions for the application of a moral concept, either strictly sufficient conditions or else "hedged" *ceteris paribus* conditions (Holton 2002; McKeever and Ridge 2005; Väyrynen 2006). Thus construed, the principle of utility, for example, tells us that an action is properly counted as morally right if and only if it has the best consequences among the available alternatives.

This initial characterization of principles as standards must be more narrowly tailored to remain plausible. First, moral principles should be necessary, not contingent. They must help to identify the extension of our moral concepts at all possible worlds. Second, the principle must be substantive and explanatory, not trivial. Two cases are relevant here. First, take the case of seemingly trivial generalizations, such as, "Any action that is not wrong is permissible." Such a principle gives sufficient conditions for permissibility, and it is arguably necessary, but it is merely formal. Perhaps it is a valid theorem of deontic logic, but it is not the kind of generalization over which particularists and generalists disagree.

Second, consider the implications of supervenience. According to supervenience there can be no moral difference between two objects of evaluation without some non-moral difference. If supervenience is true (as most philosophers would be willing to assume), and if some moral concept ever properly applies to some object, then there must be generalizations that provide sufficient conditions for the application of that moral concept. Given an exhaustive characterization of the world in which the moral concept applies to some object supervenience will entail that whenever matters are like that, the moral concept also properly applies. These generalizations (sometimes called "supervenience functions") should not count as moral principles, however. First, even if we could know such generalizations, they contain far too much irrelevant information since many aspects of the characterization of the world they contain will have no bearing on whether the moral concept does or does not apply.

This failure to exclude irrelevant information undermines the idea that such generalizations are explanatory – a traditional role for moral principles conceived as standards. Furthermore, such supervenience functions are unknowable because we are never in possession of a complete characterization of the world (Little 2000). Being unknowable also undermines their ability to guide the actions of finite agents like ourselves, which brings us to our next way of understanding moral principles – as guides.

Conceived as guides, moral principles are valuable deliberative tools in the hands of a conscientious moral agent; they help one to more reliably perform morally valuable actions and avoid immoral actions. The distinction between principles as standards and principles as guides is interesting in its own right but also because there are grounds for thinking that a sound standard might be a poor guide and that an excellent guide might prove to be a deeply flawed standard. First, if particularists are right to characterize morality as highly complex and context-dependent, then even if we succeed in articulating sound standards, these might prove to be cumbersome and difficult to employ in deliberation. Second, a highly valuable guide might be valuable precisely because it directs our attention to easy-to-grasp features that, while not directly morally relevant themselves are tightly correlated with features that are of direct moral relevance.

By way of analogy, the standard for success in playing the stock market is given by the imperative, "buy low and sell high" but depending on an investor's ability to determine when a given stock is not going any lower or higher, this might be a fairly useless guide. Whereas the imperative "follow your broker's advice" might be an excellent guide but is of course hopeless as a standard – even if your broker were omniscient and infallible, such a norm would not be *explanatory* in the right way. A version of Plato's *Euthyphro* point is telling here – an infallible broker would advise you to buy or sell because this will maximize profits – it does not maximize profits because the broker advises it.

Of course, even if we distinguish principles as standards from principles as guides, it remains possible that a single generalization might successfully play both roles. Such a principle would be an action-guiding standard. Indeed, unlike the case of something as crass as playing the stock market, some traditions in moral philosophy can be understood as implicitly insisting that in the moral case a generalization cannot be an adequate moral standard unless it is also an adequate guide. In particular, Kantian traditions which derive morality "from the inside out" – that is, starting from the perspective of the deliberating agent – try to derive moral standards from suitable moral guides which they argue reflect our autonomy and to which we are rationally committed (Darwall 1986). By contrast, those working in the consequentialist tradition are typically willing to allow that guides and standards may well come apart (Railton 1984).

What about the application of a moral principle to a particular case? Neither thinking of principles as standards nor as guides entails that principles are "mere algorithms" which can be mindlessly applied to particular cases without judgment or insight. To take an example, suppose one were trying to articulate a principle (conceived as a standard) expressing that and why rape is morally wrong. One might think that rape is itself, a moral concept, that it can be defined as a kind of wrongful sexual assault. As particularists rightly point out it would be very difficult (if not impossible) to specify in clearly non-moral terms when a sexual encounter constitutes rape. As Margaret Little puts it, "[T]hink of trying to isolate that instantiation conditions of consent without help of moral notions like fair, or of force at the level of physical mechanics" (Little 2000: 284). We should distinguish two issues here, each of which is important. The first, which Little points to, is the evident difficulty of articulating standards for value-laden concepts which do not themselves employ other equally contested value-laden concepts. The second, which would arguably persist even if the first task were completed, is the judgment required in the application of any concepts, including non-moral ones. Even if consent were properly characterized as expressed willingness, it would still require judgment to know, in a particular case, whether willingness had been expressed.

This point is relevant because some defenses of particularism have been inspired, in part, by Wittgenstein's famous discussion of rule-following. Wittgenstein's original discussion and the subsequent literature devoted to it are notoriously complex. That said, any bearing Wittgenstein's discussion has for the debate between particularists and generalists is highly uncertain. For if Wittgenstein's point is a general one about all conceptual competence, and if the point is that conceptual competence cannot be explained as the grasp of rules or principles, then Wittgenstein's discussion threatens to establish particularism about everything. In so far as moral particularism is meant to express something distinctive about morality (or about the normative, more generally), particularists may need to eschew reliance on Wittgenstein or else show how the argument can be appropriated without colonizing unwanted territory.

On some accounts, moral principles are analytic or conceptual truths, and on some accounts, our knowledge of moral principles is *a priori*. The forgoing account of moral principles, however, leaves open the semantic and epistemic status of moral principles. Dialectically, this is important because the twentieth century saw the development of a great diversity of meta-ethical accounts of the semantic and epistemic status of moral claims, many of which cast doubt on the analyticity and/or *a priori* status of moral claims. Nevertheless, even if these meta-ethical issues were settled, that should not settle the debate between particularism and generalism. For example, we take it as obvious that no particularist would be assuaged if told that the principle of utility is true, though neither analytic nor *a priori*.

A further distinction between different kinds of principles concerns the concepts they deploy. While virtually all particularists would reject principles that purport to express, in entirely non-evaluative terms, sufficiency conditions for moral concepts, particularists are less agreed whether morality is patterned in some less robust way. W. D. Ross, for example, is commonly taken to be a proto-particularist. For while Ross held that there were exceptionless principles specifying when one has a *prima facie* duty, he distinguished between an agent's *prima facie* duties and the agent's duty overall. This latter is determined, Ross claimed, by the relative significance, in the context, of all the agent's *prima facie* duties, and cannot be deduced by further self-evident principles (Ross 1930). This last component of Ross's view is particularist in spirit, though Ross's view as a whole is founded upon a generalist account of *prima facie* duties. Contemporary particularism, by contrast, stands opposed to principles governing concepts like ought, duty (all things considered), and wrong but also to principles governing so-called contributory moral concepts, such as the concept of a moral reason.

Though contemporary particularists would not accept principles connecting the moral and the non-moral even at the contributory level, there is disagreement about the possibility of intra-moral principles, for example, principles connecting thick and thin evaluative concepts. Those defending an affirmative answer argue that, while the conditions of justice cannot be spelled out in principled and non-normative terms, we can say that the justice of an institution always counts in its moral favor (McNaughton and Rawlings 2000). More radical particularists deny even these intra-moral principles (Dancy 2004).

Having distinguished several conceptions of a moral principle, let us turn to the variety of negative theses one might advance about them. One straightforward and ambitious thesis denies that there are any true moral principles. This eliminativism about moral principles can be contrasted with a more open-ended skepticism, according to which we have no adequate grounds for believing there are any true principles. Third, one might recommend abstinence when it comes to the use of principles in arriving at judgment and choice. In effect, this is to take a skeptical or eliminitivist attitude towards moral principles as guides. In either its elimintivist or its skeptical guise, however, particularism should be read as a thesis that specially applies to principles and not simply as a consequence of a broader rejection of morality. For example, a nihilist would agree that there are no true moral principles, but only on grounds that there are no moral values at all. Particularism, by contrast, must hold that, setting aside arguments against morality *tout court*, there are additional reasons to reject or be skeptical of moral principles.

A final possibility that deserves independent consideration is Jonathan Dancy's most recent statement of particularism. According to Dancy, particularism holds that, "The possibility of moral thought and judgment do not depend upon the provision of a suitable supply of moral principles" (Dancy 2004: 7). Particularism in this sense is apparently consistent with eschewing eliminativism, skepticism, and abstinence about principles. This characterization may have the advantage of allowing the particularist to concede that morality might be, in some respects, patterned while insisting that we are not entitled to think that it must be so. Just how much weaker this doctrine is than other versions of particularism turns on how one interprets the relation of dependence that it denies and on what falls under the heading of "moral thought and judgment." Some generalists charge that this version of particularism represents a dramatic weakening of the doctrine since, even if true, it may imply only that moral principles cannot be derived in a certain way.

While some philosophers, such as Kant and Hare, have tried to derive substantive moral principles from the very conditions of moral thought and judgment, others defend substantive moral principles while conceding that it is possible to engage in moral thought and judgment without accepting or even implicitly relying upon them. It is not clear, for example, that Mill would claim moral thought and judgment depend upon the principle of utility (or on any other principle), but it would be surprising if Mill could lay claim to being a particularist. One might say the same about contemporary meta-ethical naturalists who understand morality as one of the natural sciences (Boyd 1988).

Arguments for particularism and generalism

Let us turn now to a brief review of some of the major arguments for and against particularism. One way to settle the debate between particularists and generalists would be by establishing the validity of a specific moral principle. For example, if Mill's proof of the principle of utility succeeds, then this would seem to settle matters in favor of generalism. Mill's argument, moreover, would carry dialectical weight even without a prior specification of what a moral principle is or what its role is to be. After all, it is in part by reference to such paradigmatic principles as the principle of utility that philosophers try to explain more specifically what a moral principle is and what its role is to be. By the same token, refuting a candidate moral principle, such as the principle of utility, might erode confidence in generalism. The case would be stronger still if it were established that the history of attempts to articulate moral principles is a history of successive failure. This argument, however, is dialectically weak since many of those who are not confident that, for example, the categorical imperative is a valid moral principle will still not accept the premise that the categorical imperative has been refuted. This is especially true if one is appropriately cautious about regarding purported refutations by counter-example as sound and decisive. It is hardly indisputable that utilitarianism implies that we should sometimes punish the innocent, and many Kantians deny that the categorical imperative implies that we should never lie even to prevent murder. Contemporary discussions of particularism, however, have tended to revolve not around arguments for or against specific moral principles, but instead around those general considerations which bear upon the importance of moral principles to morality and thus to moral theory.

The most influential and widely discussed argument for particularism is based upon the holism of reasons, a doctrine which is supposed to capture an important kind of context sensitivity. According to holism about reasons, a consideration that is a reason in one context may be no reason at all in another context or even a reason with a different valence. By contrast, atomism about reasons holds that what is a reason in one case must also and similarly be a reason in any other case. To take one example, holists claim that the fact that an action brings pleasure is often a reason in favor of the action. In some cases, though – the pleasure of a sadist to take one example – the fact that an action brings pleasure is no reason at all or even a reason against the action. Holism depends critically on sharply distinguishing considerations that are reasons from broader features of the context that can affect whether some consideration is a reason. Discussions of holism have given rise to a rich vocabulary for describing these salient aspects of context. There are "defeaters," "enablers," "intensifiers," and "diminishers" that lead respectively to a consideration not being a reason when otherwise it would have been, to a consideration being a reason when otherwise it would not have been, and to a consideration being a reason of greater or lesser force than it otherwise would have been. Particularists argue that, given the holism of reasons, the prospects for moral principles are bleak.

Generalists challenge both the soundness and validity of this argument. Some argue that holism is false (Raz 2000; Crisp 2000). They argue that the full reason favoring action includes those contextual features which holists distinguish as enablers and defeaters. Once these are seen as a part of the reason we can reclaim the view that what is a reason in one case must always be similarly a reason in other cases where it is present. Debate about the soundness and proper formulation of holism is ongoing. Consensus has proved elusive, perhaps because arguments on both sides tend either to appeal to intuitions about what is the reason in a particular case or else to appeal to other concepts, e.g. explanation or causation, where the proper characterization of salient background conditions is similarly contested. For further discussion, see Dancy (2004) and Väyrynen (2006).

Others have urged that even if holism is true it is entirely compatible with principles (Jackson et al. 2000; McKeever and Ridge 2005). If principles can include as part of their content the very context sensitivity upon which holists insist, then, it is argued, holism does not support particularism. For example, one might advance as a principle the claim that the fact that an action brings pleasure is always a reason in favor unless that pleasure is sadistic in which case it is a reason against. This toy example maintains the sharp distinction between reasons and defeaters upon which holists insist, but still implies that there is a robust pattern to morality of the sort that particularists typically deny. Moreover, some historically significant moral doctrines are holistic in just this way. For example, Kant claimed that the fact that an action would advance our happiness is a reason to perform it but only on the condition that the act itself is compatible with having a good will.

Some particularists urge that even if holism and particularism are strictly compatible, the sheer amount of context sensitivity in moral matters renders generalism implausible (Little 2000). Critics charge that this begs the question since the degree of context sensitivity that must be assumed is precisely that amount that would render capture by principles implausible. Others claim that the argument from holism is indirect and that while holism is consistent with generalism it would render any principles "cosmic accidents" (Dancy 2004). Just how such an indirect argument is to proceed is not entirely clear (McKeever and Ridge 2006: 32–41). At any rate, the argument from holism continues to occupy a central place in discussions of particularism.

A second line of support for particularism proceeds from moral epistemology. Moral knowledge, the argument goes, is properly likened to perceptual knowledge (McNaughton 1988; McDowell 1979, 1985). In the perceptual case, moreover, principles are neither used nor even presupposed. We can know that a canary is yellow without deploying any principles that specify in non-chromatic terms when an object is yellow. Indeed, it seems largely an empirical matter whether yellow objects even share a common reflective property that can be picked out without deploying color concepts. If moral knowledge is acquired in a way akin to perception, then perhaps principles are equally unnecessary in the moral case.

While one might question whether our ordinary perceptual knowledge does depend upon law-like generalizations connecting color and non-color properties, critics of the perceptual argument have tended, instead, to put pressure on the analogy being drawn between moral and perceptual knowledge. First, basic moral knowledge is arguably *a priori*, as some particularists agree (Dancy 2004). One reason for thinking so is that our knowledge of moral matters can extend to hypothetical cases. We can know not only that an act was wrong, but also that some act would be wrong. This is a salient difference between the moral and the ordinary perceptual case. Moreover, it seems that this is an essential and not merely a curious feature of moral knowledge since only then can we have advance knowledge of the morality of our would-be actions. Of course, *a priori* intuitions are often described in perceptual terms, but the areas where *a priori* intuitions have been most persuasively defended, e.g. mathematics, are paradigmatically rule-governed. A second salient difference between the moral and the ordinary perceptual case is the significance of some basing relation. In the moral case, we seem to presuppose that objects acquire a moral status on the basis of their other features. In the terms Dancy borrows from Ross, moral properties are resultant. This appears to be a salient difference between ordinary perceptual judgments of, for example, color and moral judgments.

The arguments thus far considered are best understood as attempts to support principle eliminativism, principle skepticism, or anti-transcendental particularism about standards. But what about principle abstinence? Should principles be used as guides? If morality is variable and context dependent in ways that principles simply cannot capture, as the original argument from holism maintains, then any agent who relied exclusively on principles for guidance would be apt to err. But even if the argument from holism fails, there are other avenues to principle abstinence. Particularists have urged that reliance on principles leads to rigidity and narrow-mindedness (Dancy 1993; McNaughton 1988). Principles direct our attention only to those features already countenanced as relevant by whatever principle we are trying to apply. Consequently we miss entirely or disregard morally relevant features that we would not have ignored had we not relied on principles in the first place. Of course, this argument assumes that the agent is not perfectly applying a perfect set of standards, but, dialectically, this is a fair assumption. Generalists are not entitled to assume a perfect set of normative principles.

Generalists have cautioned that this argument cannot establish a strong doctrine of principle abstinence since there are plausible competing advantages to being guided by moral principles, such as the benefits of interpersonal coordination and assurance (Hooker 2000; Väyrynen 2009). They have also questioned whether it supports even a modest version of principle abstinence. A critical issue concerns both the content of our moral principles and the attitudes we have in being guided by them. While it is true, generalists will agree, that dogmatically accepting a highly rigid principle is apt to lead us astray, this is not a model of guidance to which generalism must be committed. Generalists can allow for various hedged principles and can allow that even as we rely on a principle for guidance we should regard it as potentially fallible (McKeever and Ridge 2006) and even cultivate the very sensitivity to reasons that particularists urge is necessary (Väyrynen 2009). One challenge for this route is to show that this greater flexibility does not simply leave us ready to abandon our principles anytime they seem mistaken and so compromise what is initially attractive about principled guidance.

Having reviewed several arguments for particularism, let us turn now to arguments for generalism. Some generalists argue that principles connecting the moral and the non-moral are conceptual truths the implicit grasp of which is constitutive of our competence with moral concepts (Jackson et al. 2000). The argument does not rely on any specific conceptual truth, but rather claims that there must be some such truth if our moral judgments are to count as the deployment of genuine concepts. Whether one counts this argument successful will depend upon one's view of analytic truths in general and the prospect for them in the moral case, especially in light of G. E. Moore's open question argument and its philosophical descendants (Moore 1903; Hare 1952; Horgan and Timmons 1992).

Other generalists argue from what they take to be common ground between generalists and particularists. One strategy is to argue from claims about the need for moral explanation. While particularism may suggest an intuitionist moral epistemology, particularists agree that the moral status of some object of evaluation (e.g. the rightness of some act) is not an explanatorily opaque fact. Objects have the moral status they do because of their other features. Furthermore, we might think there must be some further explanation of how those other features can confer the moral status they do. For example, we might think that some act is right because it is done for a friend, while also thinking that there must be some explanation of how being done for a friend can confer rightness on an action. Some generalists argue that the best account of this kind of explanation just is the existence of some moral principle (Väyrynen 2006).

Other generalists argue that moral principles are presupposed by moral knowledge and practical wisdom (McKeever and Ridge 2006). Again, this argument proceeds from initially common ground since particularism, as normally defended, is a non-skeptical doctrine. The thought here is that, even if a fact's status as a moral reason can be defeated by further features of our circumstances, as holism maintains, our claim to know that a fact is a reason presupposes that it is not, in fact, defeated. If the variability and context dependence of morality were so extensive as to never be captured by finite principles, then we, as limited and finite beings, could never reliably judge that that consideration had not been defeated, and so could never have moral knowledge. One worry about this argument is that it may prove too much, namely that principles are required in any case where knowledge is possible. This, critics charge, is implausible since some ways of acquiring knowledge, for example, ordinary empirical induction, seem not to presuppose a prior grasp of principles (Schroeder 2008).

Recent developments

Though particularism and generalism are logically incompatible doctrines, much recent work has been devoted to exploring middle ground. The middle ground in question agrees that there are law-like generalizations governing features that have moral significance whilst insisting that such generalizations are exception-laden, and ineliminably so (Little 2000; Lance and Little 2004). For example, it may be a law that pain is bad, even while there are exceptions to this, cases in which some identifiable departure from the normal case has as a consequence that pain is not bad (say, in the case of just punishment). The status of the exception as an exception is what, as the saying goes, proves the rule. Pain is "defeasibly" bad. The key particularist element in this story is that while the exceptions may be categorized into types, they cannot be exhaustively identified. Thus when we appeal to such laws in explanation or deploy them in deliberation we are relying on a non-principled skill of identifying relevant exceptional circumstances. Whether such law-like but exception-laden generalizations should be called "principles" may be a largely terminological question.

Conclusion

Generalists and particularists have waged a wide-ranging and fruitful debate. Historically, the most radical forms of particularism emerged in opposition to R. M. Hare's seemingly radical generalist view that principles are essential to moral thought and judgment. More recently generalists and particularists alike have sought a plausible synthesis which preserves the best insights of each of the opposing doctrines. As such work continues, it seems likely to uncover novel ideas, insights and distinctions which will be of use not only to the defenders of compromise views, but should also enrich the views of those who defend more radical positions.

See also Aristotle (Chapter 4); Reasons for action (Chapter 24); Reasons, values, and morality (Chapter 36); Ethical intuitionism (Chapter 39).

References

Aristotle (1999) *Nicomachean Ethics*, trans., ed. Terence Irwin, Indianapolis, IN: Hackett.
Boyd, R. (1988) "How to Be a Moral Realist," in Sayre-McCord 1988, pp. 181–228.
Crisp, R. (2000) "Particularizing Particularism," in Hooker and Little 2000, pp. 23–47.
Dancy, J. (2003) *Moral Reasons*, Oxford: Blackwell.
——(2004) *Ethics Without Principles*, Oxford: Oxford University Press.
Darwall, S. (1986) "Agent-Centred Restrictions from the Inside-Out," *Philosophical Studies* 50: 291–319.
Hare, R. M. (1952) *The Language of Morals*, Oxford: Oxford University Press.
Hooker, B. (2000) "Moral Particularism: Wrong and Bad," in Hooker and Little 2000, pp. 1–22.
Hooker, B. and Little, M. (2000) *Moral Particularism*, Oxford: Oxford University Press.
Horgan, T. and Timmons, M. (1992) "Troubles on Moral Twin Earth: Moral Queerness Revived," *Synthese* 92: 221–60.
Jackson, F., Pettit, P., and Smith, M. (2000) "Ethical Particularism and Patterns," in Hooker and Little 2000, pp. 79–99.
Lance, M. and Little, M. (2004) "Defeasibility and the Normative Grasp of Context," *Erkenntnis* 61, nos 2–3: 435–55.
Little, M. (2000) "Moral Generalities Revisited," in Hooker and Little 2000, pp. 276–304.
McDowell, J. (1979) "Virtue and Reason," *Monist* 62: 331–50.
——(1985) "Values and Secondary Qualities," in T. Honderich (ed.) *Morality and Objectivity*, London: Routledge, pp. 110–29; repr. in Sayre-McCord 1988, pp. 166–80.
McKeever, S. and Ridge, M. (2005) "What Does Holism Have to Do with Particularism?," *Ratio* 18: 93–103.
——(2006) *Principled Ethics: Generalism as a Regulative Ideal*, Oxford: Oxford University Press.
McNaughton, D. (1988) *Moral Vision*, Oxford: Blackwell.
McNaughton, D. and Rawlings, P. (2000) "Unprincipled Ethics," in Hooker and Little 2000, pp. 256–75.
Moore, G. E. (1903) *Principia Ethica*, New York: Cambridge University Press.
Railton, P. (1984) "Alienation, Consequentialism, and the Demands of Morality," *Philosophy & Public Affairs* 13: 134–71.

Raz, J. (2000) "The Truth in Particularism," in Hooker and Little 2000, pp. 48–78.
Ross, W. D. (1930) *The Right and the Good*, Oxford: Clarendon Press.
Sayre-McCord, G. (1988) *Essays in Moral Realism*, Ithaca, NY: Cornell University Press.
Schroeder, M. 2008 (Forthcoming) "An Issue of Principle," *Noûs*.
Väyrynen, P. (2006) "Moral Generalism: Enjoy in Moderation," *Ethics* 116: 707–41.
——2009 "A Theory of Hedged Moral Principles," in Russ Shafer-Landau (ed.) *Oxford Studies in Metaethics*, vol. 4, New York: Oxford University Press, pp. 91–132.

Further reading

Dancy, J. (1981) "On Moral Properties," *Mind* 90: 367–85.
Holton, R. (2002) "Principles and Particularisms," *Proceedings of the Aristotelian Society*, Supplementary Volume 67, no. 1: 191–209.
Lance, M., Potrč, M., and Strahovnik, V. (2008) *Challenging Moral Particularism*, Routledge Studies in Ethics and Moral Theory, New York: Routledge.
Stratton-Lake, P. (2002) *Ethical Intuitionism: Re-Evaluations*, Oxford: Oxford University Press.

Part VI

DEBATES IN ETHICS

(i)

GOALS AND IDEALS

54
WELFARE

Christopher Heathwood

The question of welfare, and its importance

Things go better for some people than they do for other people. Some people's lives are quite good; if someone we cared about were to live such a life, this would please us. Other lives are not worth living at all; if there is no prospect for improvement in such a life, it may be rational for the person living it to end it. In virtue of what are such things true? What makes a life a good or a bad life for the person living it? What must we get in life if things are to go well for us? What does welfare or well-being consist in? What makes for quality of life? What things is it ultimately in our interest to get? These are different ways of asking the philosophical question of welfare.

Our question is not the question of what things *cause* a person's life to be going well. Psychologists, economists, and self-help books often offer advice on this question. They might tell us that things are likely to go better for us if we are married, get regular exercise, and stay in touch with friends. This may be good advice, but it does not answer the question that interests philosophers. If these things are good for us, this is due to their effects, but philosophers of welfare want to know what things are good in themselves for a person, independent of any effects. They want to know, in other words, what things are *intrinsically good* (or bad), as opposed to merely *instrumentally good* (or bad), for a person. These philosophical questions are more fundamental than the causal question; a complete justification of a claim of instrumental value must eventually appeal to some claim of intrinsic value, but not vice versa.

Nor is our question the question of what makes a situation better, or makes things go better, or makes the world a better place. In other words, the question of what things are intrinsically good *for a person* is not the question of what things are intrinsically good *period*. To illustrate, it may be that some people deserve to be badly off, and that their being badly off is a good thing. What makes such a person's life go worse for him makes the world better. Or it may be that beauty is intrinsically good, in that the existence of something beautiful, even when no one will ever enjoy it, is itself a good thing. It is easy to fail to distinguish the question of what things are intrinsically good for a person from the question of what things are intrinsically good because when someone is getting something that is intrinsically good for her, this is usually an intrinsically good thing. According to *welfarism*, it is the only thing that makes a situation a good one.

Finally, the question of welfare is not the question of what makes a life a *morally good* life. For surely it is possible for bad things to happen to good people, for the wicked to prosper, and for nice guys to finish last. Even if we became persuaded, as many ancient philosophers were, that there is some necessary connection between moral virtue and well-being, it would still not follow that *what it is* to be a good person is the same thing as what it is to get a good life.

The question of welfare is inherently interesting and important, and worth our attention in its own right. But the concept of welfare plays important roles in moral and evaluative thought, and deserves our interest for this reason, too. The two most intuitively plausible principles of conduct – those of *beneficence* and *non-maleficence* – instruct us, respectively, to benefit others (raise their welfare) and to refrain from harming others (from diminishing their welfare). Principles of *justice* that enjoin us to distribute according to desert, often enjoin us to distribute *welfare* according to desert. In similar fashion, welfare will play a role in explicating the *personal virtues* of benevolence and justice, not to mention compassion, kindness, mercy, and prudence. Welfare is often thought to be the *object of moral consideration*, in that, when we are taking someone (or something, such as an animal) into account morally, it is her (or its) welfare we are looking after. The promotion of our own welfare is what *rational self-interest* demands, and the promotion of the general welfare is what, according to *utilitarianism*, morality demands. When we want to *reward* or *punish* a person, it is his welfare that we ultimately want to affect. When we *envy* a person, we envy the good things in his life. Finally, a person's welfare is what those who *care* about him will look after. We cannot hope to have a full understanding of any of these important topics or concepts in ethics without an understanding of the nature of welfare. Furthermore, appreciating the ties the notion of welfare has to these central concepts in our moral thinking helps us to identify in the first place the notion that this chapter is about.

The main kinds of answer

A reasonable way to begin answering the question of welfare may be to produce a list of initially plausible intrinsic goods and bads, the presence of which seems to make a life more or less desirable to live. A first pass at a list of goods might include happiness, knowledge, friendship, freedom, rational activity, creative activity, and being respected (cf. the lists in Ross 1988/1930: 134–41; and Frankena 1973: 87–88). It seems sensible to want such things in our lives. This pluralistic (partial) theory of welfare is an instance of the *objective list theory*, so-called because the items on the list are put forth as good for a person independently of her particular predilections (Parfit 1984: 4).

One concern for objective list theories, at least if they are pluralistic, is that of comparability between the different goods on the list. A complete theory of welfare should include principles specifying how the value of a whole life is determined by the values of the various goods in the life. This seems to require that all the goods in life be measurable on a single scale so that, for instance, the knowledge acquired from reading some newspaper article might have the same intrinsic value for the person in question as the freedom gained each day when speed limits are raised. Even if we put aside the question of how we might come to know the relative values of such goods, some philosophers doubt whether there is even any fact of the matter here to be known.

A second issue is a challenge to explain why just these items are the ones that belong on the list. What makes them so special? The most satisfying answer would involve a criterion for inclusion on the list. Such a principle would reveal in virtue of what the things that are good for us are good for us. It would also give the theory a kind of unity it otherwise lacks. Although it is worth trying to meet this challenge, we should be open to the possibility that there are just several basic human goods whose status as goods cannot be explained in terms of any overarching principle.

One kind of objective list theory that answers this challenge is *perfectionism*, which contends (on some versions) that what is fundamentally good for us is to cultivate those features essential to and/or distinctive of human beings (Hurka 1993). On one reading of Aristotle, the very best human life is a life of contemplation, and this is so because the ability to engage in intellectual contemplation is a central facet of human nature.

A deeper problem for objective theories of well-being arises when we consider people who haven't the slightest interest in the items on the objective list, and seem, when they receive these things, to get nothing out of it. Imagine a person who finds the highest forms of intellectual activity completely hollow. He is much happier doing carpentry, which he does for a living, and playing softball, which he does after work. It is hard to believe that such a person gets a life that is in any way better *for him* if he goes through the motions and studies organic chemistry for its own sake. It doesn't seem that those who love him and are concerned about his quality of life would encourage him to do this.

Another way to get at this point is to consider the notions of punishment and reward, which seem bound up with the notions of harm and benefit. If an objective list theory is true, then although one way to reward a person may be to give him something he would love (since an objective list can include the subjective good of getting something one loves, so long as it also includes objective goods), another perfectly good way to reward a person is to give him an objective good he couldn't care less about. But this is not how we go about rewarding people.

This objection to the objective list theory of welfare should not be confused with analogous objections to objective theories of other phenomena in ethics, such as impersonal value, or moral obligation. If, for example, it is an intrinsically good thing for there to be people who are morally virtuous, the fact that some person would not regard his own virtue as any kind of reward is no objection to this view. It very well may be no reward for him, but this is no objection to the view that it is an intrinsically good thing, impersonally speaking, that he be virtuous. The problem arises for objective theories of welfare because welfare is a subject-relative kind of value: it is value *for* some subject. For this reason, it seems plausible that something can contribute to a person's well-being only if it bears some connection to what the person cares about.

One of the most popular arguments, historically, concerning welfare is the argument from psychological hedonism. Psychological hedonism is the doctrine that the only thing human beings ever desire or care about for its own sake ("intrinsically desire") is their own pleasure, and the only thing to which human beings are ever intrinsically averse is their own pain. This empirical thesis is to be contrasted with the evaluative thesis of *welfare hedonism*, the view that the only thing that is fundamentally intrinsically good for us is our own pleasure and the only thing intrinsically bad for us is our own pain. The great historical hedonists – Epicurus, Bentham, Mill – believe that the psychological claim establishes the evaluative claim: the fact that our own pleasure is the sole object of our intrinsic desire shows that our own pleasure is our sole intrinsic good (Bentham 1907/1789: 1–2; Mill 2002/1863: 35–6).

The argument from psychological hedonism seems to rely on the criterion that whatever a person intrinsically desires is intrinsically good for that person. This thought fits naturally with (perhaps it just is) the thought that motivated the main problem above for objective list theories, which is the idea that what is good for a person must connect up in some important way with her particular interests.

Hedonism is one of the simplest, oldest, and historically most popular answers to the question of what makes a person's life go well for him or her. In its simplest form, it holds

- that all pleasures are intrinsically good and all pains intrinsically bad for the person experiencing them;
- that the value of an episode of pleasure or pain for the person experiencing it is a function of the intensity and duration of the pleasure or pain; and
- that how good a life is for the person who lives it is equal to the balance of pleasure over pain in the life (Feldman 2004: 25–30).

Because it is a form of monism about welfare, hedonism is a satisfyingly unified theory. Hedonists can account for the apparent plurality of goods in life (such as appear on the sample objective list above) by appeal to the instrumental value of these things. Knowledge, friendship, freedom, etc. are good because it makes us happy to have these things. But, the hedonist will insist, for the rare individuals who derive no pleasure from such things, they are worthless.

Also because hedonism is a form of monism, there is less of a problem of comparability between goods. We can compare the value for some person of gaining some piece of knowledge with the value of gaining some amount of freedom by determining the effect of each on the person's pleasure and pain. Although such determinations are difficult in practice, fewer people doubt that there are facts of the matter here to be discovered.

In the popular imagination, hedonists are people devoted to sensual pleasures and instant gratification. But the philosophical doctrine of hedonism does not imply that we ought to live this way. Most hedonists believe that we ought to look out for the welfare of others in addition to our own. Furthermore, it is far from clear that a dedication to instant bodily gratification is the best way to maximize, in the long run, the balance of pleasure over pain in one's life. Hedonists emphasize the greater reliability of intellectual pleasures, as well as the tendency of bodily indulgence to bring with it hangovers, bellyaches, addiction, and other sources of suffering. Some hedonists have even maintained that intellectual pleasures are *intrinsically* more valuable than bodily pleasures of equal intensity and duration (Mill 2002/1863: 7–11), though critics have doubted whether such a claim is in fact consistent with hedonism (Moore 1903: §48).

We should distinguish hedonism, the view that the good life is the pleasurable life, from *eudaimonism*, the view that the good life is the happy life. If to be happy just is to have a favorable balance of pleasure over pain, then hedonism and eudaimonism are equivalent (Mill 2002/1863: 7). But on another popular theory of the nature of happiness, to be happy is to be satisfied with one's life as whole (Sumner 1996: 145–6). If this or another non-hedonistic theory of happiness is true, hedonism and eudaimonism about welfare diverge.

One of the oldest objections to hedonism is the argument from base pleasures (Aristotle 1998/c. 330 BCE: 253). Imagine the pleasure received by a member of the Ku Klux Klan during a lynching or a child molester during a rape. Such pleasures seem positively bad. Hedonists may reply, however, that while such pleasures are reprehensible morally speaking, and come with horrific causes and effects, this is compatible with the pleasure, just considered in itself, being good for the person experiencing it. Furthermore, the view that such pleasures are good for the person experiencing them may actually help explain why these cases are so offensive: the person is receiving a *good* he doesn't deserve.

Another problem for hedonism has been made vivid with a science-fiction device called an experience machine, which gives its users perfect replicas of real-life experiences (Nozick 1974: 42–5). Consider some fine human life, replete with real relationships, real achievements, and a real awareness of what is going on. Compare it to a life on the experience machine that is indistinguishable "from the inside." Which life would you prefer to lead, just taking yourself into account? Which life would you prefer your child to lead? Although the lives are on a par hedonically, many people believe the first life to be preferable to the second. This intuition is not universal, however; some insist that "what you don't know can't hurt you," and that our intuitions may here be distorted by the fact that if one knew one was on the experience machine, one would be upset, and this would make one's life worse (as hedonism of course recognizes). Critics reply, however, that hedonists are unable to explain why such a discovery *should* make us upset (Nagel 1970: 76).

The final problem for hedonism we will discuss is a version of the main problem we discussed for objective list theories. Imagine a person who has little interest in pleasure, and who is prepared to forgo it for the sake of the things she really wants in life. Suppose, for example, she wants to climb all of the tallest peaks in the world. It seems plausible that how well things go for this person is a function not of how much pleasure and pain her life contains – she doesn't care about that – but of the extent to which she achieves this and other goals. The original complaint against objective list theories – that they fail to respect people's differing interests in life – may therefore be a double-edged sword for hedonists. If it moves us from an objective theory to hedonism, shouldn't it also move us away from hedonism, since it is possible for people to be interested in things other than pleasure (the argument from psychological hedonism notwithstanding)?

Recall the criterion that the argument from psychological hedonism assumes: that whatever a person intrinsically desires is intrinsically good for that person. Some hedonists believe this claim helps establish hedonism. But if such a claim is true, it seems we should instead maintain that welfare has to do most fundamentally with desire rather than with pleasure. Even if psychological hedonism is true, surely this is just a contingent fact about our psychology, making welfare hedonism a contingent truth at best. The deep truth about welfare would still be that welfare consists in getting what one wants. This is *preferentism* about welfare.

Preferentism is emphatically not the view that welfare consists in the feelings of satisfaction one has when one gets what one wants. For a desire to be satisfied, all that need happen is that the state of affairs desired in fact comes about. When a desire is satisfied, this often gives rise to feelings of satisfaction, and we often prefer to experience such feelings rather than not. So this will be a further good according to preferentism. But such feelings will have no value in themselves, apart from being desired.

Preferentism epitomizes the idea we have been discussing that one's good must be connected to what one cares about. It thus avoids the objection that applies to both hedonism and the objective list theory. Preferentism also nicely handles the experience machine problem. It does not imply that the two lives considered above in connection with this case are equally good, for the life on the machine contains far less desire satisfaction. This person will have desires for real relationships and really to do certain things, but, hooked up to the machine, these desires will go unsatisfied. Preferentism has also been attractive to empirically minded theorists of welfare, such as economists, who seek a theory that makes welfare amenable to measurement. The thought is that one's preferences, unlike private feelings of pleasure and pain, are observable relatively directly, through one's choices.

But preferentism faces problems, too. One problem is that we have desires for things so remote from our lives that it seems implausible to hold that having them satisfied makes any difference to how well our lives go (Parfit 1984: 494; Griffin 1986: 16–17). Consider some random person, past, present, or future, who will remain forever unknown to you, and ask which you prefer: that he suffers from migraine headaches, or that he doesn't. I assume you prefer that he doesn't. Suppose, as a matter of fact, the person you picked doesn't suffer in this way. Preferentism implies that this fact is good *for you* and makes *your* life go better, but that is hard to believe. Some preferentists believe this shows that the theory should be restricted to count only those preferences that are about our own lives, or are "self-regarding" (Overvold 1982; Parfit 1986: 494–5). But when Red Sox fans got their heart's desire as their team won the World Series, surely this was a good thing in these fans' lives, even though the desire involved – that the Red Sox win – was not self-regarding.

A different solution holds that it is of no value to us when the stranger avoids migraines because, although we prefer that he doesn't have migraines, it is no *goal* or *aim* of ours that he not suffer in this way. This is in fact not a preferentist solution – it is a move to a different, albeit similar, theory: *aim achievementism* (Scanlon 1998: 118–23). This theory holds that welfare consists not in satisfying one's desires but in achieving one's aims. Aim achievementism seems particularly well-suited to respect our intuitions about what would make things turn out well for the rock climber we imagined earlier.

Aim achievementism, however, may face the Red Sox objection just discussed, since it doesn't seem correct to say that it is an aim or goal of Red Sox fans that the Red Sox win – it is just a very strong desire. Aim achievementists also seem poorly suited to accommodate a certain datum concerning welfare: that suffering is bad for those who suffer. Hedonism obviously accommodates this datum. Preferentists can, too, by appealing to the desire theory of the nature of pleasure and pain, according to which, roughly, for an experience to be a painful experience is for it to be one its subject has a desire not to be having. Since, given this view, pain and suffering always involve desire frustration, preferentists can accommodate, and even explain, the badness of suffering. But since it doesn't seem that suffering typically constitutively involves the frustration of aims, aim achievementism may be unable to make room for the seemingly undeniable truth that suffering is intrinsically bad for those who suffer. It should be noted that neither of these objections to aim achievementism is an objection to the more modest thesis that the achievement of aims is merely *one of* the intrinsic personal goods.

Returning to preferentism, another problem for preferentists concerns desires based on false beliefs or on failures to appreciate properly the objects of one desires. Suppose I have a desire to drink the stuff in the glass before me. I believe it to be water, but in fact it is sulfuric acid. Surely satisfying this desire would not be good for me. The most common way preferentists deal with this problem is by modifying the theory to count only the desires one would have if one were fully informed, thinking clearly, vividly appreciating the relevant facts, and in other ways idealized. This modification brings with it a new problem, however. My ideal self, with his other-worldly powers of appreciation, might prefer things – caviar, experimental music – that my actual self hates. Surely it is of no benefit to me as I actually am to receive such things (Griffin 1986: 11).

A third problem for preferentism mirrors a problem for hedonism. If base pleasures don't make us better off, then neither should the satisfaction of base desires. Preferentists may be tempted to appeal again to the idealization strategy to avoid this problem. They may want to say that no one who was thinking clearly and appreciating the relevant facts would have racist or pedophilic desires. They might further add that those who appreciate matters aright want things like knowledge, friendship, creative activity, etc. Two problems arise here. First, one of the main motivations for preferentism – that what is good for us must be connected to what we actually care about – has evidently been abandoned. Second, one can't help but suspect that purveyors of such theories are just closet objective list theorists. Driving their view about when a desire is ideal may be intuitions about when what is desired would be a good thing to get.

We have thus come full circle, back to the objective list theory. One way we can stop the dialectic repeating itself is to introduce yet another option, *the hybrid theory*, which combines objective and subjective elements (Parfit 1984: 501–2; Adams 1999: 93–101; Darwall 1999: 176–96; Feldman 2004: 119–22). On this approach, things are going well for us when we are enjoying (or having some other specified attitude towards) things that have some value independent of this attitude. The hybrid theorist cannot say, as a pure objective list theorist will say, that the items on her objective list are the things that are intrinsically good for the people who get them. But she might instead say that the items on her objective list are the things that are, say, inherently worthy of being enjoyed. Combine something inherently worthy of being enjoyed with enjoyment of it, and this is a good thing for the person doing the enjoying.

Evaluating the hybrid theory involves, among other things, assessing to what degree it is open to any of the original objections against the theories it is hybridizing. Two concerns for pure objective list theories – comparability between items on the list and criteria for inclusion on the list – remain. The third problem we discussed for objective list theories – the one concerning the plausible connection between what is good for one and what one cares about – is certainly mitigated in the hybrid theory. But it may not be eliminated entirely. Imagine a hybrid theory according to which the music of Miles Davis is most worthy of being enjoyed while the music of Madonna is only somewhat worthy. Suppose that we want to reward a friend for some favor, and that our friend would be ecstatic to attend a performance of Madonna's music but would only mildly enjoy attending a performance of Miles Davis's music. We want to do what would give our friend the best evening for her. So long as we describe the case properly, the hybrid theory will imply that we benefit our friend most by sending her to hear Miles Davis's music rather than Madonna's. But that seems wrong, and is not how we conceive of rewarding people and benefiting friends. Although the hybrid theory avoids much of the objectionable paternalism of pure objective list theories, it may not avoid all of it.

There is no consensus among philosophers which, if any, of the six broad approaches described above,

- objective list theory
- hedonism
- eudaimonism
- preferentism
- aim achievementism
- the hybrid theory,

is correct. But this disagreement should not worry us unduly. Serious, sustained inquiry into this topic by a relatively large group of people is a new phenomenon in human intellectual history. The deep disagreement of today may not be a sign of intractable disagreement. Also, it's not as if the many inquiries in moral philosophy in which welfare figures need to be put on hold until the true theory of welfare has been discovered. We don't need to know the correct theory of welfare to know, for instance, that malnutrition and disease are bad for people and that eliminating such evils is praiseworthy.

How should I live my life?

Moral philosophy's first question is, How should one live? Most of us agree that, in living our lives, we ought to be concerned with how our choices affect others – and not only because of the effects that this, in turn, will have on us. But even if we set this factor aside, there remains the question of what I ought to do, just taking myself into account. One answer is that I ought to do whatever would benefit me most, or maximize my own well-being. Indeed, the claim that, just taking myself into account, I ought to promote my own well-being, may seem to be something of a tautology. But in fact it is a substantive claim, for an alternative answer is that I ought, say, to become the best person I can be (and that this is not exhausted by the effects I have on others). Fleshing this idea out somewhat, perhaps it would make me a more excellent person if there was some worthwhile intellectual activity – e.g. chess – I did well and if there was some worthwhile physical pursuit – e.g. rock climbing – at which I excelled. An advocate of this view might say that doing things like these is what we should be doing in life (again, putting aside our duties to others). But they need not say that we should be doing such things because such things are the ingredients of well-being.

This view is a kind of perfectionism, not about well-being (as was discussed earlier), but about "how I should live my life, just taking myself into account." Advocates of this approach may even want to describe it as a view about "the good life," or as a view about what makes a life most worth choosing – as against a view about what well-being, welfare, or benefit consists in (Scanlon 1998: 131). Proponents of this view may hold that hedonism, say, is the correct theory of well-being, but that well-being is only one ingredient, and perhaps not even a very important ingredient, of the good life. The life most worth our while is not one in which we are most well-off but in which we have the highest possible level of excellence.

All of this suggests a potential way to resolve some of the disagreement described earlier. Perhaps the advocates of the more objective theories discussed earlier disagree so deeply with the advocates of more subjective theories because the two parties are in fact offering theories of different phenomena (see Kagan [1994] for discussion of a different but related claim). Advocates of the objective theories may be telling us which sort of life is most worth choosing, while advocates of the subjective theories may be telling us in which sort of life one would be most well-off. This distinction is subtle, but assuming it is genuine, then, of any proposed theory, we must ask, before evaluating it, what it is a theory of. Its proponent should be prepared to identify what roles its target notion is meant to play. The notion may, for example, play a role in a principle of beneficence, or in defining rational self-interest; or the theory may simply be an analysis of a concept of ordinary language. The most ambitious and satisfying theories will offer a unified account meant to play all the roles in the neighborhood. Some hedonists mean to be doing this; they think not only that well-being consists in pleasure, but that the pleasant life is the one most worth choosing. More modest proposals will attempt to capture less. Increased sensitivity to exactly which phenomena one's proposed theory is meant to capture may be a way for future theorizing about welfare to make further progress.

See also Aristotle (Chapter 4); Utilitarianism to Bentham (Chapter 13); John Stuart Mill (Chapter 16); Consequentialism (Chapter 37); Evil (Chapter 49); Ideals of perfection (Chapter 55); Life, death, and ethics (Chapter 59).

References

Adams, R. M. (1999) *Finite and Infinite Goods*, Oxford: Oxford University Press.

Aristotle (1998/c. 330 BCE) *Nicomachean Ethics*, trans. W. D. Ross, Oxford: Oxford University Press.

Bentham, J. (1907/1789) *An Introduction to the Principles of Morals and Legislation*, Oxford: Clarendon Press.
Darwall, S. (1999) "Valuing Activity," *Social Philosophy and Policy* 16: 176–96.
Feldman, F. (2004) *Pleasure and the Good Life*, Oxford: Oxford University Press.
Frankena, W. K. (1973) *Ethics*, 2nd edn, Englewood Cliffs, NJ: Prentice-Hall.
Griffin, J. (1986) *Well-Being*, Oxford: Clarendon Press.
Hurka, T. (1993) *Perfectionism*, Oxford: Oxford University Press.
Kagan, S. (1994) "Me and My Life," *Proceedings of the Aristotelian Society* 94: 309–24.
Mill, J. S. (2002/1863) *Utilitarianism*, Indianapolis, IN: Hackett.
Moore, G. E. (1903) *Principia Ethica*, Cambridge: Cambridge University Press.
Nagel, T. (1970) "Death," *Noûs* 4: 73–80.
Nozick, R. (1974) *Anarchy, State and Utopia*, New York: Basic Books.
Overvold, M. C. (1982) "Self-Interest and Getting What You Want," in H. B. Miller and W. H. Williams (eds) *The Limits of Utilitarianism*, Minneapolis, MN: University of Minnesota Press.
Parfit, D. (1984) *Reasons and Persons*, Oxford: Clarendon Press.
Ross, W. D. (1988/1930) *The Right and the Good*, Indianapolis, IN: Hackett.
Scanlon, T. M. (1998) *What We Owe to Each Other*, Cambridge, MA: Harvard University Press.
Sumner, L. W. (1996) *Welfare, Happiness, and Ethics*, Oxford: Oxford University Press.

Further reading

Carson, T. L. (2000) *Value and the Good Life*, Notre Dame, IN: University of Notre Dame Press.
Crisp, R. (2008) "Well-Being," in E. N. Zalta (ed.) *Stanford Encyclopedia of Philosophy*, <http://plato.stanford.edu/archives/win2008/entries/well-being/>
Haybron, D. (2008) *The Pursuit of Unhappiness*, Oxford: Oxford University Press.
Kraut, R. (1994) "Desire and the Human Good," *Proceedings and Addresses of the American Philosophical Association* 68: 39–54.
——(2007) *What Is Good and Why*, Cambridge, MA: Harvard University Press.
Nussbaum, M. (2000) Chapters 2 and 3 of *Women and Human Development*, Cambridge: Cambridge University Press.
Parfit, D. (1984) "What Makes Someone's Life Go Best," Appendix 1 of *Reasons and Persons*, Oxford: Clarendon Press.
Raz, J. (2004) "The Role of Well-Being," *Philosophical Perspectives* 18: 269–94.
Sen, A. (1993) "Capability and Well-Being," in M. Nussbaum and A. Sen (eds) *The Quality of Life*, Oxford: Clarendon Press.
Sidgwick, H. (1907) *The Methods of Ethics*, London: Macmillan & Co.

55
IDEALS OF PERFECTION

Vinit Haksar

Introduction

According to perfectionism we should strive for what is best. The self-regarding version tells us to concentrate on our own perfection. The impartial version stresses that we should aim at the fullest realization of what is best in ourselves and others. There is also the version which has as its goal the maximization of intrinsic value in the world rather than human flourishing or well-being. Intrinsic value here is understood objectively as something that is of value independently of human desires or choices. Things such as knowledge or beauty are not intrinsically valuable because human beings desire them or choose them. Rather, human beings should choose such things because they are intrinsically valuable. On a weaker version of perfectionism human beings should pursue excellences such as knowledge and artistic achievements because by doing so they develop their true nature. Such a view involves a sort of conditional perfectionism. Assuming that we need to pursue human excellences in order to fulfill our nature and flourish, we should set as our goal the promotion of human excellences. If, however, it turns out that human nature requires something quite different, such as the pursuit of security or solidarity, then we should pursue these other activities in order to flourish, even if this involves an abandonment of the pursuit of excellence. The idea that the best for an individual consists *only* in perfectionist achievements is controversial. Welfare considerations also seem relevant as constituents of human flourishing.

Perfectionist ideals can be moral or non-moral. The moral ideals require us to be virtuous and to strive for excellence in morals. Non-moral ideals include the pursuit of excellence in arts, science and culture. The pursuit of ideals, especially of moral ones, can sometimes lead to considerable self-sacrifice. On some views the self-sacrifice is really required for self-realization. Moral perfectionists tend to regard the pursuit of perfection in morality as intrinsically good. Kant thought that the good will is the only thing that is unconditionally good. Some others would claim that perfection in non-moral areas too can be unconditionally good in the sense of intrinsically good. Kant thought that non-moral skills and achievements can be abused for evil purposes. But this only shows that when this occurs they are instrumentally evil, not that they are intrinsically evil. Not everyone thinks that the pursuit of moral ideals is of more value than the pursuit of other ideals. Aristotle thought that the life of contemplation had greater worth and for him the pursuit of moral virtue was a second best, as most people were not capable of proper contemplation.

Oscar Wilde said, "We are all in the gutter. But some of us are looking at the stars"(Wilde 1995: Act 3). Ideals of living can provide us with a vision, not only to look at but to be inspired by. If our lives are to be significant it is necessary that we commit ourselves to ideals and follow them with zest (James 1908/1899). This view is very plausible; those who simply drift from day to day hardly lead meaningful lives. But which ideals one is attracted to may vary with one's temperament, talents and social environment, and one's beliefs about human nature and the afterlife. Ideals of living that some find awesome, others may find repulsive. Moral ideals can be evaluated by appealing to moral, factual and metaphysical considerations. The ideal of perfection to be reached through renunciation and self-sacrifice, as preached by Christ, Gandhi and others has been criticized by those who think that there is no afterlife. Humanists insist that we should only appeal to this world and this life in constructing our ideals. Even if we confine ourselves to this world, there would be much disagreement about which ideals are worth pursuing in morals as well as in other areas; the perfection that Nietzsche favored was to be attained by the self-assertion (rather than self-denial), in this world, of those who had superior talents, and he was dismissive of what he called the ascetic ideal (Nietzsche 1969: Essay 3). There is also much disagreement regarding the weight to be attached to moral ideals compared with non-moral ideals.

Liberal perfectionists in the West tend to be Aristotelians who stress a high level of excellence in knowledge and conduct, but there are other perfectionists worth mentioning. Gandhi thought his ideal of the good life could be followed by the simple peasant; indeed, he thought that villages were less corrupting of the human spirit than much of modernity. Admittedly, existing villages have their own vices (such as untouchability in India), many of which may be less prevalent in the big cities. But the villages that Gandhi admired were to be modeled on ideals of Truth and Love and Non-violence. Excellence in non-moral areas such as science, art, sports may be much more difficult to achieve if one leads a simple peasant life, but Gandhi would say that such excellences are much less important than purity of heart and moral excellence.

Ideals of excellence can be attainable or unattainable. Some people think that we should be realistic and pursue ideals that are attainable. Unattainable ideals are unnecessarily demanding and can lead to the ideals getting discredited. Others such as Tolstoy and Gandhi (Gandhi 1986–: Vol. 2, 284–5) believe in the pursuit of perfection even though it can never be attained in this world. Complete perfection has an awesome quality and can stir us to action in a way in which moderate perfection cannot. Though we can never hope to attain it totally, the ideal provides us with a vision that can inspire us; our job is to make progress on the road to perfection. A person on a lower level but moving towards perfection "lives a more moral and better life than one who, though on a much higher level of morality is not advancing towards perfection." Therefore "the movement towards perfection ... of the woman who was a sinner or of the thief on the cross is a higher degree of life than the stagnant righteousness of the Pharisee" (Tolstoy 1935: Ch. 3).

On some inegalitarian versions of perfectionism lives that are higher on the scale of perfection should be regarded as having greater worth: "the lower well being – it may be ultimately the very existence – of countless Chinamen or Negroes must be sacrificed that a higher life may be possible for a much smaller number of white men" (Rashdall 1924: Vol. 1, 238–9). There are non-racist variants of such inegalitarian perfectionism. According to Nietzsche ordinary human beings should when necessary be sacrificed for the great achievements of super-individuals like Napoleon and Goethe. The Tolstoy–Gandhi version of the pursuit of perfection is much easier to reconcile with ideals of human equality. For it is possible for us all to strive towards perfection.

Versions of perfectionism that tell us to maximize the sum of intrinsic value are inherently prone to sacrifice the interests of the less talented. Even the interests of the gifted can be sacrificed; a person may excel in morals or in other areas at the expense of his overall well-being. One possibility is to adopt moral pluralism and to commend perfectionism and respect for persons as two ultimate principles. Another possibility would be to construct an egalitarian (or respect-for-persons) theory and to use perfectionist considerations (along with welfare considerations) to work out its implications (Haksar 1979). Thus Frankena suggests that the state should make the same proportionate contribution to the best life of everyone, so that everyone has the same chance to enjoy the best life he is capable of (Frankena 1976). On such views perfectionist considerations, as well as welfare considerations, are brought in for the good of the individual person rather than the individual being used as a mere means for increasing perfection and/or welfare in the world.

Moral rules, moral ideals and the second best

The pursuit of excellence sometimes leads to smugness, arrogance and fanaticism, to expecting too much from oneself and from others and to the looking down on the less talented and the unfortunate, but these are dangers to guard against rather than an essential part of the pursuit of excellence. It is not only ideals of perfection that have been criticized for being too demanding. The utilitarian ideal too has been subject to such criticisms. Those who advocate such difficult ideals point out that ideals are not to be confused with moral rules. It is important to distinguish the basic moral rules and principles which we can all be expected to obey from moral ideals that are desirable but cannot be demanded from us. Without such a distinction morality would indeed become too demanding and as a result people would not comply with its precepts.

Some moralists contend that people are required to follow moral rules (at least the basic ones), whereas they are admired for following moral ideals but not criticized for not following them (Gert 1989). Some others argue that pressure can be applied to a person to go some way beyond the basic duty in the direction of kindliness and forbearance (Urmson 1958: 214). Basic moral rules lay down the minimum requirements for living together: we have an absolute or perfect duty to obey them, for without them society would not survive. Moral ideals are relatively optional. Society is enriched when people follow them, but they are supererogatory in the sense that they go beyond the call of duty. Saintly and heroic actions are ones that typically involve going beyond the call of duty. The Ten Commandments are examples of moral rules that tell us our duties. The Sermon on the Mount provides us with moral ideals. We are not criticized for not turning the other cheek or for not loving our enemies. Therefore, moral ideals, even when unattainable, need not be too demanding.

For some the Christian ideal of universal love and the Gandhian ideal of non-violence are indeed noble ideals but they involve supererogatory acts that go beyond the call of duty. Gandhi did regard non-violence as a supreme duty (rather than supererogatory) but he believed that there is room for saintly and heroic acts in his system; these would be acts that are done by people in situations when most people would run away from performing their duties. At times Gandhi too allowed for noble acts, such as the noblest form of civil disobedience that went beyond the call of duty.

Since ideals, especially ideals of perfection, are so difficult to attain, they need a theory of the second best to complement them. The second best is something that can be demanded of those of us who believe in the ideal. The precepts regarding the second best do not aspire as high as the corresponding ideals. They provide the minimum below which an individual must not fall in his quest for perfection; typically they go beyond and aim higher than the basic moral rules that lay down the minimum demands without which society would not be possible.

Typically, the second best may be perfectly permissible, though not as noble as following the ideal. Thus Gandhi preached the ideal of voluntary poverty. Gandhi claimed to have flourished as a result of voluntary poverty. But he was aware that the renunciation of wealth can be very demanding for the average person, so he advocated as a second best that the wealthy can legitimately keep their wealth but must use it as trustees for society. Again both Gandhi and Tolstoy advocated celibacy as an ideal. They were aware that this could be very demanding and as a second best they insisted that sex should be confined to marriage. And in the case of civil disobedience, Gandhi thought that ideally it should not be rights based but duty based. He did not deny that civil disobedience to assert one's rights, as in the case of the non-cooperation movement to get rid of the British Raj and the boycott of British goods, could be legitimate, but it was a second best which was not as noble (nor as effective in the long run) as the civil disobedience that is motivated by the duty to promote the highest ideal which includes the love of the opponent (Haksar 2008).

In some cases however Gandhi thought that the second best may involve us in excusable wrongdoing. For Gandhi non-violence is an ideal that we have a duty to approach though we can never attain it fully. He also regarded it as a moral principle in the sense that it is wrong to depart from it. He could not deny that sometimes we have to use violence. The ideal is not always attainable or is only attainable at too great a cost, so he advocated a second best according to which violence is better than cowardice when that involves running away from duty. Violence may sometimes be necessary and excusable and even honorable, but it is always wrong and can never be justified (Gandhi 1986–: Vol. 2, 307). The distinction between excuses and justification can enable us to deal with the objection that even the second best may sometimes be too demanding.

Even when the violation of the precept is not justifiable, it can sometimes be excused. For instance, under certain extreme situations, extramarital sex may be excusable, even killing may be.

Ideals and self-sacrifice

Perfectionism is sometimes understood as a high-minded version of utilitarianism. It distinguishes between higher goods such as virtue, knowledge and beauty, and lower ones such as the pleasures of eating and drinking. It is utilitarian in the sense that it tells us that it is right to maximize the good, but it attaches greater intrinsic weight to the higher goods. It is sometimes called ideal utilitarianism. Many critics of utilitarianism complain that it does not treat persons as ends in themselves: a person's interests can be sacrificed when that is required by utility. The ideal version (e.g. as developed by Nietzsche or Rashdall) is if anything even more prone to such sacrifices. This point can be reinforced by the following. There are many sacrifices that are made in the hope of achieving some kind of Utopia or paradise on earth. On the traditional utilitarian view there is the consideration that the sacrifices that are made now are certain, whereas the Utopia for the sake of which they are made is uncertain in the sense that it may never be achieved to the degree required to offset the disutility of sacrifices. We therefore need to be cautious before making sacrifices. However, if sacrifice itself is virtuous and if virtue is intrinsically good then this could sometimes tip the scale in favor of making the sacrifice (Green 2003/1883: Para. 376).

Renunciation or self-sacrifice can have instrumental worth when it leads to good results. The idea that self-sacrifice has intrinsic worth is much more controversial. Classical utilitarians deny that self-sacrifice is intrinsically good; they argue that there is nothing inherently good or virtuous about making a sacrifice; sacrifices can only have instrumental worth (Mill 1957: Ch. 2). Green, a perfectionist, admitted that self-sacrifice is not good when it does not tend to promote the total good of humanity, but he thought that when it does tend to promote the overall good, it reflects virtue which is intrinsically good (Green 2003/1883: Paras 261–78).

Even when self-sacrifice is virtuous and virtue is intrinsically good, this would only show that the world is better off because of the sacrifice, quite apart from any instrumental effects; it would not show that the individuals who sacrificed themselves would be better off. Similar points apply to sacrifices made by an individual in the pursuit of non-moral ideals such as the promotion of knowledge or culture. Utilitarians, including ideal utilitarians, neglect the fact that the promotion of the good may be at the expense of the individual sacrificed. But there are versions of perfectionism which are not variants of utilitarianism.

Some believe that persons are ends in themselves and have an (imperfect) duty to follow moral or non-moral ideals of excellence. Some others believe that persons are ends in themselves and therefore have a right to choose their ways of life, and that in making such choices they should be guided to some extent by the highest ideals of excellence. To follow ideals of excellence in morals or science or art does not have to lead to the sacrifice of other human beings, especially if one agrees that they should be followed within the constraints provided by the view that persons are ends in themselves. It can, as we shall see in the case of the pursuit of virtue, involve the sacrifice of one's own well-being. Some would argue that if people, such as saints and heroes, voluntarily agree to sacrifice their well-being in the interests of a noble cause, this is not evil but praiseworthy.

According to the Gospel those who lose their life gain life; and those who gain it lose it. One way of removing the paradox here is to distinguish the higher life from the lower one. Sometimes self-sacrifice is required for the development of one's worthwhile capacities. Self-improvement may sometimes require abandonment or modification of some materialistic goals. Even within the higher life, development of some capacities may only be possible at the expense of neglecting others. A life devoted to service may be at the expense of developing one's talents in non-moral areas. And excellence in some non-moral fields may only be possible by neglecting one's moral or non-moral development in other areas. Such are the perils of specialization! Even if we grant that self-improvement through self-sacrifice is good for one it is not the only thing that is good for one; it can sometimes be achieved at too great a cost to oneself.

If we grant that virtue is good in itself does it follow that it is good for the individual who behaves virtuously? Similar questions arise for other intrinsic goods such as knowledge or beauty. The pursuit of excellence, whether in morals or in other areas, can involve much self-sacrifice. People like Tolstoy and Gandhi advocated a life of renunciation and self-sacrifice. They were against violence, but is self-sacrifice, especially when it involves sacrifice of life, not a kind of violence against oneself even when it is for a good cause? Gandhi himself claimed that he was much better off as a result of voluntarily embracing poverty and celibacy. He became full of joy and free of the burdens that go with material possessions and with sexual cravings.

Even though sexual abstinence may suit some people, it can cause havoc in the lives of others. It is true that if celibacy is an ideal rather than a rule, it does not have to be achieved totally by all of us; we need only to strive towards it. But it is not at all obvious that we should strive for abstinence for its own sake. Gandhi appealed to the controversial factual claim that the energy released as a result of sexual abstinence can be transformed to achieve higher aims. It is probably true that Gandhi's well-being was increased as a result of his renunciation. But can we generalize from his example?

Aristotle stressed that human nature is such that the exercise of virtue tends to the well-being of the agent. But he was aware that in some cases this tendency could be overcome by the costs of virtuous conduct (Aristotle 1963: 72–3). Even when the agent voluntarily chooses to incur the costs, his well-being may be adversely affected. People sometimes voluntarily make great sacrifices for the sake of a noble cause; these sacrifices could involve loss of well-being as well as loss of self-development. A brave person may in a war lose the use of limbs, as well as be mentally damaged, he may also go through such traumas that even his moral well-being is seriously impaired. Similar points apply in a non-violent struggle. For the opponents of the peaceful volunteers could be so ruthless and cruel that they inflict great injuries and degradations on the volunteers, even upon their spiritual and moral welfare. Some people may be so strong morally that they can resist any attempt to corrupt them. But this is not true of all. This is one reason why Gandhi would impose stringent tests before allowing a person to join him in the non-violent struggle.

Some high-minded philosophers think that happiness is not even part of what is good for a person: "the good for the individual is to be good … and to be good is to contribute disinterestedly … to the perfecting of man" (Green 2003/1883: Para. 280). It would follow from this view that if a person's happiness (or even his life?) are sacrificed for the sake of a noble ideal, this need not be a cause for great concern. When a person's life is sacrificed, his own perfection in the sense of betterment in terms of development of his capabilities (e.g. his scientific or artistic or other worthwhile talents) would then be sacrificed. Should this not be a cause for concern? Sometimes (as in the above quote) Green talks as if nothing matters compared with moral perfection, at other times he admits that non-moral perfection is important, though there is no intrinsic value in it unless it is accompanied by some minimum degree of moral attainment (Green 2003/1883: Para. 381).

Some people, such as some martyrs, suffer a lot in this world voluntarily. Some people bear all their suffering cheerfully because they have faith in God; they follow the road to moral perfection because they see it as their duty to do so. They do not seek any material reward. Gandhi said that the only reward he wanted was to be given more and more opportunities for serving humanity. Green and Gandhi use the ideal of moral perfection to show that the person who sacrifices even his life for the sake of humanity does not really lose out even in this world. They argue that though the person may have renounced his material goods, suffered much and sacrificed even his life, he has progressed morally and so his real interests harmonize with the interests of others who have gained by his renunciation. But it is implausible to regard happiness and suffering as irrelevant to what is really in one's interest; even if a person's virtue is a constituent of his well-being it is not the whole of it. Consider the example of "a man who has enjoyed twenty years of unbroken virtue in a loathsome dungeon, cut off from books or human society, and afflicted by perpetual toothache or a succession of other tortures. Such a man has not attained the true end of his being" (Rashdall 1924: Vol. 2, 39).

A world where the good suffer a lot and the wicked prosper is not just bad on the pragmatic grounds that it will encourage wickedness. It is also bad intrinsically; it is unfair. But why would it be unfair if suffering and happiness were irrelevant to what is good for the virtuous? Even Kant, who was a great champion of the view that we should do our duty for the sake of duty, said that the complete good requires that the virtuous should be happy. Similar considerations apply to the recognition of achievement. Recognition of the right kind is important not just as an encouragement for further achievement but also as an ingredient in the flourishing of the person who has pursued ideals of excellence.

Green claimed that perfectionism is an improvement on hedonism which only offers a succession of pleasures. He thought that those who sacrifice themselves and their lives for the sake of betterment of fellow human beings achieve a kind of permanent good by identifying with humanity. By such identification one's well-being can be increased even when one's life is sacrificed. He promises us that humanity of which we are a part will continue its march towards perfection. There is in a sense a permanent (collective?) self which survives one's death and he talks of the abiding satisfaction of this permanent self with which we identify (Green 2003/1883: Bk 3, ch. 4). His arguments for this view will leave many unconvinced, but it is important to note that here he implicitly acknowledges that perfection of our capabilities, including moral ones, does not by itself ensure well-being; we also need some kind of abiding satisfaction. Whether we get it will, as Aristotle was aware, depend upon human nature and also on good fortune. But also perhaps on social conditions and on whether this is our only life.

Many people postulate a just God who ensures the just rewards in the next life if not in this world. Perhaps the high-minded do not need an abundance of material rewards, but they too could do without too much suffering if their well-being is not undermined. And even when they may have little use for material pleasures, their well-being can be increased if their life is full of joy and bliss.

The Sermon on the Mount does not just praise the life of renunciation. It also says that the people who follow the ideals are blessed.

Gandhi thought that the true end of our being is moksha or spiritual salvation. Moksha is not easy to understand, but it does not involve extinction of our true self, and it does seem to imply some very profound and high-quality experiential reality; it is not just the height of perfection but also a state of blissful consciousness. Most religions offer great rewards for the virtuous in the afterlife. Suppose there is no such afterlife, would the virtuous who have voluntarily suffered a lot in this world not be worse off? They are even worse off than the people who are blissfully unaware that their friends are deceiving them. Ignorance can sometimes make one happy in this world, though it may be at the cost of one's well-being because one's life is not really objectively going as well as one thinks. But in the case of those who voluntarily suffer in this world in the belief that there are rewards in the next life, there is the added problem that often the comfort they get from this belief is nothing compared with the suffering that they undergo in this world; that is one reason why they are regarded as saints. The person who never discovers that his spouse deceives him may not suffer as a result of this ignorance; but the person who undergoes tortures and martyrdom in the belief that there is a God looking after the virtuous, may have suffered a lot in the service of a God that never delivers the compensating goods.

Gandhi's ideal involves promoting the well-being of others but critics argue that this is achieved by the practitioners sacrificing their own well-being. Gandhi denies this, partly by appealing to their well-being after this life but partly by appealing to the view that they are ennobled even in this life and by appealing to the fact that the sacrifice was voluntary. Their moral grandeur and the beauty of their sacrifice enrich this world. But does it enrich the volunteers themselves, enough to offset all their suffering? If not, we have to be careful that their well-being is not sacrificed for the sake of the greater good. The fact that they are volunteers does not mean that their sacrifice should not be a serious cause for concern; though other things being equal it is true that there should be even greater cause for concern if they were conscripts.

In a free country we do not believe we should prevent sane adults from voluntarily sacrificing their well-being for the sake of noble ideals. But we have to be careful before we encourage them to do so, especially if they are doing so in the belief that they will get their rewards in the next life which may not exist. If we agree that they get their rewards eventually we can be less cautious. This is one of the many ways in which one's beliefs (including metaphysical beliefs such as the existence of the afterlife) influence the evaluation of an ideal.

Much of the debate regarding ideals of living revolves around beliefs about human nature. Gandhi appealed to what he regarded as psychological truths on which his ideals were based; for instance in the power of genuine suffering and self-sacrifice to reform the opponent; and he would maintain that these work even on opponents who do not have any use for the afterlife. Gandhian ideals have been adapted by people like Martin Luther King to empower the oppressed. Critics point out that the self-sacrifice of the oppressed only promotes the noble cause when the opponents have the right kind of conscience that responds to such displays of suffering. There are other brutal opponents who are left unmoved or even react with disgust at the sight of defenseless people courting the infliction of physical injuries upon themselves.

Gandhi admits that often his ideal does not give good results in the short run, but he claims that in the long run non-violence triumphs. Violence breeds more violence in a vicious circle while non-violence and love breed more non-violence and love in the long run. Christ may have been crucified and appear to be on the losing side in the short run but in the long run he has won. His critics would reply that in such a long run we are dead, and if there is no immortality then even when there is success it is achieved at the expense of the well-being of those who made sacrifices while following non-violent ideals.

Such debates suggest that perhaps there is no standpoint from which we can evaluate ideals of living that will be regarded as impartial by all, not even by all reasonable people.

See also Ethical thought in India (Chapter 2); Sidgwick, Green, and Bradley (Chapter 17); Nietzsche (Chapter 18).

References

Aristotle (1963) *The Nicomachean Ethics of Aristotle*, trans. David Ross, London: Oxford University Press.

Frankena, W. (1976) "Some Beliefs about Justice," in *Perspectives on Morality*, ed. K. Goodpaster, London: University of Notre Dame Press.

Gandhi, M. K. (1986–) *The Moral and Political Writings of Mahatma Gandhi*, vols 1–3, ed. R. Iyer, Oxford: Clarendon Press.

Gert, B. (1989) *Morality: A New Justification of the Moral Rules*, New York: Oxford University Press.

Green, T. H. (2003/1883) *Prolegomena to Ethics*, Oxford: Clarendon Press.

Haksar, V. (1979) *Equality, Liberty and Perfectionism*, Oxford: Clarendon Press.

——(2008) "Satyagraha and the Right to Civil Disobedience," in D. Allen (ed.) *The Philosophy of Mahatma Gandhi for the Twenty First Century*, Lanham, MD: Rowman & Littlefield.

James, William (1908/1899) *Talks to Teachers on Psychology and to Students on Some of Life's Ideals*, New York: Henry Holt.

Mill, J. S. (1957) *Utilitarianism, On Liberty, Representative Government*, Letchworth: Aldine Press.

Nietzsche, F. (1969) *On the Genealogy of Morals*, trans. W. Kaufmann, New York: Vintage Books.

Rashdall, H. (1924) *The Theory of Good and Evil*, vols 1 and 2, London: Oxford University Press.

Tolstoy, L. (1935) *The Kingdom Of God Is within You*, trans. Aylmer Maude, New York: Oxford University Press.

Urmson, J. (1958) "Saints and Heroes," in A. Melden (ed.) *Essays in Moral Philosophy*, Seattle: University of Washington Press.
Wilde, O. (1995) *Lady Windermere's Fan*, London: Penguin Popular Classics.

Further reading

Hurka, T. (1993) *Perfectionism*, Oxford: Oxford University Press. (An Aristotelian approach, identifying the human good with the development of human nature.)

(ii)
JUSTICE

56
RIGHTS
Tom Campbell

Rights have become the dominant concept in the moral and political discourse of contemporary democracies, displacing to some extent, at least where moral issues are concerned, talk of the common good, general well-being, and social justice. We live in an age in which right and wrong are approached through reflection, debate and dispute about whose and what rights are at stake. This development is part of the post-Second World War emergence of *human* rights as the principal vehicle for articulating the ethical dimensions of law and politics, both domestic and international. More recently it has become commonplace to associate rights with responsibilities, although it is often not clear whether this is meant to curtail the scope of rights by making people's rights conditional on the fulfillment of their duties, or to strengthen the impact of rights by emphasizing the duties of various parties to uphold the rights of others.

Despite their popularity, the meaning and the foundations of rights in general, and human rights in particular, are unclear and controversial, with little evident philosophical agreement or underlying common usage to be found either within or beyond cultural boundaries. This chapter explores some philosophical attempts to bring clarity to, and enhance understanding of, both what it means to have a right and the proper content of rights. It starts by asking what is distinctive about the idea of rights, goes on to relate rights to the social functions of rules and then outlines a typology of different sorts of rights. Arguing that so-called "moral rights" are best thought of as the rights that ought to, but often do not, exist, the chapter considers how specific rights may be justified and concludes by dealing with these issues in relation to human rights.

The right to do wrong

One way of bringing out what is distinctive about the idea of rights is to distinguish rights from right or rightness. This may be done by noting that it makes perfect sense to say that sometimes a person has a right to do that which is wrong, or to say that there are occasions in which it is wrong for a person to do that which they have a right to do (Waldron 1981; Edmundson 2004: 133–42). Moreover, we usually accept that it is morally right that people ought to be allowed to exercise their rights even when this entitles them to do what we think is wrong. The juxtaposition of rights and right may seem rather strange, especially as in general we assume that it is right to let a person do what they have a right to do and wrong to violate the rights of others. However, examining the difference between rights and rightness helps to clarify the distinctive role of rights in normative discourse.

We might explain the difference between rights and right by drawing on the distinction between law and morality. Perhaps it is acting on your legal rights that may sometimes be morally (not legally) wrong. However, the difference between rights and rightness can be found within both law and morality. Thus, in the moral realm, we may possess moral rights that we sometimes (morally) ought to waive. And in the legal realm there is more to determining what is the legally right thing to do than simply deciding which legal rights are relevant to the matter at hand. Indeed the emergence of the very idea of rights, even in legal contexts, is a relatively recent phenomenon (Griffin 2008).

A better approach to explaining "the right to do wrong" is to consider the function of rules within a society or social group. For instance, law is a system of rules which authoritatively determines how people must or may act towards each other in the specified circumstances. Legal rules have a variety of social functions, including preventing harmful and promoting beneficial conduct and enabling cooperation between individuals and groups by the general adoption of agreed rules, an arrangement which enables us to predict or control the conduct of other people. Thus, stopping at a red light not only prevents car drivers from harming each other, it also enables them to proceed on their way in a coordinated manner, to their mutual benefit. Having such rules saves us from the damaging chaos that would follow if we all individually decided as we go what is the right or wrong thing to do on a public road. Having rules of the road means that we know what is right to do on the road without making our own mind up about what is right or wrong to do in a particular situation. Within philosophy, such rules are said to be "exclusionary" in that their function is to exclude, within their sphere, the application of other reasons for action in such circumstances (Raz 1975: 35–48, 1986: 186–7; Schauer 1999: 74–82).

It is illuminating to think of both rights and duties as part and parcel of the operation of social rules. In general, duties are what the rules say *must* be done and (at least some) rights are what rules say *may* be done. However, rights are not involved in all social rules. We need, therefore, to identify which sorts of rules involve rights.

What's so special about rights?

There is long and complex debate about what is distinctive about rights and how they relate to other normative concepts, such as duties. Even if we go along with the thesis that both rights and their correlative duties involve having social rules we still have to identify more clearly when it is that a rule establishes rights (on this see Kramer et al. 1998). On one account, rights are special in that they relate to those who benefit from the rule, whereas rules that disadvantage persons impose responsibilities or duties on the persons who are disadvantaged. In fact, the coincidence of the benefit and the exercising of rights is not universal: I may, for instance, have the right to inherit a business that is in debt. The same applies to the link between disadvantages and duties. I have a duty to stop at a red light even when I want to stop (for instance, to put on my sun-glasses) and am not therefore disadvantaged by so doing. Nevertheless, it may be broadly true that rights are generally ascribed to persons whom a rule benefits and responsibilities to those it disadvantages. This is the thesis put forward in the "interest" or "benefit" analysis of rights. The interest theory gains further credence from the common criticism of rights that they encourage self-interest and even selfishness, an argument which takes it for granted that there is at the very least a close association of rights and interests.

That said, the interest theory does not hold that simply having an interest automatically generates a right, only that the function of rights is to protect, and further, selected interests. Nor does the theory hold that, if one person's interests happen to be advanced by another person fulfilling an obligation, this means that the first person has a right. The obligation in question may derive from a rule adopted to protect quite a different interest.

Burdens don't go with duties in quite the way that benefits go with rights. The benefits in having rights are very varied, whereas the disadvantage of duties is tied to the disadvantage of a particular sort: namely, having to perform an onerous action. More generally, just because a rule disadvantages someone doesn't mean it imposes a duty on them, although imposing a duty is generally disadvantageous to the person concerned. Critics of the "benefit" or "interest" approach to identifying the rules that create rights make a similar point about the connection between rights and benefits, their point being that, merely because a rule happens to benefit someone, this does not mean that it gives them a right to that benefit. For instance, in the case of "third party beneficiaries," such as a person who receives a benefit as a result of a promise made by the donor to someone else (as when a sister receives a gift from her brother as a result of a promise he made to their father), we attribute the right to the promisee (the father) not to the beneficiary (the daughter). Nor are such critics satisfied by the more restricted variation of the approach, according to which rights exist only where the rules are *intended* to confer a benefit.

The principal alternative to the "rule-protected interest" analysis of rights is the "will" or "choice" theory of rights, according to which what is so special about rights is that they confer power on the right-holders to control the actions of others, should the right-holder choose to exercise this power. This theory sees rights as a social mechanism whereby one person can require or permit other people to behave in certain ways. This happens most clearly when we demand, claim, or waive our rights.

One problem for the will theory is that it does not cover all standard examples of rights. For instance, it does not apply to those who, by reason of age or non-competence, cannot make demands or waive claims, yet young children, for instance, do have rights. Perhaps, however, these persons would make such demands and grant such waivers if they could. Or, maybe other people can do these things on their behalf. Yet it is difficult for the will theory to explain routine examples where the performance of the correlative duty is not required only "on demand" and ought to be carried out whether or not it is claimed or enforced. Moreover, the interest theorists can point out that the fact that many rights can be demanded and waived fits neatly with their theory that the purpose of rights is to benefit the right-holder. It is precisely because it is the rights-holders' interests that are at stake that they claim their rights and are sometimes given the power to enforce their correlative duties, and it is precisely because rights are in the interests of rights-holders that they are often given the power of waiver. Furthermore, waivers, like demands, do not apply in every case. Thus the right to life correlates with the duty of others not to kill the right-holder but does not entail the right to allow oneself to be killed.

A typology of rights

Arriving at a general theory as to what constitutes a right is made more difficult by the variety of normative relationships that are involved in the discourse of rights. While the interest theory of rights applies in general to most of these relationships, more detailed analysis requires us to take account of the different sorts of rights that have been recognized in actual systems of social rules. The diversity of rights is well captured in a typology of rights developed in a legal context by Wesley Hohfeld (1919) but is presented here in slightly different terminology.

First, "pure liberty rights" exist when people have no duties not to do the action in question and so are "at liberty" to do it even although other people do not have the duty to allow them so to act. Pure liberty rights feature in competitive situations where the right-holder may attain something but no one has a duty to permit him to do so. A pure liberty right indicates simply the absence of a duty not to do what the right-holder has a right to do. For example, according to the seventeenth-century political philosopher Thomas Hobbes, such a condition of obligation-free liberty existed in a pre-social "state of nature," when individuals had "natural rights" to do whatever they liked. In actual societies, pure liberty rights continue to have considerable importance in cultures where it is assumed that in the absence of a duty not to act in a certain way a person is entitled so to act. Also, in situations where an existing rule is relaxed with respect to some people then those people may be said to have a "privilege," the term Hohfeld applies to pure liberty rights.

In contrast to pure liberty rights, "substantive liberty rights" are one form of what Hohfeld calls "claim rights," that is, rights which correlate either with the duty of others to refrain from preventing someone from acting (negative claim rights), or with the duty to assist someone in doing or achieving what they have the right to do (positive claim rights). Claim rights are the paradigm type of rights. In most cases the analysis of a right involves identifying who is the person that has the right, whether the correlative duty is negative or positive, and who has that duty. This is the prime way in which rights relate to duties. It is not that my right depends on the fulfillment of my duties (although in some cases it may do so) but that my right correlates with someone else's duty.

The term "claim rights" suggests that these rights function as the basis for making and pursuing claims against other people, the correlative duty-holders, in line with the will theory. Here it is helpful to distinguish what may be called "option rights" which exist when the requirement to perform the correlative duty depends on the right-holder actually making a claim against the duty-holder. Another, rather different, conception of an option right is one that the right-holder is permitted to waive, thereby releasing the person from their existing correlative duty. However, in most claim rights the existing correlative duties do not depend on the trigger of a claim being made, and in some claim rights the correlative duties may not be waived by the right-holder.

The typology of rights does not end here, for many rights are neither pure liberties nor claim rights. For instance, some rights are facilitative powers that can be exercised by the right-holder in order to affect the rights and duties on others, as when a person enters into a contract, thereby binding not only himself but the other party as well. These "power rights" do not correlate with duties but with what Hohfeld calls "liabilities." The fact that someone has a power right means that someone (perhaps the right-holder himself) is liable to have their rights and responsibilities changed by the act of that power right-holder. The term is inept to the extent that the change might be for the benefit of the person who is "liable" but it does capture an essential difference between claim rights and power rights, namely that the latter are rights which enable their holders to create or annul other rights and duties.

Usefully, Hohfeld also notes the existence of "immunity rights" whereby individuals are protected from being liable to having their other rights and duties changed by the exercise of the power rights of others, as, for instance, when a foreign diplomat cannot be convicted of a criminal offense. Such immunities can provide important protections for holders of claim rights when there exists an immunity right that prevents the annulment of their claim right.

It should be noted that there are other duties that arise within the normal context of most rights, whether they are claim rights or powers, namely the responsibility to see to it that any correlative duties or other legal consequences are in fact adhered to. Such indirect duties of enforcement often adhere to governments, and need to be carefully distinguished from the direct correlative duties and liabilities themselves. Typically people have such implementation rights against governments or other authorities, such as employers.

In actual social situations rights and duties come in complex bundles involving the different types of rights, all of which can have a bearing on complex circumstances.

Moral rights

It may be thought that the typology of rights offered above applies only to legal rights and not to the standard rights that arise in moral and political discourse. Outside the legal context, perhaps there are less well-defined types of rights. Thus some people may speak of there being a "moral right" whenever it is believed that a person's interests ought to be protected or furthered by other people. This assumes that, if I ought to be kind to my mother because it will be hurtful to her if I am not, then I may be said to have a duty to be kind to her and she to have a (moral) right that I be kind to her. Yet, unless there is a hidden appeal to an established social custom or convention, it seems unnecessary to think of there being a right in play here, although perhaps there ought to be.

There is no doubt that we sometimes do use the language of rights in this rather loose way, even though it is something that can be expressed without speaking in terms of rights, simply by saying that it is right to act in such a way. It is certainly the case that the moral significance of the interests of others may be a ground for establishing and sustaining a rule and hence a right that this is how they ought to be treated. But this does not identify the distinctive uses of rights discourse and may be discouraged in the interests of clarifying normative discourse.

Nevertheless, insisting that rights be conceptually tied to rules does not require that the rule in question is a legal rule. It may be that a non-legal social or "societal" rule – that is, a rule which is widely recognized and enforced through the general opinion of members of that society or groups in which the right exists – constitutes a "societal (or social) right." Very often this is the phenomenon to which the term "moral rights" refers, and it is important to note that our typology of rights does apply to such societal rights. Indeed, many legal rights and duties are developed from such bases, although legalization usually involves more precise formulations and the imposition of other modes of sanction for non-compliance.

In the jargon of philosophy, "positivists" put forward a conceptual scheme in which all actual rights are either legal or societal rights. Positivists contend that

> so called "moral rights" are either to be construed as referring to societal rights or as the "positive" or actual rights that morally ought to exist.
>
> (Nagel 2002: 33)

The term "positivist" derives from the fact that rights are based on rules that are in some way "posited" or created, so that their existence is a matter of social fact and open to observation. On the positivist view, the existence of a right is dependent on the prior existence of a legal or societal rule. In theory, this approach can be extended to cover those rights which are established by rules that are posited by divine commands or in sacred texts.

The positivist analysis of rights runs up against the counter-view that we have moral knowledge of certain matters on which we can base our judgments of rights and their correlative duties without drawing on such so-called "positivist" rights as do or might exist. Thus some "natural law" theorists argue that the normative force of positive rights derives from the moral force of the "natural rights" that are part of "natural law." In its religious forms this natural law is part of the divine order to be found in God's creation. In its more secular forms natural law is thought to be known through the exercise of human reason reflecting on our experience of human nature and society. We know, for instance, that we ought not to tell lies and therefore that people have a right to be told the truth. We know that we ought never to kill other people, except in self-defense, which means that everyone has the right to life.

Some forms of secular natural law theory fit well with the positivist analysis of societal rights as rights deriving from commonly held beliefs that are enforced through public opinion as well as through positive law. In this case natural laws are the social norms the content of which is known to every rational person. However, natural law theory meets with difficulties if it claims that there is moral knowledge accessible to some members of a society but not to others so that it makes sense to say that certain moral rights exist even though most people do not agree about their content. Such disagreements, normally the subject of much moral and political debate, cast doubt on the existence of natural law and natural rights, and, positivists argue, create the need for actual, that is, positive, rights to provide an agreed framework for stable social relationships between people who hold very divergent moral views as to moral right and wrong (Waldron 1999).

Justifying rights

Whatever analysis of rights we adopt it is necessary to ask what justification can be offered for recognizing or adopting specific rights. Some natural law approaches to justifying rights assert the existence of certain basic rights of which we have moral knowledge independent of actual social norms. This is an example of what is called a "rights-based" morality, according to which questions of moral right and wrong come down to identifying certain basic rights and then asking whether the situation being morally assessed has come about in a way which violates any of these rights. If there has been such violation then the situation is morally bad, indeed unacceptable. If there has been no such violation then the situation in question is morally acceptable and, indeed, cannot be coercively changed without a rights violation, which is itself morally unacceptable (Nozick 1974).

Rights-based theories contend that it is a moral fact that people have basic rights and that it is morally wrong to violate these rights even when it would be in the general interest to do so. Drawing on the "exclusionary" function of rights noted by positivists, rights are said to operate as vetoes which prohibit what we may do to other people. In the terminology of Ronald Dworkin, rights are "trumps" in that they override all other considerations, including moral ones, such as the utilitarian objective of acting so as to maximize the well-being of the greatest number of people (Dworkin 1977: 90–4).

In the natural law tradition, basic rights standardly derive from the existence of certain properties of human beings in virtue of which they possess these rights. Characteristically, these properties are said to relate to the fact that human beings are moral agents with the capacity to choose how to conduct themselves (Griffin 2008). This makes people intrinsically valuable, or, in Kantian terms, "ends in themselves," from which it follows that they ought to be treated with "concern and respect" (Dworkin 1977) so that certain things cannot rightly be done to them.

Rights-based theories use this conception of basic rights in order to justify and limit the actions of governments and individuals, including the systems of rules that establish the less basic rights that are established by positive law and social convention. These underlying rights constitute the independently known "moral rights" which are a prime ingredient in justifying rights in general and provide the framework within which people are entitled or at liberty to pursue other morally acceptable goals, such as doing whatever it is that they want to do according to their own views as to what is good or worthwhile in life.

Rights-based theories are classified as "deontological" because they hold that morality is a matter of obeying certain imperatives, no matter what the consequences. "Consequentialists," on the other hand, make moral assessments purely in terms of the outcomes of certain types of conduct. These goal- or output-based approaches to the justification of rights accept that there are certain things of intrinsic value, such as life, happiness and moral goodness, and argue that we should have a system of positive rights and responsibilities that protects and promotes such values. One simplistic type of output-based or consequentialist theory is that we should adopt those rights and responsibilities which promote the greatest happiness of the greatest number. Others draw upon a variety of desirable outputs, such as creativity, fairness, beauty and the natural environment.

In many cases both rights-based and output-based theories arrive at the same recommendations, such as the right to life and the right to a fair trial. Both approaches also draw on the idea that rights are to some extent "exclusionary" in practice, however they may be established or justified, in that they take precedence over other considerations, moral or otherwise. However, a rights-based approach focuses on a much smaller range of rights, basic rights, and tends to give them a near absolute exclusionary force when it comes to the justification of rights in general.

One way of trying to harmonize these two approaches is to distinguish between "intrinsic rights" – that is, those rights, such as the right to health care, which protect the interests of the right-holder – and "extrinsic rights" that have a wider social purpose, like the right to freedom of speech which is of benefit to society in general and not just to the individual right-holder. Rights-based theories can then be said to be concerned with intrinsic rights, and output-based theories with extrinsic rights.

However, there are in fact very few basic rights which are justified on purely intrinsic grounds. The right not to be tortured may be one such, but even that may be justified in part on extrinsic grounds, in that torture does not produce reliable information, as well as on intrinsic grounds, in that it is degrading to the person tortured.

Even if we accept rights-based justifying theories, there may be disagreement concerning what it is about human beings that is of intrinsic value. Using the torture example again, the intrinsic right not to be tortured might be that it is demeaning to and destructive of that intrinsically valuable property, moral agency. But the prohibition of torture may also be based on the intrinsic disvalue of extreme physical pain and psychological distress.

Moreover, just because a right is justified by reference to an intrinsically valued property like personhood, this does not automatically give it the force of an absolute right – that is, a right which cannot be taken away or diminished by any other intrinsically valuable property, such as sentience – either of the right-bearer or of other persons. Intrinsic value is not necessarily, indeed it rarely is, absolute value.

Human rights

Rights-based theories of morality fare best in relation to what used to be called natural rights but are now referred to as human rights. These rights are attributed to all human beings in virtue of their humanity. They are also rights which have priority over other considerations, and are therefore described as absolute and inalienable. In this context what is intrinsically valuable about all human beings and is also of overriding importance to them, such as life, liberty and happiness are identified as human rights (Donnelly 1989).

Normally, but not always, human rights are classified as the negative claim rights of all persons, correlating with the duties of all others, particularly governments, not to damage that to which the person has the right, be it their life, their liberty or their happiness. Further the exclusionary force of such rights is paramount and can be overridden, if at all, only by the same or another human right of others and, in most cases, are not forfeited or diminished by their failure to respect the rights of others.

In the early Enlightenment these rights were held to be "natural" in part because they were held to exist in the "state of nature" before there were governments, positive laws or even societies, and in part because they were believed to be derived from facts about human nature. Sometimes they were held to be sacred or divine in that they were taken to be conferred by God as the creator of human beings. Others held that they were known to "reason," either as a matter of direct moral insight or because they could be shown to be necessary for the survival and flourishing of human societies (Finnis 1980).

Historically the idea of natural or human rights was used to justify obedience to governments that protect and respect the rights of their subjects, or to justify disobedience to those governments which did violate these rights. They also served as a legitimation for establishing new forms of government, in particular democratic ones, which were seen as an expression of the equal worth of all members of a society.

More recently human rights have come to be associated with the idea of constitutional rights, which are applied by courts to override legislation which the judges consider to be violations of these constitutional rights. They are also used to justify forceful intervention in the internal affairs of those states which violate the human rights of their citizens, and also to justify demands for international humanitarian aid, limitations on the activities of multinational corporations, and as the basis for an international criminal law which prohibits and punishes gross violations of human rights, such as genocide.

Another feature of human rights is that they are usually stated in very broad and abstract terms with little specification of the locus and content of the correlative duties, so much so that they are better viewed as assertions of fundamental values which may be used to justify positive rights but are not themselves rights at all. This analysis makes sense in view of the extensive disagreement about the content and practical implications of human rights, about who has the correlative responsibilities and about how "absolute" they are. In practice such disagreements are settled by determining which institution in a polity has the authority (or power right) to determine the specific content of the constitutional rights as they are to be applied within that polity, some giving this role to courts and others to elected governments and legislatures.

See also Ethics and reason (Chapter 9); Freedom and responsibility (Chapter 23); Ethics and law (Chapter 35); Ethical intuitionism (Chapter 39); Responsibility: Act and omission (Chapter 51); The ethics of free speech (Chapter 64).

References

Donnelly, J. (1989) *Universal Human Rights in Theory and Practice*, Ithaca, NY: Cornell University Press.

Dworkin, R. M. (1977) *Taking Rights Seriously*, London: Duckworth.
Edmundson, W. A. (2004), *Introduction to Rights*, Cambridge: Cambridge University Press.
Finnis, J. (1980) *Natural Law and Natural Rights*, Oxford: Oxford University Press.
Griffin, J. (2008) *On Human Rights*, Oxford: Oxford University Press.
Hohfeld, W. (1919) *Fundamental Legal Conceptions as Applied in Legal Reasoning*, New Haven, CT: Yale University Press.
Kramer, M., Simmonds, N. and Steiner, H. (1998) *Rights, Wrongs and Responsibilities*, Oxford: Oxford University Press.
Nagel, T. (2002) *Concealment and Exposure*, Oxford: Oxford University Press.
Nozick, R. (1974) *Anarchy, State and Utopia*, Oxford: Blackwell.
Raz, J. (1975) *Practical Reason and Norms*, London: Hutchinson.
——(1986) *The Morality of Freedom*, Oxford: Oxford University Press.
Schauer, F. (1991) *Playing by the Rules: A Philosophical Analysis of Rule-Based Decision-Making*, Oxford: Clarendon Press.
Waldron, J. (1981) "A Right to Do Wrong," *Ethics* 92 : 21–39.
——(1999) *Law and Disagreement*, Oxford: Oxford University Press.

Further reading

Campbell, T. (2006) *Rights: A Critical Introduction*, London: Routledge.
Dworkin, R. (1997) *Taking Rights Seriously*, London: Duckworth.
Finnis, J. (1980) *Natural Law and Natural Rights*, Oxford: Oxford University Press.
Waldron, J. (ed.) (1984) *Theories of Rights*, Oxford: Oxford University Press.

57
JUSTICE AND PUNISHMENT

John Tasioulas

Punishment in the perspective of justice

Friedrich Nietzsche famously declared that concepts with a history, like that of punishment, are indefinable. For this reason and others, the quest for necessary and sufficient conditions governing the use of the word "punishment" may be a futile one. Still, the legitimate need to demarcate our subject matter can be met by isolating the features exemplified by focal or paradigmatic cases of punishment. On one moderately uncontroversial account, punishment is a practice that involves (a) the deliberate infliction of hard treatment, (b) on an alleged wrongdoer, (c) because of the alleged wrongness of their conduct, (d) by someone who claims the authority to inflict it for that reason, where (e) the hard treatment is intended to communicate to the wrongdoer justified censure of their wrongdoing. Activities that may closely resemble some forms of punishment – quarantining people with lethal contagious diseases, taking vulnerable children into care, fining those who commit parking violations – all fail to qualify as punishment because they do not instantiate one or more of these elements.

But why confer salience on the rubric of "justice" in relation to punishment? Of course, the habit of linking justice and punishment is not a philosophical idiosyncrasy, as common expressions like "just deserts" and "criminal justice system" amply attest. But it still requires an explanation. One possibility is that "justice" is being used to refer not to a subset of moral considerations, but to morality itself. And surely it is obvious that the practice of punishment cries out for moral justification. In virtue of feature (a), it involves doing things to people – depriving them of life, liberty and property without their consent, and so on – that we normally take to be morally reprehensible. Moreover, in virtue of feature (e), the infliction of hardship is intended as censure for wrongdoing, which presumably also requires a specifically moral justification. A related explanation is that justice is that component of morality which, as H. L. A. Hart put it, is "concerned with the adjustment of claims between a multiplicity of persons" (Hart 2008/1968: 21). The persons in question will be, in the first instance, the wrongdoer and their victim (where the latter is a person), but also any community that has a requisite stake in the wrongdoer's conformity with the relevant standards. Both construals of justice are acceptable, so far as they go, but they are rather unspecific, failing to isolate a subset of considerations in terms of which the moral justifiability of punishment is primarily to be determined.

Consider, then, two alternative ways of making the nexus with justice yield more. One line of thought is that justice – conceived as a "set of principles for assigning rights and duties and for determining ... a proper distribution of the benefits and burdens of social cooperation" (Rawls 1971: 5) – is the "first virtue of social institutions," and that its salience in justifying punishment arises from the fact that only the state satisfies condition (d). This characterization of justice is more determinate, but the link it forges with punishment through its statist assumption about condition (d) is question-begging. There appear to be many contexts in which punishment occurs that cannot readily be described as social institutions, and certainly not as state-based institutions: in relations among spouses, family members, friends, co-workers, and so on.

Still, one might drop the controversial statist restriction on (d) while retaining the focus on *rights* in specifying justice. After all, the domain of justice is often identified with that of rights, where rights are broadly understood as grounding duties that are owed by the duty-bearers to identifiable individuals (the right-holders), as opposed to imperfect duties (e.g. of charity) that are not. One way of developing the connection between rights and punishment is by holding it to be at least a necessary condition for the justifiability of punishment that the wrongdoer is punished for violating another's rights. But this has the peculiar upshot that wrongs which arguably are not rights violations, such as cruelty to animals, the wanton destruction of the natural environment or beautiful artifacts, fall beyond the scope of justified punishment.

Rather more promising is the intriguing but initially strikingly counter-intuitive idea, endorsed by G. W. F. Hegel (1967/1821) and Simone Weil (1996) among others, that punishment is morally justified because *wrongdoers* themselves have a right to be punished. The observation that rights are typically beneficial to the right-holder is not immediately fatal to this view. To begin with, some philosophers contend that rights are grounded not in the interests of right-holders but in their status as members of the moral community. But even on an interest-based conception of rights, it is hardly obvious that a wrongdoer's interests are not served (even if not served overall) through undergoing punishment. For example, punishment involves recognizing the wrongdoer's status as a responsible moral agent, and it can work as a penance that affords them the opportunity to give vivid expression to their repentance, thus enabling them to be reconciled with the victim and the community to which they belong. Still, given the costs that the punishment of wrongdoers typically exacts from those who inflict it, it is doubtful that the status or interests of the wrongdoer can normally of themselves generate a duty to punish them.

Retributive justice

Now, there is a different way of bringing punishment under the rubric of justice that has been historically influential and increasingly popular in recent years. Retributive theories treat desert as both central and basic in the justification of punishment, where principles of desert along with those of rights are conceived as demarcating the domain of justice. The essential retributive idea is that punishment is to be justified as what (some) wrongdoers deserve in virtue of their wrongdoing. For some, call them negative retributivists, the centrality of desert consists in the fact that it is a necessary condition of justified punishment that must be supplemented by other, independent reasons. In this section, I focus on the stronger, positive thesis that desert is not only necessary but can be sufficient to justify punishment. What the "basic" character of retributive desert amounts to, however, is not always clear. It does not necessarily mean "underived" with respect to any other moral premise, since many prominent retributivists hold that the principle of retributive desert itself must be justified by an underlying moral principle, such as Immanuel Kant's categorical imperative. But they nonetheless insist that compliance with the principle of retributive desert is intrinsically valuable, and not simply valuable in virtue of the consequences of inflicting deserved punishment, and so basic in that sense.

Introductory writings on punishment often illustrate the retributive idea with the following passage from Kant's *Metaphysics of Morals*:

> Even if a civil society were to be dissolved by the consent of all its members (e.g., if a people inhabiting an island decided to separate and disperse throughout the world), the last murderer remaining in prison would first have to be executed, so that each has done to him what his deeds deserve and blood guilt does not cling to the people for not having insisted upon his punishment; for otherwise the people can be regarded as collaborators in this public violation of justice.
>
> (Kant 1991/1797: 142/333)

Although undeniably memorable, this passage is not ideally suited to conveying the gist of retributivism. It drags in the red herring of capital punishment, whereas retributivists are not as such committed to the view that all (or any) murderers deserve to be executed. The passage also appears to assume that retributive desert imposes a (quasi-)absolute requirement, one (almost) never overridden by competing considerations. But the contention that retributive desert has intrinsic value is compatible with the defeasibility of the reasons it generates, e.g. when punishment would be ruinously costly or when mercy justifies more lenient treatment. And, of course, the doctrine of "blood-guilt," according to which one is retrospectively implicated in a murderer's crime by the failure to punish them, is also not entailed by retributivism.

Now, consider Kant's passage shorn of these extraneous commitments. Is some demand of justice left unfulfilled in virtue of the very fact – as opposed to the causal consequences – of permitting a murderer to escape punishment, even if all things considered there are compelling reasons for doing so? Those inclined towards retributivism will answer "Yes"; others, notably those who believe that any justification for punishment must lie in the value of its consequences, will answer "No." Are we then left with a hopeless philosophical stand-off involving rival intuitions in response to the same hypothetical case? And if we are, must not the onus of proof work against the retributivist, since only they countenance a reason to inflict censure and hard treatment in the contested cases? One response is that retributivism does not rest on anything so frail as a stand-alone and contested intuition, but has deep roots in our ordinary moral outlook.

One development of this line of thought appeals to supposedly ordinary and appropriate emotional responses to (certain kinds of) wrongdoing. These responses of resentment or blame on the part of the victim or an onlooker, or guilt and remorse on the part of the wrongdoer, typically involve the thought that the latter deserves to be punished for the wrong that they have committed and a desire that they should be so punished (Murphy and Hampton 1988: Chs 1 and 3; Moore 1997: Ch. 4). Only in this way is the distinctive gravity of the relevant kind of wrongdoing registered, e.g. the fact that it is a transgression of another's rights or a violation of a communal obligation.

A radically skeptical response to this argument admits that our moral outlook embodies these retributive emotions, but then calls that whole outlook into question. One kind of skepticism targets the presupposition of free will – that the agent who deserves to be punished could have acted otherwise than they did – that retributivism seemingly involves. Another, Nietzschean variety offers a debunking genealogy of the retributive emotions, portraying them as remnants of a cankered "slave morality" that is deeply inimical to human flourishing. One plausible retort to both is a common sense-respecting, Strawsonian line, according to which the ordinary moral outlook is something we cannot feasibly abandon while living a recognizably human life (Strawson 1962). And even if we could give it up, it would be undesirable to do so, as is shown by the fact that the evaluative outlook that anti-moralists put in its place is invariably deeply unattractive – whether because it is chillingly inhuman (Meursault in Camus' *The Outsider*) or absurdly (even comically) superhuman (Nietzsche's *Übermensch*).

But, as a justification of punishment, the Strawsonian argument falters. It is one thing to conclude that it is neither feasible nor desirable to extirpate retributive emotions from human life. It is quite another to treat this as sufficient reason for establishing the practice of punishment, especially the institution of legal punishment, with the onerous burdens, such as imprisonment, it imposes on wrongdoers and the great social cost of operating it. Nor would abandoning punishment be tantamount to abolishing the criminal law, since institutions aimed at publicly prohibiting crimes and authoritatively identifying and denouncing those who commit them may be retained without the vital added ingredient of hard treatment. Wherein lies the *intrinsic* value of expressing retributive emotions specifically through punishment, given the hardship this entails for wrongdoers and the cost it imposes on the community? Two retributive theories of punishment that have been prominent in recent years can be interpreted as offering competing answers to this question.

According to the first, the wrongdoer deserves punishment because they have gained an unfair advantage of which only the infliction of hard treatment can deprive them. But isn't it straightforwardly morally corrupt to regard the sadistic murderer, child molester or rapist as gaining an advantage just by having committed those heinous acts? The standard reply is that the criminal has benefited from the self-restraint of law-abiding citizens while exempting his or her self from the burden of obedience, and surely the exercise of free choice is a genuine human good. Punishment is justified insofar as it cancels out the wrongdoer's ill-gotten gain (Morris 1968; Murphy 1973; for criticism, see Duff 1986: Ch. 8). Even if this response fully allays the concern about moral corruption, and even if there is a means of quantifying the magnitude of the advantage gained and convincing ourselves that it will reliably correspond to our sense of the relative gravity of the wrongdoing, a deeper problem looms. For the idea that punishment is justified as a restoration of a just balance of advantages between the wrongdoer and the law-abiding involves a fundamentally misplaced focus. It fails to grasp that the wrongdoer deserves punishment, first and foremost, because of the wrong that they have perpetrated against their victim, not their defection from a just scheme for distributing burdens and benefits among members of a society. A related shortcoming is that the theory cannot even begin to justify punishment in the absence of a legal or conventional scheme for the distribution of advantages or where the relevant sort of wrongdoing is not prohibited within such a scheme.

The second line of response, represented by the communicative theory of punishment, strikes me as more promising. It builds a retributive justification of punishment on element (e) of our initial characterization: hard treatment is justified as a means of communicating deserved censure to the wrongdoer (Feinberg 1970; Duff 1986: Ch. 9, and 2001; Hampton 1984). But it faces an obvious and, for many, devastating objection: given the existence of purely symbolic means of communicating censure, such as a solemn reprimand, why should the deserved censure take the form of hard treatment – imprisonment, fines, community service orders, and so on (Hart 2008/1968: 66)? If no adequate reply is available, the communicative theory gets us no further than the original Strawsonian line of thought it was supposed to rescue. One tempting answer, which I consider later (the third section, "Consequentialist and Hybrid Theories"), is that the communication of censure through hard treatment is justified by its valuable preventative consequences (von Hirsch 1993). But this entails abandoning the positive retributivist claim that desert can, by itself, constitute a sufficient justification for punishment.

However, the following points can be made in defense of the latter claim. The first is just to try to impress upon the objector the sheer inadequacy of a purely symbolic mode of censure as a response to such grave wrongdoing as murder, rape and grievous assault. Only hard treatment can suitably convey our sincere commitment to the important values that the wrongdoer has transgressed in such cases. To the objection that this is tantamount to a foot-stamping insistence on the original claim, one can try to show how the communication of deserved censure through hard treatment illuminates and integrates with other aspects of our moral experience. First of all, it does not exclusively reflect the perspective of a putative inflicter of punishment. For the wrongdoer, the appropriate emotional response in such cases is one of guilt, which typically involves the judgment that they deserve punishment and, ideally, a preparedness to undergo it. Moreover, willingly undergoing the punishment can serve as a penance that makes vivid to the victim and the broader community the wrongdoer's repentance, thereby enabling them to make moral (as opposed to merely material) reparation for their wrongdoing and to restore their broken relationship with both victim and community. Looking further afield, the communication of deserved censure through hard treatment is bound up with a number of other valuable activities, e.g. emphatically dissociating the community from the wrongdoing, vindicating the victim's standing as a full member of the relevant community, reassuring other members of the community that certain forms of wrongdoing will not be tolerated, and sending a message of appreciation and encouragement to law-enforcement officials.

Of course, the communicative account remains deeply controversial. Among the numerous objections it faces is a mirror-image of one that confronts its unfair advantage cousin. Whereas the latter seems incapable of justifying punishment outside an institutional framework for allocating benefits and burdens, there is a serious question whether the former's stress on punishment as a vehicle of repentance precludes it from justifying punishment by a liberal state (as opposed to punishment in a family or monastic community, say). Does it not license a level of intrusiveness by the state in assessing and influencing the moral responses of wrongdoers that is incompatible with a due regard for their autonomy? (For contrasting views, see von Hirsch and Ashworth [2005] and Tasioulas [2007]). In any case, this objection highlights the fact that a complete theory of punishment must offer answers to questions beyond the justificatory issue on which we have focused. It must also address such questions as the conditions under which an agent has the *authority* to punish, how the justified *amount* of punishment is to be determined, what are the appropriate *modes* of punishment given the rationale for the practice, among others.

Consequentialist and hybrid theories

What about those who replied "No" to the question posed about the revised Kantian case in the previous section (p. 683), and who have not been swayed by the arguments subsequently adduced in favor of positive retributivism? Their guiding thought is that the retributivist tradition overlooks the vital significance of the consequences of punishment for its justification. Punishment involves censure and hard treatment – these are painful or burdensome for the wrongdoer and, contrary to positive retributivism, possess no countervailing intrinsic value grounded in desert. Moreover, maintaining the institution of punishment, especially legal punishment, is very costly to society as a whole. So, the practice of punishment can only be justified if the value of its consequences outweighs its evident costs.

Now, the idea that consequences are relevant to the justification of punishment, whether in a particular case or in general, is common ground among many theories of punishment. The non-absolutist versions of positive retributivism discussed in the previous section, for example, allow that sufficiently detrimental consequences can outweigh the reasons of retributive desert for punishing a wrongdoer. But an emphasis on the consequences of punishment can also reflect an underlying commitment to a general consequentialist moral principle, according to which it is only the consequences of an action, policy or institution that are relevant to its moral evaluation. On this view, the idea that the practice of punishment must be assessed primarily by reference to a specific standard of *justice* tends to go by the board or, if it does not, justice is being interpreted in the first two, unspecific, senses identified in the first section.

Different proponents of "consequentialist" theories offer differing prescriptions for assessing the value of consequences, depending on the theory of the good to which they subscribe. For example, utilitarians evaluate consequences exclusively by reference to well-being, which in turn may be understood in varying ways. Whatever their deeper philosophical disagreements, consequentialist theorists of legal punishment tend to accept crime prevention as the proximate end in terms of which the justification of that institution should be assessed. This is on the assumption that the provisions of the criminal law itself should comply with the relevant consequentialist principle, so that preventing crime conduces to the best overall outcome.

This leaves us with the large, perhaps intractable, empirical question of whether the most efficient method of crime prevention involves punishment. Pending its resolution, the consequentialist must keep an open mind as to the possibility that non-punitive methods of crime prevention, such as a therapeutic approach to criminal offenders, are more efficient. It is a disconcerting feature of many consequentialist defenses of punishment that they tend to skirt the heavily contested empirical issues that their theory officially deems salient to the justification of punishment. Instead, armchair reflection is usually thought to yield the conclusion that punishment is broadly morally justifiable, because it serves the end of crime prevention through such means as incapacitation, deterrence (both of the wrongdoer who is being punished [special deterrence] and other potential wrongdoers [general deterrence]), and reformation.

This relative neglect of the empirical question reflects the widespread sense that the deepest challenges to consequentialist theories of punishment are moral rather than empirical. If all that matters is the consequences, why not punish the innocent (e.g. the mothers of tender-hearted gangsters), when this will lead to the maximally valuable outcome? Alternatively, why not punish the guilty disproportionately (e.g. the electric chair for shoplifting, small fines for murder)? Retributivists, by contrast, do not face these difficulties. First, because they hold that punishment must be deserved for wrongdoing. And secondly, because the severity of the punishment that is deserved is proportionate to the gravity of the wrongful conduct, where the latter is usually taken to be some function of the harm it causes or risks and the moral culpability it manifests.

Consequentialists have well-rehearsed replies to such objections. They might claim that, in light of the empirical facts and a due appreciation of the values in terms of which outcomes are to be assessed, the likelihood of policies favoring punishing the innocent or punishing the guilty disproportionately being endorsed by the consequentialist principle in the real world is negligible. They may proceed to buttress this point by drawing on the familiar distinction between a decision procedure and a criterion of rightness, arguing that the most effective means of complying with the consequentialist criterion is by general adherence to retributive standards. Indeed, some consequentialists press further, contending that a form of rule consequentialism (as opposed to act consequentialism) would validate rules along retributivist lines, albeit for ultimately consequentialist reasons. These maneuvers are not to be dismissed, but their interest for the justification of punishment is secondary, since what they fundamentally bear on is the tenability of consequentialism as a general moral theory. In any case, they are all susceptible to a general objection: that they make the justification of punishment unduly hostage to the play of contingent circumstances, giving no regard to the fact that there is in all cases an independent reason of justice against punishing the innocent or punishing the guilty disproportionately.

This is why the most interesting and powerful consequentialist justifications of punishment are arguably not of the pure variety, which appeal to nothing other than an underlying general consequentialist principle of morality, but rather hybrid theories that combine consequentialist and retributivist considerations. The most famous hybrid theory, at least on one interpretation, is that developed by H. L. A. Hart (2008/1968: Ch. 1). On this view, the general justifying aim of punishment remains the consequentialist one of crime prevention, but the pursuit of that aim is subject to compliance with retributivist norms that prohibit the punishment of the innocent or the disproportionate punishment of the guilty. The retributivism invoked here is of the negative, rather than positive, variety, since it does not generate positive reasons for punishment. Any such theory faces a number of objections. One is that of giving a cogent justification for the retributivist constraints. Another is showing that conjoining retributivism with consequentialism comes to more than an *ad hoc* compromise, aimed at generating more palatable practical outcomes, but incoherent at the level of underlying philosophical theory.

Yet another focuses on the problems with consequentialism even of this muted sort. Admittedly, the theory avoids the problems of punishing the innocent, or punishing the guilty disproportionately, that afflicted its purer consequentialist cousin. But the question remains whether a wrongdoer punished on these grounds may not rightly feel aggrieved that they are being instrumentalized to the pursuit of valuable social goals, such as crime prevention, i.e. that they are treated only as a means to those ends and not with the respect due to a responsible moral agent. To this the response will be that they are not being treated *merely* as means to valuable ends, since their punishment is justified only on condition that they have committed a wrong and the severity of the punishment is proportionate to the gravity of that wrong. But the hybrid theory that is arguably most sensitive to the vague, but persistent, concern about illegitimate instrumentalization is that developed by Andrew von Hirsch (1993; von Hirsch and Ashworth 2005).

This is a communicative theory of punishment that justifies the communication of censure through hard treatment by invoking the preventative function of sanctions. In contrast with the positive retributivist version of the communicative theory, von Hirsch contends that nothing so onerous as the punishments meted out by the state can be justified purely as censure. On this "two-pronged" justification, the moral reason to refrain from wrongdoing grounded in the wrongfulness of the conduct, which is expressed by the reprobative function of the sanction, is supplemented by a prudential reason created by the threat of hard treatment. Potential offenders are therefore addressed as responsible agents capable of grasping the moral reasons behind criminal law prohibitions, while being given a supplementary prudential reason for conformity. The theory may be regarded as reversing the priorities of the Hartian hybrid account – the communication of censure to responsible moral agents being the central function of punishment, one which is only to be fulfilled when doing so has sufficient preventative value – in such a way as to address more effectively the concern about instrumentalization.

Now, the positive retributivist will question whether the case for punishing a murderer, for example, really must turn in part on anything so contestable as the preventative pay-off of doing so. And in light of the importance the theory confers on crime prevention, it is not clear how or why the amount of punishment that is justified in a given case can be constrained by a principle of retributive justice. Moreover, given that there is no case for punishing anyone in the absence of a showing of a suitable preventative outcome, it is not obvious that the problem of instrumentalization has been truly laid to rest. Still, it is worth observing that, in pursuing both the "Yes" and "No" responses to our initial Kantian conundrum, we have arrived, by means of argumentative pathways that are hopefully not overly contrived, at two versions of the communicative theory of punishment.

Beyond punishment? Beyond justice?

It would be seriously misleading to give the impression that all philosophers believe that the institution of punishment is in principle justifiable, let alone that its justification lies in (a communicative rendering of) retributive justice. Some are abolitionists who believe that no such justification exists (see Boonin 2008); others are pure consequentialists who hold that retributive justice plays no role in it. Another group of thinkers that has been influential in recent years advocates the displacement of the institution of punishment, to varying degrees, by practices more in tune with the demands of "restorative justice." This focuses on the need for reparation by the wrongdoer and the importance of restoring the relationship between them, their victim and the wider community, that their wrongdoing has disrupted. Members of this movement advocate "repentance rituals" – such as family group or "community accountability" conferences – as an alternative to punishment. If the offender successfully undergoes such a ritual, any case for punishing them may evaporate (Braithwaite 2002).

Defenders of the communicative theory of punishment have tried to deflect the challenge posed by the restorative justice movement by arguing that its legitimate aims can be adequately pursued within their own theory. After all, restoration can only be achieved when the wrongdoer suitably acknowledges the *wrong* they have committed, and not just by their making reparation for the material harm they have caused. Undergoing deserved punishment as a secular penance is precisely what enables such a restoration to be effected, at least in the case of the most serious crimes. The value of restoration, therefore, can only be pursued in light of a prior acknowledgment that some wrongdoers deserve to be punished (Duff 2001: Ch. 3.4–6). This response is cogent, so far as it goes. But there is a real question whether the standard versions of the communicative theory go far enough in defusing the challenge of restorative justice by accommodating the significance of repentance.

Consider, for example, the case of "antecedent repentance," i.e. when the wrongdoer has already repented of their wrongdoing prior to sentencing. Consumed by painful feelings of guilt, they may have turned themselves in to the authorities, made material reparation to their victim, and sincerely expressed their willingness to undergo the deserved punishment. What difference, if any, does their repentance make to whether, or how much, they should be punished? It is arguable that traditional versions of the communicative theory go awry in responding to this question by making a common assumption: that it is to be answered exclusively by reference to considerations of retributive desert. On the basis of this assumption, some argue that they deserve a milder punishment than one who is unrepentant. But this threatens to distort the retributive norm, since it is doubtful that repentance can lessen the gravity of one's original wrongdoing by retrospectively diminishing the culpability or harm it involved. Others, making the same assumption, argue that antecedent repentance has no bearing on whether, or how much, punishment is justified within the communicative theory, precisely because it has no bearing on retributive desert. But this view seems unduly severe, since there appears to be a reason to treat the repentant offender more leniently.

A deeper rapprochement between restorative justice and the communicative theory can be achieved by adopting a third, formal version of the latter. According to this, the communication of justified censure is merely the formal end of punishment, an end to which a number of distinct values, and not only retributive justice, may contribute. Another such value is mercy, understood in its classic formulation, as a source of reasons, grounded in charity (a proper concern for the wrongdoer's welfare) for punishing them less severely than they deserve. This pluralistic approach preserves the integrity of the retributive norm, while allowing antecedent repentance to play an integral role within the communicative theory as one of the grounds for mercy. It thereby enables the institution of punishment to speak to the offender in a more nuanced, and compassionate, manner than would be permitted by strict adherence to the vocabulary of retributive justice (Tasioulas 2006; for criticism, Duff 2007).

See also Ethics and Law (Chapter 35); Consequentialism (Chapter 37); Blame, remorse, mercy, forgiveness (Chapter 48).

References

Boonin, D. (2008) *The Problem of Punishment*, Cambridge: Cambridge University Press.

Braithwaite, J. (2002) "Repentance Rituals and Restorative Justice," *Journal of Political Philosophy* 8: 115–31.

Duff, R. A. (1986) *Trials and Punishments*, Cambridge: Cambridge University Press.

——(2001) *Punishment, Communication, and Community*, New York: Oxford University Press.

——(2007) "The Intrusion of Mercy," *Ohio State Journal of Criminal Law* 4: 361–87.

Feinberg, J. (1970) "The Expressive Function of Punishment," in *Doing and Deserving*, Princeton, NJ: Princeton University Press, pp. 95–118.

Hampton, J. (1984) "The Moral Education Theory of Punishment," *Philosophy & Public Affairs* 13: 208–38.

Hart, H. L. A. (2008/1968) *Punishment and Responsibility*, 2nd edn, ed., introduction by John Gardner, Oxford: Oxford University Press.

Hegel, G. W. F. (1967/1821) *The Philosophy of Right*, trans. T. M. Knox, Oxford: Oxford University Press.

Kant, I. (1991/1797) *The Metaphysics of Morals*, trans. M. Gregor, Cambridge: Cambridge University Press.

Moore, M. S. (1997) *Placing Blame: A Theory of Criminal Law*, Oxford: Oxford University Press.

Morris, H. (1968) "Persons and Punishment," *Monist* 52: 475–501.

Murphy, J. G. (1973) "Marxism and Retribution," *Philosophy & Public Affairs* 2: 217–43.

Murphy, J. G. and Hampton, J. (1988) *Forgiveness and Mercy*, Cambridge: Cambridge University Press.

Rawls, J. (1971) *A Theory of Justice*, Oxford: Oxford University Press.

Strawson, P. F. (1962) "Freedom and Resentment," *Proceedings of the British Academy* 48: 1–25.

Tasioulas, J. (2006) "Punishment and Repentance," *Philosophy* 81: 279–322.

——(2007) "Repentance and the Liberal State," *Ohio State Journal of Criminal Law* 4: 487–521.

von Hirsch, A. (1993) *Censure and Sanctions*, Oxford: Oxford University Press.

von Hirsch, A. and Ashworth, A. (2005) *Proportionate Sentencing*, Oxford: Oxford University Press.

Weil, S. (1996) *The Need for Roots: Prelude to a Declaration of Duties towards Mankind*, trans. A. Wills, London: Routledge.

Further reading

Braithwaite, J. and Pettit, P. (1990) *Not Just Deserts*, Oxford: Oxford University Press. (Sophisticated consequentialist approach to punishment.)

Duff, R. A. (2001) *Punishment, Communication, and Community*, New York: Oxford University Press. (Systematic overview of the subject area and a leading presentation of the communicative theory of punishment.)

Hart, H. L. A. (2008/1968) *Punishment and Responsibility*, 2nd edn, ed., introduction by John Gardner, Oxford: Oxford University Press. (Classic defense of a hybrid approach to punishment.)

von Hirsch, A. and Ashworth, A. (2005) *Proportionate Sentencing*, Oxford: Oxford University Press. (Sophisticated defense of a hybrid approach.)

58
JUSTICE AND DISTRIBUTION

Matthew Clayton

Should income tax for high earners be raised or lowered? Is the availability of expensive private schooling justified? To what extent must the present generation reduce its carbon emissions for the sake of future generations? These are just a few of the questions that lead us to consider more abstract and general questions about justice and distribution.

Rawls's "justice as fairness"

Since the publication of John Rawls's *A Theory of Justice* (1971), distributive justice has been perhaps the most debated issue within political philosophy. Much of this debate proceeds on the basis of a critical assessment of Rawls's own influential conception of social justice, "justice as fairness." Rawls limits himself to certain questions by framing the problem of justice as one that concerns how the significant social, economic and political institutions of a single society (what he calls "the basic structure of society") should be regulated. The aim of a theory of justice is to propose principles to guide these institutions in such a way that each individual receives a fair share of social benefits and burdens. In his landmark book, the importance of which has been compared to Plato's *Republic* and Hobbes's *Leviathan* (Cohen 2008: 11), Rawls defends both a particular *approach for addressing* distributive justice and *a set of principles of justice* for the regulation of society's basic structure.

Rawls begins his theory by expressing concerns about two alternative approaches to distributive justice. First, when dealing with a distributive problem, such as choosing a principle to allocate a sum of money, it is common for people to appeal to a number of different concerns that move them: that the money should go to the person who *deserves* it as a reward, or to those who *need* it most, or to those who would *benefit most* from having it, or that it should be divided *equally*. One worry about this manner of appealing to our common intuitions about justice is that it is unclear in which contexts considerations of desert, need, beneficence or equality apply, and it is not obvious how much weight should be attached to each consideration. Ideally, a conception of justice will supply a set of principles of justice that will deliver determinate answers to distributive questions, by justifying the rejection of certain common intuitions of justice and by ordering our relevant intuitions in a way that yields clear prescriptions. Rawls's additional aspiration is to articulate a conception of justice that generates "reflective equilibrium" between our different convictions. We have beliefs about distributive justice at various levels of generality and abstraction – concrete beliefs about the wrongness of employment discrimination on grounds of color or sex, for example, but also an adherence to the more abstract ideals of freedom and equality – and one aim of an account of justice is to provide a conception that enables us to see how our (duly revised) beliefs at various levels are mutually supportive.

Utilitarianism is the second approach to distributive justice that Rawls rejects. Rawls's central complaint is that utilitarianism wrongly countenances the sacrifice of some people's interests if that would generate greater offsetting benefits for others: it proposes that we ought to maximize the total or average sum of net benefits, rather than attend to the interests of each considered separately. Friends of utilitarianism have responded in several ways to Rawls's criticisms. One response is that utilitarianism is an egalitarian conception of justice, because each person's interests count equally in the determination of public policy (Griffin 1986: 167–70). However, the worry remains that when considering *how* persons' interests matter, utilitarians are concerned only with the *size* of the overall benefits that would follow from the operation of di fferent policies; they have no principled objection to policies that generate substantial inequalities or are detrimental to the interests of the worst off in society.

Rawls's alternative to intuitionist and utilitarian approaches to distributive justice considers the issue by asking which principles follow from the ideals of freedom and equality. More specifically, citizens are viewed as having equal status and Rawls argues that this supports the claim that valid principles of justice are ones that can be accepted by every reasonable person. His famous and widely discussed "original position" models his thought that valid principles of justice are ones that everyone would choose from a position of equality. In this thought experiment, individuals' representatives are charged with the responsibility of advancing their respective clients' interests. These interests are understood in terms of a range of "primary goods," including various democratic and civil liberties, educational and occupational opportunity, wealth and income, and "the social bases of self-respect." However, to ensure that the choice of principles is not influenced by differences in bargaining power – differences that generate problems of injustice for traditional social contract theories of the kind offered by Lockeans and Hobbesians – Rawls deploys the device of a "veil of ignorance." Under the veil, while a representative has some knowledge of her client's interests supplied by the list of primary goods and a general understanding of social and economic processes, she lacks knowledge of her client's particular characteristics such as her sex, skin color, class origin, biological endowment, and even her convictions about sexuality and religion. The veil of ignorance is a device that is designed to ensure that political principles are chosen in a way that does not reflect what Rawls calls "morally arbitrary" factors, such as skin color. Because of the veil, representatives are forced to attend to the interests of every citizen considered separately.

In the absence of information about their clients' particular characteristics, Rawls claims that representatives would reject utilitarian principles in favor of his "two principles of justice," the first of which guarantees a familiar set of political and civil rights – including the right to democratic participation and the freedoms of conscience, expression and association – and has priority over the second principle, which permits inequalities of wealth and income if and only if those inequalities are (a) not detrimental to the interests of those with least wealth and income (the "difference principle") and (b) consistent with the maintenance of equal opportunity in the provision of education and allocation of occupation and political office (the principle of "fair equality of opportunity"). Because the two principles are clearly ordered and generate reasonably determinate policy objectives, Rawls regards them as preferable to the unfortunate balancing of conflicting concerns about justice that is characteristic of the intuitionist approach. The two principles constitute a philosophical defense of liberal democratic constitutional states in which the significant social and economic inequalities that characterize contemporary industrial societies are considerably reduced. Indeed, the difference principle, which condemns economic inequalities that are not *maximally* beneficial to the least advantaged, represents a more radical view of distributive justice than that embodied in many social democratic regimes in which the concern is to ensure only that no one falls below a certain threshold of socioeconomic advantage.

Rawls's conception has received considerable critical attention. Some have questioned the relevance of hypothetical agreements for a conception of justice; others challenge his derivation of his two principles of justice from the original position or other arguments he offers in favor of them. Rawls has, in turn, revised his conception of justice and provided further defense of it (Rawls 2001). In addition, his second major work, *Political Liberalism* (1993), explores the ideal of political legitimacy, the conditions under which the exercise of political power is justified, and clarifies how his conception of justice can be viewed as one that can command the allegiance of citizens who disagree about religion or what makes one's life a success.

To explore debates about distributive justice further it is useful to distinguish between accounts that reject the egalitarian foundations of Rawls's conception and those that accept those foundations but interpret them in ways that depart from justice as fairness.

Libertarian justice

In *Anarchy, State and Utopia*, Robert Nozick, a libertarian critic of Rawlsian justice, proclaims that "taxation of earnings from labor is on a par with forced labor" (Nozick 1974: 169). Nozick's rejection of taxation for the purposes of redistribution or welfare provision is premised on the thought that individuals own themselves. Leaving aside cases in which property in oneself can be forfeited (by violating the rights of others) or transferred (through voluntary self-enslavement), self-ownership is the right that I and only I may justly control how my body is used. It would be a violation of my self-ownership if others take my blood without my consent, irrespective of the benefits others might reap from it.

The principle of self-ownership generates a set of rights that make it impermissible for others, individually or collectively through state institutions, to force an individual to supply her labor for the benefit of others. However, the extent of different individuals' wealth is a product not only of the exercise of their talents, but their work with external resources. Consequently, Nozick's argument for a "minimal" state and his permissive attitude with respect to inequality depend on the combination of self-ownership with principles that specify justice with respect to the distribution of the external world.

For Nozick, justice is historical in the sense that a just distribution of resources is simply the distribution that is the product of people's different choices with respect to investment, consumption and giving within certain specified rules. These rules are supplied by the principles of "acquisition" and "transfer." The former spells out how individuals may justly appropriate items that are not owned by others, and asserts that appropriation is just if it does not harm anyone in comparison with her position had the item in question remained unowned. Acquisition generates property rights. In a world in which items, such as tracts of land, are unowned everyone is at liberty to use them. Once an item is owned, however, others have rights to use it only with the permission of the owner. Nevertheless, because having exclusive rights over an item might motivate its owner to improve it, which might in turn benefit others in various ways, property rights might not worsen the position of others. True, others cannot use that item without the owner's consent. But that loss might be outweighed by the benefits of living in an environment in which property is put to productive use.

Nozick specifies the nature of property rights further through the principle of transfer, which spells out how one person's property can justly become someone else's property. Here, he appeals to a consent-based rule: that the owner's free consent to a transfer as a gift or in exchange for other items or labor, for example, generates an entitlement for the recipient. By contrast, theft, fraud or breach of contract violate the principle of transfer. Justice is served, in this libertarian conception, if the principles of acquisition and transfer are respected regardless of the outcome in terms of equality, need satisfaction, or rewarding individuals according to their deservingness.

Nozick's view is sometimes interpreted as a defense of the moral permissibility of individuals exclusively pursuing their own economic advantage, but this is a misreading. It is consistent with Nozick's view to claim that individuals have a moral duty to spend much, perhaps most, of their money in the service of the poor or vulnerable. The key claim of Nozick's libertarianism is that if there is such a duty it must be understood as a *non-enforceable* one, that is, it is unjust for others to force individuals to spend the money to which they are entitled in any particular way.

One kind of criticism of Nozick's libertarianism accepts his commitment to self-ownership but rejects his principles that deal with natural resources. In particular, "left-libertarians" treat the external world as belonging to everyone. Property rights over natural resources in this view are conditional upon everyone receiving a just share of the world's assets. There are certain disagreements within left-libertarianism with respect to how to specify the notion of a "just share." One simple view is that everyone should receive an equal share of the value of the external world calculated in monetary terms, i.e., what the world would fetch if it were efficiently auctioned (Steiner 1994). A different account argues that property rights should be distributed in a manner that compensates individuals for their disabilities or their inability to generate welfare as well as others do (Otsuka 2003: 11–40).

A more thoroughgoing critique of many versions of right- and left-libertarianism rejects the thought that justice requires a distribution of *property* rights understood as conferring rights to control and transfer items that one owns. Consider two implications of libertarianism that are widely questioned. First, self-ownership permits individuals voluntarily to give or sell their labor to others on any terms. Voluntary slavery is permissible and, consequently, our legal institutions have a reason to enforce contracts in which individuals sell themselves into slavery even when the individual later regrets her self-enslavement. And, second, it is a violation of an individual's ownership of her talents if others or state officials interfere in the exchange of her labor for income: taxation of purchases or income on this view is unjust. The libertarian preoccupation with property ownership has been criticized for failing to make appropriate distinctions between the different *interests* individuals have. For example, while we might have an interest in preserving our bodily integrity that generates a right to prohibit others from taking our organs without our consent, many deny that we have an interest in being free permanently to sell our bodies to others. And, while we might have weighty interests that support a right of occupational choice that, in normal circumstances, prevents others from forcing us to work in particular occupations, this right is compatible with our labor being taxed in the service of everyone's interest in having the wherewithal to live a decent life or in living in a society in which inequalities are limited to ensure that no one is vulnerable to domination by others. Conceptualizing justice in terms of an allocation of property rights, the criticism asserts, is insufficiently sensitive to our different interests and the different implications of those interests for public policy (Nagel 1975).

Egalitarian justice

A number of recent political philosophers accept the egalitarian foundations on which Rawls builds his conception of justice but elaborate them in ways that depart from justice as fairness.

Luck egalitarianism

One influential conception of equality, labeled "luck egalitarianism," exhibits a qualified commitment to reduce inequalities in society. In this conception, it is prima facie unjust for some to be worse off than others if the inequality in question has its origin in differences of biological endowment or family circumstance, for example, but it might not be unjust if the inequalities stem from different choices individuals make given equally valuable options (Dworkin 2000; Cohen 1989).

The most prominent egalitarianism of this kind is Dworkin's conception of "equality of resources." Dworkin insists that justice demands that individuals should enjoy equal resources, where resources are understood not just in terms of land and other external items but also include one's natural endowments, such as the abilities or disabilities with which one is born or one's propensity to ill health.

To elaborate equality of resources, Dworkin makes use of two devices. Leaving aside differences of biological endowment, what economists call the "envy test" identifies an equal distribution of the external world as one in which no one would prefer anyone else's set of resources to her own. For example, if Alan possesses a sandy beach which both he and Biff prefer to her rocky outcrop then there is an inequality which calls for a redistribution of land or other resources, such as money, to compensate Biff for her disadvantage. If, however, neither would prefer to have what the other has, then there is no unjust inequality, even though Alan and Biff lead very different lives and are unequally happy. In the same vein as justice as fairness, it is not part of equality of resources to ensure that everyone enjoys equal welfare, where "welfare" is understood in terms of preference satisfaction or some objective measure of happiness.

The envy test can also be used to identify inequalities that arise in virtue of differences of endowment. If the blind prefer to be sighted, they have a claim to compensation. For Dworkin, the central question is how we are to determine the appropriate extent of that compensation. One view is that other resources, such as wealth and income, should be redistributed from the sighted to the blind until, taking every kind of resource into account, the envy test is satisfied.

Dworkin rejects this view in favor of a conception of egalitarian compensation that is sensitive to individuals' ambitions and, particularly, their attitudes towards risk. Suppose Colin and David decide to set out to climb a high mountain and their expedition carries with it the possibility of frostbite. Colin decides to take out insurance that would compensate him generously for losing his toes while David does not. Now suppose that both suffer frostbite. In Dworkin's view, if both individuals enjoyed an equal and fully informed opportunity to insure at different levels of coverage, then any inequality that exists after the event is a product of their different ambitions or attitudes towards risk-taking and is, therefore, not unjust.

This simple example illustrates Dworkin's "ambition-sensitive" approach to dealing with inequalities in endowment. For example, individuals are beset by different kinds of ill health at different points in their lives. How many resources should be devoted to trying to rectify ill health or compensate for it when these resources might be put to other uses, such as educating the next generation or funding the pursuit of people's projects? Furthermore, when deciding how the health-care budget should be spent, should priority be given to those whose condition is more debilitating or to those whose health can be improved to a greater extent? In response to these distributive questions, Dworkin asks us to imagine what kinds of insurance decisions individuals would make if they enjoyed equal opportunity to insure. Actual insurance markets in medical care are a poor guide to answering that question, because they reflect unjust inequalities in income and penalize the disabled by refusing them insurance or by pricing their premiums more highly compared with those offered to the healthy. By contrast, Dworkin asks us to imagine what kinds of insurance decisions would be made by individuals who enjoyed a fair share of wealth and income, had complete information about the costs and benefits of different types of medical intervention, and, crucially, were ignorant of whether they are more or less likely to suffer ill health than the average individual. The just level of compensation for ill health is determined by the insurance choices that would be made in that hypothetical context (Dworkin 2002, 2000: 307–19). Dworkin also deploys the hypothetical insurance scheme to defend rights for the unemployed and a progressive system of taxation for income and bequests (2000: 320–50).

While Dworkin has proposed the most elaborate version of luck egalitarianism, alternative conceptions, which advocate compensating individuals for their unchosen expensive tastes, have been defended (Arneson 1989; Cohen 1989, 2004). Furthermore, a number of forceful objections have been raised against the central distinction on which luck egalitarianism trades, namely, the distinction between the influence of choice and chance in shaping individuals' fates. For example, some insist that ensuring that everyone has the opportunity to relate to each other as equal citizens is a requirement of justice regardless of whether some have willfully wasted their earlier opportunities. And, some argue that compensation is not owed in every case of an involuntary disadvantage. On this view individuals who like playing the piano are not owed compensation for their small hands even though these clearly disadvantage them in resource or welfare terms compared with others with similar ambitions: redistribution is appropriate only if one's standing as an equal citizen is threatened (see Anderson 2000; Scheffler 2003).

Egalitarianism and personal conduct

Both justice as fairness and resource egalitarianism affirm what Nagel calls a "moral division of labor" (Nagel 1991: 53–62). On these conceptions, distributive justice is served by state institutions guaranteeing various freedoms and redistributing opportunities and resources to compensate for the effects of unequal luck. Individuals are permitted to serve their own interests in the knowledge that their duties of justice are satisfied by the laws that constrain them. Our duty to promote justice, then, requires that we vote for governments that will constrain us according to the right principles, but does not require us to make particular choices in our daily lives. One notable critique of this position is summarized in the feminist claim that "the personal is political." On this view, women are denied justice in virtue of the unequal division of labor within the family, which sees them working a "double-day" as homemaker and waged worker that disadvantages them in comparison to the working lives of men. An adequate account of distributive justice, the argument goes, demands more than fair legislation; it requires a thoroughgoing revision of customary expectations and, according to certain feminists, the development of "genderless" families in which men and women are motivated to share both waged and unwaged work equally (Okin 1989).

The idea of an egalitarian "ethos" in which individuals are motivated by a concern to promote economic equality through their daily choices has also been defended by certain socialist philosophers (Carens 1986; Cohen 2000, 2008). G. A. Cohen's defense proceeds on the basis of a critique of Rawls's conception of economic justice. Rawls rejects certain conceptions of justice that either permit or require economic inequality, such as libertarian accounts of distributive justice or accounts that claim that the more productive *deserve* greater than average income as a reward. However, he allows unequal incomes to be earned if the inequality generates incentives for the more productive to work harder than they otherwise would or to take socially beneficial jobs they would otherwise avoid. Such inequalities can be justified, according to Rawls, because they are beneficial for everyone and, in particular, the least advantaged.

While this *incentive-based* argument for inequality justifies less economic inequality compared with other accounts, Cohen objects that it permits too much inequality. His argument is that the reasons that justify the selection of laws and public policies that are favorable to the interests of less advantaged citizens also justify the development of an ethos that guides the productive to take socially beneficial jobs and to work for everyone's benefit without the allure of financial inducements. In Cohen's view, one attractive feature of an egalitarian ethos is that it renders equality and economic efficiency compatible and thereby responds to a long-standing critique that equality "levels down" and makes everyone worse off.

Cohen's egalitarian ethos represents a demanding conception of distributive justice and has generated considerable debate on the question of what is the appropriate "site" of justice, that is, how to characterize the range of items that are to be evaluated from the point of view of justice (see, for example, Williams 1998).

Equality, priority and sufficiency

Egalitarian conceptions of justice are concerned about the *gap* between the more and less advantaged. The "leveling down objection" asserts that egalitarians are implausibly committed to the claim that a distribution that reduces inequality but which makes everyone worse off is, at least in one respect, preferable from the point of view of justice: "how can a society in which all are poor be, in any respect, preferable to a society in which half are rich and half are very rich?" (see Parfit [2002] for a discussion, though not an endorsement, of the objection).

Egalitarians have responded in various ways to this objection. Some, like Temkin (2002), have argued for the non-derivative value of equality on the grounds that the implicit assumption that motivates the leveling down objection – that a distributive principle is plausible only if its application benefits someone – is mistaken. In other parts of our ethical thought, Temkin insists, this assumption is rejected. For example, depriving the undeserving of a good, even when that good cannot be transferred to benefit the more deserving, is widely regarded as just. If Temkin is right, then equality cannot be rejected just in virtue of its status as an impersonal value, since the presence of such values is a common feature of ethical reasoning. However, even if this is accepted, the question remains whether and why we should value equality, in particular, as an impersonal good.

A different egalitarian response that sees the force of the leveling down objection involves a *qualified* endorsement of equality. *Paretian egalitarianism* treats Pareto efficiency as a necessary condition of distributive justice: a principle is to be rejected if there is an alternative principle that benefits some while leaving no one worse off. Paretian egalitarians, then, favor the most equal distribution among those distributions that are efficient. Rawls's argument for the Difference Principle appeals to this kind of reasoning (Rawls 2001: 61–4, 122–4).

In contrast to the egalitarian concern about the gap between, or the *relative* advantage of, different individuals, some philosophers affirm *prioritarianism*. This conception of justice directs our concern to those who are less advantaged, not because they are worse off than others but simply because of their low *absolute* level of advantage. Public policy should be directed to the satisfaction of the needs of less advantaged individuals, on this view, and sometimes even when we can benefit them less than we can someone who is better off. In practice, prioritarians agree with egalitarian proposals to transfer wealth from rich to poor, but they do so on the basis of different reasons (Parfit 2002).

One view that is sometimes allied with prioritarianism is that of *sufficientarianism*, which, as the term suggests, is a conception of justice that stresses the importance of individuals having enough. Several sufficientarian proposals have been developed (Frankfurt 1987; Crisp 2003). The more interesting and controversial conceptions reject the relevance of other distributive principles if everyone has enough. For example, they claim that the gap between the rich and very rich does not generate concerns of justice and neither is it more important to give priority in distributing resources to the rich over the very rich. Nevertheless, sufficientarianism faces a number of objections. For example, many claim that if a number of individuals make competing claims for a particular resource, a sum of money or job opportunity, for example, the fact that everyone has enough to lead a decent or good life does not make the allocation of that resource a matter of indifference from the point of view of justice: arbitrary, discriminatory or unequal treatment might remain unjust even when it does not prevent someone from leading a good life (see Casal [2007] for discussion of this and further objections).

Pluralist justice

As noted above, Rawls's account of justice was motivated, in part, by his worry that appealing to common intuitions about justice, which involve a number of commitments including equality, liberty, desert, need, efficiency, renders distributive justice indeterminate. His solution is to prioritize liberty and equality and to derive principles of justice that reflect the constraints imposed by those ideals.

A rather different account of distributive justice seeks to accommodate the wide variety of commitments that people commonly hold while avoiding indeterminacy. Two conceptions of justice of this kind are Walzer's *Spheres of Justice* (1983) and Miller's *Principles of Social Justice* (1999). Walzer believes that different distributive principles can be derived from the "shared understanding" of a citizenry with respect to the distributive requirements of different *goods* such as medical care, education, citizenship, and so on. For example, our shared understanding of medical care, he claims, includes the principle that it should be distributed according to need, while our understanding of honors, prizes, and jobs involves distribution according to merit or deservingness. It would be unjust, Walzer claims, to distribute prizes according to need or to distribute health care in a way that prioritizes the care of the talented over those who have greater medical need. Accordingly, distributive justice is satisfied if each good is distributed according to the principle that is suited to it according to our shared understanding. In particular, there are certain goods that money cannot or should not be permitted to buy: distribution according to ability to pay is appropriate for certain goods such as televisions and cars, but not for other goods like health care, jobs, or political office.

Miller's pluralist conception proceeds on the basis that different "modes of relationship" call for different distributive principles. Whereas citizenship involves relating to each other as equals, what he calls "solidaristic" relationships such as those exhibited in families, religious associations, local communities, and, to some extent, nations generate obligations to share the costs of meeting each other's needs as defined by the communal ethos. And, finally, economic relationships that are generally instrumental in nature call for distribution according to desert in which each is rewarded in proportion to contribution (1999: 25–41). The task of a theory of justice, for Miller, is to identify or clarify the different kinds of relationship that are relevant in particular contexts and to propose distributive principles that are suited to those relationships.

One of the valuable features of these conceptions is that they have encouraged a renewed interest in particular distributive issues: the problems that are distinctively raised by global inequality, climate change, migration, health care, or education. However, whether pluralist accounts can offer more satisfying solutions to these problems than the more abstract accounts outlined by Rawls or Dworkin, for example, remains an open question.

See also Contemporary Kantian ethics (Chapter 38); Ethical intuitionism (Chapter 39); Contractualism (Chapter 41); Feminist ethics (Chapter 43); Population ethics (Chapter 61); The environment (Chapter 63); World poverty (Chapter 66).

References

Anderson, E. (2000) "What Is the Point of Equality?," *Ethics* 109: 287–337.

Arneson, R. (1989) "Equality and Equal Opportunity for Welfare," *Philosophical Studies* 56: 77–93.

Carens, J. (1986) "Rights and Duties in an Egalitarian Society," *Political Theory* 14: 31–49.

Casal, P. (2007) "Why Sufficiency Is Not Enough," *Ethics* 117: 296–326.

Cohen, G. A. (1989) "On the Currency of Egalitarian Justice," *Ethics* 99: 906–44.

——(2000) *If You're an Egalitarian, How Come You're So Rich?*, Cambridge, MA: Harvard University Press.

——(2004) "Expensive Taste Rides Again," in J. Burley (ed.) *Dworkin and His Critics*, Oxford: Blackwell.

——(2008) *Rescuing Justice and Equality*, Cambridge, MA: Harvard University Press.

Crisp, R. (2003) "Equality, Priority, and Compassion," *Ethics* 113: 745–63.

Dworkin, R. (2000) *Sovereign Virtue: The Theory and Practice of Equality*, Cambridge, MA: Harvard University Press.

——(2002) "Justice in the Distribution of Health Care," in M. Clayton and A. Williams (eds) *The Ideal of Equality*, London: Palgrave.

Frankfurt, H. (1987) "Equality as a Moral Ideal," *Ethics* 98: 21–43.
Griffin, J. (1986) *Well-Being: Its Meaning, Measurement and Moral Importance*, Oxford: Clarendon Press.
Miller, D. (1999) *Principles of Social Justice*, Cambridge, MA: Harvard University Press.
Nagel, T. (1975) "Libertarianism without Foundations," *The Yale Law Journal* 85: 136–49.
——(1991) *Equality and Partiality*, New York: Oxford University Press.
Nozick, R. (1974) *Anarchy, State and Utopia*, Oxford: Blackwell.
Okin, S. M. (1989) *Justice, Gender and the Family*, New York: Basic Books.
Otsuka, M. (2003) *Libertarianism without Inequality*, Oxford: Oxford University Press.
Parfit, D. (2002) "Equality or Priority?," in M. Clayton and A. Williams (eds) *The Ideal of Equality*, London: Palgrave.
Rawls, J. (1971) *A Theory of Justice*, Cambridge, MA: Harvard University Press.
——(1993) *Political Liberalism*, New York: Columbia University Press.
——(2001) *Justice as Fairness: A Restatement*, Cambridge, MA: Harvard University Press.
Scheffler, S. (2003) "What Is Egalitarianism?," *Philosophy & Public Affairs* 31: 5–39.
Steiner, H. (1994) *An Essay on Rights*, Oxford: Blackwell.
Temkin, L. (2002) "Equality, Priority, and the Levelling Down Objection," in M. Clayton and A. Williams (eds) *The Ideal of Equality*, London: Palgrave.
Walzer, M. (1983) *Spheres of Justice: A Defense of Pluralism and Equality*, Oxford: Blackwell.
Williams, A. (1998) "Incentives, Inequality, and Publicity," *Philosophy & Public Affairs* 27: 225–47.

Further reading

Brighouse, H. (2004) *Justice*, Cambridge, UK: Polity Press. (A short introduction to the subject.)
Clayton, M. and Williams, A. (eds) (2004) *Social Justice*, Oxford: Blackwell. (A collection of extracts and essays on distributive justice.)
Kymlicka, W. (2002) *Contemporary Political Philosophy: An Introduction*, 2nd edn, Oxford: Oxford University Press. (An extended introduction to the issue of distributive justice and its place within contemporary political philosophy.)

(iii)
HUMAN LIFE

59
LIFE, DEATH, AND ETHICS

Fred Feldman

Introduction

Serious reflection on life and death is a remarkably rich gateway into ethics. As soon as we start thinking carefully about life and death, we are drawn into a web of related topics in ethics. Some of these questions are axiological. Death seems to be a great evil for the one who dies. We may wonder how this can be possible, given that the one who dies cannot suffer while being dead. Furthermore, since the deceased may not exist after she dies, it may be difficult to see how she can be harmed in any way by her own death. Other questions concern the rationality of emotions. Some have argued that the fear of death must be irrational. After all, it would seem quite irrational for a person to fear (or otherwise be emotionally agitated about) his own prenatal non-existence. How is post-mortem non-existence any different? A final class of questions concerns the moral rights and wrongs of causing death. It seems intuitively clear that it is morally wrong to kill a thriving innocent human being. But other cases are much less clear. What shall we say about the killing of a miserable, suffering elderly person who is begging for death? What shall we say about a microscopic human fetus? What shall we say about the case of a person who decides to kill himself in order to avoid unremitting pain? To answer these questions we must consider the deeper question: Precisely what makes an act of killing morally wrong, when it is wrong? Thus, before we can answer questions about the moral rights and wrongs of killing, we must face more fundamental questions in the normative ethics of behavior.

Death and non-existence

Many philosophers endorse the idea that people go out of existence when they die. This so-called "termination thesis" has been hotly debated. Critics point out that familiar ways of speaking and thinking about death conflict with this notion. For example, no one would find anything odd in this exchange: "We finally found Saddam!" "Great! Is he dead or alive?" Nor should anyone be surprised to discover that there are websites containing lists of "famous dead people." Ordinary language is filled with talk that suggests that people go on existing after they have died (Feldman 1992, 2000, 2001).

Some philosophers, however, insist that these familiar forms of speech should not be taken seriously. Perhaps common-sense thought about the metaphysics of death is simply wrong. Furthermore, they point out that there are other familiar forms of speech that suggest that common-sense metaphysics presupposes the termination thesis. For example, we often say that we have found "the remains" of a deceased person, rather than that we have found the person himself (now dead) (Johansson 2005).

According to the termination thesis, when a person dies he literally ceases to exist. On one version of this view, at death the person goes out of existence and a new entity – her corpse – comes into existence in her place (Rosenberg 1998). Other even more radical views have been defended. Consider a case in which a person first loses her capacity to distinguish herself from others; then falls into a coma; then lingers near death for a while; then dies and is buried; and then years later her body disintegrates. Some apparently want to claim that the person went out of existence when she lost her "first-person perspective" (Baker 1999, 2000). On this view, if a person becomes seriously and permanently mentally deranged, she is "gone." Even if her body is walking around, eating and drinking, and talking, the former person is no longer in existence. Others claim that the person goes out of existence when she falls into an irreversible coma. Yet others would say that the person persists through these psychological changes, but goes out of existence when she dies (Olsen 1997, 2004; Johansson 2005). And yet others would say that since the person is her body, the thing that was the person goes on existing as a corpse until that body disintegrates (Feldman 1992, 2000, 2001; Mackie 1999).

The termination thesis figures prominently in the debate about the evil of death.

The Epicurean argument

A substantial portion of the philosophical literature on death is stimulated by a line of argument due to Epicurus and subsequently defended by Lucretius. Epicurus said:

> death is nothing to us. For all good and evil consists in sensation, but death is deprivation of sensation. … So death, the most terrifying of ills, is nothing to us, since so long as we exist death is not with us; but when death comes, then we do not exist. It does not then concern either the living or the dead, since for the former it is not, and the latter are no more.
>
> (Epicurus 1994: 29)

In a related passage Epicurus said that "the wise man" does not fear the cessation of life. This has been taken to mean that it is irrational to fear death.

Some have maintained that the argument essentially presupposes the "experience condition" (Silverstein 1980; Rosenbaum 1993). In its simplest form, this principle asserts that something is an evil for a person only if the person experiences it. The argument, under this interpretation, might go like this:

(1) No one experiences his own death.
(2) If no one experiences his own death, then his own death is not an evil for the one who dies.
(3) If his own death is not an evil for the one who dies, then it is irrational for anyone to fear his own death.
(4) Therefore, it is irrational for anyone to fear his own death.

Critics have been quick to point out a variety of familiar counter-examples to the experience condition. For example, it might be bad for me to be secretly betrayed by my supposed friends, even if I am never aware of the betrayal (Fischer 1997). Thus, premise (2) is objectionable.

A weaker form of the experience condition would not be refuted by examples of this sort. We might maintain that something can be evil for a person only if the person *could have experienced it*. Although I did not actually experience any acts of betrayal, it seems reasonable to suppose that such acts *could have been experienced*. One's own death, on the other hand, could not have been experienced. This generates a slightly modified version of the argument:

(1) No one can experience his own death.
(2) If no one can experience his own death, then his own death is not an evil for the one who dies.
(3) If his own death is not an evil for the one who dies, then it is irrational for anyone to fear his own death.
(4) Therefore, it is irrational for anyone to fear his own death.

But further reflection makes it clear that even in this weaker form, the experience condition remains problematic. Part of the trouble emerges when we reflect on fundamental theories of welfare. If a simple form of preferentism is true, then a person's welfare is ultimately determined by the extent to which her desires are satisfied. Anything that frustrates a person's desires would therefore count as being bad for her. In typical forms, this theory conflicts with the experience condition even in the revised form. Suppose a seafarer desires to be buried at sea (*the burial to take place after he dies, of course!*). Suppose that after he dies, he is buried on land. The imagined form of preferentism implies that being buried on land was bad for this seafarer, since it served to frustrate one of his desires. However, since he was dead at the relevant time, he did not and could not have experienced that burial.

Some theories of welfare imply that the ultimate determinants of a person's welfare are things that the person must experience. Sensory hedonism is a familiar example of such a theory. If this theory is true, then a person's welfare is ultimately determined by his own experiences of pleasure and pain. Such a view would imply that nothing can be an ultimate determinant of a person's welfare unless he could experience it. But even this theory leaves room for unexperienceable evils. Consider a "silent stroke." By definition, the victim of a silent stroke is not aware of the stroke when it occurs. But of course even a hedonist can acknowledge that the occurrence of the stroke may be a great evil for the victim. The stroke itself is *extrinsically bad* for the victim in virtue of its consequences. If the victim is worse off in terms of pleasure and pain as a result of the stroke, then (though he does not experience the stroke itself) the stroke is still declared to be bad for him. Thus, premise (2) is still open to doubt.

The experience condition seems, then, to be indefensible (Fischer 1997). Furthermore, the Epicurean texts do not make any explicit mention of it. Thus, some philosophers have sought a different interpretation of the argument.

Some commentators have understood the argument to turn essentially on certain features of *harm*. They have said that something can harm a person only if it harms him *at a time*. They take it that Epicurus's point was that death cannot harm a person at any time before he dies (since it hasn't yet happened); nor can death harm a person at any time after he dies (since he does not exist at those times). Thus, the argument may look more like this:

(1) His own death cannot harm a person before he dies (because it has not yet occurred).
(2) His own death cannot harm a person after he dies (because the victim does not then exist).
(3) If (1) and (2) are true, then there is no time at which his own death can harm a person.
(4) If there is no time at which his own death can harm a person, then his own death is not an evil for the one who dies.
(5) If his own death is not an evil for the one who dies, then it is irrational for anyone to fear his own death.
(6) Therefore, it is irrational for anyone to fear his own death.

While it is obvious that in some cases a person is harmed because he has actually received certain evils (on a hedonistic assumption, this would always ultimately be understood to be some sort of pain), it should also be obvious on reflection that in other cases a person is harmed because he has failed to receive certain goods. This might happen, for example, in a case in which a person is harmed because he never got an education, or the opportunity to vote, or the chance to travel freely. In the case of these "harms of deprivation," the identification of a precise date of the harm seems far more problematic. Precisely when, we may ask, did the uneducated person suffer the harm of *not getting an education?* Thus, there is doubt about the notion that every harm must have a date. So premise (4) is questionable.

Others have in effect rejected premise (2). They have suggested that a person may suffer the harm of early death at many times after he has died. For example, one may claim that the victim of an early death is harmed at all post-mortem times when he would have been happy if that early death had not taken place (Bradley 2004, 2009; Feit 2002). It is reasonable to suppose that if his early death actually harmed him, then there must be such times.

Another suggestion is that harms of deprivation have a kind of "universal" occurrence. Suppose a person would have been happier if he had lived longer. Then since every time is a time when it is correct to say that he would have been happier if he had lived longer, we can say that every time is a time when he is harmed by dying young. This yields another way to defend the rejection of premises (1) and (2) (Feldman 2002). Many find this implausible (Bradley 2009, forthcoming).

According to a standard version of the "deprivation approach," a person's death may be bad for her, and worthy of fear, because her death deprives her of all the goods she would have enjoyed if she had lived longer (Nagel 1979). One difficulty for those who adopt the deprivation approach concerns the rationality of emotions. If we focus on "positive" harms, such as sufferings of pain, we might think that there is no problem about the rationality of our fear or hatred of harms. Thus, it might be quite rational for a certain prisoner to fear being sent to a foreign country to be tortured. After all, it might turn out to be a horrible experience. Some deprivations seem to be suitable objects for fear. For example, if someone threatens to steal my car, or to kidnap my child, then I may reasonably fear the threatened loss. But other instances of deprivation seem troublesome. Suppose I know quite well that I will not be granted magical powers, such as the power to fly. Suppose I believe (correctly, let us imagine) that as a result of not being able to fly, I will miss out on a remarkable sequence of very enjoyable experiences that I would have had if I had been granted the power to fly. Thus, not being granted the power to fly deprives me of some great goods. Yet it would be completely irrational for me to fear this deprivation, or to allow myself to fall into despair because of it. The question, then, is this: How are we to distinguish between (a) deprivations (such as those resulting from early death) that seem to merit a strong emotional response and (b) deprivations (such as those resulting from the failure to be given magical powers) that do not seem to merit a strong emotional response? Why is fear rational in one case but not in the other (Draper 1999, 2004)? This puzzle has not yet been satisfactorily solved.

Lucretius and the mirror of time

In a widely quoted passage in *On the Nature of Things*, Lucretius says:

> Look back at the eternity that passed before we were born, and mark how utterly it counts to us as nothing. This is a mirror that Nature holds up to us, in which we may see the time that shall be after we are dead. Is there anything terrifying in the sight – anything depressing – anything that is not more restful than the soundest sleep?
>
> (Lucretius 1965)

It seems pretty clear that Lucretius means to be presenting an argument here; and it seems pretty clear that the argument somehow involves the notion that there is nothing terrifying about the long stretch of non-existence that a person "suffered" before she was born. It also involves the notion that the long stretch of non-existence that a person will suffer after she dies is somehow the "mirror image" of that prenatal time. The conclusion is not precisely stated, but some have taken it to be this: it is irrational for a person to fear her own death.

Let us assume that the argument can be understood in this way:

(1) It would be irrational for a person to be emotionally upset about her prenatal non-existence.
(2) If it would be irrational for a person to be emotionally upset about her prenatal non-existence, then it would be irrational for a person to be emotionally upset about her post-mortem non-existence.
(3) Therefore, it would be irrational for a person to be emotionally upset about her post-mortem non-existence.

Replies to this argument take several forms. Some have (in effect) rejected (2). They have said that post-mortem times are not the mirror image of prenatal times. The failure of symmetry (it has been alleged) makes it irrational to fear prenatal non-existence, but allows it to be rational to fear post-mortem non-existence. One alleged difference between these two periods of time might be this: whereas those post-mortem times are times at which a person might have existed (after all, the person could have survived his disease; he could have died later), the prenatal times are not times at which the person might have existed (because he could not have been born earlier than he in fact was born) (Nagel 1979).

This sort of reply seems to turn on indefensible metaphysical assumptions about time and personal identity. As several critics have pointed out, even if a person essentially arose from the union of a specific sperm and egg, still it is metaphysically possible that that sperm and egg could have combined at an earlier date. This is especially clear in cases involving frozen sperm and egg that are chosen for *in vitro* fertilization. Such fertilizations may occur earlier or later, at the discretion of parents and doctors. If earlier fertilization had happened, the person would have come into existence earlier (Feldman 1991: 222; Breuckner and Fischer 1993: 215).

Others (e.g. Parfit 1984) have pointed out that we seem to care deeply about future harms and benefits, but to be nearly indifferent to past harms and benefits. The "amnesiac patient" example illustrates this. Suppose you wake up in a hospital. Your memory is a blank; you have no idea how you got there. The nurse informs you that either you had a very painful operation last night but have forgotten it as a result of some amnesia-inducing drugs, or else you will be getting a somewhat less painful operation later today. If you have the operation later today, you will get an amnesia-inducing drug and as a result you won't remember the pain afterwards. It seems perfectly natural for you to prefer that the painful operation be in the past and forgotten. This suggests that, other things being equal, we prefer that our pains be in the past – "over and done with." A corresponding thought experiment would suggest that we prefer that our pleasures be in the future.

These thoughts suggest a different way in which the future and the past are not mirror images of each other. We fear dying prematurely because we care about future pleasures. Failing to receive those pleasures seems to be contrary to our welfare. On the other hand, we don't care about having been born late because we don't care about any pleasures that we lost as a result of being born later than we might have been (Fischer 2006a, b; Breuckner and Fischer 1986, 1993).

Critics may acknowledge that in fact we do have the temporal bias that Parfit describes; but they may go on to say that this does not constitute a refutation of Lucretius's point. The point, after all, concerned the *rationality* of our attitudes. Lucretius seems to have claimed that in light of the metaphysical symmetry of past and future, there is no justification for our asymmetrical attitudes. He reminded us that it would be irrational to fear past non-existence. He wanted to know how, given the metaphysical symmetry of past and future, it could be rational to fear future non-existence while it is irrational to fear past non-existence. Merely pointing out that in fact we do have these asymmetrical attitudes seems not to be a reply at all (Kaufman 2009/1999).

A different sort of reply to Lucretius would involve rejecting premise (1). Perhaps we can agree that most of us are indifferent to the pleasures we lost as a result of being born too late. But we might claim that there would be nothing irrational about it if someone were distressed about these lost pleasures. Perhaps the bias toward the future is common but unjustified. Maybe it would be reasonable to be unhappy about all lost pleasures, whether past or future (see also McMahan 2006).

The conquest of death

Whether the fear of death is rational or not, it appears that this is a fear that people have experienced throughout history. Some religious traditions seem almost to be built upon this fear, since those traditions claim that true believers will gain a chance to evade death. For some it seems obvious that an eternal life would be vastly preferable to a short life followed by an endless stretch of non-existence.

Of course, no reasonable person would prefer an eternal life of suffering in hell. But what shall we say about an eternal life filled with typical earthly pleasures and pains? Would this be better than a finite life followed by non-existence? Those who fear and hate death apparently would prefer to go on living their ordinary lives no matter how old they may become. But is this preference rational?

Bernard Williams (1973) claimed that it is not obvious that eternal earthly life is an attractive prospect. After a sufficiently long time, the victim of eternal life would become bored. He would have done everything that a person with his tastes and preferences could possibly enjoy doing. It would be no fun to have to do it again. On the other hand, if he were to change his tastes and preferences, further enjoyment might be possible, but then it would be unclear whether the original person had survived. For with the imagined dramatic change in tastes and preferences, the previous person would have been transformed into a new person. Thus, if a given person retains his identity long enough, he will eventually become bored. Eternal life *for a persisting person* is thus seen to be unattractive.

Critics have pointed out two main problems with Williams' argument. First, it appears that Williams has underestimated the individual's capacity for growth. Surely a person can retain his identity while gradually coming to enjoy new experiences (Fischer 1994; Rosenberg 2006). Second, there seem to be some pleasures that enhance the value of life even when they have been repeated thousands of times. Surely a person might enjoy (for example) a fresh sexual encounter every day *forever*. Thus, while Williams may be right to point out that not every eternal life would be desirable, he seems to have gone too far when he claimed that every such life would have to become painfully boring.

The ethics of killing

Suppose we think, following Epicurus, that early death cannot harm a person. Suppose we think, following Lucretius, that early death is no more to be feared than late birth. Then we seem to put ourselves into an odd position with respect to killing. For if we can kill a person painlessly, and if his death will not make others unhappy, it is not clear why there would be anything wrong with killing him.

But this result is in direct conflict with a deeply entrenched component of common-sense morality. We all find something intuitively plausible about the idea that killing another person is morally impermissible. Of course, we recognize that there are some circumstances in which it may be morally permissible to kill another person – as, for example, in cases of justified self-defense when there is no other way to save oneself from a vicious criminal assault. Some philosophers maintain that while it is generally wrong to kill others, it may be morally permissible to kill oneself in order to avoid unremitting, pointless suffering. Others seem to think that it may be morally permissible to kill (or to allow to die) a person who has fallen into a horrible state in which continued existence is of great disvalue. This is especially compelling in the case of someone who repeatedly and emphatically has asked for help in ending his life. There are also questions about killing enemy combatants in a justified war and questions about executing convicted murderers, rapists, and traitors. But in the standard case not involving any of these exceptions, it seems wrong to kill people. This gives rise to a profound question: Precisely when (if ever) is it morally permissible to kill a person? To answer this question, it seems that we must answer a yet more fundamental question: When it is morally wrong to kill a person, precisely *why* is it wrong?

Some philosophers proceed as if they think that these questions about the morality of killing can be studied more-or-less in isolation, but a more reasonable assumption is that one's view about the morality of killing should be a corollary of one's view about the morality of behavior in general. If we don't know what makes actions in general wrong, it's hard to see how we can know what makes acts of killing wrong.

Act consequentialism of the simplest variety is the view that an action is morally right (permissible) if and only if no alternative would lead to a better outcome for all affected. This theory offers a simple explanation of the wrongness of killing, when it is wrong. According to the theory, it is wrong to kill someone (when it is wrong) precisely because killing him leads to an outcome that is on the whole worse than the outcome of some alternative course of behavior. Familiar examples involving killing have been thought to prove this view untenable. Consider a case in which several decent people are in need of organs for transplantation. If they get those organs, they and their friends will be happier. Suppose a healthy but not very happy person is available. Suppose he has very few friends. If he is killed and his organs are transplanted several others will be happy. Very few will be made unhappy. In this case, act consequentialism seems to imply that it would be morally permissible (even *obligatory*) to kill the innocent victim so as to keep several others alive. This implication is widely seen as repugnant, and so the act consequentialist approach has been rejected.

More extreme objections have been raised. It has been thought, for example, that act consequentialism implies that there is a moral obligation to kill any person whose unhappiness is dragging down the collective welfare level. It may appear that the community as a whole would be better off with such people out of the way, provided that it is possible to kill them painlessly (Henson 1971).

The theory also seems to imply, somewhat implausibly, that we have a moral obligation to bring new people into existence whenever the community as a whole will be better off with such people in existence. This obligation would persist even in cases in which the introduction of the new people would decrease the welfare of everyone already in existence, provided that the total welfare of the community as a whole (including the new people) would be increased. In response to cases of this sort, some have been moved to consider "person-affecting" forms of consequentialism. On these theories, the utility of an action is determined by the pleasures and pains of people who would exist whether the action is performed or not. Thus, the hypothetical pleasures of people who would be brought into existence if the action were performed, but who otherwise would never exist, would be disregarded. This sort of view faces new difficulties of its own. It seems to permit the creation of a new person who would lead a miserable life, provided that his introduction would make already existing people happier. Other versions of the person-affecting form of consequentialism have been proposed, but all are currently controversial (Arrhenius 2003; Roberts 2003).

Advocates of the deprivation approach may claim that acts of killing are wrong (when they are wrong) because they inflict serious harms of deprivation on their victims. This view is open to many objections. Suppose an innocent victim is being brutally attacked by a vicious killer. Suppose the victim can defend himself only by killing his attacker. But suppose that the attacker would be harmed by being thus killed. Surely in such a case it would be morally permissible for the victim to defend himself, even though such defense would impose a serious harm (early death) on the attacker. Harm to the one killed cannot be the sole determinant of the normative status of acts of killing.

Some have suggested (perhaps following Kant) that every person, merely in virtue of the fact that he is a person, deserves a certain sort of moral respect. Killing anyone is thus morally wrong because it inevitably involves a violation of that demand for respect.

When formulated in this stark way, this view seems to violate some very intuitive general principles about moral obligation in general. Consider a case in which some agent has a choice of killing one unfortunate person or another. He can't avoid killing someone or other. The view in question would then imply that the agent is doomed to do something morally wrong no matter what he does. Each alternative involves a violation of the alleged demand for respect. This seems to conflict with the well-grounded moral intuition that there is always something that morality permits. Perhaps morality permits whichever act would involve the smaller total amount of disrespect for humanity.

In some cases morality seems to require killing. For example, in an otherwise just war, military decision-makers may correctly see that on balance far more lives will be saved if a certain target is destroyed. They may foresee that innocent civilians will die as an undesired and unintended result of their attack. Yet for all that, it may still be the morally right thing for the military decision-makers to do. This seems to show that the moral status of an act of killing depends upon considerations beyond mere harm to the victim or respect for the victim's humanity.

We may imagine an eclectic view. Suppose we say, first, that harm to the victim constitutes one reason to avoid killing someone; but suppose we say, in addition, that harm to the community as a whole constitutes another reason to avoid killing someone. And suppose we say, furthermore, that potential violation of the demand for respect of persons is yet a third source of reasons to avoid killing. Each of these considerations, we may say, constitutes some defeasible reason to avoid killing. Each consideration may thus be seen as helping to make such acts of killing *prima facie* wrong. In any specific case, the overall moral status of an act of killing would be determined by the weights in that case of all of these factors (and perhaps others) somehow taken together (McMahan 1988, 2002).

While this approach may have the virtue of accommodating a variety of intuitions about the morality of killing, it confronts a serious objection. The view seems hardly more than a restatement of the problem rather than a solution. It reminds us that we have conflicting pre-theoretic intuitions about the morality of killing. It then tells us that the actual moral status of any act of killing is somehow determined by some unexplained interactions among the factors that pre-theoretically seemed relevant. This seems to leave us with precisely the problem with which we started. We still don't have any general account of what makes acts of killing all things considered wrong when they are wrong. We still don't have a helpful explanation of what makes acts of killing morally right in those unusual cases where they are morally right (if any).

It seems, then, that moral philosophers have not yet managed to explain clearly and precisely why it is wrong to kill people in those cases in which it is wrong.

See also Later ancient ethics (Chapter 5); Utilitarianism to Bentham (Chapter 13); John Stuart Mill (Chapter 16); Consequentialism (Chapter 37); Contemporary Kantian ethics (Chapter 38); Respect and recognition (Chapter 47); Ideals of perfection (Chapter 55); Rights (Chapter 56); Ending life (Chapter 60); Population ethics (Chapter 61); War (Chapter 67).

References

Arrhenius, Gustaf (2003) "The Person-Affecting Restriction, Comparativism, and the Moral Status of Potential People," *Ethical Perspectives* 10: 185–95.

Baker, Lynne (1999) "What Am I?" *Philosophy and Phenomenological Research* 59: 151–9.

——(2000) *Persons and Bodies: A Constitution View*, Cambridge: Cambridge University Press.

Bradley, Ben (2004) "When Is Death Bad for the One Who Dies?," *Noûs* 38: 1–28.

——(2009) *Well-Being and Death*, Oxford: Oxford University Press.

——(Forthcoming) "Eternalism and Death's Badness," in Joseph Campbell, Michael O'Rourke and Harry Silverstein (eds) *Time and Identity*, Cambridge, MA: MIT Press.

Brueckner, A. L. and Fischer, J. M. (1986) "Why Is Death Bad?," *Philosophical Studies* 50: 213–23.
——(1993) "The Asymmetry of Early Birth and Late Death," *Philosophical Studies* 71: 327–31.
Draper, Kai (1999) "Disappointment, Sadness, and Death,"*Philosophical Review* 108: 387–414.
——(2004) "Epicurean Equanimity Towards Death," *Philosophy and Phenomenological Research* 69: 92–114.
Epicurus (1994) *The Epicurus Reader: Selected Writings and Testimonia*, trans., ed. Brad Inwood and L. P. Gerson, Indianapolis, IN: Hackett.
Feit, Neil (2002) "The Time of Death's Misfortune," *Noûs* 36: 359–83.
Feldman, Fred (1991) "Some Puzzles About the Evil of Death," *Philosophical Review* 100: 205–27.
——(1992) *Confrontations with the Reaper: A Philosophical Study of the Nature and Value of Death*, New York: Oxford University Press.
——(2000) "The Termination Thesis," in Peter French and Howard Wettstein (eds) *Life and Death: Metaphysics and Ethics*, Special issue, *Midwest Studies in Philosophy* 24: 98–115.
——(2001) "What to Do About Dead People," in Dan Egonsson, Jonas Josefsson, Björn Petersson and Toni Ronnow-Rasmussen (eds) *Exploring Practical Philosophy: From Action to Values*, Aldershot, UK: Ashgate, pp. 41–58.
Fischer, John (ed.) (1993) *The Metaphysics of Death*, Stanford, CA: Stanford University Press.
——(1994) "Why Immortality Is Not So Bad," *International Journal of Philosophical Studies* 2: 257–70.
——(1997) "Death, Badness, and the Impossibility of Experience," *Journal of Ethics* 1: 341–53.
——(2006a) "Epicureanism about Death and Immortality," *Journal of Ethics* 10: 355–81.
——(2006b) "Earlier Birth and Later Death," in McDaniel et al. 2006, pp. 189–201.
Henson, R. G. (1971) "Utilitarianism and the Wrongness of Killing," *Philosophical Review* 80: 320–37.
Johansson, Jens (2005) *Mortal Beings: On the Metaphysics and Value of Death*, Stockholm: Almqvist & Wiksell International.
Kaufman, Frederik (2009/1999) "Pre-Vital and Post-Mortem Nonexistence," in David Benatar (ed.) *Life, Death, and Meaning: Key Philosophical Readings on the Big Questions*, 2nd edn, Lanham, MD: Rowman & Littlefield, pp. 241–64; originally published in *American Philosophical Quarterly* 36, no. 1 (January 1999): 1–19.
Lucretius (1965) *On the Nature of Things*, trans., introduction and notes by Russell Geer, New York: Bobbs-Merrill.
Mackie, D. (1999) "Personal Identity and Dead People," *Philosophical Studies* 95: 219–42.
McDaniel, Kris, Raibley, Jason, Feldman, Richard and Zimmerman, Michael (eds) (2006) *The Good, the Right, Life and Death: Essays in Honor of Fred Feldman*, Burlington, VT: Ashgate.
McMahan, Jeff (1988) "Death and the Value of Life," *Ethics* 99: 32–61.
——(2002) *The Ethics of Killing: Problems at the Margins of Life*, New York: Oxford University Press.
——(2006) "The Lucretian Argument," in McDaniel et al. 2006, pp. 213–26.
Nagel, Thomas (1979) *Mortal Questions*, New York: Cambridge University Press.
Olsen, E. T. (1997) *The Human Animal: Personal Identity without Psychology*, New York and Oxford: Oxford University Press.
——(2004) "Animalism and the Corpse Problem," *Australasian Journal of Philosophy* 82: 265–74.
Parfit, Derek (1984) *Reasons and Persons*, New York: Oxford University Press.
Roberts, Melinda (2003) "Is the Person-Affecting Intuition Paradoxical?," *Theory and Decision* 55: 1–44.
Rosenbaum, Stephen (1993) "How to Be Dead and Not Care: A Defense of Epicurus," *American Philosophical Quarterly* 23: 217–25; repr. in Fischer 1993, pp. 119–34.
Rosenberg, Jay (1998) *Thinking Clearly about Death*, Indianapolis, IN: Hackett.

——(2006) "Reassessing Immortality: The Makropulos Case Revisited," in McDaniel et al. 2006, pp. 227–40.

Silverstein, Harry (1980) "The Evil of Death," *The Journal of Philosophy* 77: 401–24.

Williams, Bernard (1973) "The Makropulos Case: Reflections on the Tedium of Immortality," in *Problems of the Self*, Cambridge: Cambridge University Press; repr. in Fischer 1993, pp. 73–92.

Further reading

Benatar, David (ed.) (2004) *Life, Death, & Meaning: Key Philosophical Readings on the Big Questions*, Lanham, MD: Rowman & Littlefield.

Bradley, Ben, Feldman, Fred and Johansson, Jens (eds) (Forthcoming) *Oxford Handbook of Death and Philosophy* Oxford: Oxford University Press.

Campbell, Joseph, O'Rourke, Michael and Silverstein, Harry (eds) (Forthcoming) *Time and Identity*, Cambridge, MA: MIT Press.

Fischer, John (ed.) (1993) *The Metaphysics of Death*, Stanford, CA: Stanford University Press.

French, Peter and Wettstein, Howard (eds) (2000) *Midwest Studies in Philosophy*, Vol. 24: *Life and Death: Metaphysics and Ethics*, Malden, MA: Blackwell.

McDaniel, Kris, Raibley, Jason, Feldman, Richard and Zimmerman, Michael (eds) (2006) *The Good, the Right, Life and Death: Essays in Honor of Fred Feldman*, Burlington, VT: Ashgate.

60
ENDING LIFE

R. G. Frey

A part of life is death. For some years, concerns at the beginning of life, typically to do with serious disease in or radical deformity to the fetus or infant, brought into prominence discussion of abortion and, to a lesser extent, infanticide. More recently, concerns at the end of life, typically to do with serious disease, radical deterioration in the quality of life, and permanently vegetative states, have brought into prominence discussions of suicide, physician-assisted suicide, and euthanasia. All of these topics, of course, involve the taking of life and require, philosophically, some statement of the reasons for and against this taking. They have become battlegrounds for the playing out of certain kinds of consequentialist reasoning over intending and causing or bringing about death.

Suicide is the intentional ending of one's own life. Often, the person is gravely and terminally ill and, in modern settings, either in hospital or under a doctor's care. Of course, there remains the possibility that a patient can store up pills and then take a lethal dose to end their existence, though this still, to some, has an unsavory aspect to it. But in modern medical settings the most direct way of ending one's own life is simply to refuse treatment.

We value autonomy, and autonomously choosing to refuse treatment, either by word of mouth or by advanced directive, is part of what we think of as choosing how to live. To have a doctor impose his view or a hospital to impose its view of whether we should continue to live appears a direct violation of our autonomy. Surely we should have a say in the matter! It is not uncommon for others to oppose one's decision to refuse treatment or, if treatment has begun, to terminate treatment; they urge that one is (mentally) ill or, much more commonly, depressed and so is unable to think clearly about the matter. Psychiatric intervention is urged on all sides, as a matter of course. But it is no longer obvious, if it ever was, that one cannot rationally decide that one does not wish to live with pancreatic cancer and so endure the life to which that disease condemns one. This is certainly true in the case of progressively degenerative diseases, such as amyotrophic lateral sclerosis, where one can detect the creeping yet inexorable deterioration in one's condition. To say to someone that they must live out the life to which disease has condemned them or to insist that such a person must always be deranged in their thinking or depressed seems, all other things being equal, a direct assault on their autonomy.

Euthanasia is the intentional ending of another's life from a benevolent or kind motive. Again, the person is typically gravely and terminally ill. But, as with suicide, in contemporary debates over the morality of these activities, the person need not be in imminent danger of dying. They simply do not wish to continue to live the life to which disease and illness have condemned them. Accordingly, they require assistance in dying. Obviously, to those who object to the intrusion of quality-of-life concerns into a discussion of ending life, the fact that a life has plummeted in quality to a disastrous extent does not provide a reason for seeking to end it. One must live it out, whatever its quality, with whatever ameliorative possibilities that are available, even though one does not wish to live it out and even though the life to which those possibilities further condemn one, such as morphine addiction and mental disorientation, are themselves anathema to the individual. Before going further it is necessary to comment on several associated lines of argument.

Can we mark off genuine moral differences between cases by distinguishing between intending death and merely foreseeing death, as a side effect of one's act? This question has proved central to the moral debate over taking life; it is the main concern in the debate over the viability of the doctrine of double effect, and it is, when allied with an array of concerns to do with whether the act/omission and active/passive distinctions are morally significant ones, part of the killing/letting die debate. Generally speaking, consequentialists dispute the moral significance of these distinctions. With a patient who has received ever larger doses of morphine to relieve pain, suppose a doctor now proposes to administer the minimum dosage necessary to relieve pain, in the (practically certain) knowledge, however, that that dosage will likely prove fatal through respiratory depression or at least hasten death: Is the doctor's act permissible? To some, it is, since the doctor intends the relief of pain, not death, and only foresees as a side effect of his act that death will occur or be hastened. If the doctor came to intend the death, either as end or as means, she would be held to have murdered her patient. So, some want to distinguish between the doctor's intentionally killing her patient and her knowingly bringing about her patient's death.

Consequentialists dispute that any such distinction can be drawn; in both cases, the patient ends up dead as the result of causal steps that the doctor takes. If the doctor injects the morphine and "brings about" his patient's death, that death cannot be attributed to accident, mistake, or ignorance; it is in part the result of the doctor's choice to inject the morphine and he is a causal agent in the patient's death. The choice by the doctor to administer the drug cannot be ignored, since it in part determines what happened to the patient. And this is true, even if the patient's death forms no part of the doctor's intention. It is not the case that the only way morality can be injected into the doctor's case is through what he intends; for that fails to take account of the fact that the patient's death is brought about by the doctor. Unplugging ventilators, turning off machines, etc., are all things that the doctor does, in the course of bringing about the patient's death.

Similarly, withdrawing treatment or food and hydration is something the doctor does. It is sometimes said (for example, by most state medical and legal authorities in the United States) that a doctor may not permissibly supply the means of death to a competent, informed patient who is terminally ill, who has voluntarily requested the doctor's assistance in dying, and whose request has survived depression therapy. Yet, the doctor may, it is claimed (by these same medical and legal authorities), withdraw food and hydration if, say, the patient makes a valid refusal of further treatment. Consequentialists do not concede a moral difference between these cases. The doctor can supply a pill and produce death or she can withdraw feeding tubes and produce death; how can one be permissible and the other not? Causally, the doctor appears to be a factor in the patient's death in both cases. Moreover, in the withdrawal case as described, the patient's autonomous, voluntary decision to forgo treatment is not the only morally or causally relevant fact; for death is only produced if the doctor withdraws feeding tubes. Nor in this case can it be maintained that what kills the patient is his underlying illness; he dies, not of this illness, but through starvation, as the result of withdrawal of the feeding tube. What one causes is relevant to one's moral responsibility. To be sure, we may want the doctor to pay attention to the patient's autonomous, voluntary decision to forgo further treatment, but this does not mean that withdrawing feeding tubes did not help cause the death by starvation. So the contrast suggested, between supplying pills that produce death and withdrawing feeding tubes, is not thus far a substantive one, so far as causality is concerned. Nor need it be substantive with regard to intention; for the pill may be supplied by the doctor not with the intention that the patient decide to take it and die but merely for comfort, as the patient realizes he always has it available to him, should he come to feel its necessity. So withdrawal of feeding tubes does not form an alternative to supplying pills, either causally or morally.

Importantly, the alleged contrast between supplying the pills and withdrawal of treatment needs to be seen in a certain light. If the patient decides to take the pills, he commits suicide, whereas if he refuses treatment (and insists that the doctor honor his refusal by withdrawal of feeding tubes), he also commits suicide. Why, if suicide is permissible, is one way of committing suicide more acceptable than another? If suicide is not permissible, then the one case cannot be used by way of contrast to the other.

We can now apply these causal points directly to our discussion of euthanasia and physician-assisted suicide. Three distinctions are typically observed in the discussion of euthanasia. First, active euthanasia involves taking steps to end a life; passive euthanasia involves taking no steps to save a life and/or withdrawing treatment. The former is deeply objectionable to many, whereas the latter is a not infrequent occurrence in our hospitals. Turning off a ventilator in a patient whose further treatment is deemed futile is said to be a passive death, whereas supplying a patient with pills which she takes and ends her life is said to be an active death. The former is said to be permissible, the latter to be impermissible. But, as our earlier discussion has shown, the patient will die if a large enough dose of morphine is injected, in the attempt to relieve pain, but the patient will also die if her ventilator is turned off or her feeding tubes are removed. In the case of this patient whose further treatment is held to be futile, what is the moral difference among these ways of producing death? In none of these cases is it true that the patient's underlying illness kills them; in the morphine case, what kills them is respiratory depression, in the ventilator case, suffocation, and in the feeding tubes case, starvation.

It is held by some that, if a doctor intentionally kills her patient, she is a causal agent in the patient's death, whereas if she knowingly brings about her patient's death, she is not a causal agent in that death. If she is not a cause of death, she cannot through causation be, even in part, morally responsible for a death. But in the morphine, ventilator, and withdrawal cases we are dealing with positive actions on the doctor's part (not, for example, with omissions on her part). The patient may request and consent to what is done, but that does not mean that the doctor does not do the injecting, unhooking, withdrawing, etc. It just means that, while the doctor is a causal factor in the patient's death, we think her moral reasons for causing what she did pass muster. Consent here goes towards establishing that the doctor had no moral responsibility, though her patient ends up dead; it does not go towards establishing that she was not a causal factor in that death.

Second, a distinction can be drawn between voluntary, involuntary, and non-voluntary forms of euthanasia. In voluntary euthanasia, the steps taken to end life are taken with the consent of the patient and often at their request; in involuntary euthanasia, the steps taken are not taken with the patient's consent, are not taken at their request, and, indeed, may even be something they would reject; and in non-voluntary euthanasia, the steps taken to end life are taken in connection with someone deemed by the appropriate authorities to be incompetent and whose trustee is authorized to consent or not to consent to what is proposed to be done. Involuntary and non-voluntary euthanasia are typically not held to be live options in ethical debate. The fear that allowing voluntary euthanasia might lead to these, through a slippery slope, is debatable, since in all cases where active voluntary euthanasia has been implemented, as in the Netherlands and in the state of Oregon, safeguards have been implemented to prevent involuntary and non-voluntary euthanasia.

Third, a distinction can be drawn between physician-assisted suicide and euthanasia. The distinction is to be drawn in terms of who acts last, causally; in physician-assisted suicide, the patient acts last; in active voluntary euthanasia, the doctor.

Physician-assisted suicide is a form of suicide; if one objects to suicide, one will object to this variety of it. But if one does not object to suicide, there appears to be no difference between producing one's death by refusing treatment (say, through withdrawal) and producing one's death through swallowing pills provided by another.

Now it is sometimes maintained, by medical authorities and others that withdrawal of food and hydration is a permissible alternative to physician-assisted suicide and active voluntary euthanasia. The crux of this permissibility lies in the claim that the doctor is not, in the first alternative, but is in the second and third alternatives, responsible for a death. I take the essence of this opposition to amount to the claim that a doctor may not permissibly supply the means of death to a competent, informed patient who is terminally ill, who has voluntarily requested the doctor's assistance in dying, and whose request has survived depression therapy. Yet, these very same opponents insist that, while the doctor cannot supply the pill, he can withdraw food and hydration if, e.g., the patient makes a valid refusal of further treatment. Death ensues. Notice, then, that the case is unlike some ventilator cases, where the patient sometimes survives withdrawal. Starvation inevitably kills the patient. Thus, by withdrawing feeding tubes, the doctor must at the very least be prepared that starvation overtake and kill his patient. Since withdrawal and ensuing starvation would be painful in this case, a sedative is administered, and withdrawal takes place while the patient is under its effect. (This is what is called in the popular press "terminal sedation.")

Plainly, what doctors who support withdrawal of feeding tubes but not physician-assisted suicide or active voluntary euthanasia want is that, in the former case, they be held not to be legally or morally responsible for the patient's death. However, even if a particular jurisdiction were legally to permit withdrawal or even require it (if the patient's refusal were valid) we have not thereby settled the moral issue. Legally, it may be permissible for a doctor to withdraw feeding tubes under certain conditions, but we would not thereby have settled the issue of whether, if he does, he is partially morally responsible for a death. Nor can the case be construed as one in which, if the patient refuses further treatment, the doctor is, as it were, not present. The doctor, of course, is present, and only if he withdraws feeding tubes does the patient die of starvation. In fact, the doctor's act of withdrawal is morally significant; it helps cause the patient's death. So the only way a doctor can claim to be neither legally nor morally responsible for a death in the withdrawal case is if he can show, *per impossible*, that he is not a cause, either wholly or partly, of the patient's death. Put differently, the causal relation in which the withdrawal of feeding tubes stands to death may be held to be different from the causal relation in which the supply of the pill stands to death; but this differing causal relation, given that morality is in question, cannot consist in the claim that the law permits withdrawal, because that does not show that withdrawal does not cause death.

Again, were we to ask in this case "How did starvation come to kill this patient?," it would obviously be relevant to mention the patient's valid refusal of further treatment, and it would obviously be relevant to mention as well, if, indeed, it turns out to be the case, that in the particular jurisdiction in question the law demands that the doctor take this valid refusal seriously. But the death of this patient is produced by starvation only if the doctor withdraws feeding tubes. To pretend that the doctor's act of withdrawal is not part of this general picture of the outcome in this patient's case is to wrongly characterize the case.

In using causal responsibility for a death to get at moral responsibility for a death, we do not cast guilt upon the doctor. We simply affirm that what one causes to occur in the world is relevant to what one is morally responsible for. Of course, we want the doctor to take seriously the autonomous, voluntary decision of the patient to refuse further treatment and to take seriously as well the various laws pertaining to the case in her jurisdiction, and we think well of her if she does these things. But the fact that we do not think ill of her does not settle the issue of whether withdrawing feeding tubes caused death by starvation. Notice two further points. First, the doctor's intention in withdrawing feeding tubes may be relevant to further things we want to say about her act, but that intention, whatever it is, does not affect the issue of whether the doctor's act of withdrawal of feeding tubes caused death by withdrawal. Second, the patient's consent to this withdrawal goes towards the issue of whether a moral (and legal) charge should be brought against the doctor for doing to the patient something that he did not want done; it does not go to the issue of whether the withdrawal of feeding tubes causes death. In sum, there is no substantive moral or causal difference between the withdrawal and pills cases, so that withdrawal is not an alternative to physician-assisted suicide or active voluntary euthanasia.

It is important to distinguish withdrawing cases of the above sort from a withholding case of a certain kind and for an important reason. Suppose a competent, informed patient, exercising a valid refusal of treatment, instructs their physician that, should they fall into a certain condition, they do not want food and hydration given them in an attempt to sustain them. Here, should the patient now fall into that condition, the doctor honors the patient's autonomy not by withdrawing treatment but by withholding treatment. The patient's instruction to the doctor goes towards explaining and justifying why the doctor withheld treatment, and it seems obvious to many that the case is one of the patient and the doctor cooperating to produce the death of the patient. But withholding is a form of omitting or refraining from action, and it might be asked how failing to act on the doctor's part can be regarded causally in just the way that, above, acting on his part has been regarded. This raises the important issue of whether omissions are causes, an issue that lies far beyond any discussion here of end-of-life cases. Yet, it is easy to see why that discussion is crucial here. For if asked what produced the patient's death in the present case, it seems evident that the patient's instruction to the doctor and the doctor's withholding treatment as a result of that instruction are the explanation, so that the patient's death can be viewed as occurring as a cooperative outcome on the part of the patient and the doctor This makes withholding appear as a part cause of a death, or, at the very least, as having a hand in producing death. Notice here, too, that it falsely describes the situation to suggest that in this withholding case it is as if the doctor is not there, that the patient's instruction to the doctor is alone what determines the outcome. This is not the case: the doctor must honor the patient's instruction to him. (If that instruction takes the form of an advanced directive, he must honor it. And it must not be assumed that there cannot be reason on the doctor's part to hesitate: if he thinks, as the result of conversation with his patient, that the patient changed her mind over her advanced directive, the doctor might hesitate before honoring it.)

Slippery-slope concerns always arise in discussions of taking life, and it may be held that, if we permit certain instances of physician-assisted suicide or active voluntary euthanasia, we shall descend the slope of taking life to some unthinkable abyss. One needs to present arguments about what compels us, despite safeguards, to descend such a slope and why safeguards are always thought to be inadequate, no matter how they are drawn. Interestingly, the legislation in the Netherlands and Oregon permitting assisted suicide has not produced a great rush to make use of it, nor has there been a great rush either to extend such legislation to include involuntary and non-voluntary euthanasia. But this does not mean that we do not need to be sensitive to consequentialist arguments of the slippery-slope variety. For suppose we allow physician-assisted suicide and that the procedure is put into operation as the result of a competent, informed patient requesting assistance in dying; suppose further that in the present case the person becomes incapacitated before they can request assistance; can we cite the patient's best interests and resort to active non-voluntary euthanasia? This, of course, will no longer be a case of physician-assisted suicide or active voluntary euthanasia, but it shows why sensitivity to slippery-slope concerns is important. Of course, this kind of case is particularly vexing, since there are likely to be cases in which we allow duly appointed trustees or surrogates for people to make vital decisions for them, as well as cases in which we want to take into account the "best interests" of patients in deciding their treatment, where we can no longer consult these patients as to their "best interests." But where the choice by the trustee or surrogate is one of death for the patient, we exercise great caution.

Increasingly, in discussion of end-of-life cases, two principles thus far not mentioned are frequently cited as worthy of helping to determine our views of these cases. One is the claim that we should be allowed to die with dignity. Here, the driving thought seems to be an image of someone forced to live out a life in a condition in which they do not want to live. Sometimes, this image is made to depend upon the presence of serious pain and suffering, but, increasingly, the image takes a different form. Suppose one has contracted the AIDS virus and the virus has moved into the full-blown illness: one decides that one does not want to live with all the ancillary illnesses and ultimately unpalatable death that that implies. So, while one is still able to take action, one arranges for one's death or insists upon one's right to refuse further treatment or makes out an advanced directive that instructs one's trustee to have all treatment stopped at a certain juncture. What in this sort of case, dying with dignity seems to mean has not so much to do with pain and suffering as with having one's wishes satisfied, and this is a version of having one's autonomy recognized. To exercise one's autonomy in life is in part to exercise it over one's death, and a part of exercising it in the cases being discussed is to have other people recognize and take heed of our wishes. To be sure, some regard this kind of image as one of autonomy run wild, as if it were a value that had been inflated into a super value, dwarfing all others; but those who think this usually think that our lives are not things we have the right to decide to end.

Second, and even more controversially, with the advent of quality-of-life concerns has come discussion of someone having a life "not worth living." For those in sympathy with these concerns, the value of a life is a function of its quality, and the quality of life is a function of a life's content. Some lives lack the scope and capacities for richness of life that make other lives so extraordinary, and this issue of content can reach such desperate levels as we find in the lives of anencephalic infants, those fully in the grip of Alzheimer's disease, and those in a permanently vegetative state, where even the capacities for having a rich life are impaired or, worse yet, missing. The result is that such lives on a quality-of-life view of the value of a life are judged to be of deficient quality and so of deficient value, as compared with the lives of ordinary people. This clashes radically with the principle, espoused by many, of the equal value of all human lives, whatever their quality. The equal-value view can seem difficult to accept, when we come across lives so deficient in quality that virtually everyone would seek to avoid them. Nor is it made more plausible, as we find people who are condemned to live out such lives often asking for release from them, through physician-assisted suicide or active voluntary euthanasia. In such cases, it is not other people saying to someone "your life is not worth living"; it is the person whose life it is saying "I no longer want to live this life to which illness has condemned me."

Of course, the equal-value view of the value of life was dominant when medical and ethical discussions all took place under a religious umbrella; for we could say of all lives, whatever their quality, that they were equal in the eyes of God. But if such discussions no longer take place under such an umbrella, in whose eyes are all lives equal? We see tragic lives all around us, lives whose quality has plummeted to terrible depths; we see what they once were but what, through Huntington's disease or cancer or senile dementia, they have become. The unequal value of lives, however, seems almost inevitably to put some very deficient lives at risk. Obviously, what counts as "very deficient" is open to challenge, as we see today among the physically handicapped, who do not see themselves as "disadvantaged." But an elderly person fully in the grip of Alzheimer's disease, who has lost meaningful sense of who they are, or a person who has fallen into a permanently vegetative state, who has lost, so far as we know, experience of the world, or an anencephalic infant, who never has had nor ever will have experience of the world, all seem far beyond the kinds of lives we think of as of equal value to normal human lives. Of these lives, it is common in private conversation for people to say that they "would not want to live like that."

One often encounters the view that some life is better than no life, that some life of however deficient quality is better than no life at all; so even if unequal-value views were to be acceptable, there would still be protection for lives of radically deficient quality. Life is a good, and any of it, under whatever condition, is better than none of it. So, when a person decides to end their life, because they no longer want to live a life of that quality, they make a kind of error. But this is simply to insist that life, not quality of life, is what is crucially important. Suppose we could add ten additional years to the life of a person fully in the grip of Alzheimer's disease: far from this being a good, it could be seen as cruel, as adding to the already dreadful burden on that life. More is not better.

See also Consequentialism (Chapter 37); Contemporary Kantian ethics (Chapter 38); Rights (Chapter 56); Life, death, and ethics (Chapter 59).

Further reading

Beauchamp, Tom L. (ed.) (1996) *Intending Death: The Ethics of Assisted Suicide and Euthanasia*, Englewood Cliffs, NJ: Prentice-Hall.

Dworkin, Gerald, Frey, R. G. and Bok, Sissela (1998) *Euthanasia and Physician-Assisted Suicide*, Cambridge: Cambridge University Press.

Kamm, Frances (1993) *Morality, Mortality*, vol. 1: *Death and Whom to Save from It*, Oxford: Oxford University Press.

Rachels, James (1986) *The End of Life: Euthanasia and Morality*, Oxford: Oxford University Press.

Singer, Peter (1996) *Rethinking Life and Death: The Collapse of Traditional Ethics*, New York, St. Martin's Press.

——(2002) *Unsanctifying Human Life*, ed. Helga Kuhse, Oxford: Blackwell.

Tooley, Michael (2007) "Physician-Assisted Suicide and Voluntary Euthanasia," in C. Wellman and A. Cohen (eds) *Contemporary Debates in Applied Ethics*, Oxford: Blackwell, pp. 87–105.

(iv)

OUR WORLD

61
POPULATION ETHICS

Tim Mulgan

Population ethics brings together abstract value theory, practical ethics, economics, and public policy. Population ethics is often joined with the ethics of individual reproduction into a single topic: obligations to future generations. This chapter seeks to provide a taste of the relevant issues and approaches in contemporary philosophical population ethics.

This chapter comprises three sections. The first deals with the optimum population problem, with a focus on utilitarian value theory. The second deals with practical issues in population policy, with a focus on the issue of coercion. The final section deals with the impact of an inter-generational dimension on political philosophy, with a focus on the social contract tradition.

The pure optimum-population problem

There are two optimum-population problems, which we might call the pure and the practical. These concern, respectively, the comparative evaluation of (logically) possible worlds, and of (practically) possible futures. Moral philosophers who discuss optimum population often focus on the pure problem. They seek a general account of what makes one possible population more valuable than another. Suppose you could create any possible world, with any possible population. Which should you choose? The answer to this abstract question can then be combined with practical information to generate policy advice. On the other hand, as we will see, some philosophers regard this abstract question – along with the whole idea of a pure optimal population – as an irrelevant and dangerous distraction.

Most discussion of the optimum-population problem has taken place within the utilitarian ethical tradition. Because they base morality on the maximization of happiness, utilitarians obviously need to know what counts as "the greatest happiness of the greatest number." Utilitarians need a *theory of aggregation* – taking us from the values of individual lives to the value of a population as a whole. The prominence of the optimum-population problem in the philosophical literature is due to the prominence of utilitarianism itself in the philosophical landscape. As far as possible, when constructing a theory of aggregation, utilitarians seek to remain neutral as to the nature of happiness. In these discussions, "happiness" is often used as a generic placeholder – it refers to whatever makes life worth living.

Utilitarians focus on two contrasting approaches to aggregation.

The total view. One outcome is better than another if and only if it contains a greater total amount of happiness.
The average view. One outcome is better than another if and only if it contains a higher average level of happiness.

The total view is the simplest theory of aggregation. It has been the most popular account of value in the utilitarian tradition. (At least among philosophers. Economists often favor the average view.) The basic argument for the total view is simple. If we value happiness, then presumably we should aim to produce as much happiness as possible.

Unfortunately, the total view has problems. The most famous of these is highlighted by Derek Parfit (1984). Parfit distinguishes two kinds of moral choice. In a *same-people choice* our actions affect what will happen to people in the future, but not who will exist. If our actions do affect who will come to exist, then we are making a *different-people choice*.

Parfit also distinguishes two kinds of different-people choices: *same number* (where our choice affects who exists, but not how many people exist), and *different number* (where we decide how many people ever exist). This second distinction is especially relevant for population ethics, because most puzzles in population ethics arise in different number choices – where the total and average views diverge.

Parfit argues that the total view implies the following:

> *The repugnant conclusion*. For any possible population of at least ten billion people, all with a very high quality of life, there must be some much larger imaginable population whose existence, if other things are equal, would be better, even though its members have lives that are barely worth living.
> (Parfit 1984: 388)

To see why the total view implies the repugnant conclusion, begin with a world where ten billion people all have extremely good lives. Call it *A*. Imagine a second world, with twice as many people, each of whom is more than half as happy as the people in *A*. Call this new world *B*. Total happiness in *B* exceeds that in *A*. Now repeat this process until we reach a world where a vast population of people each have a life that is barely worth living. Call this world *Z*. As each step increases total happiness, *Z* must be better than *A*.

Parfit finds this conclusion "intrinsically repugnant" (Parfit 1984: 390). If this is a consequence of the total view, then the total view is unacceptable. The repugnant conclusion is one of the organizing problems of contemporary philosophical population ethics – most philosophers begin their discussions by saying how they will deal with it. They either reject Parfit's intuition that A is better than Z (in those cases where the total view prefers Z to A), or they reject the total view.

Some philosophers reject intuitions altogether. What does it matter if a conclusion "appears" repugnant, so long as it follows from well-established premises? However, it is difficult to see what could justify those premises other than a moral intuition of some kind. Other philosophers defend the total view by rejecting all intuitions regarding large numbers. John Broome says: "We have no reason to trust anyone's intuitions about very large numbers, however excellent their philosophy. Even the best philosophers cannot get an intuitive grasp of, say, tens of billions of people" (Broome 2004: 57–8). Broome doesn't think we should abandon population ethics – or abandon moral intuitions altogether. We should rely instead on a *theory* built on our everyday intuitions. That theory is the total view.

An even less radical response is to reject Parfit's particular intuition. For instance, Yew-Kwan Ng objects that, when we consider the repugnant conclusion, we privilege our own perspective and are guilty of "misplaced partiality" (Ng 1989). We picture the A-lives as similar to our own, and imagine the A-people choosing between A and Z. If we were more impartial, we might see that Z contains more total value than A, and is thus better.

Alternatively, we might reconsider the repugnant conclusion by examining the Z-world more closely. By definition, the Z-lives are just worth living. So we need to know what such lives are like. On the total view, we should create an extra life whenever doing so would raise the total happiness. Setting aside the impact on already existing people, we raise total happiness if and only if the extra life itself is worth living. If we imagine a numerical scale of well-being, then the lives in Z must be above zero. If the zero level is higher than Parfit thinks, then the Z-lives may be better than his discussion suggests.

Parfit himself describes the Z-lives as consisting of nothing but muzak and potatoes. If they are *human* lives, then it is natural to suppose that such lives also contain negative elements – such as boredom, frustration, or lack of accomplishment and friendship. These features reduce the value of a life. A friendless underachieving human is badly off in a way that a friendless slug is not. We may well feel that a muzak-and-potatoes life is well *below* zero.

Think about what it means to say that a life is "barely worth living," as the Z-lives are meant to be. This phrase can evocate a life of frustration and pain – one that we would rather not live at all. But, if the Z-lives are like *that*, then the total view does not conclude that Z is better than A. Rather, Z (as pictured by Parfit) will be much *worse* than A. So the *real* Z-lives must be much better than Parfit says.

Some philosophers distinguish two values of a life: its *general* value and its *personal* value. Personal value is the value of a life to the person who lives it; while general value is that amount that a life increases the value of a state of affairs in which that life is lived. The general zero level may be higher than the personal zero. A person's life could then be worth living from her point of view, but not good enough to ensure that adding her life increases the value of the world. To reach the general zero level, a life would have to be very good in personal terms. Z would then be a world where each person's life was well worth living, from her own perspective.

Utilitarians who reject the total view need an alternative account of aggregation. The most popular has been the average view. This easily avoids the repugnant conclusion, as A has a higher average happiness than Z.

We begin with an obvious objection. If we average over everyone *alive in the future*, then the average view tells us to kill anyone whose happiness is below average. We should then kill anyone below the new average and so on – until two people remain and the happier one should kill the other. To avoid this repellent consequence, we must average over *all those who will ever live*. Killing someone merely makes their life go worse; it does not make it the case that they never existed. Killing *lowers* the average – unless it improves the welfare of the person killed.

Unfortunately, the average view faces real problems of its own. One of the most discussed is the following:

> *The hermit problem.* Everyone in the cosmos is extremely happy. On a distant uninhabited planet, we create a new person. His life, while very good, is slightly below the cosmic average.

The average view says that we have made things worse. It also says that what we ought to do depends on the happiness of people in distant corners of the cosmos, with whom our hermit will never interact – as the value of those distant lives affects the cosmic average. Both claims seem intuitively implausible. As Parfit puts it, the *mere addition* of lives worth living cannot make things worse (Parfit 1984: 420).

Another popular alternative among contemporary philosophers is the *lexical view*. Suppose you enjoy both Mozart and muzak. Someone offers you a choice between one day of Mozart and as much muzak as you like. You opt for the former, because *no amount* of muzak could match the smallest amount of Mozart. Philosophers would say you believe that Mozart is *lexically superior* to muzak.

We can use lexicality to avoid the repugnant conclusion. Suppose the creatures in A and Z belong to different species. Perhaps A contains flourishing human beings while Z is full of slugs. Lexicality seems plausible here, as it says that ten billion human lives are more valuable than any number of slug lives.

The most pressing question for any lexical account is where to draw the line. How do we decide that some possible lives are lexically more important than others?

The philosophical literature contains many other theories of aggregation. However, these all face problems similar to those affecting the three theories we have discussed. Some philosophers conclude that it is impossible to construct an intuitively plausible theory, because our intuitions themselves are inconsistent. The pure population problem cannot be solved. One focus of debate is Parfit's *mere addition paradox*, which shows that we cannot avoid the repugnant conclusion and at the same time claim that the mere addition of happy lives never makes things worse (Parfit 1984: 419–41).

All these problems arise because we seek to rank all possible worlds on a single objective scale of betterness. Some philosophers propose relativized models of value, where we evaluate different possible worlds relative to the interests of the people who live in them. This can yield the result that *A* is better than *B* (from the perspective of those who live in *A*) while *B* is also better than *A* (from the perspective of those who live in *B*) (Dasgupta 1994; Roberts 2002).

Some utilitarians would defend the shift to relativist models by appealing to a *person-affecting restriction*. Instead of seeking to maximize happiness as an end-in-itself, utilitarians should focus on the impact of their actions on the happiness of particular individuals. One situation is better than another if and only if it is better for persons. Instead of asking what population is best *per se*, we should seek the best population for those who exist.

One set of problems for the person-affecting restriction arises from another puzzle due to Parfit:

> *The non-identity problem*. Not only do our decisions affect what will happen to people in the future, they also affect which people (if any) will exist. When choosing a population policy for our society, we face a different people choice, as different policies bring different people into existence.
> (Parfit 1984: 351–79)

Some argue that non-identity undermines the person-affecting approach. If different people exist in different possible futures, then we cannot compare those futures from the point of view of the people who will exist – as this would require us to compare existence with non-existence from the point of view of a particular person. This is impossible, as it makes no sense to ask what it would be like to have never existed. These philosophers conclude that we can only compare possible futures from the point of view of those who exist *now*. But this would give the present generation free rein to despoil the environment in pursuit of their own happiness. Therefore, we must return to impersonal theories such as the total view or the average view.

Others reply that we *can* compare different possible futures from the point of view of those who will exist – *even if* different futures contain different people.

Phrases such as "the British people of the twenty-second century" can be used to refer to whoever is alive then and there. We can then see that a future with clear air and drinkable water is better *for those people* than one without.

We introduced the person-affecting restriction as a variation within a utilitarian framework. But it can also lead beyond utilitarianism. In particular, the person-affecting restriction is often cited by those who wish to ignore the optimum-population question entirely. They argue that there is no *ethical* point in asking what you should do if you can choose any possible world. This bizarre thought experiment bears no relation to real-life ethics. Instead, philosophers should ask how changes in population patterns impact on actual human beings. This impact depends primarily on empirical factors. The pure optimum-population problem is thus irrelevant.

Population policy

Practical population ethics covers a vast array of topics, ranging across politics, law, reproductive technology, climate change, and many other issues. Instead of attempting to survey these, we focus on three key questions. How does population impact on the ethics of aid? Is coercion a necessary feature of population policy? How does environmental ethics impact on population ethics?

A central question in global ethics is what affluent people owe to those in less fortunate lands. One influential argument suggests that population issues undermine all charitable obligations. This *Malthusian argument* (pioneered by the nineteenth-century economist Robert Malthus) grants the (controversial) empirical premise that we are able to improve and safeguard the lives of those who are currently starving, but concludes that this would be an undesirable result. If we aid those who are starving, then more of them will live to maturity. As the birth rate in poor countries is often very high, this will lead to a population explosion. The result is an unsustainably high population in future, with more people starving. Unpleasant as it may seem, a high rate of infant mortality is necessary in the long term.

If it were sound, the Malthusian argument would have radical implications for the ethics of aid. However, the evidence suggests that Malthus was wrong. Increases in the standard of living tend to be followed by *decreases* in the birth rate, so that population growth is reduced. This suggests that, *if* aid can succeed in raising living standards, then it will also complement a sustainable population policy. (Of course, if aid will not succeed, then there is presumably no obligation to provide it.) Population ethics and development ethics are thus supporters, not rivals.

Suppose we have chosen the optimal population size for our society. Our population policy then aims at that population. The simplest policy will dictate how many children each citizen may have. Coercive policies regarding fertility have been adopted in many countries. The Chinese government's one-child-family policy is a striking example. One key issue in population ethics is whether such coercion is necessary.

If we aim at *any* precise population size, then we will need a very prescriptive policy. It is almost certainly impossible to achieve a global population of precisely six billion (or precisely ten billion, or any other specific target). To approximate any precise population would require enormous cooperation, and a large degree of coercion. This suggests that utilitarians – and others who treat the optimum population question as ethically significant – must favor coercive population policy. The threat of coercion is one reason why many people are suspicious of utilitarian approaches to population ethics.

The standard utilitarian reply appeals to the value of *freedom*. On many accounts of what makes human lives worth living, a freely chosen life is vastly superior to one without choice. If the best future is one where six billion people enjoy freedom, then the best future cannot (by definition) be reached via coercion. Population ethics thus illustrates a general feature of utilitarianism. The best behavior (from a utilitarian point of view) is often not simply to aim directly to bring about the best possible result (from a utilitarian point of view).

The person-affecting restriction offers the same response in a stronger form. A world where people enjoy freedom is likely to be better *for those people* than one where central life choices, such as reproductive decisions, are taken out of people's hands.

Proponents of coercion reply that freedom is inefficient, as it takes too long to reduce the birth rate to a sustainable level. We cannot reach a sustainable world of happy, free people. We must be realistic, and use coercion to ensure a sustainable future. In the developing world, the threat to sustainability typically comes in the form of *overpopulation*. Some countries in the developed world face the opposite problem. Reproductive freedom, combined with increasing employment opportunities and education for women, threatens to make the birth rate unsustainably low. In either case, proponents of coercion argue that, however intrinsically desirable freedom may be, it is unsustainable.

This objection applies both to those who seek an optimum population, and to those who adopt a person-affecting approach. The argument is that, without coercion to control the population size, we cannot ensure that future people will be able to enjoy such basic necessities as drinkable water and breathable air. The threat of coercion is present even for those who reject the whole notion of optimum population.

Given the complexities involved, non-coercive policies cannot *guarantee* an optimum population, a sustainable population, or a high average level of happiness. However, we must ask if coercive alternatives fare any better. Recent work by the Nobel Prize-winning economist Amartya Sen highlights the unreliability of coercion. Because it largely leaves people's underlying inclinations unchanged, a coercive policy must continually be enforced to defeat people's determined efforts to avoid it. For instance, Sen quotes the architects of China's family policy as admitting that "the birth concept of the broad masses has not changed fundamentally" (Sen 1999: 220).

Sen also questions the evidence supporting coercion. He notes that correlation is not causation. Changes in fertility in China followed significant improvements in education, health care, and female job opportunities. In fact, general development policy in China shares many of the features of the socialist government in the Indian state of Kerala. Yet Kerala's fertility rate has declined even faster than China's, despite the fact that coercive policies are not followed in Kerala (Sen 1999: 219–26).

This brief discussion of two issues illustrates the interplay between philosophical and empirical questions in the practical application of population ethics. It also illustrates the general possibility that very different theoretical views may agree in their practical recommendations. The population policies of optimum-population utilitarians, person-affecting utilitarians, and those who attach intrinsic value to freedom, may all coincide.

Environmental issues impact on population policy in many complex practical ways. They also give population policy a new urgency. While some environmental problems affect us now, many of the most worrying arise only in the distant future. Climate change, environmental degradation, and pollution all impact primarily on future people.

More fundamentally, environmental problems also undermine two assumptions that are shared by almost all traditional approaches to population policy. The first is the assumption that the present population level is sustainable. Economists, philosophers, and policymakers often ask whether increases in population would be good for society or the economy. While we are familiar with the idea that rapid population increase may be undesirable, it is usually taken for granted that there is no harm in maintaining the population at its present level indefinitely. However, if climate change is as bad as some estimates suggest, then perhaps we should focus instead on the question of how large a reduction in population is required, and how quickly.

One sense in which the present population may not be sustainable is that it may not be possible to maintain six billion people at the present global average standard of living. This brings us to the second implicit assumption that environmental issues call into question. Traditional political philosophy often asks whether, and to what extent, we are obliged to enable future generations to be better off than ourselves. We take it for granted that, at the very least, we can leave our descendants no worse off than ourselves – and that we can do so at relatively little cost to ourselves. The threat of environmental catastrophe raises serious doubts about this assumption. It may turn out that the question before us is much bleaker. How much worse off should we leave future people, and at what cost to ourselves (Mulgan 2006)?

The intersection of population ethics and environmental ethics thus raises new and urgent ethical questions.

Social contract theory

Traditional theories of justice concern a single generation. Attempts to extend them to future generations face the problem of *power imbalance*. The lives of future people depend on our decisions. By contrast, our lives are unaffected by their decisions. We can do a great deal to (or for) posterity but posterity cannot do anything to (or for) us.

One influential strand of Western political philosophy models justice on a contract between rational individuals. But how can we bargain with future people when their very existence is in our hands? To see how contract theorists answer this question, we examine two contemporary exponents: David Gauthier and John Rawls.

Gauthier's (1986) *contractarianism* sees justice as a mutually advantageous bargain between self-interested agents. Such a bargain is possible between overlapping generations, because they can interact and bargain. But consider a *time bomb* that devastates people in the distant future but has no direct impact until then. Intuitively, planting a time bomb is very wrong. But self-interested overlapping generations will see no reason to ban time bombs, as they will not be affected. So, according to the contractarian, planting a time bomb is not wrong.

One common response is the *zipper argument*. Suppose we have only three generations: G1, G2, and G3. G1 leaves a bomb that will devastate G3. G1 and G3 do not interact, but G2 and G3 do. G3 will want G2 to disconnect the bomb. The bomb thus weakens G2's bargaining position with G3. G2 will be aware of this in advance, and will thus ask G1 not to plant the bomb. Each contract between overlapping generations will prohibit time bombs (Gosseries 2001). However, a time bomb might *strengthen* G2's position against G3. ("If you don't give us what we want, we will not defuse the time bomb.") G2 would then ask G1 to plant such a bomb – and so contractarians would have to regard time bombs as morally desirable (Mulgan 2006: 28–32).

Rawls's *justice as fairness* asks what people *would* agree to under certain idealized circumstances (Rawls 1971). The aim is to find principles of justice everyone can recognize as a fair basis for mutual interaction. Principles of justice are chosen in an *original position*, from behind a *veil of ignorance*. The choosers know *what* their society will look like if any given principle is adopted, but they do not know *who* they will be in that society. Imagine a very simple society with two groups: rich and poor. We seek the principles a rational person would choose if they did not know whether they would be rich or poor.

Those in the original position belong to the same generation. As their rational egoism rules out concern for future people, intergenerational justice will have no place in the principles they choose. Nothing we do to future people – however devastating – could count as unjust. Given his strong egalitarian commitments, this result is not palatable to Rawls. He attempts to bring future generations into his framework.

Rawls originally added a motivational assumption. Those in the original position care about their descendants, at least for the next generation or two

(Rawls 1971: 284–93). This solution is *ad hoc*. Why allow concern for descendants, when we allow no concern for contemporaries? Furthermore, any motivational assumption only works for a few generations. It thus cannot remove the threat of time bombs. Rawls focuses on savings from one generation to the next, not on longer term issues such as environmental pollution. This focus was controversial even at the time (1971) – and seems much more problematic now.

Rawls abandoned this solution, and stipulated instead that those in the original position must behave in a way that they would want previous generations to have behaved (Rawls 1993: 273–4). Total self-sacrifice is ruled out, as the cost of our sacrifice outweighs the benefits of the sacrifices of others. Total selfishness also fails, as the damage of earlier selfishness outweighs our own freedom to behave as we wish. We need something in-between. Unfortunately for Rawls, it is very hard to say what that something will be.

Contract theory is not the only approach to political philosophy. Some of its opponents will argue that its difficulties are caused by its *individualism*. Instead of imagining contracts or bargains between isolated, independent individuals, we do better to think of any human society as a single entity extending across many generations. In other areas of political philosophy, this *communitarian* approach often emphasizes the importance of obligations to one's predecessors, and the value of continuing traditional ways and relationships. The notion of intergenerational ties also extends into the future. Some communitarians argue that obligations regarding future people are owed, not to those future people themselves, but to the earlier generations who themselves make sacrifices to provide cultural and other resources for ourselves (de Shalit 1994).

Of course, communitarians face problems of their own, especially in any modern liberal society. How do we determine what "our" cultural traditions are? How do we extend them into the future, and apply them to changing circumstances such as environmental problems? These problems have not received as much attention from philosophers as the problems facing utilitarian and social contract theories. It is thus too soon to say whether population ethics favors one approach over others.

See also Formal methods in ethics (Chapter 34); Consequentialism (Chapter 37); Contractualism (Chapter 41); Welfare (Chapter 54); Justice and distribution (Chapter 58); Life, death, and ethics (Chapter 59); The environment (Chapter 63); World poverty (Chapter 66).

References

Broome, J. (2004) *Weighing Lives*, Oxford: Oxford University Press.

Dasgupta, P. (1994) "Savings and Fertility: Ethical Issues," *Philosophy& Public Affairs* 23: 99–127.

de Shalit, A. (1994) *Why Posterity Matters*, London: Routledge.

Gauthier, D. (1986) *Morals by Agreement*, Oxford: Clarendon Press.
Gosseries, A. (2001) "What Do We Owe the Next Generation(s)?," *Loyola of Los Angeles Law Review* 35: 293–354.
Mulgan, T. (2006) *Future People*, Oxford: Oxford University Press.
Ng, Y.-K. (1989) "What Should We Do about Future Generations? Impossibility of Parfit's Theory X," *Economics and Philosophy* 5: 235–53.
Parfit, D. (1984) *Reasons and Persons*, Oxford: Oxford University Press.
Rachels, S. (1998) "Counterexamples to the Transitivity of 'Better Than'," *Australasian Journal of Philosophy* 76: 71–83.
Rawls, J. (1971) *A Theory of Justice*, Cambridge, MA: Harvard University Press.
——(1993) *Political Liberalism*, New York: Columbia University Press.
Roberts, M. (2002) "A New Way of Doing the Best We Can: Person-based Consequentialism and the Equality Problem," *Ethics* 112: 315–50.
Sen, A. (1999) *Development as Freedom*, Oxford: Oxford University Press.

Further reading

Barry, B. (1989) *Theories of Justice*, Berkeley: University of California Press.
Gosseries, A. (2001) "What Do We Owe the Next Generation(s)?," *Loyola of Los Angeles Law Review* 35: 293–354. (A very good introduction to contract theory and intergenerational justice.)
Parfit, D. (1984) *Reasons and Persons*, Oxford: Oxford University Press. (Remains the best introduction to the puzzles in contemporary value theory.)
——(1986) "Overpopulation and the Quality of Life," in P. Singer (ed.) *Applied Ethics*, Oxford: Oxford University Press.
Sen, A. (1999) *Development as Freedom*, Oxford: Oxford University Press. (Covers a wide range of relevant empirical and economic issues.)

62
ANIMALS
Alan Carter

While containing notable exceptions, such as the work of Henry Salt in the nineteenth century, the history of Western thought, never mind of its behavior, has displayed marked disregard for the interests of non-human animals, with a tendency to view them as mere resources for human use – a view that is explicit in the philosophies of such influential thinkers as Aristotle, Augustine and Thomas Aquinas. Today, however, choosing to become a vegan or a lacto-vegetarian has been one of the fastest growing lifestyle changes in developed countries, and the moral status of non-human animals is now a core topic within applied ethics.

Peter Singer and animal liberation

The initial impetus for the growing interest among philosophers in the moral status of non-human animals were the activities of a small group of graduate students working at the University of Oxford in the late 1960s and early 1970s. A symposium on the maltreatment of non-human animals was organized by three of those students, Ros and Stan Godlovitch and John Harris, and the papers presented there were published as a book, which contained the first modern philosophical discussion of the moral status of non-human animals. This volume (Godlovitch et al. 1971) was later reviewed by Peter Singer, also a graduate student at Oxford, in the *New York Review of Books* on 5 April 1973. Singer's review met such an enthusiastic response that he expanded part of the content into an article in *Philosophical Exchange*, which was later abridged as the now widely anthologized "All Animals Are Equal," and then greatly expanded into his 1975 book *Animal Liberation*, which is frequently referred to as "the bible" of the Animal Liberation Movement.

Now, most of us like to believe that we are morally enlightened. Whereas many have been extremely prejudiced in the past, whether against people of a different sexual orientation or of other races or of the other sex, we think that we are now, by and large, free of prejudice. However, as Singer observes, people are usually blind to just how prejudiced they are until a liberation movement springs up and exposes the true extent of their prejudices, as the histories of the Gay Liberation Movement, the Black Liberation Movement and Women's Lib demonstrated. And in Singer's view, many of us are still highly prejudiced, and against a very large group indeed: namely, the members of other animal species. And to combat this prejudice, Singer argued that a new liberation movement was required: Animal Liberation.

But why regard non-human animals as meriting a liberation movement? In order to avoid misunderstanding Singer, it is important to note that he was a student of the demi-vegetarian R. M. Hare, White's Professor of Moral Philosophy at Oxford at that time, and Hare argues that (1) moral terms possess the property of universalizability (Hare 1952), and, in his view, (2) this implies some form of utilitarianism (Hare 1963). According to (1), moral imperatives are such that they apply to all relevantly similar agents in relevantly similar situations. But, as Singer observes, many assume that it is morally permissible to treat non-human animals in a very different manner to how we may permissibly treat humans. For example, we do not rear humans for food and serve them up as a Sunday roast. If this is an impermissible way of treating humans, then there must be some morally relevant and morally significant difference between human and non-human animals that would justify such a major difference in treatment. But what is it? The challenge that Singer poses is that any characteristic we might pick to differentiate human from non-human animals will either include those non-humans we currently mistreat or exclude some humans (Singer 1977: 250–1). Take intelligence. If we set the bar high enough so that pigs, which we rear for food, or chimpanzees, upon which we conduct painful experiments, possess insufficient intelligence to be included within the class of those who are thereby deemed morally considerable, many humans will no longer count within our moral calculations, for very young children, to take one example, are less intelligent than adult pigs. But if we set the bar low enough to include those humans who are far less intelligent than most of their species, then adult pigs, say, will also have to be included within our moral calculations. It might be thought that potential will do the trick. But young chimpanzees possess far greater potential than certain brain-damaged humans. And the real sting in the tale of this argument, often referred to as "the argument from marginal cases," is that if we exclude or devalue the interests of non-human animals from our moral calculations simply because they differ from us biologically without that resulting in arguably morally relevant differences, such as intelligence or potential, then we are inconsistent in criticizing racists or sexists for excluding or devaluing the interests of other races or the other sex simply on the basis of a biological difference (Singer 1977: 9). Put another way, the price of rejecting racism and sexism is the rejection of, what Singer (following Richard Ryder) terms, "speciesism" – the unjustifiable privileging of one's own species over another.

But where are we to draw the line? For it is surely not immoral to kick a stone around the street, even if it is immoral to do that to a cat. By virtue of what characteristic should an entity be included within our moral calculations? In his early work, as a hedonistic utilitarian, Singer follows Jeremy Bentham in regarding the capacity for pleasure and pain as the morally relevant characteristic (Singer 1977: 7–8). If a being is capable of suffering, then that being has interests. Stones cannot suffer, so they lack interests. And this is why kicking a cat is morally wrong, but kicking a stone is not. So, if a being suffers, then that suffering should be taken into account regardless of which species the suffering being is a member. Indeed, morality requires that like suffering should count equally, regardless of species membership. In brief, Singer holds that the equal consideration of interests has often been proposed by philosophers as a basic moral principle, but the vast majority have failed to realize that consistency requires that the interests of those non-humans that possess them – those that can feel pleasure or pain – should be taken just as much into account as the interests of humans (Singer 1977: 7).

How, then, do we disregard or devalue non-human interests in our actions, thereby displaying speciesism? We do so primarily when we rear non-human animals for food, which inflicts a great deal of suffering on them (see Singer 1977: Ch. 3), and in conducting painful experiments upon them (see Singer 1977: Ch. 2). Consequently, in his early work, as a welfarist utilitarian seeking to minimize suffering, Singer advocates both vegetarianism and a prohibition on a great deal of research on non-human animals.

Regan on animal rights

But what if greater (human) suffering can be prevented by conducting painful experiments on non-human animals, say in the course of finding treatments for painful diseases? Or what if animals could be reared in a significantly less painful manner, and what if they could be killed painlessly? Might the pleasure that humans gain from eating non-human animals outweigh, and thus justify, whatever pain animals reared for food might experience? That one or more sentient being's pleasures can outweigh another's pains and thereby ostensibly justify maltreatment is a standard concern that deontologists (who hold that actions can be morally wrong even if they bring about good consequences) raise in rejecting consequentialist doctrines, such as utilitarianism. (Consequentialists hold that actions are morally right in virtue of their bringing about good consequences, and actions are morally wrong in virtue of their bringing about bad consequences.) Deontologists who advocate rights-based theories often argue that rights are required to protect morally considerable beings from an otherwise unconstrained pursuit of the general welfare. Tom Regan, however, differs from the vast majority of deontologists in regarding not just humans but also certain non-human animals as morally considerable beings who should be viewed as rights-holders.

Like Singer, Regan – the leading advocate of animal rights – has also deployed the argument from marginal cases. Many humans possess abilities that non-human animals lack. But some humans lack them, too (Regan 1985: 22). And we do not use that as a reason for regarding those humans as lacking moral considerability. Importantly, many believe that human infants have a right not to be harmed. But as they have yet to develop the capacities necessary for them to act as moral agents, human infants, if they are indeed rights-holders, cannot be so in virtue of being moral agents. The actions of moral agents are subject to moral constraints, but moral constraints, it would seem, extend beyond our treatment of other moral agents. They include our treatment of moral patients – those rights-holders, such as human infants, or so many believe, that are not moral agents. So, what is it that makes humans, whether they are moral agents or merely moral patients, morally considerable? For Regan, it is not the capacity to suffer. And though he is a deontologist working within the Kantian tradition, Regan does not follow Immanuel Kant in thinking that it is the capacity for rationality. Rather, it is the fact that their lives matter to them. In other words, what makes the moral agent or the moral patient morally considerable is his or her property of being an experiencing subject of a life, where that is to be understood as the capacity for having

> beliefs and desires; perception, memory, and a sense of the future, including their own future; an emotional life together with feelings of pleasure and pain; preference- and welfare-interests; the ability to initiate action in pursuit of their desires and goals; a psychological identity over time; and an individual welfare in the sense that their experiential life fares well or ill for them, logically independently of their utility for others and logically independently of their being the object of anyone else's interests.
>
> (Regan 1983: 243)

So, why, precisely, is it that you should be treated with respect? According to Regan, it is because you are an experiencing subject of a life. By virtue of being such a subject, you possess what Regan refers to as inherent value. Those who possess inherent value merit respect, and that is shown by respecting their rights. And in Regan's views, all who possess inherent value possess it equally. But not only humans but also certain non-human animals, including all normal, adult mammals over a year in age, are experiencing subjects of a life. All those animals, both human and non-human, that satisfy the subject-of-a-life criterion are therefore rights-holders.

As rights-holders, certain non-human animals, just like humans, must not be sacrificed in the furtherance of the general welfare. To sacrifice such non-human animals for the greater good would be to violate their rights, and that is no more permissible than is the violation of the rights of humans. How do we violate the rights of certain animals? We do so when we use them for sport, such as when we hunt them, when we use them in commercial agriculture and when we experiment on them. And in Regan's view, it is not the infliction of pain that makes such practices immoral, although it might make matters worse. Rather, it is the failure to treat an experiencing subject of a life as inherently valuable. It is the using of such beings as mere means to one's ends, rather than regarding them as ends-in-themselves.

Now, Regan is at pains to distinguish his position from Singer's (who, as a utilitarian, does not subscribe to a rights-based moral theory), even though many of their practical conclusions are similar. In Regan's view, Singer, when he argued as a hedonistic utilitarian, was concerned with quantities of pleasure and pain, and not, Regan claims, with those who feel pleasure and pain. To the utilitarian, Regan charges, we are like receptacles of something valuable – pleasure – and not something of value in itself. In order to regard morally considerable beings as valuable in themselves, their rights need to be recognized and protected. This prevents aggregative considerations, such as the summing of pleasure, from overriding a morally considerable individual's interests. Consequently, the pleasure obtained from eating animals reared in more humane conditions cannot justify such agricultural practices. Rearing animals for food, no matter how humane the conditions, is to treat them as mere means to the satisfaction of human interests, and constitutes a violation of their rights.

However, it will be recalled that Regan argues that all experiencing subjects of a life possess equal inherent value. This makes inherent value a binary property. An entity either possesses it or that entity does not. But the properties by virtue of which an entity counts as an experiencing subject of a life differ in degree. As Mary Anne Warren (2001: 47) asks: "why should we believe that there is a sharp line between creatures that are subjects-of-a-life and creatures that are not? Isn't it more likely that 'subjecthood' comes in degrees, that some creatures have only a little self-awareness, and only a little capacity to anticipate the future, while some have a little more, and some a good deal more?" The capacity for forming beliefs, forming desires, having perceptions, having memories, having a sense of the future, and so on, can all, surely, be greater or less. It is, therefore, a scalar property. But this means that at some point on the scale an entity suddenly acquires the same inherent value as every other inherently valuable entity, but before reaching that point an entity possesses no inherent value whatsoever. Many are likely to find this sudden transition implausible (see Alexander 2008).

The problem of conflicts between species

This also pertains to a problem that is evident in both Regan's deontological approach and Singer's early welfarism: namely, that of justifiably taking sides with other humans against non-humans when their interests conflict.

Consider an example made famous by Regan: A lifeboat capable of supporting four individuals has five on board. Four are human; one is a dog. Regan concurs with the widespread human intuition that the dog should be sacrificed rather than one of the humans. But how is this to be justified, given his advocacy of animal rights, and given that every entity that possesses inherent value possesses it equally?

Regan holds that the innocent have a right of self-defense against aggressors. But this right will not help in all cases. We can easily imagine a scenario where the dog is not attacking any of the humans. So, some further consideration is required. And according to Regan, when rights conflict, there are two principles to which we can appeal. The first is "the miniride principle," which is short for "the minimize overriding principle" (Regan 1983: 305): If one course of action would violate the rights of many, while the only alternative course of action would violate the rights of fewer rights-holders, and if the rights violated by either course of action are, individually, of the same degree of seriousness, then the rights of the few should be violated in preference to violating the rights of the many. But when one rights violation is a more serious violation than another, a different principle applies: "the worse-off principle" (Regan 1983: 308). According to this principle, we should violate the lesser right rather than the greater. Indeed, we should violate a countless number of lesser rights rather than violate one greater right. And the seriousness of the rights violation is to be understood in terms of the degree of harm involved. In short, we should harm many individuals slightly rather than harming one severely.

There is intuitive support for this. Wouldn't it be worse to torture one person to death than to cause a million people to suffer a mild headache? In such a case, classical utilitarianism seems flawed, for the greater pain of the million would outweigh the pain of the one tortured to death. So, the utilitarian should conclude that we ought to torture the one individual to death. Regan's rights view seems preferable in this case, for it insists that this would be immoral. It would be a greater rights violation to torture the one individual to death, and avoiding the lesser rights violations of the million cannot justify it. In short, when it comes to the worse-off principle, the numbers do not count. One rights violation is worse than one lesser rights violation, and one rights violation is worse than a million lesser rights violations. Put another way, the more serious rights violation is the one that should always be avoided when one has no choice but to engage in one or more rights violations.

How does this apply to the lifeboat case? Regan argues that a human has more to lose by dying than a dog does, therefore death is a greater harm to a human than it is to a dog. Hence, the killing of a dog is a lesser rights violation than is the killing of an innocent human. Consequently, we are justified in saving the humans by throwing the dog overboard.

But recall: according to the worse-off principle, the numbers do not count. Thus, as Regan (1983: 325) argues:

> Let the number of dogs be as large as one likes; suppose they number a million. … Then the rights view still implies that, special considerations apart, the million dogs should be thrown overboard and the four humans saved. To attempt to reach a contrary judgment will inevitably involve one in aggregative considerations – the sum of the losses of the million dogs over and against the losses for one of the humans – an approach that cannot be sanctioned by those who accept the respect principle.

And the "respect principle" enjoins us "to treat those individuals who have inherent value in ways that respect their inherent value" (Regan 1983: 248). Now, the sacrifice of a million dogs for one human might appear to be a rather extreme concession on the part of the leading defender of animal rights. One challenge that might be offered is that while it is plausible that the numbers do not count when the differences in harm are great, it is not so when they are not so great. For it might well be wrong to torture one person rather than inflict a mild headache on a million people. But it is far from obvious that we should cause a million people to lose one arm each rather than cause one person to lose both arms. The difficult question then arises: Is a human's death *that* much worse to that human than a dog's death is to that dog?

Singer's response to the problem of conflicts between members of different species changed along with a change in his philosophical position. At the time of writing *Animal Liberation*, he argued as a hedonistic utilitarian. But one objection that can be raised against hedonistic utilitarianism concerns "the replacement problem." What if the painless death of one person allowed the bringing into being of an equally happy person. There would be no loss of pleasure in the world and no increase in pain by killing the one in order to replace him or her with the other, so why would killing that person be wrong? In order to avoid such difficulties, Singer, in *Practical Ethics* (1979), advocated preference, in contrast to hedonistic, utilitarianism, where, rather than maximize the balance of pleasure over pain for all those who are morally considerable, we are to maximize the satisfaction of their preferences. This seems to solve the replacement problem because killing the one person would frustrate his or her very strong preference to go on living and accomplish his or her various projects. And preference utilitarianism also appears to offer a solution to the lifeboat case: for if a human has greater preferences than a dog, then we are justified in throwing the dog overboard rather than a human. But this would not seem to justify throwing a million dogs overboard in preference to one human.

However, if non-human animals lack certain preferences, this might also be used to justify rearing them for food in certain cases, for the non-human animal might be replaceable in a way that a human, given his or preferences, is not. This seems *prima facie* consistent with the view that some hold that it is permissible to eat meat if the animal has been reared humanely and killed painlessly. Singer, however, holds that it is wholly unrealistic to think that this is possible on the kind of scale that mass meat-eating requires. In his view, large-scale animal husbandry will inevitably involve considerable suffering on the part of non-human animals. Moreover, Singer believes that there is reason for being vegan or vegetarian that exclusively concerns human interests: Rearing non-human animals for meat is extremely wasteful of food, for several pounds of feed are required to produce one pound of flesh. Hence, more hungry people in poor countries could be comfortably fed if we changed our diets and stopped consuming meat.

Some other core problem areas

While many have found either Singer's or Regan's arguments compelling, others have remained unconvinced. Leslie Pickering Francis and Richard Norman (1978) agree that there is no intrinsic property that separates all humans from non-humans other than species membership, but they argue that Singer ignores relational properties. Humans can form political, economic, communicative and familial relations with one another that they cannot form to the same degree with non-human animals; and "liberation" is a political concept, while "equality" is an economic and political one. Moreover, these relations together comprise a network, and it is a human's ability to enter into them that constitutes a morally significant difference that sets the humans apart from non-humans. In a nutshell, humans count because of their relations with each other, and non-humans do not count, because they are excluded from those relations.

However, taking relations as the sole basis of moral concern might be thought problematic. Surely there are some relations that we believe ought to be criticized. But if the relations that presently obtain determine who counts, how do we criticize certain relations if it is the relations themselves that constitute the yardstick? We might want to say that the relations are bad because certain persons within those relations merit better treatment. But we cannot say that if the relations determine those persons' moral standing. Perhaps we could criticize exploitative relations, say, because it is possible for humans to enter into less exploitative ones. In other words, we might argue that it is not the relations that currently obtain that determine moral standing, but the relations that could obtain. But humans are capable of entering into far better relations with non-human animals than those between experimenters and their subjects, say. Moreover, not all humans can enter into decent political, economic and communicative relations. And this means that the capacity to enter into such relations is prey to the argument from marginal cases. A response that one could take, and Francis and Norman seem prepared to take it, is to bite the bullet. One can simply deny that very young or certain brain-damaged humans are directly morally considerable. And if we need to take them into account, it is only indirectly. If a parent would be upset by someone harming her infant, then that provides a reason for not harming the child. While the infant does not count directly, the infant's parents do. But that infants do not count in themselves will seem highly counter-intuitive to many.

However, there is a way in which the argument from marginal cases might be countered. Carl Cohen (1986) argues that all humans are morally considerable because they are members of a kind – a species – whose standard members are morally considerable. Because the vast majority of humans are morally considerable, they form a kind that is morally considerable. And any member of that kind, including very young and brain-damaged humans, should count in our moral deliberations by virtue of their being of that kind. The moral standing of all humans is therefore determined by some property that is normal for humans, even if not all humans possess that property.

But it can be argued that this, too, is problematic. As James Rachels (1990: 187) points out, Cohen's argument "assumes that we should determine how an individual is to be treated, not on the basis of *its* qualities, but on the basis of *other* individuals' qualities." To take an example that is not Rachels', imagine a job that requires a tall person to perform it: say stacking high shelves. To employ a short man rather than a tall woman because men are normally taller than women would be irrational, and many would deem it immoral. It seems bizarre to ascribe a status to a being on the basis of a property possessed by others typical of its kind which that individual does not actually possess.

Now, Kantians have tended to argue that, while non-human animals do not count morally in themselves, one should, nevertheless, refrain from gratuitous cruelty towards them. Kant argued that non-human animals lack the rationality that is required for acting according to moral principles. Whereas humans are moral agents, non-human animals are not. But we have already seen that we regard moral patients as counting, even if they are not moral agents. In any case, why would it be morally wrong gratuitously to inflict suffering on non-human animals if, lacking rationality, they were not morally considerable? Kant's answer is that cruelty to non-human animals is more likely to lead to cruelty to humans, and as human moral agents count, one has reason to avoid being cruel to non-human animals.

But while most of us agree that we should not be cruel to non-human animals, this surely cannot be a good reason for it. If cruelty to humans is morally wrong, one should not engage in it. If one ensures that one does nothing that is morally wrong, why should doing something that is not directly morally wrong – being cruel to non-human animals – make one more likely to do something that is morally wrong? As Robert Nozick (1974: 36) asks: "If I enjoy hitting a baseball squarely with a bat, does this significantly increase the danger of my doing the same to someone's head? Am I not capable of understanding that people differ from baseballs, and doesn't this understanding stop the spillover?" It seems likely that if non-human animals are morally considerable, and if being cruel to them is therefore directly morally wrong, then one's being willing to act immorally towards non-humans might increase the likelihood that one will act immorally towards humans. But it is far from obvious that being willing to act in a manner that is not immoral increases the likelihood that one will act immorally.

Of course, both Singer's and Regan's arguments fail if non-human animals lack consciousness, and, correlatively, do not experience pain. It might be thought that Occam's Razor could justify dismissing claims that any non-human possesses consciousness, for we could, perhaps, claim that all of their behavior is a machine-like response. If consciousness is not required to explain non-human animal behavior, then a more parsimonious account would leave out all mention of non-human consciousness. However, Singer has argued that, given the similarity between human and many non-human animals in not just behavior but also in physical responses and in physiology, it is more parsimonious to assume that other mammals, for example, react to certain stimuli as we do for the same reason that we do – namely, as a response to feeling pain – than to assume a different mechanism, which is what denying that they feel pain would require.

Peter Carruthers (1989), however, has argued that we perform all sorts of actions without our being conscious of performing them. For example, when driving a car one engages in numerous actions and maneuvers without being conscious of engaging in them. If we can behave in complex ways without being conscious of what we are doing, then it is possible that non-human animals behave in complex ways while lacking all consciousness. And this sidesteps the Occam's Razor objection. But it seems far too weak a purported justification for subjecting non-human animals to experiments that would be incredibly painful if those animals feel pain. We do not believe that we can just go around blowing up large islands because it is possible that no one is there. Rather, there has to be a very high probability, at least, that there is no one around before we start blowing things up. Similarly, the fact that we can tell a story such that it is possible that animals lack consciousness will not suffice. We would need, at least, good reason for thinking that it is highly unlikely that an animal can feel pain before we would be justified in acting in a manner that, were the animal capable of feeling pain, would cause that animal great suffering.

However, even if it is the case that non-human animals can be harmed, R. G. Frey (1980) has argued that they nevertheless still lack morally significant interests. Such interests, Frey contends, concern the satisfaction of desires. But that requires beliefs, and a belief concerns the truth of a declarative sentence. For example, an animal cannot desire that an experimenter stop an experiment that is inflicting pain on her because she wants that pain to stop unless she believes that "Stopping the experiment will end my pain" is true. But that belief depends upon a linguistic capacity that, Frey believes, non-human animals lack.

Bernard Rollin (1992) argues, however, that humans communicate not only linguistically by means of conventional signs but also by natural signs, and non-human animals are quite capable of the latter. Moreover, Rollin argues that there is no clear dividing line between natural and conventional signs. To this we might add that we are all well aware of how important "body language" is.

But we observe it in non-human animals just as clearly as in humans; for example, we know when a dog is scared just as we know when a human is, without either having to say anything. But what if Frey is right to argue that desires require a conventional language? We would have to conclude that human infants lack desires, and hence have no interests. This seems to go against the grain of common sense, but we could claim that there is a technical sense of "interests" that does not apply to infants. But surely there is *something* that we act against when we torture babies? Babies try to stop us torturing them. There is something at least like an urge, that they possess, to stop what is happening to them. As they lack a conventional language, call it a "proto-desire." This could ground a "proto-interest." There seems no good reason for denying that certain non-human animals also possess proto-interests. And if it is wrong to torture babies, then it would appear that proto-interests are morally significant. But then it would be wrong to torture adult mammals even if they lack "interests."

Other approaches and later developments

A later wave of philosophers arguing in favor of animal welfarism or animal rights eschewed the system-building from core philosophical principles that was characteristic of Singer and Regan. David DeGrazia (1996) argues that recognizing that we have obligations to non-human animals is what a coherence model of ethical justification requires, while Steve Sapontzis (1987) engages in detailed responses to arguments against animal liberation and animal rights. The philosophical approach that has seemed least conducive to taking non-human animals seriously is contractarianism, which construes morality as a form of agreement. However, by arguing that John Rawls' contractarianism is premised upon a revisable intuition regarding equality, Mark Rowlands (1997) has claimed that even contractarianism, when properly construed, is compatible with animal rights.

Given the interests that some humans have in animal experimentation or in the pleasure obtained from eating meat, the ongoing debate between those arguing in favor of animal welfarism or animal rights, on the one hand, and their detractors, on the other, is unlikely to end, at least in the foreseeable future.

See also Utilitarianism to Bentham (Chapter 13); Kant (Chapter 14); Consequentialism (Chapter 37); Contemporary Kantian ethics (Chapter 38); Rights (Chapter 56); Life, death, and ethics (Chapter 59); The environment (Chapter 63).

References

Alexander, L. (2008) "Scalar Properties, Binary Judgments," *Journal of Applied Philosophy* 25, no. 2: 85–104.

Carruthers, P. (1989) "Brute Experience," *Journal of Philosophy* 86: 258–69.
Cohen, C. (1986) "The Case for the Use of Animals in Biomedical Research," *New England Journal of Medicine* 315: 865–70.
DeGrazia, D. (1996) *Taking Animals Seriously: Mental Like and Moral Status*, Cambridge: Cambridge University Press.
Francis, L. P. and Norman, R. (1978) "Some Animals Are More Equal Than Others," *Philosophy* 53: 507–27.
Frey, R. G. (1980) *Interests and Rights: The Case against Animals*, Oxford: Clarendon Press.
Godlovitch, R., Godlovitch, S. and Harris, J. (eds) (1971) *Animals, Men and Morals: An Inquiry into the Maltreatment of Non-Humans*, New York: Grove Press.
Hare, R. M. (1952) *The Language of Morals*, Oxford: Oxford University Press.
——(1963) *Freedom and Reason*, Oxford: Oxford University Press.
Nozick, R. (1974) *Anarchy, State and Utopia*, New York: Basic Books.
Rachels, J. (1990) *Created from Animals: The Moral Implications of Darwinism*, Oxford: Oxford University Press.
Regan, T. (1983) *The Case for Animal Rights*, Berkeley: University of California Press.
——(1985) "The Case for Animal Rights," in P. Singer (ed.) *In Defence of Animals*, Oxford: Blackwell.
Rollin, B. E. (1992) *Animal Rights and Human Morality*, rev. edn, Buffalo, NY: Prometheus Books.
Rowlands, M. (1997) "Contractarianism and Animal Rights," *Journal of Applied Philosophy* 14, no. 3: 235–47.
Sapontzis, S. F. (1987) *Morals, Reason and Animals*, Philadelphia, PA: Temple University Press.
Singer, P. (1977) *Animal Liberation: A New Ethics for Our Treatment of Animals*, New York: Avon Books; first published 1975.
——(1979) *Practical Ethics*, Cambridge: Cambridge University Press.
Warren, M. A. (2001) "A Critique of Regan's Animal Rights Theory," in L. P. Pojman (ed.) *Environmental Ethics: Readings in Theory and Application*, Belmont, CA: Wadsworth.

Further reading

DeGrazia, D. (2002) *Animal Rights: A Very Short Introduction*, Oxford: Oxford University Press.
Regan, T. (1985) "The Case for Animal Rights," in P. Singer (ed.) *In Defence of Animals*, Oxford: Blackwell.
Singer, P. (1986) "All Animals Are Equal," in P. Singer (ed.) *Applied Ethics*, Oxford: Oxford University Press.
Taylor, A. (2003) *Animals and Ethics: An Overview of the Philosophical Debate*, Peterborough, ON, Canada: Broadview Press.

63
THE ENVIRONMENT

Andrew Brennan and Norva Y. S. Lo

Despite significant resonances between earlier thought and the work of twentieth-century philosophers, the natural environment as such became the explicit topic of philosophical theorizing only in the second half of the twentieth century. Some of that work drew on earlier work – for example, the writings of the pre-Enlightenment thinkers Giordano Bruno and Benedict Spinoza on *natura naturans* and *natura naturata*, and the love of nature evoked by the work of Jean-Jacques Rousseau. While some contemporary writers on environmental philosophy have referred to Rousseau, Spinoza and even Shakespeare as sources of philosophical and ethical inspiration, the multiple ambiguity of the term "nature" makes it difficult to trace any clear lineage in Western philosophy for the key doctrines that have dominated the recent emergence of environmental philosophy as a thriving field of applied philosophy.

The primary theoretical focus of the field has been the moral status and value of natural objects, processes and systems. One central question over the last four decades of work in the field has been: Do we have moral duties towards, and owe moral respect to, natural things? That question was itself the product of a social and intellectual context in which other questions of value and duty were also pressed – questions about animals, civil rights, power and patriarchy. The rise of environmental ethics and philosophy was one aspect of a complex response to the sense of crisis and doom pervading the late 1950s and 1960s, reflecting fears about the Cold War and the threat of nuclear annihilation – well represented in the music of protest songs characteristic of counter-cultural currents in the 1960s. The *New Yorker* magazine published a series of essays by Rachel Carson, later reprinted in her best-selling book, *Silent Spring* (1963), documenting the accumulation of dangerous pesticides and chemical toxins throughout planetary food webs, a theme echoed in the folk songs of Bob Dylan and the poetry of Lawrence Ferlinghetti. In 1968, the journal *Science* published "The Tragedy of the Commons" by Garrett Hardin, arguing that human self-interest and a growing population inevitably tend to resource destruction and environmental degradation (see Hardin 1972). In the same year, another best-seller, Paul Ehrlich's *Population Bomb*, (wrongly) anticipated hundreds of millions of deaths in the coming decades, due directly to failure of food supply to keep pace with an ever-expanding global population. Ehrlich also claimed to foresee an imminent and dramatic decline in US population and life expectancy, and some of these gloomy predictions were echoed in Donnella and Dennis Meadows' book *Limits to Growth* (Meadows et al. 1972).

In the academy, many reputable scientists and economists were quick to critique these Jeremiah oracles, yet the sense of crisis out of which these works had emerged was not readily dispelled. After the 1962 Cuban Missile Crisis, the quick retreat of the 1968 Prague Spring, and the continuing posturing associated with the Cold War it seemed that the world was in need of a new set of values. In a seminal essay that appealed to increasingly disenchanted Marxist and left-leaning thinkers, Murray Bookchin remarked that ecology was a critical science with "explosive implications," because "in the final analysis, it is impossible to achieve a harmonization of man and nature without creating a human community that lives in a lasting balance with its natural environment" (Bookchin 1978/1965). For Bookchin, ecological thinking would be the answer to the challenge Carson had set out explicitly when she wrote: "The road we have long been travelling is deceptively easy, a smooth superhighway on which we progress with great speed, but at its end lies disaster. The other fork of the road – the one 'less travelled by' – offers our last, our only chance to reach a destination that assures the preservation of our earth" (Carson 1963: 226).

When historian Lynn White Jr published an essay in the journal *Science* claiming that Judeo-Christian thought was itself a major driver of environmental destruction (White 1967), the scene was set for full-scale philosophical and ethical soul-searching aimed at answering Carson's challenge to find a road less travelled. The first answers appeared in three different countries at almost the same time. In the United States and Australia direction and inspiration came from the earlier twentieth-century American literature of the environment. The Scottish emigrant John Muir (founder of the Sierra Club and "father of American conservation") and subsequently the forester Aldo Leopold advocated a concern for natural values, and for conservation of things "natural, wild and free." Their concerns were motivated by a combination of both ethical and aesthetic responses to nature and a rejection of crudely economic approaches. Leopold's *Sand County Almanac* (1949), in particular, advocated the adoption of a "land ethic": "that land is a community is the basic concept of ecology, but that land is to be loved and respected is an extension of ethics" (Leopold 1949: vii–ix).

The land ethic was drawn on explicitly by the Australian philosopher Richard Routley (later naming himself Richard Sylvan) in his argument that the mainline principles of western liberal thinkers were committed to what he called "human chauvinism." This view – he argued – was a prejudice in favor of one species, human beings, over all others. "Whether the blue whale survives," he wrote, "should not have to depend on what humans know or what they see on television. Human interests and preferences are far too parochial to provide a satisfactory basis for deciding on what is environmentally desirable" (Routley 1973: 210). In a case that anticipates the fears of those who now warn about the risks of runaway global warming, he imagined the last people on earth choosing to eliminate all other living things after their own demise. If humans are the only morally valuable things on the planet, then such an action involves no moral wrong. Yet, Routley pointed out, there is a strong intuition, shared by many people, that such a destructive final act would be morally abhorrent. Routley's essay raised two questions at the same time: first, whether the main approaches in western moral thinking (Routley called this the "dominant western view" or "the western superethic") could permit the recognition that natural things have their own intrinsic value; second, whether the western liberal tradition required overhaul of a significant kind. Since in his view the dominant western view denied that natural things have intrinsic value, he suggested that an ethic of environmental concern challenged many of the widely shared assumptions of the utilitarianism then popular in Australian philosophy. As a result, he gave an affirmative answer to the second question – proposing that the liberal tradition needed serious overhaul.

For Leopold's land ethic "a thing is right when it tends to preserve the integrity, stability and beauty of the biotic community. It is wrong when it tends otherwise" (Leopold 1949: 224–5). In the United States, Holmes Rolston III followed this idea up by proposing that we have duties, not only to individual humans and animals, but also to larger wholes – species, and ecosystems, for example. Like Routley's last-people argument, Rolston's ideas were illustrated by imagined cases – for example, the butterfly collector who considers eliminating the last members of a rare *Papilio* species to enhance the value of his own specimens (Rolston 1975). On Rolston's natural theological view, biological processes are deserving of respect, as are species and as also are natural individuals because they all have a nature that is intrinsically valuable. For him, all biologists are religious, in a sense, and our experience of nature is numinous, or mystical, in the way that some religious experience is.

The third answer came from Arne Næss, based in Norway. Pleased to find, during a climbing expedition in Nepal, that Sherpa people would not venture onto sacred mountains, Næss and two of his Norwegian friends discussed formulating a new philosophy that would extend such reverence for mountains to all of nature in general, emphasizing the interconnectedness of each thing in larger webs of value. In place of the isolated or atomic individual, Næss asks us to think of people and other things as constituted by their relationships with others – as knots in a larger web of life (Næss 1995/1973). While such a relational conception of the self might be thought to resonate with animist, Confucian or Buddhist traditions (ones to which Næss was open) Næss usually claimed to draw his philosophical inspiration in large measure from Spinoza. Taking relationships seriously, he argued, meant that we should care for the extended – or ecological – self, since each of us is larger than his or her body. While in his early work, Næss seemed to regard all living things as having equal value, by the 1980s he dropped the equality constraint and was prepared to support only the weaker claim that the flourishing of all life – human and non-human alike – has value in its own right. In collaboration with George Sessions, Næss also formulated a deep ecology platform in 1984, listing the eight points on which deeply committed conservation philosophies would agree, while leaving up to individuals how best to interpret such principles in specific cases (the platform statements are reprinted in Sessions 1995: 151–5). By the mid-1980s, then, three possible answers to Carson's challenge seemed to be available. Those following Routley and Rolston rejected the human-centered bias of conventional moral theory, finding a place for animals, plants and even rocks in the scheme of things to which intrinsic or inherent value might be attached. On the other hand, followers of Næss's deep ecology were moved to rethink the notion of the ethical subject, querying what they saw as the individualistic and decontextualized nature of much western philosophical and moral theory.

In all cases, a common target for criticism was the conception of the specialness of humankind – a doctrine usually labeled as "anthropocentrism." In environmental philosophy, the thesis of anthropocentrism has generally been taken to be one about value: that only human beings have intrinsic value, which makes them worthy of direct moral consideration. In its strong form, anthropocentrism limits intrinsic value solely to human beings. Weak anthropocentrism, by contrast, allows the possibility of intrinsic value to be present in some animals and also some other non-human things – but always to a very much lower degree than it is present in humans. By contrast, the non-anthropocentrist holds that intrinsic value can be found equally, or at least nearly equally, in all sorts of non-human things – the lives of animals, animals themselves, plants, trees, populations and species, and even in rocks and mountains (Taylor 1981, 1986; Brennan 1984, 1988). Some non-anthropocentrists argue that there is more value in non-human things simply by their being non-human (Elliot 1997; Katz 1997). A challenge has been how to develop a non-misanthropic version of this view.

Conceptual challenges

Since the 1980s it has become commonplace to classify environmental philosophies in terms of various positions or movements – for example, wise use, social ecology, a variety of feminist approaches (Plumwood 1993), the land ethic, reverence for life, deep ecology, bioregionalism, ethics of place, radical activism, wilderness ethics, and animist or panpsychist metaphysics (for examples of the latter see Harvey 2005; Mathews 2005). These approaches deploy for the most part the very ideas and concepts already introduced. One cluster of ideas involves the expansion of moral concern, and the corresponding extension of the vocabulary of *intrinsic value*, *respect* and *duty*, to things other than human moral agents, particularly to animals, plants, mountains, ecosystems and even the biosphere as a whole. Alongside the adoption of this strategy was the rejection of human-centered approaches to ethics. One problem for all such theories is to find a plausible criterion of moral value or at least of moral standing (where by "moral standing" was meant the status something has if it, or some aspect of its existence, well-being, etc., should enter directly into our moral deliberations).

The traditional view of moral standing is associated with the more familiar concept of legal standing (Stone 1987). To have standing in law is to be able to be recognized and protected by law, and such standing is attributed to people and some non-human entities – for example, companies, governments and various other "merely legal persons." Standing in this sense is attributed to things, not their properties. So in virtue of what properties does a thing attain standing? Citizenship, or corporate registration, can be properties that confer legal standing. But what about moral standing? The search was on for some property or aspects that would provide a criterion for moral standing. In the framework of Christianity, being loved by God would be an explanation for the moral standing of human beings. Those influenced by Kant held that the ability for self-reflection and self-rule justified the claim for humans – and maybe some animals – to have standing in morality. Utilitarians, following Bentham, canvassed the idea that the capacity to suffer, to feel pleasures or pains might be a significant criterion of moral standing and impose on us a responsibility to consider our actions towards animals in the light of this fact. The focus on moral standing in environmental philosophy became a search for a wider criterion to include many more things than human beings and sentient animals in the domain of objects appropriate for direct moral consideration. Proposals for such criteria – including having some form of awareness (e.g. being a "subject of a life" as in Regan 1983), being alive (or a teleological center of life as in Taylor 1981), being natural (variously construed as not being interfered with by humans [Katz 1977] or by rational beings [Elliot 1997]), being endangered, being in a relation of a certain kind to valuers (Callicott 1989), even a holistic entity of a certain kind such as species, populations and ecosystems (Callicott 1989).

The challenge of finding some criterion of moral standing is often equated with the problem of finding a criterion of intrinsic value. Such an equation is not particularly harmful. The common implication of possessing moral standing, on the one side, and intrinsic value, on the other, is that the thing in question deserves moral protection. It can be helpful to distinguish entities from properties. The latter are aspects possessed by things. For example, being sentient is an aspect, or property, of an animal. Traditionally the term "moral standing" has been used to describe things, not their properties. So the animal would be a candidate for moral standing, not its property of being in pain. However, intrinsic value is often attributed to the properties and aspects of things as well as to the things themselves. Both the experiences of animals, and the animals themselves, can have intrinsic value (or disvalue).

For utilitarians like Peter Singer, the experiences of all sentient beings have intrinsic value or disvalue. The rat's experience of pain is something which is intrinsically bad, and therefore we should be morally concerned to reduce or eradicate it, he claims (Singer 2003). By so arguing, he extends the kind of view which was held by G. E. Moore that the only intrinsically valuable things in the world were human experiences. One dispute between utilitarians on the one hand, and rights theorists on the other is whether – say – an animal itself is intrinsically valuable, or is merely a vessel that contains experiences that themselves may or may not be valuable. According to the latter view, the painless killing of an animal is morally acceptable if doing so reduces the amount of unhappiness in the world, especially if we are going to replace it with a happier animal. For the rights-theorist, by contrast, questions of whether it is right or wrong to kill an animal is not settled by considerations about the balance of happiness and unhappiness in the world. This is why Regan, for example, accuses utilitarians of being concerned only with what is in the vessel, not with the value of the vessel itself (Regan 1983).

The debate regarding what things apart from human have intrinsic value is further complicated by the fact that the notion of intrinsic value itself is multiply ambiguous. Much confusion can be avoided by adopting the following terminology:

(i) *x* has *non-instrumental value*: *x* has value independent of its usefulness, that is, regardless of whether *x* is a means to some other end. Human beings may be the prime example of things of non-instrumental value.

(ii) *x* has *non-subjective value* (i.e., *objective value*): *x* has value independent of subjects' attitudes. Some writers argue that natural objects and processes have just such value: for example, a world with a diversity of plant species, but without any valuing subjects in it, would be objectively valuable in this sense (e.g. Routley 1973; Rolston 1975).

(iii) *x* has *non-relational value* (sometimes called *non-extrinsic value)*: *x* has value independent of any relation *x* may or may not have to anything else (Moore 1903). Some writers argue that every animal has equal value, whether the species to which it belongs is endangered or not, whether endemic or not. This would be because each animal is a center of life and experience – a property that depends on no relations to other things (Regan 1983).

In much of the literature, the term "intrinsic value" is often used simply to mean "non-instrumental value." Using it this way does not exclude its opposite: trees may be valued for their own sake as well as for their uses (such as providing timber or supplying windbreaks). However, it is easy to slide from sense (i) to a stronger sense such as (ii) or (iii). Key writers in the field, such as Baird Calliott and Holmes Rolston, have argued both for the intrinsic (non-instrumental) value of nature and for the objectivity of value in nature. In this way, they follow

Leopold's exhortations to show "love" and "respect" for the land – attitudes that make sense if the land is regarded as having value in both senses (i) and (ii).

Extending the notion of intrinsic value to sense (iii) raises real problems, however, for conservation biology and much everyday thinking about the value of endangered species. When non-native (or "exotic") species threaten the indigenous populations in an area, there is often a strong response in favor of the native. In Australia, for example, foxes and other species introduced by European settlers have been the subject of control and extermination often through methods such as poisoning that inflict a high toll of pain and suffering on the target animals. Here is an issue where animal welfare considerations drive a wedge between animal liberation, on the one hand, and environmental ethics, on the other – a rift that has not been satisfactorily resolved so far (see Callicott's essay "Animal Liberation: A Triangular Affair," reprinted in Callicott 1989). Some writers (Rolston 1989, for example) have claimed that the species has value above the individual and the ecosystem above the species. The resulting conception of a value hierarchy has been condemned by animal liberationists. If an individual should be sacrificed when this is necessary to protect the good of the larger community, then an analogy with totalitarian thought becomes possible. In some of his early work, Callicott maintained that if culling a population of deer was necessary for the protection of larger ecosystemic goods, then it was clearly a Leopoldian, land-ethical requirement that such culling take place. The extension of such a requirement to populations of humans, rather than deer, would seem to be a consistent application of the land ethic, albeit one that would be unacceptable as a general policy recommendation and untenable as a serious ethical position. Two issues, however, should be separated out in this case. First is the disagreement between holistically oriented environmental philosophers and more individualistically oriented defenders of animal rights and animal liberation. Treating wholes such as the land, the species or the ecosystem as entities with moral value does raise new possibilities for value ranking and value conflicts – ones that have not been satisfactorily resolved in the ongoing debate between animal liberation theorists and environmental ethicists.

On the other hand, the charge of environmental totalitarianism was also associated with rejection of a claim that is common to totalitarian political philosophies, that some master principle or overarching set of values can be found, and that all other values are subservient to these. Sometimes this charge was linked to the charge that environmental ethics was inherently conservative and hostile to the relief of poverty (see Rolston 1996, and the response by Guha 1999) or a vision of the world propagated by comfortable westerners (see the essays in Guha and Martinez-Alier 1997). Philosophical critiques claimed that a rigidly monistic or hierarchic conception of value does scant justice to the complexity of our moral situation. The philosophical debate largely recapitulated an earlier debate over moral pluralism that has recently re-emerged as a contested matter in moral theory. One of the twentieth century's best-known moral theorists, W. D. Ross, outlined a pluralistic ethic in which our various moral duties – such as those of keeping promises, of self-improvement, of acting justly, and so on – are not reducible to any single duty or principle. Ross's original argument for pluralism made use of an intuition about "what we really think." Even if some systematic moral theory based on a single overarching principle, a single core duty, or a set of such duties, were to yield satisfying answers to our moral problems, Ross argued that such a system would not match "what we really think" when we engage in moral reflection. According to him, "what we really think" is that we have many different – and irreducible – sources of moral obligation (Ross 2002/1930).

Ever since Ross put forward the case for moral pluralism, theorists have worried that such an account of moral duties leaves us with a disparate set of duties without internal connection among them. In response to defenses of pluralism in environmental ethics by a variety of writers (including Christopher Stone [1987], Gary Varner [1991] and Andrew Brennan [1992]), Callicott has maintained that pluralist ethics fails to provide a consistent systematization of moral decision-taking, and might even lead to relativism and nihilism (Callicott 1990). For Callicott, an environmental ethic should ideally be monistic, that is, committed to a single system of values. More precisely, it should provide clear principles for action, and where there is conflict among these it should provide guidance on which principle has priority over the others.

Over time, Callicott has modified his views in order to try to give weight to different scales and degrees of obligation that humans might have to the individuals and groups with whom they interact and share the planet. By so doing, he attempts to maintain a non-pluralist ethic, while avoiding the charge of eco-fascism. What, then, of the situation when, as members of the multilayered communities to which we belong, we are faced with conflicts among competing interests? Callicott argues that in such cases, we should give preference to the interests of those communities (and individuals) to whom we are closely related, and give attention to communities and individuals at a greater emotional distance from us only when some very strong interest of theirs is at stake (Callicott 1990; Lo 2001). As critics have pointed out, Callicott's own proposal itself seems to lead to a kind of pluralism and may lead to support for the very anthropocentrism he was trying to avoid in the first place. These arguments echo familiar puzzles elsewhere in moral theory over how to bring coherence and unity to our ethical reflections. Echoing a complaint forcefully put by Bernard Williams, we can ask whether the appearance of systematicity in some parts of our moral thinking itself fools us into believing that we can one day hope for a complete systematization and structuring of all of ethics (Williams 1985).

The conceptual and the empirical

Given that ethics is deeply concerned with issues about how to live flourishing lives, what reasons are appropriate to move us to action, and with other practical matters, ethical theorizing itself has developed in tandem with sensitivity to matters of fact, questions of means and ends and concern with the practical application of principles. Although recent concern with climate change and energy use has brought environmental issues to the forefront of debate in many countries, there has often been a perceived gap between the rhetoric of environmental care, respect and protection and the actual behavior of individuals and governments in the face of declining environmental quality and increasing scarcity of environmental goods. Theorists have been quick to identify failure to protect the environment as itself a symptom of a deeper intellectual or conceptual malaise. The historian Lynn White Jr (1967) suggested that Christianity itself may be the source of environmental destruction, while feminists have suggested that patriarchy has encouraged anti-environmental attitudes and the deep ecology movement, as described above, has put the blame at least partly on the atomized, individualistic bias of standard western thought.

What has not been much recognized is that all of these diagnoses of our environmental problems have themselves depended on factual claims that have so far not been subject to test or much scrutiny. White's original argument about the religious sources of human environmental destructiveness has a structure that is typical of many different diagnoses. At heart his argument was very simple: first, that Christianity itself encourages a kind of anthropocentrism; second, that anthropocentrism is bad for the environment, and thus – in conclusion – that Christianity is the source of environmental destruction. White's article, originally published in the journal *Science* in 1967, provoked vigorous responses from a variety of authors, several of whom argued that Christianity itself can be the source of an ethic of environmental stewardship which could motivate care, protection and preservation of the environment (Passmore 1980; Attfield 1983). The focus of much critique of White's argument has not been so much the claim that Christianity encouraged anthropocentric ways of thinking (perhaps a surprising claim in terms of the value Christianity gives to the non-human realm of God and the angels) but rather the association made between anthropocentric thought and environmental damage.

Exactly the same argument structure also underpins the claims of some feminists and deep ecologists. For the former, patriarchal thought is male-centered and such androcentrism is itself just a narrower version of anthropocentrism. For the latter, individualistic modes of thought themselves encourage a particular emphasis on human rights and human value, a kind of human-centeredness or chauvinism, that makes it hard to give proper weight to the value of nature and the individuals and systems it embraces. In these cases, human-centeredness is linked to attitudes and behaviors that are either anti-environmental, or too weak to provide the kind of protection of which the environment stands in dire need. But at the heart of all these theories is a real unclarity over empirical and conceptual matters.

The widespread rejection of anthropocentrism by many environmental philosophers is capable of two readings, a point that has passed largely unnoticed in the literature. The first reading is an evaluative one: that natural non-human things have intrinsic value, that is, value in their own right independent of any use they have for humans. Easily confused with this is a second – but empirically debatable – claim: that people who believe in anthropocentrism (the ones who think humans are special) are more likely to have un-environmental attitudes, and to be environmentally damaging in their behavior, than those who hold non-anthropocentrism as a value stance. This second claim is a socio- or psycho-behavioral one, which may look obviously true, but whose truth can be tested by empirical means.

For example, it is not a conceptual truth that agricultural people who worship and value nature, who pray to nature spirits, or who make offerings to forest gods before cutting down trees are always less damaging to their natural surroundings than those who try to farm in ways that provide a steady income stream to the family and who have no particularly anti-anthropocentric value stance. Indeed, some evidence from the study of Latin American farming groups has suggested that the latter sometimes practice more sustainable forms of agriculture than the former (Durham 1995; Martinez-Alier 2002).

The assumption that the factual, psycho-behavioral thesis is true explains why so much of environmental philosophy can be seen as a mission to secure converts to non-anthropocentrism about value. Indeed, some of the main theorists of environmental philosophy – especially Callicott – have been emphatic in claiming that only a non-anthropocentric ethic can deserve the label "environmental." If the psycho-behavioral thesis turned out to be false, then not only the discipline itself, but also several of the leading diagnostic theories of the origin of the environmental predicament will be seriously undermined. Now there is plainly a problematic core to the psycho-behavioral thesis given its dependence on empirical claims that cannot be answered by purely philosophical reasoning. In fact, to be credible, they must be able to stand up to empirical testing. The same is true for a range of other diagnostic claims as well. Feminists sometimes claim that patriarchal thought is characterized by dualism and value hierarchies: dualisms which oppose male with female, reason with emotion, mind with body, and so on, privileging one side of the dualism (the male side) as superior to the other. Again, it is an empirical question whether people who think in dualistic and hierarchical ways are in fact more likely to have anthropocentric attitudes and more likely to act harmfully towards the environment. As social science research has often shown, common-sense notions about attitudes and behavior developed separately from empirical studies cannot be relied on to deliver the truth about the relation of thought to action.

Just as the debate on moral pluralism in environmental philosophy echoes the wider philosophical debate about ethical theory, so the question about the empirical assumptions of deep ecology, feminist theories and other positions resonates with the emerging interest in empirical matters that bear on philosophy of mind, consciousness studies and applied ethics. In the case of theories about the environment, the relation between the conceptual and evaluative components of theories and their alleged factual implications may be clear enough to encourage some interdisciplinary studies of the material just discussed.

See also Reasons, values, and morality (Chapter 36); Population ethics (Chapter 61); Animals (Chapter 62).

References

Attfield, Robin (1983) *The Ethics of Environmental Concern*, Oxford: Basil Blackwell.

Bookchin, Murray (1978/1965) "Ecology and Revolutionary Thought," *Antipode* 10: 21–32. (Originally written under the pseudonym Lewis Herber.)

Brennan, Andrew (1984) "The Moral Standing of Natural Objects," *Environmental Ethics* 6: 35–56.

——(1988) *Thinking About Nature*, Athens, GA: University of Georgia Press.

——(1992) "Moral Pluralism and the Environment," *Environmental Values* 1: 5–33.

Callicott, J. Baird (1989) *In Defense of the Land Ethic: Essays in Environmental Philosophy*, Albany: State University of New York Press.

——(1990) "The Case Against Moral Pluralism," *Environmental Ethics* 12: 99–124.

Carson, R. (1963) *Silent Spring*, London: Hamish Hamilton.

Durham, W. (1995) "Political Ecology and Environmental Destruction in Latin America," in M. Painter and W. Durham (eds) *The Social Causes of Environmental Destruction in Latin America*, Ann Arbor: University of Michigan Press.

Elliot, Robert (1997) *Faking Nature*, London: Routledge.

Guha, Ramachandra (1999) "Radical American Environmentalism Revisited," in Witoszek and Brennan 1999.

Guha, Ramachandra and Martinez-Alier, Joan (eds) (1997) *Varieties of Environmentalism: Essays North and South*, London: Earthscan Publications.

Hardin, G. (1972) *Exploring New Ethics for Survival*, New York: Viking.

Harvey, Graham (2005) *Animism: Respecting the Living World*, New York: Columbia University Press.

Katz, Eric (1997) *Nature as Subject*, New York: Rowman & Littlefield.

Leopold, Aldo (1949) *A Sand County Almanac*, Oxford: Oxford University Press.

Lo, Y. S. (2001) "The Land Ethic and Callicott's Ethical System (1980–2001): An Overview and Critique," *Inquiry* 44: 331–58.

Martinez-Alier, Joan (2002) *The Environmentalism of the Poor: A Study of Ecological Conflicts and Valuation*, Cheltenham: Edward Elgar.

Mathews, Freya (2005) *Reinhabiting Reality: Towards a Recovery of Culture*, Sydney, Australia: University of New South Wales Press.

Meadows, D. H., Meadows, D. L., Randers, J. and Behrens, W. W. (1972) *The Limits to Growth*, New York: Universe Books.

Moore, G. E. (1903) *Principia Ethica*, Cambridge: Cambridge University Press.

Næss, Arne (1995/1973) "The Shallow and the Deep, Long-Range Ecology Movement," *Inquiry* 16; repr. in George Sessions (ed.) *Deep Ecology for the 21st Century*, Boston, MA: Shambhala, pp. 151–5.

Passmore, J. (1980/1974) *Man's Responsibility for Nature*, 2nd edn, London: Duckworth.

Plumwood, Val (1993) *Feminism and the Mastery of Nature*, London: Routledge.

Regan, Tom (1983) *The Case for Animal Rights*, London: Routledge & Kegan Paul.

Rolston, Holmes (1975) "Is There an Ecological Ethic," *Ethics* 85: 83–109.

——(1988) *Environmental Ethics: Duties to and Values in the Natural World*, Philadelphia, PA: Temple University Press.

——(1996) "Feeding People versus Saving Nature?," in W. Aiken and H. LaFollette (eds) *World Hunger and Morality*, Englewood Cliffs, NJ: Prentice-Hall, pp. 248–67.

Ross, W. D. (2002/1930) *The Right and the Good*, Oxford: Oxford University Press.

Routley, Richard (1973) "Is There a Need for a New, an Environmental Ethic?" *Proceedings of the 15th World Congress of Philosophy*, vol. 1, Sophia: Sophia Press, pp. 205–10.

Sessions, George (ed.) (1995) *Deep Ecology for the 21st Century*, Boston, MA: Shambhala.

Singer, Peter (2003) "Animal Liberation at 30," *New York Review of Books* 50, no. 8.

Stone, Christopher D. (1987) *Earth and Other Ethics*, New York: Harper & Row.

Taylor, Paul (1981) "The Ethics of Respect for Nature," *Environmental Ethics* 3: 197–218.

——(1986) *Respect for Nature*, Princeton, NJ: Princeton University Press.

Varner, Gary E. (1991) "No Holism without Pluralism," *Environmental Ethics* 13: 175–9.

White, L. (1967) "The Historical Roots of Our Ecological Crisis," *Science* 155: 1203–7.

Williams, B. (1985) *Ethics and the Limits of Philosophy*, London: Fontana.

Witoszek, N. and Brennan, A. (eds) (1999) *Philosophical Dialogues: Arne Næss and the Progress of Eco-Philosophy*, New York: Rowan & Littlefield.

Further reading

Bookchin, M. (1980) *Toward an Ecological Society*, Montreal, Canada: Black Rose Books.

Brennan, A. and Lo, Y. S. (Forthcoming in 2010) *Understanding Environmental Philosophy*, London: Acumen. (A detailed treatment of the key issues in contemporary environmental philosophy.)

Elliot, R. and Gare, A. (eds) (1983) *Environmental Philosophy: A Collection of Readings*, Milton Keynes, UK: Open University Press. (A useful collection of influential early essays.)

Jamieson, Dale (ed.) (2003) *A Companion to Environmental Philosophy*, Oxford: Blackwell. (Comprehensive descriptions of the history of environmental philosophy, contemporary issues, and connections with other branches of philosophy.)

Norton, Bryan (1991) *Toward Unity among Environmentalists*, New York: Oxford University Press.

Pojman, L. and Pojman, P. (2007) *Environmental Ethics: Readings in Theory and Application*, New York: Barnes & Noble. (One of many comprehensive anthologies of key readings in the subject.)

Sagoff, Mark (1988) *The Economy of the Earth: Philosophy, Law and the Environment*, Cambridge: Cambridge University Press. (A classic study of the difference between ethical and economic valuation of nature.)

(v)
CURRENT ISSUES

64
THE ETHICS OF FREE SPEECH

Mary Kate McGowan

Most liberal societies are deeply committed to a principle of free speech. As a result, we sometimes tolerate very disagreeable speech. This is as it should be. After all, people have the right to say false things and they even have the right to say false and obnoxious things. Even more than this, though, some speech (e.g. racist hate speech) appears to be *harmful*. Arguably, racist hate speech undermines equality by causing things like racial discrimination. In this way, it looks as if allowing such speech means that one values the right to free speech even more than equality. Might our commitment to free speech be so strong that it is more important than our commitment to equality?

Since a commitment to free speech is so important, it is prudent to be as clear as possible about what this commitment involves. For one thing, it does *not* mean that a person is free to say whatever that person wants to say. As we shall see, plenty of speech is regulated (e.g. insider trading, defamation, contracts). Furthermore, regulating such speech is perfectly compatible with a commitment to free speech. What a commitment to free speech does, rather, is make it *more difficult* to regulate speech. This means that the justifications offered for regulating speech must meet raised standards. In this way, a principle of free speech extends special protections to speech that make it more difficult to regulate.

Why should it be more difficult to regulate speech than it is to regulate other actions? What is it about speech that warrants these special protections? In other words, what makes speech so valuable? Theorists disagree about the right answer to this question but most offer one (or a combination) of the following three sorts of answers. The first answer maintains that speech ought to be protected because the free flow of ideas is the best (or only) way to access the truth (or knowledge). By saying what we think and by attending to the opinions and reactions of others, we, as a society, are more likely to form better-justified and hence true beliefs (Mill 1978). The second answer contends that speech must be protected in order for a democracy to function well. A society will be genuinely democratic only if we are free to criticize the government, tell our representatives what we want them to do and freely discuss matters of public concern (Meiklejohn 1960). Finally, the third sort of answer maintains that speech must be free in order for persons to be genuinely autonomous by deciding for themselves what to think and do. If the state limits expression, then we are prevented from *even considering* some possibilities when deciding what to do and think. In this way then, the free expression of ideas is a requirement of autonomy (Scanlon 1972). As one can see, there are really two important questions about value here. First, what is so valuable about speech and, second, what is so valuable about the alleged good (e.g. truth, democracy, autonomy) that speech seems to serve?

Another important question concerns what counts as speech for the purposes of a free speech principle. To exactly which class of actions will the special protections be extended? One might think that the answer to this question is straightforward: Everything that is speech (in the ordinary sense) is harder to regulate because of the special protections extended to it in virtue of a free speech principle. Although this answer is simple and intuitive, it is not correct. To see this, notice that burning a flag or wearing an armband, for example, is not speech in the ordinary sense but such actions do count as speech for the purposes of a free speech principle. Moreover, plenty of speech in the ordinary sense (e.g. "I hereby hire you to kill my boss" or "It is henceforth against company policy to hire women") is regulated without raising any free speech concerns at all. Although this is a somewhat controversial way to put the point, it seems that such utterances do not even count as speech for the purposes of a free speech principle. When it comes to free speech then, the word "speech" seems to be being used in a special technical sense and this raises a question about precisely what this special technical sense is. Unfortunately, only a handful of scholars have explicitly addressed this question (Greenawalt 1989; Braddon-Mitchell and West 2004; Schauer 2004; Maitra and McGowan 2007). Despite the neglect of this question, this much seems clear. This question (about what counts as speech) is related to the above question (about what makes speech valuable). In particular, it seems that what ought to count as speech should have the property (or properties) that make speech valuable in the first place.

Regulation

Suppose that Johnny is on trial for hiring an assassin to kill his wife and the prosecution actually has a videotape of Johnny hiring the assassin. On this tape, Johnny can clearly be heard saying to a known assassin: "Now, once you kill her, you'll be sure to hide the body where no one will find it, right? I don't want this coming back on me, you know. So, you'd better do it right, 'cause I'm sure paying you enough!" Suppose that, in his defense, Johnny admits that it is he on the tape but he insists that he has a free speech right to say what he said.

According to Johnny, since his alleged crime merely involves the uttering of words, the government cannot punish him because the government is committed to free speech. As clever as this defense may be, it will not be taken seriously by the courts. Some speech is regulated without raising any free speech concerns at all and hiring an assassin is a case in point. I think this is because Johnny's utterance does not even count as speech in the technical sense of a free speech principle. On this view, his utterance is easy to regulate exactly because the special protections extended to speech (in the technical sense) are not extended to utterances like his.

Other categories of speech (e.g. defamation) are regulated even though they do count as speech in the free speech sense. Although special protections are extended to such utterances, the justifications for regulating the speech in question meet the raised standards. The justifications (or arguments) for regulation typically involve the "balancing of harms" approach. On this approach, it is alleged that the harms associated with failing to regulate the speech in question outweigh any harms that would be associated with regulating it. Since this characterization is rather abstract, an example may help. When Peter said that George is a pedophile, for example, Peter said something he knew to be false. Furthermore, what Peter said also damaged George's reputation in certain measurable ways. (Let's say that George lost his job and his wife divorced him because of what Peter said.) As a result, Peter's utterance constitutes defamation and it is thereby an unprotected, and hence regulable, form of speech.

Defamation is regulable, in part, because the harms that would be caused by failing to regulate it outweigh any harms that may be caused by its regulation. To see this, imagine what it would be like if individuals had the legal right to say false and damaging things about one another. In such a case, reputations would be wrongly damaged. Even worse than that, though, we would probably stop believing each other. After all, if people could get away with undermining their enemies (accusers or competitors) with defamatory speech, then we would probably eventually stop trusting what people say about each other. In this way, one can see that *failing* to regulate defamation would undercut what is so valuable about speech. Moreover, since regulating defamatory speech does little to undermine our commitment to free speech, it is clearly less harmful, and therefore better, to regulate it.

Note that, depending on the system of free speech in question, there may be various levels of protection. In other words, it may be that some categories of speech (e.g. political speech) are more valuable, and hence more difficult to regulate, than other categories of speech (e.g. commercial speech). Whether or not some particular kind of speech is regulated will depend on whether the justifications for regulating it meet the relevant (raised) standard (and this will typically involve demonstrating that it is less harmful to regulate it than it is to fail to regulate it).

Strictly speaking, the legitimate regulation of speech requires more than just showing that the balancing of harms turns out a certain way. Given that important values (e.g. autonomy, truth, democracy) justify the special protections that we extend to speech, we should expect that the cost–benefit calculus of this balancing of harms approach is insufficient to restrict the free speech right. In what follows, I identify two further conditions that legitimate regulations must meet.

Although there are differences in free speech law between different countries, certain principles seem to guide the legitimate regulation of speech. First, any legitimate regulation of speech must carefully identify the precise class of speech to be regulated. To get a sense of this, consider the following example. Suppose that a young member of the Aryan Nation burns a cross on the lawn of an African American family in the very white community of Mattapoisett, Massachusetts. The residents of Mattapoisett are, quite rightly, very upset by this action and they demand that a new law be enacted to prohibit such things in the future. Suppose that, in response, the town enacts a law prohibiting the burning of crosses. This law would be problematic because it is "over broad." It would, after all, prohibit actions that should not be prohibited. In particular, it would prohibit Helen, for example, from burning a cross as a political protest against the (recent pedophile-priest-protecting actions of the) Catholic Church. Good legislation will take care to target all and *only* the speech that ought to be targeted. (Of course, it may prove difficult *in practice* to pinpoint the *exact* class of speech in question.)

Second, legitimate regulations of speech are also content-neutral. To see this, suppose next that the town enacts a law prohibiting all racist cross-burnings. Although this might do a better job of targeting the right cases, it violates the principle of content (or viewpoint) neutrality which states that the reasons for regulating a certain category of speech should not be based on the viewpoint expressed by that speech. Since the government should not be in the business of deciding what we ought to think, the government should not regulate speech based on the views expressed. As a result, it would be illegitimate to ban cross-burning because it expresses racist views. Of course, this leaves it open whether it might be legitimate to ban (some) cross-burnings on other grounds. Perhaps the instances of cross-burnings that ought to be regulated are all and only those instances that constitute a serious threat of death or bodily injury. Perhaps instead they are all and only those instances that constitute a certain sort of intimidation.

As one can see, regulations of speech (in this technical sense) are justified only if the harms associated with the speech clearly outweigh the harms that would be associated with its regulation. Although demonstrating this is *necessary* for regulation, it is not sufficient. Further conditions are, first, that the regulation carefully identify the exact class of speech to be regulated and, second, that the basis for the regulation be content-neutral. I here leave it open whether there are further conditions as well.

In certain especially controversial cases, it can be quite difficult to assess the merits of any particular argument for regulation. This is because such arguments often rely on controversial empirical claims (e.g. the consumption of pornography causes rape, regulating racist hate speech would chill too much race-related political speech, regulating pornography would ultimately harm homosexuals). In the following section, I present some of the controversies regarding the free speech status of pornography.

Pornography

There are many different kinds of pornography and it is very difficult, if not impossible, to define. Thus, in order to simplify our discussion, I will begin by excluding some pornographic materials from our discussion. We will not be concerned with the types of pornography that are already illegal. Snuff films (i.e. films of actual rape–murders) and child pornography (i.e. films or pictures of sexual acts with minor children) involve crimes in their very production. As a result, the creation and possession of such material is illegal. Also, we will not be concerned with erotica (i.e. sexually explicit images of mutually consenting and mutually respectful adults). Erotica is importantly different from pornography (or from the sort of pornography that concerns us here) because pornography depicts and *endorses* degrading or abusive sexual behavior (Longino 1980). Thus, for the purposes of our discussion and to fix ideas, we shall be concerned with sexually explicit materials that endorse degrading and/or abusive sexual activity.

Certainly, some disagreements about the alleged harm of pornography arise because theorists have different materials in mind when they make their respective claims about it. Suppose, for example, that Les maintains that pornography is liberating because it presents and celebrates healthy gay sexual relations while Catharine maintains that pornography is oppressive because it portrays women as mere sexual objects. It seems that, in this case, Les and Catharine have different materials in mind. Les appears to be making a claim about gay erotica while Catharine is concerned with a certain sort of heterosexual pornography. Thus, when discussing pornography (or when evaluating a discussion about it), it is prudent to keep this possibility in mind.

That said, not all disagreements about pornography arise in this manner. People certainly do disagree about the harmfulness of pornography even when they are talking about the very same materials. In what follows, I briefly survey some of the positions taken on pornography and I assume, even if only to make the discussion manageable, that all theorists are talking about the same sorts of materials (i.e. sexually explicit materials that endorse degrading and/or abusive sexual acts).

Some theorists argue for the regulation of pornography on the grounds that it encourages promiscuity and other aberrant sexual behaviors. Such arguments, which sometimes appeal to obscenity law, typically appeal to shared (moral) standards of decency and are concerned primarily with the alleged immoral content of the sexual activity depicted (Devlin 1965; Clor 1970).

Others see pornography as liberating exactly because it presents a wide variety of sexual behaviors as both legitimate and enjoyable. Pro-porn feminists, for example, see porn as an important form of cultural expression with a multiplicity of meaning and they are also typically quite critical of claims that pornography causes harm (Williams 1989; Kipnis 1996). Although it is clear that pornography offends people, it is significantly less clear that pornography actually harms anyone.

Pornography is alleged to cause a wide variety of harms. Some claim that women are abused in various ways in the very making of pornography (MacKinnon and Dworkin 1997). Others allege (typically in addition) that consuming pornography causes harms like rape, gender discrimination and even the political disenfranchisement of women generally (Russell 2000). Some feminists even claim that pornography "silences" women in a way that violates women's right to free speech (MacKinnon 1987a; Hornsby 1993; Langton 1993; Maitra 2009). Note that if this silencing claim is correct, then *failing* to regulate pornography damages free speech.

Despite all this, some maintain that, even if pornography causes these harms, attempting to regulate it would be even more harmful (Easterbrook 1985; Carse 1995). The main worry seems to be that attempting to regulate pornography would inevitably lead to the regulation of speech that ought to remain protected. In this way, it is alleged that regulating pornography would undermine free speech. Moreover, since other remedies are available (e.g. educating people about the harmful effects of pornography or promoting the political power of women), regulation is thought to be unnecessary and hence unwarranted.

Unsurprisingly, others claim that the balancing of harms works out differently. According to such theorists, the harms caused to women by pornography outweigh any harms that might be caused by its regulation. Such theorists also claim that the alleged remedies are inadequate and that careful legislation would minimize (or even avoid) damage to free speech anyway.

There are also feminists who contend that, in addition to *causing* harm to women, pornography actually *constitutes* harm. According to MacKinnon (1987b), for example, pornography ought to be legally actionable because it constitutes an otherwise illegal act of gender discrimination.

Another radical argument claims that pornography is more like prostitution than expression and so it should not be treated as speech in this technical sense (Schauer 1982: 181–2). Note that, in the United States, it is illegal to hire a prostitute and it is illegal to hire a prostitute to have sex with somebody else. Schauer then asks why pornography is legal in the United States when it involves paying people to have sex with each other and then recording and distributing their "performance."

As one can see, the free speech status of pornography is no simple matter. Whether it is (or ought to be) regulated depends, first, on whether it counts (or ought to count) as speech in this technical sense. Second, if it does count as speech, then it ought to be regulated only if the harms it causes (or constitutes) outweigh the harms that would be caused (or constituted) by its regulation.

Note that even if one has the *legal* (free speech) right to participate in pornography, it certainly does not follow that doing so is the *morally* right thing to do. Remember that the law is not in the business of enforcing morality. Plenty of immoral things are legally permissible (e.g. cheating on one's spouse, lying, cheating while playing gin rummy with one's friends). So, just because the law permits participation in pornography does not mean that such participation is morally OK. In fact, there is reason to believe that such participation is, at least sometimes, morally problematic. After all, acting in a pornographic film (or posing for a pornographic photograph) might be extremely damaging to people you love. Doing so could harm your spouse, your parents or even your (current or future) self. Furthermore, being involved in the production of pornography is morally suspect, if, for example, the "actors" involved are abused, exploited or coerced. Moreover, distributing or selling pornography is morally problematic if, for example, its consumption really does cause the harms alleged. (Of course, there are complicated issues here regarding when an agent is responsible for such causal consequences.)

In fact, some argue that the real issue with pornography is moral, as opposed to legal. Altman (2007), for example, argues that we have a moral right to (even violent) pornography and this right is grounded in our right to sexual autonomy (as opposed to our free speech right). Brison (2007) argues against this right to pornography. According to her, autonomy can be respected without protecting such harmful pornography (1998). Finally, Dwyer (2005) argues that, even though one has a legal right to consume (cyber)pornography, one ought to refrain from doing so because of the damage to one's moral character that results.

Racist hate speech

The free speech status of racist hate speech is also controversial. Like pornography, it too is extremely difficult (if not impossible) to define. Following Matsuda (1993), let's say that racist hate speech is a persecutory, hateful and degrading message of racial inferiority aimed directly at a member of a racialized group. Some of it is clearly illegal. If such an utterance incites a crime, for example, then it would be punishable. Suppose, for instance, that Charlie utters racist hate speech to Peter knowing full well that doing so will make Peter so mad that Peter will certainly assault him. In a case like this, Charlie's "fighting words" are regulable (Greenawalt 1995).

Arguably, though, most instances of racist hate speech are not like this. Whether racist hate speech is (or ought to be) regulable seems to depend on how the balancing of harms works out. Since the free speech status of racist hate speech depends on this balancing of harms, let us now turn to a consideration of the alleged harms involved.

Racist hate speech is alleged to cause many different sorts of harm. According to Delgado (1993), for example, racist hate speech causes both immediate (e.g. anxiety, fear) and long-term (e.g. high blood pressure, low self-esteem) harm to the person addressed. Racist hate speech is also alleged to cause more widespread social harms (e.g. racial violence, racial discrimination, and the political disempowerment of people of color). Some theorists claim that, in addition to causing various harms, racist hate speech also *is* the harm of racial subordination (Lawrence 1993; Matsuda 1993). Such speech is alleged to mark persons of color as socially inferior. Finally, if racist hate speech silences people of color and if that silencing violates the free speech right, then *failing* to regulate racist hate speech will harm free speech.

On the other side of this balancing act, it is alleged that regulating racist hate speech would (or could) cause various harms. Some believe, for example, that by regulating such speech, we would thereby be prevented from identifying the racists. Moreover, such a result would be harmful because we would thereby be prevented from making the world a better place by, for example, educating them about race or avoiding them (and their racial abuse). Some contend that regulating racist hate speech would actually *increase* racial violence because the uttering of racist hate speech allows racists to let off steam thereby preventing such violence. Still others maintain that since freedom of speech is required to gain rights for minorities, anything that regulates speech will thereby harm freedom of speech and ultimately undermine the rights of minorities. For a response to such arguments, see Delgado and Yun (1995). Similarly, some express a distrust for the government and insist that any governmental regulation on racist hate speech would ultimately backfire and be used against members of racial minority groups (Butler 1997). Perhaps the most common concern is that any regulation of racist hate speech would eventually lead to the regulation of speech that ought to remain protected. The concern seems to be that if racist *hate* speech is regulated then so eventually will *all* discussions of race and, since so many issues of public concern involve race, such a result would seriously undermine free speech.

As one can see, the free speech status of racist hate speech is a fairly complex affair. There are subtle and difficult to assess causal claims involved and, even if such claims could be established one way or the other, settling how to weigh the various harms is a further complication. As things currently stand in the United States, most racist hate speech is protected. Although it is generally agreed that racist hate speech causes various harms, it is the official opinion of the US courts that regulating it would be even more harmful. It is interesting to note that the United States here departs from the rest of the international community which has criminalized all racist hate propaganda (Matsuda 1993). In the United Kingdom, for example, speech that incites racial hatred is regulable on the grounds that it is more harmful than its regulation. As one can see, different systems of free speech can yield different conclusions about what ought to be regulated.

Keep in mind, however, that even if one has a legal right to utter racist hate speech, it certainly does not follow that doing so is morally right. After all, if such speech causes *any* of the harms alleged, then engaging in it is morally suspect.

Lies, promises and disrespectful speech

Lying is a fairly familiar immoral form of speech. Some lies are even illegal. When one is under oath, for example, one is legally obligated to tell the truth. As a result, lying in a court of law can constitute the crime of perjury. Although there are such illegal lies, most lies are perfectly legal. Suppose, for example, that during the course of a casual conversation with a total stranger in the supermarket, I lie and claim to be a corporate attorney from Philadelphia. While one might wonder why anyone would bother to do this, such a lie is perfectly legal. Maybe such a lie is harmless. Maybe it is not. Maybe such a lie is immoral whether or not it is harmful. Maybe it is not.

Other legal lies, however, are clearly immoral. Consider the following whopper of a lie. Cindy meets Carl and they immediately feel a deep mutual connection. Just two weeks after meeting, Carl informs Cindy that he has been diagnosed with an inoperable form of stomach cancer. They mourn together. Carl then tells Cindy that he wants to spend what little time he has left making love with the woman of his dreams. Wanting desperately to support the man she loves, Cindy works desperately to satisfy his every sexual whim. Eventually Cindy discovers that the perfectly healthy Carl lied about the stomach cancer in order to gain sympathy and lots of sex. Supposing that Cindy does not suffer financially, the harm of Carl's lie is not legally recoverable. Although Carl's lie is perfectly legal, he nevertheless did something seriously awful to Cindy. As one can see, even when issues of legality are beside the point, mere words can be incredibly harmful.

Notice also that words are often involved in the undertaking of obligations. When I promised my neighbor that I would watch her child swimming, for example, I thereby undertook an obligation by saying what I said. If I subsequently fail to watch her child, I have done something immoral. Had I not promised to do so, however, I would not have been under any such obligation and so my failure to watch the child would not be a moral failing. As one can see, it is the speech act of promising that creates the obligation and thus the possibility of moral failure.

Finally, speech plays a pivotal role in the construction and perpetuation of social hierarchies. If such hierarchies are unjust then there is a moral component to the speech associated with them. To see what I have in mind, consider the following simplified example. Joe is the coolest kid in fifth grade. Most of his classmates take their cues from Joe since his actions indicate how to act, dress and talk. His actions also indicate who is cool and who is not. Suppose now that a new kid comes to town and, with contempt, Joe calls him a "wuss." By calling the new kid a "wuss," Joe marks the new kid as uncool and thereby makes it socially acceptable for everyone else to treat him accordingly. As a result, the new kid *is* uncool and he is consequently excluded, bullied and mocked. As one can see, Joe's words have the power to affect one's social position (and thus one's treatment).

Now, of course, the social hierarchies in the adult world are considerably more complex and they are also more subtle. Despite this, one ought to be mindful of the possibility that one's words function somewhat like Joe's. By using disparaging terms about another person, for example, one thereby expresses one's disrespect. Doing so is morally suspect (assuming, of course, that such disrespect is unwarranted). Using such terms does more than just express disrespect, though, it also signals to others that such disrespect is in accord with that person's social status. In other words, using such terms marks that person as inferior and this, in turn, licenses further mistreatment (Tirrell 1999; McGowan 2009). While most would no doubt agree that telling racist jokes (or making sexist comments) is morally wrong, most people probably think this is because doing so causes offense. If what I am suggesting here is correct, though, such disrespectful speech may be significantly more harmful than that. As a result, even if one has (or ought to have) the legal right to engage in such speech, anyone interested in social justice should think twice before doing so.

Conclusion

As one can see, being committed to free speech does not mean that one is free to say whatever one wants. Rather, it means that speech is valuable in a way that warrants extending special protections to it so that it is more difficult to regulate. We have also seen that free speech theory is more complex than generally recognized. What makes speech valuable and even what counts as speech are important open questions. Finally, we have seen that different systems of free speech can yield different verdicts regarding which categories of speech ought to be regulated.

Even when one has the legal right to say a certain thing, it does not follow that one is morally right to do so. Although one has the legal right to neglect one's elderly and ailing parents, doing so is wrong. What is legally permissible is one thing. What is morally right is another. Thus, even if the law maintains that one has the right to utter racist hate speech with legal impunity, it does not follow from this that doing so is morally defensible. Similarly, even if the law contends that Charlie has the right to hang a pornographic poster in his locker at work, Charlie may nevertheless be quite wrong to do so.

See also Ethics and law (Chapter 35); Feminist ethics (Chapter 43); Rights (Chapter 56).

References

Altman, A. (2007) "The Right to Get Turned On: Pornography, Autonomy, Equality," in H. LaFollette (ed.) *Ethics in Practice*, 3rd edn, Malden, MA: Blackwell, pp. 387–97; originally published in A. Cohen and C. Wellman (eds) *Contemporary Debates in Applied Ethics*, Malden, MA: Blackwell, 2004, pp. 223–35.

Braddon-Mitchell, D. and West, C. (2004) "What Is Free Speech?," *Journal of Political Philosophy* 12: 437–60.

Brison, S. (1998) "The Autonomy Defense of Free Speech," *Ethics* 108: 312–39.

——(2007) "'The Price We Pay?' Pornography and Harm," in H. LaFollette (ed.) *Ethics in Practice*, 3rd edn, Malden, MA: Blackwell, pp. 377–86; originally published in A. Cohen and C. Wellman (eds) *Contemporary Debates in Applied Ethics*, Malden, MA: Blackwell, 2004, pp. 236–50.

Butler, J. (1997) *Excitable Speech: The Politics of the Performative*, New York: Routledge.

Carse, A. (1995) "Pornography: An Uncivil Liberty," *Hypatia* 10, no. 1: 155–82.

Clor, H. (1970) *Obscenity and Public Morality*, Chicago, IL: University of Chicago Press.

Delgado, R. (1993) "Words That Wound: A Tort Action for Racial Insults, Epithets and Name Calling," in Matsuda et al. 1993, pp. 89–110.

Delgado, R. and Yun, D. (1995) "Pressure Valves and Bloodied Chickens: An Assessment of Four Paternalistic Arguments Resisting Hate-Speech Regulation," in L. Lederer and R. Delgado (eds) *The Price We Pay: The Case Against Racist Hate Speech, Hate Propaganda, and Pornography*, New York: Hill & Wang, pp. 290–300.

Devlin, P. (1965) *The Enforcement of Morals*, London: Oxford University Press.

Dwyer, S. (2005) " 'Enter Here' – At Your Own Risk: The Moral Dangers of Cyberporn," in R. Cavalier (ed.) *The Impact of the Internet on Our Moral Lives*, Albany: State University of New York Press, pp. 69–94.

Easterbrook, F. (1985) *American Booksellers, Inc. v. Hudnut*, 771 F. 2nd 323th Circuit.

Greenawalt, K. (1989) *Speech, Crimes and the Uses of Language*, Oxford: Oxford University Press.

——(1995) *Fighting Words: Individuals, Communities, and Liberties of Speech*, Princeton, NJ: Princeton University Press.

Hornsby, J. (1993) "Speech Acts and Pornography," *Women's Philosophy Review* 10: 38–45.

Kipnis, L. (1996) *Bound and Gagged*, New York: Grove Press.

Langton, R. (1993) "Speech Acts and Unspeakable Acts," *Philosophy & Public Affairs* 22: 293–330.

Lawrence, C. (1993) "If He Hollers Let Him Go: Regulating Racist Speech on Campus," in Matsuda et al. 1993, pp. 53–88.

Longino, H. (1980) "Pornography, Oppression and Freedom: A Closer Look," in L. Lederer (ed.) *Take Back the Night: Women and Pornography*, New York: William & Morrow, pp. 40–54.

MacKinnon, C. (1987a) "Linda's Life and Andrea's Work," in *Feminism Unmodified: Discourses on Life and Law*, Cambridge, MA: Harvard University Press, pp. 127–33.

——(1987b) "Francis Biddle's Sister: Pornography, Civil Rights and Speech," in *Feminism Unmodified: Discourses on Life and Law*, Cambridge, MA: Harvard University Press, pp. 163–97.

MacKinnon, C. and Dworkin, A. (eds) (1997) *In Harm's Way: The Pornography Civil Rights Hearings*, Cambridge, MA: Harvard University Press.

Maitra, I. (2009) "Silencing Speech," *Canadian Journal of Philosophy* 39, no. 2: 309–38.

Maitra, I. and McGowan, M. K. (2007) "The Limits of Free Speech: Pornography and the Question of Coverage," *Legal Theory* 13: 41–68.

Matsuda, M. (1993) "Public Response to Racist Speech: Considering the Victim's Story," in Matsuda et al. 1993, pp. 17–51.

Matsuda, M., Lawrence, C., Delgao, R. and Crenshaw, K. (eds) (1993) *Words That Wound: Critical Race Theory, Assaultive Speech and the First Amendment*, Boulder, CO: Westview Press.
McGowan, M. K. (2009) "Oppressive Speech," *Australasian Journal of Philosophy* 87: 389–407.
Meiklejohn, A. (1960) *Free Speech and its Relation to Government* in *Political Freedom: The Constitutional Powers of the People*, New York: Harper.
Mill, J. S. (1978) *On Liberty*, ed. E. Rapaport, Indianapolis, IN: Hackett.
Russell, D. (2000) "Pornography and Rape: A Causal Model," in D. Cornell (ed.) *Feminism and Pornography*, Oxford: Oxford University Press, pp. 48–93.
Scanlon, T. (1972) "A Theory of Freedom of Expression," *Philosophy & Public Affairs* 1: 204–26.
Schauer, F. (1982) *Free Speech: A Philosophical Enquiry*, Cambridge: Cambridge University Press.
——(2004) "The Boundaries of the First Amendment: A Preliminary Exploration of Constitutional Salience," *Harvard Law Review* 117, no. 6: 1765–1809.
Tirrell, L. (1999) "Derogatory Terms: Racism, Sexism and the Inferential Role of Meaning," in C. Hendricks and K. Oliver (eds) *Language and Liberation: Feminism, Philosophy and Language*, Albany: State University of New York Press, pp. 41–79.
Williams, L. (1989) *Hard Core: Power, Pleasure and the "Frenzy of the Invisible,"* Berkeley, CA: University of California Press.

Further reading

Langton, R. (1993) "Speech Acts and Unspeakable Acts," *Philosophy & Public Affairs* 22: 293–330. (This paper develops some of Catharine MacKinnon's arguments for the regulation of pornography.)
Lawrence, C. (1993) "If He Hollers Let Him Go: Regulating Racist Speech on Campus," in M. Matsuda, C. Lawrence, R. Delgao and K. Krenshaw (eds) *Words that Wound: Critical Race Theory, Assaultive Speech and the First Amendment*, Boulder, CO: Westview Press, pp. 53–88. (This paper argues for the regulation of racist hate speech.)
Longino, H. (1980) "Pornography, Oppression and Freedom: A Closer Look," in L. Lederer (ed.) *Take Back The Night: Women and Pornography*, New York: William & Morrow, pp. 40–54. (This paper distinguishes pornography from erotica.)
Scanlon, T. (1972) "A Theory of Freedom of Expression," *Philosophy & Public Affairs* 1: 204–26. (This paper articulates the autonomy approach to free speech.)
Schauer, F. (1982) *Free Speech: A Philosophical Enquiry*, Cambridge: Cambridge University Press. (This book introduces free speech issues from both a legal and philosophical perspective.)
Sunstein, C. (1993) *Democracy and the Problem of Free Speech*, New York: The Free Press. (This book introduces free speech issues and argues for a new Madisonian system of free speech.)

65
THE ETHICS OF RESEARCH

Julian Savulescu and Tony Hope

Introduction

The ethics of scientific research is one of the most important issues in applied ethics today. We are a part of radical scientific revolution that promises untold benefits for humans, but also threatens our existence in new and profound ways. How we should proceed is an ethical question of the deepest significance. To answer it we require understanding of the reasons for a particular piece of research, and the concept of reasonable risk.

During the Second World War, the Nazi doctors placed healthy, innocent people in freezing water until they froze to death and amputated healthy limbs to test surgical procedures. These appalling experiments, among other atrocities, led to the first internationally agreed guidelines on research involving people – the Nuremberg Code (established in 1946), which was incorporated by the medical profession into the Declaration of Helsinki in 1964. Two influential publications in the 1960s identified several hundred allegedly unethical experiments involving people as the participants in the research (Beecher 1966; Pappworth 1967). These experiments were considered unethical either because they put research participants at unacceptable risk of harm or because they were performed without adequate consent.

Examples of such research were:

- The Tuskegee syphilis study 1932–72
- The Jewish Chronic Disease Hospital New York study 1963
- The Willowbrook study 1956
- The human radiation experiments 1945–72 (Hope et al. 2003).

The Declaration of Helsinki stated that research involving human participants should be clearly formulated in an experimental protocol and reviewed by a committee independent of the researcher. This has led to such review committees being established in most Western countries and these committees can effectively prevent research considered unethical from being carried out. Researchers and review committees are constrained by: professional guidance issued by various bodies, which in the United Kingdom include the Royal College of Physicians (1996), General Medical Council (guidelines established in 2002), British Medical Association (guidelines established in 2004), Medical Research Council (guidelines established in 2004); the common law; a number of statutes such as the *Human Rights Act 1998*, the *Human Tissue Act 2004*, and the *Mental Capacity Act 2005*.

Three ethical principles relevant to human research

There are three main ethical principles relevant to research involving human participants.

Principle 1: Respect for the autonomy of the research participant

One dominant ethical principle in the ethics of research is to respect participant autonomy. This normally requires participants to give valid consent, i.e. the consent must be voluntary (obtained without duress or undue influence), informed (following full and detailed disclosure) and competent.

Principle 2: Minimizing the risk of harm to the research participants

A second principle is that participants should not be put at undue risk of harm through taking part in the research. Current guidelines are paternalistic, limiting the risk to "minimal risk" even if the potential participant gives fully informed consent, and even if she wishes, perhaps from altruistic motives, to take part in such risky research.

Principle 3: Maximizing the overall consequences of the research

On a consequentialist view, the risk of harm to research participants may be justified by the good to people in the future who will benefit from the research. Some consequentialist perspectives would give equal weight to the interests of research participants and those in the future who might benefit from the research. The Declaration of Helsinki and national guidelines reject this position and give much greater weight to the interests of the research participants, although some guidelines suggest that the greater the expected value of the research the greater the risk of harm to the participants that can be justified. No guideline, however, allows significant risk of harm to the research participants for the sake of those in the future. And no guideline considers risk of technologies derived from the knowledge arising from research to future people as a ground for prohibiting research. We will return to this latter point below.

Key ethical considerations in carrying out research

These three ethical principles lead to three major ethical considerations for researchers and review committees.

Consideration 1: Scientific validity

The Declaration of Helsinki (Principle 11) emphasizes the importance of research conforming to "generally accepted scientific principles" (World Medical Association 2000). Research that is scientifically poor is unethical for two reasons: it will not benefit people in the future and so any risk of harm to participants cannot be justified; and it may harm people in the future because the results are misleading.

Consideration 2: The risk of harm to research participants

The Declaration of Helsinki (Principle 5) states:

> In medical research on human subjects, considerations related to the well-being of the human subject should take precedence over the interests of science and society.
>
> (World Medical Association 2000)

A central ethical position taken by international and national guidelines is that research participants must be protected from being at much risk of harm, even if the benefit of the research to people in the future is considerable. There are two relevant components: the probability of the harm and the degree of harm. These are combined in the single term "risk of harm," and the phrase "minimal risk of harm" is often used to describe an acceptable level. Few guidelines specify what probability of serious harm (e.g. death) corresponds with "minimal harm." This nettle has been grasped by the Royal College of Physicians, London (1990: §7.2) which states that: "Minimal risk could include everyday risks such as travelling on public transport or a private car ... but would not include travel by pedal or motorcycle."

Two points are noteworthy about the position taken by these and other guidelines. First, they markedly restrict the degree of risk that competent adults can take voluntarily when participating in medical research. The maximum degree of risk allowed is in marked contrast with many areas of life such as sports. Second, within the acceptable limits of risk, some trade-off is allowed (in some guidelines) between risk to participants and the value of research to those in the future.

Consideration 3: Consent, information and competent adults

The Declaration of Helsinki (Principle 22) states:

> the physician should obtain the subject's freely-given informed consent, preferably in writing.
>
> (World Medical Association 2000)

The relevant "key information" would include the purpose of the research, what is involved in taking part, the risks and benefits, and its general methodology. Some guidelines, and the *Mental Capacity Act 2005*, do allow research with participants lacking capacity to consent to the research but only if the risk of harm is very low and in most guidelines only if consent is given by a proxy.

New ethical challenges

Benefit to others

The complexity, novelty and power of current scientific research provides a considerable challenge in balancing the three major ethical principles that we have discussed. In this section, we examine the balancing of risk of harm to participants with the value of the research to people in the future using the example of large randomized controlled trials (experimenting on people with possible cures, using large, random samples of patients from the general population) as a focus. In the following section we consider the issue of consent and risk of harm to participants. In the final section we discuss some implications of research that might be of great benefit but could also be harmful to people in the future.

The requirement that participants be exposed only to minimal risk may be too stringent and not consistent with accepted existing research practice. We will illustrate this through consideration of the "gold standard" of clinical trials: those which showed that thrombolytic drugs ("clot busters") improved outcome after heart attack.

In 1982, the first analysis combining all the results of different existing experiments on people of "clot busters" (called a "meta-analysis" – Stampfer et al. 1982) was performed. It showed these very likely reduced the rate of death after heart attack. So a very large trial was designed to test one version of these clot busters (streptokinase): the 1986 trial of the Italian Group for the Study of the Survival of Myocardial Infarction (Gruppo Italiano per lo Studio della Streptochinasi nell'Infarto Miocardico, GISSI 1986). Before the data from this trial were available, another large meta-analysis was performed which showed that these drugs reduced the risk of death by approximately 20 percent with a very high level of statistical accuracy and confidence (in statistical terms, at the $p < 0.001$ level) (Yusuf et al. 1985). The results of the GISSI trial subsequently confirmed that these drugs reduced mortality by 18 percent (with even more statistical certainty, $p = 0.0002$).

While the GISSI trial was in progress, yet another large trial was commenced to evaluate the effectiveness of these drugs: the 1988 trial of the Second International Study of Infarct Survival (ISIS-2) Collaborative Group (1988). It might seem unobjectionable to continue to experiment on such drugs until one is certain that they are effective. The problem is that to understand whether they are effective, such trials often employ a placebo or dummy drug given to half the patients. This is important until it becomes clear the drug is doing more benefit than harm. So, over the span of this study, there were 238 more deaths in the group receiving placebo compared with the group receiving streptokinase. This study found that these drugs (streptokinase) reduced the risk of death by 23 percent.

Should the ISIS-2 trial have been stopped as soon as the GISSI trial results were available? Was the continuation of the ISIS-2 trial unnecessarily denying people life-saving treatment? Was the increase in certainty that streptokinase is effective worth the deaths of more than 100 people? Should the ISIS-2 trial have even been started given that the GISSI was under way? These are value judgements, not scientific judgements. Participants recruited later in the trial were probably exposed to more than "minimal risk" by being given the placebo. Indeed the same might be said of those in the GISSI trial given that the trial was continued to very high levels of accuracy or significance. Without such high levels of accuracy or statistical significance, however, occasionally the conclusions from trials will be wrong, which could lead to very large numbers of patients subsequently receiving the wrong treatment when such treatment goes onto the market.

Once such (randomized controlled) trials are under way, data are constantly collected, as part of the trial, which may provide evidence that one drug is better than the other. Indeed that is the point of the trial. The question then arises: at what point should the trial be stopped?

Four main issues arise:

(1) How are the interests of research participants to be balanced against the interests of future patients? In general, future patients benefit from very large trials that provide highly reliable information. However, large trials involve continuing the trial when half of those participating will receive what is almost certainly the inferior treatment.

(2) What is "against the best interests" of those participating in the trial given that:
   - It is probabilities not certainties with which we are dealing?
   - There are known and unknown short- and long-term side effects? Thus, simply focusing on the main, and relatively short-term, outcomes measured as part of the trial is not sufficient.

   Different clinicians (doctors) and patients will be persuaded by different types and amounts of evidence.

(3) What are the responsibilities of those running the trial compared with those of the clinicians who enter patients into the trial?
(4) How should patients be informed and involved?

Eight strategies for determining when to stop large randomized trials and how to define reasonable risk

There are many quite different answers that can be given to the question of what should the principle be for stopping a clinical trial, each of these based on different value judgements. There seems to be no general agreement on this issue. We outline briefly eight possible "stopping rules" (Hope et al. 2003).

STRATEGY 1: WHEN THE TRUTH IS KNOWN

One approach is to say that the trial should be continued until the right answer is known. However, this criterion is an illusion. All we invariably have is greater or lesser degrees of probability that the two treatments being compared do not differ in efficacy.

STRATEGY 2: UTILITARIANISM – TO MINIMIZE DEATHS OVERALL

According to this rule, the trial should be stopped at the point that would lead to the best outcome (e.g. fewest deaths) overall – taking both trial subjects and future patients whose treatment is affected by the trial into account and giving equal consideration to people in both groups. This rule is likely to favor running trials until accuracy or significance levels are very high (at least if the treatment of very large numbers of patients is likely to be affected by the trial results) since if we make a mistake and conclude that drug *A* is better than drug *B* when in fact *B* is better than *A*, a large number of people in the future will die through getting the worse treatment.

STRATEGY 3: WHEN THE EVIDENCE FAVORS ONE DRUG – THE MINIMAL EVIDENCE CONDITION

The central criticism for following the "utilitarian" view is that it harms those in the trial for the sake of people in the future, thus conflicting with the Declaration of Helsinki.

Should a clinician who puts the interest of his patients above all other concerns pull out of the trial as soon as there is a reasonable minimum evidence that one drug is better, that is, with any greater than chance probability, statistically defined by a $p < 0.05$)?

STRATEGY 4: WHERE THERE IS NO LONGER "REASONABLE UNCERTAINTY"

Strategies 2 and 3 assume no side effects. In practice, drugs can have both short- and long-term unwanted effects. Because of this, different clinicians (and patients) might reasonably differ in their judgement as to when it is in their patients' best interests to receive treatment *A* or *B*; and when a clinician is justified in entering a patient into a trial, on the grounds that there is reasonable uncertainty as to which is better overall. This may be the case even if the "minimal evidence condition" is met with regard to the central outcome measure of the trial, and might justify running a trial for longer than would be the case using Strategy 3.

STRATEGY 5: CLINICAL AUTONOMY

According to Yusuf et al, "patients can only be entered [in a clinical trial] if the responsible clinician is substantially uncertain as to which of the trial treatments would be most appropriate for this particular patient" ("the uncertainty principle" or "clinician's equipoise") (1985).

This position is about who is responsible for the decision to enter a patient into a trial and simply transfers the question of what the correct stopping rule is from the researcher to the clinician. More crucially, if individual clinicians are responsible for deciding whether it is right to enter a patient into a trial they need to be provided with the latest data from the trial. But this is not generally done. If clinicians are only given the evidence at the time before the start of the trial, all they can decide is whether they believe that the trial should have been started. They do have available the data crucial to the question of whether the trial should be stopped.

STRATEGY 6: PRAGMATISM – WHAT CHANGES PRACTICE

Richard Doll gave two justifications for large clinical trials:

> (1) they provide evidence that is "much more readily accepted by clinicians."
> (2) "Involving large numbers of clinicians in the trial predisposes them to accept the results … Participation in a large-scale controlled trial constitutes, in practice, one of the best means of continuing medical education."
> (Doll 1993 : 311).

But this, we believe, is putting the cart before the horse. We should first decide on what, epistemologically and ethically, are the correct criteria for stopping the trial and then tackle the question of how clinicians' prescribing can be affected. It is wrong to continue trials beyond reasonable evidence and expose participants to inferior treatment simply as a means of correcting clinicians' poor prescribing habits.

STRATEGY 7: WHEN POTENTIAL SUBJECTS ARE BETTER OFF OUTSIDE THE TRIAL

The pragmatic argument could be applied more convincingly in considering only the best interests of those in the trial. Different clinicians make different judgments about when to switch to a new treatment. Such differences might be reasonable given uncertainties over the longer term side effects of the new treatment. According to Strategy 7, when the data part way through a trial suggest that the measured effect of the drug *B* is real and unlikely to have arisen by chance (that is, when the interim analysis shows that the p value is < 0.05), the trial leaders should ask the following question to the clinicians involved: "Given this information, if the trial were stopped now, which treatment would you recommend for your patients?" If the clinician answered *A* – but was still willing to enter his or her patients in the trial (and so risk being randomized to receive the other treatment) – then it would be best to continue the trial recruiting patients from this clinician. If the clinician answered *B* then it would be best to discontinue the trial, even if the clinician were willing to continue to enter the randomized trial.

STRATEGY 8: THE AUTONOMY OF PATIENTS

All the strategies so far have concentrated on the question of when those running the trial, or clinicians, should stop it. The interests of the patients taking part in the trial have been considered but not their views. From the perspective of enhancing patient autonomy the question arises as to how patients should be involved in the decision concerning their entry into the trial. Almost always, a minimum standard should be that patients are informed about the trial and the fact that it is a randomized controlled trial. But they are rarely given emerging evidence from a trial. One response to the problem of when to terminate trials is to allow participants to access emerging data and decide whether to participate.

The example of when to stop large clinical trials raises complex questions about balancing the interests of those in a trial with those who may benefit in the future, and in a context in which epistemological issues to do with evidence are far from self-evident. We now turn to a different issue: that of the relative importance of informed consent vis-à-vis risk.

Autonomy and reasonableness of risk

For many the most important ethical issue in research is whether the participant has given valid consent. This focus on consent, however, at the expense of concerns about risk can, we believe, lead to wrong decisions.

Consider the following case:

> Jesse Gelsinger was an 18 year old man with a mild form of ornithine transcarbamylase (OTC) deficiency which could be controlled by diet

> and drug treatment. A more severe form of the disease occurs in the newborn which is normally lethal. Gelsinger was recruited into a trial of gene therapy: he was injected with virus vector particles containing a gene to correct the genetic defect. He died four days later. This was the first death directly attributed to gene therapy.
>
> (Savulescu 2001: 148)

In designing the trial the researchers had decided, on ethical advice, to recruit adult participants who could consent, but who had a mild form of the disease, rather than newborns who could not consent, but had a lethal form of the disease (Savulescu 2001). Consent was considered more important than harm.

This case illustrates the importance of distinguishing between two concepts: the chances of a bad outcome occurring and expected harm. The magnitude of the expected harm to adult participants with milder forms of this disease was significantly greater than to newborns with the severe form of the disease. Gelsinger had something to lose while the seriously affected newborn did not.

Determining ***reasonable risk***

In determining whether the risks of participation in research are reasonable, the following factors are relevant (Savulescu 1998):

(1) Is there a known risk to participants prior to commencing the study and what is its magnitude, based on evidence available at the time?
(2) Should any non-human or epidemiological research, systematic overview or computer modeling have been performed prior to the study to better estimate the risk to participants or obviate the need for the use of human participants?
(3) Could the risk have been reduced in any other way? Is it as small as possible?
(4) Are the potential benefits (in terms of knowledge, improvement of welfare of trial participants or other people) of this study worth the risks?
(5) Could this research generate knowledge which is likely to significantly harm either participants or others outside the research, now or in the future?

Radical new challenges

Most discussion, and the majority of guidelines, that address the ethics of medical research are principally concerned with the protection of research participants. It is generally assumed that the research is likely to benefit people in the future. In the final part of this chapter, we focus on an issue that is of increasing significance: the possibility that a research project while carried out in the hope of benefiting mankind might turn out to do more harm than good, and indeed do catastrophic harm.

There are at least two ways in which this might occur. First, medical research might lead to the development of methods that could be used, either through accident or with malicious intent, to cause enormous numbers of human deaths. For example, the development of a strain of mousepox virus turned out to be quite unexpectedly lethal and similar techniques might be used to develop a highly lethal bioweapon (Jackson et al. 2001).

Second, there are many developments that might lead to radical alterations in what future humans will be like, or even raise the question of whether the future beings are indeed human. For example, synthetic biology techniques aim to create new forms of life from scratch (Smith et al. 2003). Scientists have developed new bases that can be incorporated into DNA and are replicated by natural enzymes. The development of DNA with such new characteristics might lead to humans with radically new features or even lead to radically new life forms. More disturbing for some is the possibility of creating novel human–non-human animals.

In the United Kingdom a substantial majority of members of the House of Commons rejected an attempt to ban the use of "human admixed embryos," which combine human and animal genetic material for scientific research (*Human Fertilisation and Embryology Bill*, House of Lords 2007–8). There are several ways in which such mixed embryos can be created. For example, human nuclear DNA can be transferred into the cytoplasm from the egg of an animal (cybrids); or animal DNA can be introduced into cells of a human embryo; or one or more animal cells can be added to a human embryo (chimeras); or hybrid embryos can be formed from a human egg and animal sperm or vice versa.

Should such research be allowed to go ahead? We will consider the example of cybrids, introducing human genetic material into animal eggs as a source of embryonic stem cells.

Cybrids could prove to be a valuable research tool. Human eggs for research are in short supply and their use is ethically problematic because of the risks related to the surgical procedure and superovulation. Research using cybrids might be a first step in developing effective ways in which organs for transplants could be created from a patient's own tissues, thus overcoming problems of rejection. They might also be used in the development of models of human diseases, for example, by creating tissues with a human disease which could be used to test potential treatments.

Given these possible important results from research involving cybrids there is a strong argument for enabling such research. Indeed to prevent potentially lifesaving research for no good reason is wrong. A consequentialist view goes further: to fail to carry out research that will save 100,000 lives is morally equivalent to killing 100,000 people.

There are, however, several objections to research involving cybrids, and indeed embryonic stem cell research more generally. We will outline these objections and counter-arguments to them.

Pragmatic or "scientific" issues

Some argue that such novel embryo research is not needed because of other developments such as the use of pluripotent stem cells (iPS cells) from human skin cells without using an embryo. These iPS cells are in some ways like embryonic stem cells, capable of forming different types of tissues in the body. For example, such iPS cells might be successfully converted into nerve and heart cells. This argument depends on predicting what types of research – cybrid or iPS – will prove fruitful and there is reasonable disagreement over such predictions. Given such disagreement it might be argued that all promising lines of research should be pursued including the use of embryos, and of mixed human and animal organisms such as cybrids.

Destruction of embryos

Many believe all embryo research is wrong because human cloned embryos are created with the intention of destroying them. Two responses to this objection are, first, that in a society that allows some destruction of embryos and fetuses for various purposes (such as fertility treatment or termination of pregnancy) the onus of argument should be on justifying why such destruction is not permissible for research. Second, it is disputable whether cybrids are human embryos and whether they could develop into live-born offspring.

Absolute deontological constraints

Some argue that there should be an absolute deontological constraint (or a "moral taboo" (Karpowicz et al. 2004) proscribing such research whatever its utility, just as we might proscribe torture. This, however, is not an argument but a conclusion. Further reasons are required to justify such an absolute constraint.

Animal welfare

Obtaining animal eggs by ovarian stimulation and surgical removal would present the same risks and discomfort for animals as these procedures do for humans. This raises the question of when, to what extent, and how much animal suffering is justified for human good. This objection appears weak within a society that generally allows considerably more animal suffering for medical research (and food) than is likely to be caused in creating cybrids.

Human dignity; against "Nature"

Some people are concerned that forming embryos with human and animal genetic material that might develop into a living creature is unnatural and therefore morally wrong; or that it offends human dignity.

Such objections require further justification since the fact that something is unnatural does not, of itself, explain why it is immoral, and it is not clear in what way human dignity is offended. Furthermore, human genes have been introduced into animals for over twenty-five years to create animal models of human diseases, and cows and goats with human genes have produced human blood-clotting factors in their milk. The legislation requiring the destruction of transgenic or chimeric embryos after fourteen days has proved effective in preventing the development of independent living creatures.

Uncertain moral status

A final objection is that the moral and legal status of mixed human and animal life forms is uncertain, and this uncertainty might lead to bad consequences. In such circumstances it is wise to be cautious and indeed not to proceed.

This objection could be met through legislation prohibiting such life forms from developing beyond the early stages. People might, however, break the law. This objection might also be met by arguing that any risks from uncertainty over moral status (and it is not clear quite what kind of risks these are, nor how important) are outweighed by the potential tangible benefits in overcoming human disease.

Should we create human–non-human life forms for research?

The question of whether research involving human–non-human life forms should be banned is an issue faced by all societies that undertake significant medical research and different countries approach this issue differently. It is our view, based on the above considerations, that as long as there is legislation limiting the age to which such life forms can be allowed to develop they should not be banned. The arguments against this position outlined above are not in our view convincing and the potential benefits of such research are significant. The main purpose, however, of our discussing this example in the context of this chapter is not to argue for one position but to show that the traditional issues discussed in the ethics of medical research do not exhaust the ethical issues to which modern science gives rise. Research ethics is not a static topic and doubtless new issues will continue to surface that require new analyses.

Conclusion

Whether research is reasonable turns on its risks, both to participants and others, and its benefits, to participants and others. We must evaluate the reasons for each piece of research. This requires a radically different kind of review from that which is currently undertaken by research ethics committees. It requires a knowledge of normative ethics and moral argument.

There are three ground-level ethical principles governing research which are founded on higher order or overarching ethical principles or values such as the value of liberty and autonomy, beneficence, perfectionism, respect for the moral status of living beings, justice, and the promotion of public interest. These three ground-level principles are:

(1) *A Principle of Permission.* Research should be permitted where it imposes justifiable risks on those who participate and those who are affected by it.
(2) *A Principle of Facilitation.* Research should be facilitated and promoted where there are justifiable expected benefits to those who participate and will be affected by it.
(3) *A Principle of Restriction.* Research should be prevented or restricted where it imposes unjustifiable risks either on individuals who participate or on those affected by the results.

The concepts of "unjustifiable risk" and "unjustifiable benefit" are the products of vectors of reasons derived from higher order ethical principles and values, that is, these principles or values provide reasons to permit, facilitate or restrict research. These higher order principles can generate reasons which conflict. The justifiability of research turns on the balance or prioritization of these reasons.

Specific research which should be restricted is best restricted by law. But because of the globalization of research, this must be international law, which is currently lacking.

At present, we have no adequate procedure for evaluating radical research except on a case-by-case basis, examining the reasons for and against it, and no way of internationally implementing decisions. Research remains in a free space which could be to our great benefit or existential detriment.

See also Ethics and reason (Chapter 9); Utilitarianism to Bentham (Chapter 13); Ethics, science, and religion (Chapter 22); Reasons for action (Chapter 24); Social anthropology (Chapter 31); Ethics and psychology (Chapter 32); Biology (Chapter 33); Formal methods in ethics (Chapter 34); Ethics and Law (Chapter 35); Reasons, values, and morality (Chapter 36); Consequentialism (Chapter 37); Feminist ethics (Chapter 43); Conscience (Chapter 46); Respect and recognition (Chapter 47); Evil (Chapter 49); Responsibility: Intention and consequence (Chapter 50); Responsibility: Act and omission (Chapter 51); Partiality and impartiality (Chapter 52); Moral particularism (Chapter 53); Welfare (Chapter 54); Ideals of perfection (Chapter 55); Rights (Chapter 56); Justice and distribution (Chapter 58); Life, death, and ethics (Chapter 59); Animals (Chapter 62); The ethics of free speech (Chapter 64).

References

Beecher, H. K. (1966) "Ethics and Clinical Research," *New England Journal of Medicine* 274: 1354–60.

GISSI (Gruppo Italiano per lo Studio della Streptochinasi nell'Infarto Miocardico [Italian Group for the Study of the Survival of Myocardial Infarction]) (1986) "Effectiveness of Intravenous Thrombolytic Treatment in Acute Myocardial Infarction," *Lancet* 1: 397–402.

Doll, R. (1993) "Summation of the Conference," *Doing More Good Than Harm: The Evaluation of Health Care Interventions*, Special issue *Annals of the New York Academy of Science* 703: 310–13.

House of Lords (2007–8) *Human Fertilisation and Embryology Bill*, Norwich, UK: Her Majesty's Stationery Office.

Hope, T., Savulescu, J. and Hendrick, J. (2003) *Medical Ethics and Law: The Core Curriculum*, London: Churchill Livingstone.

ISIS-2 (Second International Study of Infarct Survival Collaborative Group) (1988) "Randomised Trial of Intravenous Streptokinase, Oral Aspirin, Both, or Neither among 17,187 Cases of Suspected Acute Myocardial Infarction: ISIS-2," *Lancet* 2: 349–60.

Jackson, R. J., Ramsay, A. J., Christensen, C., Beaton, S., Hall, D. F. and Hamshaw, I. A. (2001) "Expression of Mouse Interleukin-4 by a Recombinant Ectromelia Virus Suppresses Cytolytic Lymphocyte Responses and Overcomes Genetic Resistance to Mousepox," *Journal of Virology* 75, no. 3: 1205.

Karpowicz, P., Cohen, C. B. and van der Kooy, D. (2004) "It Is Ethical to Transplant Human Stem Cells into Nonhuman Embryos," *Nature Medicine* 10, no. 4: 331–5.

Pappworth, M. H. (1967) *Human Guinea Pigs: Experimentation on Man*, London: Routledge & Kegan Paul.

Royal College of Physicians (1990) *Royal College of Physicians Guidelines on the Practice of Ethics Committees in Medical Research Involving Human Subjects*, 2nd edn, London: Royal College of Physicians.

——(1996) *Royal College of Physicians Guidelines on the Practice of Ethics Committees in Medical Research Involving Human Subjects*, 3rd edn, London: Royal College of Physicians.

Savulescu, J. (1998) "Safety of Participants of Non-Therapeutic Research Must Be Ensured," *British Medical Journal* 16: 891–2.

——(2001) "Harm, Ethics Committees and the Gene Therapy Death," *Journal of Medical Ethics* 27: 148–50.

Smith, H. K., Hutchison, C. A., 3rd, Pfannkoch, C. and Venter, J. C. (2003) "Generating a Synthetic Genome by Whole Genome Assembly: φX174 Bacteriophage from Synthetic Oligonucleotides," *Proceedings of the National Academy of Science* 100, no. 26: 15440–45.

Stampfer, M. et al. (1982) "Effect of Intravenous Streptokinase on Acute Myocardial Function: Pooled Results from Randomized Trials," *New England Journal of Medicine* 307: 1180–2.

World Medical Association (2000) "World Medical Association Declaration of Helsinki: Ethical Principles For Medical Research Involving Human Subjects," Edinburgh: World Medical Association.

Yusuf, S., Collins, R., Peto, R., Furberg, C., Stampfer, M. J., Goldhaber, S. Z. and Hennekens, C. H. (1985) "Intravenous and Intracoronary Fibrinolytic Therapy in Acute Myocardial Infarction: Overview of Results on Mortality, Reinfarction and Side-Effects from 33 Randomized Trials," *European Heart Journal* 7: 556–85.

Further reading

A useful website to guidelines about the ethical conduct of medical research with links to other relevant sites is the Department of Health website. Several key guidelines and Web links are given in the references to this chapter. The General Medical Council (GMC) guidelines to doctors taking part in research ("Research: The Role and Responsibilities of Doctors") are available on the GMC website at: <http://www.gmc-uk.org/guidance/current/library/research.asp>

Brody, B. A. (1998) *The Ethics of Biomedical Research: An International Perspective*, New York: Oxford University Press.

Doyal, L. and Tobias, J. S. (eds) (2001) *Informed Consent in Medical Research*, London: BMJ Books, pp. 266–76. (A detailed examination of the ethical issues surrounding consent to participate in medical research.)

Eckstein, S. (2003) *Manual for Research Ethics Committees*, Cambridge: Cambridge University Press. (Provides both background discussion of the issues and practical materials relevant to ethics committee members.)

Elliot, D. and Stern, J. E. (eds) (1997) *Research Ethics: A Reader*, Hanover, NH: University of New England. (Deals with more general issues arising from research, with several case studies.)

Evans, D. and Evans, M. (1996) *A Decent Proposal: Ethical Review of Clinical Research*, Chichester: John Wiley. (A very detailed and practical guide to the evaluation of clinical research.)

Foster, C. (2001) *The Ethics of Medical Research on Humans*, Cambridge: Cambridge University Press. (Looks at research from goal-based, duty-based and right-based perspectives. Many case studies.)

Grayson, L. (2000) *Animals in Research: For and Against*, London: British Library. (This is a useful introduction and sourcebook to further reading. Grayson's book addresses the issue of animals used in research, a topic not covered in this chapter.)

Murphy, T. F. (2004) *Case Studies in Biomedical Research Ethics*, Boston, MA: MIT Press.

Smith, T. (1999) *Ethics in Medical Research: A Handbook of Good Practice*, Cambridge: Cambridge University Press. (A very detailed and practical guide to evaluating all types of clinical research. Useful for ethics committee members and researchers.)

66
WORLD POVERTY

Thomas Pogge

Poverty is most serious when people are not merely poor relative to other people, but also poor in a narrow, absolute sense. Today, a majority of the world's population is poor in this sense: unable securely to meet their most basic needs. This has been so throughout human history. Yet, the moral situation has changed dramatically, insofar as huge gains in productivity have made severe poverty easily avoidable. There is now a grotesque incongruity between the human and the economic magnitude of the world poverty problem.

In human terms, this problem is unimaginably large, as is shown by the reports of deprivations due to poverty. For the first time in human history, the number of chronically undernourished people has broken above a billion (FAO 2009); 884 million live without safe drinking water and 2.5 billion without improved sanitation (www.wssinfo.org/en/40_MDG2008.html); 924 million lack adequate shelter (UN Habitat 2003) and 1.6 billion have no electricity (UN Habitat n.d.); 2 billion lack access to essential medicines (FIC n.d.); 774 million adults are illiterate (UIS n.d.). Some 218 million children between 5 and 17 do wage-work outside their household – often under slavery-like and hazardous conditions: as soldiers, prostitutes or domestic servants, or in agriculture, construction, textile or carpet production (ILO 2006).

People suffering such deprivations are highly vulnerable to even minor changes in natural or social conditions as well as to many forms of exploitation and abuse. Each year, some 9 million children under 5 years of age (Unicef 2009) and over twice as many human beings altogether (WHO 2004) die prematurely from poverty-related causes, treatable diseases mostly – accounting for about one-third of all human deaths. Hundreds of millions more suffer grievously from avoidable diseases. The lives of even more are shattered by severe illnesses or premature deaths in their families. These medical problems weigh down the economies of many poor countries, thereby perpetuating their poverty which in turn contributes to the ill-health of their populations.

In economic terms, the world poverty problem is the gap between the current economic standing of the poor and the economic standing they would require in order to meet their basic needs. Thanks to increasing global productivity, this gap has become tiny. World poverty persists so massively nonetheless because of enormous and still rising global inequality. Looking at private household wealth, we find that the poorer half of humankind owns about 1.1 percent, as compared with 40 percent owned by the richest 1 percent (Davies et al.: >Table 10a). In 2007, the 1,125 billionaires had about three times as much wealth as the poorest 3,400 million people put together. Inequalities in per capita household income and consumption are smaller but still dramatic as Table 66.1 shows.

With a shift of only 2 percent of global household income, all the great deprivations of the poorer half of humankind could be avoided. The poorer half would then have 5 rather than 3 percent of global household income. This extra 2 percent would amount to only one-third of the *gain* in income share that the top ventile (twentieth) achieved in the 1988–2002 period. Had they expanded their own share of global household income a little less for the sake of poverty avoidance, the top ventile of the human population would still have captured 46.8 percent of that income.

We see here the incongruity mentioned in the opening paragraph. Even while rising global income renders the cost of eradicating poverty ever more trivial, its huge human cost persists. World poverty today causes death and suffering at over twice the rate of the Second World War at its worst. Yet the effort required to end severe poverty would be very much smaller. Ending the Second World War required the sacrifice of 15 million Allied soldiers as well as financial outlays around half of the combined GDP (gross domestic product) of the United Kingdom, United States, and Soviet Union in 1943–45. To end poverty, no lives would need to be sacrificed, and the financial opportunity cost (the cost to other expenditures) would barely be felt among the affluent. It is for the sake of trivial gains that the world's affluent, and their governments and international organizations, are keeping the poorer half in severe and often life-threatening poverty.

This plain truth about world poverty today is creatively obscured by the world's elite: by their politicians, officials, and economists. Winning world poverty the moral attention it deserves therefore requires a Sisyphean effort of analyzing and deflating the many rationalizations that misrepresent the human or economic magnitude of the problem, its evolution over time, the causes of its persistence, and the elite's willingness to respond to it. This task will end only when poverty itself has ended: when the world no longer needs or rewards these efforts to rationalize world poverty.

One important way of obscuring the problem involves the use of purchasing power parities (PPPs), comparing incomes on the basis of buying power. The income shares shown in Table 66.1 are calculated on the basis of actual currency exchange rates. Orthodox economists would reject this table on the ground that it ignores the fact that poor people face much lower prices. Once this fact is taken into account, the incomes and income shares of the poor are two to three times higher, and income inequality correspondingly lower by a slightly larger factor (slightly larger because the income share of the rich also declines a little).

Table 66.1 Distribution of global household income converted at current market exchange rates.

Segment of the population	Global household income share 1988 (%)	Global household income share 2002 (%)	Absolute change in income share (%)	Relative change in income share (%)
Richest ventile	42.87	48.80	+5.93	+13.8
Next four ventiles	46.63	42.78	−3.85	−8.3
Second quarter	6.97	5.44	−1.53	−22.0
Third quarter	2.37	2.06	−0.31	−13.1
Poorest quarter	1.16	0.92	−0.24	−20.7

Source: Data from Branko Milanovic, World Bank, personal communication, 18 August 2009.
Note: Figures in the fourth column are calculated by subtracting the second column from the third. Figures in the fifth column reflect the ratio of the third to the second.

While economists have thus far used PPPs mainly to revise exchange rates between national currencies, the World Bank is currently introducing analogous adjustments even within countries – by considering a Chinese yuan, for example, to be worth 37 percent more when earned or spent in a rural rather than an urban area. This adjustment enables the Bank to report much lower domestic inequality in many countries.

But is it plausible to use PPPs to tone down economic inequalities within or across countries? Suppose money bought twice as much of everything among the poor as among the rich. Should we then conclude that the income inequality between those in the top ventile and those in the bottom quarter is only 133:1 rather than 265:1? Drawing this conclusion overlooks the fact that rich and poor alike much prefer to live among the affluent rather than among the poor. To be sure, poor people cannot afford to act on this preference. But affluent people could live in the cheapest part of town and could, after retirement, move to the cheapest part of their country or even to rural Bangladesh. How can we tell poor people that they are not so much worse off where they live, when this difference in price levels would never motivate us to move there?

The main point of Table 66.1 is to document not global inequality as such, but the avoidability of absolute poverty narrowly defined. Applied to absolute poverty, the use of PPPs distorts the picture by making the problem look economically much more foreboding than it is. The true opportunity cost to the rich of allowing the poor to meet their basic needs depends on what the missing necessities cost where poor people actually live – not on what these necessities would cost in affluent countries. To be sure, the cost of these necessities among the poor might be slightly higher if the poor had more income. But this effect would not be large enough to render insufficient the contemplated 2 percent shift in the distribution of global household income in favor of the poor.

The World Bank measures and tracks absolute poverty in monetary terms. To do so, one must indeed take account of the prices that households are actually facing. Yet PPPs are not the right way to do this, because they emphasize the various national prices of each commodity depending on its share in international expenditure by households. By using PPPs, the Bank gives far too much weight to the commodities such as real estate and consumer electronics that are irrelevant to poverty avoidance and far too little to those such as basic foodstuffs and medicines, which the poor absolutely need to survive. As it happens, the use of PPPs makes the situation of the poor look better than it is. Especially cheap among the poor are so-called non-tradables, such as services, which the poor barely need and barely consume. Tradables, such as foodstuffs, by contrast are not nearly so much cheaper among the poor as PPPs would suggest. We can see this by comparing the Bank's household consumption PPPs with those based, much more narrowly, on the prices of food and non-alcoholic beverages alone. We find that the latter, more poverty-relevant PPPs are higher in each and every poor country, and by about 50 percent on average (World Bank 2008: Table 1). This means that, after PPP conversion, the dollar incomes that the Bank attributes to poor people overstate the amount of food that poor people can actually buy by about one half.

To illustrate. The World Bank counts as non-poor all people whose daily consumption cost in local currency would have at least as much purchasing power as $1.25 had in the United States in 2005. In 2005, about 75 Pakistani rupees were needed to buy $1.25 at the prevailing exchange rate. Appealing to household consumption PPPs, the Bank takes 25.89 rupees for each person each day to be enough to avoid poverty. But nearly twice as much, 41.81 rupees, was actually needed in Pakistan to buy as much food and non-alcoholic beverages in 2005 as $1.25 could buy in the United States. Subsisting right at the Bank's poverty line, a "non-poor" Pakistani could buy only as much daily food in 2005 as could be bought in the United States for $0.77. Of course, such a person would actually have to spend even less on food, because the daily 25.79 rupees had to cover not merely nutrition, but also clothing, shelter, medical care, water, and other basic utilities.

Clearly, the World Bank's official poverty line is far too low to reflect an income or consumption level sufficient to meet people's basic needs. As a result, the Bank undercounts the poor and thereby makes the human cost of global poverty appear much smaller than it is. More importantly, the level of the Bank's poverty line also greatly affects the reported poverty trend. For instance, the Bank reports that over the full 1981–2005 period of World Bank statistics the number of poor people declined by 27 percent (from 1,896 to 1,377 million) relative to the official international poverty line of $1.25 at 2005 PPPs. However, it also reports a rise in poverty for the same period, where it applies a higher poverty line of 2.00 or 2.50 (Chen and Ravallion 2008: Table 7). With the use of the $2.50 line, the number of poor increased by 13 percent (from 2,732 to

3,085 million). Such sensitivity of the poverty trend to the level of the poverty line is extremely important because governments are using the Bank's statistics in interpreting their repeated promises to halve poverty by 2015.

A very prominent such promise was made at the 1996 World Food Summit in Rome, where 186 governments pledged themselves "to achieving food security for all and to an ongoing effort to eradicate hunger in all countries, with an immediate view to reducing the number of undernourished people to half their present level no later than 2015" (FAO 1996). Using the Bank's official poverty line, we find that the number of poor declined by 16.9 percent in the first half (1996–2005) of the plan period. Using the more adequate doubled poverty line, we find only a 4.5-percent decline. Either way, fulfillment of this promise is unlikely.

Perhaps for this reason, the world's governments soon substituted a different promise. Unanimously adopting the Millennium Declaration in September 2000, the United Nations General Assembly solemnly promised "to halve, by the year 2015, the proportion of the world's people whose income is less than one dollar a day and the proportion of people who suffer from hunger." This formulation retains the idea of halving the problem by 2015, and yet smartly dilutes the goal by focusing, not on the actual number, but on the proportion of poor in the world population. With world population expected to increase to 120 percent of what it was in 2000, cutting the proportion of the poor by half would only require reducing the actual number of the poor to 60 percent, not half, of what it was in 2000.

Since its unanimous adoption by the UN General Assembly, the so-called First Millennium Development Goal (MDG-1) has undergone further dramatic dilution. The current UN interpretation and tracking of MDG-1 expresses the number of poor as a proportion, not of the world population, but of the faster growing population of the developing countries, and it also backdates the baseline to 1990, thereby capturing a huge poverty reduction reported for China in the 1990s. (This backdating of the MDG-1 baseline has its comical side: causing the UN to report that the 2015 target was met in the world's most populous region – East Asia and the Pacific – already in 1999, a full year *before* this goal had even been adopted!) Because the population of the developing countries in 2015 is expected to be 146 percent of what it was in 1990, to meet the goal of "halving poverty by 2015" it is now deemed sufficient to reduce the actual number of poor people to an even less impressive 73 percent of what it was in 1990. The aim now is to reduce the number of extremely poor people by 27 percent over a 25-year period. Imagine if Roosevelt had responded analogously to the much more costly task of eradicating the harms the Axis powers were causing all over Europe in 1942: calling for a 27 percent reduction in the rate of victimization by 1967.

How much progress has been made toward this 27 percent reduction in the number of poor? Using the Bank's official poverty line, we find that the actual number of the poor already fell by 24 percent during 1990 to 2005 – MDG-1 as officially tracked is almost certain to be achieved. We would be way behind schedule, however, if the more adequate, doubled poverty line were used. Relative to it, the Bank reports a slight *increase* in the number of poor during the same period (Table 66.2).

Statistics matter. We are on target for achieving MDG-1 only because we are using an absurdly low poverty line that is insufficient to allow "non-poor" persons to meet their basic needs – and only because governments revised their promise from halving between *1996* and 2015 the *number* of poor people to halving between *1990* and 2015 the *proportion* of poor people in the population of the developing countries. Table 66.2 also shows how the revisions of the promise affect the number of people whose extreme poverty ($1.25) in 2015 is deemed morally acceptable. The revisions add 496 million to this acceptable number of people living on less than 1.25 international dollars per person per day and thereby several million to the number of accepted poverty deaths in 2015 and in each year thereafter.

The story of how the world's governments keep revising their promise to "halve world poverty by 2015" illustrates one main reason for the persistence of massive poverty: the poor have no allies among the global elite. Hundreds of officials in many governments and international agencies were involved in shifting the goalposts to the detriment of the poor. Thousands of economists and other academics understood what was happening. So did thousands of people in the media, who had been reporting on the Rome Summit and the MDGs – with some of them expressly denying that the revisions were worth reporting. Most of these people harbor no ill-will toward the poor. They merely have other

Table 66.2 Consequences of choosing a level and baseline year for the international poverty line.

Poverty line in 2005†	Baseline year	Reduction in number of poor required by 2015 (%)	Number of poor in baseline year (millions)	Target number of poor in 2015 (millions)	Change required by 2005 to be "on track" (%)	Actual change reported by 2005 (%)	Percentage ahead or behind schedule (%)
1.25	1996	50	1,656	828	−28.0	−16.9	40 behind
2.50	1996	50	3,231	1,616	−28.0	−4.5	84 behind
1.25	2000	40	1,665	999	−15.7	−17.3	11 ahead
2.50	2000	40	3,301	1,981	−15.7	−6.6	58 behind
1.25	1990	27	1,813	1,324	−17.2	−24.1	40 ahead
2.50	1990	27	3,071	2,242	−17.2	+0.45	103 behind

Note: The figures in the sixth column are based on a uniform percentage reduction from the baseline year to 2015. The figures in the last column reflect the ratio of the seventh to the sixth.

† In international dollars, equal to the purchasing power of 1 United States dollar.

Source: Chen and Ravallion 2008: Table 7.

priorities. And they don't care how their pursuit of these priorities may affect the global poor.

This widespread lack of attention to world poverty becomes morally indefensible once we understand that its human cost is enormous, that its economic magnitude is pathetically small by comparison, and that it persists despite healthy global economic growth. This is clearly a problem that any moral person must pay serious attention to.

Those who begin to pay attention often easily content themselves with the thought that we simply cannot avoid world poverty, at least not at reasonable cost. We have already seen that the financial cost of overcoming severe poverty is tiny. But many think of the millions of annual poverty deaths as necessary to avoid an overpopulated, impoverished, and ecologically unsustainable future for humanity. While this view once had prominent academic defenders (Hardin 1974), it is now discredited by abundant empirical evidence across regions and cultures, showing that, when poverty declines, fertility rates also decline sharply (Sen 1994). Wherever people have gained access to contraceptives and associated knowledge and have gained some assurance that their children will survive into adulthood and that their own livelihood in old age will be secure, they substantially reduced their rate of child birth. We can see this in the dramatic declines in total fertility rates (average number of children per woman) in areas where poverty has declined. In the last 55 years, this rate has dropped from 5.42 to 1.72 in Eastern Asia, for instance, and from 3.04 to 1.38 in Portugal and from 3.18 to 1.83 in Australia. In economically stagnant poor countries, by contrast, there has been little change over the same period: Equatorial Guinea went from 5.50 to 5.36, Mali from 6.23 to 5.49, Niger from 6.86 to 7.15, and Sierra Leone from 5.52 to 5.22 (United Nations 2008). The correlation is further confirmed by synchronic comparisons. Currently, the total fertility rate is 4.39 for the 50 least developed countries versus 1.64 for the more developed regions, and 2.46 for the remaining countries (*ibid.*). The complete list of national total fertility rates also confirms a strong correlation with poverty and shows that already some 95 of the more affluent countries have reached total fertility rates below 2 (CIA n.d.), foreshadowing future declines in population. Taken together, these data provide overwhelming evidence that reduced poverty is associated with large fertility declines.

These data also discredit the claim that we should accept world poverty for the sake of the environment, which would be gravely damaged if billions of presently poor people began consuming at the rate we do. The short-term ecological impact of eradicating world poverty would be dwarfed by its long-term ecological impact through a lower human population. Eradicating poverty with all deliberate speed would make a huge contribution to an early peaking of the human population, which would bring enormous ecological benefits for the rest of the third millennium and beyond. At current projections, massive eradication of severe poverty can achieve, by 2100, a declining population of 7 billion as compared with a still rising population of 10–14 billion otherwise. It should also be noted that the short-term harm from poverty eradication is often overstated. It is true that if the poorer half of humankind had an additional 2 percent of global household income (i.e. 5 instead of 3 percent), then their ecological footprint would expand. But it is also true that the richer half of humankind would then have 2 percent less of global household income (i.e. 95 instead of 97 percent) with a consequent contraction of their much larger ecological footprint. There is still a net harm to the environment as ecological footprint per unit of income tends to decline with rising income. But this effect is very small compared with the long-term ecological benefit of poverty eradication. And it can be avoided by small incremental reductions in the ecological burdens which the more affluent produce.

Having disposed of the claim that world poverty is a morally necessary evil, we more affluent confront the question what, and how much, we are duty-bound to "sacrifice" toward reducing severe poverty worldwide. Most of us believe that these duties are feeble, that it is not very wrong to give no help at all. Against this view, some philosophers have argued that the affluent have positive duties that are quite stringent and quite demanding: if people can prevent much hunger, disease, and premature death at little cost to themselves, then they ought to do so even if those in need are distant strangers. Peter Singer (1972) famously argued for this conclusion by likening the global poor to a drowning child: affluent people who give no aid to the hungry behave no better than a passer-by who fails to save a drowning child from a shallow pond in order not to muddy his pants.

One problem with Singer's view is to work out how much an affluent person is required to give when there are always yet further urgent needs she might help meet. On reflection, the assumption of such a cut-off point seems odd. It seems more plausible to assume that, as an affluent person expands her assistance, the moral reason to give even more becomes less stringent. We tend to talk in binary terms, to be sure, about whether some effort is morally required or else beyond the call of duty. But there is no plausible formula that would allow us to compute, from data about a person's financial situation, exactly how much she is required to give toward helping those to whom an extra dollar would bring much greater benefit.

Still, as she keeps giving, the moral reasons to give yet more do become weaker, less duty-like and more discretionary. The strength of these moral reasons may thus fade for three reasons. First, the needs of the poor may become less urgent. Second, giving an extra dollar becomes more of a burden as the donor's assets decline. Third, the dollars she has already given continuously build a case that she has already done a lot. These three reasons do not coincide precisely. The third reason is sensitive to whether her current financial situation reflects the fact that she has already given a lot. Singer and his followers have no algorithm for assessing the strength of these reasons or for determining with any precision whether someone has done her duty or not. Nonetheless, they have a plausible case for concluding that we ought to relieve life-threatening poverty so long as we can do so without giving up anything really significant.

Other philosophers have challenged the terms of this debate and, in particular, the shared suggestion that people in affluent countries are as innocent in regard to world poverty as Singer's passer-by is in regard to the child in the pond. This challenge can be formulated in different ways (Pogge 2008: 205–10). One can question the legitimacy of the existing highly uneven global distribution of income and wealth – which has emerged from a historical process that was pervaded by grievous wrongs (genocide, colonialism, slavery) and has left many of the living without a fair share of the world's natural resources or an adequate equivalent. One can criticize the negative externalities affluent populations are imposing upon the world's poor: greenhouse gas emissions that are spreading desertification and tropical diseases, for example, or highly efficient European fishing fleets that are decimating fish stocks in African waters.

One can also critique the increasingly dense and influential web of global institutional arrangements that foreseeably and avoidably perpetuates massive poverty. It does so, for example, by permitting affluent states to protect their markets through tariffs and anti-dumping duties and through huge subsidies to domestic producers amounting to some $300 billion annually in agriculture alone. It does so by requiring all WTO (World Trade Organization) members to grant 20-year product patents, thereby causing important new medicines that can be produced very cheaply to be priced out of reach of a majority of the world's population. The existing international institutional order also fosters corrupt and oppressive government in the poorer countries by recognizing any person or group holding effective power – regardless of how they acquire or exercise it – as entitled to sell the country's resources and to dispose of the proceeds of such sales, to borrow in the country's name and thereby to impose debt service obligations upon it, to sign treaties on the country's behalf, and thus to bind its present and future population, and to use state revenues to buy the means of internal repression. This practice of recognition is beneficial to many a putschist and oppressive ruler, who can gain and keep political power even against a large majority of his compatriots and then greatly enrich himself at their expense. This practice is also beneficial to affluent populations who can, for instance, buy natural resources from an African strongman regardless of how he came to power and regardless of how badly he rules. But this practice is devastating for the populations of such countries by strengthening their oppressors as well as the incentives toward coup attempts and dictatorial rule. Bad governance in so many poor countries (especially those rich in natural resources) is a foreseeable effect of the privileges our international order bestows upon any person or group that manages to bring a country under its control.

The common conclusion suggested by all these considerations is that the moral challenge world poverty poses to the affluent is not merely to help more, but also to harm less. They are not merely failing to fulfill their positive duties to assist and protect, but also violating negative duties: the duty not to impose or take advantage of an unjust distribution of holdings, or the duty not to contribute to or take advantage of unjust international practices and institutional arrangements that foreseeably and avoidably keep billions trapped in life-threatening poverty.

A violation of the latter duty presupposes that it is reasonably possible for the affluent collectively to shape the international practices and a institutional arrangements they design and uphold to be more poverty-avoiding. This presupposition is hard to deny in regard to the examples just provided: it is reasonably possible for us not to deplete African fish stocks, not to distort world markets through massive subsidies and other protectionist measures that hamper exports from poor countries, not to insist on pharmaceutical monopolies that deprive the poor of access to cheap generic versions of advanced medicines, not to recognize and arm rulers who oppress their poor compatriots and steal their resources. Insofar as alternative, more poverty-avoiding practices and rules are reasonably possible, the existing practices and institutional order must count as unjust and their continued imposition as a harm done to the world's poor.

There is no agreement on how much inequality and poverty just international practices and institutional arrangements may maximally engender. But no precise answer to this question is required for concluding that existing levels of poverty and inequality are excessive. When basic human rights of a large proportion of humanity are avoidably unfulfilled, then international practices and institutional arrangements must count as unjust insofar as they contribute to this human rights deficit. The more powerful countries especially have, then, responsibilities to reform these practices and institutional arrangements so as to make them comply with human rights – a responsibility that falls, in the last analysis, upon these countries' citizens. They cannot reform international practices and institutions single-handedly, to be sure, but they can work politically toward such reform and can also make individual efforts to protect poor people from the effects of the unjust arrangements imposed upon them. Such efforts, though active, are required by their negative duty to do no harm: insofar as you contribute to and benefit from the imposition of unjust arrangements, you are responsible for a share of the harm these arrangements cause unless you take compensating action that prevents this share of the harm from materializing.

To conclude: world poverty is the morally most important issue of our time. It is not an avoidable disaster on the horizon, like nuclear war or catastrophic climate change, but an avoidable disaster now actually blighting the lives of billions and killing some 50,000 people every day. Most of the more affluent people who could do something about this problem do not even pay attention. If they did, they would find that we have strong positive and negative duties to make considerable efforts toward eradicating severe poverty with all deliberate speed.

See also Responsibility: Act and omission (Chapter 51); Welfare (Chapter 54); Justice and distribution (Chapter 58); Population ethics (Chapter 61); The environment (Chapter 63).

References

Chen, S. and Ravallion, M. (2008) "The Developing World is Poorer than We Thought, But no Less Successful in the Fight against Poverty," World Bank Policy Research Working Paper WPS 4703, <econ.worldbank.org/docsearch>

CIA (Central Intelligence Agency) (n.d.) "Country Comparison Total Fertility Rate," *World Fact Book*, <www.cia.gov/library/publications/the-world-factbook/rankorder/2127rank.htm> (data for 2009).

Davies, James B., Sandstrom, Susanna, Shorrocks, Anthony and Wolff, Edward N. (2006) "The World Distribution of Household Wealth," Ottawa, Canada: International Association for Research in Income and Wealth, 5 December,<www.iariw.org/papers/2006/davies.pdf>

FAO (Food and Agriculture Organization) (1996) *Rome Declaration on Food Security*, World Food Summit, 13–17 November 1996, <Rome, www.fao.org/docrep/003/w3613e/w3613e00.htm>

——(2009) "1.02 Billion People Hungry: One Sixth of Humanity Undernourished – More Than Ever Before," *Media Centre*, Rome: FAO, <www.fao.org/news/story/en/item/20568/icode/>

FIC (Fogarty International Center for Advanced Study in the Health Sciences) (n.d.) Strategic Plan: Fiscal Years 2000–2003, Bethesda, MD: National Institutes of Health, <www.fic.nih.gov/about/plan/exec_summary.htm>

Hardin, G. (1974) "Lifeboat Ethics: The Case Against Helping the Poor," *Psychology Today* 8, no. 4: 38–43.

ILO (International Labour Office) (2006) The End of Child Labour: Within Reach, Geneva, Switzerland: ILO, <www.ilo.org/public/english/standards/relm/ilc/ilc95/pdf/rep-i-b.pdf>

Milanovic, B. (2005) *Worlds Apart: Measuring International and Global Inequality*, Princeton, NJ: Princeton University Press.

Pogge, T. (2008) *World Poverty and Human Rights*, 2nd edn, Cambridge: Polity Press.

Reddy, S. and Pogge, T. (2010) "How *Not* to Count the Poor," in S. Anand, P. Segal and J. Stiglitz (eds) *Debates in the Measurement of Global Poverty*, Oxford: Oxford University Press, <www.socialanalysis.org>

Sen, A. (1994) "Population: Delusion and Reality," *New York Review of Books* 41, no. 15 (22 September): 62–71.

Singer, P. (1972) "Famine, Affluence and Morality," *Philosophy & Public Affairs* 1, no. 3: 229–43.

UIS (UNESCO Institute for Statistics) (n.d.) "Literacy Topic," UIS webpage, <www.uis.unesco.org/ev.php?URL_ID=6401&URL_DO=DO_TOPIC&URL_SECTION=201>

UN Habitat (United Nations Human Settlements Program) (2003) The Challenges of Slums: Global Report on Human Developments 2003, London: Earthscan, <www.unhabitat.org/pmss/listItemDetails.aspx?publicationID=1156>

——(n.d.) "Urban Energy," UN Habitat website, <www.unhabitat.org/content.asp?cid=2884&catid=356&typeid=24&subMenuId=>

United Nations (2009) *World Populations Prospects: The 2008 Revision Population Database*, New York: United Nations Population Division, New York, <www.who.int/whr/2004>

UNDP (United Nations Development Program) (2007) *Human Development Report 2007–08*, Basingstoke: Palgrave Macmillan, <hdr.undp.org/en/reports/global/hdr2007–8)>

Unicef (2009) "Global Child Mortality Continues to Drop," Unicef website, <www.unicef.org/media/media_51087.html>

WHO (World Health Organization) (2008) The Global Burden of Disease, Geneva, Switzerland: WHO, <www.who.int/healthinfo/global_burden_disease/2004_report_update/en/index.html>

World Bank (2008) *Global Purchasing Power Parities and Real Expenditures: 2005 International Comparison Program*, Washington, DC: World Bank, <http://siteresources.worldbank.org/ICPINT/Resources/icp-final.pdf>

Further reading

Dasgupta, Partha (1993) *An Inquiry into Well-Being and Destitution*, Oxford: Oxford University Press. (Still the most comprehensive work exploring the empirical and economic aspects of world poverty.)

Pogge, Thomas (ed.) (2007) *Freedom from Poverty as a Human Right: Who Owes What to the Very Poor?*, Oxford: Oxford University Press; and Paris: UNESCO. (Fifteen new essays by a very international group of authors discussing why freedom from poverty is a human right and what duties this right might create in the affluent.)

——(2008) *World Poverty and Human Rights: Cosmopolitan Responsibilities and Reforms*, 2nd, exp. edn, Cambridge: Polity Press. (Develops and defends two claims. The existing global institutional order is gravely unjust by foreseeably perpetuating a massive deficit in social and economic human rights that is reasonably avoidable by a modified design of that order. Affluent people who contribute to designing or upholding the present global order or benefit from its injustice are thereby violating human rights unless they take sufficiently compensating action to reduce some of the harm global institutional arrangements are producing.)

——(2010) *Politics as Usual: What Lies behind the Pro-Poor Rhetoric*, Cambridge: Polity Press. (This book examines some of the ways in which world poverty is misrepresented in order to make it appear that reasonable efforts are being made to end it. It discusses specifically the various dilutions of the promise to halve poverty by 2015, as well as the distortions inherent in the World Bank's method of measuring world poverty.)

Pogge, Thomas and Horton, Keith (eds) (2008) *Global Ethics: Seminal Essays*, St Paul, MN: Paragon House. (Essays from the last 30 years on our personal responsibilities toward the global poor, including [chronologically] Peter Singer, Garrett Hardin, Charles Beitz, Onora O'Neill, Amartya Sen, Henry Shue, Samuel Scheffler, Richard Rorty, Peter Unger, John Rawls, David Miller, Richard Miller, Thomas Pogge, and Alison Jaggar.)

Pogge, Thomas and Moellendorf, Darrel (eds) (2008) *Global Justice: Seminal Essays*, St Paul, MN: Paragon House. (Essays from the last 30 years on the responsibility to design global institutional arrangements to be poverty-avoiding, including (chronologically) Onora O'Neill, Charles Beitz, Tom Nagel, Amartya Sen, Henry Shue, Brian Barry, Robert Goodin, John Rawls, Thomas Pogge, Martha Nussbaum, Hillel Steiner, and Michael Blake.)

67
WAR

Henry Shue

War is an extraordinary form of human activity in which organized groups of human beings attempt to inflict death, injury, suffering, and devastation upon the members of opposing groups. Yet, this social competition in the infliction of harms that are utterly prohibited in all other circumstances is remarkably a partly rule-governed activity for which elaborate systems of prohibitions and permissions have evolved. To understand the ethics of war one must first comprehend the utter strangeness of the notion that an enterprise within which people are to some degree unleashed to try to kill or wound each other can have rules at all, much less specific legal rules that are in some instances ethically justified.

"To some degree unleashed" is a key to the function of the ethics of war. The ethics of war, mainly expressed in the laws of war, are attempts to limit the organized use of violence: to retain any customary restraints on violence and to control burgeoning new technologies for killing (Prokosch 1995). The most natural thought about the assessment of war, once one appreciates the ferocity and frequency of the crippling and killing which constitute military action (Bourke 1999), is that war consists predominantly of the commission of wrongful acts and ought therefore to be morally prohibited and legally outlawed. The evident response to war would, then, simply be: no! The violent constitutive features of war seem at an absolute minimum to invite "a strong presumption against war" (National Conference of Catholic Bishops 1983: 30).

Four responses to the presumption against war

Four fundamentally quite different responses arise to this proposed presumption, beginning with the two opposite extremes: (1) to reject any strong presumption against war largely on empirical grounds by contending that warfare, while terrible, is a regular and sometimes unavoidable component of an anarchic non-system of international affairs, although the violence of war should be employed only as necessary and prudent when other forms of statecraft fail;

(2) to accept the presumption as indefeasible on any grounds and to treat all forms of war, in whatever circumstances fought and however fought, simply as all inexcusably wrong; (3) to contend that the presumption against war can sometimes be overridden on moral grounds so that particular wars can be on the whole justified, provided they are sufficiently limited; and (4) to accept the presumption against war as indefeasible on any grounds but to contend that even if all wars are unjustified, more limited wars are less inexcusable than less limited wars. The ethics of war is thought to be relatively simple by both the extreme positions: (1) self-styled "realist" theory, and (2) one kind of pacifist theory.

The central question about self-described "realism" is how realistic it actually is, which is an empirical matter. "Realist" theory turns on such empirical contentions as that some war will always be inevitable because an arena like the international one in which there is no central executive or judicial authority is virtually guaranteed to produce conflicts that can be settled only by force of arms. It further depends on an unacknowledged ethical premise that it is sometimes better to use military force oneself than to allow others who use it to have their way. As a matter of fact, I am convinced, the international system is not the kind of anarchy assumed by the "realist" argument, and the web of international laws and norms is becoming far more deeply influential than "realism" assumes (Hurrell 2007; Reus-Smit and Snidal 2008), but the empirically correct characterization of international affairs cannot be explored here.

The relations among these four fundamental positions are surprising and important. The views assigned to category (2) normally show the least interest in our theme, ethical limits on war. All pacifists conclude that all war is inexcusable and that consequently all war ought to be opposed. Nevertheless, it is not incoherent to believe that while all war is inexcusable, some wars are more inexcusable than others, so that one ought to oppose most strongly the most inexcusable wars; and some pacifists modulate their opposition to wars accordingly. A pacifist thus willing to rank wars according to their excusability falls into my category (4). I designate the other, purer pacifists "renunciatory": they utterly renounce violence. Category (2), then, is for renunciatory pacifist theory. Since the basis of much pacifism is the conviction that all wars involve the commission of acts of violence against other human beings that are never justifiable, any ranking of wars according to the extent of their intolerable acts tends to feel to these renunciatory pacifists like a betrayal in practice of the fundamental conviction that all wars are wrong and ought all to be condemned, even if the wars are not equally wrong. Some renunciatory pacifists argue as well, in an appeal to consequences, that any acknowledgment of rules for war, including limiting rules, is liable to have the political and psychological effect of suggesting that some war is acceptable – to dignify it by regulating it (Holmes 1989).

Like the purer, renunciatory pacifists, none of the people in category (4), including the non-renunciatory pacifists, are committed to thinking that any war is, all things considered, justified; and they may not even consider any war to be, all things considered, excused. They may simply believe that war is at least in the short and medium term ineradicable and that the important difference that can be made by the application of ethical principles is in the limitation of the wars that are now in any case going to be fought. The focus is, thus, on whether a war is nuclear or conventional, terroristic or discriminate, and in other respects more or less limited. What matters most for now, it is thought, is the formulation of the ethical limits on war. So position (4) will be labeled the least-inexcusable war theory.

Category (3) differs sharply from (2) and (4) in believing that some wars are, all things considered, morally justified, and includes much of the historic Western tradition of just war thinking – hence, the label just war theory. These positions maintain that it can be not only right but a duty to go to war and wrong not to go to war (Johnson 1975, 1981). But the grounds of the resort to war (*jus ad bellum*) and the methods of the conduct of war (*jus in bello*) matter decisively, so the correct formulation of the limits on both resort and conduct is a preoccupation. Consequently, just war theory and least-inexcusable war theory share an intense concern with the proper limits on war, although it is an open question to what extent they can agree on the specific content of these limits, given the differences in their premises.

Adherents of "realist" theory notably share with just war theory the conviction that wars are sometimes fully justified. The substance of the justifications they respectively offer differ enormously, however, with "realists" emphasizing putative necessities grounded in the nature of the international arena and just war adherents claiming that respect for rights can mean using force to defend rights against those who use force to violate rights. Once again, the shared interest in specifying limits may not yield shared understanding of the particular content of the limits, given the divergent premises. All this makes it especially fruitful to examine specific proposed ethical limits on war and the grounds offered for them.

Limited resort

The most obvious means for limiting the ethically objectionable activities that constitute war appears to be to limit the resort to war. Against pacifists who would prevent all war, theorists of just war and of least-inexcusable war maintain that if the evils that can be prevented or stopped by military action are sufficiently great, the acknowledged evils of war may be the lesser evils. Traditional theories of just war had fairly long lists of individually necessary and jointly sufficient conditions for just war. The most influential exponent of just war theory during the last half century effectively reduced explicit conditions for going to war to a single necessary and sufficient condition: defense against aggression (Walzer 2006). This shrinkage of the list reflected the post-Second

World War political consensus embodied in the legal requirement for Security Council approval for any military action not in self-defense (*Charter of the United Nations*, United Nations 1945: Art. 2:4 and articles 39 and 51).

Apart from challenges to the analogy presupposed between individual self-defense and national self-defense (Rodin 2002), this relatively simple picture has been complicated by two proposed exceptions to any requirement that justified military action consist solely of self-defense against prior aggression. "Humanitarian" military intervention, conceived of as the defense, not of oneself, but of vulnerable third parties incapable of defending themselves, has become widely, but far from universally, accepted (Wheeler 2000: 21–52). And preventive war specifically to eliminate weapons of mass destruction prior to their actual use for terrorist purposes has been far less widely accepted, but insistently propounded (Doyle 2008; Luban 2007). Our focus here will, however, be on limits on the conduct of war, which have been subject to the most vigorous recent philosophical controversy.

Limited conduct of war: military necessity

The evident coherence of least-inexcusable war theory has already provided one answer to the general question how anyone could propose ethical limits on the conduct of an activity that consists largely or entirely of wrongful acts: one might try to promote the least-inexcusable form of an inexcusable type of enterprise, especially if one saw no prospect of preventing it completely in the short term. The overall wisdom of each of the four general approaches to war naturally depends on the specific content of the limits each proposes. How, then, should one think about ethical limits on the actual conduct of the violent enterprise of war?

One natural line of thought is this. On the one hand, if war cannot be justified, it ought if possible to be prevented; and if a particular war cannot be prevented, then its violence ought to be minimized as a kind of second-best partial prevention. Adherents of the least-inexcusable war positions, including non-renunciatory pacifism, agree with this; renunciatory pacifism insists that evil of this violent kind is to be avoided entirely, not merely minimized. On the other hand, even if some wars can be justified by the ends served, their violence still ought to be minimized because the means involved – violent and often lethal or crippling assault upon other human beings and their property – are inherently objectionable even where justified (or excused). "Realist," just war, and least-inexcusable war theory all agree on the general project of war limitation. Therefore, except for renunciatory pacifism, all positions agree that the violence of war should be kept to the minimum necessary. This yields the fundamental underlying principle of military necessity: violence may be employed only if it is necessary to the achievement of a military success that is itself necessary.

Needless to say, any judgement about when some form of military success is necessary to resolve a given conflict is a difficult and complex military, political, and moral decision.

A common error is to substitute the converse of the principle for the genuine principle. The principle of military necessity says that contributing to the achievement of a reasonable conception of military success is a necessary condition for the justifiability of an employment of violence, that is, violence may be employed only if it is necessary to the achievement. By contrast, one treats being necessary to the military goal as a sufficient condition if one asserts: if the violence is necessary to the achievement, it may be employed. This radically transforms the meaning of the principle and distorts it into a virtual license to do whatever works from a military point of view. It is in opposition to this distorting reversal that the "basic rule" of international treaty law governing military conflict insists: "In any armed conflict, the right of the Parties to the conflict to choose methods or means of warfare is not unlimited" (Geneva Protocol I, see ICRC 1977: Art. 35[1]). International law insists that warfare is to be limited because war consists of morally objectionable activities. And the principle of military necessity is certainly one compelling limit because it minimizes the morally objectionable activity, given a decision to resort to war at all.

Limited conduct of war: distinction

A second widely endorsed limit is the principle of discrimination, or distinction. One fundamental legal expression of this moral principle is Rule 1 of the customary international law of armed conflict: "The parties to the conflict must at all times distinguish between civilians and combatants. Attacks may only be directed against combatants. Attacks must not be directed against civilians" (Henckaerts and Doswald-Beck 2005: 3). Chinese, European, Indian, and other cultures contain from their early histories broadly similar examples of formulations of a principle of distinction prohibiting attacks on non-combatants. What can be the basis of this second limit? This is the subject of ongoing controversy.

I believe that the most natural understanding of the principle of distinction is that it is an extension of the principle of military necessity. The principle of military necessity limits violence generally to what is necessary. Necessity can be assessed in a number of different respects, the most important of which has long been targets. Which people is it necessary to try to kill or disable in order to be successful in a military effort? The principle of distinction provides the compelling answer: only those who are directly participating in the opposing military efforts – those directly involved in attempting to thwart your own campaign. But is it not possible – this is one of the perennial myths of war – that if, instead of confronting the fighters on the opposing side, one could manage to kill their families and destroy their property one could undermine their will to fight and they would give up the battle without needing to be defeated militarily? Many reasons tell against the myth of easy victory through the undermining of morale by attacks on civilians. One reason is simply that it has turned out in fact that, like many mythical short cuts, this one does not lead to the intended destination; the "total war" constituted by the bombings targeted against German and Japanese civilians in the Second World War, which was the most extreme attempt in history to force the short cut to work, was not in the case of either country a significant factor in bringing victory but was instead a highly wasteful diversion of scarce air power from more effective military uses that might have actually shortened the European and Pacific wars (Pape 1996). But the response to the myth that civilian suffering undermines military morale provided by the principle of military necessity is: even if attacks on non-combatants and civilian society were in reality one path to victory, they would still not be necessary. One can succeed by confronting only the opposing forces. To at least some extent this limits the death, injury, and destruction to those actively participating in the fighting on the opposing sides. The nature of the violence of war makes its limitation highly desirable, and the relative clarity of the military/civilian line makes this limitation feasible.

In traditional Western just war theory the criterion of who could be attacked was precisely in accord with this rationale. One was permitted to attack those who were engaged (*nocent*) in the military effort on the opposing side, and was prohibited from attacking those who were not engaged (*innocent* – privative of *nocent*). People unfamiliar with Latin have often mistakenly assumed that a correct translation of "*innocent*" is the English cognate "innocent" as if the criterion of who can be attacked were some kind of guilt. But the *innocent* were simply those who are in fact not involved in military action. The criterion is active involvement in military operations, not moral responsibility for the occurrence of the fighting. International law, as we have seen, refers to those immune to attack as civilians, and they can also be called non-combatants, alternative terminology that also reflects the fact that the issue is engagement or non-engagement in combat. Civilians may not be attacked because it is not necessary to attack them in order to defeat the opposing military forces, who are more effectively attacked directly, and because limitation of human losses is ethically required. In the just war tradition whether civilians were morally responsible for unjustified fighting was irrelevant to their immunity from attack as non-combatants.

In recent decades some philosophers have launched a critique of this standard view of the distinction between military and civilian that is entrenched in international law and have advocated its replacement by a more moralized account of who may permissibly be targeted. I believe this alternative proposal rests on a deep conflation between issues about who deserves to be held responsible and perhaps punished for the occurrence of wars and issues about who is best targeted for the death and injury during wars. It is also not clear whether the advocates of the moralization of the rules of war would like to see the laws of war replaced by other supposedly ethically better laws or would be content to see the laws of war often be ignored in the name of an overriding morality.

The advocates of this moralization correctly point out that many civilians bear much greater moral responsibility for the initiation of wars than the combatants who fight in them. They also correctly note that the military personnel fighting on a fully justified side of a war may rightfully be participating in self-defense while the military fighting on the opposing side may wrongfully be participating in aggression. The argument, then, is that it is an ethical mistake simply to draw the generally accepted line between civilians and military because some civilians are implicated in wrongdoing and some are not, while some military too are implicated in wrongdoing and some are not (McMahan 2004, 2008). Consequently civilians need to be separated into those who are as individuals ethically liable to attack and those individuals who are not, while the military too need to be similarly divided on the basis of their individual ethical liability to being attacked. The underlying assumption is: only wrongdoers may properly suffer during war.

The crucial mistakes in this argument are the assumptions that there can be some coherent notion of ethical liability to military attack (somewhat analogous to ethical liability to punishment or other forms of accountability) and that individuals have moral features that provide the appropriate basis for targeting during military conflict, as if military action could function as a fair procedure for the distribution of death and wounds so that the morally guilty, or ethically liable, would be the ones to die, while those who were justified in fighting would go safely home (Shue 2008). If war could thus be made to function like a fair trial in which the guilty perished or were wounded and the innocent soundly survived, war would no longer be the horror that it always is. Why do we not, then, reform war by moralizing the rules so that it becomes such a fair process in which death and wounds are allocated more nearly according to the ethical standing of each individual?

First, the principles of military necessity and distinction, and the international laws embodying them in which combatants are now instructed, are the crucial constraints that at present function to prevent total war in which utterly anyone besides combatants and civilians on your own side is treated as a legitimate target. Anything that undermines these principles and the distinction on which they rest, the distinction between military and civilian, is highly dangerous unless it is at least as likely to function effectively as they do. The standard principles do not function especially well, but they are the only effective barriers now between us and barbarity, including terrorism. We undercut functioning constraints at great peril. If soldiers are encouraged to decide for themselves which civilians and which combatants are worthy of immunity and which are properly liable to be shot, it is hard to see why the principle of distinction will not severely erode or collapse.

Second, the project for the moralization of the rules for fighting rests on a very attractive appeal to individual accountability, but it is completely impossible for soldiers engaged in deadly combat, often with literally unseen adversaries who are firing at them from a great distance, to assess, individual by individual, the ethical status of those engaged in trying to kill them. Discrimination among opposing combatants according to individual ethical features is in reality impossible. One of the sorrows of war is indeed that relatively inexperienced and often well-intentioned young people slaughter other similar young people whom they have never met and know very little about. This is a powerful reason to be a pacifist, but the wish to continue to tolerate wars but somehow to use them as fair distributive mechanisms for the allocation of death and wounds is an incoherent dream. War can be limited somewhat. By far the most successful limit now, as weak as it is, is the principle of distinction which permits combatants on each side to attack all the combatants on the other side, and no one else. This is a distinction that it is in practice possible to observe during most combat. Distinctions based on individual ethical characteristics cannot be implemented outside orderly peacetime conditions.

Third, the advocates of moralization themselves are trying to formulate rules that should be followed only by those who were morally justified in fighting. Much of their argument rests on the idea that a military that is justifiably defending against aggression, or otherwise in the right, ought to be allowed to do things that a military unjustifiably committing aggression, or otherwise in the wrong, is not allowed to do. The rules for the justified would be less restrictive than the rules for the unjustified (Rodin 2008). Objectively, this is appropriate. But another of the tragedies of war is that most people on both sides of most wars appear to believe that they are the ones who are justified. Consequently, practically everyone will in fact follow the less restrictive rules that the advocates of moralization correctly argue are applicable only to the objectively right. Few will restrict themselves to the actions, if any, that are correctly said to be objectively permitted to those who are not justified. So the work of the advocates of moralization will lose all effect on the actual conduct of war because few who are fighting with conviction in their own cause will believe that the restrictive rules apply to themselves.

If these arguments are correct, the conclusions take a striking shape. The morally best justified rules for the conduct of war are laws of war the content of which is in many respects disanalogous to the content of the rules, legal and moral, of ordinary peaceful life. Arguments that ignore the profound differences between the circumstances of peace and the circumstances of war and attempt to draw simple analogies, such as comparing a justified side in a war to a police officer and an unjustified side to a burglar, produce irrelevantly moralistic standards that will not be, because they cannot be, followed during combat.

Any side that is not justified in fighting, which includes both sides in many wars, ought not to be assaulting any other human beings at all, much less killing and wounding people who are only defending themselves. The rule for any side that is not justified in departing from the ethical principles that govern ordinary life – that is, not justified in going to war – is: do not employ violence against other human beings whom you do not know. The rule for any side that is justified is: employ violence only against combatants on the unjustified side because this so far appears to be one of the few workable limits on permissible attacks during war. The terrible reality is that the rule for justified sides will, in fact, often be followed by unjustified sides as well, because often they believe they are justified. This tendency toward predictable misapplication of the rules cannot be changed by reforming the rules themselves. If the current situation is ethically unacceptable, as it may well be, war is ethically unacceptable.

The principle of distinction is under assault in practice as well as in theory. Much of the death and destruction in recent international wars has been inflicted by air power, and the struggle over the applicability of the principle of distinction to aerial bombing has been under way for more than half a century. In the Second World War the principle of distinction was flagrantly violated as a matter of Allied policy (Schaffer 1985), being ridiculed by Winston Churchill, for example, as simply out of fashion for the bombing of cities, like the wrong length of women's skirts (Garrett 1993: 45). But the post-war Geneva Conventions vigorously reasserted the principle of distinction (Geneva Convention IV, see ICRC 1949). In the Korean War the principle was again systematically violated, but this time not publicly challenged (Conway-Lanz 2006); some of the various bombing campaigns in the Vietnam War were similar (Pape 1996: 176–95). Then, once again, the principle was reaffirmed by the international community in treaty law (Geneva Protocol I, ICRC 1977).

Now the struggle focuses on how to interpret the provisions of Geneva Protocol I that govern bombing (Shue and Wippman 2002), especially the provisions applicable to the social infrastructure and, above all, to a society's sources of energy like electricity-generating plants and oil refineries. The party with the greatest capacity for destruction, the US military, interprets these provisions as allowing the destruction of all infrastructure that contributes to the military effort of the opposing side, irrespective of how much that infrastructure also contributes to essential civilian functions like water purification, sewage treatment, medical care, food preservation and transportation, and all the other vital operations for which any modern society needs energy. On this interpretation, while civilians are protected from direct attack, they are subject to equally lethal indirect attack by means of the crippling of indispensable social services. Consequently, this interpretation of the distinction between military and civilian thwarts the fundamental purpose of protecting civilian lives (Thomas 2006). If this American interpretation triumphs, the principle of distinction will have lost much of its critical bite.

Limited conduct of war: proportionality

The principles of military necessity and distinction apply to what one intends to result from military action. Much of what happens in war (as in life generally) is unintended, although some of what is unintended is foreseeable. One's responsibility for the foreseeable but unintended consequences of one's actions is less than one's responsibility for the intended consequences, but one bears significant responsibility nevertheless. The third of the three main principles governing the conduct of war, the principle of proportionality, applies to the foreseeable but unintended results of military action. The principle of proportionality is embodied in international treaty and customary laws that prohibit military attacks that may be expected to cause civilians losses that "would be excessive in relation to the concrete and direct military advantage anticipated" (Geneva Protocol I,ICRC 1977: Art. 57; Henckaerts and Doswald-Beck 2005: 46). Comparing the civilian losses to "military advantage" has the great merit of isolating judgements about the proportionality of particular attacks from beliefs about the importance of the causes for which the war is being fought, since such beliefs tend in fact to be highly subjective and often self-serving.

Some suggest, on the contrary, that judgements of proportionality could rest on the importance of a war's goal, and one could choose between an objective conception of the importance of the war's goal and a subjective conception (Hurka 2005: 44–5). Every commander ought to rely on an objectively correct understanding of whether it is important that his war be fought and won. If in truth he ought not to be fighting it, any foreseeable civilian losses inflicted by any attack he is considering will be utterly excessive, serving no good purpose at all and in fact only inflicting unjustified harm. Every battlefield commander ought to be urged to base all his judgements only on true beliefs about whether the war is justified and the importance of the reasons for fighting.

In the end, nevertheless, if he were permitted to weigh the war's goal at all, there is no alternative to allowing the commander to base his judgement on his own conception. This will be his subjective conception, which may not have the same content as the objective conception. In the end people act on the beliefs they actually have. Commanding officers tend to believe that it is not only justified but extremely important that they launch attacks that will contribute to military success for their own side. If a military commander making a judgement of proportionality could appeal to what he believed was the importance of his war's goal, any commander who believed his goal to be highly significant would be inclined to consider relatively large civilian losses not to be excessive. It appears dangerous to civilians to permit commanders to assess civilian losses in light of what they take to be the importance of the war rather than appealing, as international law now requires, to some relatively standard and professional understanding of the military usefulness of a particular type of operation in any military effort, whatever its political and moral goals.

As with the principle of distinction, proportionality is seriously threatened in practice. The US and UK governments, for instance, refuse as a matter of policy to count the civilians who are unintentionally killed by their military operations (Sloboda 2008), making any genuine consideration of proportionality impossible (Shamash 2005–6).

See also Relativism (Chapter 30); Ethics and Law (Chapter 35); Responsibility: Intention and consequence (Chapter 50); Life, death, and ethics (Chapter 59); Torture and terrorism (Chapter 68).

References

Bourke, J. (1999) *An Intimate History of Killing: Face-to-Face Killing in Twentieth-Century Warfare*, London: Granta.

Conway-Lanz, S. (2006) *Collateral Damage: Americans, Noncombatant Immunity, and Atrocity after World War II*, New York and London: Routledge.

Doyle, M. W. (2008) *Striking First: Preemption and Prevention in International Conflict*, ed. S. Macedo, Princeton, NJ, and Oxford: Princeton University Press.

Garrett, S. A. (1993) *Ethics and Airpower in World War II: The British Bombing of German Cities*, New York: St Martin's Press.

Henckaerts, J.-M. and Doswald-Beck, L. (2005) *Customary International Humanitarian Law*, vol. 1: *Rules*, Cambridge: Cambridge University Press.

Holmes, R. (1989) *On War and Morality*, Princeton, NJ, and Oxford: Princeton University Press.

Hurka, T. (2005) "Proportionality in the Morality of War," *Philosophy & Public Affairs* 33: 34–66.

Hurrell, A. (2007) *On Global Order: Power, Values, and the Constitution of International Society*, Oxford: Oxford University Press.

ICRC (International Committee of the Red Cross) (1949) *Geneva Convention (IV) Relative to the Protection of Civilian Persons in Time of War*, ICRC website, <http://www.icrc.org/ihl.nsf/FULL/380?OpenDocument>

——(1977) *Protocol Additional to the Geneva Conventions of 12 August 1949, and Relating to the Protection of Victims of International Armed Conflicts (Protocol I)*, ICRC website, <http://www.icrc.org/ihl.nsf/FULL/470?OpenDocument>

Johnson, J. T. (1975) *Ideology, Reason, and the Limitation of War: Religious and Secular Concepts, 1200–1740*, Princeton, NJ, and Oxford: Princeton University Press.

——(1981) *Just War Tradition and the Restraint of War: A Moral and Historical Inquiry*, Princeton, NJ, and Oxford: Princeton University Press.

Luban, D. (2007) "Preventive War and Human Rights," in H. Shue and D. Rodin (eds), *Preemption: Military Action and Moral Justification*, Oxford: Oxford University Press.

McMahan, J. (2004) "The Ethics of Killing in War," *Ethics* 114: 693–733.

——(2008) "The Morality of War and the Law of War," in Rodin and Shue 2008, pp. 19–43.

National Conference of Catholic Bishops (1983) *The Challenge of Peace: God's Promise and Our Response, A Pastoral Letter*, Washington, DC: United States Catholic Conference.

Pape, R. A. (1996) *Bombing to Win: Air Power and Coercion in War*, Ithaca, NY: Cornell University Press.

Prokosch, E. (1995) *The Technology of Killing: A Military and Political History of Antipersonnel Weapons*, London: Zed.

Reus-Smit, C. and Snidal, D. (eds) (2008) *The Oxford Handbook of International Relations*, Oxford: Oxford University Press.

Rodin, D. (2002) *War & Self-Defense*, Oxford: Oxford University Press.

——(2008) "The Moral Inequality of Soldiers: Why *jus in bello* Asymmetry Is Half Right," in Rodin and Shue 2008, pp. 44–68.

Rodin, D. and Shue, H. (eds) (2008) *Just and Unjust Warriors: The Moral and Legal Status of Soldiers*, Oxford: Oxford University Press.

Schaffer, R. (1985) *Wings of Judgment: American Bombing in World War II*, Oxford: Oxford University Press.

Shamash, H. E. (2005–6) "How Much Is Too Much? An Examination of the Principle of *Jus in Bello* Proportionality," *Israeli Defense Forces Law Review* 2: 103–48.

Shue, H. (2008) "Do We Need a 'Morality of War'?," in Rodin and Shue 2008, pp. 87–111.

Shue, H. and Wippman, D. (2002) "Limiting Attacks on Dual-Use Facilities Performing Indispensable Civilian Functions," *Cornell International Law Journal* 35: 559–79.

Sloboda, J. (2008) "Can There Be Any 'Just War' If We Do Not Document the Dead and Injured?," Oxford: Oxford Research Group.

Thomas, W. (2006) "Victory by Duress: Civilian Infrastructure as a Target in Air Campaigns," *Security Studies* 15: 1–33.

United Nations (1945) *Charter of the United Nations*, New York: United Nations, <http://www.un.org/aboutun/charter/>

Walzer, M. (2006/1977) *Just and Unjust Wars: A Moral Argument with Historical Illustrations*, 4th edn, New York: Basic Books.

Wheeler, N. J. (2000) *Saving Strangers: Humanitarian Intervention in International Society*, Oxford: Oxford University Press.

Further reading

Bao, N. (1998) *The Sorrow of War*, London: Vintage. (For those who have not experienced war, the best novels can convey some of the reality. The novelist was a Vietnamese soldier during the Vietnam War; to be read in conjunction with novel by Tim O'Brien.)

Coady, C. A. J. (2008) *Morality and Political Violence*, Cambridge: Cambridge University Press. (Recent comprehensive treatment by outstanding philosopher.)

O'Brien, T. (1998) *The Things They Carried*, New York: Broadway Books. (The novelist was an American soldier during the Vietnam War; to be read in conjunction with novel by Bao Ninh.)

Reichberg, G. M., Syse, H. and Begby, E. (eds) (2006) *The Ethics of War: Classic and Contemporary Readings*, Oxford: Blackwell. (Best collection of classic sources, including fresh translations.)

68
TORTURE AND TERRORISM

David Rodin

Terrorism and torture are connected on a number of levels. Both are generally accepted to be heinous crimes. Both have loomed large in the moral consciousness of the early twenty-first century. The readiness of George W. Bush's administration to instigate what many consider a policy of torture was triggered by the terrorist attacks of September 11, and philosophical defenses of torture typically begin from a thought experiment involving a "ticking bomb" terrorist. Conversely there is evidence that American torture at Abu Ghraib and Guantánamo Bay have played a role in sustaining the murderous practices of Al-Qaida and its affiliates. Torture and terrorism clearly feed off one another, linked by more than their shared commitment to a strategy of coercion through fear.

It is perhaps surprising that these topics have re-emerged as significant areas of philosophical debate. As Jeremy Waldron points out, the question of torture's permissibility had been considered closed in the civilized world for over a century (Waldron 2005: 1683). To have to return to a debate about the legitimacy of torture and terrorism is dispiriting. Despite this, recent discussion of both topics has been rich and has undoubtedly shed light on two of the darkest facets of the human condition. In this chapter I will focus on issues of meaning and definition and on the related question of moral assessment, in particular of whether there can be such thing as morally justified torture and terrorism.

The definition of torture

Torture, like terrorism, is difficult to define. There is no consensus on the distinction between torture and other forms of coercion and manipulation, or between torture and cruel, inhuman or degrading treatment, of which torture is a species. The legal definition is contained in the United Nations Convention against Torture and Other Cruel, Inhuman or Degrading Treatment or Punishment which defines torture as follows:

> torture means any act by which severe pain or suffering, whether physical or mental, is intentionally inflicted on a person for such purposes as obtaining from him or a third person information or a confession, punishing him for an act he or a third person has committed or is suspected of having committed, or intimidating or coercing him or a third person, or for any reason based on discrimination of any kind, when such pain or suffering is inflicted by or at the instigation of or with the consent or acquiescence of a public official or other person acting in an official capacity. It does not include pain or suffering arising only from, inherent in or incidental to lawful sanctions.
>
> (Art. 1.1)

The convention makes clear that the prohibition of torture is absolute, that is to say it admits of no justifying exceptions: "No exceptional circumstances whatsoever, whether a state of war or a threat of war, internal political instability or any other public emergency, may be invoked as a justification of torture" (Art. 2.1). This extraordinarily stringent treatment is underlined by the fact that the prohibition of torture has the status of *jus cogens*, that most central and important part of international law which is taken to be binding even on states that are not party to the treaty in question.

The UN Convention definition is broad in the sense that it includes the infliction of both mental and physical pain, but in other respects it is too narrow. For example, it limits torture to acts committed by or with the consent of public officials. While state-sanctioned torture is the most common and important case, it seems clear that torture may also be inflicted by non-state criminal or paramilitary groups or indeed by a private individual acting alone. The Convention definition limits torture to pain intentionally inflicted by a person on another person. The focus on the intentional seems right. While one can unintentionally kill or maim, it does not make sense to talk of unintentional torture. It is less clear whether humans are the only beings who can be the victims or perpetrators of torture. In common usage we talk of children torturing insects and of cats torturing mice. However, though such acts certainly involve the intentional infliction of pain, these acts may possess a different moral structure to paradigm cases of torture proper. On David Sussman's account (discussed below) torture can only occur when the victim has rich cognitive and affective abilities like those of a human.

One significant definitional issue is whether there is a moral distinction between torture proper and so-called "torture lite" – techniques such as sleep deprivation, forced standing and stress positions, isolation, manipulation of heat and cold, noise bombardment, and mock execution. This distinction was utilized by members of the Bush administration to justify interrogational techniques used at the Guantánamo Bay detention center. But not only is the distinction not recognized in law, Jessica Wolfendale has argued that there is no significant moral difference between torture and "torture lite": both cause intense suffering and both can have extremely severe long-term physical and mental consequences for victims (Wolfendale 2009). On the contrary the most important differences seem to be that torture lite does not leave physical evidence and it can be inflicted without the intimate proximity of traditional methods, features which can increase the distress of victims by making it harder to establish the *post facto* truth about their ordeal.

Why is torture morally wrong?

Torture has a number of obvious wrong-making features. It consists in the intentional infliction of extreme pain and associated mental states of terror, disorientation, isolation, humiliation and despair. The experience of torture often leaves its victims physically, mentally and emotionally scarred for long periods of time, if not for life. Characteristically the torturer's intention is to inflict pain beyond the point at which it can be borne by the human will, in order to "break" the subject and shatter their mental integrity and autonomy. These are all moral evils of the highest order.

And yet these features do not seem sufficient to explain the moral revulsion with which torture is typically held or the stringency of its prohibition. After all killing can cause immense pain, and death deprives its victim of autonomy – indeed of all goods – permanently. In this sense death may be considered a greater harm even than torture and a person may rationally prefer a measure of torture to death. Yet killing is not absolutely prohibited – most notably it is permissible to kill an unjust aggressor in self-defense and also to kill enemy combatants in war. Why the difference?

Henry Shue locates the greater wrongness of torture in the fact that it violates a primitive norm against attacking the defenseless (Shue 1978). Killing an enemy combatant in war is at least the outcome of a minimally fair process in the sense that the enemy is armed and able to defend himself. But one of the most striking features of torture is the absolute asymmetry in power between the torturer and the tortured. The tortured exists in an environment which is totally controlled by the torturer. The victim exists in a state of utter helplessness, unable to defend himself in even the most trivial way. This feature of attacking the defenseless does seem to account for some of the particular moral horror with which we hold torture.

David Luban and Seth Kreimer have offered consonant arguments which locate the wrongness of torture in the way that it manifests a perversion of minimally decent political relations as understood within the liberal tradition. Liberals are committed to the development and preservation of human liberty and dignity as the highest values of political and personal relations. Yet torture deliberately sets out to destroy both the dignity and the autonomy of its victims as a means to some other goal (information, political control, intimidation or mere recreation). In Luban's words:

> the self-conscious aim of torture is to turn its victim into someone who is isolated, overwhelmed, terrorized, and humiliated. Torture aims, in other words, to strip away from its victim all the qualities of human dignity that liberalism prizes ... torture is a microcosm, raised to the highest level of intensity, of the tyrannical political relationships that liberalism hates the most.
>
> (Luban 2005: 1430)

One of the most philosophically sophisticated discussions of the moral structure of torture is that of David Sussman (2005). Beginning from broadly Kantian premises Sussman argues that what is distinctively wrong with torture is not simply that it fails to respect the dignity and rational agency of its victims. Rather torture turns the victim's agency against his or her self by making the torture victim feel complicit in his or her own suffering. What makes this possible is the ambiguous affective status of pain which presents both as something external and alien, but at the same time as our own, a product of our own body. Through the pain of torture the victim is made to feel that their own body and their own emotional and rational responses to it have betrayed them by colluding with the will of the torturer. In this sense torture is not simply a violation of autonomy; it is a deep perversion of it.

Is the prohibition of torture absolute?

We have seen that in international law the prohibition of torture is absolute. Yet philosophers have questioned whether the use of interrogational torture might not be justified in certain exceptional circumstances. Nor is this simply a theoretical matter of interest only within the academy. The Bush administration, supported by senior legal officials, instigated and attempted to legitimize the use of a number of torture practices euphemistically termed "enhanced interrogation procedures." Typically the starting point for those who wish to justify some form of torture has been the "ticking bomb" hypothetical. Imagine that a terrorist has planted a large bomb in the heart of a crowded city and the only way to diffuse the bomb is to torture the terrorist who had planted it. Would it not then be permissible to torture? This simple thought experiment has had a significant effect both in the public and academic debate.

The argument behind the thought experiment can be elaborated in a number of different ways. The simplest employs a straightforward welfare consequentialism: if torturing the terrorist yields greater aggregate welfare than abstaining, then on this view it is justifiable to torture. Few would be persuaded by the argument in this form, however, because most people accept that there is a right not to be tortured which is sufficiently stringent to trump claims of superior aggregate welfare. Many are persuaded, however, by a "threshold deontology" interpretation of the case. On this view the right against torture may be justifiably overridden if the welfare gains of doing so exceed a certain extraordinary threshold (significantly, there is no agreement – even in terms of an order of magnitude – as to where this threshold lies).

A subtle interpretation of the ticking bomb case is provided by Michael Walzer's "dirty hands" argument, which we will encounter again below in the form of his "supreme emergency" defense of targeting civilians in war. On this view the ticking bomb scenario presents an inescapable moral dilemma. This is because the moral repulsiveness of torture is such that it is always wrong to undertake it, yet at the same time a leader or public official is morally obliged to defend and protect fellow citizens when they are threatened with massive avoidable harm. These irreducibly conflicting imperatives create a tragic situation in which the official is morally obliged to do what is morally wrong. Thus for Walzer, while the official is morally required to undertake the torture, this does not expunge the wrong of committing it. There is an irreducible moral remainder which he describes with the term "dirty hands" (Walzer 1973).

Each of these interpretations of the ticking bomb case starts from the assumption that the terrorist has a right or legitimate interest in not being tortured which is in some sense overridden or outweighed by competing moral considerations. But there is another interpretation of the case which denies that the terrorist even has a right not to be tortured in the circumstances. This argument invokes the right to use necessary, proportionate force against an imminent unjust attack in self-defense or the defense of others (McMahan 2006). According to one prominent account of self-defense an aggressor, by engaging in an unjust attack, has forfeited his right to life and hence made himself liable to the defensive force. The self-defense interpretation of the ticking bomb case seeks to extend this idea to interrogational torture. According to this argument if the terrorist is responsible for placing the bomb and is deliberately withholding information in order that the bomb may go off, and if the use of torture is both necessary and proportionate to prevent the detonation then the torture would be justified. The justification in this case arises from the fact that the terrorist no longer possesses a right against being tortured. The justification for torture yielded by the self-defense argument (if successful) is considerably stronger than that yielded by the various consequentialist arguments. On the self-defense argument, torturing the detainee involves no rights infringement at all (not even justified infringement), and therefore can apparently be done without any color of wrongdoing or *post hoc* obligations of redress or compensation. Moreover the self-defense variant of the argument could potentially justify torture when far less is at stake than an overwhelming catastrophe, because the defensive harm inflicted need only be "proportionate" to the harm averted.

The ticking bomb argument in each of its variants has been subject to significant criticism (for a representative discussion see Bufacchi and Arrigo 2006). First, the extreme artificiality of the case has been attacked. The case relies on a number of suppressed assumptions: that the detainee is indeed the responsible terrorist, that he has the required information, that he is the only viable source of the information, that the torture will be successful and will yield results in a timely manner, that evacuation or other mitigation strategies are not available, and many others. These suppressed features of the case clearly help to strengthen the intuition in favor of torture, but they equally distance the case from any real-life interrogation which always involves ambiguity and uncertainty.

Related to this is the narrowness of the consequences considered by consequentialist variants of the argument. Torture is a notoriously unreliable method of interrogation. False information generated under torture may impede rather than assist in locating the bomb. Moreover the use of torture in counter-terrorism and counter-insurgency operations has often proved counter-productive, sapping government legitimacy and generating resentments that feed the very attacks one is seeking to avert. Even if torturing a ticking bomb terrorist yields a tactical success, it may generate a strategic failure. Indeed the act-consequentialist arguments in favor of torture seem vulnerable to a more general rule-consequentialist rejoinder. We know that torture tends to spread and become entrenched within organizations that consent to its practice. This leads not only to harm inflicted on the victims of proliferating torture, but to a corruption and degradation of the legal, political and social institutions that are complicit in it. In a related vein Jeremy Waldron has argued that the absolute prohibition of torture plays a vital role as a "legal archetype" helping to sustain, inform and unify adjacent areas of the law, including the prohibition on cruel and unusual punishment, the requirements of procedural and substantive due process, and the general culture of rejecting police brutality in law enforcement (Waldron 2005). Though difficult to quantify, these kinds of normative consequences argue strongly in favor of maintaining an absolute prohibition and not allowing justifications for torture.

The self-defense version of the ticking bomb argument has also been criticized. Some authors have argued that the theory of self-defense upon which it is based is deficient and should be abandoned (Kaufman 2008). As a practical argument for torture in the real world it is vulnerable to the same charge of artificiality as the consequentialist argument. Indeed it may be more vulnerable, because self-defense is subject to the inherent limitations of proportionality, necessity and imminence. On a forfeiture of rights account of self-defense, these limits have an evidentiary, rather than a welfare-maximizing function: their role is to ensure that defensive force is only used against those who are genuinely liable. Yet it is hard to see how this evidentiary burden could be met in a putative case of defensive torture. How can we tell a detainee who is culpably withholding information under torture from one who is simply ignorant and innocent?

Defining terrorism

Even more than torture, terrorism has remained an extraordinarily contested and difficult concept. The reasons for this are obvious: "terrorism" is a highly charged term often used in rhetorical and inconsistent ways (as suggested by the old saw that "one man's terrorist is another man's freedom fighter").

A bewildering number of definitions of terrorism have been proposed in the academic literature. However, the issues involved can be largely organized into four major areas of debate:

(1) Who are the victims of terrorism?
(2) Who are its agents or perpetrators?
(3) What are the distinctive ends or goals of terrorism?
(4) What are its tactical or operational features?

(1) There is considerable agreement that terrorism centrally involves an attack on those who (at least presumptively) ought to be immune from attack. Such a definition makes terrorism an explicitly normative concept and raises the question, considered below, of whether terrorism can ever be justified or whether it is wrong as a matter of definition. While many subscribe to this normative conception of terrorism, it is less clear how to specify the morally immune class of victims in concrete terms. It is often said that terrorism involves an attack on civilians. But this cannot be quite right because some attacks on uniformed soldiers who are not engaged in fighting a war seem to be clear cases of terrorism (for example, the 1983 truck bomb attack on a US military base in Lebanon and the bombing of *the USS Cole* in Aden in 2000).

The key point seems not to be whether the victims are soldiers or civilians, but whether they are legitimate targets of attack in the course of an ongoing war or conflict. For this reason many philosophers define terrorism as an attack on non-combatants as distinguished from combatants. Non-combatants may include soldiers during peacetime and military doctors during war, whereas combatants may include certain civilian officials and support staff who are an integral part of the war effort.

But why is targeting combatants in war legitimate, while targeting non-combatants presumptively constitutes terrorism? Traditional just war theory holds that targeting non-combatants is illegitimate because, unlike combatants, non-combatants are "innocent," and that it is always wrong intentionally to kill the innocent (Anscombe 1981). This has led to much confusion because, according to just war theory, a soldier fighting lawfully in a legitimate war of self-defense is morally innocent even though he is a combatant. In fact just war theory uses the term "innocent" in a somewhat technical way. The term does not refer to the moral innocence of putative targets, but to whether or not they are currently engaged in threatening behavior (the Latin term "nocents" means those who are threatening, hence to be innocent in this sense is to be non-threatening). Just combatants are held to be legitimate targets, despite being morally innocent, because they are materially non-innocent (i.e. they are currently threatening others).

But this account, invoking the idea of material non-innocence, has been powerfully criticized because it does not cohere with our beliefs about the use of force in non-war situations (McMahan 2009; Rodin and Shue 2008). For example, if a victim of attack uses lawful force in self-defense against an aggressor, the victim does not become a legitimate target of attack even though at this point in time the victim is posing a threat to the aggressor, and hence is materially non-innocent in the technical sense of just war theory. This example and others like it suggest that material non-innocence is not sufficient to make one a legitimate target, and that some form of moral responsibility for a wrongful attack is the crucial determinant of who is and who is not a legitimate target.

This conclusion suggests two things for the debate on terrorism. First, it may be that some non-combatants have equal (or greater) moral responsibility for wrongful acts of aggression than combatants. If so, then it may be possible to argue that they should no longer be immune from attack, and hence using force against them would not constitute terrorism (McMahan 2009). Some attempts have been made to show that in democratic societies, voting citizens are responsible for the unjust wars of their governments and hence may be liable to attack. This line of thought does not seem persuasive, however, because the moral responsibility required to become a legitimate target of attack is normally thought to be much stronger than the rather tenuous responsibility established by collective political decision-making processes such as voting.

Second, if moral responsibility for a wrongful attack is a necessary condition for becoming a legitimate target, then (contra traditional just war theory) soldiers lawfully fighting a just war should be considered morally immune to attack by the enemy. Though attacks on such "just soldiers" by the enemy in wartime would not normally be described as terrorism, this analysis suggests that, morally speaking, killing "just soldiers" in war shares important similarities with terrorism.

Some authors have claimed that a distinctive feature of terrorism is that it has two sets of victims or targets: the immediate or direct victims of the attack, which are of secondary importance, and an indirect, though more important, target, namely the broader group or society. Terrorism on this account involves attacking the broader target through the direct targets (Primoratz 1990).

(2) If terrorism is defined by a distinctive class of victims is it also defined by a distinctive class of agents? Many state governments maintain that terrorism is restricted to acts performed by non-state actors. Most philosophers reject this claim as *ad hoc* and morally unjustifiable. Attacking someone who ought to be immune from attack seems equally bad whether it be done by agents of the state or by a non-state actor. If one rejects an agent-centered definition of terrorism,

then many acts of states may turn out to be forms of terrorism. Plausible examples would include the bombing of the Greenpeace ship "Rainbow Warrior" by French secret agents in New Zealand in 1985, the area bombing of German cities by Britain during the Second World War, and the nuclear bombing of Japan by the United States.

(3) Teleological considerations. Most philosophers claim that terrorism has distinctive goals or ends, and thus is distinguished from common crime or aimless violence. Many philosophers claim that terrorism is necessarily directed to political goals. This definition is probably acceptable as long as one interprets "political goals" in a broad way so as to include the religious, ideological, racist and messianic goals that have motivated different terrorist groups.

Many writers, drawing on the principle of double effect, have assumed that terrorism must involve a direct or intentional attack on those with moral immunity. This has been challenged by work which claims that some forms of foreseen but unintended harm to non-combatants (so-called "collateral damage") which is reckless or negligent can be properly classed as terrorism (Rodin 2004).

"Terrorism" is etymologically connected to "terror," and some authors have argued that the creation of terror among a given community is definitional of terrorism. Although some state of fear or anxiety related to terror is a characteristic effect of terrorist attacks, it seems too strong to make this a definitional feature because it seems possible that communities could react to terrorism with stoic resolve rather than terror. A more plausible claim is that terrorism always involves the intention on the part of the terrorist to create fear and anxiety.

Finally, some philosophers argue that terrorism is necessarily coercive, aiming to get people or groups to do things they would not otherwise do (Wellman 1979). Such a definition would rule out seemingly purposeless attacks such as the 2001 Washington "sniper" attacks from being defined as terrorism.

(4) There are weapons and tactics that we think of as characteristic of terrorism, such as plane hijacking and suicide attacks. But it seems wrong to make this part of the definition of terrorism because, first, such tactics could be used strictly against legitimate targets in which case they would not constitute terrorism, and second, conventional military practices may be terrorist if used against those who are morally immune from attack.

Michael Walzer claims that randomness is the crucial feature of terrorist activity, not in the sense that terrorist attacks are unplanned or untargeted, but rather that the violence comes unpredictably, often without warning and people are killed or escape death by merest chance (Walzer 1977: ch. 12).

It seems plausible that terrorism must involve the use of violence against persons. But this has been challenged in a number of ways. Some philosophers allow violence against property, or threats of violence to count as terrorism. Some philosophers have denied a necessary connection with physical violence, claiming that certain kinds of extreme psychological harm may count as terrorism (Wellman 1979).

Moral assessment of terrorism

It is almost universally agreed that terrorism is morally wrong. A core question is whether terrorism is wrong by definition and, if not, whether there are extreme cases in which its practice might be justified or excused.

There is clearly a sense in which moral condemnation is built into the concept of terrorism, in the same way that it is built into the closely related concept of murder. This is implied, for example, by the analysis suggested in the first section (above) that terrorism is an attack on those who morally should be immune from attack. But it seems odd to claim that we can know *a priori* and merely as a matter of conceptual analysis that any given act of terrorism is all-things-considered wrong. Rather the moral assessment of particular terrorist acts seems to require substantive judgement. Just as in the case of murder, the possibility that an act of terrorism could be justified as the lesser evil in a particular circumstance cannot be foreclosed simply by conceptual analysis.

For utilitarians, of course, there is no conceptual difficulty in conceiving of justified acts of terrorism. For utilitarians the moral evil of terrorism consists in the suffering and harm it inflicts, but one can readily imagine cases in which this evil is outweighed by important goods that can be achieved in no morally less costly way. In practice utilitarians often argue that terrorism is almost universally morally wrong. The reasons for this may have an act-utilitarian form (for example, because terrorism's ability to achieve important goods in a utility-efficient manner is historically very dubious), or they may have a rule-utilitarian form (for example, because the harmful effects of undermining the convention of non-combatant immunity are thought to outweigh the goods that may be achieved by particular acts of terrorism).

The most prominent non-utilitarian defense of terrorism arises from Michael Walzer's "supreme emergency argument" (Walzer 1977: ch. 16). This is a variant of the "dirty hands" argument discussed above. It claims that if a nation or community faces the extreme threat of complete destruction and the only way it can preserve itself is by intentionally targeting non-combatants (arguably the position of the United Kingdom when it commenced area bombing of German cities in the early years of the Second World War), then it is morally entitled to do so. As in the case of an official engaging in torture to diffuse a ticking bomb, Walzer believes that the killing of non-combatants in such a situation remains morally wrong, even though the leader of a community is morally permitted to do it.

The supreme emergency argument is not normally regarded as a defense of terrorism and Walzer is strongly critical of terrorism in other contexts. However, Walzer explicitly invokes the argument to justify acts that clearly constitute terrorism on most definitions (including Walzer's own). There is no principled reason why the argument could not be used to justify more common terrorist activities such as suicide bombings and plane hijacking. Once the connection between supreme emergency and terrorism is made explicit, many people find the supreme emergency argument, and the communitarian assumptions that underlie it, much less attractive.

See also Consequentialism (Chapter 37); Contemporary Kantian ethics (Chapter 38); Responsibility: Intention and consequence (Chapter 50); Rights (Chapter 56); War (Chapter 67).

References

Anscombe, G. E. M. (1981) "War and Murder," Chapter 6 in her *Ethics, Religion and Politics*, vol. 3 of *The Collected Philosophical Papers of G. E. M. Anscombe*, Oxford: Basil Blackwell, pp. 51–61; essay first published in 1961.

Bufacchi, Vittorio and Arrigo, Jean Maria (2006) "Torture, Terrorism and the State: A Refutation of the Ticking-Bomb Argument," *Journal of Applied Philosophy* 23, no. 3: 355–73; repr. in David Rodin (ed.) *War Torture and Terrorism: Ethics and War in the 21st Century*, Oxford, Blackwell, 2007.

Kaufman, Whitley (2008) "Torture and the 'Distributive Justice' Theory of Self-Defense: An Assessment," *Ethics and International Affairs* 22, no. 1: 93–115.

Luban, David (2005) "Liberalism, Torture, and the Ticking Bomb," *Virginia Law Review* 91: 1425–61.

McMahan, Jeff (2004) "The Ethics of Killing in War," *Ethics* 114, no. 4: 693–733.

——(2006) "Torture, Morality and the Law," *Case Western Reserve Journal of International Law* 37: 241–48.

——(2009) *Killing in War*, Oxford, Oxford University Press.

Primoratz, Igor (1990) "What is Terrorism?," *Journal of Applied Philosophy* 7, no. 2: 129–38.

Rodin, David (2004) "Terrorism without Intention," *Ethics* 114, no. 4: 752–71.

Rodin, David and Shue, Henry (eds) (2008) *Just and Unjust Warriors, the Moral and Legal Status of Soldiers*, Oxford: Oxford University Press.

Shue, Henry (1978) "Torture," *Philosophy & Public Affairs* 7, no. 2: 124–43.

Sussman, David (2005) "What's Wrong with Torture?," *Philosophy & Public Affairs* 33, no. 1: 1–33.

Waldron, Jeremy (2005) "Torture and Positive Law: Jurisprudence for the Whitehouse," *Columbia Law Review* 105, no. 6: 1681–1750.

Walzer, M. (1973) "Political Action: The Problem of Dirty Hands," *Philosophy & Public Affairs* 2, no. 2: 160–80; repr. in Marshall Cohen, Thomas Nagel and Thomas Scanlon (eds) *War and Moral Responsibility*, Princeton, NJ: Princeton University Press, 1974, pp. 62–82.

——(1977) *Just and Unjust Wars*, New York: Basic Books.

Wellman, C. (1979) "On Terrorism Itself," *Journal of Value Enquiry* 13: 250–58.

Wolfendale, Jessica (2009) "The Myth of 'Torture Lite'," *Ethics and International Affairs* 23, no. 1: 47–61.

Further reading

Coady, C. A. J. (1985) "The Morality of Terrorism," *Philosophy* 60: 47–69. (Classic article on the definition of terrorism.)

Scheffler, Samuel (2006) "Is Terrorism Morally Distinctive?," *Journal of Political Philosophy* 14, no. 1: 1–17.
Sinnott-Armstrong, Walter (1991) "On Primoratz's Definition of Terrorism," *Journal of Value Enquiry* 8, no. 1: 115–20.
Teichman, J. (1989) "How to Define Terrorism," *Philosophy* 64: 505–17.

INDEX